CASES AND MATERIALS ON

CORPORATIONS

INCLUDING PARTNERSHIPS AND LIMITED LIABILITY COMPANIES

Sixth Edition

By

Robert W. Hamilton

Minerva House Drysdale
Regents Chair in Law
The University of Texas at Austin

AMERICAN CASEBOOK SERIES®

WEST
GROUP

ST. PAUL, MINN., 1998

COPYRIGHT © 1976, 1981, 1986, 1990, 1994 WEST PUBLISHING CO.
COPYRIGHT © 1998 By WEST GROUP
610 Opperman Drive
P.O. Box 64526
St. Paul, MN 55164–0526
1–800–328–9352

Library of Congress Cataloging-in-Publication Data

Hamilton, Robert W., 1931–
    Cases and materials on corporations, including partnerships and limited partnerships / by Robert W. Hamilton. — 6th ed.
      p.   cm. — (American casebook series)
    Includes index.
    ISBN 0–314–22774–1 (hardcover : alk. paper)
    1. Corporation law—United States—Cases. 2. Partnership—United States—Cases. I. Title. II. Series.
KF1413.H35 1997
346.73'066—dc21   97–39229
                                        CIP

ISBN 0–314–22774–1

 *TEXT IS PRINTED ON 10% POST CONSUMER RECYCLED PAPER*

Preface

This book is designed for introductory courses in the law of business associations or corporations. With a minimum of adjustment it may be used in courses covering anywhere from three to six semester hours. It is not designed for use in advanced courses such as securities regulation, mergers and acquisitions, or corporation finance. While it contains materials on agency and partnership, it is not well suited for an introductory course devoted exclusively to these subjects.

Today, limited liability is available in general partnerships, limited partnerships, and limited liability companies on nearly as broadly a basis as it is in the corporate form. As a result, these business forms are often attractive alternatives to corporations and the sharp lines between corporations and unincorporated business forms are becoming blurred. The first three chapters of this book describe these important developments.

I am strongly of the view that the modern law of business organizations can be most effectively taught only in the context of a specific set of statutes. The statutory supplement contains the full text of the Uniform Partnership Act (1914), the Uniform Partnership Act (1994)(colloquially often referred to as "RUPA"), the Uniform Limited Partnership Act (1976) with the 1985 Amendments (colloquially often referred to as "RULPA"), the Uniform Limited Liability Company Act of 1995, and the Model Business Corporation Act (1984)(except for transition provisions). The statutory supplement also contains the financial provisions of the 1969 Model Business Corporation Act if the mysteries of par value and legal capital are to be covered.

Students are encouraged to become familiar with these statutes in the statutory supplement by the simple practice of referring to, but not quoting, the relevant provisions of these statutes throughout this casebook.

In the preparation of this book, numerous citations and footnotes have been omitted without specification. All footnotes have been renumbered in each chapter. In a few instances the location of footnotes taken from original sources has been changed; these changes are noted in the footnote itself). In order to identify the source of footnotes, the bracketed phrases "[By the Court]" or "[By the Author]" appear at the beginning of footnotes that appear in the original source while footnotes beginning "[By the Editor]" were prepared by the undersigned.

Ellipsis ("* * *"} may indicate the omission of single words in a paragraph or entire paragraphs.

Finally, I would like to thank Judy Dodson, my patient secretary, who prepared the original text of this book, recorded innumerable changes, ensured consistency of form through, checked galleys and page proofs, and obtained the necessary permissions from the publishers and authors listed below.

Acknowledgments

Permission to use copyrighted materials is gratefully acknowledged from Academy of Legal Studies in Business, Donna D. Adler, Albany Law Review, Barbara B. Aldave, William T. Allen, American Bar Association, American Bar Foundation, American Business Law Journal, American Enterprise Institute, American Law Institute, Arizona Law Review, Aspen Law & Business, Joseph W. Bishop, Bernard S. Black, Dennis Block, Andrew E. Bogen, Wayne N. Bradley, Douglas Branson, Brooklyn Law Review, Victor, Brudney, Bureau of National Affairs, James R. Burkhard, Cardozo Law Review, William L. Cary, Case Western Reserve Law Review, Catholic University Law Review, Pat Chew, Cincinnati Law Review, Robert C. Clark, Cleveland State Law Review, John C. Coffee, Columbia Law Review, Cornell Law Review, Delaware Journal of Corporate Law, Dow Jones & Co., Inc., Duke Law Journal, Frank H. Easterbrook, Melvin A Eisenberg, Emory Law Journal, Richard A. Epstein, Edward A. Fallone, Daniel Fischel, Fordham Law Review, Fred B. Rothman & Co., Milton Freeman, Geoffrey D. Genz, George Mason Law Review, Jeffrey Gordon, Susan P. Hamill, James J. Hanks, Charles Hansen, Harper Collins, Harvard Business School Publishing, Harvard Law Review Association, Harry J. Haynsworth, Leo Herzel, Allan H. Ickowitz, Thomas M. Jones, Journal of Corporate Finance, Journal of Corporation Law, Journal of Small and Emerging Business Law, Leo Katz, Edmund W. Kitch, Richard H. Koppes, Jake Krocheski, Reinier Kraakman, Bayless Manning, Patricia A. McCoy, Minnesota Law Review, National Law Journal, New York Times, North Carolina Law Review, Northwestern University School of Law, Andrew Orrick, Penguin, U.S.A., Playboy Magazine, Michael J. Powell, Adam H. Prussin, Roberta Romano, Chuck Santangelo, Texas Law Review, The Journal of Corporation Law, The Michigan Law Review Association, The New York Law Publishing Co., The Practical Accountant, The University of Chicago Press, University of Chicago Press, University of Chicago Law Review, University of Florida Law Review, University of Illinois Law Review, University of Miami Law Review, University of Michigan Journal of Law Reform, University of Pennsylvania Law Review, Vanderbilt Law Review, Norman Veasey, Virginia Law Review Association, Wake Forest Law Review, Washington Law Review, West Publishing Co./West Group, Ralph Winter, Wisconsin Law Review, Yale Law Journal, Yale Journal on Regulation.

ROBERT W. HAMILTON

Austin, Texas
February 16, 1998

Summary of Contents

---

*

Table of Contents

Page

Table of Cases

The principal cases are in bold type. Cases cited or discussed in the text are roman type. References are to pages. Cases cited in principal cases and within other quoted materials are not included.

*

CASES AND MATERIALS ON

CORPORATIONS

INCLUDING PARTNERSHIPS AND LIMITED LIABILITY COMPANIES

Sixth Edition

*

Chapter One

INTRODUCTION

A. THE SUBJECT IN GENERAL

The subject of this book is the means and devices by which business in the United States is conducted either by a single individual or cooperatively by a few or many individuals. "Business" is a broad term describing all kinds of profit-making activity, excluding the performance of services for another in an employment relationship. As so defined, the subject covers an extremely broad range of activities: From the summer lemonade stand opened for one afternoon by a twelve-year-old, at one extreme, to General Motors Corporation, a corporation that in 1995 had more than 1,000,000 shareholders, sales of more than 168 billion dollars, profits of more than 6.8 billion dollars, and about 700,000 employees, at the other.

This subject may be broken down in different ways for purposes of analysis and classification. A very traditional classification is by legal form. The lemonade stand is an example of a sole *proprietorship*, a business owned by a single person. General Motors is, of course, a *corporation*. Other traditional forms of business are the *general partnership* and the *limited partnership*. In the 1990s, new forms of business have been created with names confusingly similar to the limited partnership: the *limited liability company*, the *limited liability partnership*, and in some states, the *limited liability limited partnership*. These new business forms are discussed in chapter 3. Classification by business form naturally breaks into two categories: (1) *unincorporated* associations, e.g., proprietorships, partnerships, limited partnerships, and the new forms of business developed in the 1990s, and (2) *corporations*. Some law school curricula have separate courses broken down in this manner, and it provides a natural, if somewhat artificial, development of the subject.

Another method of classification, and the one basically followed in this book, is to divide business firms on the basis of whether they are *closely held*, that is, whether they have one or a few owners, or *publicly held*, with hundreds or thousands of owners.[1] A major advantage of this approach is that it permits a comparative examination of alternative business forms for closely

---

1. [By the Editor] There is obviously a continuum in the number of owners of businesses. From a technical standpoint, the most useful dividing line between "closely held" and "publicly held" is not some arbitrary number of owners but whether an active market exists for ownership interests in the business, a clear indicia that the business is "publicly held."

held firms. Almost all unincorporated firms are closely held; the new business forms developed in the 1990s currently are suitable only for closely held firms. At the same time many closely held firms do business in corporate form, so that the selection of business form for a closely held firm runs over the gamut of business forms discussed above. In many ways, publicly held firms are quite different. They are virtually all incorporated, and the problems of management, control, economics, and social responsibilities, as well as the legal requirements specifically imposed on them, have little in common with closely held firms. This classification does have disadvantages: First, it ignores the fact that in the real world there is a continuum of business size, complexity, and ownership; it views the world of business basically as polar rather than continuous. Second, it tends to hide the fact that closely and publicly held firms to a surprising extent draw from a common reservoir of principles and tradition, particularly with respect to the use of the corporate form, and each therefore to some extent influences the other.

Developments during the last decade have greatly increased the attractiveness of unincorporated forms of business for closely held firms. The most important of these developments are (1) the universal recognition of new unincorporated business forms that grant the advantage of limited liability for all owners of the business, particularly the limited liability company (or "LLC," as it is usually called), and (2) changes in the Internal Revenue Code income that permit unincorporated firms in effect to elect how they are to be taxed. The net result of these developments is to encourage use of unincorporated business forms for firms with a few owners.

As the immediately preceding paragraph should make clear, trends in the modern law of business associations can be understood only if one has passing familiarity with the modern federal income tax structure. Chapter Three of this casebook provides a basic introduction to this subject for the benefit of students who have little or no exposure to this subject.

B. THE STATUTES

Unlike subjects such as property and torts, the subject of business associations is largely governed by statute. This is true not only in the large commercial states such as New York, Texas, and California but in the smaller states as well. Answers to many but not all questions must be found in the statutes and cannot be answered solely on the basis of common sense. In this respect the law of business associations is similar to many other areas of the law in the modern commercial and government-oriented society.

An experienced attorney does not attempt to memorize the detailed provisions of the numerous complex statutes with which he or she must be familiar. Rather, the attorney becomes generally familiar with the provisions and keeps copies of them available for easy reference. Each student should follow approximately the same process. To encourage this process, the materials that follow refer to but do not quote the basic statutory materials.[2]

---

2. [By the Editor] This statement refers to the basic statutory codification of the model and uniform statutes set forth in the Supplement. Relevant federal statutes and individual statutes of specific states discussed in the text that differ from the uniform or model statutes in the Supplement are quoted in the text or footnotes.

Statutory references should be looked up in the Supplement, since the materials cannot be fully understood without doing so.

The Supplement to this book contains the text of the following statutes:

(1) The Uniform Partnership Act [UPA (1914)].

(2) The Uniform Partnership Act (1994) [UPA (1994)];[3]

(3) The Uniform Limited Partnership Act of 1976 with 1985 amendments [ULPA];[4]

(4) The Uniform Limited Liability Company Act of 1996 [ULLCA];

(5) The Model Business Corporation Act (1984), with amendments through December, 31, 1996 [MBCA];[5] and

(6) The financial provisions of the Model Business Corporation Act of 1969 [MBCA (1969)].[6]

The Supplement briefly describes the background of each of these statutes and gives an indication of the extent of uniformity actually achieved by them.

This book may be used either with the uniform and model statutes in the Supplement or with the statutes of a particular state. If the latter are assigned, it will be necessary to master the numeration of the specific statutes and to locate the most analogous provisions to the model and uniform statutes cited in the following materials. This is "a good thing" since it doubtless will speed your mastery of the statutory materials.

To repeat: A lawyer does not need to memorize the detailed provisions of statutes. Rather, he or she keeps them close at hand, is generally familiar with what is in them, and, most importantly, knows about where in the statutes the specific provision is so that the precise language can be located quickly.

It is particularly important, as you study from this casebook, that you have your copy of the relevant statutes open and at hand.

The statutes in most jurisdictions today are modern, and drawn from the common core of these model and uniform statutes. However, it should not be assumed that statutes always clarify and simplify. In specific circumstances, statutory language may appear to require an unjust or unreasonable result; where this occurs, the statute must be viewed as an obstacle to overcome rather than a rule to be followed. This is probably more likely to be true in jurisdictions that have not drawn from the common core of the model and

---

3. [By the Editor] In some academic commentary, this statute is referred to as the "Revised Uniform Partnership Act" or "RUPA." For example, the Reporters responsible for the development of this statute used this terminology in their semi-official explanation of this statute. See Donald J. Weidner and John W. Larson, The Revised Uniform Partnership Act: The Reporters' Overview, 49 Bus. Law. 1 (1993).

4. [By the Editor] This statute was originally referred to as the "Revised Uniform Limited Partnership Act" (or "RULPA") but was renamed the "Uniform Limited Partnership Act of 1976 with 1985 amendments" in 1985.

5. [By the Editor] This statute was referred to as the "Revised Model Business Corporation Act" (or "RMBCA") until 1987 when it was renamed the "Model Business Corporation Act (1984)." It continues to be referred to as the RMBCA in some academic literature.

6. [By the Editor] Even earlier versions of the Model Business Corporation Act are referred to by following "MBCA" with the date of the edition, e.g. "MBCA (1950)".

uniform statutes, but it is also true in some circumstances under these statutes as well.

C. THE BASIC BUSINESS FORMS

Consider the following simple situation:

A and B are planning to go into the retail furniture business. A will invest $100,000 while B will make no cash contributions but will operate the store on a day-to-day basis. A desires first, assurance that he will not be called upon to increase his investment and second, a veto power over basic decisions made by B in order to protect his investment. Profits are to be divided equally after B is paid a "salary" of $1500 per month.

What is the legal relationship if, without legal advice or any additional discussion, A and B shake hands on the deal, A gives B a check for $100,000 and B proceeds to rent a store, buy stock and commence business?

RESTATEMENT (SECOND) OF AGENCY[7]
§§ 1, 2, 220 (1958).

§ 1. Agency; Principal; Agent

(1) Agency is the fiduciary relation which results from the manifestation of consent by one person to another that the other shall act on his behalf and subject to his control, and consent by the other so to act.

(2) The one for whom action is to be taken is the principal.

(3) The one who is to act is the agent.

§ 2. Master; Servant; Independent Contractor

(1) A master is a principal who employs an agent to perform service in his affairs and who controls or has the right to control the physical conduct of the other in the performance of the service.

(2) A servant is an agent employed by a master to perform service in his affairs whose physical conduct in the performance of the service is controlled or is subject to the right to control by the master.

(3) An independent contractor is a person who contracts with another to do something for him but who is not controlled by the other nor subject to the other's right to control with respect to his physical conduct in the performance of the undertaking. He may or may not be an agent.

§ 220. Definition of Servant

* * * (2) In determining whether one acting for another is a servant or an independent contractor, the following matters of fact, among others, are considered:

(a) the extent of control which, by the agreement, the master may exercise over the details of the work;

7. Copyright 1958 by The American Law   The American Law Institute.
Institute. Reprinted with the permission of

(b) whether or not the one employed is engaged in a distinct occupation or business;

(c) the kind of occupation, with reference to whether, in the locality, the work is usually done under the direction of the employer or by a specialist without supervision;

(d) the skill required in the particular occupation;

(e) whether the employer or the workman supplies the instrumentalities, tools, and the place of work for the person doing the work;

(f) the length of time for which the person is employed;

(g) the method of payment, whether by the time or by the job;

(h) whether or not the work is a part of the regular business of the employer;

(i) whether or not the parties believe they are creating the relation of master and servant; and

(j) whether the principal is or is not in business.

---

(1) A servant, in the foregoing definitions, is not limited to a menial position but includes all relationships usually described as involving "employment." Can the relationship between A and B be analyzed as an "employment" of B by A? What elements are present in the relationship between A and B which are missing in the usual employer-employee relationship? Is B working for another or for himself? Or for both? If B is not A's "servant," can B be viewed as an "independent contractor"?

(2) Is the relationship between A and B that of creditor and debtor? Did A lend B $100,000? Is there, for example, a promise to repay and a repayment date?

(3) Are A and B partners? Consider UPA (1914) §§ 6(1), 7; UPA (1994) § 202. Assuming so, can A be assured that he will not be called upon to increase his investment against his will despite the agreement? Consider the implications of UPA (1914) § 15; UPA (1994) § 306.

(4) Can A be considered a limited partner and B a general partner in a limited partnership? Consider ULPA §§ 101(7), 201, 303(a). However, even assuming that the necessary certificate has been filed in the proper form (see ULPA §§ 201, 206), can the control arrangements desired by A be worked out in light of ULPA § 303? The problem of the limited partner who wished to keep a "hand" in the business (as did A) was even more uncertain under the 1916 Uniform Limited Partnership Act. Section 7 of that Act merely stated "A limited partner shall not become liable as a general partner unless, in addition to the exercise of his rights and powers as a limited partner, he takes part in the control of the business." The bare phrase "takes part in the control of the business" without the enumeration and embroidery of section 303 of ULPA provided little guidance as to what controls a limited partner might safely retain and therefore greatly decreased the attractiveness of the limited partnership form of business, at least from the standpoint of the risk-adverse investor. For a case that dramatically shows the risks that a limited partner

may take when a business turns sour and he tries to save it, see Continental Waste Systems, Inc. v. Zoso Partners, p. 121, infra.

(5) Can A obtain what he desires through the device of a corporation? A corporation is formed by following the relatively simple procedures set forth in the corporation statute. See MBCA §§ 2.01–2.03, 2.05. Section 2.03 states that "the corporate existence begins" upon the filing of articles of incorporation. This language accepts the traditional theory that incorporation results in the creation of a new legal entity, a fictitious person, so to speak. In the above hypothetical, the "corporation" would be liable for business debts of the furniture store and neither A nor B would be liable. The "corporation" might enter into contracts, borrow money, sue and be sued, and otherwise conduct the furniture store business. It may also own real estate in its own name and may own property free and clear of claims of the spouses of A and B or other claims of creditors or shareholders. However, the shares of stock of the corporation owned by the shareholder might be subject to such claims.

A corporation offers advantages in internal management structure over the traditional partnership forms of business enterprise discussed above. Unlike a limited partnership, management powers and limited liability may co-exist in a single individual in a corporation. Theoretically, a corporation consists of three layers or tiers: (1) the shareholders who are traditionally viewed as the ultimate owners of the enterprise, (2) the board of directors, who are the managers of the corporation's affairs (see MBCA § 8.01(b)), and (3) the officers, who act for the corporation to implement the decisions of the directors (compare MBCA § 8.41). A single individual may simultaneously act as an officer, a director, and a shareholder. It is possible, for example, for A and B each to own 50 percent of the shares and to be the directors of the corporation; A may be president of the corporation with power to approve or disapprove of all expenditures, while B may be vice president, secretary, "general manager," and whatever other office the parties desire to create. In this way, profits may be shared equally in the form of dividends without personal liability for corporate obligations, B is entitled to a salary, and A has the veto power he desires. The essentials of the desired control arrangement are therefore achieved.

Of course, in the above hypothetical, a corporation was not actually formed since A and B did not take the simple but essential steps to form a corporation. See MBCA § 2.02.

(6) Can A and B form a limited liability company for their furniture store enterprise? See ULLCA § 112. Like a limited partnership or a corporation, an LLC is formed by filing a document with a state official. See ULLCA §§ 202, 203. A major difference between an LLC and a traditional corporation is that the LLC has much greater internal flexibility than a corporation. An LLC may be "member managed," and operated much as though it were a partnership but without personal liability, or as "manager managed" much as though it were a corporation. See ULLCA §§ 203(a)(6), 301, 404. Again, of course, an LLC was not actually formed in the above hypothetical since A and B did not take the simple but essential steps to form an LLC.

(7) Assuming that A and B have entered into an informal partnership as they shake hands on the deal, may they thereafter elect to be a limited liability partnership (LLP)? See UPA (1994) §§ 1001–1003, 306(c), 101(5). If

they do make this election, how does an LLP differ from a general partnership? From a limited partnership? Compare ULPA §§ 303, 403.

(8) A final new type of business form, a limited liability limited partnership (LLLP) is a limited partnership that has elected to be an LLP for the benefit and protection of its general partners.

Notes

(1) The general partnership is the default form for businesses that are owned by more than one person. In other words, a partnership is formed if two or more persons go into a co-owned business without any thought or planning or understanding of what the relationship is. All other business forms require some planning and an official filing of some kind. Many general partnerships, of course, are also carefully planned, formal affairs with a professionally drafted written partnership agreement which contains explicit provisions dealing with most aspects of the relationship.

(2) A relevant question is why has the American legal system developed so many unincorporated business forms that appear to be to some extent overlapping, repetitious, and redundant? There is no simple answer to this question, but the following comments may shed some light.

(a) First of all, the proliferation of overlapping business forms is a very recent development. Until the late 1980s the only business forms generally available were the general partnership, the limited partnership, and the corporation. LLC statutes in most states were enacted between 1990 and 1994 following a favorable tax ruling in 1988. The LLP was first introduced in Texas in 1991 and other states quickly adopted the concept. The LLLP was introduced in 1993 but has received less than universal acceptance.

(b) The development of these new unincorporated business forms in the 1990s obviously reflects dissatisfaction with the traditional business forms. Aspects of this dissatisfaction are discussed in chapter 3; they relate to federal income tax rules; state income and franchise taxes; state filing fees; differences in managerial rules applicable to various business forms; and ethical limitations that many states impose on lawyers, physicians, and other professionals. Also contributing were tax and accounting rules that made it difficult and expensive to convert an ongoing business from one business form to another.

(c) Because the development of new business forms has occurred so recently, future developments are difficult to predict. It may be that some forms may become obsolete or used only rarely; it may be that practices and usages will develop differently in one state than in another. Indeed the whole area today is in a state of flux.

(3) As is described at length in later chapters of this book, there is a great deal of law relating to closely held corporations that has potential applicability by analogy to unincorporated business forms that provide for limited liability and permit the concentration of management in some but not all the owners. These include doctrines such as "piercing the corporate veil" (Chapter 6) and fiduciary duties arising from the power to manage (Chapter 8). However, there is virtually no law relating to the newer forms of unincorporated business entities and there is no way to know in advance whether these corporate doctrines will be applied to unincorporated business forms that have characteristics similar to those of a corporation.

In late 1996, the Internal Revenue Service promulgated its "check the box" regulations[8] that make the income tax treatment of unincorporated business forms virtually elective and independent of the specific business form chosen. These regulations may lead to a "shake out" of unincorporated business forms as federal income taxation becomes a less important factor in their selection. "Check the box" may also discourage the use of closely held corporations and encourage the use of unincorporated business forms that provide for limited liability and centralized management. Chapter 3 discusses "check the box" as part of an introduction to federal income tax rules generally.

Complicating all these matters further, is the fact that it is possible to utilize combinations of business forms to own and manage a single business, thereby creating novel combinations of characteristics. The most common combination, discussed in chapter 3, is a limited partnership in which the sole general partner is a corporation or limited liability company and the limited partners are either inactive investors or shareholders of the corporate general partner. If the corporate general partner has only relatively nominal assets, a de facto limited liability entity has been created for all investors in a limited partnership. One also sometimes sees a limited partnership in which the sole general partner is another limited partnership which has a corporation or limited liability company as its sole general partner. The reasons for creating these complex multi-tiered businesses are usually economic or business concerns.[9]

D. ROLE OF THE LAW OF AGENCY IN BUSINESS ASSOCIATIONS

Many problems that arise in connection with business associations involve simple and direct application of principles of agency. Assume, for example, that B decides it is necessary to hire a third person, C, to assist him in running the store. One of C's principal duties is to be the sales person in charge of the store when B cannot be present. C also is to be a truck driver, assembler of furniture, and so forth. C is paid a salary based on the number of hours he works each week. Is C a "servant"? If so, who is his "master"? A? B? The AB Furniture Store? The answer is "the partnership." See UPA (1994) § 201.[10]

8. [By the Editor] 26 C.F.R. § 301.7701–1 et seq. (effective January 1, 1997).

9. [By the Editor] For example, if one assumes that both the "operating" limited partnership and the "managing" limited partnership raise capital by selling limited partnership interests, the economic risks to the investors in the "managing" limited partnership are entirely different than the risks of investors in the "operating" limited partnership. Because the two investments are attractive to investors with different objectives, it is possible that the venture may be able to raise more capital than if it were a single limited partnership.

10. [By the Editor] It may be noted that UPA (1914) does not contain a provision simi-

lar to UPA (1994) § 201. Earlier this century, most courts viewed a partnership as an aggregate of the individual partners and not an entity in its own right, but more recent cases generally accept the entity approach. Admittedly, at first blush, it may be difficult to conceptualize an informal, hand-shake partnership such as the AB Furniture Store as an entity distinct from the individual partners. However, if one examines carefully the provisions of UPA (1914) it is apparent that there are many entity concepts embodied in that statute. See e.g. UPA (1914) § 18(b)["*the partnership* must indemnify *every partner*"]; § 9(1)[each partner is an "agent of *the partnership*"].

A major question is whether C's "master," the AB Furniture Store, is liable for a variety of possible problems created by C's activities: contracts entered into by C in the name of the AB Furniture Store, injuries caused by C's negligence, liability for C's intentional torts committed in the course of his employment, and so forth. Such questions are usually thought of as involving primarily agency principles that are not dependent on whether the AB Furniture Store is doing business as a proprietorship, partnership, limited partnership, limited liability company, or corporation. Other questions also addressed by the law of agency include whether C may be personally liable to persons with whom he dealt on behalf of the AB Furniture Store, whether the AB Furniture Store may enforce promises or commitments made by third persons to C, and whether AB Furniture Store may sue C if C is disloyal or disobeys instructions so that the store becomes liable to a third person as a result of C's unauthorized activities.

Many law students are not exposed to a systematic analysis of agency principles during the first year of law school. For the benefit of such students, Appendix One (pages 1098–1110, infra) sets forth a brief introduction to agency principles. If you are uncertain about the answers to the questions set forth in the preceding paragraph or the following notes, you should read this chapter carefully.

Notes

Under the agency principles described in the appendix, what is the responsibility of the AB Furniture Store if—

(a) C is the "office manager" who, contrary to specific instructions, buys 10 variety tables from a visiting "manufacturer's rep"?

(b) C is the delivery truck operator who negligently runs into a pedestrian while delivering furniture? Does it make any difference whether C is normally a careful driver and whether the store owners investigated his driving record before hiring him?

(c) C is the store's "security officer" who wrongly accuses X of being a shoplifter and holds X against his will for an hour until the police arrive?

E. THE CORPORATION AS A "PERSON"

A corporation has been treated as an entity separate and distinct from its owners for centuries. Indeed, in England, acceptance of the concept that a corporation is an entity separate from its shareholders or members long antedates the development of limited liability for shareholders, which occurred in the middle of the nineteenth century. Consult Phillip I. Blumberg, The Law of Corporate Groups: Procedural Law 1–2 (1983). It is a short step from this acceptance of the corporation to its further reification as an "artificial person," with many of the rights and privileges of individuals. In the United States, this reification has led to the corporation being given many of the constitutional protections available to flesh-and-blood individuals. As described by Justice Sandra Day O'Connor:

> In the words of Chief Justice Marshall, a corporation is "an artificial being, invisible, intangible, and existing only in contemplation of law." *Dartmouth College v. Woodward*, 4 Wheat. 518, 636, 4 L.Ed. 629 (1819).

As such, it is not entitled to " 'purely personal' guarantees" whose " 'historic function' . . . has been limited to the protection of individuals." *First National Bank of Boston v. Bellotti,* 435 U.S. 765, 779, n. 14, 98 S.Ct. 1407, 1417, n. 14, 55 L.Ed.2d 707 (1978). Thus, a corporation has no Fifth Amendment privilege against self-incrimination, *Wilson v. United States,* 221 U.S. 361, 31 S.Ct. 538, 55 L.Ed. 771 (1911), or right to privacy, *United States v. Morton Salt Co.,* 338 U.S. 632, 70 S.Ct. 357, 94 L.Ed. 401 (1950). On the other hand, a corporation has a First Amendment right to freedom of speech, *Virginia Pharmacy Bd. v. Virginia Citizens Consumer Council, Inc.,* 425 U.S. 748, 96 S.Ct. 1817, 48 L.Ed.2d 346 (1976), and cannot have its property taken without just compensation, *Penn Central Transportation Co. v. New York City,* 438 U.S. 104, 98 S.Ct. 2646, 57 L.Ed.2d 631 (1978). A corporation is also protected from unreasonable searches and seizures, *Marshall v. Barlow's, Inc.,* 436 U.S. 307, 98 S.Ct. 1816, 56 L.Ed.2d 305 (1978), and can plead former jeopardy as a bar to a prosecution, *United States v. Martin Linen Supply Co.,* 430 U.S. 564, 97 S.Ct. 1349, 51 L.Ed.2d 642 (1977). Furthermore, a corporation is entitled to due process, *Helicopteros Nacionales de Colombia v. Hall,* 466 U.S. 408, 104 S.Ct. 1868, 80 L.Ed.2d 404 (1984), and equal protection, *Metropolitan Life Ins. Co. v. Ward,* 470 U.S. 869, 105 S.Ct. 1676, 84 L.Ed.2d 751 (1985), of law.

Whether a particular constitutional guarantee applies to corporations "depends on the nature, history, and purpose" of the guarantee. First National Bank, 435 U.S., at 779, n. 14, 98 S.Ct., at 1417, n. 14. * * *

Browning–Ferris Industries of Vermont, Inc. v. Kelco Disposal, Inc., 492 U.S. 257, 284–85, 109 S.Ct. 2909, 2925, 106 L.Ed.2d 219, 244 (1989) (concurring in part and dissenting in part). See also Elizabeth S. Warren, The Case for Applying the Eighth Amendment to Corporations, 49 Vand.L.Rev. 1313 (1996); Charles D. Watts, Jr., Corporate Legal Theory Under the First Amendment: *Bellotti* and *Austin,* 46 U.Miami L.Rev. 317 (1991).

This approach should not disguise the true nature of a corporation. Consider W. Hohfeld, Fundamental Legal Conceptions 197 (1923):

> Strangely enough, it has not always been perceived with perfect clearness that transacting business under the forms, methods, and procedure pertaining to so-called corporations is simply another mode by which *individuals* or *natural persons* can enjoy their property and engage in business. Just as several individuals may transact business collectively as partners, so they may as members of a corporation—the corporation being nothing more than an association of such individuals. * * *

Hohfeld represented the "realist" approach toward law that was popular before World War II. Despite the general recognition and usefulness of the entity theory (and the almost irresistible temptation to reify the corporation in specific contexts), the fictional nature of this approach should be recognized, as Hohfeld suggests.

F. OTHER THEORIES OF CORPORATENESS: THE "NEXUS OF CONTRACTS" THEORY

Many commentators have speculated on the proper way to analyze a corporation. "[W]hat is the nature of a corporation?" Professor Alfred Conard writes. "Is it a fund of property, a band of investors, a crew of workers, a place, an entry in official records, or a mere figment of legislative and judicial imaginations? What principle of justice grants it the same capacities to sue and be sued, to convey and to receive conveyances, to promise and receive promises, to trespass and be trespassed against, as a free and mature human individual?" Alfred F. Conard, Corporations in Perspective 416 (1976). These possible approaches appear to be more suitable for a publicly held corporation with many shareholders and employees than a corporation with only a few shareholders.

The economist has evolved a unique and increasingly important theory of corporateness that permits analysis of the corporation within the confines of that discipline, and harks back to the realism of Hohfeld, but rejects the notion that the shareholders are the ultimate owners of the enterprise.

STEPHEN M. BAINBRIDGE, BOOK REVIEW: COMMUNITY AND STATISM: A CONSERVATIVE CONTRACTARIAN CRITIQUE OF PROGRESSIVE CORPORATE LAW SCHOLARSHIP
82 Cornell L. Rev. 856, 859–70 (1997).

* * * Most law and economics scholars embrace a model of business organizations known as the "nexus-of-contracts theory of the firm." These so-called "contractarians" model the firm not as a single entity, but as an aggregate of various inputs acting together with the common goal of producing goods or services. Employees provide labor. Creditors provide debt capital. Shareholders provide equity capital, bear the risk of losses, and monitor the performance of management.[11] Management monitors the performance of employees and coordinates the activities of all the firm's inputs. The firm is simply a legal fiction representing the complex set of contractual relationships between these inputs. In other words, the firm is not an individual thing, but rather a nexus or web of explicit and implicit contracts establishing rights and obligations among the various inputs making up the firm. * * *

The nexus of contracts model has important implications for a range of corporate law topics, the most obvious of which is the debate over the proper role of mandatory legal rules. Contractarians contend that corporate law is generally comprised of default rules, from which shareholders are free to depart, rather than mandatory rules. As a normative matter, contractarians argue that this is just as it should be.[12]

* * * Douglas Branson rejects this contractarian view and argues instead

11. [By the Author] * * * [N]exus-of-contracts theory rejects traditional entity-based theories. Because shareholders are simply one of the inputs bound together by the web of voluntary agreements, ownership should not be a particularly meaningful concept in nexus-of-contracts theory. Someone owns each input, but no one owns the totality. Instead, the corporation is an aggregation of people bound together by a complex web of contractual relationships. The contractarian account thus rests not on an out-moded reification of the corpora-

tion, but on the presumption of validity a free market society accords voluntary contracts. [This footnote has been moved from another portion of Professor Bainbridge's text.]

12. [By the Author] See, e.g., Frank H. Easterbrook & Daniel R. Fischel, The Economic Structure of Corporate Law 15 (1991); Larry E. Ribstein, The Mandatory Nature of the ALI Code, 61 Geo. Wash. L. Rev. 984, 989–91 (1993).

that mandatory rules pervade corporate law.[13] This attack is far from fatal. In the first instance, most contractarians probably regard the theory's normative claim as being the more important of the two. As such, we cheerfully concede the existence of mandatory rules, while deploring that unfortunate fact. In the second, as Bernard Black persuasively argues, many mandatory corporate law rules are trivial in nature.[14] Finally, nontrivial mandatory rules are often subject to evasion by choice of form and jurisdiction. Thus, the progressives' focus on mandatory legal rules is little more than a red herring.[15] * * *

* * * William Bratton's essay[16] * * * [argues] that the nexus-of-contracts model "has a significant shortcoming" in that it "gives us ex ante contracts across-the-board and thereby makes corporate governance entirely contractual without providing a description of the process by which corporate actors make contracts." Here we confront the distinction between actual and hypothetical bargaining. Contractarians concede, or at least should concede, that actual bargaining over rules such as limited liability is precluded by transaction cost barriers, but they contend that this is precisely why corporate statutes provide a set of off-the-rack rules amounting to a standard-form contract.

If transaction costs are zero, the substantive content of a corporate law rule does not matter greatly. If, for example, the law imposed full personal liability on shareholders, but limited liability is the efficient rule, shareholders and creditors would contract around the rule through private bargaining. In the face of transaction costs, however, the rule's substantive content begins to matter very much. Indeed, if transaction costs are high, bargaining around

---

13. [By the Author] Douglas M. Branson, The Death of Contractarianism and the Vindication of Structure and Authority in Corporate Governance and Corporate Law, published in Progressive Corporate Law (Lawrence E. Mitchell ed., 1995) 94–5.

14. [By the Author] Bernard S. Black, Is Corporate Law Trivial?: A Political and Economic Analysis, 84 Nw. U. L. Rev. 542 passim (1990). The triviality argument provides a partial response to William Bratton's observation that most contractarian scholars do not propose a sweeping repeal of mandatory fiduciary duties. Bratton attributes this failure to "doubts about both contractarian assumptions and their underlying ethical presuppositions." William W. Bratton, Game Theory and the Restoration of Honor to Corporate Law's Duty of Loyalty, in Progressive Corporate Law, supra note 1, at 139, 152. Yet, the contractarian position on mandatory fiduciary duties may simply indicate a belief that such rules are subject to evasion through choice of form or, to the extent that some duties appear across the spectrum of possible organizational forms, that they are trivial in the sense that they embody rules virtually everyone would demand in the event of actual bargaining. * * *

15. [By the Editor] Corporation statutes are studded with provisions that are mandatory and cannot be modified by contract among the participants. As Professor Black argues, many of them are trivial, but some are not. See, for example, MBCA §§ 8.03(b),

16.02(d); John A. MacKerron, A Taxonomy of the Revised Model Business Corporation Act, 61 U.M.K.C.L.Rev. 663 (1993). Further, the federal securities laws, and particularly the regulations promulgated by the Securities and Exchange Commission under them, contain literally thousands of significant mandatory rules with respect to disclosure, insider trading, proxy solicitations, and other subjects. Economic theorists may of course respond that such mandatory provisions are archaic and should be eliminated. However, some may accept the idea that some mandatory regulation may be necessary even under the "nexus of contracts" approach. The latter appears to be the position taken in Frank H. Easterbrook and Daniel R. Fischel, The Corporate Contract, 89 Colum. L. Rev. 1416 (1989), though it is unlikely that those authors would accept the types of mandatory regulation currently being imposed. A revised version of this article appears as chapter 1 of Frank H. Easterbrook and Daniel R. Fischel, The Economic Structure of Corporate Law (1991). See generally Symposium, Contractual Freedom in Corporate Law, 89 Colum. L. Rev. 1395 (1989); William W. Bratton, The "Nexus of Contracts" Corporation: A Critical Appraisal, 74 Cornell L. Rev. 407 (1989).

16. [By the Editor] William W. Bratton, Game Theory and the Restoration of Honor to Corporate Law's Duty of Loyalty, in Progressive Corporate Law, supra at 139, 152.

the rule becomes wholly impractical, forcing the parties to live with an inefficient rule. Because the public corporation setting gives rise to prohibitively high transaction costs, parties cannot depend on private contracting to achieve efficient outcomes. Instead, a legally-imposed rule must function as a substitute for private bargaining. Identifying the party for whom getting one's way has the highest value thus becomes the critical question. In effect, corporate legal scholars ask: " 'If the parties could costlessly bargain over the question, which rule would they adopt?' "[17] By imposing a rule to which parties would agree if they could bargain, society facilitates private ordering. * * *

Contractarians treat the corporation's organic rules as if they arose through the trading of rights and duties among the corporation's various constituencies and, accordingly, treat those rules as though they represent a bargain in which claims on the corporation were sold to their highest-valuing user. The bargains struck will vary from firm to firm, depending on a variety of factors, including the risk preferences of each of the firm's constituencies and the thickness of the markets in which the bargain is struck. Because the various contracts making up the firm thus differ little from contracts created through voluntary exchange, they enjoy a presumption in their favor, and ought to be enforced in the same way other mutually beneficial contracts are enforced.

Lawrence Mitchell rejects the contractarian account because the corporation's constituencies do not and cannot bargain:

> The idea that the bylaws of a public corporation were somehow bargained for by the stockholders in a manner that can be said to give rise to intent is troubling. In the first place, most public corporation stockholders have never read the corporation's bylaws, if they even are aware of their existence. While it is possible to argue that the stockholders should have read the bylaws, to which they became bound by their purchasing stock, this in no way suggests any sort of bargaining process that gives rise to mutual intent. At best they can be said to have accepted the bylaws as one characteristic of the entire corporation, within the context of corporate laws holding that directors are fiduciaries of the corporation and its stockholders.[18]

This argument fundamentally misconceives the contractarian project by ignoring the distinction between outcome and process bargaining. A bargain can be understood in two distinct ways: as a process, which is how Mitchell appears to understand it, or as an outcome. As Mitchell correctly notes, there is no bargaining process between a shareholder and the public corporations in which he invests. But there is an outcome—the set of organic rules contained in the articles and bylaws as drafted by the corporation's founders or directors—that can fairly be described as a bargain. A bargain involving only an outcome is just as much a contract as a bargain involving both a process and an outcome. * * *

---

17. [By the Author] * * * As I have argued elsewhere, a rule of limited liability plausibly emerges from this hypothetical bargaining process.

18. [By the Author] * * * Lawrence E. Mitchell, Trust, Contract, Process, in Progressive Corporate Law, supra at 185, 186–187.

HENRY N. BUTLER, THE CONTRACTUAL THEORY OF THE CORPORATION

11 Geo. Mason U.L.Rev. 99, 100–123 (Summer 1989).

The contractual theory of the corporation is in stark contrast to the legal concept of the corporation as an entity created by the state. The entity theory of the corporation supports state intervention—in the form of either direct regulation or the facilitation of shareholder litigation—in the corporation on the ground that the state created the corporation by granting it a charter. The contractual theory views the corporation as founded in private contract, where the role of the state is limited to enforcing contracts. In this regard, a state charter merely recognizes the existence of a "nexus of contracts" called a corporation. Each contract in the "nexus of contracts" warrants the same legal and constitutional protections as other legally enforceable contracts. Moreover, freedom of contract requires that parties to the "nexus of contracts" must be allowed to structure their relations as they desire.

The contractual theory of the corporation should be of practical as well as academic interest. * * * Recently, corporation law scholars antagonistic to the contractual theory have adopted the methodology and terminology of the contractual theory, but have misapplied it in a way that reaches contrary policy positions. * * * [T]hese mistakes might be due to something other than a mere misunderstanding of the contractual theory[.] * * *

It is reasonable to assume that the parties to the nexus of contracts that form a firm anticipate the numerous problems associated with specialization, delegation, team production, and agency relationships. Freedom of contract allows the parties to structure their relations in a manner that ameliorates most of the agency problems inherent in the large corporation. * * *

[T]he contractual theory of the corporation offers a new perspective on the corporation and the role of corporation law. The corporation is in no sense a ward of the state; it is, rather, the product of contracts among the owners and others. Once this point is fully recognized by the state legislators and legal commentators, the corporate form may finally be free of unnecessary and intrusive legal chains.

Notes

(1) Professor Bainbridge begins his article with the claim that "[o]ver the last few decades, law and economics scholars have mounted a largely successful hostile takeover of the corporate legal academy." He states:

> The law and economics movement remains the most successful example of intellectual arbitrage in the history of corporate jurisprudence. It is virtually impossible to find serious corporate law scholarship that is not informed by economic analysis. Even those corporate law scholars who reject economic analysis spend most of their time responding to those of us who practice it * * *. Perhaps the most telling evidence of the success of law and economics in our field, however, is that many leading corporate law judges and lawyers now rely upon economic analysis extensively. Both judicial opinions and practitioner publications are filled with the jargon of law and economics. This is a claim no other modern school of jurisprudence can make.

82 Cornell L.Rev., at 857. In a subsequent letter Professor Bainbridge qualifies somewhat this broad claim of success ("in retrospect, I probably should have limited my 'victory' comments to the law review/law school context") but adds a new and stronger claim: "[L]aw and economics is also taking over the law schools. My sense is that it is getting very hard to get a job as a corporate law teacher without having a law and economics background. At least this seems to be true among the 'top' schools." Letter to Robert W. Hamilton, dated August 19, 1997, at 6.

(2) Consider an investor who purchases 100 shares of General Motors Co. common stock in a transaction executed on the New York Stock Exchange. In what sense has that investor entered into a contract with General Motors in order to become part of that "nexus of contracts?" If "contract" is understood in its normal legal sense, it seems clear that she has not. See Victor Brudney, Corporate Governance, Agency Costs, And The Rhetoric Of Contract, 85 Colum.L.Rev. 1403, 1412 (1985):[19]

> It stretches the concept "contract" beyond recognition to use it to describe either the process of bargaining or the arrangements between investors of publicly held corporations and either theoretical owners first going public or corporate management. Scattered stockholders cannot, and do not, negotiate with owners who go public (or with management—either executives or directors) over hiring managers, over the terms of their employment, or over their retention.

See Jeffrey n. Gordon, The Mandatory Structure of Corporate Law, 89 Colum.L.Rev. 1549–50 (1989):[20]

> [T]he economists' conception of a "contract" as an arrangement between two or more actors supported by reciprocal expectations and behavior is far broader than the lawyer's conception, which focuses on the existence of judicially cognizable duties and obligations. Thus the lawyer, but not the economist, will pay particularly close attention to the indicia of contract formation—offer and acceptance, an exchange of promises—ideally reflected in an explicit bargaining process. This difference in perspective becomes acute in the case of an "implied" contract. To a lawyer, an implied contract is one that does not actually exist, but because of some overriding principle of justice is judicially enforceable nonetheless. To an economist, an implied contract is one that is enforced through marketplace mechanisms such as reputation effects rather than in a court, a means of enforcement that may not bring relief to the aggrieved party but will over time penalize parties who welsh.

(3) As should be evident from the tenor of Professor Butler's analysis, proponents of the "nexus of contracts" analysis are strong believers in laissez faire, the absence of governmental regulation of or intervention in economic activity. Indeed, the "nexus of contracts" appears to be a proprietary invention of laissez faire economists. Suggestions that even if the corporation is viewed as a "nexus of contracts" there may be problems because some parties to these contracts may lack full cognition and volition about risks and benefits, or that the relationships within a large corporation may not successfully prevent self-aggrandizing behavior by managers, are sternly rejected: In the words of Professor Butler, "[r]ecently, corporation-law scholars antagonistic to the contractual theory

---

19. This article originally appeared at 85 Colum.L.Rev. 1403 (1985). Reprinted by permission.

20. This article originally appeared at 89 Colum.L.Rev. 1549 (1989). Reprinted by permission.

have adopted the methodology and terminology of the contractual theory, but have misapplied it in a way that reaches contrary policy positions." Henry N. Butler, The Contractual Theory of the Corporation, 11 Geo. Mason U.L.Rev. 99, 100 (Summer 1989). Good examples of "misapplications" to reach a "contrary policy position" are Marleen O'Connor, Restructuring the Corporation's Nexus of Contracts: Recognizing a Fiduciary Duty to Protect Displaced Workers, 69 N.C.L.Rev. 1189 (1991); Marleen O'Connor, The Human Capital Era: Reconceptualizing Corporate Law to Facilitate Labor–Management Cooperation, 79 Cornell L.Rev. 899 (1993). Professor Bainbridge describes the book he was reviewing as containing many articles that "claim to sound in economic theory * * * [but] deny contractarianism's validity and/or its utility as an economic model." 82 Cornell L.Rev., at 858.

(4) For a generally critical appraisal of the usefulness of the "nexus of contracts" theory as a basis for determining public policy, see Robert W. Hamilton, Business Organizations: Unincorporated Businesses and Close Corporations, § 8.6 (1997). For an interesting effort to apply the theory to establish the importance of worker involvement in management, see Stephen M. Bainbridge, Participatory Management Within a Theory of the Firm, 21 J.Corp.L. 857 (1996). For criticisms of the theory within the context of "law and economics" generally, see Michael Klausner, Corporations, Corporate Law, and Networks of Contracts, 81 Va.L.Rev. 757 (1995); G.T. Garvey and P.L. Swan, The Economics of Corporate Governance: Beyond the Marshallian Firm, 1 J.Corp.Fin. 139 (1994).

(5) The notion that a corporation should be viewed essentially as contractual in nature is not original with the economic theorists of the late Twentieth Century. The corporate charter was viewed as a "contract" between the state and the corporation in the famous Dartmouth College case in 1819 (Trustees of Dartmouth College v. Woodward, 17 U.S. (4 Wheat.) 518, 4 L.Ed. 629 (1819)). The conclusion reached in that case was that this contract could not be unilaterally amended by New Hampshire since that would constitute an unconstitutional impairment of contract in violation of Section 10 of Article I of the United States Constitution. By the middle of the Twentieth Century this "contract" analysis had been modified into a tripartite analysis: the corporate charter was not only a contract between the corporation and the state but also a contract between the corporation and its shareholders and a contract among the shareholders themselves. These modifications of a "contract" theory arose because of the general recognition that many rights of shareholders may be modified by agreement, traditionally embodied in provisions in articles of incorporation.

(6) *Trustees of Dartmouth College* appears at first blush to prohibit all amendments to state corporation statutes from affecting already-formed corporations. This result has been largely avoided by the practice of including reservations of the power to amend in virtually all general corporation statutes enacted after 1819. For a modern example of a reservation of power to amend see MBCA § 1.02. Mr. Justice Story originally suggested in the *Dartmouth College* case that such a provision—or rather such a provision in a charter granted directly by the legislature—would avoid the application of Section 10 of Article I of the Constitution.

Chapter Two

THE PARTNERSHIP

A. THE NEED FOR A WRITTEN AGREEMENT

Returning to the furniture store partnership between A and B referred to in Chapter 1, let us assume that the business is to be conducted as a partnership. Is it necessary for A and B to enter into a written agreement? If not, is it desirable for them to do so?

One major advantage of having a written agreement is that it may avoid future disagreements over what the arrangement actually was. It avoids litigation similar to that involved in Fulbright v. Culbertson, 429 S.W.2d 179, 182 (Tex.Civ.App.1968), where the Court stated:

> The case on appeal exhibits an example of a situation where two persons have entered into a "relationship" without any clearly defined understanding of either as to duties, if any, of one to the other, or rights, if any, of one against the other.

Second, a written agreement is readily proved in court while proof of an oral agreement may involve substantial factual controversy. Third, a written agreement may focus attention on potential trouble spots in the relationship which may be unnoticed if the partners proceed on a "handshake" deal. Fourth, the Internal Revenue Code treatment of partnerships permits partners by agreement to allocate the tax burdens among themselves within limits, and a written agreement is clearly desirable where advantage of such provisions is taken. Fifth, UPA (1914) and UPA (1994) both contemplate that upon the death or retirement of a partner, the business is either to be disposed of or the interest of the deceased partner is to be purchased by the partnership or by the other partners. It is usually sensible for the partners to agree on what should happen in advance of such an event, and such provisions should be in writing since they may affect surviving spouses, executors, heirs, and others who are strangers to the agreement and are unfamiliar with their rights. Sixth, a partner may wish to lend rather than contribute specific property to a partnership. A written agreement clearly identifying which property is contributed and which is loaned is necessary to protect the partner's interest in the loaned property. Seventh, where real estate is to be contributed as partnership property or the agreement includes a term of more than one year, a written agreement may be necessary to comply with the statute of frauds. In Gano v. Jamail, 678 S.W.2d 152 (Tex.App.1984), for example, Gano claimed that he was made a partner by oral agreement in Jamail's one-person law practice in 1969 on a fifty percent participation basis; the firm was thereafter known as "Jamail and Gano." In 1978, Jamail terminated the arrangement, and Gano brought suit on the alleged partnership agreement; he lost because of the one-year provision of the statute of frauds, the court accepting the argument that the firm "was involved almost exclusively in a personal injury practice in which cases were based on contingent fee contracts, and almost always took more than a year to conclude," and the agreement contemplated that the partnership was to last until all of the cases signed up during the partnership were resolved. (678 S.W.2d, at 154) Finally, a written partnership agreement is advantageous to the attorney: not only may it justify a higher fee but also it places suggestions and advice in concrete form so that there is less possibility of misunderstanding.

Even though the advantages of a written agreement are undeniably substantial, it should be recognized that many successful partnerships have operated for years without a written agreement. Included within this group are many law partnerships.

B. SHARING OF PROFITS AND LOSSES

One important non-tax issue is how the profits and losses of the business are to be shared. In the absence of agreement, how are profits and losses shared? See UPA (1914) § 18(a); UPA (1994) § 401(b). Does it make any difference if the partners contributed unequal amounts of capital? See Dunn v. Summerville, 669 S.W.2d 319 (Tex.1984).

Profits of a business may be divided by agreement in numerous possible ways including:

(a) The partners may share on a flat percentage basis without regard to any other factor. Profit sharing ratios for each partner may be established in the partnership agreement itself. They may also be established by issuing "partnership units" to each partner and determining the profit-or loss-sharing ratio for each partner by dividing the number of units owned by that partner by the total number of units outstanding. In this way, if new partners are added dilution of existing interests occurs automatically without any need to amend the agreement; if old partners depart without new ones being added the remaining interests are also automatically concentrated. Partnership units also permit the creation of incentive options or unit appreciation rights that permit successful partners to increase their percentage interest in the firm.

(b) One or more partners may be entitled to a fixed weekly or monthly "salary." This payment may be treated as a "cost" and subtracted before the "profit" is computed for division on some other basis, or it may be considered an advance to be credited against the amount the partner is otherwise entitled to after division of the profit. In the latter case, the agreement should consider the responsibility of the partner receiving the "salary" if the "salary" exceeds the actual profit allocable to him or her during any period.

(c) The partners may share on a percentage basis, with the percentages recomputed each year on the basis of the average amount invested in the business during the year by each partner. This type of arrangement is appropriate where the business is largely dependent on capital for generation of income.

(d) The partners may share on a percentage basis, with the percentages recomputed each year on the basis of total income, the sales or billings by each partner, time devoted to the business, or on the basis of some other factor.

(e) In large partnerships, each partner may be entitled to a fixed percentage applied against perhaps 80 percent of the income. The remaining 20 percent is allocated among the junior partners as a form of incentive compensation by a committee of senior partners on the basis of productivity, billings, or some other factor. Usually committee members are not themselves eligible to share in the "incentive pie."

(f) The agreement may remain silent on the division of profits, it being contemplated each year that the partners will work out the division of profits by agreement on a mutually acceptable basis.

The division of profits is, of course, basically a function of the relative bargaining power of each partner. An attorney may be helpful in suggesting techniques to divide the income on a reasonable basis which may not have occurred to the partners. Also, he or she may be able to formulate precisely the vague ideas that the partners may have expressed as to how profits should be shared.

In what types of business would the various ways of sharing profits described above be most appropriate?

Assume that in ABC Law Firm, A is responsible for bringing 70% of the year's business to the firm. As the principal business-getter, A spends most of his time entertaining potential clients on the local golf course so that his office time billed to clients constitutes only 10% of the total. B brings 30% of the business and her time billings constitute 35% of the total. C brought no business to the firm, but handled the bulk (55%) of the actual legal work. What formula might be used to divide the year's profits? Or might it be better not to have a fixed formula, and negotiate the division of the pie each year? (As a matter of political power in a small law firm, A in such a situation is likely to have the predominant voice in any such negotiation, and C the smallest voice.)

DENIS ORME, PAYING PARTNERS FOR NEW BUSINESS: AN EQUITABLE LAW FIRM PARTNER COMPENSATION SCHEME
70 A.B.A.J. 60 (Dec. 1984).[1]

In recent years, possibly because of economic pressure, law firms have begun to swing away from lock-step systems of partner compensation. Less emphasis is being placed on tenure and seniority, and more consideration is being given to merit performance and attraction of new business.

In a true partnership all income derived from the practice of law goes first to the firm and then is divided among the members on the basis of

1. Reprinted with permission from the ABA Journal, The Lawyer's Magazine.

individual performance, which is a measure of the individual's contribution to the prosperity of the firm. A generally accepted principle is that not all partners are equal in income distribution.

An equitable partner compensation system should divide profits primarily according to a partner's percentage of equity ownership in the firm, but it also should set apart a portion of profits into a "bonus pool" to be distributed according to new business brought in.

Compensation Factors

Among the various compensation schemes several factors govern the size of individual allocations. The following are perhaps the most common:

● **Productivity and billable hours.** Given that all partners achieve a threshold level of performance, special recognition should be given to those who regularly contribute the most billed and collected hours.

● **New business.** If a partner's activities produce new business for the firm, the compensation scheme should give that partner credit. This credit usually is a percentage of the total fees generated by the new business. The credit continues for a predetermined time period.

● **Client liaison.** Recognition should be given to efforts to retain the larger clients, although those efforts may not produce discernible, tangible results.

● **Practice economics.** Credit should be given to such efforts as client matter planning and control, prompt billing, accounts receivable follow-up and cash collection, fees received from clients, other fees directly resulting from partners' work, profitability by type of law, avoiding write-offs and overhead control.

● **Management, administration, training and supervision.** Recognition should be given for effective work delegation, supervision and good staff relations. Those contributions are hard to quantify, but they are essential to a true partnership.

● **Marketing advancement.** This includes firm promotion, enhancement of the firm's public and professional image and the pursuit of specific marketing opportunities.

A starting point in choosing a compensation scheme is to decide which factors to use and their relative weight. Regardless of which method is chosen, the goal is to arrive at a plan that will enable the partners to deal fairly with each other and to let them work together without friction.

Notes

(1) Reginald Heber Smith, a Boston lawyer, wrote extensively on compensation schemes within firms. He developed a rather mechanical "value produced" system that weighted three major factors: (a) productivity and billable hours, (b) the development of new business ("rainmaking") and (c) practice management, which included client liaison and the various other miscellaneous contributions to the firm bulleted in the Orme excerpt. He suggested that total compensation of each individual partner should be based 50–70 percent on productivity, 30 percent on rainmaking, and 0–30 percent on the less tangible contributions of practice management. While many law firms adopted variations of this system (either because of Mr. Smith's writings or because they independently evolved a similar

system), it never achieved complete acceptance. Other firms adopted a wide variety of compensation systems for partners, ranging from virtual lock-step distributions based on seniority to a "you-eat-what-you-kill" approach in which compensation is based exclusively on billings or earnings each year.

(2) The 1990s have seen major changes in traditional patterns of law firm compensation. "The old systems often pay all partners equally or based rewards on rainmaking and billing. The new compensation plans * * * are more likely to be tailored to fit long term goals. That usually includes bonuses or raises for lawyers who bring in clients or bill a lot of hours. But it also may mean valuing work that does not add to a firm's income immediately but which can help it expand over the long run. * * * And, in a bow to client preferences, some law firms are paying lawyers based on their ability to achieve results in an efficient way rather than the number of hours they bill. * * * Still, competitive pressures are forcing many firms to pay rainmakers more to keep them from defecting. 'Rainmakers are still sought after and rewarded,' says Leonard Hirsch, a director of Ernst & Young's legal services and benefits consulting division. 'This has always been true but it has accelerated since the early 1990s. It's more so now than before.'" Erik Milstone, Slicing the Pie: Business Realities Force Some Firms to Change Partner Pay Structures, ABA Journal, April 1996, 26. These more flexible compensation plans usually involve relatively subjective annual evaluations of the performance of individual partners by a committee of senior partners.

(3) A 1995 survey by the Law Firm Services Association of law firms with more than 25 lawyers showed that 3 percent distributed earnings equally among the partners, 32 percent based distributions on a fixed salary plus amounts based on units of ownership, 13 percent on the basis of partner profitability ("you-eat-what-you-kill"), 29 percent solely on units of ownership, and 3 percent on seniority. A significant fraction of those surveyed did not respond.

WARD BOWER, RETHINKING LAW FIRM ORGANIZATION—THE NEW PYRAMID

75 A.B.A.J. 90 (April 1989).

Conventional wisdom suggests that the successful law firm is structured as a pyramid, with the partners (profit sharers) at the top and the associates (profit contributors) at the bottom. Each associate produces sufficient income to pay himself, defray his overhead and generate profit to be distributed among the partners. This is the essential rationale behind group law practice: Lawyers can make more money in a law firm, provided they make partner, than they can in solo practice.

The leveraging of profits from associates is the structure upon which many successful law firms have built. The dynamics of the pyramid in the not-so-distant past provided for an expected 33 percent return on associates, as leveraged assets. Under a commonly accepted doctrine, the "Rule of Three," one-third of expected revenue was used to pay the associate, one-third to defray overhead, and the remaining one-third inured to partners as profit.

Under the conventional model, law firm profitability became a "Ponzi scheme": Adding a partner lowered the line of demarcation on the pyramid between profit sharer and profit contributors. This reduced average partner income unless productive associates (profit contributors) were added in a ratio equal to that existing before the admission of the new partner.

In the embryonic legal services marketplace of the past, in which the demand for services exceeded the supply, this presented little problem. There was enough work to keep new associates productive while maintaining partner incomes, despite the fact that profits were divided among an increased number of partners.

The logical extension of the conventional wisdom of the past was a law firm that continually grew at practically geometrical proportions. Associates were recruited with the expectation of becoming partners. It was the exception, rather than the rule, not to admit an associate to partnership after a specified number of years.

Developments of the past decade, however, have introduced a new reality to the conventional law firm profitability model. The legal services profession has matured from an embryonic to a fully mature marketplace, in which there is an oversupply of services. * * *

ROBERT W. HAMILTON AND RICHARD BOOTH, BUSINESS BASICS FOR LAW STUDENTS: ESSENTIAL TERMS AND CONCEPTS

2d Ed. (1998).*
Pages ——-——

Because the supply of legal services has increased while the realistic demand has not, many law firms find themselves in increasingly competitive circumstances. They must scramble and discount if they wish to keep desirable clients and attract new ones. In an earlier period, commercial enterprises usually paid legal fees that were billed without serious question; these enterprises themselves now face serious competition, and they realize that they must control costs to remain competitive. As a result, legal fees have come under the microscope of cost-cutting or cost-saving. Alternative billing techniques that depart from the simple hourly rate are very common, and are offered by law firms both to existing clients and important new ones. In an earlier era, businesses usually relied primarily or exclusively on a single firm for legal services; today, large business divide their legal work among several different large firms, increasing the sense of competition among the chosen firms and enabling the business to "shop" specific cases or problems so as to obtain the best price. As a result, the practice of law has become much more of a "business" and less of a "profession" than it was a couple of generations ago. In a word, it is much more cut-throat out there than it used to be.

At one time, many lawyers prided themselves that they practiced law in "the grand manner," to benefit mankind and not with an eye on their personal pocketbooks. While most of these statements probably should be taken with a grain of salt no matter what period is involved, it seems clearly to be true that lawyers were more willing two decades ago to take cases without the hope or expectation of a substantial fee than they are today. This

* Reprinted with the permission of Aspen Law & Business/Panel Publishers, a division of Aspen Publishers, Inc. The text set forth above is subject to further revision.

is in large part a product of the changing economics—the increased commercialization—of the business of the practice of law.

Notes

(1) "The enormous economic changes that have rocked law firms for the past four years have resulted in a dramatic reversal of * * * one of the most fundamental elements of large law firm structure—partner leverage—according to data from The National Law Journal's annual surveys of the nation's 250 largest law firms." Rita Henley Jensen, Partner Leverage Changes, The National Law Journal, Monday, May 11, 1992, p. 1, col. 2. "It is well-known that during the past several years, many of the largest law firms have increased their partnership ranks and decreased their number of associates. Some firms that once had a 2–to–1 associate-to-partner ratio now have more partners than associates. A few large firms now have twice as many, or even three times as many, partners as associates. * * * [T]he benefits once derived from leveraging associates has dried up. This is due to the declining volume of associate-intensive work, such as exhaustive research that a partner wouldn't normally do. As a result, the value of leveraging associates has decreased, as associates who once might have been considered 'profit centers' by their firms have become 'cost centers.'" Joel A. Rose, Firms Rethink Partners' Pay, The National Law Journal, February 15, 1993, p. 24, col. 1.

(2) Law students are acutely aware that the job market has tightened significantly in the 1990s. The decline in leverage in large law firms has been perhaps the most important single contributor to this tightening since it directly reduced the number of job offers being made to new lawyers for several years.

(3) Other factors have also contributed to the decline in hiring of new associates by law firms: (a) the movement of legal work away from outside law firms and to "inside" counsel of major companies, (b) the decline of certain areas of corporate practice, particularly takeover, merger and public capital raising, that are extremely labor-intensive from the legal standpoint, (c) the elimination of the traditional "up or out" approach toward associates, and (d) to a lesser extent, the use of temporary lawyers ("temps") rather than hiring permanent associates because of concerns of overstaffing.

(4) The decline in leverage has also had significant effects on the compensation of some partners. Leverage hid the fact that some individual partners were not paying their own way. As leverage declined, earnings per partner became flat or declining in many large law firms. Compensation committees were forced to widen the spread of compensation within the firm between the most productive and least productive partners. Traditionally, the compensation ratio between the highest-and lowest-paid law firm partners was in the range of 2–1 to 3–1, with the most junior partners naturally in the lowest ranges and the most senior in the highest ranges. In some firms, the ratio is now closer to 5–1 (or even higher) and seniority has declined as a major factor in determining compensation. If a firm fails to correct inequities as perceived by the most productive partners, of course, those partners are apt to negotiate a more favorable compensation arrangement with a competing firm or leave and open their own firm.

(5) A final result of the increased competitiveness in law firms is that partners have considerably less security than they had in an earlier era. In the 1960s, an associate who "made" partner could expect to spend the rest of his productive career with the firm so long as he continued to be reasonably productive. Today, firms are much more hard-nosed. If a partner is not a

substantial producer he may be told he must leave. The mechanics by which a partnership compels a partner—theoretically a co-owner of the firm—to withdraw from the firm are described in Section H of this chapter. If he is permitted to stay his "draw" may be significantly reduced. Needless to say, these tactics have caused a significant increase in litigation between lawyers and their former law firms.

JAKE KROCHESKI AND CHARLES J. SANTANGELO, TWO–TIERED PARTNERSHIPS PROLIFERATE[2]

Nat'l L. J., July 5, 1993, at p. 36, col. 1.

Many law firms have had to rethink their strategy of how and when—or even if—to promote associates to partners. The downswing in the economy has caused law firms increasingly to adopt two-tiered partnerships.

A two-tiered structure consists of income partners and equity partners. Income partners are paid a salary that is not contingent on their firms' profits. Equity partners are owners of their firms and share in the profits.

Many law firms are finding that a two-tiered structure is an alternative to terminating talented, well-regarded associates simply because they do not meet all of the criteria for becoming full equity partners. As partners find themselves challenged by a growing range of responsibilities—including management, business development and training—it can be unrealistic for firms to expect their associates to develop strengths in all these areas while improving their legal skills.

Income partners are entitled to many of the same benefits as equity partners, but there are differences. Income partners attain partnership status without assuming any risk. Typically, their privileges include:

- The right to attend firm meetings, except on specific topics that are overseen only by equity partners.

- The right to serve on most firm committees, except the compensation and management committees.

- The right to receive paid benefits-which equity partners typically have to pay for themselves.

- The right to see the firm's financial picture.

A law firm may promote some individuals to income partner as an interim step.[3] Others may remain at this level because of lifestyle decisions or an inability to meet all the expectations required of equity partners.

Notes

(1) Are "income partners" really partners if they are paid a fixed salary plus discretionary bonus? Or are they merely employees with a fancy title? In general partnerships each partner is jointly (or jointly and severally) liable for the actions

2. Reprinted with the permission of the National Law Journal, copyright 1993. The New York Law Publishing Company.

3. [By the Editor] In Winston & Strawn v. Nosal, 279 Ill.App.3d 231, 664 N.E.2d 239 (Ill. App.1996), for example, Nosal began as an associate with Winston & Strawn in 1970, was promoted to income partner in 1977, and became a capital partner in 1984. In 1992, he received notice that he was being "outplaced" or discharged by the firm, an action which he challenged in the courts.

of all partners. Krocheski and Santangelo state that in a two-tiered firm equity (or capital) partners "are liable for the debts of the firm, whereas income partners normally are indemnified." Id. at col. 2. Does that indicate that the firm itself believes they are partners for liability purposes? Is a promise to indemnify income partners—presumably by the partnership—an indication that they are truly partners? If so, does indemnification provide adequate protection from the standpoint of income partners? The issue whether income partners should be viewed as partners or as employees also arises in a number of other contexts, for example, whether their salary is subject to withholding for income tax purposes and whether they are entitled to participate in employee retirement plans.

(2) In some firms, income and equity partners have essentially the same responsibility toward clients, the difference being that an "equity" partner is expected to be a rainmaker while an income partner is not. In many law firms, a management committee and a managing partner actually make decisions on behalf of the firm, with other partners being entitled to vote only on specific matters. In some law firms, the partner in charge of office management—hiring and firing of support staff, ordering of supplies, keeping the books, etc.—is designated the "managing partner" and the true managers of the firm are a committee.

(3) The income/equity partner distinction is not the only recent development in law firm practices. Many firms have quietly lengthened the period between initial hiring of associates and the partnership decision. Four to six years was once common; now it is more likely to be eight to ten years. Furthermore, if it seems clear that a young associate has little future with the firm, he or she may be informally so advised relatively early in the relationship. At an earlier time, such an associate might wait until the partnership decision to learn that he or she must seek another job.

(4) As part of the process of delaying promotion to full partner, some firms have created classes of associates as well as classes of partners. The titles for the more senior positions may be "of counsel," "senior counsel," "senior attorney," "participating associate," "staff attorney," or some similar phrase. An associate may be promoted to senior attorney and then face the partnership decision several years later or may remain permanently in the senior associate status. Thus, in some firms there may be four steps between entering associate and full-scale partner but at the same time there may be permanent jobs for associates who, for one reason or another, do not "make" partner but who are valuable to the firm. Many law firms have thus abandoned the traditional "up or out" approach for associates who do not "make" partner.

(5) Some firms have created a "part time partnership" or "part time associate" status usually for attorneys with child care demands. Usually, the part time attorney may return to a full-time status at a later date, but may also remain on a part time status indefinitely.

(6) Even though partners have joint (or joint and several) liability for firm obligations, it was assumed until relatively recently that the risk that individual lawyers in large law firms might have to dip into personal assets to satisfy law firm obligations was entirely theoretical. The major risk, malpractice claims, could be protected against by insurance. That assumption is not true today. There have been at least three recent failures of major law firms in which firm liabilities exceeded firm assets. For example, when the well-known Boston, Massachusetts firm of Gaston and Snow dissolved, potential firm liabilities exceeded firm assets by over $50 million. In 1992, the Office of Thrift Supervision sued New York's

Kaye, Scholer, Fierman, Hays and Handler for $275 million based on its earlier representation of Lincoln Savings & Loan Association, and at the same time imposed a limited freeze on the law firm's assets. The freeze threatened the continued existence of Kaye Scholer since clients questioned the ability of the law firm to continue to function under the freeze; a prompt settlement of the law suit was reached under which Kaye Scholer agreed to settle for $41 million with an immediate payment of $25 million and the balance payable at the rate of $4 million per year for the next four years. Malpractice insurance covered only $21.5 million of this settlement; the balance is the responsibility of the present and former partners. In 1993, another nationally known law firm, Jones, Day, Reavis & Pogue, settled another set of claims arising out of the Lincoln collapse for $51 million, $19.5 million of which was to be paid by the Jones Day partners over six years. In light of events such as these it is not surprising that large law firms today routinely purchase the maximum amount of malpractice insurance available and increasingly are selecting forms of business that (hopefully) shield partners from massive malpractice claims. For example, a 1995 study of 191 Texas law firms with more than ten lawyers showed that 95 percent of them had elected a limited liability form of business. Susan S. Fortney, Are Law Firm Partners Islands Unto Themselves? An Empirical Study of Law Firm Peer Review and Culture, X Georgetown Journal of Legal Ethics 271, 278–79 (1996). See Part C below.

(7) The traditional view is that the goal of all young associates in a law firm is to become (or "make") partner. Is that true today? In a multi-tiered law firm, is that still the principal goal?

(8) Personal liability for law firm obligations is not uncommon in small firms. A typical liability that haunts many small firms is a long-term lease of expensive office space which was originally entered into on the incorrect assumptions that the firm would continue to grow in size, that the short-term market for office space would at least remain stable so that excess space could be sublet until it was needed, and that the long term market for office space would continue to tighten so that even if the firm closed down, someone would be willing to take over the lease. Another, less common source of personal liability are guaranteed payments to laterals or senior partners that turn out to be over-optimistic. These contract liabilities, of course, cannot be insured against, and as a result smaller firms also are selecting forms of business that may shield their members from personal liability.

(9) Changes in the economics of large firm law practice have led to a variety of new hiring and employment practices. These include:

(a) Contract attorneys. Law firms may hire lawyers at the associate level on a contract basis—e.g., for two years or for a specific matter—with the possibility but not the assurance that the contract may be renewed. If business improves, a contract attorney may be "promoted" to the associate category.

(b) Temps. "The use of temporary attorneys by law firms and corporate law departments through placement agencies is booming, as is the pool of available qualified attorneys. The number of temporary lawyers nationally is estimated by the U.S. Department of Labor's Bureau of Labor Statistics to be more than 40,000, up from only 10,000 in 1992. * * * Traditional temporary hirings may be short-term, prompted by on-staff illness, vacation, family/medical leave, special project demands or seasonal increases in workload. However, contract lawyers are increasingly called on for long-term assignments that include protracted complex litigation and sophisticated transactional work. * * * [The use of temporary legal staff] reduces operating and labor costs associated with permanent employment, including the costs of recruitment, payroll taxes and benefits. One particular advantage of using temporary paralegals is that regular staff members are freed from putting in costly overtime, which typically results in reduced productivity." Lisa Moore Turano and Antje Buelte Dolido, The Ethics of Using Temporary Lawyers, Texas Lawyer, May 20, 1996, 29. Legal placement firms—"headhunters"—advertise for temporary placements as well as permanent hires. Individual lawyers who work as temps include new parents who need flexible work hours, former associates at firms who have been laid off or terminated, and recent graduates with limited legal experience (usually summer clerkships or part-time work while in law school) who failed to find permanent employment. Presumably some readers of this note will at some time find themselves in one of these categories. It should be pointed out that working as a "temp" has some advantages (other than the obvious one of survival): One gets exposed to real world legal work, gains legal experience, and works with a firm or lawyer who may consider the temp as a suitable permanent hire, or at least be willing to provide a favorable recommendation. It is not at all uncommon for recent law school graduates who find no permanent job immediately after graduation, to work as a temp for one or two years, and then locate a permanent job either at or through the law firms that used the recent graduate as a temp.

(c) Of counsel. The traditional "of counsel" (or "senior counsel") was a senior partner who has provided many years of services and has essentially retired. His name remains on the firm letterhead; he retains his office, a part-time secretary, and may come in once or twice a week "to pick up his mail." Of course, becoming of counsel was not always voluntary; firms sometimes compelled senior attorneys to accept reduction in profit sharing or complete removal from the profit sharing group. Today, firms use these designations to cover a wide variety of other situations. Many of the permanent non-equity partners within a modern law firm may be designated "of counsel," a phrase which is becoming a reference to any senior permanent lawyer who is not an equity or income partner. A lawyer who has spent a decade or more working for an operating company may join a firm as "of counsel" to reflect the fact that he has experience but no billings. Part time lawyers may also be given the title "of counsel." Active lawyers who are of counsel in these new categories may be compensated by a fraction of their billings or by a guaranteed minimum payment from the firm. In addition, the firm normally covers overhead expenses and malpractice insurance premiums.

(10) Many law firms have programs by which senior partners reaching the age of 58 or 60 are permitted or encouraged to retire, thereby leaving the profit sharing group. Some firms have an intermediate pre-retirement status in which the senior partner's compensation and work load is reduced at ages 58, 60 or 62 in preparation for retirement. Until relatively recently, most law firms did not have formal pension plans or programs for partners. The assumption was that each partner would set aside funds for savings and retirement during his or her productive years at the firm. Retirement payments of course might be informally negotiated when a senior partner agreed to leave the firm.

(11) The first pension plans for partners were unfunded plans: Retirement payments to former partners were to be made out of future earnings of the firm. These plans almost invariably led to inter-generational conflict, as younger partners in their most productive years resented losing a portion of their earnings in order to benefit retired partners. In many instances, this issue led to the most productive junior partners leaving the firm in order to be free of unfunded retirement obligations to senior partners. Are such benefits liabilities of the firm

and of the individual partners? Increasingly, law firms now provide funded retirement plans so that the future cost of retirement is paid for during the years the beneficiaries of the plan are partners or associates in the firm. In many firms, partners are expected to provide for their own retirement by the creation of tax deferred Keogh plans that permit the accumulation of substantial retirement benefits over a career.

———

Turning to the unfortunate situation where the venture does not prove to be profitable, who is responsible for losses? Consider first UPA (1914) § 18(a), compared with UPA §§ 13–15. Why is § 18 modified by the phrase "subject to any agreement between them," while §§ 13–15 are not? Is it clear that an individual partner may be held personally liable on a partnership obligation even if the partnership is solvent and able to satisfy all its obligations? If so, why might a creditor elect to sue a partner and ignore a solvent partnership? May a creditor sue a partner individually even if the partner had nothing to do with the creation of the obligation and indeed was unaware that it was created? If so, and one partner is compelled to pay an entire claim, how does the Act contemplate the working out of the financial relations among the partners so that the losses or reduction of profit resulting from that claim are allocated as provided by the partnership agreement? Consider UPA (1914) §§ 18(b), 40(d); compare UPA (1994) §§ 401(a)-(e), 807(c)-(d).

With respect to a partner's liability for a partnership obligation, consider UPA (1994) §§ 305–307. UPA (1994) makes one radical, and three important, substantive changes from UPA (1914): (1) § 306(c) is the radical change; it reverses the general rule of individual partner responsibility for most partnership debts if the partnership has elected to be a "limited liability partnership," a status that is obtained by following the relatively simple procedural requirements set forth in §§ 1001 through 1004; (2) § 306(a) makes all liability joint and several and all reference to partners being "jointly" liable for contract and related claims is eliminated, (3) § 307(d) provides that a judgment creditor is first required to exhaust partnership assets (with certain exceptions) before proceeding directly against one or more partners individually, and (4) §§ 307(a), (b) and (c) set forth rules about the naming of partnerships and partners in lawsuits. Each of these developments deserve brief description:

(1) Limited liability partnerships (LLPs) authorized by § 306(c) are discussed in greater detail in the following section of this chapter. The first LLP statute was enacted in 1991 so that experience with this type of partnership is quite limited. However, it is clear that the entity is still a partnership despite the limited liability: It must be organized for profit, it must have two or more members, it is subject to dissolution or dissociation as any other general partnership, and so forth. Its unique feature is that by electing LLP status partners may avoid *personal* liability for partnership claims that cannot be satisfied from partnership assets. The assets they have invested in the partnership remain at risk, and there is always some possibility that partners may become liable to third persons because of their own conduct. Nevertheless, the elimination of personal liability of partners in some general partnerships is a radical change that essentially creates a new type of business form.

Diff b/t UPA (1914) + UPA (1944)

(2) "Joint" liability, as contemplated by UPA (1914) § 15(b) requires joinder of all partners as defendants in litigation; this joinder requirement may create serious practical enforcement problems where process cannot readily be served on some partners. "Joint and several" liability permits suit to be brought against one or more of the partners without suing them all. Presumably, in 1914 most partnerships were small and local in character, and joint liability did not create the practical problem faced, for example, by a plaintiff seeking to sue a large law firm with 150 partners located in a dozen offices in major American cities with additional offices in London, Hong Kong, and Zurich. The decision to make all liability joint and several in UPA (1994) is important but not revolutionary: About a dozen states previously had amended section 15 of UPA (1914) to provide for joint and several liability for all claims.

(3) The requirement that judgment creditors should first be required to exhaust partnership assets before proceeding directly against the assets of one or more partners is an important change that was suggested by an ABA committee in 1986. The Committee stated that the new rule "would respect the concept of the partnership as an entity and would provide that the partners are more in the nature of guarantors than principal debtors on every partnership debt. We believe that this result would be most consistent with general business expectations today." UPA Revision Subcommittee of the Committee on Partnerships and Unincorporated Business Organizations. Should the Uniform Partnership Act Be Revised? 43 Bus. Law. 121, 143 (1987).

(4) Paragraphs (a), (b) and (c) of UPA (1994) § 307 dealing with procedural requirements for suits brought by or against partnerships also clearly strengthen the view that a partnership is an entity separate from the original partners. The issue of how partnerships should sue or be sued was not addressed by the UPA (1914) but was addressed by codes or rules of civil procedure in the various states. Many states evolved rules quite similar to those set forth in § 307, so that these changes are largely consistent with modern practice.

It is not uncommon in informal ventures for the parties to agree on a sharing of the profits but not discuss the sharing of losses. There is often some judicial sympathy for the unfortunate investor who is unexpectedly caught in a losing venture with the threat of personal liability for the venture's obligations that were incurred by others. In these cases, a court may be willing to accept the argument that the absence of an express agreement to share losses indicates that no partnership was ever created in the first place. See, e.g., In re Tingle, 34 B.R. 676 (Bankr.S.D.Fla.1983); Grimmett v. Higginbotham, 907 S.W.2d 1 (Tex.App.1994); FDIC v. Claycomb, 945 F.2d 853 (5th Cir.1991). Many cases, however, recognize that an express agreement to share losses is not essential for the existence of a partnership, a result that seems clear from the language of UPA (1914) § 7 and UPA (1994) § 202(c)(3). Parks v. Riverside Ins. Co., 308 F.2d 175 (10th Cir.1962).

Notes

(1) In the AB Furniture Store, can A obtain protection against possible future liabilities by requiring B to execute a written agreement that provides: "It is understood and agreed that the parties hereto are not partners and that no partnership is formed by this agreement?" See UPA (1994) § 202(a), last clause. What about a clause that states that A will not be liable for any losses incurred in the business' in excess of A's $100,000 investment? Would such an agreement have any legal effect at all? If so, what?

(2) Assume that the XYZ Real Estate Company is formed in a state that has adopted § 307 of UPA (1994). XYZ owns seven different rental properties; each property is subject to one or more separate mortgages but the fair market value of each property is somewhat greater than the sum of the outstanding balances owed on the mortgages applicable to that property. Your client, a bank, is considering making a loan to XYZ to permit it to do substantial repair and renovation work on its properties. Your client knows that X, a partner in XYZ, is independently wealthy and is relying on X to pay off the loan if XYZ is not able to do so. What provisions should you include in the loan agreements to ensure that your client is able to collect directly and immediately from X in the event of a default? See UPA (1994), §§ 307(c), 307(d)(3). Indeed, while you are at it, would it not be a good idea to revise the bank's form loan documents to include such provisions whenever a partnership is the borrower?

(3) In the AB Furniture Store, could A obtain the desired protection by being a "silent" partner? For example, the store might be known as B Furniture Store; A might advance the money but never appear in the store or participate in any public way in the management of the store. Assuming that creditors extend credit without knowing of A's interest in the business, can A escape liability? Should a negative inference be drawn from UPA (1914) § 35(2) a provision applicable only "after dissolution," or UPA (1994) § 703(b)(1), a provision applicable after "dissociation"? How might a creditor learn that A is a silent partner?

RICHERT v. HANDLY

Supreme Court of Washington, 1957.
50 Wash.2d 356, 311 P.2d 417.

ROSELLINI, JUSTICE.

This is an action for an accounting, wherein the plaintiff alleged that he entered into a partnership agreement with the defendant husband (hereafter referred to as the defendant), under the terms of which he, the plaintiff, was to purchase a stand of timber and the defendant was to log it, using his equipment, and the two were to share equally in the profits or losses resulting from the venture. He further alleged that the undertaking was unsuccessful; that after the payment of all operating expenses, the partnership suffered a loss of $9,825.12; that he had advanced $26,842 but had been repaid only $10,000 for his advances; and that he was entitled to $16,842 less $4,912.56 (one half of the net loss), or $11,929.44. In his amended answer, the defendant admitted that the parties had contracted with each other, but alleged that "there was no settled agreement between the partners as to recovery by the plaintiff for loss upon his capital contribution, nor as to the priority of any right to recover upon his capital contribution." In addition, he claimed certain offsets and asked that the complaint be dismissed.

The cause was tried to the court, which found in favor of the defendant in the amount of $1,494.51, plus costs. * * *

The facts found by the trial court are as follows:

"I   That defendants C.C. Handly and Mildred Handly are husband and wife constituting a marital community resident in Mason County, Washington.

"II   During the month of April 1953 plaintiff Richert advised defendant Handly that he had available for purchase according to his cruise 1,700,000 feet of timber in the State of Oregon, that he, Richert proposed to purchase said timber with his funds and requested Handly to log said timber on the basis that the two of them would share the profit or loss on the transaction.

"III   Prior to the purchase of the timber by the plaintiff the parties inspected the same and defendant Handly advised Richert that there was no more than approximately 1,000,000 feet of timber on the tract in question, and that the cruise was in error.

"IV   The plaintiff Richert purchased the timber for a price of $24,-300.00 after the parties had inspected it as aforesaid, and Handly proceeded to log the same under an oral working agreement. The essential elements of this agreement were as follows: Handly was to furnish a tractor for which he was to be paid rental at the rate of $13.00 per hour and was to haul the logs on his trucks at the rate of $8.00 per thousand. He was also to manage the operation, keep the records and handle and account for the funds received and expended during the course of the same. The profit or loss resulting from this single logging venture was to be borne equally. There was no requirement that Handly contribute to Richert for the purchase price of the timber in the event of loss.

"V   The tract involved yielded between 800,000 and 900,000 feet of timber and the transaction resulted in a loss, the loss being caused by the deficiency in timber.

"VI   The defendant Handly employed a bookkeeper and accountant in the State of Oregon to keep the records of this venture.

"VII   The gross receipts of the venture amounted to $41,629.83. These funds were banked and accounted for by Handly. There was no concealment nor unlawful withholding or conversion of any of the funds.

"VIII   Handly drew from the proceeds of the sale of the timber the sum of $7,016.88. Richert received from the proceeds of the sale of the timber the sum of $10,000.00.

"IX   There was no agreement express or implied on the part of Handly to repay Richert for his investment in the timber.

"X   A partnership income tax was prepared for the year 1953 by Elliott B. Spring, accountant in Shelton, Washington. This return was signed by Handly after he protested the accounting shown thereon. The accounting appearing on said return was set up on the basis of Spring's understanding and opinion as to what the legal relationship of the parties was with reference to this single logging transaction.

"XI   The $10,000.00 received by Richert and the $7,016.88 drawn by Handly are unexpended gross revenues of the undertaking."

Upon these facts, the court entered the following conclusions of law:

"I   The arrangement of the parties hereto with reference to the single transaction involved constitutes a joint venture.

"II   The defendant Handly is in no way responsible for plaintiff's loss on the purchase of the timber involved.

"III   Of the total amount of $17,016.88 heretofore identified as unexpended gross revenue of the undertaking each party hereto is entitled to $8,508.44. Richert has been overpaid in the amount of $1491.56, and Handly is entitled to judgment against him in the amount of $1491.56.

"IV   Plaintiff is entitled to take nothing by his complaint. * * *"

Although the plaintiff maintains that the court erred in holding the undertaking to be a "joint venture" rather than a "partnership," we think the distinction is immaterial in this action. Deciding whether the relationship between the parties was that of partners or joint venturers does not determine their rights and duties under their contract or the status of their account. We will disregard, therefore, the conclusion of law that the arrangement constituted a joint venture.

On the other hand, it is manifest that the findings are inadequate to support the judgment entered, or any other judgment. There is a finding that the parties to the contract had agreed to share the profits or losses equally; but there is a further finding that the defendant had not agreed to contribute to the plaintiff for his investment in the timber in the event of loss; in other words, that they had not agreed to share the losses equally. Aside from the finding that the profit or loss was to be borne equally, which is inconsistent with the further finding that the defendant was not to contribute to the plaintiff for the purchase price of the timber in the event of loss, the findings are silent as to the basis on which the profit or loss was to be shared, whether proportionately to the contribution of each party, or otherwise. The mere fact that the defendant was not to be personally liable to the plaintiff for his losses does not mean that the plaintiff was not to be reimbursed out of the proceeds of the venture.

The findings also fail to reveal whether there was an understanding that the defendant was to be compensated for his services in managing the operation, apart from his share in the profits, and if so, in what amount. The only allegation contained in the amended answer pertaining to an agreement to reimburse the defendant for his services, was that he was owed $400 for maintaining fire watch and $25 for running property lines; and yet inherent in the court's disposition of the matter is a finding that these services were worth the full amount of the plaintiff's investment, or $26,842; for the court treated all of the "unexpended gross revenues" as profits and divided them equally between the parties, one of whom had lost nothing (unless his claimed offsets in the total amount of $4,800 were valid), while the other had lost an investment of $26,842.

The court appears to have lost sight of the fact that there could be no profits until the expenses of the operation were paid, including the cost of the timber. The conclusion that all of the "unexpended gross revenues" were to be divided equally between the parties could only be reached if it had been agreed that the plaintiff would not be reimbursed for his contribution. Such an intention cannot be inferred from any of the findings entered.

Since the findings are inadequate to support the conclusions and judgment, or any judgment on the matter in question, the cause must be remanded with directions to make findings regarding the basis on which the parties agreed that the losses were to be shared and whether the claims of one partner were to take priority over the claims of the other; the amount contributed by each (including cost of timber, and equipment rental, and also including services if there was an agreement that the defendant was to be compensated for his services, in addition to his share in the profits, if any); the total receipts and the authorized disbursements; the amount which each of the parties has received to date; and the amount due each on the basis of their agreement.

The judgment is reversed and the cause is remanded with directions to enter findings on the matters indicated above, conclusions, and judgment based thereon. * * *

RICHERT v. HANDLY

Supreme Court of Washington, 1958.
53 Wash.2d 121, 330 P.2d 1079.

HUNTER, JUSTICE. * * *

At the hearing on this matter pursuant to the remittitur, counsel for the respective parties agreed that no additional proof would be produced. Therefore, the trial court, after hearing argument of counsel, entered the following additional findings of fact in compliance with the remittitur:

"XII. The parties *did not agree upon or specify the basis* upon which losses were to be shared, nor whether the claims of *one partner* were to take priority over the claims of *the other*.

"XIII. Richert [appellant] contributed a total of $26,842 for cost of timber and incidental advancements. Handly [respondent husband] used his own equipment to haul logs, as agreed by the parties, and was paid $8,673.84 for this service. Handly used his own tractor, as agreed by the parties, and was paid $9,240 for this service. *There was no agreement that Handly was to be compensated for his services*, in addition to his share in the profits, if any, (and except for the equipment and tractor services as last hereinbefore stated), and the accounting between the parties does not disclose any such compensation.

"XIV. The gross receipts from the sale of logs were $41,629.83. The disbursements were hauling (as per Finding XIII), $8,673.84; falling and bucking, $3,474.21; tractor (as per Finding XIII), $9,240.00; payroll and taxes, $4,786.56; cruising, $35.00; right of way, $200.00; commission, $500.00; paid to Richert, $10,000.00; withdrawn by Handly, $7,016.88; Total $43,926.49.

"XV. *There was no agreement* of the parties as to how a loss of the capital contributed by Richert in the amount of $26,842.00 was to be borne, and *accordingly it cannot be determined the amount due each on the basis of their agreement.*" (Italics ours.)

On the basis of such findings, the court concluded neither party was entitled to judgment against the other, that the complaint should be dismissed, and that the costs should abide the ultimate outcome of the case as provided by remittitur.

Mr. Richert has again appealed to this court from the judgment entered.

Since the trial court found that the parties had not agreed upon or specified the basis upon which losses were to be shared, or whether the claims of *one partner* were to take priority over the claims of the *other*, the provisions of the uniform partnership act are controlling. [The court quotes UPA (1914) §§ 18(a), 18(f).]

Therefore, applying the statute to the additional facts found by the trial court, to which no error was assigned, we find the following account established:

Capital Contribution:	
Appellant Richert..	$26,842.00
Respondent Handly	None
Gross Receipts From Sale of Timber.........................	41,629.83
Expenses:	
Tractor	9,240.00
Hauling...	8,673.84
Falling & Bucking	3,474.21
Payroll & Taxes	4,786.56
Cruising	35.00
Right of Way	200.00
Commission	500.00
	$26,909.61
Gross Receipts	41,629.83
Less Expenses...	26,909.61
Net Receipts	$14,720.22
Appellant's Capital Contribution	26,842.00
Less Net Receipts	14,720.22
Net Loss...	$12,121.78
Appellant has received $10,000 from the venture leaving a balance due on his Capital Contribution of	$16,842.00
Less ½ of net loss ($12,121.78)	6,060.89
Amount respondent must reimburse appellant for loss resulting from logging venture......................................	$10,781.11

It follows that the judgment of the trial court is incorrect, as a matter of law, under the facts found. Therefore, the judgment is reversed, and the cause remanded with directions to enter judgment in favor of the appellant in accordance with the views expressed herein.

Notes

(1) What was the theory adopted by the trial court in its first judgment?

(2) What was the theory adopted by the Supreme Court of Washington in its second opinion? Is this conclusion logically and irresistibly compelled by UPA

(1914)? Not all cases accept the result of *Richert*; the leading case rejecting this approach is Kovacik v. Reed, 49 Cal.2d 166, 315 P.2d 314 (Cal.1957). These cases rejecting *Richert* essentially adopt the arguments suggested in the balance of these notes.

(3) The problem in *Richert* potentially arises whenever partners make unequal contributions of capital and services and decide precisely how they will split the profits but do not consider the possibility that the venture will result in a loss. UPA (1914) § 18(a) provides a rule of thumb for such situations that seems inconsistent with the parties' probable intention where one person is providing only capital and the other only services. In the AB Furniture Store, assume there is a fire shortly after B has invested A's $100,000 in inventory and fixtures, and there is a total loss not covered by insurance. Following the theory of *Richert,* would it not follow that B is liable to A for $50,000 (or $100,000, if the agreement is construed to allocate all losses to B)? In a sense, A is risking his capital and B is risking his services; it probably never occurred to B that he might have to restore a portion of A's risk capital. Cannot the same argument be made in Richert v. Handly? Or should the solution be to recognize that Handly made a "capital contribution" by providing his services in the form of his knowledge and skill in cutting and marketing the timber (other than the costs of the tractor and trucks for which he was entitled to compensation under the agreement)? But see UPA (1914) § 18(f); UPA (1994) § 401(h).

(4) During the course of development of UPA (1994), the Reporter suggested adding a provision that a court might award compensation "in other appropriate circumstances" to address the basic problem of *Richert* but the Committee rejected this language on the ground that it was too much an invitation to litigation. As a result, UPA (1994) does not squarely address the issue. See UPA (1994) §§ 401, 807(b).

(5) In Kessler v. Antinora, 279 N.J.Super. 471, 653 A.2d 579 (App.Div.1995), Antinora entered into a written agreement to build a house on a lot to be purchased by Kessler. Kessler agreed to provide the necessary funds and Antinora the knowledge and skill to build the house which was to be put on the market and sold with the parties dividing profits on a 60–40 basis. No provision was made with respect to the sharing of losses. The house was sold at a loss and Kessler sought to require Antinora to contribute toward the losses. Relying on language in the agreement that stated that upon the sale of the house *"and after deducting all monies expended by Robert Kessler"* the remaining profits would be divided, the court concluded that the agreement contemplated that no contribution was required from the services partner. Of course, this victory was obtained only after a trial and an appeal; furthermore, it was based on language in the contract that was apparently inserted with a different problem in mind. If you were drafting a partnership agreement where one partner is contributing capital and the other services, how would you phrase a provision to effectuate the intent of the partners that the service partner is not to be required to contribute toward losses that is sufficiently clear that it does not require a law suit?

C. LIMITED LIABILITY PARTNERSHIPS (LLPS)

ROBERT W. HAMILTON, REGISTERED LIMITED LIABILITY PARTNERSHIPS: PRESENT AT THE BIRTH (NEARLY)

66 Colo.L.Rev. 1065, 1069–1071 (1995).

The LLP is a direct outgrowth of the collapse of real estate and energy prices in the late 1980s, and the concomitant disaster that befell Texas's banks and savings and loan associations. Texas led the nation in bank and savings and loan failures during the 1980s. More than one-third of all the bank failures in the United States occurred in Texas.

Ever since the collapse of these financial institutions across the state, the Federal Deposit Insurance Corporation ("FDIC") and the Resolution Trust Corporation ("RTC") (and its predecessor, the Federal Savings and Loan Insurance Corporation ("FSLIC")) have devoted a significant part of their total resources to the recovery of funds lost in the collapse of Texas institutions. Suit was brought against hundreds of shareholders, directors and officers of failed financial institutions. However, the amounts recovered from the principal wrongdoers were only a tiny fraction of total losses and attention quickly turned to the roles of the lawyers and accountants who had represented the failed financial institutions before their collapse. "Where were the lawyers?" and "Where were the public accountants?" were cries figuratively heard across the state. Claims against lawyers and accountants for malpractice and breach of duty were attractive because the individual professionals sometimes had been deeply involved in the affairs of their clients. Also, these lawyers and accountants were usually associated with partnerships that had substantial malpractice insurance and numerous wealthy partners. As a result, several highly reputable law firms in Texas found themselves in deep trouble because of their bank and thrift work during the "salad days" of the 1980s.

The most vivid example is provided by a major Dallas law firm (hereafter referred to as the "Dallas Law Firm").[4] Long recognized as one of the leading corporate law firms in the state, the Dallas Law Firm in the early 1980s was a traditional general partnership.[5] One Dallas Law Firm partner, Laurence Vineyard, along with four associates, did legal work for three savings and loan associations. * * * In addition to providing legal services, it turned out that Vineyard sat on the board of directors of at least one of the S & Ls and had profitable financial arrangements with the others. These three S & Ls were among the more flagrant "high fliers" which paid little attention to principles of sound financial management and provided lavish benefits and large unsecured loans for their owners. Losses from the collapse of these three S & Ls ran over one billion dollars. Vineyard was deeply involved. He was criminally

---

4. [By the Author] The firm continues in business today under its original name and has requested that it not be specifically identified in this paper.

5. [By the Author] The present Dallas Law Firm is a professional corporation.

prosecuted, convicted, sentenced to two five year prison terms, and disbarred.[6] His personal assets were insubstantial in light of the losses incurred by the S & Ls, and the FSLIC and FDIC turned their attention to the malpractice insurer for the Dallas Law Firm and to all persons who were partners during the period the firm represented the S & Ls. Caught within the FSLIC/FDIC net were retired partners, partners who had since left the Dallas Law Firm to join other firms,[7] partners who had been promoted from associate to partner, persons who had become "of counsel" to the Dallas Law Firm, and the forty-some partners who had nothing at all to do with representation of the various thrift institutions. The total claims asserted by the FSLIC greatly exceeded the liability insurance available to the firm and the assets of the firm itself. To emphasize this point, in one particularly chilling meeting, FSLIC personnel used an overhead projector to show a slide listing the names of each Dallas Law Firm defendant with estimates of total net worth and the amount likely to be available from each of them to satisfy the government's claims.

Needless to say, the Dallas Law Firm litigation caught the attention of the hundreds of law firms that had represented banks or thrifts during the 1980s. Thousands of lawyers in hundreds of Texas law firms watched this litigation closely as it unfolded in the late 1980s with a "there but for the grace of God go I" reaction. The lawsuit against the Dallas Law Firm was ultimately settled for approximately the amount of malpractice insurance carried by the firm.

Notes

(1) The LLP statute enacted by Texas in 1991 was designed to meet this precise perceived liability crisis. It differs in several significant respects from UPA (1994) § 306(c) [a provision that was added to UPA (1994) in 1996]: (a) The Texas statute was limited only to acts of negligence or malpractice and did not cover contract or other liabilities; (b) It required each electing LLP to maintain either a fidelity bond or liquid assets of at least $100,000 for the protection of malpractice creditors; (c) It did not expressly cover obligations of a partner to indemnify other partners [UPA (1914) § 18(b)] or to contribute to the assets of the partnership on winding up [UPA (1914) § 40(d)]; and (d) It expressly imposed liability on partners who had a responsibility of oversight of partners or associates that committed acts of negligence or malpractice. Similar statutes were promptly enacted in Delaware and other states.

---

6. [By the Author] Vineyard was actually convicted in connection with transactions involving a Colorado S & L that occurred after he left the Dallas Law Firm. He was also convicted for diverting loan proceeds from an approved S & L project to the purchase of his personal residence, a transaction that also occurred after he had left the Dallas Law Firm. However, the government cited and relied upon these criminal convictions when raising questions about the validity of transactions he performed for the S & Ls while a partner with the Dallas Law Firm. See United States v. Vineyard, 699 F. Supp. 103 (N.D.Tex.1988) (ordering Vineyard to pay millions of dollars restitution for the damage caused by these loans).

7. [By the Author] FSLIC made a major effort to recover a portion of the losses from the malpractice insurers of the firms to which former Dallas Law Firm partners had moved. Malpractice insurance is written on a "claims made" basis, and notice was given after these lawyers had joined their new firms. Some of these firms had independent potential exposure to S & L liability because of their own representation of S & Ls as well as derivative exposure arising from the claims being asserted against former partners of the Dallas Law Firm. Global settlements were negotiated with some of these firms, involving substantial payments to the federal agencies.

(2) The limited liability provided by LLP statutes is usually called the "shield of limited liability." Almost from the outset, when states followed the lead of Texas they adopted statutes that broadened the limited shield of the Texas statute. The first "fixes" to the LLP statute related to the problems of indemnification and contribution and also concern about whether the shield of limited liability could be "evaded" by artful pleading of a malpractice claim as breach of contract rather than tort. The initial justification for broadening the shield to cover contract claims was concern about contractual malpractice claims. However, as states continued to enact these statutes, the shield of limited liability was steadily broadened until in about 17 states today it covers all liabilities of every kind, as in § 306(c) of UPA (1994). About 30 states have "tort only" statutes of the Texas type, though several states that originally adopted limited shields have amended, or are considering amending, their statutes to broaden them. Some states today have "full shield" statutes that require no minimum capitalization.

(3) It is true, of course, that even under broad shield LLP statutes, individual partners who themselves commit acts of malpractice or negligence remain personally liable because of their own conduct. It is also possible that partners with oversight responsibility over other professionals may have personal responsibility for the malpractice or negligence of persons they supervise. In addition, there may be other arguments to pierce the broad shield of limited liability based on theories of fraudulent transfers or analogies with doctrines such as the "piercing the corporate veil doctrine" in corporate law discussed in chapter 6.

(4) Given the long history of unlimited liability in partnership law, was the introduction of the LLP a good idea? The elimination of personal liability of innocent partners for malpractice or negligence of co-partners may reduce their incentive to monitor the performance of other partners. On the other hand, how important is this incentive in a firm, such as the Dallas Law Firm, with over 40 partners? In very large professional partnerships, it is quite possible that an individual partner will not even know the names of all of her copartners, and arguments based on monitoring do not seem very persuasive.

(5) The narrow shield statutes (like the original Texas statute) do not affect basic partnership rules except in the case of firms that actually face substantial malpractice claims in excess of their malpractice insurance plus the undistributed assets in the partnership. In all other situations, the traditional partnership rules continue to apply. Thus, of all the millions or billions of partnership transactions that occur each year in the United States, only a very few would be affected by the narrow shield statutes.

(6) The same cannot be said of the modern broad shield LLP statute, which make all electing partnerships into limited liability entities, and which potentially affect basic partnership rules whenever the partnership is unable to satisfy all of its obligations. Is there any policy justification for broadening the shield to cover liability arising from transactions voluntarily entered into? Law and economics scholars, exemplified by Professor Larry Ribstein, have put forth a normative argument that limited liability is the preferred policy for contractual obligations of business entities and therefore the broad shield statutes "get it right." See Larry E. Ribstein, The Deregulation of Limited Liability and the Death of Partnership, 70 Wash.U.L.Q. 417 (1992). Limited liability is preferable, he argues, because it encourages passive investments in firms as well as protecting inadvertent or unwary partners from unexpected and crushing liabilities. Furthermore, the shield may be easily "contracted around," so that sophisticated persons always may obtain personal liability by express agreement. Thus, in Professor Ribstein's

view, it is not very important which default rule is adopted (i.e., liability or no-liability) with respect to contractual obligations because parties may negotiate either for nonrecourse liability (to avoid an unlimited liability default rule) or for personal guarantees by owners (to avoid a limited liability rule). In addition, Professor Ribstein argues that persons dealing with a partnership should prefer the limited liability default rule because they would then know how much the benefit of personal liability costs (when they negotiate for it). In this view, limited liability with respect to contract claims is desirable, and the difficult question is whether there should be limited liability for malpractice and tort claims.

(7) Consider the following response to the law and economics arguments described in the previous note:

I simply do not agree that the desirable default rule for general partnerships in contract matters is limited liability or that partnership default rules are unimportant in the real world. The law and economics scholarship is based on the assumption that the world consists of persons who act rationally, with full information, and with alternative choices. The real world doubtless has many such people and these people will adjust their behavior to either default rule without difficulty. * * * [However,] the real world contains a tremendous number of people who lack basic sophistication. There are about one and a half million partnerships in the United States; most of them are very small and involve primarily relatively unsophisticated people. Indeed, when one thinks about the population of persons who contract with partnerships, the number of unsophisticated people far, far exceeds the number of sophisticated ones. And, it is this population of persons who contract with partnerships that is adversely affected as a group by the quiet reversal of the default rule * * * of personal liability * * * that has existed for centuries. * * * There is a wide gulf, in short, between the theoretical model used by law and economics scholars in which all persons are sophisticated and the real world in which we live where most individuals may not even know what a default rule is, much less that it might be in their interest to seek to negotiate a special deal to change it in the unlikely event that something unexpected happens. The great bulk of society relies, without realizing it, on whatever default rule the legal system provides. * * * How many people are dimly aware that when they deal with a partnership that the personal credit of each partner stands behind the firm? A great many, I suspect. How many will understand that the little letters "L.L.P." on the door means that the rule of personal liability has been changed for that partnership? Not very many, I suspect.

I would like to make one concluding comment about all this. Bills proposing the creation of LLPs will inevitably be viewed as "legislation for lawyers" even though they cover other types of general partnerships as well. It is no secret that the legal profession is not held in the highest regard and esteem in many areas of society. Indeed, lawyers are viewed by many as generally greedy, shifty, tricky, and untrustworthy folk. I am afraid that widespread enactment of [broad shield] LLP statutes * * * will, in the long run, cause further erosion of the image of the legal profession. We will be viewed as having "pulled a fast one" on society by the enactment of this legislation without any real justification or any real discussion. I do not have the same fear about statutes of the [narrow shield] * * * type, since they will be applied only very rarely.

Robert W. Hamilton, Registered Limited Liability Partnerships: Present at the Birth (Nearly), 66 Colo.L.Rev. 1065, 1092–1094, 1103 (1995). For an extended discussion of the assumptions that underlie these conflicting perspectives, see Robert W. Hamilton and Larry E. Ribstein, Limited Liability and the Real World, 54 Wash. & Lee L.Rev. 687 (1997). Contrast the conclusion of Robert P. Keatinge, et al., Limited Liability Partnerships: The Next Step in the Evolution of the Unincorporated Business Organization, 51 Bus.Law. 147, 180 (1995): "There is no policy justification not to provide a complete limitation on vicarious individual liability similar to that applicable to shareholders in a corporation or members in an LLC. That determination avoids the debate about whether a particular claim— such as malpractice, breach of contract, or environmental liability—is excluded and eliminates the confusion as to the payment priority of different claims."

(8) Might the LLP election affect the distribution of profits within a law firm? Consider Jennifer J. Johnson, Limited Liability for Lawyers: General Partners Need Not Apply, 51 Bus.Law. 85, 139–140 (1995):

> The shift from a general partnership to a limited liability enterprise could have a major impact upon the culture of a law firm. Practicing law in a limited liability environment can lead to conflicts of interest among the firm members and may necessitate the renegotiation of traditional partnership arrangements. For example, firm members may need to rethink their compensation structures with limited liability in mind. The practice of law in high risk areas such as regulated industries often yields higher rewards commensurate with the increased risk of liability. Partners now practicing in these areas usually share the risk related gains with their partners who share in the risk. If a shift to a limited liability enterprise causes a firm member to individually shoulder the increased risk of liability, he or she may demand a higher share of the rewards. A similar concern arises due to the provisions in many statutes that professionals remain liable not only for their personal misconduct but for the acts of those "under their direct supervision and control." Fairness issues could arise among firm members when some members supervise less experienced lawyers and others do not.

(9) Robert R. Keatinge, et al, Limited Liability Partnerships: The Next Step in the Evolution of the Unincorporated Business Organization, 51 Bus.Law 147, 184 (1995):

> Where different partners have different individual liability with respect to different partnership obligations, there will be a question of prioritizing the payment of these liabilities. These differences can arise in several ways. For example, all partners will be individually liable for obligations that arose before the registration, while only negligent or responsible partners will be liable for certain claims arising after registration. If there are insufficient assets within the partnership to pay all obligations, may the non-negligent partners determine to apply those assets to the payment of liabilities for which they are individually liable? If general firm debts, such as a lease or line of credit, are paid, the negligent partner will be required to use separate assets to pay any liability arising from such partner's negligence. Whether such a decision would constitute a breach of fiduciary duty to the negligent partner remains to be determined. If the liability for malpractice is paid with partnership assets, all the partners will be liable for the remaining firm obligations.

This problem is sometimes referred to as the "stacking" problem. In addition to stacking, the LLP creates a number of other issues that have not been resolved.

For example, consider the meaning of the phrase "obligation of a partnership *incurred while* the partnership is a limited liability partnership" in UPA(1994) § 306(c). Assume that a partnership signs a long term lease before it elects to be an LLP. Was this "obligation" incurred when the lease was signed or when the rent comes due each month? Or, consider an LLP that consists of four partners. In the middle of the year, they decide to split into two different law firms of two partners each. Has the LLP election been lost? See UPA (1994) § 1001(e), last sentence. Does it now cover both firms? Neither firm? The firm that uses the same office space?

D. MANAGEMENT

NATIONAL BISCUIT CO. v. STROUD
(Nabisco)

Supreme Court of North Carolina, 1959.
249 N.C. 467, 106 S.E.2d 692.

PARKER, JUSTICE.

C.N. Stroud and Earl Freeman entered into a general partnership to sell groceries under the firm name of Stroud's Food Center. There is nothing in the agreed statement of facts to indicate or suggest that Freeman's power and authority as a general partner were in any way restricted or limited by the articles of partnership in respect to the ordinary and legitimate business of the partnership. Certainly, the purchase and sale of bread were ordinary and legitimate business of Stroud's Food Center during its continuance as a going concern.

Several months prior to February 1956 Stroud advised plaintiff that he personally would not be responsible for any additional bread sold by plaintiff to Stroud's Food Center. After such notice to plaintiff, it from 6 February 1956 to 25 February 1956, at the request of Freeman, sold and delivered bread in the amount of $171.04 to Stroud's Food Center.

In Johnson v. Bernheim, 76 N.C. 139, this Court said: "A and B are general partners to do some given business; the partnership is, by operation of law, a power to each to bind the partnership in any manner legitimate to the business. If one partner go to a third person to buy an article on time for the partnership, the other partner cannot prevent it by writing to the third person not to sell to him on time; or, if one party attempt to buy for cash, the other has no right to require that it shall be on time. And what is true in regard to buying is true in regard to selling. What either partner does with a third person is binding on the partnership. It is otherwise where the partnership is not general, but is upon special terms, as that purchases and sales must be with and for cash. There the power to each is special, in regard to all dealings with third persons at least who have notice of the terms." There is contrary authority. 68 C.J.S. Partnership § 143, pp. 578–579. However, this text of C.J.S. does not mention the effect of the provisions of the Uniform Partnership Act.

The General Assembly of North Carolina in 1941 enacted a Uniform Partnership Act, which became effective 15 March 1941. G.S. Ch. 59, Partnership, Art. 2. * * *

[The Court quotes UPA (1914) §§ 9(1), 9(4), 18(e), 18(h) and the North Carolina version of UPA (1914) § 15, which reads, "All partners are jointly and severally liable for the acts and obligations of the partnership."]

Freeman as a general partner with Stroud, with no restrictions on his authority to act within the scope of the partnership business so far as the agreed statement of facts shows, had under the Uniform Partnership Act "equal rights in the management and conduct of the partnership business." Under [UPA (1914) § 18(h)] Stroud, his co-partner, could not restrict the power and authority of Freeman to buy bread for the partnership as a going concern, for such a purchase was an "ordinary matter connected with the partnership business," for the purpose of its business and within its scope, because in the very nature of things Stroud was not, and could not be, a majority of the partners. Therefore, Freeman's purchases of bread from plaintiff for Stroud's Food Center as a going concern bound the partnership and his co-partner Stroud. * * *

In Crane on Partnership, 2d Ed., p. 277, it is said: "In cases of an even division of the partners as to whether or not an act within the scope of the business should be done, of which disagreement a third person has knowledge, it seems that logically no restriction can be placed upon the power to act. The partnership being a going concern, activities within the scope of the business should not be limited, save by the expressed will of the majority deciding a disputed question; half of the members are not a majority." * * *

At the close of business on 25 February 1956 Stroud and Freeman by agreement dissolved the partnership. By their dissolution agreement all of the partnership assets, including cash on hand, bank deposits and all accounts receivable, with a few exceptions, were assigned to Stroud, who bound himself by such written dissolution agreement to liquidate the firm's assets and discharge its liabilities. It would seem a fair inference from the agreed statement of facts that the partnership got the benefit of the bread sold and delivered by plaintiff to Stroud's Food Center, at Freeman's request, from 6 February 1956 to 25 February 1956. But whether it did or not, Freeman's acts, as stated above, bound the partnership and Stroud.

The judgment of the court below is affirmed.

RODMAN, J., dissents.

SMITH v. DIXON

Supreme Court of Arkansas, 1965.
238 Ark. 1018, 386 S.W.2d 244.

HOLT, JUSTICE.

The appellee, as purchaser, brought this action against appellants, as sellers, for the specific performance of a contract for the sale of realty and in the alternative sought damages for nonperformance of the contract.

The appellants are E.F. Smith, his wife, and their children and spouses. This entire family constitutes a business firm known as E.F. Smith & Sons, A Partnership. The "Contract For Sale of Realty With Lease" was signed by one of the appellants, W.R. Smith, on behalf of the family partnership.

By the terms of the contract, executed in March 1962, the partnership agreed to sell the 750 acre "Cracraft" plantation for $200,000.00 and convey title to the appellee on January 3, 1963. In the interim, by the lease provisions, the appellee took possession, farmed, and improved a portion of the property. Upon refusal of the appellants to convey the land as recited in the contract, the appellee instituted this action. The chancellor denied specific performance and awarded appellee special damages in the amount of $11,-512.73. * * *

The partnership was created a short time after the lands in controversy were acquired by the family in 1951. The court found that:

> "Soon after the purchase of 'Cracraft' [the lands in question] and the 'Sterling Place,' the Smiths, at the suggestion and on the recommendation of the financial institutions, who were to finance the farming operations for them on the farms, organized and formed a partnership known as E.F. Smith & Sons. They term the partnership an 'operating partnership'. The general purpose of the firm was to engage in farming operations on the farms, including direct cultivation and renting to others. The operation was later expanded to engage in the general farming business in the area. The partnership agreement was oral and has never been reduced to writing. Mr. W.R. Smith is the predominant member of both the partnership and the Smiths. He serves as the managing partner with general powers, with Mr. Charles Smith in charge of production. The other members of the partnership did not, nor at the present time, appear to have any direct participation or responsibility in the operation. * * *

> "The firm, by and through its managing partner, Mr. W.R. Smith, has acted as agent for or under contract with, the Smiths, in the sale of the 'Sterling Place' to Mr. Rankin, in a similar capacity in another land conveyance and as trustee for another purchase."

It appears undisputed that appellant W.R. Smith was authorized by the members of the partnership to negotiate for the sale of the lands in question to the appellee. However, it is claimed that his authorization was based upon different terms of sale, mainly, a price of $225,000.00 instead of $200,000.00. Therefore, it is urged that the contract is unenforceable since it was not signed nor ratified by other members of the family.

In the case of May v. Ewan, 169 Ark. 512, 275 S.W. 754, we held that a partnership is bound by the acts of a partner when he acts within the scope or *apparent* scope of his authority. There we quoted with approval:

> " * * * In order to determine the apparent scope of the authority of a partner, recourse may frequently be had to past transactions indicating a custom or course of dealing peculiar to the firm in question".

See, also [UPA (1914) §§ 8–10]. In the case at bar it was customary in past transactions, as in the present one, for the partnership to rely upon the co-partner, W.R. Smith, to transact the business affairs of the firm. We agree with the chancellor that appellant W.R. Smith was acting within the apparent scope of his authority as a partner when he signed the contract and that it is binding and enforceable upon the partnership. * * *

Notes

(1) Is National Biscuit Co. v. Stroud a case of actual authority or apparent authority? What about Smith v. Dixon? For a description of the differences between these two types of authority, see Appendix One, pp. 1103–1107, infra.

(2) Many agency relationships may involve simultaneously actual and apparent authority. For example, if Freeman had been an employee or agent of Stroud rather than a partner, it is clear that Stroud could revoke any actual authority that Freeman might have to bind him to a purchase of bread simply by notifying Freeman. However, despite such notice, Freeman might still have the power under concepts of apparent authority to bind Stroud to a purchase of bread unless Nabisco is advised of the revocation of authority. In the actual case, of course, Stroud actually advised Nabisco that he did not intend to be bound by further purchases by Freeman yet he was held liable as a result of the court's decision. How can this be?

(3) Would the result in Smith v. Dixon be changed if W.R. Smith had been an agent or employee of E.F. Smith & Sons rather than the "predominant member" or "managing partner with general powers?"

(4) To what extent do the basic concepts of actual authority and apparent authority appear in UPA (1914) §§ 9(1), 9(2), and 9(4)? In UPA (1994) § 301?

(5) What should a person in Stroud's position do if he or she no longer trusts the co-partner and wishes to avoid liability for future bread purchases by the partnership?

(6) How does one ascertain the scope of the phrase "for apparently carrying on in the usual way the business of the partnership" in UPA (1914) § 9(1) or UPA (1994) § 301?

(a) Many partnership agreements contain a recitation of the business to be carried on. For example, "The purpose of the Partnership is to engage in the sale, service, and repair of all types of outboard and inboard motor boats, outboard and inboard motors, and all characters of marine equipment and accessories." Alan R. Bromberg, Crane and Bromberg on Partnership 599 (1968). Are such recitations relevant?

(b) Consider Burns v. Gonzalez, 439 S.W.2d 128, 131 (Tex.Civ.App.—San Antonio 1969, writ ref'd n.r.e.):

> As we interpret [UPA (1914) § 9(1)], the act of a partner binds the firm, absent an express limitation of authority known to the party dealing with such partner, if such act is for the purpose of "apparently carrying on" the business of the partnership in the way in which other firms engaged in the same business in the locality usually transact business, or in the way in which the particular partnership usually transacts its business. In this case, there is no evidence relating to the manner in which firms engaged in the sale of advertising time on radio stations usually transact business. Specifically, there is no evidence as to whether or not the borrowing of money, or the execution of negotiable instruments, was incidental to the transaction of business, "in the usual way," by other advertising agencies or by this partnership, Inter–American Advertising Agency. It becomes important, therefore, to determine the location of the burden of proof concerning the "usual way" of transacting business by advertising agencies.

The Court concluded that there was no reason to depart from the normal rule that the party who asserts that the particular act of an agent is within the scope of the agent's authority has the burden of proving the extent of that authority.

(7) To what extent may the management rights of partners be varied by agreement? It is important to note that UPA (1914) § 18 is qualified by the phrase "subject to any agreement between them." Does that mean that anything goes? Can management of a partnership be vested solely in one partner or in a

person who is not a partner? Or to put the same question in the most extreme way, what is the legal effect of a partnership agreement between A and B that states "X shall have the sole power to manage the business and affairs of the partnership and A and B shall have no power to participate in partnership decisions or to bind the partnership to third persons?" Given the potential responsibility of A and B for partnership liabilities, why would they ever agree to such a provision? Is this not an attempt to eliminate the authority granted partners in UPA (1914) § 9 by agreement? Yet § 9 does not contain the phrase "subject to any agreement among them." If despite such a provision, B obtains a loan from a bank in the partnership name, is the partnership liable to the bank even though B subsequently misappropriates the money? Compare UPA (1914) §§ 9(1), 13, 14, 15; UPA (1994) §§ 103(a), 301. If B obtains a loan in the partnership name and the proceeds are used appropriately to benefit the partnership business, has B nevertheless committed a breach of the partnership agreement? If so, who might be the plaintiff in a breach of contract suit and how might damages be measured?

(8) The partnership agreement is often referred to as "the law of the partnership" for that particular partnership. This statement reflects that a partnership is a consensual arrangement and that the substantive rules governing the internal affairs of a partnership may generally be altered by agreement. But see UPA (1994) § 103(b). Third parties are not bound by provisions in the agreement and may enforce rights and liabilities created by UPA (1914) or UPA (1994) without regard to the agreement. See UPA (1994) § 103(b)(9). May the authority granted partners in UPA (1914) § 9 or UPA (1994) § 301 itself be eliminated by agreement if potential creditors are given notice?

(9) As previously discussed, law firms may designate certain partners as "senior counsel," "of counsel," "capital partners," "equity partners," "income partners," or the like. There is statutory authority confirming this practice in a few states. Do such designations have any legal effect on the scope of authority of those partners? Does designation of B as "managing partner" or a committee of senior partners as "the management committee" have the effect of limiting the agency of other partners to bind the partnership under UPA (1914) § 9(1) or UPA (1994) § 301? Might an "equity" or "capital" partner have greater actual or apparent authority to bind the partnership than an "income partner" or a person who is designated as "of counsel?" Consider also UPA (1914) § 9(3), a provision that has no precise counterpart in UPA (1994). Might a "managing partner" (or all of the "managing partners") have authority to do any of these acts? What about an "equity partner" or all of the "equity partners?" Should not they have power to confess a judgment [see UPA (1914) § 9(3)(d)] without the consent of the income partners? UPA (1914) § 9(3) was not carried over into UPA (1994). Why not?

(10) UPA (1994) authorizes partnerships and partners to make a public filing of a "statement of partnership authority.". See, UPA (1994) § 303 UPA (1994) § 105. UPA (1914) contains no similar provisions. This innovation is patterned upon provisions in the Georgia statute. See Ga. Code Ann. § 14–8–10.1. Does § 303 mean that Nabisco would have to check the public filings before it can safely sell bread on credit to a business such as Stroud's Food Center? With respect to real estate transfers, does not § 303 simply create one more piece of paper that a title examiner must examine in connection with transfers of real estate by partnerships?

ROUSE v. POLLARD

Court of Chancery of New Jersey, 1941.
129 N.J.Eq. 47, 18 A.2d 5, affirmed 130 N.J.Eq. 204, 21 A.2d 801 (1941).

BIGELOW, VICE CHANCELLOR.

The seven defendants were partners engaged in the general practice of law, their firm well-known and enjoying a high reputation for skill and integrity. Complainant was their client. The member of the firm who took care of her legal business was Thomas E. Fitzsimmons. At almost her first interview with him, she disclosed that she owned valuable securities, whereupon he immediately suggested that she sell them and turn the money over to the firm, saying that they would invest for her in good mortgages, and send her the interest every six months. Accordingly, on June 21, 1927, complainant endorsed to Fitzsimmons a check for the proceeds of her securities, $28,253, which he deposited in his personal bank account. Out of this sum, he gave the firm's bookkeeper $350 on account of complainant, for legal services unconnected with this transaction. He paid to her or on her order $403, retaining the balance. For several years he sent her a check every January and July for an amount equal to three percent of the principal sum. In 1931, at her request, he paid complainant $7,000 and thereafter through 1937 continued to pay her interest on $20,500. Meanwhile, the law firm, of which defendants were members, was dissolved at the end of 1932.

In January, 1938, Fitzsimmons was arrested for embezzlement, was found to have defrauded a large number of persons and was sentenced to the State Prison. No mortgages or other securities representing complainant's $20,500 have been discovered and from the vagueness of Fitzsimmons' testimony, I am satisfied that immediately upon receipt of her money in 1927, he converted it to his own use. She may, of course, have a decree against Fitzsimmons but he is insolvent. The question is whether the other defendants as well are liable to her.

Until after Fitzsimmons' exposure, his co-defendants were entirely ignorant that complainant had entrusted him with any money, or had any dealings with him except for ordinary law work. Neither the payment to the firm of $350 by Fitzsimmons on complainant's account, nor any other circumstance which has been proved, was sufficient to put the partners on notice that he held other funds of complainant. They did not suspect or have reason to suspect him of improper conduct in this or other matters until long after the partnership was dissolved. Complainant can recover only if the partners are answerable for Fitzsimmons' malfeasance. They are responsible only if he was acting as their agent in accepting complainant's money. Certainly he had no express authority to act for his co-defendants in this regard. If there were authority, it existed only by implication from the fact that he and they were partners.

As a general rule, each partner is, by virtue of the partnership relation, authorized to act as the general agent for his co-partners in all matters coming within the scope of the business of the firm, in the same manner and to the same extent as if he had full power of attorney from his co-partners. All the partners are responsible for the act of one of their number as agent, even though he acts for some secret purpose of his own, and not really for the benefit of the firm. Restatement–Agency [2d], sec. 165. [Appendix One] Where one partner, by fraudulent promises made in a transaction within the scope of the partnership business, obtains money from a third person and misappropriates it, the other partners are liable. While the agency of a partner extends to all matters connected with the business in which the partnership is engaged, his authority extends no further. If the transaction is outside the partnership business, the other partners are not liable and they are not bound by a statement of the partner who conducts such transaction that he is acting on behalf of the firm.

So we come to the question whether the receipt of complainant's money by Fitzsimmons was a transaction within the scope of defendant's business. The scope of any line of business may be gauged by the usual and ordinary course in which such business is carried on by those engaged in it in the locality where the partnership has its seat. But the scope may be broadened by the actual though exceptional course and conduct of the business of the partnership itself, as carried on with the knowledge, actual or presumed, of the partner sought to be charged.

In their practice, defendants frequently had in their hands moneys belonging to clients, held for a particular purpose such as investment in a certain mortgage. But they were not in the habit of receiving, and indeed never received, money from a client to place on mortgage at their discretion. Fitzsimmons, doubtless in other cases besides the present one, received money for general investment and represented when doing so that he was acting for the firm. But the other members of the firm had no knowledge of such actions or representations on his part.

In England, although the receipt of money to be invested on a particular security may be considered an incident of an attorney's or solicitor's business, the receipt of money for the purpose of investment generally, or to invest it in mortgage as soon as a good mortgage can be found, is not so considered. No proof has been presented to show how the practice of law is usually carried on in New Jersey, and none is necessary, for that is a subject with which the court is familiar. Some few lawyers have made a habit of receiving money for general investment, and such practice has too often led to disastrous results. The prudent lawyer never retains funds or securities of his client in his hands longer than is necessary. He does not accept money until an investment has been found and approved by his client. The receipt of money for the purpose of investing it as soon as a good mortgage can be found, as was done by Fitzsimmons in the case at bar, is not part of the practice of law according to the usual and ordinary course pursued in New Jersey.

It follows that Fitzsimmons' partners are not answerable to complainant and as to them the bill will be dismissed.

Notes

(1) If Rouse v. Pollard arose under UPA (1914), which sections would be decisive? § 9? § 13? § 14? § 15?

(2) The opinion of the Court of Errors and Appeals of New Jersey affirming the principal case contains a somewhat fuller description of what happened (130 N.J.Eq. at 205–06, 21 A.2d at 802–03):

In the course of the incidental conferences Fitzsimmons asked Mrs. Rouse what money she possessed and was informed by her of the amount thereof and the manner in which it was invested. According to Mrs. Rouse:

> "He said that securities was a bad thing for a woman in my position to have and he suggested that I turn over my securities and sell them and turn the money over to the firm, that they dealt in gilt edge mortgage bonds, as he said. He said that they did that for their clients and it was perfectly secure. I asked if it was all right for me and he said that is the only way they would take care of it and I would get my check every six months. He said if I handed it at once they would place it the first of July and I did place it the 15th and the 15th of January was the first check."

Mrs. Rouse wrote to her brokers directing them to sell her securities and to "forward a check for the same payable to me to my attorney, Mr. Thomas E. Fitzsimmons, c/o Riker & Riker, 24 Commerce Street, Newark, N.J.". A check for $28,252.67 was sent as directed, was endorsed by Mrs. Rouse "Pay to the order of Thos. E. Fitzsimmons" and was deposited by Fitzsimmons in his personal bank account. No part ever came to the firm except $350, or thereabouts, which was paid by Fitzsimmons to the firm for the legal services rendered, and no member of the firm, other than Fitzsimmons, knew of the transaction. The bill of complaint specifically exonerates the remaining members from any fraud, deceit or misappropriation. On January 16, 1928, Fitzsimmons wrote Mrs. Rouse: "Enclosed herewith find my check for $825., being six months' interest at 6% on the $27,500., which I have invested for you." On July 19, 1932, Fitzsimmons wrote: "I enclose herewith check for $615., representing six months' interest on the money which I have invested for you." For more than ten years interest payments went to Mrs. Rouse by Fitzsimmons' personal check. $7,000 of the principal was returned to her, likewise by Fitzsimmons' check, and the receipt was by Mrs. Rouse to Fitzsimmons, personally. The letter from Fitzsimmons to Mrs. Rouse accompanying the check reads:

> "As requested, I enclose herewith check for $7,000, which sum is to be deducted from the amount which I have invested for you on bond and mortgage. I am also enclosing a receipt for such amount which I would request you to sign and return to me."

So, too, the receipt to Mrs. Rouse showing a balance retained to invest is by Fitzsimmons, personally. That was in October of 1931. On December 31, 1932, Fitzsimmons retired from the firm of Riker and Riker, and complainant had actual notice of this fact at that time or shortly thereafter. From then on Fitzsimmons' letters to Mrs. Rouse were written on his own stationery from his new office address, and Mrs. Rouse never thereafter went to, or communicated with, the Riker firm until after she had learned, in the early spring of 1938, of Fitzsimmons' defalcations and arrest.

Do these facts suggest an alternative ground for the decision in Rouse v. Pollard?

(3) The opinion of the Court of Errors and Appeals also gives additional information and detail about the nature of the firm practice of Riker and Riker (130 N.J.Eq. at 208–09, 21 A.2d at 803–04):

> The firm did engage extensively in what is known as a "real estate practice"; it represented banks, building and loan associations and estates; it examined titles, closed mortgages and drew necessary documents relating to mortgage investments by clients; it had clients' funds and trust funds on

deposit awaiting the closing or other requirements of transactions for which such funds were held; it did not do a general investment business and it did not accept funds for future, unspecified investment, at the firm's discretion, in mortgages or otherwise.

> It has long been a recognized incident to the general practice of law, more extensively developed in some offices than in others, to make note of such clients as have moneys to invest on bond and mortgage, to bring the attention of those clients to the applications of proposed borrowers and, after the principals come to an agreement, to search the title, draw the necessary documents, even hold the money against the event, place the recordable papers on record and in general superintend the closing of the transaction. But we do not understand that it is a characteristic function of the practice of law to accept clients' money for deposit and future investment in unspecified securities at the discretion of the attorney, and we find to the contrary. It is possible that attorneys in isolated instances have done this; just as it is possible that a person of any profession or occupation has done so. It has not, however, been done by lawyers, in this jurisdiction at least, with such frequency or appropriateness as to become a phase of the practice.

Assuming that a person knowledgeable about law firms would understand this, should Mrs. Rouse be held to this standard? If she goes to a well-known law firm for assistance in a divorce settlement, is introduced to a partner, Mr. Fitzsimmons, and is told by him what the business of the firm is, can't she rely on the accuracy of this information?

(4) What would you suggest an attorney do if he or she learns that a partner has accepted money under the circumstances Fitzsimmons accepted Mrs. Rouse's funds in the principal case? Obviously the selection of a law partner is a serious matter since, even if the scope of the agency is limited to legal matters, there is unlimited liability for losses caused by negligence or incompetence as well as willful defalcation.

ROACH v. MEAD

Supreme Court of Oregon, 1986.
301 Or. 383, 722 P.2d 1229.

Before Peterson, C.J., and Lent, Linde, Campbell, Carson and Jones, JJ.

Jones, Justice.

* * * At trial, defendant, David J. Berentson, moved for a directed verdict, contending that he was not vicariously liable for the negligent acts of his partner, Kenneth E. Mead, because the negligent acts were outside the scope of the partnership's business. The trial court denied the motion, and the jury found defendant liable for $20,000 damages * * *. The Court of Appeals held that defendant attorney was vicariously liable for his former partner's negligence. We affirm the Court of Appeals. * * *

Mead, defendant's former law partner, first represented plaintiff in December 1974 on a traffic charge and later represented plaintiff on several occasions. On November 1, 1979, Mead and defendant formed a law partnership. Mead continued to advise plaintiff on other traffic charges and on business dealings. Defendant prepared plaintiff's income tax returns.

In June 1980, plaintiff sold his meter repair business for $50,000. On November 25, 1980, plaintiff asked for Mead's advice on investing $20,000 in proceeds from the sale. Plaintiff testified that Mead told plaintiff that "he would take [the money] at 15 percent. So, I let him have it. * * * I trusted him and felt he would look out for me." Plaintiff considered Mead's advice to be legal advice; he testified that otherwise he would not have consulted an attorney.

After plaintiff agreed to the loan, Mead executed a promissory note for $20,000 payable on or before November 25, 1982, at 15 percent interest. Mead said that he would be receiving a large sum of money with which he would repay plaintiff. Mead offered to secure the loan with a second mortgage on his house, and plaintiff replied that he should do "whatever you think is best." Mead did not secure the loan.

On May 1, 1981, Mead went to plaintiff's home and requested a $1,500 loan, telling plaintiff he was in financial trouble but "had big money coming in." Plaintiff agreed to the loan and Mead added the $1,500 to the amount due on the promissory note.[8] Mead did not repay any money to plaintiff and later was declared bankrupt.[9]

Plaintiff sued defendant's partnership for negligence, alleging that the partnership failed to disclose the conflicting interests of plaintiff and Mead, to advise plaintiff to seek independent legal advice, to inform plaintiff of the risks involved in an unsecured loan, and to advise plaintiff that the loan would not be legally enforceable because the rate of interest was usurious. * * *

I. VICARIOUS LIABILITY

Plaintiff contends that Mead negligently advised him about the loan and that defendant should be vicariously liable for Mead's negligent legal advice. Defendant, while conceding that Mead was negligent, argues that the transaction between plaintiff and Mead was a personal loan outside the scope of the partnership, and that the evidence did not prove that soliciting personal loans was within Mead's express, implied or apparent authority as defendant's law partner. * * *

[The Court quotes UPA (1914) §§ 9(1), 9(2), 9(4), 13, and 15(a).]

Liability of partners for the acts of co-partners is based on a principal-agent relationship between the partners and the partnership. "Partners are jointly and severally liable for the tortious acts of other partners if they have authorized those acts or if the wrongful acts are committed 'in the ordinary course of the business of the partnership.' [UPA (1914) §§ 13, 15]" *Wheeler v. Green,* 286 Or. 99, 126, 593 P.2d 777 (1979). The issue in this case is whether Mead's failure to advise plaintiff on the legal consequences of the loan was "in the ordinary course of the business of the partnership."

---

8. [By the Court] The jury found defendant not liable for [this] additional $1,500 loan, presumably because it determined that the loan was personal and that giving legal advice concerning the loan was not within the scope of the partnership's business.

9. [By the Court] On January 18, 1983, this court accepted Mead's resignation from the bar. He stated that he had chosen not to con-

test disciplinary charges alleging that he had "borrowed $45,000 from a client, that he misrepresented the priority of the security given for the loan and that he subsequently forged a satisfaction of the mortgage given as security." 43 Or.St.B.Bull., June 1983, at 42. Mead was convicted of theft by deception because of the loan referred to in the disciplinary charges.

In *Croisant v. Watrud,* 248 Or. 234, 432 P.2d 799 (1967), this court confronted a similar issue of the vicarious liability of a partnership for the wrongful acts of a partner. In *Croisant,* the client of an accountant sued the accounting partnership, claiming damages for the accountant's breach of trust. The accountant collected income from the client's property and then made unauthorized payments to the client's husband from the money. The defendant partnership contended that the collection services were personal dealings of the accountant with the client and not part of the partnership's business. This court held:

> "If a third person reasonably believes that the services he has requested of a member of an accounting partnership is undertaken as a part of the partnership business, the partnership should be bound for a breach of trust incident to that employment even though those engaged in the practice of accountancy would regard as unusual the performance of such services [collecting and disbursing funds] by an accounting firm." 248 Or. at 242, 432 P.2d 799.

The court stated that the reasonableness of the third person's belief that "the service he seeks is within the domain of the profession is a question which must be answered upon the basis of the facts in the particular case." *Id.* at 243, 432 P.2d 799.

Defendant contends that *Croisant* may be distinguished from the case at bar because in *Croisant* "the misconduct occurred in the course of * * * activities which the court held could reasonably be viewed as within the scope of the accounting firm's business," while in this case "[t]here was no evidence that the act of an attorney in taking a personal loan from a client could reasonably be viewed as part of the business of a law firm." However, defendant admits that "the evidence most favorable to Plaintiff was simply that Plaintiff thought Mead was giving him investment advice and that the giving of advice regarding legal aspects of loans and investments in general is a normal part of law practice." Defendant thus concedes the validity of plaintiff's argument that plaintiff reasonably believed that investment advice was within the scope of the partnership's business; plaintiff does not contend that soliciting loans from clients was partnership business.

In the case at bar, the jury determined that plaintiff reasonably believed that the partnership's legal services included investment advice. We agree with the Court of Appeals that:

> "* * * There is expert and other testimony from which the jury could have found that plaintiff relied on Mead for legal advice concerning the loan, that a lawyer seeking a loan from a client would be negligent if the lawyer did not tell the client to get independent legal advice and that a lawyer advising a client about this particular loan would seek to secure it and would warn the client of the risks involved in providing a usurious interest rate." 76 Or.App. at 85, 709 P.2d 246.

The Court of Appeals' rationale is buttressed by our decisions in bar disciplinary proceedings concerning loans from clients to lawyers. * * *

When a lawyer borrows money from a client, this court requires that the lawyer advise the client about the legal aspects of the loan. Mead's failure to advise plaintiff to seek independent legal advice, that loans usually should be secured and the debtor's financial status checked, and that the rate of interest was usurious were all failures of Mead as a lawyer advising his client. Because these failures occurred within the scope of the legal partnership, responsibility for Mead's negligence was properly charged to defendant as Mead's law partner. The trial court did not err in submitting the negligence issue to the jury. * * *

The Court of Appeals is affirmed.

Notes

(1) Can this case be distinguished from *Rouse v. Pollard?* There were several cases during the 1980s in which liability was imposed on the partnership or copartners in situations similar to *Roach v. Mead*. See Stephen E. Kalish, When a Law Firm Member Borrows From a Client—The Law Firm's Responsibility: A Professional Model Replaces a Club Model, 37 Kan.L.Rev. 107 (1988). Professor Kalish views *Rouse v. Pollard* as illustrative of the "club model" of law partnerships and *Roach v. Mead* as illustrative of a "professional model."

(2) In the principal case, what differences are there, if any, between the $20,000 loan on which liability was found and the $1500 loan, on which it was not?

(3) Model Rules of Professional Conduct, Rule 1.8:

(a) A lawyer shall not enter into a business transaction with a client or knowingly acquire an ownership, possessory, security or other pecuniary interest adverse to a client unless:

(1) the transaction and terms on which the lawyer acquires the interest are fair and reasonable to the client and are fully disclosed and transmitted in writing to the client in a manner which can be reasonably understood by the client;

(2) the client is given a reasonable opportunity to seek the advice of independent counsel in the transaction; and

(3) the client consents in writing thereto.

Is a law firm liable for malpractice if a partner fails to obtain the written consent required by Rule 1.8(a)(3) for a personal loan from a client?

(3) What principles determine the liability of a partner for the negligence or incompetence of an associate, e.g., a staff attorney employed by a law firm?

(4) In *Fanaras Enterprises, Inc. v. Doane*, 423 Mass. 121, 666 N.E.2d 1003 (1996), Fanaras had entered into a retainer arrangement with Doane, an attorney. Under the retainer, Fanaras alleged, Doane was paid fees of $25,000 per quarter "in return for full, total and immediate access to Mr. Doane's legal advice, and so that [Fanaras] would always receive devoted priority service from Attorney Doane." While this arrangement continued, Fanaras also loaned Doane over $400,000, an amount that was to be repaid, with interest of 11 per cent "as soon as Doane obtained sufficient funds by way of selling [two properties he owned] or by way of obtaining a mortgage loan against either or both of those properties." However, Doane secretly placed mortgages against the two properties of over $1,800,000, diverted the funds, defaulted on the mortgages, and declared personal bankruptcy. Fanaras recovered nothing from the properties or from Doane. In an effort to collect from Doane's malpractice insurer, Fanaras sued Doane, alleging that Doane was negligent in failing to advise Fanaras "to seek independent legal advice and or to secure the loans with a mortgage" and that it "relied on Attorney

Doane, at all times, to protect my interests in connection with these loans, and he failed to do that." (423 Mass., at 122–24, 666 N.E.2d, at 1004–05) Doane's liability insurer intervened and successfully moved for summary judgment. Held, affirmed:

> The fact that the plaintiff paid Doane a substantial retainer "in return for full, total, and immediate access to Mr. Doane's legal advice, and so that Fanaras Enterprises, Inc., would always receive devoted priority service from Attorney Doane," * * * is of no consequence. That arrangement clearly contemplated the plaintiff's right to Doane's prompt legal advice on request. Nowhere * * * in any of the summary judgment materials is there the slightest suggestion that the plaintiff, through Fanaras or otherwise, requested Doane's advice or assistance with respect to the loans to Doane and obtaining security for their repayment, or with respect to managing the plaintiff's money. To the contrary, the clear implication of the affidavit is that Fanaras did not seek such advice or assistance but merely "relied" on Doane to protect him. That reliance may or may not have been reasonable, but it did not establish an attorney-client relationship or legal malpractice with respect to the loans. It is not enough that, with respect to other matters, the parties were in an attorney-client relationship.

Three Justices dissented:

> I believe that in light of the materials the plaintiff has presented, it may well be able to prove at trial that Doane owed it a duty as an attorney in respect to the loans Doane obtained from it. * * * If Doane had been advising Fanaras about Fanaras's dealings with a building owner for whom Fanaras was doing construction work, and that building owner, in Doane's earshot, had solicited a business loan from Fanaras, a jury would surely have been warranted in finding that the "devoted priority" service, for which Fanaras was paying such a high price, extended—even without an explicit request—to Doane's advising Fanaras about any legal aspects of the loan. Similarly here, the jury might have concluded that Fanaras had put itself in Doane's hands, as far as legal advice went, and that it was a violation of the relationship (if not an attorney-client relationship, then what?) for Doane neither to have advised Fanaras of the need to obtain some security nor, because Doane was now in a conflict of interest situation, to seek outside counsel. Nor would a finding of a conflict somehow preclude a finding of an attorney-client relationship. Much more likely, the conflict was itself a potential breach of Doane's duty, and it would be brazen for Doane to urge that, because of the conflict, there was no relationship on which Fanaras might rely. (423 Mass., at 126–27, 666 N.E.2d, at 1006–07).

Is the result reached in *Doane* consistent with Roach v. Mead?

(5) In a well-known novel of a few years ago, an incoming partner in a law partnership learns that a senior partner handling estate accounts has a substantial shortage of assets in his accounts which he is covering by commingling accounts and robbing Peter to pay Paul. What is the new partner's liability with regard to the original shortage? See UPA (1914) § 17; UPA (1994) § 306(b). On the above facts is the new partner entirely safe? Might the last clause be inoperative if the new partner arguably assumes liability for existing or future obligations, e.g., by letting the practice continue?

(6) Robert W. Hamilton and Richard A Booth, Business Basics for Law Students: Essential Terms and Concepts (1998), ___:[10]

---

10. Reprinted with permission of Aspen Law & Business/Panel Publishers, a division of Aspen Publishers, Inc. The text set forth above is subject to further revision.

[I]f a lawyer is representing an unsophisticated client, the lawyer often gradually assumes the roles of both legal and business adviser. Where an unsophisticated client is involved, business risks should be pointed out clearly, forcefully, and without hesitation. To take an extreme example, a lawyer who is handling the estate of a corporate executive may learn that a securities broker has suggested to the widow that she attempt to augment the size of the estate by engaging in options trading (a highly speculative and sophisticated market * * * in which it is easy to lose one's entire capital investment in a very brief period). Probably every lawyer in this situation would feel compelled to speak up and warn the widow of the dangers of following the advice of the securities broker. This general type of situation is probably more common than many people realize: Most sophisticated business lawyers at one time or another represent relatively unsophisticated clients. In these situations, the client may end up relying on the lawyer for both financial and legal advice. Usually the lawyer should try to persuade the client that he or she should seek appropriate business advice, and that reliance on a lawyer for advice on such matters is not desirable. Often, however, the client is happy with the lawyer's advice or is unwilling to incur the cost of direct business advice or does not know who to ask.

It is perhaps unnecessary to point out that there is a difference between a lawyer warning a client that a proposed business transaction with third persons is risky or inappropriate, and the lawyer engaging in a direct business transaction with a client. However, what happens if the advice turns out badly? For example, the value of the recommended options may increase dramatically; can the client then sue the attorney for bad advice or for advice that is beyond the competence of a lawyer to give? If the lawyer fails to warn the client about the risk of options and significant losses are incurred, might the lawyer be liable on the theory that attorneys of ordinary competence would have warned the client under such circumstances?

E. DUTIES OF PARTNERS TO EACH OTHER

MEINHARD v. SALMON

Court of Appeals of New York, 1928.
249 N.Y. 458, 164 N.E. 545.

CARDOZO, C.J.

On April 10, 1902, Louisa M. Gerry leased to the defendant Walter J. Salmon the premises known as the Hotel Bristol at the northwest corner of Forty–Second street and Fifth avenue in the city of New York. The lease was for a term of 20 years, commencing May 1, 1902, and ending April 30, 1922. The lessee undertook to change the hotel building for use as shops and offices at a cost of $200,000. Alterations and additions were to be accretions to the land.

Salmon, while in course of treaty with the lessor as to the execution of the lease, was in course of treaty with Meinhard, the plaintiff, for the necessary funds. The result was a joint venture with terms embodied in a writing. Meinhard was to pay to Salmon half of the moneys requisite to reconstruct, alter, manage, and operate the property. Salmon was to pay to

Meinhard 40 percent of the net profits for the first five years of the lease and 50 percent for the years thereafter. If there were losses, each party was to bear them equally. Salmon, however, was to have sole power to "manage, lease, underlet and operate" the building. There were to be certain preemptive rights for each in the contingency of death.

The two were coadventurers, subject to fiduciary duties akin to those of partners. King v. Barnes, 109 N.Y. 267, 16 N.E. 332. As to this we are all agreed. The heavier weight of duty rested, however, upon Salmon. He was a coadventurer with Meinhard, but he was manager as well. During the early years of the enterprise, the building, reconstructed, was operated at a loss. If the relation had then ended, Meinhard as well as Salmon would have carried a heavy burden. Later the profits became large with the result that for each of the investors there came a rich return. For each the venture had its phases of fair weather and of foul. The two were in it jointly, for better or for worse.

When the lease was near its end, Elbridge T. Gerry had become the owner of the reversion. He owned much other property in the neighborhood, one lot adjoining the Bristol building on Fifth avenue and four lots on Forty-Second street. He had a plan to lease the entire tract for a long term to some one who would destroy the buildings then existing and put up another in their place. In the latter part of 1921, he submitted such a project to several capitalists and dealers. He was unable to carry it through with any of them. Then, in January, 1922, with less than four months of the lease to run, he approached the defendant Salmon. The result was a new lease to the Midpoint Realty Company, which is owned and controlled by Salmon, a lease covering the whole tract, and involving a huge outlay. The term is to be 20 years, but successive covenants for renewal will extend it to a maximum of 80 years at the will of either party. The existing buildings may remain unchanged for seven years. They are then to be torn down, and a new building to cost $3,000,000 is to be placed upon the site. The rental, which under the Bristol lease was only $55,000, is to be from $350,000 to $475,000 for the properties so combined. Salmon personally guaranteed the performance by the lessee of the covenants of the new lease until such time as the new building had been completed and fully paid for.

The lease between Gerry and the Midpoint Realty Company was signed and delivered on January 25, 1922. Salmon had not told Meinhard anything about it. Whatever his motive may have been he had kept the negotiations to himself. Meinhard was not informed even of the bare existence of a project. The first that he knew of it was in February, when the lease was an accomplished fact. He then made demand on the defendants that the lease be held in trust as an asset of the venture, making offer upon the trial to share the personal obligations incidental to the guaranty. The demand was followed by refusal, and later by this suit. A referee gave judgment for the plaintiff, limiting the plaintiff's interest in the lease, however, to 25 percent. The limitation was on the theory that the plaintiff's equity was to be restricted to one-half of so much of the value of the lease as was contributed or represented by the occupation of the Bristol site. Upon cross-appeals to the Appellate Division, the judgment was modified so as to enlarge the equitable interest to one-half of the whole lease. With this enlargement of plaintiff's interest, there went, of course, a corresponding enlargement of his attendant obligations. The case is now here on an appeal by the defendants.

Joint adventurers, like copartners, owe to one another, while the enterprise continues, the duty of the finest loyalty. Many forms of conduct permissible in a workaday world for those acting at arm's length, are forbidden to those bound by fiduciary ties. A trustee is held to something stricter than the morals of the market place. Not honesty alone, but the punctilio of an honor the most sensitive, is then the standard of behavior. As to this there has developed a tradition that is unbending and inveterate. Uncompromising rigidity has been the attitude of courts of equity when petitioned to undermine the rule of undivided loyalty by the "disintegrating erosion" of particular exceptions. Wendt v. Fischer, 243 N.Y. 439, 444, 154 N.E. 303. Only thus has the level of conduct for fiduciaries been kept at a level higher than that trodden by the crowd. It will not consciously be lowered by any judgment of this court.

The owner of the reversion, Mr. Gerry, had vainly striven to find a tenant who would favor his ambitious scheme of demolition and construction. Baffled in the search, he turned to the defendant Salmon in possession of the Bristol, the keystone of the project. He figured to himself beyond a doubt that the man in possession would prove a likely customer. To the eye of an observer, Salmon held the lease as owner in his own right, for himself and no one else. In fact he held it as a fiduciary, for himself and another, sharers in a common venture. If this fact had been proclaimed, if the lease by its terms had run in favor of a partnership, Mr. Gerry, we may fairly assume, would have laid before the partners, and not merely before one of them, his plan of reconstruction. The pre-emptive privilege, or, better, the pre-emptive opportunity, that was thus an incident of the enterprise, Salmon appropriated to himself in secrecy and silence. He might have warned Meinhard that the plan had been submitted, and that either would be free to compete for the award. If he had done this, we do not need to say whether he would have been under a duty, if successful in the competition, to hold the lease so acquired for the benefit of a venture then about to end, and thus prolong by indirection its responsibilities and duties. The trouble about his conduct is that he excluded his coadventurer from any chance to compete, from any chance to enjoy the opportunity for benefit that had come to him alone by virtue of his agency. This chance, if nothing more, he was under a duty to concede. The price of its denial is an extension of the trust at the option and for the benefit of the one whom he excluded.

No answer is it to say that the chance would have been of little value even if seasonably offered. Such a calculus of probabilities is beyond the science of the chancery. * * *

We have no thought to hold that Salmon was guilty of a conscious purpose to defraud. Very likely he assumed in all good faith that with the approaching end of the venture he might ignore his coadventurer and take the extension for himself. He had given to the enterprise time and labor as well as money. He had made it a success. Meinhard, who had given money, but neither time nor labor, had already been richly paid. There might seem to be something grasping in his insistence upon more. Such recriminations are not unusual when coadventurers fall out. They are not without their force if conduct is to be judged by the common standards of competitors. That is not to say that they have pertinency here. Salmon had put himself in a position in which thought of self was to be renounced, however hard the abnegation. He was much more than a coadventurer. He was a managing coadventurer. For him and for those like him the rule of undivided loyalty is relentless and supreme. Wendt v. Fischer, supra, Munson v. Syracuse, etc., R.R. Co., 103 N.Y. 58, 74, 8 N.E. 355. A different question would be here if there were lacking any nexus of relation between the business conducted by the manager and the opportunity brought to him as an incident of management. For this problem, as for most, there are distinctions of degree. If Salmon had received from Gerry a proposition to lease a building at a location far removed, he might have held for himself the privilege thus acquired, or so we shall assume. Here the subject-matter of the new lease was an extension and enlargement of the subject-matter of the old one. A managing coadventurer appropriating the benefit of such a lease without warning to his partner might fairly expect to be reproached with conduct that was underhand, or lacking, to say the least, in reasonable candor, if the partner were to surprise him in the act of signing the new instrument. Conduct subject to that reproach does not receive from equity a healing benediction.

A question remains as to the form and extent of the equitable interest to be allotted to the plaintiff. The trust as declared has been held to attach to the lease which was in the name of the defendant corporation. We think it ought to attach at the option of the defendant Salmon to the shares of stock which were owned by him or were under his control. The difference may be important if the lessee shall wish to execute an assignment of the lease, as it ought to be free to do with the consent of the lessor. On the other hand, an equal division of the shares might lead to other hardships. It might take away from Salmon the power of control and management which under the plan of the joint venture he was to have from first to last. The number of shares to be allotted to the plaintiff should, therefore, be reduced to such an extent as may be necessary to preserve to the defendant Salmon the expected measure of dominion. To that end an extra share should be added to his half.

Subject to this adjustment, we agree with the Appellate Division that the plaintiff's equitable interest is to be measured by the value of half of the entire lease, and not merely by half of some undivided part. A single building covers the whole area. Physical division is impracticable along the lines of the Bristol site, the keystone of the whole. Division of interests and burdens is equally impracticable. Salmon, as tenant under the new lease, or as guarantor of the performance of the tenant's obligations, might well protest if Meinhard, claiming an equitable interest, had offered to assume a liability not equal to Salmon's, but only half as great. He might justly insist that the lease must be accepted by his coadventurer in such form as it had been given, and not constructively divided into imaginary fragments. What must be yielded to the one may be demanded by the other. The lease as it has been executed is single and entire. If confusion has resulted from the union of adjoining parcels, the trustee who consented to the union must bear the inconvenience. Hart v. Ten Eyck, 2 Johns. Ch. 62. * * *

The judgment should be modified by providing that at the option of the defendant Salmon there may be substituted for a trust attaching to the lease a trust attaching to the shares of stock, with the result that one-half of such shares together with one additional share will in that event be allotted to the defendant Salmon and the other shares to the plaintiff, and as so modified the judgment should be affirmed with costs.

ANDREWS, J. (dissenting). * * *

Were this a general partnership between Mr. Salmon and Mr. Meinhard, I should have little doubt as to the correctness of this result, assuming the new lease to be an offshoot of the old. Such a situation involves questions of trust and confidence to a high degree; it involves questions of good will; many other considerations. As has been said, rarely if ever may one partner without the knowledge of the other acquire for himself the renewal of a lease held by the firm, even if the new lease is to begin after the firm is dissolved. Warning of such an intent, if he is managing partner, may not be sufficient to prevent the application of this rule.

We have here a different situation governed by less drastic principles. I assume that where parties engage in a joint enterprise each owes to the other the duty of the utmost good faith in all that relates to their common venture. Within its scope they stand in a fiduciary relationship. I assume prima facie that even as between joint adventurers one may not secretly obtain a renewal of the lease of property actually used in the joint adventure where the possibility of renewal is expressly or impliedly involved in the enterprise. I assume also that Mr. Meinhard had an equitable interest in the Bristol Hotel lease. Further, that an expectancy of renewal inhered in that lease. Two questions then arise. Under his contract did he share in that expectancy? And if so, did that expectancy mature into a graft of the original lease? To both questions my answer is "No." * * *

What then was the scope of the adventure into which the two men entered? It is to be remembered that before their contract was signed Mr. Salmon had obtained the lease of the Bristol property. Very likely the matter had been earlier discussed between them. The $5,000 advance by Mr. Meinhard indicates that fact. But it has been held that the written contract defines their rights and duties. Having the lease, Mr. Salmon assigns no interest in it to Mr. Meinhard. He is to manage the property. It is for him to decide what alterations shall be made and to fix the rents. But for 20 years from May 1, 1902, Salmon is to make all advances from his own funds and Meinhard is to pay him personally on demand one-half of all expenses incurred and all losses sustained "during the full term of said lease," and during the same period Salmon is to pay him a part of the net profits. There was no joint capital provided.

It seems to me that the venture so inaugurated had in view a limited object and was to end at a limited time. There was no intent to expand it into a far greater undertaking lasting for many years. The design was to exploit a particular lease. Doubtless in it Mr. Meinhard had an equitable interest, but in it alone. This interest terminated when the joint adventure terminated. There was no intent that for the benefit of both any advantage should be taken of the chance of renewal—that the adventure should be continued beyond that date. Mr. Salmon has done all he promised to do in return for Mr. Meinhard's undertaking when he distributed profits up to May 1, 1922. Suppose this lease, nonassignable without the consent of the lessor, had contained a renewal option. Could Mr. Meinhard have exercised it? Could he have insisted that Mr. Salmon do so? Had Mr. Salmon done so could he insist that the agreement to share losses still existed, or could Mr. Meinhard have claimed that the joint adventure was still to continue for 20 or 80 years? I do not think so. The adventure by its express terms ended on May 1, 1922. The contract by its language and by its whole import excluded the idea that the tenant's expectancy was to subsist for the benefit of the plaintiff. On that date whatever there was left of value in the lease reverted to Mr. Salmon, as it would had the lease been for thirty years instead of twenty. Any equity which Mr. Meinhard possessed was in the particular lease itself, not in any possibility of renewal. There was nothing unfair in Mr. Salmon's conduct. * * *

The judgment of the courts below should be reversed and a new trial ordered, with costs in all courts to abide the event.

POUND, CRANE, and LEHMAN, JJ., concur with CARDOZO, C.J., * * *

ANDREWS, J., dissents in opinion in which KELLOGG and O'BRIEN, JJ., concur.

Notes

(1) Consider UPA (1914) §§ 20–22. Does § 21 incorporate the broad fiduciary duty of *Meinhard*? An ABA Committee, commenting on this section, states that while it "is often cited as establishing a broad fiduciary duty, in fact, as presently worded, [it] is basically merely an anti-theft provision." UPA Revision Subcommittee of the Committee on Partnerships and Unincorporated Business Organizations, Should the Uniform Partnership Act Be Revised? 43 Bus. Law. 121, 151 (1987). However, many partnership cases cite *Meinhard* and § 21 as establishing a broad fiduciary duty among partners. Indeed, some cases state that this is "one of the highest fiduciary duties recognized in the law." Huffington v. Upchurch, 532 S.W.2d 576, 579 (Tex.1976).

(2) Is this duty affected by whether or not the partners are dealing with each other at arms length? In Johnson v. Peckham, 132 Tex. 148, 120 S.W.2d 786 (1938), strained relations had developed between two partners and a suit for an accounting and dissolution was pending in a court. Peckham agreed to purchase Johnson's interest in two oil leases that constituted the partnership property for $1,500. Shortly after this transaction was completed, Peckham resold the leases for $10,500. Upon a showing that negotiations for this resale had begun prior to the time Peckham purchased Johnson's interest, Peckham was required to share the profitable resale with Johnson. A judgment for $3,750 (one-half of $10,500 minus $1,500) was entered, the Court quoting the ringing language of Mr. Justice Cardozo in Meinhard v. Salmon. Same result under UPA (1914)?

(3) A partner secretly takes $1,000 from the partnership and invests it in another venture. What rights do his copartners have if the other venture fails? If it is profitable?

(4) An important issue under UPA (1914) is whether the broad fiduciary duties contemplated by that statute may be modified by an express agreement among the parties. (The same issue under UPA (1994) is discussed below.) Singer v. Singer, 634 P.2d 766 (Okla.App.1981) involved a written partnership agreement for a family oil and gas partnership which stated:

8.   Each partner shall be free to enter into business and other transactions for his or her own separate individual account, even though such business or other transaction may be in conflict with and/or competition with the business of this partnership. Neither the partnership nor any individual member of this partnership shall be entitled to claim or receive any part of or interest in such transactions, it being the intention and agreement that any partner will be free to deal on his or her own account to the same extent and with the

same force and effect as if he or she were not and never had been members of this partnership. (634 P.2d, at 768)

Members of the partnership discussed the purchase of a tract of land, but before the partnership could act, two members of the family formed their own separate partnership and purchased the land in question. They refused to share the purchase with the original partnership, citing paragraph 8. The court held this conduct permissible:

> We find the defendants had a contract right to do precisely what they did * * *. [P]aragraph 8 is designed to allow and is uniquely drafted to promote spirited, if not outright predatory competition between the partners. Its strong wording leaves no doubt in our minds that its drafters intended to effect such a result. * * * We construe it to legitimize and extend free competition between the partners to partnership prospects and opportunities * * *. (634 P.2d at 772–73)

> From a fiduciary aspect, the permissible boundaries of intra-partnership competition, under paragraph 8, are limited only after the threshold of actual partnership acquisition has been crossed. Had Stanley and Andrea pirated an existing partnership asset or used partnership funds or encumbered [the family partnership] financially, our decision would be different.

Does this case stand for a general proposition that under UPA (1914) basic partnership duties be waived? For arguments that it does, see J. Dennis Hynes, Fiduciary Duties and RUPA: An Inquiry Into Freedom of Contract, 58–SPG Law & Contemp. Probs. 29 (Spring 1995); Larry E. Ribstein, Fiduciary Contracts in Unincorporated Firms, 54 Wash. & Lee L.Rev. 537 (1997). What if the agreement, instead of being limited to permitting competition with the partnership, stated that "each partner hereby waives all fiduciary duties owed by other partners in connection with partnership affairs"? Might such a provision mean that the relationship created is not a partnership despite the use of the terms "partners" and "partnership"? The overwhelming—though not universal—consensus is that under UPA (1914) fiduciary duties are mandatory, part of the status of being partners, and therefore not a matter purely of contractual choice. Consult Allan W. Vestal, Advancing The Search For Compromise: A Response To Professor Hynes, 58–SPG Law & Contemp. Probs. 55 (1995).

(5) UPA (1994) approaches the fiduciary duty issue very differently from UPA (1914). Consider carefully UPA (1994) § 404, particularly the word "only" in § 404(a) and the phrase "is limited to" in § 404(b). This language was inserted because of "a sense that vague, broad statements of a powerful duty of loyalty cause too much uncertainty. * * * [E]ven if there are no bad holdings, overly broad judicial language has left practitioners uncertain about whether their negotiated agreement will be voided. * * * [P]racticing attorneys want to be able to reach a deal, put it down on paper and know that it will not be undone by the application of fiduciary duties." Donald J. Weidner, The Revised Uniform Partnership Act Midstream: Major Policy Decisions, 21 U. Tol. L. Rev. 825, 856 (1990). A description of the last-minute changes made in the language of § 404 is described in J. Dennis Hynes, Fiduciary Duties and RUPA: An Inquiry Into Freedom of Contract, 58–SPG Law & Contemp. Probs. 29 (1995).

(a) Does not UPA (1994) § 404(b)(1) incorporate most of the essence of UPA (1914) § 21? However, UPA (1914) § 21 refers to the "formation, conduct, or liquidation" of the partnership while UPA (1994) § 404(b)(1) refers only to the "conduct or winding up" of the partnership. Under UPA (1994) there is no duty of loyalty in connection with the formation of the partnership. Does that make sense? Should the negotiation of a partnership contract be subject to a broader fiduciary duty than the negotiation of a contract, say, for employment or to purchase a new automobile? Might not a relationship of trust and confidence exist while a partnership agreement is being drafted? See also UPA (1994) § 404(d). There is no similar provision in UPA (1914). Does the combination of UPA (1914) §§ 404(b), (c), and (d), taken together, equal the broadly phrased duty established by *Meinhard* and UPA (1914) § 21 (except with respect to partnership formation)?

(b) Might there be aspects of a duty of loyalty that are not encompassed within the three subsections of UPA (1994) § 404(b)? If so, what?

(c) Does not UPA (1994) § 404(e) significantly undercut § 404(b)? Cannot most breaches of fiduciary duty be justified on the theory that the conduct "furthers the partner's own interest?" What function, if any, does the word "merely" in § 404(e) serve?

(d) The duty of care defined in UPA § 404(c) essentially adopts the duty of care applicable in the corporate context (see Chapter 10 pp. 663–706, infra) for partnerships. UPA (1914) did not attempt to define a duty of care for partners. For an argument that the relaxed corporate concepts of duty of care are "inappropriate" for partnerships, see Claire Moore Dickerson, Is It Appropriate to Appropriate Corporate Concepts: Fiduciary Duties and the Revised Uniform Partnership Act, 64 U. Colo. L.Rev. 111, 151–56 (1993).

(6) What is "the right to a formal account" referred to in UPA (1914) § 22? Alan R. Bromberg, Crane and Bromberg on Partnership 410–412 (1968):*

> A formal account or (as it is sometimes called) an accounting is more than a presentation of financial statements. It encompasses a review of all transactions, including alleged improprieties, which should be reflected in the financial statements. It resembles a trustee's accounting.
>
> If a partner asks his co-partners for an account and does not get it, or is not satisfied with it, he may bring an action for an accounting. This is a comprehensive investigation of transactions of the partnership and the partners, and an adjudication of their relative rights. It is conducted by the court or, more commonly, by an auditor, referee or master, subject to the court's review. Equitable throughout most of its long history, this action is well adapted to the complexity of partners' relations. But its origins lie in the mutual fiduciary obligations of the partners.
>
> An accounting action is designed to produce and evaluate all testimony relevant to the various claims of the partners. It results in a money judgment for or against each partner according to the balance struck. Ancillary relief, like injunction, receivership, and partition may be granted in appropriate cases. Since all activities related to the partnership are subject to scrutiny, a wide variety of matters may be determined * * *.
>
> At common law an action for an accounting was generally denied except incident to dissolution. The feeling was that partners should not seek to have the courts operate their affairs; if they cannot get along together amicably, they should dissolve and wind up. * * *

The language of UPA (1914) § 22 (particularly § 22(c)) softens the common law rule that an action for an accounting can occur only upon dissolution and winding up, but it is unusual to have a formal accounting within the context of an ongoing partnership. See Alan R. Bromberg and Larry E. Ribstein, Bromberg and Ribstein

* Reprinted with permission from West Publishing Corporation.

on Partnership, § 6.08. One consequence of permitting an accounting only upon the termination of a partnership is that the court is required to inquire into all matters during the life of the partnership, including old and stale claims without concern about statutes of limitation or laches. UPA (1994) does not retain this aspect of the common law concept of a formal accounting; see UPA (1994) §§ 405 and 807, particularly § 405(c).

(7) From the facts of Meinhard v. Salmon it appears likely that the written joint venture agreement entered into by those individuals was drafted by a lawyer. Assume that this lawyer was Salmon's personal attorney, and that he continued to render legal assistance from time to time, both to Salmon individually and to the Meinhard–Salmon joint venture without seriously considering whether there might be a potential conflict of interest between these two roles. Does that lawyer then have two clients, Salmon and the joint venture? ABA Formal Ethics Opinion 91–361 (July 12, 1991) concludes that a partnership is an "organization" under Model Rule 1.13[11] and that a lawyer who represents the partnership does not thereby represent any (or all) of the individual partners. Such a lawyer today thus has a dual representation. Assume further that Salmon's lawyer became involved in Salmon's negotiations with Gerry near the end of the joint venture. Did he do so as Salmon's lawyer or as the joint venture's lawyer? As a lawyer for the joint venture, might he have an obligation to disclose to Meinhard what he has learned without regard to who he represents?

ABA Commission on Ethics and Professional Responsibility, Formal Opinion 91–361 (1991), suggests the following procedure be followed when a lawyer for the partnership elects to also represent one or more partners:

> If an attorney retained by a partnership explains at the outset of the representation, preferably in writing, his or her role as counsel to the organization and not to the individual partners, and if, when asked to represent an individual partner, the lawyer puts the question before the partnership or its governing body, explains the implications of the dual representation, and obtains the informed consent of both the partnership and the individual partners, the likelihood of perceived ethical impropriety on the part of the lawyer should be significantly reduced.

Is it a fair conclusion that today a lawyer should not simultaneously represent both a partnership and an individual partner, at least with respect to his dealings with other partners?

(8) 6 Del. Code Ann. § 17–1101(d) provides that in limited partnerships, "[t]o the extent that, at law or in equity, a partner has duties (including fiduciary duties) and liabilities relating thereto to a limited partnership or to another

---

11. [By the Editor] Rule 1.13 provides in part: "(a) A lawyer employed or retained by an organization represents the organization acting through its duly authorized constituents. (b) If a lawyer for an organization knows that an officer, employee or other person associated with the organization is engaged in action, intends to act or refuses to act in a matter related to the representation that is a violation of a legal obligation to the organization, or a violation of law which reasonably might be imputed to the organization, and is likely to result in substantial injury to the organization, the lawyer shall proceed as is reasonably necessary in the best interest of the organization. * * * (d) In dealing with an organization's directors, officers, employees, members, shareholders or other constituents, a lawyer shall explain the identity of the client when it is apparent that the organization's interests are adverse to those of the constituents with whom the lawyer is dealing. (e) A lawyer representing an organization may also represent any of its directors, officers, employees, members, shareholders or other constituents, subject to the provisions of Rule 1.7. If the organization's consent to the dual representation is required by Rule 1.7, the consent shall be given by an appropriate official of the organization other than the individual who is to be represented, or by the shareholders."

partner * * * (2) the partner's duties and liabilities may be expanded or restricted by provisions in a partnership agreement." Does "restrict" mean "eliminate"? For an argument that this is the "appropriate rule" for partnerships generally, see Larry E. Ribstein, Fiduciary Duty Contracts in Unincorporated Firms, 54 Wash. & Lee L.Rev. 537 (1997).

F. PARTNERSHIP PROPERTY

OFFICIAL COMMENT TO SUBDIVISIONS (1) AND (2–B) OF SECTION 25 OF THE UNIFORM PARTNERSHIP ACT

6 Uniform Laws Annotated: Uniform Partnership Act 327 (1969).*

Subdivision (1). One of the present principal difficulties in the administration of the law of partnerships arises out of the difficulty of determining the exact nature of the rights of a partner in specific partnership property. That the partners are co-owners of partnership property is clear; but the legal incidents attached to the right of each partner as co-owner are not clear. When the English courts in the seventeenth century first began to discuss the legal incidents of this co-ownership, they were already familiar with two other kinds of co-ownership, joint tenancy and tenancy in common. In joint tenancy on the death of one owner his right in the property passes to the other co-owners. This is known as the right of survivorship. The incident of survivorship fits in with the necessities of partnership. On the death of a partner, the other partners and not the executors of the deceased partner should have a right to wind up partnership affairs. (See [UPA (1914) § 25(d).].) The early courts, therefore, declared that partners were joint tenants of partnership property, the consequence being that all the other legal incidents of joint tenancy were applied to partnership co-ownership. Many of these incidents, however, do not apply to the necessities of the partnership relation and produce most inequitable results. This is not to be wondered at because the legal incidents of joint tenancy grew out of a co-ownership of land not held for the purposes of business. The attempt of our courts to escape the inequitable results of applying the legal incidents of joint tenancy to partnership has produced very great confusion. Practically this confusion has had more unfortunate effect on substantive rights when the separate creditors of a partner attempt to attach and sell specific partnership property than when a partner attempts to assign specific partnership property not for a partnership purpose but for his own purposes.

The Commissioners, however, believe that the proper way to end the confusion which has arisen out of the attempt to treat partners as joint tenants, is to recognize the fact that the rights of a partner as co-owner with his partners of specific partnership property should depend on the necessities of the partnership relation. In short, that the legal incidents of the tenancy in partnership are not necessarily those of any other co-ownership.

In the clauses of this section these incidents of tenancy in partnership are stated with several practical results of value. In the first place the law is greatly simplified in expression. In the second place the danger of the courts

* Reprinted with permission from West Publishing Corporation.

reaching an inequitable conclusion by refusing to modify the results of applying the legal incidents of joint tenancy to the partnership relation is done away with. Finally, ground is laid for the simplification of a procedure in those cases where the separate creditor desires to secure satisfaction out of his debtor's interest in the partnership. (Compare [UPA (1914) § 25(2)(c)] with [UPA (1914) § 28(1).].)

Subdivision (2–b). Clause (b) asserts that the right of a partner as co-owner in specific partnership property is not separately assignable. This peculiarity of tenancy in partnership is a necessary consequence of the partnership relation. If A and B are partners and A attempts to assign all his right in partnership property, say a particular chattel, to C, and the law recognizes the possibility of such a transfer, C would pro tanto become a partner with B; for the rights of A in the chattel are to possess the chattel for a partnership purpose. But partnership is a voluntary relation. B cannot have a partner thrust upon him by A without his, B's, consent.

A cannot confer on C his, A's, right to possess and deal with the chattel for a partnership purpose. Neither can he confer any other rights which he has in the property. A partner has a beneficial interest in partnership property considered as a whole. As profits accrue, he has a right to be paid his proportion, and on the winding up of the business, after the obligations due third persons have been met, he has a right to be paid in cash his share of what remains of the partnership property. These rights considered as a whole are his interest in the partnership; and this beneficial interest he may assign in whole or fractional part, as is indicated in [UPA (1914) § 27]. In a sense, each partner, having thus a beneficial interest in the partnership property considered as a whole, has a beneficial interest in each part, and such beneficial interest might be regarded as assignable if it were not impossible, except by purely arbitrary and artificial rules, to measure a partner's beneficial interest in a specific chattel belonging to the partnership, or any other specific portion of partnership property.

Notes

(1) As indicated in the official comment, the problem of ownership of property, the rights of partners, and the rights of creditors of the partnership and of individual partners are covered in some detail in UPA (1914) §§ 24–28. These sections should be read carefully since they provide firm (and sometimes startling) answers to questions. For example, a person dies leaving a will that provides that son A inherits all his personal property and daughter B inherits all his real estate. His only asset on his death is a one-half interest in a partnership whose sole asset is a valuable piece of real estate. Who is entitled to his interest in that real estate? See UPA (1914) § 26.

(2) Are not the complexities of property ownership in UPA (1914) a consequence of the unwillingness of the draftsmen of that statute to accept the notion that a partnership was an entity separate from the partners? Consider the much simpler property ownership rules adopted by UPA (1994) §§ 203, 204, 501, 502, 503. Section 502 defines the partner's "transferable interest" in a partnership; What is the analogous property interest defined in UPA (1914) § 24? How does UPA (1994) treat the "property interest" that is defined in UPA (1914) § 24 as "the right to participate in management"?

(3) The ability of a *partnership* creditor to proceed against the *individual* property of a partner is dependent only on naming and serving the partner as a defendant in the suit (and possibly obtaining a judgment against both the partner and the partnership and exhausting the assets of the partnership). If these steps are taken, the partner's individual property may be subject to execution, attachment or other process. However, the ability of an *individual* creditor to proceed against *partnership* property is sharply circumscribed. See UPA (1914) §§ 25(2)(c), 28; UPA (1994) §§ 501, 504. Why are individual creditors seeking to recover from partnership assets treated differently from partnership creditors seeking to recover from individual assets?

(4) What is a "charging order"? See UPA (1914) § 28; UPA (1994) § 504. Precisely what must an individual creditor do in order to obtain such an order? What rights or powers does such a creditor get when she obtains such an order. Is it a "lien" on the partnership interest? Consult Kerry v. Schneider, 239 F.2d 896 (9th Cir.1956); UPA (1994) § 504(b). What other rights does the creditor have or what can he thereafter obtain? J. Gordan Gose, The Charging Order Under the Uniform Partnership Act, 28 Wash.L.Rev. 1, 15–18 (1953), describes the relationship between creditor, debtor, and partnership as follows:

> In the somewhat doubtful state of the law,[12] the following propositions seem to accord best with the language and purpose of the statute and the philosophy of the American courts with respect thereto.
>
> First, the charging order may enjoin the members of the partnership from making further disbursements of any kind to the debtor partner, except such payments as may be permissible under a legal exemption right properly asserted by the debtor.
>
> Second, the charging order may formally require the members of the partnership to pay to the creditor any amounts which it would otherwise pay to the debtor partner, exclusive of any amounts payable to the latter under a properly asserted legal exemption right.
>
> Third, the appointment of a receiver is not indispensable to the collection of the claim out of the debtor partner's share. A receiver should be appointed only where he has some useful function to serve such as the maintenance of a lawsuit, the conduct of a sale or the representation of competing creditors of the debtor partner. It may be that even in such a case, no receiver is necessary since there is no insuperable reason why these services cannot be obtained by some other method. Certainly the court should not appoint a receiver where he would serve no useful purpose while adding to the expense of the proceeding.
>
> Fourth, the debtor's interest should be sold if, and only if, the court is convinced that the creditor's claim will not be satisfied with reasonable expedition by the less drastic process of diverting the debtor's income from the partnership to the payment of the debt.[13] Even in the case of a wholly solvent partnership, the creditor's claim may be so large in relation to the

12. [By the Author] No substantial aid to specific interpretations of the statute is obtained from the texts or other non-judicial literature. * * *

13. [By the Author] There is actually no authority whatsoever as to when a sale should be ordered. Necessarily the order must fall in the area of those "which the circumstances of the case require." The apparent situations in which sale would be necessary are those in which, owing to the size of the claim or the absence of current liquid income, an order to pay over the debtor partner's share of current income and other moneys would not be effective.

current income of the debtor from the firm as to require sale as the only alternative to long delay in payment.

Fifth, the courts should liberally employ the general language of the act concerning "orders, directions, accounts and inquiries * * * which the circumstances of the case may require." By this means information as to the nature and extent of the debtor's interest in the partnership can be obtained and the whole range of unusual problems which are bound to arise may be dealt with as the occasion demands. Included in this general power should be the power to prescribe the manner in which a sale of the partnership interest is to be made.[14]

One other question prominently posed by both the English and American statutes and not touched upon by any decision in either country since the adoption of the respective acts goes to the rights of a non-debtor partner who redeems or purchases the interest of a debtor partner. Both statutes expressly recognize the right to redeem and, in the event of a sale being ordered, the right to purchase at the sale. The American statute is somewhat more detailed, specifying that the right to redeem exists "before foreclosure."[15] and that a purchase or redemption may be made with separate property of the redemptioner or, if all of the non-debtor partners consent, with partnership property. Both statutes present the question whether a non-debtor partner who redeems or purchases thereby acquires the interest of the debtor partner free and clear of the latter's claim or in trust for him.

Considering the statute only, a possible distinction between the redemption and purchase situations can be urged. The price realized on a competitive sale theoretically represents the full value of the thing sold, although in practice this ideal result is seldom achieved. Upon a redemption before sale, however, there is not even a theoretical logical connection between the redemption price and the value of the redeemed interest. Normally the redemption price would be the amount of the creditor's claim and any identity between the amount of the claim and the value of the interest would be merely a coincidence.

Under these circumstances it might be maintained with some force that the non-debtor partners who purchase at a sale held under the statute acquire the debtor partner's interest absolutely[16] whereas the non-debtor partner who redeems has merely advanced moneys for the benefit of the debtor and holds the interest in trust for him. The theory would be that, in the former situation, the debtor's interest is entirely represented by the purchase money while, in the latter case, the value of the interest and its relation to the redemption price can be determined only by an accounting.

---

14. [By the Author] The statute is utterly silent as to the procedure to be followed in making a sale. * * * Whether [a sheriff] can be called on to make judicial sales in the absence of a special statutory provision is questionable. Unless the receiver contemplated by Section 28 is to be regarded as limited to the express duties mentioned in the statute, the logical procedure would be for him to conduct the sale on such notice and terms as the court might fix. * * *

15. [By the Author] No definition of these words appears elsewhere in the Act or in the cases decided thereunder. Doubtless the language would mean before sale or before the expiration of a redemption period fixed by the Court in its order of sale. There appears to be no unqualified right to a redemption period extending after sale, the matter being controlled by the Court's discretion.

16. [By the Author] Upon this theory, it would be immaterial whether separate or partnership funds were used by the non-debtor partners. The debtor would have received the full value of his interest in either event.

More likely, however, the courts would in all cases invoke principles of fiduciary relationship which are so deeply rooted in the law of partnership and would in every instance require the non-debtor partners to account for the full value of the debtor partner's interest, less the amount paid by way of redemption or purchase. * * *

(5) Where the partnership or a partner is insolvent UPA (1914) § 40(h) and (i) establish the "jingle rule" for priority of payment: individual creditors have priority with regard to individual property and partnership creditors have priority with regard to partnership property. For many years the federal Bankruptcy Act followed the same pattern, but in 1978 it was changed to provide, essentially, that partnership creditors have priority as to partnership property and equivalence with individual creditors as to individual property. 11 U.S.C.A. § 723(c). The most serious criticism of the old "jingle rule" was that partnership creditors consider the net worth of both the partnership and the individual partners in deciding to extend credit to the partnership and should not therefore be subordinated to individual creditors with respect to individual assets. UPA (1994) does not seek to define the priorities between partnership and individual creditors, presumably leaving the matter to the federal Bankruptcy Act.

(6) What is the status of an assignee or transferee of a partnership interest? Is she a partner? Is she liable for partnership obligations? Can she compel dissolution and winding up of the partnership? What rights does she have? See UPA (1914) §§ 18(g), 27, 32(2); UPA (1994) § 503. What are the rights and duties of an assignor or transferor of a partnership interest? Is he still a partner? Is he entitled to participate in management? Is he personally liable for partnership obligations incurred after the assignment?

G.   PARTNERSHIP ACCOUNTING

From an accounting standpoint, the business of the partnership is almost universally recognized as being distinct from the financial affairs of the individual partners. The interests of the partners are usually reflected in capital accounts which are adjusted periodically for income, drawings, and contributions or withdrawals of capital. A capital account essentially sets forth the partner's ownership interest in the partnership. UPA (1994) § 401 describes how each partner's capital account is constructed and maintained: that account equals the capital contributed by the partner less the amount of any distributions to the partner plus the partner's share of the profits less the partner's share of the losses. A partner's capital account may be negative from time to time; upon the final settlement of accounts when the partnership is terminated, a partner with a negative capital account must pay the partnership that amount. UPA (1994) § 807(b). It is not essential that the partnership actually maintain a formal capital account for each partner but all except the most informal partnerships do so. Because the tax accounting rules with respect to partnerships differ from general accounting principles for partnerships, most partnerships also maintain a second set of books to record transactions for tax purposes.

Financial accounting for partnerships in most respects closely resembles corporate accounting for profits and losses, assets and liabilities. A simple illustration based on the first year's successful operation of the AB Furniture Store might be helpful.

(1) Income Statement

AB FURNITURE STORE

Statement of Profit and Loss for Year Ending December 31, 19___

Sales	$417,000	
Cost of Sales	270,000	
GROSS PROFIT		$147,000
Other Expenses:		
Advertising	8,000	
Rentals..	24,000	
Depreciation	5,000	
Salaries	32,000	
Miscellaneous	18,000	87,000
NET PROFIT		$60,000

(2) Balance Sheet

AB FURNITURE STORE

Balance Sheet, December 31, 19___

Assets		Liabilities	
Cash	$19,000	Accounts Payable	$73,000
Accounts Receivable	93,000	Note Payable to A	25,000
Inventory	95,000		
Fixtures (Net of depreciation)	42,000		
Truck (Net of depreciation)	9,000	**Equity**	
		Partner's Capital	160,000
	$258,000		$258,000

(3) Capital Accounts for 19___

	Opening	Income for Year	Drawing for Year	Closing
A	$100,000	$30,000	–0–	$130,000
B	–0–	30,000	–0–	30,000
				$160,000

ROBERT W. HAMILTON AND RICHARD A BOOTH, BUSINESS BASICS FOR LAW STUDENTS: ESSENTIAL TERMS AND CONCEPTS

Pages ___–___ (1998).*

The starting point of the whole subject of accountancy is a very simple equation:

$$\text{Equity} = \text{Assets} - \text{Liabilities}$$

Equity in this equation has nothing to do with the historical courts of equity or with notions of fairness or simple justice: It means *ownership* or *net worth*. This equation simply states that the net worth of a business is equal to its assets minus its liabilities.

A *balance sheet* is in many ways the most fundamental financial statement: It is simply a restatement of this fundamental equation in the form:

$$Assets = Liabilities + Equity$$

A balance sheet simply is a presentation of this equation in a chart form:

Assets:	Liabilities + Equity
_____	_____

Every balance sheet, whether it is for General Motors or the smallest retail grocery store, is based on this format. * * *

The asset side of a balance sheet is usually referred to as the *left hand side* [and] the liability/equity side is usually called the *right hand side* * * *.

There are four fundamental premises underlying financial accounting that can readily be grasped from this simple introduction. First, *financial accounting assumes that the business that is the subject of the financial statements is an entity*. A person may own several different businesses; if each maintains its own records, it will be on the assumption that it is independent from the person's other businesses. The equity referred to in that business's balance sheet will be limited to the person's investment in that single business. If a person owns two businesses that keep separate financial records, a debt owed by one business to the other will be reflected as an asset on one balance sheet and a liability on the other. Second, *all entries have to be in terms of dollars*. All property, tangible or intangible, shown on a balance sheet, must be expressed in dollars, either *historical cost* or *fair market value* or some other method of valuation. Many "assets" or "liabilities" of a business, however, are not reflected at all. A person's friendly smile may be an asset in a sense, but will not appear on a balance sheet since a dollar value is not normally given to a smile. Intangible assets, such as a debt owed to the company or rights to a patent, on the other hand, are assets that appear in balance sheets. * * * Similarly, a company may have a reputation for sharp practices or questionable dealing; while that reputation is doubtless a liability in a sense, it is not the type of liability that appears on a balance sheet. A liability in the balance sheet sense is a recognized debt or obligation to someone else, payable either in money or in something reducible to money. Not all liabilities that in the legal or lay sense meet this test are recognized as liabilities in the accounting sense. * * * Third, *a balance sheet has to balance*. The fundamental accounting equation itself states an equality: The two sides of the balance sheet restate that equality in somewhat reorganized form. A balance sheet therefore is itself an equality and the sum of the left hand side of the balance sheet must precisely equal the sum of the right hand side. Indeed, when accountants are involved in auditing a complex business, they take advantage of this characteristic by running *trial balances* on their work to make sure that they have not inadvertently transposed or omitted figures: The mathematical equality of the two sides of the balance sheet provides a check on the accuracy of the accountant's labors. In short, if a balance sheet doesn't balance, somewhere there is a mistake. Fourth, *every transaction entered into by a business must be recorded in at least two ways if the balance sheet is to continue to balance*. This last point underlies the concept of that mysterious subject, *double entry bookkeeping*, and is the cornerstone on which modern accounting is built.

Assume that we have a new business, just starting out, in which the owner has invested $10,000 in cash (for this purpose it makes no difference whether the business is going to be conducted in the form of a proprietorship, partnership, or corporation; all that is important is that it will be accounted for as an entity separate from the owner). The opening balance sheet will look like this:

Assets:		Liabilities	–0–
Cash	10,000	Owner's Equity	10,000

Now let us assume that the owner buys a used truck for $3,000 cash. The effect of this transaction is to reduce cash by $3,000 and create a new asset on the balance sheet:

Assets:		Liabilities	–0–
Cash	7,000	Owner's Equity	10,000
Used Truck	3,000		
	10,000		10,000

Voila! The balance sheet still balances. Let us assume next that the owner goes down to the bank and borrows an additional $1,000. This also has a dual effect: it increases cash by $1,000 (since the business is receiving the proceeds of the loan) and increases liabilities by $1,000 (since the business thereafter has to repay the loan). Yet another balance sheet can be created showing the additional effect of this second transaction:

Assets:		Liabilities	
Cash	8,000	Debt to Bank	1,000
Used Truck	3,000	Owner's Equity	10,000
	11,000		11,000

A couple of further insights should be evident from these two examples: First, *a balance sheet records a situation at one instant in time*. It is a static concept, an equilibrium that exists at one point in time rather than a record of change from an earlier period. Put another way, every transaction potentially creates a different or new balance sheet when the transaction is recorded. Second, *the bottom line of a balance sheet—$11,000 in this example—is not itself a meaningful figure*, since transactions such as the bank loan that do not affect the real worth of the business to the owners may increase or decrease it. * * *

The two transactions described above—the purchase of a used truck and a short-term bank loan—involve a reshuffling of assets and liabilities. From an accounting standpoint, the owner of the business is neither richer nor poorer as a result of them. However, most transactions that a business enters into are of a different type: They involve ordinary business operations leading to a profit or loss in the current accounting period. Let us take a simple example: The business involves hauling things in the truck for customers. The day that it opens for business, it hires a truck driver at a cost of $200 per day to drive the truck and pick up and deliver for it. During that first day the truck driver works very hard and for long hours making deliveries for which the business is paid $500. It is simple to create a *profit and loss statement* or *income statement* for the business for the one day of operation. "Profit and loss" and "income" are synonyms for this purpose. The basic formula is:

$$\text{Income} = \text{Revenues} - \text{Expenses}$$

Obviously, the business had income of $300 ($500 of revenue minus $200 of expense for the truck driver) for its first day of operation. There may have been other expenses as well that arguably should be charged to that first day of operation, but for simplicity we are ignoring that possibility.

At first glance the income statement appears to have nothing to do with the balance sheet described in the previous section. However, one should not jump too quickly to conclusions. It is possible to create a new balance sheet to reflect each of these transactions as well:

First, the payment of the $200 to the truck driver involves a cash payment of $200 by the business; it is easy to record that. But where should the offsetting entry be? The balance sheet cannot look like this:

Assets:			Liabilities	
Cash		7,800	Debt to Bank	1,000
Used Truck		3,000	Equity	10,000
		10,800		11,000

Something is obviously wrong since this balance sheet does not balance. There has to be an offsetting entry. It certainly should not be a reduction of liabilities (since the amount of the bank loan is unchanged) or an increase in value of the truck. Perhaps one could view the services as an asset something like the truck, but that does not make much sense since the services are transient and performed at the time the payment is made. One could perhaps argue that no balance sheet should be created until the payment to the truck driver is offset by whatever he earns during the rest of the day, but that cannot be correct either, because the balance sheet should balance after every transaction, not just at the end of a sequence of transactions. The only possible solution is to reduce "owner's equity" by the payment:

Assets:			Liabilities	
Cash		7,800	Debt to Bank	1,000
Used Truck		3,000	Equity	9,800
		10,800		10,800

Second, the $500 payment for the services rendered:

Assets:			Liabilities	
Cash		8,300	Debt to Bank	1,000
Used Truck		3,000	Equity	10,300
		11,300		11,300

Admittedly, these two balance sheets are not very helpful in showing the relationship between the balance sheet and the income statement. What is needed is a segregation of income items *within the equity account* so that the permanent investment and the transient changes are shown separately. If we take as the period of time the one-day period in which the truck driver was hired and his services were performed, the following balance sheet at the end of the period is much more illuminating:

Assets:			Liabilities	
	Cash	8,300	Debt to Bank	1,000
	Used Truck	3,000	Original capital	10,000
			Earnings	300
		11,300		11,300

The important point at present is that *the statement of income or profit and loss is itself a right-hand entry on the balance sheet.*

The balance sheet is a static concept showing the status of a business at a particular instant in time while the income statement describes the results of operations over some period of time: daily, monthly, quarterly, or annually. In a sense, the balance sheet is a photograph, the income statement a motion picture. However, the income statement for a period provides the bridge between the balance sheet at the beginning of the period and the balance sheet at the end of the period because positive income items (revenues) increase the owner's equity account while negative income items (expenses) reduce that account. Logically, the balance sheet is the basic document around which all financial statements are constructed while the income statement is a bridge between successive balance sheets.

Notes

(1) It is important for every law student to understand enough of the rudiments of accounting principles to be able to distinguish between the balance sheet and profit and loss statement set forth above.

(2) Turning to AB Furniture Store partnership financial statements, how would the partners' capital accounts look if the store had spent $10,000 rather than $8,000 on advertising in the year in question without any increase in sales? How would they look if both A and B had drawn $5,000 each out of the business at the end of the year in question? If the partnership had lost $6,000 rather than showing a profit of $60,000?

(3) While AB Furniture Store has had a smashing first year income-wise, it is not blessed with an overabundance of cash. In this respect it is like many new, struggling businesses. Do you look at the profit and loss statement or balance sheet to determine the cash position of the business? Why? The year-end balance sheet shows that the bulk of the current assets of the business are tied up in inventory and accounts receivable (amounts representing goods sold on credit). However, the AB Furniture Store, like most businesses, can safely work on the assumption that there will be continuous sales from inventories and payments by customers on account so that a cash crisis is unlikely even though the business's current liabilities significantly exceed its cash on hand.

(4) A, despite his desire to limit his financial investment to $100,000, agreed to lend the partnership an additional $25,000, presumably because the store was successful. He therefore has the status both of creditor and of partner. What are his rights as against other general creditors with respect to his loan if the partnership goes under? See UPA (1914) § 40.

(5) In actual operation, a small business such as the AB Furniture Store would likely use its "cash flow" as a measure of its success or failure. Accounting

for cash flow differs from traditional accounting in that it considers only transactions that involve dollars in and dollars out. Traditional accounting, as set forth above, includes some expenses that do not reduce the amount of available cash of the business. An example is the item "depreciation" in AB Furniture's financial statements. When assets are purchased by a business they are usually recorded in a business's accounting records at their purchase price ("historical cost") with no subsequent adjustment for variations in market value but with an annual charge for "depreciation" to reflect the gradual "wearing out" or "using up" of the asset. See Robert W. Hamilton and Richard A. Booth, Business Basics for Law Students: Essential Terms and Concepts § __.__ (1998), for a fuller discussion. The AB Furniture Store has adopted this practice and has deducted from its earnings $5,000 for depreciation of its fixtures and its equipment. Obviously, there was no payment of $5,000 to anyone involved in this transaction. Hence, if everything else were equal, cash flow of the AB Furniture Store for the first year will be $5,000 higher than its reported earnings. However, there are many items that do not affect earnings but have the opposite effect of reducing cash flow. An obvious example is the repayment of a debt. Most businesses prepare "cash flow" financial statements for internal purposes and to make sure that there will be cash available when foreseeable payments become due. In modern financial analysis, there is usually more emphasis on analysis of cash flow than on accounting earnings. Assume that AB Furniture Store decides to liquidate and wind up after one year—all the assets are sold, the proceeds used to discharge debts, and the balance distributed to the partners. Given the conventions described in this note, can one determine from the balance sheet how much will be available for distribution to A and B?

(6) Also, neither A nor B withdrew any portion of the profit for the year, though, of course, B received his "salary." Where does B's salary appear in the financial statements? Is that a proper treatment for those payments? Also, why didn't A and B distribute funds at the end of the year? Do you think A would object if B proposed to pay himself an additional $10,000 as a distribution of his share of the profits? After all, it is his money, isn't it? In deciding whether or not to make distributions to partners, should one look at the profit and loss statement or a cash flow statement? If more cash is distributed to B than the amount set forth in his capital account, his capital account will become negative. Is there anything wrong with that?

(7) Rather than winding up the AB Furniture Store, A and B decide they will sell the business as an operating unit to a third person, X. Presumably, X is buying the business in order to continue to operate it, not to close it down. Can one use the financial statements set forth above to determine how much X should offer for the business? How might they be used to estimate the value of the AB Furniture Store? See Robert W. Hamilton and Richard A. Booth, Business Basics for Law Students, Ch. 8 (1998). Does the value of the business depend in part on whether B is willing to remain as manager?

H. PARTNERSHIP DISSOLUTION

The dissolution provisions of the two versions of the Uniform Partnership Act differ significantly from each other and were an area of significant controversy in the drafting of UPA (1994). Dissolution provisions are the most complicated sections in both of these statutes. The cases and materials in the balance of this Section primarily deal with UPA (1914). The changes made by UPA (1994) are described in a note at the end of this Section.

In § 29 of UPA (1914), "dissolution" is defined as a change in legal relationship "caused by any partner ceasing to be associated in the carrying on * * * of the business." It should be apparent that this definition of the word "dissolution" differs considerably from the lay understanding of that word. It refers to a change in personal relationships among partners within the partnership and has nothing to do with the disposition of assets or closing down or selling the business. As a result of this peculiar definition, for the last eighty-odd years there has been a considerable risk of misunderstanding and confusion whenever the word "dissolution" is used in the partnership context. UPA (1914) § 30 defines two additional concepts: Following "dissolution" there is a period of "winding up," which leads to the "termination" of the partnership. Early drafts of UPA (1994) attempted to avoid the basic confusion over the word "dissolution" by not using the "d word" at all; however, it crept back into § 603 and article 8 of UPA (1994). UPA (1994) consistently uses the word "dissociation" to refer to an event that causes a partner to cease being a participant in the partnership; it is therefore very close to the technical concept of "dissolution" that was used in UPA (1914) § 29. In UPA (1994), "dissolution" is used only when referring to an event that leads to the termination of the partnership.

Notes

(1) Whatever the provisions of UPA (1914), partnership agreements prepared by attorneys usually make careful provision for the continuation of the business following dissolution. The most common provision is that upon any withdrawal of a partner ("dissolution" in the language of UPA (1914) § 29) the business of the partnership is not to be wound up and terminated but is to be continued by the remaining partners with the interest of the withdrawing partner being paid off in cash on some basis. Where the partnership is continued by agreement, is it not clear under UPA (1914) that "dissolution" has occurred and that a "new" partnership has instantaneously been formed to continue the business? For a court that refused to apply the language of UPA § 29 literally in this very common situation, see Adams v. Jarvis, page 82, infra.

(2) Even in the absence of express agreement, the withdrawal of one or more partners usually does not lead to the closing of the doors of the business. For example, in a partnership of three doctors, A, B, and C, that do not have a partnership agreement providing for the continuation of the business, assume that C withdraws but A and B decide to continue the same practice at the same location under the same name. C may well acquiesce in this decision by A and B since continuation is usually more sensible as a matter of simple business economics than a piecemeal liquidation and sale of the business. UPA (1914) contains elaborate provisions defining the rights and responsibilities of C if the business is continued after his withdrawal. See Cauble v. Handler, page 78, infra. However, in the absence of an agreement to continue, C may compel the winding up of the business. UPA (1914) § 38(1).

(3) The issue whether a change in membership of a partnership constitutes a "dissolution" that leads to a "new" partnership rather than merely the continuation of the old one, is not entirely academic. For example, leases usually prohibit assignments by tenants without the landlord's consent and may also authorize the landlord to cancel the lease if a prohibited assignment occurs. May a landlord use C's withdrawal from the partnership as a ground to cancel a lease that provides for rent at below current market prices?

(4) Under UPA (1914), does a technical dissolution occur when one or more new partners are admitted but no existing partner withdraws? See UPA (1914) §§ 17, 29.

COLLINS v. LEWIS

Texas Court of Civil Appeals, 1955.
283 S.W.2d 258, writ ref'd n.r.e.

HAMBLEN, CHIEF JUSTICE.

This suit was instituted in the District Court of Harris County by the appellants, who, as the owners of a fifty percent (50%) interest in a partnership known as the L–C Cafeteria, sought a receivership of the partnership business, a judicial dissolution of the partnership, and foreclosure of a mortgage upon appellees' interest in the partnership assets. Appellees denied appellants' right to the relief sought, and filed a cross-action for damages for breach of contract in the event dissolution should be decreed. Appellants' petition for receivership having been denied after a hearing before the court, trial of the issues of dissolution and foreclosure, and of appellees' cross-action, proceeded before the court and a jury. At the conclusion of such trial, the jury, in response to special issues submitted, returned a verdict upon which the trial court entered judgment denying all relief sought by appellants.

The facts are substantially as follows:

In the latter part of 1948 appellee John L. Lewis obtained a commitment conditioned upon adequate financial backing from the Brown–Bellows–Smith Corporation for a lease on the basement space under the then projected San Jacinto Building for the purpose of constructing and operating a large cafeteria therein. Lewis contacted appellant Carr P. Collins, a resident of Dallas, proposing that he (Lewis) would furnish the lease, the experience and management ability for the operation of the cafeteria, and Collins would furnish the money; that all revenue of the business, except for an agreed salary to Lewis, would be applied to the repayment of such money, and that thereafter all profits would be divided equally between Lewis and Collins. These negotiations * * * culminated in the execution between the building owners, as lessors, and Lewis and Collins, as lessees, of a lease upon such basement space for a term of 30 years. Thereafter Lewis and Collins entered into a partnership agreement to endure throughout the term of the lease contract. This agreement is in part evidenced by a formal contract between the parties, but both litigants concede that the complete agreement is ascertainable only from the verbal understandings and exchanges of letters between the principals. It appears to be undisputed that originally a corporation had been contemplated, and that the change to a partnership was made to gain the advantages which such a relationship enjoys under the internal revenue laws. The substance of the agreement was that Collins was to furnish all of the funds necessary to build, equip, and open the cafeteria for business. Lewis was to plan and supervise such construction, and, after opening for business, to manage the operation of the cafeteria. As a part of this undertaking, he guaranteed that moneys advanced by Collins would be repaid at the rate of at least $30,000, plus interest, in the first year of operation, and $60,000 per year, plus interest, thereafter, upon default of which Lewis would surrender his interest to Collins. In addition Lewis guaranteed Collins against loss to the extent of $100,000. * * *

Immediately after the lease agreement had been executed Lewis began the preparation of detailed plans and specifications for the cafeteria. Initially Lewis had estimated, and had represented to Collins, that the cost of completing the cafeteria ready for operation would be approximately $300,000. Due to delays on the part of the building owners in completing the building, and delays in procuring the equipment deemed necessary to opening the cafeteria for business, the actual opening did not occur until September 18, 1952, some 2½ years after the lease had been executed. The innumerable problems which arose during that period are in part reflected in the exchange of correspondence between the partners. Such evidence reflects that as to the solution of most of such problems the partners were in entire agreement. It further reflects that such disagreements as did arise were satisfactorily resolved. It likewise appears that the actual costs incurred during that period greatly exceeded the amount previously estimated by Lewis to be necessary. The cause of such increase is disputed by the litigants. Appellants contend that it was brought about largely by the extravagance and mismanagement of appellee Lewis. Appellees contend that it resulted from inflation, increased labor and material costs, caused by the Korean War, and unanticipated but necessary expenses. Whatever may have been the reason it clearly appears that Collins, while expressing concern over the increasing cost, and urging the employment of every possible economy, continued to advance funds and pay expenses, which, by the date of opening for business, had exceeded $600,000.

Collins' concern over the mounting costs of the cafeteria appears to have been considerably augmented by the fact that after opening for business the cafeteria showed expenses considerably in excess of receipts. Upon being informed, shortly after the cafeteria had opened for business, that there existed incurred but unpaid items of cost over and above those theretofore paid, Collins made demand upon Lewis that the cafeteria be placed immediately upon a profitable basis, failing which he (Collins) would advance no more funds for any purpose. There followed an exchange of recriminatory correspondence between the parties, Collins on the one hand charging Lewis with extravagant mismanagement, and Lewis on the other hand charging Collins with unauthorized interference with the management of the business. Futile attempts were made by Lewis to obtain financial backing to buy Collins' interest in the business. Numerous threats were made by Collins to cause Lewis to lose his interest in the business entirely. This suit was filed by Collins in January of 1953.

The involved factual background of this litigation was presented to the jury in a trial which extended over five weeks * * *. At the conclusion of the evidence 23 special issues of fact were submitted to the jury. The controlling issues of fact, as to which a dispute existed, were resolved by the jury in their answers to Issues 1 to 5, inclusive, in which they found that Lewis was competent to manage the business of the L–C Cafeteria; that there is not a reasonable expectation of profit under the continued management of Lewis; that but for the conduct of Collins there would be a reasonable expectation of profit under the continued management of Lewis; that such conduct on the part of Collins was not that of a reasonably prudent person acting under the same or similar circumstances; and that such conduct on the part of Collins materially decreased the earnings of the cafeteria during the first year of its operation. * * * [W]e conclude not only that there is ample support for the findings of the jury which we consider to be controlling, but further that upon the entire record, including such findings, the trial court entered the only proper judgment under the law, and that judgment must be in all things affirmed. * * *

As we understand appellants' position * * * they contend that there is no such thing as an indissoluble partnership; that it is not controlling or even important, in so far as the right to a dissolution is concerned, as to which of the partners is right or wrong in their disputes; and finally, that whenever it is made to appear that the partners are in hopeless disagreement concerning a partnership which has no reasonable expectation of profit, the legal right to dissolution exists. In support of these contentions appellants cite numerous authorities, all of which have been carefully examined. We do not undertake to individually distinguish the authorities cited for the reason that in no case cited by appellants does a situation analogous to that here present exist, namely, that the very facts upon which appellants predicate their right to a dissolution have been found by the jury to have been brought about by appellant Collins' own conduct, in violation of his own contractual obligations.

We agree with appellants' premise that there is no such thing as an indissoluble partnership only in the sense that there always exists the power, as opposed to the right, of dissolution. But legal right to dissolution rests in equity, as does the right to relief from the provisions of any legal contract. The jury finding that there is not a reasonable expectation of profit from the L–C Cafeteria under the continued management of Lewis, must be read in connection with their findings that Lewis is competent to manage the business of L–C Cafeteria, and that but for the conduct of Collins there would be a reasonable expectation of profit therefrom. In our view those are the controlling findings upon the issue of dissolution. It was Collins' obligation to furnish the money; Lewis' to furnish the management, guaranteeing a stated minimum repayment of the money. The jury has found that he was competent, and could reasonably have performed his obligation but for the conduct of Collins. We know of no rule which grants Collins, under such circumstances, the right to dissolution of the partnership. The rule is stated in Karrick v. Hannaman, 168 U.S. 328, 18 S.Ct. 135, 138, 42 L.Ed. 484, as follows: "A court of equity, doubtless, will not assist the partner breaking his contract to procure a dissolution of the partnership, because, upon familiar principles, a partner who has not fully and fairly performed the partnership agreement on his part has no standing in a court of equity to enforce any rights under the agreement." It seems to this Court that the proposition rests upon maxims of equity, too fundamental in our jurisprudence to require quotation.

The basic agreement between Lewis and Collins provided that Collins would furnish money in an amount sufficient to defray the cost of building, equipping and opening the L–C Cafeteria for operation. As a part of the agreement between Lewis and Collins, Lewis executed, and delivered to Collins, a mortgage upon Lewis' interest in the partnership "until the indebtedness incurred by the said Carr P. Collins * * * has been paid in full out of income derived from the said L–C Cafeteria, Houston, Texas." * * *

Collins' right to foreclose [the mortgage on Lewis' interest] depends upon whether or not Lewis has met his basic obligation of repayment at the rate agreed upon. Appellees contend, we think correctly, that he has, in the following manner: the evidence shows that Collins advanced a total of $636,-720 for the purpose of building, equipping and opening the cafeteria for business. The proof also shows that Lewis contended that the actual cost exceeded that amount by over $30,000. The litigants differed in regard to such excess, it being Collins' contention that it represented operating expense rather than cost of building, equipping and opening the cafeteria. The jury heard the conflicting proof relative to these contentions, and resolved the question by their answer to Special Issue 20, whereby they found that the minimum cost of building, equipping and opening the cafeteria for operation amounted to $697,603.36. Under the basic agreement of the partners, therefore, this excess was properly Collins' obligation. Upon the refusal of Collins to pay it, Lewis paid it out of earnings of the business during the first year of its operation. Thus it clearly appears that Lewis met his obligation, and the trial court properly denied foreclosure of the mortgage.

In their brief, appellants repeatedly complain that they should not be forced to endure a continuing partnership wherein there is no reasonable expectation of profit, which they say is the effect of the trial court's judgment. The proper and equitable solution of the differences which arise between partners is never an easy problem, especially where the relationship is as involved as this present one. We do not think it can properly be said, however, that the judgment of the trial court denying appellants the dissolution which they seek forces them to endure a partnership wherein there is no reasonable expectation of profit. We have already pointed out the ever present inherent power, as opposed to the legal right, of any partner to terminate the relationship. Pursuit of that course presents the problem of possible liability for such damages as flow from the breach of contract. The alternative course available to appellants seems clearly legible in the verdict of the jury, whose services in that connection were invoked by appellants.

Judgment affirmed.

Notes

(1) The principal case arose before Texas enacted its version of UPA (1914). Would the result have been the same under that Act? See UPA §§ 31(1)(b), 31(2), 38(2).

(2) Assuming the case had arisen under that Act, would Collins' rights have been different if he could have dissolved the partnership under § 31(1)(b) rather than under § 32? In what way?

(3) Apparently Collins and Lewis are locked into a partnership that is, as a practical matter, not dissolvable. What happens next?

CAUBLE v. HANDLER

Texas Court of Civil Appeals, 1973.
503 S.W.2d 362, writ ref'd n.r.e.

BREWSTER, JUSTICE.

This is a suit brought by the administratrix of the estate of a deceased partner against the surviving partner for an accounting of the partnership assets. No jury was involved and the trial court did not file findings of fact and conclusions of law. Tom Handler, the defendant, was the surviving partner and Thomas Cauble was the deceased partner. The partnership was engaged in selling at retail furniture and appliances and each partner owned a 50% interest.

The trial court awarded the plaintiff, the administratrix of the estate of the deceased partner, a judgment against the surviving partner for $20.95 plus six percent interest thereon from February 2, 1973, the date of the judgment. The judgment also awarded the court appointed auditor a fee in the sum of $1,800.00 for his services in auditing the partnership accounts, taxed the item as court costs, and then taxed the entire court costs against plaintiff. It is from this judgment that plaintiff is appealing. We will refer herein to the parties as they appeared in the court below.

We reverse and remand the case for a new trial.

The plaintiff's first point is that the trial court erred in basing its judgment upon the book value of the partnership assets that were arbitrarily established by defendant. Her eighth point of error is that the court erred in refusing to consider the cash market value of the partnership assets in arriving at its judgment.

We sustain both of these points of error.

It is apparent from the record that the trial court determined the value of the partnership inventory by using the cost or book value thereof. Thomas Cauble died on May 18, 1971. * * * Handler kept the partnership books and took a physical inventory that was used by the partnership tax man in preparing [the] final partnership income tax return. In preparing the inventory Handler testified that he priced each item in the inventory "According to the invoices, according to cost." Again he stated: "Take the count first and then you * * * go back to the invoice and pick up the amount."

The value of the partnership inventory, arrived at as above indicated, was used by the accountant in preparing the final income tax return and was used by the court in determining the value of the plaintiff's interest in the partnership at the date of Cauble's death.

The court erred when he used the cost price or book value of the partnership assets in determining the value of the inventory. The following is from the opinion in the case of Johnson v. Braden, 286 S.W.2d 671 (San Antonio, Tex.Civ.App., 1956, no writ hist.), at page 672: "The judgment must be reversed. Market values of the company assets are wholly absent from the record, and Johnson, on cross-examination, demonstrated that the plaintiff's audit was based on book values. *It should have been based on market value.*" (Emphasis ours.)

See also * * * Hurst v. Hurst, 1 Ariz.App. 227, 401 P.2d 232 (1965). This Hurst case holds that book values are simply arbitrary values and cannot be used. The case also holds that the amount for which the partnership assets were sold four years after the date of dissolution is also not proper evidence to be considered on the issue of market value of the partnership property at date of dissolution. * * *

Much of plaintiff's argument under her first three points of error is devoted to her contention that the trial court erred in failing and refusing to allow her a share of the profit made by Handler by continuing the partnership business between date of dissolution and date of judgment.

We sustain this contention.

The undisputed evidence shows that Handler continued to operate and to control the partnership business after the death of Cauble and down to the trial date, and that he used and sold the assets of the partnership during all that period. The record does not show that this was done with the consent of the administratrix of the deceased's estate.

Exhibit E of the court appointed auditor's report was offered into evidence and it showed that during the period from May 19, 1971, to May 21, 1972, Handler made a net profit of $40,163.42 out of operating the partnership business after dissolution. The fact that this net profit was made is undisputed. As demonstrated above this auditor's report was legitimate evidence of the amount of those profits.

The defendant * * * admits that plaintiff tried this case on the theory that she was entitled to recover, after the accounting, one-half of the value of the partnership assets, plus a share of the profits from the date of Cauble's death to date of judgment.

The trial court, in its judgment, refused to allow the plaintiff to recover one-half of the profits that were made by Handler after the dissolution of the partnership by his continued operation of the business. Instead the trial court awarded plaintiff a recovery of some interest in the amount of $3,764.89.

It is section 38(1) of [UPA (1914)] that gave the representative of the estate of the deceased partner the right to elect, if she so desired, to have the partnership assets liquidated, the debts paid, and the share of each partner in the surplus paid to him in cash.

The plaintiff in this case did not elect to have this done.

If that election is made it many times results in the sacrifice of going concern values. See "Law of Partnership" by Crane and Bromberg, page 474, note 43.

The following quotation explains the several elections that were open to the plaintiff under the fact situation that we have here. It is from "Law of Partnership" by Crane and Bromberg, Section 86(c), pages 495–496, and is as follows:

> "If a partnership is seasonably wound up after dissolution, profits and losses during the liquidation are shared by the partners in proportion to their pre-dissolution ratios, unless they have agreed otherwise. * * *
>
> "*The situation changes if the business is not wound up, but continued, whether with or without agreement.* In either case, the noncontinuing partner (or his representative) has a first election between two basic alternatives, either of which can be enforced in an action for an accounting. He can force a liquidation, taking his part of the proceeds and thus sharing in profits and losses after dissolution. Alternatively, he can permit the business to continue (or accept the fact that it has continued) and claim as a creditor (though subordinate to outside creditors) the value of his interest at dissolution. This * * * means he is unaffected by later changes in those values. *If he takes the latter route, he has a second*

election to receive in addition either interest * * * *or profits from date of dissolution.* This second election shields him from losses, * * *

"The second election may seem one-sided. It serves as 'a species of compulsion * * * to those continuing the business * * * to hasten its orderly winding up.' In part it is compensation to the outgoing partner for his liability on partnership obligations existing at dissolution; this liability continues until satisfaction, which would normally occur in the process of winding up. * * *

"The second election rests partly on the use of the outgoing partner's assets in the conduct of the business * * * his right to profits ends when the value of his interest is properly paid to him." (Emphasis ours.)

[UPA (1914)] Section 42 * * * gives the representative of the estate of a deceased partner a right to share in the profits, if he elects to do so, if the other partner continues to operate the business after dissolution.

The great weight of authority is to the effect that Sec. 42, giving the option to take profits to the non-continuing partner is applicable regardless of whether the business is continued with or without the consent of the non-continuing partner or the representative of his estate. For a full discussion of this see the law review article in 63 Yale Law Journal 709, entitled "Profit Rights and Creditors' Priorities After a Partner's Death or Retirement: Section 42 of the UPA" and the additional article on this subject in 67 Harvard Law Review 1271.

It is manifestly clear that the plaintiff in this case elected, as she had a right to do under Sec. 42 to have the value of Cauble's partnership interest at the date of dissolution ascertained and to receive from the surviving partner, Handler, as an ordinary creditor, an amount equal to the value of Cauble's interest in the dissolved partnership at date of dissolution, plus the profits attributable to his right in the property of the dissolved partnership.

The following proceedings that occurred during the trial show that this election was made by plaintiff:

"THE COURT: You think they're making an election for the profits, is that correct, sir?

"MR. OWENS: The way they've been introducing their evidence and talking here I presume they have.

"MR. SCHATTMAN: That's correct.

"THE COURT: If you have not done so that is your election?

"MR. SCHATTMAN: Right.

"THE COURT: All right, then that disposes of that point."

Although the undisputed evidence showed that Handler made over $40,-163.42 by operating the partnership business after dissolution the Court refused to allow plaintiff to recover from Handler the Cauble estate's share of those profits, which plaintiff had a right to do. In lieu of profits, which plaintiff elected to recover, the Court awarded her six percent interest on what he found to be the cost or book value of the Cauble interest in the partnership at date of dissolution. This interest amounted to $3,764.89, which sum was considerably less than a one-half interest in the $40,163.42 in profits that Handler made out of his operation of the partnership business after dissolution.

This error was obviously prejudicial to plaintiff.

In plaintiff's fifth point of error she contends that the trial court erred in taxing all the costs incurred in connection with the accounting case, including the court appointed auditor's fee of $1,800.00, against the plaintiff. * * *

The record does not reveal the court's reason for taxing all the court costs, including the $1,800.00 court appointed auditor's fee, against just one of the two partners involved in this accounting suit. * * *

We recognize that the trial court does have a broad discretion in taxing the costs in a case like this and there are occasions where the costs have been taxed against just one partner. But, as a general rule, the costs that are incurred in an accounting case are ordered paid out of the partnership estate. This results in the costs being paid by the partners in proportion to their interest in the business.

It would seem that in the ordinary case both partners would benefit by having the state of the account between them legally adjudicated so that the partnership can be terminated. One partner is not obligated to accept the adverse party's word for the state of the partnership account. * * *

Reversed and remanded for a new trial.

Notes

(1) In addition to the basic elections provided by UPA (1914) described in the principal case, the Act also provides answers for a number of other questions that may arise when a partnership business is simply continued after dissolution. For example:

(a) What are the rights of creditors of the old partnership with respect to the assets of the continuing business? See UPA (1914) § 41.

(b) In view of the agency that exists between partners, what must a retiring partner do to avoid liability for subsequent partnership obligations? See UPA (1914) § 35(1)(b).

(c) If a creditor knows that a partner has retired and deals with the successor partnership, does that release the retired partner from preretirement partnership obligations? See UPA (1914) § 36(2).

(2) In general, the dissolution provisions of UPA (1914) are complicated because they deal with a number of possible variations and a number of possible problems. They are also arranged in a sequence which complicates the process of tracing through how each specific situation should be handled.

ADAMS v. JARVIS

Supreme Court of Wisconsin, 1964.
23 Wis.2d 453, 127 N.W.2d 400.

Action for declaratory judgment construing a medical partnership agreement between three doctors. Plaintiff-respondent withdrew from the partnership seven years after it was formed. * * *

The dispute concerns the extent of the plaintiff's right to share in partnership assets, specifically accounts receivable. The relevant portions of the agreement provide:

"12. Books of Account. Proper books of account shall be kept by said partners and entries made therein of all matters, transactions, and things as are usually entered in books of account kept by persons engaged in the same or similar business. Such books and all partnership letters, papers and documents shall be kept at the firm's office and each partner shall at all times have access to examine, copy, and take extracts from the same.

"13. Fiscal Year—Share of Profits and Losses. The partnership fiscal year shall coincide with the calendar year. Net profits and losses of the partnership shall be divided among the individuals in the same proportion as their capital interests in the partnership, except as hereinafter provided for partners who become incapacitated or have withdrawn from the partnership, or the estates of the deceased partners. * * *

"15. Conditions of Termination. Partnership shall not terminate under certain conditions. The incapacity, withdrawal or death of a partner shall not terminate this partnership. Such partner, or the estate or heirs of a deceased partner shall continue to participate in partnership profits and losses, as provided in this agreement, but shall not participate in management, the making of partnership decisions, or any professional matters. On the happening of any of the above events, the books of the partnership shall not be closed until the end of the partnership fiscal year.

"16. Withdrawal. No withdrawal from the firm shall be effective until at least thirty (30) days have elapsed from the date on which written notice of such intention is given the other partners by registered mail to their last known address.

"As used herein 'withdrawal' shall refer to any situation in which a partner leaves the partnership, at a time when said partnership is not dissolving, pursuant to a written agreement of the parties to do so. The withdrawing partner shall be entitled to receive from the continuing partners the following:

"(1) Any balance standing to his credit on the books of the partnership;

"(2) That proportion of the partnership profits to which he was entitled by this agreement in the fiscal year of his withdrawal, which the period from the beginning of such year to the effective date of withdrawal shall bear to the whole of the then current fiscal year. Such figure shall be ascertained as soon as practicable after the close of the current fiscal year and shall be payable as soon as the amount thereof is ascertained. All drawings previously made during the then fiscal year shall be first charged against the share in net partnership profits as above computed. If there shall have been losses for such fiscal year, or overdrawings, or losses and the whole of any overdrawings or loans, shall be determined and charged against his capital account, and if in excess thereof, shall be paid by him or his estate promptly after the close of the fiscal year, plus

"(3) The amount of his capital account on the effective date of his withdrawal (after deduction of any losses required to be paid in subdivision (2) above).

"In the event such withdrawing partner dies prior to receiving any or all of the above payments, his personal representative, heirs or assigns shall receive the same payments at the same time as those to which he would have been entitled by the terms had he lived. Payment of the items set forth in subdivisions (1) and (3) above shall be made according to and evidenced by a promissory note, executed by the remaining partners, payable in twelve (12) equal quarterly installments, the first of which shall be payable at the end of the six (6) months following the effective date of such withdrawal. Acceleration of said note shall be permitted at the sole discretion of the two remaining partners. Such note shall bear interest at Two (2) Percent, payable with each installment.

"It is further agreed that in the event of the withdrawal of any partner or partners, any and all accounts receivable for any current year and any and all years past shall remain the sole possession and property of the remaining member or members of THE TOMAHAWK CLINIC. * * *

"18. Dissolution. Should this partnership be dissolved by agreement of the parties, all accounts and notes shall be liquidated and all firm assets sold or divided between the partners at agreed valuations. The books of the partnership shall then be closed and distribution made in proportion to the capital interests of the partners as shown by the partnership books. No drawings should be paid once the partnership has begun to wind up its affairs, although liquidating dividends based on estimates may be paid from time to time. No dissolution shall be effective until the end of the then fiscal year, and until ninety (90) days have elapsed from the date on which written agreement to such dissolution shall have been executed by the parties hereto.

"This agreement shall be binding not only upon the parties hereto, but also upon their heirs, executors, administrators, successors, and assigns, and the wives of said partners have signed this agreement as witnesses, after being advised of the terms of this agreement."

The trial court decided that the withdrawal of the plaintiff worked a dissolution of the partnership under [UPA (1914) §§ 29, 30]; that the partnership assets should be liquidated and applied to the payment of partnership interests according to the scheme set forth in [UPA (1914) § 38] for the reason that paragraphs 15 and 16 of the partnership agreement did not apply in the case of a statutory dissolution; that plaintiff's interest was one-third of the net worth, including therein accounts receivable of the partnership as of May 31, 1961; that plaintiff should recover from defendants the value of his partnership interest; and gave judgment accordingly, but retained jurisdiction for supplementary proceedings. Defendants appeal.

BEILFUSS, JUSTICE.

1. Does a withdrawal of a partner constitute a dissolution of the partnership under [UPA (1914) §§ 29, 30], notwithstanding a partnership agreement to the contrary?

2. Is plaintiff, as withdrawing partner, entitled to a share of the accounts receivable?

WITHDRAWAL

* * * [The court quotes UPA (1914) §§ 29, 30.]

The partnership agreement as set forth above (paragraph 15) specifically provides that the partnership shall not terminate by the withdrawal of a partner. We conclude the parties clearly intended that even though a partner withdrew, the partnership and the partnership business would continue for the purposes for which it was organized. Paragraph 18 of the agreement provides for a dissolution upon agreement of the parties in the sense that the partnership would cease to function as such subject to winding up of its affairs.

While the withdrawal of a partner works a dissolution of the partnership under the statute as to the withdrawing partner, it does not follow that the rights and duties of remaining partners are similarly affected. The agreement contemplates a partnership would continue to exist between the remaining partners even though the personnel constituting the partnership was changed.

Persons with professional qualifications commonly associate in business partnerships. The practice of continuing the operation of the partnership business, even though there are some changes in partnership personnel, is also common. The reasons for an agreement that a medical partnership should continue without disruption of the services rendered is self evident. If the partnership agreement provides for continuation, sets forth a method of paying the withdrawing partner his agreed share, does not jeopardize the rights of creditors, the agreement is enforceable. The statute does not specifically regulate this type of withdrawal with a continuation of the business. The statute should not be construed to invalidate an otherwise enforceable contract entered into for a legitimate purpose.

The provision for withdrawal is in effect a type of winding up of the partnership without the necessity of discontinuing the day-to-day business. [UPA (1914) § 38] contemplates a discontinuance of the day-to-day business but does not forbid other methods of winding up a partnership.

The agreement does provide that Dr. Adams shall no longer actively participate and further provides for winding up the affairs insofar as his interests are concerned. In this sense his withdrawal does constitute a dissolution. We conclude, however, that when the plaintiff, Dr. Adams, withdrew, the partnership was not wholly dissolved so as to require complete winding up of its affairs, but continued to exist under the terms of the agreement. The agreement does not offend the statute and is valid.

ACCOUNTS RECEIVABLE

* * * [The Court quotes UPA (1914) § 38(1).]

The trial court concluded that the withdrawal constituted a statutory dissolution; that partnership assets shall be liquidated pursuant to the statute and that the plaintiff was entitled to a one-third interest in the accounts receivable.

[UPA (1914) § 38(1)], applies only "unless otherwise agreed." The distribution should therefore be made pursuant to the agreement.

Paragraphs 15 and 16 of the contract as set forth above provide for the withdrawal of a partner and the share to which he is entitled. Subject to limitations not material here, paragraph 16 provides that a withdrawing partner shall receive (1) any balance to his credit on partnership books, (2) his proportionate share of profits calculated on a fiscal year basis, and (3) his capital account as of the date of his withdrawal. Paragraph 16 further provides that in event of withdrawal "any and all accounts receivable for any current year and any and all years past shall remain the sole possession and property of the remaining member or members of THE TOMAHAWK CLINIC."

The plaintiff contends that provision of the agreement denying him a share of the accounts receivable works a forfeiture and is void as being against public policy.

We conclude the parties to the agreement intended accounts receivable to be restricted to customer or patient accounts receivable.

The provision of the agreement is clear and unambiguous. There is nothing in the record to suggest the plaintiff's bargaining position was so unequal in the negotiations leading up to the agreement that the provision should be declared unenforceable upon the grounds of public policy. Legitimate business and good will considerations are consistent with a provision retaining control and ownership of customer accounts receivable in an active functioning professional medical partnership. We hold the provision on accounts receivable enforceable.

Because of our determination that the partnership agreement is valid and enforceable the judgment of the trial court insofar as it decrees a dissolution of the partnership and a one-third division of the accounts receivable to the plaintiff must be reversed and remanded to the trial court with directions to enter judgment in conformity with this opinion.

The trial court properly retained jurisdiction for the purpose of granting supplementary relief to plaintiff to enforce a distribution to the plaintiff. The trial court may conduct such proceedings as are necessary to effectuate a distribution pursuant to the agreement.

The parties have stipulated that the plaintiff ceased to be an active partner as of June 1, 1961. The agreement provides that the partnership fiscal year shall coincide with the calendar year. It further provides that his share of the partnership profits upon withdrawal shall be calculated upon the whole year and in proportion to his participation of the whole fiscal year. He is, therefore, entitled to $5/12$ of $1/3$, or $5/36$ of the profits for the fiscal year ending December 31, 1961.

Such of the accounts receivable as were collected during the year 1961 do constitute a part of the profits for 1961. The plaintiff had no part of the management of the partnership after June 1, 1961; however, his eventual distributive share of profits is dependent, in some degree, upon the management of the business affairs and performance of the continuing partners for the remainder of the fiscal year. Under these circumstances the continuing partners stand in a fiduciary relationship to the withdrawing partner and are obligated to conduct the business in a good faith manner including a good faith effort to liquidate the accounts receivable consistent with good business practices.

Judgment reversed with directions to conduct supplementary proceedings to determine distributive share of plaintiff and then enter judgment in conformity with this opinion.

Notes

(1) If the business is to be continued after dissolution, a critical problem that must be addressed in the partnership agreement is how the interest of the departed partners is to be liquidated. As the principal case holds, such an agreement will be enforced in lieu of rights otherwise given by statute in the absence of agreement.

(2) What was the potential problem with year-end accounts receivable that caused the court in the next-to-last paragraph of its opinion to refer to the partners' fiduciary duties to each other?

(3) The manner of liquidating a former partner's interest in The Tomahawk Clinic set forth in the partnership agreement probably worked reasonably fairly, given the economics of most medical practices. Would you recommend that similar provisions be used in say, a law partnership specializing in plaintiff personal injury litigation?

(4) A drafter of a continuation agreement must resolve several basic questions that are not unlike the problems faced by a drafter of share transfer restrictions in closely held corporations. See, pp. 470–480, infra. Generally, fair treatment of the retiring interest is the ultimate aim; there is often an element of Russian roulette in drafting these provisions since clauses are usually reciprocal and it cannot be determined in advance which partner will be the first to withdraw. How were the following matters handled by the agreement in Adams v. Jarvis?

(a) First, a determination must be made as to the types of dissolution which trigger the clause. The most common provision covers death or retirement, but other types of dissolution, such as expulsion or bankruptcy may also be covered.

(b) Second, what is to happen to the outgoing interest? There are several alternatives which have widely varying income tax consequences. The other partners may simply purchase the interest. They may arrange to have the interest purchased by an acceptable third person. Or the partnership may purchase the interest. Or the assets of the partnership may be sold as a unit to the remaining partners who are to continue the business. Or the outgoing interest may continue to share in future earnings on a more or less permanent basis.

(c) Third, is the disposition to be optional or mandatory from the standpoint of the remaining partners? In other words, may the remaining partners elect to terminate, ignoring the provision in the agreement?

(d) Fourth, how much is the withdrawing interest to receive? Valuation is usually a complex task and there is no one best method. Much depends on the nature of the business. Appraisal of each asset by an independent appraiser may be most appropriate in the case of a real estate partnership, but hopelessly inadequate in a law firm where most of the assets are represented by contingent work in progress. What would be a fair basis for valuing an interest in a large law firm?

The following suggestions cover the most popular techniques of valuation:

(i) A fixed sum, usually with provision for periodic adjustment;

(ii) Book value, perhaps with supplemental appraisals of real estate, marketable securities, and inventory (which may be written down for tax purposes);

(iii) Appraisal;

(iv) Capitalization of earnings in the past;

(v) A fraction of future earnings over a specified period of time, often with provision of specific accounting rules to determine profits;

(vi) Negotiation after the fact, perhaps with a provision for arbitration if agreement cannot be reached;

(vii) A right of first refusal to meet the best offer obtainable elsewhere by the withdrawing interest; and

(viii) A sum based on a fraction of the partner's income from the partnership during the previous year or an average of several years.

(e) Fifth, is the payment to be made in a lump sum, or over a period of time?

(f) Sixth, how is the cash to be raised to meet the required payments? If a lump sum payment is required, life insurance may be the answer, or the business may create a reserve by regularly setting aside a portion of earnings, despite the unfavorable tax consequences. Borrowing may be possible. If the payment is to be made over a period of time, funds may be generated from the regular operations of the business.

(g) Seventh, may the retiring interest compete with the partnership interest? If not, how much of the consideration is to be allocated to the covenant not to compete? This allocation is important for federal income tax purposes.

(h) Eighth, should the retiring interest have power to inspect books and records or demand an audit?

(5) Even where it is desired to wind up a business on the dissolution of a partnership, e.g., on the retirement of a senior partner, it may be desirable to establish a pattern for the liquidation in the agreement rather than relying on the skeletal provisions of UPA (1914).

MEEHAN v. SHAUGHNESSY

Supreme Court of Massachusetts, 1989.
404 Mass. 419, 535 N.E.2d 1255.

Before HENNESSEY, C.J., and WILKINS, LIACOS, LYNCH and O'CONNOR, JJ.

HENNESSEY, CHIEF JUSTICE.

* * * Parker, Coulter, Daley & White is a large partnership which specializes in litigation on behalf of both defendants and plaintiffs. Meehan joined the firm in 1959, and became a partner in 1963; his practice focuses primarily on complex tort litigation, such as product liability and aviation defense work. Boyle joined Parker Coulter in 1971, and became a partner in 1980; he has concentrated on plaintiffs' work. Both have developed outstanding reputations as trial lawyers in the Commonwealth. Meehan and Boyle

each were active in the management of Parker Coulter. They each served, for example, on the partnership's executive committee and, as members of this committee, were responsible for considering and making policy recommendations to the general partnership. Boyle was also in charge of the "plaintiffs department" within the firm, which managed approximately 350 cases. At the time of their leaving, Meehan's interest in the partnership was 6% and Boyle's interest was 4.8%.

Meehan and Boyle had become dissatisfied at Parker Coulter. On June 27, 1984, after unsuccessfully opposing the adoption of a firm-wide pension plan, the two first discussed the possibility of leaving Parker Coulter. Another partner met with them to discuss leaving but told them their proposed firm would not be suitable for his type of practice. On July 1, Meehan and Boyle decided to leave Parker Coulter and form their own partnership.

Having decided to establish a new firm, Meehan and Boyle then focused on whom they would invite to join them. The two spoke with Cohen, a junior partner and the de facto head of Parker Coulter's appellate department, about joining the new firm as a partner. They arranged to meet with her on July 5, and told her to keep their conversations confidential. The day before the July 5 meeting, Boyle prepared two lists of what he considered to be his cases. The lists contained approximately eighty to 100 cases, and for each case indicated the status, fee arrangement, estimated settlement value, and potential fee to [the new firm]. Boyle gave these lists to Cohen for her to examine in preparation for the July 5 meeting.

At the July 5 meeting, Meehan and Boyle outlined to Cohen their plans for the new firm, including their intent to offer positions to [Steven H.] Schafer, Peter Black (Black), and Warren Fitzgerald (Fitzgerald), who were associates at Parker Coulter. Boyle stated that he hoped the clients he had been representing would go with him to the new firm; Meehan said he would take the aviation work he had at Parker Coulter with him. Both stated that they felt others at Parker Coulter were getting paid as much as or more than they were, but were not working as hard. Cohen decided to consider the offer from Meehan and Boyle, and agreed to keep the plans confidential until formal notice of the separation was given to the partnership. Although the partnership agreement required a notice period of three months, the three decided to give only thirty days' notice. They chose to give shorter notice to avoid what they believed would be an uncomfortable situation at the firm, and possible retaliatory measures by the partnership. Meehan and Boyle had agreed that they would leave Parker Coulter on December 31, 1984, the end of Parker Coulter's fiscal year.

During the first week of August, Cohen accepted the offer to join the new firm as a partner. [The new firm was then named Meehan, Boyle & Cohen, P.C. (MBC).] Her primary reason for leaving Parker Coulter to join MBC was that she enjoyed working with Meehan and Boyle.

In July, 1984, Boyle offered a position at MBC to Schafer, who worked closely with Boyle in the plaintiffs department. Boyle told Schafer to organize his cases, and "to keep an eye towards cases to be resolved in 1985 and to handle these cases for resolution in 1985 rather than 1984." He also told Schafer to make a list of cases he could take with him to MBC, and to keep all their conversations confidential.

Late in the summer of 1984, Meehan asked Black and Fitzgerald to become associates at MBC. Fitzgerald had worked with Meehan in the past on general defense work, and Black worked with Meehan, particularly in the aviation area. Meehan was instrumental in attracting Black, who had previously been employed by U.S. Aviation Underwriters (USAU), to Parker Coulter. Although Black had already considered leaving Parker Coulter, he was concerned about whether USAU would follow him to a small firm like MBC, and wanted to discuss his leaving Parker Coulter with the vice president of USAU. In October, 1984, Black and Meehan met with the USAU vice president in New York. They later received assurances from him that he would be interested in sending USAU business to the proposed new firm. Black then accepted the offer to join MBC. Fitzgerald also accepted. Schafer, Black, and Fitzgerald were the only associates Meehan, Boyle, and Cohen approached concerning the new firm.

During July and the following months, Meehan, Boyle, and Cohen made arrangements for their new practice apart from seeking associates. They began to look for office space and retained an architect. In early fall, a lease was executed on behalf of MBC in the name of MBC Realty Trust. They also retained an attorney to advise them on the formation of the new firm.

Boyle was assigned the task of arranging financing. He prepared a personal financial statement and obtained a bank loan in September, 1984. During that fall, two other loans were made on MBC's credit. Cohen, at the request of an accountant, had been trying to develop projections of MBC's expected revenue in order to obtain long-term financing. The accountant requested a list of cases with indications as to MBC's expected fees for this purpose. In November, Boyle updated and revised the list of cases he expected to take to MBC which he had compiled in July. The November list contained approximately 135 cases. The increase in Boyle's caseload from July to November resulted in part from the departure of a Parker Coulter attorney in early September, 1984. Boyle was in charge of reassigning the cases this attorney worked on. Although another attorney requested transfer of some of these cases, Boyle assigned none to that attorney, and assigned most of the cases to himself and Schafer. Meehan, Cohen, and Black also prepared lists of cases which they anticipated they would remove, and included the potential fee each case would generate for MBC.

Toward the end of November, Boyle prepared form letters to send to clients and referring attorneys as soon as Parker Coulter was notified of the separation. He also drafted a form for the clients to return to him at his home address authorizing him to remove cases to MBC. An outside agency typed these materials on Parker Coulter's letterhead. Schafer prepared similar letters and authorization forms.

While they were planning their departure, from July to approximately December, Meehan, Boyle, Cohen, Schafer, Black, and Fitzgerald all continued to work full schedules. They settled cases appropriately, made reasonable efforts to avoid continuances, tried cases, and worked on discovery. Each generally maintained his or her usual standard of performance.

Meehan and Boyle had originally intended to give notice to Parker Coulter on December 1, 1984. Rumors of their leaving, however, began to circulate before then. During the period from July to early fall, different

Parker Coulter partners approached Meehan individually on three separate occasions and asked him if the rumors about his leaving were true. On each occasion, Meehan denied that he was leaving. On November 30, 1984, a partner, Maurice F. Shaughnessy (Shaughnessy), approached Boyle and asked him whether Meehan and Boyle intended to leave the firm. Shaughnessy interpreted Boyle's evasive response as an affirmation of the rumors. Meehan and Boyle then decided to distribute their notice that afternoon, which stated, as their proposed date for leaving, December 31, 1984. A notice was left on the desk of each partner. When Meehan, Boyle, and Cohen gave their notice, the atmosphere at Parker Coulter became "tense, emotional and unpleasant, if not adversarial."

On December 3, the Parker Coulter partners appointed a separation committee and decided to communicate with "important sources of business" to tell them of the separation and of Parker Coulter's desire to continue representing them. Meehan and Boyle asked their partners for financial information about the firm, discussed cases and clients with them, and stated that they intended to communicate with clients and referring attorneys on the cases in which they were involved. Sometime during the week of December 3, the partners sent Boyle a list of cases and requested that he identify the cases he intended to take with him.

Boyle had begun to make telephone calls to referring attorneys on Saturday morning, December 1. He had spoken with three referring attorneys by that date and told them of his departure from Parker Coulter and his wish to continue handling their cases. On December 3, he mailed his previously typed letters and authorization forms, and by the end of the first two weeks of December he had spoken with a majority of referring attorneys, and had obtained authorizations from a majority of clients whose cases he planned to remove to MBC.

Although the partners previously were aware of Boyle's intention to communicate with clients, they did not become aware of the extent of his communications until December 12 or 13. Boyle did not provide his partners with the list they requested of cases he intended to remove until December 17. Throughout December, Meehan, Boyle, and Schafer continued to communicate with referring attorneys on cases they were currently handling to discuss authorizing their transfer to MBC. On December 19, 1984, one of the partners accepted on behalf of Parker Coulter the December 31 departure date and waived the three-month notice period provided for by the partnership agreement. Meehan, Boyle, and Cohen formalized their arrangement as a professional corporation on January 1, 1985.

MBC removed a number of cases from Parker Coulter. Of the roughly 350 contingent fee cases pending at Parker Coulter in 1984, Boyle, Schafer, and Meehan removed approximately 142 to MBC. Meehan advised Parker Coulter that the 4,000 asbestos cases he had attracted to the firm would remain, and he did not seek to take certain other major clients. Black removed thirty-five cases; Fitzgerald removed ten; and Cohen removed three. A provision in the partnership agreement in effect at the separation provided that a voluntarily retiring partner, upon the payment of a "fair charge," could remove "any matter in which the partnership had been representing a client who came to the firm through the personal effort or connection of the retiring partner," subject to the right of the client to stay with the firm. Approximately thirty-nine of the 142 contingent fee cases removed to MBC came to Parker Coulter at least in part through the personal efforts or connections of Parker Coulter attorneys other than Meehan, Boyle, Cohen, Schafer, Black, or Fitzgerald. In all the cases removed to MBC, however, MBC attorneys had direct, existing relationships with the clients. In all the removed cases, MBC attorneys communicated with the referring attorney or with the client directly by telephone or letter. In each case, the client signed an authorization.

Schafer subsequently separated his practice from MBC's. He took with him a number of the cases which had been removed from Parker Coulter to MBC.

Based on these findings, the judge determined that the MBC attorneys did not manipulate cases, or handle them differently as a result of their decision to leave Parker Coulter. He also determined that Parker Coulter failed to prove that the clients whose cases were removed did not freely choose to have MBC represent them. Consequently, he concluded that Meehan and Boyle neither violated the partnership agreement nor breached the fiduciary duty they owed to their partners. In addition, the judge also found that Meehan and Boyle did not tortiously interfere with Parker Coulter's relations with clients or employees. He similarly rejected Parker Coulter's claims against Cohen and Schafer. * * *

The Parker Coulter partnership agreement provided for rights on a dissolution caused by the will of a partner which are different from those [UPA (1914)] provides.[17] Because going concerns are typically destroyed in the dissolution process of liquidation and windup, see J. Crane & A. Bromberg, Partnership 419 (1968), the agreement minimizes the impact of this process. The agreement provides for an allocation to the departing partner of a share of the firm's current net income, and a return of his or her capital contributions. In addition, the agreement also recognizes that a major asset of a law firm is the expected fees it will receive from unfinished business currently being transacted. Instead of assigning a value to the departing partner's interest in this unfinished business, or waiting for the unfinished business to be "wound up" and liquidated, which is the method of division [UPA (1914)] provides, the agreement gives the partner the right to remove any case which came to the firm "through the personal effort or connection" of the partner, if the partner compensates the dissolved partnership "for the services to and expenditures for the client."[18] Once the partner has removed a case, the agreement provides that the partner is entitled to retain all future fees in the case, with the exception of the "fair charge" owed to the dissolved firm.[19]

---

17. [By the Court] [UPA (1914)] is intended to be a type of "form contract." See 1 A.R. Bromberg & L.E. Ribstein, Partnership § 1.01(d) (1988). Parties are therefore allowed the freedom to provide for rights at dissolution and during the wind-up period which are different from those provided for in the statute. See [UPA (1914)] § 38(1).

18. [By the Court] The agreement expressly protects a client's right to choose his or her attorney, by providing that the right to remove a case is "subject to the right of the client to

direct that the matter be retained by the continuing firm of remaining partners."

19. [By the Court] The agreement provides that this "fair charge" is a "receivable account of the earlier partnership * * * and [is] divided between the remaining partners and the retiring partner on the basis of which they share in the profits of the firm at the time of the withdrawal." This fair charge is thus treated as an asset of the former partnership. Because the partnership, upon the receipt of the fair charge, gives up all future rights to income

Although the provision in the partnership agreement which divides the dissolved firm's unfinished business does not expressly apply to the removal of cases which did not come to Parker Coulter through the efforts of the departing partner, we believe that the parties intended this provision to apply to these cases also. We interpret this provision to cover these additional cases for two reasons. First, according to the Canons of Ethics and Disciplinary Rules Regulating the Practice of Law, a lawyer may not participate in an agreement which restricts the right of a lawyer to practice law after the termination of a relationship created by the agreement. One reason for this rule is to protect the public. The strong public interest in allowing clients to retain counsel of their choice outweighs any professional benefits derived from a restrictive covenant. Thus, the Parker Coulter partners could not restrict a departing partner's right to remove any clients who freely choose to retain him or her as their legal counsel. Second, we believe the agreement's carefully drawn provisions governing dissolution and the division of assets indicate the partners' strong intent not to allow the provisions of [UPA (1914)] concerning liquidation and windup to govern any portion of the dissolved firm's unfinished business. Therefore, based on the partners' intent, and on the prohibition against restrictive covenants between attorneys, we interpret the agreement to provide that, upon the payment of a fair charge, any case may be removed regardless of whether the case came to the firm through the personal efforts of the departing partner. This privilege to remove, as is shown in our later discussion, is of course dependent upon the partner's compliance with fiduciary obligations.

Under the agreement, therefore, a partner who separates his or her practice from that of the firm receives (1) the right to his or her capital contribution, (2) the right to a share of the net income to which the dissolved partnership is currently entitled, and (3) the right to a portion of the firm's unfinished business, and in exchange gives up all other rights in the dissolved firm's remaining assets. As to (3) above, "unfinished business," the partner gives up all right to proceeds from any unfinished business of the dissolved firm which the new, surviving firm retains. Under the agreement, the old firm's unfinished business is, in effect, "wound up" immediately; the departing partner takes certain of the unfinished business of the old, dissolved Parker Coulter on the payment of a "fair charge," and the new, surviving Parker Coulter takes the remainder of the old partnership's unfinished business.[20] The two entities surviving after the dissolution possess "new business," unconnected with that of the old firm, and the former partners no longer have a continuing fiduciary obligation to windup for the benefit of each other the business they shared in their former partnership.

In sum, * * * the partners have fashioned a division method which immediately winds up unfinished business, allows for a quick separation of the surviving practices, and minimizes the disruptive impact of a dissolution. * * *

from the removed case, the partnership's collective interest in the case is effectively "wound up." The fair charge, therefore, is a method of valuing the partnership's unfinished business as it relates to the removed case.

20. [By the Court] A more equitable provision would require that the new, surviving partnership also pay a "fair charge" on the cases it takes from the dissolved partnership. This "fair charge" from the new firm, as is the "fair charge" from the departing partner, would be an asset of the dissolved partnership, in which the departing partner has an interest.

We now consider Parker Coulter's claims of wrongdoing. Parker Coulter claims that the judge erred in finding that Meehan, Boyle, Cohen, and Schafer fulfilled their fiduciary duties to the former partnership. In particular, Parker Coulter argues that these attorneys breached their duties (1) by improperly handling cases for their own, and not the partnership's benefit, (2) by secretly competing with the partnership, and (3) by unfairly acquiring from clients and referring attorneys consent to withdraw cases to MBC.[21] We do not agree with Parker Coulter's first two arguments but agree with the third. We first address the claims against Meehan and Boyle, and then turn to those against Cohen and Schafer.

It is well settled that partners owe each other a fiduciary duty of "the utmost good faith and loyalty." As a fiduciary, a partner must consider his or her partners' welfare, and refrain from acting for purely private gain. Partners thus "may not act out of avarice, expediency or self-interest in derogation of their duty of loyalty." *Donahue v. Rodd Electrotype Co. of New England, Inc.*, 367 Mass. 578, 593, 328 N.E.2d 505 (1975). Meehan and Boyle owed their copartners at Parker Coulter a duty of the utmost good faith and loyalty, and were obliged to consider their copartners' welfare, and not merely their own.

Parker Coulter first argues that Meehan and Boyle violated their fiduciary duty by handling cases for their own benefit, and challenges the judge's finding that no manipulation occurred.[22] * * *

We have reviewed the record, and conclude that the judge was warranted in determining that Meehan and Boyle handled cases no differently as a result of their decision to leave Parker Coulter, and that they thus fulfilled their fiduciary duty in this respect.

Parker Coulter next argues that the judge's findings compel the conclusion that Meehan and Boyle breached their fiduciary duty not to compete with their partners by secretly setting up a new firm during their tenure at Parker Coulter. We disagree. We have stated that fiduciaries may plan to compete with the entity to which they owe allegiance, "provided that in the course of such arrangements they [do] not otherwise act in violation of their fiduciary duties." *Chelsea Indus. v. Gaffney*, 389 Mass. 1, 10, 11–12, 449 N.E.2d 320 (1983). Here, the judge found that Meehan and Boyle made certain logistical arrangements for the establishment of MBC. These arrangements included executing a lease for MBC's office, preparing lists of clients expected to leave

---

21. [By the Court] Parker Coulter does not claim that Meehan and Boyle wrongfully dissolved the partnership by leaving prematurely. The partnership agreement, although providing that the firm "shall continue indefinitely," required that a partner who leaves to continue practicing elsewhere give three-months' advance notice. This, therefore, may not have been a purely "at will" partnership which a partner has a right to dissolve at any time without triggering the remedies of [UPA (1914)] § 38(2). See [UPA (1914)] §§ 31(1), 38. Here, Parker Coulter waived compliance with the agreement's three-month notice provision. Meehan and Boyle, therefore, dissolved the partnership "[w]ithout violation of the agreement between the partners." [UPA (1914)] § 31.

22. [By the Court] The judge found, specifically, that: "MBC, Schafer, Black and Fitzgerald worked full schedules from July to November 30, 1984, and some beyond. There was no manipulation of the cases nor were the cases handled differently as a result of the decision by MBC to leave Parker Coulter. They tried cases, worked on discovery, settled cases and made reasonable efforts to avoid continuances, to try their cases when reached, and settle where appropriate and in general maintain the same level of industry and professionalism that they had always demonstrated."

Parker Coulter for MBC, and obtaining financing on the basis of these lists. We believe these logistical arrangements to establish a physical plant for the new firm were permissible under *Chelsea Indus.*, especially in light of the attorneys' obligation to represent adequately any clients who might continue to retain them on their departure from Parker Coulter. Canons of Ethics and Disciplinary Rules Regulating the Practice of Law, Canon 7. There was no error in the judge's determination that this conduct did not violate the partners' fiduciary duty.[23]

Lastly, Parker Coulter argues that the judge's findings compel the conclusion that Meehan and Boyle breached their fiduciary duties by unfairly acquiring consent from clients to remove cases from Parker Coulter. We agree that Meehan and Boyle, through their preparation for obtaining clients' consent, their secrecy concerning which clients they intended to take, and the substance and method of their communications with clients, obtained an unfair advantage over their former partners in breach of their fiduciary duties.

A partner has an obligation to "render on demand true and full information of all things affecting the partnership to any partner." [UPA (1914)] § 20. On three separate occasions Meehan affirmatively denied to his partners, on their demand, that he had any plans for leaving the partnership. During this period of secrecy, Meehan and Boyle made preparations for obtaining removal authorizations from clients. Meehan traveled to New York to meet with a representative of USAU and interest him in the new firm. Boyle prepared form letters on Parker Coulter's letterhead for authorizations from prospective MBC clients. Thus, they were "ready to move" the instant they gave notice to their partners.

On giving their notice, Meehan and Boyle continued to use their position of trust and confidence to the disadvantage of Parker Coulter. The two immediately began communicating with clients and referring attorneys. Boyle delayed providing his partners with a list of clients he intended to solicit until mid-December, by which time he had obtained authorization from a majority of the clients.

Finally, the content of the letter sent to the clients was unfairly prejudicial to Parker Coulter. The ABA Committee on Ethics and Professional Responsibility, in Informal Opinion 1457 (April 29, 1980), set forth ethical standards for attorneys announcing a change in professional association.[24]

---

23. [By the Court] Parker Coulter also argues that Meehan and Boyle impermissibly competed with the firm by inducing its employees to join MBC. Because Parker Coulter identifies no specific loss resulting from this claimed breach, see, e.g., *Chelsea Indus., supra* 389 Mass. at 19 n. 23, 449 N.E.2d 320, (costs of retraining new employees), we need not address this issue.

24. [By the Court] These standards provide the following guidelines for notice to clients:

"(a) the notice is mailed; (b) the notice is sent only to persons with whom the lawyer had an active lawyer-client relationship immediately before the change in the lawyer's professional association; (c) the notice is clearly related to open and pending matters for which the lawyer had direct professional responsibility to the client immediately before the change; (d) the notice is sent promptly after the change; (e) the notice does not urge the client to sever a relationship with the lawyer's former firm and does not recommend the lawyer's employment (although it indicates the lawyer's willingness to continue his responsibility for the matters); (f) the notice makes it clear that the client has the right to decide who will complete or continue the matters; and (g) the notice is brief, dignified, and not disparaging of the lawyer's former firm."

Because this standard is intended primarily to protect clients, proof by Parker Coulter of a technical violation of this standard does not aid them in their claims. We will, however, look to this standard for general guidelines as to what partners are entitled to expect from each other concerning their joint clients on the division of their practice. The ethical standard provides that any notice explain to a client that he or she has the right to decide who will continue the representation. Here, the judge found that the notice did not "clearly present to the clients the choice they had between remaining at Parker Coulter or moving to the new firm." By sending a one-sided announcement, on Parker Coulter letterhead, so soon after notice of their departure, Meehan and Boyle excluded their partners from effectively presenting their services as an alternative to those of Meehan and Boyle.

Meehan and Boyle could have foreseen that the news of their departure would cause a certain amount of confusion and disruption among their partners. The speed and preemptive character[25] of their campaign to acquire clients' consent took advantage of their partners' confusion. By engaging in these preemptive tactics, Meehan and Boyle violated the duty of utmost good faith and loyalty which they owed their partners. Therefore, we conclude that the judge erred in deciding that Meehan and Boyle acted properly in acquiring consent to remove cases to MBC.

We next consider Parker Coulter's claims against Cohen and Schafer. We have determined that "[e]mployees occupying a position of trust and confidence owe a duty of loyalty to their employer and must protect the interests of their employer." *Chelsea Indus., supra,* 389 Mass. at 11, 449 N.E.2d 320. Cohen was a junior partner, and acting head of Parker Coulter's appellate department. Schafer was an associate responsible for a substantial case load. Both had access to clients and information concerning clients and therefore occupied positions of trust and confidence. We conclude that their participation in the preemptive tactics of Meehan and Boyle violated the duty they owed the partnership. * * *

Before we examine the consequences of the MBC attorneys' breach of duty, we briefly outline what is at stake. If there had been no breach of duty, the assets of the partnership upon dissolution would be divided strictly according to the partnership agreement. Under the agreement, Meehan and Boyle would be entitled to the return of their capital contributions and their share of the dissolved firm's profits. They would also possess the right to remove cases from the old partnership, and to retain all future fees generated by these cases in excess of the fair charge owed to the partnership for work performed there on the removed cases. Because the fair charge is an asset of the dissolved firm under the agreement, Meehan and Boyle would share in this amount according to their respective interests in the former partnership. Thus, of the fair charges returned to their former partnership, Meehan and

See also ABA Committee on Ethics and Professional Responsibility Informal Opinion 1466 (Feb. 12, 1981) (extending Informal Opinion 1457 to departing associates as well as partners).

25. [By the Court] We repeatedly * * * refer to "preemptive conduct" of Meehan and Boyle, as well as their "breach of duty." Undoubtedly these are accurate descriptions, but we do not wish to leave the impression that the MBC attorneys were unfair in the totality of their conduct in departing from the firm. For instance, * * * Meehan and Boyle left undisturbed with their partners, and made no attempt to claim, a very large amount of business which Meehan had attracted to Parker Coulter.

Boyle would receive their combined 10.8% partnership share, and their former partners would receive the remainder.

Parker Coulter essentially argues that, because of their breach of fiduciary duty, Meehan and Boyle forfeit all rights under the partnership agreement. * * * There is no conceivable connection between the attorneys' breach of duty and Parker Coulter's claims to the capital contributions and profit shares of Meehan and Boyle. * * * These amounts are not a form of liquidated damages to which partners can resort in the event of a breach. We conclude, therefore, that Parker Coulter is not entitled to recover these amounts. The judge correctly found that Meehan and Boyle are entitled to a return of their capital contributions (their interest, as determined by the judge, in the partners' reserve account and the partners' capital account), and to the receipt of a portion of the old firm's profits (their interest in the income earned but not distributed account).

We similarly reject Parker Coulter's claims that the MBC attorneys should be required to forfeit all compensation during the period of their breach. * * * For Parker Coulter to recover any amount in addition to what it would be entitled to receive upon dissolution under the partnership agreement or the statute, there must be a causal connection between its claimed losses and the breach of duty on the part of the MBC attorneys. We have concluded that the MBC attorneys unfairly acquired consent from clients. Parker Coulter, therefore is entitled to recover only those amounts which flow from this breach of duty. * * * Here, the judge found that throughout the period in question the MBC attorneys worked as hard, and were as productive as they had always been. This finding was warranted, and is unchallenged by Parker Coulter. In these circumstances, we conclude that the value of the MBC attorneys' services was equal to their compensation. Parker Coulter, therefore, is not entitled to this relief. * * *

In these circumstances, it is appropriate to place on the party who improperly removed the case the burden of proving that the client would have consented to removal in the absence of any breach of duty. * * * [Thus] Meehan and Boyle had the burden of proving no causal connection between their breach of duty and Parker Coulter's loss of clients. Cf. *Energy Resources Corp. v. Porter,* 14 Mass.App.Ct. 296, 302, 438 N.E.2d 391 (1982) (fiduciary who secretly acquires corporate opportunity barred from asserting that corporation would have been unable to exploit opportunity). Proof of the circumstances of the preparations for obtaining authorizations and of the actual communications with clients was more accessible to Meehan and Boyle than to Parker Coulter. Furthermore, requiring these partners to disprove causation will encourage partners in the future to disclose seasonably and fully any plans to remove cases. This disclosure will allow the partnership and the departing partner an equal opportunity to present to clients the option of continuing with the partnership or retaining the departing partner individually.[26]

---

26. [By the Court] As between the attorneys, a mutual letter, from both the partnership and the departing partner, outlining the separation plans and the clients' right to choose, would be an appropriate means of opening the discussion between the attorneys and their clients concerning the clients' choice of continuing representation.

We remand the case to the Superior Court for findings consistent with our conclusion that the MBC attorneys bear the burden of proof. * * *

To guide the judge on remand in his reexamination of the record and his subsidiary findings, we briefly outline factors relevant to determining whether a client freely chose MBC and, thus, whether the MBC attorneys met their burden of disproving a causal relationship between their preemptive tactics and the removal of the case. * * *

Although the record contains no evidence as to the actual preference of a particular client, expressed and unaffected by the MBC attorneys' improper communications, the record is replete with circumstantial evidence bearing on this issue. * * *

In those cases, if any, where the judge concludes, * * * that Meehan and Boyle have met their burden, we resolve the parties' dispute over fees solely under the partnership agreement. Under the agreement's terms, as we have interpreted them, Meehan and Boyle owe a fair charge to their former partnership for its "services to and expenditures for" the clients in these matters. Meehan and Boyle are entitled to their combined 10.8% partnership share of this amount, and their former partners are entitled to the remainder. We agree with the judge that a "fair charge" on a removed case consists of the firm's unreimbursed expenses plus the rate billed per hour by members of the firm multiplied by the hours expended on the case.[27] In fixing this hourly rate, the firm made a determination that the time charged was reasonable and fair compensation for the services rendered. We conclude, therefore, that, in accordance with the partnership agreement, Meehan and Boyle must reimburse their former partnership for time billed and expenses incurred at that firm on all cases which were fairly removed. We further conclude that, under the agreement, Meehan and Boyle have the right to retain all fees generated by these cases in excess of the fair charge.

We now address the correct remedy in those cases, if any, which the judge determines Meehan and Boyle unfairly removed. In light of a conclusion that Meehan and Boyle have failed to prove that certain clients would not have preferred to stay with Parker Coulter, granting Parker Coulter merely a fair charge on these cases pursuant to the partnership agreement would not make it whole. We turn, therefore, to [UPA (1914). The Court quotes § 21.] * * *

Meehan and Boyle breached the duty they owed to Parker Coulter. If the judge determines that, as a result of this breach, certain clients left the firm, Meehan and Boyle must account to the partnership for any profits they receive on these cases pursuant to [UPA (1914)] in addition to paying the partnership a fair charge on these cases pursuant to the agreement. The "profit" on a particular case is the amount by which the fee received from the case exceeds the sum of (1) any reasonable overhead expenses MBC incurs in

---

27. [By the Court] MBC attorneys removed from Parker Coulter a number of insurance company cases, where the fee is determined on an hourly basis, and a number of contingent fee cases, where the fee does not depend on the time involved. Deciding that billable hours is a fair charge on contingent fee cases has two effects which are arguably unfair both to Parker Coulter and to MBC. If the client is unsuccessful, MBC will nonetheless have reimbursed Parker Coulter for services which generated no contingent fee. Conversely, if the client is successful, MBC will retain all the potential "windfall" of the amount by which the contingent fee exceeds MBC's investment of time in the case and its payment of a fair charge to Parker Coulter. Treating a contingent fee case as if the fee were determined on an hourly basis is justified here, however, because the parties did not bargain otherwise.

resolving the case, and (2) the fair charge it owes under the partnership agreement. We emphasize that reasonable overhead expenses on a particular case are not the equivalent of the amount represented by the hours MBC attorneys have expended on the case multiplied by their hourly billing rate. Reasonable overhead expenses are to include only MBC's costs in generating the fee, and are not to include any profit margin for MBC. We treat this profit on a particular case as if it had been earned in the usual course of business of the partnership which included Meehan and Boyle as partners. Failing to treat this profit as if it had been earned by Meehan or Boyle while at their former partnership would exclude Meehan and Boyle from participating in the fruits of their labors and, more importantly, would provide Parker Coulter with an unjustified windfall. Parker Coulter would receive a windfall because there is no guarantee that the profit would have been generated had the case not been handled at MBC. Meehan's and Boyle's former partners are thus entitled to their portion of the fair charge on each of the unfairly removed cases (89.2%), and to that amount of profit from an unfairly removed case which they would have enjoyed had the MBC attorneys handled the case at Parker Coulter (89.2%). * * *

We now address the consequences to Cohen and Schafer of their breach of fiduciary duty. The judge found that Cohen participated in the removal of some insurance defense cases, and that Schafer participated in the removal of a number of contingent fee cases. Therefore, we conclude that Schafer must hold in a constructive trust for the benefit of the former partnership any profits, as we have defined this term, which he has received or may receive in his separate practice from cases which the judge determines were unfairly removed. Cohen also must hold any profits she has received or may receive from unfairly removed cases in a similar constructive trust. Although Cohen and Schafer were not parties to the partnership agreement, and thus were not contractually bound to remove cases fairly, we believe their fiduciary duties require this result.

* * * In sum, we conclude that the MBC attorneys' breach of duty consisted of their method of acquiring consent from clients to remove cases. We therefore limit Parker Coulter's recovery to only those losses which were caused by this breach of duty, but place on the MBC attorneys the burden of disproving causation. On remand, the judge is to determine, based on the record and his findings as they now stand, whether the MBC attorneys have met their burden as to each case removed from Parker Coulter. A constructive trust for the benefit of the former partnership is to be imposed on any profits which Meehan, Boyle, Cohen, or Schafer receive on cases which the judge determines they unfairly removed. Because the fair charge which Meehan and Boyle owe on all removed cases is an asset of the former partnership, and because the constructive trust we impose is for the benefit of the former partnership, each former partner is entitled to his or her partnership share of these amounts. The Parker Coulter defendants are thus entitled to 89.2% of the fair charges on all removed cases, and 89.2% of the profits from the unfairly removed cases; Meehan and Boyle are entitled to 6% and 4.8%, respectively, of these amounts. Additionally, under the agreement's terms, Meehan and Boyle are to receive the return of their capital contributions and their profit shares.

The judgment below is reversed and the case is remanded to the Superior Court (1) for findings, in accordance with the factors we have identified, as to which cases were unfairly removed, (2) for a further evidentiary hearing to determine the reasonable overhead and thus the "profits" on the cases, if any, which were unfairly removed, and (3) for entry of a new judgment dispositive of all issues.

SO ORDERED.

Notes

(1) According to news reports following this decision, both litigants agreed that the amount of the "fair charge" in dispute for cases moved to MBC was in excess of $1,000,000. Anthony Flint, Breaking Up Not So Hard Now, Boston Globe, April 3, 1989, at 12. Also, in the years following the MBC split, other groups of partners decided to leave Parker Coulter, which decided to liquidate in April, 1995. Maria Shao, Law Firm Liquidating, Boston Globe, November 2, 1995, at 51.

(2) The Parker Coulter agreement relating to the withdrawal of partners differs significantly from the provisions in the partnership agreement of The Tomahawk Clinic. What considerations dictated the use of the Parker Coulter type of agreement for a large law partnership and The Tomahawk Clinic type of agreement for a small medical partnership?

(3) Assume that after several years as partner in the law firm you join after law school, you decide to strike out on your own. Assuming that the partnership agreement is similar to that of Parker Coulter, what should you do in order to make sure that your withdrawal does not violate the partnership agreement?

(4) Are not the associates who left Parker Coulter treated more harshly than the partners who instigated the split and whose conduct breached the partnership agreement? How can that be?

(5) The partnership agreement of Lord, Day & Lord (LDL), a well-known New York law firm, provided that a withdrawing partner was entitled to a share of the firm profits, representing unpaid fees and fees for services performed but not yet billed, at the time of departure. To avoid expense and bookkeeping complications, the agreement provided that this amount would be calculated as one-third of the withdrawing partner's average percentage of the firm's profits for the three fiscal years preceding the date of withdrawal multiplied by the profits earned by LDL in each of the three years following withdrawal. The agreement also provided, however:

> Notwithstanding anything in this Article * * * to the contrary, if a Partner withdraws from the Partnership and without the prior written consent of the Executive Committee continues to practice law in any state or other jurisdiction in which the Partnership maintains an office or any contiguous jurisdiction, either as a lawyer in private practice or as a counsel employed by a business firm, he shall have no further interest in and there shall be paid to him no proportion of the net profits of the Partnership collected thereafter, whether for services rendered before or after his withdrawal. * * *

Cohen, the head of LDL's tax department, withdrew from the firm and joined a competing law firm in New York. When LDL refused to pay him the amount based on subsequent earnings of LDL, Cohen sued. Held: The provision is unenforceable since it unreasonably restricts Cohen's right to practice law and therefore deprives the public of free choice of legal advisers. Three justices dissented. Cohen v. Lord, Day & Lord, 75 N.Y.2d 95, 551 N.Y.S.2d 157, 550 N.E.2d 410 (1989). The Court argued:

> We hold that while the provision in question does not expressly or completely prohibit a withdrawing partner from engaging in the practice of law, the significant monetary penalty it exacts, if the withdrawing partner practices competitively with the former firm, constitutes an impermissible restriction on the practice of law. The forfeiture-for-competition provision would functionally and realistically discourage and foreclose a withdrawing partner from serving clients who might wish to continue to be represented by the withdrawing lawyer and would thus interfere with the client's choice of counsel. 75 N.Y.2d at 98, 551 N.Y.S.2d at 158, 550 N.E.2d at 411.

Is not the consequence of the Court's decision that Cohen is entitled to share in a portion of LDL's earnings for three years while he is practicing in direct competition with LDL? Is that a plausible or reasonable result? Contra to *Lord, Day & Lord* is Howard v. Babcock, 6 Cal.4th 409, 25 Cal.Rptr.2d 80, 863 P.2d 150 (1993). See also Jacob v. Norris, McLaughlin & Marcus, 128 N.J. 10, 607 A.2d 142 (1992); Vincent R. Johnson, Solicitation of Law Firm Clients by Departing Partners and Associates: Tort, Fiduciary, and Disciplinary Liability, 50 U.Pitt.L.Rev. 1 (1988).

(6) The firm of Fordham & Stewart consisted of three founding partners. Shortly thereafter a fourth lawyer, Starr, joined the firm also as a partner. The partnership agreement provided that the founding partners had authority to determine, both prospectively and retrospectively, each partner's share of the firm's profits. Starr was concerned about this clause but did not object to it. A year later he left the firm. He then brought suit complaining of the allocation of the firm's profits to him for the period he was with the firm. A judgment in his favor for more than $75,000 was affirmed, the court stating that the founding partners' decision involved their self interest and therefore they "had the burden of proving their distribution was fair and reasonable," citing Meehan v. Shaughnessy. Starr v. Fordham, 420 Mass. 178, 648 N.E.2d 1261, 1265 (1995). In a similar case, Stuart v. Lane & Mittendorf, 235 A.D.2d 294, 652 N.Y.S.2d 951 (1997), a judgment in favor of the departed partner for more than $100,000 was affirmed, the court stating that the firm had "deviated from its long-standing custom and practice in distributing its profits so as to deprive plaintiff former partner of the compensation to which he was entitled, thereby breaching its fiduciary obligations to him and the covenant of good faith and fair dealing implicit in the partnership agreement."

(7) The law firm of Graubard Mollen Dannett & Horowitz was created in 1949. In 1982 it adopted a written "Phasing Out and Retirement Program" to provide for transition of management to more junior partners and the retirement of the senior partners. The Program included the following "Clarifications:"

> 3. It is the spirit of the program that, during retirement, and even afterward, each of the retirees will not do anything to impair the firm's relationship with its existing clients and business.

> 4. The partners recognize that efforts towards institutionalization of the business of the firm is essential to the firm's continuing prosperity. In particular, the partners approaching phase-down and retirement will integrate to the extent possible, relationships between the firm's clients and the other partners.

Is this a binding obligation on the part of retired partners? Or is it merely hortatory? In 1987, Moskovitz, a 73-year-old partner, became of counsel to the firm. Shortly thereafter he became dissatisfied with his status and contacted another law firm in New York about joining that firm. In order to do so, he contacted a Graubard Mollen client, Roche, who agreed to shift its account to the other firm. Upon learning of this. Graubard Mollen immediately locked Moskovitz out of his office and brought suit alleging breach of fiduciary duty and fraud. In denying summary judgment to both parties, the Court set forth the following "general guidelines:"

Both sides acknowledge the principle that law partners, no less than any other business or professional partners, are bound by a fiduciary duty requiring "the punctilio of an honor the most sensitive." Both sides acknowledge as well the principle that an attorney stands in a fiduciary relation to the client. Translating principles into practice, however, presents a far greater problem.

One respected commentator opines that, while a departing partner's preresignation negotiations with firm clients in most businesses would probably constitute breach of the common-law obligation of loyalty to the firm, in the case of law practice, "the public policy favoring client freedom of choice in legal representation should override the firm's proprietary interest in holding its clientele" (Hazard, Ethical Considerations in Withdrawal, Expulsion, and Retirement, printed in Withdrawal, Retirement and Disputes, [What You and Your Firm Need to Know [Berger ed. 1988], at 36]).

* * * As a matter of principle, preresignation surreptitious "solicitation" of firm clients for a partner's personal gain is actionable. Such conduct exceeds what is necessary to protect the important value of client freedom of choice in legal representation, and thoroughly undermines another important value—the loyalty owed partners (including law partners), which distinguishes partnerships (including law partnerships) from bazaars. What, then, is the prohibited "solicitation"? As the trial court recognized, in classic understatement, the answer to that question is not "self-evident" (149 Misc.2d, at 486, 565 N.Y.S.2d 672). * * *

At one end of the spectrum, where an attorney is dissatisfied with the existing association, taking steps to locate alternative space and affiliations would not violate a partner's fiduciary duties. That this may be a delicate venture, requiring confidentiality, is simple common sense * * *. As a matter of ethics, departing partners have been permitted to inform firm clients with whom they have a prior professional relationship about their impending withdrawal and new practice, and to remind the client of its freedom to retain counsel of its choice (New York County Lawyers Assn, Ethics Opn 679 [1991]; Assn of Bar of City of NY, Ethics Opn 80-65 [1982]. Ideally, such approaches would take place only after notice to the firm of the partner's plans to leave.

At the other end of the spectrum, secretly attempting to lure firm clients (even those the partner has brought into the firm and personally represented) to the new association, lying to clients about their rights with respect to the choice of counsel, lying to partners about plans to leave, and abandoning the firm on short notice (taking clients and files) would not be consistent with a partner's fiduciary duties (see, Meehan v. Shaughnessy, 404 Mass. 419, 535 N.E.2d 1255).

Graubard Mollen Dannett & Horowitz v. Moskovitz, 86 N.Y.2d 112, 116, 118–121, 629 N.Y.S.2d 1009, 1011, 1012–1014, 653 N.E.2d 1179, 1181, 1182–84 (1995).

(8) Rosenfeld, Meyer, and Susman was a 19–partner law firm; the firm was an at-will partnership without a written partnership agreement; each partner's profit percentage was fixed by a committee at the beginning of each year. In 1968 it was retained by a client to bring a major antitrust case under a one-third contingent fee arrangement. Since the case involved extensive discovery and would take several years to complete, the fee arrangement contemplated that the client would make certain annual payments to the firm to cover a portion of the firm's costs, these payments ultimately to be offset against the firm's share of any recovery. Cohen and Riordan, two partners with extensive trial experience were assigned responsibility for the antitrust case and they worked on the case full-time for six years. During this period they received shares of general partnership income even though they produced virtually no revenue. By 1974 it had become clear that the antitrust case would be settled for more than $20,000,000. May Cohen and Riordan dissolve the partnership and form a new law firm in the expectation that it would be retained by the client to pursue the antitrust case? Does Rosenfeld, Meyer and Susman have a claim against Cohen and Riordan if the client exercises its unquestioned power to terminate its representation by the Rosenfeld firm and retain Cohen and Riordan? Is this a "wrongful dissolution"? Can there be a "wrongful dissolution" of a partnership at will under UPA (1914)? See Rodney M. Confer and Cheryl R. Zwart, "Disintegrating Erosion" of Fiduciary Duty in the Dissolution of a Partnership at Will, 70 Neb.L.Rev. 107, 120–23 (1991). Or should the issue be resolved under UPA (1914) § 21? See Rosenfeld, Meyer & Susman v. Cohen, 146 Cal.App.3d 200, 194 Cal.Rptr. 180 (1983). The departure of Cohen and Riordan, of course, automatically dissolved Rosenfeld, Meyer & Susman, thereby requiring a determination under UPA (1914) of the value of the partnership interests in that law firm at the time of the split-up. In 1987, the court of appeals resolved a number of complex issues arising from this litigation, Rosenfeld, Meyer & Susman v. Cohen, 191 Cal.App.3d 1035, 237 Cal.Rptr. 14 (1987), and remanded Rosenfeld, Meyer & Susman's suit for an accounting for trial. Clearly, resolution of disputes arising from a law firm break-up are as difficult under the UPA (1914) default provisions as they are under Parker Coulter's carefully-crafted partnership agreement.

(9) See generally Robert W. Hillman, Hillman on Lawyer Mobility (1994).

GELDER MEDICAL GROUP v. WEBBER

Court of Appeals of New York, 1977.
41 N.Y.2d 680, 394 N.Y.S.2d 867, 363 N.E.2d 573.

BREITEL, CHIEF JUDGE.

In an action by a medical partnership for a permanent injunction to enforce a restrictive covenant not to compete, defendant physician appeals. He had been expelled as a partner pursuant to the partnership agreement. Special Term granted the injunction on summary judgment under CPLR 3212, and dismissed defendant's counterclaim for a declaratory judgment and damages resulting from plaintiff's alleged breach of the partnership agreement. A divided Appellate Division affirmed.

At issue is whether a partner who has been forced out of a partnership as permitted by the partnership agreement may be held to his covenant not to compete within a restricted radius of 30 miles for a five-year period.

There should be an affirmance. Having joined a partnership governed by articles providing for the expulsion without cause of a member on terms that are not oppressive, and including a reasonable restrictive covenant, defendant may not complain of its enforcement.

The Gelder Medical Group, a partnership engaged in practicing medicine and surgery in Sidney, New York, was first formed in 1956. Some 17 years later, defendant Dr. Webber, then 61 years old and a newcomer to Sidney, a village of 5,000 population, was admitted to the small partnership following a one-year trial period in which he was employed by the group as a surgeon. Previously, after having entered the field of surgery, he had drifted from one professional association to another in two different provinces of Canada and in at least four different States of this country in the northeast and midwest. He came to the group from Columbus, Indiana.

As had the other members of the group who had joined since its inception, and critical to plaintiff's complaint, Dr. Webber had agreed that he "will not for five years after any [voluntary or involuntary] termination of his association with said Gelder Medical Group, practice his profession within a radius of 30 miles of the Village of Sidney, as a physician or surgeon * * * without the consent, in writing, of said Gelder Medical Group." The partnership agreement also provided a procedure for the involuntary withdrawal of partners. Thus, it was, in pertinent part, provided that "In the event that any member is requested to resign or withdraw from the group by a majority vote of the other members of the group, such notice shall be effective immediately and his share of the profits to the date of termination shall be computed and he shall be paid in full to the date of termination of his employment pursuant to his agreement with the association."

Dr. Webber's association turned out to be unsatisfactory to his partners. His conduct, both professional and personal, assertedly became abrasive and objectionable to his partners and their patients, a cause of "intolerable" embarrassment to the group. Revealing is a letter of a psychiatrist who, after his formal termination, examined Dr. Webber a number of times on the referral of the partnership. In the psychiatrist's words, Dr. Webber initially "appeared clinically with what would be termed an adjustment reaction of adult life with anxiety and depression". While the psychiatrist concluded that the adjustment reaction soon cleared, he summed up his description of Dr. Webber as a perfectionist who was a "rather idealistic sincere, direct, frank individual who quite possibly could be perceived at times as being somewhat blunt." In fact, Dr. Webber, in one of his affidavits, conceded, commendably, that he is probably "more of a perfectionist and idealist than he should be."

Although during the association difficulties were from time to time discussed with Dr. Webber, the unhappy relationship persisted. In October, 1973, the discord culminated with the group's unanimous decision to terminate Dr. Webber's association with the partnership. After Dr. Webber refused to withdraw voluntarily, the group, in writing, formally notified him of the termination. It was effective immediately, and, on the basis of an accounting, Webber was paid $18,568.41 in full compliance with the articles of agreement which, it is notable, provided for voluntary or involuntary termination on substantially the same terms. But that did not end the unpleasantness.

In about two months, the expelled partner, disregarding the restrictive covenant, resumed his surgical practice as a single practitioner in Sidney. The group, to protect its practice, promptly brought this action to enjoin Dr.

Webber's violation of the restrictive covenant and obtained a temporary injunction. Dr. Webber instituted his own action for a declaratory judgment and for damages in allegedly wrongfully expelling him. The actions were consolidated.

The plain meaning and intended effect of the restrictive covenant and the provisions for expulsion are not now in dispute. Dr. Webber urges, however, that the court superimpose a good faith requirement on the partnership's right to expel and to enforce the restrictive covenant. Also urged is the inevitable argument that the restrictive covenant is unreasonable under the circumstances.

The applicable law is straightforward. Covenants restricting a professional, and in particular a physician, from competing with a former employer or associate are common and generally acceptable (see, e.g., Karpinski v. Ingrasci, 28 N.Y.2d 45, 47–49, 320 N.Y.S.2d 1, 2–5, 268 N.E.2d 751, 752–753. As with all restrictive covenants, if they are reasonable as to time and area, necessary to protect legitimate interests, not harmful to the public, and not unduly burdensome, they will be enforced.

Similarly common and acceptable are provisions in a partnership agreement to provide for the withdrawal or expulsion of a partner. While there is no common-law or statutory right to expel a member of a partnership, partners may provide, in their agreement, for the involuntary dismissal, with or without cause, of one of their number.

Turning to the Gelder Group agreement, no acceptable reason is offered for limiting the plainly stated provisions for expulsion, freely subscribed to by Dr. Webber when he joined the group, and none is perceived. When, as here, the agreement provides for dismissal of one of their number on the majority vote of the partners, the court may not frustrate the intention of the parties at least so long as the provisions for dismissal work no undue penalty or unjust forfeiture, overreaching, or other violation of public policy.

Assuming, not without question, that bad faith might limit the otherwise absolute language of the agreement, the record does not reveal bad faith. Embarrassing situations developed, affecting the physicians and their patients, as a result of Dr. Webber's conduct, however highly motivated his conduct might have been. It was as important, therefore, in the group's eyes, as anything affecting survival of the group that it be disassociated from the new member's conflict-producing conduct. Indeed, at the heart of the partnership concept is the principle that partners may choose with whom they wish to be associated.

Even if bad faith on the part of the remaining partners would nullify the right to expel one of their number, it does not follow that under an agreement permitting expulsion without cause the remaining partners have the burden of establishing good faith. To so require would nullify the right to expel without cause and frustrate the obvious intention of the agreement to avoid bitter and protracted litigation over the reason for the expulsion. Obviously, no expulsion would ever occur without some cause, fancied or real, but the agreement provision is addressed to avoiding the necessity of showing cause and litigating the issue. On the other hand, if an expelled partner were to allege and prove bad faith going to the essence, a different case would be presented. As with any contractual agreement, in the time-honored language of the law, there is an implied term of good faith. In his affidavits Dr. Webber has not shown even a suggestion of evil, malevolent, or predatory purpose in the expulsion. Hence, he raises no triable issue on this score.

Insofar as the restrictive covenant is concerned, its reasonableness must be measured by the circumstances and context in which enforcement is sought. * * * [The Court concluded that the covenant was reasonable].

Hence, defendant's attempts to free himself from the covenant not to compete, which, it is notable, will expire by its own provisions in less than two years, must be rejected. It is true, as the group stated in its letter of termination to Dr. Webber, that the termination was a tragedy which it regretted. But the expulsion clause was designed to function when the conflict between the group and one of its members was insoluble, and the necessity for its use must always be unfortunate. Such use is free of fault to remedy an intolerable situation, a situation which would not be less intolerable because the "blame" for its occasion could be pointed in one direction rather than another.

Accordingly, the order of the Appellate Division should be affirmed, with costs.

JASEN, GABRIELLI, JONES, WACHTLER, FUCHSBERG and COOKE, JJ., concur.

Order affirmed.

Notes

(1) Consider UPA (1914) §§ 31(1)(d), 38(2). What is the relationship between "wrongful dissolution" and "expulsion"? Could the Gelder group have viewed Webber's conduct as wrongful dissolution? Does "expulsion" have any meaning in partnerships at will? Consult Robert W. Hillman, Misconduct as a Basis for Excluding or Expelling a Partner: Effecting Commercial Divorce and Securing Custody of the Business, 78 Nw.U.L.Rev. 527 (1983).

(2) Does UPA (1914) contemplate that a partner may be expelled "without cause"? What then, does the phrase "bona fide" mean in § 31(1)(d)? UPA (1994) § 601(3) omits these words. Is that significant?

(3) Why isn't the restrictive covenant enforced against Webber contrary to public policy since it restricts the citizenry of Sidney, New York in their choice of medical services? Compare Cohen v. Lord, Day, & Lord, abstracted supra note (6), at 100. Or are the rules different for doctors and for lawyers?

(4) As indicated earlier, with the change in the economics of law practice, the number of cases involving expulsion of arguably under-performing partners in law firms has increased dramatically in recent years. Examples include:

(a) The partnership agreement of Cadwalader, Wickersham & Taft, a well-known New York firm, did not contain a provision involving expulsion of partners. In 1993 the share value of the firm declined, and a branch office located in Palm Beach, Florida, operated at a loss. 1994 saw an even larger decline in share value. A group of fifteen younger partners and the management committee developed a plan, "Project Right Size," which aimed at identifying and eliminating less productive partners. As part of this project the Palm Beach office was closed and an armed guard posted. Negotiations with one Palm Beach partner, Beasley, broke down and he was expelled from the firm. He thereafter brought suit, claiming that his expulsion violated the partnership agreement and breached fiduciary duties owed to him. In Beasley v. Cadwalader, Wickersham & Taft, 1996 WL 438777

(Fla.Cir.Ct., Jul 23, 1996) the court, in an opinion highly critical of the firm's conduct, awarded Beasley substantial compensatory and exemplary damages. The case is discussed in Allan W. Vestal, "Assume a Rather Large Boat:" The Mess We Have Made of Partnership Law, 54 Wash. & Lee L.Rev. 487 (1997).

(b) The partnership agreement of White & Case, another well-known New York law firm, also did not contain an express expulsion provision. The firm commenced negotiations with a partner, Evan Dawson, seeking his retirement. Dawson, who had been with the firm for twenty years, refused to retire voluntarily. The firm then dissolved and immediately reformed but without Dawson as a partner. The New York Court of Appeals upheld this procedure, relying on the statement in *Gelder* "that partners may choose with whom they wish to be associated." Dawson v. White & Case, 88 N.Y.2d 666, 649 N.Y.S.2d 364, 672 N.E.2d 589 (1996). The principal issue discussed was how Dawson's interest in the partnership should be valued. If that is the way to do it, should not Cadwalder simply have dissolved and reconstituted itself?

(c) In Winston & Strawn v. Nosal, 279 Ill.App.3d 231, 215 Ill.Dec. 842, 664 N.E.2d 239 (1996), the firm had decided to "downsize" by eliminating 19 partners ("outplacing" was the term used); Nosal was not included in the initial list of "outplaced" partners that was posted, and indeed thereafter received an increase in point allocation. He thereafter requested information about possible allocations of points and distributions to members of the management committee without disclosure to other members. This request was denied, but Nosal persevered. Within a month, Nosal's name appeared on a new list of partners to be "outplaced." According to deposition testimony by managing partners, "Nosal was outplaced because his interest in building a two-pronged tax and international trade practice was incompatible with the interests and resources of the firm, and because he had engaged in 'disturbing' conduct." The court held that summary judgment in favor of the firm should be reversed and the issue whether Nosal's termination was in bad faith should be tried: the "steadfast refusal of Nosal's access to records * * * and the fact that it occurred just after Nosal's threatened lawsuit, raise an inference that Nosal was expelled solely because he persisted in invoking rights belonging to him under the partnership agreement and that the reasons advanced by the firm were pretextual." (279 Ill.App.3d at 239, 215 Ill.Dec. at 847, 664 N.E.2d at 244)

(5) Assume a law firm's partnership agreement does not contain an express provision authorizing expulsion but provides that the agreement may be amended by a vote less than unanimity. May a law firm amend its partnership agreement to include an expulsion clause and then immediately apply it to expel a specific partner? If so, do fiduciary duties or the duty of good faith require there be disclosure as to the identity of the target?

———

Dissolution Under UPA (1994). The technical definition of "dissolution" set forth in UPA (1914) may be traced to the partial acceptance in that Act of the view that a partnership was an aggregate of the partners. By the time the development of UPA (1994) began, it had become clear that the entity theory of partnership was generally accepted and that a new approach toward dissolution was called for. An influential article by Professor Larry E. Ribstein (A Statutory Approach to Partner Dissociation, 65 Wash. U. L.Q. 357 (1987)) not only added the word "dissociation" to the partnership lexicon but also pointed out that "cessation of partner status" was an event that was independent of the question whether the business should be "dissolved" and wound up. In other words, it should be possible for a partner to leave—to be "dissociated"—and yet have the partnership continue if the value of the withdrawing partner's interest is paid to him. UPA (1994) adopts this approach.

The dissolution provisions of UPA recognize specifically that partners need not be individuals; they may be corporations, trusts, other partnerships, limited liability companies, and other types of entities.

The major features of the dissolution provisions of UPA (1994) are as follows:

(1) The death, withdrawal, cessation of existence, or expulsion of a partner is a "dissociation." UPA (1994) § 601. Events causing dissociation of a partner who is an individual were broadened from similar provisions relating to "dissolution" under UPA (1914) in various ways, most notably by broadening the power to expel partners without express authorization in the partnership agreement (§ 601(4)) or by judicial order (§ 601(5)). Events causing dissociation of a partner which is not an individual (e.g., a corporation, partnership, trust or estate) are identified (§ 601(4), (8)–(10)).

(2) The basic distinction between "rightful" and "wrongful" dissociation (see p. 75) is retained, but the definition of "wrongful" dissociation in a partnership for a term or particular undertaking is broadened (§ 602(b)).

(3) A partnership continues in existence despite dissociation of a partner. It may continue in existence indefinitely with the dissociated partner becoming entitled to the value of her partnership interest in cash under article 7, or it may be dissolved and wound up pursuant to the provisions of article 8.

(4) Dissolution and winding up are required in only the limited circumstances set forth in § 801. Two provisions are of particular importance in terms of the continuity of the enterprise: a) in a partnership at will, any partner who dissociates by his express will may compel dissolution and winding up; and, b) in a partnership for a definite term or particular undertaking, if one partner dissociates wrongfully (or a dissociation occurs because of death or dissolution of a partner), a dissolution and winding up of the partnership occurs only if one-half of the remaining members agree to dissolve the partnership within 90 days after the dissociation. Once an event requiring dissolution and winding up occurs, the partnership is to be wound up unless all the partners (including any dissociated partner other than a wrongfully dissociating partner) agree.

(5) If a partner dissociates, but the business is not dissolved and wound up, the partner is entitled to receive the "buyout price." § 701(a). This price is defined in § 701(b). If the dissociation was wrongful, damages may offset the buyout price, § 701(c), and the payment may be deferred until the expiration of the term or completion of the undertaking, "unless the partner establishes to the satisfaction of the court that earlier payment will not cause undue hardship to the business of the partnership." § 701(h). A deferred payment must be "adequately secured and bear interest."

(6) UPA (1994) does not contain the election in § 42 of UPA (1914) that permits a former partner in a partnership that does not wind up to take

either a share of post-dissolution profits or interest on his capital account (see page 78, supra) as compensation for the use of his capital. Under UPA (1994) § 701(b), last sentence, a dissociated partner is entitled only to interest on the amount to be paid the dissociated partner from the date of dissociation to the date of payment.

(7) A dissociated partner has apparent authority to bind the partnership, § 702, and may be liable for post-dissociation partnership liabilities incurred within two years after the dissociation. § 703. A dissociated partner, or the partnership, may file a public statement of dissociation to limit this apparent authority and potential liability. § 704.

(8) A partnership *"is dissolved"* when one of the events requiring winding up listed in § 801 occur, but this list is exclusive. After dissolution, the partnership continues in existence for the purpose of winding up. § 802(a). The apparent authority of partners to bind the partnership continues after dissolution, but any partner who has not wrongfully dissociated may file a public statement of dissolution to give notice that the partnership is in the winding up process. § 806. Section 807 describes the final settlement of partnership accounts upon winding up. Partnership assets must be applied to the discharge of partnership liabilities, and if the assets are insufficient, individual partners are required to contribute in accordance with their respective loss sharing ratios. Partners with negative balances in their accounts are required to restore those balances to zero to ensure that all partners receive the amounts in their accounts. Any excess assets remaining are distributable to the partners in accordance with their profit sharing ratios. In general, section 807 is considerably more precise about the winding up process than the corresponding provisions of UPA (1914).

I. INADVERTENT PARTNERSHIPS

A recurring issue in partnership law is whether an arrangement between persons may unintentionally constitute a partnership so that a creditor who dealt with A may force B to pay its claim. At common law, a sharing of profits was often deemed conclusive of the existence of a partnership. Consider UPA (1914) §§ 6, 7. Section 7(4) states that such sharing is "prima facie evidence" of a partnership except that in certain cases "no such inference shall be drawn." May "prima facie evidence" be rebutted? If so, what kind of "evidence" might do so? If no "inference" of partnership is to be drawn in certain situations, does that mean no partnership exists, or does it mean that a partnership might be found to exist on the basis of other information? If so, what information? Finally, what is the significance of the co-ownership requirement in § 6 in this context? Does this definition help in determining when an arrangement is a partnership as compared to something else? Is § 7 more helpful than § 6?

UPA (1994) § 202(c)(3) states that a person who receives a share of the profits of a business "is presumed to be a partner" unless the payments were received in some other capacity. Is a "presumption" of partnership any different than "prima facie evidence" of a partnership? Is this simply an instance where the drafters of UPA (1994) cleaned up some rather archaic language in UPA (1914)?

MARTIN v. PEYTON

Court of Appeals of New York, 1927.
246 N.Y. 213, 158 N.E. 77.

ANDREWS, J.

Much ancient learning as to partnership is obsolete. Today only those who are partners between themselves may be charged for partnership debts by others. [UPA (1914) § 7] There is one exception. Now and then a recovery is allowed where in truth such relationship is absent. This is because the debtor may not deny the claim. [UPA (1914) § 16]

Partnership results from contract, express or implied. If denied, it may be proved by the production of some written instrument, by testimony as to some conversation, by circumstantial evidence. If nothing else appears, the receipt by the defendant of a share of the profits of the business is enough. [UPA (1914) § 7]

Assuming some written contract between the parties, the question may arise whether it creates a partnership. If it be complete, if it expresses in good faith the full understanding and obligation of the parties, then it is for the court to say whether a partnership exists. It may, however, be a mere sham intended to hide the real relationship. Then other results follow. In passing upon it, effect is to be given to each provision. Mere words will not blind us to realities. Statements that no partnership is intended are not conclusive. If as a whole a contract contemplates an association of two or more persons to carry on as co-owners a business for profit, a partnership there is. [UPA (1914) § 6] On the other hand, if it be less than this, no partnership exists. Passing on the contract as a whole, an arrangement for sharing profits is to be considered. It is to be given its due weight. But it is to be weighed in connection with all the rest. It is not decisive. It may be merely the method adopted to pay a debt or wages, as interest on a loan or for other reasons.

An existing contract may be modified later by subsequent agreement, oral or written. A partnership may be so created where there was none before. And again, that the original agreement has been so modified may be proved by circumstantial evidence—by showing the conduct of the parties.

In the case before us the claim that the defendants became partners in the firm of Knauth, Nachod & Kuhne, doing business as bankers and brokers, depends upon the interpretation of certain instruments. There is nothing in their subsequent acts determinative of or indeed material upon this question. And we are relieved of questions that sometimes arise. "The plaintiff's position is not," we are told, "that the agreements of June 4, 1921, were a false expression or incomplete expression of the intention of the parties. We say that they express defendants' intention and that that intention was to create a relationship which as a matter of law constitutes a partnership." Nor may the claim of the plaintiff be rested on any question of estoppel. "The plaintiff's claim," he stipulates, "is a claim of actual partnership, not of partnership by estoppel, and liability is not sought to be predicated upon [§ 16] of the [1914 Uniform] Partnership [Act]."

Remitted then, as we are, to the documents themselves, we refer to circumstances surrounding their execution only so far as is necessary to make them intelligible. And we are to remember that although the intention of the parties to avoid liability as partners is clear, although in language precise and definite they deny any design to then join the firm of K.N. & K.; although they say their interests in profits should be construed merely as a measure of compensation for loans, not an interest in profits as such; although they provide that they shall not be liable for any losses or treated as partners, the question still remains whether in fact they agree to so associate themselves with the firm as to "carry on as co-owners a business for profit."

In the spring of 1921 the firm of K.N. & K. found itself in financial difficulties. John R. Hall was one of the partners. He was a friend of Mr. Peyton. From him he obtained the loan of almost $500,000 of Liberty bonds, which K.N. & K. might use as collateral to secure bank advances. This, however, was not sufficient. The firm and its members had engaged in unwise speculations, and it was deeply involved. Mr. Hall was also intimately acquainted with George W. Perkins, Jr., and with Edward W. Freeman. He also knew Mrs. Peyton and Mrs. Perkins and Mrs. Freeman. All were anxious to help him. He therefore, representing K.N. & K., entered into negotiations with them. While they were pending a proposition was made that Mr. Peyton, Mr. Perkins, and Mr. Freeman, or some of them, should become partners. It met a decided refusal. Finally an agreement was reached. It is expressed in three documents, executed on the same day, all a part of the one transaction. They were drawn with care and are unambiguous. We shall refer to them as "the agreement," "the indenture," and "the option."

We have no doubt as to their general purpose. The respondents were to loan K.N. & K. $2,500,000 worth of liquid securities, which were to be returned to them on or before April 15, 1923. The firm might hypothecate them to secure loans totaling $2,000,000, using the proceeds as its business necessities required. To insure respondents against loss K.N. & K. were to turn over to them a large number of their own securities which may have been valuable, but which were of so speculative a nature that they could not be used as collateral for bank loans. In compensation for the loan the respondents were to receive 40 percent of the profits of the firm until the return was made, not exceeding, however, $500,000, and not less than $100,000. Merely because the transaction involved the transfer of securities and not of cash does not prevent its being a loan, within the meaning of section 11. The respondents also were given an option to join the firm if they, or any of them, expressed a desire to do so before June 4, 1923.

Many other detailed agreements are contained in the papers. Are they such as may be properly inserted to protect the lenders? Or do they go further? Whatever their purpose, did they in truth associate the respondents with the firm so that they and it together thereafter carried on as co-owners a business for profit? The answer depends upon an analysis of these various provisions.

As representing the lenders, Mr. Peyton and Mr. Freeman are called "trustees." The loaned securities when used as collateral are not to be mingled with other securities of K.N. & K., and the trustees at all times are to be kept informed of all transactions affecting them. To them shall be paid all dividends and income accruing therefrom. They may also substitute for any of the securities loaned securities of equal value. With their consent the firm may sell any of its securities held by the respondents, the proceeds to go, however, to the trustees. In other similar ways the trustees may deal with these same securities, but the securities loaned shall always be sufficient in value to permit of their hypothecation for $2,000,000. If they rise in price, the excess may be withdrawn by the defendants. If they fall, they shall make good the deficiency.

So far, there is no hint that the transaction is not a loan of securities with a provision for compensation. Later a somewhat closer connection with the firm appears. Until the securities are returned, the directing management of the firm is to be in the hands of John R. Hall, and his life is to be insured for $1,000,000, and the policies are to be assigned as further collateral security to the trustees. These requirements are not unnatural. Hall was the one known and trusted by the defendants. Their acquaintance with the other members of the firm was of the slightest. These others had brought an old and established business to the verge of bankruptcy. As the respondents knew, they also had engaged in unsafe speculation. The respondents were about to loan $2,500,000 of good securities. As collateral they were to receive others of problematical value. What they required seems but ordinary caution. Nor does it imply an association in the business.

The trustees are to be kept advised as to the conduct of the business and consulted as to important matters. They may inspect the firm books and are entitled to any information they think important. Finally, they may veto any business they think highly speculative or injurious. Again we hold this but a proper precaution to safeguard the loan. The trustees may not initiate any transaction as a partner may do. They may not bind the firm by any action of their own. Under the circumstances the safety of the loan depended upon the business success of K.N. & K. This success was likely to be compromised by the inclination of its members to engage in speculation. No longer, if the respondents were to be protected should it be allowed. The trustees therefore might prohibit it, and that their prohibition might be effective, information was to be furnished them. Not dissimilar agreements have been held proper to guard the interests of the lender.

As further security each member of K.N. & K. is to assign to the trustees their interest in the firm. No loan by the firm to any member is permitted and the amount each may draw is fixed. No other distribution of profits is to be made. So that realized profits may be calculated the existing capital is stated to be $700,000, and profits are to be realized as promptly as good business practice will permit. In case the trustees think this is not done, the question is left to them and to Mr. Hall, and if they differ then to an arbitrator. There is no obligation that the firm shall continue the business. It may dissolve at any time. Again we conclude there is nothing here not properly adapted to secure the interest of the respondents as lenders. If their compensation is dependent on a percentage of the profits, still provision must be made to define what these profits shall be.

The "indenture" is substantially a mortgage of the collateral delivered by K.N. & K. to the trustees to secure the performance of the "agreement." It certainly does not strengthen the claim that the respondents were partners.

Finally we have the "option." It permits the respondents, or any of them, or their assignees or nominees to enter the firm at a later date if they desire to do so by buying 50 percent or less of the interests therein of all or any of the members at a stated price. Or a corporation may, if the respondents and the members agree, be formed in place of the firm. Meanwhile, apparently with the design of protecting the firm business against improper or ill-judged action which might render the option valueless, each member of the firm is to place his resignation in the hands of Mr. Hall. If at any time he and the trustees agree that such resignation should be accepted, that member shall then retire, receiving the value of his interest calculated as of the date of such retirement.

This last provision is somewhat unusual, yet it is not enough in itself to show that on June 4, 1921, a present partnership was created, nor taking these various papers as a whole do we reach such a result. It is quite true that even if one or two or three like provisions contained in such a contract do not require this conclusion, yet it is also true that when taken together a point may come where stipulations immaterial separately cover so wide a field that we should hold a partnership exists. As in other branches of the law, a question of degree is often the determining factor. Here that point has not been reached.

The judgment appealed from should be affirmed, with costs.

CARDOZO, C.J., and POUND, LEHMAN, KELLOGG, and O'BRIEN, JJ., concur.

Notes

(1) The indenture in Martin v. Peyton contained the following provision:

> The parties of the first part shall not be interested in 'profits' as such. Their interest in profits shall be construed merely as a measure of compensation for loaning said active securities to said firm and granting permission to the firm to hypothecate the same, and for the services to be rendered by the trustees. The parties of the first part shall not be responsible for any losses that may be made by said firm. The parties of the first part shall not in any way be deemed or treated or held as partners in said firm. No one of the parties of the first part shall be under any partnership liability or obligation. It is not the intention of any of the parties of the first part to assume any of the liabilities of the said firm * * *.

219 App.Div. 297, 220 N.Y.S. 29, 34 (1927). To what extent should provisions of this nature be given effect as against third parties?

(2) Many modern financing arrangements involve a sharing of profits. Leases of stores in shopping centers often contain provisions for increasing the rent based on increased sales or, more rarely, profits. A large institutional investor making a loan for a real estate venture may insist on a "piece of the action." Elaborate provisions are necessary to protect the investor's interest in such arrangements. For example, in a percentage rent shopping center lease, the lease may permit the landlord to establish (uniform) hours of operation, advertising programs, and the like. The lessee may be required to open its books on demand, to keep its store fully stocked and staffed, and so forth. Is there any danger that such arrangements may be deemed to constitute a partnership rather than a lease?

SMITH v. KELLEY

Appellate Court of Kentucky, 1971.
465 S.W.2d 39.

CLAY, COMMISSIONER.

Appellant brought this suit for a partnership accounting. The Chancellor adjudged no partnership existed and dismissed appellant's claim. Appellant contends on appeal that the judgment is "erroneous".

With one exception, there is little dispute about the facts. In 1964 appellees Kelley and Galloway were partners in an accounting business. Appellant left another firm and came to work for them. For three and one-half years appellant drew $1,000 a month, plus $100 a month for travel expenses. At the end of each year he was paid a relatively small additional sum as a bonus out of the profits of the business. Not until appellant left the Kelley–Galloway firm in 1968 did he make any claim that he was entitled to a fixed percentage of the profits. In this lawsuit he asserts he had a twenty-percent interest therein.

There was no writing evidencing a partnership agreement. However, during the years appellant worked for the firm he was held out to the public as a partner. In a contract entered into between Kelley, Galloway, appellant and a third party, appellant was designated a partner. Partnership tax returns listed him as such; so did a statement filed with the Kentucky Board of Accountancy. In a suit filed in the circuit court against a third party he was designated a partner.

On the other hand, Kelley, Galloway and another employee of the firm testified there was no agreement that Smith would be a partner or have a right to share in the profits; he made no contribution to the assets of the partnership; he took no part in the management; he had no authority to hire or fire employees or to make purchases for the firm; he did not sign any notes when the firm was borrowing money; and he was not obligated to stand any losses of the firm.

A partnership is a contractual relationship and the intention to create it is necessary. As to third parties, a partnership may arise by estoppel, but our question is whether the parties intended to and did create such a relationship as would entitle appellant to share in the profits.

The Chancellor found that the original partners had at no time agreed that appellant would be entitled to share in a percentage of the profits. This was a matter of credibility and the Chancellor, who heard the evidence, chose to believe appellees. His finding on this point was not clearly erroneous and would seem to be dispositive of the case. In addition however, the conduct of the parties over a three-and-one-half-year period confirms the conclusion that, though appellant was held out to the public as a partner, between themselves a partnership relationship was not intended to be and was not created. We find no error in the court's findings of fact or conclusions of law.

Appellant relies on Guthrie v. Foster, 256 Ky. 753, 76 S.W.2d 927 (1934), wherein the Chancellor's finding that a partnership existed was based on certain facts similar to those we have in this case. However, there were other considerations in the cited case that do not appear here and it is not controlling.

We have examined the [1914] Uniform Partnership Act, and particularly [§§ 6, 7(1), 7(4), 18(a), 18(e), 18(g)], and find the trial court's decision took cognizance of the essential elements of a partnership therein prescribed.

The judgment is affirmed.

YOUNG v. JONES

United States District Court, District of South Carolina, 1992.
816 F.Supp. 1070.

HAWKINS, CHIEF JUDGE.

[Price Waterhouse, Chartered Accountants (PW–Bahamas) is a Bahamian general partnership. Price Waterhouse–United States (PW–US) is a New York general partnership, one of the "big six" accounting firms. Suit was brought in South Carolina against both of these partnerships, the partners of PW–US who reside in South Carolina, and certain other persons and entities. The opinion set forth here relates to motions to dismiss filed by PW–Bahamas and PW–US.]

* * * As background, this suit arises from an investment transaction. Plaintiffs are investors from Texas who deposited over a half-million dollars in a South Carolina bank and the funds have disappeared.

PW–Bahamas issued an unqualified audit letter regarding the financial statement of Swiss American Fidelity and Insurance Guaranty (SAFIG). Plaintiffs aver that on the basis of that financial statement, they deposited $550,000,00 in a South Carolina bank. Other defendants, not involved in the motions herein, allegedly sent the money from the South Carolina Bank to SAFIG. The financial statement of SAFIG was falsified. The plaintiffs' money and its investment potential has been lost to the plaintiffs and it is for these losses that the plaintiffs seek to recover damages. * * *

The first cause of action alleged in the amended complaint is that the Bahamian accounting firm negligently performed an audit and negligently released an audit letter upon which the plaintiffs relied to their detriment. There are no allegations that PW–US, or any individual U.S. partner who resides in South Carolina, was involved in the subject transaction. The only connection between the allegations of negligence and the U.S. firm are conclusory allegations that the Bahamian partnership and the U.S. partnership operate as a partnership, or in the alternative, are a partnership by estoppel. * * *

Plaintiffs allege that an unqualified audit letter concerning a financial statement of an association, SAFIG, was issued by a Bahamian accounting office. The letterhead identified the Bahamian accounting firm only as "Price Waterhouse." The audit letter also bore a Price Waterhouse trademark and was signed "Price Waterhouse."

Plaintiffs assert that it was foreseeable to the accounting firm that issued the letter that third-parties would rely upon the financial statement, the subject of the audit letter. According to the plaintiffs, the stamp of approval created by Price Waterhouse's audit letter of SAFIG's financial statement lent credence to the defrauders' claims so that plaintiffs were induced to invest to their detriment. * * *

Plaintiffs assert that PW–Bahamas and PW–US operate as a partnership, i.e., constitute an association of persons to carry on, as owners, business for profit. In the alternative, plaintiffs contend that if the two associations are not actually operating as partners they are operating as partners by estoppel.

Defendants PW–US and PW–Bahamas flatly deny that a partnership exists between the two entities and have supplied, under seal, copies of relevant documents executed which establish that the two entities are separately organized. Counsel for plaintiffs admits that he has found nothing which establishes that the two entities are partners in fact. The evidence presented wholly belies plaintiffs claims that PW–Bahamas and PW–US are operating as a partnership in fact.[28] Thus, the court finds that there is no partnership, in fact, between PW–Bahamas and PW–US.

Then, plaintiffs make a double-edged argument that PW–US is a partner by estoppel of PW–Bahamas. On the one hand, the argument is that if the two partnerships are partners by estoppel, then the court has personal jurisdiction over PW–Bahamas, as PW–US's partner by estoppel, because PW–US has at least "minimum contacts" with South Carolina. On the other hand, the argument for estoppel seems to be that if the two partnerships are partners by estoppel then PW–US can be held liable for the negligent acts of its partner PW–Bahamas, so the claim against PW–Bahamas operates as a claim against PW–US. * * *

As a general rule, persons who are not partners as to each other are not partners as to third persons. [UPA (1914) § 7]. However, a person who represents himself, or permits another to represent him, to anyone as a partner in an existing partnership or with others not actual partners, is liable to any such person to whom such a representation is made who has, on the faith of the representation, given credit to the actual or apparent partnership. [UPA (1914) § 16]. This exception to the general rule for liability by partners by estoppel is statutorily created under the Uniform Partnership Act in the version adopted by the State of South Carolina.

Generally, partners are jointly and severally liable for everything chargeable to the partnership. S.C.Code Ann. § 33–41–370.[29] In South Carolina, a partnership is an entity separate and distinct from the individual partners

---

28. [By the Editor] The relationship between PW–US and PW–Bahamas is described as follows in Young v. F.D.I.C., 103 F.3d 1180, 1191, n. 6 (4th Cir.1997):

PW–Bahamas is part of a world-wide organization of separate and independent Price Waterhouse firms that practice accountancy in various countries. The members of each Price Waterhouse firm hold shares in Price Waterhouse World Firm Limited (PW–World Firm), a limited liability company incorporated under the Laws of Bermuda. PW–World Firm assists the various Price Waterhouse firms in advancing their respective practices, and it facilitates the maintenance of uniform standards of practice. It does not conduct or supervise client engagements,

however. Nor does it play a part in the day-to-day management of the Price Waterhouse firms.

PW–World Firm's bylaws designate twenty-six separate "member firms" in the Price Waterhouse organization. Those member firms include PW–US and Price Waterhouse North Caribbean (PW–North Caribbean), a Cayman Islands partnership authorized to use the Price Waterhouse name pursuant to an agreement with PW–World Firm. PW–North Caribbean sub-licenses PW–Bahamas to use the Price Waterhouse name.

29. [By the Editor] S.C. Code Ann. § 33–41–370, states "all partners are liable jointly and severally for everything charged to the partnership."

who compose it. *South Carolina Tax Comm. v. Reeves*, 278 S.C. 658, 300 S.E.2d 916 (1983). Therefore, plaintiffs' argument is that if the court would find that PW–Bahamas and PW–US are partners by estoppel, PW–US would be jointly and severally liable with PW–Bahamas for everything chargeable to the partnership of the two firms. Moreover, if the two partnerships are partners by estoppel, the individual partners of PW–US would then be jointly and severally liable for the negligent acts of the PW–Bahamas partnership.

Plaintiffs maintain that Price Waterhouse holds itself out to be a partnership with offices around the world. According to the plaintiffs, the U.S. affiliate makes no distinction in its advertising between itself and entities situated in foreign jurisdictions. The foreign affiliates are permitted to use the Price Waterhouse name and trademark. Plaintiffs urge the conclusion of partnership by estoppel from the combination of facts that Price Waterhouse promotes its image as an organization affiliated with other Price Waterhouse offices around the world and that it is common knowledge that the accounting firm of Price Waterhouse operates as a partnership.

Plaintiffs offer for illustration that PW–Bahamas and PW–US hold themselves out to be partners with one another, a Price Waterhouse brochure, picked up by plaintiffs' counsel at a litigation services seminar, that describes Price Waterhouse as one of the "world's largest and most respected professional organizations." The brochure states: "[O]ver 28,000 Price Waterhouse professionals in 400 offices throughout the world can be called upon to provide support for your reorganization and litigation efforts." Plaintiffs assert that assurances like that contained in the brochure cast Price Waterhouse as an established international accounting firm and that the image, promoted by PW–US, is designed to gain public confidence in the firm's stability and expertise.

However, the plaintiffs do not contend that the brochure submitted was seen or relied on by them in making the decision to invest. In addition, plaintiffs point to nothing in the brochure that asserts that the affiliated entities of Price Waterhouse are liable for the acts of another, or that any of the affiliates operate within a single partnership. * * *

PW–US points out that the South Carolina statute, which was cited by plaintiffs in support of their argument for partnership by estoppel, speaks only to the creation of liability to third-persons who, in reliance upon representations as to the existence of a partnership, "[give] credit" to that partnership. [UPA (1914) § 16]. There is no evidence, neither has there been an allegation, that credit was extended on the basis of any representation of a partnership existing between PW–Bahamas and the South Carolina members of the PW–US partnership. There is no evidence of any extension of credit to either PW–Bahamas or PW–US, by plaintiffs. Thus, the facts do not support a finding of liability for partners by estoppel under the statutory law of South Carolina.

Further, there is no evidence that plaintiffs relied on any act or statement by any PW–US partner which indicated the existence of a partnership with the Bahamian partnership. Finally, there is no evidence, nor is there a single allegation that any member of the U.S. partnership had anything to do with the audit letter complained of by plaintiffs, or any other act related to the investment transaction.

The court cannot find any evidence to support a finding of partners by estoppel. * * * [The court granted the motions of PW–Bahamas, PW–US, and the South Carolina partners of PW–US to dismiss the suit.]

Notes

(1) In Smith v. Kelley, assume that a customer of the accounting firm of Kelley & Galloway sues the partnership for malpractice and adds Smith as a defendant. Is Smith liable? In light of the argument of the Court in Young v. Jones about the specific reliance that is needed to establish liability under UPA (1914) § 16, what would that customer have to show?

(2) Would Smith be liable if a customer of Kelley & Galloway was injured in a slip-and-fall accident in the waiting room of the partnership?

(3) Do you agree with the result reached in Young v. Jones that Price Waterhouse is not liable for the actions of its overseas office despite (1) the use by the Bahamian partnership of letterhead that referred only to "Price Waterhouse" and (2) the advertising of its overseas offices by Price Waterhouse that was cited by plaintiffs in that case?

(4) UPA (1994) § 308 uses the phrase "purported partner" rather than "partner by estoppel." Is that phrase an improvement?

(5) Simpson v. Ernst & Young, 100 F.3d 436 (6th Cir.1996), cert. den. ___ U.S. ___, 117 S.Ct. 1862, 137 L.Ed.2d 1062 (1997) involved a claim by Simpson, a "partner" of the Ernst & Young accounting firm, that he had been released in violation of the Age Discrimination in Employment Act (ADEA). To recover under ADEA, Simpson had to establish that he was in fact an employee and not a partner. Simpson was one of 2,200 persons who had been designated as "partners." The evidence showed that Ernst & Young's business, assets, and affairs were directed exclusively by a 10 to 14 member Management Committee. Simpson "had no authority to direct or participate in the admission or discharge of partners or other firm personnel; participate in determining partners or other personnel compensation predicated upon performance levels, responsibility, and years of service with the firm, including his own; participate in the firm's profits and losses or share in unbilled uncollected client accounts. Simpson had no right to examine the books and records of the firm except to the extent permitted by the Management Committee. * * * He had no authority to sign promissory notes on behalf of the firm, or pledge, transfer, or otherwise assign his interest in the firm. He was refused access to data concerning various client accounts. He was denied participation in annual performance reviews and other indicia of partnership status." 100 F.3d, at 441. The Court concluded that Simpson was an "employee" and not a "partner." Sixteen major law firms unsuccessfully urged the Supreme Court to review this holding. Contrast Rhoads v. Jones Financial Companies, 957 F.Supp. 1102 (E.D.Mo.1997).

Chapter Three

OTHER UNINCORPORATED BUSINESS FORMS

A. IN GENERAL

As described in chapter 1, the last decade has seen the development of novel business form—particularly, the limited liability company and the limited liability partnership—that appear to overlap not only existing business forms but each other as well. Today, most ventures may select their desired business form from a complex menu:

(1) The proprietorship (for a single-owner business) or the general partnership (for a multi-owner business);

(2) The general partnership which elects to be a limited liability partnership (LLP);[1]

(3) The limited partnership with one or more individuals as general partners;

(4) The limited partnership with a corporation or other limited liability entity as general partner;

(5) The limited partnership which elects to be a limited liability limited partnership;

(6) A "member managed" limited liability company;

(7) A "manager managed" limited liability company;

(8) A corporation which for tax purposes may be (a) a "C corporation" or (b) an "S corporation" (if it is eligible and an election is made); and

(9) A professional corporation (if the owners are engaged in a profession which is prohibited from incorporating under the general business corporation statute).

Even this list is not exhaustive. Some states authorize business trusts, joint stock companies, and a variety of other business forms. However, the forms listed above are the most important ones.

---

1. [By the Editor] It is not possible for a proprietor to elect limited liability status. A proprietor, however, may elect to conduct business as a corporation, or, in some states, as a one person limited liability company, and obtain the benefits of limited liability in that fashion.

Parts B and C of this chapter consider the two most important alternative business forms to the corporation that provide limited liability to some or all participants: the limited partnership and the limited liability company. Part D discusses the impact of federal income taxation on business forms and describes a major—indeed, almost revolutionary—change in tax regulations that was effective January 1, 1997.

B. THE LIMITED PARTNERSHIP

ROBERT W. HAMILTON, BUSINESS ORGANIZATIONS: UNINCORPORATED BUSINESSES AND CLOSELY HELD CORPORATIONS (1997)*
Pages 102–104 (1997).

The cooperative enterprise on which general partnerships are based appears to be a fundamental aspect of cooperative human enterprise and can be traced back to ancient times. The same is not so with respect to limited partnerships. The idea that some persons should be able to contribute capital to an enterprise and share in its profits, but not be responsible for its debts developed comparatively recently. The history of limited partnerships may be traced back to medieval Europe where a *society comandita* was developed primarily to permit the nobility and the Church to quietly invest their wealth in mercantile enterprises. In England and the United States, limited partnerships were first authorized by statute in the late Nineteenth and early Twentieth centuries. Today, the limited partnership form of business is exclusively a creature of statute; in the absence of statute (or the failure to comply with the mandatory provisions of an applicable statute), all partners are general partners no matter what their private understanding is or how they are designated in the partnership agreement. Thus, there is no general common law of limited partnerships as there is a common law of general partnerships, and limited partnerships are not a default form of business.

During most of the Twentieth Century the law of limited partnership was based on the Uniform Limited Partnership Act of 1916,[2] which, like the Uniform Partnership Act of 1914, achieved virtually universal acceptance. * * * There are internal indications that ULPA (1916) was prepared on the assumption that the traditional limited partnership was a small local business that desired to raise capital from local risk-adverse investors.[3] What comes to mind is a local hardware store in a small town with two general partners and two or three limited partners, perhaps bankers or other persons of substance in the community, who are willing to invest the necessary capital for the hardware store to operate in exchange for a share of its profits but who are unwilling to assume the risk of personal liability for the hardware store's debts. A major emphasis of ULPA (1916) was to ensure that creditors of the hardware store not be misled as to who was responsible for partnership obligations.[4]

* Reprinted with the permission of Aspen Law & Business/Panel Publishers, a division of Aspen Publishers, Inc.

2. [By the Editor] The 1916 Act is abbreviated here as "ULPA (1916)."

3. [By the Author] For example, ULPA makes no reference at all to the possibility that a limited partnership might conduct a business in more than one state.

4. [By the Author] * * * ULPA (1916) prohibited limited partners from providing services as their capital contribution to the limited partnership, prohibited the limited partnership from adopting a name that in-

Whether or not that original conception accurately described the use of the limited partnership in the early years of this Century, the typical limited partnership today bears little resemblance to that hardware store. The typical modern limited partnership is a federal income tax driven business in which there are scores or hundreds of limited partners and one or two general partners that are usually corporations or other limited partnerships rather than individuals. * * * [The modern] limited partnership seems economically closer to a corporation than to a general partnership.

CONTINENTAL WASTE SYSTEM, INC. v. ZOSO PARTNERS

United States District Court, N.D. Illinois, 1989.
727 F.Supp. 1143.

ASPIN, DISTRICT JUDGE.

[Ivo Zoso, an individual referred to as "Ivo," had previously invested in hazardous waste treatment facilities with Charles McKiel. McKiel learned that a waste treatment facility owned by Continental Waste Systems ("Continental") was for sale in Indiana and persuaded Ivo and Frederick Cook, Ivo's accountant and advisor, to purchase this facility. McKiel created a limited partnership called "I. Jones Partners" with himself as general partner and "Zoso Partners," as the sole limited partner. Zoso Partners was itself a newly-created general partnership between Ivo and Cook. Ivo and Cook collectively contributed $900,000 to Zoso Partners which in turn contributed the funds to I. Jones Partners to make the down payment on the facility. I. Jones Partners also executed promissory notes for the balance of the purchase price and agreed to assume certain obligations that Continental owed to the Hanchars, the family that owned Continental.]

[At the time of this transaction, limited partnerships in Illinois were governed by ULPA (1916). Illinois had adopted the Uniform Limited Partnership Act (1976) with the 1985 Amendments[5] in 1987 but that statute was made applicable only to transactions occurring on or after January 1, 1990.]

* * * I. Jones Partners began to experience severe financial difficulties. Various environmental hazards were discovered on the Indiana site; these hazards represented enormous cleanup costs. During this time, Ivo invested additional capital in I. Jones. McKiel was eventually removed as general partner of I. Jones and replaced by Cook, who attempted to continue operations at the Indiana facility. Plaintiffs allege that Ivo, through Cook, con-

cluded the name of a limited partner, and provided that a limited partner who participated in the conduct of the business became a general partner. Many states adopting this older statute provided that limited partnership certificates had to be filed in the county or city in which the limited partnership conducted its business. Multiple filings in each locali-

ty in which the limited partnership conducted business might be required. Also, no provision was made for the possibility that a limited partnership might engage in business in more than one state.

5. [By the Editor] This is the statute referred to as ULPA in the balance of this chapter and printed in the Statutory Supplement.

trolled the business of I. Jones both before and after this change in management. * * *

This is an action for breach of contract, failure to pay promissory notes, misappropriation and * * * damage to personal property, for which plaintiffs seek to recover against defendants Zoso Partnership and Ivo Zoso. Plaintiffs claim that the defendants should each be treated as a general partner and be held liable for the debts of I. Jones partnership. Plaintiffs claim this liability exists because of several violations of the Uniform Limited Partnership Act [ULPA (1916)], and because the defendants engaged in active participations and control of the partnership business. * * * [Defendants have moved for summary judgment in their favor.]

III.

* * *In Counts I through V, plaintiffs seek to hold Ivo Zoso liable as a general partner for debts of I. Jones partnership owed to the Hanchars. Ivo was nominally a [general partner of a] limited partner of I. Jones. However, the Hanchars contend that there are two grounds on which to assess personal liability against Ivo. First, plaintiffs argue that filing defects precluded the lawful creation of a limited partnership. Second, plaintiffs allege that Ivo participated in the control of I. Jones, thus rendering him personally liable as a general partner. Ivo moves for summary judgment, claiming that these allegations present no genuine issues of material fact.

The Hanchars maintain that several violations of the recording and registration requirements of the Uniform Limited Partnership Act ([ULPA (1916)]), preclude Ivo from claiming limited partner status in I. Jones. First, the I. Jones certificate of limited partnership was not filed until September 12, 1985; this was six weeks after the closing of the purchase agreement. Second, the Hanchars' maintain that the certificate was filed in the wrong county. Section 2 of the [ULPA (1916)] provides that the certificate should be filed "in the office of the recorder of the county where the principal office of such limited partnership is located." The Hanchars claim that the certificate should have been filed in Allen County, Indiana, rather than in Cook County, Illinois. Third, I. Jones failed to file an amendment to the certificate when Cook became the new general partner. * * *

Under Illinois law, these filing defects precluded the formation of a limited partnership. "Limited partnerships are creatures of statute. * * * Unlike a general partnership, a limited partnership cannot be created by informal agreement; its existence depends on compliance with the Uniform Limited Partnership Act. A certificate of incorporation must be signed by all the partners and filed in the county of the partnership's principal place of business." Inland Real Estate Corporation v. Christoph, 107 Ill.App.3d 183, 63 Ill.Dec. 9, 13, 437 N.E.2d 658, 662 (1st Dist.1982) (citations omitted). See also Allen v. Amber Manor Apartments Partnership, 95 Ill.App.3d 541, 51 Ill.Dec. 26, 32, 420 N.E.2d 440, 446 (1st Dist.1981) ("The certificate is a statutory prerequisite to the creation of a limited partnership and until it is filed, the partnership is not formed as a limited partnership.").

A corollary to the principle that filing defects preclude the formation of a limited partnership is that such filing defects affect the liability of the ostensible limited partners. Until a proper certificate of limited partnership is filed, "the partnership is not formed as a limited partnership and all partners will be treated as general partners." Deporter–Butterworth Tours Inc. v. Tyrrell, 151 Ill.App.3d 949, 104 Ill.Dec. 821, 827, 503 N.E.2d 378, 384 (3d Dist.1987). "Any contracts entered into prior to * * * the date on which the limited partnership certificate was filed and made of record, would be contracts entered into by a general partnership and all partners involved would be liable as general partners." Id. 104 Ill.Dec. at 827, 503 N.E.2d at 384.

Applied to the present case, these principles would suggest that Ivo may be subject to personal liability beyond his capital contribution to I. Jones. I. Jones did not even attempt to comply with the filing requirements of the [ULPA (1916)] until September 12, 1985. Even assuming, for present purposes, that this filing constituted "substantial compliance in good faith" for purposes of [ULPA (1916)] § 2(2)[6], I. Jones entered into a contract with the Hanchars six weeks prior to this filing. Ivo would be liable as a general partner for this pre-filing contract under Illinois law.

Ivo seeks to avoid the effect of these filing defects and obtain summary judgment in his favor through § 11 of the [ULPA (1916)]. This section provides:

A person who has contributed to the capital of a business conducted by a person or partnership erroneously believing that he has become a limited partner in a limited partnership, is not, by reason of his exercise of the rights of a limited partner, a general partner with the person or in the partnership carrying on the business, or bound by the obligations of such person or partnership; provided that on ascertaining the mistake he promptly renounces his interest in the profits of the business, or other compensation by way of income.

Ivo states that the Hanchars first raised the defective filing issues on January 21, 1987 * * *. On January 29, 1987, Ivo sent Cook a letter renouncing any interest in the profits of I. Jones. Ivo contends that this renunciation is sufficient to bring him within [ULPA (1916)] § 11 as a matter of law.

However, Ivo's attempted application of § 11 raises substantial issues of material fact. First, § 11 is available only to those individuals who limit their participation in the partnership to the exercise of rights held by limited partners. See Giles v. Vette, 263 U.S. 553, 44 S.Ct. 157, 161, 68 L.Ed. 441; [ULPA (1916)] § 7. There is a substantial question of fact as to whether Ivo participated in the control of I. Jones, thereby exercising the rights of a general partner. Second, there is a question of fact as to whether Ivo could have believed in good faith that he was a limited partner until January of 1987. The Hanchars suggest at least two dates, far in advance of the January 29, 1987 renunciation, when Ivo should have had notice of the filing defects. * * * At a minimum, there is an issue of fact as to whether Ivo was or should have been aware of the filing defects on one or both of these dates. Furthermore, the possibility that Ivo had notice of filing defects far in advance of the renunciation creates a material issue of fact as to whether this renunciation was prompt. See Vidricksen v. Grover, 363 F.2d 372 (9th Cir.1966) (holding that a six-month delay in renunciation was not "prompt" for purposes of

6. [By the Editor] Section 2(2) of ULPA (1916) stated "A limited partnership is formed if there has been substantial compliance in good faith with the requirements of paragraph (1)."

[ULPA (1916)] § 11). Together, these issues of fact render summary judgment inappropriate.

Ivo also contends that he is entitled to summary judgment on the issue of whether he exercised control over I. Jones, rendering him liable under § 7 of the [ULPA (1916)]. This section provides that, "A limited partner shall not become liable as a general partner unless, in addition to the exercise of his rights and powers as a limited partner, he takes part in the control of the business." Ivo makes two arguments in favor of his motion for summary judgment. First, Ivo argues that he is entitled to summary judgment because in order to make a limited partner liable under § 7, a creditor must show that in extending credit to the partnership, he relied upon the fact that the limited partner acted as a general partner. Ivo claims that there is no issue of fact as to whether the Hanchars relied on Ivo's status as a general partner. Second, Ivo contends that no reasonable juror could conclude that he participated in the control of I. Jones.

Courts are split as to whether creditor reliance is a requirement under § 7. Illinois, however, has not considered this question. A federal court recently discussed the underlying rationales that have driven courts to reach divergent views on the issue.

> Although undoubtedly in conflict with one another, these dichotomous lines of authority can be explained by recognizing that the different courts had different focuses. Those which required reliance as an element of control were concentrating upon the external relationship between the plaintiff and the limited partner, and were concerned with the equities arising from that relationship. The Delaney [v. Fidelity Lease Ltd., 526 S.W.2d 543 (Tex.1975)] Court, in contrast, appears to have been concerned with the broader public policy of requiring those who choose to accept the benefits of the limited partnership form to preserve the integrity of the partnership's internal relationships.

Mt. Vernon Sav. and Loan v. Partridge Assoc., 679 F.Supp. 522, 527 (D.Md. 1987). Because Illinois courts have consistently affirmed the importance of complying with the strict formation requirements of the [ULPA (1916)], it seems likely that Illinois courts would side with those courts that have chosen not to import a reliance requirement into § 7.[7] However, we need not decide the issue at this time, as there are facts in the record that indicate that the Hanchars may have relied on the assets of Ivo when entering into the purchase agreement. * * *

The question of whether Ivo participated in the control of I. Jones also involves issues of fact wholly inappropriate for summary judgment. * * * [I]t is sufficient to cite a few of the facts that might lead a jury to conclude that Ivo controlled I. Jones. First, the record is replete with alleged assertions of control over both Chemisphere[8] and I. Jones by Cook.[9] Cook admitted that he had Ivo's authority to act as his agent with respect to Chemisphere, and it

---

7. [By the Court] See, e.g., Inland Real Estate v. Christoph, 63 Ill.Dec. 9, 437 N.E.2d 658; Deporter–Butterworth Tours, Inc. v. Tyrrell, 104 Ill.Dec. 821, 503 N.E.2d 378; Allen v. Amber Manor Apts. Partnership, 51 Ill.Dec. 26, 420 N.E.2d 440.

8. [By the Editor] The court does not identify this entity, but the context indicates that this was the name under which another waste treatment facility was operated.

9. [By the Court] Many of these assertions are included in the deposition testimony of McKiel. * * *

would be reasonable for a jury to conclude that Cook also acted as Ivo's agent with respect to I. Jones. Cook and Ivo had weekly meetings at which Cook would report on the status of I. Jones and received directions regarding I. Jones' business. Ivo participated in the decision to remove McKiel as general partner and install Cook in his place. Finally, Cook has stated that he felt Ivo controlled the business of I. Jones through him.

In conclusion, determinations regarding the existence, extent and duration of Ivo's alleged control over the business of I. Jones are issues for the trier of fact, not for a court deciding a motion for summary judgment. For this reason, and the reasons stated above, the defendant's motion for summary judgment on Counts I through V is denied.

Notes

(1) Section 7 of ULPA (1916), in its entirety, stated, "A limited partner shall not become liable as a general partner unless, in addition to the exercise of his rights and powers as a limited partner, he takes part in the control of the business." There was considerable doubt under the sparse language of this section as to how much activity by the limited partner would constitute "taking part" in control. This uncertainty of itself made the limited partnership form of business unattractive, since, as in Mr. Zoso's case, there are always possible crisis situations in which even inactive investors would expect to be able to change or participate in management in an effort to save their investment. May limited partners retain the power to remove the general partner and substitute another person in that position? Under ULPA (1916) one could not be sure. Many similar issues also arose. May a limited partner also act as an employee or agent of the limited partnership? As a surety for the limited partnership? What if the limited partners retain the power to approve or disapprove amendments to the limited partnership agreement or fundamental changes in the nature of the limited partnership's business? Under the case law arising under ULPA (1916) the test appeared to depend on whether the limited partner had actually exercised the powers he had reserved, but the actual decisions were not very illuminating. For example:

(a) In Silvola v. Rowlett, 129 Colo. 522, 272 P.2d 287 (1954), a limited partner was held not generally liable for partnership obligations even though he "express[ed] opinions as to the advisability of transactions when his suggestions or opinion was sought by the general partner."

(b) In Rathke v. Griffith, 36 Wash.2d 394, 218 P.2d 757 (1950), a limited partner was named to the "board of directors" of the limited partnership but did not actually participate in the day-to-day decisions of the business. Even though the limited partner had also signed a few documents on behalf of the limited partnership, the court refused to hold the limited partner liable to creditors who were unaware of such documents.

(2) The extent limited partners may participate in the affairs of the limited partnership is significantly broadened by § 303 of ULPA (1976), a section which should be read carefully. The first sentence of § 303(a) is taken directly from ULPA (1916). There are then two major additions:

(a) Section 303(b) creates a series of "safe harbors" for actions by limited partners. For example, in *Continental Waste*, it was alleged that Mr. Zoso "had weekly meetings with Cook at which Cook would report on the status of I. Jones and received directions regarding I. Jones' business." Would that conduct be protected by the safe harbor of § 303(b)(1)? Mr. Zoso also "participated in the decision to remove McKiel as general partner and install Cook in his place." Would that be protected by § 303(b)(6)(v)? If the answer to both of these questions is "yes," might Mr. Zoso nevertheless be held liable as a general partner under the first sentence of § 303(a) if the court believed Cook's testimony "that he felt Ivo controlled the business of I. Jones through him?"

(b) The second major change is the addition of the last sentence of § 303(a). Is Mr. Zoso safe if the Hanchars were unaware that he was acting through Mr. Cook? The Commissioner's Comments to § 303 states that "[t]he second sentence of Section 303(a) reflects a wholly new concept in the 1976 Act that has been further modified in the 1985 Act. It was adopted partly because of the difficulty of determining when the "control" line has been overstepped, but also (and more importantly) because of a determination that it is not sound public policy to hold a limited partner who is not also a general partner liable for the obligations of the partnership except to persons who have done business with the limited partnership reasonably believing, based on the limited partner's conduct, that he is a general partner." 6 U.L.A. 392 (Supp. 1993). Do you believe that the "wholly new concept" introduced in § 303(a) of ULPA is a good idea? Did the earlier versions of ULPA encourage creditors of limited partnerships to investigate the prior activities of limited partners (of which they were unaware when they extended credit) in order to find a deeper pocket? Does not the current version of ULPA encourage the sale of T-shirts stating "I am a limited partner" to limited partners who want to participate publicly and actively in the control of the limited partnership's business?

(3) What about the fact that the certificate of limited partnership of I. Jones Partnership was not filed until a couple of weeks after the purchase of the waste treatment facility? Assume that Mr. Zoso was aware that no certificate had been filed at the time the purchase of the waste treatment facility. It seems clear that he is not entitled to the protection of § 11 of ULPA (1916), discussed in the opinion, since that section protects only persons who "erroneously believe" a filing was made. Is it logical to conclude that I. Jones Partnership is a general partnership with respect to liabilities arising before the certificate is filed if the other party to the transaction is unaware that no filing was made?. Does ULPA (1976) § 304(b), last clause, change this result? What about liabilities arising after the certificate was filed? Is Mr. Zoso protected against those?

(4) Assume that a general partner falsely represents to investors who have agreed to be limited partners that a limited partnership certificate has been or will be filed, but no such filing is or has been made. Precisely what should such an investor do after discovering this unpleasant fact? Can he or she wait a month or so to see whether the venture will "pan out"? In Vidricksen v. Grover, 363 F.2d 372 (9th Cir.1966), a physician learned in March that a Chevrolet car agency business in which he had invested had never filed a certificate. A renunciation was filed in September. Commenting that "the shoemaker strayed from his last," the Court held the physician to be a general partner. See also Direct Mail Specialist, Inc. v. Brown, 673 F.Supp. 1540 (D.Mont.1987). For cases involving a happier result see Graybar Elec. Co. v. Lowe, 11 Ariz.App. 116, 462 P.2d 413 (1969); Voudouris v. Walter E. Heller & Co., 560 S.W.2d 202 (Tex.Civ.App.1977). The leading case stating that the purpose of the 1916 ULPA § 11 was broadly remedial is Giles v. Vette, 263 U.S. 553, 44 S.Ct. 157, 68 L.Ed. 441 (1924).

(5) Under ULPA (1916) § 11 a putative limited partner must renounce "his interest in the profits of the business, or other compensation by way of income." Does that mean the partner gets his or her invested capital back but without

interest or profits? Does ULPA (1976) § 304(a)(2) provide any greater guidance? May a putative limited partner under that section himself prepare, execute, and file a certificate of limited partnership or a certificate of amendment under ULPA (1976) § 304(a)(1) if the general partner refuses to do so? See ULPA (1976) § 204. Why not permit a putative limited partner to file a certificate stating in effect "I am only a limited partner" if the general partners fail to execute an appropriate certificate on request?

(6) In addition to § 7, ULPA (1916) imposed further restrictions on limited partners. Section 4 provided that the contributions of a limited partner may be "cash or other property, but not services." Compare ULPA (1976) § 501. Section 4 did not identify the consequences of a limited partner agreeing to contribute services to a limited partnership but presumably it was the loss of the shield of limited liability. Section 5 of ULPA (1916) sharply limited the use of the surname of the limited partnership as part of the name of the limited partnership. Compare ULPA (1976) § 102(2). What is the consequence under § 102 of the use of the name of a limited partner in the name of a limited partnership? Is a "name" and a "surname" the same thing?

ROBERT W. HAMILTON, CORPORATE GENERAL PARTNERS OF LIMITED PARTNERSHIPS

1 Jnl. of Small and Emerging Business Law 73, 78–87, No. 1 (1997).

A limited partnership with a corporation as the sole general partner creates a totally different kind of entity than the traditional limited partnership. If the general partner is only marginally capitalized, the limited partnership becomes a limited liability entity not unlike a corporation. No individual is personally liable for the firm's debts. Most of the capital is provided by passive investors who, as limited partners, have no right to participate in management. Furthermore, control of the limited partnership is vested solely in the hands of the corporate general partner; in turn, control of that entity may be vested exclusively in the persons who organize the venture but provide only a small fraction of the capital needed by the enterprise. Since there is no legal prohibition against limited partners serving as shareholders, directors, or officers of the corporate general partner, organizers of the venture may also participate in the sharing of profits and losses as limited partners as well as through the corporate general partner.[10]

10. [By the Author] The conceptual problem of whether a limited partner could retain his shield of limited liability while participating in the management of the corporate general partner created problems in Texas in the 1970s. In *Delaney v. Fidelity Lease Ltd.,* 526 S.W.2d 543, 545–46 (Tex.1975) the Texas Supreme Court imposed personal liability on those limited partners basically on a "too many hats" approach. Shortly thereafter, the Texas Attorney General, relying primarily on *Delaney,* opined that a corporation could not be the sole general partner of a limited partnership. Op. Tex. Att'y Gen. H–1229 (1978). This opinion flew so squarely in the face of the partnership statutes and widespread current practice that six law professors teaching corporation law objected in a letter to the Attorney General. 16 Bull. of Sec. on Corp., Bank. & Bus. L. 24

(No. 1 Sept. 1978). The Attorney General then backed down. Op. Tex. Att'y Gen. No. H–1229A (1978). By this time the tax shelter business discussed below was in full swing, and the Texas Legislature in 1979 adopted amendments that made it perfectly clear (1) that corporations could be general partners and (2) that limited partners had a safe harbor from liability if they participated in the management of the general partner. 1979 Tex. Gen. Laws 1781, now codified in Tex. Rev. Civ. Stat. Ann. art. 6132b §§ 6–A, 15 (West Supp. 1997). When the same issue arose in other states, decisions usually rejected the *Delaney* approach. *See* Frigidaire Sales Corp. v. Union Properties, Inc., 562 P.2d 244, 246 (Wash.1977); Western Camps, Inc. v. Riverway Ranch Enters., 138 Cal. Rptr. 918, 927 (Cal.Ct.App.1977). The issue was ultimately laid to rest by ULPA (1976)

What was the incentive that gave rise to the rather sudden development of corporate general partners beginning in about 1970? The answer, in a word, was taxes; federal income taxes, to be precise. The 1970s were the era of tax shelters. A business form was needed that assured that losses could be passed through to investors, that investors had no personal responsibility for losses, and that the promoters of the tax shelter could run things without personal responsibility for debts and losses arising when the business ultimately collapsed. The limited partnership with a corporate general partner filled this need perfectly.[11] During the 1970s many thousands of real estate and oil and gas ventures were created in the limited partnership form primarily to provide tax deductions for affluent professionals and investors based on tax deductions for depreciation in real estate ventures, and for tangible and intangible drilling expenses and depletion in oil and gas ventures.

The era of tax shelters ended with the enactment of the Tax Reform Act of 1986.[12] However, the changes in marginal tax rates for individuals and corporations made in that statute opened up entirely new tax saving devices which utilized limited partnerships with corporate general partners. * * *

* * * [W]here limited partnerships are used today, it is the norm to use a corporation as the sole general partner. Probably the most common allocation of financial benefits is 99% to the limited partners and 1% to the general partner. In these situations, the general partner is usually under the direct control of some but not all of the limited partners. The 99/1 division minimizes the tax disadvantages * * *.

II. DIFFERENCES BETWEEN CORPORATE AND INDIVIDUAL GENERAL PARTNERS

A corporate general partner differs from an individual general partner in several basic respects. * * *

First, a corporate general partner is subject to the control of somebody else. With an individual as a general partner, there is no doubt as to whose decisions will be evaluated under applicable principles of fiduciary duty. Where a corporate general partner is involved, the decision-maker may be a panel of individuals or a single person whose identity may or may not be known to limited partners and whose financial interest in the limited partnership may be great or may be small.[13]

Second, it is relatively easy to control transfers of managerial authority to third persons when individual general partners are involved. Restrictions on transfers of general partnership interests without the consent of the limited partners appear in both statutes[14] and limited partnership agreements, and, while it may be possible to evade these limitations through a delegation of duties rather than an assignment of interest itself, such a delegation does not

§ 303(b)(1) which created a "safe harbor" for limited partners who were "an officer, director or shareholder of a general partner that is a corporation."

11. [By the Author] Various other business forms were sometimes used as tax shelters. * * *

12. [By the Author] Tax Reform Act of 1986, Pub. L. No. 99–514, 100 Stat. 2085

(1986) (codified as amended in scattered sections of 26 U.S.C.).

13. [By the Author] The financial interest of the general partner in the limited partnership may be known, but the economic interest of the decision maker in the corporate general partner may be small or unknown.

14. [By the Author] *See* [ULPA (1976)] §§ 401–402.

eliminate the continuing responsibility of the general partner. However, a corporate general partner is inherently an economic entity which itself may be the subject of purchase or sale. The individuals involved in the ownership and management of the business of the corporate general partner may change without a change in the identity of the general partner itself. The simplest example is the sale of shares by the shareholders of the general partner to an unrelated third person. Further, the same result can be achieved through mergers or other transactions that arguably may not involve a sale or transfer at all. Thus, a corporate general partner is unlike an individual general partner in the basic respect that control may be shifted from one group to another without apparently affecting the continuous existence of the corporate general partner. From the standpoint of inactive investors who are limited partners, of course, the identity of those in control of the general partner is usually more important than the formal identity of the general partner itself.

Third, a corporate general partner may be entirely acceptable and responsible as a general partner even though its assets are nominal or relatively insignificant in comparison to the size of the business it is managing. This is likely where the shareholders or managers of the corporate general partner also own substantial limited partnership interests. A claim of breach of fiduciary duty against a general partner is not worth very much if the general partner itself is a corporation with nominal assets. Recovery, if there is to be recovery, must come from finding some theory to hold the parties that manage the general partner liable for the general partner's breach of duty.

Fourth, even if a corporate general partner is reasonably capitalized at the outset, subsequent transactions may largely bleed off these assets to the owners of the corporation without the consent of the limited partnership and without involving a fraudulent conveyance, but greatly increasing potential risks to limited partners.

Finally, there are potential conflicts of fiduciary duty whenever a corporation (as contrasted with an individual) is the general partner of a limited partnership. The general partner obviously owes fiduciary duties to the limited partnership and to the limited partners. Corporate officers and directors also owe fiduciary duties to the shareholders of a corporate partner. These fiduciary duties may conflict. This conflict is likely to be particularly intense when there are shareholders of the corporate general partner who have no direct financial interest in the limited partnership. Indeed, one can argue that these duties have the same degree of intensity: If the shareholders of the corporate general partner gain more from a breach of fiduciary duty than the limited partners lose, it should be the duty of the managers of the corporate general partner to breach duties to the limited partners and maximize the gain to the corporate general partner. However, the rhetoric of fiduciary duties in this situation appears to indicate the contrary: That the duties owed by the corporate general partner to the limited partners trump the duties owed by the officers and directors of the corporate general partner to the shareholders. Cases state that a corporation that is the sole general partner owes "the duty * * * to exercise the utmost good faith, fairness, and loyalty" for the benefit of the limited partnership.[15] This statement seems to require that officers and directors of the corporate general partner favor the duties to the limited partnership and the limited partners above any duty to the shareholders.

IN RE USACAFES, L.P. LITIGATION

Court of Chancery of Delaware, 1991.
600 A.2d 43.

ALLEN, CHANCELLOR.

These consolidated actions arise out of the October 1989 purchase by Metsa Acquisition Corp. of substantially all of the assets of USACafes, L.P., a Delaware limited partnership (the "Partnership") at a cash price of $72.6 million or $10.25 per unit. Plaintiffs are holders of limited partnership units. They bring these cases as class actions on behalf of all limited partnership unitholders except defendants. The relief sought includes, inter alia, the imposition of constructive trusts on certain funds received by defendants in connection with the Metsa sale and an award of damages to the class resulting from the sale.

The Partnership was formed in the 1986 reorganization of the business of USACafes, Inc., a Nevada corporation. Also formed as part of that reorganization was USACafes General Partner, Inc. (the "General Partner"), a Delaware corporation that acts as the general partner of the Partnership. Both the Partnership and the General Partner are named as defendants in this action. A second category of defendants is composed of Sam and Charles Wyly, brothers who together own all of the stock of the General Partner, sit on its board, and who also personally, directly or indirectly, own 47% of the limited partnership units of the Partnership. Sam Wyly chairs the Board of the General Partner. * * *

The * * * most central theory [of the amended complaint] involves an alleged breach of the duty of loyalty. In essence, it claims that the sale of the Partnership's assets was at a low price, favorable to Metsa, because the directors of the General Partner all received substantial side payments that induced them to authorize the sale of the Partnership assets for less than the price that a fair process would have yielded. Specifically, it is alleged that, in connection with the sale, (1) the Wylys received from Metsa more than $11 million in payments (or promises to pay in the future) which were disguised as consideration for personal covenants not to compete; (2) the General Partner (which the Wylys wholly own) received a $1.5 million payment right in consideration of the release of a claim that plaintiffs assert was non-existent; * * * In sum, it is alleged that between $15 and $17 million was or will be paid to the directors and officers of the General Partner by or with the approval of Metsa; those payments are alleged to constitute financial induce-ments to the directors of the General Partner to refrain from searching for a higher offer to the Partnerships. Plaintiffs add that, even assuming that

---

15. Boxer v. Husky Oil Co., 429 A.2d 995,   1984).
997 (Del.Ch.1981), *aff'd*, 483 A.2d 633 (Del.

Metsa was the buyer willing to pay the best price, some part at least of these "side payments" should have gone to the Partnership. * * *

* * * [T]he Wyly defendants and the other director defendants move under Rule 12(b)(6) to dismiss the breach of fiduciary duty claims in the amended complaint asserting that, while the General Partner admittedly did owe fiduciary duties to the limited partners, they as directors of the General Partner owe no such duties to those persons. The whole remedy of the limited partners for breach of the duties of loyalty and care, it is said, is against the General Partner only and not its directors. * * *

I turn first to the director defendants' motion to dismiss for failure to state a claim with respect to the sale of the Partnership's assets. The gist of this motion is the assertion that the directors of the General Partner owed the limited partners no duty of loyalty or care. In their view their only duty of loyalty was to the General Partner itself and to its shareholders (i.e., the Wyly brothers). Thus, in alleging that the director defendants breached duties of loyalty and care running to them, the directors say the limited partners have asserted a legal nullity.

In my opinion the assertion by the directors that the independent existence of the corporate General Partner is inconsistent with their owing fiduciary duties directly to limited partners is incorrect. Moreover, even were it correct, their position on this motion would have to be rejected in any event because the amended complaint expressly alleges that they personally participated in the alleged breach by the General Partner itself, which admittedly did owe loyalty to the limited partners.

The first basis of this holding is the more significant. While I find no corporation law precedents directly addressing the question whether directors of a corporate general partner owe fiduciary duties to the partnership and its limited partners, the answer to it seems to be clearly indicated by general principles and by analogy to trust law. I understand the principle of fiduciary duty, stated most generally, to be that one who controls property of another may not, without implied or express agreement, intentionally use that property in a way that benefits the holder of the control to the detriment of the property or its beneficial owner. There are, of course, other aspects—a fiduciary may not waste property even if no self interest is involved and must exercise care even when his heart is pure—but the central aspect of the relationship is, undoubtedly, fidelity in the control of property for the benefit of another.[16] See generally Robert Flannigan, The Fiduciary Obligation, 9 Oxford J. Legal St. 285 (1989).

While the parties cite no case treating the specific question whether directors of a corporate general partner are fiduciaries for the limited partnership, a large number of trust cases do stand for a principle that would extend a fiduciary duty to such persons in certain circumstances. The problem comes up in trust law because modernly corporations may serve as trustees of express trusts. Thus, the question has arisen whether directors of a corporate trustee may personally owe duties of loyalty to cestui que trusts of the corporation. A leading authority states the accepted answer:

---

16. [By the Court] Thus, for example, a borrower of money is not considered a fiduciary for the lender simply because she is bound to return the principle [*sic*] sum plus interest. The "property" is held by the borrower for her own benefit.

The directors and officers of [a corporate trustee] are certainly under a duty to the beneficiaries not to convert to their own use property of the trust administered by the corporation * * *. Furthermore, the directors and officers are under a duty to the beneficiaries of trusts administered by the corporation not to cause the corporation to misappropriate the property * * *. The breach of trust need not, however, be a misappropriation * * *. Any officer [director cases are cited in support here] who knowingly causes the corporation to commit a breach of trust causing loss * * *. is personally liable to the beneficiary of the trust.

Moreover, a director or officer of a trust institution who improperly acquires an interest in the property of a trust administered by the institution is subject to personal liability. He is accountable for any profit * * *. Even where the trustee [itself] is not liable, however, because it had no knowledge that the director was making the purchase, the director * * * is liable to the beneficiaries * * *. The directors and officers are in a fiduciary relation not merely to the [corporation] * * * but to the beneficiaries of the trust administered by the [corporation].

4 A. Scott & W. Fratcher, The Law of Trusts § 326.3, at 304–306 (4th ed. 1989) (citing cases).

The theory underlying fiduciary duties is consistent with recognition that a director of a corporate general partner bears such a duty towards the limited partnership. That duty, of course, extends only to dealings with the partnership's property or affecting its business, but, so limited, its existence seems apparent in any number of circumstances. Consider, for example, a classic self-dealing transaction: assume that a majority of the board of the corporate general partner formed a new entity and then caused the general partner to sell partnership assets to the new entity at an unfairly small price, injuring the partnership and its limited partners. Can it be imagined that such persons have not breached a duty to the partnership itself? And does it not make perfect sense to say that the gist of the offense is a breach of the equitable duty of loyalty that is placed upon a fiduciary? It appears true that the same result might be rationalized as aider and abettor liability, but I am unsure what such indirection would add that is useful where a self-dealing transaction or other diversion of partnership property is alleged. Indeed in some instances, for example the use by a director of confidential information concerning the partnership's business not yet known by the board of the general partner, there may be no breach of loyalty or care by the general partner itself to abet, yet there may be director liability to the partnership by the director. * * * It is not necessary here to attempt to delineate the full scope of that duty. It may well not be so broad as the duty of the director of a corporate trustee.[17] But it surely entails the duty not to use control over the partnership's property to advantage the corporate director at the expense of the partnership. That is what is alleged here. * * *

The motions of the individual defendants, the General Partner, and the Partnership to dismiss the claims arising out of the sale of the Partnership's assets is denied. * * *

17. [By the Court] For example, I imply nothing on such questions as whether a director of a corporate general partner might be held liable directly to the partnership on a "corporate" opportunity theory or for waste of partnership assets (two possible consequences of characterizing such persons as fiduciaries for the partnership).

Notes

(1) The basic issue addressed by Chancellor Allen in *USACafes* has arisen in a significant number of cases. See generally, Robert W. Hamilton. Corporate General Partners of Limited Partnerships, 1 Jnl. of Small and Emerging Business Law 73, No. 1 (1997). Most cases impose a fiduciary duty on the controllers of the corporate general partner on some theory or other, see e.g. Wilson v. Friedberg, 323 S.C. 248, 473 S.E.2d 854 (App.1996)("corporate veil" of corporate general partner pierced because sole shareholder intermingled partnership assets and failed to keep adequate records). Some cases impose liability without discussion of the theory but simply state that X was in complete control of the corporate general partner and therefore was responsible for breaches of duty by the general partner.

(2) A basic principle of partnership law is that no partner can be compelled to accept another person as a partner against his will. For example, an attempt by a general partner to assign his interest in a partnership to a person who is not a partner is effective to transfer only his financial interest unless the other partners are willing to accept the assignee as a partner. See UPA (1914) § 27; UPA (1994) § 502. Should the same rule be applicable to direct transfers of partnership interests by *general*[18] partners of limited partnerships? From a statutory standpoint, the answer is clearly "yes" on the theory that where the limited partnership statute is silent, rules applicable to general partnerships control. See ULPA (1976) § 1105. (This is usually referred to as the "linkage" problem.)

(a) The transfer of *shares in a corporate general partner* is not of itself a transfer of a *partnership* interest. If this approach is followed, the limited partners have no basis for objecting when the shareholders of the corporate general partner decide to sell all or a controlling block of their shares in the corporation to someone else. However, the limited case law is to the contrary:

> * * * *In re Integrated Resources, Inc.*[19] * * * involved a petition by a corporation (Integrated) that was in bankruptcy reorganization and wished to sell the shares of its wholly-owned subsidiary, American Property Investors (API), to a third party. API itself was the sole general partner of a limited partnership, American Real Estate Partnership, L.P. (AREP), and its interest in that partnership was its sole asset. Neither API nor AREP were involved in the bankruptcy proceeding. AREP's limited partnership interests were widely held and publicly traded on the New York Stock Exchange. AREP was a valuable asset: An outside bid of $40 million for the stock of API had been received by Integrated; shortly thereafter other bids were submitted, the highest of which was $44 million. This bid was submitted by Meadowstar Holding Co., Inc. (Meadowstar), a newly formed corporation, that listed among its investors the well known financier, Carl Icahn. Integrated desired to accept the Meadowstar offer, and requested court approval of the sale as required by the Bankruptcy Act.
>
> Several limited partners objected to the proposed sale on a variety of grounds. Their principal argument was that it was likely that Meadowstar planned to loot API since Meadowstar had no business plan and had refused to guarantee the continuation of distributions to the limited partners. In support of this assertion, the limited partners argued that the market value of API's interest

---

18. [By the Editor] Transfers by limited partners involve only transfers of financial interests and therefore are generally permitted. See ULPA §§ 702, 704.

19. [By the Author] No. 90–B–10411(CB), 1990 WL 325414 (Bankr.S.D.N.Y.1990) (opinion by Cornelius Blackshear, United States Bankruptcy judge).

in AREP was only $13 million, so that Meadowstar was paying a premium of $30 million solely for control.[20]

Because the case required judicial approval of a proposed transaction, the court found it necessary to consider what test should be applied to such a transaction. It concluded that Integrated, the sole shareholder of API, owes a duty to the limited partners of AREP which is essentially the same duty that is owed by controlling shareholders of a corporation to minority shareholders when they plan to sell the controlling shares to a third person. This fiduciary duty, the court held, runs directly from *Integrated* to the limited partners of AREP. Phrased another way, the court concluded that Integrated owes the same duties to the limited partners of AREP that it would have owed to them had they been minority shareholders of API itself. The court therefore examined the "sale of control" cases involving the capture of a "control premium" by the seller of a controlling block of stock to a third person.[21]

Robert W. Hamilton, Corporate General Partners of Limited Partnerships, 1 Jnl. of Small and Emerging Business Law 73, 92–3 (1997).

(b) The identity of corporate general partners also may change through mergers or similar transactions without a transfer of the general partnership interest itself. Such a transaction (unlike a sale of controlling shares) does involve a change in the corporate form of the general partner and arguably may therefore constitute either a "transfer" or "assignment" in violation of prohibitions against assignment in limited partnership agreements or in breach of the general prohibition against assigning management powers by general partners. The leading case is *Star Cellular Tel. Co., Inc. v. Baton Rouge CGSA, Inc.*, Civ. A. No. 12507, 1993 WL 294847 (Del.Ch.1993) (per Jacobs, Ch.), aff'd, 647 A.2d 382 (Del.1994). The agreement provided that:

> The General Partner may transfer or assign its General Partner's Interest only after written notice to all the other Partners and the unanimous vote of all the other Partners to permit such transfer and to continue the business of the Partnership with the assignee of the General Partner as General Partner. * * * Withdrawal of the General Partner (which will also be deemed its withdrawal as a Limited Partner) will cause the dissolution and termination of the Partnership * * * unless it is continued by the unanimous consent of the remaining Partners * * *.

The importance of the court's decision lies in its analysis, not in its conclusion: It did not base its decision on the meaning of the words "transfer" or "assign" or on the question whether a merger under the applicable corporation statutes was or was not defined to be a transfer. Rather it applied a test whether the transaction was of a type that could adversely affect the interests of the non-assigning parties. In other words, the test was not a mechanical or linguistic one but rather whether or not the specific transaction might adversely affect the non-assigning parties. The court concluded that the merger of subsidiaries into a new subsidiary involved in that case did not adversely affect the interests of the limited partners. However, there have been surprisingly few reported cases dealing with the

---

20. [By the Author] The objectors also argued that the proposed sale of API shares constituted an implicit sale of API's general partnership interest and therefore required the approval of a majority in interest of the holders of the limited partnership interests of AREP.

21. [By the Editor] This duty is described in section E of Chapter 12 of this Casebook.

The court cited classic "sale of control" cases, including Swinney v. Keebler Co., 480 F.2d 573 (4th Cir.1973); Essex Universal Corp. v. Yates, 305 F.2d 572 (2d Cir.1962); and Zetlin v. Hanson Holdings Inc., 48 N.Y.2d 684, 421 N.Y.S.2d 877, 397 N.E.2d 387 (N.Y. 1979).

question whether transfers of managerial control over the general partner constitute violation of anti-assignment clauses or general partnership duties.

(3) As described in Chapter One, A "limited liability limited partnership" (LLLP) is a limited partnership in which the general partners have elected the shield of limited liability provided by LLP statutes, while the limited partners retain their shield as limited partners. Because of the "linkage" between UPA and ULPA it is quite possible that a limited partner may become liable for partnership obligations by participating in control (e.g. Mr. Zoso's case) in a way that is not protected by the various safe harbors of § 303. In an LLLP, limited partners who take part in control of the business may have greater potential liability for partnership obligations than the general partners who are protected by the LLLP election. Does that make any sense? Problems created by this linkage appear to be so intractable that NCCUSL in 1997 began the development of a revised ULPA that will be a free-standing statute not linked to the UPA.

C. THE LIMITED LIABILITY COMPANY

Between 1988 and 1997, every state adopted limited liability company statutes that authorize the creation of a new business form, the "limited liability company" or "LLC." This unanimous acceptance of the LLC in a relatively brief period indicates that there is a strong demand for this new and more flexible business form.

There is a wide variation in the LLC statutes that have been enacted by the various states. The Uniform Limited Liability Company Act (ULLCA) was approved by NCCUSL in 1995, after most states had enacted LLC statutes.

SUSAN PACE HAMILL, THE LIMITED LIABILITY COMPANY: A CATALYST EXPOSING THE CORPORATE INTEGRATION QUESTION

95 Mich.L.Rev. 393, 446 (1996).*

The rise of the domestic limited liability company (LLC)[22] from obscurity to its present position as a viable, mainstream alternative to the corporation or partnership was met with enormous enthusiasm by the business community and the practicing bar. * * * [T]the LLC offers for the first time a domestic entity that combines the tax advantages of a partnership with limited liability protection for all members, an advantage commonly associated with corporations. * * *

By combining the best of both worlds, partnership taxation and limited liability, the LLC revolution can be characterized as tax driven. Nevertheless, some commentators believe that it is the LLC's superior business provisions

* Reprinted with permission from The Michigan Law Review Association.

22. [By the Author] The LLC is an unincorporated business organization that contains dissolution, management, and transferability provisions similar to those of a general partnership but that can easily be altered to resemble the limited partnership or to approach the corporate model. A related unincorporated business entity that appeared in 1991, the limited liability partnership (LLP), essentially operates as a general partnership for business purposes, while offering the partners either partial or total limited liability protection. The articles written on LLCs and LLPs are too numerous to cite completely.

that will cause LLCs to continue to rise in popularity. Although the LLC's business provisions may be characteristic of either partnerships or corporations, in toto they produce a truly unique and new business entity that cannot be aligned categorically with either of the more traditional forms. For example, the statutory provisions addressing the management and control of the LLC generally vest agency authority and governance rights in all members, as if they were partners in a general partnership. However, LLC members, unlike general partners, can adopt a management structure resembling those of corporations or limited partnerships by appointing managers. The LLC's managers, holding the power to make important policy decisions and to bind the LLC in day-to-day business transactions, take on the roles held both by general partners of limited partnerships and by corporate directors and officers.

Regardless of whether the motivation is tax or business related, the use and acceptance of LLCs as a serious alternative to the partnership and the corporation exponentially increased between 1988 and 1995 and will probably grow more each year. Indeed, some commentators believe the LLC will largely replace the partnership and the closely held corporation and emerge as the dominant form of business for nonpublicly traded entities.

The rise of the LLC, however, has not been greeted with uniform zeal. Said one critic: "The federal government has opened up a candy store."[23] This pithy comment metaphorically sums up the underlying and often unarticulated concern hidden in the shadows of the LLC euphoria. * * *

Notes

(1) The author estimates that as of December 31, 1995, more than 210,000 business ventures across the United States had chosen the LLC business form.

(2) Larry E. Ribstein, The Emergence of the Limited Liability Company, 51 Bus.Law. 1, 2–3, 6–10 (1995):*

The LLC is, fundamentally, a hybrid of the corporate and partnership forms. The LLC is best understood in terms of four general characteristics: (i) limited liability; (ii) partnership tax features; (iii) chameleon management—that is, the ability to choose between centralized and direct member-management; and (iv) creditor-protection provisions. These characteristics, in turn, are best understood in light of the development of the LLC as an alternative to existing business forms.

All LLC statutes provide that LLC members are not liable as such for the debts of the LLC. Although it is an important feature of LLCs, limited liability is not the whole LLC story. Firms long have had other ways of obtaining limited liability—most notably, by incorporating. But incorporating may be costly. * * * A second problem with the corporate form is that it is not well-suited to closely held firms. * * * These problems of the corporate form suggest the need for a new business form that combines corporate-type limited liability with partnership tax and organizational characteristics. This straightforward idea underlies the LLC. * * *

23. [By the Author] New York Contemplates Cost of Partnership Treatment for Limited Liability Companies, 1992 Tax Notes Today, 243–10 (quoting from James W. Wetzler, New York State Commissioner of Taxation and Finance).

* Reprinted with permission from the American Bar Association.

(a) The Scope of Liability

All of the LLC statutes provide that members, like corporate shareholders, are not liable as such for the debts of the LLC. LLC statutes do not protect members from liability for agreed contributions and excessive distributions, for members' own wrongs, or for debts the members contractually assume or guarantee. The New York statute and the ULLCA include a variation on the guarantee by providing that a member may agree to be held liable for all or some of the LLC's debts if, in addition to the member's agreement, the liability is stated in the articles of organization This lets members broadly erase the liability limitation without having to contract with individual creditors. In such a firm, some members have limited liability and others have personal liability like a limited partnership only without the control rule.

(b) The Two–Member Requirement

* * * [Many] LLC statutes either explicitly require the LLC to have two members or require that at least two people form the LLC at the time of creation, and do not permit the LLC to have only one member.[24] The status of a one-member LLC under a statute that requires two members is unclear. If there were two members at formation but one member later dissociated, this presumably would result only in dissolution of the firm and not nonenforcement of the agreement from the beginning. Even a dissolution, however, would likely come as a surprise and inconvenience to the remaining members because, rather than merely permitting the remaining member to buy out the dissociating member, dissolution would require a liquidation and a paying off of debts.

The main question concerning one-member firms under state law is whether the liability shield is enforced as against third parties in this situation. The two-member requirement is probably best explained as a carryover from the partnership origins of the LLC. Partnership is inherently an "association," which implies multiple members, and the partnership statutes require two or more members. * * *

(c) Piercing the Veil

One of the most important open questions about the liability of LLC members concerns the grounds on which courts will "pierce the veil"[25] of LLCs and impose liability on members of LLCs that have complied with statutory formalities. In general, veil-piercing in corporate law is based on basic equitable and common-sense principles that should apply equally to LLCs. * * *

Despite the large number of LLCs that have been formed in the 1990s, the third issue discussed by Professor Ribstein has not been definitively resolved. In Ditty v. CheckRite, Ltd., 973 F.Supp. 1320, 1335–36 (D.Utah 1997), the Court, citing nine law review articles, concluded that "[w]hile there is little case law discussing veil piercing theories outside the corporate context, most commentators assume that the doctrine applies to limited liability companies." The court concluded however, that "[p]laintiffs have not produced evidence sufficient to

---

24. [By the Editor] Following the adoption of "check-the-box" regulations, many states have amended their statutes expressly to recognize one-member LLCs.

25. [By the Editor] Veil-piercing in the corporate context is discussed in chapter 6.

permit a finding, as a matter of law, that the protective veil of DeLoney & Associates should be pierced to hold Richard DeLoney personally liable * * *''.

(3) While the LLC provides limited liability for all investors, it does not involve an "incorporation" in the traditional sense of that term as used in corporation statutes; rather a closer analogy is to the limited liability of partners achieved by a public filing under the limited partnership statutes. Indeed, from a liability standpoint, an LLC may be readily conceptualized as a limited partnership in which there is no general partner. However, many provisions in LLC statutes are modeled after corporate statutes. The following provisions, for example, are all drawn directly from the corporate model: An LLC is formed by filing "articles of organization" with a public officer. ULLCA §§ 202, 203. The name of the LLC must contain words or abbreviations indicating that the entity is an LLC. ULLCA § 105(a). Provisions are made for reserved [ULLCA § 106] and registered [ULLCA § 107] names. The LLC must maintain a registered agent for service of process. ULLCA § 108.

(4) In other respects, the LLC is clearly based on a partnership model. LLC statutes provide extreme flexibility with respect to all aspects of internal organization and financing of an LLC; there are relatively few mandatory statutory requirements, and internal relationships are largely governed by contract rather than by statutory provision. In contrast, traditional corporation statutes are notoriously specific particularly with respect to financial matters. As described in chapter 5, many state corporation statutes have mandatory and complex provisions respecting the issuance of securities and legal capital. An LLC is free to adopt much simpler financial structures. With respect to management, corporate statutes traditionally required compliance with a formal structure that was not well suited for small, closely held businesses. While these rules have been relaxed in many states,[26] they continued to exist in some. Another difference—perhaps important theoretically—is that in a corporation the articles of incorporation control over bylaws in case of a conflict; an LLC is based more on the theory of a contract among members, and the rule adopted in most statutes is that the operating agreement controls over the articles of incorporation in case of conflict. ULLCA § 203(c).

(5) ULLCA goes much further in adopting partnership-like default provisions than most LLC statutes. ULLCA provides that internal rules may be set forth in a written or oral "operating agreement" that is modeled upon a partnership agreement. ULLCA § 103. Partnership concepts of "dissociation" and "dissolution" are applicable to LLCs. ULLCA §§ 601, 701, 801. Membership interests are patterned after interests in a partnership. For example, transferees are admitted as members only with the unanimous consent of the remaining members (though the operating agreement may make such interests more freely transferable). ULLCA § 503. ULLCA, like most other LLC statutes, provide the option of being manager-managed rather than member-managed, but an affirmative election to be manager-managed must be made in the articles of organization; the default rule is that LLCs are member managed. ULLCA § 203(a)(6). In many states, the default rule is exactly the opposite: centralized, corporate-type management is the default rule. The operating rules for member-managed LLCs in ULLCA are very closely based on the partnership analogy. For example, voting in a member-managed LLC is on a per capita basis as in a general partnership. ULLCA § 404(a). Indeed, as one leafs through provisions of ULLCA, one spots many provisions clearly based on UPA (1994) and ULPA. While broad generalization is hazardous, most LLC

26. [By the Editor] See chapter 8, section D.

statutes enacted prior to ULLCA do not place the same reliance on the partnership model; rather they rely more on the "corporate" analogy.

(6) The law and commentary relating to LLCs refer, rather confusingly, to "*member*-managed" and "*manager*-managed" LLCs. These two forms of management, of course, are quite different, one based roughly on the partnership model and the other based roughly on the corporate model. Might this linguistic similarity lead to serious misconceptions on the part of unsophisticated third parties? Might the flexibility in management structure create practical problems for LLCs when they enter into transactions with third parties who may not be familiar with the internal structure of the specific LLC? To take a simple example, when an LLC wishes to open a bank account, the bank officer must decide whether to use a partnership-type or corporate-type form, i.e. whether to require a resolution of the managers or to rely on the authority of the single member making the application. Will banks have two different kinds of forms for LLCs? What happens if the bank officer uses the wrong form? What happens if the person making the application is himself confused and uses the wrong form? Presumably issues of this type will tend to work themselves out as individuals and commercial entities become more familiar with the LLC.

(7) Assume that you are advising A and B as to the form of business enterprise they should select for the retail furniture store discussed in chapter 1. Would you recommend that they select an LLC? Should such an enterprise be member-managed or manager-managed? If it is member-managed, can you ensure that A's veto power will be effective?

(8) Despite numerous predictions that in the long run LLCs will become the predominant business form for closely held businesses, data on the number of LLC formations indicate that growth has been steady but not overwhelming. In part this may be due to the fact that some states impose different filing fees that in effect discriminate against the LLC. For example, in Illinois, the filing fee for a corporation is $100 but $500 for an LLC. The annual filing fee in Illinois is $50 for a corporation but $300 for an LLC. Symposium, Check-the-Box and Beyond: The Future of Limited Liability Entities, 52 Bus.Law 605, 625 (1997)(comment of Hanson). More seriously, several states provide for state income or franchise taxes directly on LLCs and corporations, but not on partnerships or limited partnerships. For example, Florida imposes a 5.5 percent corporate income tax on LLCs but not on partnerships; Texas imposes a 4.5 percent franchise tax on LLC net receipts but partnerships are not subject to this tax. There also may be differences in the application of federal social security and similar taxes between these forms of business. So long as these economic differences continue to exist, the choice is likely to be driven by dollars rather than by the inherent usefulness of the business forms.

(9) Other factors that may limit the acceptance of LLCs are (1) uncertainty over applicable legal rules in areas such as bankruptcy and the application of the Federal securities acts and state Blue Sky laws, (2) concern over the complexity of the federal tax rules that are applicable to partnerships (which may require the services of a tax specialist), (3) potential problems of interstate operation of an LLC, and (4) as indicated above, concern as to whether members may have inherent agency powers to bind the LLC despite provisions in the operating agreement to the contrary. Particularly where the owners are relatively unsophisticated, the greater certainty and familiarity with traditional business forms may dictate avoidance of the LLC. There also may be resistance to the LLC on the part of some lawyers who are not familiar with this new business form or who are

concerned that it is a fad that may not last. Many lawyers may feel more comfortable with the customary corporation or limited partnership than with a new and untried business form for which there are not many tested forms, very little case law, and not much experience with specific provisions. Again, these problems and issues are likely to be worked out in the long run.

POORE v. FOX HOLLOW ENTERPRISES

Superior Court of Delaware, 1994.
1994 WL 150872.

STEELE, JUDGE.

Pursuant to Superior Court Civil Rule 12(f), Tammy Poore filed a Motion to Strike Appellee's Answering Brief for failure to properly file an answer in Superior Court through Delaware counsel. * * * During the oral arguments concerning this Motion, Douglas E. Campbell admitted he drafted the answering brief himself. Although Mr. Campbell stated he did not have a license to practice law in Delaware, he believed because Fox Hollow Enterprises is a Limited Liability Company and not a corporation, he could represent this company in Superior Court without a Delaware licensed attorney. * * *

The Delaware Supreme Court has held a corporation cannot appear or conduct business in court without representation by Delaware counsel. Transpolymer Industries, Inc. v. Chapel Main Corp., Del.Supr., No. 284, 1990, Horsey, J. (Sept. 18, 1990) (ORDER). The Supreme Court reasoned "[a] corporation, though a legally recognized entity, is regarded as an artificial or fictional entity, and not a natural person. While a natural person may represent himself or herself in court even though he or she may not be an attorney licensed to practice, a corporation being an artificial entity, can only act through its agents and, before a court only through an agent duly licensed to practice law." Id. (citations omitted).

The threshold question presented to this Court concerns whether or not it should apply this theory of corporate representation to Delaware Limited Liability Companies. As an alternative business entity under Delaware law, the Court must decide if a Limited Liability Company more closely resembles a partnership, which may represent itself in Court, or a corporation, which requires representation by legal counsel. * * *

The Court recognizes the Delaware General Assembly enacted the DLLCA to serve as an alternative business entity which allows the combination of the best features of both partnerships and corporations. The Delaware statute treats a properly structured LLC as a partnership for federal income tax purposes while affording limited liability for members and managers similar to the limited liability afforded to shareholders and directors of a Delaware corporation. 6 Del.C. § 18–303, 18–1106(a).

Although the statute treats an LLC as a partnership for federal income tax purposes, an LLC is largely a creature of contract—with management, economic, voting and other rights and obligations being primarily specified in the LLC agreement. Walter C. Tuthill & Denison H. Hatch, Jr., Delaware Limited Liability Companies, March 5, 1993, at 3. An LLC formed under the DLLCA constitutes a separate legal entity. 6 Del.C. § 18–201(b). Additionally, the interest of a member in the LLC is analogous to shareholders of a corporation. A member usually contributes personal property and has no interest in specific assets owned by the LLC. 6 Del.C. § 18–701. Moreover, a member or manager of an LLC cannot be held liable for the company's debts or obligations above his or her contribution to the company. 6 Del.C. § 18–303.

The Court finds these aspects of the LLC constitute a distinct, but artificial entity under Delaware law. Because of the limited liability inherent in the LLC and the contractual nature of this entity, the Court finds the Delaware Legislature did not intend a member or manager of an LLC could appear in Court to represent the entity without representation by Delaware legal counsel. Ultimately, regulation of the practice of law rests in the Delaware Supreme Court, not the legislature. The underlying purpose of the rule prohibiting the appearance of a corporation by anyone other than a member of the Delaware Bar also applies to the representation of Limited Liability Companies.

Because Fox Hollow Enterprises did not obtain Delaware legal counsel to represent its interests in this appeal, the Court grants Appellant's Motion to Strike Appellee's Answering Brief pursuant to Superior Court Civil Rule 12(f).

MEYER v. OKLAHOMA ALCOHOLIC BEVERAGE LAWS ENFORCEMENT COMMISSION

Court of Appeals of Oklahoma, 1995.
890 P.2d 1361.

Stubblefield, Judge.

This is an appeal from the district court's reversal of the declaratory ruling of the Oklahoma Alcoholic Beverage Laws Enforcement Commission (ABLE) that a newly created form of business entity, a limited liability company (LLC), is not entitled to receive and hold a retail package store license. Wanda L. Meyer, holder of a retail package store license, initiated these proceedings when she petitioned ABLE requesting a declaratory judgment that she could hold the license as an LLC, a business entity authorized by the Oklahoma Legislature in 1992 through the adoption of the Oklahoma Limited Liability Company Act (OLLC Act), 18 O.S.Supp.1992 §§ 2000 through 2060. ABLE denied the petition, thus holding that an LLC is not eligible to hold a retail package store license.

Meyer * * * appealed the ABLE decision to the district court. That court focused on two provisions of the law: (1) The Oklahoma constitutional provision, which only prohibits licensing of "corporations, business trusts, and secret partnerships," Okla. Const. art. 28, § 10; and, (2) The provision in the LLC Act that authorized LLCs to "conduct business in any state for any lawful purpose, except the business of banking and insurance," 18 O.S.Supp. 1992 § 2002 (emphasis added) (footnote omitted). Based upon those provisions, and a conclusion that the provisions of the Oklahoma Alcoholic Beverage Control Act "do not prohibit an LLC from holding a package store license," the trial court reversed the ABLE ruling and ordered it to "issue such license to petitioner as a limited liability company."

ABLE appeals, claiming that the order of the lower court is contrary to law in that an LLC is not authorized to hold a package store license. ABLE further claims that it could not be ordered to grant a license when no application by Meyer, as an LLC, was made. * * *

The issue is one of first impression—whether an LLC, created pursuant to the OLLC Act, is eligible for issuance of a retail package store liquor license. Indeed, the issue could only have arisen after the 1992 legislative creation of the new form of business entity. LLCs were not a recognized business entity in this state at the time of adoption of our Constitution or at the time of adoption of the Oklahoma Alcoholic Beverage Control Act. However, both the Constitution and the Oklahoma Alcoholic Beverage Control Act do address qualifications of an applicant for a package store license. We conclude that the constitutional directives do prohibit the holding of a license by an LLC and, thus, the lower court did err in its conclusion.

The pertinent constitutional provisions are Okla. Const. art. 28, §§ 4 and 10. Section 4, in pertinent part, provides: "Not more than one retail package license shall be issued to any person or general or limited partnership." Section 10, in pertinent part, provides:

No retail package store or wholesale distributor's license shall be issued to:

(a) A corporation, business trust or secret partnership.

(b) A person or partnership unless such person or all of the copartners including limited partners shall have been residents of the State of Oklahoma for at least ten (10) years immediately preceding the date of application for such license.

(c) A person or a general or limited partnership containing a partner who has been convicted of a violation of a prohibitory law relating to the sale, manufacture, or the transportation of alcoholic beverages which constituted a felony or misdemeanor.

(d) A person or a general or limited partnership containing a partner who has been convicted of a felony.

It is true, as noted by the trial court in its decision, that the specific constitutional prohibitions regarding license holders includes only corporations, business trusts, and secret partnerships. Of course, neither the framers nor amenders of the Constitution could have addressed the qualification or disqualification of LLCs as retail package store licensees, because the business entity did not exist in this state until 1992. Indeed, the testimony before ABLE indicated that the business form did not exist in this country until 1977. However, the Constitution did address all of the business formats as they existed at the time of adoption of the article on alcoholic beverage laws and enforcement and, significantly, section 4 names only individuals and partnerships as those entities to which a license may be issued.

Likewise, it is true that the Oklahoma Alcoholic Beverage Control Act does not prohibit an LLC from holding a license. However, what the Act does or does not prohibit is not dispositive because [i]t appears that qualification as a license holder, with regard to types of business entities, was left to the constitutional pronouncement. * * *

Meyer argues that an LLC is essentially a partnership. However, the act creating the business form is in Title 18, which is entitled "Corporations."

Furthermore, a provision in our Uniform Partnership Act states that "any association formed under any other statute of this state * * * is not a partnership under this act, unless such association would have been a partnership in this state prior to adoption of this act." 54 O.S.1991 § 206(2).

Meyer claims that its expert witness, the only witness in all the proceedings, testified that an LLC was a partnership. However, contrary to Meyer's contention, the witness's testimony was not so unequivocal. The totality of the testimony was that an LLC is a hybrid that has attributes of both corporations and partnerships. The witness indicated an LLC is more like a partnership, but noted the primary difference is that all owners/members have limited liability in an LLC—something not found in partnerships. We conclude that the limitation of liability of all LLC members is a substantial difference especially relevant to the provisions of our liquor laws.

Our examination of the pertinent constitutional provisions leads us to conclude that their evident purpose was the assignment of personal responsibility for compliance with the liquor laws. Thus, business forms that did not insure such personal responsibility were excluded from eligibility for licensing.

The OLLC Act does exactly what its name indicates. It creates a form of business that has as its most important feature the limitation of liability of its members. This liability limitation is also a shield from the very responsibility and accountability that the constitutional provisions regarding alcoholic beverage laws and enforcement sought to impose. * * *

The judgment of the trial court is REVERSED.

GOODMAN, P.J., and REIF, J. (sitting by designation), concur.

Notes

(1) These two cases are symptomatic of basic classification problems that are created by the development of any new business form. There are many issues in which there are different rules applicable to partnerships and to corporations, but no specific rule for LLCs. It should be noted that neither of these early cases relied on the member-managed/manager-managed distinction, but treated the LLC as a unitary business form. Is that a reasonable approach? Might it be reasonable to treat an LLC as a corporation only when issues relating to limited liability of members are involved on the theory that limited liability is inherently a corporate concept, but as a partnership when other types of issues are involved? Is *Fox Hollow* consistent with that approach?

(2) The Oklahoma constitutional provision and statutes involved in *Meyer* were drafted at a time when the only business forms available were a partnership or a corporation. There must be hundreds or thousands of federal and state statutory and regulatory provisions that are based on the same premise. Indeed, the Internal Revenue Code and the federal tax regulations are studded with administrative provisions that are based on the assumption that all taxable businesses entities are either a corporation or a partnership. Doubtless in many situations significant tax liabilities will ride on the issue whether an LLC should have complied with some administrative provision or other. Might it be possible to develop a statutory "fix" by a provision that states, e.g., that for administrative purposes an LLC should always be treated as a partnership? Is there is a danger of developing such a fix without first examining each provision of the Internal Revenue Code.

(3) Among the numerous open issues with respect to LLCs is the scope of fiduciary duties owed by members and managers. The statutes of many states are silent on this basic issue, and the choice ranges from the strong fiduciary duty owed by general partners Under UPA (1914) to the somewhat lower duty owed under UPA (1994) to the much lower duty owed in connection with corporations (see chapters 8, 10, and 11), or quite possibly to something in-between. See ULLCA § 103(b). See also J. William Callison, Blind Men and Elephants: Fiduciary Duties Under the Revised Uniform Partnership Act, Uniform Limited Liability Company Act, and Beyond, 1 Jnl. Small and Emerging Business Law, 109, 163–4 (1997):

> * * *[T]he ULLCA should not slavishly adhere to RUPA. Instead, consideration should be given to whether LLCs more resemble close corporations and whether the corporate body of law, and not the partnership body of law, should apply. * * * Since the members of an LLC have less to lose through their co-members' and managers' actions than do partners in a general partnership (at least one that is not registered as an LLP), it is arguable that the fiduciary standards should be corporate-like. On the other hand, it seems to make little sense for there to be one set of rules for LLPs and LLLPs and a different set of rules for LLCs. We need to learn to see clearly before we adopt rules.

For a more doctrinaire view see Larry E. Ribstein, Fiduciary Duty Contracts in Unincorporated Firms, 54 Washington & Lee Law Review 537 (1997).

D. FEDERAL INCOME TAXATION OF BUSINESS FORMS: HEREIN OF "CHECK–THE–BOX"

Many readers may have the quite erroneous notion that limited liability is the first and most basic priority in selecting a business form. It is not. The highest priority is the manner in which the income of (or loss from) the business is taxed under the Internal Revenue Code. In this regard, one must consider not only the taxation of the closely held business itself but also the interrelationship with the taxation of the individual owners. Therefore, an excursion into the tax treatment of individuals—the ultimate owners of businesses—is necessary as well as into the method of taxation of businesses generally. While a complete discussion of this interesting topic must await courses in Federal Income Taxation and Business Planning, knowledge of the fundamentals of the subject is essential.

Initially, all businesses compute income for tax purposes in basically the same manner, deducting expenses of doing business from receipts in order to compute taxable income. After determination of the business's taxable income, however, the tax treatment to some extent depends on the business form.

In broad terms, the Internal Revenue Code recognizes two distinct methods of taxing business income which are generally described as "corporate" and "partnership" taxation. Corporate income taxation is described in Subchapters C and S of the Internal Revenue Code, while partnership income taxation is described in Subchapter K. The differences between these two basic methods of taxing business income, and the troublesome issue of whether business entities such as LLCs and limited partnerships with corporate general partners should be taxed as corporations or as partnerships, has largely driven the selection of business form for specific enterprises in the past.

(a) Corporate Tax Rates

Corporations historically have been treated as separate taxable entities under the Internal Revenue Code with their own sets of rules and their own tax schedules In 1997, corporations are subject to tax on income at the following rates:[27]

Table 1

Corporate Tax Rates

If Taxable Income Is Over	But Not Over	The Tax Is	Of the Amount Over
–0–	$50,000	15%	–0–
$50,000	75,000	$7,500 + 25%	$50,000
75,000	100,000	13,750 + 34%	75,000
100,000	335,000	22,250 + 39%	100,000
335,000	10,000,000	113,900 + 34%	335,000
10,000,000	15,000,000	3,400,000 + 35%	10,000,000
15,000,000	18,333,333	5,150,000 + 38%	15,000,000
18,333,333	———	6,416,667 + 35%	18,333,333

Notes

(1) It is important to distinguish between *marginal* tax rates and *effective* tax rates. The *marginal* tax rate applicable to a corporation with exactly $75,000 of income is 34 percent because that is the rate applicable to each additional dollar of taxable income the corporation earns above $75,000 (up to $100,000). However, the *effective* tax rate on such income is 18 percent since a corporation's tax bill on exactly $75,000 of taxable income is $13,750 (15 percent of $50,000 plus 25 percent of $25,000). A corporation with precisely $100,000 of taxable income owes $22,250; that is an effective rate of 22.25 percent, but the marginal tax rate on each addition dollar of income is 39 percent up to $335,000.

(2) Where do the mysterious numbers $7,500, $13,750 come from? Hint: calculate the precise tax due on $50,000 of income taxed at 15%; then calculate the precise tax due on an additional $25,000 of income taxed at 25%.

(3) The tax structure for corporations in general is mildly progressive; it is "progressive" because additional income is taxed at increasingly higher effective rates. A tax structure is "regressive" if lower amounts of income are taxed at higher rates than higher amounts of income. When a corporation's income is in the $100,000–$335,000 range, it is subject to a marginal rate of 39 percent; above $335,000 the tax rate reverts to 34 percent. (At the $15,000,000–$18,333,333 level, there is a similar pattern: the tax rate rises to 38 percent and then drops back to 35 percent.) These declines in marginal rates may be viewed as regressive even though the effective rate of taxation on corporate income can never exceed 34 percent at any level of income up to $10,000,000 or 35 percent at any level of income. These special surtaxes on corporations are designed to gradually eliminate

27. [By the Editor] This table is a composite table building in special surtaxes at the $100,000 and $15,000,000 levels.

the benefit of the lower brackets for corporations that have incomes over $100,000 and $15,000,000 respectively.

(4) Classic examples of regressive taxes on individuals are state sales taxes and federal social security taxes, since these taxes take up a larger percentage of the income of low income taxpayers than for higher income taxpayers.

(5) A "qualified personal service corporation" is defined in I.R.C. § 448(d)(2) as a corporation "substantially all of the activities of which involve the performance of services in the fields of health, law, engineering, architecture, accounting, actuarial science, performing arts, or consulting" and substantially all of the stock of the corporation is owned by present or former employees or their distributees. The income of a qualified personal service corporation is taxed at a flat 35 percent rate. The purpose of this provision is to prevent personal service suppliers from incorporating solely to take advantage of corporate rates that may be lower than individual rates.

(6) Corporations subject to the tax rates set forth in Table 1 are called C corporations, named after Subchapter C of the Internal Revenue Code.

(b) Individual Tax Rates

Individual income tax rates are considerably more complex than the corporate rate schedules described above. There are four different rate schedules based primarily on marital status, plus elaborate sets of tax tables for use by persons with relatively small amounts of income. In addition, there is a special tax schedule for the income of trusts and estates. For purposes of considering the interaction of personal and corporate tax rates upon business income, however, a detailed consideration of this complex structure is unnecessary. It is simplest to use the most generally applicable tax schedule, married taxpayers filing joint tax returns, in 1997 and later years:

Table 2

Individual Income Tax Rates
(Married Taxpayer Filing Joint Return)

If taxable income is	The tax is:
Not over $41,200	15% of taxable income
Over $41,200 but under $99,600	$6,180 + 28% of excess over $41,200
Over $99,600 but under $151,750	$22,532 + 31% of excess over $99,600
Over $151,750 but under $271,050	$38,698.50 + 36% of excess over $151,750
Over $271,050..............................	$81,646.50 + 39.6% of excess over $271,050.[28]

28. [By the Editor] Other provisions of the Internal Revenue Code "phase out" taxpayers' personal exemptions and a portion of taxpayers' personal deductions for high income taxpayers, beginning at specified threshold amounts (approximately $150,000 of taxable income for taxpayers filing a joint return). These phase out provisions may be viewed as a type of surtax (similar to that applicable to corporations at the $100,000 and $15,000,000 levels of income) that create interim rates higher than those set forth in the above table at certain levels of income. However, for technical reasons these phase out provisions cannot be simply reflected in this Table in the same way that the effect of the corporate surtaxes was reflected in Table 1.

Other individual tax rate schedules all involve higher tax rates than the schedule for married taxpayers filing joint returns.

Notes

(1) The calculation of individual income taxes, once taxable income is determined, is similar to the method followed by corporations subject to the rate schedule of Table 1. In the case of individuals, however, there are a variety of profit-related and personal deductions that may be claimed, or a standard deduction in lieu of personal deductions (which is phased out for high income taxpayers).

(2) In the years during and after World War II, marginal rates on individual taxpayers were extremely high by modern standards, rising above 90 percent in some years. As late as 1980, the highest marginal rate for joint returns was 70 percent for taxable income in excess of $215,400. (The aggregate tax due in 1980 on exactly $215,400 of taxable income was $117,504; at 1993 rates, the aggregate tax due on the same amount of taxable income was "only" $63,072, though major differences in allowable deductions, tax shelters, and other tax benefits deprives this comparison of most of its apparent significance.) A major policy implemented by the Reagan administration in the 1980s was to reduce high marginal rates. This policy resulted in a maximum marginal rate of 28 percent in 1986, a date which is a watershed in much of the discussion that follows. Since 1986, however, the trend has been toward the return of higher marginal rates, culminating in the 39.6 percent maximum rate currently in effect.

(c) *The Taxation of Capital Gains or Losses*

Before 1986, at the same time that the maximum individual tax rates of 70 percent or more were in effect, the maximum tax rate on a different form of income-long-term capital gains arising from the sale or exchange of capital assets held for more than 6 months—was only 25 percent. Capital assets are assets held for profit making or investment purposes and not for personal use. This dramatic difference in rates created strong incentives to structure transactions or establish long-term strategies so as to transmute ordinary income into long-term capital gain in order to make the 25 percent rather than the 70 percent rate applicable. To a somewhat lesser extent, this same incentive exists today.

The technical rules with respect to the treatment of capital gains were relatively complex before 1986 and are even more complex today. Today, long term capital gains or losses are defined to be gains or losses on assets held for more than one year, and the maximum tax rate on long term capital gains is 20 percent.[29] Short term capital gains are taxed at ordinary income tax rates. Capital losses are available to offset capital gains plus up to $3,000 of ordinary income in any year; excess capital losses may be carried over to offset capital gains in future years. In making these various calculations and determining the net amount of gain or loss, and its character as short term or long term,

---

29. [By the Editor] Tax legislation enacted in 1997 made a number of important changes in capital gains rules. It established a 20 percent rate for capital assets held for more than eighteen months while retaining a 28 percent rate for capital assets held for between twelve and eighteen months. It also eliminated a preferential capital gains rate for corporations and made a number of other changes. These changes reduced taxes but increased the complexity of the tax structure.

short term gains and losses are separately netted to determine the net short term capital gain or loss and long term capital gains and losses are netted in the same manner to establish the net long term gain or loss; the two are then combined to determine the net capital gain or loss for the year.

ROBERT W. HAMILTON AND RICHARD A. BOOTH, BUSINESS BASICS FOR LAW STUDENTS: ESSENTIAL TERMS AND CONCEPTS (1998)*

The calculation of the amount of the gain from sales or exchanges [of property] involves the use of technical language that is fundamental to any understanding of the tax laws:

a. *Basis* is the investment the seller of the property has in the property. It is the cost or purchase price of the property paid or incurred by the seller in acquiring the property. In the case of property acquired by gift, the basis in the hands of the donee is usually the same as the basis in the hands of the donor (a *substituted basis*); in the case of property acquired by inheritance, it is generally the fair market value of the assets on the death of decedent (a *stepped up basis*).

b. *Adjusted basis* is the basis of the property, (1) plus capital improvements made by the seller, purchase commissions originally paid by the seller, legal costs for defending or perfecting title, and so forth, and (2) minus returns of capital, particularly depreciation claimed as tax deductions, depletion, deducted casualty losses, insurance reimbursements, and the like.

c. The *amount realized* includes the cash received for the property on a sale or the fair market value of the property received in exchange for the property. Selling expenses, including brokerage commissions paid by the seller, reduce the amount realized. In the case of property subject to a mortgage, the amount realized also includes the amount of mortgage debt which the seller is relieved from paying as a result of the sale. For example, if an owner of real estate that is encumbered by a $50,000 mortgage sells the property for $10,000 cash over and above the mortgage, which the buyer agrees to assume and pay, the amount realized from the sale is $60,000, not $10,000. If the property is sold with the seller giving the buyer $5,000 for assuming the mortgage of $50,000, the amount realized is $45,000.

d. *Gain* on a transaction equals the amount realized minus the adjusted basis. If the adjusted basis is greater than the amount realized, the difference is the loss.

The rule that on the death of a taxpayer the tax on unrealized gain is in effect forgiven (by giving the estate or heirs a stepped up basis) is a significant benefit that may well dictate business strategy. For example, if an elderly taxpayer owns a piece of property that has appreciated significantly in value, it makes sense to borrow against that property rather than selling it outright if the taxpayer needs additional funds for living expenses. In the case of an elderly shareholder owning stock that has appreciated significantly in value, it makes sense to retain that property until death in order to avoid the 28 percent capital gains tax.

(d) The Taxation of Partnerships and Corporations

When personal and corporate income tax rates are compared, the differences at first blush seem modest or insignificant. Both individual and corporate rates begin at 15 percent of taxable income and then progress to a maximum of 35 percent for corporations and 39.6 percent for individuals. There does not seem to be a great deal of difference between them. However, that turns out not to be the case.

(1) Proprietorships. Consider first the tax treatment of a proprietorship, a business wholly owned by a single individual, and conducted in her own name.

ROBERT W. HAMILTON, BUSINESS ORGANIZATIONS: UNINCORPORATED BUSINESSES AND CLOSELY HELD CORPORATIONS*
Pages 46–49 (1997).

A proprietorship is not a separate taxable entity. Its income or loss is reported on the proprietor's personal income tax return. For example, if a proprietor files a joint return with his or her spouse, the business income or loss of each proprietorship owned by either or both of them must be included in that joint return.

The manner of reporting the income and expenses of a proprietorship is interesting because it reflects a pragmatic compromise between the legal view that a proprietorship is not a separate entity from its owner and the economic view that the proprietorship's financial affairs should not be intermixed with the proprietor's personal affairs. The Internal Revenue Code requires an individual taxpayer who is also an entrepreneur to file the long-form personal income tax return—the form 1040. The Internal Revenue Code also requires a separate tax form, Schedule C, to be prepared to record the gain or loss from each business owned by the taxpayer. Schedule C must be attached to the taxpayer's form 1040 and the income or loss of the proprietorship is added to or subtracted from the proprietor's other income in order to determine her final liability to Uncle Sam. A separate Schedule C must be filed for each business. State income taxation works much the same way (though many states base their tax on the taxpayer's federal tax return and do not require a completely separate accounting of income or loss). * * *

Every entrepreneur operating a sole proprietorship must also take into account the requirements of the Self Employment Contributions Act of 1954, imposing a tax on Schedule C income equal (in 1995) to 12.4 percent of proprietorship income up to $61,200 for old age survivors and disability insurance (OASI) and an additional uncapped 2.9 percent for Medicare. If the

* Reprinted with the permission of Aspen   Aspen Publishers, Inc.
Law & Business/Panel Publishers, a division of

entrepreneur is also an employee of another firm, the OASI tax is applied first against the salary of the employee and the proprietorship income is taxed only to the extent the salary is less than $61,200.

———

(2) **Partnerships.** The taxation of both general and limited partnerships is set forth in Chapter K of the Internal Revenue Code. It is a logical extension of the manner of taxation of a proprietorship:

> The method of taxation applicable to a partnership is usually referred to as *pass through* (or conduit) taxation. A partnership must prepare an information return[30] each year that shows partnership income and expenses, but it does not itself pay any tax. Rather, it then allocates the income or loss of the partnership among the individual partners in accordance with the partnership agreement. Each partner must then include in his or her personal income tax return the amount of each item so allocated.[31]

Robert W. Hamilton, Business Organizations: Essential Terms and Concepts 85 (1997). It is important to appreciate that while, both the proprietorship and the traditional partnership are taxed as extensions of the individual taxpayers who are the owners of the enterprise, the amounts allocated are based on the income calculations of the proprietorship or partnership and not on the amounts actually distributed in cash or property to the proprietor or partner.

In general terms the Self Employment Contributions Act tax is imposed on general partners, I.R.C. § 1402(a), but not on limited partners (I.R.C. § 1402(a)(13)). The application of this tax to individual members of limited liability companies creates obvious problems. See Prop.Treas.Reg. § 1.1402(a)(18), 59 Fed.Reg. 67253 (1994).

(3) **Corporations.** As described above, corporations have their own special tax schedule. However, when comparing the tax consequences of conducting a business in corporate or partnership form, it is essential to recognize that the corporate rate is not in lieu of, but is in addition to, the tax on the ultimate shareholders. In other words, the corporate tax is applicable to the corporation; if corporate income is then distributed to the shareholders, that distribution is itself subject to income tax as dividends to the shareholders. There is, in short, double taxation of business earnings if a corporation makes distributions to shareholders. An example should make this clear. If the corporation has taxable income of precisely $75,000, the corporation must pay a corporate income tax of $13,750, leaving $61,250 available for distribution to the shareholders; if the corporation then distributes the $61,250 to its shareholders, all of whom are in the 36 percent bracket, the shareholders will owe another $22,050, for a total tax bill at both levels of $35,800. The effective combined tax rate on $75,000 of corporate income is 48 percent. In contrast, if the business were conducted as a proprietorship or partnership,

30. [By the Author] This information return is form 1065.

31. [By the Author] The partnership must send each individual partner a statement on form K–1 as to the amount of each item of income, deduction, or loss allocated to him or her for the year.

there is no tax at all at the entity level, and the maximum additional tax (calculated at the rate of 36 percent) would be $27,000. In other words, on the assumption that all income is to be distributed to shareholders, the failure to obtain conduit or pass-through tax treatment results in $8,800 in additional federal income taxes in a single year!

Indeed, if the corporate and individual taxpayers are both at the highest marginal rates, 35 percent and 39.6 percent respectively, the combined tax rate on a C corporation and its shareholders (assuming the distribution of all income) is 74.6 percent. The maximum rate on individuals is 39.6 percent. There is thus a 35 percent differential or bias against C corporation tax status at the highest levels of income.

* * * The double tax treatment of closely held C corporations is widely viewed by shareholders in those corporations as unfair and discriminatory. In the 1950s, Subchapter S was added to the Internal Revenue Code to give some relief from the double tax treatment. Subchapter S requires an affirmative election by the corporation and is not available to all closely held corporations. A corporation that makes this election is call an "S corporation" or a "sub S corporation."

The S corporation election is a tax election and not a corporate law election: an S corporation possesses all of the normal attributes of a corporation under state law, but is taxed in a different way than C corporations. To be eligible for S corporation treatment, corporations must have fewer than 75 individual shareholders; the maximum number of shareholders in an S corporation was originally set at ten and gradually increased over the years. A corporation, in addition to meeting the maximum 75 shareholder requirement, may not have shareholders who are nonresident aliens or certain artificial entities, and may not have issued more than one class of stock (except for classes of common stock that differ only in voting rights). Before 1996, S corporations were not permitted to have corporate shareholders or own stock in another corporation; these restrictions have been eliminated. There is no maximum size limitation for S corporations, though doubtless most of them are very small. Most S corporations have only one shareholder. A few S corporations have assets in excess of $1,000,000,000—large businesses by any standard—but these are atypical. These various requirements are fleshed out in considerable detail in the Internal Revenue Code and the regulations issued thereunder.

S corporations are taxed on a modified conduit basis that is similar in many respects to that applicable to partnerships: the corporation files a return showing the earnings allocable to each shareholder, who must include that amount in his or her personal income tax return. That amount is includible whether or not any distributions are made by the corporation. However, the tax treatment of S corporations is not identical to that of partnerships in all respects, and in several respects is less advantageous to the taxpayer than the conduit tax provided by partnerships. These technical difference are set forth in the note.[32] However, an S corporation does have the basic feature of conduit or pass-through taxation that is typical of partnership

---

32. [By the Editor] Robert W. Hamilton, Corporate General Partners of Limited Partnerships, 1 J. Small Bus.L. 101, 109 n. 23 (1997):

S corporation tax treatment is superficially similar to partnership tax treatment in that the tax in each case is imposed directly on the owners and not on the business entity

and proprietorship forms of business, and as a result is a plausible alternative to a partnership from a tax standpoint.

Notes

(1) The tax treatment of C corporations has been the subject of considerable theoretical discussion, both historically and at the present time. One basic

itself. However, the two forms of taxation differ in a number of technical respects that favor partnership tax treatment. A partial list of these differences include:

(1) A shareholder of an S corporation must include in her taxable income the amount of the income of the S corporation allocated to her based on her proportional interest in the corporation. See I.R.C. § 1366. The tax rules applicable to partnerships, on the other hand, give the business entity some discretion as to how income or loss are to be allocated among the participants, allocations that may produce significant net tax savings. See I.R.C. § 705; Treas. Reg. 1.704–1.

(2) S corporation and partnership tax treatment differ in the manner in which gain is recognized when a participant in the business contributes appreciated property to the business and the property is thereafter sold. (This type of gain is called "built-in gain.") See I.R.C. § 1374 In a partnership, built-in gain from any sale of property within two years must be allocated back to the contributing partner. See I.R.C. § 704(c). In an S corporation the gain must be allocated strictly in accordance with ownership interests. See I.R.C. § 1366. For example, assume that A contributes $10,000 in cash and B contributes a piece of real estate having a tax basis of $4,000 and a fair market of $10,000. Each has a fifty percent interest in the business. There is "built-in gain" of $6,000. Shortly thereafter, suppose that the business sells the real estate for $10,000. If the business is subject to partnership tax treatment, the $6,000 gain must be allocated to B, who must pay tax on this gain (presumably as a capital gain). B's basis in the partnership becomes $10,000. If the business is subject to S corporation tax treatment, on the other hand, $3,000 of the gain must be allocated to A and $3,000 to B. A in effect will be taxed on a portion of the gain attributable to B's contribution of property, and the tax bases of A's and B's interests in the corporation will not be equal even though each contributed property of equal value.

(3) Another difference in tax treatment arises if an S corporation or partnership owns property that has appreciated in value while owned by the business, and distributes that property to its shareholders or partners, respectively. In the case of a

partnership, no gain is recognized on the transfer, see I.R.C. § 731, and the basis of each partner in the property is carried over from the partnership's basis. In an S corporation, on the other hand, the distribution of appreciated property results in recognition of gain, its allocation to the shareholders, and a tax on the gain is due, even if the appreciated property has not been sold to third parties. See I.R.C. § 311(b).

(4) Another difference between S corporation and partnership tax treatment relates to adjustments to basis for liabilities incurred by the business itself. Losses are deductible by partners and S corporation shareholders only to the extent of the tax basis of their interests in the firm. See I.R.C. §§ 704(d), 1366(d). If a partnership borrows money for purposes of its business, the tax basis of each partner's interest in the partnership is immediately increased by his proportionate share of the new liability. See I.R.C. § 752(a). In an S corporation, if money is borrowed by the shareholder and contributed to the corporation, his basis is also increased by the amount of the loan. See Estate of Leavitt v. Commissioner, 875 F.2d 420, 422–23 (4th Cir.1989); Harris v. United States, 902 F.2d 439, 443 (5th Cir.1990). However, if the indebtedness is incurred directly by the S corporation, there is no adjustment in the shareholders' basis in the stock, see I.R.C. § 1367, and a valuable tax attribute is lost (since it is always advantageous to increase one's basis in S corporation shares)

(5) Finally, the I.R.C. permits a step-up of basis in partnership assets to reflect the partners' bases in the partnership whenever a partner's interest is redeemed or liquidated. See I.R.C. § 754. This privilege is not available to S corporation shareholders, again with the result that valuable tax benefits may be lost in the S corporation business form.

While these differences between partnership and S corporation taxation are rather technical, they involve real dollars in the real world. Since the rules favor the partnership form of taxation over the S corporation, practitioners have naturally gravitated toward the limited partnership in preference to the S corporation, even when the S corporation election is available to the firm.

problem is that it is unclear where the ultimate incidence of the corporate income tax falls, whether on consumers, employees, shareholders, or other businesses. At the beginning of President Reagan's second term in 1985 there was a brief flirtation with the idea that the corporate income tax should be abolished; however, as the compromises that eventually became the Tax Reform Act of 1986 were hammered out, this idea was abandoned. Instead, there was increased reliance on the corporate income tax as a revenue raiser—investment tax credits, accelerated depreciation deductions, and similar revenue reducing items were either eliminated entirely or cut back. To some extent the economic effect of these changes were offset by unanticipated consequences of the changes in tax rates.

(2) There have been numerous proposals over the years to "integrate" the corporate and individual income tax structures and thereby eliminate the "double tax" on corporate shareholders. Other industrialized countries generally do not have a double tax structure. President Reagan's proposal to repeal the corporate income tax was one example of such a proposal. Alternatively, one could eliminate dividends from the taxable income of shareholders. Yet another approach would treat the payment of tax by a corporation as a kind of withholding tax with respect to income ultimately distributed to shareholders. Yet another approach would in effect extend S corporation tax treatment to all corporations. These proposals, however, all have formidable problems created by different types of taxpayers. tax-exempt entities, foreign shareholders, and the like. For interesting analyses of the double tax structure and the problems of integration proposals, see American Law Institute, Federal Income Tax Project; Alvin C. Warren, Jr., Reporter's Study of Corporate Tax Integration (1993); Alvin C. Warren, Jr., Corporate Integration Proposals and ACRS, 22 San Diego L.Rev. 325 (1985); Peter L. Faber, Taxation of Corporations and Shareholders: Premises of the Present System, 22 San Diego L.Rev. 5 (1985).

(3) In 1997 even more radical changes in the federal income tax structure are being considered: a flat tax, a national sales tax, and a variety of other proposals.

(e) Tax planning strategies

Tax planning for businesses involves several considerations:

First, everyone has to pay, or at least account to the United States by filing returns for, income taxes. In this respect, taxation is more immediate and certain than the risk of unlimited liability for owners. The danger that a business may incur a liability in excess of business assets may or may not materialize depending on what happens in the future; but liability for taxes is a certainty, not a possibility. Hence tax planning is a routine and often dominant aspect of every significant business venture.

Second, taxpayers quite legitimately expect to minimize their tax liability to the extent they may legally do so. There is a basic distinction between legitimate tax avoidance [usually called "tax planning"] on the one hand and tax evasion that may lead to fraud penalties, or worse, on the other.[33] The

---

33. [By the Editor] The claiming of personal exemptions for household pets is an example of criminal tax evasion while electing S corporation status is an example of acceptable tax avoidance. While this may seem obvious, the line between legitimate avoidance and improper evasion is often shadowy. In addition to criminal sanctions, the Internal Revenue Service possesses authority to impose civil sanc-

tions in situations where criminal prosecution is thought to be inappropriate.

The IRS possesses power to review and reject specific tax avoidance transactions. For example, the IRS has statutory power to compel accounting changes so as "to clearly reflect income" (I.R.C. § 446) that may result in significant tax liability arising from apparently selection of business forms in order to take advantage of differences in tax schedules or the S corporation election is clearly permissible tax planning.

Third, in tax planning one must usually concentrate on the marginal rate of taxation, not the effective rate. As a practical matter, most individuals considering an investment in a business venture will already have income from other sources that exceeds $36,900, so that every dollar of income obtained from the business venture will be taxed at 28 percent or more; the 15 percent individual tax rate is simply irrelevant in most situations.[34] Where there are several different investors or owners, they are likely to be in different tax brackets. Generally, the strategy that minimizes the tax obligations of the owner or investor who is in the highest tax bracket will be followed, though that is not always true.[35]

Fourth, in selecting the form of business, the total tax liabilities of both business and owners must be taken into account. Under current tax rates, it is usually advantageous to conduct a small business in a form that permits conduit tax treatment. But that is not true at all tax rates. In some tax regimes, the widespread use of the C corporation minimizes effective taxes.

Before 1986, corporate tax rates were lower than individual tax rates at most levels of income; Corporate tax rates were capped at 48 or 52 percent of income while individual marginal tax rates were 80 percent or higher. As a result, total taxes were minimized if a C corporation was employed and a policy was adopted of never paying dividends which were taxable as such to shareholders. To minimize tax bills before 1986, therefore, profitable corporations often accumulated large amounts of undistributed earnings.[36] Of course, at some point the owners will wish to enjoy the fruits of their successful enterprise. One widely followed strategy was to accumulate the maximum amount possible within the corporation at the favorable corporate rates and then sell all the stock in the business at a price that presumably reflected the accumulated income within the corporation. Alternatively, the corporation might redeem all the stock of a shareholder. Properly structured, the gain on either the sale or the redemption of the stock would be taxed to the

proper tax avoidance transactions. The IRS may also take advantage of a court-created doctrine relating to "step transactions" that permits it to treat a series of transactions as a single transaction so as to clearly reflect income. Many courts have also accepted an argument often made by the IRS that form should not be elevated over substance, and that the substance should determine how a transaction is taxed. Review of tax avoidance transactions under these various doctrines typically arise in audits of tax returns and do not normally lead to the imposition of penalties (other than the payment of interest on tax deficiencies) on the taxpayer.

34. [By the Editor] The same is not true of a newly formed corporation. That entity will be taxed at the 15 percent rate for its income up to $75,000, though the 5 percent surtax will wipe out the benefit of that lower tax rate after the corporation's taxable income grows. Since new businesses may be placed in several different corporations, multiple use of the 15 per-

cent bracket may be available in many situations.

35. [By the Editor] A revised version of the "Golden Rule" for business is "He who has the gold, rules." Typically, the person in the highest tax bracket will be contributing capital that is essential for the success of the enterprise, and hence his tax minimization becomes the goal of tax planning.

36. [By the Editor] The Internal Revenue Code contains a penalty tax aimed at unreasonable accumulations of income in a corporation for the purpose of avoiding the taxation of dividends to shareholders. See chapter 7, Section H. While this tax did limit the strategy described in the text, it was only applicable to large accumulations unrelated to the reasonable needs of the enterprise, and could often be avoided as a practical matter. This penalty tax has become much less important as a result of the current marginal rates applicable to corporations and individuals.

shareholder at favorable capital gains tax rates. This basic strategy was so common in pre–1986 tax strategy that it had its own name: the "accumulation-bail out" strategy. Its success was based ultimately on the combined effect of the favorable income tax rate on corporations coupled with the equally favorable tax rate applicable to capital gains.

The S corporation election was less attractive than the accumulation-bail out strategy in the era of very high marginal individual tax rates. For a profitable corporation, the S corporation election was disastrous, since it moved taxable income away from the corporation with its lower rates and into the returns of the individual shareholders to be taxed at the much individual marginal rates. However, with the lower marginal individual rates now in effect, the S corporation election may be more advantageous than the accumulation-bail out strategy if the owners wish to withdraw income from the business for their own use.

A second pre–1986 tax strategy that enabled a corporation to minimize the impact of double taxation of corporate income involved "zeroing out" a C corporation's taxable income. This strategy relied on the fact that, while distributions in the form of dividends are not deductible by corporations, payments to shareholders in the form of salaries, rent, and interest are deductible by the corporation (so long as the payments are reasonable in amount).[37] The distribution of income in the form of salaries, rent, and interest to shareholders thus eliminated the corporate tax on that income and in effect shifted it to the shareholders, since such payments are taxable as ordinary income to the shareholders who receive them. One could minimize the total tax bill of a corporation by a judicious determination of how much salary and related benefits could be paid to the shareholders. The goal was to reduce the taxable income of the corporation and increase the taxable income of the shareholder by the amount of the deductible payments so that the total tax bill was minimized. However, the process of "zeroing out" was often not precise and if the corporation was extremely successful, it might not be possible to shift the optimal amount of taxable income to shareholders and sustain as reasonable those deductions.[38] As a result, under pre–1986 tax rates, the "zeroing out" process was often not carried to its ultimate, but the payments to shareholders were structured so as broadly to minimize the combined corporation/shareholders tax obligations. Partial "zeroing out" might be combined with the accumulation-bail out strategy.

A final strategy popular in the pre–1986 period involved start-up businesses which expected losses temporarily. In this situation, it was attractive to have the business be taxed on a conduit or pass-through basis, since that

37. [By the Editor] The suggestion was sometimes made that the corporation should not pay dividends but provide living benefits indirectly or secretly; the corporation might pay shareholders' grocery bills or provide automobiles at no expense to shareholders. Such suggestions may move across the shadowy line between permissible tax planning and improper tax evasion. Certainly if the Internal Revenue Service learned that excessive benefits were being provided (as it might, for example, from an audit of the corporate books), it would, at the least, insist that deductions by the corporation be disallowed. If the recipient did not include the value of the benefits as income subject to taxation, benefits would also be taxed to the individual shareholders as informal dividends. In addition, tax fraud penalties might be assessed and criminal prosecution pursued in egregious cases.

38. [By the Editor] A more serious problem often was that distributions in these forms sometimes led to friction within the corporate family since payments were usually not made in proportion to shareholdings.

enabled the shareholders to take advantage of the losses to shield other income from taxation. In effect, the loss business served as a kind of tax shelter for its shareholders. A common pattern then was initially to conduct a business as a partnership or proprietorship until it became profitable and then incorporate, or to elect S corporation status during the period losses continued and then revoke that election when the corporation became profitable. The accumulation-bail out strategy would then be followed thereafter.

The 1986 Tax Reform Act changed these various strategies in fundamental ways. First of all, it imposed significant restrictions on the deductibility of passive losses in an effort to stamp out "abusive" tax shelters and these restrictions continue to prevent the widespread use of loss businesses as tax shelters. Secondly, and much more fundamentally, it reduced the marginal rates on individuals to a maximum of 28 percent, a rate that was lower than the corporate tax rate. Overnight, tax strategies changed dramatically. For a profitable enterprise, a partnership business form provided dramatic tax savings over a traditional corporation. Subchapter S suddenly became an attractive tax strategy for profitable as well as loss corporations. The result, inevitably, was a move to "disincorporate" American business, leading to an unexpected and unplanned for decline in revenues. And, rather predictably, this caused a backlash, leading to a statute that made it crystal clear that large corporations could not reduce their tax bills by electing to be taxed as partnerships.

(f) Publicly Held Limited Partnerships

DONNA D. ADLER, MASTER LIMITED PARTNERSHIPS[39]
40 U.Fla.L.Rev. 755, 756–58, 763–65, 774, 777, 779, 783–85 (1988).

The term "master limited partnership" * * * refers * * * to large partnerships that are widely held and whose ownership interests are frequently traded. * * * The debate over the proper treatment of master limited partnerships resulted in the enactment of a provision in the Revenue Act of 1987 that will cause certain "publicly traded partnerships" to be taxed as corporations. * * *

Between 1981 and 1987, the number of master limited partnerships grew markedly. * * * [By] 1985 forty-eight master limited partnership had been formed and were being traded on established exchanges. In 1986 alone, thirty-eight additional exchange traded master limited partnerships were formed, and in the first six months of 1987, another forty had been marketed. * * * Among the new master limited partnership offerings were such established businesses as Burger King, Mauna Loa Macadamia, and the Boston Celtics. * * *

* * * [T]he Kintner regulations set forth the test of whether a master limited partnership would be treated as an association taxable as a corporation or as a partnership.[40] These regulations identify six characteristics that are "found in a pure corporation which, taken together, distinguish it from other organizations." These characteristics are: "(i) associates, (ii) an objec-

---

39. Reprinted with permission from the University of Florida Law Review. Copyright 1989.

40. [By the Author] Treas.Reg. § 301.7701–2 (as amended in 1983).

tive to carry on a business and divide the gains therefrom, (iii) continuity of life, (iv) centralization of management, (v) liability for corporate debts limited to corporate property, and (vi) free transferability of interests." A partnership will be treated as an association taxable as a corporation if it "more nearly resembles a corporation than a partnership." Because both corporations and partnerships have as common characteristics associates and an objective to carry on a business and divide the gains therefrom, those traits will be disregarded in determining whether the partnership will be taxed as a corporation. If a partnership lacks two of the four remaining characteristics, its status as a partnership will be respected for tax purposes. Most limited partnerships, including master limited partnerships, do not possess the characteristic of continuity of life because death, insanity, or bankruptcy of the general partner will cause the termination of the partnership. In addition, liability for partnership debts is not limited to partnership property if the general partner is not a "dummy" or has a substantial amount of assets.[41]

Master limited partnerships can fulfill the necessary requirements to avoid being treated as associations taxable as corporations rather easily. Most states have adopted partnership laws that provide for the termination of the partnership on the death, insanity, or bankruptcy of the general partner. Case law has held that even if the limited partners can replace the general partner, the possibility that the partnership could terminate under state law precludes the partnership from having the characteristic of continuity of life. Furthermore, a general partner that either has a substantial amount of assets or plays an active managerial role in the partnership business will be considered as having unlimited liability. The classification rules consider only the above-listed characteristics, and the determination does not turn on whether the partnership interests are publicly traded. Through careful planning, many businesses could, in effect, choose whether to be treated as partnerships by forming a master limited partnership that complied with a state's uniform limited partnership act or as a corporation merely by incorporating under state law. * * *

Large partnerships that are listed and publicly traded on established securities markets are, in many respects, indistinguishable from publicly traded corporations. The partners of a master limited partnership are generally investors that are not concerned with the identity of the other partners; rather, they view investment in these partnerships much the same way they view corporate stock. Commentators and planners have noted that "[t]here is * * * another type of business entity, the [publicly traded] limited partnership, which can be structured essentially to embody the salient features of a corporation from the investor's point of view."[42] Master limited partnerships, therefore, are competing for the same capital investment as corporations but can promise higher yields because of the competitive edge created by the tax advantages of operating in partnership form. * * *

Congress responded to the concerns and complexities raised by master limited partnerships in the Revenue Act of 1987.[43] The major thrust of the

41. [By the Author] *Id.* § 301.7701–2.

42. [By the Author] Million & Bolding [Metamorphosis: Liquidation of the Corporation into a Publicly Traded Limited Partnership, 38 Bus.Law.], at 1487.

43. [By the Author] Revenue Act of 1987, Pub.L.No. 100–203.

changes in the Revenue Act is to treat certain "publicly traded partnerships" as corporations.[44] Generally, publicly traded partnerships are defined as any partnership with interests that are "traded on an established securities market," or has interests that "are readily tradeable on a secondary market (or the substantial equivalent thereof)."[45] * * * On the first day a partnership is treated as a corporation, the partnership will be considered to have transferred all its assets to a newly formed corporation in exchange for its stock and distributed the stock to the partners in liquidation of their partnership interests. * * *

By selecting public trading as the dividing line, Congress has undercut its own efforts at correcting the tax equity and neutrality problems. Congress has chosen public trading as the sole characteristic that makes the Burger King master limited partnership qualitatively different from a Mom and Pop burger stand that operates as a general partnership. Neither the statutory language nor the legislative history presents a convincing argument that public trading is the characteristic that differentiates the two.

The justification for treating publicly traded partnerships as corporations for tax purposes is that they are essentially no different from corporations. Using public trading as the overriding factor in classifying partnerships as corporations, however, ignores the wide diversity among corporations. Most corporations are not publicly traded, but they still incur a corporate-level tax. * * *

Notes

(1) As a result of the 1987 Tax Act, there is one invariant rule about conduit-type taxation. If a business has ownership interests that are publicly traded, that business will be taxed as a C corporation no matter what business form is adopted.

(2) Under the tax rates in effect in 1997, the name of the game for most closely held businesses is to continue to take advantage of conduit or pass-through taxation. This means the use of unincorporated business forms that provide conduit tax treatment, the election of subchapter S if the corporation is eligible, and the "zeroing out" of income as much as possible—to 100 percent if that can be defended in a tax audit. Taxation as a C corporation is usually to be avoided, though the reduction of the capital gains tax rate to 20 percent may make the "accumulate and bail out strategy" again attractive in specific situations. A business owned by one or more elderly shareholders may also be conducted in corporate form to take advantage of the anticipated step-up in basis on the death of shareholders.

(g) Check-the-Box: The End of the Kintner Regulations

The *Kintner* regulations, summarized in the Adler excerpt, were originally developed by the Internal Revenue Service in response to the development of limited partnerships with corporate general partners that provided limited liability to all the owners of the business. The IRS considered taking the position that unlimited personal liability was the touchstone of partnership taxation, but eventually moved to the tax classification based on the presence of "corporate" characteristics as defined in the *Kintner* regulations. The desire that there be economic meaning and substance in these corporate

---

44. [By the Author] I.R.C. § 7704(a).   **45.** [By the Author] *Id.* § 7704(b).

"characteristics" led to extremely detailed substantive regulations for limited partnerships and limited liability companies, numerous private rulings by the Service as new twists were developed, and the creation of a cottage industry in large law firms as individual attorneys specialized in the nuances of the application of the *Kintner* regulations to LLCs and limited partnerships. This approach toward classification was widely criticized by commentators. See e.g. Larry E. Ribstein, The Deregulation of Limited Liability and the Death of Partnership, 70 Wash. U.L.Q. 417, 451 (1992)("there is no normative basis for the tax distinction between 'corporations' and 'partnerships,'" and "the classification is unsuitable as an arbitrary line because it entails significant costs"); see also Rebecca S. Rudnick, Who Should Pay the Corporate Tax in a Flat Tax World?, 39 Case W. Res. L.Rev. 965, 1047–61 (1988–89).

Effective January 1, 1997, the Internal Revenue Service adopted new regulations for the classification of business forms. 26 C.F.R. Parts 1, 301, 602, TD 8697, 61 Fed.Reg. 66,584 (1996). These new regulations, popularly known as "check the box," state that the *Kintner* rules had become "increasingly formalistic," and that the new regulations replace those rules "with a much simpler approach that generally is elective."

While the detailed "check the box" regulations are relatively complex, the basic principles can be simply stated:

(1) An entity will be classified as a corporation for tax purposes if it is created under a statute that "describes or refers to the entity as incorporated as a corporation, body corporate, or body politic" or as "a joint-stock company or joint stock association." Such an entity must be taxed as a C corporation or as a sub S corporation (if it qualifies).

(2) An entity that is not classified as a corporation and has at least two members can elect to be classified for tax purposes either as a corporation or as a partnership by making an election at the time it files its first tax return. If the entity does not formally elect to be taxed as a corporation it will be taxed as a partnership. Existing entities with two or more members retain the tax status they had immediately before the new regulations go into effect.

(3) An entity that has only one member may elect to be taxed as a corporation or it will be taxed as a "nothing," i.e. as though it has no separate existence from its owner.

(4) If an entity elects to change its classification, it may not change its classification back within five years without permission of the Commissioner. The conversion of an entity that is currently taxable as a corporation to a partnership is itself a taxable event, treated as though the corporation dissolved and reconstituted itself as a partnership. The conversion the opposite direction, i.e. from a partnership to a corporation will usually (though not always) be tax-free.

Notes

(1) This regulation made a major simplification of what formerly was a complex and arcane area of business law and was generally received with shouts of joy by practitioners (though one suspects that the lawyers who were "classification experts" and whose expertise suddenly became completely irrelevant along with the *Kintner* regulations were less than happy). One comment captures the general euphoria: "Surfs up. An unincorporated entity can look, walk and quack

like a corporation in every respect—have officers and a board of managers, uninterruptible life, certificates that are freely transferable as well as limited liability—without risking classification as a corporation. However, don't organize the entity under any statute that refers to the entity as a joint stock company or association." Comment of John Debruyn by electronic mail, August 31, 1996. In the same message his one word response to the treatment of one member limited liability companies as a "nothing," was "Hooray!"

(2) Under check-the-box closely held corporations must be taxed as corporations. Of course, most such corporations may elect S corporation treatment but they will never be eligible for the more flexible subchapter K treatment unless they go through the tax-costly process of dissolving the corporation and reforming as an LLC or limited partnership.

(3) Does check-the-box spell the end of the S corporation for business organizations formed in the future? At first blush, the answer would appear to be "yes," given the tax advantages that partnership taxation has over S corporation treatment. See n. 32, page 151, supra. However there are countervailing factors that indicate S corporations are likely to continue to be used for the indefinite future. See Symposium: Check-the-Box and Beyond: The Future of Limited Liability Entities (Larry E. Ribstein and Mark A. Sargent, Editors), 52 Bus. Law. 605 (1997):*

(a) "[Bernard] Black asked why a lawyer would saddle clients with the restrictions of an S corporation when you don't have to. I've asked the same question of friends and colleagues who (unlike me) purport not to specialize in tax. Their general response as to small business is that lawyers are comfortable with S corporations. They know the applicable tax and non-tax rules well at this point. LLCs are a little scary. The law is still developing; why put your clients in the position of being the ones to have to make the law (in litigation)? Over time, I suppose, lawyers and clients will become more comfortable with the new world. I understand, however, that for the time being, many lawyers are taking the safe course, with all of its extra requirements." (Linda Galler, at 629)

(b) "I agree. Drafting the allocation and distribution provisions of LLC agreements, for example, can be daunting for the lawyer who is not a tax specialist. It is certainly daunting to try and explain them in plain English to a client. I think Subchapter S is more easily understood and applied by the nontax specialist than Subchapter K. Clients seem to comprehend Subchapter S more easily as well." (Jude Lemke, at 630)

(c) "S corporations will have a role with respect to old C corporations that prefer pass-through treatment. Conversion to a partnership would require recognition of gain under [I.R.C. section 1374]."[46] (Daniel L. Simmons, at 631)

(d) "One advantage an S corporation will continue to have is in going public. It is a fairly straight-forward matter to switch to a C corporation and make a public offering. An LLC would have to incorporate. While this typically can be done tax-free at the federal level, there can be federal as well as state problems upon the incorporation. Thus, S corporations can be

---

* Reprinted with permission from the American Bar Association.

46. [By the Editor] In other words, all previously unrealized appreciation in value of as-

sets owned by the corporation would be viewed as realized upon the conversion and subject to tax.

preferable, for example, if the parties want a short term loss pass-through and anticipate a quick public offering." (Walter D. Schwidetzsky, at 632)

(4) What effect will check-the-box have on the proliferation of unincorporated business forms under state law? In the symposium on check-the-box a number of predictions were made: that limited partnerships will fall into disuse, that states will adopt a single unincorporated business form, that states will adopt a "hub-and-spoke" configuration for statutory provisions relating to business forms, that entirely different business forms, such as limited partnership associations or business trusts, will become dominant, and so forth. Persons also suggested that the flexibility of the LLC will ultimately lead to its being the principal if not the sole business form. As this is written, it is too early to tell how accurate any of these predictions are. However, there are reasons to believe that change will come relatively slowly, See Symposium: Check-the-Box and Beyond: The Future of Limited Liability Entities (Larry E. Ribstein and Mark A. Sargent, Editors), 52 Bus. Law. 605 (1997):

(a) "I don't think we 'real lawyers' necessarily need more time to digest what's already out there, but I do think in terms of giving practical 'choice of entity' business advice, we necessarily tend to recommend those things that have a body of established law behind them. While a new type of entity may be way cool from an intellectual point of view, I would not normally encourage its use to a client in the commonplace situation—better not to be on the leading edge of the law in a commonplace situation. It's not so much that flexibility is a burden ('Gee, I don't have a form for that') as it is a matter of predictability of result ('Gee, I don't know the answer to that'). (William R. Asbell, at 618)

(b) "Yesterday, while all of this discussion was progressing I received a call from a real estate [lawyer] who was trying to form an LLC to own a vacation condo. She is very bright (law review and federal judicial clerkship), with many years of experience. Her client did not want her to bring in a tax or LLC expert so she was trying to form the entity by herself. She was totally befuddled by our default rules, flexibility, and tax provisions. It is a malpractice case waiting to happen. * * * We need some time to digest all of these entity laws, or something much simpler that small businesses and nonspecialist lawyers can deal with efficiently and economically." (Anthony K. Mallgren, at 618)

Of course, as experience with LLCs no longer constrained by the Kintner rules increases, the LLC may become as commonplace and familiar to lawyers, accountants, and the general public as partnerships and corporations are today. Only then will the full impact of "check-the-box" on business forms be known.

(5) Check-the-box is also having an influence on state statutes dealing with business forms. Many LLC statutes contained substantive requirements for LLCs that were designed to ensure that LLCs formed under that statute qualified for partnership taxation under the old Kintner rules. These substantive provisions became unnecessary with check-the-box, and are gradually being eliminated, increasing the freedom of choice for LLCs. As of 1997, 16 states were considering amendments permitting one-person LLCs, 12 states were considering eliminating term limits for LLCs and providing for perpetual existence, 10 states were considering eliminating membership dissociation as a default dissolution event, and so forth. Most, if not all, of this legislative activity can be traced to the new-found freedom under check-the-box.

(6) The recognition of one-person LLCs combined with the check-the-box rule that such an entity is a "nothing" for tax purposes, permits proprietors to obtain immunity from proprietorship liabilities coupled with pass-through taxation of income or loss at a relatively nominal cost.

(h) *Concluding Thoughts on Limited Liability*

Historically, the corporation was the business form that minimized the likelihood that the entrepreneurs would be personally liable for debts of the business should it fail. The corporation was a well understood business form but its lack of flexibility and adverse tax treatment increased its cost to owners of closely held businesses. In the last few years new types of business forms permit limited liability to be introduced into unincorporated entities that combine limited liability and partnership tax treatment: LLCs, LLPs, and limited partnerships with corporate general partners. The costs of forming these entities are typically less than the cost of forming a corporation, though that varies from state to state.

Superficially, it might appear that the advantages of limited liability are so great (and the cost of obtaining such protection today is so small) that all businesses should automatically elect a business form that provides limited liability for the owners. Surprisingly, many experienced attorneys tend toward the opposite conclusion. Writing in 1977 (when incorporation was the only sure route to limited liability), George C. Seward and W. John Nauss, Jr. in Basic Corporate Practice 1 (2d Ed. 1977) began their treatise with the statement, "When in doubt, do not incorporate. Many small corporations are formed inadvisedly. The corporate form * * * is probably disadvantageous for a small, new venture." The same point may be made today about any business form that requires compliance with technical rules, written documentation, and the periodic filing of documents with the state.

The risks involved in operating a business form such as a proprietorship or general partnership that does not provide a shield of limited liability depends to a very large extent on the nature of the business. If the business is in a low risk area, the cost of obtaining limited liability may not be justified. New businesses are often marginally funded at best; it may well be sensible for the business to devote all of its assets to opening and operating the business rather than spending some portion of them on lawyers, on preparing formal documents, and on filing fees.

The importance of limited liability depends primarily on possible exposure to tort liability. Consider several typical small businesses:

(1) A retail furniture, clothing, appliance or hardware store;

(2) A law firm;

(3) A restaurant and bar;

(4) An automobile distributorship;

(5) An apartment complex;

(6) An advertising, insurance or employment agency; and

(7) A wholesale supply firm.

As a practical matter, how significant is limited liability to each of these businesses?

Some of these businesses obviously involve a greater risk of tort liability than others, e.g. for malpractice in a law partnership or for an accident involving a delivery truck owned by a wholesale or retail business. Individuals, of course, assume a risk of unlimited liability whenever they drive a car, have a dinner party, or what have you. An individual or partner routinely obtains considerable protection against individual liability simply by the purchase of insurance. Businesses may do likewise. Do limited liability business forms purchase less insurance than those with unlimited liability? Why do limited liability entities purchase insurance at all? To what extent does insurance fail to give complete protection to a partner or individual? It is likely that most businesses will purchase insurance to provide adequate protection against most plausible tort liabilities without regard to whether or not the business form provides limited liability for owners.

What about liability on important contracts such as bank loans, real estate contracts, leases, inventory finance plans, and the like? Doing business in a limited liability form avoids individual responsibility for these often-substantial liabilities in theory. However, the other parties to such contracts are usually sophisticated and well understand the implications of limited liability; if they are concerned about the possibility that a limited liability entity may not have adequate resources to meet its obligations they will demand personal guarantees; as a result, they almost routinely require some or all of the owners of the business (and often their spouses as well) to enter into such guarantees. A wealthy investor (such as A in the hypothetical used in chapter 1) may demand the protection of a limited liability entity, but such an investor is exactly the type of person that a sophisticated third party wants to guarantee an obligation. Typically in these situations the third party has the more powerful bargaining position and the limited liability entity may be faced with the unpleasant choice between foregoing the transaction entirely or persuading the affluent investor to personally guarantee the obligation. In these situations, the advantages of limited liability disappear.

In some instances, secured creditors may rely exclusively on their secured positions and as a matter of policy choose not to pursue individual owners of the business whether or not they are personally liable on the obligation. (These creditors do not seek personal guarantees and the use of a limited liability form may therefore provide some peace of mind to owners).

There remain a variety of business liabilities that may cumulatively be substantial and for which a limited liability form of business may provide protection: e.g. claims of customers, tax claims, wage claims, warranty claims, claims of service providers such as accountants and lawyers, and claims of small suppliers. Probably the most common justification for using a limited liability entity is protection against these types of claims. As a practical matter, however, considerable protection against personal liability on such claims may be obtained in proprietorships or general partnerships by careful oversight of business activities engaged in by agents, employees and partners. Also, a timely decision to close down a marginal business may significantly reduce exposure to excessive and unacceptable liabilities in a proprietorship or general partnership.

Some people, of course, are more risk adverse than others. Inactive investors are likely to be risk averse and may be unwilling to accept an even-remote risk of exposure to liability for business obligations. In large part this is because they are not actively engaged in monitoring the performance of the managers and employees of the business and are less able to police things. Also, there are a wide variety of alternative investment opportunities in modern society that carry no risk of liability (and may also have the advantage of instant liquidity). As a result, if outside capital from inactive investors is sought, a business form that provides them with limited liability will almost always be necessary. If a business needs the capital of an outside investor who demands limited liability, the business will have to provide it one way or another, or find a less risk-adverse source of capital.

The growth of malpractice claims against professionals, particularly lawyers, accountants, doctors, and dentists, during the 1980s and 1990s has obviously increased concern about exposure to unlimited liability. While malpractice insurance may alleviate this concern to some extent, this insurance is expensive and, more seriously, may some immense claims have been asserted that exceed the maximum amount of insurance that is available. As a result there is a strong trend among professionals today both to carry malpractice insurance and to utilize business forms that provide (or hopefully may provide) some limitation on exposure to claims based on malpractice by others.

While corporations are viewed as providing the strongest shield against the imposition of personal liability on owners, subsequent chapters of this book point out that judicially-created doctrines such as "piercing the corporate veil" makes it clear that the shield is not impenetrable. There is some doubt in many states whether these judicially-created doctrines will be applied by analogy to other limited liability business forms. It is likely that they will, but one cannot be sure.

Notes

(1) Would you recommend that the AB Furniture Store discussed in Chapter 1 operate as partnership? A limited partnership? A limited liability partnership? A limited liability company? A corporation? If it incorporates, should it elect to be taxed as an S corporation?

(2) Assume that you have represented A on legal matters for several years but you have never represented B. B does not have a lawyer. When A asks you to give advice on the best form of business for the furniture store, B indicates that he relies on your judgment and will accept your recommendation. Do you have to take B's interest into account as well as A's? In some circumstances, a choice may be more favorable to A than to B. See Chapter 7, Part E, page 328, infra. Does B become your client if he relies on you but you fail to warn him about possible problems? Are you "counsel for the venture"? Consider Model Rules of Professional Conduct 1.7 (1983):

> (a) A lawyer shall not represent a client if the representation of that client will be directly adverse to another client, unless:
>
> (1) the lawyer reasonably believes the representation will not adversely affect the relationship with the other client; and
>
> (2) each client consents after consultation.

(b) A lawyer shall not represent a client if the representation of that client may be materially limited by the lawyer's responsibilities to another client or to a third person, or by the lawyer's own interests, unless:

(1) the lawyer reasonably believes the representation will not be adversely affected; and

(2) the client consents after consultation. When representation of multiple clients in a single matter is undertaken, the consultation shall include explanation of the implications of the common representation and the advantages and risks involved.

Does that rule apply to your situation? If so, how do you explain "the implications of the common representation and the advantages and risks involved" to B in making the decision of the business form to adopt?

Chapter Four

THE DEVELOPMENT OF CORPORATION LAW IN THE UNITED STATES

In England the power to award corporate charters was first assumed by the King and later by Parliament. In post-revolutionary America, state legislatures assumed the power to award charters. For many years, this power was exercised sparingly, usually limited to ventures of a public or quasi-public nature. Charters often contained numerous restrictions. Perhaps as a result of the English heritage (which often combined corporate charters with grants of monopoly power), corporations were viewed with suspicion and mistrust. Also, since charters were issued on a case-by-case basis by the legislature, these decisions were directly involved in the political process.

Industrialization and the development of very large business entities during the Nineteenth Century spelled the end of that era. The corporation proved to be an ideal vehicle for the development of large business entities since it combined firm, centralized direction with limited financial commitment by a theoretically limitless number of passive investors. As commerce developed during the Nineteenth Century, the charters issued to corporations became increasingly standardized, and the restrictions became less onerous. See generally Herbert Hovenkamp, Enterprise and American Law 1836–1937, ch. 11 (1991). The enactment of the first general and unlimited corporation statute by New Jersey, closely followed by Delaware, touched off an unseemly race among states, which is vividly described in the following excerpt.

LOUIS K. LIGGETT CO. v. LEE

Supreme Court of the United States, 1933.
288 U.S. 517, 548–65, 53 S.Ct. 481, 490–96, 77 L.Ed. 929, 944–54.

Mr. Justice Brandeis, dissenting. * * *

* * * The prevalence of the corporation in America has led men of this generation to act, at times, as if the privilege of doing business in corporate form were inherent in the citizen; and has led them to accept the evils attendant upon the free and unrestricted use of the corporate mechanism as if these evils were the inescapable price of civilized life, and, hence, to be borne with resignation. Throughout the greater part of our history a different view prevailed. Although the value of this instrumentality in commerce and indus-

try was fully recognized, incorporation for business was commonly denied long after it had been freely granted for religious, educational, and charitable purposes. It was denied because of fear. Fear of encroachment upon the liberties and opportunities of the individual. Fear of the subjection of labor to capital. Fear of monopoly. Fear that the absorption of capital by corporations, and their perpetual life, might bring evils similar to those which attended mortmain. There was a sense of some insidious menace inherent in large aggregations of capital, particularly when held by corporations. So at first the corporate privilege was granted sparingly; and only when the grant seemed necessary in order to procure for the community some specific benefit otherwise unattainable. The later enactment of general incorporation laws does not signify that the apprehension of corporate domination had been overcome. The desire for business expansion created an irresistible demand for more charters; and it was believed that under general laws embodying safeguards of universal application the scandals and favoritism incident to special incorporation could be avoided. The general laws, which long embodied severe restrictions upon size and upon the scope of corporate activity, were, in part, an expression of the desire for equality of opportunity.

(a) Limitation upon the amount of the authorized capital of business corporations was long universal. The maximum limit frequently varied with the kinds of business to be carried on, being dependent apparently upon the supposed requirements of the efficient unit. Although the statutory limits were changed from time to time, this principle of limitation was long retained. Thus in New York the limit was at first $100,000 for some businesses and as little as $50,000 for others. Until 1881 the maximum for business corporations in New York was $2,000,000; and until 1890, $5,000,000. In Massachusetts the limit was at first $200,000 for some businesses and as little as $5,000 for others. Until 1871 the maximum for mechanical and manufacturing corporations was $500,000; and until 1899, $1,000,000. The limit of $1,000,000 was retained for some businesses until 1903.

In many other states, including the leading ones in some industries, the removal of the limitations upon size was more recent. Pennsylvania did not remove the limits until 1905. * * * Michigan did not remove the maximum limit until 1921. * * * Missouri did not remove its maximum limit until 1927. Texas still has such a limit for certain corporations.

(b) Limitations upon the scope of a business corporation's powers and activity were also long universal. At first, corporations could be formed under the general laws only for a limited number of purposes—usually those which required a relatively large fixed capital, like transportation, banking and insurance, and mechanical, mining, and manufacturing enterprises. Permission to incorporate for "any lawful purpose" was not common until 1875; and until that time the duration of corporate franchises was generally limited to a period of 20, 30, or 50 years. All, or a majority, of the incorporators or directors, or both, were required to be residents of the incorporating state. The powers which the corporation might exercise in carrying out its purposes were sparingly conferred and strictly construed. Severe limitations were imposed on the amount of indebtedness, bonded or otherwise. The power to hold stock in other corporations was not conferred or implied. The holding company was impossible.

(c) The removal by the leading industrial states of the limitations upon the size and powers of business corporations appears to have been due, not to their conviction that maintenance of the restrictions was undesirable in itself, but to the conviction that it was futile to insist upon them; because local restriction would be circumvented by foreign incorporation. Indeed, local restriction seemed worse than futile. Lesser states, eager for the revenue derived from the traffic in charters, had removed safeguards from their own incorporation laws.[1] Companies were early formed to provide charters for corporations in states where the cost was lowest and the laws least restrictive.[2] The states joined in advertising their wares.[3] The race was one not of diligence but of laxity. Incorporation under such laws was possible: and the great industrial States yielded in order not to lose wholly the prospect of the revenue and the control incident to domestic incorporation.

The history of the changes made by New York is illustrative. The New York revision of 1890, which eliminated the maximum limitation on autho-

---

1. [By the Justice] The traffic in charters quickly became widespread. In 1894 Cook on Stock and Stockholders (3d Ed.) Vol. II, pp. 1604, 1605, thus described the situation: "New Jersey is a favorite state for incorporations. Her laws seem to be framed with a special view to attracting incorporation fees and business fees from her sister states and especially from New York, across the river. She has largely succeeded in doing so, and now runs the state government very largely on revenues derived from New York enterprises." * * *

In 1906 John S. Parker thus described the practice, in his volume Where and How—A Corporation Handbook (2d Ed.) p. 4: "Many years ago the corporation laws of New Jersey were so framed as to invite the incorporation of companies by persons residing in other states and countries. The liberality and facility with which corporations could there be formed were extensively advertised, and a great volume of incorporation swept into that state. * * *

"The policy of New Jersey proved profitable to the state, and soon legislatures of other states began active competition. * * *

"Delaware and Maine also revised their laws, taking the New Jersey act as a model, but with lower organization fees and annual taxes. Arizona and South Dakota also adopted liberal corporation laws, and contenting themselves with the incorporation fees, require no annual state taxes whatever.

"West Virginia for many years has been popular with incorporators, but in 1901, in the face of the growing competition of other states, the legislature increased the rate of annual taxes." And West Virginia thus lost her popularity. See Conyngton and Bennett, Corporation Procedure (Rev.Ed.1927), p. 712. On the other hand, too drastic price cutting was also unprofitable. The bargain prices in Arizona and South Dakota attracted wild cat corporations. Investors became wary of corporations organized under the laws of Arizona or South Dakota and both states fell in disrepute among them and consequently among incorporators. See Conyngton on Corporate Organizations (1913) c. 5.

2. [By the Justice] Thus, in its pamphlet "Business Corporations Under the Laws of Maine" (1903), the Corporation Trust Company enumerated among the advantages of the Maine laws: The comparatively low organization fees and annual taxes; the absence of restrictions upon capital stock or corporate indebtedness; the authority to issue stock for services as well as property, with the judgment of the directors as to their value conclusive; and, significantly enough, "the method of taxation, which bases the annual tax upon the stock issued, does not necessitate inquiry into or report upon the intimate affairs of the corporation." * * * See, also, the Red Book on Arizona Corporation Laws (1908), published by the Incorporating Company of Arizona, especially page 5:

"The remoteness of Arizona from the Eastern and Southern States has in a measure delayed the promulgation of the generousness of its laws. New Jersey, Delaware and West Virginia have become widely known as incorporating states. More recently Arizona, [South] Dakota, New Mexico and Nevada have come into more or less prominence by the passage of laws with liberal features."

3. [By the Justice] Thus, in an official pamphlet containing the corporation laws of Delaware (1901), the secretary of state wrote in the preface: "It is believed that no state has on its statute books more complete and liberal laws than these"; and the outstanding advantages were then enumerated. * * * See, also, "The General Corporation Act of New Jersey" (1898), edited by J.B. Dill, issued by the secretary of state: "Since 1875 it has been the announced and settled policy of New Jersey to attract incorporated capital to the State. * * *" P. xvii.

rized capital, and permitted intercorporate stockholding in a limited class of cases, was passed after a migration of incorporation from New York, attracted by the more liberal incorporation laws of New Jersey. But the changes made by New York in 1890 were not sufficient to stem the tide. In 1892, the Governor of New York approved a special charter for the General Electric Company, modelled upon the New Jersey act, on the ground that otherwise the enterprise would secure a New Jersey charter. Later in the same year the New York corporation law was again revised, allowing the holding of stock in other corporations. But the New Jersey law still continued to be more attractive to incorporators. By specifically providing that corporations might be formed in New Jersey to do all their business elsewhere, the state made its policy unmistakably clear. Of the seven largest trusts existing in 1904, with an aggregate capitalization of over two and a half billion dollars, all were organized under New Jersey law; and three of these were formed in 1899. During the first seven months of that year, 1336 corporations were organized under the laws of New Jersey, with an aggregate authorized capital of over two billion dollars. The Comptroller of New York, in his annual report for 1899, complained that "our tax list reflects little of the great wave of organization that has swept over the country during the past year and to which this state contributed more capital than any other state in the Union." "It is time," he declared, "that great corporations having their actual head-quarters in this State and a nominal office elsewhere, doing nearly all of their business within our borders, should be brought within the jurisdiction of this State not only as to matters of taxation but in respect to other and equally important affairs." In 1901 the New York corporation law was again revised.
* * *

Able, discerning scholars have pictured for us the economic and social results of thus removing all limitations upon the size and activities of business corporations and of vesting in their managers vast powers once exercised by stockholders—results not designed by the states and long unsuspected. They show that size alone gives to giant corporations a social significance not attached ordinarily to smaller units of private enterprise. Through size, corporations, once merely an efficient tool employed by individuals in the conduct of private business have become an institution—an institution which has brought such concentration of economic power that so-called private corporations are sometimes able to dominate the state. The typical business corporation of the last century, owned by a small group of individuals, managed by their owners, and limited in size by their personal wealth, is being supplanted by huge concerns in which the lives of tens or hundreds of thousands of employees and the property of tens or hundreds of thousands of investors are subjected, through the corporate mechanism, to the control of a few men. Ownership has been separated from control; and this separation has removed many of the checks which formerly operated to curb the misuse of wealth and power. And, as ownership of the shares is becoming continually more dispersed, the power which formerly accompanied ownership is becoming increasingly concentrated in the hands of a few. The changes thereby wrought in the lives of the workers, of the owners and of the general public are so fundamental and far-reaching as to lead these scholars to compare the evolving "corporate system" with the feudal system; and to lead other men of insight and experience to assert that this "master institution of civilised life" is committing it to the rule of a plutocracy. * * *

___

The problems discussed by Mr. Justice Brandeis largely relate to the role of large corporations with many shareholders rather than the small, closely held corporation that might operate a retail store. The competition for the incorporation business of larger corporations continues. Delaware particularly has found it profitable to maintain a hospitable climate for corporations. The success of this small state in attracting and retaining corporation business has been the subject of considerable study.

COMMENT, LAW FOR SALE: A STUDY OF THE DELAWARE CORPORATION LAW OF 1967
117 U.Pa.L.Rev. 861, 863–64, 866–70 (1969).[4]

The three groups responsible for the 1899 law are still active in shaping Delaware's corporation law. They are the corporation service companies, which have grown considerably since their inception in 1899; the legislature, which seems to have become more docile; and the Delaware bar, which consists of approximately 500 lawyers, about 425 of whom practice in Wilmington. Approximately twenty-five of these Wilmington lawyers comprise the full-time corporate bar. It is a very friendly bar, considered by outsiders to be quite competent in dealing with the Delaware corporation law, and headed by three firms—Morris, Nichols, Arsht & Tunnell, Richards, Layton & Finger, and Potter, Anderson & Corroon.

The 1963 statute calling for a revision of Delaware's corporation law empowered the Secretary of State, Elisha Dukes, to spend the appropriated money [Ed.—$25,000] "for consultants and assistance in such manner as will, in his discretion, most expeditiously accomplish" the revision. He decided to form the Delaware Corporation Law Revision Commission, made up of himself and nine others. * * *

Several decisions were made quickly. The first problem was whether to scrap the existing statute and start over again or simply to amend and revise the present one. * * * The Commission decided to preserve as much of the present wording as possible so as to keep the body of precedents that had been built up over the years. This is not, of course, an unsound decision for a legislative draftsman to make. Statutes should be written to make their meaning as clear as possible, and using phrases which have already been interpreted furthers this goal. But the decision not to scrap the existing statute may have been made with other considerations in mind. A wealth of judicial decisions helps Delaware attract corporations; to do away with this body of precedent could very well lessen Delaware's salability. Thus the "comprehensive revision" of an 1899 bill began by rejecting thorough change of what can only be termed a tortured statute. Delaware began its business by borrowing New Jersey's wording so as to insure settled judicial interpretation, and it was not about to tamper lightly with part of the formula for its success.

___

4. Copyright 1969 by the University of Pennsylvania Law Review.

For a similar reason, it was also decided that the revision should not follow the Model Act. The reason was stated simply by Mr. Jackman, President of the United States Corporation Company, who "emphasized that Delaware should not adopt the Model Act because we do not want to be a 'me too' state in view of the fact that in the past most of the other States had copied our laws and that we should be a leader not a follower." * * *

The new statute was not written as rapidly as had been planned. The ten-member Commission proved unwieldy, so Chief Justice Southerland split up assignments among the members. A drafting committee of three was formed—Corroon, Canby, and Arsht. Through late 1966 and early 1967 they met to draft the actual statute, usually meeting on Saturdays in Arsht's office. Their job was far from mechanical. They considered many things the entire Commission never did, and felt they had broad authority and full responsibility.[5] Although they rejected some of Folk's recommendations, and although he never attended any of their meetings, much of his wording was adopted *in toto,* a result which seems to frighten him.

Since the product being manufactured is a law, the legislature (remember the legislature?) is supposed to have something to do with it. But it is clear that this was not the case. Simply stated, the Commission never expected the legislature to do anything with this law except pass it. One member of the Commission referred to the legislature as "just a bunch of farmers." Corroon did attend a caucus of Democratic Senators, and Canby did attend a caucus of Republican Senators. But Corroon was out in fifteen minutes, Canby in three, and neither was asked any questions about the law. The legislature did have one concern (besides tax revenues)—jobs. While it makes little sense to have certificates of incorporation filed with the Secretary of State *and* with county Recorders, to eliminate the Recorders would mean putting people out of jobs and the legislature might not have accepted that. So at the fourth meeting of the Commission, we find that "[i]t was moved by Mr. Jackman and seconded by Judge Herrmann that recordation as presently practiced should be continued * * *." There is no evidence that the legislature had any other influence on the actual content of the law.

5. [By the Editor] Mr. Arsht later described this portion of the statutory development process as follows:

A drafting subcommittee, consisting of myself and Messrs. Canby and Corroon, assisted by three young lawyers from our respective law firms who had also been serving as law clerks for the Revision Committee, began the task of putting the Revision Committee's decisions into bill form. As soon as this project began, it became clear that much work remained to be done and that a satisfactory bill could not be drafted without making numerous substantive decisions that the full Committee had not made and reversing some that it had made. In making the necessary changes, the subcommittee looked again to the Folk Report, to the minutes of the Revision Committee and to other sources such as the Model Business Corporation Act for guidance.

After meeting each Saturday for the better part of a year, the subcommittee presented a draft bill to the full Revision Committee for its consideration. The Revision Committee unanimously approved the draft bill without change. Subsequently, the proposed bill was approved by the Bar Association and the legislature and became effective July 3, 1967.

S. Samuel Arsht, A History of Delaware Corporation Law, 1 Del.J.Corp.L. 1, 16 (1976). Compare Joel Seligman, A Brief History of Delaware's General Corporation Law of 1889, 1 Del.J.Corp.L. 249, 282 (1976):

Ultimately, the revisions to the Delaware General Corporation Law, the most influential business statute in the country, the closest thing we have to a national corporate law, were drafted in the law office of one S. Samuel Arsht.

The bill was passed unanimously by the legislature and became effective on July 3, 1967; amendments were worked through their "normal" course, the Delaware Bar Association's Committee on Corporation Law, and became effective on January 2, 1968. There were no official documents explaining the statute's provisions, no legislative hearings, and no publications by the Revision Commission. Folk's Report, Review of the Delaware Corporation Law, may not prove extremely helpful on key points and, in any event, it may be hard to find. The Commission originally made only one copy publicly available (in the New Castle County Law Library), but xerographic reproductions can now be bought from the Corporation Service Company for $25.00. Despite the fact that the Commission had about $15,000 left over, Secretary of State Dukes did not want to spend the money to reproduce the report. Thus, the participants are left free to write their own "legislative history," an invaluable opportunity for a lawyer. This can be done through writing books and articles "explaining" the law, or through argument in litigation.

It is difficult to believe that the process just described represents the way legislation should be drafted. State legislatures may not be noted for thoroughgoing consideration of proposed bills, but the Delaware legislature's lack of concern seems extraordinary. The legislature simply abdicated its responsibility to consider the merits of its corporation law. It made no attempt to go outside the Commission and determine whether the statute served that "public interest" a legislature is supposed to represent. It was content to leave its work entirely to an appointed commission. It was content to leave this commission free to do what it pleased; and it pleased to solicit the views only of corporate interests and then to write a statute without one official word to guide future interpretation.

Notes

(1) S. Samuel Arsht, A History of Delaware Corporation Law, 1 Del.J.Corp.L. 1, 17–18 (1976):

> The present position of Delaware's General Corporation Law as the most popular of such laws in the United States is attributable to many factors, some of which have their roots in the distant past. The authors of a number of recent articles critical of the General Corporation Law,[6] to the extent they have traced the history of corporation law in Delaware, have alluded to sinister motives and methods in its development. It is not the thesis of this article to rebut such allegations and the arguments for federal chartering, nor is it my purpose to deny that the motivation for change in Delaware's corporation laws over their 189–year history is unrelated to the interests of American business and industry. On the other hand, I do not believe that enough emphasis has been given to the positive aspects of the development of the Delaware law. * * *
>
> Following the enactment of technical amendments to the corporation law in 1968, the Revision Committee's work came to an end and the Delaware Bar Association's standing committee on the General Corporation Law resumed its traditional role as the initiator of amendments to the law. Although the

6. [By the Author] William L. Cary, A Proposed Federal Corporate Minimum Standards Act, 29 Bus.Law 1101 (1975); William L. Cary, Federalism and the Corporate Law: Reflections Upon Delaware, 83 Yale L.J. 663 (1974); Law for Sale: A Study of the Delaware Corporation Law of 1967, 117 U.Pa.L.Rev. 861 (1969).

Bar Association has had a standing committee on the General Corporation Law during my forty plus years at the bar, the Committee is now quite large when compared to its predecessors in the years prior to the 1967 revision. At present, the Committee includes twenty-three private practitioners from all three Delaware counties and inside counsel from two large Delaware-based corporations. In addition, representatives of the Corporation Department of the Secretary of State's office and of the corporation service companies regularly attend Committee meetings.

In discharging their responsibility to improve the corporation law, Committee members draw on their own experience as practitioners, on suggestions received by them from corporate attorneys throughout the United States and on experience gained as members of American Bar Association committees such as the Committee on Corporate Laws and the Committee on Securities Laws.

It has been the practice of the Committee since 1967 to seek amendments to the corporation law on a yearly basis.[7] Amendments proposed by the Committee are first approved by the Bar Association and then submitted to the legislature in bill form.[8] Within the Committee, suggested changes in the law are, in most cases, first raised by a letter from a Committee member to the Chairman. The Chairman then places the suggested change on the agenda for a forthcoming meeting. If the change is one of substance rather than a minor change in language and if the Committee does not disapprove the suggested change on initial consideration, the Chairman usually names a subcommittee to draft a suggested revision to the statute. On a major substantive change, the subcommittee will meet separately from the full Committee and work through numerous drafts before presenting its proposal to the full Committee.

(2) Joel Seligman, A Brief History of Delaware's General Corporation Law of 1899, 1 Del.J.Corp.L. 249, 282–83 (1976):

[The revised Delaware General Corporation Law] became effective on July 3, 1967. It was an immediate financial success. According to the January 12, 1969 *New York Times,*

Delaware began chartering new companies at a record-breaking clip after it revised and liberalized its corporation laws to meet modern needs. Before the revisions were made in July 1967, Delaware was signing up new corporations at an average of 300 a month. * * * [Delaware is now] chartering new corporations at a record rate of 800 a month. * * *

The article concluded with Secretary of State Dukes' statement. "The franchise tax will bring the state about $21 million in the fiscal year ending June 30."

---

7. [By the Author] Some members of the Committee have suggested that the yearly amendment process may detract from the perceived stability of the Delaware General Corporation Law.

8. [By the Author] Beginning with the proposed 1973 amendments to the General Corporation Law, the Committee prepared a brief commentary for distribution to the members of the Bar Association and, in turn, to the legislature. In 1973 several corporation service companies asked the Committee for permission to publish the commentary for distribution to the

corporate bar throughout the United States. The Committee granted those requests with the proviso that publication of the text of the commentary reflect that it is the product of the Committee on the General Corporation Law. Unlike the comments accompanying the Delaware version of the Uniform Commercial Code, the Committee's commentary is not official nor was it intended to be. Its purpose is to aid in the legislative process and not to function as a definitive guide to statutory construction.

That was just the beginning. By 1971 corporation franchise taxes and related corporate income represented $55.5 million out of $246 million in state revenue collections, approximately 23 percent of the total—the result of a stampede of the leading industrial corporations to Delaware. Of *Fortune* magazine's 1000 largest industrial corporations, 134 reincorporated or incorporated for the first time in Delaware in the years 1967–1974. This meant that by late 1974, Delaware was "home" for 448 of the 1,000 largest corporations—including 52 of the largest 100, and 251 out of the largest 500. These 448 corporations accounted for over 52 percent of the sales of the largest 1,000 manufacturers.

A 1974 Report to the Governor of Delaware further highlighted the special relationship between Delaware and the largest corporations. Although Delaware had chartered 76,000 corporations by June, 1974, franchise tax revenues received from the largest 556 corporations equaled 64 percent of all franchise tax revenues; revenues received from the largest 950 corporations equaled nearly 80 percent of the total.

(3) All this does not entirely explain Delaware's spectacular success in the incorporation business. Professor Seligman suggests that the advantage of Delaware lies "not [in] her statute alone, but rather [in] the manner in which her judiciary interprets it." Id. at 284. In reaching this conclusion Professor Seligman relies primarily on an earlier article by Professor William L. Cary, a former chairman of the SEC, who, after reviewing a number of Delaware decisions, concludes that "there is no public policy left in Delaware corporate law except the objective of raising revenue. * * * Consciously or unconsciously, fiduciary standards and standards of fairness generally have been relaxed. In general, the judicial decisions can best be reconciled on the basis of a desire to foster incorporation in Delaware." William L. Cary, Federalism and Corporate Law: Reflections Upon Delaware, 83 Yale L.J. 663, 670, 684 (1974). Professor Cary attributes this attitude to the relationship between the Delaware bench, bar, and state government:[9]

What is striking about the membership of the court in the last 23 years is that almost all the justices were drawn from the group responsible for the 1967 revision of the corporation law. In fact, two of them were members of the Commission. A majority of the justices practiced law in the firms which represent the important corporations registered in Delaware. Justices Southerland and Wolcott had been partners in a distinguished firm. Justice Tunnell eventually joined another, and Justice Herrmann was the senior partner of still another bearing his name. Three left the bench, two of them to return to leading firms in Delaware, and one to become Governor. With the exception of Justice Carey, who served from 1945 on the bench in various roles, all but two of the justices have been directly involved in major political positions in the state. The three chief justices have been chronologically (1) Attorney General, (2) Secretary of State and Governor, and (3) the Democratic candidate for Attorney General. Two other justices were Chairman of the State Planning Commission and attorney for the Delaware Senate. The whole process is reminiscent of musical chairs. In such a small state as Delaware, with a population of 548,000 and a bar of 733, of whom 423 are in private practice, we have in microcosm the ultimate example of the relationship between politics, the bar, and the judiciary. There is certainly nothing "wrong" or

9. Reprinted by permission of The Yale Law Journal Company and Fred B. Rothman & Company from *The Yale Law Journal*, Vol. 83, pp. 690–92.

surprising about these relationships. Yet it is clear that Delaware may be characterized as a tight little club in which the corporate bar cites unreported decisions before the courts in which they practice. Thus major participation in state politics and in the leading firms inevitably would align the Delaware judiciary solidly with Delaware legislative policy. Indeed, as outstanding members of the bar they may have contributed to its formulation before they became judges and at any rate might be disloyal to their state to pursue any other course.

This is harsh criticism and it is not surprising that defenders of the Delaware Corporation Act reacted sharply and with outrage. E.g. S. Samuel Arsht, Reply to Professor Cary, 31 Bus.Law. 1113 (1976):

> Professor Cary premises his advocacy of a Federal Corporate Minimum Standards Act upon the alleged deficiencies of state law, particularly focusing upon Delaware, its statutes, bench and bar. I submit that Professor Cary's analysis of the Delaware experience is biased, unscholarly and wholly unfair. If his articles had to measure up to the required standards of an SEC disclosure document, they would be found woefully deficient.

(4) Whatever the merits of Professor Cary's complaints about the "cozy" relationship between the Delaware judiciary, the Bar, and the legislature in the 1970s, it is clear that the Delaware judiciary is highly regarded today. Because of the importance of Delaware as the preferred state of incorporation for publicly held corporations, the Delaware Supreme Court today is the most powerful corporation court in the United States. It is respected for the quality of its opinions in the business area, and its decisions are often followed by courts in other states. The Delaware Chancery Court, the trial court in which most corporation issues are litigated, is a specialized business and corporation court that is the envy of other states.[10] This court sits without a jury and handles local equity matters as well as major commercial disputes. Because of the sophistication and experience of the Chancellor and the four Vice Chancellors on corporate matters, corporations often prefer to litigate issues in Delaware rather than elsewhere. The turnover of judges in Delaware is relatively slow. In the chapters that follow, a number of decisions by Delaware courts are included. The reader should reserve final judgment on the merits of Professor Cary's criticism until after reading these opinions, and particularly the opinions since 1974.

(5) Bayless Manning, State Competition: Panel Response, 8 Cardozo L.Rev. 779, 785–6 (1987):

> We, as practitioners, do not go to Delaware to incorporate and to litigate primarily because the law is "favorable" (whatever that may mean). We go to Delaware because there is a vast corpus of sophisticated law there and a lot of people in the right positions who know what it is all about.
>
> I happen to be particularly fond of the State of Idaho. I have a home and spend a good bit of time there. I am prepared to rise to the defense of that great state for a good many purposes. But even I would not argue that one should choose that jurisdiction for litigation of a complex question of corporation law. In the forum of Delaware, I may lose, I may win, I may have a bad day, or whatever. But when people from my law firm go to Delaware, or when

---

10. [By the Editor] The trend toward establishing specialized business courts "is in its inception but is gaining strength." Report of Ad Hoc Committee on Business Courts, Business Courts: Toward a More Efficient Judicia-ry, 52 Bus. Law. 947, 960 (1997). This report indicates that three states (New York, Illinois, and North Carolina) have established business courts since 1992, and that studies are underway in at least six additional states.

I talk on the phone to the Delaware Secretary of State's office, we are confident that we will encounter someone who already knows what a preemptive right is, and we will not have to start from zero.

Why, as a lawyer, am I inclined to recommend to a client that his new company be formed in Delaware? My answer is more grounded in that jurisdiction's unique human capital that in anything else. In Delaware, I will be dealing with pros. In many circumstances, speed of administrative and legal response will be important and in Delaware I will find that. And if one able Delaware corporation lawyer should be barred by a conflicting engagement from helping me, I know I will have available an array of other talented, experienced counsel to choose from.

Further, my Delaware counsel and I will have a wide ranging and sophisticated body of corporation law—a jurisprudence if you will—to bring to bear on almost any problem that will arise. No other jurisdiction can provide so much. And that is why Delaware is, in fact, national, and why its own gravitational pull tends to attract more companies each year and thereby further reinforce its preeminence.

(6) Ralph Winter, Government and the Corporation 9 (1978):

Rejecting full federal chartering as "politically unrealistic," Cary calls for federal minimum-standards legislation. He claims this legislation, designed to "raise" the standards of management conduct, would increase public confidence—and investment—in American corporations. This last claim, it is absolutely critical to note, is not that an overriding social goal is sacrificed by state law but that Delaware is preventing *private* parties from optimizing their *private* arrangements.

With all due respect to Cary and to the almost universal academic support for his position, it is implausible on its face. The plausible argument runs in exactly the opposite direction. (1) If Delaware permits corporate management to profit at the expense of shareholders and other states do not, then earnings of Delaware corporations must be less than earnings of comparable corporations chartered in other states; therefore, shares in the Delaware corporations must trade at lower prices. (2) Corporations with lower earnings will be at a disadvantage in raising debt or equity capital. (3) Corporations at a disadvantage in the capital market will be at a disadvantage in the product market, and their share price will decline, thereby increasing chances of a takeover that would replace management. To avoid this result, corporations must seek legal systems more attractive to capital. (4) States desiring corporate charters will thus try to provide legal systems that optimize the shareholder-corporation relation. * * *

(7) Roberta Romano, Competition for Corporate Charters and the Lesson of Takeover Statutes, 61 Fordham L.Rev. 843, 848–50 (1993):

Since the publication of the Cary and Winter articles, empirical studies have sought to arbitrate the debate over who benefits from state corporation codes by determining the economic impact of managerial discretion to choose among alternative corporation codes by changing a firm's incorporation state. They conclude that the choice benefits rather than harms shareholders. The conclusion rests on widely-accepted financial econometric techniques known as event studies, which examine whether particular information events—discrete public events introducing new information to financial markets, such as a firm's decision to reincorporate—produce a significant effect on a firms' stock prices.[11] If an information event is considered beneficial to shareholders (that is, if investors believe that it enhances the value of their equity investment), then stock prices will significantly increase upon the public announcement of the event. If an event is perceived as detrimental to shareholder wealth, then stock prices will significantly decline. Such stock price effects are typically referred to as abnormal returns. The posited relationships between changes in stock price and reincorporation announcements restate the Winter and Cary theses in testable event study form. The implication of Cary's thesis that shareholders are harmed by Delaware's code is that firms should experience a significant negative price effect when they announce a reincorporation in Delaware. Similarly, Winter's hypothesis predicts a significant positive effect.

There have been five event studies of reincorporations. While several have found significant positive price effects upon reincorporation in Delaware, no study found a negative stock price effect as Cary would have predicted. The data are therefore most consistent with Winter's hypothesis of the efficacy of competition.

Some advocates of national corporation laws question the usefulness of event studies. Melvin Eisenberg and Lucian Bebchuk contend that event studies do not indicate investors' evaluation of the new state's regime because of the possibility of confounding signals if a reincorporation announcement is accompanied by disclosure of a new corporate strategy. In such a situation, a positive stock price reaction may be the result of investors' assessment of the new strategy and not the value of the new statutory domicile. It is, however, improbable that such information could swamp an otherwise significantly negative stock price effect of a reincorporation. If this offsetting effect hypothesis is correct and reincorporation has a wealth-decreasing effect, we should observe a significant negative stock price effect for firms changing domicile to engage in activities that are perceived to favor managers over shareholders. The stock price effect is not, however, significantly different across firms reincorporating for different business purposes—that is, for those planning to undertake activities that commentators consider adverse to shareholder interests (fortifying takeover defensive tactics) and those which they do not criticize (implementing a mergers and acquisitions program or reducing taxes). Shareholders also must approve a reincorporation, and the SEC requires detailed disclosure of differences in legal regimes in proxy materials. It is not credible to contend that informed shareholders will approve a destination state whose regime is adverse to their interests. * * *

Bebchuk further questions whether event studies can ever resolve the state competition debate. He asserts that even if the findings of positive or insignificant stock price effects upon reincorporation are bolstered by further studies finding even stronger positive stock price effects, this will not arbitrate the Cary–Winter debate because there could always be some code provision that disadvantages shareholders but whose negative impact is netted out by greater positive price effects of other code provisions. However, it should be noted that Bebchuk's contention, while cast as a criticism of the empirical basis for supporting a federal system of state corporation laws, acknowledges that state competition is on the whole beneficial for shareholders because the effect of good provisions outweighs the bad. Far from shifting

---

11. [By the Author] The researcher examines whether the average residuals of a regression of observed stock price on predicted stock price are significantly different from zero.

the burden of proof from advocates of national regulation to advocates of state competition, this argument implies that state competition generally benefits shareholders. Thus, those who would promote Cary's position have the burden of demonstrating empirically which particular code provisions harm shareholders and why national legislation would be more likely to alleviate the problem.

For a fuller analysis of the role of Delaware in the corporation laws area, see Roberta Romano, The Genius of American Corporate Law (1993). Delaware's franchise tax supplies approximately fifteen percent of state governmental income. Professor Romano argues that this is an "intangible asset that precommits it not to renege on contracts with its corporate customers, for it renders the state equally vulnerable to breach. Delaware is thereby a hostage to its success in the chartering market." Id., at 38.

(8) Are you satisfied by the economists' analysis of the role of Delaware in the incorporation business? Are studies based on stock price changes an appropriate measure for evaluating the "race to the bottom" thesis? Are there social policies other than shareholder profit-maximization involved, and if so, how should they be weighed?

DOUGLAS M. BRANSON, COUNTERTRENDS IN CORPORATION LAW: MODEL BUSINESS CORPORATION ACT REVISION, BRITISH COMPANY LAW REFORM, AND PRINCIPLES OF CORPORATE GOVERNANCE AND STRUCTURE

68 Minn.L.Rev. 53, 62–63, 67–70 (1983).[12]

The proposed Revised Model Business Corporation Act (RMA)[13] has features which represent an improvement over prior MBCA versions. The proposed statute's organization alone is an improvement. Some of its substantive provision, as well, seem to provide workable, creative solutions, even in an absolute sense.

Even so, in order to evaluate the RMA, "you must," in Justice Holmes' words, "look at it as a bad man, who cares only for the material consequences * * * knowledge enables him to predict" and "not as a good one, who finds his reasons for conduct * * * in the vaguer sanctions of conscience."[14] The RMA's drafters predicate the overwhelming majority of their revisions on a need for yet more flexibility, and apparently find justification for those revisions in notions of good faith, fiduciary duty, and "the vaguer sanctions of conscience" in those to whom they would entrust that flexibility. * * *

[S]hareholders have never had complete protection against a squeeze or freeze-out by means of a share issuance. Fifteen years ago, however, the shareholders did have several statutory and common law shields, none of which afforded complete protection. In combination, though, the protection

12. Copyright (1983) by the Minnesota Law Review.

13. [By the Editor] Professor Branson was working from an intermediate version of the MBCA, now called the "Exposure Draft." His comments, however, are equally pertinent to the MBCA, as finally approved.

14. [By the Author] O.W. Holmes, *The Path of the Law,* in COLLECTED LEGAL PAPERS 171 (1920).

afforded would in most cases prevent management from achieving nefarious ends. Tomorrow under the RMA, or even today under the MBCA, all or most of these shareholder protections are gone. In addition, the RMA will give corporate management a proliferating choice of swords to use, although, perhaps, no one of them may be capable of striking a death blow to the minority. In combination, though, the RMA provisions give, and have as an avowed aim the bestowal of, an almost infinite range of choices for corporate management to use for good or for evil as they wish. * * *

Many other RMA provisions also purposefully eliminate all substantive or other control over corporate entities.[15] Some of these provisions have surface appeal. Others run flatly counter to well-developed state or federal policy.[16] * * *

All of this elimination is done in the name of flexibility. Repeatedly, the RMA official comments reason that this or that relaxation or elimination of a formerly required procedure or substantive command is required because "flexibility" is needed and "discretion" is necessary. Curiously, in their comments the RMA drafters use the passive voice. The question that arises is flexibility and discretion for whom. The answer is flexibility and discretion for corporate managements and, secondarily, for their counsel. At a minimum, the RMA could forthrightly use the active voice in telling legislators and opinion makers that it is management who purportedly needs additional flexibility.

The RMA is a lawyers' product. Members of the ABA Committee on Corporate Laws are corporate lawyers. When faced with a choice between substantive commands or "flexible" organizational guidelines, they consider the former but adopt the latter. They do so not because of any ulterior motive, but rather because they understandably believe the corporate bar to be comprised of persons of rectitude and ability. Naturally, such individuals would not allow the flexibility the statute grants to be used for mean or sharp dealing. Coincidentally, however, that flexibility also may make easier counsel's task of advising management, structuring a transaction, or authoring an opinion letter. Under older MBCA versions, attorneys sometimes found it difficult to defend the legality of a transaction because a substantive prohibition or command directly or indirectly impinged on the transaction. Yet the RMA drafters fail to heed Justice Holmes's admonition to approach and evaluate the proposed statute from the perspective of a "bad man." Undoubtedly, there exist some members of the corporate bar with only a modicum, or

15. [By the Author] See e.g., RMA §§ 2.03 (secretary of state or analogous official no longer required to ascertain upon filing if articles of incorporation conform to law), [6.02(a)] (directors may be granted blank check authority to determine relative rights and preferences of new issuances of preferred shares), 6.40(d) (directors have power to revalue corporate assets for purposes of declaring a dividend or making other distributions), 11.03(g) (in surviving corporation, no shareholder vote required on merger if merger will not cause more than 20% increase in shares outstanding).

16. [By the Author] See e.g., RMA § 7.28 (elimination of cumulative voting). * * * Seven

state constitutions mandate cumulative voting. Ten other states statutorily mandate cumulative voting in all corporations. See § 3.02[16] comment (permitting corporate "contributions * * * that may not be charitable such as for political purposes or to influence elections"). Federal law, of course, makes criminal direct corporate contributions to political campaigns. See 2 U.S.C.A. § 441b, *construed in* Cort v. Ash, 422 U.S. 66, 95 S.Ct. 2080, 45 L.Ed.2d 26 (1975). Indirect corporate support for elections, such as through political action committees, is also currently a matter of some debate.

less, of integrity. There are also corporate managers whom even the "vaguer sanctions of conscience" do not affect. * * *

In truth, though, the seemingly infinite flexibility the RMA will grant is not infinite. Corporate directors have independent fiduciary duties of care and loyalty. Time and again the RMA official comments, and occasionally the proposed statute itself, remind the reader that exercise of this flexibility remains subject to fiduciary duty. * * *

Considered together with the ever-escalating degree of flexibility the statute grants, all of this RMA effort to remind of fiduciary duty * * * [makes it appear] that the entire edifice of corporate law has begun to totter on the head of a pin. Every issue comes directly or indirectly to fiduciary duty. Moreover, that fiduciary duty is not the strict common law variety which even at its best produced inconsistent results. Instead, it has become a much weakened statutory variety designed, in the main, as a safe harbor into which corporate managements may sail.

ROBERT W. HAMILTON, REFLECTIONS OF A REPORTER

63 Tex.L.Rev. 1455, 1455, 1458–59, 1464–69 (1986).[17]

For the last five years I have served as the Reporter for the project that led to the development of the [1984 Model Business Corporation Act]. This new Act * * * is a model statute designed for use by states in revising and updating their corporation statutes. It is intended to be a "convenient guide for revision of state business corporation statutes, reflecting current views as to the appropriate accommodation of the various commercial and social interests involved in modern business corporations."[18] The initial reception of the new Act has been extremely favorable. * * *

The Committee on Corporate Laws of the ABA's Section on Corporation, Banking, and Business Law has complete responsibility for developing and updating the MBCA. This Committee is unusual in several respects. Unlike practically all other ABA standing committees, its membership is closed and is currently limited to twenty-five persons; membership is by invitation only. Furthermore, the Committee on Corporate Laws has authority to make final decisions with reference to the MBCA solely on its own motion without prior approval from the Section on Corporation, Banking, and Business Law or the ABA's Board of Governors. * * *

The Committee on Corporate Laws is widely viewed as one of the most prestigious committees in the Section on Corporation, Banking, and Business Law: no attempt has been made, however, to require it to be representative of all the various constituencies that might have an interest in state corporation laws. In the early years of the Committee's history, it was considerably less representative than now: until the early 1970s, the members were almost exclusively lawyers from a handful of big cities and from major firms whose clients were predominantly large, publicly held corporations. It was, in short,

17. Published originally in 63 Texas Law Review 1455, 1455–70 (1985). Copyright 1985 by the Texas Law Review Association. Reprinted by permission.

18. [By the Author] Revised Model Business Corp. Act (1985).

management-and defense-oriented. Members, furthermore, were appointed for indefinite terms. As a result, the Committee experienced relatively little turnover in membership. As late as 1974, the Committee was described as follows: "[M]anagement lawyers apparently filled every one of the Committee's seats during the twenty-year period ending in 1969; filled all but one seat from 1969 through 1972, and still fill virtually all the Committee's seats even today."[19]

While the present Committee continues to have a strong predominance of management-oriented attorneys, diversification has occurred. Members serve for six-year terms and are rotated off the Committee at the conclusion of their terms. One or two attorneys who principally represent plaintiffs in derivative litigation and two or three law professors regularly serve on the Committee.[20] Diversity of viewpoints has also been enhanced by appointing attorneys from smaller cities and in a more geographically diverse manner. However, even with these changes, corporate attorneys from large firms continue their numerical dominance of the Committee on Corporate Laws membership.
* * *

Professor Eisenberg's 1974 article, the first external examination of the procedures followed by the Committee on Corporate Laws in revising the MBCA, made serious and fundamental criticisms. The Committee did not regularly follow basic notice-and-comment procedures, which prevented interested persons from commenting upon proposed changes. Further, even when notice of proposed changes was given, the Committee appeared to exhibit little interest in obtaining public comment or willingness to consider carefully comments that were made.[21] Promptly following that critical analysis, however, the Committee made procedural changes and since then has consistently published proposed changes to the Model Act in *The Business Lawyer* with requests for comment. Final changes are promulgated only after consideration of all comments received. * * *

There is a widespread belief that an academic Reporter has broad power in major revision or codification projects to determine what is included and what is excluded. The committee or governing authority has ultimate power, but, in reality, the real power rests in the capable hands of the Reporter. Whatever may be the case in other projects, that is an inaccurate perception of the relation I had with the Committee on Corporate Laws. That Committee was fully in charge of all decisions. Preliminary drafts were prepared by me and screened by subcommittees that sometimes did not reflect the sentiment of the full Committee; statutory provisions or official comments, after being hammered out in extended (and sometimes excruciating) debate, were includ-

19. [By the Author] Melvin A. Eisenberg, *The Model Business Corporation Act and the Model Business Corporation Act Annotated*, 29 Bus.Law. 1407, 1410 (1974).

20. [By the Author] It should be noted that I was invited to join the Committee in 1977 and served until 1983. Since then my only association with the Committee has been in my capacity as Reporter for the [1984 MBCA].

21. [By the Author] Professor Eisenberg stated:

[T]he severe imbalance in the Committee's composition has been compounded, over the years, by the Committee's failure to adopt adequate procedures for circulating draft provisions among relevant sectors of the profession for comment. The values of such circulation hardly need explication and the procedure is so common in projects of this kind that one would think it routine. Yet until recently the Committee failed to do anything of the sort.

Id.

ed only with the express and considered judgment of the Committee. The [MBCA] is the product of the Committee, and not of my own views.

There were several reasons for the dominance of the Committee in this project. For one thing, the Committee participants were very capable. Each was a successful practitioner with many years of experience in the best corporate practice; the members are accustomed to dealing squarely with major transactions and difficult issues. They were not deferential, to say the least, to the views of a mere academic on issues they have been dealing with for years. Second, most Committee members welcomed the opportunity to put aside the parochial interests of their clients and develop the "best" principles.[22] Discussions were spirited, the level of interest was high, and the willingness to spend time away from the meeting room to review drafts, prepare memoranda, or write substitute sections was remarkable. No one will ever know the number of uncompensated hours spent on this project by these leading attorneys, but the total must run into the tens of thousands of hours. In short, the Committee controlled the product because its members were intelligent, they had broad practical experience, they were very interested in the project, and they worked hard. * * *

Because most Committee members had backgrounds in large-firm corporate practice, one might be tempted to dismiss the [MBCA] as an exercise in improving "flexibility" so that corporate management can do what it wishes as efficiently as possible.[23] I believe this is a misleading oversimplification. The Committee members generally *were* trying to develop the "best" statute they could in a jurisprudential sense. They were trying to meld principles of fairness and equity with a system of management that permitted efficiency in operation.

In approaching this task, two factors strongly influenced the Committee members' perspectives on the issues that arose. The first was that they had a wealth of practical experience which no academic could reasonably hope to match. As a result, issues were not approached as theoretical or logical questions but as real-life problems. The second was the geographic diversity of the Committee members. This diversity allowed attorneys from more than ten states to bring their experience to bear on statutory issues that arose. Furthermore, their experience involved practical application of various corporate statutes to numerous diverse situations. From the vantage of these perspectives, a provision superficially desirable in one setting could be seen as increasing the complexity of transactions in a variety of other situations. The weighing of these advantages and disadvantages obviously involved practical questions about the frequency of events. After listening to and participating in this process, on a number of occasions I was persuaded that provisions I had openly criticized in class and in published writing had more support in

---

22. [By the Author] This was probably not uniformly true: In a few instances, I sensed that positions taken at meetings or in memoranda might have been influenced by the interests of clients or, in the case of corporate general counsels, by their employers. These positions generally did not survive the review process that led to the final statute.

23. [By the Author] Indeed, one early assessment of the Exposure Draft takes precisely this position. Branson, Countertrends in Corporation Law: Model Business Corporation Act Revision, British Company Law Reform, and Principles of Corporate Governance and Structure, 68 Minn.L.Rev. 53 (1983). * * *

fact than I had previously supposed.[24] * * *

In drafting a new corporate statute it is necessary to determine what goals the statute is designed to achieve. Traditionally, the watchwords of the Model Act have been "flexibility" and "modernization." From this perspective, corporation statutes should be designed to assure efficiency and economy of management and to avoid unnecessary costs. In contrast, some academics have criticized most modern corporation statutes on the ground that they are too "permissive"—that they do not provide adequate protection for interests other than incumbent corporate management. This view would make the basic goal of corporation statutes the "protection of shareholders" or "strong" regulatory goals.[25]

Economists have developed quite a different theory of state corporation statutes.[26] According to them, the purpose of a corporation statute is to serve as a substitute for private contract * * *. The economist's approach toward corporation statutes is certainly not the theory on which the [MBCA] was drafted. This theory was never expressly considered or explored by the Committee on Corporate Laws during the drafting process. Further, I suspect that most practicing attorneys would not accept the underlying premise of

24. [By the Author] A good example of this is the provision in most indemnification statutes that a director is entitled to indemnification as a matter of right if he or she "is successful on the merits *or otherwise*." The "or otherwise" language, from an academic viewpoint, is objectionable because it may require indemnification of a director who has a valid procedural defense—for example, that the statute of limitations has run—even though his conduct concededly violates every conceivable duty that directors or officers owe to a corporation. Accepting this reasoning, the California statute does not contain the "or otherwise" phrase. Cal.Corp.Code § 317(d) (West Supp. 1985). When revisions to the indemnification statutes were being considered in 1980, I unsuccessfully urged the committee to follow the California approach on the grounds that the statute should not condone indemnification that violates basic concepts of public policy. The argument against its elimination was a very practical one: If a director has a valid procedural defense, he or she should not be required to go through the expense of preparing for what was essentially a second trial in order to establish his or her right to indemnification. The implicit premise was that the cost of all such second proceedings exceeds the injuries suffered by corporations when a procedural defense shields improper conduct. It was also argued that the cost of the second proceeding might adversely affect the litigation decision of a defendant with a valid procedural defense and a plausible substantive defense. While I do not agree that these arguments carry the day, I believe the issue is a much closer one than I originally thought.

25. [By the Author] There are many provisions in modern corporation statutes that arguably fail to provide adequate protection to minority interests in unregistered corporations. As Reporter, I raised many of these issues, among them the modest proposal to extend minimal proxy disclosure requirements to unregistered corporations to cover, for instance, recommendations on issues management knows will arise at an annual meeting. This suggestion and other similar ones were rejected in large part because the Model Act had never contained analogous provisions, the need for them had not been demonstrated, and most states had not seen fit to adopt them. The response to suggestions such as these was sometimes sympathetic ("We will study that idea further") but more often negative ("In my experience, cumulative voting is almost always a nuisance and usually has no effect on what happens"). Sometimes suggestions such as these were rejected on the ground of precedent ("We talked about that several years ago [i.e. before I had joined the committee] and there was no interest in including such provisions"). However, given the history of the Committee, it is possible that some of these suggestions may be considered further at a later date. On the other hand, in order not to give a misleading impression, many new suggestions I made on various issues were accepted. They appear, for example, in relaxation of involuntary dissolution requirements for deadlocked corporations, for liability for preincorporation transactions, and for requiring shareholders' lists to be available before meetings of shareholders. In these instances, support seemed to turn on whether Committee members had experienced situations where such provisions would have been useful.

26. [By the Author] R. Winter, Government and the Corporation (1978); Fischel, The Corporate Governance Movement, 35 Vand. L.Rev. 1259 (1982).

this argument that corporations are purely contractual in nature. Contract-type arguments were raised by Committee members in a number of contexts, * * * [b]ut all members appeared to recognize that although corporation law obviously does have contractual aspects, some regulation was necessary. The Committee generally accepted, for example, that some actions authorized by articles of incorporation or other corporate documents can and should be subject to judicial invalidation. The powers and duties of corporate officers and directors are only partially contractual, and some duties may not be contracted away by simple agreement. * * *

Given a regulatory premise for corporation statutes, opinions will differ about whether the [MBCA] pursues "flexibility" and "modernization" too aggressively, at the cost of "shareholder protection." My own view is that the new Act strikes a plausible balance between the two goals, though I personally disagree with some of the choices made by the Committee.

The advantages of many traditional "shareholder protection" devices urged by proponents of a regulatory statute are more apparent than real. The devices that might be cited as falling within this category include cumulative voting, preemptive rights, shareholder approval of certain transactions, and many traditional restrictions on the issuance of shares, such as the prohibition against issuing shares for promissory notes or future services. The protection afforded by these traditional "shareholder protection" devices is illusory because they do not prevent harmful transactions if the corporation is willing to structure the transaction in a manner that circumvents the statute. To dismiss such provisions as harmless and simply view them as ineffective regulatory devices however, would be a mistake: they have a real capacity for harm because a statute may, by containing such provisions, create the impression that it affords greater protection than really exists. * * *

TRITON ENERGY CORPORATION PROXY STATEMENT
April 3, 1995.

PROPOSAL NO. 2 REINCORPORATION IN DELAWARE
BACKGROUND

Triton Energy Corporation (the 'Company' or 'Triton Texas') was incorporated under the laws of the State of Texas in 1962. The Company believes that it would be in the best interests of the Company's shareholders for the Company to become incorporated under the laws of the State of Delaware.

At the Annual Meeting, shareholders will be asked to approve a change in the state of incorporation of the Company by adopting and approving the Merger Agreement in the form of Appendix A to this Proxy Statement. After the shareholders have approved the proposed Merger Agreement, Triton Texas will be merged (the 'Reincorporation') into a wholly owned Delaware subsidiary ('Triton Delaware'), which has been organized for that purpose. The Board of Directors is recommending that shareholders approve the proposed Merger Agreement and Reincorporation of the Company from Texas to Delaware. * * * The Certificate of Incorporation and Bylaws of Triton Delaware are substantially identical to the Articles of Incorporation and Bylaws of Triton Texas. Particularly, the provisions of the Certificate of Incorporation of Triton Delaware relating to the authorized number and classes of stock and the characteristics thereof and the management of the affairs of the Company are substantially identical to the corresponding provisions currently contained in the Articles of Incorporation of Triton Texas.

REASONS FOR CHANGE IN THE STATE OF INCORPORATION

As part of the Company's strategy to focus on its international oil and gas exploration business, the implementation of which to date has resulted in a substantial majority of the Company's assets being located outside the United States, management is continually evaluating the Company's corporate structure. The Company proposes to reincorporate as a Delaware corporation for several reasons. First, the General Corporation Law of the State of Delaware (the 'DGCL') is generally recognized as one of the most comprehensive and progressive of the state corporation statutes. Accordingly, because, in the opinion of the Board and management of the Company, the DGCL addresses matters of corporate concern more thoroughly than does the Texas Business Corporation Act (the 'TBCA') and is more reflective of current trends and developments in the business community than is the TBCA, by reincorporating as a Delaware corporation, the Company will be better suited to take advantage of business opportunities as they arise and to provide for changing business needs. Second, there exists a more substantial body of case law construing the DGCL concerning corporate matters, such as the governance of a corporation's internal affairs and its relationships and contacts with others, than is found construing the TBCA. This substantial body of case law contributes to greater predictability under the DGCL and reduces uncertainties and risks commonly associated with resolving corporate matters. See 'Certain Differences Between the Corporation Statutes of Texas and Delaware.' In making its recommendation, the Board of Directors considered a number of jurisdictions in which to reincorporate, including a number of offshore jurisdictions. Although the Company may give further consideration to an offshore migration, the Company has not yet concluded, and may not conclude, that an offshore migration would be advisable. * * *

CONVERSION OF SHARES

At the effective date of the Reincorporation (the 'Effective Date'), (i) each outstanding share of the Company's Common Stock, par value $1.00 per share, will be converted on a one-for-one basis into a share of common stock, par value $1.00 per share, of Triton Delaware and (ii) each outstanding share of the Company's 5% Convertible Preferred Stock, no par value, will be converted on a one-for-one basis into a share of 5% Convertible Preferred Stock, no par value, of Triton Delaware. Such conversion of shares will not result in any change in the present ownership of shares of stock of the Company. Triton Texas stock certificates outstanding will automatically be deemed to represent the same number of Triton Delaware shares as represented by the Triton Texas certificates prior to the Reincorporation. * * * Following the Reincorporation, previously outstanding Triton Texas stock certificates may be delivered in effecting sales, through a broker or otherwise, of shares of Triton Delaware. The Triton Delaware Common Stock is expected to be listed on the NYSE, as a successor to the Triton Texas stock. * * *

NO CHANGE IN BUSINESS PLAN, MANAGEMENT, ASSETS, LIABILITIES, NET WORTH OR CAPITALIZATION

The proposed Reincorporation will not result in any change in the business, management, assets, liabilities, net worth or capitalization of the

Company. Upon completion of the Reincorporation, the name of the Company will continue to be Triton Energy Corporation * * *.

Company Employee Benefit Plans

The Company's employee benefit plans will not be changed in any material respect by the Reincorporation. Each option and Debenture exercisable for or convertible into the Company's Common Stock outstanding immediately prior to the Reincorporation will be automatically adjusted so that such options and Debentures will become exercisable for or convertible into the same number of shares of Triton Delaware Common Stock upon the same terms and conditions as in effect immediately prior to the Effective Date. * * *

Certain Differences Between the Corporation Statutes of Texas and Delaware

After the Reincorporation, the shareholders of the Company, a Texas corporation, will become shareholders of Triton Delaware, a Delaware corporation. Consequently, because of differences between the TBCA and the DGCL, rights of shareholders will be changed in certain respects. Certain changes are summarized below:

Required Vote for Certain Transactions—shareholder Approval of Business Combinations

Under the TBCA, a merger or consolidation, a sale, lease, exchange or other disposition of all or substantially all of the property of the corporation (a 'Disposition') not in the usual and regular course of the corporation's business, or a dissolution of the corporation, must be approved by at least two-thirds of the shares entitled to vote thereon, unless the charter requires the vote of a different number of shares. If the holders of any class of shares are entitled to vote as a class thereon, such a transaction must be approved by two-thirds of the outstanding shares of such class and at least two-thirds of the outstanding shares otherwise entitled to vote thereon.

Under the DGCL, such transactions are required to be approved by the holders of a majority of the shares entitled to vote thereon unless the charter provides otherwise. In addition, under the DGCL, class voting rights exist with respect to amendments to the charter that adversely affect the terms of the shares of a class. * * * Such class voting rights do not exist as to other extraordinary matters, unless the charter provides otherwise; the Certificate of Incorporation of Triton Delaware does not provide otherwise. * * *

The Board of Directors believes that it is in the best interests of the Company and its shareholders to change the Company's state of incorporation from Delaware to California (the 'Reincorporation'), and therefore the Board of Directors has unanimously approved the Reincorporation. * * *

Notes

(1) Demetrios G. Kozyris, Is Delaware Still a Haven for Incorporation? 20 Del.J.Corp.L. 965, 1010 (1995) states, without supporting authority, that over eighty percent of the corporations seeking to reincorporate chose Delaware as their new corporate domicile. Of course, some corporations do the reverse. In one example of a reincorporation from Delaware to another state, the proxy statement sets forth the following "Principal Reasons for the Reincorporation:"

The decision by the Company to [originally] incorporate in Delaware, despite the fact that the Company's principal executive offices were located in California, was made at a time when Delaware corporate law contained several benefits not then provided under California corporate law. In recent years, however, California law has been modified such that many of these benefits are now provided to California corporations. In particular, Delaware, to a larger extent than California, authorized the limitation of liability of corporate directors in situations not involving personal gain, dishonesty or other wrongful acts. In addition, Delaware law authorized broader indemnification for directors and officers than did California. In recent years, California's legislature has adopted provisions regarding limitation of directors' liability and indemnification of corporate officers and directors similar to those previously adopted by the Delaware legislature. Consequently, one of the principal reasons for being incorporated in Delaware is no longer applicable. Additionally, Delaware law contained certain provisions regarding control of the Company, largely absent from California law, that made it more difficult for an individual to undertake a hostile takeover of the Company at the expense of its other shareholders, such as the right to establish a classified board of directors with staggered terms of office and to permit the removal of directors only for cause. The California legislature has in recent years adopted some of these provisions. Thus, another principal reason for being incorporated in Delaware is no longer as compelling. Whereas the major benefits of being a Delaware corporation vis-à-vis being a California corporation have to a large extent disappeared, certain drawbacks of being a Delaware corporation have appeared. Principally, under Delaware's system of taxation, certain franchise taxes are assessed against the Company based on the number of shares authorized. This formula of taxation has resulted in increased tax costs to the Company. For the year ended December 31, 1994, the Company paid Delaware franchise taxes totaling approximately $50,000. On the other hand, the tax imposed on California corporations by virtue of being incorporated in California is only $800 per year. Thus, had the Company been incorporated in California in 1994, it would have paid approximately $50,000 less in taxes. * * *

Proxy Statement, Bell Industries, Inc., March 25, 1995, at 58–61.

(2) The importance of the law of the state of incorporation (in addition to such mundane matters as differences in franchise taxes) is greatly enhanced by the so-called "internal affairs rule," which provides that foreign courts will apply the law of the state of incorporation to issues relating to the internal affairs of a foreign corporation. Consult MBCA § 15.05(c); Restatement of Conflict of Laws (2d) § 302. See generally Phaedon J. Kozyris, Corporate Wars and Choice of Law, 1985 Duke L.J. 1; Deborah DeMott, Perspectives on Choice of Law for Corporate Internal Affairs, 48 Law & Contemp.Probs. 161 (Summer 1985).

(3) California is the principal state that has sought to apply specific provisions of its corporation statutes to corporations formed in other states but whose principal business activities are in California. West's Ann.Cal.Corp.Code § 2115 requires corporations with "specified minimum contacts" in California to comply with designated provisions of the California statute: among others, sections dealing with cumulative voting, limitations on distributions, inspection rights of shareholders, and dissenters' rights. The section is not applicable to corporations with shares listed on national securities exchanges or NASDAQ. The constitutionality of this approach has not been definitively resolved. Wilson v. Louisiana–Pacific Resources, Inc., 138 Cal.App.3d 216, 187 Cal.Rptr. 852 (1982) upheld the

imposition of the California cumulative voting provisions upon a Utah corporation that was subject to § 2115; the California shareholders' inspection statute was applied to a foreign corporation in Valtz v. Penta Inv. Corp., 139 Cal.App.3d 803, 188 Cal.Rptr. 922 (1983). But see Arden–Mayfair, Inc. v. Louart Corp., 385 A.2d 3 (Del.Ch.1978), holding the California statute inapplicable under "generally recognized choice of law principles" and discussing an unreported California lower court decision holding § 2115 unconstitutional. For a further discussion of litigation with respect to § 2115 and similar statutes, see Norwood P. Beveridge Jr., The Internal Affairs Doctrine: The Proper Law of a Corporation, 44 Bus. Law 693, 702–09 (1989).

BAYLESS MANNING, THE SHAREHOLDER'S APPRAISAL REMEDY: AN ESSAY FOR FRANK COKER

72 Yale L.J. 223, 245 n. 37 (1962).[27]

One result of this break-through is that corporation law, as a field of intellectual effort, is dead in the United States. When American law ceased to take the "corporation" seriously, the entire body of law that had been built upon that intellectual construct slowly perforated and rotted away. We have nothing left but our great empty corporation statutes—towering skyscrapers of rusted girders, internally welded together and containing nothing but wind. But that is a broader thesis best saved for another day.

Those of us in academic life who have specialized in corporation law face technological unemployment, or at least substantial retooling. There is still a good bit of work to be done to persuade someone to give a decent burial to the shivering skeletons. And there will be plenty of work overseas for a long time to come, for in Latin America, and to a lesser extent on the Continent, the "corporation" yet thrives and breeds as it did in this country eighty years ago.

Notes

(1) In contrast with Manning's gloomy assessment, consider Melvin A. Eisenberg, The Modernization of Corporate Law: An Essay for Bill Cary, 37 U. Miami L.Rev. 187, 209–10 (1983):*

Within the last ten years or so, there has been a remarkable amount of ferment in the area of corporate law. For the moment, the American Law Institute's *Principles of Corporate Governance: Analysis and Recommendations* is at center stage, but the ferment precedes that project. * * * This ferment was precipitated in large part by several developments in the mid–1970s. One was the general reexamination of our institutions that followed in the wake of Watergate. An element of Watergate was the revelation that some of our largest corporations had been engaged in widespread violation of domestic law, and some others had paid bribes to persons at the highest levels of foreign governments and thereby recklessly endangered our national security by putting at risk the political stability of our closest allies. In the short

27. Reprinted by permission of The Yale Law Journal Company and Fred B. Rothman & Company from *The Yale Law Journal*, Vol. 72, p. 245.

* Reprinted from the *University of Miami Law Review,* 51 U.Miami L. Rev. 579 (1997), which holds copyright on this article.

term, these disclosures led to the Foreign Corrupt Practices Act of 1977.[28] In the long term, they needlessly shook the public's confidence in one of the pillars of legitimacy of the American corporate system—the premise (which I regard as correct) that placing control of the factors of production and distribution in the hands of privately appointed managers maximizes our national wealth without entailing substantial nonfinancial costs.

(2) The Corporate Governance Project referred to by Professor Eisenberg was finally completed in 1992 and published in final form in early 1994. The American Law Institute, Principles of Corporate Governance: Analysis and Recommendations. Professor Eisenberg served as chief reporter for this project during most of its development. The project was awash in controversy throughout its development, and its influence on the long term development of corporation law is still unclear. As of the Summer of 1997 it had been cited only 29 times by state appellate courts and 13 times by Federal appellate courts. For discussions, see, e.g. A Symposium on the ALI Corporate Governance Project, 37 Miami L.Rev. 169, 169–349 (1983); American Law Institute's Corporate Governance Project, 52 Geo. Wash. L.Rev. 495, 495–871 (1984); Symposium on Corporate Governance, 8 Cardozo L.Rev. 657, 657–839 (1987); Symposium: The American Law Institute's Principles of Corporate Governance, 61 Geo.Wash.L.Rev. 871 (1993); Carol B. Swanson, Juggling Shareholder Rights and Strike Suits in Derivative Litigation: The ALI Drops the Ball, 77 Minn. L.Rev. 1339 (1993); Charles Hansen, A Guide to the ALI Corporate Governance Project (1995). Consideration of the Corporate Governance Project within the ALI involved an apparently unprecedented amount of lobbying-type activities by members from firms representing corporate management, a large number of close votes at the plenary session, and extensive consideration and reconsideration of many provisions.

One active participant in the ALI debates describes the controversy as follows:

In the field of corporate governance, the economic and political interests concerned were not, of course, as visible or sensitive as they would be in a project dealing with the regulation of banks, unions, or farmers. But interests that would be affected by the Project existed and they soon manifested themselves in the floor debate and elsewhere—some from the quarter of the plaintiffs' bar and others from the quarter of the organized executives of large corporations.

These manifestations of interest apparently came as a complete surprise to some at the ALI. Senior figures in the ALI were incensed, even outraged, that the corporate community displayed a sensitive concern with the course of the Project. Some in the ALI saw this development as a first-time defiling invasion of crass economic interests into a temple of debate in search of the truth. But it is hard to understand what else could have been expected, given (i) the subject matter of the Project and (ii) the new pro-active role assumed by the Reporters.[29]

At the same time, one must wonder at the quality of the tactical, negotiatory, and legal advice given to the interested corporate executive community that

28. [By the Author] Pub.L. No. 95–213, 91 Stat. 1494 (codified at 15 U.S.C.A. §§ 78a note, 78m, 78dd–1, 78dd–2, 78ff).

29. [By the Author] One wonders what the response of judges, law professors, and law practitioners would be if the Chamber of Commerce were to organize a project the objective of which is for an assembly of executives, managers, and business school professors to proclaim how courts, law schools, and law firms should be run and the penalties that will attach to non-compliance with the Chamber's proclamation.

led it to choose to express its understandable concerns in a hobnailed confrontational style within and outside the ALI forum—a style that was certain to produce not course-correction, but outrage on the part of the ALI.

Bayless Manning, Principles of Corporate Governance: One Viewer's Perspective on the ALI Project, 48 Bus. Law. 1319, 1325 (1993).[30] The ABA appointed an ad hoc committee to oversee and attempt to influence the course of the Project. This committee, known as CORPRO ended up with a unique relationship within the ALI. "[It] became more deeply involved in the drafting of the Project than the Advisers and Consultants to the Project who were appointed by the ALI. Its members recognized that, if the Project were to express the thoughts of the ALI as to what the law should be, their thoughts should be communicated to and considered by the Reporters." Elliott Goldstein, CORPRO: A Committee That Became an Institution, 48 Bus. Law. 1333, 1335 (1993). See also Rita H. Jensen, Navigating Turbulent Waters at ALI, Nat'l L.J., Aug. 9, 1993, at 1. The headline on the continuation of this article is "Business Twisted Arms In ALI Conflict Over Corporate Governance." However, the final conclusion of the article is that "the score is about six all."

(3) For a variety of different views and perspectives on this epochal clash within the American Law Institute (which ultimately led to a change in the rules of Institute requiring members to disclose their financial interest in the positions they were taking), see Symposium on Corporate Governance, 48 Bus. Law. 1267, 1267–1483 (1993).

(4) The ferment in corporation law noted by Professor Eisenberg has continued unabated since the early 1980s. A variety of publicly discussed and highly controversial issues has kept corporation law at center stage. Many of these issues were directly involved in the debates over the Corporate Governance Project. These issues include:

(a) The takeover movement that started in the 1970s but reached an apogee during the 1980s, declined to practically zero in the early 1990s, and then rose to new heights in the mid–1990s. See Chapter 14, infra. The takeover movement raises major corporate governance issues in several areas. For example, should the proper goal of the board of directors of a corporation be solely to maximize the financial wealth of the corporation's shareholders? May management appropriately consider the interests of other constituencies, such as employees, communities in which plants are located, and so forth? See Chapter 9, Section A. Should courts review changes in bylaws or financial structure that appear to have the principal purpose of entrenching management and making third party takeovers impractical, and, if so, what standards should courts apply?

(b) Articulation of the duty of care of directors of publicly held corporations, and the attendant "business judgment rule" which modifies this duty. See chapter 10, infra.

(c) The development of litigation committees. This topic is also discussed in Chapter 10, infra. Litigation committees raise sharply the issue of the scope of judicial review of business decisions with respect to shareholder-instituted litigation and the duties owed by outside directors to the corporation and to shareholders.

(d) Executive compensation. The American economy entered a recessionary period in the late 1980s leading to layoffs, salary and wage reductions, closing of

---

plants, and unprecedented losses by many well-known publicly held corporations. Yet at the same time, many of these corporations granted their top executives significant increases in compensation. In the 1990s, "incentive compensation" became the rage, and as stock prices rose to new highs, compensation levels for senior executives correspondingly rose to unprecedented levels. In a number of instances, executives received incentive stock options that led to aggregate compensation in a single year of amounts that were widely viewed as astronomical—tens of millions of dollars in many cases, and hundreds of millions of dollars in a few. In one widely publicized incident, Michael Eisner, the CEO of Disney, received a ten year contract at a base pay of $750,000 per year plus new stock options that had a then current value of $195 million. This was on top of outstanding stock options previously granted that had a then current market value of $358 million. Consult Ronald Grover, At Disney, Grumpy Isn't Just a Dwarf, Business Week, February 24, 1997, at 39. The primary focus of this article was on the fact that Michael Ovitz, the former president of Walt Disney, had received a $94.5 million severance payment from Walt Disney after working at Disney for only about one year. The size of the severance payment drew protests at Walt Disney's annual meeting, a significant number of shareholders withheld their votes in favor of directors, and subsequently became the subject of a law suit. See Chapter 11, infra.

(5) The emphasis on *state* corporation law in this Chapter should not be misinterpreted. A significant portion of the modern law of corporations is federal in origin. There is a significant amount of federal regulation based primarily on two New Deal era statutes, the Securities Act of 1933 and the Securities Exchange Act of 1934. In a sense, of course, these statutes were originally a response to the perceived inadequacy of state regulation of corporations in the period before the Great Depression, but they did not create a pervasive scheme of federal regulation. The relationship between federal and state law has not been stable.

(a) During the 1960s and early 1970s there was a trend toward the gradual expansion of federal law at the expense of state law under these two statutes, largely based on expansive construction of antifraud concepts in the 1934 Act and Rule 10b–5 promulgated thereunder, but this trend had stabilized by the mid–1970s. In the early 1980s another movement toward federalization of state corporation law developed from the conservative "law and economics" movement's theory that there existed a national market for "corporate control" of publicly held corporations with which states were powerless to interfere. The United States Supreme Court abruptly dismantled this theory in CTS Corp. v. Dynamics Corp. of America, 481 U.S. 69, 107 S.Ct. 1637, 95 L.Ed.2d 67 (1987). Justice Powell's majority opinion strongly restates the traditional role of states in the regulation of state-created publicly held corporations:

> We think the Court of Appeals failed to appreciate the significance for Commerce Clause analysis of the fact that state regulation of corporate governance is regulation of entities whose very existence and attributes are a product of state law. As Chief Justice Marshall explained:
>
> > "A corporation is an artificial being, invisible, intangible, and existing only in contemplation of law. Being the mere creature of law, it possesses only those properties which the charter of its creation confers upon it, either expressly, or as incidental to its very existence. These are such as are supposed best calculated to effect the object for which it was created." *Trustees of Dartmouth College v. Woodward,* 4 Wheat. 518, 636, 4 L.Ed. 629 (1819).

* * * Every State in this country has enacted laws regulating corporate governance. By prohibiting certain transactions, and regulating others, such laws necessarily affect certain aspects of interstate commerce. This necessarily is true with respect to corporations with shareholders in States other than the State of incorporation. Large corporations that are listed on national exchanges, or even regional exchanges, will have shareholders in many States and shares that are traded frequently. The markets that facilitate this national and international participation in ownership of corporations are essential for providing capital not only for new enterprises but also for established companies that need to expand their businesses. This beneficial free market system depends at its core upon the fact that a corporation—except in the rarest situations—is organized under, and governed by, the law of a single jurisdiction, traditionally the corporate law of the State of its incorporation.

These regulatory laws may affect directly a variety of corporate transactions. Mergers are a typical example. In view of the substantial effect that a merger may have on the shareholders' interests in a corporation, many States require supermajority votes to approve mergers. See, *e.g.,* * * * (requiring approval of a merger by a majority of all shares, rather than simply a majority of votes cast) * * *. MBCA § 11.03. By requiring a greater vote for mergers than is required for other transactions, these laws make it more difficult for corporations to merge. State laws also may provide for "dissenters' rights" under which minority shareholders who disagree with corporate decisions to take particular actions are entitled to sell their shares to the corporation at fair market value. See, *e.g.,* * * * MBCA § 13.02. By requiring the corporation to purchase the shares of dissenting shareholders, these laws may inhibit a corporation from engaging in the specified transactions.[31]

It thus is an accepted part of the business landscape in this country for States to create corporations, to prescribe their powers, and to define the rights that are acquired by purchasing their shares. A State has an interest in promoting stable relationships among parties involved in the corporations it charters, as well as in ensuring that investors in such corporations have an effective voice in corporate affairs.

481 U.S. at 89–91, 107 S.Ct. at 1649–51, 95 L.Ed.2d at 85–86.

(b) In Kamen v. Kemper Fin. Services, Inc., 500 U.S. 90, 111 S.Ct. 1711, 114 L.Ed.2d 152 (1991), the court refused to fashion a federal procedural rule for determining whether a shareholder was required to make a demand on directors before commencing a derivative suit against an investment company based on the federal Investment Company Act of 1940 (ICA), 15 U.S.C.A. § 80a–1(a) et seq. The Court stated:

---

31. [By the Court] Numerous other common regulations may affect both nonresident and resident shareholders of a corporation. Specified votes may be required for the sale of all of the corporation's assets. See * * * MBCA § 12.02. The election of directors may be staggered over a period of years to prevent abrupt changes in management. See * * * MBCA § 8.06. Various classes of stock may be created with differences in voting rights as to dividends and on liquidation. See * * * MBCA § 6.01(c). Provisions may be made for cumulative voting. See * * * MBCA § 7.28. Corporations may adopt restrictions on payment of dividends to ensure that specified ratios of assets to liabilities are maintained for the benefit of the holders of corporate bonds or notes. See MBCA [§ 6.40] (noting that a corporation's articles of incorporation can restrict payment of dividends); * * *. Where the shares of a corporation are held in States other than that of incorporation, actions taken pursuant to these and similar provisions of state law will affect all shareholders alike wherever they reside or are domiciled. * * *

It is clear that the contours of the demand requirement in a derivative action founded on the ICA are governed by *federal* law. Because the ICA is a federal statute, any common law rule necessary to effectuate a private cause of action under that statute is necessarily federal in character.

It does not follow, however, that the content of such a rule must be wholly the product of a federal court's own devising. Our cases indicate that a court should endeavor to fill the interstices of federal remedial schemes with uniform federal rules only when the scheme in question evidences a distinct need for nationwide legal standards or when express provisions in analogous statutory schemes embody congressional policy choices readily applicable to the matter at hand. Otherwise we have indicated that federal courts should 'incorporat[e] [state law] as the federal rule of decision,' unless 'application of [the particular] state law [in question] would frustrate specific objectives of the federal programs.' *United States v. Kimbell Foods, Inc.*, 440 U.S. 715, 728, 99 S.Ct. 1448, 1458, 59 L.Ed.2d 711 (1979). The presumption that state law should be incorporated into federal common law is particularly strong in areas in which private parties have entered legal relationships with the expectation that their rights and obligations would be governed by state-law standards.

Corporation law is one such area. * * *

500 U.S. at 90, 111 S.Ct. at 1717, 114 L.Ed.2d at 165. The Court concluded that the demand rule of Maryland (the state of incorporation) should be applied rather than a federal rule based on § 7.03 of the Principles of Corporate Governance or MBCA § 7.42. Two subsequent cases involved claims arising out of the collapse of financial institutions in the late 1980s. In O'Melveny & Myers v. F.D.I.C., 512 U.S. 79, 114 S.Ct. 2048, 129 L.Ed.2d 67 (1994), the Court held that the question whether the FDIC was subject to imputed knowledge from the Bank for which it was acting as receiver should be resolved by the state law of California and not by a federal rule. And, in Atherton v. F.D.I.C., ___ U.S. ___, 117 S.Ct. 666, 136 L.Ed.2d 656 (1997), the Court held that the standard of care for officers and directors of federally insured savings institutions should be governed by state law so long as the state standard was consistent with a " 'gross negligence' floor" provided by 12 U.S.C. § 1821(k)(usually called the Financial Institutions Reform, Recovery, and Enforcement Act or "FIRREA").[32]

---

32. [By the Editor] This section, a model for ambiguity, provided that a director or officer "may be held personally liable for monetary damages * * * for gross negligence [or] similar conduct * * * that demonstrates a greater disregard of a duty of care * * *. Nothing in this paragraph shall impair or affect any right of the [RTC] under other applicable law."

Chapter Five

THE FORMATION OF A CLOSELY HELD CORPORATION

A. WHERE TO INCORPORATE

Selection of the state of incorporation involves an appraisal of two factors: (a) a dollars-and-cents analysis of the relative cost of incorporating, or qualifying as a foreign corporation, under the statutes of the states under consideration, and (b) a consideration of the advantages and disadvantages of the substantive corporation laws of these states. As a practical matter the choice often comes down to the jurisdiction where the business is to be conducted, or Delaware, the most popular outside jurisdiction.

If the corporation is closely held and its business is to be conducted largely or entirely within a single state, local incorporation is almost always to be preferred. The cost of forming a Delaware corporation and qualifying it to transact business in another state will be greater than forming a local corporation in that state. In addition, the probable cost of legal assistance in forming a Delaware corporation must be considered. The cost of operating a Delaware corporation also will be greater than the cost of operating a local corporation. Income and franchise taxes are usually the same for both domestic and qualified foreign corporations, but again the Delaware taxes must be added. In 1991, the Delaware franchise taxes were increased significantly, thereby reducing the attractiveness of that state for small out-of-state corporations. Another disadvantage of Delaware incorporation is the possibility of being forced to defend a suit in that distant state rather than where the corporation has its principal place of business. While the Delaware statute may offer some flexibility not available in other states, most desired control arrangements can be worked out under most states' current statutes. In addition, a number of states give specific statutory recognition to the close corporation or have adopted § 7.32 of the MBCA. These statutes are discussed in Chapter 8, infra. Despite these disadvantages, data indicates that substantial numbers of Delaware corporations are formed each year, way in excess of the number of publicly held corporations incorporating or reincorporating in that state.

How does an attorney in, say, California, go about forming a Delaware corporation? One possibility, of course, is to make a crash study of Delaware's statutory and case law, but there are obvious risks in that as well as a substantial (and perhaps uncompensated) expenditure of time. Another possibility is to contact a Delaware attorney, though that may raise a question in the client's mind as to whether an attorney is needed in California. A third, and often most attractive, possibility is to use the services of a "corporation service company." For a fee, these companies provide a variety of services to assist lawyers in forming and representing corporations in other states and foreign countries. One such corporation, CT Corporation System, has been in business since 1892. Its promotional brochures announce that "CT corporation provides statutory representation for more than 600,000 business entities in the United States and abroad, including 80% of the Fortune 1000." In order to handle more than 400,000 law suits each year, "CT has 75 Service of Process specialists, all of whom are trained in the proper receipt, logging, and forwarding of these critical legal documents." It has provided an electronic data base since 1992 that permits subscribers to access documents from all state jurisdictions and, through a series of "interactive questions," to create actual filings either for a single state or a multi-state filing. It also offers world-wide document retrieval, corporate filing services and statutory representation to customers doing business internationally for more than 150 companies. While direct electronic filing is generally not permitted for corporate documents, it is likely to become more widely available in the future, and CT plans to offer it as and whenever it becomes available.

CT Corporation System also provides proxy and ballot counting services for shareholders meetings. In connection with its Delaware office, CT provides additional services for "single purpose" corporations:

> When you need to incorporate a separate entity for a single purpose, such as a conduit corporation for a sale-leaseback agreement, CT will incorporate, staff, and maintain the company for you. We can also provide staffing for a special purpose corporation to suit the specific needs you outline for your client. As a special service, CT also maintains a limited number of Delaware "shelf" corporations for purchase. They are inactive, in good standing, and can generally be made available within 24 hours.

In short, for a fee, a corporation service company will provide standardized documents for forming or qualifying a corporation in any state and in most foreign countries.

B. HOW TO INCORPORATE

The process of corporate formation in most states is essentially a very simple one, and much (though not all) of it may be performed by a legal secretary. There are two significant pitfalls in the corporation-formation process. The first is the danger of overlooking some obvious matter. This danger can be largely avoided by the routine use of a decent checklist of steps to be followed. The second danger is the use of "boiler plate" forms which may contain some provision that was suitable for the last corporation but is egregiously inappropriate for this corporation. Some corporations may be stamped from a single mold and be perfectly satisfactory, but many cannot. Depending on such matters as the nature of the business, the agreements among the shareholders, and their degree of trust and confidence, a considerable amount of individual tailoring may be necessary. Read MBCA §§ 2.01–

2.03, 2.05–2.06; 7.32. The drafting of a shareholders' agreement may easily involve the same degree of difficulty as drafting a partnership agreement, articles of limited partnership or an operating agreement for a limited liability company.

The formal requirements for filing of documents are set forth in MBCA, Chapter 1, particularly §§ 1.20–1.26. These minimal requirements are similar to those adopted by a substantial number of states, and the trend is towards limiting the procedures for forming a corporation to those specified in the MBCA. Generally, the trend in most states is towards the simplification of the process of incorporation wherever possible, and "incorporation by postcard" is feasible in some states. However, about a dozen states still require the filing or recording of the articles of incorporation in one or more counties as well as with a state official. About a half-dozen states still require publication of the articles of incorporation as well as filing with a state official. Double filing and/or publication of the articles appear to serve little purpose. Why are they preserved in face of the general trend toward simplification?

Consider again MBCA §§ 2.02, 1.20. Would the following document, submitted to the secretary of state with the appropriate fee (a) be accepted for filing under the MBCA, and (b) result in the formation of a corporation?

ARTICLES OF INCORPORATION

1. The name of the corporation is AB Furniture Store, Inc.

2. The corporation is authorized to issue 1,000 shares of stock.

3. The street address of the corporation's registered office is 125 Main Street, City of _____, State of _____ and the name of the corporation's registered agent at that address is Robert B_____.

4. The name and address of the incorporator is Robert B_____, 125 Main Street, City of _____, State of _____.

> /s/ Robert B_____
> Robert B_____, Incorporator

Whatever minor technical defects may exist in this form, incorporation under the MBCA appears to be a very simple process that hardly requires the services of an attorney (if a "plain vanilla" corporation such as that described above is desired).[1] This apparent simplicity is somewhat deceptive since articles of incorporation usually will have to contain express provisions on additional topics if the desires of the interested parties are to be fully carried out. Consider, for example, MBCA § 6.01 in the situation where it is contemplated that the corporation will issue shares of stock of more than one class. If it is contemplated that the corporation may have a significant number of shareholders, careful consideration should also be given to limiting the

---

1. [By the Editor] Also, it should be obvious that modern articles of incorporation provide relatively little useful information to third persons about the owners of the corporation, its assets, or the nature of its business. For example, the incorporator, "Robert B_____," might be an attorney, an employee of a law firm, or an employee of a corporation service company. Somewhat more meaningful information may sometimes be obtained from other filed documents. See for example, MBCA § 16.22.

liability of directors (MBCA § 2.02(b)(4), discussed in Chapter 10) and adjusting the scope of the right of directors and officers to indemnification (MBCA §§ 8.50 et seq., discussed in Chapter 13). The Official Comment to MBCA § 2.02 contains a two-page list of provisions "that may be elected only in the articles of incorporation" and a shorter list of provisions "that may be elected either in the articles of incorporation or in the bylaws."

Notes

(1) So far as formal requirements for filing are concerned, the Committee on Corporate Laws in 1997 amended Chapter 1 of the MBCA to authorize electronic filing of documents as a guide for the adoption of such procedures by states. Among the numerous technical changes made by these amendments is definitions of the concepts of "delivery," of "electronic transmissions," and of "signatures." MBCA § 1.40(5), (7A), 22A. At the same time, the Committee recognized that the development of reliable and inexpensive copying machines made unnecessary the filing requirement that a copy of a document to be filed accompany with the document itself. These are innovative provisions: State statutes continue to require the filing of physical documents and actual signatures. Many states also impose additional requirements, such as that documents be acknowledged or verified, steps that usually involve presentment to a notary public and the attachment of his or her acknowledgement and notarial seal. These older formal requirements serve little real purpose as a practical matter, and should gradually disappear.

(2) The processing of filed documents by the secretary of state is described in § 1.25, a section that was also significantly amended in 1997. The date the existence of the corporation so formed begins is described in § 2.03, as is the legal effect of the decision by the secretary of state to file the document. Chapter 1 of the MBCA does not reflect a very expansive approach to the powers of the office of secretary of state. For example, the secretary of state may not prescribe a mandatory form for articles of incorporation (§ 1.21(b)), his or her filing duty is expressly defined as "ministerial" (§ 1.25(d)), and he or she is expressly commanded to file a document if it "satisfies the requirements of section 1.20" (MBCA § 1.25(a)). The Official Comment to MBCA § 1.25[2] expands upon this language:

> This language should be contrasted with earlier versions of the Model Act (and many state statutes) that required the secretary of state to ascertain whether the document "conformed with law" before filing it. The purpose of this change is to limit the discretion of the secretary of state to a ministerial role in reviewing the contents of documents. If the document submitted is in the form prescribed and contains the information required by section 1.20 and the applicable provision of the Model Act, the secretary of state under section 1.25 must file it even though it contains additional provisions the secretary of state may feel are irrelevant or not authorized by the Model Act or by general legal principles.

This restrictive view of the powers of the secretary of state rests on the experience of attorneys in a number of states where the office of secretary of state viewed its powers broadly, purported to adopt rules or regulations in addition to the

---

2. Reprinted from 1 *Model Business Corporation Act Annotated* (3d Ed.) 1–51 with the permission of the American Bar Association.

requirements of the corporation statute,[3] and often conducted wide-ranging review of the propriety of specific provisions of documents filed with it. One can envision the frustration of an attorney who, after negotiating a complex provision for inclusion in a proposed articles of incorporation (or other document), is faced with the task of persuading a relatively low-level employee in the office of the secretary of state that the provision is consistent with the secretary of state's view of the meaning of the corporation statute.

Of course, the office of secretary of state has considerable political "clout" in the legislatures of most states, and therefore these provisions may not be accepted in some states. In Virginia, the first state to largely adopt the MBCA, for example, § 1.25 was simply not adopted. As of 1995, seventeen states that generally followed the MBCA in revising their corporation statutes had granted the secretary of state greater review power than provided by § 1.25.

(3) There is a great deal of history and some substantive complexity behind the requirements for articles of incorporation that now appear (or no longer appear) in the MBCA. The following notes describe some of this history.

(4) *Names.* Consider, for example, the requirement that the corporation have a name, and the requirements relating to that name in MBCA § 4.01. Consider also MBCA §§ 4.02, 4.03.

(a) The critical language in § 4.01(b) is that a corporate name "must be distinguishable upon the records of the secretary of state" from other corporate names. Earlier versions of the MBCA required that a corporate name "not be the same as, or deceptively similar to, the name" of an existing corporation. MBCA (1969) § 8. Many secretaries of state construed this or similar language to require a determination whether the proposed name constituted unfair competition with existing corporations. The Official Comment to § 4.01 states that "confusion in an absolute or linguistic sense is the appropriate test under the Model Act, not the competitive relationship between the corporations, which is the test for fraud or unfair competition." The Official Comment adds that "the secretary of state does not generally police the unfair competitive use of names and, indeed, usually has no resources to do so," and that he or she typically does not know what businesses a corporation is actually engaged in or the names a corporation may be using in conducting those businesses. In enforcing whatever statutory standard is applicable, the secretary of state "simply maintains an alphabetical list of 'official' corporate names as they appear from corporate records and makes his decision * * * by comparing the proposed name with those on the list." Official Comment to § 4.01. Today, this list is usually maintained electronically, and in some states may be accessible by the public.

(b) Is the new test a desirable one for determining name availability? The "distinguishable upon the records of the secretary of state" language was taken from § 102(1) of the Delaware General Corporation Law. In Trans–Americas Airlines, Inc. v. Kenton, 491 A.2d 1139 (Del.1985), Transamerica Corporation, the nationally-known conglomerate, had long associated the name "Transamerica" with the activities of a wholly owned subsidiary named "Trans International Airlines, Inc.," which operated a worldwide air charter service. This association took the form of national advertising by Transamerica and using the word "Transamerica" on many of the airplanes operated by the subsidiary. Trans

---

3. [By the Editor] In this connection, consider also MBCA § 1.30. Contrast this narrow grant of authority with § 139 of the 1969 Model Act, which granted the secretary of state the power and authority "reasonably necessary to enable him to administer this Act efficiently and to perform the duties therein imposed upon him."

International Airlines, Inc. was permitted by the Delaware Secretary of State to change its name to "Transamerica Airlines, Inc." An entirely unrelated corporation named "Trans–Americas Airlines, Inc." complained to the Secretary of State and filed suit after the Secretary of State refused to revoke the registration of the name "Transamerica Airlines, Inc." The Delaware Supreme Court accepted the lower court's conclusion that " 'Transamerica Airlines, Inc.' is distinguishable from the name 'Trans–Americas Airlines, Inc.,' on the records of the [Secretary of State]," and held that the statute did not authorize the Secretary of State to reject a name on the ground that it was "confusingly similar" to a name or names already in use.

(c) Because of the widespread adoption of earlier versions of the Model Act, the statutes of many states today contain a "deceptively similar" standard (though sometimes phrased in different words) that makes it clear that prevention of unfair competition is at least partially the objective of corporate name regulation. The extent to which secretaries of state actually attempt to police against unfair competition apparently varies widely from state to state. Many secretaries of state have also evolved "house rules" about name availability that may lead to rather peculiar results. For example, in Texas (which has a "deceptively similar" statute) the names "AGX Corporation" and "A*G*X Corporation" would be viewed as "deceptively similar" but the names "AAA Corporation" and "AAAA Corporation" would not.

(d) As noted in MBCA § 4.01(e), corporations may generally conduct business under an assumed or fictitious name to the same extent that an individual may. (The general test for the lawfulness of doing business under an assumed or fictitious name is that it is proper to do so if the purpose is not to defraud. See e.g. United States v. Dunn, 564 F.2d 348, 354 n. 12 (9th Cir.1977).) Many states, however, have "assumed name" statutes requiring a person conducting business under an assumed or fictitious name to make a public filing disclosing his or her real identity. The use of assumed or fictitious names by corporations is usually not a matter of record with the secretary of state, since filing is normally in local offices rather than statewide. See also MBCA § 15.06(a)(2). As a result, no matter what the secretary of state does, unfair competition through the use of unfairly similar assumed or fictitious names may readily occur. Of course, injured businesses have common law or statutory causes of action against such competition independent of the provisions of the corporation statutes.

(e) Despite this, there is litigation from time to time over corporate names as they are filed with the secretary of state. Most of that litigation is presumably based on the presence or fear of unfair competition by existing businesses.

(f) What purposes are served by "reserved names" (MBCA § 4.02) and "registered names" (MBCA § 4.03)?

(5) *Duration.* MBCA § 3.02 automatically grants every corporation "perpetual duration and succession in its corporate name," unless its articles of incorporation provide otherwise. Earlier versions of the Model Act required that the articles of incorporation affirmatively set forth "[t]he period of duration, which may be perpetual." MBCA (1969) § 54(b); see also id. § 4(a). Many state corporation acts today contain provisions similar to the 1969 Act. Since almost all corporations elected perpetual status under these provisions, MBCA § 3.02 does not reflect a significant change. Why might a corporation with less than a perpetual duration ever be created?

(6) *Purposes.* Historically, a great deal of importance was attached to the statement of purposes in the articles of incorporation. It "is undoubtedly the most

important part of the corporate charter, for this clause, together with the general act under which it is drawn, is the true measure of the powers of the corporation." Louis S. Berkoff, The Object Clause in Corporate Articles, 4 Wis.L.Rev. 424 (1928). During the nineteenth and early twentieth centuries, corporations were formed for a specific "purpose" that had to be "fully stated;" general purpose and multiple purpose clauses were not accepted in many states. As a result, a great deal of litigation involved the question whether a corporation had exceeded its purposes in some transaction. See the discussion of *ultra vires* in part C in this Chapter. This problem has just about disappeared under modern statutes. See MBCA § 3.01(a). Indeed, the disappearance of litigation over the scope of purpose clauses is one of the more visible and sensible changes in corporation law in the last half-century.

(a) The first step in this development was recognition that a corporation may list multiple purposes without any limitation on the number of purposes specified and without any obligation that the corporation actually pursue all the purposes contained in its articles. The result was that formbooks were developed that contained hundreds of possible purposes clauses. A couple chosen at random from an old Pennsylvania formbook give their flavor:

(i) To clean by chemical, machinery or other means, boilers, tanks, heat exchangers, cooling towers, coils, condensers, piping, evaporators, kettles, compressor jackets, innercoolers, aftercoolers, wells, water softeners, filters, septic tanks, all pressure vessels and heat exchange attachments; to manufacture, repair and maintain any and all types of heat exchange or pressure vessels, together with all attachments pertaining thereto.

(ii) To carry on the business of brewers and maltsters in all its branches.

* * *

To manufacture, brew, buy, sell, deal in, distribute, store, warehouse, and export malt, beers, ales, alcohol and other spirituous and fermented and distilled products and by-products thereof and all kinds of brewery products and by-products, and such other commodities as are or may be handled, used and employed in and about such manufacture, distribution and sale.

To carry on the business of distillers in all its branches and to manufacture, buy, sell and deliver in any and all such commodities and products as are or may be handled, used and employed in and about such business.

To manufacture, buy, sell, deal in, distribute and store ice and refrigerated products.

To build, construct, purchase or lease, or otherwise acquire, and to own, hold, operate, sell, lease or otherwise dispose of breweries, factories, plants, warehouses, works and machinery, and any and all other property and things of whatsoever kind and character, real, personal or mixed, tangible or intangible, including good will necessary or desirable in connection with any of the objects hereinbefore or hereinafter set forth.

15 Purdon's Penn.Forms, 15 Penn.Stat. § 1201, Forms 51, 55.

Such clauses were generally drafted on the theory that they should be as broad as possible consistently with the idea of describing some line or kind of business. Since the number of purposes was unlimited, furthermore, it was possible to string together a large number of such clauses to produce an impressively long and unreadable articles of incorporation. Purpose clauses in this era often ran pages in length but usually gave little or no information as to what precise business the corporation planned to engage in.

(b) The next step, quite logically, was to eliminate the excessive verbiage of purposes clauses by permitting incorporation "for the transaction of any lawful business," or similar language that did not require specification of particular lines or kinds of business. These clauses, however, were not quickly accepted; their use did not become widespread until the second half of the twentieth century. The 1969 Model Act permitted this streamlined language (which, after all, did little more than what a long statement of specific purposes did), but it continued to require an affirmative statement of the purposes of the corporation in the articles of incorporation "which may be stated to be, or to include, the transaction of any or all lawful business for which corporations may be incorporated under this Act." MBCA (1969) § 54(c). Where such general statements of purpose were acceptable, they were usually used as a routine matter in most articles of incorporation. Thus, the decision reflected in MBCA § 3.01(a) to eliminate purposes clauses unless a narrow purpose is desired was analogous to the similar decision made in connection with the duration clause.

(c) Why might articles of incorporation today ever include a narrow purposes clause? There are several possible explanations: (1) some types of corporations may be engaged in businesses subject to state regulation that permits incorporation under general business statutes (see MBCA § 3.01(b)) but requires limitations on corporate activities; (2) some persons may be uncomfortable with the complete lack of useful information about the purpose of the corporation permitted by the MBCA, preferring that some description of the principal business of the corporation appear in the articles of incorporation (without restricting the corporation to that business); and (3) in closely held corporations, a limited purposes clause may be used where one or more persons interested in the corporation (but not controlling its affairs) wish to restrict the lines of business the corporation may enter. Other justifications may exist as well.

(7) *Powers.* Historically, one often encountered provisions in articles of incorporation that dealt with corporate "powers" as well as corporate "purposes." The distinction between "powers" and "purposes" is not self-evident; it can best be appreciated by comparing the list of "general powers" in MBCA § 3.02 with a "purpose" such as operating a furniture store. The distinction between "purposes" and "powers" certainly was not understood by many practitioners, since articles of incorporation clauses dealing with "powers" were often indiscriminately mixed in with "purposes." A useful psychological device that aids in distinguishing "powers" from "purposes" is mentally to precede each statement with the phrase "to engage in the business of * * * "and then to use the present participle form of the applicable verb. Thus, instead of saying, "The purpose for which the corporation is organized is to operate a retail furniture store," say "The purpose for which the corporation is organized is *to engage in the business of* operating a retail furniture store." By transposing the verb form from the infinitive to the present participle form, the distinction between powers such as "to sue and be sued" and purposes such as "to operate a furniture store" becomes accentuated.

(a) Is it necessary or desirable to make any references to corporate powers in modern articles of incorporation? Consider MBCA § 2.02(c). Most attorneys agree that it is preferable to take this subsection at face value, at least in states where the statutory powers are sufficiently broad to encompass various acts that raised *ultra vires* problems in an earlier era, such as the power of a corporation to enter into a general partnership or to guarantee the debts of customers or third persons. A listing of powers will be partial rather than complete, and inclusion of express powers may give rise to an inference that it was intended that unlisted powers be denied. Adverse inferences may also arise from any variation between the language of the statute and the listed powers. Where, however, a question exists under the law of a state whether corporations generally possess a specific power, an appropriate provision in the articles may resolve all doubt and avoid possible problems. Thus, it is necessary to examine the substantive issue whether the corporation statute in a specific state provides that all corporations have specified powers.

(b) Today, all statutes contain a list of general powers analogous to those found in MBCA § 3.02. In addition, provisions relating to specific powers may be "tucked away" in substantive provisions themselves. See, e.g. MBCA § 8.51. Section 3.02 contains several changes from earlier versions of similar sections in earlier Model Acts. Perhaps most important is the addition of the introductory phrase "has *the same powers as an individual* to do all things necessary or convenient to carry out its business and affairs" (emphasis added). As of 1995, twenty-three states include this phrase in their corporation statutes. If this language really is effective in giving corporations the same powers as an individual, why is it necessary or desirable for the section also to contain a relatively long traditional list of specific powers found in varying form in most state corporation statutes?

MBCA § 3.02 begins with the phrase "[u]nless its articles of incorporation provide otherwise." Why might it be desired to preclude a corporation from exercising specific powers? Consider, for example, § 3.02(15), which according to the Official Comment was included in addition to § 3.02(13) to permit "contributions for purposes that may not be charitable, such as for political purposes or to influence elections." Might an investor wish to preclude such contributions? What other kinds of restrictions on powers might a cautious investor wish to impose on a corporation in which he or she is making an investment as a minority shareholder?

(8) *Registered office and registered agent.* The designation of a registered office and registered agent, and the statutory provisions relating thereto (see MBCA §§ 5.01–5.04) are designed to ensure that every corporation has publicly stated a current place where it may be found for purposes of service of process, tax notices, and the like. Often a corporation designates its registered office to be its principal business office. In such a case, the registered agent usually is a corporate officer or employee. The principal disadvantage of this is the possibility that legal documents or communications may be mixed in with routine business mail and not receive the attention they deserve. For this reason, many attorneys suggest that they be designated as registered agent and their office be designated as the registered office. Corporation service companies also routinely provide registered offices and registered agents for a fee.

The provisions of the MBCA deal with several mundane questions that may arise in connection with registered offices and registered agents. For example: (a) What happens when a process server goes to the designated street address and finds no office and/or no registered agent on which process may be served? (b) How can a corporation service company effectively discontinue acting as a registered agent when its annual fee is not paid? (c) What is to prevent a person from being named a registered agent without his knowledge or consent? (d) Assume that a corporate service company wishes to change the location of its office in a major city; its old address is the registered office for several thousand corporations. Can it change its office address without seeking the consent of every corporation for which it maintains a registered office? Does it have to obtain the signature of corporate officers for every one of those corporations?

(9) *"Initial directors" and "incorporators."* Under earlier versions of the Model Act the organization of the corporation was accomplished by "initial directors" named in the articles of incorporation; the "incorporators" executed the articles of incorporation but did not meet. MBCA (1969) § 57. A number of states, however, provided that the incorporators were to complete the organization of the corporation, and therefore did not require that initial directors be named in the articles of incorporation. MBCA § 2.05 in effect gives the drafter of articles of incorporation an option as to how the organization of the corporation is to be completed. Factors that might be considered in this regard include (a) will it be necessary for shareholders to meet shortly after the formation of the corporation to elect permanent directors and conduct other business, and (b) do the real parties in interest desire anonymity?

Should an attorney serve as incorporator or initial director? In most states it is clear that no liability attaches to the role of incorporator; the same may not necessarily be true of the position of director, which, as discussed in a later chapter, may carry with it certain fiduciary duties and potential liabilities. Some cautious attorneys refuse as a matter of principle to serve as directors of corporations they form, though there appears to be no ethical objection to doing so.

(10) *The number of incorporators, directors or shareholders.* Blackstone noted that "Three make a corporation." Until mid-century, statutes required that there be at least three incorporators and three directors. Further, there were often residency requirements, shareholding requirements, and the like. So far as incorporators are concerned, the trend is clearly to reduce the minimum number to one and to allow corporations or other artificial entities to serve as incorporators; all but a handful of states now follow the Model Act in this regard. Of course, in view of the limited role of incorporators, this result is probably reasonable.

What about a minimum number of shareholders and directors? There apparently has never been in recent history a requirement that a corporation have at least three shareholders. One North Carolina case that appears to have so held, Park Terrace v. Phoenix Indem. Co., 243 N.C. 595, 91 S.E.2d 584 (1956), was promptly overruled by statute. Assuming this is so, what then about directors? See MBCA § 8.03(a). As of 1995, about eleven states still required a board of at least three directors, though a number of these states permit a corporation with one or two shareholders to reduce the size of the board to the number of shareholders. As a matter of policy, should the privilege of having a board of one or two persons be limited to corporations with one or two shareholders, or should it be extended to all corporations? Is there anything magical about the number three? Assume that you are practicing in one of the three states that continues to require at least three directors in all circumstances. If you are forming a corporation which will have only one shareholder, who should be the directors? Is there any device by which their loyalty to the single shareholder can be assured? Consider, for example, MBCA § 8.08. Assume that your client is incorporated in a state that requires three directors except where there are one or two shareholders, in which case the board of directors may consist of the same number of members as there are shareholders. After a few years of operation, the sole shareholder wishes to begin making gifts of shares of stock to her three minor children. If she does so, will the corporation have to add two directors to its board?

(11) *Initial Capital.* One interesting aspect of the articles of incorporation set forth above is that there is no reference to dollars: no dollar figure is associated with the shares of stock (i.e. no minimum issuance price is established) and no minimum capitalization of the corporation is set forth.

(a) The matter of the issuance price for shares is discussed in Chapter 7 and discussion of that issue is deferred until then.

(b) Shouldn't a new corporation be required to have at least some minimum amount of capital before it is launched into the business world? Until relatively recently there was such a requirement in most states. Prior to 1969, the Model Act prohibited a corporation from transacting any business or incurring any indebtedness "until there has been paid in for the issuance of shares consideration of the value of at least one thousand dollars." MBCA (1966) § 51. The articles of incorporation also had to contain a recitation to the same effect. Id. § 48(g). These provisions have largely disappeared: As of 1995, minimum capital provisions appeared in the statutes of only seven states.

It is probably true that in most states there was never a serious attempt to enforce these minimum capitalization requirements by holding up the certificate of incorporation, though some states did require the submission of an affidavit or certificate that the required amount had been contributed. Much more important was the question whether initial or subsequent directors who acquiesced in the conduct of business before the minimum capital was in fact paid in might be personally liable either for the $1,000 or for all debts of the corporation incurred before the required capital was paid in. The Model Act (MBCA (1966 Ed.) § 43(e)) minimized the potential impact of the minimum capitalization requirement by providing that directors who assent to the commencement of business are "jointly and severally liable to the corporation for such part of one thousand dollars as shall not have been received before commencing business, but such liability shall be terminated when the corporation has actually received one thousand dollars as consideration for the issuance of shares." Not all states followed this provision. In Tri–State Developers, Inc. v. Moore, 343 S.W.2d 812 (Ky.1961), for example, a corporation began business with $500 rather than the required minimum of $1,000. In upholding a judgment for $10,180.34 under such a statute, the court said:

> The state extends to the members of a corporation organized under Chapter 271 personal immunity from corporate liabilities, but only if and when the requirements of KRS 271.095 are satisfied. Those requirements are quite minimal. Anyone can launch a corporate enterprise with $1,000. It may seem harsh that personal immunity should be withheld for a mere $1,000 (in this case $500), but that is a legislative prerogative, and we can find no lesser meaning in the plain words of the statute. One may start business on a shoestring in Kentucky, but if it is a corporate business the shoestring must be worth $1,000.

Kentucky eliminated entirely the minimum capital requirement in 1972. See Ky.B.C.A. § 271B.2–020 (1989). Do you think that it was sensible to eliminate all minimum capital requirements? Considering today's prices and today's conditions, shouldn't the move be in the opposite direction? Or is this simply an illustration of the race of laxity?

———

What happens after the articles of incorporation are filed? See MBCA §§ 2.05, 2.06. In addition to preparing and filing the articles of incorporation, attorneys often handle a number of other details in connection with the formation of a corporation. They may:

(1) Prepare the corporate bylaws;

(2) Prepare the notice calling the meeting of the initial board of directors, minutes of this meeting, and waivers of notice if necessary;

(3) Obtain a corporate seal and minute book for the corporation;

(4) Obtain blank certificates for the shares of stock, arrange for their printing or typing, and ensure that they are properly issued;

(5) Arrange for the opening of the corporate bank account;

(6) Prepare employment contracts, voting trusts, shareholder agreements, share transfer restrictions, and other special arrangements which are to be entered into with respect to the corporation and its shares;

(7) Obtain taxpayer identification numbers, occupancy certificates, and other governmental permits or consents to the operation of the business; and

(8) Evaluate whether the corporation should file an S corporation election, assuming that election is available.

Where there are to be several shareholders, consideration should be given to the manner of governance of the corporation after it is formed. There are numerous "boiler plate" forms for articles of incorporation and bylaws. But these forms create a corporation that may not be well suited for a closely held corporation with multiple shareholders. A carefully crafted shareholders' agreement may be necessary to provide appropriate protections for shareholders both in terms of participation in management and the power to "exit" in case of controversy. In some cases, these appropriate provisions may be effective if they are placed in the bylaws or articles of incorporation, but it is a mistake to assume that participants in a corporation automatically have the same freedom as partners in a partnership or members in an LLC to structure the form of governance in any manner they wish. The traditional rule was that the governance structure set forth in the corporation statute was mandatory—even a corporation with a single shareholder was required to have a board of directors, officers, meetings, and so forth. The gradual erosion of this rule is described in Chapter 8, Section A.

MBCA § 7.32 was added to the MBCA in 1991 (see Changes in the Revised Model Business Corporation Act—Amendments Pertaining to Closely Held Corporations, 46 Bus. Law. 297 (1990)). This section represents a new approach toward the problem of governance in corporations with a few shareholders. As of 1995, eight states had adopted § 7.32, though some with minor variations or limitations. In addition to § 7.32, most states have adopted some provisions designed to ameliorate to some extent the traditional rules of corporate management when applied to small corporations. In deciding what form of governance should be adopted for such a corporation, care must be taken to work within the confines of provisions authorized in the specific state, since failing to do so runs the risk that the manner of governance selected may later be held invalid. Indeed, in some states, it may be preferable to utilize a limited liability company, with its virtually unlimited flexibility, rather than a corporation if the corporation statutes do not provide sufficient management flexibility.

Different considerations apply if the corporation contemplates that it will make a public offering of its shares after its formation. Not only must the number of authorized shares be adjusted appropriately, but additional provisions appropriate for a publicly held corporation must be included, e.g., proxy voting, registration of securities ownership, and similar matters. It is relatively uncommon, but certainly possible, for a newly formed business to contemplate an initial public offering shortly after its formation. More likely, a corporation will operate as a closely held entity for at least several years before considering "going public." In this situation, specialized securities counsel should be retained; review and, if necessary, amendment of articles of incorporation is a normal part of the duties of securities counsel in preparing such a corporation for a public offering. In addition, there must be a review of pre-offering transactions and arrangements between the corporation and its shareholders to determine whether disclosure of specific transactions may be required.

MINUTES OF ORGANIZATIONAL MEETING OF DIRECTORS OF ABC CORPORATION

The organizational meeting of the Board of Directors of ABC Corporation was duly convened in _____, _____ on _____, __, 19__, at _____ __.M.

All directors were present at the meeting and each director waived notice of the time, place of the meeting and of the purposes for which it was held, as evidenced by execution of a waiver of notice, which is attached hereto.

By unanimous consent, Ms. Barbara Brown served as chairperson of the meeting and Mr. Walter White served as secretary of the meeting.

The secretary presented and read to the meeting a copy of the articles of incorporation of the corporation. He reported that an original and a copy of the articles of incorporation had been duly filed with the office of the Secretary of State, together with the required filing fee, and that the Secretary of State had issued a fee receipt dated _____.

The secretary presented to the meeting a minute book for the corporation. Thereupon motion duly made, seconded and unanimously adopted, it was:

RESOLVED, That the minute book presented to this meeting be adopted as the minute book for this corporation, and that the secretary of this meeting be instructed to place therein the articles of incorporation and certificate of incorporation of the corporation.

The chairperson then read to the meeting a draft of the bylaws which had been prepared for the regulation and management of the affairs of the corporation. On motion duly made, seconded and unanimously adopted, it was:

RESOLVED, That the bylaws submitted at and read to this meeting are hereby approved as the bylaws of this corporation, and the secretary of this meeting is hereby instructed to copy such bylaws, at length, in the minute book of the corporation.

The chairperson then presented a form of stock certificate to be used to represent shares issued by the corporation. On motion duly made, seconded and unanimously adopted, it was:

RESOLVED, That the form of stock certificate presented to this meeting is hereby approved and adopted, and the secretary of this meeting is hereby instructed to insert a specimen of such stock certificate in the minute book of the corporation.

The chairperson then presented to the meeting a form of corporate seal for use by the corporation. On motion duly made, seconded and unanimously adopted, it was:

RESOLVED, That the corporate seal, an impression of which is affixed in the margin of the bylaws, is hereby approved and adopted as the official corporate seal of this corporation.

The chairperson then called for the election of officers of the corporation. On motion duly made, seconded and unanimously adopted, the following persons were elected to the offices set opposite their respective names:

Barbara Brown	President
George Green	Vice President and Treasurer
Walter White	Vice President and Secretary

each such officer to serve in accordance with the provisions of the bylaws and until his or her successor shall have been elected and shall have qualified.

Thereupon, on motion duly made, seconded and unanimously adopted, Ms. Brown not voting, it was resolved that Ms. Brown be paid a salary of $_____ per month, payable monthly, but that the other officers of the corporation not be paid any regular salary.

Barbara Brown, George Green and Walter White each submitted written offers to purchase one thousand (1,000) shares of the corporation at a price of ten dollars ($10) per share. On motion duly made, seconded and unanimously adopted, it was:

RESOLVED, That this corporation accept the following offers to purchase shares of the corporation:

Name	Number of Shares	Total Price
Barbara Brown	1,000	$10,000.00
George Green	1,000	$10,000.00
Walter White	1,000	$10,000.00

FURTHER RESOLVED, That upon payment to this corporation of the respective sums payable to this corporation, the officers of this corporation are hereby authorized and directed to issue to the respective purchasers certificates representing fully paid and nonassessable shares of this corporation for the shares so purchased.

Ms. Brown reported to the meeting that she had incurred and paid the following sums to the following persons for the following purposes in connection with the formation of the corporation:

$100.00   to the secretary of state of _____ as the statutory fee for filing the articles of incorporation.

$277.20   to Mr. Jones for legal services in connection with drafting the articles of incorporation, bylaws and other matters directly related to the formation of the corporation.

It was thereupon resolved that Ms. Brown should be reimbursed for such expenses in the total sum of $377.20 and the treasurer was instructed to pay Ms. Brown such sum as soon as possible out of corporate funds.

On motion duly made, seconded and unanimously adopted, it was

RESOLVED that the _____ Bank be chosen as the depository of the funds of the corporation, and the _____ and the _____ were each authorized to draw checks on the corporation's bank account in such bank. A form of resolution furnished by such bank was then presented to the meeting and, after being read and fully understood, such form of resolution was adopted and is attached to these minutes as an exhibit.

There being no further business, on motion duly made, seconded and unanimously adopted, the meeting was adjourned.

_____

Secretary

We consent to the foregoing actions

_____

_____

_____

Alternate form:

WAIVER

We, the undersigned, being all the original directors of ABC Corporation named in the articles of incorporation, do hereby waive notice and the call by the incorporators of said corporation of the organization meeting of the directors of said corporation, and agree that the organization meeting shall be held at _____, in the city of _____, _____ _____ o'clock __.M. on the _____ day of _____, 19__.

_____

_____

_____

Notes

(1) Under the MBCA, there may be only one initial director or one incorporator who organizes the corporation. Where only a single person is acting, much of the "playacting" flavor of these minutes should disappear and a simpler formulation followed, e.g. "The original director determined that ..." On the other hand, many attorneys continue to draft minutes that have a "playacting" flavor even though only one person is acting.

(2) Most of the miscellaneous matters relating to the launching of a new corporation are accomplished at a meeting of the incorporators or initial directors. The attorney will normally draft the minutes of this meeting. In some circumstances it may be necessary to have a meeting of the shareholders to elect permanent directors; the attorney normally drafts the minutes of this meeting also.

(3) If the corporation is small and closely held, it is not necessary to actually hold meetings of incorporators, directors, or shareholders. See MBCA §§ 2.05, 7.04, 8.21. Similar provisions appear in all corporation statutes. Thus, a consent signed by all the incorporators, directors, or shareholders is effective as a legal matter. If the consent procedure is not utilized (as may be the case, for example, where one individual is absent, or where the number of persons involved is large), it is generally desirable to actually hold a meeting, using the minutes as a form of script. Some attorneys object to the playacting nature of such a meeting, but there is some question of validity of actions taken without a meeting and without taking advantage of the consent procedure. Of course, the consent procedure should be followed where a single incorporator or initial director is acting.

(4) At the very early stages of corporate formation, there is unlikely to be significant disagreement, dissent, or controversy. See, however, Walsh v. Search Exploration, Inc., 16 Del.J.Corp.L. 1640 (Del.Ch.1990). Del.Gen.Corp.L. § 211, provides in part that "[i]f there be a failure to hold the annual meeting * * * for a period of 13 months after the organization of the corporation * * * the Court of Chancery may summarily order a meeting to be held * * *." Compare MBCA § 7.03(a)(1). Search Exploration was incorporated on April 24, 1989, but did not hold its organizational meeting until some time in October, 1989. Shares were issued but no meeting of shareholders held. On August 31, 1990, the court issued its opinion holding that the 13 month period began to run from April 24, 1989, rather than from the date of the organizational meeting, and directed that an annual meeting for the election of directors be held "no later than 90 days from September 3, 1990."

———

Bylaws of a corporation constitute the internal set of operating rules for the corporation. See MBCA § 2.06. They are usually prepared by the attorney overseeing the formation of a corporation. Numerous sample bylaws are available in form books; corporation service companies also provide a set of bylaws as part of their services in connection with the formation of a corporation. Bylaws may vary from a brief one or two page document to elaborate provisions covering all aspects of corporate management and operation. Since officers and directors of a corporation are usually not familiar with the provisions of the applicable corporation statute and may not be familiar with special requirements set forth in the articles of incorporation, the more common practice is to restate such provisions in the bylaws for the benefit of the corporate officers. The following excerpt from a form set of bylaws give their flavor:

ARTICLE III. BOARD OF DIRECTORS

§ 3.1 General Powers.

Unless the articles of incorporation have dispensed with or limited the authority of the board of directors by describing who will perform some or all of the duties of a board of directors, all corporate powers shall be exercised by or under the authority of, and the business and affairs of the corporation shall be managed under the direction of the board of directors.

§ 3.2 Number, Tenure, and Qualifications of Directors.

Unless otherwise provided in the articles of incorporation, the number of directors of the corporation shall be _____. Each director shall hold office until the next annual meeting of shareholders or until removed. However, if his term expires, he shall continue to serve until his successor shall have been elected and qualified or until there is a decrease in the number of directors. Directors need not be residents of the State of [name of state] or shareholders of the corporation unless so required by the articles of incorporation.

§ 3.3 Regular Meetings of the Boards of Directors.

A regular meeting of the board of directors shall be held without other notice than this bylaw immediately after, and at the same place as, the annual meeting of shareholders. The board of directors may provide, by resolution, the time and place [either within or without the State of _____,] for the holding of additional regular meetings without other notice than such resolution. (If so permitted by § 3.7, any such regular meeting may be held by telephone.)

§ 3.4 Special Meetings of the Board of Directors.

Special meetings of the board of directors may be called by or at the request of the [insert title] or any [insert number] director(s). The person or persons authorized to call special meetings of the board of directors may fix any place, either within or without the State of [name of state], as the place for holding any special meeting of the board of directors called by them, or if permitted by § 3.7, such meeting may be held by telephone.

§ 3.5 Notice of, and Waiver of Notice for, Special Director Meetings.

Unless the articles of incorporation provide for a longer or shorter period, notice of any special director meeting shall be given at least two days previously thereto either orally or in writing. If mailed, notice of any director meeting shall be deemed to be effective at the earlier of: (1) when received; (2) five days after deposited in the United States mail, addressed to the director's business office, with postage thereon prepaid; or (3) the date shown on the return receipt if sent by registered or certified mail, return receipt requested, and the receipt is signed by or on behalf of the director. Any director may waive notice of any meeting. Except as provided in the next sentence, the waiver must be in writing, signed by the director entitled to the notice, and filed with the minutes or corporate records. The attendance of a director at a meeting shall constitute a waiver of notice of such meeting, except where a director attends a meeting for the express purpose of objecting to the transaction of any business and at the beginning of the meeting (or promptly upon his arrival) objects to holding the meeting or transaction business at the meeting, and does not thereafter vote for or assent to action taken at the meeting. Unless required by the articles of incorporation, neither the business to be transacted at, nor the purpose of, any special meeting of the board of directors need be specified in the notice or waiver of notice of such meeting.

§ 3.6 Director Quorum.

[A] majority of the number of directors shall constitute a quorum for the transaction of business at any meeting of the board of directors, unless the articles require a greater number.

Any amendment to this quorum requirement is subject to the provisions of § 3.8 of this Article III.

§ 3.7 Directors, Manner of Acting.

The act of the [majority] [or greater percentage] of the directors present at a meeting at which a quorum is present when the vote is taken shall be the act of the board of directors unless the articles of incorporation require a greater percentage. Any amendment which changes the number of directors needed to take action, is subject to the provisions of § 3.8 of this Article III.

Unless the articles of incorporation provide otherwise, any or all directors may participate in a regular or special meeting by, or conduct the meeting through the use of, any means of communication by which all directors participating may simultaneously hear each other during the meeting. A director participating in a meeting by this means is deemed to be present in person at the meeting.

A director who is present at a meeting of the board of directors or a committee of the board of directors when corporate action is taken is deemed to have assented to the action taken unless: (1) he objects at the beginning of the meeting (or promptly upon his arrival) to holding it or transacting business at the meeting; or (2) his dissent or abstention from the action taken is entered in the minutes of the meeting; or (3) he delivers written notice of his dissent or abstention to the presiding officer of the meeting before its adjournment or to the corporation immediately after adjournment of the meeting. The right of dissent or abstention is not available to a director who votes in favor of the action taken.

§ 3.8 Establishing a "Supermajority" Quorum or Voting Requirement for the Board of Directors.

For purposes of this § 3.8, a "supermajority" quorum is a requirement that more than a majority of the directors in office constitute a quorum, and a "supermajority" voting requirement is any requirement that requires the vote of more than a majority of those directors present at a meeting at which a quorum is present to be the act of the directors.

A bylaw that fixes a supermajority quorum or supermajority voting requirement may be amended or repealed:

(1) if originally adopted by the shareholders, only by the shareholders (unless otherwise provided by the shareholders);

(2) if originally adopted by the board of directors, either by the shareholders or by the board of directors.

A bylaw adopted or amended by the shareholders that fixes a supermajority quorum or supermajority voting requirement for the board of directors may provide that it may be amended or repealed only by a specified vote of either the shareholders or the board of directors.

Subject to the provisions of the preceding paragraph, action by the board of directors to adopt, amend, or repeal a bylaw that changes the quorum or voting requirement for the board of directors must meet the same quorum requirement and be adopted by the same vote required to take action under the quorum and voting requirement then in effect or proposed to be adopted, whichever is greater.

§ 3.9 Director Action Without a Meeting.

Unless the articles of incorporation provide otherwise, any action required or permitted to be taken by the board of directors at a meeting may be taken without a meeting if all the directors take the action, each one signs a written consent describing the action taken, and the consents are filed with the records of the corporation. Action taken by consents is effective when the last director signs the consent, unless the consent specifies a different effective date. A signed consent has the effect of a meeting vote and may be described as such in any document.

§ 3.10 Removal of Directors.

The shareholders may remove one or more directors at a meeting called for that purpose if notice has been given that a purpose of the meeting is such removal. The removal may be with or without cause unless the articles provide that directors may only be removed with cause. If a director is elected by a voting group of shareholder, only the shareholders of that voting group may participate in the vote to remove him. If cumulative voting is authorized, a director may not be removed if the number of votes sufficient to elect him under cumulative voting is voted against his removal. If cumulative voting is not authorized, a director may be removed only if the number of votes cast to remove him exceeds the number of votes cast not to remove him.

§ 3.11 Board of Director Vacancies.

Unless the articles of incorporation provide otherwise, if a vacancy occurs on the board of directors, including a vacancy resulting from an increase in the number of directors, the shareholders may fill the vacancy. During such time that the shareholders fail or are unable to fill such vacancies then and until the shareholders act:

(1) the board of directors may fill the vacancy; or

(2) if the directors remaining in office constitute fewer than a quorum of the board, they may fill the vacancy by the affirmative vote of a majority of all the directors remaining in office.

If the vacant office was held by a director elected by a voting group of shareholders, of shares of that voting group are entitled to vote to fill the vacancy if it is filled by the shareholders.

A vacancy that will occur at a specific later date (by reason of a resignation effective at a later date) may be filled before the vacancy occurs but the new director may not take office until the vacancy occurs.

The term of a director elected to fill a vacancy expires at the next shareholders' meeting at which directors are elected. However, if his term expires, he shall continue to serve until his successor is elected and qualifies or until there is a decrease in the number of directors.

James R. Burkhard, Proposed Model Bylaws To Be Used With The Revised Model Business Corporation Act (1984), 46 Bus. Law. 189, 211–12, 214–23 (1990).[4] Numerous additional annotations, commentaries, and alternative provisions are included in these proposed bylaws which are not included here.

C. THE DECLINE OF THE DOCTRINE OF *ULTRA VIRES*

A classic English case presents the doctrine of *ultra vires* in its full rigor and glory. In Ashbury Ry. Carriage & Iron Co. v. Riche, 33 L.T.R. 450 (1875), the charter of a corporation authorized it to "sell or lend all kinds of railway plant, to carry on the business of mechanical engineers and general contractors, &c." The corporation entered into contracts with one Riche to purchase a concession to construct and operate a railway line in Belgium. Riche was apparently to construct the railroad line, and the corporation was to raise the necessary capital. After partial performance, the corporation repudiated the contract. The House of Lords concluded that the corporation was not liable to Riche because owning and operating a railway line was *ultra vires*. Lord Chancellor Cairns declared:

> * * * In a case such as your Lordships have now to deal with, it is not a question whether the contract sued upon involves that which is *malum prohibitum* or *malum in se,* or is a contract contrary to public policy, and illegal in that sense. I assume the contract in itself to be perfectly legal; to have nothing in it obnoxious to any of the powers involved in the expressions which I have used. The question is not the illegality of the contract, but the competency and power of the company to make the contract. I am of opinion that this contract was, as I have said, entirely beyond the objects of the memorandum of association. If so it was thereby placed beyond the powers of the company to make the contract. If so it is not a question whether the contract ever was ratified or not ratified. If it was a contract void at its beginning it was void for this reason—because the company could not make the contract. If every shareholder of the company had been in this room, and every shareholder of the company had said, "That is a contract which we desire to make, which we authorise [sic] the directors to make, to which we sanction the placing the seal of the company," the case would not have stood in any different position to that in which it stands now. The company would thereby by unanimous assent have been attempting to do the very thing which by the Act they were prohibited from doing.

Several things may be noted about this case. First, while it involves a purposes clause that is narrower than the activities actually engaged in by the corporation, the activities themselves were not inherently unlawful or beyond the powers of corporations generally. Presumably, the corporation could have amended its memorandum of association to permit it to operate a Belgian railroad. Modern practice in drafting articles of incorporation greatly reduces but does not eliminate the possibility that such a case will arise in the future.

---

4. Copyright (1990) by the American Bar Association. All rights reserved. Reprinted with permission of the American Bar Association and its Section of Business Law.

Such a case is unlikely ever to arise under a general "all lawful business" purposes clause, but conceivably might arise if a narrow purposes clause is included in articles of incorporation. Second, the result of the case hardly seems reasonable or fair. After entering into what appears to be an entirely reasonable business contract, and presumably receiving benefits thereunder, the corporation is permitted to avoid the contract on the basis of a defense that was entirely within its power to correct. Third, the argument that corporations simply are unable to commit *ultra vires* acts threatens to be very unsettling. It might be used, for example, to set aside completed transactions, including sales of goods and land, that the corporation now regrets. It also would appear to be a handy defense for the corporation to avoid liability to injured plaintiffs in torts cases. Thus, almost from the first, the law of *ultra vires* became, in effect, a judicial attempt to avoid the harsh and undesirable but apparently logically compelled consequences of a judicially-created doctrine.

Some courts avoided the *ultra vires* doctrine by construing purposes clauses broadly and finding implied purposes from the language used. A famous example is the conclusion by the United States Supreme Court that a railway company might engage in the business of leasing and running a seaside resort hotel. Jacksonville M.P.Ry. & Nav. Co. v. Hooper, 160 U.S. 514, 16 S.Ct. 379, 40 L.Ed. 515 (1896). Other doctrines that have found acceptance include estoppel, unjust enrichment, including quasi-contract, and waiver. In particular, these doctrines were applied to ensure that completed transactions would not be disturbed, and to permit tort claimants to recover for injuries suffered as a consequence of the corporation's conduct of an *ultra vires* business. *Ultra vires* continued to be applied, however, in connection with executory agreements and, when all is said and done, the doctrine was an undesirable one, involving harsh and erratic consequences.

In the *Ashbury Railway* case, could the House of Lords have concluded that constructing and operating a Belgian railroad was subsumed under the purpose of carrying on a "general contractors" business? This argument was strongly pressed by the plaintiff, but was rejected by the House of Lords. What do you think the effect should be of the "&c."?

One superficially plausible justification for the doctrine arises from the fact that articles of incorporation are on public file; it seems reasonable to argue that one is charged with notice of whatever unexpected provision might appear in public documents. From a business standpoint, that argument is unrealistic: it assumes people will check articles of incorporation when in fact they do not, and that when they do check the articles, they will make business judgments based on a reading of what often is essentially boilerplate legalese. Whatever the merits of the notion of being charged with notice of public documents in different contexts, the decline and elimination of the *ultra vires* doctrine prove that it should not be applied to purposes clauses of articles of incorporation.

711 KINGS HIGHWAY CORP. v. F.I.M.'S
MARINE REPAIR SERV., INC.

Supreme Court of New York, 1966.
51 Misc.2d 373, 273 N.Y.S.2d 299.

VICTOR L. ANFUSO, JUSTICE.

Defendant corporation moves pursuant to CPLR 3211, subdiv. [a], par. 7 for judgment dismissing the complaint for legal insufficiency or in the alternative for summary judgment pursuant to CPLR 3212.

The verified complaint alleges that on or about April 20, 1965 the plaintiff, owner of premises known as 711–715 Kings Highway in the County of Kings, City of New York, entered into a written lease agreement with defendant whereby plaintiff leased the aforesaid premises to defendant for a period of 15 years commencing July 1, 1966; that with the exception of a security deposit of $5,000 paid by defendant to plaintiff pursuant to the lease agreement, which sum plaintiff now tenders or offers to return to defendant, the lease remains wholly executory; that under the terms of the lease the demised premises were to be used as a motion picture theatre; that the purposes for which the defendant corporation was formed were restricted generally to marine activities including marine repairs and the building and equipment of boats and vessels, as set forth in the certificate of incorporation; that the execution of the subject lease calling for defendant's use of the demised premises as a motion picture theatre, and the conduct and operation of a motion picture theatre, and the conduct and operation of a motion picture theatre business for profit by the defendant are acts which fall completely outside the scope of the powers and authority conferred by the defendant's corporate charter, thereby rendering invalid the lease agreement entered into by the parties. The complaint then prays for a declaratory judgment declaring the lease to be invalid or in the alternative for rescission and further that the defendant be enjoined from performing, or exercising any rights, under the lease.

In the opinion of the court Section 203 of the New York Business Corporation Law embraces the situation presented by the factual allegations of the complaint and requires a dismissal of the complaint for failure to state a cause of action. This section provides as follows: That no act of a corporation and no transfer of property to or by a corporation, otherwise lawful, shall be invalid by reason of the fact that the corporation was without capacity or power to do such act or engage in such transfer except that such lack of capacity or power may be asserted (1) in an action brought by a shareholder to enjoin a corporate act or (2) in an action by or in the right of a corporation against an incumbent or former officer or director of the corporation or (3) in an action or special proceeding brought by the Attorney General. It is undisputed that the present case does not fall within the stated exceptions contained in Section 203. It is accordingly clear from the language of the statutory provision hereinabove referred to that there is no substance to plaintiff's argument, in opposition to the instant motion, which is predicated on a want of corporate power to do an act or enter into an agreement beyond the express or implied powers of the corporation conferred by the corporate charter.

Neither is there merit to the plaintiff's contention that Section 203 applies only where ultra vires is raised as a defense. Notwithstanding the fact that this section is entitled "Defense of ultra vires" it seems that except in the three stated situations set forth in the section, which are not applicable to the instant case, ultra vires may not be invoked as a sword in support of a cause of action any more than it can be utilized as a defense. To hold otherwise would render meaningless those provisions in Section 203 which permit ultra vires to be invoked in support of the actions or proceedings set forth as exceptions to the general language of this section.

Finally plaintiff's contention that the ultra vires doctrine still applies fully to executory contracts must be rejected. By virtue of Section 203 the doctrine may not be invoked even though the contract which is claimed to be ultra vires is executory, as in the instant case. See Revisers' Notes and Comments on Section 203 of the Business Corporation Law.

Accordingly the defendant's motion for judgment dismissing the complaint for insufficiency is granted. So much of the defendant's motion as seeks in the alternative summary judgment based on the amendment of defendant's certificate of incorporation subsequent to the commencement of the instant action, so as to include in the powers granted to the corporation the power to exhibit motion pictures, need not be considered in view of the determination herein made on the motion to dismiss for insufficiency.

Notes

(1) Consider MBCA § 3.04. Does this give the court the needed flexibility to protect legitimate and reasonable business relationships on the one hand while protecting shareholders who may have relied on a narrow purposes clause as protection against undesired business expansion on the other?

(2) Do not MBCA §§ 3.04(b)(1) and (c) give shareholders greater rights to set aside executory transactions than the corporation itself? Might not a corporation, having entered into a disadvantageous *ultra vires* transaction, enlist a shareholder to intervene and seek the cancellation of the contract? Of course, if it is advantageous for the corporation to avoid a transaction, it probably will be advantageous from the standpoint of the shareholder also, since it will increase the value of the shares. In Inter–Continental Corp. v. Moody, 411 S.W.2d 578 (Tex.Civ.App.1966), a shareholder intervened in a suit brought against the corporation on an *ultra vires* promissory note, and sought to enjoin payment of the note. In permitting the intervention, the court said:

> Upon the above evidence it may well be concluded that the intervening stockholder was acting in his own interest at the urging of another stockholder * * *. The mere fact that a corporation representative may have given notice of the suit and suggested it might be wise for the stockholder to intervene does not make such stockholder an agent of the corporation. As a practical matter today when corporate stock is so widely held by different persons in varying and small amounts, the average stockholder can hardly be expected to keep himself informed of corporate operations except for information afforded him by corporate representatives or those associated with them. There might in some particular case be facts establishing such an agency so that in a trial on the merits he would not be entitled to the relief sought. However, whether the stockholder is in fact but the agent of the corporation is to be determined at a trial on the merits. We note that under all facts

shown here no such agency is established, * * *. We do not know what a fuller development of the facts will show. In this connection we think it material to show who is paying Mr. Hicks' attorney's fee. He may be required to disclose this though it may not be required that he show the amount.

If on trial the trier of the facts, on evidence of probative force, finds that Richardson is but the agent of Inter–Continental, then he would not be entitled to the relief sought. If intervenor is found not to be the mere agent of Inter–Continental, then he will be entitled to * * * some relief * * *. [A]ppellee will be entitled to a judgment against the corporation, not for the full amount of the note, but only to the extent that the stockholder is held not to be entitled to relief. This is not because of a right in the corporation, but because of the rights of the stockholder.

Does the court's cryptic comment mean that the corporation can resist payment of the note only in proportion to the shareholder's relative interest in the corporation? If not, what did the court mean?

(3) In Cucchi v. New York City Off–Track Betting Corp., 818 F.Supp. 647, 657–58 (S.D.N.Y.1993), plaintiff contended that she had been fired as an employee of defendant in violation of the statutory provisions regulating the defendant, and that therefore her firing was *ultra vires*. This argument was rejected by the court on the ground that the doctrine of *ultra vires* as embodied in § 203 could be invoked only by a shareholder or by the state through its attorney-general.

THEODORA HOLDING CORP. v. HENDERSON

Court of Chancery of Delaware, 1969.
257 A.2d 398.

MARVEL, VICE CHANCELLOR:

Plaintiff, which was formed in May of 1967 by the defendant Girard B. Henderson's former wife, Theodora G. Henderson, is the holder of record of 11,000 of the 40,500 issued and outstanding shares of common stock of the defendant Alexander Dawson, Inc. It sues derivatively as well as on its own behalf for an accounting by the individual defendants for the losses allegedly sustained by the corporate defendant and the concomitant improper gains allegedly received by the individual defendants as a result of certain transactions of which plaintiff complains. * * *

The individual defendant Henderson by reason of the extent of his combined majority holdings of common and preferred stock of Alexander Dawson, Inc., each class of which has voting rights, exercises effective control over the affairs of such corporation, the net worth of the assets of which, at the time of the filing of this suit, was approximately $150,000,000.

It is claimed and the evidence supports such contention that on December 8, 1967, the defendant Girard B. Henderson, by virtue of his voting control over the affairs of Alexander Dawson, Inc., caused the board of directors of such corporation to be reduced in number from eight to three persons, namely himself, the defendant Bengt Ljunggren,[5] an employee of the corporate defendant, and Mr. Henderson's daughter, Theodora H. Ives. It is alleged that

---

5. [By the Court] Mr. Ljunggren, whose forte appears to be that of public relations, joined Alexander Dawson, Inc. in 1966 at a salary of $12,000 per annum. He has since been rewarded with substantial raises and bonuses which have more than doubled his starting salary.

thereafter the defendant Girard B. Henderson (over the objection of the director, Mrs. Ives) caused the board and the majority of the voting stock of Alexander Dawson, Inc., improperly to contribute stock held by it in the approximate value of $550,000 to the Alexander Dawson Foundation, a charitable trust, the affairs of which were then controlled and continue to be controlled by Mr. Henderson. * * *

Alexander Dawson, Inc. has functioned as a personal holding company since 1935 when Mr. Henderson's mother exchanged a substantial number of shares held by her in a company which later became Avon Products, Inc., for all of the shares of her own company known as Alexander Dawson, Inc. Mr. Henderson and a brother later succeeded to their mother's interest in Alexander Dawson, Inc., the brother thereafter permitting his shares to be redeemed by the corporation. As noted earlier, Mr. Henderson, by reason of his combined holdings of common and preferred stock of the corporate defendant, is in clear control of the affairs of such corporation, which, for the most part, has been operated informally by Mr. Henderson with scant regard for the views of other board members. Some seventy-five percent of its assets consist of shares of Avon Products, Inc. stock, there having been some diversification, particularly in 1967, largely through the urging of officers of the United States Trust Company of New York who have served as advisors. Through exercise of such control, Mr. Henderson has, since 1957, caused the corporate defendant to donate varying amounts to a charitable trust organized in that year by Mr. Henderson, namely the Alexander Dawson Foundation. In 1957, $10,610 was donated to such trust. From 1960 to 1966 (except for the year 1965) gifts were in the range of approximately $63,000 to $70,000 or higher in each year other than 1963 when $27,923 was donated. In 1966, however, a gift in the form of a large tract of land in Colorado, having a value of some $467,750, was made. All of these gifts through 1966 were unanimously approved by all of the stockholders of Alexander Dawson, Inc., including Mrs. Theodora G. Henderson. The gift now under attack, namely one of the shares of stock of [*sic*: owned by (?)] the corporate defendant having a value of some $528,000, was made to the Alexander Dawson Foundation in December of 1967. Such gift was first proposed by Mr. Henderson in April, 1967 before the board of the corporate defendant was reduced in number from eight to three. However, director reaction was thereafter confused, one of the directors, Mrs. Henderson's daughter, Theodora H. Ives, having expressed a desire that a corporate gift also be made to her own charitable corporation and that of her mother, Theodora G. Henderson. Accordingly, the matter was not pressed by Mr. Henderson until late December when the reduced board had taken over management of the corporate defendant. It is claimed and admitted that such gift had an effect on the equity and dividends of shareholders of the corporate defendant although the tax consequences of such gift clearly soften the apparent impact of such transaction. It is significant, however, as noted above, that the 1966 corporate gift, consisting of a ranch located in Colorado, had been approved by all of the directors and stockholders of the corporate defendant, and that the gift here under attack was apparently intended to be a step towards consummation of the purpose behind such grant of land, namely to provide a fund for the financing of a western camp for underprivileged boys, particularly members of the George Junior Republic, a self-governing institution which has served the public interest for some seventy-five years at a school near Freeville, New York. Thus, in the summer of 1967, a small group of underprivileged children had enjoyed the advantages of such camp in a test of the feasibility of such an institution. However, it is apparently Mr. Henderson's intention to continue and expand his interest in such camp where he maintains an underground home which he occupies at a $6,000 rental per annum, such house being occupied by him during some three months of the year. * * *

The next matter to be considered is the propriety of the December 1967 gift made by Alexander Dawson, Inc. to the Alexander Dawson Foundation of shares of stock of [*sic*: owned by (?)] the corporate defendant having a value in excess of $525,000, an amount within the limits of the provisions of the federal tax law having to do with deductible corporate gifts, Internal Revenue Code of 1954 §§ 170(b)(2), 545(b)(2).

Title 8 Del.C. § 122 provides as follows:

"Every corporation created under this chapter shall have power to-* * *

(9) Make donations for the public welfare or for charitable, scientific or educational purposes, and in time of war or other national emergency in aid thereof."

There is no doubt but that the Alexander Dawson Foundation is recognized as a legitimate charitable trust by the Department of Internal Revenue. It is also clear that it is authorized to operate exclusively in the fields of " * * * religious, charitable, scientific, literary, or educational purposes, or for the prevention of cruelty to children or animals * * *." Furthermore, contemporary courts recognize that unless corporations carry an increasing share of the burden of supporting charitable and educational causes that the business advantages now reposed in corporations by law may well prove to be unacceptable to the representatives of an aroused public. The recognized obligation of corporations towards philanthropic, educational and artistic causes is reflected in the statutory law of all of the states, other than the states of Arizona and Idaho.

In A.P. Smith Mfg. Co. v. Barlow, 13 N.J. 145, 98 A.2d 681, 39 A.L.R.2d 1179, appeal dismissed, 346 U.S. 861, 74 S.Ct. 107, 98 L.Ed. 373, a case in which the corporate donor had been organized long before the adoption of a statute authorizing corporate gifts to charitable or educational institutions, the Supreme Court of New Jersey upheld a gift of $1500 by the plaintiff corporation to Princeton University, being of the opinion that the trend towards the transfer of wealth from private industrial entrepreneurs to corporate institutions, the increase of taxes on individual income, coupled with steadily increasing philanthropic needs, necessitate corporate giving for educational needs even were there no statute permitting such gifts, and this was held to be the case apart from the question of the reserved power of the state to amend corporate charters. The court also noted that the gift tended to bolster the free enterprise system and the general social climate in which plaintiff was nurtured. And while the court pointed out that there was no showing that the gift in question was made indiscriminately or to a pet charity in furtherance of personal rather than corporate ends, the actual holding of the opinion appears to be that a corporate charitable or educational gift to be valid must merely be within reasonable limits both as to amount and purpose.

The New Jersey statute in force and effect at the time of the Smith case gift provided that directors might cause their corporation to contribute for charitable and educational purposes and the like " * * * such reasonable sum or sums as they may determine * * * "provided, however, that such contributions might not be made in situations where the proposed donee owned more than 10% of the voting stock of the donor and provided further that such gifts be limited to 5% of capital and surplus unless " * * * authorized by the stockholders."

Whether or not these statutory limitations on corporate giving were the source of the limiting language of the New Jersey Supreme Court is not clear, the point being that the Delaware statute contains no such limiting language and therefor must, in my opinion, be construed to authorize any reasonable corporate gift of a charitable or educational nature. Significantly, Alexander Dawson, Inc. was incorporated in Delaware in 1958 after 8 Del.C. § 122(9) was cast in its present form, therefor no constitutional problem arising out of the effect on a stockholder's property rights of the State's reserved power to amend corporate charters is presented.

I conclude that the test to be applied in passing on the validity of a gift such as the one here in issue is that of reasonableness, a test in which the provisions of the Internal Revenue Code pertaining to charitable gifts by corporations furnish a helpful guide. The gift here under attack was made from gross income and had a value as of the time of giving of $528,000 in a year in which Alexander Dawson, Inc.'s total income was $19,144,229.06, or well within the federal tax deduction limitation of 5% of such income. The contribution under attack can be said to have "cost" all of the stockholders of Alexander Dawson, Inc. including plaintiff, less than $80,000, or some fifteen cents per dollar of contribution, taking into consideration the federal tax provisions applicable to holding companies as well as the provisions for compulsory distribution of dividends received by such a corporation. In addition, the gift, by reducing Alexander Dawson, Inc.'s reserve for unrealized capital gains taxes by some $130,000, increased the balance sheet net worth of stockholders of the corporate defendant by such amount. It is accordingly obvious, in my opinion, that the relatively small loss of immediate income otherwise payable to plaintiff and the corporate defendant's other stockholders, had it not been for the gift in question, is far out-weighed by the overall benefits flowing from the placing of such gift in channels where it serves to benefit those in need of philanthropic or educational support, thus providing justification for large private holdings, thereby benefiting plaintiff in the long run. Finally, the fact that the interests of the Alexander Dawson Foundation appear to be increasingly directed towards the rehabilitation and education of deprived but deserving young people is peculiarly appropriate in an age when a large segment of youth is alienated even from parents who are not entirely satisfied with our present social and economic system. * * *

Notes

(1) *Ultra vires* issues have arisen in the past with respect to a number of transactions that, like charitable contributions, provide no immediate direct benefit to the corporation. Such transactions include contracts of guaranty and suretyship, purchases of the corporation's own shares, the building of homes for corporate employees (or the financing of such homes at below-market interest

rates), and the building of entire villages for employees, including sanitation, water, electrical banking, educational, religious, and recreational facilities. Most of these transactions are now specifically authorized by powers clauses of modern statutes, or at least seem clearly to fall within the general language of such clauses. MBCA § 3.02 also states that a corporation "has the same powers as an individual to do all things necessary or convenient to carry out its business and affairs," and MBCA § 3.04 provides that the validity of corporate action may not be challenged on the ground that the corporation "lacks or lacked power to act." These provisions should clearly dispel any possibility that corporations lack power to do specific acts in furtherance of their purposes; however, they may not foreclose arguments similar to those put forth in *Theodora Holding Corp.* that such transactions involve self-dealing or improper conduct by directors or officers.

(2) In First Nat'l. Bank v. Bellotti, 435 U.S. 765, 98 S.Ct. 1407, 55 L.Ed.2d 707 (1978) and Consolidated Edison Co. v. Public Serv. Comm'n, 447 U.S. 530, 100 S.Ct. 2326, 65 L.Ed.2d 319 (1980), the Supreme Court recognized that corporate political speech had constitutional protection. The most recent decision in this line of cases, Austin v. Michigan Chamber of Commerce, 494 U.S. 652, 110 S.Ct. 1391, 108 L.Ed.2d 652 (1990), held that because of the essential nature of a corporation, "narrowly drawn" limitations on corporate political speech were constitutionally permissible. See Charles D. Watts, Jr., Corporate Legal Theory Under the First Amendment: *Belloti* and *Austin*, 46 U.Miami L.Rev. 317 (1991). In this line of cases, commercial speech—speech directly affecting the property, business, or assets of the corporation—is not involved. At the time of these decisions, applicable state law generally did not expressly authorize corporate political contributions or payments to influence public elections; indeed, the statutes of some states prohibited them specifically. The "black letter" rule has long been that corporations are state creations with limited powers granted by the states. Head & Amory v. Providence Ins. Co., 6 U.S. (2 Cranch) 127, 169, 2 L.Ed. 229 (1804). If the power to make political contributions or payments to influence public elections on matters unrelated to the business of the corporation was not expressly granted by the statutes of the state of incorporation, where did corporations obtain the basic power to exercise these constitutional rights established by the Supreme Court? Does MBCA § 3.02(15) authorize these expenditures?

(3) Is there risk in broadly authorizing corporate powers in statutes such as MBCA § 3.02 without any kind of restriction or limitation? Or does the holding in *Theodora Holding Corporation* itself provide a suitable restriction?

(4) Charitable contributions by corporations, particularly publicly held corporations, have been the subject of some criticism. Are you impressed by the argument that the function of business corporations is profit, and that charitable contributions are inconsistent with that function since they involve gifts of corporate assets? What about the argument that shareholders, rather than corporate management, should be permitted to decide which charities to support since that choice is essentially a personal rather than a business related one? Should a distinction be drawn between charitable contributions that may benefit the corporation directly (e.g., General Motors making contributions to support hospitals in areas close to General Motors plants), and more general contributions (e.g., to Harvard University)? Would it affect your evaluation of this issue if the General Motors' executive with authority to decide which charities receive GM's contributions had a daughter at Harvard?

D. PREMATURE COMMENCEMENT OF BUSINESS

1. PROMOTERS

The term "promoter" includes a "person who, acting alone or in conjunction with one or more other persons, directly or indirectly takes initiative in founding and organizing the business or enterprise of an issuer."[6] A promoter is often referred to as the "founder" or "organizer" of an enterprise. S.E.C. Rule 405, 17 C.F.R. § 230.405 (1992). The formation of a business enterprise largely involves business rather than legal problems. If the new business needs a plant, the promoter must locate one and rent or buy it. If a key person is essential for the success of the venture, the promoter must negotiate a contract of employment with him. If a distributive network for the business' product or a source of raw materials is necessary, the promoter must make the necessary arrangements. In any event, capital must be raised, either through the sale of equity interests in the business, or through loans, or commonly, a combination of both.

One of the promoter's duties is to arrange for the formation of the corporation to conduct the business. The process of incorporation, however, as described in a preceding section, is now so simple and routine that this is usually considered a small and relatively unimportant part of the promoter's role.

Some opprobrium may attach to the word "promoter." In the sense the word is used here, however, a promoter is usually an individual engaging in a useful and desirable economic function.

One important aspect of the promoter relationship is that the promoter owes significant fiduciary duties to other participants in the venture. The scope of these duties is described in Post v. United States, 407 F.2d 319, 328 (D.C.Cir.1968), cert. denied, 393 U.S. 1092, 89 S.Ct. 863, 21 L.Ed.2d 784 (1969), as follows:

> By elementary legal principles, promoters stand in a fiduciary relationship exacting good faith in their intracompany activities and demanding adherence to a high standard of honesty and frankness. Not the lesser of the promoter's manifold responsibilities outlaw secret profit-making and command the dedication of corporate funds to corporate purposes. And it cannot be doubted that promoters of stock corporations who employ the mails in deceitful violation of their fiduciary obligations may incur the full condemnation of the law.

In *Post*, defendants were convicted of conspiracy and mail fraud stemming from their activities in promotion of a country club in the Washington metropolitan area. The court upheld the following jury instruction as an accurate statement of both what a promoter does and what his fiduciary duty entails:

---

6. [By the Editor] According to S.E.C. Rule 405, 17 C.F.R. § 230.405 (1992), the term "promoter" also includes a person "who, in connection with the founding and organizing of the business or enterprise of an issuer, directly or indirectly receives in consideration of services or property, or both services and property, or both services and property, ty, 10 percent or more of any class of securities of the issuer or 10 percent or more of the proceeds from the sale of any class of such securities or proceeds."

The jury are instructed that a promoter is a person who sets in motion machinery that brings about the incorporation and organization of a corporation, brings together the persons interested in the enterprise to be conducted by the corporation, aids in inducing persons to become members of the corporation, and in procuring from them membership fees to carry out purposes set forth in the corporation's articles of incorporation. If from the evidence in this case the jury should find beyond a reasonable doubt that the defendants were promoters of Lakewood Country Club, Inc., then you are instructed that the defendants stood in a fiduciary relation to both the corporation as a separate legal entity and the members, including those persons who it was to be anticipated would make application to and would become members in Lakewood Country Club, Inc. Such a fiduciary relationship on the part of the defendants, should you find them to be the promoters of the Lakewood Country Club, Inc., required that they exercise the utmost good faith in their relations with the corporation and the members, including fully advising the corporation and members and persons who it was to be anticipated would become members, of any interest which the defendants had that would in any way affect the corporation, the members and anticipated members. Such a full disclosure requirement, if you should find the defendants to be promoters, would obligate them to faithfully make known all facts which might have influenced prospective members in deciding whether or not to purchase memberships. And this full disclosure would include the duty to refrain from misrepresenting any material facts, as well as the duty to make known any personal interest the defendants had in any transaction relating to the country club enterprise.

Also you are instructed that if you should find beyond a reasonable doubt that the defendants were promoters of the Lakewood Country Club, Inc., and that the funds obtained by them from members of the club corporation to accomplish the purposes of the corporation were used by them for the club's benefit, they were properly used. On the other hand, if you should find beyond a reasonable doubt that the defendants were the promoters of the club corporation, and that they had intentionally converted those funds to their own personal use, such would be a fraud on the members of the club corporation, since such funds were in the nature of trust funds as to which the defendants had a fiduciary obligation. And in that connection you are further instructed that for promoters to knowingly use their fiduciary position to obtain secret profits at the expense of the corporation of its members would not only be a breach of that fiduciary duty but an act of fraud.

407 F.2d 319, 328, n. 51.

Notes

(1) *Post v. United States* is unusual in that it involved a criminal prosecution of a promoter; most reported promoter cases involve civil suits brought against the promoter by injured parties. In *Post*, however, civil suits against the promoters were foreclosed because the promoters voluntarily agreed to relinquish control of the Lakewood Country Club project in exchange for a general release from civil liability. Presumably, representatives of the Club agreed to this settlement be-

cause prospects of recovering the converted funds from the promoters were not good. The language in the instruction, "beyond a reasonable doubt," was obviously included only because it was a criminal case.

(2) If a subsequent investor has dealt directly with the promoter in connection with the investment, there is little doubt that the promoter is liable for common law fraud in the event of misrepresentation. An additional federal remedy for fraud, or for mere nondisclosure of a material fact, may be available under Rule 10b–5, 17 C.F.R. § 240.10b–5, promulgated by the S.E.C. under § 10 of the Securities Exchange Act of 1934. A rule 10b–5 case must be brought in the federal courts. Rule 10b–5 is applicable only if the fraud or nondisclosure is "in connection with the purchase or sale of a security" and the transaction involves use of a "telephone or other interstate means of communication or any other interstate facility." See chapter 12, section B.

(3) In addition to subsequent investors in the enterprise, who else may attack transactions between a promoter and the corporation on the ground the transaction violates the promoter's fiduciary duty? At least the following possibilities exist:

(a) *General creditors* of the corporation or their representatives, *usually trustees in bankruptcy or receivers*. These suits are based on a theory that the promoters converted corporate assets to their own use in fraud of creditors. See, e.g., Frick v. Howard, 23 Wis.2d 86, 126 N.W.2d 619 (1964).

(b) *Co-promoters*. It is clear that a promoter is in a fiduciary relationship with his or her co-promoters, Geving v. Fitzpatrick, 56 Ill.App.3d 206, 14 Ill.Dec. 175, 371 N.E.2d 1228 (1978). Co-promoters may be viewed as partners in a venture to create the business. However, if the venture is incorporated, complications may arise from the injection of the corporation into the picture, and the substitution of corporate relationships for joint venture relationships.

(c) *The corporation*. The corporation itself may bring suit against its promoters after it has come under the control of subsequent investors or other persons. Two classic cases involving this issue arise out of the same promotional scheme at the beginning of this century. In this scheme, the promoters had sold property to the corporation formed by them for shares with a par value equal to about three times what they had paid for the property, and about twice what the property was worth at the time of the transfer. The United States Supreme Court in Old Dominion Copper Mining & Smelting Co. v. Lewisohn, 210 U.S. 206, 28 S.Ct. 634, 52 L.Ed. 1025 (1908), an action by the corporation against one of the principal promoters, concluded that since the promoters and the shareholders were identical at the time of the transaction, there were no members of the corporation who were not informed of the facts at the time of the fraud, and corporate assent was therefore given with full knowledge. As a result there was no breach of duty or wrong to the corporation. It was immaterial, the court said, that thereafter outsiders subscribed for shares in ignorance of the true facts because "of course, legally speaking, a corporation does not change its identity by adding a cubit to its stature." In Old Dominion Copper Mining & Smelting Co. v. Bigelow, 203 Mass. 159, 89 N.E. 193 (1909), an action by the corporation against the other principal promoter, on the other hand, the Massachusetts court argued that promoters stand in the same fiduciary position to the corporation when uninformed shareholders are expected to be brought in after the wrong has been perpetrated as they do when there are current shareholders to whom no disclosure is made. While a wrong is committed immediately against the corporation, there is no one to enforce the remedy until the new shareholders come in. The views of the

Massachusetts court appear to have gained ascendancy where the promoters plan to invite the public to become subscribers for shares. See Northridge Co-op. Section No. 1, Inc. v. 32nd Avenue Constr. Corp., 2 N.Y.2d 514, 161 N.Y.S.2d 404, 141 N.E.2d 802 (1957).

(4) In recent years, litigation involving promoters' fraud has declined. This is partly due to the Federal Securities Act of 1933, which makes it unlawful to use means of interstate commerce or the mails to sell publicly a security unless a registration statement has been filed with the S.E.C. setting forth required information. Among the required disclosures are the following:

> *Transactions with promoters.* Registrants that have been organized within the past five years and that are filing a registration statement * * * shall:

> (1) State the names of the promoters, the nature and amount of anything of value (including money, property, contracts, options or rights of any kind) received or to be received by each promoter, directly or indirectly, from the registrant and the nature and amount of any assets, services or other consideration therefore received or to be received by the registrant; and

> (2) As to any assets acquired or to be acquired by the registrant from a promoter, state the amount at which the assets were acquired or are to be acquired and the principle followed or to be followed in determining such amount and identify the persons making the determination and their relationship, if any, with the registrant or any promoter. If the assets were acquired by the promoter within two years prior to their transfer to the registrant, also state the cost thereof to the promoter. * * *

17 C.F.R. § 229.404(d) (1997). Many state Blue Sky laws also require similar disclosure.

STANLEY J. HOW & ASSOC., INC. v. BOSS

United States District Court, Southern District of Iowa, 1963.
222 F.Supp. 936.

[Editor: This was an action to recover on a contract for the performance of architectural services. The plaintiff alleged that it had performed the required services and was entitled to a fee of $38,250, of which it had received only $14,500. It seeks to collect the difference from Boss, a promoter of a corporation. The pertinent parts of the contract (with italics added) are as follows:

> This agreement made as of the twentieth (20th) day of April in the year Nineteen Hundred and Sixty–One by and between *Boss Hotels Company, Inc. hereinafter called the Owner,* and Stanley J. How and Associates, Inc. hereinafter called the Architect * * *.

> The Owner agrees to pay the Architect for such services a fee of six (6) percent of the construction cost of the Project, with other payments and reimbursements as hereinafter provided.

> The Owner and the Architect each binds himself, his partners, successors, legal representatives and assigns to the other party to this Agreement and to the partners, successors, legal representatives and assigns of such other party in respect to all covenants of this Agreement.

> Except as above, neither the Owner nor the Architect shall assign, sublet or transfer his interest in this Agreement without written consent of the other.

IN WITNESS WHEREOF the parties hereto have made and executed this Agreement the day and year first above written.

Owner: /s/ Edw. A. Boss

By: Edwin A. Boss, agent for a Minnesota corporation to be formed who will be the obligor.

Architect:

Stanley J. How and Associates, Inc.

/s/ Stanley J. How

This contract is the Standard Form of Agreement Between Owner and Architect printed by the American Institute of Architects. The blanks were originally filled in by a representative of the plaintiff; as originally prepared, the signature clause as well as the caption referred to "Boss Hotels Co., Inc." as the "owner." However, when the contract was presented to Boss, he erased the words "Boss Hotel Co., Inc." and inserted the language "By: Edwin A. Boss, agent for a Minnesota corporation to be formed who will be the obligor." He then asked Mr. How, "Is this all right?" or "Is this acceptable, this manner of signing?" or words to that effect. How said "Yes," and the contracts were then signed by defendant and Stanley J. How. Defendant caused an Iowa corporation named Minneapolis–Hunter Hotel Co. to be formed to construct the project. The checks sent to plaintiff for partial payments under the contract bore the name of this corporation. The project was ultimately abandoned after a substantial amount of architectural work had been performed under the contract.]

HANSON, DISTRICT JUDGE.

* * * To what extent [the Minneapolis–Hunter Hotel Co.] actually came into being is not clear in the record. No corporate charter, by-laws, or resolutions were offered into evidence. At any rate, if this new corporation exists, there are no assets in it to pay the amount due on the contract.

There really is not much debate as to what the law is on the questions raised. Both parties site [*sic*] King Features Syndicate, Dept. of Hearst Corp. International News Service Division v. Courrier, 241 Iowa 870, 43 N.W.2d 718, 41 A.L.R.2d 467, for the proposition that a promoter, though he may assume to act on behalf of the projected corporation and not for himself, will be personally liable on his contract unless the other party agreed to look to some other person or fund for payment. * * *

[The court then summarizes Comment b to Section 326 of the Restatement of Agency. This comment, as revised in the Restatement of Agency, Second, reads:

b. *Promoters.* The classic illustration of the rule stated in this Section is the promoter. When a promoter makes an agreement with another on behalf of a corporation to be formed, the following alternatives may represent the intent of the parties:

(1) They may understand that the other party is making a revocable offer to the nonexistent corporation which will result in a contract if the corporation is formed and accepts the offer prior to withdrawal. This is the normal understanding.

(2) They may understand that the other party is making an irrevocable offer for a limited time. Consideration to support the promise to keep

the offer open can be found in an express or limited promise by the promoter to organize the corporation and use his best efforts to cause it to accept the offer.

(3) They may agree to a present contract by which the promoter is bound, but with an agreement that his liability terminates if the corporation is formed and manifests its willingness to become a party. There can be no ratification by the newly formed corporation, since it was not in existence when the agreement was made.

(4) They may agree to a present contract on which, even though the corporation becomes a party, the promoter remains liable either primarily or as surety for the performance of the corporation's obligation.

Which one of these possible alternatives, or variants thereof, is intended is a matter of interpretation on the facts of the individual case.]

[The third] possible interpretation is not very important in this case because a novation was not pleaded or argued. * * *

In the present case, the contract was signed: "Edwin A. Boss, agent for a Minnesota corporation to be formed who will be the obligor." The defendant argues that this is an agreement that the new corporation is solely liable. The problem here is what is the import of the words "who will be the obligor." It says nothing about the present obligor. The words "will be" connote something which will take place in the future. * * *

About the closest case to the present in terms of signature is O'Rorke v. Geary, 207 Pa. 240, 56 A. 541, where the contract was signed "D.J. Geary for a bridge company to be organized and incorporated as party of the second part." The payments were to be made monthly and work was to be done before it was possible for the corporation to make the payments. The court held the promoter personally liable. * * *

* * * [T]his is a situation where the parties used ambiguous words to describe their intentions. To resolve this ambiguity, it is helpful to resort to the usual rules of interpretation of ambiguous contracts. * * *

Mr. How's testimony and his business record * * * show that he did not intend that the new corporation was the sole obligor on the contract. He stated that he believed Boss Hotel Co., Inc. or Boss Hotels was liable on the contract. This is not inconsistent with thinking Mr. Boss was liable on the contract but it is inconsistent with intending that the new corporation was to be solely liable on the contract. Promoters other than the one signing the contract may be liable on the contract also. In this case, Boss Hotel Co., Inc. was not made a party but this does show a reason why Mr. How might state that he felt Boss Hotel Co., Inc. was liable on the contract. The oral testimony on this point was only generally to the effect that the parties agreed that the contract was all right as written, but did tend to support the conclusion that Mr. Boss was intended to be the present obligor on the contract. * * *

It might well be that the parties were thinking about an understanding such as the [third] type wherein there would be a future novation. However, the defendant didn't feel this was the situation. He did not plead or argue novation or agreement to that effect. Therefore, the only issue was whether the contract was a continuing offer to the then nonexistent corporation or was an agreement that Mr. Boss was a present obligor. While the agreement was not completely clear, the words "who will be the obligor" are not enough to offset the rule that the person signing for the nonexistent corporation is normally to be personally liable. This is especially true when considered in the light of other circumstances of this case and would be true even without the inference that the law puts on this situation. * * *

The defendant argues that a practical construction has been put on the contract to the effect the plaintiff agreed to look solely to the credit of the new corporation. For this construction, the defendant relies upon the fact that the two checks which were given to Mr. Boss carried the letterhead of the new corporation and were signed by Edwin Hunter. * * * This would be an attempt to penalize the plaintiff for being patient and not demanding strict compliance. The court feels there was no waiver of rights and none was pleaded. * * *

In this case, the defendant was the principal promoter, acting for himself personally and as President of Boss Hotels, Inc. The promoters abandoned their purpose of forming the corporation. This would make the promoter liable to the plaintiff unless the contract be construed to mean: (1) that the plaintiff agreed to look solely to the new corporation for payment, and (2) that the promoter did not have any duty toward the plaintiff to form the corporation and give the corporation the opportunity to assume and pay the liability. * * *

At the time the specifications and drawings were completed, the amount owed the plaintiff was 75% of 6% of $850,000.00 (the reasonable cost estimate). This would amount to $38,250.00. $14,500.00 of this amount has been paid leaving an amount of $23,750.00 due to the plaintiff.

Accordingly the court concludes that the plaintiff, Stanley J. How & Associates, Inc., should have and recover judgment against the defendant, Edwin A. Boss, in the sum of $23,750.00, with interest and costs and, accordingly, a judgment will be entered. * * *

Notes

(1) Is it not a fair inference from the circumstances surrounding the execution of the contract in this case that both parties probably contemplated that the architect was to look solely to some corporation for payment, that neither party thought that Boss was to be *personally* liable, and that therefore the holding of the court in effect gives the plaintiff an unjustified windfall? In light of this argument, how persuasive is the Court's reliance on O'Rorke v. Geary, holding that where performance is called for before the corporation is formed, there is an inference that the promoter intended to be personally liable?

(2) Consider the following sections of the Restatement (Second) of Agency. Do they suggest alternative grounds by which a promoter might be held liable if he executes a contract in the name of a not-yet-formed corporation but without including the phrase "a corporation to be formed"?

§ 329. Agent Who Warrants Authority

A person who purports to make a contract, conveyance or representation on behalf of another who has full capacity but whom he has no power to bind, thereby becomes subject to liability to the other party thereto upon an implied warranty of authority, unless he has manifested that he does not make such warranty or the other party knows that the agent is not so authorized.

§ 330.   Liability for Misrepresentation of Authority

A person who tortiously misrepresents to another that he has authority to make a contract, conveyance, or representation on behalf of a principal whom he has no power to bind, is subject to liability to the other in an action of tort for loss caused by reliance upon such misrepresentation.

§ 331.   Agent Making No Warranty or Representation of Authority

A person who purports to make a contract, conveyance or representation on behalf of a principal whom he has no power to bind thereby is not subject to liability to the other party thereto if he sufficiently manifests that he does not warrant his authority and makes no tortious misrepresentation.

(3) Presumably, it would have been entirely feasible for Boss to have formed a new corporation to construct the project under the corporation laws of either Minnesota or Iowa. If he had done so, and thereafter the contract had been entered into in the name of the new corporation, the possibility of a successful suit by the architect against Boss personally would have been very slight. The fact that cases involving promoter liability on contracts continue to rise with some regularity probably indicates that many promoters do not have legal advice in the early stages of the promotion, since presumably an attorney would insist that basic rights and obligations be expressed reasonably clearly, and that some provision should be made for obvious contingencies such as a total failure of the promotion. An attorney representing the promoter would normally recommend that a corporation be formed and that all contracts be taken in the name of the corporation exclusively. Alternatively, the attorney might recommend that the agreement expressly provide that the other party should look only to the corporation for payment. Of course, counsel for the other party would doubtless recommend that the promoter expressly assume personal responsibility for performance of the contract.

QUAKER HILL, INC. v. PARR

Supreme Court of Colorado, 1961.
148 Colo. 45, 364 P.2d 1056.

DOYLE, JUSTICE.

The plaintiff in error, to which we will refer as Quaker Hill or plaintiff, was plaintiff in the trial court in an action to recover the sum of $14,503.56 from defendants, defendants in error here. Judgment was in favor of the defendants, and Quaker Hill seeks review.

In May, 1958, the plaintiff, a New York corporation with offices in Newark, New York, sold a large quantity of nursery stock to the Denver Memorial Nursery, Inc. A sales contract, together with a promissory note was executed on May 19, 1958, and the Denver Memorial Nursery, Inc. was named as the contracting party in the sales contract and as the maker of the promissory note. The form of the signature on the note was as follows:

"Denver Memorial Nursery, Inc.

E.D. Parr, Pres.

James P. Presba, Sc'y.–Treas."

The contract shows the Denver Memorial Nursery, Inc. as purchaser and is signed:

"E.D. Parr, Pres."

From the evidence it appears that in the year 1958, prior to this transaction, Parr, Presba and others formed a corporation having the name "Denver Memorial Gardens, Inc." Its purpose was to operate a cemetery. In May of 1958 Parr and Presba, while in the course of negotiations with plaintiff to purchase nursery stock, undertook to organize a separate corporation called "Denver Memorial Nursery, Inc." On May 14, 1958, an order was signed by Parr on behalf of Denver Memorial Nursery, Inc. which, to the knowledge of plaintiff, was not yet formed, that fact being noted in the contract. Subsequently another order dated May 16, 1958, together with the mentioned note, was executed and was delivered to the plaintiff, together with a down payment in the amount of $1,000. Under the contract the balance of the purchase price was not due until the end of the year. The nursery stock was shipped immediately and arrived on May 26, 1958. It was temporarily planted with the assistance of plaintiff. After this temporary planting had occurred, a substitute order was sent to Quaker Hill which was similar in all respects to the previous order except that it contained the name "Mountain View Nurseries" instead of "Denver Memorial Nursery, Inc." as the purchaser. During the course of the ensuing winter and spring and prior to the due date of the balance of the purchase price, the nursery stock all died. The contract contained a guarantee providing for replacement of stock which died.

The Denver Memorial Nursery, Inc. was never formed. Because of name confusion, this corporation was called Mountain View Nurseries, Inc. Its articles were executed on May 27, 1958, and were subsequently filed with the Secretary of State. Neither the Denver Memorial Nursery, Inc. nor the Mountain View Nurseries, Inc. ever functioned as going concerns.

The explanation given at the trial for failure to form the corporation prior to entering into the first contract stemmed from insistence of Quaker Hill that the deal be consummated at once because the growing season was rapidly passing. Barker, who was salesman for Quaker Hill at the time of the sale, testified that the transaction was consummated in this form as a result of his insistence.

After Mountain View Nurseries, Inc. was formed, a new note and contract, prepared by the Division Manager of plaintiff and containing the name "Mountain View Nurseries, Inc." as contracting party, was submitted to defendants, signed in the name of Mountain View Nurseries, Inc. and returned to plaintiff. The plaintiff company thereafter used the designation "Mountain View Nurseries" in its communications. The present action seeks to subject defendants to *personal* liability in view of the defunct financial condition of the corporation, based upon the fact that the corporation was not formed at the time the contract was made and on the further ground that the defendants as promoters were individually liable. * * *

In summary, the facts disclose that Quaker Hill, a New York corporation acting through a local agent, made a sale to a corporation to be formed, and later accepted still another corporation after formation of the latter. The contract imposed no obligation on defendants to form the corporation nor did it name them as obligors on the note or as promisees in the contract. The question is whether under these circumstances personal liability can be imposed.

In urging that the trial court erred and that the cause should be reversed, plaintiff argues:

    1.   That promoters who enter a contract in the name of a proposed corporation are personally liable in the absence of an agreement that they should not be liable.

    2.   That the subsequent formation of a corporation and the ratification of the contract does not operate to release the promoters.

    3.   That the failure of the nursery stock, the subject matter of this contract, is not a defense because the contractual remedy was replacement.

    4.   That there should be liability on a quantum meruit basis.

The general principle which plaintiff urges as applicable here is that promoters are personally liable on their contracts, though made on behalf of a corporation to be formed. * * * A well recognized exception to this general rule, however, is that if the contract is made on behalf of the corporation and the other party agrees to look to the corporation and not to the promoters for payment, the promoters incur no personal liability.

In the present case, according to the trial court's findings, the plaintiff, acting through its agent, was well aware of the fact that the corporation was not formed and nevertheless urged that the contract be made in the name of the proposed corporation. There is but little evidence indicating intent on the part of the plaintiff to look to the defendants for performance or payment. The single fact supporting plaintiff's theory is the obtaining of an individual balance sheet. On the contrary, the entire transaction contemplated the corporation as the contracting party. Personal liability does not arise under such circumstances. See 41 A.L.R.2d 477, where the annotation recognizes the noted exception that personal liability does not attach where the contracting party is shown to be looking solely to the corporation for payment and not to the promoters or officers. * * *

In the case at bar, the findings of the trial court clearly establish intent on the part of the plaintiff to contract with the corporation and not with the individual defendants.

The curious form of this transaction is undoubtedly explainable on the basis of the long distance dealing, the great rush to complete it, the heavy emphasis on completion of the sale rather than on securing payment or a means of payment. No effort was made to expressly obligate the defendants and this present effort must be regarded as pure afterthought.

Being convinced that the trial court's determination was proper under the circumstances, we conclude that the judgment should be and it is affirmed.

Notes

(1) In Coopers & Lybrand v. Fox, 758 P.2d 683 (Colo.App.1988), Garry Fox was in the process of forming a new business to be called "Fox and Partners, Inc."

On November 3, 1981 he met with a representative of Coopers & Lybrand and arranged for a tax opinion and other accounting services. Articles of incorporation were filed on December 4, 1981. After rendering the services, Coopers & Lybrand sent a bill for $10,827 to "Mr. Garry R. Fox, Fox and Partner, Inc." When the bill was not paid, suit was brought against Garry Fox individually. The Court held that Fox was not entitled to the protection provided by Quaker Hill, Inc. v. Parr:

> As a general rule, promoters are personally liable for the contracts they make, though made on behalf of a corporation to be formed. The well-recognized exception to the general rule of promoter liability is that if the contracting party knows the corporation is not in existence but nevertheless agrees to look solely to the corporation and not to the promoter for payment, then the promoter incurs no personal liability. *Quaker Hill, Inc. v. Parr.* * * * In the absence of an express agreement, the existence of an agreement to release the promoter from liability may be shown by circumstances making it reasonably certain that the parties intended to and did enter into the agreement.

> Here, the trial court found there was *no* agreement, either express or implied, regarding Fox's liability. Thus, in the absence of an agreement releasing him from liability, Fox is liable.

> Coopers also contends that the trial court erred in ruling, in effect, that Coopers had the burden of proving any agreement regarding Fox's personal liability for payment of the fee. We agree. Release of the promoter depends on the intent of the parties. As the proponent of an alleged agreement to release the promoter from liability, the promoter has the burden of proving the release agreement. * * * The trial court found that there was no agreement regarding Fox's liability. Thus, Fox failed to sustain his burden of proof, and the trial court erred in granting judgment in his favor.

> It is undisputed that the defendant, Garry J. Fox, engaged Coopers' services, that G. Fox and Partners, Inc., was not in existence at that time, that Coopers performed the work, and that the fee was reasonable. The only dispute, as the trial court found, is whether Garry Fox is liable for payment of the fee. We conclude that Fox is liable, as a matter of law, under the doctrine of promoter liability.

Does this holding help to reconcile *Quaker Hill* and *Stanley J. How?*

(2) How explicit does the agreement to look only to the not-yet-formed corporation have to be to release the promoter? Consider Goodman v. Darden, Doman & Stafford Assoc., 100 Wash.2d 476, 670 P.2d 648, 652–53 (1983):

> We do not believe the agreement to release a promoter from liability must say in so many words, "I agree to release." Where the promoter cannot show an express agreement, existence of the agreement to release him from liability may be shown by circumstances. Of course, where circumstantial evidence is relied on, the circumstances must be such as to make it reasonably certain that the parties intended to and did enter into the agreement. * * * From its oral opinion it is clear that the trial court relied on three considerations in holding that the parties agreed to release Goodman from the contract: (1) DDS knew of the corporation's nonexistence; (2) Goodman told Doman that he was forming a corporation to limit his personal liability; and (3) the progress payments were made to the corporation.

> The fact that DDS knew of the corporation's nonexistence is not dispositive in any way of its intent. The rule is that the contracting party may know

of the nonexistence of the corporation *but nevertheless* may agree to look solely to the corporation. The fact that a contracting party knows that the corporation is nonexistent does not indicate any agreement to release the promoter. To the contrary, such knowledge alone would seem to indicate that the members of DDS intended to make Goodman a party to the contract. They could not hold the corporation, a nonexistent entity, responsible and of course they would expect to have recourse against someone (Goodman) if default occurred. This consideration also relates to another factor the trial court apparently had in mind—that the members of DDS were all educated people. Goodman argues that as such they should have expressly requested that he be personally liable. This was unnecessary because under the law as set out above, Goodman was liable until the partners of DDS agreed otherwise. Thus, they were not required to specify personal liability.

The fact that Goodman expressed a desire to form the corporation to limit his liability also is not dispositive of the intentions of the members of DDS. No one from DDS objected to his incorporating but this failure to object does not indicate an affirmative assent to limit Goodman's personal liability. Apparently Goodman believed that incorporation would automatically limit his liability thus misunderstanding the rules regarding promoter liability. * * * The only other evidence of the parties' intent to make the corporation the sole party to the contract is that the progress payments were made payable to the corporation. However, they were so written only at the instruction of Goodman and in fact the first check written by DDS after the signing of the contract was written to the corporation *and* Goodman as an individual. This evidence does not show by reasonable certainty that DDS intended to contract only with the corporation.

Three Justices dissented.

(3) Assume that Quaker Hill, Inc. defaulted on its obligation to deliver the nursery stock before any corporation was formed. Could Parr act as plaintiff in a suit against Quaker Hill for breach of contract? Or would he have to form a "shell" corporation for the sole purpose of bringing suit? Or should Quaker Hill's default be deemed the revocation of a mere offer so that no contractual liability exists?

(4) A "head count" of the numerous cases involving the personal liability of promoters would doubtless show that a majority of the cases hold the defendant-promoter personally liable on one theory or another. Prediction of result in a specific case, however, is hazardous.

McARTHUR v. TIMES PRINTING CO.

Supreme Court of Minnesota, 1892.
48 Minn. 319, 51 N.W. 216.

MITCHELL, J.

The complaint alleges that about October 1, 1889, the defendant contracted with plaintiff for his services as advertising solicitor for one year; that in April, 1890, it discharged him, in violation of the contract. The action is to recover damages for the breach of the contract. * * * Upon the trial there was evidence reasonably tending to prove that in September, 1889, one C.A. Nimocks and others were engaged as promoters in procuring the organization of the defendant company to publish a newspaper; that, about September

12th, Nimocks, as such promoter, made a contract with plaintiff, in behalf of the contemplated company, for his services as advertising solicitor for the period of one year from and after October 1st,—the date at which it was expected that the company would be organized; that the corporation was not, in fact, organized until October 16th, but that the publication of the paper was commenced by the promoters October 1st, at which date plaintiff, in pursuance of his arrangement with Nimocks, entered upon the discharge of his duties as advertising solicitor for the paper; that after the organization of the company he continued in its employment in the same capacity until discharged, the following April; that defendant's board of directors never took any formal action with reference to the contract made in its behalf by Nimocks, but all of the stockholders, directors, and officers of the corporation knew of this contract at the time of its organization, or were informed of it soon afterwards, and none of them objected to or repudiated it, but, on the contrary, retained plaintiff in the employment of the company without any other or new contract as to his services.

There is a line of cases which hold that where a contract is made in behalf of, and for the benefit of, a projected corporation, the corporation, after its organization, cannot become a party to the contract, either by adoption or ratification of it. This, however, seems to be more a question of name than of substance; that is, whether the liability of the corporation, in such cases, is to be placed on the grounds of its adoption of the contract of its promoters, or upon some other ground, such as equitable estoppel. This court, in accordance with what we deem sound reason, as well as the weight of authority, has held that, while a corporation is not bound by engagements made on its behalf by its promoters before its organization, it may, after its organization, make such engagements its own contracts. And this it may do precisely as it might make similar original contracts; formal action of its board of directors being necessary only where it would be necessary in the case of a similar original contract. That it is not requisite that such adoption or acceptance be express, but it may be inferred from acts or acquiescence on part of the corporation, or its authorized agents, as any similar original contract might be shown. * * * That the contract in this case was of that kind is very clear; and the acts and acquiescence of the corporate officers, after the organization of the company, fully justified the jury in finding that it had adopted it as its own.

The defendant, however, claims that the contract was void under the statute of frauds, because, "by its terms, not to be performed within one year from the making thereof," which counsel assumes to be September 12th,—the date of the agreement between plaintiff and the promoter. This proceeds upon the erroneous theory that the act of the corporation, in such cases, is a ratification, which relates back to the date of the contract with the promoter, under the familiar maxim that "a subsequent ratification has a retroactive effect, and is equivalent to a prior command." But the liability of the corporation, under such circumstances, does not rest upon any principle of the law of agency, but upon the immediate and voluntary act of the company. Although the acts of a corporation with reference to the contracts made by promoters in its behalf before its organization are frequently loosely termed "ratification," yet a "ratification," properly so called, implies an existing person, on whose behalf the contract might have been made at the time. There cannot, in law, be a ratification of a contract which could not have been made binding on the ratifier at the time it was made, because the ratifier was not then in existence. What is called "adoption," in such case, is, in legal effect, the making of a contract of the date of the adoption, and not as of some former date. The contract in this case was, therefore, not within the statute of frauds. * * *

Order affirmed.

Notes

(1) The position taken in the principal case, that a corporation is not liable on a promoter's contract unless it expressly or impliedly adopts (or "ratifies") it, appears to be generally accepted, though the issue has arisen in only a few litigated cases. For an example of implied adoption, see Stolmeier v. Beck, 232 Neb. 705, 441 N.W.2d 888 (1989) [subsequently-formed corporation was obligated to return funds to an investor since funds were later used by the corporation in operation of its business]. In Framingham Sav. Bank v. Szabo, 617 F.2d 897 (1st Cir.1980) the Court applied the "extreme minority" rule of Massachusetts that a newly formed corporation "could not become bound to the contract by ratification or adoption of the putative agent's bargain. Rather, to bind itself the corporation must introduce 'into the transaction such elements as would be sufficient foundation for a new contract.' The corporation can become liable on the terms of the original contract, but only if its post-incorporation acts are sufficient independently to bind it to a new contract." 617 F.2d at 898. Considering that corporations act only through agents, do you think results will often differ if a court applies the general rule or the "extreme minority" rule applied in Massachusetts?

(2) Both the general rule and the narrower rule applied in Massachusetts require newly formed corporations to do something before they are bound on contracts made on their behalf by promoters. Can this requirement be justified on policy grounds as well as conceptual grounds? Why not adopt a rule that newly formed corporations automatically become bound on all contracts entered into on their behalf by promoters?

(3) 2 Williston on Contracts § 306, at 431 (3d ed. 1959) states that "it seems more nearly to correspond with the intentions of the parties to suggest that when the corporation assents to the contract, it assents to take the place of the promoter—a change of parties to which the other side of the contract assented in advance." Is that true? If this inference were adopted, might promoters facing an unwanted pre-formation contractual liability form a corporation with nominal assets and arrange to have that corporation adopt the contract?

(4) A peculiar problem arises in connection with a contract between a promoter and an attorney pursuant to which the attorney agrees to form the corporation. If a straightforward theory of implied adoption through the acceptance of benefits is followed, the mere existence of the corporation constitutes acceptance of the benefits of the attorney's services, and an agreement to pay whatever fee was agreed upon between the promoter and the attorney. However, in Kridelbaugh v. Aldrehn Theatres Co., 195 Iowa 147, 149, 191 N.W. 803, 804 (1923), the Court refused to follow this logic: "This is not a case in which the corporation can accept or refuse the benefits of a contract. Under the instant record it had no choice. Like a child at its birth, it must be born in the manner provided. There is no volition on its part." See also David v. Southern Import Wine Co., 171 So. 180, 182 (La.App.1936): "A corporation brought into existence—given its life—by the service of an attorney, may not be heard to say that the service was unauthorized because rendered prior to incorporation. When the

benefit of such service is received and accepted by the corporation, it cannot be heard to question the authority through which the service was employed. It may be that in such case the corporation may not be held to the express terms of a contract for such employment; in other words, it may not be held to the contract itself, but it may not repudiate the service entirely and yet reap the benefits therefrom. It may repudiate the contract price if a price has been agreed upon, but it may not refuse to pay for the service on the basis of the value of the benefits received; in other words on a quantum meruit." Of course, an informal adoption of the contract terms will be given effect if it appears to be truly voluntary. See, e.g. Indianapolis Blue Print & Mfg. Co. v. Kennedy, 215 Ind. 409, 412, 19 N.E.2d 554, 555 (1939).

2.   DEFECTIVE INCORPORATION

ROBERTSON v. LEVY

Court of Appeals, District of Columbia, 1964.
197 A.2d 443.

HOOD, CHIEF JUDGE.

On December 22, 1961, Martin G. Robertson and Eugene M. Levy entered into an agreement whereby Levy was to form a corporation, Penn Ave. Record Shack, Inc., which was to purchase Robertson's business. Levy submitted articles of incorporation to the Superintendent of Corporations on December 27, 1961, but no certificate of incorporation was issued at this time. Pursuant to the contract an assignment of lease was entered into on December 31, 1961, between Robertson and Levy, the latter acting as president of Penn Ave. Record Shack, Inc. On January 2, 1962, the articles of incorporation were rejected by the Superintendent of Corporations but on the same day Levy began to operate the business under the name Penn Ave. Record Shack, Inc. Robertson executed a bill of sale to Penn Ave. Record Shack, Inc. on January 8, 1962, disposing of the assets of his business to that "corporation" and receiving in return a note providing for installment payments signed "Penn Ave. Record Shack, Inc. by Eugene M. Levy, President." The certificate of incorporation was issued on January 17, 1962. One payment was made on the note. The exact date when the payment was made cannot be clearly determined from the record, but presumably it was made after the certificate of incorporation was issued. Penn Ave. Record Shack, Inc. ceased doing business in June 1962 and is presently without assets. Robertson sued Levy for the balance due on the note as well as for additional expenses incurred in settling the lease arrangement with the original lessor. In holding for the defendant the trial court found that [§ 139 of the 1950 Model Act], relied upon by Robertson, did not apply and further that Robertson was estopped to deny the existence of the corporation.

The case presents the following issues on appeal: Whether the president of an "association" which filed its articles of incorporation, which were first rejected but later accepted, can be held personally liable on an obligation entered into by the "association" before the certificate of incorporation has been issued, or whether the creditor is "estopped" from denying the existence of the "corporation" because, after the certificate of incorporation was issued, he accepted the first installment payment on the note.

The Business Corporation Act of the District of Columbia, Code 1961, is patterned after the Model Business Corporation Act which is largely based on the Illinois Business Corporation Act of 1933. On this appeal, we are concerned with an interpretation of [§§ 50 and 139 of the 1950 Model Act]. Several states have substantially enacted the Model Act, but only a few have enacted both sections similar to those under consideration. A search of the case law in each of these jurisdictions, as well as in our own jurisdiction, convinces us that these particular sections of the corporation acts have never been the subject of a reported decision.

For a full understanding of the problems raised, some historical grounding is not only illuminative but necessary. In early common law times private corporations were looked upon with distrust and disfavor. This distrust of the corporate form for private enterprise was eventually overcome by the enactment of statutes which set forth certain prerequisites before the status was achieved, and by court decisions which eliminated other stumbling blocks. Problems soon arose, however, where there was substantial compliance with the prerequisites of the statute, but not complete formal compliance. Thus the concepts of de jure corporations, de facto corporations, and of "corporations by estoppel" came into being.

Taking each of these in turn, a de jure corporation results when there has been conformity with the mandatory conditions precedent (as opposed to merely directive conditions) established by the statute. A de jure corporation is not subject to direct or collateral attack either by the state in a *quo warranto* proceeding or by any other person.

A de facto corporation is one which has been defectively incorporated and thus is not de jure. The Supreme Court has stated that the requisites for a corporation de facto are: (1) A valid law under which such a corporation can be lawfully organized; (2) An attempt to organize thereunder; (3) Actual user of the corporate franchise. Good faith in claiming to be and in doing business as a corporation is often added as a further condition. A de facto corporation is recognized for all purposes except where there is a direct attack by the state in a *quo warranto* proceeding. The concept of de facto corporation has been roundly criticized.[7]

Cases continued to arise, however, where the corporation was not de jure, where it was not de facto because of failure to comply with one of the four requirements above, but where the courts, lacking some clear standard or guideline, were willing to decide on the equities of the case. Thus another concept arose, the so-called "corporation by estoppel." This term was a complete misnomer. There was no corporation, the acts of the associates having failed even to colorably fulfill the statutory requirements; there was no estoppel in the pure sense of the word because generally there was no holding out followed by reliance on the part of the other party. Apparently estoppel can arise whether or not a de facto corporation has come into existence. Estoppel problems arose where the certificate of incorporation had been issued as well as where it had not been issued, and under the following general conditions: where the "association" sues a third party and the third

---

7. [By the Court] Ballantine § 20 ("a baffling and discouraging maze,"); Stevens, Corporations, pp. 135–6 (1949) ("inaccurate and confusing,"); Frey, Legal Analysis and the De Facto Doctrine, 100 U.Pa.L.Rev. 1153, 1180 (1952) ("legal conceptualism at its worst,").

party is estopped from denying that the plaintiff is a corporation; where a third party sues the "association" as a corporation and the "association" is precluded from denying that it was a corporation; where a third party sues the "association" and the members of that association cannot deny its existence as a corporation where they participated in holding it out as a corporation; where a third party sues the individuals behind the "association" but is estopped from denying the existence of the "corporation"; where either a third party, or the "association" is estopped from denying the corporate existence because of prior pleadings.

One of the reasons for enacting modern corporation statutes was to eliminate problems inherent in the de jure, de facto and, estoppel concepts. Thus [§§ 50 and 139 of the MBCA (1950)] were enacted as follows:

[§ 50. Effect of issuance of certificate of incorporation]

Upon the issuance of the certificate of incorporation, the corporate existence shall begin, and such certificate of incorporation shall be conclusive evidence that all conditions precedent required to be performed by the incorporators have been complied with and that the corporation has been incorporated under this Act, except in a proceeding to cancel or revoke the certificate of incorporation or for involuntary dissolution of the corporation.

[§ 139. Unauthorized assumption of corporate powers]

All persons who assume to act as a corporation without authority so to do shall be jointly and severally liable for all debts and liabilities incurred or arising as result thereof.

The first portion of [§ 50] sets forth a *sine qua non* regarding compliance. No longer must the courts inquire into the equities of a case to determine whether there has been "colorable compliance" with the statute. The corporation comes into existence only when the certificate has been issued. Before the certificate issues, there is no corporation de jure, de facto or by estoppel. After the certificate is issued under [§ 50], the de jure corporate existence commences. Only after such existence has begun can the corporation commence business through compliance with section [§ 48(g) of MBCA (1950)] by paying into the corporation the minimum capital, and with [§ 51 of that Act], which requires that the capitalization be no less than $1,000. These latter two sections are given further force and effect by [a non-Model Act section] which declares that directors of a corporation are jointly and severally liable for any assets distributed or any dividends paid to shareholders which renders the corporation insolvent or reduces its net assets below its stated capital.

The authorities which have considered the problem are unanimous in their belief that [MBCA (1950) §§ 50 and 139] have put to rest de facto corporations and corporations by estoppel. Thus the Comment to [§ 50], * * * after noting that de jure incorporation is complete when the certificate is issued, states that:

"Since it is unlikely that any steps short of securing a certificate of incorporation would be held to constitute apparent compliance, the possibility that a de facto corporation could exist under such a provision is remote."[8]

---

8. [By the Editor] The comment to § 56 of MBCA (1969) was even more unambiguous:

Under the unequivocal provisions of the Model Act, any steps short of securing a

Similarly, Professor Hornstein in his work on Corporate Law and Practice (1959) observes at § 29 that: "Statutes in almost half the jurisdictions have virtually eliminated the distinction between de jure and de facto corporations [citing § 139 of the Model Act]." * * *

The portion of [§ 50] which states that the certificate of incorporation will be "conclusive evidence" that all conditions precedent have been performed eliminates the problems of estoppel and de facto corporations once the certificate has been issued. The existence of the corporation is conclusive evidence against all who deal with it. Under [§ 139], if an individual or group of individuals assumes to act as a corporation before the certificate of incorporation has been issued, joint and several liability attaches. We hold, therefore, that the impact of these sections, when considered together, is to eliminate the concepts of estoppel and de facto corporateness under the Business Corporation Act of the District of Columbia. It is immaterial whether the third person believed he was dealing with a corporation or whether he intended to deal with a corporation.[9] The certificate of incorporation provides the cut off point; before it is issued, the individuals, and not the corporation, are liable.

Turning to the facts of this case, Penn Ave. Record Shack, Inc. was not a corporation when the original agreement was entered into, when the lease was assigned, when Levy took over Robertson's business, when operations began under the Penn Ave. Record Shack, Inc. name, or when the bill of sale was executed. Only on January 17 did Penn Ave. Record Shack, Inc. become a corporation. Levy is subject to personal liability because, before this date, he assumed to act as a corporation without any authority so to do. Nor is Robertson estopped from denying the existence of the corporation because after the certificate was issued he accepted one payment on the note. An individual who incurs statutory liability on an obligation under [§ 139] because he has acted without authority, is not relieved of that liability where, at a later time, the corporation does come into existence by complying with section [§ 50]. Subsequent partial payment by the corporation does not remove this liability.

The judgment appealed from is reversed with instructions to enter judgment against the appellee on the note and for damages proved to have been incurred by appellant for breach of the lease.

Reversed with instructions.

Notes

(1) Several decisions in states that have adopted both §§ 50 and 139 of the MBCA (1969) accept the result reached in Robertson v. Levy, holding that there can be no limited liability before the certificate of incorporation is filed. E.g., Booker Custom Packing Co., Inc. v. Sallomi, 149 Ariz. 124, 716 P.2d 1061

certificate of incorporation would not constitute apparent compliance. Therefore a de facto corporation cannot exist under the Model Act.

The comment to § 146 (identical to § 139 of the 1950 Act) added "Abolition of the concept of de facto incorporation, which at best was fuzzy, is a sound result. No reason exists for its

continuance under general corporate laws, where the process of acquiring de jure incorporation is both simple and clear. The vestigial appendage should be removed."

9. [By the Court] In the present case, Robertson admitted intending to deal with a corporation.

(App.1986); Thompson & Green Mach. Co., Inc. v. Music City Lumber Co., Inc., 683 S.W.2d 340 (Tenn.App.1984).

(2) In Sherwood & Roberts–Oregon, Inc. v. Alexander, 269 Or. 389, 525 P.2d 135 (1974), the Court refused to apply §§ 50 and 139 when no attempt was made at all to incorporate. The Court further held that the promoters were not liable on the ground that the third person had agreed not to look to the promoter for payment of the note that had been executed in the name of the nonexistent corporation. See also Frontier Ref. Co. v. Kunkel's Inc., 407 P.2d 880 (Wyo.1965).

(3) When applying §§ 50 and 139 should a distinction be drawn between active participants and inactive investors? Can such a distinction be justified under the common law of de facto corporations? Under the language of § 139? What does "assume to act" mean in that section? Does it refer to all participants in an active promotion? Only the active promoter? Consider the following analysis:

> We find the language ambiguous. Liability is imposed on "[a]ll persons who assume to act as a corporation." Such persons shall be liable "for all debts and liabilities incurred or arising as a result thereof."

> We conclude that the category of "persons who assume to act as a corporation" does not include those whose only connection with the organization is as an investor. On the other hand, the restriction of liability to those who personally incurred the obligation sued upon cannot be based upon logic or the realities of business practice. When several people carry on the activities of a defectively organized corporation, chance frequently will dictate which of the several active principals directly incurs a certain obligation or whether an employee, rather than an active principal, personally incurs the obligation.

> We are of the opinion that the phrase, "persons who assume to act as a corporation" should be interpreted to include those persons who have an investment in the organization and who actively participate in the policy and operational decisions of the organization. Liability should not necessarily be restricted to the person who personally incurred the obligation.

Timberline Equip. Co., Inc. v. Davenport, 267 Or. 64, 72–76, 514 P.2d 1109, 1113–14 (1973). Shoreham Hotel Ltd. Partnership v. Wilder, 866 F.Supp. 1 (D.D.C. 1994), refused to apply a statute applicable to non-profit corporations that is identical to § 139 to members of a planning committee who did not intend to participate in the ultimate management of the not-yet-formed corporation.

(4) Before the development of the Model Act provisions set forth in the principal case, there was a tendency to hold all participants in a corporation that was neither de facto nor de jure personally liable. See Harry G. Henn and John R. Alexander, Laws of Corporations and Other Business Associations 343 (3d 3d. 1983):*

> Under the old rule, all of the associates were held liable as partners, the theory being that the associated group was either a corporation or a partnership with its mutual agency. This viewpoint failed to take into account the differentiation between active and inactive members of the group, as well as the objection that the shareholders did not intend to act as a partnership.

> The more modern approach has been to examine each situation and thereby determine whether the too-defectively-incorporated enterprise should be treated as a partnership. Associates who assumed an inactive role and who

* Reprinted with permission from West Publishing Corporation.

believed that they were members of a valid corporation ought not to be held liable as partners. Factors such as vesting authority in a "board of directors" and the absence of any holding out as partners (which might give rise to estoppel) assume importance under the modern view.

CANTOR v. SUNSHINE GREENERY, INC.

Superior Court of New Jersey, 1979.
165 N.J.Super. 411, 398 A.2d 571.

Before JUDGES MICHELS and LARNER.

The opinion of the court was delivered by LARNER, J.A.D.

This appeal involves the propriety of a personal judgment against defendant William J. Brunetti for the breach of a lease between plaintiffs and a corporate entity known as Sunshine Greenery, Inc., and more particularly whether there was a *de facto* corporation in existence at the time of the execution of the lease.

Plaintiffs brought suit for damages for the breach of the lease against Sunshine Greenery, Inc. and Brunetti. Default judgment was entered against the corporation and a nonjury trial was held as to the liability of the individual. The trial judge in a letter opinion determined that plaintiffs were entitled to judgment against Brunetti individually on the theory that as of the time of the creation of the contract he was acting as a promoter and that his corporation, Sunshine Greenery, Inc., was not a legal or *de facto* corporation.

The undisputed facts reveal the following: Plaintiffs prepared the lease naming Sunshine Greenery, Inc. as the tenant, and it was signed by Brunetti as president of that named entity. Mr. Cantor, acting for plaintiffs, knew that Brunetti was starting a new venture as a newly formed corporation known as Sunshine Greenery, Inc. Although Cantor had considerable experience in ownership and leasing of commercial property to individuals and corporations, he did not request a personal guarantee from Brunetti, nor did he make inquiry as to his financial status or background. Without question, he knew and expected that the lease agreement was undertaken by the corporation and not by Brunetti individually, and that the corporation would be responsible thereunder.

At the time of the signing of the lease on December 16, 1974 in Cantor's office, Brunetti was requested by Cantor to give him a check covering the first month's rent and the security deposit. When Brunetti stated that he was not prepared to do so because he had no checks with him, Cantor furnished a blank check which was filled out for $1,200, with the name of Brunetti's bank and signed by him as president of Sunshine Greenery, Inc. The lease was repudiated by a letter from counsel for Sunshine Greenery, Inc. dated December 17, 1974, which in turn was followed by a response from Cantor to the effect that he would hold the "client" responsible for all losses. The check was not honored because Brunetti stopped payment, and in any event because Sunshine Greenery, Inc. did not have an account in the bank.

The evidence is clear that on November 21, 1974 the corporate name of Sunshine Greenery, Inc. had been reserved for Brunetti by the Secretary of State, and that on December 3, 1974 a certificate of incorporation for that company was signed by Brunetti and Sharyn N. Sansoni as incorporators. The certificate was forwarded by mail to the Secretary of State on that same date with a check for the filing fee, but for some unexplained reason it was not officially filed until December 18, 1974, two days after the execution of the lease.[10]

In view of the late filing, Sunshine Greenery, Inc. was not a *de jure* corporation on December 16, 1974 when the lease was signed. See N.J.S.A. 14A:2–7(2). Nevertheless, there is ample evidence of the fact that it was a *de facto* corporation in that there was a *bona fide* attempt to organize the corporation some time before the consummation of the contract and there was an actual exercise of the corporate powers by the negotiations with plaintiffs and the execution of the contract involved in this litigation. When this is considered in the light of the concession that plaintiffs knew that they were dealing with that corporate entity and not with Brunetti individually, it becomes evident that the *de facto* status of the corporation suffices to absolve Brunetti from individual liability. Plaintiffs in effect are estopped from attacking the legal existence of the corporation collaterally because of the nonfiling in order to impose liability on the individual when they have admittedly contracted with a corporate entity which had *de facto* status. In fact, their prosecution of the claim against the corporation to default judgment is indicative of their recognition of the corporation as the true obligor and theoretically inconsistent with the assertion of the claim against the individual.

The trial judge's finding that Sunshine Greenery, Inc. was not a *de facto* corporation is unwarranted under the record facts herein. The mere fact that there were no formal meetings or resolutions or issuance of stock is not determinative of the legal or *de facto* existence of the corporate entity, particularly under the simplified New Jersey Business Corporation Act of 1969, which eliminates the necessity of a meeting of incorporators. See N.J.S.A. 14A:2–6 and Commissioners' Comment thereunder. The act of executing the certificate of incorporation, the *bona fide* effort to file it and the dealings with plaintiffs in the name of that corporation fully satisfy the requisite proof of the existence of a *de facto* corporation. To deny such existence because of a mere technicality caused by administrative delay in filing runs counter to the purpose of the *de facto* concept, and would accomplish an unjust and inequitable result in favor of plaintiffs contrary to their own contractual expectations. * * *

Since the trial judge erred in negating the *de facto* existence of the corporation herein, the consequent imposition of individual liability on the thesis that Brunetti was a "promoter" is also unwarranted. Since plaintiffs looked to the corporation for liability on the lease, and since we find that Sunshine Greenery, Inc. had a *de facto* existence, there can be no personal liability of Brunetti on the theory that he was a "promoter."

In view of the foregoing, the judgment entered against defendant William J. Brunetti is reversed and set aside, and the matter is remanded to the Law Division to enter judgment on the complaint in favor of William J. Brunetti.

---

10. [By the Court] We note that the letter enclosing the certificate of incorporation is addressed to "Mortimer G. Newman, Jr., Secretary of State, State House Annex, Trenton, New Jersey." Whether this misidentification of the person holding the office of Secretary of State accounts for the filing delay we are unable to say from the record.

Notes

(1) Can you see any factual differences between this case and Robertson v. Levy that might justify the difference in result?

(2) One obvious basis for reconciling the two cases is the difference in statutory provisions in the District of Columbia and New Jersey. As indicated in *Robertson,* the critical provisions in the District of Columbia were drawn directly from §§ 50 and 139 of the 1950 Model Act. New Jersey is not basically a Model Act jurisdiction; the relevant portion of N.J.Stat.Ann. § 14A:2–7(2) reads as follows:

> * * * The corporate existence shall begin upon the effective date of the certificate, which shall be the date of the filing or such later time, not to exceed 90 days from the date of filing, as may be set forth in the certificate. Such filing shall be conclusive evidence that all conditions precedent required to be performed by the incorporators have been complied with and, after the corporate existence has begun, that the corporation has been incorporated under this act, except as against this State in a proceeding to cancel or revoke the certificate of incorporation or for involuntary dissolution of the corporation.

New Jersey has not enacted anything comparable to § 139 of the 1969 Model Act. Despite this, the Commissioner's Comment to the New Jersey statute states that "the last sentence of subsection 14A:2–7(2) * * * is adapted from section 50 of the Model Act. Such a provision, * * * virtually eliminates the distinction between *de jure* and *de facto* corporations * * *." This comment was not cited or referred to by the Court in *Cantor.*

(3) Prior to the promulgation in 1984 of the MBCA, every state had enacted a provision somewhat similar to § 50 of the 1969 Model Act, defining when the corporate existence commences. Only about 20 Model Act states had enacted § 139 of that Act. If Robertson v. Levy were to arise in a jurisdiction that had enacted § 50 but not § 139, how should the case be decided?

(4) As noted in footnote 7 of the Court's opinion in *Robertson,* the common law de facto doctrine has been the subject of much criticism. In 1952, Professor Alexander Frey of the University of Pennsylvania Law School attempted to classify all *de facto* corporation cases arising prior to 1952 on the basis of the nature of the defect, whether there had been dealings on a corporate basis (roughly, whether the suit was based on contract or tort), and whether the suit sought to hold active or inactive investors personally liable. Alexander Hamilton Frey, Legal Analysis and the "DeFacto" Doctrine, 100 U.Pa.L.Rev. 1153, 1174 (1952). The year 1952 antedates all of the cases discussed in this section arising under sections 50 and 139 of the old Model Act. The following table is the result of Professor Frey's analysis of these common law cases. Does it shed any light on what is really going on in this area?

ANALYSIS OF CASES CONCERNING INDIVIDUAL LIABILITY OF MEMBERS OF DEFECTIVELY INCORPORATED ASSOCIATIONS

Nature of Defect	Dealings on Corporate Basis				Totals		Dealings Not On Corporate Basis				Totals	Total Cases
	Inactive Associates Liable	Inactive Associates Not Liable	Managing Associates Liable	Managing Associates Not Liable	Liability v. Non-Liability		Inactive Associates Liable	Inactive Associates Not Liable	Managing Associates Liable	Managing Associates Not Liable	Liability v. Non-Liability	Liability v. Non-Liability
Articles Not Recorded at All	10	9	4	2	14–11		3	0	6	1	9–1	23–12
No Attempt to Incorporate	4	2	7	0	11–2		2	0	2	0	4–0	15–2
Articles Not Recorded with Secretary of State	5	6	2	3	7–9		0	0	0	0	0–0	7–9
Articles Not Recorded Locally	2	7	0	4	2–11		2	0	3	0	5–0	7–11
Insufficient Capital Paid In	3	9	8	13	11–22		4	0	1	0	5–0	16–22
Miscellaneous	12	30	12	25	24–55		4	0	3	1	7–1	31–56
Total Cases	36	63	33	47	69–110		15	0	15	2	30–2	99–112

Source: Frey, Legal Analysis and the De Facto Doctrine, 100 U.Pa.L.Rev. 1153, 1174 (1952).*

[B2963]

(5) Wayne N. Bradley, An Empirical Study of Defective Incorporation, 39 Emory L.J. 523 (1990), brings the Frey analysis up to 1989. This study was of course complicated by the enactment since 1950 of statutes dealing with defective incorporation in many states. The author concludes that despite these statutes, cases continue to arise with regularity, that contract cases ("Dealings on a Corporate Basis") continue to outnumber tort and tax cases ("Dealings not on a Corporate Basis"), that liability continues to be imposed much more regularly on the latter class than in the former class, and that personal liability is almost universally imposed where there is no attempt at all to incorporate. The author also concludes that application of sections 39 and 146 of the Model Act "often leads to results which are contrary to the intent of the parties and thus provides one party with a windfall." 39 Emory L.J. at 573. One example he cites is this:

> The legacy of Timberline and MBCA section 146 can be seen in Thompson and Green Machinery Co. v. Music City Lumber Co.[12] In January 1982, the defendant signed a promissory note and security agreement with the plaintiff. The next day the defendant's certificate of incorporation was issued. The note was signed in the corporate name, each party dealt with the other as if the defendant were an existing corporation, and neither party knew the defendant was not formally incorporated. When the plaintiff sued on the note, it discovered the one-day incorporation delay and attempted to hold the defendant individually liable on the debt. The court quoted Timberline extensively, as well as other cases[13] and the Tennessee versions of MBCA sections 56 and 146. The court imposed personal liability on the defendant,

12. [By the Author] 683 S.W.2d 340 (Tenn. App.1984).

13. [By the Editor] The court cited three cases, including *Robertson v. Levy*.

reasoning that it could not rewrite the statute, and it cited Robertson v. Levy for authority that it must simply apply a bright-line test and not inquire into the equities of the case.[14] A strict reading of the statute led the court to a result that disregard the intent of the parties.

39 Emory L.J., at 554. In a sense, a windfall occurs whenever an individual is held personally liable on a transaction which was negotiated on a corporate basis, whether or not any steps toward incorporation had actually been taken. If a general "no windfall" rule were adopted as the standard for personal liability, what motivation would there be for persons to file articles of incorporation and pay filing fees to the state? Could they not secure personal immunity from liability simply by conducting all negotiations in the name of non-existent corporation?

(6) Professor Bradley also points out that arguments about de facto corporations arise in a variety of other contexts. For example, he cites thirty-one cases in which the *defendant* attempted to escape liability claiming *plaintiff* was not a valid corporation at the time of the transaction; this argument failed in twenty-four cases. In nine cases the defendant attempted to escape liability by asserting that it was not itself a properly formed corporation; not surprisingly, this defense failed in all nine cases. 39 Emory L.J., at 560–66. The concept of a *de facto* corporation also appears in other contexts. The franchise tax statutes of many states provide for administrative forfeiture of the charter for nonpayment of taxes. Some statutes also provide for reinstatement of the charter upon correction of all delinquencies. Of course, many corporations fail to pay franchise taxes from inadvertence and continue actively in business despite the dissolution. A corporation whose charter has been forfeited has been described as a "de facto corporation"—i.e. only the state may attack it. It should be added that franchise tax statutes often provide sanctions during the period the charter is forfeited. Officers, directors, and shareholders may be made personally liable for obligations incurred by the corporation, the courts of the state may be closed to the corporation, and there may be civil or criminal penalties levied. In Moore v. Occupational Safety & Health Review Comm'n, 591 F.2d 991 (4th Cir.1979), officers of Life Science Products Company were held personally liable for penalties imposed on the corporation for kepone contamination occurring after the corporation was administratively dissolved for temporary nonpayment of franchise taxes. Consult generally Note, Dissolution and Suspension as Remedies for Corporate Franchise Tax Delinquency: A Comparative Analysis, 41 N.Y.U.L.Rev. 602 (1966).

(7) As noted previously, the statutes of many states contain procedural and substantive requirements for forming a corporation in addition to the filing of articles of incorporation with a central state authority. The most common such requirements are that the articles of incorporation be recorded in a local county office, that there be newspaper publication of the fact that articles of incorporation have been filed, or that a corporation have a minimum capitalization before commencing business. The effect of a failure to comply with one or more of these requirements is sometimes expressly specified in the statute; more often, however, the statute is silent. In this situation should the court rely on general statutes such as section 50 of the (1969) MBCA and conclude that the corporation is validly formed despite the failure to comply with statutory requirements? Arguably, the failure to follow post-incorporation formalities may be relevant to the question whether shareholders should be held liable on corporate obligations on the theory of "piercing the corporate veil," discussed in the following chapter.

14. [By the Author] * * * 683 S.W.2d at 344–45.

CRANSON v. INTERNATIONAL BUSINESS MACHINES CORP.

Court of Appeals of Maryland, 1964.
234 Md. 477, 200 A.2d 33.

HORNEY, JUDGE.

On the theory that the Real Estate Service Bureau was neither a *de jure* nor a *de facto* corporation and that Albion C. Cranson, Jr., was a partner in the business conducted by the Bureau and as such was personally liable for its debts, the International Business Machines Corporation brought this action against Cranson for the balance due on electric typewriters purchased by the Bureau. At the same time it moved for summary judgment and supported the motion by affidavit. In due course, Cranson filed a general issue plea and an affidavit in opposition to summary judgment in which he asserted in effect that the Bureau was a *de facto* corporation and that he was not personally liable for its debts.

The agreed statement of facts shows that in April 1961, Cranson was asked to invest in a new business corporation which was about to be created. Towards this purpose he met with other interested individuals and an attorney and agreed to purchase stock and become an officer and director. Thereafter, upon being advised by the attorney that the corporation had been formed under the laws of Maryland, he paid for and received a stock certificate evidencing ownership of shares in the corporation, and was shown the corporate seal and minute book. The business of the new venture was conducted as if it were a corporation, through corporate bank accounts, with auditors maintaining corporate books and records, and under a lease entered into by the corporation for the office from which it operated its business. Cranson was elected president and all transactions conducted by him for the corporation, including the dealings with I.B.M., were made as an officer of the corporation. At no time did he assume any personal obligation or pledge his individual credit to I.B.M. Due to an oversight on the part of the attorney, of which Cranson was not aware, the certificate of incorporation, which had been signed and acknowledged prior to May 1, 1961, was not filed until November 24, 1961. Between May 17 and November 8, the Bureau purchased eight typewriters from I.B.M., on account of which partial payments were made, leaving a balance due of $4,333.40, for which this suit was brought.

The fundamental question presented by the appeal is whether an officer[15] of a defectively incorporated association may be subjected to personal liability under the circumstances of this case. We think not.

Traditionally, two doctrines have been used by the courts to clothe an officer of a defectively incorporated association with the corporate attribute of limited liability. The first, often referred to as the doctrine of *de facto* corporations, has been applied in those cases where there are elements showing: (1) the existence of law authorizing incorporation; (2) an effort in

---

15. [By the Court] Although we are concerned with the liability of an "officer" in this case, the principles of law stated herein might under other circumstances be applicable to a determination of the liability of a member or shareholder of a defectively organized corporation.

good faith to incorporate under the existing law; and (3) actual user or exercise of corporate powers. The second, the doctrine of estoppel to deny the corporate existence, is generally employed where the person seeking to hold the officer personally liable has contracted or otherwise dealt with the association in such a manner as to recognize and in effect admit its existence as a corporate body.

It is not at all clear what Maryland has done with respect to the two doctrines. There have been no recent cases in this State on the subject and some of the seemingly irreconcilable earlier cases offer little to clarify the problem.[16] * * *

[Discussion of Maryland cases omitted.]

When summarized, the law in Maryland pertaining to the *de facto* and estoppel doctrines reveals that the cases seem to fall into one or the other of two categories. In one line of cases, the Court, choosing to disregard the nature of the dealings between the parties, refused to recognize both doctrines where there had been a failure to comply with a condition precedent to corporate existence, but, whenever such non-compliance concerned a condition subsequent to incorporation, the Court often applied the estoppel doctrine. In the other line of cases, the Court, choosing to make no distinction between defects which were conditions precedent and those which were conditions subsequent, emphasized the course of conduct between the parties and applied the estoppel doctrine when there had been substantial dealings between them on a corporate basis. * * * [Insofar as two Maryland cases hold] that the doctrine of estoppel cannot be invoked unless a corporation has at least *de facto* existence, both cases * * * should be, and are hereby, overruled to the extent of the inconsistency. There is, as we see it, a wide difference between creating a corporation by means of the *de facto* doctrine and estopping a party, due to his conduct in a particular case, from setting up the claim of no incorporation. Although some cases tend to assimilate the doctrines of incorporation *de facto* and by estoppel, each is a distinct theory and they are not dependent on one another in their application. Where there is a concurrence of the three elements necessary for the application of the *de facto* corporation doctrine, there exists an entity which is a corporation *de jure* against all persons but the state. On the other hand, the estoppel theory is applied only to the facts of each particular case and may be invoked even where there is no corporation *de facto*. Accordingly, even though one or more of the requisites of a *de facto* corporation are absent, we think that this factor does not preclude the application of the estoppel doctrine in a proper case, such as the one at bar.

I.B.M. contends that the failure of the Bureau to file its certificate of incorporation debarred *all* corporate existence. But, in spite of the fact that the omission might have prevented the Bureau from being either a corpora-

16. [By the Court] Apparently because it was not requested to do so, the lower court did not undertake to prepare and file a memorandum of its reasons for deciding the problem as it did. But, inexcusably, the briefs were for the most part of no practical use to this Court in arriving at a decision of the intricate question of law presented by the appeal. While the appellant cited three Maryland cases for the proposition that a *de facto* corporation was created and the appellee cited one Maryland case for the proposition that a corporation cannot be created by estoppel, neither made an attempt to analogize or distinguish the numerous other Maryland cases touching the problem.

tion *de jure* or *de facto*,[17] we think that I.B.M. having dealt with the Bureau as if it were a corporation and relied on its credit rather than that of Cranson, is estopped to assert that the Bureau was not incorporated at the time the typewriters were purchased. * * *

Since I.B.M. is estopped to deny the corporate existence of the Bureau, we hold that Cranson was not liable for the balance due on account of the typewriters.

Judgment reversed; the appellee to pay the costs.

Notes

(1) What is the difference in factual pattern that results in *Robertson* and *Cantor* being classified as "corporation de facto" cases while *Cranson* is classified as a "corporation by estoppel" case? Do these types of cases differ from cases such as Quaker Hill v. Parr (See supra p. 229), which are classified as "promoters' transactions" cases?

(2) The Court in *Cranson* treated the question as one involving only Maryland case law, and in this regard it made a rather caustic reference to the inadequacy of the briefs before it. Neither the Court nor the attorneys apparently considered the possibility that Maryland statutory law might be relevant. At least, there is no reference to Maryland statutory law in the court's opinion. When *Cranson* was decided, Maryland had not yet adopted its version of the old MBCA. However, Art. 23, § 131(b) of the Maryland corporation statute (Md.Code 1957), provided:

> Upon acceptance for record by the Department of any articles of incorporation, the proposed corporation shall, according to the purposes, conditions and provisions contained in such articles of incorporation, become and be a body corporate by a name therein stated. Such acceptance for the record shall be conclusive evidence of the formation of the corporation except in a direct proceeding by the State for the forfeiture of the charter.

Do the differences between the D.C. and Maryland statutes explain the difference in result between Robertson v. Levy and Cranson v. I.B.M.? If *Cranson* had arisen in a state which had enacted MBCA (1960) §§ 50 and 139, should not Cranson have been held liable? After all, he "assumed to act" on behalf of the Real Estate Service Bureau even though no certificate of incorporation had been issued.

(3) In Harry Rich Corp. v. Feinberg, 518 So.2d 377 (Fla.App.1987), Feinberg found himself in essentially the same position that Cranson did in the principal case. He had been shown articles of incorporation which he believed had been properly filed. Florida had adopted § 139 of MBCA (1969); the Court, however, held that Feinberg was not liable under that section since "assume to act" should be construed to permit recovery "only where the individual acts with actual or constructive knowledge that no corporation exists." 518 So.2d, at 381. The Court also relied on a non-Model Act statute enacted in Florida that prohibits a

17. [By the Court] Those states which recognize the *de facto* doctrine are not in accord as to whether a corporation *de facto* may be created in spite of the failure to file the necessary papers. Some courts, without making clear in every instance whether a *de facto* corporation was meant or not, have stated that failure to file the required papers prevented the organizations from becoming a corporation and have held in effect that the persons acting as a corporation are a mere association or partnership. Other courts, without expressly deciding whether a *de facto* corporation was created, hold that the statutes of the state imply corporate existence prior to the filing of articles of incorporation. Still other courts hold that a *de facto* existence is not precluded by failure to file the articles of incorporation.

defectively formed corporation from using its lack of legal organization as a defense against claims brought by third persons.

(4) Consider MBCA § 2.03. The Official Comment to this section makes it clear that this provision was designed to preserve the concept of corporation by estoppel only in situations like *Cranson* and *Harry Rich Corp.*

(5) If the suit in Cranson v. I.B.M. was based on a tort rather than on a contract, is there any possible way for Cranson to avoid liability? Does it make any difference, as the Court notes, that I.B.M. was seeking to hold Cranson as an "officer" rather than as a "member" or "shareholder"?

(6) In Goodwyne v. Moore, 170 Ga.App. 305, 316 S.E.2d 601 (1984), a promissory note was executed in the form "C & N Industries, Inc., By Charles Goodwyne, Pres." The plaintiffs thereafter accepted payments made by "C & N Industries, Inc." and issued receipts for those payments addressed to that corporation. Following default on the remaining payments, an attempt was made to hold Goodwyne individually liable. It turned out that at the time the note was executed there was no corporation named "C & N Industries, Inc." in existence. Goodwyne, however, had earlier formed a corporation under the name "C & N Bottle Shop, Inc.," and four days before signing the promissory note had also obtained a certificate reserving the name "C & N Industries, Inc." Two months after the execution of the promissory note, "C & N Bottle Shop, Inc." filed articles of amendment changing its name to "C & N Industries, Inc." The Court held that the plaintiffs had "admitted the legal existence of C & N Industries, and are estopped from denying its legal existence in a suit to enforce the note." Is this type of problem covered by MBCA § 2.03? Two other Georgia cases reach the same result on roughly analogous facts. In Pinson v. Hartsfield Int'l Comm. Ctr., Ltd., 191 Ga.App. 459, 382 S.E.2d 136 (1989), Pinson was held not personally liable on a lease executed in the name "Pinson Air Freight, Inc." when there was no corporation by that name; Pinson's corporation was actually named "Pinson Air Freight of Chattanooga, Inc." In Hawkins v. Turner, 166 Ga.App. 50, 303 S.E.2d 164 (1983), Hawkins was held not liable on a contract executed in the name "Hawkins Plumbing Co., Inc." when he was an officer and major shareholder in a corporation named "Hawkins Heating & Plumbing Co." In both of these cases there was evidence of a considerable degree of casualness on the part of Pinson and Hawkins in other transactions as to the name of the corporation, and as to whether the business was owned on an individual or corporate basis.

(7) Are cases described in the preceding note distinguishable from yet another Georgia case, Echols v. Vienna Sausage Mfg. Co., 162 Ga.App. 158, 290 S.E.2d 484 (1982)? In this case the individual was held personally liable on a "corporate" obligation; he had reserved the corporate name but had not taken any additional steps to complete the incorporation at the time of the transaction in question.

Chapter Six

DISREGARD OF THE CORPORATE ENTITY

BARTLE v. HOME OWNERS COOP.

Court of Appeals of New York, 1955.
309 N.Y. 103, 127 N.E.2d 832.

FROESSEL, JUDGE.

Plaintiff, as trustee in bankruptcy of Westerlea Builders, Inc., has by means of this litigation attempted to hold defendant liable for the contract debts of Westerlea, defendant's wholly owned subsidiary. Defendant, as a co-operative corporation composed mostly of veterans, was organized in July, 1947, for the purpose of providing low-cost housing for its members. Unable to secure a contractor to undertake construction of the housing planned, Westerlea was organized for that purpose on June 5, 1948. With building costs running considerably higher than anticipated, Westerlea, as it proceeded with construction on some 26 houses, found itself in a difficult financial situation. On January 24, 1949, the creditors, pursuant to an extension agreement, took over the construction responsibilities. Nearly four years later, in October, 1952, Westerlea was adjudicated a bankrupt. Meanwhile, defendant had contributed to Westerlea not only its original capital of $25,000 but additional sums amounting to $25,639.38.

Plaintiff's principal contention on this appeal is that the courts below erred in refusing to "pierce the corporate veil" of Westerlea's corporate existence; as subordinate grounds for recovery he urged that the defendant equitably pledged its assets toward the satisfaction of the debts of the bankrupt's creditors, and that the doctrine of unjust enrichment should apply.

The trial court made detailed findings of fact which have been unanimously affirmed by the Appellate Division, 285 App.Div. 1113, 140 N.Y.S.2d 512, which are clearly supported by the evidence, and by which we are bound. It found that while the defendant, as owner of the stock of Westerlea, controlled its affairs, the outward indicia of these two separate corporations was at all times maintained during the period in which the creditors extended credit; that the creditors were in no wise misled; that there was no fraud; and that the defendant performed no act causing injury to the creditors of Westerlea by depletion of assets or otherwise. The trial court also held that the creditors were estopped by the extension agreement from disputing the separate corporate identities.

We agree with the courts below. The law permits the incorporation of a business for the very purpose of escaping personal liability. Generally speaking, the doctrine of "piercing the corporate veil" is invoked "to prevent fraud or to achieve equity", International Aircraft Trading Co. v. Manufacturers Trust Co., 297 N.Y. 285, 292, 79 N.E.2d 249, 252. But in the instant case there has been neither fraud, misrepresentation nor illegality. Defendant's purpose in placing its construction operation into a separate corporation was clearly within the limits of our public policy.

The judgment appealed from should be affirmed, without costs.

VAN VOORHIS, JUDGE (dissenting).

The judgment of the Appellate Division should be reversed on the law, as it seems to me, and plaintiff should have judgment declaring defendant to be liable for the debts of the bankrupt, Westerlea Builders, Inc., and that defendant holds its real property subject to the claims of creditors of Westerlea. Not only is Westerlea a wholly owned subsidiary of defendant Home Owners, having the same directors and management, but also and of primary importance, business was done on such a basis that Westerlea could not make a profit. Home Owners owned a residential subdivision; Westerlea was organized as a building corporation to erect homes for stockholders of Home Owners upon lots in this tract. Home Owners arranged with Westerlea for the construction of houses and then would sell the lots on which such houses had been erected to Home Owners' stockholders—at prices fixed by Home Owners' price policy committee in such amounts as to make no allowance for profit by Westerlea. The object was to benefit Home Owners' stockholders by enabling them to obtain their houses at cost, with no builder's profit.

The consequence is that described by Latty, Subsidiaries and Affiliated Corporations at pages 138–139: "The subsidiaries had, to begin with, nothing, made nothing, and could only end up with nothing. It is not surprising that the parent was held liable in each case." And again: "This set-up is often, though not necessarily, found in combination with a scheme whereby the corporation cannot possibly make profits (or can at the most make only nominal profits), and whereby all the net income in the course of the corporation's business is drained off as operating charges of one sort or another. The presence of this additional factor should remove any doubt that may remain as to the right of the creditor of the corporation not to be limited to the corporate assets for the satisfaction of his debt."

In the present instance, Westerlea was organized with a small capital supplied by Home Owners, which soon became exhausted. Thereafter, it had no funds and could acquire none over and beyond the actual cost of the houses which it was building for stockholders of Home Owners. Those stockholders obtained the entire benefit of Westerlea's operations by obtaining these houses at cost. Not only was Westerlea allowed no opportunity to make money, but it was placed in a position such that if its business were successful and times remained good, it would break even, otherwise it would inevitably become insolvent. The stockholders of Home Owners became the beneficiaries of its insolvency. This benefit to the stockholders of Home Owners was analogous to dividends, at least it was something of value which was obtained by them from Home Owners by virtue of their stock ownership. Under the circumstances, this benefit to its stockholders was a benefit to Home Owners as a corporation.

It follows that Westerlea was merely an agent of Home Owners to construct houses at cost for Home Owners stockholders, and therefore Home Owners is rendered liable for Westerlea's indebtedness.

CONWAY, C.J., and DESMOND, DYE, FULD and BURKE, JJ., concur with FROESSEL, J.

VAN VOORHIS, J., dissents in an opinion.

Judgment affirmed.

DEWITT TRUCK BROKERS v. W. RAY FLEMMING FRUIT CO.

United States Court of Appeals, Fourth Circuit, 1976.
540 F.2d 681.

Before RUSSELL and WIDENER, CIRCUIT JUDGES, and THOMSEN, SENIOR DISTRICT JUDGE.[1]

DONALD RUSSELL, CIRCUIT JUDGE:

In this action on debt, the plaintiff seeks, by piercing the corporate veil under the law of South Carolina, to impose individual liability on the president of the indebted corporation individually.[2] The District Court, making findings of fact which may be overturned only if clearly erroneous, pierced the corporate veil and imposed individual liability. The individual defendant appeals. We affirm.

At the outset, it is recognized that a corporation is an entity, separate and distinct from its officers and stockholders, and that its debts are not the individual indebtedness of its stockholders. This is expressed in the presumption that the corporation and its stockholders are separate and distinct. And this oft-stated principle is equally applicable, whether the corporation has many or only one stockholder. But this concept of separate entity is merely a legal theory, "introduced for purposes of convenience and to subserve the ends of justice," and the courts "decline to recognize [it] whenever recognition of the corporate form would extend the principle of incorporation 'beyond its legitimate purposes and [would] produce injustices or inequitable consequences.' " Krivo Industrial Supp. Co. v. National Distill. & Chem. Corp. (5th Cir.1973), 483 F.2d 1098, 1106. Accordingly, "in an appropriate case and in furtherance of the ends of justice," the corporate veil will be pierced and the corporation and its stockholders "will be treated as identical." 18 Am.Juris.2d at 559.

This power to pierce the corporate veil, though, is to be exercised "reluctantly" and "cautiously" and the burden of establishing a basis for the disregard of the corporate fiction rests on the party asserting such claim. Coryell v. Phipps (5th Cir.1942), 128 F.2d 702, 704, aff., 317 U.S. 406, 63 S.Ct. 291, 87 L.Ed. 363 (1943).

1. [By the Court] Sitting by designation.

2. [By the Court] The corporate defendant, it is conceded, is not responsive to judgment.

The circumstances which have been considered significant by the courts in actions to disregard the corporate fiction have been "rarely articulated with any clarity." Swanson v. Levy (9th Cir.1975), 509 F.2d 859, 861–2. Perhaps this is true because the circumstances "necessarily vary according to the circumstances of each case," and every case where the issue is raised is to be regarded as *"sui generis* [to] * * * be decided in accordance with its own underlying facts." Since the issue is thus one of fact, its resolution "is particularly within the province of the trial court" and such resolution will be regarded as "presumptively correct and [will] be left undisturbed on appeal unless it is clearly erroneous."

Contrary to the basic contention of the defendant, however, proof of plain fraud is not a necessary element in a finding to disregard the corporate entity. * * * [E]qually as well settled * * * is the rule that the mere fact that all or almost all of the corporate stock is owned by one individual or a few individuals, will not afford sufficient grounds for disregarding corporateness. But when substantial ownership of all the stock of a corporation in a single individual is combined with other factors clearly supporting disregard of the corporate fiction on grounds of fundamental equity and fairness, courts have experienced "little difficulty" and have shown no hesitancy in applying what is described as the "alter ego" or "instrumentality" theory in order to cast aside the corporate shield and to fasten liability on the individual stockholder. Iron City S. & G. Div. of McDonough Co. v. West Fork Tow. Corp., [N.D.W.Va. 1969] 298 F.Supp. at 1098.

But, in applying the "instrumentality" or "alter ego" doctrine, the courts are concerned with reality and not form, with how the corporation operated and the individual defendant's relationship to that operation. * * * [T]he authorities have indicated certain facts which are to be given substantial weight in this connection. One fact which all the authorities consider significant in the inquiry, and particularly so in the case of the one-man or closely-held corporation, is whether the corporation was grossly undercapitalized for the purposes of the corporate undertaking. Mull v. Colt Co. (S.D.N.Y.1962), 31 F.R.D. 154, 163; Automotriz Del Golfo De Cal. v. Resnick (1957), 47 Cal.2d 792, 306 P.2d 1, 63 A.L.R.2d 1042, 1048, with annotation.[3] And, "[t]he obligation to provide adequate capital begins with incorporation and is a continuing obligation thereafter * * * during the corporation's operations." Other factors that are emphasized in the application of the doctrine are

---

3. [By the Court] * * * In *Mull,* supra, 31 F.R.D. at 163, the Court quoted from Ballentine, Corporations, 303 (rev. ed. 1946):

" * * * It is coming to be recognized as the policy of the law that shareholders should in good faith put at the risk of the business unincumbered capital reasonably adequate for its prospective liabilities. If the capital is illusory or trifling compared with the business to be done and the risks of loss, this is a ground for denying the separate entity privilege."

In Note, Disregard of the Corporate Entity: Contract Claims, 28 Ohio S.L.J. 441 (1967), the author argues that under capitalization as a factor in determining whether to pierce the corporate veil should be inapplicable in contract cases; cf., however, Note, Limited Liability: A Definite Judicial Standard for the Inadequate Capitalization Problem, 47 Temple L.Q. 32 (1974). The reasoning is that when one extends credit or makes any other contractual arrangement with a corporation, it is to be assumed he acquaints himself with the corporation's capitalization and contracts on such basis, and not on the individual credit of the dominant stockholder. In this case, however, that reasoning would be inapplicable, since the plaintiff did not rely on the corporation's capitalization but received an assurance from Flemming of personal liability.

failure to observe corporate formalities,[4] non-payment of dividends, the insolvency of the debtor corporation at the time, siphoning of funds of the corporation by the dominant stockholder,[5] non-functioning of other officers or directors, absence of corporate records, and the fact that the corporation is merely a facade for the operations of the dominant stockholder or stockholders. The conclusion to disregard the corporate entity may not, however, rest on a single factor, whether undercapitalization, disregard of corporation's formalities, or what-not, but must involve a number of such factors; in addition, it must present an element of injustice or fundamental unfairness. * * *

If these factors, which were deemed significant in other cases concerned with this same issue, are given consideration here, the finding of the District Court that the corporate entity should be disregarded was not clearly erroneous. Certainly the [W. Ray Flemming Fruit Company] was, in practice at least, a close, one-man corporation from the very beginning. Its incorporators were the defendant Flemming, his wife and his attorney. It began in 1962 with a capitalization of 5,000 shares, issued for a consideration of one dollar each. In some manner which Flemming never made entirely clear, approximately 2,000 shares were retired. At the times involved here Flemming owned approximately 90% of the corporation's outstanding stock, according to his own testimony, though this was not verified by any stock records. Flemming was obscure on who the other stockholders were and how much stock these other stockholders owned, giving at different times conflicting statements as to who owned stock and how much. His testimony on who were the officers and directors was hardly more direct. He testified that the corporation did have one other director, Ed Bernstein, a resident of New York. It is significant, however, that, whether Bernstein was nominally a director or not, there were no corporate records of a real directors' meeting in all the years of the corporation's existence and Flemming conceded this to be true. Flemming countered this by testifying that Bernstein traveled a great deal and that his contacts with Bernstein were generally by telephone. The evidence indicates rather clearly that Bernstein was * * * "nothing more than [a] figurehead[s]," who had "attended no directors meeting," and even more crucial, never received any fee or reimbursement of expenses or salary of any kind from the corporation.

The District Court found, also, that the corporation never had a stockholders' meeting. * * * It is thus clear that corporate formalities, even rudimentary formalities, were not observed by the defendant.

---

4. [By the Court] House of Koscot Dev. Corp. v. American Line Cosmetics, Inc. (5th Cir.1972), 468 F.2d 64, 66–7 (" * * * Turner ignored normal corporate formalities * * * "); Lakota Girl Scout C., Inc. v. Havey Fund–Rais. Man., Inc. (8th Cir.1975), 519 F.2d 634, 638 (" * * * corporate formalities [were] not followed * * * "). While disregard of corporate formalities is a circumstance to be considered, it is generally held to be insufficient in itself, without some other facts, to support a piercing of the corporate veil.

Cf., Zubik v. Zubik (3d Cir.1967), 384 F.2d 267, 271, cert. denied, 390 U.S. 988, 88 S.Ct.

1183, 19 L.Ed.2d 1291 (1968), n. 4, where the Court stated that "[i]n the context of an attempt by an outside party to pierce the corporate veil of such a closely-held corporation, the informalities are considered of little consequence." * * *

See, however, Harrison v. Puga (1971), 4 Wash.App. 52, 480 P.2d 247, 254, where the Court said that if the defendants disregarded the corporate formalities, they could hardly complain if the court did likewise.

5. [By the Court] Chatterley v. Omnico, 26 Utah 2d 88, 485 P.2d 667, 670.

Beyond the absence of any observance of corporate formalities is the purely personal matter in which the corporation was operated. No stockholder or officer of the corporation other than Flemming ever received any salary, dividend, or fee from the corporation, or, for that matter, apparently exercised any voice in its operation or decisions. In all the years of the corporation's existence, Flemming was the sole beneficiary of its operations and its continued existence was for his exclusive benefit. During these years he was receiving from $15,000 to $25,000 each year from a corporation, which, during most of the time, was showing no profit and apparently had no working capital. Moreover, the payments to Flemming were authorized under no resolution of the board of directors of the corporation, as recorded in any minutes of a board meeting. Actually, it would seem that Flemming's withdrawals varied with what could be taken out of the corporation at the moment: If this amount were $15,000, that was Flemming's withdrawal; if it were $25,000, that was his withdrawal. * * *

That the corporation was undercapitalized, if indeed it were not without any real capital, seems obvious. Its original stated "risk capital" had long since been reduced to approximately $3,000 by a reduction in the outstanding capital, or at least this would seem to be inferable from the record, and even this, it seems fair to conclude, had been seemingly exhausted by a long succession of years when the corporation operated at no profit. The inability of the corporation to pay a dividend is persuasive proof of this want of capital. In fact, the defendant Flemming makes no effort to refute the evidence of want of any capital reserves on the part of the corporation. It appears patent that the corporation was actually operating at all times involved here on someone else's capital. This conclusion follows from a consideration of the manner in which Flemming operated in the name of the corporation during the year when plaintiff's indebtedness was incurred.

The corporation was engaged in the business of a commission agent, selling fruit produce for the account of growers of farm products such as peaches and watermelons in the Edgefield, South Carolina, area. It never purported to own such products; * * * it (always acting through Flemming) sold the products as agent for the growers. Under the arrangement with the growers, it was to remit to the grower the full sale price, less any transportation costs incurred in transporting the products from the growers' farm or warehouse to the purchaser and its sales commission. An integral part of these collections was * * * represented by the plaintiff's transportation charges. Accordingly, during the period involved here, the corporation had as operating funds seemingly only its commissions and the amount of the plaintiff's transportation charges, for which the corporation had claimed credit in its settlement with its growers. At the time, however, Flemming was withdrawing funds from the corporation at the rate of at least $15,000 per year; and doing this, even though he must have known that the corporation could only do this by withholding payment of the transportation charges due the plaintiff, which in the accounting with the growers Flemming represented had been paid the plaintiff. And, it is of some interest that the amount due the plaintiff for transportation costs was approximately the same as the $15,000 minimum annual salary the defendant testified he was paid by the corporation. Were the opinion of the District Court herein to be reversed, Flemming would be permitted to retain substantial sums from the operations of the corporation without having any real capital in the undertaking, risking nothing of his own and using as operating capital what he had collected as due the plaintiff. Certainly, equity and fundamental justice support individual liability of Flemming for plaintiff's charges, payment for which he asserted in his accounting with the growers that he had paid and for which he took credit on such accounting. This case patently presents a blending of the very factors which courts have regarded as justifying a disregard of the corporate entity in furtherance of basic and fundamental fairness.

Finally, it should not be overlooked that at some point during the period when this indebtedness was being incurred—whether at the beginning or at a short time later is not clear in the record—the plaintiff became concerned about former delays in receipt of payment for its charges and, to allay that concern, Flemming stated to the plaintiff, according to the latter's testimony as credited by the District Court, that "he (i.e., Flemming) would take care of [the charges] personally, if the corporation failed to do so * * *." On this assurance, the plaintiff contended that it continued to haul for the defendant. The existence of this promise by Flemming is not disputed. * * * This assurance was given for the obvious purpose of promoting the *individual* advantage of Flemming. This follows because the only person who could profit from the continued operation of the corporation was Flemming. When one, who is the sole beneficiary of a corporation's operations and who dominates it, as did Flemming in this case, induces a creditor to extend credit to the corporation on such an assurance as given here, that fact has been considered by many authorities sufficient basis for piercing the corporate veil. Weisser v. Mursam Shoe Corporation (2d Cir.1942), 127 F.2d 344, 145 A.L.R. 467. The only argument against this view is bottomed on the statute of frauds. But reliance on such statute is often regarded as without merit in a case where the promise or assurance is given "at the time or before the debt is created," for in that case the promise is original and without the statute. Goldsmith v. Erwin (4th Cir.1950), 183 F.2d 432, 435–6, 20 A.L.R.2d 240, with annotation. A number of courts, including South Carolina, however, have gone further and have held that, where the promisor owns substantially all the stock of the corporation and seeks by his promise to serve his personal pecuniary advantage, the question whether such promise is "within the statute of frauds" is a fact question to be resolved by the trial court and this is true whether the promise was made before the debt was incurred or during the time it was being incurred. Amer. Wholesale Corp. v. Mauldin (1924), 128 S.C. 241, 244–5, 122 S.E. 576. This is that type of case and may well have been resolved on this issue.

For the reasons stated, we conclude that the findings of the District Court herein are not clearly erroneous and the judgment of the District Court is

Affirmed.

Notes

(1) One should not let the talismanic phrase, "piercing the corporate veil," obscure reality. The issue in piercing the corporate veil cases is whether a shareholder should be held personally liable for a corporate obligation. The decision to "pierce" in *DeWitt* does not mean that the Fruit Company was no longer a corporation. It remains in business, its name remains in the records of the Secretary of State, it has the privilege of filing federal and state income tax

returns, and so forth. Further, it does not necessarily mean that *all* the shareholders are personally liable for *all* the obligations of the corporation. While DeWitt may be able to "pierce," other creditors may not; Fleming may be held personally liable on a "piercing" theory but the other shareholder (if there in fact was one) may continue to be protected by the shield of limited liability. Basically, the principal cases only involve the question whether a specific shareholder is personally liable for a specific corporate obligation, and the court's conclusion uses "piercing the corporate veil" as a theory on which to impose or refuse to impose liability.

(2) The rhetoric and reasoning in *DeWitt* is typical of many "piercing the corporate veil" cases: Long on rhetoric and contradictory general principles but short on reasoning. Indeed, perhaps in no other area are courts more prone to decide real life disputes by characterization, epithet, and metaphor: "alter ego," "instrumentality," "sham," "subterfuge," or "tool," to select a few. Various terms are often combined in artful phraseology. Philip L. Blumberg, The Law of Corporate Groups: Procedural Law 8 (1983)[6] states, "This is jurisprudence by metaphor or epithet. It does not contribute to legal understanding because it is an intellectual construct, divorced from business realities. * * * Courts state that the corporate entity is to be disregarded because the corporation is, for example, a mere "alter ego." But they do not inform us why this is so, except in very broad terms that provide little general guidance. As a result, we are faced with hundreds of decisions that are irreconcilable and not entirely comprehensible. Few areas of the law have been so sharply criticized by commentators."

(3) Piercing the corporate veil is entirely a phenomenon of closely held corporations, and predominantly one-person corporations. Robert B. Thompson, The Limits of Liability in the New Limited Liability Entities, 32 Wake Forest L.Rev. 1, 9–10 (1997):

> * * * In an earlier empirical study, I reported that among the 1600 reported cases of piercing the veil, there was no case in which shareholders of a publicly held corporation were held liable. After additional analysis of that data base, I can make a broader statement. Piercing occurs only within corporate groups or in close corporations with fewer than ten shareholders. None of the close corporations in which piercing occurred had more than nine shareholders.

> * * * Those who are only passive investors, as the shareholders of a large corporation, will be insulated from the liability of the enterprise, while those who take a more active role in the business are subject to liability. Piercing the corporate veil is usually described as imposing liability on shareholders, but that is misleading because the activity required to pierce the veil goes well beyond the typical shareholder role as a passive provider of capital. Most successful piercing cases involve either individuals who serve as both shareholders and managers, or corporate groups in which the parent corporation was the shareholder and could name the individuals who managed the subsidiary.

(4) Several cases involving contractual liability accept the argument that a third party who knowingly and voluntarily agrees to deal with a marginally financed corporation without requesting assurances from the shareholders personally cannot hold the shareholders personally liable. In O'Hazza v. Executive Credit Corp., 246 Va. 111, 431 S.E.2d 318, 323 (1993), for example, the court stated:

6. Reprinted with permission of Aspen Publishing Co.

[T]he record does not show that ECC was the victim of fraud, of any type, perpetrated by the O'Hazzas or by anyone else. Hughes had been involved with the corporation on at least 10 previous deals. * * * Hughes knew the financial situation of the corporation prior to advancing Guy O'Hazza the money for the hotel project. Hughes was a voluntary creditor who had the knowledge and opportunity to investigate the corporation before he agreed to loan the funds. We agree with the O'Hazzas' position that ECC "knowingly made a risky loan to a corporation on shaky financial footing with the hope of making a profit."

See also Consumer's Co–op. of Walworth County v. Olsen, 142 Wis.2d 465, 419 N.W.2d 211 (1988) (sophisticated creditor continued to extend credit despite delinquencies in payment in violation of its own internal policies with respect to extension of credit). A nominally capitalized corporation may be an ideal device for allocating the risk of loss between sophisticated parties. If X extends credit to a venture operated by A, the risk of loss is normally on A; however, if it is agreed that X is to look for repayment only to the profits of the venture rather than to A personally, a nominally capitalized corporation organized to operate the venture allocates the risk as desired. At least this is true if A can persuade the court that X was reasonably sophisticated. In these types of cases refusal to pierce is necessary if the bargain that was apparently in fact struck when the contract was entered into is to be enforced. Where, however, the third party lacks sophistication, courts often indulge in the opposite presumption: that a party dealing with a corporation normally does not assume the risk that the corporation is inadequately capitalized. In Laya v. Erin Homes, Inc., 177 W.Va. 343, 352 S.E.2d 93, 100 (1986), for example, the court said: "parties are [generally] entitled to rely upon certain assumptions, one being that the corporation is more than a mere shell— that it has substance as well as form." However, some cases concentrate on the "misconduct" of the plaintiff and have pierced the corporate veil on behalf of a sophisticated plaintiff. Kinney Shoe Corp. v. Polan, 939 F.2d 209 (4th Cir.1991). Might DeWitt be viewed as sophisticated in this regard? The trustee in bankruptcy in *Bartle* represents all unsatisfied creditors, presumably at least some of them were unsophisticated. On this standard, isn't it plausible to conclude that both cases might have been decided in the opposite way?

(5) In chapter 5 there was discussion of the formalities required for the creation and operation of a corporation. There was a reference there to silly "play acting," particularly when one person owns all the shares of a corporation. Does *DeWitt* put a different perspective on the importance of play acting? Consider Robert W. Hamilton, The Corporate Entity, 49 Tex.L.Rev. 979, 989–91 (1971)[7]:

> Anyone reading * * * cases dealing with shareholder liability for corporate obligations will be struck by the emphasis of the courts on failure to follow the requisite corporation formalities as a ground for imposing shareholder liability. In most opinions, a failure to follow normal corporate routine appears a most significant consideration in deciding whether a corporation is the "alter ego" of the shareholder or whether the "corporate veil should be pierced." * * *
>
> It is difficult to see, as a matter of logic, why corporate confusion and informality have been given the importance that they have. In most cases, the confusion and informality are not related to the claim advanced by either tort or contract plaintiffs. As a matter of fact, evidence of informality or comming-

---

7. Published originally in 49 Texas Law Review 979, 979–1009 (1971). Copyright 1971   by the Texas Law Review Association. Reprinted by permission.

ling of affairs is first sought long after the transaction giving rise to the particular litigation took place. A judgment against shareholders based on these activities, which are unrelated to the plaintiff's claim, is a windfall. * * *

The use of confusion as an important part of the test for determining whether the corporation's separate existence will be recognized also tends to create a trap for the unwary shareholder in the closely held corporation. Shareholders in a small business often find managing the business a full-time occupation; formal corporate affairs are put off or ignored because there is full agreement in fact by all interested parties regarding what should be done and who should do it. Also, the play-acting aspects of corporate meetings, elections, and the like, may strike businessmen as rather silly. Insistence by an attorney that formal corporate procedures be followed may be dismissed as a subtle attempt at an additional fee. This attitude invites disaster.

When failure to follow appropriate corporate procedures tends to injure third persons, there can be little objection to holding the shareholder liable. Procedures within the corporation may be so undifferentiated that a person may believe he is dealing with a shareholder individually when he is dealing with the corporation. Similarly, intermingled personal and corporate assets may disappear into the personal coffers of the shareholder to the detriment of corporate creditors.

(6) Is it sound to argue that public policy requires attention to be paid to corporate formalities, and that ignoring the corporate entity where formalities have been ignored furthers this policy? Or may one argue that a shareholder should be liable because he may not be permitted first to ignore the rules of corporate behavior and then to claim the advantage of the corporate shield? In other words, the apparent theory is to punish an errant shareholder, punishment that, depending on the vagaries of the case, may involve a draconian liability for a relatively minor infraction.

(7) Consider how Flemming apparently ran his business. Flemming caused the Fruit Company to make distributions to himself out of funds that were earmarked for the payment of plaintiff's transportation charges on the statements of account with growers. Whether or not this constitutes "plain fraud" is perhaps open to question but it is clearly an improper diversion of assets that effectively disabled the Fruit Company from ever being able to pay the plaintiff. The force of theoretical arguments that the fruit company was a "separate legal person" may well unravel in the light of such inequitable conduct. Many piercing cases involve similar misconduct. For example, consider the pricing policy described in the dissent to the *Bartle* case. If that description is accurate, is that conduct any less objectionable than what was done in *DeWitt*? In the light of this analysis, was it really necessary for the court in *DeWitt* to get involved in the rhetoric of piercing the corporate veil at all?

(8) In *DeWitt*, Flemming at some point also made an oral promise that he would pay the plaintiff's transportation charges personally if the corporation could not pay them. Despite the Court's discussion, is not the statute of frauds a bar to a direct suit on that promise? If so, can one avoid the statute of frauds by arguing that the oral promise (presumably made to encourage DeWitt to continue dealing with the corporation on credit) should permit the Court to pierce the corporate veil because it involves misconduct by the shareholder? In some cases, such an oral promise may mislead or trick the third person into dealing with the corporate

"shell." Arguably, Weisser v. Mursam Shoe Corp., 127 F.2d 344 (2d Cir.1942), relied upon by the Court in *DeWitt,* is such a case:

In 1926, Murray Rosenberg approached the plaintiffs to negotiate the terms of a lease of certain premises in Paterson, New Jersey. Their version of the negotiations is as follows: "When we had agreed upon the terms of the lease, Murray M. Rosenberg told us that the tenant was to be the Mursam Shoe Corporation. I asked him who was the Mursam Shoe Corporation. Murray M. Rosenberg represented to me that the name Mursam was an abbreviation for Murray and Samuel, and that he and his brother were the corporation and 'stood behind' the lease. He told us that the store to be opened at the leased premises by them, was to be part of the chain of stores which he and his brother were then operating. Relying upon these representations, the plaintiffs entered into a lease with Mursam for a term of fifteen years." The Mursam Shoe Corporation was organized by the Rosenbergs the day the lease was signed and sealed by the plaintiffs, and two days later it signed and sealed the lease as tenant. According to its books, the original capital investment in Mursam was $1; apart from paying legal and similar fees arising out of the organization of Mursam, the Rosenbergs paid nothing for their stock, and it does not appear that subsequently they made any contributions to capital. Mursam was, therefore, a corporation without assets. Its obligation under the lease was $10,000 annually, for the first five years, $11,000 for the next five and $12,000 for the last five years, or $165,000 for the entire term.

For fourteen years Mursam met its obligations on this lease. It was able to do so because of payments made to it by Murray M. Rosenberg, Inc., which occupied the leased premises under short term subleases. In March 1940, Murray M. Rosenberg, Inc., terminated the sublease then in effect (made February 1, 1939), which was of unspecified duration on a monthly basis, and vacated the premises. Mursam having no assets, this action for damages caused by breach of the lease by failing to pay rent was brought against the other individual and corporate defendants as well.

Id. at 345. On these facts, the Court concluded that it was error to grant summary judgment in favor of the Rosenbergs, and that the statute of frauds was not a defense available to the Rosenbergs. In both this case and *DeWitt,* the plaintiff could easily have declined credit or refused to enter into the lease unless the guarantee was in writing. If they fail to do so, why should they be able to recover despite the statute of frauds?

BAATZ v. ARROW BAR

Supreme Court of South Dakota, 1990.
452 N.W.2d 138.

SABERS, JUSTICE.

Kenny and Peggy Baatz (Baatz), appeal from summary judgment dismissing Edmond, LaVella, and Jacquette Neuroth, as individual defendants in this action. * * * Kenny and Peggy were seriously injured in 1982 when Roland McBride crossed the center line of a Sioux Falls street with his automobile and struck them while they were riding on a motorcycle. McBride was uninsured at the time of the accident and apparently is judgment proof.

Baatz alleges that Arrow Bar served alcoholic beverages to McBride prior to the accident while he was already intoxicated. Baatz commenced this action in 1984, claiming that Arrow Bar's negligence in serving alcoholic beverages to McBride contributed to the injuries they sustained in the accident. Baatz supports his claim against Arrow Bar with the affidavit of Jimmy Larson. Larson says he knew McBride and observed him being served alcoholic beverages in the Arrow Bar during the afternoon prior to the accident, while McBride was intoxicated. * * *

Edmond and LaVella Neuroth formed the Arrow Bar, Inc. in May 1980. During the next two years they contributed $50,000 to the corporation pursuant to a stock subscription agreement. The corporation purchased the Arrow Bar business in June 1980 for $155,000 with a $5,000 down payment. Edmond and LaVella executed a promissory note personally guaranteeing payment of the $150,000 balance. In 1983 the corporation obtained bank financing in the amount of $145,000 to pay off the purchase agreement. Edmond and LaVella again personally guaranteed payment of the corporate debt. Edmond is the president of the corporation, and Jacquette Neuroth serves as the manager of the business. Based on the enactment of SDCL 35–4–78 and 35–11–1 and advice of counsel, the corporation did not maintain dram shop liability insurance at the time of the injuries to Kenny and Peggy.[8]

In 1987 the trial court entered summary judgment in favor of Arrow Bar and the individual defendants. Baatz appealed that judgment and we reversed and remanded to the trial court for trial. * * * Shortly before the trial date, Edmond, LaVella, and Jacquette moved for and obtained summary judgment dismissing them as individual defendants. Baatz appeals. We affirm.

A trial court may grant summary judgment only when there are no genuine issues of material fact. * * * When determining whether a genuine issue of material fact exists, the evidence must be viewed most favorably to the non-moving party and reasonable doubts are to be resolved against the moving party. Groseth Int'l, Inc. v. Tenneco, Inc., 410 N.W.2d 159 (S.D.1987). * * *

Baatz claims that even if Arrow Bar, Inc. is the licensee, the corporate veil should be pierced, leaving the Neuroths, as the shareholders of the corporation, individually liable. A corporation shall be considered a separate legal entity until there is sufficient reason to the contrary. Mobridge Community Indus., Inc. v. Toure, Ltd., 273 N.W.2d 128 (S.D.1978); cf. Hamaker v. Kenwel–Jackson Mach., Inc., 387 N.W.2d 515 (S.D.1986). When continued

---

8. [By the Editor] Section 35–4–78(2) makes it a misdemeanor for any licensed bar to sell an alcoholic beverage to "any person who is obviously intoxicated at the time." In Walz v. City of Hudson, 327 N.W.2d 120 (S.D.1982) the Court held that this section created a private cause of action for persons injured by patrons who were sold alcoholic beverages in violation of this section. In 1985, the South Dakota Legislature attempted to overrule Walz by (1) adding a sentence to 35–4–78(2) stating that "no licensee is civilly liable to any injured person * * * for any injury suffered * * * because of the intoxication of any person due to the sale of any alcoholic beverage in violation of the provisions of this section," and (2) adding 35–11–1 which made a formal legislative finding that "the consumption of alcoholic bev-

erages, rather than the serving of alcoholic beverages, is the proximate cause of any injury inflicted upon another by an intoxicated person" and therefore "abrogated" the Walz holding. Apparently while this legislation was pending, the attorney recommended that the Arrow Bar not obtain dram shop insurance even though the Baatz law suit had been filed in 1984. However, in Baatz v. Arrow Bar, 426 N.W.2d 298 (1988) the South Dakota Supreme Court held that the attempted abrogation was invalid both retrospectively and prospectively. The court's opinion does not make clear how the attorney's recommendation not to purchase dram shop insurance presumably in 1985 affected the Baatz litigation filed in 1984 for injuries that occurred in 1982.

recognition of a corporation as a separate legal entity would "produce injustices and inequitable consequences," then a court has sufficient reason to pierce the corporate veil. Farmers Feed & Seed, Inc. v. Magnum Enter., Inc., 344 N.W.2d 699, 701 (S.D.1984). Factors that indicate injustices and inequitable consequences and allow a court to pierce the corporate veil are:

1) fraudulent representation by corporation directors;

2) undercapitalization;

3) failure to observe corporate formalities;

4) absence of corporate records;

5) payment by the corporation of individual obligations; or

6) use of the corporation to promote fraud, injustice, or illegalities.

When the court deems it appropriate to pierce the corporate veil, the corporation and its stockholders will be treated identically. Mobridge, supra.

Baatz advances several arguments to support his claim that the corporate veil of Arrow Bar, Inc. should be pierced, but fails to support them with facts, or misconstrues the facts.

First, Baatz claims that since Edmond and LaVella personally guaranteed corporate obligations, they should also be personally liable to Baatz. However, the personal guarantee of a loan is a contractual agreement and cannot be enlarged to impose tort liability. Moreover, the personal guarantee creates individual liability for a corporate obligation, the opposite of factor 5), above. As such, it supports, rather than detracts from, recognition of the corporate entity.

Baatz also argues that the corporation is simply the alter ego of the Neuroths, and, in accord with Loving Saviour Church v. United States, 556 F.Supp. 688 (D.S.D.1983), aff'd, 728 F.2d 1085 (8th Cir.1984), the corporate veil should be pierced. Baatz' discussion of the law is adequate, but he fails to present evidence that would support a decision in his favor in accordance with that law. When an individual treats a corporation "as an instrumentality through which he [is] conducting his personal business," a court may disregard the corporate entity. Larson v. Western Underwriters, Inc., 77 S.D. 157, 163, 87 N.W.2d 883, 886 (1958). Baatz fails to demonstrate how the Neuroths were transacting personal business through the corporation. In fact, the evidence indicates the Neuroths treated the corporation separately from their individual affairs.

Baatz next argues that the corporation is undercapitalized. Shareholders must equip a corporation with a reasonable amount of capital for the nature of the business involved. See Curtis v. Feurhelm, 335 N.W.2d 575 (S.D.1983). Baatz claims the corporation was started with only $5,000 in borrowed capital, but does not explain how that amount failed to equip the corporation with a reasonable amount of capital. In addition, Baatz fails to consider the personal guarantees to pay off the purchase contract in the amount of $150,000, and the $50,000 stock subscription agreement. There simply is no evidence that the corporation's capital in whatever amount was inadequate for the operation of the business. Normally questions relating to individual shareholder liability resulting from corporate undercapitalization should not be reached until the primary question of corporate liability is determined.

Questions depending in part upon other determinations are not normally ready for summary judgment. See Van Knight Steel Erection, Inc. v. Housing and Redev. Auth. of the City of St. Paul, 430 N.W.2d 1 (Minn.Ct.App.1988); see also Candee Constr. Co., Inc. v. South Dakota Dep't of Transp., 447 N.W.2d 339, 346 (S.D.1989) (Sabers, J., dissenting). However, simply asserting that the corporation is undercapitalized does not make it so. Without some evidence of the inadequacy of the capital, Baatz fails to present specific facts demonstrating a genuine issue of material fact. Ruane, supra.

Finally, Baatz argues that Arrow Bar, Inc. failed to observe corporate formalities because none of the business' signs or advertising indicated that the business was a corporation. Baatz cites SDCL 47–2–36 as requiring the name of any corporation to contain the word corporation, company, incorporated, or limited, or an abbreviation for such a word. In spite of Baatz' contentions, the corporation is in compliance with the statute because its corporate name—Arrow Bar, Inc.—includes the abbreviation of the word incorporated. Furthermore, the "mere failure upon occasion to follow all the forms prescribed by law for the conduct of corporate activities will not justify" disregarding the corporate entity. Larson, supra, 77 S.D. at 164, 87 N.W.2d at 887 (quoting P.S. & A. Realties, Inc. v. Lodge Gate Forest, Inc., 205 Misc. 245, 254, 127 N.Y.S.2d 315, 324 (1954)). Even if the corporation is improperly using its name, that alone is not a sufficient reason to pierce the corporate veil. This is especially so where, as here, there is no relationship between the claimed defect and the resulting harm.

In addition, the record is void of any evidence which would support imposition of individual liability by piercing the corporate veil under any of the other factors listed above in 1), 4) or 6).

In summary, Baatz fails to present specific facts that would allow the trial court to find the existence of a genuine issue of material fact. There is no indication that any of the Neuroths personally served an alcoholic beverage to McBride on the day of the accident. Nor is there any evidence indicating that the Neuroths treated the corporation in any way that would produce the injustices and inequitable consequences necessary to justify piercing the corporate veil. In fact, the only evidence offered is otherwise. Therefore, we affirm summary judgment dismissing the Neuroths as individual defendants.

Wuest, C.J., and Morgan and Miller, JJ., concur.

Henderson, Justice (dissenting).

This corporation has no separate existence. It is the instrumentality of three shareholders, officers, and employees. * * *

A corporate shield was here created to escape the holding of this Court relating to an individual's liability in a dram shop action. * * * As a result of this holding, the message is now clear: Incorporate, mortgage the assets of a liquor corporation to your friendly banker, and proceed with carefree entrepreneuring.

In both of these briefs, the parties argue, all in all, about the facts. One may reasonably conclude that there exists questions of fact. * * * [The] Baatzes had their case thrown out of court when many facts were in dispute. I am reminded of the old lawyer, before a jury, who expressed his woe of corporations. He cried out to the jury: "A corporation haveth no soul and its hind end you can kicketh not." * * *

Peggy Baatz, a young mother, lost her left leg; she wears an artificial limb; Kenny Baatz, a young father, has had most of his left foot amputated; he has been unable to work since this tragic accident. Peggy uses a cane. Kenny uses crutches. Years have gone by since they were injured and their lives have been torn asunder.

Uninsured motorist was drunk, and had a reputation of being a habitual drunkard; Arrow Bar had a reputation of serving intoxicated persons. (Supported by depositions on file). An eyewitness saw uninsured motorist in an extremely intoxicated condition, shortly before the accident, being served by Arrow Bar. * * * This evidence must be viewed most favorably to the nonmoving party. American Indian Agr. Credit Consortium, Inc. v. Ft. Pierre Livestock, Inc., 379 N.W.2d 318 (S.D.1985). A police officer testified, by deposition, that uninsured motorist was in a drunken stupor while at the Arrow Bar.

* * * Arrow Bar, Inc. is being used to justify any wrongs perpetrated by the incorporators in their individual capacity. Conclusion: Fraud is perpetrated upon the public. At a deposition of Edmond Neuroth (filed in this record), this "President" of "the corporation" was asked why the Neuroth family incorporated. His answer: "Upon advice of counsel, as a shield against individual liability." The corporation was undercapitalized (Neuroths borrowed $5,000 in capital). * * * In Loving Saviour Church, it was held that a chiropractor could not use a church to escape income taxes; here, a corporation conceived in undercapitalization as "a shield," in the words of "the President," should not be used as an artifice to avoid the intent of SDCL 35–4–78(2). * * *

Therefore, I respectfully dissent.

Notes

(1) The tort cases involving the "piercing" doctrine have a different flavor than the contracts cases. Consider Robert W. Hamilton, The Corporate Entity, 49 Tex.L.Rev. 979, 983–85 (1971).[9]

> Secondly, a major consideration in determining whether the shareholders or the third party should bear the loss is whether the third party dealt voluntarily with the corporation or whether he is an involuntary creditor, typically a tort claimant. In a contract case, the plaintiff has usually dealt in some way with the corporation and should be aware that the corporation lacks substance. In the absence of some sort of deception, the creditor more or less assumed the risk of loss when he dealt with a "shell"; if he was concerned, he should have insisted that some solvent third person guarantee the performance by the corporation. In tort cases, on the other hand, there is usually no element of voluntary dealing, and the question is whether it is reasonable for businessmen to transfer a risk of loss or injury to members of the general public through the device of conducting business in the name of a corporation that may be marginally financed. The issues of public policy raised by tort claims bear little relationship to the issues raised by a contract

9. Published originally in 49 Texas Law Review 979, 979–1009 (1971). Copyright 1971 by the Texas Law Review Association. Reprinted by permission.

claim. It is astonishing to find that this fundamental distinction is only dimly perceived by many courts, which indiscriminately cite and purport to apply, tort precedents in contract cases and vice versa.

(2) Robert B. Thompson, Piercing the Corporate Veil: An Empirical Study, 76 Cornell L.Rev. 1036 (1991),[10] examines 1,583 cases involving the piercing the corporate veil doctrine decided before 1985. The conclusions reached from this massive survey include the following:

* * *

b) The corporate veil was pierced in about 40 percent of the reported cases. This percentage remained stable over more than four decades, was about the same in state and federal courts, and variations from state to state did not appear to be statistically significant.

c) Corporations with a single individual shareholder were pierced in nearly 50 percent of all cases involving those corporations. This dropped to 46 percent for corporations with two or three individual shareholders, and 35 percent for corporations with more than three individuals. The veil of subsidiary corporations was pierced in about 28 percent of all cases involving those corporations and in 42 percent of all cases involving sibling corporations.

d) 779 cases in the survey involved contract claims and 226 involved tort claims.[11] The corporate veil was pierced in 327 of the contracts cases (42 percent) and 70 of the torts cases (31 percent).

e) Undercapitalization was a factor in 19 percent of the contracts cases in which the corporate veil was pierced (61 of 327) but was a factor in only 13 percent of the tort cases in which piercing occurred (9 of 70). A failure to follow corporate formalities was cited in 20 percent of the contracts cases and 11 percent of the torts cases.

(3) Thompson's study, of course was limited to litigated cases, and mostly appellate litigated cases. He points out that this type of study has certain inherent limitations:

As with any empirical study, it is worthwhile to keep in mind what the study can and cannot do. These results are based on reported cases that may not be a representative sample: of all piercing the veil cases actually decided (since many opinions are not reported); of all piercing the veil cases actually filed (since most cases are settled); or of the total number of transactions in which a "piercing" question comes up (since many questions are resolved without litigation). These limitations make it inappropriate to draw conclusions as to the number of corporations in which the question of piercing the corporate veil arises. * * *

The literature on selection bias (including the work by Priest and Klein[12] and Priest alone[13] suggests that disputes selected for litigation will constitute neither a random nor representative sample of the set of all disputes. Any

---

10. Copyright 1991 by Cornell University. All rights reserved.

11. [By the Editor] The remaining cases were classified as "criminal" or "statute" cases.

12. [By the Author] George L. Priest & Benjamin Klein, *The Selection of Disputes for Litigation*, 13 J. Legal Stud. 1, 4 (1984) (developing a model that suggests "disputes selected

for litigation (as opposed to settlement) will constitute neither a random nor a representative sample of the set of all disputes").

13. [By the Author] George L. Priest, *Selective Characteristics of Litigation*, 9 J. Legal Stud. 399 (1980); George L. Priest, Measuring Legal Change (1987) (Yale Law School working paper, Program in Civil Liability).

relative comparison of various factors, such as the one done here, can be affected to the extent that litigants understand the prior learning on a legal issue and use that knowledge to decide which cases to file, to continue on appeal, or to settle. While that type of selection might be occurring in this set of reported opinions, other factors suggest that the bias is not so great as to prevent meaningful uses of differences in the results. First, * * * the law in this area has not crystallized. Case results are very fact specific, and the fact patterns that cause a court to pierce or not to pierce are not clearly understood. The area of uncertainty is broad enough that litigants have continued to bring a large number of cases. Second, the lack of any significant change over time in the percentage of cases in which courts pierce the veil, or any significant difference between results in state and federal court cases or between results in trial, appellate, and supreme court cases, suggests that the sample has stayed within the same broad range. Finally, to the extent that these results are used to evaluate theories in prior commentary, this study uses a data set broader than the sample of reported cases that form the basis for the comments previously put forward.

(4) In an often quoted passage, Frank H. Easterbrook and Daniel R. Fischel, Limited Liability and the Corporation, 52 U.Chi.L.Rev. 89 (1985) stated, "Limited liability is a fundamental principle of corporate law. Yet liability has never been absolutely limited. Courts occasionally allow creditors to 'pierce the corporate veil,' which means that shareholders must satisfy creditors' claims. 'Piercing' seems to happen freakishly. Like lightning, it is rare, severe, and unprincipled. There is a consensus that the whole area of limited liability, and conversely of piercing the corporate veil, is among the most confusing in corporate law." The authors then go on to "argue to the contrary that economic analysis—in particular the theory of the firm and the economics of insurance—explains the legal treatment of limited liability. Both the rules and the exceptions serve valuable functions." In their book, The Economic Structure of Corporate Law, ch. 2 (1991) the authors develop their thesis at greater length.

(5) As discussed in chapter 5, most state corporation statutes do not require any minimum amount of capital. It is literally possible today to form a corporation with one cent or one dollar of capital. Of course, to actually form a corporation with essentially zero capital to engage in a risky business would be extremely dangerous in light of the rhetoric in many piercing cases about "inadequate capital." In *Baatz*, the corporation began with $5,000 in cash and some personal guarantees, which the majority held was sufficient to avoid the inadequate capitalization argument. However, should that really be the test? The cash plus the personal guarantees was sufficient to permit the Neuroths' to purchase the Arrow Bar but certainly not sufficient to cover possible unexpected liabilities, let alone the serious injuries to the members of the Baatz family. If the test should be some amount of "free" capital sufficient to cover unexpected liabilities, the question becomes, how much? Is the problem in *Baatz* the conscious decision not to purchase dram shop insurance? Might there be malpractice on the part of the attorney who recommended that the purchase of such insurance was unnecessary?

RADASZEWSKI v. TELECOM CORP.

United States Court of Appeals, Eighth Circuit, 1992.
981 F.2d 305.

Before RICHARD S. ARNOLD, CHIEF JUDGE, HEANEY, SENIOR CIRCUIT JUDGE, and MAGILL, CIRCUIT JUDGE.

RICHARD S. ARNOLD, CHIEF JUDGE.

This is an action for personal injuries filed on behalf of Konrad Radaszewski, who was seriously injured in an automobile accident on August 21, 1984. Radaszewski, who was on a motorcycle, was struck by a truck driven by an employee of Contrux, Inc. The question presented on this appeal is whether the District Court had jurisdiction over the person of Telecom Corporation, which is the corporate parent of Contrux. This question depends, in turn, on whether, under Missouri law, Radaszewski can "pierce the corporate veil," and hold Telecom liable for the conduct of its subsidiary, Contrux, and Contrux's driver. The District Court held that it lacked jurisdiction. We agree, though for different reasons.

In general, someone injured by the conduct of a corporation or one of its employees can look only to the assets of the employee or of the employer corporation for recovery. The shareholders of the corporation, including, if there is one, its parent corporation, are not responsible. This is a conscious decision made by the law of every state to encourage business in the corporate form. Obviously the decision has its costs. Some injuries are going to go unredressed because of the insolvency of the corporate defendant immediately involved, even when its shareholders have plenty of money. To the general rule, though, there are exceptions. There are instances in which an injured person may "pierce the corporate veil," that is, reach the assets of one or more of the shareholders of the corporation whose conduct has created liability. In the present case, the plaintiff seeks to hold Telecom Corporation liable for the conduct of an employee of its wholly owned subsidiary, Contrux, Inc.

Under Missouri law, a plaintiff in this position needs to show three things. The leading case is *Collet v. American National Stores, Inc.*, 708 S.W.2d 273 (Mo.App.1986). The Missouri Court of Appeals had this to say:

A tripartite test has been developed for analysis of the question. To "pierce the corporate veil," one must show;

(1) Control, not mere majority or complete stock control, but complete domination, not only of finances, but of policy and business practice in respect to the transaction attacked so that the corporate entity as to this transaction had at the time no separate mind, will or existence of its own; and

(2) Such control must have been used by the defendant to commit fraud or wrong, to perpetrate the violation of a statutory or other positive legal duty, or dishonest and unjust act in contravention of plaintiff's legal rights; and

(3) The aforesaid control and breach of duty must proximately cause the injury or unjust loss complained of.

Id. at 284.

It is common ground among all parties that Telecom, as such, has had no contact with Missouri. If it is subject to jurisdiction over its person in Missouri courts, it is only because of the conduct of Contrux, its subsidiary. So the issue of jurisdiction over the person depends on whether the corporate veil of Contrux can be pierced to bring Telecom into the case. As it happens, this is also the question upon which Telecom's substantive liability depends. (We assume for present purposes that Contrux is liable—this has not yet been proved.) * * *

Undercapitalizing a subsidiary, which we take to mean creating it and putting it in business without a reasonably sufficient supply of money, has become a sort of proxy under Missouri law for the second *Collet* element. On the prior appeal, for example, we said that "Missouri courts will disregard the existence of a corporate entity that is operated while undercapitalized." 891 F.2d at 674. *Collet, supra,* 708 S.W.2d at 286–87. The reason, we think, is not because undercapitalization, in and of itself, is unlawful (though it may be for some purposes), but rather because the creation of an undercapitalized subsidiary justifies an inference that the parent is either deliberately or recklessly creating a business that will not be able to pay its bills or satisfy judgments against it. This point has been made clear by the Supreme Court of Missouri. In *May Department Stores Co. v. Union Electric Light & Power Co.,* 341 Mo. 299, 327, 107 S.W.2d 41, 55 (1937), the Court found an improper purpose in a case where a corporation was "operating it without sufficient funds to meet obligations to those who must deal with it." Similarly, in *Consolidated Sun Ray, Inc. v. Oppenstein,* 335 F.2d 801 (8th Cir.1964), we said: "Making a corporation a supplemental part of an economic unit and operating it without sufficient funds to meet obligations to those who must deal with it would be circumstantial evidence tending to show either an improper purpose or reckless disregard of the rights of others." *Id.* at 806–07.

Here, the District Court held, and we assume, that Contrux was undercapitalized in the accounting sense. Most of the money contributed to its operation by Telecom was in the form of loans, not equity, and when Contrux first went into business, Telecom did not pay for all of the stock that was issued to it. This is a classic instance of watered stock, of putting a corporation into business without sufficient equity investment. Telecom in effect concedes that Contrux's balance sheet was anemic, and that, from the point of view of generally accepted accounting principles, Contrux was inadequately capitalized. Telecom says, however, that this doesn't matter, because Contrux had $11,000,000 worth of liability insurance available to pay judgments like the one that Radaszewski hopes to obtain. No one can say, therefore, the argument runs, that Telecom was improperly motivated in setting up Contrux, in the sense of either knowingly or recklessly establishing it without the ability of pay tort judgments.

In fact, Contrux did have $1,000,000 in basic liability coverage, plus $10,000,000 in excess coverage. This coverage was bound on March 1, 1984, about five and one-half months before the accident involving Radaszewski. Unhappily, Contrux's [excess liability] insurance carrier became insolvent two years after the accident and is now in receivership. (This record does not show the financial status of the receivership. We thus do not know whether any money would ever be available from the insurance company to pay a judgment in favor of Radaszewski, if he obtains one.) But this insurance, Telecom points out, was sufficient to satisfy federal financial-responsibility requirements. Under 49 C.F.R. § 387, motor carriers must maintain "financial reserves (e.g., insurance policies or surety bonds) sufficient to satisfy liability amounts set forth in this subpart covering public liability." 49 C.F.R. § 387.5. It is undisputed that the amount of insurance maintained by Contrux exceeded federal requirements, and that Contrux, at all times during its operations, was considered financially responsible by the relevant federal agency, the Interstate Commerce Commission.

The District Court rejected this argument. Undercapitalization is undercapitalization, it reasoned, regardless of insurance. The Court said: "The federal regulation does not speak to what constitutes a properly capitalized motor carrier company. Rather, the regulation speaks to what constitutes an appropriate level of *financial responsibility." Konrad Radaszewski v. Contrux, Inc.*, No. 88–0445–CV–W–1 (W.D.Mo. Oct. 26, 1990), slip op. 7 n. 6 (emphasis in original). This distinction escapes us. The whole purpose of asking whether a subsidiary is "properly capitalized," is precisely to determine its "financial responsibility." If the subsidiary is financially responsible, whether by means of insurance or otherwise, the policy behind the second part of the *Collet* test is met. Insurance meets this policy just as well, perhaps even better, than a healthy balance sheet. * * *

The doctrine of limited liability is intended precisely to protect a parent corporation whose subsidiary goes broke. That is the whole purpose of the doctrine, and those who have the right to decide such questions, that is, legislatures, believe that the doctrine, on the whole, is socially reasonable and useful. We think that the doctrine would largely be destroyed if a parent corporation could be held liable simply on the basis of errors in business judgment. Something more than that should be shown, and *Collet* requires something more than that. In our view, this record is devoid of facts to show that "something more." * * *

We * * * affirm the judgment of the District Court dismissing the complaint for want of jurisdiction, but modify that judgment to provide that it is with prejudice as to Radaszewski's complaint against Telecom.

Heaney, Senior Circuit Judge, dissenting.

I respectfully dissent. * * * In my view, Contrux's liability insurance is a relevant factor to be considered, but a fact finder after a trial might well find that this factor alone does not require a verdict for the defendant. * * *

Notes

(1) Do you agree that the piercing doctrine should not apply in a tort case if the corporation has acquired liability insurance against that risk even if, under the circumstances, the plaintiff is unable to recover under that insurance?

(2) What is meant by "undercapitalization"? If a corporation is adequately capitalized when it is formed, but thereafter suffers operating losses, is it then undercapitalized? If so, does that mean the shareholders must infuse additional capital in that corporation or suffer the possible application of the piercing the corporate veil doctrine? For a negative answer, see Consumer's Co–op. of Walworth County v. Olsen, 142 Wis.2d 465, 419 N.W.2d 211, 218–19 (1988); CNC Service Center, Inc. v. CNC Service Center, 753 F.Supp. 1427 (N.D.Ill.1991). What about a corporation that was formed some time ago, and is reactivated by shareholders to go into a new business? Should undercapitalization be measured at the time it goes into the new business or when it was originally incorporated? What about a corporation that is adequately capitalized for its continuing business A, but then goes into a new business B? If the capital is inadequate for businesses A and B combined, is it thereafter undercapitalized with respect to a claim arising from business A?

(3) What should count as capital? Liability insurance? Should such insurance be relevant in contracts cases? Capital invested by the shareholders in the form of loans to an otherwise undercapitalized business? Should it make any difference if the shareholders plan to have the corporation repay those loans or whether they plan to leave the funds in the corporation indefinitely? In O'Hazza v. Executive Credit Corp., 246 Va. 111, 431 S.E.2d 318 (1993), the Court concluded that a corporation was adequately capitalized when the shareholders contributed $10,000 in initial capital and then loaned the corporation approximately $140,000 "without expectation of repayment." Should such subjective intentions play any role in the piercing the corporate veil doctrine? See also Arnold v. Phillips, 117 F.2d 497, 501–02 (5th Cir.1941)(distinction made between loans before the enterprise was launched and loans thereafter to keep the business afloat).

(3) Corporations with a common shareholder or set of shareholders are called "brother-sister" or "sibling" corporations. In Walkovszky v. Carlton, 18 N.Y.2d 414, 276 N.Y.S.2d 585, 223 N.E.2d 6 (1966), a famous New York case, the complaint alleged "that the plaintiff was severely injured four years ago in New York City when he was run down by a taxicab owned by the defendant Seon Cab Corporation and negligently operated at the time by the defendant Marchese. The individual defendant, Carlton, is claimed to be a stockholder of 10 corporations, including Seon, each of which has but two cabs registered in its name, and it is implied that only the minimum automobile liability insurance required by law (in the amount of $10,000) is carried on any one cab. Although seemingly independent of one another, these corporations are alleged to be 'operated * * * as a single entity, unit and enterprise' with regard to financing, supplies, repairs, employees and garaging, and all are named as defendant.[14] Does the diffusion of what appears to be a single business enterprise into eleven different corporations constitute a stratagem or device that itself justifies piercing the corporate veil even though there is no parent/subsidiary relationship? See Adolph Berle, The Theory of Enterprise Entity, 47 Colum.L.Rev. 343, 348 (1947):

> Another illustration of judicial erection of a new entity occurs in situations where the corporate personality (as embodied in its charter, books and so forth) does not correspond to the actual enterprise, but merely to a fragment of it. The result is to construct a new aggregate of assets and liabilities. Typical cases appear where a partnership or a central corporation owns the controlling interest in one or more other corporations, but has so handled them that they have ceased to represent a separate enterprise and have become, as a business matter, more or less indistinguishable parts of a larger enterprise. The decisions disregard the paper corporate personalities and base liability on the assets of the enterprise. The reasoning by which courts reach this result varies: it is sometimes said that one corporation has become a mere "agency" of another; or that its operations have been so intermingled that it has lost its identity; or that the business arrangements indicate that it has become a "mere instrumentality."

It is unlikely that recovery against the eleven corporations would satisfy any judgment obtained by the plaintiff. Should Carleton be personally liable? If so, on what theory? Should it be on the ground that the statutorily mandated insurance of $10,000 was inadequate[15] and therefore the corporate veil of Seon should be

---

14. [By the Court] The corporate owner of a garage is also included as a defendant.

15. [By the Editor] This issue evoked a lively debate between the majority and the dissenters. The majority argued:

pierced? The majority of the court in *Walkovszky* concluded that the complaint did not state a claim against Carleton individually because it was "barren of any 'sufficiently particular[ized] statements' that the defendant Carlton and his associates are actually doing business in their individual capacities, shuttling their personal funds in and out of the corporations 'without regard to formality and to suit their immediate convenience.' (Weisser v. Mursam Shoe Corp., * * *supra.)" Is this an appropriate test for piercing the corporate veil in a torts case? Walkovszky then amended his complaint to allege that Carlton was "conducting the business of the taxicab fleet in [his] individual capacity." This complaint was upheld on motion to dismiss for failure to state a cause of action, one judge dissenting. Walkovszky v. Carlton, 29 A.D.2d 763, 287 N.Y.S.2d 546 (1968), aff'd 23 N.Y.2d 714, 296 N.Y.S.2d 362, 244 N.E.2d 55 (1968). The case then settled.

④ Frank H. Easterbrook and Daniel R. Fischel, The Economic Structure of Corporate Law 57 (1991):[16]

> [Parent corporations should not always] be liable for the debts of those in which they hold stock. Far from it. Such general liability would give unaffiliated firms a competitive advantage. Think of the taxicab business. Taxi firms may incorporate each cab or put just a few cabs in a firm. If courts routinely pierced this arrangement and put the assets of the full venture at risk for the accidents of each cab, then "true" single-cab firms would have lower costs of operation because they alone could cut off liability. That would create a perverse incentive because, as we have emphasized, larger firms are apt to carry more insurance. Potential victims of torts would not gain from a legal rule that promoted corporate disintegration. As a result, courts properly disregard the corporate form only when the corporate arrangement has increased risks over what they would be if firms generally were organized as separate ventures.

Do you agree? Do Easterbrook and Fischel correctly state "the law" in the last sentence that is quoted?

* * * [W]e agree with the court at Special Term that, if the insurance coverage required by statute "is inadequate for the protection of the public, the remedy lies not with the courts but with the Legislature." * * * [T]he responsibility for imposing conditions on the privilege of incorporation has been committed by the Constitution to the Legislature and it may not be fairly implied, from any statute, that the Legislature intended, without the slightest discussion or debate, to require of taxi corporations that they carry automobile liability insurance over and above that mandated by the Vehicle and Traffic Law.

The dissenters responded:

The Legislature in requiring minimum liability insurance of $10,000, no doubt, intended to provide at least some small fund for recovery against those individuals and corporations who just did not have and were not able to raise or accumulate assets sufficient to satisfy the claims of those who were injured as a result of their negligence. It certainly could not have intended to shield those individuals who organized corporations, with the specific intent of avoiding responsibility to the public, where the operation of the corporate enterprise yielded profits sufficient to purchase additional insurance. Moreover, it is reasonable to assume that the Legislature believed that those individuals and corporations having substantial assets would take out insurance far in excess of the minimum in order to protect those assets from depletion. Given the costs of hospital care and treatment and the nature of injuries sustained in auto collisions, it would be unreasonable to assume that the Legislature believed that the minimum provided in the statute would in and of itself be sufficient to recompense "innocent victims of motor vehicle accidents * * * for the injury and financial loss inflicted upon them".

16. Reprinted by permission of the publishers from *The Economic Structure of Corporate Law* by Frank H. Easterbrook and Daniel Fischel, Cambridge, Mass.: Harvard University Press, Copyright © 1991 by the President and Fellows of Harvard College.

(5) In <u>Minton v. Cavaney,</u> 56 Cal.2d 576, 15 Cal.Rptr. 641, 364 P.2d 473 (1961), Cavaney, an attorney, duly incorporated the Seminole Hot Springs Corporation, a corporation that thereafter leased and operated a public swimming pool. No stock was ever issued by the corporation and no capital was ever paid in. Cavaney served as a director and as secretary and treasurer of Seminole; the corporate records were stored in his office. Cavaney testified on deposition that he was only a "temporary" or "accommodation" director and officer, but there was also testimony that he expected to receive a portion of the corporation's stock. During the first year of the pool's operation, the plaintiffs' daughter drowned in the pool. Cavaney died sometime thereafter. The plaintiffs obtained a $10,000 default judgment against Seminole and, since that corporation had no assets, sought to hold Cavaney's estate personally liable on the judgment. Held: Cavaney's estate could be held personally liable on the plaintiffs' claim on a theory of alter ego, but his estate can relitigate the issues of Seminole's negligence and the amount of damages, since Cavaney was not a party to the original proceeding. The Court rejected Cavaney's claim that he should not be liable because he was merely a temporary or accommodation director with the understanding that he would not exercise any of the duties of a director: "A person may not in this manner divorce the responsibilities of a director from the statutory duties and powers of that office." 15 Cal.Rptr. at 644, 364 P.2d at 476. This and similar cases illustrate the dangers of an attorney agreeing to serve even briefly as a director or officer of a corporation created by the attorney.

(6) Minton v. Cavaney is cited in <u>California</u> for the proposition that inadequate initial capitalization alone is sufficient to pierce the corporate veil. In Slottow v. American Cas. Co., 10 F.3d 1355, 1360 (9th Cir.1993), for example, the court stated "FNT's initial capitalization of $500,000 was woefully inadequate for a corporation that handled trust agreements of the magnitude involved here. The investors claimed damages in the range of $10,000,000; * * * Under California law, inadequate capitalization of a subsidiary may alone be a basis for holding the parent corporation liable * * *." But see Paul Steelman, Ltd. v. Omni Realty, 110 Nev. 1223, 885 P.2d 549, 550 (1994) ["Although undercapitalization is one criterion considered by courts in deciding whether to set aside the corporate barrier to shareholder liability for corporate debts, it is usually an insufficient ground, of itself * * *."]

(7) The conflict between corporate limited liability and the uncompensated tort victim has been the subject of considerable theoretical discussion. Henry Hansmann and Reinier H. Kraakman, Toward Unlimited Shareholder Liability for Corporate Torts, 100 Yale L.J. 1879 (1991), proposed that a rule of pro rata or proportionate liability—each shareholder is liable only for that proportion of the plaintiff's recovery that her shares bear to the total number of outstanding shares—be substituted for the current rule of (usually) no shareholder liability for corporate torts. This article caused a flurry of academic criticism, and defense by the original authors, but whatever the merits of the economic, social and legal arguments put forth, the Hansmann–Kraakman proposal appears to suffer from at least one major defect: There is no practical way to implement it. Any state that has the temerity to impose proportionate corporate tort liability on shareholders would presumably witness the immediate migration of corporations formed in that state to more hospitable climes.

FLETCHER v. ATEX, INC.

United States Court of Appeals, Second Circuit, 1995.
68 F.3d 1451.

Before: KEARSE, CALABRESI, and CABRANES, CIRCUIT JUDGES.

JOSE A. CABRANES, CIRCUIT JUDGE:

* * * The plaintiffs-appellants filed suit against Atex, Inc. ("Atex") and its parent, Eastman Kodak Company ("Kodak"), to recover for repetitive stress injuries that they claim were caused by their use of computer keyboards manufactured by Atex. * * * [A summary judgment was entered dismissing Kodak as a defendant and plaintiff's appeal.]

* * * From 1981 until December 1992, Atex was a wholly-owned subsidiary of Kodak. In 1987, Atex's name was changed to Electronic Pre–Press Systems, Inc., ("EPPS"), but its name was changed back to Atex in 1990. In December 1992, Atex sold substantially all of its assets to an independent third party and again changed its name to 805 Middlesex Corp., which holds the proceeds from the sale. Kodak continues to be the sole shareholder of 805 Middlesex Corp. * * *

The district court correctly noted that "[u]nder New York choice of law principles, '[t]he law of the state of incorporation determines when the corporate form will be disregarded and liability will be imposed on shareholders.'" * * * Because Atex was a Delaware corporation, Delaware law determines whether the corporate veil can be pierced in this instance.

Delaware law permits a court to pierce the corporate veil of a company "where there is fraud or where [it] is in fact a mere instrumentality or alter ego of its owner." Geyer v. Ingersoll Publications Co., 621 A.2d 784, 793 (Del.Ch.1992). Although the Delaware Supreme Court has never explicitly adopted an alter ego theory of parent liability for its subsidiaries, lower Delaware courts have applied the doctrine on several occasions, as has the United States District Court for the District of Delaware. * * *[U]nder an alter ego theory, there is no requirement of a showing of fraud. Id. at 1085. To prevail on an alter ego claim under Delaware law, a plaintiff must show (1) that the parent and the subsidiary "operated as a single economic entity" and (2) that an "overall element of injustice or unfairness * * * [is] present." Harper v. Delaware Valley Broadcasters, Inc., 743 F.Supp. 1076, 1085 (D.Del. 1990), aff'd, 932 F.2d 959 (3d Cir.1991).(internal quotation marks omitted).

To prevail on an alter ego theory of liability, a plaintiff must show that the two corporations "'operated as a single economic entity such that it would be inequitable * * * to uphold a legal distinction between them.'" * * * Among the factors to be considered in determining whether a subsidiary and parent operate as a "single economic entity" are:

"[W]hether the corporation was adequately capitalized for the corporate undertaking; whether the corporation was solvent; whether dividends were paid, corporate records kept, officers and directors functioned properly, and other corporate formalities were observed; whether the dominant shareholder siphoned corporate funds; and whether, in general, the corporation simply functioned as a facade for the dominant shareholder."

Harco Nat'l Ins. Co. v. Green Farms, Inc., No. CIV.A. 1331, 1989 WL 110537, at *4, (Del.Ch. Sept. 19, 1989) (quoting United States v. Golden Acres, Inc., 702 F.Supp. 1097, 1104 (D.Del.1988)). As noted above, a showing of fraud or wrongdoing is not necessary under an alter ego theory, but the plaintiff must demonstrate an overall element of injustice or unfairness. Harco, 1989 WL 110537, at *5.

A plaintiff seeking to persuade a Delaware court to disregard the corporate structure faces "a difficult task." Harco, 1989 WL 110537, at *4. Courts have made it clear that "[t]he legal entity of a corporation will not be disturbed until sufficient reason appears." Id. Although the question of domination is generally one of fact, courts have granted motions to dismiss as well as motions for summary judgment in favor of defendant parent companies where there has been a lack of sufficient evidence to place the alter ego issue in dispute. See, e.g., Akzona, Inc. v. Du Pont, 607 F.Supp. 227, 237 (D.Del.1984) (rejecting plaintiffs' alter ego theory of liability on a motion to dismiss). * * *

Kodak has shown that Atex followed corporate formalities, and the plaintiffs have offered no evidence to the contrary. Significantly, the plaintiffs have not challenged Kodak's assertions that Atex's board of directors held regular meetings, that minutes from those meetings were routinely prepared and maintained in corporate minute books, that appropriate financial records and other files were maintained by Atex, that Atex filed its own tax returns and paid its own taxes, and that Atex had its own employees and management executives who were responsible for the corporation's day-to-day business. The plaintiffs' primary arguments regarding domination concern (1) the defendant's use of a cash management system; (2) Kodak's exertion of control over Atex's major expenditures, stock sales, and the sale of Atex's assets to a third party; (3) Kodak's "dominating presence" on Atex's board of directors; (4) descriptions of the relationship between Atex and Kodak in the corporations' advertising, promotional literature, and annual reports; and (5) Atex's assignment of one of its former officer's mortgage to Kodak in order to close Atex's asset-purchase agreement with a third party. The plaintiffs argue that each of these raises a genuine issue of material fact about Kodak's domination of Atex, and that the district court therefore erred in granting summary judgment to Kodak on the plaintiffs' alter ego theory. We find that the district court correctly held that, in light of the undisputed factors of independence cited by Kodak, "the elements identified by the plaintiffs * * * [were] insufficient as a matter of law to establish the degree of domination necessary to disregard Atex's corporate identity."

First, the district court correctly held that "Atex's participation in Kodak's cash management system is consistent with sound business practice and does not show undue domination or control." The parties do not dispute the mechanics of Kodak's cash management system. Essentially, all of Kodak's domestic subsidiaries participate in the system and maintain zero-balance bank accounts. All funds transferred from the subsidiary accounts are recorded as credits to the subsidiary, and when a subsidiary is in need of funds, a transfer is made. At all times, a strict accounting is kept of each subsidiary's funds.

Courts have generally declined to find alter ego liability based on a parent corporation's use of a cash management system. See, e.g., In re Acushnet River & New Bedford Harbor Proceedings, 675 F.Supp. 22, 34 (D.Mass.1987) (Without "considerably more," "a centralized cash management system * * * where the accounting records always reflect the indebtedness of one entity to another, is not the equivalent of intermingling funds" and is insufficient to justify disregarding the corporate form.); United States v. Bliss, 108 F.R.D. 127, 132 (E.D.Mo.1985) (cash management system indicative of the "usual parent-subsidiary relationship"); Japan Petroleum Co. (Nigeria) v. Ashland Oil Inc., 456 F.Supp. 831, 838, 846 (D.Del.1978)(finding segregation of subsidiary's accounts within parent's cash management system to be "a function of administrative convenience and economy, rather than a manifestation of control"). The plaintiffs offer no facts to support their speculation that Kodak's centralized cash management system was actually a "complete commingling" of funds or a means by which Kodak sought to "siphon[ ] all of Atex's revenues into its own account."

Second, the district court correctly concluded that it could find no domination based on the plaintiffs' evidence that Kodak's approval was required for Atex's real estate leases, major capital expenditures, negotiations for a sale of minority stock ownership to IBM, or the fact that Kodak played a significant role in the ultimate sale of Atex's assets to a third party. Again, the parties do not dispute that Kodak required Atex to seek its approval and/or participation for the above transactions. However, this evidence, viewed in the light most favorable to the plaintiffs, does not raise an issue of material fact about whether the two corporations constituted "a single economic entity." Indeed, this type of conduct is typical of a majority shareholder or parent corporation. See Phoenix Canada Oil Co. v. Texaco, 842 F.2d 1466, 1476 (3d Cir.1988) (declining to pierce the corporate veil where subsidiary required to secure approval from parent for "large investments and acquisitions or disposals of major assets"), cert. denied, 488 U.S. 908, 109 S.Ct. 259, 102 L.Ed.2d 247 (1988); Akzona v. Du Pont, 607 F.Supp. 227, at 237 (D.Del.1984), (same, where parent approval required for expenditures exceeding $850,000); Japan Petrol., 456 F.Supp. at 843 (finding no parent liability where parent approval required for expenditures exceeding $250,000). In Akzona, the Delaware district court noted that a parent's "general executive responsibilities" for its subsidiary's operations included approval over major policy decisions and guaranteeing bank loans, and that that type of oversight was insufficient to demonstrate domination and control. Akzona, 607 F.Supp. at 238 (internal quotation marks omitted). Similarly, the district court in the instant case properly found that the presence of Kodak employees at periodic meetings with Atex's chief financial officer and comptroller to be "entirely appropriate." 861 F.Supp. at 245 (citing Akzona, 607 F.Supp. at 238); see Acushnet, 675 F.Supp. at 34 ("The quarterly and annual reports made [to the parent] do not represent an untoward intrusion by the owner into the corporate enterprise. The right of shareholders to remain informed is similarly recognized in many public and closely held corporations.").

The plaintiffs' third argument, that Kodak dominated the Atex board of directors, also fails. Although a number of Kodak employees have sat on the Atex board, it is undisputed that between 1981 and 1988, only one director of Atex was also a director of Kodak. Between 1989 and 1992, Atex and Kodak had no directors in common. Parents and subsidiaries frequently have overlapping boards of directors while maintaining separate business operations. In Japan Petroleum, the Delaware district court held that the fact that a parent and a subsidiary have common officers and directors does not necessarily demonstrate that the parent corporation dominates the activities of the subsidiary. 456 F.Supp. at 841; see Scott–Douglas Corp. v. Greyhound Corp., 304 A.2d 309, 314 (Del.Super.Ct.1973) (same). Since the overlap is negligible here, we find this evidence to be entirely insufficient to raise a question of fact on the issue of domination.

Fourth, the district court properly rejected the plaintiffs' argument that the descriptions of the relationship between Atex and Kodak and the presence of the Kodak logo in Atex's promotional literature justify piercing the corporate veil. The plaintiffs point to several statements in both Kodak's and Atex's literature to evidence Kodak's domination of its subsidiary. For example, plaintiffs refer to (1) a promotional pamphlet produced by EPPS (a/k/a Atex) describing Atex as a business unit of EPPS and noting that EPPS was an "agent" of Kodak; (2) a document produced by Atex entitled "An Introduction to Atex Systems," which describes a "merger" between Kodak and Atex; (3) a statement in Kodak's 1985 and 1986 annual reports describing Atex as a "recent acquisition[ ]" and a "subsidiar[y] * * * combined in a new division"; and (4) a statement in an Atex/EPPS document, "Setting Up TPE 6000 on the Sun 3 Workstation," describing Atex as "an unincorporated division of Electronic Pre–Press Systems, Inc., a Kodak company." They also refer generally to the fact that Atex's paperwork and packaging materials frequently displayed the Kodak logo.

It is clear from the record that Atex never merged with Kodak or operated as a Kodak division. The plaintiffs offer no evidence to the contrary, apart from these statements in Atex and Kodak documents that they claim are indicative of the true relationship between the two companies. Viewed in the light most favorable to the plaintiffs, these statements and the use of the Kodak logo are not evidence that the two companies operated as a "single economic entity." See Coleman v. Corning Glass Works, 619 F.Supp. 950, 956 (W.D.N.Y.1985) (upholding corporate form despite "loose language" in annual report about "merger" and parent's reference to subsidiary as a "division"), aff'd, 818 F.2d 874 (1987); Japan Petrol., 456 F.Supp. at 846 (noting that representations made by parent in its annual reports that subsidiary serves as an agent "may result from public relations motives or an attempt at simplification"); American Trading & Prod. Corp. v. Fischbach & Moore, Inc., 311 F.Supp. 412, 416 (N.D.Ill.1970) ("boastful" advertising and consideration of subsidiaries as "family" do not prove that corporate identities were ignored). * * *

Finally, even if the plaintiffs did raise a factual question about Kodak's domination of Atex, summary judgment would still be appropriate because the plaintiffs offer no evidence * * * of an "overall element of injustice or unfairness" that would result from respecting the two companies' corporate separateness. * * *

Notes

(1) Philip I. Blumberg, The Multinational Challenge to Corporation Law: The Search for a New Corporate Personality viii (1993):

Under traditional law, the fragmentation of an integrated business among a number of affiliated companies as a matter of legal form * * * achieves legal consequences of great importance. In sanctioning this result, the traditional law ignores the fact that despite the legal restructuring, only one business is involved—a business being conducted collectively by interlinked companies under common ownership and control.

Blumberg's basic thesis—extended over six volumes entitled "The Law of Corporate Groups"—is that a parent corporation with numerous subsidiaries should be viewed as a single economic enterprise for liability and other purposes. Do you agree? Despite Professor Blumberg's efforts to develop a "law" applicable to all corporate groups judicial decisions lend scant support to his thesis in the liability area.

(2) Large publicly held corporations usually have numerous wholly owned subsidiaries. The number of subsidiaries of a single major company such as Exxon Corporation may easily run into the hundreds. Subsidiaries are created to operate in separate geographic areas, to operate businesses acquired by the parent corporation that are not closely related to the principal business, to provide services to other subsidiaries, and, generally, to operate in business areas in which the corporate management believes the business may be run most efficiently by a separately organized corporation. In many instances a corporation acquires one or more subsidiaries almost by accident in a transaction to acquire some desired business. The opinion in *Atex* does not indicate how Kodak happened to acquire a wholly owned subsidiary that was involved in the manufacture of computer keyboards, but it might easily have occurred as part of Kodak's interest in the computer business or as the result of an acquisition of an unrelated business that happened to own Atex.

(3) A parent corporation may operate a business either as a separate subsidiary or as a division or department of the parent corporation itself. If the business is operated as a division or department, there is no legal separation between the parent and the business, and the parent is personally liable for the obligations of that business. If it is operated as a subsidiary, on the other hand, there is legal separation and the parent probably will not be liable on the subsidiary's obligations. The managerial differences between a subsidiary and a division are not as clear as might be thought, since a "division" can be set up with a board of directors and other "corporate" characteristics. Usually, the limitation of parental liability is not the dominant factor in a decision to conduct a specific business in the form of a subsidiary rather than a division. More important is the perceived benefit by the parent in terms of operational efficiency, e.g, to give the managers of a subsidiary in an unrelated business a greater degree of independence or to have outsiders on the subsidiary's board of directors. However, where the subsidiary's business seems unduly risky (or is of a type for which it is difficult to assess the risk), the element of limited liability may become a factor. And no matter why the subsidiary was originally incorporated, when unexpected potential or actual liabilities arise, it is quite likely that the parent corporation may seek to avoid direct responsibility by relying on the separate existence of the subsidiary. The plaintiffs in turn usually argue that the subsidiary's corporate veil should be pierced in order to impose liability directly on the parent.[17]

---

17. [By the Editor] Piercing arguments may of course may be made for other reasons as well. A plaintiff may seek to add the parent corporation as a defendant even though the subsidiary is clearly able to respond in damages if exemplary damages are being sought on the theory that such damages may be larger if the assets of the parent are considered along

(4) Many subsidiaries of large publicly held corporations are themselves immense businesses, with sales and assets in the billions of dollars, and profits in the millions of dollars. They have their own work force, their own managers, and their own board of directors (usually comprised of executives of the subsidiary and parent corporations and, sometimes, individuals not affiliated with either). Large subsidiaries are almost certain to have almost complete operational freedom in their day-to-day activities. However, they are subject to control by the parent corporation in non-operational areas similar to areas in which Atex was subject to direct control by Kodak; these areas of control may be justified by economic or legal considerations:

(i) A parent corporation must file a consolidated income tax return including its subsidiaries and accounting rules require that published financial statements consolidate the operations of all wholly and majority-owned subsidiaries. Uniform accounting principles and practices for all subsidiaries are therefore highly desirable. Accounting personnel may be provided by the parent to do all the bookkeeping for each subsidiary, for which a charge usually is imposed by the parent.

(ii) Routine legal services are likely to be provided by the parent for all subsidiaries, though subsidiaries may be authorized to hire local counsel in areas in which the parent has no other operations. The subsidiary may be charged for the value of these services.

(iii) Subsidiaries usually are not permitted to borrow money from banks or third parties. The parent corporation is usually able to borrow larger amounts of money on more favorable terms than any subsidiary so that central financing of major capital improvements is sensible from an economic standpoint. Such a policy also permits the parent corporation to allocate capital funds among its various subsidiaries so as to maximize the overall return of the enterprise.

(iv) Employees may from time transfer or be transferred from one subsidiary to another or to or from the parent. In order to facilitate these transfers, the parent corporation usually creates common pension, profit sharing, and retirement plans for all employees of both parents and subsidiaries; it also may establish salary scales so that transfers are simplified and inter-corporate competition for salaries and "percs" eliminated. Employees may be regularly "lent," "borrowed", or "assigned" on a temporary basis to or by the various corporations that make up the corporate family, though employee transfers appear usually to be worked out on a consensual basis. The advantage of having easy transferability of employees within the corporate family is particularly apparent with respect to specialists since it avoids each subsidiary having to employ its own.

(v) Cash concentration systems, similar to that described in the principal case permits the corporation to receive a higher return on excess funds than

with those of the subsidiary. Piercing arguments also arise in other contexts as well. In the wake of the stranding of the Exxon Valdez in Alaska, issues arose over the interpretation of excess liability insurance policies issued by Lloyds of London. It turned out that the Exxon Valdez was owned and operated by a wholly-owned Exxon subsidiary, Exxon Shipping Company. While Exxon did not attempt to limit its responsibility for the costs of the Exxon Valdez disaster to Alaska residents, it did argue strenuously that Exxon Shipping Company was a separate insured for purposes of the Lloyds' policies; the insurers, in turn, attempted to pierce the corporate veil and claim there was only a single insured. This single issue, which involved hundreds of millions of dollars of insurance coverage, was ultimately settled with the insurers accepting substantial responsibility for Exxon's claims.

would be possible if each subsidiary maintained its own separate banking accounts. It also makes sure that idle funds are not left in non-interest bearing accounts even for a brief period. Cash concentration systems function in a manner very similar to a bank, with the parent and its various subsidiaries being its customers.

(vi) Because large corporations usually have internal legal staffs, the documentation with respect to separate subsidiaries is usually maintained with a care and fastidiousness to detail that is unusual in a corporation with human shareholders. Minutes, consents, waivers, and so forth are usually routinely generated in great detail. Rules exist in some corporate families about careful identification of which "hat" each employee is wearing when he or she takes specific actions. Companies also may have policies limiting the use of corporate stationery. Despite these efforts, however, there usually can be found extemporaneous comments or statements which blur the legal existence between parent and subsidiary. The incidents described in the principal case are fairly typical in this regard.

Should these various factors be enough to persuade a court to pierce the subsidiary's corporate veil? If they are, it will be difficult to find any wholly owned operating subsidiary of a corporation that is immune from veil-piercing, and Blumberg's vision will be borne out. However, the case law as epitomized by the principal case is not so generous to plaintiffs, though one cannot be sure that other courts will be as respectful of the corporate entity as was the Second Circuit in this case.

————

The cases set forth above give a flavor of the piercing the corporate veil jurisprudence. As of about 1980, it was fair to say that there appeared to exist a national jurisprudence on piercing the corporate veil. Courts usually cited cases from various jurisdictions without discrimination in their attempts to apply whatever standards and doctrines that existed in this area to the specific facts before them, and there was general agreement on what the underlying standards were. However, doctrines in this area have shown a considerable capacity to grow and mutate, and there are many indications that states are "going their own way" and developing individualized tests for piercing the corporate veil. See generally Stephen B. Presser, Piercing the Corporate Veil (1991) (state by state analysis of precedents relating to piercing the corporate veil, updated by annual supplements).

Texas. The Texas law of piercing the corporate veil took a bizarre turn in Castleberry v. Branscum, 721 S.W.2d 270 (Tex.1986), a case decided by a five-to-four vote. The court rewrote the traditional piercing rhetoric so broadly that it appeared likely that thereafter shareholders' protection from liability on both contract and tort corporate obligations had become entirely dependent on a jury's determination that the transaction met some undefined and abstract standard of fairness. The Court held, first, that the corporate veil may be pierced if the corporate fiction is used "as a means of perpetrating fraud" or as "a sham to perpetrate a fraud," and either "actual fraud" or "constructive fraud" was sufficient: The difference between "actual" and "constructive" fraud is that "[a]ctual fraud usually involves dishonesty of purpose or intent to deceive, whereas constructive fraud is the breach of some legal or equitable duty which, irrespective of moral guilt, the law declares fraudulent because of its tendency to deceive others, to violate confidence, or to injure public interest." Archer v. Griffith, 390 S.W.2d 735, 740 (Tex.1964). Furthermore, the distinction between tort and contract claimants (a distinction which several earlier Texas opinions had accepted) was expressly rejected; in either type of case, plaintiffs may hold shareholders personally liable if they can establish "a sham to perpetrate a fraud" which involves "a flexible fact-specific approach focusing on equity." Castleberry v. Branscum, 721 S.W.2d at 273.

Probably equally as troubling, the issue whether the corporate veil should be pierced was a question of fact for the jury rather than a question of law for the judge. If the plaintiff presented evidence sufficient to permit the issue to be submitted to the jury, the jury decision controlled. Finally, the doctrine of piercing the corporate veil was subdivided into a multi-tiered classification comprised of seven or eight independent categories. However, the classification created by the Court was highly confusing, with overlapping requirements and vague definitional provisions, and "alter ego" was found to be "separate from" the other listed categories and "only one of the bases for disregarding the corporate fiction." Alter ego involves "such unity between corporation and individual that the separateness of the corporation has ceased and holding only the corporation liable would result in injustice." Id. at 272.

The *Castleberry* opinion caused grave concern within the Texas business community since it appeared that it might no longer be safe to conduct business in corporate form in Texas. These concerns, in turn, almost immediately gave rise to calls for legislative correction. The Texas Legislature responded by enacting a statute in 1989 that is apparently the first legislative attempt to codify, or partially codify, the piercing the corporate veil doctrine. Vernon's Ann. Texas Bus. Corp. Act art. 2.21 now reads[18] as follows:

A. A holder of shares, an owner of any beneficial interest in shares, or a subscriber for shares * * *, or any affiliate thereof or of the corporation shall be under no obligation to the corporation or to its obligees with respect to: * * *

(2) any contractual obligation of the corporation or any matter relating to or arising from the obligation on the basis that the holder, owner, subscriber, or affiliate is or was the alter ego of the corporation, or on the basis of actual fraud or constructive fraud, a sham to perpetrate a fraud, or other similar theory, unless the obligee demonstrates that the holder, owner, subscriber, or affiliate caused the corporation to be used for the purpose of perpetrating and did perpetrate an actual fraud on the obligee primarily for the direct personal benefit of the holder, owner, subscriber, or affiliate; or

(3) any obligation of the corporation on the basis of the failure of the corporation to observe any corporate formality, including without limitation: (a) the failure to comply with any requirement of this Act or of the articles of incorporation or bylaws of the corporation; or (b) the failure to observe any requirement prescribed by this Act or by the articles of incorporation or bylaws for acts to the taken by the corporation, its board of directors, or its shareholders.

18. [By the Editor] This statute was amended in 1993 and 1997.

B. The liability of a holder, owner, or subscriber of shares of a corporation or any affiliate thereof or the corporation for an obligation that is limited by Section A of this article is exclusive and preempts any other liability imposed on a holder, owner, or subscriber of shares of a corporation or any affiliate thereof or of the corporation for that obligation under common law or otherwise, except that nothing contained in this article shall limit the obligation of a holder, owner, subscriber, or affiliate to an obligee of the corporation when:

(1) the holder, owner, subscriber, or affiliate has expressly assumed, guaranteed, or agreed to be personally liable to the obligee for the obligation; or

(2) the holder, owner, subscriber, or affiliate is otherwise liable to the obligee for the obligation under this Act or another applicable statute.

Do you believe this statute limits too narrowly the scope of the piercing the corporate veil doctrine? What law in Texas should apply to piercing issues in tort cases under this legislation? *Castleberry*? The former "general" law of piercing the corporate veil?

Subsequent developments in Texas reveal that judges and lawyers apparently read cases more often than they read statutes. In several cases courts have continued to cite and rely on the broad language of *Castleberry* as authority in contracts cases without referring to Art. 2.21. See, e.g. Gonzales County Water Supply Corp. v. Jarzombek, 918 S.W.2d 57 (Tex.App.1996). It is possible, of course, that this is the fault of the lawyers or the judge's law clerks rather than the judges themselves. In Western Horizontal Drilling, Inc. v. Jonnet Energy Corp., 11 F.3d 65, 69, n. 5 (5th Cir.1994), the Court noted, "We recognize that the Texas Supreme Court seems to be ignoring the amendments to article 2.21 and continues to permit a failure to observe corporate formalities as a means of proving alter ego. * * *."[19] And, in one unreported case, a court held that "denuding of assets" remained a ground for piercing the corporate veil under *Castleberry* not covered by article 2.21. Gradually, however, the existence of this novel statute is coming to the attention of lawyers and judges. See Mike Tanskersley, What If They Made a Law and No One Noticed? Texas Lawyer, December 16, 1996, p.3; Thomas Oldham, Piercing the corporate Veil Under Texas Law, 58 Tex.B.J. 1013 (1995).

Notes

(1) Was the *Castleberry* Court correct in holding that the issue whether a corporate veil is to be pierced is a question of fact for the jury to decide rather than a question of law for the court? Some courts state that "piercing" is an "equitable" doctrine and therefore is to be tried to the Court, e.g. Consumer's Co-op. of Walworth County v. Olsen, 142 Wis.2d 465, 419 N.W.2d 211, 213 (1988) but other courts follow the Texas position, e.g. Wm. Passalacqua Builders, Inc. v. Resnick Developers South, Inc., 933 F.2d 131, 134–36 (2d Cir.1991).

---

19. [By the Editor] The court then completely misreads the intent of article 2.21 by stating, "The amendments overruled Castleberry to the extent that a failure to observe corporate formalities is no longer a factor in proving the alter ego theory in contract claims. Thus, to pierce the corporate veil using the alter ego theory in a contract claim, the claimant must look to the remaining factors outlined in *Castleberry*." 11 F.3d, at 68.

The Second Circuit. This federal court has developed a theory about New York law (that appears to have slim basis in New York state court precedents) that in parent/subsidiary cases the corporate veil may be pierced "in two broad situations: to prevent fraud or other wrong, *or* where a parent dominates and controls a subsidiary." Carte Blanche (Singapore) Pte., Ltd. v. Diners Club Int'l, Inc., 2 F.3d 24, 26 (2d Cir.1993)(emphasis added). The disjunctive means, according to the Second Circuit, that domination and control alone is sufficient to justify piercing the corporate veil in some circumstances even in the absence of a showing of inequity or unfairness. See Wm. Passalacqua Builders, Inc. v. Resnick Developers South, Inc., 933 F.2d 131 (2d Cir.1991); Itel Containers Int'l Corp. v. Atlanttrafik Express Serv. Ltd., 909 F.2d 698, 703 (2d Cir.1990); Thomson–CSF, S.A. v. American Arbitration Ass'n, 64 F.3d 773, 777 (2d Cir.1995).[20] If one corporation owns all the stock of another, how can it avoid "dominating" and "controlling" the subsidiary? According to the Second Circuit, factors that might be considered include:

> [T]he triers of fact are entitled to consider factors that would tend to show that defendant was a dominated corporation, such as: (1) the absence of the formalities and paraphernalia that are part and parcel of the corporate existence, *i.e.*, issuance of stock, election of directors, keeping of corporate records and the like, (2) inadequate capitalization, (3) whether funds are put in and taken out of the corporation for personal rather than corporate purposes, (4) overlap in ownership, officers, directors, and personnel, (5) common office space, address and telephone numbers of corporate entities, (6) the amount of business discretion displayed by the allegedly dominated corporation, (7) whether the related corporations deal with the dominated corporation at arms length, (8) whether the corporations are treated as independent profit centers, (9) the payment or guarantee of debts of the dominated corporation by other corporations in the group, and (10) whether the corporation in question had property that was used by other of the corporations as if it were its own.

Wm. Passalacqua Builders, Inc. v. Resnick Developers South, Inc., 933 F.2d at 139. Except for number (3), are these appropriate standards for holding a parent corporation liable for the debts of a subsidiary if there is no other evidence of fraud or injustice? Recent Second Circuit decisions indicate that there may be retreat from these earlier holdings by the simple substitution of "and" for "or" at the critical point in the test for piercing the corporate veil. American Fuel Corp. v. Utah Energy Development Co., 122 F.3d 130 (2d Cir. 1997); Freeman v. Complex Computing Co., 119 F.3d 1044 (2d Cir. 1997).

Alaska. Alaska state courts have also developed a piercing standard in parent/subsidiary cases which makes it relatively easy to impose personal liability on parent corporations. In McKibben v. Mohawk Oil Co., 667 P.2d 1223 (Alaska 1983) the court described the test as follows:

---

20. [By the Editor] See, however, Campo v. 1st Nationwide Bank, 857 F.Supp. 264, 271 (E.D.N.Y.1994), where the Court without comment substitutes an "and" for the critical "or" when citing *Carte* Blanche and *Passalacqua*, and then concludes that the complaint alleges sufficient facts under both branches to state a cause of action.

Two theories may be used to justify disregarding the corporate status of a subsidiary. First, a parent corporation may be held liable for the wrongful conduct of its subsidiary when the parent uses a separate corporate form "to defeat public convenience, justify wrong, commit fraud, or defend crime." Jackson v. General Electric Co., 514 P.2d 1170, 1172–73 (Alaska 1973); Elliott v. Brown, 569 P.2d 1323, 1326 (Alaska 1977). Second, a parent corporation may be held liable on the alternative theory that the subsidiary is the mere instrumentality of the parent. Uchitel Co. v. Telephone Co., 646 P.2d 229, 234 (Alaska 1982); Jackson, 514 P.2d at 1173. In the latter instance, liability is imposed "simply because the two corporations are so closely intertwined that they do not merit treatment as separate entities." Id.

The criteria for determining when two corporations are "closely intertwined" depends on eleven factors, including the parent corporation owns all or most of the capital stock of the subsidiary, the parent and subsidiary corporations have common directors or officers, the parent corporation finances the subsidiary, the parent corporation subscribes to all the capital stock of the subsidiary or otherwise causes its incorporation, the parent corporation pays the salaries and other expenses of the subsidiary, and the subsidiary has grossly inadequate capital. However, it is not necessary that all eleven of these factors be found in order to pierce the corporate veil.

The problem with a list such as this is that it puts weight on some factors that appear relatively unimportant, and encourages a mechanical counting of those factors. As a practical matter, such a mechanical approach probably does not improve the predictability of result. However Alaska is not alone. The court in Perry v. Household Retail Services, Inc., 953 F.Supp. 1370 (M.D.Ala.1996) (involving the question whether Household International, Inc. was subject to personal service in Alabama and was responsible for an obligation of its wholly owned subsidiary, Household Retail Services, Inc.) used factors very similar to the above list, stating that these factors "are certain circumstances which are important, and which, if present in the proper combination are controlling." However, "[n]o one of these factors is dispositive; nor does the list exhaust the relevant factors."

Notes

(1) A choice of law issue arises once it is recognized that states may develop different rules with respect to piercing the corporate veil. Consider, for example, a Delaware corporation that transacts all of its business in Illinois; its shares are owned by Illinois residents and the decision to incorporate in Delaware was based on the perceived benefits of Delaware law. If this corporation enters into a contract with citizens of Illinois who later bring suit in an Illinois court for breach of contract, naming the shareholders as co-defendants, should the court apply Illinois or Delaware "veil piercing" principles in determining the liability of the shareholders? As suggested by *Fletcher*, there is a plausible argument that Delaware law should apply, since the relationship of shareholders to their corporation may be viewed as a matter of "internal affairs" of the corporation to be governed by the law of the state of incorporation under section 307 of the Restatement of Conflicts of Law (Second).[21] A number of cases support this

21. [By the Editor] "The local law of the state of incorporation will be applied to deter- mine the existence and extent of a shareholder's liability to the corporation for assessments

approach.[22] Also proceeding on this theory, Texas in 1989 amended Art. 8.02A of its Business Corporation Act to make clear that *Castleberry* should never apply to a qualified foreign corporation:

> A foreign corporation which shall have received a certificate of authority under this Act shall * * * enjoy the same, but no greater, rights and privileges as a domestic corporation * * *; provided, however, that only the laws of the jurisdiction of incorporation of a foreign corporation shall govern (1) the internal affairs of the foreign corporation, including but not limited to the rights, powers, and duties of its board of directors and shareholders and matters relating to its shares, and (2) the liability, if any of shareholders of the foreign corporation for the debts, liabilities, and obligations of the foreign corporation for which they are not otherwise liable by statute or agreement.

If an unregistered corporation is successfully sued in Texas article 8.02(a) has no application. Does that make sense? If the internal affairs rule is to apply to a foreign corporation registered in Texas, is it not *a fortiori* that it should also apply to a foreign corporation that has even lesser contacts with the state of Texas? See generally, P. Blumberg, The Law of Corporate Groups: Substantive Law, chapter 27.

(2) Choice of law in a torts case raises different problems. In § 145 of the Restatement (Second) of Conflict of Laws (1969), it is suggested that the local law of the state which has the "most significant relationship to the occurrence and the parties" should apply in a torts case. Is not § 145 fundamentally inconsistent with § 307 in this area? If, in the hypothetical referred to in note (4), suit is brought in Illinois against the Delaware corporation on an automobile accident that occurred in Illinois, should not § 145 of the Second Restatement "trump" § 307 and the "internal affairs" rule, and require the application of Illinois piercing principles? Would it make any difference if Illinois veil-piercing law gives no indication that it views torts cases differently from contracts cases? If the accident occurred in Texas involving Texas residents rather than in Illinois, would not article 8.02 of the Texas Business Corporation Act compel the application of Delaware law despite the fact that Delaware has virtually no relationship with the case?

UNITED STATES v. KAYSER–ROTH CORPORATION

United States District Court, District of Rhode Island, 1989.
724 F.Supp. 15.

FRANCIS J. BOYLE, CHIEF JUDGE.

In the somnolent village of Forestdale, Rhode Island, the ground waters run deep. Unfortunately, the waters also contain pollutants. Having long been home to machining and textile manufacturing industries, Forestdale found itself a victim of its own hospitality. Trichloroethylene, sometimes a by-product of those industries, had filtered into Forestdale's private and public residential water wells. The Government alleges that Stamina Mills, Inc., a defunct textile operation, was a source of the contaminant.

In a slight twist on a biblical passage, the Court in this case must also decide whether the sins of the son should be visited upon the father. *Cf.*

---

or contributions *and to its creditors for corporate debts.*" [emphasis added]

22. [By the Editor] In many of the cases that discuss the choice of law issue, however, the Court indicates it can find no substantive difference between the laws of the two relevant states, and applies "general" veil piercing concepts without deciding which state law is applicable.

Exodus 20:5. Specifically, the issue is whether Kayser–Roth Corporation, the parent corporation and sole shareholder of Stamina Mills, Inc., is responsible for clean-up and response costs generated at least in part by a spill of a hazardous substance on its subsidiary's property in 1969. The answer to that query requires not only a journey through the labyrinth of the Comprehensive Environmental Response, Compensation and Liability Act ("CERCLA"), but thorough examination of the relationship between the related corporations as well.

FACTS

RELEASE AND RESPONSE

Stamina Mills, Inc. was a textile manufacturing operation in North Smithfield, Rhode Island from approximately 1952 to 1975. The mill building had been on the site since some time in the last century. It is located on the north side of the Branch River. The Branch River flows west to east at the site. The company employed a soap scouring system to remove oil and dirt from newly-woven fabric. Because of complaints involving discharge into and pollution of the Branch River, Stamina Mills replaced the soap scouring system with one that used trichloroethylene ("TCE") in March 1969. Tanker trucks delivered the TCE which was pumped into a storage tank. During one delivery before November 1969, a mishap occurred; a tanker driver improperly attached a hosing coupling and spilled an indeterminate number of gallons of TCE. In addition to this accidental release of TCE, there is evidence that Stamina Mills would deposit used quantities of TCE bottoms in a landfill on its property. One witness, a Rhode Island Department of Health employee, testified that he saw a truck back up to the landfill and dump a purplish fluid with oily texture. The same witness also stated that the odor of TCE emanated from Stamina Mills' building.

In August 1979, ten years after Stamina Mills began to use TCE, the Rhode Island Department of Health conducted a survey of drinking water supplies in the Forestdale area, which is generally north and northwest of the Stamina property. The survey found that residential wells north of the Stamina Mills site had elevated levels of TCE. In September 1982, the Environmental Protection Agency ("EPA") completed a hydrogeological study of the area which concluded that the Stamina Mills site was a source of the contaminant. The study found a hydraulic connection between the Stamina Mills site and the residential wells. Although the flow of water through the bedrock aquifer was from north to south, normal pumping of the residential wells would reverse the flow. Consequently, the site was added to the National Priorities List the following September, making Superfund monies available for response actions. * * *

The EPA conducted remedial measures at both the Stamina Mills site and the residential wells. The parties have stipulated that the EPA incurred $660,612.71 in costs related to removal and enforcement activities. In addition, the parties have agreed that the Department of Justice (DOJ) spent $185,879.62 for enforcement activities. The record fails to reflect any distinction between costs related to "on-site" clean-up (at the Stamina Mills site) and "off-site" clean-up (at the residential wells).

CORPORATE RELATIONSHIPS

Stamina Mills, Inc. has expired. Its parent corporation, or more accurately, the parent's successor, remains in the form of the Kayser–Roth Corporation. Before Stamina Mills' dissolution, the two corporations shared a common history. * * * [In 1966, Kayser–Roth became the sole shareholder of Stamina Mills in a merger transaction by which Kayser–Roth acquired all the stock of Stamina Mills' parent. In the same transaction it also became the sole shareholder of Crown Mfg.] Kayser–Roth was therefore the owner of all the capital stock of both Crown Mfg. and Stamina Mills. Both subsidiaries, along with many other corporations, were part of Kayser–Roth's "Crown Division", a designation created for internal organization purposes only. Kayser–Roth remained the sole stockholder of Stamina Mills until its dissolution on December 31, 1977. Pursuant to the dissolution plan, Kayser–Roth received Stamina Mills' assets and assumed "all liabilities and obligations" of Stamina Mills.

As might well be expected, the two corporations shared common officers nominated and appointed by Kayser–Roth. * * * Moreover, and probably of greater significance, Kayser–Roth and Stamina Mills shared common directors, again nominated and appointed by Kayser–Roth, including Chester H. Roth, Alfred P. Slaner, Norman A. Jackson, Harold L. Glasser, David J. Roth, and James I. Spiegel. These individuals were officers of Kayser–Roth at the time they were also directors of Stamina Mills.

Kayser–Roth and its Crown Mfg. Division exerted practical total influence and control over Stamina Mills' operations. Kayser–Roth required Stamina Mills, after obtaining Crown Mfg. Division's approval, to obtain Kayser–Roth's approval in almost all its activities including purchase or movement of capital assets; leasing, buying, or selling real estate; borrowing money; and its budgets. The fiscal operations were completely in the control of Kayser–Roth including accounting supervision, payment of bills, collection of accounts receivable and executive compensation. Stamina Mills' officers did participate in union negotiations but this was simply a bargaining ploy since Kayser–Roth had to approve the ultimate collective bargaining agreement. Three former presidents of Stamina Mills each testified that they played little or no role in major decisions affecting Stamina Mills, except with respect to the local details of operating the factory. Kayser–Roth essentially was in charge in practically all of Stamina's operational decisions, including those involving environmental concerns. Kayser–Roth made the ultimate decision to acquire the dry cleaning process using TCE. Moreover, Kayser–Roth issued a directive requiring Stamina Mills to notify the Kayser–Roth Legal Department of any correspondence with courts or governmental agencies regarding environmental matters. The only autonomy given the officers of Stamina Mills was that absolutely necessary to operate the facility on-site from day to day such as hiring and firing hourly employees and ordering inventory. Stamina was in fact and effect the serf of Kayser–Roth.

LAW

CERCLA, enacted in 1980, allocates responsibility for the clean-up of releases and threatened releases of hazardous materials into the environment.

42 U.S.C. §§ 9601–9675.[23] A responsible party is strictly, jointly and severally liable for costs incurred for removal or remedial action as well as for damages for injury to or loss of natural resources. *Id.* at § 9607(a). Because CERCLA liability is strict, a party will be held responsible upon proof that: (1) a release or threat of a release of a hazardous substance occurred; (2) the government or other authorized party incurred response costs as a result of the release; and (3) the party falls into one of the four categories of responsible parties. *Id.* The four categories are: (1) the current owner or operator of the site; (2) any former owner or operator of the site at the time of the release or threatened release; (3) a transporter of hazardous materials which are released; and (4) a generator of hazardous waste. *Id.* The Government claims that Kayser–Roth and Crown Mfg. were owners and operators of Stamina Mills at the time of the TCE release.

CERCLA's definition of "owner or operator" is not especially illuminating. In terms of an expanded definition, it states that "in the case of an onshore facility * * *, any person owning or operating such facility" qualifies as an owner or operator. 42 U.S.C. § 9601(20)(A)(ii). The term "person" expressly includes corporations. *Id.* at § 9601(21). CERCLA does provide that the term "owner or operator" does not include "a person, who, without participating in the management of a * * * facility, holds indicia of ownership primarily to protect his security interest in the * * * facility." *Id.* at 9601(20)(A). Courts have generally concluded that these provisions confer a subsidiary's liability upon its parent in two situations. The first occurs when the parent dominates the subsidiary to such an extent that the corporate form ought to be ignored and the corporate veil pierced. The second situation takes place where a stockowner participates directly in the management of a facility, although not to the extent that allows a piercing of the corporate veil. * * *

LIABILITY WITHOUT PIERCING THE CORPORATE VEIL

A parent corporation that controls the management and operations of its wholly owned subsidiary can be held responsible for its subsidiary's CERCLA liability without piercing the corporate veil. * * * To be held directly liable as an operator, courts have considered a number of factors including: whether the person or corporation had the capacity to discover in a timely fashion the release or threat of release of hazardous substances; whether the person or corporation had the power to direct the mechanisms causing the release; and whether the person or corporation had the capacity to prevent and abate damages. * * *

PARENT LIABILITY: PARENT AS OPERATOR

* * * The evidence establishes that Kayser–Roth was indeed an operator for purposes of CERCLA. Kayser–Roth exercised pervasive control over Stamina Mills through, among other things: 1) its total monetary control including collection of accounts payable; 2) its restrictions on Stamina Mills' financial budget; 3) its directive that subsidiary-governmental contact, including envi-

23. [By the Court] CERCLA as initially enacted encompassed 42 U.S.C. §§ 9601–9657. In 1986, the Superfund Amendments and Reauthorization Act (SARA) was passed, which provided additional funding and repealed certain sections while adding certain other sections. *See* 95 Pub.L. No. 99–499, 100 Stat. 1613 (1986). The statute, as amended, now comprises 42 U.S.C. §§ 9601–9675.

ronmental matters, be funneled directly through Kayser–Roth; 4) its requirement that Stamina Mills' leasing, buying or selling of real estate first be
approved by Kayser–Roth; 5) its policy that Kayser–Roth approve any capital
transfer or expenditures greater than $5,000; and finally, 6) its placement of
Kayser–Roth personnel in almost all Stamina Mills' director and officer
positions, as a means of totally ensuring that Kayser–Roth corporate policy
was exactly implemented and precisely carried out. These are only examples
of Kayser–Roth's practical total control over Stamina Mills' operations. * * *

PARENT LIABILITY: PIERCING THE CORPORATE VEIL

CERCLA liability based upon piercing the corporate veil is a species of
owner, rather than operator, liability. While an owner may be, in most cases,
an operator, the converse is not necessarily true. Imputing CERCLA liability
upon a parent corporation by piercing the corporate veil is, in essence,
concluding that the parent is an owner for CERCLA's purposes. * * * [The
Court preliminarily concludes that federal rather than state law controls the
piercing of the corporate veil in CERCLA cases. The Court notes, however,
that "this federal common law borrows heavily from state law," and that the
"considerations do not radically differ from Rhode Island law."] Upon analysis of the factors relevant to piercing Stamina Mills' veil, and mindful of the
liberal construction CERCLA must be afforded so as not to frustrate probable
legislative intent, the Court concludes that Kayser–Roth is an owner for
CERCLA's purposes.

* * * Stamina Mills' veil should be pierced to hold Kayser–Roth liable,
not only because public convenience, fairness, and equity dictate such a result,
but also due to the all encompassing control which Kayser–Roth had over
Stamina Mills as, in fact and deed, an owner. Any other result would provide
too much solace to deliberate polluters, who would use this device as an
escape. * * *

Accordingly, Kayser–Roth is found liable for $846,492.33. In addition, the
Government shall within 10 days prepare and present a form of declaratory
judgment holding Kayser–Roth liable for future response costs related to on-
site and off-site clean-up.

SO ORDERED.

Notes

(1) Given the definition of "operator" in CERCLA, is there any need to get
into the piercing the corporate veil issue?

(2) Should Kayser–Roth's liability for the cost of the clean-up of the site be
based on a parent's liability for contractual obligations entered into by a subsidiary under the piercing doctrine? On liability for torts committed by the subsidiary? Or is this a *sui generis* issue of parent liability?

(3) The principal case was affirmed on the ground that Kayser–Roth was an
"operator" of the business because of its involvement in the management of its
subsidiary (and it was therefore unnecessary to consider whether Stamina Mills'
corporate veil should be pierced). United States v. Kayser–Roth Corp., Inc., 910
F.2d 24 (1st Cir.1990). A majority of Circuits appear to have accepted this view,
but not all. The Fifth and Sixth Circuits require a showing that the corporate veil
of the subsidiary may be pierced before liability may be imposed on a parent
corporation. In Joslyn Mfg. Co. v. T.L. James & Co., Inc., 893 F.2d 80, 82–84 (5th

Cir.1990), the Court was clearly unsympathetic to the "control" approach of *Kayser–Roth*: "Joslyn asks this court to rewrite the language of the Act significantly and hold parents directly liable for their subsidiaries' activities. To do so would dramatically alter traditional concepts of corporation law. * * * Veil piercing should be limited to situations in which the corporate entity is used as a *sham* to perpetrate a fraud or avoid personal liability." Accord: United States v. Cordova Chemical Co. of Michigan, 113 F.3d 572(6th Cir.1997)(the majority indorses the *Joslyn* approach, and, rejects a "middle ground" solution proposed by the District Court that liability might be imposed on a parent corporation simply by reason of the control it in fact exerted over the subsidiary). The Fourth and Ninth Circuits take the view that the parent may be viewed as an "operator" if it has power to control the activities of the subsidiary even though that power may not have been exercised. Nurad, Inc. v. William E. Hooper & Sons Co., 966 F.2d 837 (4th Cir.1992); Kaiser Aluminum and Chem. Corp. v. Catellus Deve. Corp., 976 F.2d 1338 (9th Cir.1992). *Cordova* makes it clear that the Federal court should look to the applicable state law of piercing under CERCLA. Is it appropriate or desirable to use state veil-piercing standards, thereby imparting a diversity of results depending on the state where the facility in question is located?

(4) Another federal program in which piercing issues arise is employment discrimination arising under title VII of the Civil Rights Act of 1964. The supervisor being complained of may be on the payroll of the parent while the employee is on the payroll of the subsidiary. In Garcia v. Elf Atochem North America, 28 F.3d 446 (5th Cir.1994) the court stated that the test was whether the parent and subsidiary were part of a "single, integrated enterprise," and there was a four-fold test to make this determination: "(1) interrelation of operations, (2) centralized control of labor relations, (3) common management , and (4) common ownership or financial control." Is this another way of describing the traditional tests for piercing the corporate veil? If not, is it more stringent or less stringent than those tests?

STARK v. FLEMMING

United States Court of Appeals, Ninth Circuit, 1960.
283 F.2d 410.

[Editor: The Secretary of Health, Education and Welfare ruled that Mrs. Stark was not entitled to old-age benefits. The District Court affirmed, 181 F.Supp. 539 (N.D.Cal.1959).]

PER CURIAM.

* * * Appellant placed her assets—a farm and a duplex house—in a newly organized corporation. Then she began to draw $400 per month as salary. The Secretary has found the corporation was a sham. There is no doubt that the corporation was set up to qualify appellant in a short time for social security payments.

But here there seems to have been proper adherence to the normal corporate routines. And it is difficult to understand how the corporate arrangement would not have to be respected by others than the Secretary. And we think he must respect it, too.

Congress could have provided that the motivation to obtain social security by organizing a corporation would defeat the end. It did not.

The Secretary is justified in taking exception to the amount paid Mrs. Stark for her services by which she sought to qualify herself for the maximum amount of social security payments. The salary left little or nothing for a return on capital, and the capital was substantial.

So we think the Secretary is entitled to make an objective reappraisal of the salary to determine what would have been a reasonable salary for Mrs. Stark for the services she performed. One legitimate approach would be: What would a commercial farm agency in the vicinity of the farm have charged? And what would a rental agency in the vicinity of the duplex have charged for the same service? And perhaps she might be allowed slightly more than such agencies. It is not for us to review such determinations within reasonable limits. When the Secretary determines a reasonable salary, then the amount of social security payments can be readily computed.

We, therefore, hold that the district court's judgment should be vacated and that the case should go back through the district court for direction to the Secretary to reevaluate the case on an approach consistent with what we have indicated herein.

Reversed.

ROCCOGRANDI v. UNEMPLOYMENT COMP. BD. OF REVIEW

Superior Court of Pennsylvania, 1962.
197 Pa.Super. 372, 178 A.2d 786.

MONTGOMERY, JUDGE.

The appellants are all members of a family who are involved in the wrecking business together. Each owns 40 shares of stock in the company which has 205 outstanding shares, and all three are officers of the company. The officers of the company, during periods of insufficient work to employ all the members of the family, hold a meeting and by majority vote decide which members shall be "laid off". It was decided by majority vote of all the stockholders that the appellants would be "laid off" because it was their respective turns. Immediately thereafter claims for unemployment compensation benefits were filed by the three appellants. The Bureau of Employment Security denied the claims on the grounds that the appellants were self-employed. Upon appeal the referee reversed the bureau and held the appellants to be entitled to benefits. The Board of Review reversed the referee's decision, holding that the appellants had sufficient control to lay themselves off and that they did just that. Therefore the appellants were self-employed and must be denied eligibility for benefits under section 402(h) and section 402(b)(1) of the law, 43 P.S. § 802(b)(1), (h).

This case is ruled by De Priest Unemployment Compensation Case, 196 Pa.Super. 612, 177 A.2d 20, in which this Court held that the corporate entity may be ignored in determining whether the claimants, in fact, were "unemployed" under the act, or were self-employed persons whose business merely proved to be unremunerative during the period for which the claim for benefits was made.

Decisions affirmed.

Notes

(1) Does the question raised by these two cases relate to the nature of corporateness, or does it merely involve an interpretation of the Federal Social Security Act or Pennsylvania Unemployment Compensation Act? If the former, is the question the same as in the cases discussed earlier involving whether a shareholder should be liable for the debts of the corporation?

(2) State unemployment compensation statutes provide an exemption from contributions for employers who employ less than a minimum number of employees, often eight. May an employer avoid liability under these statutes by splitting his business among several different corporations so that each corporation has less than the minimum number of employees? See State v. Dallas Liquor Warehouse No. 4, 147 Tex. 495, 217 S.W.2d 654 (1949).

CARGILL, INC. v. HEDGE

Supreme Court of Minnesota, 1985.
375 N.W.2d 477.

SIMONETT, JUSTICE.

Do the owner-occupants of a farm, by placing their land in a family farm corporation, lose their homestead exemption from judgment creditors? The trial court and the court of appeals said no. We agree and affirm.

On October 24, 1973, defendant-respondent Sam Hedge and his wife Annette entered into a contract for deed for the purchase of a 160–acre farm. On March 1, 1974, the Hedges assigned their vendees' interest to Hedge Farm, Inc., a Minnesota corporation qualified as a family farm corporation under Minn. Stat. § 500.24, subd. 1(c) (1973), and took possession. Between 1976 and 1979, Sam Hedge purchased farm supplies and services on account from plaintiff-appellant Cargill, Inc., totaling about $17,000. Apparently not until 1980, however, after Cargill had started suit on the account, did it become aware of the Hedges' corporation. Eventually, pursuant to a confession of judgment, judgment was entered in favor of Cargill and against Sam Hedge and Hedge Farms, Inc., for $12,707.08.

An execution sale was held on July 15, 1982, with Cargill as the successful bidder. Shortly before the 1–7 year redemption period expired, the district court, on motion of the judgment debtor, enjoined further proceedings on the execution, tolled the redemption period, and allowed Annette to join the proceedings as an intervenor. Subsequently, the trial court ruled that the Hedges had a right to exempt from the execution 80 acres constituting their homestead. The court of appeals affirmed, ruling that Annette Hedge, as sole shareholder of Hedge Farm, Inc., had an "equitable interest" in the corporate property, and that this interest, coupled with the Hedges' occupancy, satisfied the homestead statute. The court implied that it was willing to reach the same result by "piercing the corporate veil." *Cargill, Inc. v. Hedge*, 358 N.W.2d 490 (Minn.Ct.App.1984). We granted Cargill's petition for further review.

The right to a homestead exemption from execution is a constitutional right. Minn. Const. art. 1, § 12. This right exempts from seizure or sale "[t]he house owned and occupied by the debtor as his dwelling place, together with the land upon which it is situated," Minn. Stat. § 510.01 (1984); in rural areas, 80 acres may be exempted, Minn. Stat. § 510.02 (1984). Clearly, a corporation, an artificial entity needing no dwelling, is not entitled to a homestead exemption. *E.g. Sugg v. Pollard*, 184 N.C. 494, 115 S.E. 153 (1922). If there is to be a homestead exemption here, it must be one personal to the Hedges, notwithstanding the existence of their corporation.

Annette Hedge is the sole stockholder of Hedge Farm, Inc. The court of appeals felt that this gave Annette an "equitable interest" in the property which, together with occupancy, constituted the kind of ownership which would allow the Hedges to assert a homestead exemption in the corporate property. But if Annette is the sole "owner" of the farm, there is no need to assert any homestead exemption because Annette is not a debtor. In any event, the "equitable interest" rationale seems to us conceptually ill-adapted to resolving the issue of creditors' rights we have here, especially since the relationship of a shareholder to a corporation is also implicated. We decline to adopt any equitable interest theory.

We do think, however, that the approach of a reverse pierce of the corporate veil may be used. In *Roepke v. Western National Mutual Insurance Co.*, 302 N.W.2d 350 (Minn.1981), we disregarded the corporate entity to further the purposes of the No–Fault Act. Although title to six motor vehicles was in a corporation, in *Roepke* we nevertheless treated the vehicles as if they had been owned by the deceased, sole shareholder of the corporation, so that the decedent could be deemed an "insured" under the no-fault policy for the purpose of survivors' benefits. It seemed unfair to deprive the business owner of no-fault coverage he would have had if he had operated as a sole proprietorship. We stressed that the decedent had been president and sole stockholder of the corporation that all six vehicles were used as family vehicles, and that no one in the family owned any other vehicles. Later, in *Kuennen v. Citizens Security Mutual Insurance Co.*, 330 N.W.2d 886 (Minn.1983), we made clear that policy reasons for a pierce do not alone justify disregarding the corporate entity. We refused a reverse pierce in *Kuennen*, where the decedent held only 51% of the stock and used only two of the four corporate vehicles for family use. Thus the degree of identity between the individual and his or her corporation, the extent to which the corporation is an alter ego, is important. Also important is whether others, such as a creditor or other shareholders, would be harmed by a pierce.

Here there is a close identity between the Hedges and their corporation. While the Hedges maintained some of the corporate formalities, such as keeping corporate minutes, filing corporate tax returns, and dealing with the Production Credit Association as a corporation, realistically, as the trial court found, they operated the farm as their own. They had no lease with the corporation and paid no rent. The farmhouse was their family home. Annette Hedge owned all the stock. Mr. and Mrs. Hedge and their daughters were the corporate directors with Sam Hedge as president, Patricia as vice-president, and Annette as secretary-treasurer. None of the officers received any salary. The corporation was as much an alter ego for the Hedges as Mr. Roepke's corporation was for him.

In this case, too, we have strong policy reasons for a reverse pierce, much stronger than in *Roepke*, namely, furtherance of the purpose of the homestead exemption. * * *

One of the features of a corporation is limited creditor liability to the corporate assets. We are aware of the danger of a debtor being able to raise or lower his corporate shield, depending on which position best protects his property. Consequently, a reverse pierce should be permitted in only the most carefully limited circumstances. This is such a case, and we so hold. Disregarding the entity Hedge Farm, Inc., we treat the Hedge farm as if owned by Sam and Annette Hedge as vendees under their contract for deed. As a co-vendee, Sam Hedge, the debtor, is entitled to claim a homestead exemption in 80 acres of his farm, and the creditors' execution sale of the exempted 80 acres is void.

Affirmed.

KELLEY, J., took no part in the consideration or decision of this case.

Notes

(1) Gregory S. Crespi, The Reverse Pierce Doctrine: Applying Appropriate Standards, 16 J. Corp. L. 33, 36–7 (1990):

> [The traditional piercing the corporate veil jurisprudence] is almost wholly irrelevant to the interesting and diverse set of situations that are collectively referred to by the cases and commentary as involving a "reverse pierce" of the corporate veil. In a reverse pierce claim, either a corporate insider or a person with a claim against a corporate insider is attempting to have the insider and the corporate entity treated as a single person for some purpose. * * * [R]everse pierce claims implicate different policies and require a different analytical framework from the more routine corporate creditor veil-piercing attempts.

Crespi's analysis indicates, however, that reverse piercing claims have been met with skepticism and outright rejection by many courts. Does not *Cargill* simply represent judicial sympathy for a farm family that is about to lose its means of livelihood because of an ill-considered decision to incorporate? Presumably, the Hedges would seek corporate tax and limited liability benefits if the issue were to arise; should they not have to take the bitter with the sweet?

(2) Workers' Compensation statutes provide an administrative remedy for injured employees and prohibits suits brought against the "employer" of the injured employee. However, suits against third parties whose negligence contributed to the injury are not barred. In Sims v. Western Waste Industries, 918 S.W.2d 682 (Tex.App.1996), writ denied, an injured employee of a subsidiary corporation sued the parent corporation of his employer, alleging that the parent was involved in the design, manufacture and marketing of the truck involved in the employee's accident. The parent filed a motion for summary judgment arguing that it was the alter ego of the employer and therefore protected by the statutory bar against suits brought against the employer. A summary judgment in favor of the parent corporation was reversed:

> We are not persuaded that the legislature ever intended parent corporations, who deliberately chose to establish a subsidiary corporation, to be allowed to assert immunity under the Texas Workers' Compensation Act by reverse piercing of the corporate veil they themselves established. WWI has accepted the benefits of establishing a subsidiary corporation in Texas and will not be allowed to disregard that entity now that it is to their gain to do so. We hold that Texas law does not permit a parent corporation to assert the alter ego theory of piercing the corporate veil of their subsidiary and thereby assert

Workers' Compensation immunity as a defense to a suit by the subsidiary's employee. Point of error one is sustained. We reverse the judgment of the trial court and remand for trial.

918 S.W.2d, at 686. Accord: Reboy v. Cozzi Iron & Metal, Inc., 9 F.3d 1303, 1308, n. 9 (7th Cir.1993), where the court stated: "Moreover we agree with the district court and the Reboys that Cozzi's defensive use of the 'piercing the corporate veil' doctrine may simply be inappropriate under Indiana law. There are no cases in Indiana allowing the doctrine to be used to gain immunity under the Worker's Compensation Act. Moreover, the defensive use of the 'piercing the corporate veil' doctrine in the employment context has been addressed and soundly rejected in at least one other circuit. See Boggs v. Blue Diamond Coal Co., 590 F.2d 655, 662 (6th Cir.1979)."

(3) Frankel was a shoe sales representative for Bally, Inc. In 1979, he formed Harold Frankel Co. (HFC), of which he was the sole shareholder and permanent employee, in order to obtain pension benefits that were not provided to employees of Bally. Bally was aware of the incorporation of HFC; indeed, several other sales representatives had similarly formed corporations to obtain retirement benefits. Bally thereafter dealt with HFC, which in turn "employed" Frankel, and paid his salary, and provided benefits. In 1988, when Frankel was 61 years old, Bally announced that it was terminating its relationship with HFC. Frankel then brought suit against Bally under the Age Discrimination in Employment Act of 1967 (ADEA). The District Court dismissed this suit on the ground that Frankel was an employee of HFC and not of Bally. Held, reversed and remanded: The common law agency test of employment is applicable to ADEA, and while under that test "Frankel's establishment of HFC, and HFC's payment of salary and benefits to Frankel are important factors to be weighed in an analysis under the common law agency test, the corporate form under which a plaintiff does business is not dispositive in a determination of whether an individual is an employee or an independent contractor * * *." Frankel v. Bally, Inc., 987 F.2d 86, 91 (2d Cir.1993). Is that right? Is this an indirect invitation to reverse pierce?

PEPPER v. LITTON

Supreme Court of the United States, 1939.
308 U.S. 295, 60 S.Ct. 238, 84 L.Ed. 281.

[Editor: Pepper sued the Dixie Splint Coal Company for an accounting of royalties due Pepper under a lease. While this case was pending, Litton, the sole shareholder of Dixie Splint, caused Dixie Splint to confess a judgment in favor of Litton based on alleged claims for back salary. After Pepper obtained a judgment, Litton caused execution to be issued on his judgment; Litton purchased the corporate assets at the resulting sale, and then caused Dixie Splint to file a voluntary petition in bankruptcy. The trustee in bankruptcy brought suit in state court to have the judgment obtained by Litton set aside and the execution sale quashed; the trustee lost. Smith v. Litton, 167 Va. 263, 188 S.E. 214 (1936). Litton then filed a claim in the bankruptcy court based on the portion of the judgment not satisfied by the proceeds of the execution sale. The District Court disallowed Litton's claim in its entirety and directed that the trustee should recover for the benefit of the bankrupt's estate the property purchased by Litton at the execution sale. The Court of Appeals reversed on the ground that the state court decision was res judicata.]

MR. JUSTICE DOUGLAS, delivered the opinion of the Court.

This case presents the question of the power of the bankruptcy court to disallow either as a secured or as a general or unsecured claim a judgment obtained by the dominant and controlling stockholder of the bankrupt corporation on alleged salary claims. * * *

The findings of the District Court, amply supported by the evidence, reveal a scheme to defraud creditors reminiscent of some of the evils with which 13 Eliz. c. 5 was designed to cope. But for the use of a so-called "one-man" or family corporation, Dixie Splint Coal Company, of which respondent was the dominant and controlling stockholder, that scheme followed an ancient pattern. * * *

In the first place, res judicata did not prevent the District Court from examining into the Litton judgment and disallowing or subordinating it as a claim. * * *

In the second place, even though we assume that the alleged salary claim on which the Litton judgment was based was not fictitious but actually existed, we are of the opinion that the District Court properly disallowed or subordinated it.

Courts of bankruptcy are constituted by §§ 1 and 2 of the bankruptcy act, 30 Stat. 544, 11 U.S.C.A. §§ 1(8), 11, and by the latter section are invested "with such jurisdiction at law and in equity as will enable them to exercise original jurisdiction in bankruptcy proceedings." Consequently this Court has held that for many purposes "courts of bankruptcy are essentially courts of equity, and their proceedings inherently proceedings in equity". Local Loan Co. v. Hunt, 292 U.S. 234, 240, 54 S.Ct. 695, 697, 78 L.Ed. 1230, 93 A.L.R. 195. * * *

That equitable power also exists in passing on claims presented by an officer, director, or stockholder in the bankruptcy proceedings of his corporation. The mere fact that an officer, director, or stockholder has a claim against his bankrupt corporation or that he has reduced that claim to judgment does not mean that the bankruptcy court must accord it pari passu treatment with the claims of other creditors. Its disallowance or subordination may be necessitated by certain cardinal principles of equity jurisprudence. A director is a fiduciary. Twin–Lick Oil Company v. Marbury, 91 U.S. 587, 588, 23 L.Ed. 328. So is a dominant or controlling stockholder or group of stockholders. Southern Pacific Company v. Bogert, 250 U.S. 483, 492, 39 S.Ct. 533, 537, 63 L.Ed. 1099. Their powers are powers in trust. See Jackson v. Ludeling, 21 Wall. 616, 624, 22 L.Ed. 492. Their dealings with the corporation are subjected to rigorous scrutiny and where any of their contracts or engagements with the corporation is challenged the burden is on the director or stockholder not only to prove the good faith of the transaction but also to show its inherent fairness from the viewpoint of the corporation and those interested therein. Geddes v. Anaconda Copper Mining Company, 254 U.S. 590, 599, 41 S.Ct. 209, 212, 65 L.Ed. 425. The essence of the test is whether or not under all the circumstances the transaction carries the earmarks of an arm's length bargain. If it does not, equity will set it aside. While normally that fiduciary obligation is enforceable directly by the corporation, or through a stockholder's derivative action, it is, in the event of bankruptcy of the corporation, enforceable by the trustee. For that standard of fiduciary obligation is designed for the protection of the entire community of interests in the corporation—creditors as well as stockholders.

As we have said, the bankruptcy court in passing on allowance of claims sits as a court of equity. Hence these rules governing the fiduciary responsibilities of directors and stockholders come into play on allowance of their claims in bankruptcy. [I]n the exercise of its equitable jurisdiction the bankruptcy court has the power to sift the circumstances surrounding any claim to see that injustice or unfairness is not done in administration of the bankrupt estate. And its duty so to do is especially clear when the claim seeking allowance accrues to the benefit of an officer, director, or stockholder. That is clearly the power and duty of the bankruptcy courts under the reorganization sections. In Taylor v. Standard Gas & Electric Co., 306 U.S. 307, 59 S.Ct. 543, 83 L.Ed. 669, this Court held that the claim of Standard against its subsidiary (admittedly a claim due and owing) should be allowed to participate in the reorganization plan of the subsidiary only in subordination to the preferred stock of the subsidiary. This was based on the equities of the case—the history of spoliation, mismanagement, and faithless stewardship of the affairs of the subsidiary by Standard to the detriment of the public investors. Similar results have properly been reached in ordinary bankruptcy proceedings. Thus, salary claims of officers, directors, and stockholders in the bankruptcy of "one-man" or family corporations have been disallowed or subordinated where the courts have been satisfied that allowance of the claims would not be fair or equitable to other creditors. And that result may be reached even though the salary claim has been reduced to judgment. It is reached where the claim asserted is void or voidable because the vote of the interested director or stockholder helped bring it into being or where the history of the corporation shows dominancy and exploitation on the part of the claimant. It is also reached where on the facts the bankrupt has been used merely as a corporate pocket of the dominant stockholder, who, with disregard of the substance or form of corporate management, has treated its affairs as his own. And so-called loans or advances by the dominant or controlling stockholder will be subordinated to claims of other creditors and thus treated in effect as capital contributions by the stockholder not only in the foregoing types of situations but also where the paid-in capital is purely nominal, the capital necessary for the scope and magnitude of the operations of the company being furnished by the stockholder as a loan.

Though disallowance of such claims will be ordered where they are fictitious or a sham, these cases do not turn on the existence or nonexistence of the debt. Rather they involve simply the question of order of payment. At times equity has ordered disallowance or subordination by disregarding the corporate entity. That is to say, it has treated the debtor-corporation simply as a part of the stockholder's own enterprise, consistently with the course of conduct of the stockholder. But in that situation as well as in the others to which we have referred, a sufficient consideration may be simply the violation of rules of fair play and good conscience by the claimant; a breach of the fiduciary standards of conduct which he owes the corporation, its stockholders and creditors. * * *

On such a test the action of the District Court in disallowing or subordinating Litton's claim was clearly correct. Litton allowed his salary claims to lie dormant for years and sought to enforce them only when his debtor corporation was in financial difficulty. Then he used them so that the rights of another creditor were impaired. Litton as an insider utilized his strategic position for his own preferment to the damage of Pepper. Litton as the dominant influence over Dixie Splint Coal Company used his power not to deal fairly with the creditors of that company but to manipulate its affairs in such a manner that when one of its creditors came to collect her just debt the bulk of the assets had disappeared into another Litton company. Litton, though a fiduciary, was enabled by astute legal manoeuvering to acquire most of the assets of the bankrupt not for cash or other consideration of value to creditors but for bookkeeping entries representing at best merely Litton's appraisal of the worth of Litton's services over the years.

This alone would be a sufficient basis for the exercise by the District Court of its equitable powers in disallowing the Litton claim. But when there is added the existence of a "planned and fraudulent scheme", as found by the District Court, the necessity of equitable relief against that fraud becomes insistent. No matter how technically legal each step in that scheme may have been, once its basic nature was uncovered it was the duty of the bankruptcy court in the exercise of its equity jurisdiction to undo it. Otherwise, the fiduciary duties of dominant or management stockholders would go for naught; exploitation would become a substitute for justice; and equity would be perverted as an instrument for approving what it was designed to thwart. * * *

In view of these considerations we do not have occasion to determine the legitimacy of the "one-man" corporation as a bulwark against the claims of creditors.[24]

Accordingly the judgment of the Circuit Court of Appeals is reversed and that of the District Court is affirmed.

Reversed.

Notes

(1) The doctrine applied in Pepper v. Litton is usually referred to as the "Deep Rock" doctrine, after the name of the corporation involved in Taylor v. Standard Gas & Electric Co., discussed in Pepper v. Litton. Could the court have "pierced the corporate veil" of Dixie Splint Coal Co. and avoided Litton's claim on the theory that one cannot owe a debt to oneself? If the latter approach had been followed, Litton may have been personally liable for all of Dixie Splint's debts. What tests should the Court use in determining which approach to follow? Is it simply a matter of relative (and subjective) degrees of bad faith or improper conduct? The absence of reasonably objective tests in this area has led to considerable confusion and some inconsistency in results.

(2) Section 510(c) of the Bankruptcy Act of 1978, 11 U.S.C.A. § 510(c), provides that " * * * after notice and a hearing, the Court may * * * under

---

24. [By the Court] On this point the District Court said: "An examination of the facts disclosed here shows the history of a deliberate and carefully planned attempt on the part of Scott Litton and Dixie Splint Coal Company to avoid the payment of a just debt. I speak of Litton and Dixie Splint Coal Company because they are in reality the same. In all the experience of the law, there has never been a more prolific breeder of fraud than the one-man corporation. It is a favorite device for the escape of personal liability. This case illustrates another frequent use of this fiction of corporate entity, whereby the owner of the corporation, through his complete control over it, undertakes to gather to himself all of its assets to the exclusion of its creditors."

principles of equitable subordination, subordinate for purposes of distribution all or part of an allowed claim to all or part of another allowed claim or all or part of an allowed interest to all or part of another allowed interest * * *." H.R.Rep. No. 595, 95th Cong., 1st Sess., at 359 (1977) states that "[t]his section [was] intended to codify case law, such as *Pepper v. Litton,* * * *."

(3) Obligations running from a corporation to a controlling shareholder may arise in several different ways. For example, a shareholder may desire to put in a portion of his initial capital contribution in the form of debt to minimize the double taxation problem. How should such debt be treated in bankruptcy? See Arnold v. Phillips, 117 F.2d 497 (5th Cir.1941); Small v. Williams, 313 F.2d 39 (4th Cir.1963). Or, a shareholder may take preferred stock or debt in order to equalize the distribution of voting power and the original contributions of the shareholders. How should such debt be treated in bankruptcy? See Obre v. Alban Tractor Co., 228 Md. 291, 179 A.2d 861 (1962). Or, a shareholder may lend his corporation money in an unsuccessful attempt to save it from financial disaster. How should such debt be treated in bankruptcy?

(4) Do the tests for subordination under the Deep Rock doctrine differ in degree or kind from the tests applicable to piercing the corporate veil?

Chapter Seven

FINANCIAL MATTERS AND THE CLOSELY HELD CORPORATION

A. DEBT AND EQUITY CAPITAL

Every firm needs capital in order to conduct its operations. Capital may be obtained from a variety of different sources, e.g. (1) by borrowing funds from private sources, from banks, or on credit cards, (2) by capital contributions from the owners of the firm, (3) by capital contributions from outside investors who thereafter become co-owners of the firm, or (4) by retaining business earnings rather than distributing them to owners.

One basic distinction in the raising of capital is whether the funds provided are in the form of "equity capital" or "debt." Debt usually is associated with the concepts that it must at some point be repaid and that interest is to be paid periodically and is not dependent on the earnings of the business. Equity in this context is synonymous with "ownership" and has nothing to do with the word "equity" in its traditional historical or legal meaning.[1] Equity capital is composed of contributions by the original entrepreneurs in the firm, capital contributed by other investors in exchange for ownership interests in the business, and retained earnings of the enterprise. While the line between debt and equity may be blurred at its margin by the creation of interests that have some of the characteristics of equity and some of the characteristics of debt, the fundamental difference is easily grasped.

This Chapter considers primarily the raising of equity capital by corporations through the sale of its securities. It considers debt financing only to a limited extent. A word of warning at the outset is appropriate. An important federal statute, the Securities Act of 1933, 15 U.S.C.A. § 77a et seq., imposes substantial disclosure requirements on the public sale of securities using the mails or the facilities of interstate commerce. All states have statutes called "blue sky laws" that regulate the distribution of securities within the specific state. These statutes are potentially applicable whenever a business seeks funds from noncommercial sources; they are not limited to large transactions or to transactions in which capital is raised with the assistance of professional underwriters. These statutes are discussed briefly in Section F of this Chap-

---

1. [By the Editor] This use of the word "equity" is derived from the idea that the value of an owner's equity in a piece of proper-ty equals the market value of that property minus the debts that are liens against that property.

ter. In real life, potential applicability of these statutes must be considered whenever a firm is raising capital from third parties.

B. TYPES OF EQUITY SECURITIES

There is a recognized nomenclature for equity securities issued by corporations. The following brief discussion is essential background for those unfamiliar with this nomenclature; it also illustrates that while the language is sometimes arcane, the underlying ideas are not complicated.

1. COMMON SHARES

It is helpful to begin with fundamental concepts. A "class" of shares simply means all authorized shares of a corporation that have identical rights. "Shares," in turn mean the "units into which the proprietary interests in a corporation are divided," MBCA § 1.40(21). MBCA does not expressly define "common shares," but it does identify indirectly two fundamental characteristics of common shares in §§ 6.01(b) and 6.03(c):

(1) They are entitled to vote for the election of directors and on other matters coming before the shareholders, and

(2) They are entitled to the net assets of the corporation (after making allowance for debts), when distributions are made in the form of dividends or liquidating distributions.

MBCA § 6.01(b) permits these essential attributes of common shares to be placed in different classes of shares, but requires that one or more classes with these attributes must always be authorized. Section 6.03(c) adds that at least one share of each class with each of these basic attributes must always be outstanding—that is, issued to some person or persons.[2] The reasons for these abstruse provisions are described below.

"Common shares" may be defined in other ways as well. The United States Supreme Court identified the characteristics usually associated with common stock as: (i) the right to receive dividends contingent upon an apportionment of profits, (ii) negotiability, (iii) the ability to be pledged or hypothecated, (iv) the conferring of voting rights in proportion to the number of shares owned, and (v) the capacity to increase in value. United Housing Found., Inc. v. Forman, 421 U.S. 837, 95 S.Ct. 2051, 44 L.Ed.2d 621 (1975). This definition was set forth in a case involving the issue whether a "share of stock" that entitled the owner to lease an apartment in a housing cooperative was a "security"; housing cooperative shares possess virtually none of the enumerated characteristics.

---

2. [By the Editor] When a new corporation is in the process of being formed, there is a brief period between the filing of the articles of incorporation and the organizational meeting when the corporation is in existence but no shares are issued or outstanding. The assumption is that the corporation will not enter into business transactions until after the organizational meeting is held, since prior to the organizational meeting, the corporation will not have officers to act on its behalf, will not have a bank account, and will not have any assets because no stock will have been issued. It is possible, however, for a corporation to commence business without holding a formal organizational meeting. Typically, in those cases there will be no doubt as to the persons who are to own the common shares of the corporation and who therefore are in fact the shareholders. Premature commencement of business in this fashion creates a serious risk of personal liability being imposed on the shareholders.

Whatever the niceties of definition, common shares are usually viewed as representing the residual ownership interest in the corporation. The financial interests of common shares in the corporation are open-ended in the sense that as the business prospers and the corporate assets increase, the additional assets benefit the holders of the common shares. They may be paid to the shareholders in the form of dividends or other types of distributions, or may be retained by the corporation, in which case the value of the common shares should increase in value. A "dividend" is a distribution from current or retained earnings; the MBCA sets forth rules for distributions generally and does not set forth special rules for dividends. MBCA §§ 1.40(6), 6.40. It is important to recognize that decisions whether or not to make a distribution to shareholders, and if so, how much, are within the business judgment of directors. Typically, shareholders have no legal basis for complaint if distributions or dividends on common shares are omitted over extended periods of time.

Holders of common shares have other rights as well: a right to inspect books and records (see MBCA § 16.02), a right to sue on behalf of the corporation to right a wrong committed against it (see MBCA §§ 7.40–7.47), a right to financial information (see MBCA § 16.20), and so forth. But the fundamental rights of the common shareholders, as the residual owners, appear to be those identified in §§ 6.01(b) and 6.03(c): the right to vote and the right to receive excess assets, either during the life of the corporation or upon its dissolution.

Where a corporation has only one class of shares outstanding, that class obviously has the voting and distributional rights described above. They are common shares, even though they may be described in the articles of incorporation as "capital stock" or simply "stock" or "shares." The MBCA (as did earlier versions of the Model Act) consistently uses the word "shares" rather than "stock" in describing equity security interests, but the Official Comment to § 6.01 points out that "no specific designation is required by the Model Act."

Many corporations begin their life with only a modest amount of capital raised by the sale of stock. As noted earlier, the statutes in some states prescribe a minimum initial capitalization—often $1,000. The Model Act contained such a requirement until 1969 when it was eliminated on the grounds "that the protection sought to be achieved was illusory and that the provision served no useful purpose." Comment to MBCA (1969) § 56. The MBCA currently does not contain a minimum capital requirement.

Under § 2.02(a)(2) of the MBCA, the articles of incorporation must set forth "the number of shares the corporation is authorized to issue." This provision is incomplete, however, since § 6.01(a) provides that if more than one class of shares is authorized, the articles of incorporation must prescribe "the classes of shares and the number of shares of each class that the corporation is authorized to issue"; in addition the articles of incorporation "must prescribe a distinguishing designation for each class and, prior to the issuance of shares of a class the preferences, limitations, and relative rights of that class must be described in the articles of incorporation." If only one class of shares is authorized, it is not necessary to say anything about what the rights of that class are.

2. PREFERRED SHARES

What other classes of shares might a corporation issue? The traditional distinction is between common shares on the one hand and "preferred" shares on the other. "Preferred" means only that the shares entitle the holders to some preference or priority in payment as against the holders of common shares. This priority may be either in the payment of dividends or in the making of distributions in liquidation of a corporation, or very commonly in both. A "priority" or "preference" simply means that the holders of preferred shares are entitled to a specified distribution before anything can be paid on the common shares. For example, if a class of preferred shares entitles the holders to a dividend preference of $5 per year, that means only that nothing can be paid to the holders of common shares until the preferred shareholders are first paid their $5 per share. Preferred shares are often described by reference to the amount of their dividend preference, or by the percentage such preference bears to the stock's par or stated value. Thus, a "$5.00 preferred" has a dividend preference of $5.00 per year, while a "5% preferred" has a dividend preference equal to five percent of the share's par value.

The precise scope of the rights of a preferred shareholder is traditionally established by the detailed provisions in the articles of incorporation creating that class of shares. These provisions are usually called the "preferred shareholder's contract," and may not be amended without the consent of holders of some statutorily designated fraction of the preferred shares themselves. Rights and privileges usually given to publicly traded preferred shares include the following:

Cumulative Dividend Rights. The dividend preference of preferred shares may be cumulative, noncumulative, or partially cumulative. A cumulative dividend simply means that if a preferred dividend is not paid in any year, it accumulates and must be paid (along with the following years' unpaid cumulative dividends) before any dividend may be paid on the common shares in a later year. For example, if a preferred share has a $5.00 cumulative dividend preference, and that dividend is omitted in one year, not only may no dividend be paid on the common shares in that year, but also in the following year no dividend may be paid on the common shares unless the holder of the preferred share receives $10.00 in dividends, making up for the omission in the prior year. A noncumulative dividend is not carried over from one year to the next; if no dividend is declared during the year, the preferred shareholder loses the right to receive the dividend for that year. A noncumulative dividend that is not paid during the year simply disappears, and the following year is a new ball game. A partially cumulative dividend typically is cumulative to the extent there are earnings in the year, and noncumulative with respect to any excess dividend preference. Unpaid cumulative dividends are not debts of the corporation, but a right of priority in future distributions. Unlike interest on a debt, dividends on preferred shares may be paid only from funds that are legally available for the payment of distribution. Many state statutes, however, liberally permit the payment of cumulative preferred dividends from various capital accounts. Typically, publicly traded preferred shares have cumulative dividend rights.

Voting. Preferred shares are usually nonvoting shares (though many exceptions exist, particularly in closely held corporations). In order to provide some protection for preferred shareholders, it is customary to provide that nonvoting preferred shares obtain a right to vote for the election of a specified number of directors if preferred dividends have been omitted for a specified period.

Liquidation Preferences. Preferred shares usually have a liquidation preference as well as a dividend preference. The liquidation preference is often fixed at a specified price per share, payable upon the dissolution of the corporation before anything may be paid to the common shares. Like preferred dividends, a liquidation preference is not a debt but a claim to priority if funds are available. The amount of the liquidation preference is usually a fixed amount, so that the holders of the preferred do not share in any general appreciation in value of the corporation's assets.

Redemption Rights. Preferred shares may be made redeemable at the option of the *corporation*, usually at a price fixed by the articles of incorporation at the time the class of preferred shares was created. A right to "redeem" shares simply means that the corporation has the power to buy back the redeemable shares at any time at the fixed price, and the shareholder has no choice but to accept that price. (If the shareholder refuses to turn in his certificates, the corporation simply deposits the redemption price in a bank and refuses to recognize that the shares are outstanding or that they have rights with respect to the corporation other than to get the redemption price.) When a corporation elects to exercise the redemption privilege, it "calls" the stock for redemption. Typically, the power to call redeemable shares may be exercised only after a specified period of time has elapsed; also the redemption price is usually set somewhat in excess of the amount of the share's liquidation preference. For example, preferred shares which are entitled to receive $100.00 per share on liquidation may be made redeemable at any time for $105.00 plus any unpaid cumulative dividends.

Conversion Rights. Preferred shares may be made convertible at the option of the *holder* into common shares at a fixed ratio specified in the articles of incorporation; convertible preferred shares are attractive when the common shares are publicly traded, so that an active market exists for the conversion securities. A conversion privilege allows the holders of the preferred shares to obtain a part of the long term appreciation of the corporation's assets if the holders are willing to give up their preferred rights by converting their shares into common shares. Typically, the conversion ratio is established so that the common shares must appreciate substantially in price before it is profitable to convert the preferred shares. When the price of the common shares rises above this level, the preferred shares fluctuate in price with the common shares. Convertible shares are also usually redeemable, but typically the privilege to convert continues for a limited period of time after the call for redemption. A conversion is described as "forced" when shares are called for redemption at a time when the market value of the shares obtainable on conversion exceeds the redemption price.

Protective Provisions. Preferred shares may also have certain financial protections, such as sinking fund provisions, which require the corporation to set aside a certain amount each year to redeem a specified portion of the preferred stock issue. In addition, convertible preferred shares usually contain elaborate provisions protecting the conversion privilege from dilution in case of share dividends, share splits, or the issuance of additional common shares. The importance of these protections cannot be minimized since preferred shareholders have not fared well on arguments based on fiduciary duty and the like. Lawrence E. Mitchell, The Puzzling Paradox of Preferred Stock (And Why We should Care About It), 51 Bus.Law. 443. 443–44 (1996):*

> [A]ll is not well jurisprudentially with preferred stock. Several recent judicial pronouncements seemingly have clarified the preferred stockholders' relationship to the corporation, its directors, and its common stockholders. But that apparent clarity is an illusion. It is fair to say * * * that the position of the preferred stockholder in the corporate firmament, fiduciary rhetoric notwithstanding, is more vulnerable than any other financial participant. The only situation in which courts regularly apply fiduciary standards in evaluating preferred stockholders' rights is when their equity stake in the corporation is threatened by corporate control transactions involving interested directors or a controlling stockholder and even then, only in limited circumstances. By contrast, courts will not apply fairness analysis to protect preferred stockholders' return on their equity. These conclusions, when combined with the reality that most preferred stock is structured in a way that never obligates the corporation to redeem it and thus return equity, suggests that the preferred stockholders can, with impunity, be frozen out of realizing any value from the enterprise. In brief, I shall conclude that the preferred stockholder ought not think of himself or herself as a stockholder at all and should plan to rely exclusively on his or her contract as the source of rights, with all that implies in terms of evaluating the stock's pricing.* * *

Participating Preferred. The preferred shares described above are nonparticipating. Nonparticipating shares are entitled to the specified dividend payment and the specified liquidation preference, and nothing more no matter how profitable the corporation. "Participating preferred" shares are entitled to the specified dividend and, after the common shares receive a specified amount, they share with the common in additional distributions on some predetermined basis. Such shares combine some of the features of common and preferred. They are sometimes referred to as "Class A common" or by a similar designation that shows that their right to participate is open-ended and therefore that they have one of the major attributes of common shares. Preferred shares that are participating in dividend distributions usually have liquidation preferences that are tied in some way to the amounts receivable by the common shares on liquidation.

Classes of Preferred. A corporation may issue different classes of preferred shares. A corporation, for example, may issue "Class A preferred" and "Class B preferred" with different dividend rates, different rights on dissolution, and different priorities. The Class A preferred may be junior to the Class B in terms of priorities or it may be superior to or on a parity with the Class B. Both are "senior" securities, however, because both have preferential rights over common shares.

---

* Reprinted with permission from the American Bar Association.

Series of Preferred. MBCA § 6.02(a)(2) refers to "one or more series within a class." The concept of one or more "series within a class" arose because of problems of raising substantial amounts of capital over periods of time through the issuance of preferred shares. In preferred share financing, it is often advantageous to tailor the price, dividend, and other terms of the shares to the market conditions current at the time of issue. It was inconvenient and expensive to amend the articles of incorporation of a corporation with many shareholders to create a new class of preferred shares whenever a new issue was to be sold; as a result, a number of states authorized the creation of a "class" of preferred shares that contained no financial terms at all but authorized the board of directors to carve out different "series" of shares from within the class, and designate the financial terms of each series when it was issued. Preferred shares for which the board of directors is authorized to establish terms are often called "blank shares." MBCA § 6.02 is a somewhat broader "blank shares" provision since it authorizes the board to establish "classes" as well as "series." In practice, however, there is usually no economic difference between a "class" of preferred shares and a "series within a class" of preferred shares: both have unique financial terms, but all shares within the "class" or "series" have identical preferences, limitations and relative rights (see MBCA § 6.02(c)). The Official Comment to MBCA § 6.02, states that the labels "class" and "series" are "often a matter of convenience"; it does not seem sensible to limit the power of directors merely because of historical nomenclature.

The terms of one or more "series" may also be specified in the articles of incorporation if that is desired. However, the term "series" is most widely used in connection with preferred shares, the financial terms of which may be established by the board of directors following procedures similar to those set forth in MBCA § 6.02.

3. CLASSES OF COMMON SHARES

Section 6.01 of the MBCA, like all state statutes, authorizes the creation of classes of common shares by appropriate provision in the articles of incorporation; such classes may vary in terms of management, financial or voting rights. For example, classes of nonvoting common shares, classes with multiple or fractional votes per share, classes entitled to twice the dividend of another class, classes entitled to a preference or priority in distributions to another class, classes entitled to elect a specified number of directors, are all permissible. Different classes of common shares are often designated by alphabetical reference, e.g. "Class A common shares," or sometimes by description, e.g. "nonvoting common stock." Classes of common shares are widely used as planning devices in closely held corporations (as are classes of preferred stock).

————

From the foregoing description, it should be clear that the precise line between "preferred" and "common" shares, at the margin at least, was always a shadowy one. There might be little or no difference, for example, between a "participating preferred" and a "Class A common" except the title. Developments during the 1970s and early 1980s also tended to blur this distinction (as well as the distinction between "debt securities" and preferred shares). Extremely high interest rates during this period led to the development of novel financing devices. This period, for example, saw the development of "flexible rate" preferred, where the amount of the dividend was tied to interest rates or some other objective criteria, or left discretionary with the board of directors.

Faced with these developments, the drafters of the MBCA, in § 6.01, made a significant philosophical break with the past by studiously avoiding the words "preferred shares" and "common shares," and by establishing a scheme of consummate generality designed to accommodate the most innovative and ingenious creator of new classes or types of shares.

When considering classes of debt or equity securities, not too much weight should be given to the name. A class may be described as a "senior preferred" and yet be subordinate to virtually all other classes of preferred shares with much more modest titles. Modern equity and debt issues often have unique or fanciful names, such as "senior reset preferred stock" or "preferred equity redemption cumulative stock" ("PERCS") that give little or no clue as to either the nature of the securities involved or their investment quality.

Notes

(1) May a corporation create a class of *preferred* shares that is redeemable at the option of the holder? Such shares have some of the characteristics of a demand note, and are widely used as a financing device. They are not (or arguably may not be) permitted by the statutes of some states.

(2) What about creating *common* shares that are redeemable at the option of the holder? Is there any possible evil that might arise from such shares? Some states also prohibit this kind of security, except in specified limited circumstances. One well-known and universally accepted example of such shares are shares of "mutual funds" the issuer of which stands ready at any time to redeem shares at net asset value.

(3) What about creating common shares that are callable at the option of the corporation? The great majority of states impose limitations on this type of security or prohibit it entirely. In older versions of the Model Act, a right of redemption at the corporation's option could be created only in connection with shares with preferential rights; several states authorize callable or redeemable common shares only if there is another class of common shares that is not callable or redeemable. E.g. West's Ann.Cal.Corp.Code § 402; N.Y. McKinney's Bus.Corp. Law § 512(c). What possible evils might be created if the corporation had the power generally to "call" common shares at a predetermined price?

(4) Most state statutes also prohibit shares with an "upstream conversion" right, that is, the right to convert common shares into preferred shares, or to convert either common or preferred shares into debt securities or interests. What possible evils might arise if shareholders generally had the power to convert their equity interests into senior securities or into debt?

(5) The MBCA permits the creation of all types of shares referred to in the previous paragraphs without restriction or limitation. Indeed, the MBCA goes even further in some respects, permitting, for example, the creation of shares that are redeemable at the option of a third person, e.g. the holders of other classes of shares, or the creation of shares that are redeemable at a price "determined in

accordance with a designated formula or by reference to extrinsic data or events." MBCA § 6.01(c)(2). Is this total freedom a good idea? It may be justified on several grounds: (1) there is no evidence of demonstrated harm caused by these types of securities in states that permit their use; (2) the rights of classes of shares are determined in part by contractual negotiation, and elimination of restrictions may be justified on the ground of "freedom of contract"; (3) essentially the same results may usually be attained by contractual commitments between investors and the corporation independent of the articles of incorporation, and there seems to be no reason why persons cannot place their commitments in the articles of incorporation if they wish; and (4) upstream conversions and similar transactions are potentially less damaging to creditors and other senior security holders than the reacquisition of shares by the corporation for cash. Whatever the force of this reasoning, it is likely that individual states will continue to retain a variety of restrictions on the creation of specific rights in classes of shares for the indefinite future.

C. ISSUANCE OF SHARES: HEREIN OF SUBSCRIPTIONS, PAR VALUE AND WATERED STOCK

1. SHARE SUBSCRIPTIONS AND AGREEMENTS TO PURCHASE SECURITIES

Historically, the traditional method of raising capital for a new venture was by public subscriptions pursuant to which persons agreed to purchase a specified number of shares contingent upon a specified amount of capital being raised. Usually these subscriptions were "preincorporation subscriptions" solicited before the corporation was formed; the actual formation of the corporation would occur only if a sufficient number of preincorporation subscriptions had been obtained to assure the success of the venture. After being formed, the corporation would make "calls" on the subscribers for them to actually pay to the corporation the amounts they promised to pay in their subscriptions. In an agrarian society, one can envision promoters of a new mill going from farm to farm seeking to persuade shrewd and cautious farmers to subscribe for shares in the new venture that promised to be of benefit to them. The common law of subscription agreements grappled with a number of problems arising from raising capital in this fashion, including the revocability of subscriptions before acceptance, the basis on which calls are to be made, and the remedies available to the new corporation if the subscription was not paid. These issues are now usually resolved in an unambiguous way by statute. See MBCA § 6.20.

The use of preincorporation subscription agreements declined in importance with the development of the modern investment banking industry, which permitted large amounts of capital to be raised on a nationwide basis.

Subscription agreements may be used to a limited extent in connection with the capitalization of a closely held business with a small number of investors. Modern practice, however, is to use simple contractual agreements to purchase securities rather than a formal subscription agreement. In the words of the annotation to MBCA (1969), "today financing by subscription is the exception." Comment to MBCA (1969) § 17.

2. AUTHORIZATION AND ISSUANCE OF COMMON SHARES UNDER THE MODEL ACT

Assume that a corporation has been formed under the MBCA, and that it is desired to create only a single class of common shares. These shares, or some of them, are to be issued equally to two persons, A and B, for an aggregate consideration of $10,000 in cash or for specified property, the value of which is uncertain but probably about $10,000. How many shares should be authorized, how many shares should be issued, and what price should be established as the issue price for such shares?

Under the MBCA, the answers to these questions are so simple and direct that they do not merit extended consideration. From the standpoint of A and B, the number of shares to be issued and the price may be set at any combination that totals $10,000. It may be 5,000 shares each at $1 per share, 500 shares each at $10 per share, 50 shares each at $100 per share, 5 shares each at $1,000 per share, one share each at $5,000, or any combination in between. It is important that the price be the same for both A and B if they are to be equally treated, but the number of shares and the corresponding price may be set at any level. Further, the number of authorized shares must at least equal the number the corporation plans to issue; however, since it is always possible that more capital may be needed at a later date, the authorization of some excess shares may be sensible. On the other hand, it may not be desirable to authorize vastly more shares than the corporation plans to issue for a couple of reasons. First, limiting the number of shares may protect minority shareholders since a majority shareholder may be able to issue authorized but unissued shares more easily than he can secure an amendment to the articles of incorporation increasing the authorized shares. Since, as will subsequently appear, the issuance of shares in some situations may harm the minority's interest, greater protection is generally given the minority if only the number of shares actually to be issued are authorized. Second, some states impose taxes based on authorized shares: authorizing unnecessary shares may simply increase one's taxes. On balance, most attorneys recommend that some shares be authorized in excess of what is proposed to be issued, even if there is some additional tax cost.

The A–B example set forth above is elementary because A and B both are contributing cash or property. The problem involved in incorporating the AB Furniture Store is obviously more complicated because B is contributing only services, and it is unclear how his services should be balanced against A's capital. This problem is discussed more fully below.

3. PAR VALUE AND STATED CAPITAL

In about 20 states (as of 1995), the articles of incorporation must state the "par value" of the shares of each class (or state that the shares are issued "with no par value" or "without par value"). The remaining states, like the MBCA, have eliminated or made optional the concept of par value, and the current trend is toward the elimination of this concept as an historical anomaly. Par value provisions involve archaic and confusing concepts. They involve common law concepts of legal capital and watered stock and, in most jurisdictions that retain the par value concept, form the basis for restrictions on dividends, corporate share repurchases, and other transactions involving a direct or indirect distribution of corporate assets to shareholders.

The Statutory Supplement contains the provisions of MBCA (1969) relating to par value. The discussion below is tied to these individual provisions, the text of which should be carefully examined. While not all states adopted the 1969 Model Act par value provisions, they are typical of these statutes, and raise the basic issues that must be addressed under all state statutes that retain these concepts.

Perhaps one final preliminary comment should be made. Simply because the statutory par value provisions appear on their face to be logical and regulatory in nature, they are not necessarily so.

Consider MBCA (1969), §§ 54(d), 15 (second sentence), 18, 21. As these statutory provisions make clear, par value is established in the articles of incorporation as a fundamental part of the description of the shares. It is whatever amount that is designated as par value by the drafter; it may be one mill, one cent, one dollar, ten dollars, or some other amount. Originally, par value had considerable importance because it was widely viewed as the amount for which shares would be issued: shares with a par value of one hundred dollars per share could be subscribed for at one hundred dollars per share with confidence that all other identical shares would also be issued for $100. In effect, par value originally ensured proportionality of treatment of widely dispersed shareholders, increased confidence in the resale market that the shares had real value (and were not "mere pieces of paper"), and assured the population in general that corporations had in fact been capitalized as advertised by the par values of the shares they issued.

It did not take long, however, for unscrupulous promoters to turn this practice to their own advantage. In the leading case of Hospes v. Northwestern Mfg. & Car Co., 48 Minn. 174, 50 N.W. 1117, 1118 (1892), for example, the Court summarized the allegations of the complaint as follows:

Briefly stated, the allegations of the complaint are that on May 10, 1882, Seymour, Sabin & Co. owned property of the value of several million dollars, and a business then supposed to be profitable. That, in order to continue and enlarge this business, the parties interested in Seymour, Sabin & Co., with others, organized the car company, to which was sold the greater part of the assets of Seymour, Sabin & Co. at a valuation of $2,267,000, in payment of which there were issued to Seymour, Sabin & Co. shares of the preferred stock of the car company of the par value of $2,267,000, it being then and there agreed by both parties that this stock was in full payment of the property thus purchased. It is further alleged that the stockholders of Seymour, Sabin & Co., and the other persons who had agreed to become stockholders in the car company, were then desirous of issuing to themselves, and obtaining for their own benefit, a large amount of common stock of the car company, "without paying therefor, and without incurring any liability thereon or to pay therefor;" and for that purpose, and "in order to evade and set at naught the laws of this state," they caused Seymour, Sabin & Co. to subscribe for and agree to take common stock of the car company of the par value of $1,500,000. That Seymour, Sabin & Co. thereupon subscribed for that amount of the common stock, but never paid therefor any consideration whatever, either in money or property. That thereafter these persons caused this stock to be issued to D.M. Sabin as trustee, to be by him distributed among them.

That it was so distributed without receipt by him or the car company from any one of any consideration whatever, but was given by the car company and received by these parties entirely "gratuitously." * * * The common stock issued by the car company is a species of "watered stock," since the corporation did not receive the par value for the stock when it was issued. What should be done about this? Is there a danger that innocent creditors might rely on the fact that shares with a specified par value are outstanding and assume that the corporation had at least the specified amount of capital? The Court believed that this was a potential problem, and concluded that under some circumstances the recipients of watered shares should be required to pay in the par value even though they had never agreed to do so. The Court, however, had some difficulty with the rationale:

> [The plaintiff] plants itself upon the so-called "trust-fund" doctrine that the capital stock of a corporation is a trust fund for the payment of its debts; its contention being that such a "bonus" issue of stock creates, in case of the subsequent insolvency of the corporation, a liability on part of the stockholder in favor of creditors to pay for it, notwithstanding his contract with the corporation to the contrary.

> This "trust fund" doctrine, commonly called the "American doctrine," has given rise to much confusion of ideas as to its real meaning, and much conflict of decision in its application. To such an extent has this been the case that many have questioned the accuracy of the phrase, as well as doubted the necessity or expediency of inventing any such doctrine. * * * The phrase that "the capital of a corporation constitutes a trust fund for the benefit of creditors" is misleading. Corporate property is not held in trust, in any proper sense of the term. A trust implies two estates or interests,—one equitable and one legal; one person, as trustee, holding the legal title, while another, as the *cestui que trust,* has the beneficial interest. Absolute control and power of disposition are inconsistent with the idea of a trust. The capital of a corporation is its property. It has the whole beneficial interest in it, as well as the legal title. It may use the income and profits of it, and sell and dispose of it, the same as a natural person. It is a trustee for its creditors in the same sense and to the same extent as a natural person, but no further. * * *

> Another proposition which we think must be sound is that creditors cannot recover on the ground of contract when the corporation could not. Their right to recover in such cases must rest on the ground that the acts of the stockholders with reference to the corporate capital constitutes a fraud on their rights. We have here a case where the contract between the corporation and the takers of the shares was specific that the shares should not be paid for. * * * In such a case the creditors undoubtedly may have rights superior to the corporation, but these rights cannot rest on the implication that the shareholder agreed to do something directly contrary to his real agreement, but must be based on tort or fraud, actual or presumed. In England, since the act of 1867, there is an implied contract created by statute that "every share in any company shall be deemed and be taken to have been issued and to be held subject to the payment of the whole amount thereof in cash." This statutory contract makes every contrary contract void. Such a statute would be entirely just

to all, for every one would be advised of its provisions, and could conduct himself accordingly. And in view of the fact that "watered" and "bonus" stock is one of the greatest abuses connected with the management of modern corporations, such a law might, on grounds of public policy, be very desirable. But this is a matter for the legislature, and not for the courts. We have no such statute * * *.

It is well settled that an equity in favor of a creditor does not arise absolutely and in every case to have the holder of "bonus" stock pay for it contrary to his actual contract with the corporation. Thus no such equity exists in favor of one whose debt was contracted prior to the issue, since he could not have trusted the company upon the faith of such stock. Handley v. Stutz, 139 U.S. 435, 11 Sup.Ct.Rep. 530. It does not exist in favor of a subsequent creditor who has dealt with the corporation with full knowledge of the arrangement by which the "bonus" stock was issued, for a man cannot be defrauded by that which he knows when he acts. It has also been held not to exist where stock has been issued and turned out at its full market value to pay corporate debts. The same has been held to be the case where an active corporation, whose original capital has been impaired, for the purpose of recuperating itself issues new stock, and sells it on the market for the best price obtainable, but for less than par, (Handley v. Stutz, supra) although it is difficult to perceive, in the absence of a statute authorizing such a thing, (of which every one dealing with the corporations is bound to take notice) any difference between the original stock of a new corporation and additional stock issued by a "going concern." It is difficult, if not impossible, to explain or reconcile these cases upon the "trust-fund" doctrine, or, in the light of them, to predicate the liability of the stockholder upon that doctrine. But by putting it upon the ground of fraud, and applying the old and familiar rules of law on that subject to the peculiar nature of a corporation and the relation which its stockholders bear to it and to the public, we have at once rational and logical ground on which to stand. The capital of a corporation is the basis of its credit. It is a substitute for the individual liability of those who own its stock. People deal with it and give it credit on the faith of it. They have a right to assume that it has paid in capital to the amount which it represents itself as having; and if they give it credit on the faith of that representation, and if the representation is false, it is a fraud upon them; and, in case the corporation becomes insolvent, the law, upon the plainest principles of common justice, says to the delinquent stockholder, Make that representation good by paying for your stock. It certainly cannot require the invention of any new doctrine in order to enforce so familiar a rule of equity. It is the misrepresentation of fact in stating the amount of capital to be greater than it really is that is the true basis of the liability of the stockholder in such cases; and it follows that it is only those creditors who have relied, or who can fairly be presumed to have relied, upon the professed amount of capital, in whose favor the law will recognize and enforce an equity against the holders of "bonus" stock. This furnishes a rational and uniform rule, to which familiar principles are easily applied, and which frees the subject from many of the difficulties and apparent inconsistencies into which the "trust-fund" doctrine has involved it; and we think that, even when the trust-fund doctrine has been invoked, the decision in almost every well-considered case is readily referable to such a rule.

50 N.W., at 1119–21. The Court then concluded that subsequent creditors should not be required to allege and prove affirmatively that they relied on the capital represented by the bonus shares, but that lack of reliance might be a defense. In other words, the capitalization of a corporation as established by the par values of its issued shares was a public representation on which subsequent creditors might rely and compel the shareholders to make good their representation, unless the corporation could establish that the creditors extended credit knowing the represented capital was not there. Finally, the Court concluded that the particular plaintiff involved in the Hospes case (a newly formed corporation that had bought up claims against the original car company at significant discounts) had not sufficiently alleged its own bona fides to be allowed to maintain suit.

Notes

(1) The shares issued by the car company in the Hospes case are usually described as "bonus shares," because nothing was paid for them. "Watered shares" are technically shares issued for property worth less than their par value, while "discount shares" are shares issued for cash but less than par. All three types are usually lumped under the single phrase "watered stock." As indicated in *Hospes,* recipients of such shares are potentially liable to subsequent creditors of the corporation.

(2) In *Hospes*, the Court stated that watered stock "is one of the greatest abuses connected with the management of modern corporations." 50 N.W., at 1120. Of course, the Court was speaking as of 1892. Was that true even then? In that connection, draw up a balance sheet for the car company. Is it not clear that fundamental accounting principles require the creation of some fictional assets to balance things off? Is the risk of fraud increased by the presence of fictional assets on a balance sheet?

(3) The notion that funds paid in for stock constitute a "trust fund" for creditors has a strange fascination for many courts. See e.g. Wood v. Dummer, 30 Fed.Cas. 435, No. 17,944 (C.C.Me.1824). While most of these cases are old, the language appears in some fairly recent decisions, and it is possible that it may influence decisions in some cases. The idea that corporate capital constitutes a "trust fund" is a fiction for the reasons recognized in the quoted excerpts from *Hospes*. For a short and convincing explanation of why the "trust fund" argument is circular and indeterminate, see C. Robert Morris, Some Notes on "Reliance," 75 Minn. L.Rev. 815, 815–20 (1991).

HANEWALD v. BRYAN'S INC.

Supreme Court of North Dakota, 1988.
429 N.W.2d 414.

MESCHKE, JUSTICE.

Harold E. Hanewald appealed from that part of his judgment for $38,600 plus interest against Bryan's, Inc. which refused to impose personal liability upon Keith, Joan, and George Bryan for that insolvent corporation's debt. We reverse the ruling that Keith and Joan Bryan were not personally liable.

On July 19, 1984, Keith and Joan Bryan incorporated Bryan's, Inc. to "engage in and operate a general retail clothing, and related items, store

* * *." The Certificate of Incorporation was issued by the Secretary of State on July 25, 1984. The first meeting of the board of directors elected Keith Bryan as president and Joan Bryan as secretary-treasurer of Bryan's, Inc. George Bryan was elected vice-president, appointed registered agent, and designated manager of the prospective business. The Articles of Incorporation authorized the corporation to issue "100 shares of common stock with a par value of $1,000 per share" with "total authorized capitalization [of] $100,-000.00." Bryan's, Inc. issued 50 shares of stock to Keith Bryan and 50 shares of stock to Joan Bryan. The trial court found that "Bryan's, Inc. did not receive any payment, either in labor, services, money, or property, for the stock which was issued."

[The Bryans then lent Bryan's, Inc. $10,000 in cash and personally guaranteed a $55,000 loan from a local bank. These funds enabled Bryan's, Inc. to purchase from Hanewald the inventory and assets of a dry goods store in Hazen, North Dakota, partly for cash and partly for a $45,000 corporate promissory note. Bryan's, Inc. also signed a 5-year lease on Hanewald's store.]

Bryan's, Inc. began operating the retail clothing store on September 1, 1984. The business, however, lasted only four months with an operating loss of $4,840. In late December 1984, Keith and Joan Bryan decided to close the Hazen store. Thereafter, George Bryan, with the assistance of a brother and local employees, packed and removed the remaining inventory and delivered it for resale to other stores in Montana operated by the Bryan family. Bryan's, Inc. sent a "Notice of Rescission" to Hanewald on January 3, 1985, in an attempt to avoid the lease. The corporation was involuntarily dissolved by operation of law on August 1, 1986, for failure to file its annual report with the Secretary of State.

Bryan's, Inc. did not pay the $5,000 promissory note to Hanewald but paid off the rest of its creditors. Debts paid included the $55,000 loan from Union State Bank and a $10,000 loan from Keith and Joan Bryan. The Bryan loan had been, according to the trial court, "intended to be used for operating costs and expenses."

Hanewald sued the corporation and the Bryans for breach of the lease agreement and the promissory note, seeking to hold the Bryans personally liable. The defendants counterclaimed, alleging that Hanewald had fraudulently misrepresented the business' profitability in negotiating its sale. After a trial without a jury, the trial court entered judgment against Bryan's, Inc. for $38,600 plus interest on Hanewald's claims and ruled against the defendants on their counterclaim. The defendants have not cross appealed these rulings.

The trial court, however, refused to hold the individual defendants personally liable for the judgment against Bryan's, Inc., stating:

> "Bryan's, Inc. was formed in a classic manner, the $10,000.00 loan by Keith Bryan being more than sufficient operating capital. Bryan's, Inc. paid all obligations except the obligation to Hanewald in a timely fashion, and since there was no evidence of bad faith by the Bryans, the corporate shield of Bryan's, Inc. should not be pierced."

Hanewald appealed from the refusal to hold the individual defendants personally liable.

Insofar as the judgment fails to impose personal liability upon Keith and Joan Bryan, the corporation's sole shareholders, we agree with Hanewald that the trial court erred. We base our decision on the Bryans' statutory duty to pay for shares that were issued to them by Bryan's, Inc.

Organizing a corporation to avoid personal liability is legitimate. Indeed, it is one of the primary advantages of doing business in the corporate form. However, the limited personal liability of shareholders does not come free. As this court said in *Bryan v. Northwest Beverages*, 69 N.D. 274, 285 N.W. 689, 694 (1939), "[t]he mere formation of a corporation, fixing the amount of its capital stock, and receiving a certificate of incorporation, do not create anything of value upon which the company can do business." It is the shareholders' initial capital investments which protects their personal assets from further liability in the corporate enterprise. Thus, generally, shareholders are not liable for corporate debts beyond the capital they have contributed to the corporation.

This protection for corporate shareholders was codified in the statute in effect when Bryan's, Inc. was incorporated and when this action was commenced * * *. [The Court quotes MBCA (1969) § 25, first paragraph.] This statute obligated shareholders to pay for their shares as a prerequisite for their limited personal liability.

The kinds of consideration paid for corporate shares may vary. Article XII, § 9 of the state constitution says that "[n]o corporation shall issue stock or bonds except for money, labor done, or money or property actually received; and all fictitious increase of stock or indebtedness shall be void." [The Court summarizes and quotes from MBCA (1960) § 19.] The purpose of these constitutional and statutory provisions is "to protect the public and those dealing with the corporation...." *Bryan v. Northwest Beverages, supra,* 285 N.W. at 694.

In this case, Bryan's, Inc. was authorized to issue 100 shares of stock each having a par value of $1,000. Keith Bryan and Joan Bryan, two of the original incorporators and members of the board of directors, were each issued 50 shares. The trial court determined that "Bryan's, Inc. did not receive any payment, either in labor, services, money, or property, for the stock which was issued." Bryans have not challenged this finding of fact on this appeal. We hold that Bryans' failure to pay for their shares in the corporation makes them personally liable under [MBCA (1969) § 25], for the corporation's debt to Hanewald.

Drafters' comments to § 25 of the Model Business Corporation Act, * * * sketched the principles:

> "The liability of a subscriber for the unpaid portion of his subscription and the liability of a shareholder for the unpaid balance of the full consideration for which has shares were issued are based upon contract principles. The liability of a shareholder to whom shares are issued for overvalued property or services is a breach of contract. These liabilities have not been considered to be exceptions to the absolute limited liability concept.

> "Where statutes have been silent, courts have differed as to whether the cause of action on the liabilities of shareholders for unpaid consider-

ation for shares issued or to be issued may be asserted by a creditor directly, by the corporation itself or its receiver, or by a creditor on behalf of the corporation. The Model Act is also silent on the subject for the reason that it can be better treated elsewhere." 1 Model Business Corporation Act Annotated 2d, Comment to § 25, at pp. 509–510 (1971).

This court, in *Marshall–Wells Hardware Co. v. New Era Coal Co.*, 13 N.D. 396, 100 N.W. 1084 (1904), held that creditors could directly enforce shareholders' liabilities to pay for shares held by them under statutes analogous to [MBCA (1969) § 25]. We believe that the shareholder liability created by [MBCA (1969) § 25] may likewise be enforced in a direct action by a creditor of the corporation.

Our conclusion comports with the generally recognized rule, derived from common law, that "a shareholder is liable to corporate creditors to the extent his stock has not been paid for." 18A Am.Jur.2d *Corporations* § 863, at p. 739 (1985). *See also, id.* at §§ 906 and 907. One commentator has observed:

"For a corporation to issue its stock as a gratuity violates the rights of existing stockholders who do not consent, and is a fraud upon subsequent subscribers, and upon subsequent creditors who deal with it on the faith of its capital stock. The former may sue to enjoin the issue of the stock, or to cancel it if it has been issued, and has not reached the hands of a bona fide purchaser; and the latter, according to the weight of authority, may compel payment by the person to whom it was issued, to such extent as may be necessary for the payment of their claims." 11 W. Fletcher, *Cyclopedia of the Law of Private Corporations* § 5202, at p. 450 (1986).

The shareholder "is liable to the extent of the difference between the par value and the amount actually paid," and "to such an extent only as may be necessary for the satisfaction of" the creditor's claim. 11 W. Fletcher, *supra,* § 5241, at pp. 550, 551.

The defendants asserted, and the trial court ruled, that the $10,000 loan from Keith and Joan Bryan to the corporation was nevertheless "more than sufficient operating capital" to run the business. However, a shareholder's loan is a debt, not an asset, of the corporation. Where, as here, a loan was repaid by the corporation to the shareholders before its operations were abandoned, the loan cannot be considered a capital contribution.[3]

We conclude that the trial court, having found that Keith and Joan Bryan had not paid for their stock, erred as a matter of law in refusing to hold them personally liable for the corporation's debt to Hanewald. The debt to Hanewald does not exceed the difference between the par value of their stock and the amount they actually paid. Therefore, we reverse in part to remand for entry of judgment holding Keith and Joan Bryan jointly and severally liable

---

3. [By the Court] There are some circumstances in which a shareholder's loan to the corporation may be treated as a capital contribution. *See* 12B W. Fletcher, *Cyclopedia of the Law of Private Corporations* § 5739 (1984). In bankruptcy proceedings, for example, a shareholder's loans to his corporation can be treated as capital contributions when a corporation is deemed undercapitalized. *See Pepper v. Litton,* 308 U.S. 295, 60 S.Ct. 238, 84 L.Ed. 281 (1939). However, the result in this class of cases is an equitable subordination of the shareholder's claim to the claims of other creditors, which is consistent in principle with the result we reach today.

for the entire corporate debt to Hanewald. The judgment is otherwise affirmed.

Notes

(1) Is the liability imposed on the Bryans based on the theories developed in the Hospes case, or does it arise from the force of the statutes themselves? Under MBCA (1969), is there watered stock liability if:

(a) The directors fraudulently recite that property is worth $2,000 when it is really worth only $1,000, and then issue shares with a par value of $2,000 for it?

(b) The directors reasonably and nonfraudulently recite that property is worth $1,000, but then issue shares with a par value of $2,000 for it? As a practical matter, the last paragraph of MBCA § 19 eliminates many potential problems in this area?

(2) In most states watered stock liability arises only in connection with the original issuance of shares. If a corporation reacquires some of its shares after they have been lawfully issued, it may resell those shares at any price it desires without giving rise to watered stock liability. The theory is that these shares remain "issued" even though they are held in the corporation's treasury and their resale at less than par does not water the corporation's stock account. These shares (called "treasury shares") have an intermediate status under most statutes: they are not viewed as "outstanding" for purposes of dividends, quorum, and voting purposes, but are viewed as "issued" so that their "reissuance" does not violate the restrictions imposed by the par value statutes. See Brumfield v. Horn, 547 So.2d 415 (Ala.1989). There is some contrary authority. MBCA § 6.31 eliminates the concept of treasury shares (for reasons to be discussed later) and treats reacquired shares as authorized but unissued shares. However, most states still retain the concept of treasury shares.

4. ELIGIBLE AND INELIGIBLE CONSIDERATION FOR SHARES

Consider MBCA (1969) § 19. The idea that only the actual receipt of certain types of property or services by a corporation will support the issuance of shares is not technically a part of the par value structure, but it is closely aligned with it and must be taken into account whenever shares are being issued under a traditional statute. In the AB Furniture Store hypothetical, if B receives shares with a par value in exchange for his promise to perform services in the future, does he have potential "watered stock" liability under §§ 19 and 25? If so, what arrangements may be made for the issuance of B's shares to avoid this potential liability? What if the issuance is held back until some services are performed? May the directors allocate all the shares to the services already performed under § 18 and thereby avoid the creation of this liability?

What purpose is served by § 19? There are at least two possibilities: first, it was designed to protect creditors of the corporation who may rely on its capital in extending credit, since it attempts to assure that there is something "real" which can be levied against and sold; second, it may protect other investors (who invest "real" assets such as money or property) from dilution of their interests.

Obviously, in some circumstances a contract to perform services may have considerable value. If Jane Fonda enters into a contract to perform in a film, the producer could presumably borrow large sums solely on the strength of the Fonda contract. If Ms. Fonda is to receive a twenty-five percent interest in the corporation producing the film, can the corporation issue shares to her reflecting that interest when she signs the contract? If not, how can she be given the interest that her contract entitles her to at the outset of the filming?

Consider, on the other hand, John Q. Promoter, who sells 75 percent of his newly formed corporation's shares to outsiders for cash, and issues the remaining 25 percent to himself in exchange for his contract to perform services of an indefinite nature in the future. The investors determine that Promoter's future services are of no benefit to the corporation. Section 19 of MBCA (1969) may permit the corporation to cancel the shares issued to Promoter, thus allowing the investors to avoid dilution of their interests in the corporation. Is there any basis for attacking such a transaction on grounds other than § 19?

Shares issued for a promissory note are also prohibited by MBCA (1969) § 19. Again it is possible to divine an intention either to protect creditors of the corporation or to protect other investors who contribute cash while the promoter puts in an uncollectible promissory note. Courts have held that if a corporation does issue shares for a promissory note in violation of this section, the corporation may nevertheless enforce the note; the corporation, however, may be able to cancel the offending shares for failing to comply with § 19. Presumably, a note executed by John D. Rockefeller is "as good as gold," and yet shares cannot be issued to John D. in exchange for that note. On the other hand, if John D.'s note is owned by a third person, Pam Smith, may Smith be issued shares in consideration of John D.'s note?

Another problem may be raised by the language in MBCA (1969) § 19, "other property, tangible or intangible." What about claimed secret processes, formulas, conditional or contingent contract rights, "good will," capitalized research costs that have not yet led to a marketable product, and other intangible "property"? Intangibles are often not only difficult to value; their very existence may be so ephemeral as not to constitute "property" at all in the eyes of some courts, at least for purposes of § 19. There are several decisions in which this question has been raised, usually in the context of seeking to cancel shares issued in exchange for such "property."

While statutes are less than crystal clear on the matter, a good argument can be made that it is proper to resell treasury shares for a consideration that is not eligible consideration for the issuance of new shares under MBCA (1969) § 19. Brumfield v. Horn, 547 So.2d 415 (Ala.1989). One court that reached the opposite conclusion, Public Inv. Ltd. v. Bandeirante Corp., 740 F.2d 1222 (D.C.Cir.1984), was apparently influenced by the unfortunate consequences of the transaction under consideration; the result reached is probably not consistent with generally understood principles relating to treasury shares. Another decision invalidating an issuance of treasury shares for a promissory note is Place v. P.M. Place Stores Co., 857 S.W.2d 291 (Mo.App.1993).

Notes

(1) What about issuing shares for a promise to pay money in the future that is not evidenced by a promissory note? Is not that literally permitted by MBCA

(1969) § 19? The New York analogue to this section uses the phrase "obligations of the subscriber for future payments" rather than "promissory notes." N.Y.—McKinney's Bus.Corp.Law § 504(b). What about a *secured* promissory note? General Bonding & Casualty Ins. Co. v. Moseley, 110 Tex. 529, 222 S.W. 961 (1920), held that a note secured by a valid first trust lien on real estate was permissible consideration; cf., American Radiator & Standard Sanitary Corp. v. United States, 155 Ct.Cl. 515, 295 F.2d 939 (1961). For a case upholding the issue of shares for services of uncertain value previously rendered, see Haft v. Dart Group, 841 F.Supp. 549, 573 (D.Del.1993).

(2) As indicated in the text, these restrictions on eligible consideration for shares are not technically part of the par value structure. A state may abolish par value and yet decide to retain these traditional restrictions on eligible consideration (as California, for example, has done). North Dakota and several other states have placed language similar to MBCA (1969) § 19 in their state constitutions. In these states, it may not be possible to abolish par value and other aspects of the legal capital regime without constitutional amendments.

(3) Consider MBCA §§ 6.21(b), 6.21(d), 6.21(e), 16.21(b). Does § 16.21(b) provide adequate protection against a transaction like that of John Q. Promoter referred to in the text? In many cases, of course, the corporation will elect to follow the escrow procedure suggested in § 6.21(e), thereby avoiding possible dilution. MBCA § 6.21(d) may initially appear to be a completely pro-corporation provision; in fact, it was primarily intended as a pro-lawyer provision, to provide the basis for subsequent legal opinions that outstanding shares were validly issued and non-assessable without requiring a historical review of a transaction that may have occurred many years earlier. Courts have not applied this statute broadly and literally. For example, Haft v. Dart Group Corporation, 1994 WL 643185 (Del.Ch.1994), held that this section does not preclude a shareholder from attacking grants of options to purchase shares at favorable prices because they constituted gift or waste. "The legal test of corporate waste is more demanding than a peppercorn standard; it asks whether any reasonable person could conclude, in the particular circumstances, that the exchange represented a fair exchange." See also Michelson v. Duncan, 407 A.2d 211 (Del.1979).

(4) The Official Comment to § 6.21 states that the term "benefit" should be "broadly construed to include, for example, a reduction of a liability, a release of a claim, or benefits obtained by a corporation by contribution of its shares to a charitable organization or as a prize in a promotion."

(5) The Official Comment to § 6.21 also states that "[i]n the realities of commercial life, there is sometimes a need for the issuance of shares for contract rights or * * * intangible property or benefits." Do you agree? If you were drafting a new corporation statute, would you follow § 6.21 in this regard, or would you retain some or all of old § 19?

5. PAR VALUE IN MODERN PRACTICE

The early practice of creating shares with a par value equal to the proposed issuance price long ago fell into disuse. Today, the practice most often followed is to use "nominal" par value, that is one cent, ten cents, or one dollar per share when the shares are issued for several dollars or more per share. The use of no par shares—for reasons discussed below—is a distant second. The fact that a case such as Hanewald v. Bryan's Inc. arose in the 1980s can be explained only on the basis that the person forming the corporation was unaware of modern practice and the dangers of placing a high par value on shares. Under current practice, par value serves only a minor function and is in no way an indication of the price at which the shares are issued. There is, however, one significant carryover from the earlier practice: to avoid watered stock liability the issuance price for shares of stock with par value must always be equal to or greater than par value.

Several factors caused the movement away from par value as a representation of the purchase price of shares and the development of nominal par value shares. Doubtless, concern about watered stock liability, particularly where property of uncertain value is being contributed, was a factor. If high par value shares are given in exchange for such property, arguments may later arise that the property was not worth the par value of the shares received and the recipients might be sued for the difference. Another factor was the possible loss of flexibility of pricing shares. When a secondary market for previously issued shares develops, a corporation raising capital by selling shares in effect competes with that market. A corporation issuing shares with a par value of $100 may not be able to reduce the price below that figure and may have to stop selling shares if the market price of the previously-issued shares dropped below $100 per share. (At that point interested investors could get a better price by buying previously issued shares in the secondary market than they could from the corporation which may be locked into the $100 price by the par value.)

Still another factor was that nominal par shares increase corporate flexibility in making distributions in the future. Consider MBCA (1969) § 21, and its possible application to "high par," "nominal par," and "no par" alternatives when forming a corporation. Consider the following alternatives:

(i) The corporation issues 10 shares of $100 par value stock for $1,000 in cash.

(ii) The corporation issues 10 shares of $1 par value stock for $1,000 in cash.

(iii) The corporation issues 10 shares of no par value stock for $1,000 in cash.

The appropriate accounting for alternatives (i) and (ii) are as follows:

Alternative (i)

Assets			Liabilities	0
Cash		1000	Capital accounts	
			Stated Capital	1000
			Capital Surplus	0
		1000		1000

par value × amt shares issued (handwritten)

Alternative (ii)

Assets			Liabilities	0
Cash		1000	Capital accounts	
			Stated Capital	10
			Capital Surplus	990
		1000		1000

In connection with alternative (iii), MBCA (1969) § 21 provides that the entire $1,000 should be treated as stated capital unless the directors determine to allocate to capital surplus "any portion of the consideration received for the issuance of such shares." (Does "any portion" include "all"?) Not all states give the directors total freedom to allocate the proceeds from no par shares to capital surplus. Some states do not permit such allocation at all (in which case, alternative (iii) becomes identical to alternative (i)), while others permit only a partial allocation. Before 1985, Texas, for example, permitted allocation of only 25 percent of the consideration to capital surplus. Vernon's Ann.Tex.Stat.Bus.Corp.Act, art. 2.17B (1980). Assuming that such a restriction is applicable, and the directors elect to classify the maximum amount possible to capital surplus, alternative (iii) becomes:

Alternative (iii)			
Assets		Liabilities	0
Cash	1000	Capital accounts	
		Stated Capital	750
		Capital Surplus	250
	1000		1000

Now, a logical question is: What difference does it make if the capital contribution is recorded as stated capital or capital surplus? Rather surprisingly, it does make a difference, which can best be appreciated if a balance sheet is drawn up after the corporation (financed as suggested in alternative (ii)) has (1) borrowed $1,000 from a bank, and (2) had two years of operations during which it has earned and accumulated an aggregate of $2,000 from its earnings. Further, for simplicity, it will be assumed that all of the assets are held by the corporation in the form of cash. The balance sheet looks like this:

Assets		Liabilities	$1,000
Cash	$4,000	Capital accounts	
		Earned Surplus	$2,000
		Stated Capital	10
		Capital Surplus	990
	$4,000		$4,000

At this point the shareholders decide they want to distribute to themselves some or all of the $4,000. If the balance sheet is to continue to balance, every dollar taken from the left-hand column must obviously be reflected by the reduction of a right-hand column entry. The significance of the right-hand entries is that they in effect limit or monitor the distribution of assets from the left-hand column. The distributions permitted by a corporation are evaluated in accordance with MBCA (1969) §§ 45, 46, and 6.

Under these statutes, capitalizing a corporation with large amounts of capital surplus gave that corporation greater freedom and flexibility to make distributions or reacquire its own shares than it would have had if it were capitalized with large amounts of stated capital. In the above examples, the corporation, no matter how capitalized, could use the $2,000 of earned surplus to reacquire shares or make a distribution to shareholders. However, the corporation capitalized solely with stated capital (alternative (i)) would be limited to that amount; the corporation created with no par shares (alternative (iii)) would have available for distribution an additional $250 of capital surplus, for total potential distributions of $2250; the corporation capitalized most flexibly (alternative (ii)) could legally distribute $2990 out of its assets (subject, however, to the general insolvency tests in the 1969 Model Act).

Admittedly, this increase in flexibility does not seem to be of earthshaking significance, and indeed may raise policy questions about whether corporations should have the freedom to distribute virtually all their capital as permitted in alternative (ii). However, why should the persons creating a corporation needlessly impose any restriction on a corporation's freedom?

Where the consideration for no par shares may be allocated to capital surplus without limitation (as permitted by § 18 of MBCA (1969)), either no par or nominal par shares give the same amount of freedom. No par shares, however, never gained the popularity and widespread use of nominal par shares. One factor that in the past undoubtedly encouraged the use of nominal par shares, and discouraged the use of both high par and no par, was the federal excise tax statute, repealed in 1965, that imposed a documentary stamp tax on issues and transfers of securities. This tax was based on "the par or face value of each certificate" of par value stock and "the actual value of each certificate" of no-par stock. I.R.C. § 4301 (1954), repealed by Pub.L. No. 89–44, Tit. IV, § 401(a), 79 Stat. 148 (1965). Several states continue to measure their taxes on a similar basis.

Is there any public relations value in the use of high par value stock? Is such stock desirable in order to ensure protection to creditors? Of course, from the creditors' standpoint, assets reflected as stated capital are somewhat preferable to assets reflected as capital surplus since they are more "locked in" and unavailable for distribution to shareholders. Consider, however, MBCA (1969) § 58(d), (e), (h), and (i).

TED J. FIFLIS, HOMER KRIPKE, & PAUL M. FOSTER, ACCOUNTING FOR BUSINESS LAWYERS
(4th ed. 1991), p. 433.*

* * * [A] prospective creditor who inspects the balance sheet of a corporation and finds a low par or stated capital and most of the net worth embodied in capital surplus should know * * * that corporation laws to some extent permit the distribution of capital surplus as well as earned surplus to stockholders, giving creditors no protection beyond the legal capital consisting of par or stated capital.

Not equally well-known is the fact that just as lawyers minimized the effect of the rule that the legal capital must be paid-in to the corporation, by use of low par or low stated value no-par stock, so too they minimized the effect of the rule limiting distributions out of legal capital by various techniques permitting reduction of legal capital without creditors' approval. The conclusion is that corporation law provides creditors with very little actual protection * * *.

As a result creditors today do not rely upon statutory protection against shareholder distributions. Trade creditors rely instead on security interests or careful monitoring of their receivables while commercial lenders require disclosure of financial data, security interests, and contractual limitations on distributions. It is in the areas of disclosure and statutory and contractual limitations that the practitioner must understand the accounting in order to serve his clients properly. * * *

* Reprinted with permission from West Publishing Corporation.

Notes

(1) It is important to distinguish conceptually between "no par shares" in states that retain the par value structure, and shares issued in states that, like the MBCA, have eliminated par value. The issuance of "no par shares" in par value states affects the stated capital and capital surplus accounts, may create watered stock liability in certain circumstances, and may affect the distributions a corporation may lawfully make. States that have eliminated the par value structure have eliminated the watered stock concept and have also generally eliminated mandatory capital accounts. They have also established different rules relating to when distributions lawfully may be made.

(2) Of course, it is not strictly true that the MBCA has "eliminated" the concept of par value. See MBCA § 2.02(b)(2)(iv). The Official Comment explains that optional par value provisions may be of use "to corporations which are to be qualified in foreign jurisdictions in that franchise or other taxes are computed upon the basis of par value." In addition, optional par value may also be given effect "essentially as a matter of contract between the parties." In other words, the par value rules described in this chapter may be elected by the participants in a corporation, if they so desire, by creating a par value for shares in the articles of incorporation. Where a corporation formed in a state that has abolished par value contemplates multistate operations, lawyers usually recommend that an optional par value be adopted to minimize tax consequences if the corporation becomes subject to taxation in a state that uses par value as a measure of tax liability.

(3) Issues involving the legality of distributions, dividends, and reacquisition or redemption of shares are considered further in Section I of this chapter.

D. DEBT FINANCING

Evidences of indebtedness usually referred to as "securities" are bonds and debentures. Both involve unconditional promises to pay a stated sum in the future, and to pay interest periodically until then. Technically, a debenture is an unsecured corporate obligation while a bond is secured by a lien or mortgage on corporate property. However, the word "bond" is often used indiscriminately to cover both bonds and debentures. Bonds and debentures historically were payable to bearer; interest coupons reflecting the periodic obligation to pay interest were attached. A registered bond is one that has been registered in the name of a specific individual and from which the coupons have been removed; interest is paid directly to the registered owner. Virtually all new bonds are issued today in registered form. Of course, registered bonds are freely transferable.[4]

---

4. [By the Editor] Other typical characteristics of debt securities are: (1) Interest payments are usually fixed obligations, due in any event, and expressed as a percentage of the face amount of the security. However, income bonds, which condition the obligation to pay interest on adequate corporate earnings, are also used. Somewhat rarer are so-called participating bonds, where the interest obligation increases with corporate earnings. (2) Debt securities are usually subject to redemption, permitting the corporation to pay off the obligation before it is due, often at a premium over the face value. (3) Debt securities may be subordinated to the payment of other obligations. (4) Debt securities may be convertible into other classes of stock, usually common stock. Convertible debentures are treated as equity securities for many purposes. See, e.g., 15 U.S.C.A. § 78c(a)(11). (5) Some states authorize holders of bonds or debentures to participate in the selection of the board of directors upon specified contingencies. Many of these characteristics are also present in preferred shares.

In recent years, novel types of debt instruments have been created, and new words have entered the common vocabulary. Zero coupon bonds, often called "zeroes," pay no interest at all; they sell at a substantial discount from face value and upon maturity the holder receives the face value. The entire difference between original issue price and face value represents interest payable upon the maturity of the "zero." For income tax purposes, however, a holder of a "zero" must include in taxable income an allocable portion of the discount even though it is not to be received until some time in the distant future; as a result, "zeroes" are attractive investments primarily for tax-exempt or tax-deferred entities. Junk bonds, widely used in takeovers, are simply below investment-grade debt instruments. Many other novel variations exist. See generally Robert W. Hamilton and Richard A. Booth, Business Basics for Law Students: Essential Terms and Concepts, §§ 00.00–00.00.

While primary attention is paid to equity securities in this chapter, it should be pointed out that from an economic standpoint, debt financing is considerably more important than equity financing. Most established, large publicly held corporations regularly engage in debt financing but rarely raise capital through issuance of equity securities. Indeed, in recent years many of these publicly held corporations have reduced the amount of equity securities outstanding through repurchases of shares while at the same time increasing their outstanding indebtedness.

As has previously been indicated, the distinction between debt and equity may not be at all clear in many situations. The ambivalent nature of preferred shares redeemable at the option of the holder has previously been commented upon. Also, as a matter of economics, how does a subordinated 100–year income debenture differ from a class of plain vanilla preferred shares? It is obviously possible to create a variety of mixed or "hybrid" securities that have some of the characteristics of debt and some of equity.[5]

It is usually advantageous to engage to some extent in debt financing. The notion that the best business is a debt-free business, while sounding attractive, is not consistent either with the minimization of income taxes or with the maximization of profits. A sharp distinction must be drawn, however, between debt owed to third persons, and debt owed to shareholders.

1. THE CONCEPT OF LEVERAGE

Debt owed to third persons creates leverage. Leverage is favorable to the borrower when the borrower is able to earn more on the borrowed capital than the cost of the borrowing. The entire excess is allocable to the equity accounts of the corporation, thereby increasing the rate of return on the equity invested in the corporation. An example should help to make this clear. Assume that a corporation has a total invested capital of $500,000. Let us consider the earnings per share on two alternative assumptions: (a) all this capital is invested as equity capital, e.g., 50,000 shares sold at $10.00 per share, and (b) half is borrowed on a long-term basis, and the other half is contributed capital, e.g., 25,000 shares sold at $10.00 per share.

---

5. [By the Editor] The use of such securities is often questionable as a business matter, however, because of lack of certainty as to how the instruments will be treated for tax purposes. Also, unusual securities may be difficult to market publicly.

ALTERNATIVE A

Assumed net earnings	$25,000	$100,000	$150,000	$200,000
Number of shares	50,000	50,000	50,000	50,000
Earnings per share	$ 0.50	$ 2.00	$ 3.00	$ 4.00

ALTERNATIVE B

Assumed net earnings	$25,000	$100,000	$150,000	$200,000
Interest on bonds (8% on $250,000)	$20,000	$ 20,000	$ 20,000	$ 20,000
Earnings allocable to common[6]	$ 5,000	$ 80,000	$130,000	$180,000
Number of shares	25,000	25,000	25,000	25,000
Earnings per share	$ 0.20	$ 3.20	$ 5.20	$ 7.20

In alternative B, the interest represents a fixed cost, a charge for obtaining the use of $250,000 of capital. When earnings are low, debt service takes up most of the earnings: in the hypothetical above, if earnings drop below $20,000, alternative B will show losses while alternative A continues to show modest profits until earnings drop to zero. When earnings increase above $20,000, however, the per share earnings under alternative B rise much more rapidly than alternative A even though the shares are otherwise identical. In effect, in alternative B, the common shareholders are getting $500,000 to work for them even though they contributed only $250,000, at the cost of the fixed interest charge which they must meet out of their own capital if necessary. Even this fixed charge is partially offset by the tax saving resulting from the deductibility of the interest.[7] This is leverage, a device well understood by real estate syndicates and promoters who seek to obtain the largest possible mortgage and the smallest possible equity investment of their own. The risk, of course, is that the income from the project may not be sufficient to cover the fixed charges, and the investors may quickly be wiped out.[8]

Debt financing is attractive during periods of high inflation because the loans will ultimately be repaid with inflated dollars. Of course, the competition for loans in such circumstances may cause high interest charges which will offset, either wholly or partially, this advantage of debt financing.

---

6. [By the Editor] Computed simply by subtraction and without regard to reduction in income taxes as a result of the increased interest deduction.

7. [By the Editor] Nonparticipating preferred stock owned by third persons also creates leverage, which technically is a phenomenon of a senior, limited position rather than of debt. However, the tax advantage of debt—the deductibility of the interest—is lost if preferred stock is used, with the result that most leverage situations created today involve the issuance of debt. On the other hand, a corporation is entitled to a credit for dividends received, including dividends paid upon preferred stock.

8. [By the Editor] An economist might show impatience with an example such as that set forth in the text. Assuming that both the common shares and the bonds are publicly

traded (and with certain further simplifying assumptions), the economist would argue that the total value of the securities issued by the enterprise (the aggregate market value of all issued common shares plus all issued bonds) would be independent of the amount of debt in the capital structure of the enterprise. In other words, any increase in value of the common stock by reason of the corporation's capital structure would be offset by a decrease in the market price for the bonds. Even if this principle, first set forth by Miller and Modigliani, is abstractly accepted, a leveraged capital structure such as set forth in the example may benefit the common shareholders at the expense of the debtholders. Also, this relationship may not be visible to the holders of the bonds where the assumptions are not fully true, for example, where the debt is not publicly or widely held.

Leverage can generally be obtained only by the use of other people's money.[9]

2. TAX TREATMENT OF DEBT

In a C corporation, there are usually tax advantages for shareholders who are individuals to lend to the corporation a portion of their investment in the corporation rather than making a contribution to capital. Interest payments on debt are deductible by the borrower whereas dividend payments on equity securities are not.[10] A loan by a shareholder to his corporation therefore reduces the double tax problem of a C corporation. On the other hand, if the shareholder is a corporation, the shareholder may prefer to receive payments in the form of dividends rather than interest because of the dividend-received deduction,[11] even though this causes the "borrower" to lose the benefit of an interest deduction.

Because of the tax advantages of loans by individual shareholders to C corporations, there is an extensive jurisprudence as to whether debt should be reclassified as equity for tax purposes. A classic case is Slappey Drive Indus. Park v. United States, 561 F.2d 572 (5th Cir.1977), where the court stated:

> Articulating the essential difference between * * * [debt and equity] is no easy task. Generally, shareholders place their money "at the risk of the business" while lenders seek a more reliable return. That statement of course glosses over a good many considerations with which even the most inexperienced investor is abundantly familiar. A purchaser of General Motors stock may bear much less risk than a bona fide lender to a small corporation.
>
> Nevertheless, the "risk of the business" formulation has provided a shorthand description that courts have repeatedly invoked. Contributors of capital undertake the risk because of the potential return; in the form of profits and enhanced value, on their underlying investment. Lenders, on the other hand, undertake a degree of risk because of the expectancy of timely repayment with interest. Because a lender unrelated to the corporation stands to earn only a fixed amount of interest, he usually is unwilling to bear a substantial risk of corporate failure or to commit his funds for a prolonged period. A person ordinarily would not advance funds likely to be repaid only if the venture is successful without demanding the potential enhanced return associated with an equity investment.
>
> These considerations provide only imperfect guidance when the issue relates to a shareholder's purported loan to his own corporation, the usual situation encountered in debt-equity cases. It is well established that shareholders may loan money to their corporations and achieve

---

9. [By the Editor] Some leverage may also be obtained if loans by shareholders are made on a basis other than in proportion to their shareholdings.

10. [By the Editor] There are also technical differences between interest payments and dividends. For example, dividends are taxable to the provider of capital only if the corporation has earnings and profits, while interest is taxable in any event.

11. [By the Editor] In general terms, a corporation is entitled to a deduction of 70 percent of dividends received from a corporation of which the recipient owns less than 20 percent (by stock vote and value); the deduction is increased to 80 percent if the recipient corporation owns between 20 percent and 80 percent of the paying corporation, and to 100 percent if the recipient corporation owns more than 80 percent of the paying corporation.

corresponding tax treatment. When making such loans they could hardly be expected to ignore their shareholder status; their motivations will not match those of potential lenders who have no underlying equity interest. The "risk of the business" standard, though, continues to provide a backdrop for our analysis. While we should not expect a creditor-shareholder to evidence motivations and behavior conforming perfectly to those of a mere creditor, neither should we abandon the effort to determine whether the challenged transaction is in substance a contribution to capital masquerading as debt.

The Court then identified 13 factors that may be relevant in making the classification, and concluded that "[i]n the case at bar the most telling * * * factor[ ] is the corporate debtors' consistent failure to repay the debts on the due dates or to seek postponements. More generally, that failure and the corresponding absence of timely interest payments combine with * * * [the defendants'] testimony regarding the parties' view of their relationships to make clear that these transactions were in substance not at all the type arrangements for which debt treatment is appropriate."

The issue whether debt should be reclassified as equity for tax purposes arises in the S corporation context as well. It may be recalled that a corporation eligible to be taxed as an S corporation may have only one class of stock. See p. 151 supra. If an S corporation issues debt to shareholders that might be reclassified as equity under the C corporation precedents, is that corporation's S corporation status at risk? The IRS first took a rather literalistic approach in its regulations, arguing that "administrative complexities" compelled disallowance of S corporation status in all reclassification cases. Some courts accepted this view, but others did not, holding the regulations invalid. The leading case invalidating the regulations was Portage Plastics Co., Inc. v. United States, 486 F.2d 632 (7th Cir.1973). In 1982, Congress largely solved this problem by creating a "safe harbor" for "straight debt," the existence of which does not disqualify a corporation from the S corporation election. I.R.C. § 1361(c)(5) defines "straight debt" as debt that involves a written unconditional promise to pay a sum certain in money if (a) interest rates and interest payment dates are not contingent on profits, the borrower's discretion, or similar factors, (b) there is no direct or indirect convertibility into stock, and (c) the creditor is an eligible shareholder under Chapter S.

There was an irony in the attempts by the IRS to disqualify corporations from S corporation treatment on the basis of the existence of reclassifiable debt interests, since this special tax election was originally created to eliminate the double tax treatment that gives rise to the incentive for shareholders to create thin corporations to begin with.

Notes

(1) A "debt/equity ratio" is the mathematical ratio between a corporation's liabilities and the shareholders' equity. For example, a corporation with $10,000 of equity that borrows $100,000 has a debt/equity ratio of 10:1. This ratio may be calculated on an aggregate or overall liabilities basis (taking into account debts and obligations owed to persons other than shareholders) or on an "inside" basis (taking into account only debts owed to shareholders). At one time the Internal Revenue Service proposed regulations to the effect that debt would not be viewed

as "excessive" if the corporation's "outside" ratio was less than 10:1 and its "inside" ratio was less than or equal to 3:1. Is this a sensible way to create a "safe harbor" for shareholder-created debt? Would such a "safe harbor" be desirable?

(2) At one time, it was thought that under the case law an inside debt/equity ratio of 4:1 or higher would be decisive in reclassifying the debt as equity. This ratio test, originally based on a statement in John Kelley Co. v. Commissioner, 326 U.S. 521, 66 S.Ct. 299, 90 L.Ed. 278 (1946), was generally rejected by courts in favor of the more flexible approach set forth in *Slappey Drive*.

(3) A corporation with a high debt/equity ratio is sometimes referred to as a "thin corporation."

3. DEBT AS A PLANNING DEVICE

The advantages of debt as a planning device in closely held corporations are well illustrated by Obre v. Alban Tractor Co., 228 Md. 291, 179 A.2d 861 (1962). Obre and Nelson formed a new corporation, Annel Corporation, to engage in the dirt moving and road building business. Obre agreed to contribute to the corporation equipment and cash worth $65,548.10 while Nelson agreed to contribute $10,000 in cash and equipment. The equipment values were based on an independent appraisal. The parties agreed that control was to be shared equally from the outset. Acting upon the advice of "a well-known and reputable firm of certified public accountants," the parties capitalized the corporation as follows:

O → 65,548.10
N → 10,000

Obre: $10,000 par value voting common stock
        $20,000 par value non voting preferred stock
        $35,548.10 unsecured promissory note

Nelson: $10,000 par value voting common stock

The venture was an economic failure, shortly ending up in a state insolvency proceeding. In this proceeding, Obre successfully claimed the right to participate as an unsecured creditor to the extent of his $35,548.10 unsecured note. The unpaid trade creditors argued that a "subordinating equity" principle required that this note be treated as equity—a capital contribution—rather than as a valid debt. The Court rejected this argument, stating that there was no showing of undercapitalization, fraud, misrepresentation, or estoppel. In deciding that Annel Corporation was not undercapitalized, the Court treated Obre's preferred stock as an equity investment so that the corporation had begun business with $40,000 of equity and only $35,548.10 of debt. The Court held that there was no showing that $40,000 of equity capital was inadequate for a business such as Annel Corporation's. The Court also relied on the fact that Obre's "loan" to the corporation was either known to the creditors or could easily have been discovered by examining public state tax filings, by requesting a financial statement, or by obtaining a credit report.

Notes

(1) The "subordinating equity" concept is essentially the Deep Rock doctrine in a state law context. Do you think the trade creditors might have been more successful if they had placed Annel Corporation in federal bankruptcy proceedings?

(2) Was the Annel Corporation adequately capitalized? Isn't it reasonably clear that even $75,548.10 was not enough capital and that $40,000 was inadequate? Should this be a matter of proof or of presumption?

(3) Why did those certified public accountants recommend that a significant portion of Obre's contribution be in the form of debt rather than simply having a preferred stock investment of $55,548.10?

E. PLANNING THE CAPITAL STRUCTURE FOR THE CLOSELY HELD CORPORATION

Attorneys are often requested to review and make recommendations about the proposed capital structure of newly formed closely held ventures. Usually, the capital structure will be an integral part of broader control considerations in which individual participants attempt to ensure their continued right to participate in the venture and the attorney reviews the entire "package" as a single unit. Tax considerations may also be of critical importance. In reviewing proposed capital structures, an attorney will generally have several basic concerns, including:

(1) Will the structure "work"; i.e., will it stand up in the event of later disagreement and possible legal attack?

(2) Will the structure actually provide the desired result? For example, a person desiring a guaranteed, unconditional periodic payment who is asked to accept preferred stock should be made aware that the directors may usually forego declaring dividends on the preferred if they so desire.

(3) Will the desired tax treatment be available, or more likely, is the structure created one that makes the desired tax treatment probable if not certain? In this regard, the availability of the S corporation election may be of major importance to the participants.

(4) Might the structure give rise to unexpected liabilities? The most likely sources of unexpected liabilities are the possible application of the concepts of par value and watered stock (in states that still recognize such concepts) and, possibly, the ubiquitous doctrine of piercing the corporate veil.

(5) Are his or her clients' financial contributions reasonably protected and reasonably fairly treated in the event of unexpected or calamitous occurrences causing the sudden and premature termination of the venture?

This listing is only partial. Depending on the circumstances, participants will usually have additional concerns about the capital structure. For example, a person planning on contemplated periodic payments for living expenses may wish to have assurance that corporate matters are handled conservatively and not in a way that may jeopardize future distributions. Other persons may wish to have a major voice in fiscal management and future plans to raise additional capital which may affect their roles in the venture. Considerations about capital structure obviously shade over into questions relating to control over the venture in general, and indeed should be addressed as part of the broader considerations of control.

Notes

(1) These various factors may be illustrated by an analysis of the AB Furniture Store, where A is to contribute $100,000 in cash and B is to render

services in exchange for a "salary" and a 50 percent interest in the business. Further, assume that B is to have "earned out" his 50 percent interest at the end of two years. Assuming that the corporation is formed under the 1969 Model Act, consider the following alternatives:

(a) At the outset of the venture, A and B are each issued 1,000 shares of stock, par value of $100 per share. Does B have watered stock liability? What about MBCA (1969) § 19, second paragraph?

(b) At the outset of the venture, 100 shares of stock, $1 par value, are issued to A for $100,000; 100 shares are issued to B only after he has performed services for two years in consideration of such services. Does this avoid the § 19 and watered stock problems? What happens if A decides to close out the business after eighteen months? Where does B stand? (B, however, may have a breach of contract action against A if A wrongfully excludes B from the venture in violation of the agreement.)

(c) At the outset of the venture, 100 shares of stock, par value of $1, are issued to A for $100,000; B executes a promissory note for $100,000, payable in two years out of future services, and B is issued 100 shares in exchange for that note. Again consider MBCA (1969) § 19. As indicated earlier, some states permit shares to be issued in exchange for a promissory note; in those states, B presumably would be simultaneously a shareholder and a debtor.

(d) At the outset of the venture, shares of common stock are issued to A and B at different prices. For example, using $1.00 par value shares, 100 shares are issued to A for $100,000 and 100 shares are issued to B for $100. B actually pays the $100. So long as there is full disclosure, is there anything improper in issuing otherwise identical shares for different prices? Even if this is proper, what happens if there is a fire shortly after the venture is begun, covered by insurance, and the parties decide to liquidate and distribute the insurance proceeds? Would not B be entitled to $50,000, even though he invested only $100? There is also an income tax problem from B's standpoint, since the bargain purchase of shares will probably be treated as compensation to B which is fully taxable in the year in which he receives the shares. This income tax problem is involved in some of the other alternatives as well, including alternatives (b) and (c).

(e) At the outset of the venture, two classes of common shares are created with identical rights per share on dissolution, but with different voting rights:

(i) Class A common, par value $1.00 per share, one vote per share, 10,000 shares issued to A for $10.00 per share, or a total of $100,000.

(ii) Class B common, par value $1.00 per share, one thousand votes per share, 10 shares issued to B for $10.00 per share, or a total of $100.

If this technique were followed, how should the relative dividend rights of the two shares be established? (If dividend rights differ, which will probably be the case, the S corporation election is unavailable.) Generally, the MBCA permits multiple or fractional votes per share; some state statutes, however, permit only single votes per share. Obviously, essentially the same structure could be created with fractional votes per share.

(f) At the outset of the venture, a single class of shares is created with a par value of $1.00 per share, and 10 shares are issued to A for $100 and 10 shares are issued to B for $100. A then lends the corporation $99,800 to complete the capitalization. Would that loan qualify for the "straight debt" safe harbor for the S corporation election? What should be the terms of repayment? Of interest? Is it fair to B to require that a commercial rate of interest be paid to A?

(g) At the outset of the venture, two classes of shares, preferred and common, are created each with a par value of $1.00 per share; 10 shares of common stock are issued to A for $100, 10 shares of common stock are issued to B for $100, and 9,980 shares of preferred stock are issued to A at $10 per share for $99,800, completing the capitalization. How should the dividend right of the preferred stock be established? Why is this alternative less attractive than others?

(h) Combine alternatives (f) and (g) as follows: at the outset of the venture, two classes of shares, preferred and common, are created each with a par value of $1.00 per share; ten shares of common are issued to A and B for $100 each; A is also issued 5,000 shares of preferred for $50,000 and lends the corporation the remaining $49,800, completing the capitalization. Is this an improvement over both alternatives (f) and (g)? Does it resemble the structure proposed by that "well-known and reputable firm of certified public accountants" in *Obre*?

(i) Combine alternatives (d) and (f) as follows: at the outset of the venture, one class of common stock with a par value of $1.00 per share is created, and ten shares are issued to A for $50,000 and ten shares to B for $100. A then lends the corporation the remaining $49,900. Is this the best solution?

(2) What difference would the enactment of the MBCA make in the above alternatives? The elimination of par value and the restrictions on eligible consideration obviously simplify several of the alternatives, but the choices involving different classes of common shares and the mixing of debt and preferred shares in the capital structure are basically unaffected. It would be possible under the MBCA to have B sign a two-year employment contract and issue all shares immediately. This, however, is not without its disadvantages. First, there may be a bunching of B's income for tax purposes in the year the corporation is formed. Second, what is the corporation to do with the employment contract if the fire described in example 1(d) above occurs? Sell it? To whom and for how much? B's shares have been properly issued so that B is entitled to share ratably with A in the assets; A might quite justifiably object if no attempt is made to realize upon this "asset."

(3) In many instances one or more investors will contribute appreciated property to the corporation in exchange for stock. The issue raised by such a contribution is whether the contributor will be taxed on the appreciation when he receives stock for the property, or in tax terms, whether the gain will be "recognized." Section 351 of the Internal Revenue Code provides for non-recognition of gain or loss on contributions of property to a corporation solely in exchange for shares if the contributing shareholders own more than 80 percent of the shares of the corporation immediately after the transfer. If gain is not recognized, the corporation assumes the tax basis of the property in the hands of the contributor. A contributor is taxed on any "boot" he receives (as in "stock and money, to boot") or in some rare circumstances if the contributed property is subject to a lien. In most circumstances, an encumbrance on contributed property simply operates to reduce the basis of the property in the hands of the corporation.

(4) In the AB Furniture Store, A is a passive investor, putting in capital but not participating in the day-to-day affairs of the store. As indicated above, such investors often demand, and are entitled to receive, some sort of return on their investment. The choice of "how much" and "when" are obviously sensitive business decisions that must be negotiated. From the standpoint of the venture, if the S corporation election is unavailable, it is usually advantageous for such payments to be in deductible form rather than as nondeductible dividends on, say,

a special class of preferred shares. On the other hand, it is also usually desirable to give the corporation the option to defer or omit such payments if business demands dictate. That, of course, means that the debt is no longer within the "straight debt" safe harbor for the S corporation election. On such issues it is not uncommon for different participants to have different and inconsistent goals which must be accommodated, adjusted, or compromised before the venture can begin.

(5) In many of the above alternatives, the interests of A and B are potentially, if not actually, adverse. If B is without a lawyer, an attorney representing A faces essentially the same ethical problems that must be addressed when considering the more basic question of the form of the enterprise. See Chapter 3, Section D, part (h), pages 164–165, supra. As indicated there, B is very likely to resist retaining a lawyer for reasons of cost, and may wish to rely on A's lawyer to represent his interests as well as A's. If you were A's lawyer in this situation, would you feel comfortable in giving B advice as well as A? Are the problems associated with par value, classes of stock, watered stock, S corporation election, Deep Rock, and other issues arising in the capitalization area of such complexity that you should insist B retain his own lawyer? In an electronic symposium dealing with a situation similar to this, most practicing attorneys stated they would not agree to represent both parties because of concerns about mandatory disclosure, conflict of interest, and about being sued if the venture turns out badly. Several law professors argued that there should be some basis on which an attorney can give limited assistance to a party with full disclosure of the limits to the person involved without incurring liability for malpractice.

F. PUBLIC OFFERINGS

THOMAS LEE HAZEN, TREATISE ON THE LAW OF SECURITIES REGULATION
Vol. 1, pp. 6–8 (2d ed. 1990).*

Beginning in the late nineteenth century the eastern industrialists found fertile ground for securities in the developing American frontier. There were many questionable practices and as a result pressures arose to regulate the marketing of fraudulently valued securities. Accordingly in 1911 Kansas passed the first state security statutory regulation which is also known as a "blue sky law" because of its purpose to protect the Kansas farmers against the industrialists' selling them a piece of the blue sky. A number of states followed suit and blue sky laws began to spring up throughout the country; today all states have blue sky legislation. The state blue sky laws not only focused on disclosure but also required that all securities registered thereunder "qualify" on a merit basis; that is, the state securities commissioner had the power to pass on the merits of the investment. Notwithstanding the broad regulatory potential of the merit approach, the blue sky laws proved to be relatively ineffective in stamping out securities frauds, especially on a national level. For a while federal legislation was successfully resisted. The stock market crash of 1929 can be viewed as the straw that broke the camel's back.

Although the general economic condition went a long way toward causing the Wall Street crash of 1929, the number of fraudulently floated securities that contributed to the great crash cannot be underestimated. In fact, the congressional hearings are replete with examples of outrageous conduct that most certainly had a great impact on our nation's disastrous economy. As a result, Congress entered into the regulatory arena with the Securities Act of 1933 which is also known as the "Truth in Securities" Act.[12] At the time of enactment, the 1933 Act was administered by the Federal Trade Commission. The FTC's securities law jurisdiction was replaced in 1934 with the SEC. The 1933 Act * * * is directed primarily at the distribution of securities. Subject to certain enumerated exemptions, the Securities Act of 1933 generally, requires the registration of all securities being placed in the hands of the public for the first time.[13] After considerable debate, Congress decided not to follow the pattern of the state acts and eschewed the idea of a merit approach, opting instead for a system of full disclosure. The theory behind the federal regulatory framework is that investors are adequately protected if all * * * aspects of the securities being marketed are fully and fairly disclosed and thus there is no need for the more time-consuming merit analysis of the securities being offered. The Securities Act of 1933 contains a number of private remedies for investors who are injured due to violations of the Act.[14] There are also general anti-fraud provisions which bar material omissions and misrepresentations in connection with the sale of securities. The scope of the Securities Act of 1933 is limited; first, insofar as it covers only distributions of securities and second, as its investor protection reach extends only to purchasers of securities.

In 1934 Congress enacted the Securities Exchange Act of 1934[15] which is a more omnibus regulation. The extent of the regulation was so vast that Congress felt it was not possible to continue overburdening the Federal Trade

---

12. [By the Author] 15 U.S.C.A. §§ 77a–77aa.

13. [By the Author] * * * This includes not only primary distributions (sold by the issuer), but also secondary distributions wherein the securities are sold by individuals or institutions who did not acquire the securities in a public offering.

14. [By the Editor] The most important of these private remedies are the following: 1) Section 11 permits purchasers of securities in a registered offering to bring suits for losses incurred if the prospectus contains misleading statements of material facts. Reliance by the purchaser on the false statement is not required, but a purchaser cannot recover if he or she knew of the misstatement when making the purchase. The issuer is strictly liable under Section 11; officers, directors, underwriters, and other persons named in the registration statement as having prepared or certified any part of the registration statement, may also be liable unless they can establish that they made a reasonable investigation or relied on experts. 2) Section 12(1) permits any purchaser of securities that should have been registered, but were not, to rescind the purchase without regard to fault or misstatement. If the securities are no longer owned by the purchaser, the defendant is liable for damages based on the loss calculated as the difference between the plaintiff's purchase price and sales price. 3) Section 12(2) imposes liability on any seller for material misstatements or omissions in connection with the sale of securities subject only to the defense that the seller did not know and with reasonable care would not have known that the statement was false or omitted. Purchasers have the right to bring suit to recover their losses if there are incomplete or inaccurate disclosures of material facts in the prospectus, without regard to intent or negligence. Persons who may be liable include the issuer itself, its responsible directors and officers, the underwriters, holders of controlling interests, and the sellers of the securities in a secondary offering. In 1995, the Supreme Court in Gustafson v. Alloyd Co., 513 U.S. 561, 115 S.Ct. 1061, 131 L.Ed.2d 1 (1995), sharply narrowed § 12(2) by limiting it to misstatements in the public documents filed in connection with the offering. The draconian nature of these civil remedies is softened by reason of a relatively short statute of limitations: one year from the date of discovery but in no event more than three years after the public distribution.

15. [By the Editor] 15 U.S.C.A. § 78a et seq. The most important antifraud provision under this Act is Rule 10b–5, discussed at length in Chapter 12.

Commission with this new administrative responsibility and thus established the Securities and Exchange Commission which is now one of the largest federal agencies. The Exchange Act of 1934 is directed at regulating all aspects of public trading of securities. * * *

Whenever a corporation makes an offering of shares, consideration must be given to the possible application of the state and federal securities laws. If the offering is made to only a few persons, one or more exemptions will often be available, though that cannot be absolutely guaranteed simply by the size of the offering; if the offering is made in a public manner or to numerous persons, there is a presumption that compliance with both state and federal law will be necessary unless an exemption is clearly available.

———

Full compliance with the Securities Act of 1933, 15 U.S.C.A. §§ 77a–77aa, involves the filing of a registration statement with the Securities and Exchange Commission pursuant to Section 5 of the Act. A registration statement consists of two parts: 1) a "prospectus," a document that is to be distributed to potential and actual investors, and 2) additional information that must be submitted to the SEC and is publicly available but need not be included in the prospectus. Registration of an issue by an "unseasoned company," i.e. one whose shares are not widely traded in the public markets and which has never previously filed a registration statement under the 1933 Act, is an expensive, complex and often messy process. Robert W. Hamilton and Richard A. Booth, Business Basics for Law Students: Essential Terms and Concepts (1998):[16]

A registered public sale of securities will usually involve the use of professional securities underwriters and securities firms to distribute the securities to the investing public. An underwriter is a person or organization that acquires shares for resale or who arranges the direct sale of shares by the issuer. Investment bankers and securities firms regularly underwrite new securities issues on a commercial basis. Large issues are "syndicated" or broken up among a number of securities firms and sold by them to investors. There is a precept in the securities business that "shares are sold not bought" and that professional selling assistance is essential for most successful floatations of new securities. The flip side, of course, is that underwriting fees and sales commissions add significantly to the cost of the public offering. Nevertheless professional assistance may be a bargain in the long run, since a do-it-yourself public offering may not raise enough capital. * * *

There are significant advantages to a public offering. A successful public offer may create a market for the shares of the corporation: The entrepreneur may later use this market to liquidate a portion of his or her investment in the business. Further, very large amounts of capital may be raised through a public offering. * * *

There are significant disadvantages as well. The cost of a public offering for an "unseasoned" company (one that has not previously made

---

16. Reprinted with permission of Aspen Law & Business/Panel Publishers, a division of   Aspen Publishers, Inc. The text set forth above is subject to further revision.

a public offering) is so substantial that a public offering of at least $10,000,000 is necessary to justify the expense. Further, there are substantial disclosure obligations with respect to previous transactions that the entrepreneur may prefer not be made public. Finally, a public company takes on disclosure and other legal obligations that add to the cost of operation and limit the amount of information about future developments that may be kept confidential. Whether or not these disadvantages outweigh the advantages cannot be answered in the abstract.

Notes

(1) A registration statement of a company making an initial public offering (usually referred to as an "IPO") must contain information about 27 items described in Schedule A of the 1933 Act; additional disclosure requirements appear in SEC Regulation S–K and on the registration statement form (form S–1) itself. The company must also arrange to have certified financial statements prepared in accordance with Regulation S–X for the previous three years. Preparation of these financial statements by an independent auditor is usually difficult and expensive, often complicated by incomplete or misleading financial records. Virtually all closely held companies find that their existing financial statements must be significantly revised to meet the requirements of Regulation S–X even if they were originally prepared by an outside auditor and were believed to be entirely suitable for their own needs while privately held.

(2) Securities registration from the standpoint of the attorney is a highly specialized and complex matter. The "corporate check" required for an IPO usually involves the cooperation of two sets of attorneys: Those representing the issuer and those representing the underwriter. Because the 1933 Act imposes substantial civil liabilities, the attorneys must examine carefully the background of prior transactions, determine whether disclosure may be required of transactions between the issuer and the managers, determine whether prior issues of securities were lawfully made pursuant to an available exemption, and so forth. The process by which attorneys verify the accuracy and completeness of registration statements is usually referred to as a "due diligence" investigation. A sloppily prepared or incomplete registration statement may subject the attorneys to personal liability to investors as well as causing damage to their reputations if they are named as parties in a securities fraud or disciplinary proceeding. The number of suits filed against attorneys under the 1933 Act is surprisingly large, and this type of practice is viewed as a high risk practice. Insurers may be reluctant to write malpractice insurance for securities attorneys in solo practice or with small firms. This, plus the fact that the SEC disclosure requirements are complex, means that lawyers generally should not attempt a securities registration unless they are specialists in this area or they obtain the assistance of specialized counsel. Full-scale registration of an initial public offering by a closely held corporation is considered in detail in advanced law school courses in securities regulation.

The standard fee for the investment banker is seven percent of the issue; additional fees for lawyers and accountants routinely run into the hundreds of thousands of dollars. Clearly, it is a complex undertaking and for many small companies, simply out of the question. Smaller companies must structure their capital-raising activities to avoid the registration requirement. The balance of this Section deals specifically with *exemptions* from the registration requirement that may be used by small businesses.

(4) In addition to the registration requirements of the 1933 Act, public offerings traditionally had to comply with state blue sky laws in the states in which securities are to be offered. In the case of a nationwide offering, that meant compliance with 50 different blue sky laws. This process was referred to as "blue skying" an issue and was a specialized subbranch of the practice of securities law. In 1996 Congress enacted a major statute, the National Securities Markets Improvement Act "NSMIA" Pub.L. 104–290, 110 Stat. 3416 (1996), that attempted to rationalize and simplify the registration process for registered public corporations by preempting a significant portions of the state blue sky laws. For a negative preliminary review of this statute, see Rutherford B. Campbell, Jr., Blue Sky Laws and Recent Preemption Failure, 22 J.Corp.L. 175 (1997).

(5) NSMIA does preempt state blue sky laws with respect to full scale securities registrations of the type described above, and thus very materially simplifies the problems of corporations making full scale, nation-wide initial public offerings. However, it arguably does not preempt or affect the blue sky registration process for securities that are sold publicly pursuant to an *exemption* from the federal registration process, and, today, most capital raising by closely held corporations is pursuant to one or more of these exemptions (which are described below).

SECURITIES AND EXCHANGE COMM'N v. RALSTON PURINA CO.

Supreme Court of the United States, 1953.
346 U.S. 119, 73 S.Ct. 981, 97 L.Ed. 1494.

MR. JUSTICE CLARK, delivered the opinion of the Court.

Section [4(2)] of the Securities Act of 1933 exempts "transactions by an issuer not involving any public offering" from the registration requirements of § 5. We must decide whether Ralston Purina's offerings of treasury stock to its "key employees" are within this exemption. On a complaint brought by the Commission under § 20(b) of the Act seeking to enjoin respondent's unregistered offerings, the District Court held the exemption applicable and dismissed the suit. The Court of Appeals affirmed. The question has arisen many times since the Act was passed; an apparent need to define the scope of the private offering exemption prompted certiorari. 345 U.S. 903, 73 S.Ct. 643.

Ralston Purina manufactures and distributes various feed and cereal products. Its processing and distribution facilities are scattered throughout the United States and Canada, staffed by some 7,000 employees. At least since 1911 the company has had a policy of encouraging stock ownership among its employees; more particularly, since 1942 it has made authorized but unissued common shares available to some of them. Between 1947 and 1951, the period covered by the record in this case, Ralston Purina sold nearly $2,000,000 of stock to employees without registration and in so doing made use of the mails.

In each of these years, a corporate resolution authorized the sale of common stock "to employees * * * who shall, without any solicitation by the Company or its officers or employees, inquire of any of them as to how to purchase common stock of Ralston Purina Company." A memorandum sent to branch and store managers after the resolution was adopted, advised that "The only employees to whom this stock will be available will be those who take the initiative and are interested in buying stock at present market prices." Among those responding to these offers were employees with the duties of artist, bakeshop foreman, chow loading foreman, clerical assistant, copywriter, electrician, stock clerk, mill office clerk, order credit trainee, production trainee, stenographer, and veterinarian. The buyers lived in over fifty widely separated communities scattered from Garland, Texas, to Nashua, New Hampshire and Visalia, California. The lowest salary bracket of those purchasing was $2,700 in 1949, $2,435 in 1950 and $3,107 in 1951. The record shows that in 1947, 234 employees bought stock, 20 in 1948, 414 in 1949, 411 in 1950, and the 1951 offer, interrupted by this litigation, produced 165 applications to purchase. No records were kept of those to whom the offers were made; the estimated number in 1951 was 500.

The company bottoms its exemption claim on the classification of all offerees as "key employees" in its organization. Its position on trial was that "A key employee * * * is not confined to an organization chart. It would include an individual who is eligible for promotion, an individual who especially influences others or who advises others, a person whom the employees look to in some special way, an individual, of course, who carries some special responsibility, who is sympathetic to management and who is ambitious and who the management feels is likely to be promoted to a greater responsibility." That an offering to all of its employees would be public is conceded.

The Securities Act nowhere defines the scope of [§ 4(2)'s] private offering exemption. Nor is the legislative history of much help in staking out its boundaries. * * *

Decisions under comparable exemptions in the English Companies Acts and state "blue sky" laws, the statutory antecedents of federal securities legislation have made one thing clear—to be public, an offer need not be open to the whole world. In Securities and Exchange Comm. v. Sunbeam Gold Mines Co., 9 Cir., 1938, 95 F.2d 699, 701, this point was made in dealing with an offering to the stockholders of two corporations about to be merged. Judge Denman observed that:

> In its broadest meaning the term 'public' distinguishes the populace at large from groups of individual members of the public segregated because of some common interest or characteristic. Yet such a distinction is inadequate for practical purposes; manifestly an offering of securities to all redheaded men, to all residents of Chicago or San Francisco, to all existing stockholders of the General Motors Corporation or the American Telephone & Telegraph Company, is no less 'public', in every realistic sense of the word, than an unrestricted offering to the world at large. Such an offering, though not open to everyone who may choose to apply, is none the less 'public' in character, for the means used to select the particular individuals to whom the offering is to be made bear no sensible relation to the purposes for which the selection is made. * * * To determine the distinction between 'public' and 'private' in any particular context, it is essential to examine the circumstances under which the distinction is sought to be established and to consider the purposes sought to be achieved by such distinction.

The courts below purported to apply this test. The District Court held, in the language of the Sunbeam decision, that "The purpose of the selection bears a 'sensible relation' to the class chosen," finding that "The sole purpose of the 'selection' is to keep part stock ownership of the business within the operating personnel of the business and to spread ownership throughout all departments and activities of the business." The Court of Appeals treated the case as involving "an offering, without solicitation, of common stock to a selected group of key employees of the issuer, most of whom are already stockholders when the offering is made, with the sole purpose of enabling them to secure a proprietary interest in the company or to increase the interest already held by them."

Exemption from the registration requirements of the Securities Act is the question. The design of the statute is to protect investors by promoting full disclosure of information thought necessary to informed investment decisions. The natural way to interpret the private offering exemption is in light of the statutory purpose. Since exempt transactions are those as to which "there is no practical need for * * * [the bill's] application," the applicability of [§ 4(2)] should turn on whether the particular class of persons affected need the protection of the Act. An offering to those who are shown to be able to fend for themselves is a transaction "not involving any public offering."

The Commission would have us go one step further and hold that "an offering to a substantial number of the public" is not exempt under [§ 4(2)]. We are advised that "whatever the special circumstances, the Commission has consistently interpreted the exemption as being inapplicable when a large number of offerees is involved." But the statute would seem to apply to a "public offering" whether to few or many. It may well be that offerings to a substantial number of persons would rarely be exempt. Indeed nothing prevents the commission, in enforcing the statute, from using some kind of numerical test in deciding when to investigate particular exemption claims. But there is no warrant for superimposing a quantity limit on private offerings as a matter of statutory interpretation.

The exemption, as we construe it, does not deprive corporate employees, as a class, of the safeguards of the Act. We agree that some employee offerings may come within [§ 4(2)], e.g., one made to executive personnel who because of their position have access to the same kind of information that the act would make available in the form of a registration statement. Absent such a showing of special circumstances, employees are just as much members of the investing "public" as any of their neighbors in the community. * * *

Keeping in mind the broadly remedial purposes of federal securities legislation, imposition of the burden of proof on an issuer who would plead the exemption seems to us fair and reasonable. Agreeing, the court below thought the burden met primarily because of the respondent's purpose in singling out its key employees for stock offerings. But once it is seen that the exemption question turns on the knowledge of the offerees, the issuer's motives, laudable though they may be, fade into irrelevance. The focus of inquiry should be on the need of the offerees for the protections afforded by registration. The employees here were not shown to have access to the kind of information which registration would disclose. The obvious opportunities for pressure and imposition make it advisable that they be entitled to compliance with § 5.

Reversed.

THE CHIEF JUSTICE and MR. JUSTICE BURTON dissent.

Notes

(1) Assume that a corporation seeking to take advantage of the non-public offering exemption inadvertently makes one offer to a person who needs the protection of the Securities Act under the *Ralston Purina* test. Is the exemption thereby totally lost and full-scale registration required? For an affirmative answer, see Doran v. Petroleum Management Corp., 545 F.2d 893 (5th Cir.1977). See also SEC v. Murphy, 626 F.2d 633 (9th Cir.1980).

(2) Could Ralston Purina have avoided the impact of the holding in this case by structuring its stock sale plan in the form of a sale to a corporate officer (such as the president or a vice president) who clearly did not need the protection of the Act, and then having that officer sell shares to employees who asked about the possibility of stock purchases? In a word, the answer is "no." Section 2(11) of the 1933 Act, 15 U.S.C.A. § 77b, defines an "underwriter" to mean "any person who has purchased from an issuer with a view to, or offers or sells for an issuer in connection with, the distribution of any security * * *." Thus, the officer becomes an "underwriter" and the suggested transaction violates § 5 of the Act.

(3) Section 2(11) of the 1933 Act also states that the term "issuer" in the provision quoted in note (2) includes "any person directly or indirectly controlling or controlled by the issuer, or any person under direct or indirect common control with the issuer." The effect of this language is to impose on controlling or controlled persons the same obligation as is imposed on issuers under the Securities Act. Thus, the sole shareholder of a successful company cannot avoid the registration requirements of the 1933 Act simply by selling shares from his personal portfolio to the public rather than arranging for the corporation to sell shares directly. (Of course, such a transaction might be unattractive because it would divert the proceeds of the sale from the corporation to the sole shareholder.) If the sole shareholder in the above hypothetical wished to obtain personally a portion of the capital to be raised in the public offering, he may include a portion of his holdings in the registration statement prepared on behalf of the corporation, and the shares so registered would then be sold as part of the public offering. This is known as a "secondary offering."

(4) It is quite common for a corporation that has completed a sale of securities registered under the 1933 Act to also have outstanding shares that have not been registered. For example, if Ralston Purina had offered its shares only to persons who did not need the protection of the Act, those shares could be issued without registration. At the same time, Ralston Purina had many publicly traded shares outstanding, and an active market existed for Ralston Purina shares. Can a person who received unregistered shares in a nonpublic offer simply resell those shares in the public market in light of the § 2(11) definition of "underwriter"? How can a person who acquires shares in a legitimate § 4(2) transaction, ever safely resell those shares in light of this definition? The SEC has adopted Rule 144, 17 C.F.R. § 230.144, to establish guidelines for the resale of unregistered shares (often called "restricted stock") by investors without concern that the seller may be deemed to be an "underwriter" under § 2(11). Rule 144 basically establishes a one-year holding requirement; this Rule is complex, however, and cannot be simply summarized. Rule 144 is not exclusive, so resales in some circumstances within the one year period may be consistent with the original nonpublic offering exemption even though they do not comply with Rule 144. (Rule 144 probably would not permit the president or vice president to offer shares in the hypothetical set forth in note (2) above.)

(5) The § 2(11) definition of underwriter also creates problems for the issuer. Assume that Ralston Purina offers unregistered shares only to persons who do not need the protection of the Act and thus are exempt from registration under § 4(2). Nevertheless, has it violated the Act if one of the offerees unknown to Ralston Purina is a § 2(11) underwriter since he purchased "with a view to" further distribution of the shares? As a practical matter, issuers routinely take steps to prevent inadvertent sales of unregistered shares to statutory underwriters. The excerpts from Regulation D later in this Section describe devices the issuer may use to avoid such inadvertent violations of the Securities Act.

SECURITIES ACT RELEASE NO. 33–5450
39 Fed.Reg. 2353 (1974).

BACKGROUND AND PURPOSE

Section 3(a)(11) of the Securities Act of 1933 exempts "any security which is a part of an issue offered and sold only to persons resident within a single State * * * where the issuer of such security is a person resident and doing business within or, if a corporation, incorporated by and doing business within, such State." [This section] was intended to allow issuers with localized operations to sell securities as part of a plan of local financing. Congress apparently believed that a company whose operations are restricted to one area should be able to raise money from investors in the immediate vicinity without having to register the securities with a federal agency. In theory, the investors would be protected both by their proximity to the issuer and by state regulation. Rule 147 reflects this Congressional intent and is limited in its application to transactions where state regulation will be most effective. The Commission has consistently taken the position that the exemption applies only to local financing provided by local investors for local companies. To satisfy the exemption, the entire issue must be offered and sold exclusively to residents of the state in which the issuer is resident and doing business. An offer or sale of part of the issue to a single non-resident will destroy the exemption for the entire issue.

Certain basic questions have arisen in connection with interpreting section 3(a)(11). They are:

1. What transactions does the section cover;

2. What is "part of an issue" for purposes of the Section;

3. When is a person "resident within" a state or territory for purposes of the section; and

4. What does "doing business within" mean in the context of the Section?

The courts and the Commission have addressed themselves to these questions in the context of different fact situations, and some general guidelines have been developed. Certain guidelines were set forth by the Commission in Securities Act Release No. 4434 and, in part, are reflected in Rule 147. However, in certain aspects, as pointed out below, the rule differs from past interpretations.

THE TRANSACTION CONCEPT

Although the intrastate offering exemption is contained in section 3 of the Act, which section is phrased in terms of exempt "securities" rather than "transactions", the legislative history and Commission and judicial interpretations indicate that the exemption covers only specific transactions and not the securities themselves. Rule 147 reflects this interpretation.

THE "PART OF AN ISSUE" CONCEPT

The determination of what constitutes "part of an issue" for purposes of the exemption, i.e. what should be "integrated", has traditionally been dependent on the facts involved in each case. * * * [The Commission refers to the same factors that are discussed in Rule 230.502, page 000, infra.]

THE "PERSON RESIDENT WITHIN" CONCEPT

The object of the section 3(a)(11) exemption, i.e., to restrict the offering to persons within the same locality as the issuer who are, by reason of their proximity, likely to be familiar with the issuer and protected by the state law governing the issuer, is best served by interpreting the residence requirement narrowly. In addition, the determination of whether all parts of the issue have been sold only to residents can be made only after the securities have "come to rest" within the state or territory. Rule 147 retains these concepts, but provides more objective standards for determining when a person is considered a resident within a state for purposes of the rule and when securities have come to rest within a state.

THE "DOING BUSINESS WITHIN" REQUIREMENT

Because the primary purpose of the intrastate exemption was to allow an essentially local business to raise money within the state where the investors would be likely to be familiar with the business and with the management, the doing business requirement has traditionally been viewed strictly. First, not only should the business be located within the state, but the principal or predominant business must be carried on there. Second, substantially all of the proceeds of the offering must be put to use within the local area.

Rule 147 reinforces these requirements by providing specific percentage amounts of business that must be conducted within the state, and of proceeds from the offering that must be spent in connection with such business. In addition, the rule requires that the principal office of the issuer be within the state. * * *

[The text of Rule 147 is omitted.]

Notes

(1) Section 5 of the Securities Act of 1933 in effect requires registration of a public issue that is offered or sold through the "use of any means or instruments of transportation or communication in interstate commerce or of the mails." Precisely what advantage does § 3(a)(11) provide over avoidance of all use of the mails or the facilities of interstate commerce? As a practical matter, can a small business raise capital while avoiding all use of the mails or the facilities of interstate commerce? What about making an intrastate telephone call? Using an overnight delivery service? A "fax"? An "e-mail" message?

(2) The combination of *Ralston Purina* and the narrow Rule 147 construction of the § 3(a)(11) exemption obviously complicates the raising of capital by small businesses that can ill-afford the cost of a full-scale Form S–1 registration. The result was that it was widely believed that the registration process had a negative impact on capital-raising by small businesses. In 1980, Congress enacted legislation (described below) designed to minimize this impact. In 1982, the SEC adopted

Regulation D, a series of limited offering exemptions predominantly for small businesses. In 1992, it adopted a series of additional amendments to its regulations pursuant to its so-called "Small Business Initiative."

SECURITIES ACT RELEASE NO. 33–6389

47 Fed.Reg. 11251 (1982).

SUMMARY

The Commission announces the adoption of a new regulation governing certain offers and sales of securities without registration under the Securities Act of 1933 and a uniform notice of sales form to be used for all offerings under the regulation. The regulation replaces three exemptions and four forms, all of which are being rescinded. The new regulation is designed to simplify and clarify existing exemptions, to expand their availability, and to achieve uniformity between federal and state exemptions in order to facilitate capital formation consistent with the protection of investors. * * *

I. Background

Regulation D is the product of the Commission's evaluation of the impact of its rules and regulations on the ability of small businesses to raise capital. This study has revealed a particular concern that the registration requirements and the exemptive scheme of the Securities Act impose disproportionate restraints on small issuers. * * *

Coincident with the Commission's small business program, Congress enacted the Small Business Investment Incentive Act of 1980 (the "Incentive Act") [94 Stat. 2275 (codified in scattered sections of 15 U.S.C.A.)]. The Incentive Act included three changes to the Securities Act: the addition of an exemption in Section 4(6) for offers and sales solely to accredited investors,[17] the increase in the ceiling of Section 3(b) from $2,000,000 to $5,000,000,[18] and the addition of Section 19(c) which, among other things, authorized "the development of a uniform exemption from registration for small issuers which can be agreed upon among several States or between the States and the Federal Government." * * *

Commentary to the Commission criticized the complexity of the exemptive scheme as it relates to all issuers. * * *

---

17. [By the Editor] Section 4(6) provides an exemption for "transactions involving offers or sales by an issuer solely to one or more accredited investors, if the aggregate offering price of an issue of securities offered in reliance on this paragraph does not exceed [$5,000,000], if there is no advertising or public solicitation in connection with the transaction by the issuer or anyone acting on the issuer's behalf, and if the issuer files such notice with the Commission as the Commission shall prescribe."

18. [By the Editor] Section 3(b) provides:
The Commission may from time to time by its rules and regulations, and subject to such terms and conditions as may be prescribed therein, add any class of securities to the securities exempted as provided in this section, if it finds that the enforcement of this subchapter with respect to such securities is not necessary in the public interest and for the protection of investors by reason of the small amount involved or the limited character of the public offering; but no issue of securities shall be exempted under this subsection where the aggregate amount at which such issue is offered to the public exceeds $5,000,000.

REGULATION D—RULES GOVERNING THE LIMITED OFFER AND SALE OF SECURITIES WITHOUT REGISTRATION UNDER THE SECURITIES ACT OF 1933

17 C.F.R. § 230.501 et seq. (1997).

PRELIMINARY NOTES

1. The following rules relate to transactions exempted from the registration requirements of section 5 of the Securities Act of 1933 (the *Act*). * * *

2. Nothing in these rules obviates the need to comply with any applicable state law relating to the offer and sale of securities. Regulation D is intended to be a basic element in a uniform system of Federal–State limited offering exemptions consistent with the provisions of sections 18 and 19(c) of the Act. * * *

6. In view of the objectives of these rules and the policies underlying the Act, regulation D is not available to any issuer for any transaction or chain of transactions that, although in technical compliance with these rules, is part of a plan or scheme to evade the registration provisions of the Act. In such cases, registration under the Act is required. * * *

§ 230.501 Definitions and terms used in Regulation D.

As used in Regulation D, the following terms shall have the meaning indicated:

(a) *Accredited investor.* *Accredited investor* shall mean any person who comes within any of the following categories, or who the issuer reasonably believes comes within any of the following categories, at the time of the sale of the securities to that person:

(1) Any bank * * * or any savings and loan association or other institution * * * whether acting in its individual or fiduciary capacity; any [registered] broker or dealer * * * any insurance company * * * any investment company * * * or a business development company * * * any Small Business Investment Company [or certain employee benefit plans]. * * *

(3) Any organization described in section 501(c)(3) of the Internal Revenue Code, corporation, Massachusetts or similar business trust, or partnership, not formed for the specific purpose of acquiring the securities offered, with total assets in excess of $5,000,000;

(4) Any director, executive officer, or general partner of the issuer of the securities being offered or sold, or any director, executive officer, or general partner of a general partner of that issuer;

(5) Any natural person whose individual net worth, or joint net worth with that person's spouse, at the time of his purchase exceeds $1,000,000;

(6) Any natural person who had an individual income in excess of $200,000 in each of the two most recent years or joint income with that person's spouse in excess of $300,000 in each of those years and has a reasonable expectation of reaching the same income level in the current year;

(7) Any trust, with total assets in excess of $5,000,000, not formed for the specific purpose of acquiring the securities offered, whose purchase is directed by a sophisticated person as described in § 230.506(b)(2)(ii); and

(8) Any entity in which all of the equity owners are accredited investors. * * *

(e) *Calculation of number of purchasers.* For purposes of calculating the number of purchasers under §§ 230.505(b) and 230.506(b) only, the following shall apply:

(1) The following purchasers shall be excluded:

(i) Any relative, spouse or relative of the spouse of a purchaser who has the same principal residence as the purchaser;

(ii) Any trust or estate in which a purchaser and any of the persons related to him as specified in paragraph (e)(1)(i) or (e)(1)(iii) of this section collectively have more than 50 percent of the beneficial interest (excluding contingent interests);

(iii) Any corporation or other organization of which a purchaser and any of the persons related to him as specified in paragraph (e)(1)(i) or (e)(1)(ii) of this section collectively are beneficial owners of more than 50 percent of the equity securities (excluding directors' qualifying shares) or equity interests; and

(iv) Any accredited investor. * * *

§ 230.502   General conditions to be met.

The following conditions shall be applicable to offers and sales made under Regulation D (§§ 230.501–230.508):

(a) *Integration.* All sales that are part of the same Regulation D offering must meet all of the terms and conditions of Regulation D. Offers and sales that are made more than six months before the start of a Regulation D offering or are made more than six months after completion of a Regulation D offering will not be considered part of that Regulation D offering, so long as during those six month periods there are no offers or sales of securities by or for the issuer that are of the same or a similar class as those offered or sold under Regulation D * * *.

Note: The term *offering* is not defined in the Act or in Regulation D. If the issuer offers or sells securities for which the safe harbor rule in paragraph (a) of this § 230.502 is unavailable, the determination as to whether separate sales of securities are part of the same offering (i.e. are considered *integrated*) depends on the particular facts and circumstances. Generally, transactions otherwise meeting the requirements of an exemption will not be integrated with simultaneous offerings being made outside the United States in compliance with Regulation S. See Release No. 33–6863.

The following factors should be considered in determining whether offers and sales should be integrated for purposes of the exemptions under Regulation D:

    (a) Whether the sales are part of a single plan of financing;

    (b) Whether the sales involve issuance of the same class of securities;

    (c) Whether the sales have been made at or about the same time;

    (d) Whether the same type of consideration is received; and

    (e) Whether the sales are made for the same general purpose.

(b) *Information requirements*—(1) *When information must be furnished.* If the issuer sells securities under § 230.505 or § 230.506 to any purchaser that is not an accredited investor, the issuer shall furnish the information specified in paragraph (b)(2) of this section to such purchaser a reasonable time prior to sale. * * *

(c) *Limitation on manner of offering.* Except as provided in § 230.504(b)(1), neither the issuer nor any person acting on its behalf shall offer or sell the securities by any form of general solicitation or general advertising, including, but not limited to, the following:

(1) Any advertisement, article, notice or other communication published in any newspaper, magazine, or similar media or broadcast over television or radio; and

(2) Any seminar or meeting whose attendees have been invited by any general solicitation or general advertising.

(d) *Limitations on resale.* Except as provided in § 230.504(b)(1), securities acquired in a transaction under Regulation D shall have the status of securities acquired in a transaction under section 4(2) of the Act and cannot be resold without registration under the Act or an exemption therefrom. The issuer shall exercise reasonable care to assure that the purchasers of the securities are not underwriters within the meaning of section 2(11) of the Act, which reasonable care may be demonstrated by the following:

(1) Reasonable inquiry to determine if the purchaser is acquiring the securities for himself or for other persons;

(2) Written disclosure to each purchaser prior to sale that the securities have not been registered under the Act and, therefore, cannot be resold unless they are registered under the Act or unless an exemption from registration is available; and

(3) Placement of a legend on the certificate or other document that evidences the securities stating that the securities have not been registered under the Act and setting forth or referring to the restrictions on transferability and sale of the securities.

While taking these actions will establish the requisite reasonable care, it is not the exclusive method to demonstrate such care. Other actions by the issuer may satisfy this provision. * * *

§ 230.504 Exemption for limited offerings and sales of securities not exceeding $1,000,000.

(a) *Exemption.* Offers and sales of securities that satisfy the conditions in paragraph (b) of this § 230.504 * * * shall be exempt from the provisions of section 5 of the Act under section 3(b) of the Act.

(b) *Conditions to be met.* (1) To qualify for exemption under this § 230.504, offers and sales must satisfy the terms and conditions of §§ 230.501 and 230.502(a).

(2) The aggregate offering price for an offering of securities under this § 230.504, as defined in § 230.501(c), shall not exceed $1,000,000, less the aggregate offering price for all securities sold within the twelve months before the start of and during the offering of securities under this § 230.504, in

reliance on any exemption under section 3(b), or in violation of section 5(a) of the Securities Act.

Note 1: The calculation of the aggregate offering price is illustrated as follows:

> If an issuer sold $900,000 on June 1, 1987 under this § 230.504 and an additional $4,100,000 on December 1, 1987 under § 230.505, the issuer could not sell any of its securities under this § 230.504 until December 1, 1988. Until then the issuer must count the December 1, 1987 sale towards the $1,000,000 limit within the preceding twelve months.

Note 2: If a transaction under § 230.504 fails to meet the limitation on the aggregate offering price, it does not affect the availability of this § 230.504 for the other transactions considered in applying such limitation. For example, if an issuer sold $1,000,000 worth of its securities on January 1, 1988 under this § 230.504 and an additional $500,000 worth on July 1, 1988, this § 230.504 would not be available for the later sale, but would still be applicable to the January 1, 1988 sale.

§ 230.505 Exemption for limited offers and sales of securities not exceeding $5,000,000.

(a) *Exemption*. Offers and sales of securities that satisfy the conditions in paragraph (b) of this section by an issuer that is not an investment company shall be exempt from the provisions of section 5 of the Act under section 3(b) of the Act.

(b) *Conditions to be met*—(1) *General conditions*. To qualify for exemption under this section, offers and sales must satisfy the terms and conditions of §§ 230.501 and 230.502.

(2) *Specific conditions*—(i) *Limitation on aggregate offering price*. The aggregate offering price for an offering of securities under this § 230.505, as defined in § 203.501(c), shall not exceed $5,000,000, less the aggregate offering price for all securities sold within the twelve months before the start of and during the offering of securities under this section in reliance on any exemption under section 3(b) of the Act or in violation of section 5(a) of the Act. * * *

(ii) *Limitation on number of purchasers*. There are no more than or the issuer reasonably believes that there are no more than 35 purchasers of securities from the issuer in any offering under this section. * * *

§ 230.506 Exemption for limited offers and sales without regard to dollar amount of offering.

(a) *Exemption*. Offers and sales of securities by an issuer that satisfy the conditions in paragraph (b) of this section shall be deemed to be transactions not involving any public offering within the meaning of section 4(2) of the Act.

(b) *Conditions to be met*—(1) *General conditions*. To qualify for an exemption under this section, offers and sales must satisfy all the terms and conditions of §§ 230.501 and 230.502.

(2) *Specific Conditions*—(i) *Limitation on number of purchasers*. There are no more than or the issuer reasonably believes that there are no more

than 35 purchasers of securities from the issuer in any offering under this section. * * *

(ii) *Nature of purchasers.* Each purchaser who is not an accredited investor either alone or with his purchaser representative(s) has such knowledge and experience in financial and business matters that he is capable of evaluating the merits and risks of the prospective investment, or the issuer reasonably believes immediately prior to making any sale that such purchaser comes within this description.

§ 230.508 Insignificant deviations from a term, condition or requirement of Regulation D.

(a) A failure to comply with a term, condition or requirement of § 230.504, § 230.505 or § 230.506 will not result in the loss of the exemption from the requirements of section 5 of the Act for any offer or sale to a particular individual or entity, if the person relying on the exemption shows:

(1) The failure to comply did not pertain to a term, condition or requirement directly intended to protect that particular individual or entity; and

(2) The failure to comply was insignificant with respect to the offering as a whole, provided that any failure to comply with paragraph (c) of § 230.502, paragraph (b)(2) of § 230.504, paragraphs (b)(2)(i) and (ii) of § 230.505 and paragraph (b)(2)(i) of § 230.506 shall be deemed to be significant to the offering as a whole; and

(3) A good faith and reasonable attempt was made to comply with all applicable terms, conditions and requirements of § 230.504, § 230.505 or § 230.506. * * *

Notes

(1) Rule 508 was added in 1989, SEC Rel. No. 33–6825, 54 Fed.Reg. 11369 (1989), to "alleviate the draconian consequences of an innocent and insignificant defect in perfecting an exemption from registration." Stanley Keller, Securities Exemptions: The Saga of a Substantial Compliance Defense, Insights, Vol. 3, No. 8, p. 11 (Aug. 1989).[19] The author observes:

In my judgment, the substantial compliance revision will not create a significant change in practice. Nor should it result in any slackening of rigor in attempting to comply with the requirements of Regulation D and ULOE [Uniform Limited Offering Exemption]. There may be some situations where the revision may be beneficial in connection with completing a transaction— for example, when a non-accredited investor emerges late in the deal and the offering can proceed by providing the requisite information only to him. * * *

It is important to keep in mind that Rule 508 is self-executing and will give issuers and their counsel broad latitude to make a good faith determination whether relief under the rule is available. These principles will come into play and be helpful when counsel responds to the auditors, when opinions are rendered on subsequent rounds of financing regarding the exempt status of

---

19. Insights: The Corporate & Securities Law Advisor. Copyright by Prentice Hall Law & Business.

prior rounds, * * * and when the disclosure for subsequent financings has to be formulated.

The substantial compliance revisions also add a general benefit to securities jurisprudence that is somewhat less easy to define. For the first time, in a body of law that requires exemptions to be strictly construed and the burden of establishing them to be on the claiming party, a concept of substantial compliance and relief from technical violations is introduced. Also, for the first time in the case of transactional exemptions, there is the concept that only the injured party may be entitled to relief and that the entire transaction is not necessarily jeopardized. In addition, and perhaps most importantly, the substantial compliance rule invites a court to apply equitable considerations in determining what relief fits the crime.

Id. at 12. See also Carl W. Schneider, A Substantial Compliance ("I & I") Defense and Other Changes are Added to SEC Regulation D, 44 Bus.Law. 1207 (1989).

(2) The SEC's (1992) "Small Business Initiative" involved a series of new regulations and rule amendments designed to ease the regulatory burdens imposed on small businesses. SEC Rel. Nos. 33–6949, 34–30968, 39–30968, 57 Fed. Reg. 36,442 (1992). The principal changes made by this initiative are:

(a) *Regulation A.* The oldest and at one time the most widely used "small business" regulation adopted by the SEC under § 3(b) (see n. 18, p. 341, supra) is Regulation A (affectionately known as "Reg. A" by securities lawyers). 17 C.F.R. § 230.251, et seq. While technically an exemption under § 3(b), it actually involves a somewhat streamlined registration process at the regional offices of the SEC. See generally Harvey Frank, The Processing of Small Issues of Securities Under Regulation A, 1962 Duke L.J. 507. The late 1980s saw a significant reduction in Reg. A filings: from $408 million in 1981 to $34 million in 1991. The principal reasons for this decline were the $1.5 million ceiling on Reg. A issues and the cost of the Reg. A qualification process itself. The 1992 Small Business Initiative made several changes to make Reg. A more attractive: the ceiling was increased to $5 million, the information required to be disclosed was simplified and integrated to some extent with the uniform filings proposed by the North American Securities Administrators Association (NASAA) under state blue sky laws, and the information was permitted to be presented in a question-and-answer format. The SEC also simplified reporting requirements under the Securities Exchange Act of 1934 for small businesses with revenue of less than $25 million for each of two consecutive years.

(b) *Testing the Waters.* Rule 254, 17 C.F.R. § 230.254(a), permits a potential Reg. A user to publish or deliver to prospective purchasers a written document to determine whether there is investor interest in the contemplated offering. This document may be distributed without any review by the central offices of the SEC; basically the only requirement is that a copy be filed with an appropriate regional office, and include the name and telephone number of a person able to answer possible questions about the document. Testing the waters obviously permits a potential issuer to defer investing funds in the Reg. A process until after it has a pretty good idea that the offer will be successful.

(c) *Rule 504.* Perhaps the most important change was the amendment of Rule 504 of Regulation D so as to permit offerings by nonreporting issuers of up to $1 million essentially with no registration requirement at all (except for continued application of broad antifraud provisions). This change required similar action to be taken at the state level if it was to be implemented in fact.

(3) Rutherford B. Campbell, Jr., Blue Sky Laws and Recent Preemption Failure, 22 J.Corp.L. 175, 181–85 (1997) offers the following evaluation of the small offering exemptions created by the SEC:

Issuers interested in capital formation through the sale of securities have a number of generally available avenues for meeting the registration requirements of the 1933 Act. The most likely options include registration, Rule 147, Rule 504, Rule 505, Rule 506, and Regulation A. * * *

For public or private offerings up to $1 million, Rules 504 and 147 both provide attractive alternatives for an issuer. * * *

While one may quibble with certain aspects of these exemptions, fundamentally both are consistent with the need of small issuers to access the public capital market within a reasonable cost structure that does not effectively foreclose the issuer from public financing. At the same time, investors in such transactions are accorded two meaningful protections that are entirely appropriate in the circumstances. First, investors are able to protect themselves by bargaining for investment information. * * * Second, the investor is protected by the antifraud provisions of the 1933 and 1934 Acts. * * * The author's experience as a transactions lawyer * * * confirms that the obligation under antifraud provisions to disclose all material facts results in significant, affirmative disclosures to investors.

Small issuers operating in this range, if subject only to these federal limitations, may have a realistic chance to raise capital. They can, for example, identify investors through general advertising, such as newspaper advertisements. This would be enormously helpful for small issuers, who must overcome large obstacles in raising the capital they need to run their businesses. Investors, on the other hand and in light of the need of small issuers to raise capital, are appropriately protected by market forces and by the important antifraud remedies, which require issuers to disclose all material facts to all investors prior to the sale of securities. In short, the Commission struck an appropriate balance for offerings of this size. * * *

Issues between $1 million and $5 million also can satisfy the registration requirements of the 1933 Act in various ways that generally are consistent with a balance between capital formation and investor protection. In the case of public offerings within this range, the exemption provided by Regulation A is probably the most attractive for companies that are not reporting under the 1934 Act. * * * In private offerings, Rule 505 probably is the most attractive option for issuers operating in the $1 million to $5 million range and, again, is consistent with the balance notion and the idea that larger deals can support more investor protection without destroying capital formation. Thus, for example, Rule 505, unlike Rule 504, requires in most instances that purchasers be supplied with prescribed, detailed disclosures, including financial statements. This more extensive (as compared to Rule 504) disclosure requirement, which generates added offering expenses, is appropriate because of the increased size of the transaction. * * *

Issuers making public offerings in excess of $5 million most likely comply with the requirements of the 1933 Act by registering the securities on one of the Commission's S Forms. Not surprisingly, disclosure demands for such offerings are normally increased over the disclosure requirements placed on smaller public offerings effected under Regulation A or [other small business] forms. Thus, for example, Form S-l, the Commission's S Form utilized when none other is available, requires more extensive disclosures than either Regulation A or the Commission's BD forms.

Private offerings in excess of $5 million most likely will be undertaken pursuant to Rule 506. Often, such offerings require more disclosures than the smaller offerings under Rule 505. Additionally, Rule 506, unlike Rule 505, imposes purchaser qualification requirements, which specify that each purchaser must either be an "accredited investor" or sophisticated. * * *

The foregoing description suggests that over time the Commission developed a generally sensible array of methods through which issuers can comply with their registration obligations under the 1933 Act. Under this regime, the demands on the issuers to provide additional investor protection increase as the size of the offerings increase. Thus, * * * the Commission's overall approach demonstrates an appreciation of the trade-off between investor protection and capital formation.

(4) While the issue is not free from doubt, NSMIA does not apparently preempt state requirements with respect to any of these small business related exemptions. As stated by Professor Campbell, "Glaringly absent from * * * [the list of transactions preempted by NSMIA] are securities issued in transactions under Section 3(a)(11), which includes Rule 147, under Section 3(b), which includes Rule 504, 505 and Regulation A, and under the common law of Section 4(2)." 22 J.Corp.L., at 198–99. Professor Campbell argues strongly that the relief granted from overlapping blue sky regulation benefits only companies that raise large amounts of capital and leaves the smaller enterprise fully subject to the complex and sometimes-costly blue sky process.

SMITH v. GROSS

United States Court of Appeals, Ninth Circuit, 1979.
604 F.2d 639.

Before CARTER and GOODWIN, CIRCUIT JUDGES, and WATERS, DISTRICT JUDGE.

PER CURIAM:

Gerald and Mary Smith appeal from the district court's judgment dismissing their action against the defendants. The Smiths brought suit against Gross, Gaddie, and the two corporate defendants for violation of the federal securities laws. The district court dismissed the suit without prejudice for lack of subject matter jurisdiction on the ground that there was no security involved in the transactions between the parties. * * *

We reverse. The transaction between the parties involved an investment contract.[20]

---

20. [By the Editor] Section 2(1) of the Securities Act of 1933 defines "security" as follows:

The term "security" means any note, stock, treasury stock, bond, debenture, evidence of indebtedness, certificate of interest or participation in any profit-sharing agreement, collateral-trust certificate, preorganization certificate or subscription, transferable share, investment contract, voting-trust certificate, certificate of deposit for a security, fractional undivided interest in oil, gas, or other miner-

al rights, any put, call, straddle, option or privilege on any security, certificate of deposit, or group or index of securities (including any interest therein or based on the value thereof), or any put, call, straddle, option, or privilege entered into on a national securities exchange relating to foreign currency, or, in general, any interest or instrument commonly known as a "security", or any certificate of interest or participation in, temporary or interim certificate for, receipt for, guarantee of, or warrant or right to

FACTS

The following statement of facts is taken from the Smiths' amended complaint and Gerald Smith's affidavit. Seller Gross, in a promotional newsletter, solicited buyer-investors to raise earthworms in order to help Gross reach his quotas of selling earthworms to fishermen. In the newsletter, buyers were promised that the seller's growing instructions would enable buyers to have a profitable farm, that the time involved would be similar to raising a garden, that the earthworms double in quantity every sixty days, and that the seller would buy back all bait size worms produced by buyers at $2.25 per pound. After responding to the newsletter, the Smiths were told by Gross that very little work was required, that success was guaranteed by the agreement to repurchase the Smiths' production, and that Gross needed the Smiths' help in the common enterprise of supplying worms for the bait industry. The Smiths alleged that they would not have purchased the worms without Gross' promise to repurchase the Smiths' production at $2.25 per pound. The Smiths were assured that they need not be worried about the market for worms because Gross would handle the marketing.

The Smiths alleged that, contrary to Gross' representations, worms multiply at a maximum of eight rather than 64 times per year, and that they could achieve the promised profits only if the multiplication rate was as fast as represented and Gross purchased the Smiths' production at $2.25 per pound. They also alleged that $2.25 is greater than the true market price and that Gross could pay that price only by selling the worms to new worm farmers at inflated prices. The price at which Gross sold the worms to worm farmers was ten times in excess of the true market value. There is little market for worms in the Phoenix area. * * *

INVESTMENT CONTRACT

The Smiths contend that the transactions between the parties involved an investment contract type of security. In SEC v. W.J. Howey Co., 328 U.S. 293, 301, 66 S.Ct. 1100, 1104, 90 L.Ed. 1244 (1946), the Supreme Court set out the conditions for an investment contract: "[t]he test is whether the scheme involves [1] an investment of money [2] in a common enterprise [3] with profits to come solely from the efforts of others." This court in SEC v. Glenn W. Turner Enterprises, Inc., 474 F.2d 476, 482 (9th Cir.), cert. denied, 414 U.S. 821, 94 S.Ct. 117, 38 L.Ed.2d 53 (1973), held that despite the Supreme Court's use of the word "solely", the third element of the _Howey_ test is "whether the efforts made by those other than the investor are the undeniably significant ones, those essential managerial efforts which affect the failure or success of the enterprise." The _Turner_ court defined a common enterprise as "one in which the fortunes of the investor are interwoven with and dependent upon the efforts and success of those seeking the investment or of third parties." Id. at 482 n. 7.

We find this case virtually identical with Miller v. Central Chinchilla Group, Inc., 494 F.2d 414 (8th Cir.1974). In _Miller_ the defendants entered into contracts under which they sold chinchillas to the plaintiffs with the

---

subscribe to or purchase, any of the foregoing. * * *

If the interest sold to the plaintiffs is an "investment contract", the defendants have sold a security, and since that security was not registered under the Securities Act of 1933, the plaintiffs have the statutory right to rescind the transaction under § 12.

promise to repurchase the offspring. The plaintiffs were told that it was simple to breed chinchillas according to the defendants' instructions and that the venture would be highly profitable. The plaintiffs alleged that the chinchillas were difficult to raise and had a high mortality rate, and that the defendants could return the promised profits only if they repurchased the offspring and sold them to other prospective chinchilla raisers at an inflated price.

The *Miller* court focused on two features in holding that there was an investment contract: (1) the defendants persuaded the plaintiffs to invest by representing that the efforts required of them would be very minimal; and (2) that if the plaintiffs diligently exerted themselves, they still would not gain the promised profits because those profits could be achieved only if the defendants secured additional investors at the inflated prices. 494 F.2d at 417. Both of these features are present in the instant case. We find *Miller* to be persuasive and consistent with *Turner.*

The defendants argue that *Miller* is distinguishable on the ground that there the contract prohibited buyers from reselling to anyone other than the sellers; whereas here the buyers were free to resell to anyone they wanted to. The defendants contend that this distinguishing feature shows that the agreement was not a common enterprise.

The defendants' argument is without merit. There was a common enterprise as required by *Turner.* The Smiths alleged that, although they were free under the terms of the contract to sell their production anywhere they wished, they could have received the promised profits only if the defendants repurchased above the market price, and that the defendants could have repurchased above the market price only if the defendants secured additional investors at inflated prices. Thus, the fortune of the Smiths was interwoven with and dependent upon the efforts and success of the defendants.

We also find that here, as in *Miller,* the third element of an investment contract set forth in *Turner*—that the efforts of those other than the investor are the undeniably significant ones—was present here. The *Miller* court noted that the plaintiffs there had been assured by the sellers that the effort needed to raise chinchillas was minimal. The significant effort necessary for success in the endeavor was that of the seller in procuring new investors who would purchase the chinchillas at inflated prices. Here, the Smiths alleged that they were promised that the effort necessary to raise worms was minimal and they alleged that they could not receive the promised income unless the defendants purchased their harvest.

We find the analysis in *Miller* persuasive and hold that the Smiths alleged facts that, if true, were sufficient to establish an investment contract.

The defendants contend that the agreement between the parties was analogous to a franchise agreement. Franchise agreements are not securities. See, e.g., Bitter v. Hoby's International, Inc., 498 F.2d 183 (9th Cir.1974). This argument is not persuasive. The franchise cases are distinguishable. In *Bitter* this court focused on the fact that a franchisee independently determines his own success. Here, according to the Smiths' allegations, the only market in the Phoenix area for their production was the guaranteed right to resell to the sellers, and, thus, the Smiths were not solely responsible for their own success. We also note that the ultimate buyers in *Bitter* were the consuming public and not as here the offering party.

The facts as alleged in the Smiths' amended complaint and affidavit establish that an investment contract existed. * * * The judgment of the district court is reversed.

Notes

(1) King, Faded Fads, Wall St.J., Dec. 2, 1988, at R22–23:

[T]he worm-farm idea * * * reached its full flowering in the 1970s.

The lowly earthworm, said its promoters, was a gold mine. It was desperately needed as an ingredient in dog food and shampoo, and countless numbers would be employed in waste disposal. The promoters sold worms to the investors—charging, in some cases, $800 for a batch of the critters that could have been bought elsewhere for $25. The worms would quietly and effortlessly multiply (they don't make a fuss and don't eat much), and the promoters would buy back the expanded population.

Again, the promoters were nowhere to be found when buy-back time rolled around. It seems no one was crying out for shampoo earthworms, dog-food earthworms, or waste-disposal earthworms.

(2) The legal approach taken in this case permits a large number of ingenious investment schemes to be attacked successfully under the securities laws. Many of these investments are at best marginal and at worst fraudulent, though some entirely legitimate ones become ensnared in the broad definition of "security." The leading case is unquestionably SEC v. W.J. Howey Co., cited in the Court's opinion. Basically, this case involved the sale of plots of land planted in citrus; purchases were often made in narrow strips of land arranged so that an acre consisted of a single row of 48 trees. The cultivation, harvesting, and marketing of the crop were largely centrally provided through service contracts with the seller of the land; the seller was also heavily involved in citrus production on adjoining land. The Supreme Court held that this arrangement constituted a "security" and thereby established the legal principle applied in the principal case.

(3) The broad definition of "security" set forth in this line of cases may seem necessary in order to protect investors in marginal, nontraditional schemes. The SEC, in particular, has long argued for a broad and expansive definition, but courts have not always accepted this position. As stated by Professor John C. Coffee, "The SEC has generally looked at any kind of unorthodox instrument or syndicate and tried to see whether or not investors need protection. Courts have been more doctrinal and formal." Quoted in Karen Donovan, SEC Defines 'Securities' Expansively, National Law Journal, March 31, 1997, B1, at B2. Recent litigation involves several interesting issues:

(a) Is the solicitation of a settlement proposal, which "caps" the liability of "names" previously involved in insurance syndicates promulgated by Lloyd's of London in the United States, an offering of a "security"? For a negative answer, see Allen v. Lloyd's of London, 94 F.3d 923 (4th Cir.1996)

(b) Is a "ponzi scheme"[21] in which the Foundation for New Era Philanthropy Inc. solicited donations from wealthy individuals, churches, foundations, and

---

21. [By the Editor] A ponzi scheme is "a fraudulent investment scheme in which money contributed by later investors generates artifi- cially high dividends for the originally inves- tors, whose example attracts even larger in-educational institutions on the basis of a promise to double their money in six months, a sale of securities? For an affirmative answer, see SEC v. Bennett, 904 F.Supp. 435 (E.D.Pa.1995); same case, 889 F.Supp. 804 (E.D.Pa., 1995).

(c) Is the sale of life insurance policies on the lives of HIV positive individuals to investors in order to permit the insureds to receive a portion of the face value of their policies, a sale of securities? For a negative answer, see SEC v. Life Partners, Inc., 102 F.3d 587 (D.C.Cir., 1996) [one judge dissenting].

(d) Is a "pyramid scheme"[22] in which much of the sales efforts to resell interests are made by investors in the enterprise a sale of securities to those investors? For a negative answer in a criminal prosecution see United States v. Holtzclaw, 950 F.Supp. 1306(S.D.W.Va., 1997)[investors did not rely solely or primarily on the efforts of others].

(4) Consider a person who is thinking about the purchase of all the outstanding shares of a closely held corporation; such a person is clearly purchasing control of the business and will probably run it personally in an effort to make a profit. Fundamentally, the purchaser is buying assets, or control of assets, and not making a passive investment in the shares. Are shares of a closely held corporation in a control transaction a "security" under the *Howey* test applied in Smith v. Gross? This issue split the courts of appeal in the late 1970s and early 1980s, but in Landreth Timber Co. v. Landreth, 471 U.S. 681, 105 S.Ct. 2297, 85 L.Ed.2d 692 (1985), the Supreme Court rejected the so-called "sale of business doctrine" and held that the sale of all or a majority of the shares of a closely held corporation constituted the sale of a "security" subject to the federal securities acts. The principal argument of the court was a literal one based on the language of § 2(1). This holding makes available the protections of the antifraud provisions of the securities acts to all sales of closely held shares (assuming that the facilities of interstate commerce are used).

G.   ISSUANCE OF SHARES BY A GOING CONCERN: PREEMPTIVE RIGHTS AND DILUTION

STOKES v. CONTINENTAL TRUST CO. OF CITY OF NEW YORK

Court of Appeals of New York, 1906.
186 N.Y. 285, 78 N.E. 1090.

This action was brought by a stockholder to compel his corporation to issue to him at par such a proportion of an increase made in its capital stock as the number of shares held by him before such increase bore to the number of all the shares originally issued, and in case such additional shares could not be delivered to him for his damages in the premises. The defendant is a domestic banking corporation in the city of New York, organized in 1890, with a capital stock of $500,000, consisting of 5,000 shares of the par value of $100 each. The plaintiff was one of the original stockholders, and still owns all the

vestments." Black's Law Dictionary [New Pocket Edition] 487, col. 1 (1996).

22. [By the Editor] A familiar pyramid scheme is the chain letter. A pyramid scheme is "a property-distribution scheme in which a participant pays for the chance to receive compensation for introducing new persons to the scheme, as well as for when those new persons themselves introduce participants. * * *" Black's Law Dictionary, ibid., at 516, col. 2.

stock issued to him at the date of organization, together with enough more acquired since to make 221 shares in all. On the 29th of January, 1902, the defendant had a surplus of $1,048,450.94, which made the book value of the stock at that time $309.69 per share. On the 2d of January, 1902, Blair & Co., a strong and influential firm of private bankers in the city of New York, made the following proposition to the defendant: "If your stockholders at the special meeting to be called for January 29th, 1902, vote to increase your capital stock from $500,000 to $1,000,000 you may deliver the additional stock to us as soon as issued at $450 per share ($100 par value) for ourselves and our associates, it being understood that we may nominate ten of the 21 trustees to be elected at the adjourned annual meeting of stockholders." The directors of the defendant promptly met and duly authorized a special meeting of the stockholders to be called to meet on January 29, 1902, for the purpose of voting upon the proposed increase of stock and the acceptance of the offer to purchase the same. Upon due notice a meeting of the stockholders was held accordingly, more than a majority attending either in person or by proxy. A resolution to increase the stock was adopted by the vote of 4,197 shares, all that were cast. Thereupon the plaintiff demanded from the defendant the right to subscribe for 221 shares of the new stock at par, and offered to pay immediately for the same, which demand was refused. A resolution directing a sale to Blair & Co. at $450 a share was then adopted by a vote of 3,596 shares to 241. The plaintiff voted for the first resolution, but against the last, and before the adoption of the latter he protested against the proposed sale of his proportionate share of the stock, and again demanded the right to subscribe and pay for the same, but the demand was refused. On the 30th day of January, 1902, the stock was increased, and on the same day was sold to Blair & Co. at the price named, although the plaintiff formerly renewed his demand for 221 shares of the new stock at par, and tendered payment therefor, but it was refused upon the ground that the stock had already been issued to Blair & Co. owing in part to the offer of Blair & Co. which had become known to the public, the market price of the stock had increased from $450 a share in September, 1901, to $550 in January, 1902, and at the time of the trial, in April, 1904, it was worth $700 per share. Prior to the special meeting of the stockholders, by authority of the board of directors, a circular letter was sent to each stockholder, including the plaintiff, giving notice of the proposition made by Blair & Co. and recommending that it be accepted. Thereupon the plaintiff notified the defendant that he wished to subscribe for his proportionate share of the new stock, if issued, and at no time did he waive his right to subscribe for the same. Before the special meeting, he had not been definitely notified by the defendant that he could not receive his proportionate part of the increase, but was informed that his proposition would "be taken under consideration." After finding these facts in substance, the trial court found, as conclusions of law, that the plaintiff had the right to subscribe for such proportion of the increase, as his holdings bore to all the stock before the increase was made; that the stockholders, directors, and officers of the defendant had no power to deprive him of that right, and that he was entitled to recover the difference between the market value of 221 shares on the 30th of January, 1902, and the par value thereof, or the sum of $99,450, together with interest from said date. The judgment entered accordingly was reversed by the Appellate Division, and the plaintiff appealed to this court, giving the usual stipulation for judgment absolute in case the order of reversal should be affirmed.

VANN, J. (after stating the facts). * * * Thus the question presented for decision is whether according to the facts found the plaintiff had the legal right to subscribe for and take the same number of shares of the new stock that he held of the old? The subject is not regulated by statute, and the question presented has never been directly passed upon by this court, and only to a limited extent has it been considered by courts in this state. * * *

If the right claimed by the plaintiff was a right of property belonging to him as a stockholder, he could not be deprived of it by the joint action of the other stockholders, and of all the directors and officers of the corporation. What is the nature of the right acquired by a stockholder through the ownership of shares of stock? What rights can he assert against the will of a majority of the stockholders, and all the officers and directors? While he does not own and cannot dispose of any specific property of the corporation, yet he and his associates own the corporation itself, its charter, franchises, and all rights conferred thereby, including the right to increase the stock. He has an inherent right to his proportionate share of any dividend declared, or of any surplus arising upon dissolution, and he can prevent waste or misappropriation of the property of the corporation by those in control. Finally, he has the right to vote for directors and upon all propositions subject by law to the control of the stockholders, and this is his supreme right and main protection. Stockholders have no direct voice in transacting the corporate business, but through their right to vote they can select those to whom the law intrusts the power of management and control. A corporation is somewhat like a partnership, if one were possible, conducted wholly by agents where the copartners have power to appoint the agents, but are not responsible for their acts. The power to manage its affairs resides in the directors, who are its agents, but the power to elect directors resides in the stockholders. This right to vote for directors, and upon propositions to increase the stock or mortgage the assets, is about all the power the stockholder has. So long as the management is honest, within the corporate powers, and involves no waste, the stockholders cannot interfere, even if the administration is feeble and unsatisfactory, but must correct such evils through their power to elect other directors. Hence, the power of the individual stockholder to vote in proportion to the number of his shares is vital, and cannot be cut off or curtailed by the action of all the other stockholders, even with the co-operation of the directors and officers.

In the case before us the new stock came into existence through the exercise of a right belonging wholly to the stockholders. As the right to increase the stock belonged to them, the stock when increased belonged to them also, as it was issued for money and not for property or for some purpose other than the sale thereof for money. By the increase of stock the voting power of the plaintiff was reduced one-half, and while he consented to the increase he did not consent to the disposition of the new stock by a sale thereof to Blair & Co. at less than its market value, nor by sale to any person in any way except by an allotment to the stockholders. * * * The plaintiff had power, before the increase of stock, to vote on 221 shares of stock, out of a total of 5,000, at any meeting held by the stockholders for any purpose. By the action of the majority, taken against his will and protest, he now has only one-half the voting power that he had before, because the number of shares has been doubled while he still owns but 221. This touches him as a stockholder in such a way as to deprive him of a right of property. Blair & Co. acquired virtual control, while he and the other stockholders lost it. We are not discussing equities, but legal rights, for this is an action at law, and the plaintiff was deprived of a strictly legal right. If the result gives him an advantage over other stockholders, it is because he stood upon his legal rights, while they did not. The question is what were his legal rights, not what his profit may be under the sale to Blair & Co., but what it might have been if the new stock had been issued to him in proportion to his holding of the old. The other stockholders could give their property to Blair & Co., but they could not give his. * * *

We are thus led to lay down the rule that a stockholder has an inherent right to a proportionate share of new stock issued for money only and not to purchase property for the purposes of the corporation or to effect a consolidation, and while he can waive that right, he cannot be deprived of it without his consent except when the stock is issued at a fixed price not less than par, and he is given the right to take at that price in proportion to his holding, or in some other equitable way that will enable him to protect his interest by acting on his own judgment and using his own resources. This rule is just to all and tends to prevent the tyranny of majorities which needs restraint, as well as virtual attempts to blackmail by small minorities which should be prevented. * * *

[The court concluded that the plaintiff's damages should have been measured by the difference between the $450 sale price and the $550 market value of the shares rather than the difference between par value and market value of the shares.]

The order appealed from should be reversed and the judgment of the trial court modified by reducing the damages from the sum of $99,450, with interest from January 30, 1902, to the sum of $22,100, with interest from that date, and by striking out the extra allowance of costs, and as thus modified the judgment of the trial court is affirmed, without costs in this court or in the Appellate Division to either party.

HAIGHT, J. (dissenting). I agree that the rule that we should adopt is that a stockholder in a corporation has an inherent right to purchase a proportionate share of new stock issued for money only, and not to purchase property necessary for the purposes of the corporation or to effect a consolidation. While he can waive that right he cannot be deprived of it without his consent, except by sale at a fixed price at or above par, in which he may buy at that price in proportion to his holding or in some other equitable way that will enable him to protect his interest by acting on his own judgment and using his own resources. I, however, differ with Judge VANN as to his conclusions as to the rights of the plaintiff herein. Under the findings of the trial court the plaintiff demanded that his share of the new stock should be issued to him at par, or $100 per share, instead of $450 per share, the price offered by Blair & Co. and the price fixed at the stockholders' meeting at which the new stock was authorized to be sold. * * * There is no finding of fact or evidence in the record showing that he was ever ready or willing to pay $450 per share for the stock. * * * What, then, was the legal effect of the plaintiff's demand and tender? To my mind it was simply an attempt to make something out of his associates, to get for $100 per share the stock which Blair & Co. had offered to purchase for $450 per share; and that it was the equivalent of a refusal to pay $450 per share, and its effect is to waive his right to procure the stock by paying that amount. * * * But this is not all. It appears that prior to the offer of Blair & Co. the stock of the company had never been sold above $450 per share; that thereafter the stock rapidly advanced until the day of the completion of the sale on the 30th of January, when its market value was $550 per share; but this, under the stipulation of facts, was caused by the rumor and subsequent announcement and consummation of the proposition for the increase of the stock and the sale of such increase to Blair & Co. and their associates. It is now proposed to give the plaintiff as damages such increase in the market value of the stock, even though such value was based upon the understanding that Blair & Co. were to become stockholders in the corporation, which the acceptance of plaintiff's offer would have prevented. This, to my mind, should not be done. I, therefore, favor an affirmance.

CULLEN, C.J., and WERNER and HISCOCK, JJ., concur with VANN, J.; WILLARD BARLETT, J., concurs with HAIGHT, J.; O'BRIEN, J., absent.

Notes

(1) The common law preemptive right discussed in *Stokes* is now embodied in state statutes, of which there is considerable diversity. See MBCA § 6.30, which provides standard terms on an elective basis to codify many aspects of the preemptive right.

(2) It is now generally accepted that the preemptive right is not an inherent aspect of the ownership of shares but a right that may be granted or withheld by the articles of incorporation. The MBCA adopts an "opt in" clause: Under § 6.30(a), no preemptive right exists unless provision for it is expressly made. As a result, a "plain vanilla" corporation whose articles of incorporation contain the statutory minima will not have preemptive rights. Would not the converse (i.e. that a corporation has preemptive rights unless expressly denied in the articles of incorporation) be preferable? Many state statutes adopt an "opt out" rather than an "opt in" provision. Consider also the Historical Comment to MBCA § 6.30:

The 1950 Model Act followed the basic approach of the post–1930 state statutes. Section 24 made preemptive rights optional but adopted an "opt out" approach by providing that the preemptive rights of shareholders "to acquire additional or treasury shares" may be limited or denied by provision in the articles. * * *

In 1955 the Model Act was amended by adding an "[alternative] section 24," that provided an "opt in" rather than "opt out" approach: under the alternative section, no preemptive rights existed unless a specific affirmative provision granting these rights was included in the articles. * * * In the 1969 Model Act, the "[alternative] section 24," containing the "opt in" provision, was renumbered section 26 while the previous section 24 was retitled "section 26A. Shareholders Preemptive Rights [Alternative]." Thus, the alternative approach of the 1950 Model Act was retained but the preference was reversed with the "opt in" provision becoming the standard section. This change in preference reflected increased skepticism as to the value of preemptive rights coupled with increased recognition of the problems they created for many corporations. On the other hand, the Committee was unwilling to ignore the long history of preemptive rights and eliminate the "opt out" provision entirely from the statute. The decision in the 1984 Model Act to adopt an "opt in" approach is thus consistent with the long term trend in the development of this Model Act provision. * * *

(3) The Official Comment to MBCA § 6.30 states that the section "is primarily designed to protect voting power within the corporation from dilution." Was that the purpose of preemptive rights envisioned by the court in *Stokes?* The Official Comment adds, however, that preemptive rights also "may serve in part the function of protecting the equity participation of shareholders."

(4) If a corporation elects preemptive rights, should that right extend to shares issued as compensation to directors or officers? See MBCA § 6.30(b)(3)(i) and (ii). Does that not tend to frustrate the purpose of preemptive rights whenever one shareholder is an officer of the corporation and others are not? Why should shares "sold otherwise than for money" [MBCA § 6.30(b)(3)(iv)] not be subject to preemptive rights? What is the justification for the exception in MBCA § 6.30(b)(iii) for shares issued within six months of the formation of the corporation? What about shares that are offered preemptively, but not purchased? May they be sold entirely free of such rights in the future? See MBCA § 6.30(b)(6).

(5) Preemptive rights may create problems in corporations with multiple classes of shares. Consider MBCA § 6.30(b)(4) and (5). The Official Comment states that creation of (a) a class of nonvoting common shares, or (b) a class of preferential shares with general voting rights, in particular "may give rise to possible conflict between the protection of voting interests and equity participation." Why is that?

KATZOWITZ v. SIDLER + Lasker

Court of Appeals of New York, 1969.
24 N.Y.2d 512, 301 N.Y.S.2d 470, 249 N.E.2d 359.

KEATING, JUDGE.

Isador Katzowitz is a director and stockholder of a close corporation. Two other persons, Jacob Sidler and Max Lasker, own the remaining securities and, with Katzowitz, comprise Sulburn Holding Corp.'s board of directors. Sulburn was organized in 1955 to supply propane gas to three other corporations controlled by these men. Sulburn's certificate of incorporation authorized it to issue 1,000 shares of no par value stock for which the incorporators established a $100 selling price. Katzowitz, Sidler and Lasker each invested $500 and received five shares of the corporation's stock.

The three men had been jointly engaged in several corporate ventures for more than 25 years. In this period they had always been equal partners and received identical compensation from the corporations they controlled. Though all the corporations controlled by these three men prospered, disenchantment with their inter-personal relationship flared into the open in 1956. At this time, Sidler and Lasker joined forces to oust Katzowitz from any role in managing the corporations. * * *

Before the issue could be tried, the three men entered into a stipulation in 1959 whereby Katzowitz withdrew from active participation in the day-to-day operations of the business. The agreement provided that he would remain on the boards of all the corporations, and each board would be limited to three members composed of the three stockholders or their designees. Katzowitz was to receive the same compensation and other fringe benefits which the controlled corporations paid Lasker and Sidler. The stipulation also provided that Katzowitz, Sidler and Lasker were "equal stockholders and each of said parties now owns the same number of shares of stock in each of the defendant corporations and that such shares of stock shall continue to be in full force and effect and unaffected by this stipulation, except as hereby otherwise expressly provided." The stipulation contained no other provision affecting equal stock interests.

The business relationship established by the stipulation was fully complied with. Sidler and Lasker, however, were still interested in disassociating themselves from Katzowitz * * *

In December of 1961 Sulburn was indebted to each stockholder to the extent of $2,500 for fees and commissions earned up until September, 1961. Instead of paying this debt, Sidler and Lasker wanted Sulburn to loan the money to another corporation which all three men controlled. Sidler and Lasker called a meeting of the board of directors to propose that additional securities be offered at $100 per share to substitute for the money owed to the directors. The notice of meeting for October 30, 1961 had on its agenda "a proposition that the corporation issue common stock of its unissued common capital stock, *the total par value which shall equal the total sum of the fees and commissions now owing by the corporation to its * * * directors* ". (Emphasis added.) Katzowitz made it quite clear at the meeting that he would not invest any additional funds in Sulburn in order for it to make a loan to this other corporation. The only resolution passed at the meeting was that the corporation would pay the sum of $2,500 to each director.

With full knowledge that Katzowitz expected to be paid his fees and commissions and that he did not want to participate in any new stock issuance, the other two directors called a special meeting of the board on December 1, 1961. The only item on the agenda for this special meeting was the issuance of 75 shares of the corporation's common stock at $100 per share. The offer was to be made to stockholders in "accordance with their respective preemptive rights for the purpose of acquiring additional working capital". The amount to be raised was the exact amount owed by the corporation to its shareholders. The offering price for the securities was $\frac{1}{18}$ the book value of the stock. Only Sidler and Lasker attended the special board meeting. They approved the issuance of the 75 shares.

Notice was mailed to each stockholder that they had the right to purchase 25 shares of the corporation's stock at $100 a share. The offer was to expire on December 27, 1961. Failure to act by that date was stated to constitute a waiver. At about the same time Katzowitz received the notice, he received a check for $2,500 from the corporation for his fees and commissions. Katzowitz did not exercise his option to buy the additional shares. Sidler and Lasker purchased their full complement, 25 shares each. This purchase by Sidler and Lasker caused an immediate dilution of the book value of the outstanding securities.

On August 25, 1962 the principal asset of Sulburn, a tractor trailer truck, was destroyed. On August 31, 1962 the directors unanimously voted to dissolve the corporation. Upon dissolution, Sidler and Lasker each received $18,885.52 but Katzowitz only received $3,147.59.

The plaintiff instituted a declaratory judgment action to establish his right to the proportional interest in the assets of Sulburn in liquidation less the $5,000 which Sidler and Lasker used to purchase their shares in December, 1961.

Special Term (Westchester County) found the book value of the corporation's securities on the day the stock was offered at $100 to be worth $1,800. The court also found that "the individual defendants * * * decided that in lieu of taking that sum in cash [the commissions and fees due the stockholders], they preferred to add to their investment by having the corporate defendant make available and offer each stockholder an additional twenty-five shares of unissued stock." The court reasoned that Katzowitz waived his right to purchase the stock or object to its sale to Lasker and Sidler by failing to exercise his preemptive right and found his protest at the time of dissolution untimely.

On the substantive legal issues and findings of fact, the Appellate Division [two Justices dissenting, 29 App.Div.2d 955, 289 N.Y.S.2d 324] was in agreement with Special Term. The majority agreed that the book value of the corporation's stock at the time of the stock offering was $1,800. The Appellate Division reasoned, however, that showing a disparity between book value and offering price was insufficient without also showing fraud or overreaching. Disparity in price by itself was not enough to prove fraud. The Appellate Division also found that the plaintiff had waived his right to object to his recovery in dissolution by failing to either exercise his pre-emptive rights or take steps to prevent the sale of the stock.

The concept of pre-emptive rights was fashioned by the judiciary to safeguard two distinct interests of stockholders—the right to protection against dilution of their equity in the corporation and protection against dilution of their proportionate voting control. (Ballantine, Corporations [rev. ed., 1946], § 209.) After early decisions (Gray v. Portland Bank, 3 Mass. 364; Stokes v. Continental Trust Co., 186 N.Y. 285, 78 N.E. 1090, 12 L.R.A., N.S., 969), legislation fixed the right enunciated with respect to proportionate voting but left to the judiciary the role of protecting existing shareholders from the dilution of their equity (e.g., Stock Corporation Law, § 39, now Business Corporation Law, Consol.Laws, c. 4, § 622; see Drinker, The Preemptive Right of Shareholders to Subscribe to New Shares, 43 Harv.L.Rev. 586; Alexander Hamilton Frey, Shareholders' Pre-emptive Rights, 38 Yale L.J. 563).

It is clear that directors of a corporation have no discretion in the choice of those to whom the earnings and assets of the corporation should be distributed. Directors, being fiduciaries of the corporation, must, in issuing new stock, treat existing shareholders fairly. Though there is very little statutory control over the price which a corporation must receive for new shares the power to determine price must be exercised for the benefit of the corporation and in the interest of all the stockholders.

Issuing stock for less than fair value can injure existing shareholders by diluting their interest in the corporation's surplus, in current and future earnings and in the assets upon liquidation. Normally, a stockholder is protected from the loss of his equity from dilution, even though the stock is being offered at less than fair value, because the shareholder receives rights which he may either exercise or sell. If he exercises, he has protected his interest and, if not, he can sell the rights, thereby compensating himself for the dilution of his remaining shares in the equity of the corporation.[23]

When new shares are issued, however, at prices far below fair value in a close corporation or a corporation with only a limited market for its shares, existing stockholders, who do not want to invest or do not have the capacity to invest additional funds, can have their equity interest in the corporation diluted to the vanishing point.

The protection afforded by stock rights is illusory in close corporations. Even if a buyer could be found for the rights, they would have to be sold at an inadequate price because of the nature of a close corporation. Outsiders are normally discouraged from acquiring minority interests after a close corporation has been organized. Certainly a stockholder in a close corporation is at a total loss to safeguard his equity from dilution if no rights are offered and he does not want to invest additional funds.

Though it is difficult to determine fair value for a corporation's securities and courts are therefore reluctant to get into the thicket, when the issuing price is shown to be markedly below book value in a close corporation and when the remaining shareholder-directors benefit from the issuance, a case for judicial relief has been established. In that instance, the corporation's directors must show that the issuing price falls within some range which can be justified on the basis of valid business reasons. If no such showing is made by the directors, there is no reason for the judiciary to abdicate its function to a majority of the board or stockholders who have not seen fit to come forward and justify the propriety of diverting property from the corporation and allow the issuance of securities to become an oppressive device permitting the dilution of the equity of dissident stockholders.

The defendant directors here make no claim that the price set was a fair one. No business justification is offered to sustain it. Admittedly, the stock was sold at less than book value. The defendants simply contend that, as long as all stockholders were given an equal opportunity to purchase additional shares, no stockholder can complain simply because the offering dilutes his interest in the corporation.

The defendants' argument is fallacious.

The corollary of a stockholder's right to maintain his proportionate equity in a corporation by purchasing additional shares is the right not to purchase additional shares without being confronted with dilution of his existing equity if no valid business justification exists for the dilution.

A stockholder's right not to purchase is seriously undermined if the stock offered is worth substantially more than the offering price. Any purchase at this price dilutes his interest and impairs the value of his original holding. "A corporation is not permitted to sell its stock for a legally inadequate price at least where there is objection. Plaintiff has a right to insist upon compliance with the law whether or not he cares to exercise his option. He cannot block a sale for a fair price merely because he disagrees with the wisdom of the plan

---

23. [By the Court] There is little justification for issuing stock far below its fair value. The only reason for issuing stock below fair value exists in publicly held corporations where the problem of floating new issues through subscription is concerned. The reason advanced in this situation is that it insures the success of the issue or that it has the same psychological effect as a dividend.

but he can insist that the sale price be fixed in accordance with legal requirements." (Bennett v. Breuil Petroleum Corp., [34 Del.Ch. 6, 14–15, 99 A.2d 236, 241 (1953).]) Judicial review in this area is limited to whether under all the circumstances, including the disparity between issuing price of the stock and its true value, the nature of the corporation, the business necessity for establishing an offering price at a certain amount to facilitate raising new capital, and the ability of stockholders to sell rights, the additional offering of securities should be condemned because the directors in establishing the sale price did not fix it with reference to financial considerations with respect to the ready disposition of securities.

Here the obvious disparity in selling price and book value was calculated to force the dissident stockholder into investing additional sums. No valid business justification was advanced for the disparity in price, and the only beneficiaries of the disparity were the two director-stockholders who were eager to have additional capital in the business.

It is no answer to Katzowitz' action that he was also given a chance to purchase additional shares at this bargain rate. The price was not so much a bargain as it was a tactic, conscious or unconscious on the part of the directors, to place Katzowitz in a compromising situation. The price was so fixed to make the failure to invest costly. However, Katzowitz at the time might not have been aware of the dilution because no notice of the effect of the issuance of the new shares on the already outstanding shares was disclosed. In addition, since the stipulation entitled Katzowitz to the same compensation as Sidler and Lasker, the disparity in equity interest caused by their purchase of additional securities in 1961 did not affect stockholder income from Sulburn and, therefore, Katzowitz possibly was not aware of the effect of the stock issuance on his interest in the corporation until dissolution.

No reason exists at this time to permit Sidler and Lasker to benefit from their course of conduct. Katzowitz' delay in commencing the action did not prejudice the defendants. By permitting the defendants to recover their additional investment in Sulburn before the remaining assets of Sulburn are distributed to the stockholders upon dissolution, all the stockholders will be treated equitably. Katzowitz, therefore, should receive his aliquot share of the assets of Sulburn less the amount invested by Sidler and Lasker for their purchase of stock on December 27, 1961.

Accordingly, the order of the Appellate Division should be reversed, with costs, and judgment granted in favor of the plaintiff against the individual defendants.

BURKE, SCILEPPI, BERGAN, BREITEL and JASEN, JJ., concur with KEATING, J.

FULD, C.J., dissents and votes to affirm on the opinion at the Appellate Division.

Notes

(1) What is the source of the principle that the Court applied to hold improper the issuance of additional shares? If Katzowitz' preemptive rights were fully honored, as they appear to have been, why should he be permitted to complain about the dilution which he could have avoided simply by exercising that right?

(2) The transaction involved in *Katzowitz* is a type of "freezeout." A similar type of freezeout occurs when inside shareholders pay for their additional shares by canceling debts owed to them by the corporation (representing, in effect, capital that they have already invested in the business) while outside shareholders are put to the painful choice of investing fresh capital (which, of course, they may not have) over which they lose effective control or see their proportionate interest decline drastically. A classic example is Hyman v. Velsicol Corp., 342 Ill.App. 489, 97 N.E.2d 122 (1951), where an outside shareholder was given the choice of investing an additional $136,000 in order to stay even or watching his proportional interest decline from 20 percent to a fraction of one percent. What did the shareholder do? He sued, of course, but lost when the Court concluded that the plan "was not an abuse of discretion" and was not "fraudulently oppressive." As in *Katzowitz,* the shareholder's preemptive right was fully protected and shares were issued at par value, arguably below "true value." However, there was some business justification for the transaction since the majority shareholders were canceling outstanding indebtedness owed to them and the plaintiff was a former employee who was interested in a competing business.

(3) Some freezeout cases have been brought under the theory that the plan constitutes a violation of fiduciary duties, discussed in a later chapter. See generally Mark K. Kessler, Elimination of Minority Interests by Cash Merger: Two Recent Cases, 30 Bus.Law. 699 (1975). Cases have also adopted the view that transactions literally complying with statutory requirements may be set aside if they do not meet a standard of "entire fairness" since they involve conflict of interest transactions. See Weinberger v. UOP, Inc., p. 778 infra; see also Alpert v. 28 Williams St. Corp., 63 N.Y.2d 557, 483 N.Y.S.2d 667, 473 N.E.2d 19 (1984). The modern trend seems clearly to be running in the direction of imposing a fiduciary duty on dilutive transactions such as those involved in *Katzowitz*. In the words of the Mississippi Supreme Court, "[t]he traditional view that shareholders have no fiduciary duty to each other, and transactions constituting 'freezeouts' or 'squeezeouts' generally cannot be attacked as a breach of duty of loyalty or good faith to each other, is outmoded." Fought v. Morris, 543 So.2d 167, 169 (Miss. 1989). See also Johnston v. Wilbourn, 760 F.Supp. 578, 582 (S.D.Miss.1991). In the light of this trend, it is doubtful that older cases such as Hyman v. Velsicol (note (2) above) would be decided the same way if they arose today. See generally F. Hodge O'Neal, Oppression of Minority Shareholders: Protecting Minority Rights, 35 Clev.St.L.Rev. 121 (1987).

H. DISTRIBUTIONS BY A CLOSELY HELD CORPORATION

GOTTFRIED v. GOTTFRIED

Supreme Court of New York, 1947.
73 N.Y.S.2d 692.

CORCORAN, JUSTICE.

This action was brought in the early part of 1945 by minority stockholders of Gottfried Baking Corporation (hereinafter called "Gottfried"), to compel the Board of Directors of that corporation to declare dividends on its common stock. The defendants are Gottfried itself, its directors, and Hanscom Baking Corporation (hereinafter called "Hanscom"), a wholly owned subsidiary of Gottfried. Gottfried is a closely held family corporation. All of its stockholders, with minor exceptions, are children of the founder of the business, Elias Gottfried, and their respective spouses.

Both corporations are engaged in the manufacture and sale of bakery products; Gottfried for distribution at wholesale, and Hanscom for distribution at retail in its own stores. Each corporation functions separately, in the manufacture and sale of its respective products.

At the end of 1946 the outstanding capitalization of Gottfried consisted of 4500 shares of "A" stock, without nominal or par value, and 20,862 shares of common stock without par value. The "A" stock is entitled to dividends of $8 per share before any dividends may be paid upon the common stock, as well as a further participation in earnings. At the end of 1944, immediately before this action was commenced, Gottfried also had outstanding preferred stock in the face amount of $79,000, and Hanscom had outstanding $86,000 face amount of preferred stock. The plaintiffs in the aggregate owned approximately 38% of each of these classes of securities. The individual defendants owned approximately 62 percent.

From 1931 until 1945 no dividends had been paid upon the common stock, although dividends had been paid regularly upon the outstanding preferred stock and intermittently upon the "A" stock. There seems to be no question with respect to the policy of the Board of Directors in not declaring dividends prior to 1944. An analysis of the financial statements of the corporation shows a net working capital deficit at the end of 1941, in which year a consolidated loss of $109,816 had been incurred. Moreover, until the end of 1943 the earned surplus was relatively small in relation to the volume of business done and the growing requirements of the business.

Although the action was brought in the early part of 1945 to compel the declaration of dividends upon the common stock, dividends actually were declared and paid upon said stock in 1945, and subsequently. The purpose of the action now, therefore, is to compel the payment of dividends upon the common stock in such amount as under all the circumstances is fair and adequate.

The action is predicated upon the claim that the policy of the Board of Directors with respect to the declaration of dividends is animated by considerations other than the best welfare of the corporations or their stockholders. The plaintiffs claim that bitter animosity on the part of the directors, who own the controlling stock, against the plaintiff minority stockholders, as well as a desire to coerce the latter into selling their stock to the majority interests at a grossly inadequate price, and the avoidance of heavy personal income taxes upon any dividends that might be declared, have been the motivating factors that have dominated the defendants. Plaintiffs, contend, moreover, that the defendants by excessive salaries, bonuses and corporate loans to themselves or some of them, have eliminated the immediate need of dividends in so far as they were concerned, while at the same time a starvation dividend policy with respect to the minority stockholders—not on the payroll—operates designedly to compel the plaintiffs to sacrifice their stock by sale to the defendants.

There is no essential dispute as to the principles of law involved. If an adequate corporate surplus is available for the purpose, directors may not withhold the declaration of dividends in bad faith. But the mere existence of an adequate corporate surplus is not sufficient to invoke court action to compel such a dividend. There must also be bad faith on the part of the directors.

There are no infallible distinguishing ear-marks of bad faith. The following facts are relevant to the issue of bad faith and are admissible in evidence: Intense hostility of the controlling faction against the minority; exclusion of the minority from employment by the corporation; high salaries, or bonuses or corporate loans made to the officers in control; the fact that the majority group may be subject to high personal income taxes if substantial dividends are paid; the existence of a desire by the controlling directors to acquire the minority stock interests as cheaply as possible. But if they are not motivating causes they do not constitute "bad faith" as a matter of law.

The essential test of bad faith is to determine whether the policy of the directors is dictated by their personal interests rather than the corporate welfare. Directors are fiduciaries. Their cestui que trust are the corporation and the stockholders as a body. Circumstances such as those above mentioned and any other significant factors, appraised in the light of the financial condition and requirements of the corporation, will determine the conclusion as to whether the directors have or have not been animated by personal, as distinct from corporate, considerations.

The court is not concerned with the direction which the exercise of the judgment of the Board of Directors may take, provided only that such exercise of judgment be made in good faith. It is axiomatic that the court will not substitute its judgment for that of the Board of Directors.

It must be conceded that closely held corporations are easily subject to abuse on the part of dominant stockholders, particularly in the direction of action designed to compel minority stockholders to sell their stock at a sacrifice. But close corporation or not, the court will not tolerate directorate action designed to achieve that or any other wrongful purpose. Even in the absence of bad faith, however, the impact of dissension and hostility among stockholders falls usually with heavier force in a closely held corporation. In many such cases, a large part of a stockholder's assets may be tied up in the corporation. It is frequently contemplated by the parties, moreover, that the respective stockholders receive their major livelihood in the form of salaries resulting from employment by the corporation. If such employment be terminated, the hardship suffered by the minority stockholder or stockholders may be very heavy. Nevertheless, such situations do not in themselves form a ground for the interposition of a court of equity.

There is no doubt that in the present case bitter dissension and personal hostility have existed for a long time between the individual plaintiffs and defendants. The plaintiffs Charles Gottfried and Harold Gottfried have both been discontinued from the corporate payrolls.

It is true too that several of the defendants have in recent years received as compensation substantial sums. * * *

The evidence also discloses that substantial advances or loans have been made from time to time to several of the defendants, part of which still remain outstanding. Advances and loans of this character in varying amounts likewise had been made for many years to stockholders and directors. Without passing upon the propriety or legality of these transactions, the evidence does not sustain an inference that they were made with a view to the dividend policy of the corporation. They were incurred, in large part, long before any controversy arose with respect to dividends, nor is the aggregate amount thereof of sufficient magnitude to affect in a material way the capacity of Gottfried to pay dividends.

Plaintiff Charles Gottfried testified that Benjamin Gottfried, one of the defendants, told him that he and the other minority stockholders would never get any dividends because the majority could freeze them out and that the majority had other ways than declaring dividends of getting money out of the companies. Benjamin Gottfried denied that he had ever made such statements. There is no evidence, moreover, that such statements were made by any of the other defendants. The court does not believe that this disputed testimony carries much weight upon the question of a concerted policy on the part of the directors to refrain from declaring dividends for the purpose of "freezing out" the plaintiffs.

Nor does the evidence with respect to the financial condition of the corporation and its business requirements sustain the plaintiffs' claims. * * * The evidence discloses that * * * expenditures [actually made in 1945] * * * included the retirement of the then outstanding preferred stocks of Gottfried and Hanscom in the sum of $165,000. Since all the parties held these preferred stocks in the same ratio as they held Gottfried "A" stock and common stock, each of the stockholders, including the plaintiffs, participated proportionately in the benefits of such retirement. After said retirement their respective pro rata interests in Gottfried were precisely the same as before these distributions were made. From this point of view the plaintiffs were in at least as good a position as a result of this preferred stock retirement as though dividends had been paid upon the common stock in the sum of $165,000, which is almost equivalent to the entire net earnings for the year 1944. It is noteworthy in this connection, moreover, that the retirement of the preferred stock was urged by both Charles and Harold Gottfried, two of the plaintiffs, at the annual meeting of the stockholders of Gottfried held on December 5, 1944. Harold went so far as to request that funds be borrowed from a bank in order to effect such retirement. These stockholders certainly cannot complain because a sum almost equivalent to the prior year's entire net income was defrayed, in accordance with their own request, in the form of retirement of preferred stock rather than by payment of dividends on the common stock.

Other major items of expenditure in 1945, * * * were payments of dividends on Gottfried preferred stock in the sum of $5,031, dividends on Hanscom preferred stock in the sum of $5,597, and dividends on the "A" stock of $36,000. In all of these payments of dividends on stock prior to the common stock the plaintiffs were pro rata beneficiaries. In 1945 there were also payments upon outstanding mortgages in the sum of $133,626. Reduction of mortgage indebtedness seems to have been a standard policy of Gottfried when its financial condition permitted it. Payments for sites for new plants and properties deemed necessary for the corporations' operations aggregated more than $214,000.

In addition to the above-mentioned expenditures * * * Gottfried in 1945 paid $31,532 in dividends on the common stock. It may be, of course, that the payment of these dividends was stimulated by the commencement of this suit. The fact remains that they were paid. * * *

The ratio of dividends paid in 1945 to the earnings of the immediately preceding year was 44.87%.

Under these circumstances, it may not be said that the directorate policy regarding common stock dividends at the time the suit was brought was unduly conservative. It certainly does not appear to have been inspired by bad faith. * * *

The complaint is dismissed and judgment directed for the defendants. Settle judgment.

DODGE v. FORD MOTOR CO.

Supreme Court of Michigan, 1919.
204 Mich. 459, 170 N.W. 668.

OSTRANDER, C.J.

[Editor: Plaintiffs are minority shareholders in the Ford Motor Company. At the time, Henry Ford, president of the company, owned 58 percent of the outstanding capital stock.] * * *

When plaintiffs made their complaint and demand for further dividends, the Ford Motor Company had concluded its most prosperous year of business. The demand for its cars at the price of the preceding year continued. It could make and could market in the year beginning August 1, 1916, more than 500,000 cars. Sales of parts and repairs would necessarily increase. The cost of materials was likely to advance, and perhaps the price of labor; but it reasonably might have expected a profit for the year of upwards of $60,000,-000. It had assets of more than $132,000,000, a surplus of almost $112,000,-000, and its cash on hand and municipal bonds were nearly $54,000,000. Its total liabilities, including capital stock, was a little over $20,000,000. It had declared no special dividend during the business year except the October, 1915, dividend. It had been the practice, under similar circumstances, to declare larger dividends. Considering only these facts, a refusal to declare and pay further dividends appears to be not an exercise of discretion on the part of the directors, but an arbitrary refusal to do what the circumstances required to be done. These facts and others call upon the directors to justify their action, or failure or refusal to act. In justification, the defendants have offered testimony tending to prove, and which does prove, the following facts: It had been the policy of the corporation for a considerable time to annually reduce the selling price of cars, while keeping up, or improving, their quality. As early as in June, 1915, a general plan for the expansion of the productive capacity of the concern by a practical duplication of its plant had been talked over by the executive officers and directors and agreed upon; not all of the details having been settled, and no formal action of directors having been taken. The erection of a smelter was considered, and engineering and other data in connection therewith secured. In consequence, it was determined not to reduce the selling price of cars for the year beginning August 1, 1915, but to maintain the price and to accumulate a large surplus to pay for the proposed expansion of plant and equipment, and perhaps to build a plant for smelting ore. It is hoped, by Mr. Ford, that eventually, 1,000,000 cars will be annually produced. The contemplated changes will permit the increased output.

The plan, as affecting the profits of the business for the year beginning August 1, 1916, and thereafter, calls for a reduction in the selling price of the cars. It is true that this price might be at any time increased, but the plan called for the reduction in price of $80 a car. The capacity of the plant, without the additions thereto voted to be made (without a part of them at least), would produce more than 600,000 cars annually. This number, and more, could have been sold for $440 instead of $360, a difference in the return for capital, labor, and materials employed of at least $48,000,000. In short, the plan does not call for and is not intended to produce immediately a more profitable business, but a less profitable one; not only less profitable than formerly, but less profitable than it is admitted it might be made. The apparent immediate effect will be to diminish the value of shares and the returns to shareholders.

It is the contention of plaintiffs that the apparent effect of the plan is intended to be the continued and continuing effect of it, and that it is deliberately proposed, not of record and not by official corporate declaration, but nevertheless proposed, to continue the corporation henceforth as a semi-eleemosynary institution and not as a business institution. In support of this contention, they point to the attitude and to the expressions of Mr. Henry Ford.

Mr. Henry Ford is the dominant force in the business of the Ford Motor Company. No plan of operations could be adopted unless he consented, and no board of directors can be elected whom he does not favor. One of the directors of the company has no stock. One share was assigned to him to qualify him for the position, but it is not claimed that he owns it. A business, one of the largest in the world, and one of the most profitable, has been built up. It employs many men, at good pay.

"My ambition," said Mr. Ford, "is to employ still more men, to spread the benefits of this industrial system to the greatest possible number, to help them build up their lives and their homes. To do this we are putting the greatest share of our profits back in the business."

"With regard to dividends, the company paid sixty percent on its capitalization of two million dollars, or $1,200,000, leaving $58,000,000 to reinvest for the growth of the company. This is Mr. Ford's policy at present, and it is understood that the other stockholders cheerfully accede to this plan."

He had made up his mind in the summer of 1916 that no dividends other than the regular dividends should be paid, "for the present."

Q. For how long? Had you fixed in your mind anytime in the future, when you were going to pay? A. No.

Q. That was indefinite in the future? A. That was indefinite; yes, sir.

The record, and especially the testimony of Mr. Ford, convinces that he has to some extent the attitude towards shareholders of one who has dispensed and distributed to them large gains and that they should be content to take what he chooses to give. His testimony creates the impression, also, that he thinks the Ford Motor Company has made too much money, has had too large profits, and that, although large profits might be still earned, a sharing of them with the public, by reducing the price of the output of the company, ought to be undertaken. We have no doubt that certain sentiments, philanthropic and altruistic, creditable to Mr. Ford, had large influence in determining the policy to be pursued by the Ford Motor Company—the policy which has been herein referred to.

* * * There should be no confusion (of which there is evidence) of the duties which Mr. Ford conceives that he and the stockholders owe to the general public and the duties which in law he and his codirectors owe to protesting, minority stockholders. A business corporation is organized and carried on primarily for the profit of the stockholders. The powers of the directors are to be employed for that end. The discretion of directors is to be exercised in the choice of means to attain that end, and does not extend to a change in the end itself, to the reduction of profits, or to the nondistribution of profits among stockholders in order to devote them to other purposes.

There is committed to the discretion of directors, a discretion to be exercised in good faith, the infinite details of business, including the wages which shall be paid to employés, the number of hours they shall work, the conditions under which labor shall be carried on, and the price for which products shall be offered to the public.

It is said by appellants that the motives of the board members are not material and will not be inquired into by the court so long as their acts are within their lawful powers. As we have pointed out, and the proposition does not require argument to sustain it, it is not within the lawful powers of a board of directors to shape and conduct the affairs of a corporation for the merely incidental benefit of shareholders and for the primary purpose of benefiting others, and no one will contend that, if the avowed purpose of the defendant directors was to sacrifice the interests of shareholders, it would not be the duty of the courts to interfere.

We are not, however, persuaded that we should interfere with the proposed expansion of the business of the Ford Motor Company. In view of the fact that the selling price of products may be increased at any time, the ultimate results of the larger business cannot be certainly estimated. The judges are not business experts. It is recognized that plans must often be made for a long future, for expected competition, for a continuing as well as an immediately profitable venture. The experience of the Ford Motor Company is evidence of capable management of its affairs. It may be noticed incidentally, that it took from the public the money required for the execution of its plan, and that the very considerable salaries paid to Mr. Ford and to certain executive officers and employés were not diminished. We are not satisfied that the alleged motives of the directors, in so far as they are reflected in the conduct of the business, menace the interests of shareholders. It is enough to say, perhaps, that the court of equity is at all times open to complaining shareholders having a just grievance.

Assuming the general plan and policy of expansion and the details of it to have been sufficiently, formally, approved at the October and November, 1917, meetings of directors, and assuming further that the plan and policy and the details agreed upon were for the best ultimate interest of the company and therefore of its shareholders, what does it amount to in justification of a refusal to declare and pay a special dividend or dividends? The Ford Motor Company was able to estimate with nicety its income and profit. It could sell more cars than it could make. Having ascertained what it would cost to produce a car and to sell it, the profit upon each car depended upon the selling price. That being fixed, the yearly income and profit was determinable, and, within slight variations, was certain. * * *

Defendants say, and it is true, that a considerable cash balance must be at all times carried by such a concern. But, as has been stated, there was a large daily, weekly, monthly, receipt of cash. The output was practically continuous and was continuously, and within a few days, turned into cash. Moreover, the contemplated expenditures were not to be immediately made. The large sum appropriated for the smelter plant was payable over a considerable period of time. So that, without going further, it would appear that, accepting and approving the plan of the directors, it was their duty to distribute on or near the 1st of August, 1916, a very large sum of money to stockholders.

In reaching this conclusion, we do not ignore, but recognize, the validity of the proposition that plaintiffs have from the beginning profited by, if they have not lately, officially, participated in, the general policy of expansion pursued by this corporation. We do not lose sight of the fact that it had been, upon an occasion, agreeable to the plaintiffs to increase the capital stock to $100,000,000 by a stock dividend of $98,000,000. These things go only to answer other contentions now made by plaintiffs, and do not and cannot operate to estop them to demand proper dividends upon the stock they own. It is obvious that an annual dividend of 60 percent, upon $2,000,000 or $1,200,-000, is the equivalent of a very small dividend upon $100,000,000, or more.

The decree of the court below fixing and determining the specific amount to be distributed to stockholders is affirmed. * * *

STEERE, FELLOWS, STONE, and BROOKE, JJ., concurred with OSTRANDER, J.

MOORE, J. * * * I do not agree with all that is said by [JUSTICE OSTRANDER] in his discussion of the question of dividends. I do agree with him in his conclusion that the accumulation of so large a surplus establishes the fact that there has been an arbitrary refusal to distribute funds that ought to have been distributed to the stockholders as dividends. I therefore agree with the conclusion reached by him upon that phase of the case.

BIRD, C.J., and KUHN, J., concurred with MOORE, J.

WILDERMAN v. WILDERMAN

Court of Chancery of Delaware, 1974.
315 A.2d 610.

MARVEL, VICE CHANCELLOR:

Eleanor M. Wilderman, the plaintiff in this action, sues in her own right and in her capacity as a stockholder with an interest in one-half of the issued and outstanding stock of the defendant Marble Craft Company, Inc. She primarily seeks a ruling to the effect that the defendant Joseph M. Wilderman (the president of the corporate defendant and her former husband) for the fiscal years ending March 31, from 1971 through 1973, caused excessive and unauthorized payments to be made to himself out of earnings of the corporate defendant and that such payments, made in the form of unearned and unauthorized salary and bonuses, must accordingly be returned to the treasury of Marble Craft Company.

Plaintiff asks that upon the Court ordered return of such excessive payments to the corporate treasury that they be treated as corporate profits and required to be distributed as dividends, thereby opening the way to plaintiff to share in the net corporate profits as a stockholder with a 50% equity in her corporation. Plaintiff also asks that appropriate adjustments be made in the corporate defendant's pension plan so as to reflect the return to the corporate treasury of amounts found to be excessive compensation received by the defendant for the fiscal years in question. Also sought is an injunction against disbursement by the individual defendant of moneys from corporate funds or the transfer by such defendant of corporate assets without the approval of the board of directors of the corporation. Finally, plaintiff seeks an order directing the continuance of the business of the corporate defendant under a custodian as provided for under the provisions of 8 Del.C. § 226.

Marble Craft is engaged in the business of installing ceramic tile and marble facings in residences and commercial buildings, such business having been organized by the individual parties to this action some fifteen years ago, being originally operated from the family home. Defendant's initial knowledge of the tile business was gained while working briefly for his father-in-law prior to going into business with his former wife, and there is no doubt but that defendant has been the major force in the business of the corporate defendant inasmuch as he has done most of the estimating, supervising and business getting for the corporation, working up to sixty hours or more per week on corporate business. Plaintiff, on the other hand, has been primarily a bookkeeper for the business, although there is no doubt but that plaintiff is fully versed in the tile business, her father having started such a business in 1929. Significantly, in the beginning of the enterprise the parties' respective compensation was not entirely disparate, as it is now, defendant having initially drawn $125 a week compared to plaintiff's $75.

The business proved successful as a family venture, and in 1961 it was incorporated under the name of Marble Craft Company, Inc., its authorized capital shares consisting of one hundred shares of stock being issued to plaintiff and defendant as joint tenants in exchange for the assets of the business. By-laws providing for the election of two directors were adopted, and the parties, as the duly elected directors, thereupon chose themselves to fill the designated corporate offices, defendant being elected president and the plaintiff vice president, secretary, and treasurer.

The controversy here involved primarily centers around the amount of compensation which defendant has caused to be paid to himself for the fiscal years 1971, 1972 and 1973, compensation which had its origin in a policy[24]

---

24. [By the Court] This policy, however, encountered the opposition of the Internal Revenue Service which reduced the deduction allowable to Marble Craft for salary paid to defendant from $30,000 to $20,000 for 1965, from $30,000 to $25,000 for 1966, and from $60,000 to $40,000 for 1970. Presumably the effect of this action was twofold (1) the amount

designed to avoid corporate taxation by paying out the net corporate profits of Marble Craft Company in the form of executive compensation before the end of each taxable year, thus avoiding double taxation. Accordingly, dividends attributable to corporate profits have never been formally paid until ordered by the Court in the course of this litigation. Such policy of avoiding dividend payments initially worked to the advantage of both parties and their two children, the financial advantage to plaintiff in the plan having been virtually destroyed by the parties' separation and divorce. Thus, following the breakup of the home, plaintiff was largely excluded from the benefits enuring to defendant as a result of the large amounts he proceeded to pay himself. Asserting his authority as the chief executive officer of the corporate defendant, defendant caused the amount of compensation to be paid to him to be increased from $25,000 in 1963 to $60,000 in 1970, the last year for which salary payments to defendant are not questioned, such salary having concededly been authorized by corporate resolution. Next, despite the pendency of this action defendant paid himself a bonus of $71,738.71 in addition to a flat salary of $20,800 for the fiscal year 1971, the salary being based on an authorized draw of $400 per week, this being the first year after marital differences arose in which defendant could not point to at least tacit corporate authorization as to the full amount of his compensation. For the fiscal year 1972 defendant paid himself total compensation of $35,000, a year in which corporate profits were substantially lower than those of the previous year due to a building trades strike, and for the fiscal year ending March 31, 1973, defendant caused payment to himself of total compensation in the amount of $86,893.40. During this same period plaintiff received the annual sum of $7,800 for her services to the corporation.

On June 26, 1972, in an effort to work out some accommodation between the parties, a custodian was appointed by order of this Court as provided for by 8 Del.C. § 226(a)(2). However, the deadlock between the parties persisted, and on March 29, 1973, the defendant having caused the sum of $86,893.40[25] to be paid to himself as compensation for such fiscal year, an order was entered, on the recommendation of the custodian, which stipulated that such payment was without prejudice to the right to contest defendant's compensation in excess of his authorized salary of $20,800. Also authorized and paid on the custodian's recommendation was a dividend of $20,000 to be divided equally between plaintiff and defendant.

The authority to compensate corporate officers is normally vested in the board of directors, 8 Del.C. § 122(5), and the compensating of corporate officers is usually a matter of contract.

Next, while defendant's authorized compensation for the fiscal year 1970 was concededly $60,000, his readoption of a formula basis for arriving at his compensation in the years following was clearly unauthorized, thus defendant's use of the previous formula method of calculating his compensation for the fiscal years 1971, 1972 and 1973 must be reexamined. I conclude that plaintiff's March 29th, 1971 letter concerning defendant's compensation, when read in the light of the filing of this action on April 7, 1971, clearly

of disallowance was taxed as income to the corporation, and (2) the amount of disallowance less the tax due thereon became a de facto dividend.

25. [By the Court] Based on an authorized salary of $35,000 per annum plus 15% of gross receipts in excess of $300,000, a formula which was operative through the fiscal year 1970.

constituted an adequate expression of plaintiff's intention to rescind the 1970 resolution concerning defendant's compensation and hence served to revoke board authorization for the continuing payment to him of compensation on the basis recognized for 1970.

By early April 1971 the management of Marble Craft was clearly deadlocked with its owner-managers in complete disagreement as to the amount of compensation to be paid the defendant, the payment of anything above a $400 weekly salary being opposed by plaintiff. Therefore, the only amount agreed upon by the board and hence the only authorized payment to Mr. Wilderman for the fiscal years 1971, 1972 and 1973 would appear to have been at the rate of $20,800 per year, or $400 per week, and that additional compensation received by him for the years in question must find its authorization in the theory of quantum meruit.

Turning from the issue of corporate authorization of defendant's salary to the issue of the reasonableness of the compensation paid Mr. Wilderman, plaintiff contends that the compensation paid to defendant for the years in question was unreasonable, plaintiff arguing that although courts are hesitant to inquire into the reasonableness of executive compensation when it is fixed by a disinterested board, the standard for fixing executive compensation is obviously more strict when it is fixed by the recipient himself. And where, as in the case at bar, the recipient's vote as a director was necessary to the fixing of the amount of his compensation, then the burden of showing the reasonableness of such compensation clearly falls upon its recipient. This is so, of course, because of the fiduciary position which directors hold towards their corporation and its stockholders.

As to the facts to be considered in reaching a determination of the question as to whether or not defendant has met the burden he must carry there is little authority in Delaware. In Hall v. Isaacs, [37 Del.Ch. 530, 146 A.2d 602 (1958), affirmed in part 39 Del.Ch. 244, 163 A.2d 288 (1960)] the Court was of the view that evidence of what other executives similarly situated received was relevant, and in Meiselman v. Eberstadt, [39 Del.Ch. 563, 170 A.2d 720 (1961)] the ability of the executive was considered. Other factors which have been judicially recognized elsewhere are whether or not the Internal Revenue Service has allowed the corporation to deduct the amount of salary alleged to be unreasonable. Other relevant factors are whether the salary bears a reasonable relation to the success of the corporation, the amount previously received as salary, whether increases in salary are geared to increases in the value of services rendered, and the amount of the challenged salary compared to other salaries paid by the employer. See 2 Washington and Rothschild, Compensating the Corporate Executive, 848–873 (3rd Ed.1962). Dr. Seligman, an expert, testified that on the basis of a financial analysis of Marble Craft and its present earnings that reasonable compensation for defendant would range between $25,000 and $35,000. It also appears that the Internal Revenue Service proposes to permit Marble Craft a deduction of $52,000 for defendant's 1971 compensation of $92,538.

On the present record I am not convinced that defendant has discharged his burden as to the reasonableness of amounts he has drawn for all of the years in question. He has, first of all, failed to produce substantial evidence as to what other executives in the local tile business earn. Next, in light of the gross earnings of the corporate defendant and the facts concerning work of Marble Craft at Longwood Gardens there is some doubt as to whether or not defendant's work has been as truly essential and productive as he contends. Furthermore, defendant's compensation was caused by his own fiat to rise rapidly from $30,000 in 1966 to over $90,000 for 1971, although the earnings of Marble Craft rose only from about $380,000 in 1966 to approximately $680,000 for 1971.

I conclude from a consideration of all of the facts and circumstances surrounding defendant's services to his corporation, including the fact that the total number of employees of the business is about twenty, that compensation for defendant in excess of the compensation suggested by the financial analyst who testified at trial would be reasonable but that such compensation should be within the limits considered appropriate by the Internal Revenue Service. Such compensation should also constitute a reasonable increase over defendant's average salary of some $30,000 for the period 1963 through 1966 when the profits of Marble Craft were about half its 1971 earnings.

Thus, while for the fiscal years 1971, 1972 and 1973 Mr. Wilderman was technically entitled to be compensated for his services in the amount of only $20,800, I am of the opinion that in light of the nature of defendant's services to the corporation, which appear to have been important to its success, that he is entitled to compensation in the amount of $45,000 for the fiscal year 1971 and the same amount for fiscal 1973. Defendant's compensation of $35,000 for the fiscal year ending 1972 will be left undisturbed. Accordingly, he will be ordered to return $47,538 in excess compensation to the corporate treasury for fiscal 1971 and $41,893.40 for fiscal 1973, both amounts with interest.

Additionally, because payments to the Marble Craft pension fund have been tied to defendant's compensation for the years in question, defendant will be directed to repay to the defendant Marble Craft excessive payments to such fund in the same ratio as the refunds of his excessive compensation.

As to what should be appropriate dividends payable out of the reconstructed net profits of the company after the adjustments here directed to be made is, I believe, a matter for the board of directors in the first instance and in the event of deadlock for the custodian. I also decline to fix plaintiff's salary because such was not raised in the pleadings or at trial and for the reason given for declining to set a future dividend rate. * * *

An appropriate order may be submitted on notice.

Notes

(1) In Mann–Paller Found., Inc. v. Econometric Research, Inc., 644 F.Supp. 92 (D.D.C.1986), the majority shareholder of the defendant corporation received compensation in the amount of $347,745 in 1985; the minority shareholder received nothing since no dividend was declared. The minority shareholder sued to recover $191,369.10 on the theory that the compensation to the majority shareholder constituted a "de facto dividend" that had not been paid in proportion to shareholdings. The Court granted summary judgment for the defendants: The suit failed as a claim to compel the payment of a dividend since it did not allege "that the withholding of [a dividend] is explicable only on the theory of an oppressive or fraudulent abuse of discretion" (644 F.Supp. at 98); the suit also failed as a claim

alleging improper compensation to a shareholder-employee since such a suit must be brought in the name of and for the benefit of the corporation (a derivative suit) rather than directly on behalf of a minority shareholder. Compare Murphy v. Country House, Inc., 349 N.W.2d 289 (Minn.App.1984).

(2) Other courts have agreed with the basic principles of *Wilderman* that where one party in effect sets his own compensation, he then has the burden of establishing its fundamental fairness. Lynch v. Patterson, 701 P.2d 1126 (Wyo. 1985); Giannotti v. Hamway, 239 Va. 14, 387 S.E.2d 725 (1990). Cases of this type shade off into discussions of the responsibilities of directors in self-dealing cases discussed in chapter 11, section A.

ROBERT W. HAMILTON, BUSINESS ORGANIZATIONS: UNINCORPORATED BUSINESSES AND CLOSELY HELD CORPORATIONS[26]
Pp. 304–05 (1997).

Superficially, a purchase by a corporation of its own shares may not be thought of as involving a distribution at all. It may appear to be the purchase of an asset rather than the making of a distribution. That analysis, however, confuses transactions in which the corporation repurchases *its own stock* and transactions in which it purchases stock *issued by another corporation.* The former is a distribution, the latter is an investment.

When a corporation buys back its own stock, it does not receive anything of value in the hands of the corporation. The remaining shareholders continue to own 100 percent of the corporate assets (now reduced by the amount of the payment used to reacquire the shares). A corporation cannot treat stock in itself that it has purchased as an asset any more than it can treat its authorized but unissued stock as an asset. One cannot own 10 percent of oneself and have one's total worth be 110 percent of the value of one's assets. This point is so fundamental that it may be well to re-read the last few sentences.

Stock issued by another corporation is entirely different. That does not create the same circularity problem. Shares of corporation B have value based on the assets owned by corporation *B*; if shares of corporation B are purchased by corporation *A* they are an asset in the hands of corporation *A*.

The fact that a repurchase of shares constitutes a distribution can be most easily appreciated by considering a proportionate repurchase of stock by the corporation from each shareholder. Assume that three persons each own 100 shares of stock in a corporation, its entire outstanding stock. The shareholders decide that each of them will sell 10 shares back to the corporation for $100 per share, or a total of $1,000 each. When the transaction is completed, each shareholder continues to own one-third of the corporation (now represented by 90 shares rather than 100 shares), the corporation is $3,000 poorer and the shareholders are each $1,000 richer. Clearly, there has been a distribution even though the transaction was cast in the form of a repurchase of stock rather than a direct distribution of assets by the corporation. * * *

26. Reprinted with permission of Aspen Law & Business/Panel Publishers, a division of Aspen Publishers, Inc.

Under most state statutes, the 30 shares reacquired by the corporation in the previous example are called *treasury shares*. Treasury shares are viewed as being held by the corporation in a sort of twilight zone until they are either retired permanently or resold to someone else in the future. Treasury shares are not an asset of the corporation even though they are salable and may be sold at some later time. Exactly the same thing can be said of every share of authorized but unissued stock.

Assume that the corporation in the example described above decides to resell the treasury shares to X (a nonshareholder) for $3,000. The interests of each of the three original shareholders have been diluted: There are now four shareholders owning shares in the ratio 90:90:90:30. The corporation could have paid the original shareholders a cash dividend of $1,000 each and then sold 33 shares of authorized but unissued stock to X for $3,000 with * * * the same economic result. * * *

A repurchase of shares by the corporation is a distribution even if the corporation purchases only shares owned by one shareholder rather than proportionately from each shareholder. Such a transaction is a disproportionate distribution (i.e., one not shared proportionately by all shareholders). The corporation has made a distribution to a single shareholder equal to the purchase price it paid for the shares. This transaction is not all bad from the standpoint of the other shareholders, however, since it simultaneously increases their percentage interest in the corporation. For example, if the corporation with three shareholders in the above example repurchased all 100 shares owned by shareholder A for $10,000, the interests of shareholders B and C in the corporation are both increased from 33.3 percent to 50 percent. The assets of the corporation are reduced by the $10,000 purchase price paid to shareholder A to eliminate his or her interest in the corporation. Whether or not this is a "winner" for A or for B and C depends on the value of the assets in the corporation before the share repurchase.

Notes

(1) Consider the situation where one shareholder in a closely held corporation wishes to leave the enterprise, and the other shareholders are willing or committed to purchasing his or her shares. The price may be established either by negotiation or by prior agreement. How should the transaction be structured? Should the remaining shareholders each purchase their proportional number of shares? Should the corporation purchase the departing shares? Does it make any economic difference which way the transaction is structured?

(a) One can readily envision practical problems in a proportional purchase transaction. Some of the shareholders may not have readily available liquid assets to make the purchase. Some may be unwilling to increase their investment in the business with funds that were set aside for personal or family purposes. Unless the schedule of purchases is strictly adhered to, the proportional interests of the remaining shareholders will be affected; in some instances even a modest change in percentage ownership will dramatically affect a carefully balanced sharing of control. While these problems usually can be solved, perhaps by arranging for the corporation to loan funds to the reluctant shareholder, the alternative solution seems neater and cleaner: simply have the corporation purchase and retire the shares of the departing shareholder.

(b) A redemption of shares by the corporation also provides tax benefits. From the standpoint of the departing shareholder, there is no difference: a redemption of shares is treated as a sale or exchange of the shares giving rise to short-or long-term capital gain or loss equal to the difference between the redemption price of the shares and the shareholder's basis.[27] But what about the tax position of the other shareholder if the corporation is a C corporation with earnings and profits? If the corporation distributed the redemption price to the other shareholders in order for them to purchase the shares, there would clearly have been a taxable dividend. Could not the IRS argue that the redemption itself is essentially equivalent to a dividend to the remaining shareholders, particularly if the redemption was at a bargain price, so that the value of the interests of the non-redeeming shareholders was increased by the redemption? In Holsey v. Commissioner, 258 F.2d 865 (3d Cir.1958), the court held in this kind of situation that the remaining shareholders could not be taxed on the increase in wealth until the gain was realized by a sale of the shares.[28] One situation in which a tax will be imposed on the non-redeeming shareholders is where they are obligated by contract to purchase the stock of the retiring shareholder. If the corporation redeems the stock, its payment discharges a personal obligation of the nonredeemed shareholder and is a constructive dividend to him.[29]

Thus, a disproportionate redemption of stock permits the distribution of earnings of a C corporation to shareholders at a minimum tax cost.

(2) Redemptions of shares are treated by corporation statutes as a distribution subject to the legal restraints on dividends and distributions described in the following section. A redemption in violation of these restrictions probably may be enjoined. See e.g. Neimark v. Mel Kramer Sales, Inc., 102 Wis.2d 282, 306 N.W.2d 278 (App.1981). What should be done if the shareholders wish to have the corporation redeem the shares but the corporation fails to meet fully these tests for the legality of the redemption?

(3) A very common feature of disproportionate redemption transactions is that the corporation may pay only a portion of the purchase price in cash when the transaction is closed, the balance being represented by promissory notes payable over an extended period of time. The deferred purchase price may simply reflect the reality that the corporation lacks liquid assets sufficient to acquire the redeemed shares entirely for cash at the closing. The future payments may be made out of subsequent earnings or cash flow, thereby in effect making payment of the purchase price in part contingent on the future success of the business. A deferred sale may also reflect further tax planning within a C corporation, since future earnings may in effect be diverted for the benefit of shareholders without incurring the double taxation on dividends.

---

27. [By the Editor] Exceptions to the statement in the text exist. For example, if the sale is "essentially equivalent to a dividend," the redemption is treated as a dividend giving rise to ordinary income rather than as a sale or exchange giving rise to a capital gain or loss.

28. The Internal Service acquiesced in this result. Rev.Rul. 58–614, 1958–2 C.B. 920. See generally William J. Rands, Closely Held Corporations: Federal Tax Consequences of Stock

Transfer Restrictions, 7 J.Corp.Law 449, 456–57 (1982).

29. [By the Editor] An example is Sullivan v. United States, 363 F.2d 724, 729 (8th Cir. 1966) cert. denied 387 U.S. 905, 87 S.Ct. 1683, 18 L.Ed.2d 622 (1967). Such a transaction is a constructive to the remaining shareholders for exactly the same reason that use of corporate funds to pay a valid debt of a shareholder is a constructive dividend to that shareholder.

DONAHUE v. RODD ELECTROTYPE CO.

Supreme Judicial Court of Massachusetts, 1975.
367 Mass. 578, 328 N.E.2d 505.

Before TAURO, C.J., and REARDON, QUIRICO, BRAUCHER, KAPLAN and WILKINS, JJ.

TAURO, CHIEF JUSTICE.

The plaintiff, Euphemia Donahue, a minority stockholder in the Rodd Electrotype Company of New England, Inc. (Rodd Electrotype), a Massachusetts corporation, brings this suit against the directors of Rodd Electrotype, Charles H. Rodd, Frederick I. Rodd and Mr. Harold E. Magnuson, against Harry C. Rodd, a former director, officer, and controlling stockholder of Rodd Electrotype and against Rodd Electrotype (hereinafter called defendants). The plaintiff seeks to rescind Rodd Electrotype's purchase of Harry Rodd's shares in Rodd Electrotype and to compel Harry Rodd "to repay to the corporation the purchase price of said shares, $36,000, together with interest from the date of purchase." The plaintiff alleges that the defendants caused the corporation to purchase the shares in violation of their fiduciary duty to her, a minority stockholder of Rodd Electrotype.

The trial judge, after hearing oral testimony, dismissed the plaintiff's bill on the merits. He found that the purchase was without prejudice to the plaintiff and implicitly found that the transaction had been carried out in good faith and with inherent fairness. The Appeals Court affirmed with costs. Donahue v. Rodd Electrotype Co. of New England, Inc., 307 N.E.2d 8 (1974).
* * *

The evidence may be summarized as follows: In 1935, the defendant, Harry C. Rodd, began his employment with Rodd Electrotype, then styled the Royal Electrotype Company of New England, Inc. (Royal of New England). At that time, the company was a wholly-owned subsidiary of a Pennsylvania corporation, the Royal Electrotype Company (Royal Electrotype). Mr. Rodd's advancement within the company was rapid. The following year he was elected a director, and, in 1946, he succeeded to the position of general manager and treasurer.

In 1936, the plaintiff's husband, Joseph Donahue (now deceased), was hired by Royal of New England as a "finisher" of electrotype plates. His duties were confined to operational matters within the plant. Although he ultimately achieved the positions of plant superintendent (1946) and corporate vice president (1955), Donahue never participated in the "management" aspect of the business.

In the years preceding 1955, the parent company, Royal Electrotype, made available to Harry Rodd and Joseph Donahue shares of the common stock in its subsidiary, Royal of New England. Harry Rodd took advantage of the opportunities offered to him and acquired 200 shares for $20 a share. Joseph Donahue, at the suggestion of Harry Rodd, who hoped to interest Donahue in the business, eventually obtained fifty shares in two twenty-five share lots priced at $20 a share. The parent company at all times retained 725 of the 1,000 outstanding shares. One Lawrence W. Kelley owned the remaining twenty-five shares.

In June of 1955, Royal of New England purchased all 725 of its shares owned by its parent company. The total price amounted to $135,000. Royal of New England remitted $75,000 of this total in cash and executed five promissory notes of $12,000 each, due in each of the succeeding five years.

Lawrence W. Kelley's twenty-five shares were also purchased at this time for $1,000. A substantial portion of Royal of New England's cash expenditures was loaned to the company by Harry Rodd, who mortgaged his house to obtain some of the necessary funds.

The stock purchases left Harry Rodd in control of Royal of New England. Early in 1955, before the purchases, he had assumed the presidency of the company. His 200 shares gave him a dominant eighty percent interest. Joseph Donahue, at this time, was the only minority stockholder.

Subsequent events reflected Harry Rodd's dominant influence. In June, 1960, more than a year after the last obligation to Royal Electrotype had been discharged, the company was renamed the Rodd Electrotype Company of New England, Inc. In 1962, Charles H. Rodd, Harry Rodd's son (a defendant here), who had long been a company employee working in the plant, became corporate vice president. In 1963, he joined his father on the board of directors. In 1964, another son, Frederick I. Rodd (also a defendant), replaced Joseph Donahue as plant superintendent. By 1965, Harry Rodd had evidently decided to reduce his participation in corporate management. That year Charles Rodd succeeded him as president and general manager of Rodd Electrotype.

From 1959 to 1967, Harry Rodd pursued what may fairly be termed a gift program by which he distributed the majority of his shares equally among his two sons and his daughter, Phyllis E. Mason. Each child received thirty-nine shares. Two shares were returned to the corporate treasury in 1966.

We come now to the events of 1970 which form the grounds for the plaintiff's complaint. In May of 1970, Harry Rodd was seventy-seven years old. The record indicates that for some time he had not enjoyed the best of health and that he had undergone a number of operations. His sons wished him to retire. Mr. Rodd was not averse to this suggestion. However, he insisted that some financial arrangements be made with respect to his remaining eighty-one shares of stock. A number of conferences ensued. Harry Rodd and Charles Rodd (representing the company) negotiated terms of purchase for forty-five shares which, Charles Rodd testified, would reflect the book value and liquidating value of the shares.

A special board meeting convened on July 13, 1970. As the first order of business, Harry Rodd resigned his directorship of Rodd Electrotype. The remaining incumbent directors, Charles Rodd and Mr. Harold E. Magnuson (clerk of the company and a defendant and defense attorney in the instant suit), elected Frederick Rodd to replace his father. The three directors then authorized Rodd Electrotype's president (Charles Rodd) to execute an agreement between Harry Rodd and the company in which the company would purchase forty-five shares for $800 a share ($36,000).

The stock purchase agreement was formalized between the parties on July 13, 1970. Two days later, a sale pursuant to the July 13 agreement was consummated. At approximately the same time, Harry Rodd resigned his last corporate office, that of treasurer.

Harry Rodd completed divestiture of his Rodd Electrotype stock in the following year. * * * Thus, in March, 1971, the shareholdings in Rodd

Electrotype were apportioned as follows: Charles Rodd, Frederick Rodd and Phyllis Mason each held fifty-one shares; the Donahues[30] held fifty shares.

A special meeting of the stockholders of the company was held on March 30, 1971. At the meeting, Charles Rodd, company president and general manager, reported the tentative results of an audit conducted by the company auditors and reported generally on the company events of the year. For the first time, the Donahues learned that the corporation had purchased Harry Rodd's shares. According to the minutes of the meeting, following Charles Rodd's report, the Donahues raised questions about the purchase. They then voted against a resolution, ultimately adopted by the remaining stockholders, to approve Charles Rodd's report. * * *

A few weeks after the meeting, the Donahues, acting through their attorney, offered their shares to the corporation on the same terms given to Harry Rodd. Mr. Harold E. Magnuson replied by letter that the corporation would not purchase the shares and was not in a financial position to do so.[31] This suit followed.

In her argument before this court, the plaintiff has characterized the corporate purchase of Harry Rodd's shares as an unlawful distribution of corporate assets to controlling stockholders. She urges that the distribution constitutes a breach of the fiduciary duty owed by the Rodds, as controlling stockholders, to her, a minority stockholder in the enterprise, because the Rodds failed to accord her an equal opportunity to sell her shares to the corporation. The defendants reply that the stock purchase was within the powers of the corporation and met the requirements of good faith and inherent fairness imposed on a fiduciary in his dealings with the corporation. They assert that there is no right to equal opportunity in corporate stock purchases for the corporate treasury. For the reasons hereinafter noted, we agree with the plaintiff and reverse the decree of the Superior Court. However, we limit the applicability of our holding to "close corporations" * * *. Whether the holding should apply to other corporations is left for decision in another case, on a proper record. * * *

A. *Close Corporations.* In previous opinions, we have alluded to the distinctive nature of the close corporation, but have never defined precisely what is meant by a close corporation. There is no single, generally accepted definition. Some commentators emphasize an "integration of ownership and management" (Note, Statutory Assistance for Closely Held Corporations, 71 Harv.L.Rev. 1498 [1958]), in which the stockholders occupy most management positions. Others focus on the number of stockholders and the nature of the market for the stock. In this view, close corporations have few stockholders; there is little market for corporate stock. * * * We accept aspects of both definitions. We deem a close corporation to be typified by: (1) a small number of stockholders; (2) no ready market for the corporate stock; and (3) substan-

---

30. [By the Court] Joseph Donahue gave his wife, the plaintiff, joint ownership of his fifty shares in 1962. In 1968, they transferred five shares to their son, Dr. Robert Donahue. On Joseph Donahue's death, the plaintiff became outright owner of the forty-five share block. This was the ownership pattern which obtained in March, 1971.

31. [By the Court] Between 1965 and 1969, the company offered to purchase the Donahue shares for amounts between $2,000 and $10,-000 ($40 to $200 a share). The Donahues rejected these offers.

tial majority stockholder participation in the management, direction and operations of the corporation.

As thus defined, the close corporation bears striking resemblance to a partnership. Commentators and courts have noted that the close corporation is often little more than an "incorporated" or "chartered" partnership. Ripin v. United States Woven Label Co., 205 N.Y. 442, 447, 98 N.E. 855, 856 (1912) ("little more (though not quite the same as) than chartered partnerships"). The stockholders "clothe" their partnership "with the benefits peculiar to a corporation, limited liability, perpetuity and the like." In the Matter of Surchin v. Approved Bus. Mach. Co., Inc., 55 Misc.2d 888, 889, 286 N.Y.S.2d 580, 581 (Sup.Ct.1967). In essence, though, the enterprise remains one in which ownership is limited to the original parties or transferees of their stock to whom the other stockholders have agreed,[32] in which ownership and management are in the same hands, and in which the owners are quite dependent on one another for the success of the enterprise. Many close corporations are "really partnerships, between two or three people who contribute their capital, skills, experience and labor." Kruger v. Gerth, 16 N.Y.2d 802, 805, 263 N.Y.S.2d 1, 3, 210 N.E.2d 355, 356 (1965) (Desmond, C.J., dissenting). Just as in a partnership, the relationship among the stockholders must be one of trust, confidence and absolute loyalty if the enterprise is to succeed. Close corporations with substantial assets and with more numerous stockholders are no different from smaller close corporations in this regard. All participants rely on the fidelity and abilities of those stockholders who hold office. Disloyalty and self-seeking conduct on the part of any stockholder will engender bickering, corporate stalemates, and, perhaps, efforts to achieve dissolution.

In Helms v. Duckworth, 101 U.S.App.D.C. 390, 249 F.2d 482 (1957), the United States Court of Appeals for the District of Columbia Circuit had before it a stockholders' agreement providing for the purchase of the shares of a deceased stockholder by the surviving stockholder in a small "two-man" close corporation. The court held the surviving stockholder to a duty "to deal fairly, honestly, and openly with * * * [his] fellow stockholders." Id. at 487. Judge Burger, now Chief Justice Burger, writing for the court, emphasized the resemblance of the two-man close corporation to a partnership: "In an intimate business venture such as this, stockholders of a close corporation occupy a position similar to that of joint adventurers and partners. While courts have sometimes declared stockholders 'do not bear toward each other that same relation of trust and confidence which prevails in partnerships,' this view ignores the practical realities of the organization and functioning of a small 'two-man' corporation organized to carry on a small business enterprise in which the stockholders, directors, and managers are the same persons" (footnotes omitted). Id. at 486.

---

32. [By the Court] The original owners commonly impose restrictions on transfers of stock designed to prevent outsiders who are unacceptable to the other stockholders from acquiring an interest in the close corporation. These restrictions often take the form of agreements among the stockholders and the corporation or by-laws which give the corporation or the other stockholders a right of "first refusal" when any stockholder desires to sell his shares. In a partnership, of course, a partner cannot transfer his interest in the partnership so as to give his assignee a right to participate in the management or business affairs of the continuing partnership without the agreement of the other partners. [UPA (1914)] § 27. See Hazen v. Warwick, 256 Mass. 302, 308, 152 N.E. 342 (1926).

Although the corporate form provides * * * advantages for the stockholders (limited liability, perpetuity, and so forth), it also supplies an opportunity for the majority stockholders to oppress or disadvantage minority stockholders. The minority is vulnerable to a variety of oppressive devices, termed "freezeouts," which the majority may employ. See, generally, Note, Freezing Out Minority Shareholders, 74 Harv.L.Rev. 1630 (1961). An authoritative study of such "freezeouts" enumerates some of the possibilities: "The squeezers [those who employ the freezeout techniques] may refuse to declare dividends; they may drain off the corporation's earnings in the form of exorbitant salaries and bonuses to the majority shareholder-officers and perhaps to their relatives, or in the form of high rent by the corporation for property leased from majority shareholders * * *; they may deprive minority shareholders of corporate offices and of employment by the company; they may cause the corporation to sell its assets at an inadequate price to the majority shareholders * * *." F.H. O'Neal and J. Derwin, Expulsion or Oppression of Business Associates, 42 (1961). In particular, the power of the board of directors, controlled by the majority, to declare or withhold dividends and to deny the minority employment is easily converted to a device to disadvantage minority stockholders.

The minority can, of course, initiate suit against the majority and their directors. Self-serving conduct by directors is proscribed by the director's fiduciary obligation to the corporation. However, in practice, the plaintiff will find difficulty in challenging dividend or employment policies. Such policies are considered to be within the judgment of the directors. This court has said: "The courts prefer not to interfere * * * with the sound financial management of the corporation by its directors, but declare as a general rule that the declaration of dividends rests within the sound discretion of the directors, refusing to interfere with their determination unless a plain abuse of discretion is made to appear." Crocker v. Waltham Watch Co., 315 Mass. 397, 402, 53 N.E.2d 230, 233 (1944). Judicial reluctance to interfere combines with the difficulty of proof when the standard is "plain abuse of discretion" or bad faith, to limit the possibilities for relief. Although contractual provisions in an "agreement of association and articles of organization" or in by-laws have justified decrees in this jurisdiction ordering dividend declarations, generally, plaintiffs who seek judicial assistance against corporate dividend or employment policies[33] do not prevail.

Thus, when these types of "freezeouts" are attempted by the majority stockholders, the minority stockholders, cut off from all corporation-related revenues, must either suffer their losses or seek a buyer for their shares. Many minority stockholders will be unwilling or unable to wait for an alteration in majority policy. Typically, the minority stockholder in a close corporation has a substantial percentage of his personal assets invested in the corporation. Galler v. Galler, 32 Ill.2d 16, 27, 203 N.E.2d 577 (1964). The

---

33. [By the Court] Attacks on allegedly excessive salaries voted for officers and directors fare better in the courts. See Stratis v. Andreson, 254 Mass. 536, 150 N.E. 832 (1926); Sagalyn v. Meekins, Packard & Wheat, Inc., 290 Mass. 434, 195 N.E. 769 (1935). What is "reasonable compensation" is a question of fact. Black v. Parker Mfg. Co., 329 Mass. 105, 116, 106 N.E.2d 544 (1952). The proof which establishes an excess over such "reasonable compensation" appears easier than the proof which would establish bad faith or plain abuse of discretion.

stockholder may have anticipated that his salary from his position with the corporation would be his livelihood. Thus, he cannot afford to wait passively. He must liquidate his investment in the close corporation in order to reinvest the funds in income-producing enterprises.

At this point, the true plight of the minority stockholder in a close corporation becomes manifest. He cannot easily reclaim his capital. In a large public corporation, the oppressed or dissident minority stockholder could sell his stock in order to extricate some of his invested capital. By definition, this market is not available for shares in the close corporation. In a partnership, a partner who feels abused by his fellow partners may cause dissolution by his "express will * * * at any time" ([UPA (1914)] § 31[1][b] and [2]) and recover his share of partnership assets and accumulated profits.[34] [UPA (1914)] § 38. If dissolution results in a breach of the partnership articles, the culpable partner will be liable in damages. [UPA (1914)] § 38(2)(a) II. By contrast, the stockholder in the close corporation or "incorporated partnership" may achieve dissolution and recovery of his share of the enterprise assets only by compliance with the rigorous terms of the applicable chapter of the General Laws. Rizzuto v. Onset Cafe, Inc., 330 Mass. 595, 597–598, 116 N.E.2d 249 (1953). "The dissolution of a corporation which is a creature of the Legislature is primarily a legislative function, and the only authority courts have to deal with this subject is the power conferred upon them by the Legislature." Leventhal v. Atlantic Fin. Corp., 316 Mass. 194, 205, 55 N.E.2d 20, 26 (1944). To secure dissolution of the ordinary close corporation subject to G.L. c. 156B, the stockholder, in the absence of corporate deadlock, must own at least fifty percent of the shares or have the advantage of a favorable provision in the articles of organization. The minority stockholder, by definition lacking fifty percent of the corporate shares, can never "authorize" the corporation to file a petition for dissolution under G.L. c. 156B, § 99(a), by his own vote. He will seldom have at his disposal the requisite favorable provision in the articles of organization.

Thus, in a close corporation, the minority stockholders may be trapped in a disadvantageous situation. No outsider would knowingly assume the position of the disadvantaged minority. The outsider would have the same difficulties. To cut losses, the minority stockholder may be compelled to deal with the majority. This is the capstone of the majority plan. Majority "freeze-out" schemes which withhold dividends are designed to compel the minority to relinquish stock at inadequate prices. When the minority stockholder agrees to sell out at less than fair value, the majority has won.

Because of the fundamental resemblance of the close corporation to the partnership, the trust and confidence which are essential to this scale and manner of enterprise, and the inherent danger to minority interests in the close corporation, we hold that stockholders[35] in the close corporation owe one another substantially the same fiduciary duty in the operation of the enter-

---

34. [By the Court] The partnership agreement may control the amount and timing of distribution in a way which is disadvantageous to the retiring partner.

35. [By the Court] We do not limit our holding to majority stockholders. In the close corporation, the minority may do equal damage through unscrupulous and improper "sharp dealings" with an unsuspecting majority. See

prise[36] that partners owe to one another. In our previous decisions, we have defined the standard of duty owed by partners to one another as the "utmost good faith and loyalty." Cardullo v. Landau, 329 Mass. 5, 8, 105 N.E.2d 843 (1952). Stockholders in close corporations must discharge their management and stockholder responsibilities in conformity with this strict good faith standard. They may not act out of avarice, expediency or self-interest in derogation of their duty of loyalty to the other stockholders and to the corporation.

We contrast this strict good faith standard with the somewhat less stringent standard of fiduciary duty to which directors and stockholders[37] of all corporations must adhere in the discharge of their corporate responsibilities. Corporate directors are held to a good faith and inherent fairness standard of conduct (Winchell v. Plywood Corp., 324 Mass. 171, 177, 85 N.E.2d 313 [1949]) and are not "permitted to serve two masters whose interests are antagonistic." Spiegel v. Beacon Participations, Inc., 297 Mass. 398, 411, 8 N.E.2d 895, 904 (1937). "Their paramount duty is to the corporation, and their personal pecuniary interests are subordinate to that duty." Durfee v. Durfee & Canning, Inc., 323 Mass. 187, 196, 80 N.E.2d 522, 527 (1948).

The more rigorous duty of partners and participants in a joint adventure, here extended to stockholders in a close corporation, was described by then Chief Judge Cardozo of the New York Court of Appeals in Meinhard v. Salmon, 249 N.Y. 458, 164 N.E. 545 (1928): "Joint adventurers, like copartners, owe to one another, while the enterprise continues, the duty of the finest loyalty. Many forms of conduct permissible in a workaday world for those acting at arm's length, are forbidden to those bound by fiduciary ties. * * * Not honesty alone, but the punctilio of an honor the most sensitive, is then the standard of behavior." Id. at 463–464, 164 N.E. at 546.

Application of this strict standard of duty to stockholders in close corporations is a natural outgrowth of the prior case law. In a number of cases involving close corporations, we have held stockholders participating in management to a standard of fiduciary duty more exacting than the traditional good faith and inherent fairness standard because of the trust and confidence reposed in them by the other stockholders. * * *

[W]e have imposed a duty of loyalty more exacting than that duty owed by a director to his corporation (Spiegel v. Beacon Participations, Inc., 297 Mass. 398, 410–411, 8 N.E.2d 895 [1937]) or by a majority stockholder to the minority in a public corporation because of facts particular to the close corporation in the cases. In the instant case, we extend this strict duty of

Helms v. Duckworth, 101 U.S.App.D.C. 390, 249 F.2d 482 (1957).

36. [By the Court] We stress that the strict fiduciary duty which we apply to stockholders in a close corporation in this opinion governs *only* their actions relative to the operations of the enterprise and the effects of that operation on the rights and investments of other stockholders. We express no opinion as to the standard of duty applicable to transactions in the shares of the close corporation when the corporation is not a party to the transaction. Cf.

Andrews, The Stockholder's Right to Equal Opportunity in the Sale of Shares, 78 Harv. L.Rev. 505 (1965).

37. [By the Court] The rule set out in many jurisdictions is: "The majority has the right to control; but when it does so, it occupies a fiduciary relation toward the minority, as much so as the corporation itself or its officers and directors." Southern Pac. Co. v. Bogert, 250 U.S. 483, 487–488, 39 S.Ct. 533, 535, 63 L.Ed. 1099 (1919).

loyalty to all stockholders in close corporations. The circumstances which justified findings of relationships of trust and confidence in these particular cases exist universally in modified form in all close corporations. See Kruger v. Gerth, 16 N.Y.2d 802, 806, 263 N.Y.S.2d 1, 210 N.E.2d 355 (1965) (Fuld, J., dissenting). Statements in other cases which suggest that stockholders of a corporation do not stand in a relationship of trust and confidence to one another will not be followed in the close corporation context.

B. *Equal Opportunity in a Close Corporation.* Under settled Massachusetts law, a domestic corporation, unless forbidden by statute, has the power to purchase its own shares. Dupee v. Boston Water Power Co., 114 Mass. 37, 43 (1873). * * * When the corporation reacquiring its own stock is a close corporation, the purchase is subject to the additional requirement, in the light of our holding in this opinion, that the stockholders, who, as directors or controlling stockholders, caused the corporation to enter into the stock purchase agreement, must have acted with the utmost good faith and loyalty to the other stockholders.

To meet this test, if the stockholder whose shares were purchased was a member of the controlling group, the controlling stockholders must cause the corporation to offer each stockholder an equal opportunity to sell a ratable number of his shares to the corporation at an identical price.[38] Purchase by the corporation confers substantial benefits on the members of the controlling group whose shares were purchased. These benefits are not available to the minority stockholders if the corporation does not also offer them an opportunity to sell their shares. The controlling group may not, consistent with its strict duty to the minority, utilize its control of the corporation to obtain special advantages and disproportionate benefit from its share ownership. Cf. Victor Brudney and Marvin A. Chirelstein, Fair Shares in Corporate Mergers and Takeovers, 88 Harv.L.Rev. 297, 334 (1974).

The benefits conferred by the purchase are twofold: (1) provision of a market for shares; (2) access to corporate assets for personal use. By definition, there is no ready market for shares of a close corporation. The purchase creates a market for shares which previously had been unmarketable. It transforms a previously illiquid investment into a liquid one. If the close corporation purchases shares only from a member of the controlling group, the controlling stockholder can convert his shares into cash at a time when none of the other stockholders can. Consistent with its strict fiduciary duty, the controlling group may not utilize its control of the corporation to establish an exclusive market in previously unmarketable shares from which the minority stockholders are excluded. See Jones v. H.F. Ahmanson & Co., 1 Cal.3d 93, 115, 81 Cal.Rptr. 592, 460 P.2d 464 (1969).

The purchase also distributes corporate assets to the stockholder whose shares were purchased. Unless an equal opportunity is given to all stockholders, the purchase of shares from a member of the controlling group operates as a *preferential* distribution of assets. In exchange for his shares, he receives a percentage of the contributed capital and accumulated profits of the enter-

---

38. [By the Court] Of course, a close corporation may purchase shares from one stockholder without offering the others an equal opportunity if all other stockholders give advance consent to the stock purchase arrangements through acceptance of an appropriate provision in the articles of organization, the corporate by-laws or a stockholder's agreement. Similarly, all other stockholders may ratify the purchase.

prise. The funds he so receives are available for his personal use. The other stockholders benefit from no such access to corporate property and cannot withdraw their shares of the corporate profits and capital in this manner unless the controlling group acquiesces. Although the purchase price for the controlling stockholder's shares may seem fair to the corporation and other stockholders under the tests established in the prior case law, the controlling stockholder whose stock has been purchased has still received a relative advantage over his fellow stockholders, inconsistent with his strict fiduciary duty—an opportunity to turn corporate funds to personal use.

The rule of equal opportunity in stock purchases by close corporations provides equal access to these benefits for all stockholders. We hold that, in any case in which the controlling stockholders have exercised their power over the corporation to deny the minority such equal opportunity, the minority shall be entitled to appropriate relief.[39] To the extent that language in Spiegel v. Beacon Participations, Inc., 297 Mass. 398, 431, 8 N.E.2d 895 (1937), and other cases suggests that there is no requirement of equal opportunity for minority stockholders when a close corporation purchases shares from a controlling stockholder, it is not to be followed.

C. *Application of the Law to this Case.* We turn now to the application of the learning set forth above to the facts of the instant case.

The strict standard of duty is plainly applicable to the stockholders in Rodd Electrotype. Rodd Electrotype is a close corporation. Members of the Rodd and Donahue families are the sole owners of the corporation's stock. In actual numbers, the corporation, immediately prior to the corporate purchase of Harry Rodd's shares, had six stockholders. The shares have not been traded, and no market for them seems to exist. Harry Rodd, Charles Rodd, Frederick Rodd, William G. Mason (Phyllis Mason's husband), and the plaintiff's husband all worked for the corporation. The Rodds have retained the paramount management positions.

Through their control of these management positions and of the majority of the Rodd Electrotype stock, the Rodds effectively controlled the corporation. In testing the stock purchase from Harry Rodd against the applicable strict fiduciary standard, we treat the Rodd family as a single controlling group. We reject the defendants' contention that the Rodd family cannot be treated as a unit for this purpose. From the evidence, it is clear that the Rodd family was a close-knit one with strong community of interest. Harry Rodd had hired his sons to work in the family business, Rodd Electrotype. As he aged, he transferred portions of his stock holdings to his children. Charles Rodd and Frederick Rodd were given positions of responsibility in the busi-

---

39. [By the Court] Under the Massachusetts law, "[n]o stockholder shall have any preemptive right to acquire stock of the corporation except to the extent provided in the articles of organization or in a by-law adopted by and subject to amendment only by the stockholders." G.L. c. 156B, § 20. We do not here suggest that such preemptive rights are required by the strict fiduciary duty applicable to the stockholders of close corporations. However, to the extent that a controlling stockholder or other stockholder, in violation of his fiduciary duty, causes the corporation to issue stock in order to expand his holdings or to dilute holdings of other stockholders, the other stockholders will have a right to relief in court. Even under the traditional standard of duty applicable to corporate directors and stockholders generally, this court has looked favorably upon stockholder challenges to stock issues which, in violation of a fiduciary duty, served personal interests of other stockholder/directors and did not serve the corporate interest. See, e.g., Elliott v. Baker, 194 Mass. 518, 80 N.E. 450 (1907).

ness as he withdrew from active management. In these circumstances, it is realistic to assume that appreciation, gratitude, and filial devotion would prevent the younger Rodds from opposing a plan which would provide funds for their father's retirement.

Moreover, a strong motive of interest requires that the Rodds be considered a controlling group. When Charles Rodd and Frederick Rodd were called on to represent the corporation in its dealings with their father, they must have known that further advancement within the corporation and benefits would follow their father's retirement and the purchase of his stock. * * *

On its face, then, the purchase of Harry Rodd's shares by the corporation is a breach of the duty which the controlling stockholders, the Rodds, owed to the minority stockholders, the plaintiff and her son. The purchase distributed a portion of the corporate assets to Harry Rodd, a member of the controlling group, in exchange for his shares. The plaintiff and her son were not offered an equal opportunity to sell their shares to the corporation. In fact, their efforts to obtain an equal opportunity were rebuffed by the corporate representative. As the trial judge found, they did not, in any manner, ratify the transaction with Harry Rodd.

Because of the foregoing, we hold that the plaintiff is entitled to relief. Two forms of suitable relief are set out hereinafter. The judge below is to enter an appropriate judgment. The judgment may require Harry Rodd to remit $36,000 with interest at the legal rate from July 15, 1970, to Rodd Electrotype in exchange for forty-five shares of Rodd Electrotype treasury stock. * * * In the alternative, the judgment may require Rodd Electrotype to purchase all of the plaintiff's shares for $36,000 without interest. In the circumstances of this case, we view this as the equal opportunity which the plaintiff should have received. Harry Rodd's retention of thirty-six shares, which were to be sold and given to his children within a year of the Rodd Electrotype purchase, cannot disguise the fact that the corporation acquired one hundred percent of that portion of his holdings (forty-five shares) which he did not intend his children to own. The plaintiff is entitled to have one hundred percent of her forty-five shares similarly purchased.[40] * * * The case is remanded to the Superior Court for entry of judgment in conformity with this opinion.

So ordered.

WILKINS, JUSTICE (concurring).

I agree with much of what the Chief Justice says in support of granting relief to the plaintiff. However, I do not join in any implication * * * that the rule concerning a close corporation's purchase of a controlling stockholder's shares applies to all operations of the corporation as they affect minority stockholders. That broader issue, which is apt to arise in connection with salaries and dividend policy, is not involved in this case. The analogy to partnerships may not be a complete one.

---

40. [By the Court] If there has been a significant change in corporate circumstances since this case was argued, this is a matter which can be brought to the attention of the court below and may be considered by the judge in granting appropriate relief in the form of a judgment.

Notes

(1) The basic holding of *Donahue* that fiduciary relationships exist within closely held corporations has been widely cited and accepted. Courts in more than 25 states have either cited *Donahue* approvingly for this basic proposition or have cited cases that relied upon *Donahue* for this proposition. This is a major change in approach if not in results reached from earlier cases. Delaware, however, has flatly rejected the approach of *Donahue*. In Nixon v. Blackwell, 626 A.2d 1366, 1380 (Del.1993) the Delaware Supreme Court stated, "[i]t would do violence to normal corporate practice and our corporation law to fashion an ad hoc ruling which would result in a court-imposed stockholder buy-out for which the parties had not contracted." The court added, for good measure, that to do so "would be inappropriate judicial legislation." The proper standard to review the decision in question according to the Delaware court was the "entire fairness" test discussed in chapter 11, Section A, infra; see also the test applied in *Wilderman*, p. 370, supra. Do you think this decision might make Delaware a more attractive state of incorporation for closely held corporations?

(2) Even though *Donahue* talks about freezeouts, the actual transaction successfully attacked in that case involves an arguably unfair redemption of shares rather than a freezeout. Other courts have generally followed *Donahue* in this respect, and set aside a partial redemption of the majority's shares to the exclusion of the minority, e.g., Estate of Schroer v. Stamco Supply, Inc., 19 Ohio App.3d 34, 482 N.E.2d 975 (1984); Tillis v. United Parts, Inc., 395 So.2d 618 (Fla.App.1981), or the redemption of a third person's shares in order to assure the retention of control by one faction, e.g., Comolli v. Comolli, 241 Ga. 471, 246 S.E.2d 278 (1978). In Toner v. Baltimore Envelope Co., 304 Md. 256, 498 A.2d 642 (1985), the Court, while accepting the idea that fiduciary duties exist within a closely held corporation, declined to adopt "a per se equal opportunity rule" in the case of a selective redemption of shares by a closely held corporation. The Court commented that while controlling shareholders may violate fiduciary duties in such repurchases, that conclusion "should be based on all of the relevant facts." 498 A.2d at 650. The Court viewed cases such as *Donahue* and *Comolli* as establishing a "per se test." Essentially consistent with *Toner* is Delahoussaye v. Newhard, 785 S.W.2d 609 (Mo.App.1990).

(3) As might be expected, the broad language in *Donahue* has been cited often in Massachusetts cases, and clearly has influenced the development of legal principles in that state on a variety of different issues. Between 1975 and 1997, the Massachusetts appellate courts decided more than forty cases in which the *Donahue* principles were sought to be applied. For example, in Crowley v. Communications for Hospitals, Inc., 30 Mass.App.Ct. 751, 573 N.E.2d 996 (1991), the Court held that large remuneration paid to the controlling shareholders in order to "zero out" a C corporation's taxable income while not making any payments to minority shareholders violated the *Donahue* fiduciary duties; in this case evidence established that the controlling shareholders had overstated their work for the corporation in submissions to the IRS. In Puritan Medical Ctr., Inc. v. Cashman, 413 Mass. 167, 596 N.E.2d 1004 (1992), a trusted controlling shareholder was held to have violated his fiduciary duties by failing to advise the other directors that the corporation was being charged above-market rentals for space the shareholder and his sister were leasing to the corporation. In Beers v. Tisdale, 33 Mass.App.Ct. 621, 603 N.E.2d 239 (1992), two shareholders in a professional corporation were held to have violated their fiduciary duties when they failed to redeem a retired shareholder's stock as required by a redemption agreement, and instead dissolved the corporation, assigning to themselves a client

list, which was the corporation's principal asset. In Smith v. Atlantic Properties, Inc., 12 Mass.App.Ct. 201, 422 N.E.2d 798 (1981), the Court imposed liability on a minority shareholder for the claimed misuse of a veto power to prevent the payment of all dividends. In Hallahan v. Haltom Corp., 7 Mass.App.Ct. 68, 385 N.E.2d 1033 (1979), the Court ordered shares be returned to the seller at cost, where they had been secretly acquired by an equal co-owner of shares in an effort to shift the balance of control.

(4) The broad language in *Donahue* has been invoked by plaintiffs in several cases where employee-shareholders were fired for reasons that did not constitute good cause. The leading case in Massachusetts is Wilkes v. Springside Nursing Home, Inc., 370 Mass. 842, 353 N.E.2d 657 (1976), where the Court ordered the reinstatement of a minority shareholder to the corporate payroll after he had been fired in connection with an attempted freezeout. However, the Massachusetts Supreme Court in its opinion in *Wilkes* retreated to some extent from the language of *Donahue*. The Court stated:

> We are concerned that untempered application of the strict good faith standard enunciated in *Donahue* to cases such as the one before us will result in the imposition of limitations on legitimate action by the controlling group in a close corporation which will unduly hamper its effectiveness in managing the corporation in the best interests of all concerned. The majority, concededly, have certain rights to what has been termed "selfish ownership" in the corporation which should be balanced against the concept of their fiduciary obligation to the minority.

> Therefore, when minority stockholders in a close corporation bring suit against the majority alleging a breach of the strict good faith duty owed to them by the majority, we must carefully analyze the action taken by the controlling stockholders in the individual case. It must be asked whether the controlling group can demonstrate a legitimate business purpose for its action. In asking this question, we acknowledge the fact that the controlling group in a close corporation must have some room to maneuver in establishing the business policy of the corporation. It must have a large measure of discretion, for example, in declaring or withholding dividends, deciding whether to merge or consolidate, establishing the salaries of corporate officers, dismissing directors with or without cause, and hiring and firing corporate employees.

> When an asserted business purpose for their action is advanced by the majority, however, we think it is open to minority stockholders to demonstrate that the same legitimate objective could have been achieved through an alternative course of action less harmful to the minority's interest. If called on to settle a dispute, our courts must weigh the legitimate business purpose, if any, against the practicability of a less harmful alternative.

> Applying this approach to the instant case it is apparent that the majority stockholders in Springside have not shown a legitimate business purpose for severing Wilkes from the payroll of the corporation or for refusing to reelect him as a salaried officer and director. * * * There was no showing of misconduct on Wilkes' part as a director, officer or employee of the corporation which would lead us to approve the majority action as a legitimate response to the disruptive nature of an undesirable individual bent on injuring or destroying the corporation. On the contrary, it appears that Wilkes had always accomplished his assigned share of the duties competently, and that he had never indicated an unwillingness to continue to do so.

353 N.E.2d at 663–64. The Court returned to the same theme in Zimmerman v. Bogoff, 402 Mass. 650, 524 N.E.2d 849 (1988), where it said, "the *Donahue* remedy is not intended to place a strait jacket on legitimate corporate activity. Where the alleged wrongdoer can demonstrate a legitimate business purpose for his action, no liability will result unless the wronged shareholder succeeds in showing that the proffered legitimate objective could have been achieved through a less harmful, reasonably practicable, alternative mode of action." 524 N.E.2d at 853. This approach creates a potential conflict between *Donahue* and the well-accepted employment at will doctrine, which states "that an employer may terminate an at-will employee at any time with or without cause * * * [unless] the termination violates a clearly established public policy." King v. Driscoll, 418 Mass. 576, 580, 638 N.E.2d 488, 491 (1994). The public policy exception, furthermore, is interpreted "narrowly." Ibid. In three recent cases, the Massachusetts court has refused to allow *Donahue* to intrude upon the employment at will doctrine. In *King,* no breach of duty was found where an employee had been fired for agreeing to serve as a plaintiff in a derivative suit, but his shares were repurchased on terms set forth in the original contract of employment. In Blank v. Chelmsford Ob/Gyn, P.C., 420 Mass. 404, 649 N.E.2d 1102 (1995), no breach of a *Donahue* duty was found where the plaintiff's employment agreement provided that the employment could be terminated by written notice, "such notice shall be effective to terminate this contract on the last day of the sixth month following," and the plaintiff's employment was terminated in accordance with that contract. In Merola v. Exergen Corp., 423 Mass. 461, 668 N.E.2d 351 (1996), an employee/shareholder was terminated for personal non-economic reasons, but the Court held *Donahue* was not violated because the plaintiff's investment in the stock was not tied to employment in any formal way and the termination did not lead to the financial gain of the controlling shareholder.

(5) The *Donahue* principle has also not prevailed in several other Massachusetts cases. In Goode v. Ryan, 397 Mass. 85, 489 N.E.2d 1001 (1986), the Court held that *Donahue* did not permit the estate of a minority shareholder to insist that its shares be repurchased by the corporation to simplify the settlement of the estate in the absence of a contractual obligation by the corporation to repurchase the shares. The difficulty of resale, the Court said, "is merely one of the risks of ownership of stock in a close corporation," and "[i]t is not the proper function of this court to reallocate the risks inherent in the ownership of corporate stock in the absence of corporate or majority shareholder misconduct." 489 N.E.2d at 1005. Similarly, a *Donahue* argument was rejected in a suit to compel the price in a contract to sell shares to be increased so as to more closely reflect current market value or to permit the sellers in such a contract to disaffirm their contract. Evangelista v. Holland, 27 Mass.App.Ct. 244, 537 N.E.2d 589 (1989).

(6) You are an attorney that represents a closely held corporation. You also represent some but not all of the shareholders of the corporation. In light of the *Donahue* fiduciary duty, do you have any obligations with respect to the other shareholders if, for example, negotiations occur regarding the redemption of some of the outstanding shares? See Schaeffer v. Cohen, Rosenthal, et al., 405 Mass. 506, 541 N.E.2d 997 (1989), where the Court stated, "Just as an attorney for a partnership owes a fiduciary duty to each partner, it is fairly arguable that an attorney for a close corporation owes a fiduciary duty to the individual shareholders." 541 N.E.2d at 1002. However, the resolution of this issue was not necessary for the decision in the case. See also Lawrence E. Mitchell, Professional Responsibility and the Close Corporation: Toward a Realistic Ethic, 74 Cornell L.Rev. 466 (1989).

(7) Leader v. Hycor, Inc., 395 Mass. 215, 479 N.E.2d 173 (1985), involved a "reverse stock split" at the ratio of one new share for each 4,000 old shares, with fractional shares to be purchased for cash at a specified amount per share. After the reverse stock split, all of the minority shareholders owned less than a full share and thus were "cashed out." Is there anything wrong with that if the price is fair?

(8) The analogy to partnership law relied upon by the Court in *Donahue* is of course the broad and ill-defined duty described by Justice Cardozo in Meinhard v. Salmon and arguably codified in UPA (1914). Assume that Massachusetts enacts UPA (1994) with its narrower and more carefully defined fiduciary duty. See Chapter 2, Section D. Will that automatically narrow the *Donahue* fiduciary duty, or will Massachusetts have a broader fiduciary duty in close corporation cases than in partnership cases?

(9) Frank H. Easterbrook and Daniel R. Fischel, The Economic Structure of Corporate Law (1991)[41] adopts the position that corporation law is a matter of contract and the "[t]he role of corporate law * * * is to adopt a background term that prevails unless varied by contract. And the background term should be the one that is either picked by contract expressly or is the operational assumption of successful firms." Id. at 36. In the case of closely held corporations where "a court is unavoidably entwined in a dispute, it must decide what the parties would have agreed to had they written a contract resolving all contingencies." Id. at 245. Do you agree that this is the appropriate standard (a standard that is generally accepted by law and economics scholars) for determining what duties courts should imply? Easterbrook and Fischel also argue that the costs of the imposition of strict fiduciary duties are so great that "it is conceivable, nay certain, that all parties often decide that they are better off without" these duties. Id. at 238. As a result, they contend the decision in *Donahue* is totally wrong:

> Grave reflections on the plight of minority investors in closely held corporations and stirring proclamations of fiduciary duty fill the opinion. Completely overlooked in all of this rhetoric was the basic question—which outcome would the parties have selected had they contracted in anticipation of this contingency? Although no one can answer such a question with certainty * * *, it is most unlikely that they would have selected a rule requiring an equal opportunity for all. Buyouts facilitate the retirement of a manager who, by virtue of advancing and age and poor health, no longer contributes. Stock transactions on death or retirement are common in closely held corporations, mandatory in many. * * * No comparable commonly used agreement requires a firm to purchase all shares if it buys any.

Id. at 246. Do you agree with this reasoning? Of course, Donahue was an employee before he died, and his shares were not purchased at his death, a point noted by Easterbrook and Fischel. Might the Court have devised a theory that permitted the Donahues a right to be bought out without adopting the broad fiduciary duty it did?

I.   LEGAL RESTRICTIONS ON DISTRIBUTIONS

Many state statutes establish tests for the legality of distributions, principally dividends and corporate redemptions of shares, that build on

41. Reprinted by permission of the publishers from *The Economic Structure of Corporate Law* by Frank H. Easterbrook and Daniel R. Fischel, Cambridge, Mass.: Harvard University Press, Copyright © 1991 by the President and Fellows of Harvard College.

traditional accounting concepts for corporate capital. It is fair to state that the problems involved in determining the legality of dividends and redemptions, particularly under pre-MBCA statutes, are among the most complex and confusing in the entire field of corporate law. The provisions of the MBCA discussed below go a long way toward rationalizing these restrictions. It is probable that most states will ultimately revise their statutes in this area, but the older statutes will continue to be applicable in some states for many years to come. The balance of this section is designed to give a somewhat impressionistic understanding of these older dividend statutes and the MBCA.

1. "EARNED SURPLUS" DIVIDEND STATUTES

MBCA (1969) established the general tests for the legality of a dividend as (1) the availability of "earned surplus" out of which the dividend may be paid, and (2) a solvency test to be applied immediately after giving effect to the dividend. See MBCA (1969) § 45. A large number of states followed the Model Act in this regard. The definition of "earned surplus" in MBCA (1969) § 2(1), apparently contemplated the aggregation of income from all profit-and-loss statements going back to the time the corporation was organized. This approach created practical and theoretical problems that are described in William P. Hackney, The Financial Provisions of the Model Business Corporation Act, 70 Harv.L.Rev. 1357, 1368–69 (1957):[42]

> Even for a new corporation, the air of simplicity about a statutory rule allowing dividends only out of the undistributed balance of all corporate income is misleading. Actually, the correct computation of income for any one year is not only incredibly difficult but is so far from an exact science—which of course it does not purport to be—that it is meaningless to attempt to say precisely in dollars what any corporation's income actually is. The determination of income requires allocations of receipts, expenses, and losses to fiscal periods, such allocations being sometimes based on fact but sometimes estimated, or conventional, or based on assumptions as to future events which may prove invalid. Accounting principles are not fundamental truths, capable of scientific proof, but are derived from experience and reason; proved utility is the criterion. Rapidly changing accounting principles show that accounting income is not a fixed concept but one subject to both differences of opinion and variations from year to year. One "sophisticated accountant" has been quoted as defining income as "anything which good accounting practice accepts as income."
>
> Nor is it clear what is meant by the Model Act definition's repetitive terms, "net profits," "income," and "gains and losses." Paragraphs 28–34 of Accounting Terminology Bulletin No. 1 indicate that while these terms have had varying meanings in the past there is an increasing tendency to regard the terms "income" and "profit and loss" as coextensive. There is no indication of how the term "gains" might differ in meaning from "profits" or from "income," nor why the word "earnings" is left out of the definition, nor why the word "net" must precede "profits" but not "income," "gains," or "losses." * * *

---

42. Copyright © 1957 by the Harvard Law Review Association.

The earned surplus statutes raise two additional questions that are answered in various ways in specific state statutes: (1) May a corporation eliminate deficits in earned surplus by transferring amounts from capital surplus or some other surplus account to earned surplus? See MBCA (1969) § 2(1), which inferentially permits such transfers. Such a transaction is called a "quasi-reorganization," and is not permitted under the statutes of some states. (2) May a corporation with a negative earned surplus from earlier years pay a dividend out of current earnings, or must it first apply current earnings to eliminate past deficits? MBCA (1969) contained an alternative § 45(a), which allowed dividends from current earnings; such dividends, usually known as "nimble dividends," are permitted in many but not all states.

2. "IMPAIRMENT OF CAPITAL" DIVIDEND STATUTES

Many non-Model Act statutes establish a test for determining the legality of dividends that appears to be based on a balance sheet rather than income statement analysis. The Delaware statute, for example, permits a corporation to pay dividends basically "out of its surplus," Del.Gen.Corp.Law § 170, and defines "surplus" to include everything in excess of the aggregate par values of the issued shares plus whatever else the corporation has elected to add to its capital account. New York also applies a "surplus" test but adds the requirement that "the net assets of the corporation remaining after such declaration, payment or distribution shall at least equal the amount of its stated capital * * *." N.Y.—McKinney's Bus.Corp.Law § 510. Other statutes talk in terms of not "impairing capital" or of prohibiting dividends "except from surplus, or from the net profits arising from the business." This last clause in particular seems to clearly contemplate the payment of dividends out of sources other than earnings (because of the use of the disjunctive "or"). All of these impairment of capital statutes were construed to permit such distributions. For example, Randall v. Bailey, 288 N.Y. 280, 43 N.E.2d 43 (1942), arising under an earlier version of the New York statute, involved, among other issues, an attempt by a corporation to create surplus by writing up the value of appreciated assets on its books. The Court permitted the corporation to increase its dividend-paying capacity by such a bookkeeping entry. Presumably, such a "reevaluation surplus" is "surplus" under such statutes and payments out of it would not "impair capital." Could an argument be made that reevaluation surplus might be "earned surplus" as a "gain" under the definition of "earned surplus" in MBCA (1969) § 2(1)? Randall v. Bailey also involved an asset of "good will" that apparently was added to the balance sheet as a balancing entry in an earlier corporate acquisition. This entry, of course, did not represent any specific property. In applying the balance sheet tests of "surplus" for determining when a dividend can be paid, shouldn't only "real" assets be counted? The Court permitted recognition of the asset of good will under the circumstances, but the lower court commented that "[d]irectors obviously cannot create assets by fiat." 23 N.Y.S.2d 173, 177 (1940).

Cases such as Randall v. Bailey raise a basic question: to what extent should the legality of dividends be determined on the basis of accounting conventions or principles? For example, from an accounting standpoint, write-ups of assets to reflect market appreciation are generally frowned on if not flatly prohibited. Should "generally accepted principles" (which are subject to change from time to time and do not command universal respect in any event) be relevant in deciding whether a corporation may legally pay a dividend out of "reevaluation surplus"? These statutes rely on accounting concepts in establishing limitations on distributions; on the other hand, it seems odd to make the legality of dividends depend on the shifting sands of accounting rules or conventions. Further, since much of the litigation relating to the legality of dividends arose in the context of creditors seeking to surcharge directors for declaring unlawful dividends, transactions such as those involved in Randall v. Bailey also raise the question whether directors can rely on the books of the corporation as presented to them by corporate officers or on the advice of attorneys or accountants for the corporation as to the availability of funds for the payment of dividends. In this connection see MBCA §§ 6.40(d), 8.33.

3. DISTRIBUTIONS OF CAPITAL UNDER "EARNED SURPLUS" STATUTES

To complicate matters even further, MBCA (1969) freely permitted distributions out of "capital surplus" with the proper authorization. See MBCA (1969) § 46. Not all Model Act states did so, however; some included no provisions at all for distributions out of capital or other surplus, or permitted distributions out of capital or other surplus only for narrow purposes, or hedged distributions out of such surplus with substantive or procedural requirements. Some states adopted the phrase "partial liquidation" for such distributions to emphasize that they were not distributions of earnings but distributions of part of the capital of the corporation. Some statutes also imposed special limitations on capital surplus that was created by the reduction of stated capital (e.g., by amending the articles to reduce the par value of outstanding shares or canceling previously outstanding shares)—defined as "reduction surplus" in some states.

Statutes based on pre–1984 versions of the Model Act that permit distributions of capital with little or no restriction probably lead to rules of distribution not very different from the rules applicable in states such as New York or Delaware. However, the language of each statute has to be examined carefully and certainly confusion or uncertainty existed in many states.

Notes

(1) How should these legal capital restrictions be applied to a transaction in which the corporation repurchases shares on a deferred payment basis? Should the restrictions be applied only at the time of the closing of the transaction when the shares are returned to the corporation or should they be applied consecutively to each payment when made? As a practical matter, it is quite possible for a corporation to have adequate earned surplus at the time of the original closing, but that earned surplus may be dissipated through operating losses before the payments are to be made. Similarly, it is possible that a corporation may meet the solvency test at the time of the original repurchase but not at the time later payments come due. The limited case law on this issue tends in the direction of applying both standards to each payment, though that makes little sense, at least in the case of earned surplus limitations. Consult David R. Herwitz, Installment Repurchase of Stock: Surplus Limitations, 79 Harv.L.Rev. 303 (1965). For a case rejecting this conclusion, but based on the precise language of a state corporation

statute, see Williams v. Nevelow, 513 S.W.2d 535 (Tex.1974). The MBCA § 6.40(e)(2) accepts the conclusion in *Williams*. Is that the proper answer?

(2) Reacquisitions of shares on a deferred payment basis also raise a second question: should a former shareholder who holds promissory notes of the corporation for part of the purchase price of shares be treated on a parity with general trade creditors, or should his or her claim be subordinated? A leading case subordinating this debt is Robinson v. Wangemann, 75 F.2d 756 (5th Cir.1935). The MBCA squarely addresses this question in MBCA § 6.40(e)(1) and (f) and places such a creditor on a parity with general trade creditors. Is that the proper answer?

4. THE MODEL BUSINESS CORPORATION ACT

Section 6.40 of the MBCA sweeps away most of the complex issues and problems under earlier statutes. One of the major issues faced by the revisers of the Model Act was whether the validity of distributions should be measured solely by an insolvency test, or whether both an insolvency test and a balance sheet test should be retained. If a balance sheet test is retained, consideration of the underlying accounting principles is necessary if the test is to have any substance at all. The decision to retain a balance sheet test was based on several considerations: The historical reliance on balance sheet tests in state statutes, protection for senior securities interests provided by § 6.40(c)(2), and the desire for specific tests, so far as practical, in evaluating the lawfulness of distributions. There was some sentiment for the incorporation of "generally accepted accounting principles" (GAAP) into the section, at least as a "safe harbor" for directors approving a distribution, but the final compromise on this issue now appears in § 6.40(d). The decision not to include a reference to GAAP in the statute was based partially on concern that the content of GAAP principles varied over time. Is there anything wrong with a state statute incorporating by reference a changing body of principles controlled by other persons? Is that delegating lawmaking authority to a private body?

OFFICIAL COMMENT TO § 6.40

* * *

2. *Equity Insolvency Test*

[O]lder statutes prohibited payments of dividends if the corporation was, or as a result of the payment would be, insolvent in the equity sense. This test is retained, appearing in section 6.40(c)(1).

In most cases involving a corporation operating as a going concern in the normal course, information generally available will make it quite apparent that no particular inquiry concerning the equity insolvency test is needed. While neither a balance sheet nor an income statement can be conclusive as to this test, the existence of significant shareholders' equity and normal operating conditions are of themselves a strong indication that no issue should arise under that test. Indeed, in the case of a corporation having regularly audited financial statements, the absence of any qualification in the most recent auditor's opinion as to the corporation's status as a "going concern," coupled with a lack of subsequent adverse events, would normally be decisive.

It is only when circumstances indicate that the corporation is encountering difficulties or is in an uncertain position concerning its liquidity and operations that the board of directors or, more commonly, the officers or others upon whom they may place reliance under section 8.30(b), may need to address the issue. Because of the overall judgment required in evaluating the equity insolvency test, no one or more "bright line" tests can be employed. However, in determining whether the equity insolvency test has been met, certain judgments or assumptions as to the future course of the corporation's business are customarily justified, absent clear evidence to the contrary. These include the likelihood that (a) based on existing and contemplated demand for the corporation's products or services, it will be able to generate funds over a period of time sufficient to satisfy its existing and reasonably anticipated obligations as they mature, and (b) indebtedness which matures in the near-term will be refinanced where, on the basis of the corporation's financial condition and future prospects and the general availability of credit to businesses similarly situated, it is reasonable to assume that such refinancing may be accomplished. To the extent that the corporation may be subject to asserted or unasserted contingent liabilities, reasonable judgments as to the likelihood, amount, and time of any recovery against the corporation, after giving consideration to the extent to which the corporation is insured or otherwise protected against loss, may be utilized. There may be occasions when it would be useful to consider a cash flow analysis, based on a business forecast and budget, covering a sufficient period of time to permit a conclusion that known obligations of the corporation can reasonably be expected to be satisfied over the period of time that they will mature.

In exercising their judgment, the directors are entitled to rely, under section 8.30(b) as noted above, on information, opinions, reports, and statements prepared by others. Ordinarily, they should not be expected to become involved in the details of the various analyses or market or economic projections that may be relevant. Judgments must of necessity be made on the basis of information in the hands of the directors when a distribution is authorized. They should not, of course, be held responsible as a matter of hindsight for unforeseen developments. This is particularly true with respect to assumptions as to the ability of the corporation's business to repay long-term obligations which do not mature for several years, since the primary focus of the directors' decision to make a distribution should normally be on the corporation's prospects and obligations in the shorter term, unless special factors concerning the corporation's prospects require the taking of a longer term perspective. * * *

4. Balance Sheet Test

Section 6.40(c)(2) requires that, after giving effect to any distribution, the corporation's assets equal or exceed its liabilities plus (with some exceptions) the dissolution preferences of senior equity securities. Section 6.40(d) authorizes asset and liability determinations to be made for this purpose on the basis of either (1) financial statements prepared on the basis of accounting practices and principles that are reasonable in the circumstances or (2) a fair valuation or other method that is reasonable in the circumstances. The determination of a corporation's assets and liabilities and the choice of the permissible basis on which to do so are left to the judgment of its board of directors. In making a judgment under section 6.40(d), the board may rely under section 8.30(b) upon opinions, reports, or statements, including financial statements and other financial data prepared or presented by public accountants or others.

Section 6.40 does not utilize particular accounting terminology of a technical nature or specify particular accounting concepts. In making determinations under this section, the board of directors may make judgments about accounting matters, giving full effect to its right to rely upon professional or expert opinion. * * *

a. Generally accepted accounting principles

The board of directors should in all circumstances be entitled to rely upon reasonably current financial statements prepared on the basis of generally accepted accounting principles in determining whether or not the balance sheet test of section 6.40(c)(2) has been met, unless the board is then aware that it would be unreasonable to rely on the financial statements because of newly-discovered or subsequently arising facts or circumstances. But section 6.40 does not mandate the use of generally accepted accounting principles; it only requires the use of accounting practices and principles that are reasonable in the circumstances. While publicly-owned corporations subject to registration under the Securities Exchange Act of 1934 must, and many other corporations in fact do, utilize financial statements prepared on the basis of generally accepted accounting principles, a great number of smaller or closely-held corporations do not. Some of these corporations maintain records solely on a tax accounting basis and their financial statements are of necessity prepared on that basis. Others prepare financial statements that substantially reflect generally accepted accounting principles but may depart from them in some respects (e.g., footnote disclosure). These facts of corporate life indicate that a statutory standard of reasonableness, rather than stipulating generally accepted accounting principles as the normative standard, is appropriate in order to achieve a reasonable degree of flexibility and to accommodate the needs of the many different types of business corporations which might be subject to these provisions, including in particular closely-held corporations. Accordingly, the * * * Model Business Corporation Act contemplates that generally acceptable accounting principles are always "reasonable in the circumstances" and that other accounting principles may be perfectly acceptable, under a general standard of reasonableness, even if they do not involve the "fair value" or "current value" concepts that are also contemplated by section 6.40(d).

b. Other principles

Section 6.40(d) specifically permits determinations to be made under section 6.40(c)(2) on the basis of a fair valuation or other method that is reasonable in the circumstances. Thus the statute authorizes departures from historical cost accounting and sanctions the use of appraisal and current value methods to determine the amount available for distribution. No particular method of valuation is prescribed in the statute, since different methods may have validity depending upon the circumstances, including the type of enterprise and the purpose for which the determination is made. For example, it is inappropriate in most cases to apply a "quick-sale liquidation" method to value an enterprise, particularly with respect to the payment of normal dividends. On the other hand, a "quick-sale liquidation" valuation method might be appropriate in certain circumstances for an enterprise in the course of reducing its asset or business base by a material degree. In most cases, a fair valuation method or a going-concern basis would be appropriate if it is believed that the enterprise will continue as a going concern.

Ordinarily a corporation should not selectively revalue assets. It should consider the value of all of its material assets, whether or not reflected in the financial statements (e.g., a valuable executory contract). Likewise, all of a corporation's material obligations should be considered and revalued to the extent appropriate and possible. In any event, section 6.40(d) calls for the application under section 6.40(c)(2) of a method of determining the aggregate amount of assets and liabilities that is reasonable in the circumstances.

Section 6.40(d) also refers to some "other method that is reasonable in the circumstances." This phrase is intended to comprehend within section 6.40(c)(2) the wide variety of possibilities that might not be considered to fall under a "fair valuation" or "current value" method but might be reasonable in the circumstances of a particular case.

5. Preferential Dissolution Rights and the Balance Sheet Test

Section 6.40(c)(2) provides that a distribution may not be made unless the total assets of the corporation exceed its liabilities plus the amount that would be needed to satisfy any shareholder's superior preferential rights upon dissolution if the corporation were to be dissolved at the time of the distribution. This requirement in effect treats preferential dissolution rights of shares for distribution purposes as if they were liabilities for the sole purpose of determining the amount available for distributions, and carries forward analogous treatment of shares having preferential dissolution rights from earlier versions of the Model Act. * * *

8. Application to Reacquisition of Shares

The application of the equity insolvency and balance sheet tests to distributions that involve the purchase, redemption, or other acquisition of the corporation's shares creates unique problems; section 6.40 provides a specific rule for the resolution of these problems as described below.

a. Time of measurement

Section 6.40(e)(1) provides that the time for measuring the effect of a distribution under section 6.40(c), if shares of the corporation are reacquired, is the earlier of (i) the payment date, or (ii) the date the shareholder ceased to be a shareholder with respect to the shares, except as provided in section 6.40(g).

b. When tests are applied to redemption-related debt

In an acquisition of its shares, a corporation may transfer property or incur debt to the former holder of the shares. The case law on the status of this debt is conflicting. However, share repurchase agreements involving payment for shares over a period of time are of special importance in closely-held corporate enterprises. Section 6.40(e) provides a clear rule for this situation: the legality of the distribution must be measured at the time of the issuance or incurrence of the debt, not at a later date when the debt is actually paid, except as provided in section 6.40(g). Of course, this does not preclude a later challenge of a payment on account of redemption-related debt by a bankruptcy trustee on the ground that it constitutes a preferential payment to a creditor.

c.   Priority of debt distributed directly or incurred in connection with a reacquisition of shares

Section 6.40(f) provides that indebtedness created to acquire the corporation's shares or issued as a distribution is on a parity with the indebtedness of the corporation to its general, unsecured creditors, except to the extent subordinated by agreement. General creditors are better off in these situations than they would have been if cash or other property had been paid out for the shares or distributed (which is proper under the statute), and no worse off than if cash had been paid or distributed and then lent back to the corporation, making the shareholders (or former shareholders) creditors. The parity created by section 6.40(f) is logically consistent with the rule established by section 6.40(e) that these transactions should be judged at the time of the issuance of the debt.

9.   *Treatment of certain indebtedness*

Section 6.40(g) provides that indebtedness need not be taken into account as a liability in determining whether the tests of section 6.40(c) have been met if the terms of the indebtedness provide that payments of principal or interest can be made only if and to the extent that payment of a distribution could then be made under section 6.40. This has the effect of making the holder of the indebtedness junior to all other creditors but senior to the holders of all classes of shares, not only during the time the corporation is operating but also upon dissolution and liquidation. It should be noted that the creation of such indebtedness, and the related limitations on payments of principal and interest, may create tax problems or raise other legal questions.

Although section 6.40(g) is applicable to all indebtedness meeting its tests, regardless of the circumstances of its issuance, it is anticipated that it will be applicable most frequently to permit the reacquisition of shares of the corporation at a time when the deferred purchase price exceeds the net worth of the corporation. This type of reacquisition will often be necessary in the case of businesses in early stages of development or service businesses whose value derives principally from existing or prospective net income or cash flow rather than from net asset value. In such situations, it is anticipated that net worth will grow over time from operations so that when payments in respect of the indebtedness are to be made the two insolvency tests will be satisfied. In the meantime, the fact that the indebtedness is outstanding will not prevent distributions that could be made under subsection (c) if the indebtedness were not counted in making the determination.

Notes

(1) One feature of dividend statutes is that there is little litigation involving their application. They are primarily a problem for the corporate attorney striving to ensure that a directoral decision does not inadvertently give rise to personal liability. From time to time, however, they arise in unexpected fashion in litigation

having nothing to do with a simple distribution of assets to shareholders. In re C–T of Virginia, Inc., 958 F.2d 606 (4th Cir.1992), for example, the court held that a leveraged buyout (see chapter 14, Section E, infra) does not constitute a "distribution" of assets subject to § 6.40. *Contra* is Matter of Munford, Inc., 97 F.3d 456 (11th Cir.1996) arising under the Georgia statute.

(2) In Minnelusa Co. v. Andrikopoulous, 929 P.2d 1321 (Colo.1996), the court held that a corporation executing a promissory note to repurchase stock could not use the Colorado stock repurchase statute to invalidate the promissory note on the theory that its execution rendered the corporation insolvent. The court stated that the invalidity of a corporate stock repurchase agreement could be raised only by persons who are injured or prejudiced thereby and not by the corporation itself. Such a defense also was held not to be available to a shareholder who personally guaranteed the corporate performance of such a promissory note.

Chapter Eight

MANAGEMENT AND CONTROL OF THE CLOSELY HELD CORPORATION

A. THE TRADITIONAL ROLES OF SHAREHOLDERS AND DIRECTORS

McQUADE v. STONEHAM

Court of Appeals of New York, 1934.
263 N.Y. 323, 189 N.E. 234.

POUND, CHIEF JUDGE.

The action is brought to compel specific performance of an agreement between the parties, entered into to secure the control of National Exhibition Company, also called the Baseball Club (New York Nationals or "Giants"). This was one of Stoneham's enterprises which used the New York polo grounds for its home games. McGraw was manager of the Giants. McQuade was at the time the contract was entered into a city magistrate. He resigned December 8, 1930.

Defendant Stoneham became the owner of 1,306 shares, or a majority of the stock of National Exhibition Company. Plaintiff and defendant McGraw each purchased 70 shares of his stock. Plaintiff paid Stoneham $50,338.10 for the stock he purchased. As a part of the transaction, the agreement in question was entered into. It was dated May 21, 1919. Some of its pertinent provisions are

VIII. The parties hereto will use their best endeavors for the purpose of continuing as directors of said Company and as officers thereof the following:

Directors:

Charles A. Stoneham,

John J. McGraw,

Francis X. McQuade

—with the right to the party of the first part [Stoneham] to name all additional directors as he sees fit:

Officers:

Charles A. Stoneham, President,

John J. McGraw, Vice President,

Francis X. McQuade, Treasurer.

IX.   No salaries are to be paid to any of the above officers or directors, except as follows:

President	$45,000
Vice–President	7,500
Treasurer	7,500

X.   There shall be no change in said salaries, no change in the amount of capital, or the number of shares, no change or amendment of the by-laws of the corporation or any matters regarding the policy of the business of the corporation or any matters which may in anywise affect, endanger or interfere with the rights of minority stockholders, excepting upon the mutual and unanimous consent of all of the parties hereto. * * *

XIV.   This agreement shall continue and remain in force so long as the parties or any of them or the representative of any, own the stock referred to in this agreement, to wit, the party of the first part, 1,166 shares, the party of the second part 70 shares and the party of the third part 70 shares, except as may otherwise appear by this agreement. * * *

In pursuance of this contract Stoneham became president and McGraw vice president of the corporation. McQuade became treasurer. In June, 1925, his salary was increased to $10,000 a year. He continued to act until May 2, 1928, when Leo J. Bondy was elected to succeed him. The board of directors consisted of seven men. The four outside of the parties hereto were selected by Stoneham and he had complete control over them. At the meeting of May 2, 1928, Stoneham and McGraw refrained from voting, McQuade voted for himself, and the other four voted for Bondy. Defendants did not keep their agreement with McQuade to use their best efforts to continue him as treasurer. On the contrary, he was dropped with their entire acquiescence. At the next stockholders' meeting he was dropped as a director although they might have elected him.

The courts below have refused to order the reinstatement of McQuade, but have given him damages for wrongful discharge, with a right to sue for future damages.

The cause for dropping McQuade was due to the falling out of friends. McQuade and Stoneham had disagreed. The trial court has found in substance that their numerous quarrels and disputes did not affect the orderly and efficient administration of the business of the corporation; that plaintiff was removed because he had antagonized the dominant Stoneham by persisting in challenging his power over the corporate treasury and for no misconduct on his part. The court also finds that plaintiff was removed by Stoneham for protecting the corporation and its minority stockholders. We will assume that

Stoneham put him out when he might have retained him, merely in order to get rid of him.

Defendants say that the contract in suit was void because the directors held their office charged with the duty to act for the corporation according to their best judgment and that any contract which compels a director to vote to keep any particular person in office and at a stated salary is illegal. Directors are the exclusive executive representatives of the corporation, charged with administration of its internal affairs and the management and use of its assets. They manage the business of the corporation. (General Corporation Law, Consol.Laws, c. 23, § 27.) "An agreement to continue a man as president is dependent upon his continued loyalty to the interests of the corporation." Fells v. Katz, 256 N.Y. 67, 72, 175 N.E. 516, 517. So much is undisputed.

Plaintiff contends that the converse of this proposition is true and that an agreement among directors to continue a man as an officer of a corporation is not to be broken so long as such officer is loyal to the interests of the corporation and that, as plaintiff has been found loyal to the corporation, the agreement of defendants is enforceable.

Although it has been held that an agreement among stockholders whereby it is attempted to divest the directors of their power to discharge an unfaithful employee of the corporation is illegal as against public policy (Fells v. Katz, supra), it must be equally true that the stockholders may not, by agreement among themselves, control the directors in the exercise of the judgment vested in them by virtue of their office to elect officers and fix salaries. Their motives may not be questioned so long as their acts are legal. The bad faith or the improper motives of the parties does not change the rule. Manson v. Curtis, 223 N.Y. 313, 324, 119 N.E. 559, Ann.Cas.1918E, 247. Directors may not by agreements entered into as stockholders abrogate their independent judgment. Creed v. Copps, 103 Vt. 164, 152 A. 369, 71 A.L.R. 1287, annotated.

Stockholders may, of course, combine to elect directors. That rule is well settled. As Holmes, C.J., pointedly said (Brightman v. Bates, 175 Mass. 105, 111, 55 N.E. 809, 811): "If stockholders want to make their power felt, they must unite. There is no reason why a majority should not agree to keep together." The power to unite is, however, limited to the election of directors and is not extended to contracts whereby limitations are placed on the power of directors to manage the business of the corporation by the selection of agents at defined salaries.

The minority shareholders whose interest McQuade says he has been punished for protecting, are not, aside from himself, complaining about his discharge. He is not acting for the corporation or for them in this action. It is impossible to see how the corporation has been injured by the substitution of Bondy as treasurer in place of McQuade. As McQuade represents himself in this action and seeks redress for his own wrongs, "we prefer to listen to [the corporation and the minority stockholders] before any decision as to their wrongs." Faulds v. Yates, 57 Ill. 416, 417, 11 Am.Rep. 24.

It is urged that we should pay heed to the morals and manners of the market place to sustain this agreement and that we should hold that its violation gives rise to a cause of action for damages rather than base our decision on any outworn notions of public policy. Public policy is a dangerous guide in determining the validity of a contract and courts should not interfere lightly with the freedom of competent parties to make their own contracts. We do not close our eyes to the fact that such agreements, tacitly or openly arrived at, are not uncommon, especially in close corporations where the stockholders are doing business for convenience under a corporate organization. We know that majority stockholders, united in voting trusts, effectively manage the business of a corporation by choosing trustworthy directors to reflect their policies in the corporate management. Nor are we unmindful that McQuade has, so the court has found, been shabbily treated as a purchaser of stock from Stoneham. We have said: "A trustee is held to something stricter than the morals of the market place" (Meinhard v. Salmon, 249 N.Y. 458, 464, 164 N.E. 545, 546, 62 A.L.R. 1), but Stoneham and McGraw were not trustees for McQuade as an individual. Their duty was to the corporation and its stockholders, to be exercised according to their unrestricted lawful judgment. They were under no legal obligation to deal righteously with McQuade if it was against public policy to do so.

The courts do not enforce mere moral obligations, nor legal ones either, unless someone seeks to establish rights which may be waived by custom and for convenience. We are constrained by authority to hold that a contract is illegal and void so far as it precludes the board of directors, at the risk of incurring legal liability, from changing officers, salaries, or policies, or retaining individuals in office, except by consent of the contracting parties. On the whole, such a holding is probably preferable to one which would open the courts to pass on the motives of directors in the lawful exercise of their trust. * * *

[As an alternative ground for its decision, the Court held that the contract also violated public policy in light of a New York criminal statute that prohibited a city magistrate from engaging "in any other business or profession" and required him to "devote his whole time and capacity * * * to the duties of his office."]

The judgment of the Appellate Division and that of the Trial Term should be reversed and the complaint dismissed, with costs in all courts.

CRANE, KELLOGG, O'BRIEN, and HUBBS, JJ., concur with POUND, C.J.

LEHMAN, J., concurs in result in opinion in which CROUCH, J., concurs. [This concurring opinion is omitted.]

Notes

(1) 2 Model Bus.Corp.Act Ann. (3d ed.), 8–7:[1]

Business corporations in common law jurisdictions have long followed the tradition of a representative form of governance by the election of a board of directors by the shareholders, voting by interest and not per capita. The board has traditionally been charged with the duty and responsibility of managing the business and affairs of the corporation, determining corporate policies, and selecting the officers and agents who carry on the detailed administration of the business. In large, publicly held corporations, the role of directors has

---

1. Reprinted from *Model Business Corporation Act Annotated* with the permission of the   American Bar Association.

been increasingly seen as involving oversight and review rather than actual management.

Legal writers have developed various theories as to the status of directors and the source of their powers: (1) the agency theory (all powers reside in the shareholders who have delegated certain powers to the directors as their agents); (2) the concession theory (the powers of directors are derived from the state, which authorizes them to perform certain functions, so that this power does not flow from the shareholders); (3) the Platonic guardian theory (the board is an aristocracy or group of overseers created by statutory enactment); and (4) the sui generis theory (directors are not agents; they are fiduciaries whose duties run to the corporation but their relationship with the corporation is sui generis since they are not trustees). Of these various theories, the first has been generally rejected, and probably most commentators today would agree that the fourth most accurately describes the modern role of directors.

(2) Two subsequent cases have largely defined the scope of the principle originally set forth in Manson v. Curtis and articulated in the principal case:

(a) In Clark v. Dodge, 269 N.Y. 410, 199 N.E. 641 (1936), Clark owned 25 percent and Dodge owned 75 percent of the stock of each of two corporations. Clark and Dodge entered into a written agreement under seal in which it was agreed that Clark would continue to manage the business and in that connection would disclose a secret formula to Dodge's son that was necessary for the successful operation of the business. In return, Dodge agreed that he would vote his stock and also vote as director so that (i) Clark would be retained as general manager (so long as he should be "faithful, efficient and competent"), (ii) Clark would receive one-fourth of the net income either by way of salary or dividends, and (iii) no unreasonable salary would be paid to reduce the net income so as to materially affect Clark's profits. The agreement also provided that Clark would be retained as a director, and that Clark agreed to bequeath his stock—assuming no issue survived him—to Dodge's wife and children. After a falling out, Clark sought specific performance of the agreement, which was granted despite the provisions restricting Dodge's discretion as a director:

> The only question which need be discussed is whether the contract is illegal as against public policy within the decision in McQuade v. Stoneham, 263 N.Y. 323, 189 N.E. 234, upon the authority of which the complaint was dismissed by the Appellate Division.

> "The business of a corporation shall be managed by its board of directors." General Corporation Law (Consol.Laws, c. 23) § 27. That is the statutory norm. Are we committed by the McQuade Case to the doctrine that there may be no variation, however slight or innocuous, from that norm, where salaries or policies or the retention of individuals in office are concerned? There is ample authority supporting that doctrine. E.g., West v. Camden, 135 U.S. 507, 10 S.Ct. 838, 34 L.Ed. 254; Jackson v. Hooper, 76 N.J.Eq. 592, 75 A. 568, 27 L.R.A. (N.S.) 658. But cf. Salomon v. Salomon & Co. [1897] A.C. 22, 44, and something may be said for it, since it furnishes a simple, if arbitrary, test. Apart from its practical administrative convenience, the reasons upon which it is said to rest are more or less nebulous. Public policy, the intention of the Legislature, detriment to the corporation, are phrases which in this connection mean little. Possible harm to bona fide purchasers of stock or to creditors or to stockholding minorities have more substance; but such harms are absent in many instances. If the enforcement

of a particular contract damages nobody—not even in any perceptible degree, the public—one sees no reason for holding it illegal, even though it impinges slightly upon the broad provision of section 27. Damage suffered or threatened is a logical and practical test, and has come to be the one generally adopted by the courts. See 28 Columbia Law Review 366, 372. Where the directors are the sole stockholders, there seems to be no objection to enforcing an agreement among them to vote for certain people as officers. There is no direct decision to that effect in this court, yet there are strong indications that such a rule has long been recognized. * * *

Except for the broad dicta in the McQuade opinion, we think there can be no doubt that the agreement here in question was legal and that the complaint states a cause of action. There was no attempt to sterilize the board of directors, as in the Manson and McQuade Cases. The only restrictions on Dodge were (a) that as a stockholder he should vote for Clark as a director—a perfectly legal contract; (b) that as director he should continue Clark as general manager so long as he proved faithful, efficient, and competent—an agreement which could harm nobody; (c) that Clark should always receive as salary or dividends one-fourth of the "net income." For the purposes of this motion, it is only just to construe that phrase as meaning whatever was left for distribution after the directors had in good faith set aside whatever they deemed wise; (d) that no salaries to other officers should be paid, unreasonable in amount or incommensurate with services rendered—a beneficial and not a harmful agreement.

If there was any invasion of the powers of the directorate under that agreement, it is so slight as to be negligible; and certainly there is no damage suffered by or threatened to anybody. The broad statements in the McQuade opinion, applicable to the facts there, should be confined to those facts.

(b) In Long Park v. Trenton–New Brunswick Theatres Co., 297 N.Y. 174, 77 N.E.2d 633 (1948), all the shareholders of the theatre company entered into an agreement giving one shareholder "full authority and power to supervise and direct the operation and management" of certain theatres. Such shareholder could be removed as manager only by arbitration among the shareholders. The Court stated:

By virtue of these provisions the management of all theatres leased or operated by Trenton or any subsidiary is vested in Keith, without approval of the directors, and this management may not be changed by the directors but only [by arbitration]. The directors may neither select nor discharge the manager, to whom the supervision and direction of the management and operation of the theatres is delegated with full authority and power. Thus the powers of the directors over the management of its theatres, the principal business of the corporation, were completely sterilized. Such restrictions and limitations upon the powers of the directors are clearly in violation of section 27 of the General Corporation Law of this State and the New Jersey statute. * * *

We think these restrictions and limitations went far beyond the agreement in Clark v. Dodge, 269 N.Y. 410, 199 N.E. 641. We are not confronted with a slight impingement or innocuous variance from the statutory norm, but rather with the deprivation of all the powers of the board insofar as the selection and supervision of the management of the corporation's theatres, including the manner and policy of their operation, are concerned. * * *

77 N.E.2d at 634–35.

(3) Precisely what is the status of the rule of the McQuade case following these two decisions?

(4) A number of possible consequences flow from the common law concept of the independent role of the board of directors. For example:

(a) If the majority shareholder demands that the board enter into a specific transaction on behalf of the corporation, must the directors comply? The common law answer was a clear "no." See Automatic Self–Cleansing Filter Syndicate Co., Ltd. v. Cunninghame, Court of Appeal of England [1906] 2 Ch. 34.

(b) Should a majority shareholder be permitted to remove directors simply because they refuse to do as they agreed to do or as the shareholder wishes? See MBCA § 8.08 which reverses the common law rule.

(c) Are long-term management contracts entered into by the corporation with a person who is not a director enforceable? Does it make any difference if the delegation is total or partial? For five years or twenty-five? Compare Sherman & Ellis, Inc. v. Indiana Mut. Cas. Co., 41 F.2d 588 (7th Cir.1930) with Jones v. Williams, 139 Mo. 1, 39 S.W. 486 (1897).

(d) What about delegation of managerial authority to a committee of the board of directors? See MBCA § 8.25.

(e) What about one board binding a later board, e.g., by a 99–year lease? What about a two-year employment contract with the president of the corporation? Should it make any difference that bylaws of corporations usually state that the president shall be elected annually? Or should the relevance of that depend on whether the directors have authority to amend bylaws? See Realty Acceptance Corp. v. Montgomery, 51 F.2d 636 (3d Cir.1930), affirmed on other grounds 284 U.S. 547, 52 S.Ct. 215, 76 L.Ed. 476 (1932); Pioneer Specialties, Inc. v. Nelson, 161 Tex. 244, 339 S.W.2d 199 (1960). See MBCA § 10.20. What about inferences that may be drawn from MBCA § 8.43(b)?

GALLER v. GALLER

Supreme Court of Illinois, 1964.
32 Ill.2d 16, 203 N.E.2d 577.

UNDERWOOD, JUSTICE.

Plaintiff, Emma Galler, sued in equity for an accounting and for specific performance of an agreement made in July, 1955, between plaintiff and her husband, of one part, and defendants, Isadore A. Galler and his wife, Rose, of the other. Defendants appealed from a decree of the superior court of Cook County granting the relief prayed. The First District Appellate Court reversed the decree and denied specific performance, affirming in part the order for an accounting, and modifying the order awarding master's fees. (45 Ill.App.2d 452, 196 N.E.2d 5.) That decision is appealed here on a certificate of importance.

There is no substantial dispute as to the facts in this case. From 1919 to 1924, Benjamin and Isadore Galler, brothers, were equal partners in the Galler Drug Company, a wholesale drug concern. In 1924 the business was incorporated under the Illinois Business Corporation Act, each owning one half of the outstanding 220 shares of stock. In 1945 each contracted to sell 6 shares to an employee, Rosenberg, at a price of $10,500 for each block of 6 shares, payable within 10 years. They guaranteed to repurchase the shares if

Rosenberg's employment were terminated, and further agreed that if they sold their shares, Rosenberg would receive the same price per share as that paid for the brothers' shares. Rosenberg was still indebted for the 12 shares in July, 1955, and continued to make payments on account even after Benjamin Galler died in 1957 and after the institution of this action by Emma Galler in 1959. Rosenberg was not involved in this litigation either as a party or as a witness, and in July of 1961, prior to the time that the master in chancery hearings were concluded, defendants Isadore and Rose Galler purchased the 12 shares from Rosenberg. A supplemental complaint was filed by the plaintiff, Emma Galler, asserting an equitable right to have 6 of the 12 shares transferred to her and offering to pay the defendants one half of the amount that the defendants paid Rosenberg. The parties have stipulated that pending disposition of the instant case, these shares will not be voted or transferred. For approximately one year prior to the entry of the decree by the chancellor in July of 1962, there were no outstanding minority shareholder interests.

In March, 1954, Benjamin and Isadore, on the advice of their accountant, decided to enter into an agreement for the financial protection of their immediate families and to assure their families, after the death of either brother, equal control of the corporation. In June, 1954, while the agreement was in the process of preparation by an attorney-associate of the accountant, Benjamin suffered a heart attack. Although he resumed his business duties some months later, he was again stricken in February, 1955, and thereafter was unable to return to work. During his brother's illness, Isadore asked the accountant to have the shareholders' agreement put in final form in order to protect Benjamin's wife, and this was done by another attorney employed in the accountant's office. On a Saturday night in July, 1955, the accountant brought the agreement to Benjamin's home, and 6 copies of it were executed there by the two brothers and their wives. The accountant then collected all signed copies of the agreement and informed the parties that he was taking them for safe keeping. Between the execution of the agreement in July, 1955, and Benjamin's death in December, 1957, the agreement was not modified. Benjamin suffered a stroke late in July, 1955, and on August 2, 1955, Isadore and the accountant and a notary public brought to Benjamin for signature two powers of attorney which were retained by the accountant after Benjamin executed them with Isadore as a witness. The plaintiff did not read the powers and she never had them. One of the powers authorized the transfer of Benjamin's bank account to Emma and the other power enabled Emma to vote Benjamin's 104 shares. Because of the state of Benjamin's health, nothing further was said to him by any of the parties concerning the agreement. It appears from the evidence that some months after the agreement was signed, the defendants Isadore and Rose Galler and their son, the defendant, Aaron Galler sought to have the agreements destroyed. The evidence is undisputed that defendants had decided prior to Benjamin's death they would not honor the agreement, but never disclosed their intention to plaintiff or her husband.

On July 21, 1956, Benjamin executed an instrument creating a trust naming his wife as trustee. The trust covered, among other things, the 104 shares of Galler Drug Company stock and the stock certificates were endorsed by Benjamin and delivered to Emma. When Emma presented the certificates to defendants for transfer into her name as trustee, they sought to have

Emma abandon the 1955 agreement or enter into some kind of a noninterference agreement as a price for the transfer of the shares. Finally, in September, 1956, after Emma had refused to abandon the shareholders' agreement, she did agree to permit defendant Aaron to become president for one year and agreed that she would not interfere with the business during that year. The stock was then reissued in her name as trustee. During the year 1957 while Benjamin was still alive, Emma tried many times to arrange a meeting with Isadore to discuss business matters but he refused to see her.

Shortly after Benjamin's death, Emma went to the office and demanded the terms of the 1955 agreement be carried out. Isadore told her that anything she had to say could be said to Aaron, who then told her that his father would not abide by the agreement. He offered a modification of the agreement by proposing the salary continuation payment but without her becoming a director. When Emma refused to modify the agreement and sought enforcement of its terms, defendants refused and this suit followed.

During the last few years of Benjamin's life both brothers drew an annual salary of $42,000. Aaron, whose salary was $15,000 as manager of the warehouse prior to September, 1956, has since the time that Emma agreed to his acting as president drawn an annual salary of $20,000. In 1957, 1958, and 1959 a $40,000 annual dividend was paid. Plaintiff has received her proportionate share of the dividend.

The July, 1955, agreement in question here, entered into between Benjamin, Emma, Isadore and Rose, recites that Benjamin and Isadore each own 47½% of the issued and outstanding shares of the Galler Drug Company, an Illinois corporation, and that Benjamin and Isadore desired to provide income for the support and maintenance of their immediate families. No reference is made to the shares then being purchased by Rosenberg. The essential features of the contested portions of the agreement are substantially as set forth in the opinion of the Appellate Court: (2) that the bylaws of the corporation will be amended to provide for a board of four directors; that the necessary quorum shall be three directors; and that no directors' meeting shall be held without giving ten days notice to all directors. (3) The shareholders will cast their votes for the above named persons (Isadore, Rose, Benjamin and Emma) as directors at said special meeting and at any other meeting held for the purpose of electing directors. (4, 5) In the event of the death of either brother his wife shall have the right to nominate a director in place of the decedent. (6) Certain annual dividends will be declared by the corporation. The dividend shall be $50,000 payable out of the accumulated earned surplus in excess of $500,000. If 50% of the annual net profits after taxes exceeds the minimum $50,000, then the directors shall have discretion to declare a dividend up to 50% of the annual net profits. If the net profits are less than $50,000, nevertheless the minimum $50,000 annual dividend shall be declared, providing the $500,000 surplus is maintained. Earned surplus is defined. (9) The certificates evidencing the said shares of Benjamin Galler and Isadore Galler shall bear a legend that the shares are subject to the terms of this agreement. (10) A salary continuation agreement shall be entered into by the corporation which shall authorize the corporation upon the death of Benjamin Galler or Isadore Galler, or both, to pay a sum equal to twice the salary of such officer, payable monthly over a five-year period. Said sum shall be paid to the widow during her widowhood, but should be paid to such widow's children if the widow remarries within the five-year period. (11, 12) The parties to this agreement further agree and hereby grant to the corporation the authority to purchase, in the event of the death of either Benjamin or Isadore, so much of the stock of Galler Drug Company held by the estate as is necessary to provide sufficient funds to pay the federal estate tax, the Illinois inheritance tax and other administrative expenses of the estate. If as a result of such purchase from the estate of the decedent the amount of dividends to be received by the heirs is reduced, the parties shall nevertheless vote for directors so as to give the estate and heirs the same representation as before (2 directors out of 4, even though they own less stock), and also that the corporation pay an additional benefit payment equal to the diminution of the dividends. In the event either Benjamin or Isadore decides to sell his shares he is required to offer them first to the remaining shareholders and then to the corporation at book value, according each six months to accept the offer.

The Appellate Court found the 1955 agreement void because "the undue duration, stated purpose and substantial disregard of the provisions of the Corporation Act outweigh any considerations which might call for divisibility" and held that "the public policy of this state demands voiding this entire agreement".

While the conduct of defendants towards plaintiff was clearly inequitable, the basically controlling factor is the absence of an objecting minority interest, together with the absence of public detriment. * * * [Discussion of Illinois cases omitted.]

The power to invalidate the agreements on the grounds of public policy is so far reaching and so easily abused that it should be called into action to set aside or annul the solemn engagement of parties dealing on equal terms only in cases where the corrupt or dangerous tendency clearly and unequivocally appears upon the face of the agreement itself or is the necessary inference from the matters which are expressed, and the only apparent exception to this general rule is to be found in those cases where the agreement, though fair and unobjectionable on its face, is a part of a corrupt scheme and is made to disguise the real nature of the transaction. * * *

At this juncture it should be emphasized that we deal here with a so-called close corporation. Various attempts at definition of the close corporation have been made. For a collection of those most frequently proffered, see O'Neal, Close Corporations, § 1.02 (1958). For our purposes, a close corporation is one in which the stock is held in a few hands, or in a few families, and wherein it is not at all, or only rarely, dealt in by buying or selling. Moreover, it should be recognized that shareholder agreements similar to that in question here are often, as a practical consideration, quite necessary for the protection of those financially interested in the close corporation. While the shareholder of a public-issue corporation may readily sell his shares on the open market should management fail to use, in his opinion, sound business judgment, his counterpart of the close corporation often has a large total of his entire capital invested in the business and has no ready market for his shares should he desire to sell. He feels, understandably, that he is more than a mere investor and that his voice should be heard concerning all corporate activity. Without a shareholder agreement, specifically enforceable by the courts, insuring him a modicum of control, a large minority shareholder might find himself at the mercy of an oppressive or unknowledgeable majority. Moreover, as in the case at bar, the shareholders of a close corporation are often also the directors and officers thereof. With substantial shareholding interests abiding in each member of the board of directors, it is often quite impossible to secure, as in the large public-issue corporation, independent board judgment free from personal motivations concerning corporate policy. For these and other reasons too voluminous to enumerate here, often the only sound basis for protection is afforded by a lengthy, detailed shareholder agreement securing the rights and obligations of all concerned. For a discussion of these and other considerations, see Note, "A Plea for Separate Statutory Treatment of the Close Corporation", 33 N.Y.U.L.Rev. 700 (1958).

As the preceding review of the applicable decisions of this court points out, there has been a definite, albeit inarticulate, trend toward eventual judicial treatment of the close corporation as *sui generis*. Several shareholder-director agreements that have technically "violated" the letter of the Business Corporation Act have nevertheless been upheld in the light of the existing practical circumstances, i.e., no apparent public injury, the absence of a complaining minority interest, and no apparent prejudice to creditors. However, we have thus far not attempted to limit these decisions as applicable only to close corporations and have seemingly implied that general considerations regarding judicial supervision of all corporate behavior apply.

The practical result of this series of cases, while liberally giving legal efficacy to particular agreements in special circumstances notwithstanding literal "violations" of statutory corporate law, has been to inject much doubt and uncertainty into the thinking of the bench and corporate bar of Illinois concerning shareholder agreements. See e.g., Cary, "How Illinois Corporations May Enjoy Partnership Advantages: Planning for the Closely Held Firm," 48 N.W.U.L.Rev. 427; Note, "The Validity of Stockholders' Voting Agreements in Illinois," 3 U.Chi.L.Rev. 640.

It is therefore necessary, we feel, to discuss the instant case with the problems peculiar to the close corporation particularly in mind.

It would admittedly facilitate judicial supervision of corporate behavior if a strict adherence to the provisions of the Business Corporation Act were required in all cases without regard to the practical exigencies peculiar to the close corporation. West v. Camden, 135 U.S. 507, 10 S.Ct. 838, 34 L.Ed. 254. However, courts have long ago quite realistically, we feel, relaxed their attitudes concerning statutory compliance when dealing with close corporate behavior, permitting "slight deviations" from corporate "norms" in order to give legal efficacy to common business practice. See e.g., Clark v. Dodge, 269 N.Y. 410, 199 N.E. 641; Benintendi v. Kenton Hotel, 294 N.Y. 112, 60 N.E.2d 829, 159 A.L.R. 280 (dissenting opinion subsequently legislatively approved). This attitude is illustrated by the following language in Clark v. Dodge: "Public policy, the intention of the Legislature, detriment to the corporation, are phrases which in this connection [the court was discussing a shareholder-director agreement whereby the directors pledged themselves to vote for certain people as officers of the corporation] mean little. Possible harm to bona fide purchasers of stock or to creditors or to stockholding minorities have more substance; but such harms are absent in many instances. If the enforcement of a particular contract damages nobody—not even, in any perceptible degree, the public—one sees no reason for holding it illegal, even though it impinges slightly upon the broad provisions of [the relevant statute providing that the business of a corporation shall be managed by its board of directors]. Damage suffered or threatened is a logical and practical test, and has come to be the one generally adopted by the courts. See 28 Columbia Law Review 366, 372." Clark v. Dodge, 199 N.E. 641, 642.

Again, "As the parties to the action are the complete owners of the corporation, there is no reason why the exercise of the power and discretion of the directors cannot be controlled by valid agreement between themselves, provided that the interests of creditors are not affected." Clark v. Dodge, 199 N.E. 641, 643, quoting from Kassel v. Empire Tinware Co., 178 App.Div. 176, 180, 164 N.Y.S. 1033, 1035. * * *

Perhaps, as has been vociferously advanced, a separate comprehensive statutory scheme governing the close corporation would best serve here. See Note "A Plea for Separate Statutory Treatment of the Close Corporation", 33 N.Y.U.L.Rev. 700. Some states have enacted legislation dealing specifically with the close corporation.

At any rate, however, the courts can no longer fail to expressly distinguish between the close and public-issue corporation when confronted with problems relating to either. What we do here is to illuminate this problem—before the bench, corporate bar, and the legislature, in the context of a particular fact situation. To do less would be to shirk our responsibility, to do more would, perhaps be to invade the province of the legislative branch.

We now, in the light of the foregoing, turn to specific provisions of the 1955 agreement.

The Appellate Court correctly found many of the contractual provisions free from serious objection, and we need not prolong this opinion with a discussion of them here. That court did, however, find difficulties in the stated purpose of the agreement as it relates to its duration, the election of certain persons to specific offices for a number of years, the requirement for the mandatory declaration of stated dividends (which the Appellate Court held invalid), and the salary continuation agreement.

Since the question as to the duration of the agreement is a principal source of controversy, we shall consider it first. The parties provided no specific termination date, and while the agreement concludes with a paragraph that its terms "shall be binding upon and shall inure to the benefits of" the legal representatives, heirs and assigns of the parties, this clause is, we believe, intended to be operative only as long as one of the parties is living. It further provides that it shall be so construed as to carry out its purposes, and we believe these must be determined from a consideration of the agreement as a whole. Thus viewed, a fair construction is that its purposes were accomplished at the death of the survivor of the parties. While these life spans are not precisely ascertainable, and the Appellate Court noted Emma Galler's life expectancy at her husband's death was 26.9 years, we are aware of no statutory or public policy provision against stockholder's agreements which would invalidate this agreement on that ground. * * *

The clause that provides for the election of certain persons to specified offices for a period of years likewise does not require invalidation. In Kantzler

v. Benzinger, 214 Ill. 589, 73 N.E. 874, this court upheld an agreement entered into by all the stockholders providing that certain parties would be elected to the offices of the corporation for a fixed period. In Faulds v. Yates, 57 Ill. 416, we upheld a similar agreement among the majority stockholders of a corporation, notwithstanding the existence of a minority which was not before the court complaining thereof.

We turn next to a consideration of the effect of the stated purpose of the agreement upon its validity. The pertinent provision is: "The said Benjamin A. Galler and Isadore A. Galler desire to provide income for the support and maintenance of their immediate families." Obviously, there is no evil inherent in a contract entered into for the reason that the persons originating the terms desired to so arrange their property as to provide post-death support for those dependent upon them. Nor does the fact that the subject property is corporate stock alter the situation so long as there exists no detriment to minority stock interests, creditors or other public injury. It is, however, contended by defendants that the methods provided by the agreement for implementation of the stated purpose are, as a whole, violative of the Business Corporation Act to such an extent as to render it void *in toto*.

The terms of the dividend agreement require a minimum annual dividend of $50,000, but this duty is limited by the subsequent provision that it shall be operative only so long as an earned surplus of $500,000 is maintained. It may be noted that in 1958, the year prior to commencement of this litigation, the corporation's net earnings after taxes amounted to $202,759 while its earned surplus was $1,543,270, and this was increased in 1958 to $1,680,079 while earnings were $172,964. The minimum earned surplus requirement is designed for the protection of the corporation and its creditors, and we take no exception to the contractual dividend requirements as thus restricted.

The salary continuation agreement is a common feature, in one form or another, of corporate executive employment. It requires that the widow should receive a total benefit, payable monthly over a five-year period, aggregating twice the amount paid her deceased husband in one year. This requirement was likewise limited for the protection of the corporation by being contingent upon the payments being income tax-deductible by the corporation. The charge made in those cases which have considered the validity of payments to the widow of an officer and shareholder in a corporation is that a gift of its property by a noncharitable corporation is in violation of the rights of its shareholders and *ultra vires*. Since there are no shareholders here other than the parties to the contract, this objection is not here applicable, and its effect, as limited, upon the corporation is not so prejudicial as to require its invalidation.

Having concluded that the agreement, under the circumstances here present, is not vulnerable to the attack made on it, we must consider the accounting feature of this action. The trial court allowed the relief prayed, an action we deem proper except as to the master's fees which were modified by the Appellate Court. Since no question is here raised regarding them, we affirm the action of that court in this respect. The questions as to salary which the Appellate Court correctly held were improperly increased became ones of fact to be determined by the trial court.

We hold defendants must account for all monies received by them from the corporation since September 25, 1956, in excess of that theretofore authorized.

Accordingly, the judgment of the Appellate Court is reversed except insofar as it relates to fees, and is, as to them affirmed. The cause is remanded to the circuit court of Cook County with directions to proceed in accordance herewith.

Affirmed in part and reversed in part, and remanded with directions.

Notes

(1) Like *Donahue* (see page 377, supra), this decision and opinion has had a significant impact on the development of close corporation law. Its call for special legislative treatment of closely held corporations has led to statutory developments in most states. These statutes permit closely held corporations to depart dramatically from the traditional statutory scheme of shareholders/directors/officers in specified circumstances. As a result, it is possible—by appropriate planning—to create corporations that vary widely from the traditional statutory scheme envisioned in *McQuade*. It is important, however, to follow whatever statutory scheme has been adopted in the specific state, since a deviation may risk invalidation of the entire arrangement. Many states have adopted more than one of the following alternative approaches.

(2) *Modification of the Statutory Scheme by Provisions in the Articles of Incorporation.* The statutes of about 30 states permit the authority normally placed in the board of directors to be vested in other persons or organizations by an appropriate provision in the articles of incorporation (or in some instances for some types of provisions, in the bylaws). Many of these statutes also provide that if managerial authority is vested in persons or organizations other than the board of directors, those persons or organizations then have the duties, responsibilities, and liabilities of directors. Two states expressly permit shareholders to do anything that the board of directors may do so long as they act with the consent of all the shareholders.

(3) *Integrated Close Corporation Statutes.* About 17 states have followed the suggestion made by Justice Underwood in *Galler* and enacted special close corporation statutes. While these statutes vary from state to state, they share one common characteristic: they are all integrated "opt in" statutes that may be elected by a corporation that meets the statutory definition of a close corporation.

(a) The definition usually involves a numerical limit on the number of shareholders (Delaware's maximum is 30); this type of definition obviously creates problems when a corporation grows so that the number of shareholders exceed the limit, though that apparently rarely occurs as a practical matter. Some state statutes provide that the election may continue even if the number of shareholders exceed the numerical limit, apparently on the theory that a corporation with a large number of shareholders will find the close corporation election to be unwieldy. The election to take advantage of the integrated close corporation statute is usually evidenced by a provision in the corporation's articles of incorporation which simply states that "This corporation is a statutory close corporation."

(b) Delaware Gen.Corp.Law §§ 341–356, enacted in 1967, is a fairly typical Close Corporation statute, though a number of states have subsequently added novel features. With respect to the role of the board of directors, Del.Gen.Corp.

Law § 350 broadly validates agreements that restrict discretion of directors which might be invalid under *McQuade*; § 351 authorizes a corporation to dispense entirely with a board of directors and provide for direct management by shareholders; § 354 validates written agreements among shareholders that "treat the corporation as if it were a partnership or to arrange relations among the stockholders or between the stockholders and the corporation in a manner that would be appropriate only among partners." Section 352 provides for the judicial appointment of a "custodian" if the corporation is threatened with irreparable injury or deadlock while § 353 provides for the judicial appointment of a provisional director "if the directors are so divided respecting the management of the corporation's business cannot be obtained with the consequence that the business and affairs of the corporation can no longer be conducted to the advantage of the stockholders generally"; these two provisions, it should be noted, are not "opt in" provisions but rather are automatically applicable to all electing close corporations. Section 355 authorizes close corporations to adopt a provision that mandates dissolution at the request of "any stockholder, or * * * the holders of any specified number or percentage of shares of any class of stock, an option to have the corporation the corporation dissolved at will or upon the occurrence of any specified event or contingency."

(c) Close corporation statutes in other states also contain provisions that define how a corporation revokes the election to be a statutory close corporation, that encourage and simplify the use of share transfer restrictions, and, like the Delaware statute, that provide special remedies for deadlock or dissension within a close corporation. Remedies for deadlock or dissension generally are discussed in Sections C and D below.

(d) Some close corporation statutes permit a corporation to dispense with bylaws, annual meetings, and other formal requirements imposed on corporations generally. Some statutes add for good measure that the exercise of any of the powers granted to statutory close corporations "is not a ground for imposing personal liability on the shareholders for liabilities of the corporation," or provisions to the same effect.

(e) Most of the legal commentary discussing the growth of these integrated close corporation statutes has been either purely reportorial or uncritically enthusiastic. For a critical examination (and perhaps an unnecessarily negative analysis) see Dennis S. Karjala, A Second Look at Special Close Corporation Legislation, 58 Tex.L.Rev. 1207 (1980); Dennis S. Karjala, An Analysis of Close Corporation Legislation in the United States, 21 Ariz.St.L.J. 663 (1989). Several observations may be made about these statutes:

(i) They are based on little or no empirical examination of the need for such legislation. Provisions appear to be based on intuitive views as to what a close corporation probably needs; of course, as close corporation statutes have proliferated, the major source for provisions becomes statutes already enacted in other states. Do you believe that empirical investigation is necessary at all in an area such as this? After all, the surge of close corporation legislation is largely based on the problems developed in actual litigation in a few cases and on the views of influential judges in such cases. Should not that be enough?

(ii) The statutes, where available, do not appear to be widely used. Professor Karjala comments that attorneys in Arizona and California appear to take advantage of the close corporation options in only a minute fraction of the corporations that are eligible to do so. Karjala, supra, 58 Tex.L.Rev., at 1266 n. 236. Attorneys knowledgeable with filings in Arkansas, Illinois, Delaware and

Texas believe that in those states also advantage is rarely taken of the close corporation options. Indeed, in Illinois, less than 1 percent of all corporations have made the statutory election. A study of a sample of 1,033 Texas filings showed that close corporation statutes was elected in only 37 instances (3.71%). Richard A. Blunk, Analyzing Texas Articles of Incorporation: Is the Statutory Close Corporation Format Viable? 34 Sw.L.J. 941 (1980). Since this study, however, the Texas statute was considerably simplified and it is possible that its use has increased somewhat since then. In Maryland, over 50 percent of the corporations are statutory close corporations but that is apparently a result of a provision that in electing corporations, workers' compensation insurance does not have to be provided for officers and directors who are also employees. To the extent these data are reliable and indicative of practices in other states, two conclusions might be drawn: (a) close corporation statutes may not be really needed, or (b) attorneys are very cautious about trying new and untested devices. There also may be uncertainty about whether potential liability for breach of fiduciary duties might be increased by election of this new device.

(4) *Authorization of Shareholder Agreements.* MBCA § 7.32, which was added to the Model Act in 1992, was designed to be the ultimate solution to the close corporation management problem. The Official Comment states that it "rejects the older line of cases [epitomized by Long Park, Inc. v. Trenton–New Brunswick Theatres Co. and] adds an important element of predictability currently absent from the Model Act and affords participants in closely-held corporations greater contractual freedom to tailor the rules of their enterprise." See particularly §§ 7.32(a)(1), 7.32(b). When § 7.32 was approved, the Committee on Corporate Laws also withdrew a "Model Close Corporation Supplement" that was based on the Delaware model with refinements; this model close corporation supplement generally had not been enacted in states that used the MBCA as the basis for revisions of their corporation statutes. The decision to withdraw this integrated close corporation statute was also partially based on the belief of members of the Committee, that relatively few corporations actually elected close corporation status in states where that election was available.

The Official Comment to § 7.32 states:[2]

> Section 7.32 is not intended to establish or legitimize an alternative form of corporation. Instead, it is intended to add, within the context of the traditional corporate structure, legal certainty to shareholder agreements that embody various aspects of the business arrangement established by the shareholders to meet their business and personal needs. The subject matter of these arrangements includes governance of the entity, allocation of the economic return from the business, and other aspects of the relationships among shareholders, directors, and the corporation which are part of the business arrangement. Section 7.32 also recognizes that many of the corporate norms contained in the Model Act, as well as the corporation statutes of most states, were designed with an eye towards public companies, where management and share ownership are quite distinct.

What is meant by an "alternative form of corporation"? Is not the freedom to dispense entirely with the board of directors itself the creation of an "alternative form"? The Official Comment suggests the following:

2. Reprinted from *Model Business Corporation Act Annotated* with the permission of the American Bar Association.

While the outer limits of the catch-all provision of subsection 7.32(a)(8) are left uncertain, these [*sic,* there (?)] are provisions of the Model Act that cannot be overridden by resort to the catch-all. * * * [I]n defining the outer limits, courts should consider whether the variation from the Model Act under consideration is similar to the variations permitted by the first seven subsections. Subsection (a)(8) is also subject to a public policy limitation * * *. For example, a shareholder agreement that provides that the directors of the corporation have no duties of care or loyalty to the corporation or the shareholders would not be within the purview of section 7.32(a)(8) because it is not sufficiently similar to the types of arrangements suggested by the first seven subsections of section 7.32(a) and because such a provision could be viewed as contrary to a public policy of substantial importance. * * * [S]hareholder agreements otherwise validated by section 7.32 are not legally binding on the state, on creditors, or on other third parties. For example, an agreement that dispenses with the need to make corporate filings required by the Act would be ineffective. Similarly, an agreement among shareholders that provides that only the president has authority to enter into contracts for the corporation would not, without more, [be] binding against third parties, and ordinary principles of agency, including the concept of apparent authority, would continue to apply.

(6) *Galler* arose because an accountant preparing an estate plan for a client whose principal assets were shares in a closely held corporation was apparently unaware of corporate legal norms. An estate planner who has some degree of sophistication about corporation law can usually develop and effectuate an estate plan for a client within the confines of traditional corporate principles and, if not, through the use of the flexibility provided by the various statutes discussed in these notes. Under these more flexible rules, are there limitations on what the testator can do in controlling the corporation after his or her death? In the Matter of the Estate of Hirshon, 13 N.Y.2d 787, 242 N.Y.S.2d 218, 192 N.E.2d 174 (1963), the testator, who owned 68 percent of the stock of a closely held corporation, created a testamentary trust and directed the trustees to vote for themselves as directors of the corporation. His will contained detailed rules for the subsequent governance of the corporation. For example, it directed that one Arthur V. Graseck "be elected and retained in office as president of the corporation to be in charge of the general management thereof," and that the testator's widow (and, upon her death, his daughter) be named as chairman of the board of directors with a minimum compensation of $12,000 per annum plus a bonus. The Court invalidated these detailed rules under the *McQuade* principle. Would these provisions be valid under the more flexible rules described above? Are there policy considerations that militate against acceptance of such post-death instructions? What should executors or trustees faced with such detailed rules do when circumstances change, as they inevitably must?

ZION v. KURTZ

Court of Appeals of New York, 1980.
50 N.Y.2d 92, 428 N.Y.S.2d 199, 405 N.E.2d 681.

MEYER, JUDGE.

On these appeals we conclude that when all of the stockholders of a Delaware corporation agree that, except as specified in their agreement, no "business or activities" of the corporation shall be conducted without the consent of a minority stockholder, the agreement is, as between the original parties to it, enforceable even though all formal steps required by the statute have not been taken. We hold further that the agreement made by the parties to this action was violated when the corporation entered into two agreements without the minority stockholder's consent. * * *

[Editor: Harold Kurtz formed a Delaware corporation, Lombard–Wall Group, Inc. ("Group"). Group acquired all the stock of Lombard–Wall Incorporated ("L–W"), in a complex transaction in which Abraham Zion made available assets that were used as security for a loan to finance the acquisition. As part of the transaction, Zion acquired all the Class A stock of Group while Kurtz continued to own all of the Class B stock. Zion and Kurtz also executed a shareholders' agreement, which provided in § 3.01(a) that without the consent of the holders of the Class A stock, Group would not "engage in any business or activities of any kind, directly or indirectly, whether through any Subsidiary or by way of a loan, guarantee or otherwise, other than the acquisition and ownership of the stock of L–W as contemplated by this Agreement * * *." The articles of incorporation of Group did not refer to this veto power. Group's board of directors approved two agreements over the objection of Zion. Zion brought suit to cancel the two agreements as violating the shareholders' consent agreement.]

The stockholders' agreement expressly provided that it should be "governed by and construed and enforced in accordance with the laws of the State of Delaware as to matters governed by the General Corporation Law of that State", and that is the generally accepted choice-of-law rule with respect to such "internal affairs" as the relationship between shareholders and directors (cf. Greenspun v. Lindley, 36 N.Y.2d 473, 478, 369 N.Y.S.2d 123, 330 N.E.2d 79; see Restatement, Conflict of Laws 2d, § 302, Comment g). Subdivision (a) of section 141 of the General Corporation Law of Delaware provides that the business and affairs of a corporation organized under that law "shall be managed by a board of directors, except as may be otherwise provided in this chapter or in its certificate of incorporation." Included in the chapter referred to are provisions relating to close corporations, which explicitly state that a written agreement between the holders of a majority of such a corporation's stock "is not invalid, as between the parties to the agreement, on the ground that it so relates to the conduct of the business and affairs of the corporation as to restrict or interfere with the discretion or powers of the board of directors" (§ 350) * * *.

Clear from those provisions is the fact that the public policy of Delaware does not proscribe a provision such as that contained in the shareholders' agreement here in issue even though it takes all management functions away from the directors. Folk, in his work on the Delaware Corporation Law, states concerning section 350 that "Although some decisions outside Delaware have sustained 'reasonable' restrictions upon director discretion contained in stockholder agreements, the theory of § 350 is to declare unequivocally, as a matter of public policy, that stockholder agreements of this character are not invalid", that section 351 "recognizes a special subclass of close corporations which operate by direct stockholder management", and with respect to section 354 that it "should be liberally construed to authorize all sorts of internal agreements and arrangements which are not affirmatively improper or, more particularly, injurious to third parties".

Defendants argue, however, that Group was not incorporated as a close corporation and the stockholders' agreement provision was never incorporated in its certificate. The answer is that any Delaware corporation can elect to become a close corporation by filing an appropriate certificate of amendment (Del.General Corporation Law, § 344) and by such amendment approved by the holders of all of its outstanding stock may include in its certificate provisions restricting directors' authority (ibid., § 351). Here, not only did defendant Kurtz agree in paragraph 8.05(b) of the stockholders' agreement to "without further consideration, do, execute and deliver, or cause to be done, executed and delivered, all such further acts, things and instruments as may be reasonably required more effectively to evidence and give effect to the provisions and the intent and purposes of this Agreement", but also as part of the transaction by which the * * * guarantee was made and Zion became a Group stockholder, defendant Kurtz, while he was still the sole stockholder and sole director of Group, executed a consent to the various parts of the transaction under which he was "authorized and empowered to execute and deliver, or cause to be executed and delivered, all such other and further instruments and documents and take, or cause to be taken, all such other and further action as he may deem necessary, appropriate or desirable to implement and give effect to the Stockholders Agreement and the transactions provided for therein." Since there are no intervening rights of third persons, the agreement requires nothing that is not permitted by statute, and all of the stockholders of the corporation assented to it, the certificate of incorporation may be ordered reformed, by requiring Kurtz to file the appropriate amendments, or more directly he may be held estopped to rely upon the absence of those amendments from the corporate charter (see Delaney, The Corporate Director: Can His Hands Be Tied In Advance, 50 Col.L.Rev. 52, 66).[3]

The result thus reached accords with the weight of authority which textwriter F. Hodge O'Neal tells us sustains agreements made by all shareholders dealing with matters normally within the province of the directors (1 Close Corporations § 5.24, p. 83), even though the shareholders could have, but had not, provided similarly by charter or by-law provision sanctioned by statute (ibid., § 5.19, pp. 73–74). Moreover, though we have not yet had occasion to construe subdivision (b) of section 620 of the Business Corporation Law,[4] which did not become effective until September 1, 1963, it is worthy of note that in adopting that provision the Legislature had before it the Revisers'

---

3. [By the Court] The fallacy of the dissent is that it converts a shield into a sword. The notice devices on which the concept of the dissent turns are wholly unnecessary to protect the original parties, who may be presumed to have known what they agreed to. To protect an original party who has not been hurt (indeed, has expressly agreed to the limitation he is being protected against and affirmatively covenanted to see to it that all necessary steps to validate the agreement were taken) because a third party without notice could have been hurt had he been involved can only be characterized as a perversion of the liberal legislative purpose demonstrated by the Delaware statutes quoted in the text above.

4. [By the Court] That provision reads: "(b) A provision in the certificate of incorpo-

ration otherwise prohibited by law because it improperly restricts the board in its management of the business of the corporation, or improperly transfers to one or more shareholders or to one or more persons or corporations to be selected by him or them, all or any part of such management otherwise within the authority of the board under this chapter, shall nevertheless be valid: (1) If all the incorporators or holders of record of all outstanding shares, whether or not having voting power, have authorized such provision in the certificate of incorporation or an amendment thereof; and (2) If, subsequent to the adoption of such provision, shares are transferred or issued only to persons who had knowledge or notice thereof or consented in writing to such provision."

Comment that: "Paragraph (b) expands the ruling in Clark v. Dodge, 269 N.Y. 410, 199 N.E. 637 [641] (1936), and, to the extent therein provided, overrules Long Park, Inc. v. Trenton–New Brunswick Theatres Co., 297 N.Y. 174, 77 N.E.2d 633 (1948); Manson v. Curtis, 223 N.Y. 313, 119 N.E. 559 (1919) and McQuade v. Stoneham, 263 N.Y. 323, 189 N.E. 234 (1934)." Thus it is clear that no New York public policy stands in the way of our application of the Delaware statute and decisional law above referred to * * *.

For the foregoing reasons the order of the Appellate Division should be modified, as above indicated.

GABRIELLI, JUDGE (dissenting in part).

* * * I conclude that the agreement requiring plaintiff's consent was invalid under well-established public policies. * * * [It was] an illegal attempt by shareholders to deprive the board of directors of its inherent authority to exercise its discretion in managing the affairs of the corporation. * * * I would, [therefore,] reverse the determination of the Appellate Division with respect to plaintiff's * * * cause of action and hold that plaintiff cannot maintain a suit based upon defendants' failure to obtain his consent prior to executing the disputed * * * agreements.

It is beyond dispute that shareholder agreements such as the one relied upon by plaintiff in this case are, as a general rule, void as against public policy. Section 3.01 of the agreement, as interpreted both by plaintiff and by a majority of this court, would have precluded the board of directors of Group from taking any action on behalf of the corporation without first obtaining plaintiff's consent. This contractual provision, if enforced, would effectively shift the authority to manage every aspect of corporate affairs from the board to plaintiff, a minority shareholder who has no fiduciary obligations with respect to either the corporation or its other shareholders. As such, the provision represents a blatant effort to "sterilize" the board of directors in contravention of the statutory and decisional law of both Delaware and New York.

Under the statutes of Delaware, the State in which Group was incorporated, the authority to manage the affairs of a corporation is vested solely in its board of directors (Del.General Corporation Law, § 141, subd. [a]). The same is true under the applicable New York statutes (Business Corporation Law, § 701). Significantly, in both States, the courts have declined to give effect to agreements which purport to vary the statutory rule by transferring effective control of the corporation to a third party other than the board of directors (see Abercrombie v. Davies, 35 Del.Ch. 599, 604–611, 123 A.2d 893, rev'd on other grounds 36 Del.Ch. 371, 130 A.2d 338 * * *). The common-law rule in Delaware was aptly stated in Abercrombie v. Davies, 35 Del.Ch. at p. 611, 123 A.2d at p. 899, supra: "So long as the corporate form is used as presently provided by our statutes this Court cannot give legal sanction to agreements which have the effect of removing from directors in a very substantial way their duty to use their own best judgment on management matters".

True, the common-law rule has been modified somewhat in recent years to account for the business needs of the so-called "close corporation." The courts of our State, for example, have been willing to enforce shareholder agreements where the incursion on the board's authority was insubstantial (Clark v. Dodge, 269 N.Y. 410, 199 N.E. 641) or where the illegal provisions were severable from the otherwise legal provisions which the shareholder sought to enforce (Triggs v. Triggs, 46 N.Y.2d 305, 413 N.Y.S.2d 325, 385 N.E.2d 1254). Neither the courts of our State nor the courts of Delaware, however, have gone so far as to hold that an agreement among shareholders such as the agreement in this case, which purported to "sterilize" the board of directors by completely depriving it of its discretionary authority, can be regarded as legal and enforceable. To the contrary, the common-law rule applicable to both closely and publicly held corporations continues to treat agreements to deprive the board of directors of substantial authority as contrary to public policy.

Indeed, there heretofore has been little need for the courts to modify the general common-law rule against "sterilizing" boards of directors to accommodate the needs of closely held corporations. This is because the Legislatures of many States, including New York and Delaware, have enacted laws which enable the shareholders of closely held corporations to restrict the powers of the board of directors if they comply with certain statutory prerequisites (Del.General Corporation Law, §§ 350, 351; Business Corporation Law, § 620, subd. [b]). The majority apparently construes these statutes as indications that the public policies of the enacting States no longer proscribe the type of agreement at issue here in cases involving closely held corporations. Hence, the majority concludes that there is no bar to the enforcement of the shareholder agreement in this case, even though the statutory requirements for close corporations were not fulfilled. I cannot agree.

Under Delaware law, as the majority notes, the shareholders of a close corporation are free to enter into private, binding agreements among themselves to restrict the powers of their board of directors (Del.General Corporation Law, § 350). The same appears to be true under the present New York statutes (Business Corporation Law, § 620, subd. [b]). Both the Delaware and the New York statutory schemes, however, contemplate that such variations from the corporate norm will be recorded on the face of the certificate of incorporation (Del.General Corporation Law, § 351; Business Corporation Law, § 620, subd. [b]). New York additionally requires that the existence of a substantial restriction on the powers of the board "shall be noted conspicuously on the face or back of every certificate for shares issued by [the] corporation" (Business Corporation Law, § 620, subd. [g]). Significantly, in both Delaware and New York, a provision in the certificate of incorporation restricting the discretion of the board has the effect of shifting liability for any mismanagement from the directors to the managing shareholders (Del.General Corporation Law, § 351, subds. [2]–[3]; Business Corporation Law, § 620, subd. [f]).

In my view, these statutory provisions are not merely directory, but rather are evidence of a clear legislative intention to permit deviations from the statutory norms for corporations only under controlled conditions. In enacting these statutes, which are tailored for "close corporations", the Legislatures of Delaware and New York were apparently attempting to accommodate the needs of those who wished to take advantage of the limited liability inherent in the corporate format, but who also wished to retain the internal management structure of a partnership (see, generally, 1 O'Neal, Close Corporations, § 5.02). At the same time, however, the Legislatures were obviously mindful of the danger to the public that exists whenever shareholders privately agree among themselves to shift control of corporate management from independent directors to the shareholders, who are not necessarily bound by the fiduciary obligations imposed upon the board. In order to protect potential purchasers of shares and perhaps even potential creditors of the corporation, the Legislatures of Delaware and New York imposed specific strictures upon incorporated businesses managed by shareholders, the most significant of which is the requirement that restrictions on the statutory powers of the board of directors be evidenced in the certificate of incorporation. This requirement is an essential component of the statutory scheme because it ensures that potential purchasers of an interest in the corporation will have at least record notice that the corporation is being managed in an unorthodox fashion. Absent an appropriate notice provision in the certificate, there can be no assurance that an unsuspecting purchaser, not privy to the private shareholder agreement, will not be drawn into an investment that he might otherwise choose to avoid.

Since I regard the statutory requirements discussed above as essentially prophylactic in nature, I cannot subscribe to the notion that the agreement in this case should be enforced merely because there has been no showing that the interests of innocent third parties have actually been impaired. As is apparent from the design of the relevant statutes, the public policies of our own State as well as those of the State of Delaware remain opposed to shareholder agreements to "sterilize" the board of directors unless notice of the agreement is provided in the certificate of incorporation. Where such notice is provided, the public policy objections to the agreement are effectively eliminated and there is no further reason to preclude enforcement (see Lehrman v. Cohen, 43 Del.Ch. 222, 235, 222 A.2d 800). On the other hand, where, as here, the shareholders have entered into a private agreement to "sterilize" the board of directors and have failed to comply with the simple statutory prerequisites for "close corporations", the agreement must be deemed void and unenforceable in light of the inherent potential for fraud against the public. Indeed, since it is this very potential for public harm which renders these agreements unlawful, the mere fortuity that no one was actually harmed, if that be the case, cannot be the controlling factor in determining whether the agreement is legally enforceable. For the same reason, the illegality in the instant agreement cannot be cured retroactively, as the majority suggests, by requiring defendants to file the appropriate amendments to the certificate of incorporation. And, of course, it is elementary that a party to an agreement cannot be estopped from asserting its invalidity when the agreement is prohibited by law or is contrary to public policy (e.g., Brick v. Campbell, 122 N.Y. 337, 25 N.E. 493).

By its holding today, the majority has, in effect, rendered inoperative both the language and the underlying purpose of the relevant Delaware and New York statutes governing "close corporations". According to the majority's reasoning, the only requirements for upholding an otherwise unlawful shareholder agreement which concededly deprives the directors of all discretionary authority are that all of the shareholders concur in the agreement and that no "intervening rights of third persons" exist at the time enforcement of the agreement is sought. The statutes in question also recognize these factors as conditions precedent to the enforcement of shareholder agreements to "sterilize" a corporate board of directors. But the laws of both jurisdictions go further, requiring in each case that the "close corporation" give notice of its unorthodox management structure through its filed certificate of incorporation. The obvious purpose of such a requirement is to prevent harm to the public before it occurs. If, as the majority's holding suggests, this requirement of notice to the public through the certificate of incorporation is without legal effect unless and until a third party's interests have actually been impaired, then the prophylactic purposes of the statutes governing "close corporations" would effectively be defeated. It is this aspect of the majority's ruling that I find most difficult to accept.

For all of the foregoing reasons, I must respectfully dissent and cast my vote to modify the order of the Appellate Division by directing dismissal of plaintiff's first cause of action.

JASEN, JONES and FUCHSBERG, JJ., concur with MEYER, J,

GABRIELLI, J, dissents in part and votes to modify in a separate opinion in which COOKE, C.J., and WACHTLER, J., concur.

Notes

(1) Why should a court reach out like this and apply a Delaware statute when it is clear on the face of the statute that it is not applicable? Obviously, the majority was swayed by its belief that the application of close corporation statutes and the enforcement of shareholder agreements was desirable from a policy standpoint. If the result in *Zion* is accepted, what is left of the *McQuade* principle in states with close corporation statutes? Dubin v. Muchnick, 108 Misc.2d 1042, 438 N.Y.S.2d 920, 922 (1981) states that *Zion* has "apparently swept all of the earlier authorities into the realm of legal history." Do you agree? What might be the status under *Zion* of a shareholders' agreement restricting the discretion of directors that is entered into by less than all of the shareholders?

(2) In Nixon v. Blackwell, 626 A.2d 1366 (Del.1993), the Delaware Supreme Court refused to apply the Delaware close corporation statute to a nonelecting close corporation, stating that the statute "is a narrowly constructed statute which applies only to a corporation which is designated as a 'close corporation' in its certificate of incorporation, and which fulfills other requirements [set forth by the statute]." Further, it is improper to apply special provisions to a nonelecting Delaware close corporation "because the provisions of [the Delaware statute] relating to close corporations and other statutory schemes preempt the field in their respective areas." 626 A.2d at 1380. Is it not clear from these statements that the Delaware courts would reject entirely the rationale of *Zion*? Since that case is at least nominally an application of Delaware law, what is left of the holding of the principal case?

(3) Adler v. Svingos, 80 A.D.2d 764, 436 N.Y.S.2d 719 (1981) applied the *Zion* holding to a two-shareholder corporation formed under the New York Business Corporation Law. Would the holding in this case be affected by the decision in Nixon v. Blackwell? The issue apparently has not arisen in New York since *Nixon* was handed down.

MATTER OF AUER v. DRESSEL

Court of Appeals of New York, 1954.
306 N.Y. 427, 118 N.E.2d 590.

DESMOND, JUDGE.

This article 78 of the Civil Practice Act proceeding was brought by class A stockholders of appellant R. Hoe & Co., Inc., for an order in the nature of mandamus to compel the president of Hoe to comply with a positive duty imposed on him by the corporation's by-laws. Section 2 of article I of those by-laws says that "It shall be the duty of President to call a special meeting whenever requested in writing so to do, by stockholders owning a majority of the capital stock entitled to vote at such meeting". On October 16, 1953, petitioners submitted to the president written requests for a special meeting of class A stockholders, which writings were signed in the names of the holders of record of slightly more than 55% of the class A stock. The president failed to call the meeting and, after waiting a week, the petitioners brought the present proceeding. The answer of the corporation and its president was not forthcoming until October 28, 1953, and it contained, in response to the petition's allegation that the demand was by more than a majority of class A stockholders, only a denial that the corporation and the president had any knowledge or information sufficient to form a belief as to the stockholding of those who had signed the requests. Since the president, when he filed that answer, had had before him for at least ten days the signed requests themselves, his denial that he had any information sufficient for a belief as to the adequacy of the number of signatures was obviously perfunctory and raised no issue whatever. There was no discretion in this corporate officer as to whether or not to call a meeting when a demand therefor was put before him by owners of the required number of shares. The important right of stockholders to have such meetings called will be of little practical value if corporate management can ignore the requests, force the stockholders to commence legal proceedings, and then, by purely formal denials, put the stockholders to lengthy and expensive litigation, to establish facts as to stockholdings which are peculiarly within the knowledge of the corporate officers. In such a situation, Special Term did the correct thing in disposing of the matter summarily, as commanded by section 1295 of the Civil Practice Act.

The petition was opposed on the further alleged ground that none of the four purposes for which petitioners wished the meeting called was a proper one for such a class A stockholders' meeting. Those four stated purposes were these: (A) to vote, upon a resolution indorsing the administration of petitioner Joseph L. Auer, who had been removed as president by the directors, and demanding that he be reinstated as such president; (B) voting upon a proposal to amend the charter and by-laws to provide that vacancies on the board of directors, arising from the removal of a director by stockholders or by resignation of a director against whom charges have been preferred, may be filled, for the unexpired term, by the stockholders only of the class theretofore represented by the director so removed or so resigned; (C) voting upon a proposal that the stockholders hear certain charges preferred, in the requests, against four of the directors, determine whether the conduct of such directors or any of them was inimical to the corporation and, if so, to vote upon their removal and vote for the election of their successors; and (D) voting upon a proposal to amend the by-laws so as to provide that half of the total number of directors in office and, in any event, not less than one-third of the whole authorized number of directors constitute a quorum of the directors.

The Hoe certificate of incorporation provides for eleven directors, of whom the class A stockholders, more than a majority of whom join in this petition, elect nine and the common stockholders elect two. The obvious purpose of the meeting here sought to be called (aside from the indorsement and reinstatement of former president Auer) is to hear charges against four of the class A directors, to remove them if the charges be proven, to amend the by-laws so that the successor directors be elected by the class A stockholders, and further to amend the by-laws so that an effective quorum of directors will be made up of no fewer than half of the directors in office and no fewer than one third of the whole authorized number of directors. No reason appears why the class A stockholders should not be allowed to vote on any or all of those proposals.

The stockholders, by expressing their approval of Mr. Auer's conduct as president and their demand that he be put back in that office, will not be able, directly, to effect that change in officers, but there is nothing invalid in their so expressing themselves and thus putting on notice the directors who will stand for election at the annual meeting. As to purpose (B), that is, amending the charter and by-laws to authorize the stockholders to fill vacancies as to class A directors who have been removed on charges or who have resigned, it seems to be settled law that the stockholders who are empowered to elect directors have the inherent power to remove them for cause, In re Koch, 257 N.Y. 318, 321, 322, 178 N.E. 545, 546. Of course, as the Koch case points out, there must be the service of specific charges, adequate notice and full opportunity of meeting the accusations, but there is no present showing of any lack of any of those in this instance. Since these particular stockholders have the right to elect nine directors and to remove them on proven charges, it is not inappropriate that they should use their further power to amend the by-laws to elect the successors of such directors as shall be removed after hearing, or who shall resign pending hearing. Quite pertinent at this point is Rogers v. Hill, 289 U.S. 582, 589, 53 S.Ct. 731, 734, 77 L.Ed. 1385, which made light of an argument that stockholders, by giving power to the directors to make by-laws, had lost their own power to make them; quoting a New Jersey case, In re Griffing Iron Co., 63 N.J.L. 168, 41 A. 931, the United States Supreme Court said: " 'It would be preposterous to leave the real owners of the corporate property at the mercy of their agents, and the law has not done so' ". Such a change in the bylaws, dealing with class A directors only, has no effect on the voting rights of the common stockholders, which rights have to do with the selection of the remaining two directors only. True, the certificate of incorporation authorizes the board of directors to remove any director on charges, but we do not consider that provision as an abdication by the stockholders of their own traditional, inherent power to remove their own directors. Rather, it provides an additional method. Were that not so, the stockholders might find themselves without effective remedy in a case where a majority of the directors were accused of wrongdoing and, obviously, would be unwilling to remove themselves from office.

We fail to see, in the proposal to allow class A stockholders to fill vacancies as to class A directors, any impairment or any violation of paragraph (h) of article Third of the certificate of incorporation, which says that class A stock has exclusive voting rights with respect to all matters "other than the election of directors." That negative language should not be taken to mean that class A stockholders, who have an absolute right to elect nine of these eleven directors, cannot amend their by-laws to guarantee a similar right, in the class A stockholders and to the exclusion of common stockholders, to fill vacancies in the class A group of directors.

There is urged upon us the impracticability and unfairness of constituting the numerous stockholders a tribunal to hear charges made by themselves, and the incongruity of letting the stockholders hear and pass on those charges by proxy. Such questions are really not before us at all on this appeal. The charges here are not, on their face, frivolous or inconsequential, and all that we are holding as to the charges is that a meeting may be held to deal with them. Any director illegally removed can have his remedy in the courts.

The order should be affirmed, with costs, and the Special Term directed forthwith to make an order in the same form as the Appellate Division order with appropriate changes of dates.

VAN VOORHIS, JUDGE (dissenting).

* * * An examination of the request for a special meeting by these stockholders indicates that none of the proposals could be voted upon legally at the projected meeting. The purposes of the meeting are listed as A, B, C and D. Purpose A is described as "Voting upon a resolution endorsing the administration of Joseph L. Auer, as President of the corporation, and demanding his immediate reinstatement as President." For the stockholders to vote on this proposition would be an idle gesture, since it is provided by section 27 of the General Corporation Law, Consol.Laws, c. 23, that "The business of a corporation shall be managed by its board of directors". The directors of Hoe have been elected by the stockholders for stated terms which have not expired, and it is their function and not that of the stockholders to appoint the officers of the corporation, Stock Corporation Law, Consol.Laws, c. 59, § 60.

Purpose B of the special meeting is to vote upon a proposal to amend the certificate and the by-laws so as to provide "that vacancies on the Board of Directors arising from the removal of a director by stockholders or by resignation of a director against whom charges have been preferred may be filled, for the unexpired term, only by the stockholders of the class theretofore represented by the director so removed." This proposal is interwoven with the next one (C), which is about to be discussed, which is to remove four directors from office before the expiration of their terms in order to alter the control of the corporation. Proposal B must be read in the context that the certificate of incorporation provides for eleven directors, of whom the class A stockholders elect nine and the common stockholders two. So long as any class A shares are outstanding, the voting rights with respect to all matters "other than the election of directors" are vested exclusively in the holders of class A stock, with one exception now irrelevant. This means that the common stockholders are entitled to participate directly in the election of two directors, who, in turn, are authorized by the certificate to vote to fill vacancies occurring among the directors elected by the class A shareholders. This proposed amendment would deprive the directors elected by the common stockholders of the power to participate in filling the vacancies which petitioners hope to create among the class A directors, four of whom they seek to remove by proposal C which is about to be discussed. Such an alteration would impair the existing right of the common stockholders to participate in filling vacancies upon the board of directors and could not be legally adopted at this meeting demanded by petitioners from which the common stockholders are excluded. * * *

Purpose C of the special meeting is to vote "upon a proposal that the Stockholders (1) hear the charges preferred against Harry K. Barr, William L. Canady, Neil P. Cullom and Edwin L. Munzert, and their answers thereto; (2) determine whether such conduct on their part or on the part of any of them was inimical to the best interest of R. Hoe & Co., Inc., and if so (3) vote upon the removal of said persons or any of them as directors of R. Hoe & Co., Inc., for such conduct, and (4) vote for the election of directors to fill any vacancies on the Board of Directors which the Stockholders may be authorized to fill." By means of this proposal, it is sought to change the control of the corporation and to accomplish what A could not achieve, viz., remove the existing president and reappoint Mr. Joseph L. Auer as president of the corporation. Neither the language nor the policy of the corporation law subjects directors to recall by the stockholders before their terms of office have expired, merely for the reason that the stockholders wish to change the policy of the corporation. In People ex rel. Manice v. Powell, 201 N.Y. 194, 201, 94 N.E. 634, 637, this court said that "It would be somewhat startling to the business world if we definitely announced that the directors of a corporation were mere employés and that the stockholders of the corporation have the power to convene from time to time and remove at will any or all of the directors, although their respective terms of office have not expired." Fraud or breach of fiduciary duty must be shown, Matter of Koch, 257 N.Y. 318, 178 N.E. 545. In that event, directors may be removed from office before expiration of term by an action brought under subdivision 4 of section 60 of the General Corporation Law. In addition to such procedure, paragraph Fourteenth of the certificate of incorporation states: "Any director of the corporation may at any time be removed for cause as such director by resolution adopted by a majority of the whole number of directors then in office, provided that such director, prior to his removal, shall have received a copy of the charges against him and shall have had an opportunity to be heard thereon by the board. The By–Laws may provide the manner of presentation of the charges and of the hearing thereon."

Petitioners have instituted this proceeding on the theory that although no power is conferred upon the stockholders by the certificate or the by-laws to remove directors before the expiration of their terms, with or without cause, power to do so for cause is inherent in them as the body authorized to elect the directors, citing Matter of Koch, 257 N.Y. 318, 178 N.E. 545, supra. Petitioners have argued that the grant of this power to the board of directors to remove some of their number for cause after trial, does not eliminate what is asserted to be the inherent right of the stockholders to do likewise. No cases are cited in support of the latter proposition. * * * Such cases as have been cited in support of a power in the stockholders to remove directors for cause are clear in holding that such action can be taken only subject to the rule that "specific charges must be served, adequate notice must be given, and full opportunity of meeting the accusations must be afforded." Matter of Koch, 257 N.Y. 318, 322, 178 N.E. 545, 546, supra.

Although the demand by these petitioners for a special meeting contains no specification of charges against these four directors, the proxy statement, circulated by their protective committee, does describe certain charges. No point appears to be made of the circumstance that they are not contained in the demand for the meeting. Nevertheless, although this proxy statement enumerates these charges and announces that a resolution will be introduced at the special meeting to hear them, to determine whether sufficient cause exists for the removal of said persons as directors, and, if so, to remove them and to fill the resulting vacancies, the stockholders thus solicited are requested to sign proxies running to persons nominated by petitioners' protective committee. Inasmuch as this committee, with which petitioners are affiliated, has already charged in the most forceful terms that at least one of these directors has been guilty of misconduct and that "his *clique* of directors have removed Joseph L. Auer as President," it is reasonable to assume that the case of the accused directors has already been prejudged by those who will vote the proxies alleged to represent 255,658 shares of class A stock, and that the 1,200 shareholders who are claimed to have signed proxies have (whether they know it or not) voted, in effect, to remove these directors before they have been tried. The consequence is that these directors are to be adjudged guilty of fraud or breach of faith in absentia by shareholders who have neither heard nor ever will hear the evidence against them or in their behalf. Such a procedure does not conform to the requirements of Matter of Koch, supra, nor the other authorities which have been cited, and is far removed from "a law which hears before it condemns, which proceeds upon inquiry, and renders judgment only after trial." Brief by Daniel Webster in Trustees of Dartmouth Coll. v. Woodward, 4 Wheat. [U.S.] 518, 581, 4 L.Ed. 629. The charges against these directors enumerated in the proxy statement are described as having been preferred by one John Kadel and are to the effect that these four accused directors supported a resolution on July 2, 1953, that severance pay of $50,000 be granted to Mr. Auer "upon condition that he resign and that he sign an agreement not to participate, with any stockholders group or otherwise, in any action against any of the directors or officers of the Company." This money was not in fact paid to Auer. The charge based thereon against these directors is that there was a breach of trust in offering to pay $50,000 of the corporation's money in consideration of a covenant by Auer not to participate (as the minutes of the directors' meeting of July 2, 1953, actually read) in "any hostile action against the company, its officers and directors." It is not clear how this constituted actionable misconduct in view of the circumstance that none of this money actually was paid, and that there was no showing in this record any misconduct on the part of these four directors which might have furnished a basis for a stockholders' derivative action by Auer against these directors. It is not so plain that these directors should be subjected to trial by stockholders, acting through proxies who are evidently prepared to oust them with or without cause, that a mandamus order should, in any event, be issued to compel the calling of a special meeting for that purpose. The other charges, viz., that Mr. Cullom was paid $300 a month as rental for office space in his suite at 63 Wall Street, and that he engaged one of his personal friends and clients in connection with appraisal proceedings involving the common stock of the company for which the friend was paid $5,000 are not supplemented by further facts indicating that such conduct was hostile to the interest of the corporation.

It is not for the courts to determine which of these warring factions is pursuing the wiser policy for the corporation. If these petitioners consider that the stockholders made a mistake in the election of the present directors, they should not be permitted to correct it by recalling them before the expiration of their terms on charges of fraud or breach of fiduciary duty without a full and fair trial, which, if not conducted in court under section 60 of the General Corporation Law, is required to be held before the remaining directors under paragraph Fourteenth of the certificate of incorporation. The difficulty inherent in conducting such a trial by proxy may well have been the reason on account of which the incorporators delegated that function to the board of directors under paragraph Fourteenth of the certificate of incorporation. If it were to develop (the papers before the court do not contain evidence of such a fact) that enough of the other directors would be disqualified so that it would be impossible to obtain a quorum for the purpose, it may well be doubted that these directors could be tried before so large a number of stockholders sitting in person (if it were possible to assemble them in one place) or that they could sit in judgment by proxy. In ancient Athens evidence is said to have been heard and judgment pronounced in court by as many as 500 jurors known as ducats, but in this instance, if petitioners be correct in their figures, there are 1,200 class A stockholders who have signed requests or proxies, and these are alleged to hold only somewhat more than half of the outstanding shares. Since it would be impossible for so large a number to conduct a trial in person, they could only do so by proxy. Voting by proxy is the accepted procedure to express the will of large numbers of stockholders on questions of corporate policy within their province to determine, and it would be suitable in this instance if the certificate of incorporation had reserved to stockholders the power to recall directors without cause before expiration of term, as in Abberger v. Kulp, 156 Misc. 210, 281 N.Y.S. 373, but it is altogether unsuited to the performance of duties which partake of the nature of the judicial function, involving, as this would need to do if the accused directors are to be removed before the expiration of their terms, a decision after trial that they have been guilty of faithlessness or fraud. Section 60 of the General Corporation Law is always available for that purpose if the occasion requires.

The final proposal to be voted on at this special meeting (D) relates simply to an amendment to the by-laws so as to provide that a quorum shall consist of not less than one half of the number of directors holding office and in no event less than one third of the authorized number of directors. Section 8 of article II of the by-laws already provides that one half of the total number of directors shall constitute a quorum; the modification that a quorum shall in no event be less than one third of the authorized number of directors whom petitioners seek to eliminate.

Inasmuch as we consider that for the foregoing reasons none of the business for which the special meeting is proposed to be called could legally be transacted, this proceeding should be dismissed. It is not necessary to analyze whether under other circumstances an order would lie in the nature of an alternative rather than a peremptory mandamus.

The petition should be dismissed, with costs in all courts.

LEWIS, C.J., and DYE, FULD and FROESSEL, JJ., concur with DESMOND, J.

VAN VOORHIS, J., dissents in opinion in which CONWAY, J., concurs.

Notes

(1) Unlike the earlier principal cases in this Section, this case involves a publicly held corporation: At the time of this litigation, R. Hoe & Co., Inc. had 6,000 shareholders and some 460,000 Class A shares outstanding. The principal difference between a publicly held corporation and a closely held corporation from the management standpoint is that in a publicly held corporation, ownership and management are usually vested in quite different persons or groups. In a closely held corporation, the majority shareholder is likely to be the chief executive officer and possess the ability to name or remove directors virtually at will. See MBCA § 8.08. In contrast, most publicly held corporations have professional managers who in the aggregate own an insignificant fraction of the corporation's outstanding shares. Because shareholders are numerous and diffuse, the "owners" of a publicly held corporation are not a cohesive group. Indeed, the simple process of calling a shareholders meeting involves, at the least, communicating with thousands of widely scattered shareholders. Subsequent chapters of this book discuss at length the nature of control and management in the publicly held corporation. The purpose of this note is to call attention to examples of provisions in state corporation statutes that are designed primarily or exclusively for the large publicly held corporation. Many other examples might be cited.

(a) Traditional corporation statutes provide that the business and affairs of a corporation shall be managed "by" the board of directors. MBCA § 8.01(b) and the statutes of many states add "or under the direction of" following the word "by" to reflect the reality that boards of directors of publicly held corporations do not actually manage the business and affairs of a corporation.

(b) MBCA § 8.09 provides that directors may be removed by judicial proceeding in the case of "fraudulent or dishonest conduct, or gross abuse of authority or discretion, with respect to the corporation." If a director accused of serious misconduct stubbornly refuses to resign, removal by judicial proceeding is often simpler and less expensive than calling a shareholders meeting to remove the director. It is possible that this provision may also be utilized by a closely held corporation which has evenly divided voting power at the shareholder level or action is subject to a veto by a minority shareholder.

(c) MBCA § 8.03(b) and (c) limit the power of a board of directors to increase or decrease its own size. As a practical matter, major increases or decreases in board size, possibly in contravention of the wishes of a majority of the shareholders, is exclusively a phenomenon of publicly held corporations.

(d) MBCA §§ 7.23 and 7.24 contain special rules for shareholder voting by proxy that, as a practical matter, are almost exclusively a phenomenon of publicly held corporations.

(2) Consider again the practical difficulties discussed in the dissenting opinion of holding a shareholders' meeting of R. Hoe & Co., Inc. to pass on the removal of the directors for cause. If such a meeting is to be held, how should it be structured to give even minimal "due process" to the directors threatened with

removal? Do you think the conduct described in the dissenting opinion constitutes "cause" for removal?

B. SHAREHOLDER VOTING AND SHAREHOLDERS' AGREEMENTS

SALGO v. MATTHEWS

Court of Civil Appeals of Texas, 1973.
497 S.W.2d 620, writ ref'd n.r.e.

GUITTARD, JUSTICE.

This equitable proceeding involves a proxy contest for control of General Electrodynamics Corporation, a Texas corporation. Stockholders Joe W. Matthews and Paul Thorp, representing the faction opposed to current management, sought the aid of the district court in requiring the president, as chairman of the stockholders' meeting, and the election inspector appointed by him, to accept certain disputed proxies, count the votes of the stockholders cast under these proxies, and declare that the candidates supported by plaintiffs had been elected directors of the corporation. We hold that the court erred in granting injunctive relief, both temporary and final, in absence of any showing that plaintiffs could not have obtained adequate relief by the statutory remedy of quo warranto after the completion of the election. * * *

[The incumbent management faction was headed by Francis Salgo, the president of Electrodynamics. At the meeting, Salgo appointed Julian Meer, a well-known attorney, as election inspector. During the course of examining and tabulating proxy appointments,] plaintiffs presented to defendant Meer four proxy documents purporting to have been executed in plaintiffs' favor on behalf of Pioneer Casualty Company, the registered owner of 29,934 shares of stock. Beneficial title to these shares had been transferred to Don Shepherd, who was in bankruptcy, and two of the proxy documents were signed, "Pioneer Casualty Company By Don Shepherd." Plaintiffs also presented to the inspector an order of the 126th District Court of Travis County, Texas, directing Tom I. McFarling as receiver of Pioneer Casualty Company to give Shepherd a proxy to vote these shares by giving his proxy to plaintiffs Matthews and Thorp, and plaintiffs also presented a proxy document signed by the receiver in accordance with this order. Defendant Meer refused to accept any of these proxies, and their validity is the principal matter in controversy. Defendant Meer also refused to accept two telegraphic proxies aggregating 5,000 shares from stockholders Candis and Wrobliske when plaintiff Thorp presented them to him on the afternoon of November 9. * * *

* * * [W]e hold that the inspector was not subject to judicial control in the performance of his duties because he had discretionary authority to make a preliminary determination of the validity of the proxies for the purpose of tabulating them, counting the votes, and certifying the result, although the correctness of his decision was subject to review after the election by proceeding in quo warranto. * * *

Our holding that an election inspector has discretionary authority to determine the validity of disputed proxies for the purpose of declaring the result of the election should not be interpreted as meaning that he may go beyond the corporate records in determining the identity of stockholders entitled to vote. Defendants argue that the trial court's findings establish that beneficial ownership of the 29,934 shares registered in the name of Pioneer Casualty Company was not in Pioneer's receiver or in Don Shepherd, to whom these shares had been transferred, but was vested in Shepherd's bankruptcy trustee, and, consequently, that neither the receiver nor Shepherd had the right to vote. We assume that Shepherd's trustee was the beneficial owner, but, as against the corporation and its officers, beneficial ownership does not carry with it the right to vote without having the shares transferred on the books. A bylaw of General Electrodynamics Corporation provides that stock is transferable only on its books. This bylaw indicates the strong interest of the corporation and its stockholders in determining stock ownership quickly by reference to the corporate records. If beneficial title is in dispute, that dispute cannot properly be decided by the election inspector, and neither should the losing faction be able to go into court to invalidate the election on the ground that the ownership of certain shares was not correctly shown by the corporate records. For even greater reason the election should not be interrupted or suspended while complicated questions of title to stock are litigated to final judgment.

The rule that under such a bylaw, eligibility to vote at corporate elections is determined by the corporate records rather than by the ultimate judicial decision of beneficial title of disputed shares is well sustained by authority. In re Giant Portland Cement Co., 26 Del.Ch. 32, 21 A.2d 697 (Ch.1941). This rule is in accordance with Tex.Bus.Corp.Act Ann. art. 2.27(A) (1956), V.A.T.S., which provides, "The original stock transfer books shall be prima-facie evidence as to who are the shareholders entitled * * * to vote at any meeting of shareholders." According to E. Aranow & H. Einhorn, [Proxy Contests for Corporate Control (1957) at 386, although such a statute uses the term "prima-facie," it has the effect of making stock records conclusive on the inspector. The term "prima-facie" avoids any implication that the stock record is conclusive in a suit concerning title to the stock.

The binding effect of the stock record on corporate officers does not leave a beneficial owner without remedy. He may be presumed to know that the record owner can vote the stock. The beneficial owner can protect his interest by requiring a transfer on the books or by demanding a proxy from the record owner, and if voluntary compliance is not forthcoming, relief is available by injunction or mandamus. In the present case Shepherd's trustee, the beneficial owner, made no effort to vote the shares. He sought no proxy from the receiver or the receivership court. In these circumstances neither the corporate officers nor any of the other stockholders were in a position to assert that only the trustee had the right to vote.

The question presented to the inspector was, who was entitled to act for the record owner? The shares were registered in the name of Pioneer Casualty Company, which was in receivership and had no officers to act for it. The only person entitled to act for Pioneer was its receiver under orders of the 126th district court of Travis County. The receiver, acting under such an order, gave a proxy to Shepherd to act for Pioneer, with instructions to give a further proxy to plaintiffs Matthews and Thorp, and Shepherd, acting for Pioneer in accordance with the proxy to him, gave a proxy to plaintiffs. This transaction was essentially the same as if the receiver, acting under the court's order, had given the proxy directly to plaintiffs. The recitation in the order that Shepherd was the beneficial owner is of no consequence, since the beneficial owner, whether Shepherd or his trustee, had no right under the bylaws to vote the shares as against General Electrodynamics Corporation and its officers. * * * Since the stockholder of record was Pioneer Casualty Company, and the receiver was authorized by court order to act for Pioneer, the inspector's proper course was to accept the stock record as determining that the right to vote was in Pioneer Casualty Company, and to accept the proxies given by the receiver to Shepherd and by him to plaintiffs as valid.

Defendants argue that if the inspector was authorized to go behind the stock book and recognize the voting rights of the receiver for Pioneer Casualty Company, he was authorized to go further and determine the beneficial ownership of the stock for the purpose of the election. We do not agree. The inspector was bound by the stock book to consider Pioneer Casualty Company the legal owner for the purpose of the election, but he was required to determine who could act for the record owner, just as if someone had challenged the authority of a person purporting to act as an officer of a corporate stockholder. Since Pioneer was in receivership, the inspector could consider that fact and should have treated the receiver as the authorized representative of the record owner. It is quite another matter to say that the inspector should have inquired into beneficial ownership of the stock and recognized the right of Shepherd or his trustee in bankruptcy to vote the shares. * * *

Reversed and rendered.

Notes

(1) Underlying the holding in the principal case is the basic concept that shares are always registered in the name of a specific person on the records of the corporation. See MBCA §§ 6.25(b)(2), 7.07(a). The person in whose name shares are registered is called the "record holder" and may or may not be the person who is the actual owner of the shares, usually referred to as the "beneficial owner." Generally speaking, the corporation may treat the record owner as the owner of the shares for purposes such as voting, the payment of dividends or distributions, and determining to whom shares have been transferred. In *Salgo*, the record owner was a person different from the beneficial owner and the Court held that the corporation must determine who has been authorized to vote the shares by the record owner. Where the record owner and the beneficial owner are different persons it is clear, as dicta in the principal case states, that the beneficial owner can compel the record owner (by court process, if necessary) to execute a proxy appointment in the name of the beneficial owner so that the owner may vote the shares as he or she desires. The beneficial owner also has the power to compel the record owner to turn over any distributions made by the corporation and, ultimately, to reregister the shares in the name of the beneficial owner when requested to do so. Why do some beneficial owners allow shares to be held of record by someone else, sometimes for extended periods? As discussed subsequently, shares of publicly held corporations are usually held of record by nominees or by brokerage firms ("street name") in order to facilitate transfer. A large percentage of all shares publicly traded on the New York Stock Exchange are held of record by Cede & Company, the nominee of Depository Trust Company which is the central clearing house for the New York Stock Exchange. Indeed, in modern

securities practice, there usually are two or more layers of intermediaries between the record owner and the beneficial owner of publicly traded shares.

(2) The traditional practice is to issue certificates representing shares in the name of the record owner. For an example of a share certificate, see page 473, infra. See also MBCA § 6.25. Share certificates usually come attached to a "stub" that may be filled in when the certificate is actually issued by the corporation to a shareholder. In closely held corporations, the record of shareholders may simply consist of these stubs; in publicly held corporations, much more elaborate records may be kept by a "transfer agent," typically a commercial bank. These records, of course, reveal only the record owner, not the beneficial owner.

(3) MBCA § 6.26, and the statutes of many states, also authorize a corporation to issue uncertificated shares, i.e., shares that are not represented by certificates. This is a relatively recent innovation for closely held corporations, and it appears today that most corporations continue to prefer to issue certificated shares, though there is a slight saving in cost in using uncertificated shares.

(4) Shareholder voting and entitlement to distributions are determined from the records of the corporation. It is not necessary for a record shareholder to exhibit the share certificate (in the case of certificated shares) in order to vote or receive a distribution.

(5) The mechanics of establishing the date on which shareholders entitled to vote will be determined is set forth in MBCA § 7.07. See also § 7.20.

(6) Action by shareholders at a meeting requires the existence of a quorum and the approval by the requisite number of votes at a meeting at which a quorum is present. See MBCA §§ 7.25(a), 7.25(c), 7.26, 7.27, 7.28(a). These are often viewed as mundane, technical matters, but there are a number of substantive issues that may arise. For example,

(a) May a disgruntled faction of shareholders withdraw from a meeting in order to "break" a quorum? See MBCA § 7.25(b).

(b) Why should there be a different rule for determining the election of directors (MBCA § 7.28(a)) than for approval or disapproval of other matters (MBCA § 7.25(c))?

(c) What is all the statutory language concerning "voting groups" about, anyway? See, e.g., MBCA §§ 1.40(26), 8.04, 10.04.

(d) Earlier versions of the Model Act provided that the affirmative vote "of the majority of the shares represented" at a meeting at which a quorum was present was necessary to take action by shareholders. MBCA (1969) § 32. Does MBCA § 7.25(c) adopt a different test? What about shares that are present at the meeting but abstain (e.g., by casting blank ballots or by not casting ballots at all)? The Official Comment to § 7.25 offers this illustration:

> [I]f a corporation has 1,000 shares of a single class outstanding, all entitled to cast one vote each, a quorum consists of 501 shares; if 600 shares are represented and the vote on a proposed action is 280 in favor, 225 opposed, and 95 abstaining, the action is not approved [under the 1969 Model Act] since fewer than a majority of the 600 shares attending voted in favor of the action. This is anomalous since if the shares abstaining had not been present at the meeting at all a quorum would have been present and the action would have been approved. Under section 7.25(c) the action would not be defeated by the 95 abstaining votes.

Cumulative vs. Straight Voting. The workings of these two methods of voting to elect directors can be most simply described by an illustration. Let us assume a corporation with two shareholders, A with 18 shares, and B with 82 shares. Further, let us assume that there are five directors and each shareholder nominates five candidates. Directors run "at large" rather than for specific places; hence the five persons receiving the most votes are elected. If only straight voting is permitted, A may cast 18 votes for each of five candidates, and B may cast 82 votes for each of five candidates. The result, of course, is that all five of B's candidates are elected. If cumulative voting is permitted the number of total votes that each shareholder may cast is first computed and each shareholder is permitted to distribute these votes as he sees fit over one or more candidates. In the example above, A is entitled to cast a total of 90 votes (18 × 5) and B is entitled to cast 410 votes (82 × 5). If A casts all 90 votes for A_1, A_1 is ensured of election because B cannot divide 410 votes among five candidates in such a way as to give each candidate more than 90 votes and preclude A1's election. Obviously, the effect of cumulative voting is that it increases minority participation on the board of directors. In straight voting, the shareholder with 51 percent of the vote elects the entire board; in cumulative voting, a relatively small faction (18 percent in the above example) may obtain representation on the board. Whether this is good or bad depends on one's point of view.[5]

One undesirable aspect of cumulative voting is that it tends to be a little tricky. If a shareholder casts votes in an irrational or inefficient way, he may not get the directorships his position entitles him to; when voting cumulatively it is relatively easy to make a mistake in spreading votes around. The most graphic illustration of this are the cases where a majority shareholder votes in such a way that he elects only a minority of the directors.[6] This is most likely to occur when one shareholder votes "straight" and another cumulates. For example, if A has 60 shares and B only 40, with five directors to be elected, B may nevertheless elect a majority of the board if A votes "straight", and B knows that A is doing so. The result might look like this:

A_1–60, A_2–60, A_3–60, A_4–60, A_5–60; B_1–67, B_2–66, B_3–65, B_4–1, B_5–1.[7]

---

5. [By the Editor] Numerous arguments for and against cumulative voting have been made. Arguments in favor of such voting include: (1) it is democratic in that persons with large (but minority) holdings should have a voice in the conduct of the corporation; (2) it is desirable to have as many viewpoints as possible represented on the board of directors; and (3) the presence of a minority director may discourage conflicts of interest by management since discovery is considerably more likely. Arguments in opposition include: (1) the introduction of a partisan on the board is inconsistent with the notion that the board should represent all interests in the corporation; (2) a partisan director may cause disharmony which reduces the efficiency of the board; (3) a partisan director may criticize management unreasonably so as to make it less willing to take risky (but desirable) action; (4) a partisan director may leak confidential information; and (5) in practice cumulative voting is usually used to further narrow partisan goals, particularly to give

an insurgent group a toehold in the corporation in an effort to obtain control. For a comprehensive analysis of the history of cumulative voting, its advantages and disadvantages, and its possible use in publicly held corporations in the future, see Jeffrey N. Gordon, Institutions as Relational Investors: A New Look at Cumulative Voting, 94 Colum.L.Rev. 124 (1994).

6. [By the Editor] There are at least six such cases, while in several others the majority shareholder saved himself from disaster by recasting his votes on a cumulative basis before the results of the election were announced.

7. [By the Editor] The theory of B is not to create tie votes among his own candidates. If he does so, and the tie candidates come in fifth and sixth in an election for five directorships, the tie may be broken by a new election for only the fifth seat; A may be able to vote his shares in the new election for his own candi-

This is daring of B because he is spreading his vote over three persons when he can be sure only of electing two. If B decides to do this, and A knows that B will try to elect three persons, then A, by properly cumulating his votes, can elect four directors, in effect "stealing" one of B's.[8]

The following formula is useful in determining the number of shares needed to elect one director:

$$\frac{S}{D + 1} + 1.$$

where S equals the total number of shares voting, and D equals the number of directors to be elected.[9] The analogous formula to elect n directors is:

$$\frac{NS}{D + 1} + 1.$$

Notes

(1) In <u>Stancil v. Bruce Stancil Refrigeration, Inc.</u>, 81 N.C.App. 567, 344 S.E.2d 789 (1986), all the shares of stock of a North Carolina corporation were owned by two brothers: Bruce Stancil (12,500 shares) and Howard Stancil (12,500 shares). North Carolina requires cumulative voting by statute for corporations with less than 2,000 shareholders and provides that directors are elected by a "plurality of the votes cast." N.C.Gen.Stat. § 55–67(c). Before the election in question, the board of directors consisted of Bruce Stancil, Eva Stancil (Bruce's wife), and Howard Stancil. At the shareholders' meeting, each brother was represented by counsel. Bruce, "without a majority vote or consent, asserted his 'right' to act as chairman of the meeting and in fact conducted the proceedings at the meeting, acting with and upon the advice and consultation of his attorney, Wiley L. Lane, Jr." 344 S.E.2d at 790. Howard announced that he planned to vote cumulatively in conformity with the North Carolina statutes but Bruce did not acknowledge this statement (or grant the recess the North Carolina statute provides for after such an announcement is made). Bruce nominated himself, his wife, Eva, and one Sarah Barnes. Howard nominated himself, his wife, Clara, and one Henry Babb. The trial court's findings and conclusions describe what happened then:

> 15.   The Respondent, Bruce Stancil, cast his votes for his nominees for director as follows:

date, thereby causing B to lose a seat. Of course, in the above hypothetical, B might distribute his votes over only three candidates without creating a tie.

8. [By the Editor] The results of such an election might be as follows: A_1–73, A_2–74, A_3–75, A_4–76, A_5–2, B_1–67, B_2–66, B_3–65, B_4–1, B_5–1.

9. [By the Editor] A minor modification may sometimes be necessary. The first portion of the formula, $\frac{S}{D + 1}$ establishes the maximum number of shares voted for a single person which are *insufficient*

to elect that person as a director. Any share, or fraction thereof, in excess of that amount will be sufficient to elect a director. The formula in the text ignores fractional shares which sometimes may lead to a one-share error. For example, where there are 100 shares voting and five directors to be elected, the first portion of the formula is $\frac{100}{5 + 1,}$ or $\frac{100}{6}$. In this example, 16 shares will not elect a director, but 17 shares will, since the first part of the formula yields 16⅔. The formula in the text yields an answer of 17⅔.

Bruce Stancil	12,500 Votes
Sarah Barnes	12,500 Votes
Eva Stancil	12,500 Votes

The Petitioner, Howard K. Stancil, cast his votes for his nominees for director as follows:

Howard K. Stancil	18,750 Votes
Clara Stancil	18,750 Votes
Henry Babb	0 Votes

16. The Respondent, Bruce Stancil, after casting 12,500 votes for each of his three nominees (totaling 37,500 votes as allowed by law), purported to cast an additional 18,750 votes against Howard Stancil and 18,750 votes against Clara Stancil.

17. There is no provision in the North Carolina Business Corporation Act providing for the casting of shareholder votes against a nominee for director, and the purported "votes" cast by the Respondent, Bruce Stancil, subsequent to the casting of his affirmative votes totaling 37,500 for his three nominees, were void and of no lawful effect.

18. Bruce Stancil, Sarah Barnes and Eva Stancil, all being Respondents herein and recipients of 12,500 votes each, failed, as to each of them, to receive a plurality of the votes cast, as required by G.S. 55–67(c), and were not lawfully elected as directors of the Respondent corporation.

344 S.E.2d at 791. The appellate court affirmed the trial court's conclusion as to the result of the election. Do you agree with this conclusion? Does the board of directors now consist of Howard and Clara with one vacancy? What about the possible application of a statute similar to MBCA § 8.05(e)? If a vacancy exists, can Bruce demand another meeting and at that meeting elect himself to fill that vacancy? Is there any way for Bruce, at following annual meetings, to get the situation back to where it was before the election, that is, where he and his wife filled two of the three positions on the board?

(2) If you had been Wiley L. Lane, Jr., what should you have done to preserve your client's apparently dominant position on the board of directors?

HUMPHRYS v. WINOUS CO.

Supreme Court of Ohio, 1956.
165 Ohio St. 45, 133 N.E.2d 780.

BELL, JUSTICE.

It can not be disclaimed that by reason of the stock distribution of this particular corporation a classification of the three directors into three classes containing one director each effectively divests the minority shareholders of a measure of control they formerly exercised over the corporation by electing one member of the board through the expedient of cumulative voting.

The issue herein, however, is not whether a particular result was accomplished but whether, under the statutes, such a result can legally be accomplished.

Section 1701.64, Revised Code, provides, in part, as follows:

The articles or the code of regulations may provide for the term of office of all of the directors or, if classified upon the basis of the expiration of the terms of office of the directors, of each class thereof, provided that no term shall be fixed for a period of more than three years from the date of their election and until the election of their successors.

Section 1701.58, Revised Code, after providing that any shareholder may, upon giving 24 hours notice of his desire to do so, cumulate such voting power as he possesses and give one candidate as many votes as the number of directors multiplied by the number of his votes equals, then provides that "such right to vote cumulatively shall not be restricted or qualified by the articles or the code of regulations."

The Court of Appeals sustained the contention of appellees and held that, since Section 1701.58, Revised Code, was specific in character, it constituted a limitation upon the applicability of Section 1701.64, Revised Code, and that, since the classification by appellants, attempted under the authority of Section 1701.64, Revised Code, did restrict the right to vote cumulatively as specifically guaranteed by Section 1701.58, Revised Code, such classification was invalid. * * *

In enacting Section 1701.58, Revised Code, did the General Assembly intend, as urged by appellants, to guarantee only that the *right* to vote cumulatively shall not be restricted or qualified? Or did it intend to guarantee that the effectiveness of cumulative voting to ensure minority representation on the board of directors shall not be restricted or qualified? * * *

It is interesting to note that, as early as 1893, the organized bar of Ohio began to interest itself in the rights of minority shareholders. In an address before the annual meeting of the Ohio State Bar Association held at Put–in–Bay in July 1893, John H. Doyle, then president of the association, said:

> * * * While there is a unanimity of purpose and an accord of thought amongst [sic] the shareholders, the corporation moves smoothly, and its directors represent and carry out the wishes of such shareholders.

But that is not always the case, and under the present law, as it has been interpreted by the Supreme Court, a bare majority can absolutely exclude the minority from all voice in its management. To illustrate:

> In a corporation represented by 100 shares of capital stock, the owners of 51 shares could manage the corporation without the voice of the remaining 49 shares being heard, and the one odd share would be the available power; the 51 shares might be made very valuable, while the 49 could be rendered valueless, and the odd share or the balance of power receive an immense value. These suggestions will show that any statute providing for minority representation in corporations would not lead to 'absurd or improbable results,' but would be marked with wisdom and a fair regard for the rights of the parties.

The old story, so often told, of a prominent Eastern newspaperman's reply to the question of what the shares in his company were worth, is very apt:

> 'There are 51 shares,' said he, 'that are worth $250,000. There are 49 shares that are not worth a ——.'

I think the law should be so amended as to allow the 49 shares to elect two out of the five directors or three out of seven, as the case may be.

In other words, that the shareholders be allowed to cumulate their votes on one or more directors, as they see fit, so that all interests may be fairly represented, without destroying the right of the majority to control.

It would result in increased confidence in the management of such concerns, prevent the freezing-out process so often resorted to, and very often prevent fraud and corruption in the management of private corporations.

At the annual meeting of the bar association on July 20, 1897, the Committee on Judicial Administration and Legal Reform submitted the following as a part of its report to the association:

> The annual address of Judge Doyle to this association in 1893 recommended the amendment of the law respecting the management of private corporations so as to secure a representation in that management to minority stockholders, in proportion to the amount of stock held by them. * * *

> Your committee is of the opinion that our laws need amendment * * *. The minority of stockholders are entitled to such opportunity of knowledge of its business and the conduct thereof as would enable them to form judgment concerning the same, and are entitled also to have such judgment and their advice expressed in the body charged with the duty of such management. This privilege, secured by law, would be effective in preventing oppressive abuse of power by the majority of stockholders, exercised for illegitimate, selfish, and fraudulent ends. We are of the opinion that the law should be so modified as to secure these rights to a minority stockholder. * * *

If we may assume that the General Assembly was motivated by the recommendation of the bar association, it is obvious that it intended to assure minority representation on a corporate board of directors by permitting cumulative voting.

The provision for classification of directors appears for the first time in Ohio as * * * part of the General Corporation Act, effective June 9, 1927, 112 Ohio Laws, p. 32. * * *

Strangely enough, however, prior to 1955, there were only two cases which discussed the effect of classification of directors on cumulative voting. In Pittsburgh Steel Co. v. Walker (Court of Common Pleas, Allegheny County, Pennsylvania, 1944), three judges said there was doubt as to the constitutionality of the staggered system, but did not pass directly on the question. In Heeps v. Byers Co. (Court of Common Pleas, Allegheny County, Pennsylvania, 1950), one judge denied a preliminary injunction against the holding of a staggered-voting election on constitutional and other grounds. The Supreme Court of Pennsylvania, in affirming the judgment of the lower court, merely denied any right to question the granting of preliminary injunctions. Cohen v. A.M. Byers Co., 363 Pa. 618, 70 A.2d 837.

But on February 1, 1955, the Circuit Court of Cook County, Illinois, decided the case of Wolfson v. Avery. The action grew out of the much-publicized battle between Sewell Avery and Louis E. Wolfson for control of the board of directors of Montgomery Ward & Company. The Wolfson group sought a declaratory judgment that a bylaw of Montgomery Ward providing for the annual election of only one-third of the nine members of the board of directors is in violation of Section 3, Article XI of the Illinois Constitution, S.H.A., which among other things, provides for cumulative voting. Since the bylaw is specifically authorized by Section 35 of the Illinois Business Corporation Act, Illinois Revised Statutes 1953, Chapter 32, paragraph 157.35, the complaint also sought to have that portion of the statute declared unconstitutional. The Circuit Court granted the plaintiff's motion for judgment on the pleadings, declaring Section 35 of the Business Corporation Act unconstitutional.

The trial judge in the Wolfson case adopted the theory that the Constitution requires that a minority shareholder be given the right—by cumulative voting—to exercise his "maximum voting strength proportionate to his share holding." He rejected the argument that the constitutional provision merely gives minority shareholders an opportunity to have some representation on the board of directors, whether proportionate or not. 23 Law Week, 2393.

The Supreme Court of Illinois, 6 Ill.2d 78, 126 N.E.2d 701, 711, after reviewing at some length the proceedings of the constitutional convention and the publications which interpreted the constitutional provision which was ratified on July 2, 1870, concluded that "Section 35 of the Business Corporation Act, in authorizing the classification of directors, is inconsistent with the constitutional right of a stockholder to cumulate his shares through multiplying them by the 'number of directors,' and cannot be sustained."

The Illinois court, in disposing of the defendant's reliance upon the fact that a law authorizing classification was passed by the first Illinois Legislature, and that this Legislature included 13 members who had served on the Constitutional Convention, said that "that is a fact to be given some weight, but it is by no means controlling (cf. Marbury v. Madison, 1 Cranch. 137, 2 L.Ed. 60) and in this case it must yield to the evidence supplied by the constitutional debates and the contemporary accounts in the press."

* * * As distinguished from a conflict between a constitutional provision and a statutory provision as in the Wolfson case, we have here a conflict between two statutory provisions. * * *

That cumulative voting is generally accepted is evidenced by the facts that mandatory cumulative voting provisions are found in the Constitutions of 13 states and in the statutes of eight others, and that permissive cumulative voting is authorized in 18 states. Cumulative voting is provided for in [MBCA (1950) § 31], drawn by the American Bar Association, and in Section 28 of the Model Business Corporation Act, proposed by the Commissioners on Uniform State Laws. Despite the seemingly obvious conflict between classification of directors and cumulative voting, provisions for staggered elections are made in approximately 33 states. See Williams, Cumulative Voting for Directors (1951), 7; Cumulative Voting and Classification of Directors, St. John's Law Review, 83, 86.

The problem will never arise in three jurisdictions because annual election of all directors is required by statute. See Section 22, Title 10, Alabama

Code; Sections 805, 2201, California Corporation Code; Section 44–109, Wyoming Compiled Statutes.

Obviously, a provision in the articles or code of regulations to the effect that a shareholder may not vote cumulatively would restrict the right given by statute and would therefore be invalid in Ohio. Similarly a provision that a shareholder could vote cumulatively only if he held a certain percentage of the corporate stock would be invalid. But the same result might easily be accomplished without running afoul of the prohibition of Section 1701.58, Revised Code.

And majority shareholders have in many instances succeeded in curtailing or eliminating cumulative voting through a number of devices. In states where the right to vote cumulatively is permissive rather than mandatory, the charters of certain corporations have been amended to replace cumulative voting with straight voting. Cumulative voting may also be circumvented by removing minority-elected directors without cause. A third method employed to prevent effective use of cumulative voting is that of reducing the number of directors.

Other ways to circumvent effect of 2 statutes (staggered voting — cum voting)

For example, suppose in a corporation having a board of nine members a minority shareholder, by cumulating his voting power, is able to elect one member of the board. But suppose, also, at the next meeting, the code of regulations is amended to reduce the directorate from nine to seven, as permitted under Section 1701.68, Revised Code. The minority shareholder, although not deprived of his *right* to vote cumulatively, has been deprived of representation on the board just as effectively as if he had not had the right. Similar examples could be given, depending on the number of shares held by the minority and the number of directors to be elected. Can it be said that the legislative intent in enacting Section 1701.58, Revised Code, was to limit Section 1701.64, Revised Code, and not limit Section 1701.68, Revised Code, and other sections of the corporation act? We do not think so.

If effect is to be given to both enactments of the General Assembly, the guaranty provided in Section 1701.58, Revised Code, must be construed as one granting a *right* that may not be restricted or qualified rather than one *ensuring* minority representation on the board of directors.

To hold otherwise would require a complete annihilation of the provision for classification because any classification would necessarily be a restriction or qualification on the effectiveness of cumulative voting, and no corporation could ever avail itself of the privilege of classification. We do not believe the General Assembly intended any such result.

Both the Ohio State Bar Association and the General Assembly recognized that, under the law of Ohio as it existed in January 1954, the action taken here by the corporation could have been accomplished. Consequently, the bar association recommended a change in the corporation law of Ohio to the effect that any class of directors could contain not less than two directors. In commenting on the proposed change, the Corporation Law Committee of the association said: "A new provision is that the number of directors in a given class shall be not less than two. This is for the purpose of meeting the objection that has been raised to the effect that under the present law the majority shareholders may fix the number of directors at three, each director to be in a separate class so that at each annual meeting only one director is to be elected. This device would prevent the minority, even though holding 49 per cent of the shares, from electing a single director.''

Subsequently, Section 1701.57, Revised Code, was enacted, supplanting former Section 1701.64, Revised Code, to require that each class of directors must consist of not less than three directors each. 126 Ohio Laws, H70, effective October 11, 1955. Thus did the General Assembly obviate the possibility of a recurrence of the action taken by The Winous Company.

It can not be gainsaid that the action taken here effectively eliminated the minority shareholders from exercising any control over the corporation. But we are of the opinion that the throwing of an aura of uncertainty and confusion around the statutory provision for classification of directors is not required by the construction of the statutory provision for cumulative voting. We hold, therefore, that Section 1701.58, Revised Code, guarantees to minority shareholders only the right of cumulative voting and does not necessarily guarantee the effectiveness of the exercise of that right to elect minority representation on the board of directors. * * *

The judgment of the Court of Appeals is reversed and the judgment of the Court of Common Pleas is modified and, as modified, is affirmed.

Judgment reversed.

MATTHIAS, STEWART and TAFT, JJ., concur.

WEYGANDT, C.J., and HART, J., dissent.

WEYGANDT, CHIEF JUSTICE, dissents on the ground of the cogent reasoning of the Court of Appeals that "the right of a shareholder in an Ohio corporation to cumulate his vote has been provided by statute in this state for more than fifty years. The legislature in adopting the revision of the statute dealing with corporate organization in 1927, showed clearly that it intended to strengthen the cumulative voting provision by adding to existing law the provision that a corporation cannot restrict cumulative voting by its articles or code of regulations. And when in the same act the legislature, for the first time provides that there may be classification of directors when provided for by its code of regulations, it could not have been intended that the exercise of such right could be so used as to nullify the right of cumulative voting. When the minimum number of three directors is provided for, and their terms of office are for three years, one to be elected each year, the right to cumulative voting is, in such case, *completely nullified*"—an utterly futile result hardly contemplated by the emphatic language of the General Assembly in its attempt to *strengthen* the right. (Italics supplied.)

Notes

(1) Consider MBCA §§ 7.28(b), (c), (d), 8.04. Under the MBCA, cumulative voting, like preemptive rights, is an "opt in" election to be chosen by an appropriate provision in the articles of incorporation. As of 1995, twenty-eight states had adopted an "opt in" provision while thirteen states had an "opt out" election. Nine states made cumulative voting mandatory for all corporations, five by provision in state constitutions. The number of states with mandatory cumulative voting, however, is declining. In 1990 California, long the bastion of mandatory cumulative voting, made that manner of voting permissive for corporations with shares listed on a public exchange or with more than 800 shareholders of record. Cal.Gen.Corp.Law § 301.5. If a corporation has opted to grant cumulative

voting under the Model Act, may it thereafter amend the articles of incorporation by less than unanimous vote to delete that requirement? See MBCA § 10.01. What rights does a minority shareholder have who objects to such an amendment? See MBCA § 13.02(a)(4)(iv).

(2) As a practical matter, how valuable is the protection afforded by cumulative voting? In a state where cumulative voting is permissive, would you provide for such voting in the typical small, closely held corporation with, say, three or four shareholders? What if one of them has an absolute majority of shares? What about a publicly held corporation with thousands of shareholders? At the 1980 annual meeting of Exxon, a shareholder proposed that Exxon permit cumulative voting. This proposal was vigorously opposed by management on the ground that a director "elected by the cumulative votes of a particular group of shareholders might be inclined to act on the business of the corporation in accordance with the special interests of that particular group, as distinguished from the interests of shareholders as a whole." The proposal received the affirmative vote of less than 3.5 percent of the total cast. Similar proposals have been made by small shareholders in a number of other publicly held corporations, with essentially the same result. For a discussion from a policy perspective of the possible use of cumulative voting in publicly held corporations, see Jeffrey N. Gordon, Institutions as Relational Investors: A New Look at Cumulative Voting, 94 Colum.L.Rev. 124 (1994).

(3) What devices are available to minimize the impact of cumulative voting where that voting is mandatory? What about creating classes of directors consisting of one director each, such as involved in the Winous Co. case? See MBCA § 8.06. Even a decision to classify the board of directors in a permissible way may be attacked as a breach of fiduciary duty in some circumstances if made without business justification and in the midst of a proxy campaign to elect one director. Coalition to Advocate Pub. Util. Responsibility, Inc. v. Engels, 364 F.Supp. 1202 (D.Minn.1973). What about removal of a director elected by minority votes? See MBCA §§ 8.08, 8.09. What about "freezing out" the minority director by denying that director access to information, refusing to appoint him or her to any committees, and then holding "unofficial meetings" and "ramming through decisions * * * with little discussion"? It is reported that these tactics were used by a public corporation, Bunker–Ramo Corp. against a director elected by a dissident group. Kaufman, Directors of Bunker–Ramo Seek to Expel Unwelcome Suitor's Chief From Board, Wall St. J., March 31, 1980, at 10.

(4) What is the purpose of notice requirements of MBCA § 7.28(d)?

(5) One consequence of staggering of elections to the board of directors is that the term of each director is increased from one year to two or three years, depending on whether the board is classified into two or three groups. Is there any value in having longer terms for directors?

(6) Staggering of elections to the board of directors apparently arose in states with mandatory cumulative voting. Is its use to minimize the impact of cumulative voting undesirable? If so, why not mandate a minimum size for all boards of directors of corporations that have cumulative voting, so as to maximize the voting power of minority shareholders?

(7) Where a board is composed of three or more directors, several states permit the staggering of elections if the corporation does not have cumulative voting. Staggering a three-person board mens that each director serves for three years and only one director stands for election each year. Is there anything wrong with that? When coupled with a provision that permits removal of directors only

for cause, this makes outside takeovers by share purchases or proxy fights more difficult, since the successful outsider will only be able to replace one group of directors each year. During the 1980s, a number of publicly held corporations adopted a classified board of directors, coupled with a prohibition against removal of directors except for cause, as a takeover defense.

RINGLING BROS.–BARNUM & BAILEY COMBINED SHOWS v. RINGLING

Supreme Court of Delaware, 1947.
29 Del.Ch. 610, 53 A.2d 441.

PEARSON, JUDGE.

The Court of Chancery was called upon to review an attempted election of directors at the 1946 annual stockholders meeting of the corporate defendant. The pivotal questions concern an agreement between two of the three present stockholders, and particularly the effect of this agreement with relation to the exercise of voting rights by these two stockholders. At the time of the meeting, the corporation had outstanding 1000 shares of capital stock held as follows: 315 by petitioner Edith Conway Ringling; 315 by defendant Aubrey B. Ringling Haley (individually or as executrix and legatee of a deceased husband); and 370 by defendant John Ringling North. The purpose of the meeting was to elect the entire board of seven directors. The shares could be voted cumulatively. Mrs. Ringling asserts that by virtue of the operation of an agreement between her and Mrs. Haley, the latter was bound to vote her shares for an adjournment of the meeting, or in the alternative, for a certain slate of directors. Mrs. Haley contends that she was not so bound for reason that the agreement was invalid, or at least revocable.

The two ladies entered into the agreement in 1941. * * * The agreement recites that each party was the owner "subject only to possible claims of creditors of the estates of Charles Ringling and Richard Ringling, respectively" (deceased husbands of the parties), of 300 shares of the capital stock of the defendant corporation; that in 1938 these shares had been deposited under a voting trust agreement which would terminate in 1947, or earlier, upon the elimination of certain liability of the corporation; that each party also owned 15 shares individually; that the parties had "entered into an agreement in April 1934 providing for joint action by them in matters affecting their ownership of stock and interest in" the corporate defendant; that the parties desired "to continue to act jointly in all matters relating to their stock ownership or interest in" the corporate defendant (and the other corporation). The agreement then provides as follows:

Now, Therefore, in consideration of the mutual covenants and agreements hereinafter contained the parties hereto agree as follows:

1. Neither party will sell any shares of stock or any voting trust certificates in either of said corporations to any other person whosoever, without first making a written offer to the other party hereto of all of the shares or voting trust certificates proposed to be sold, for the same price and upon the same terms and conditions as in such proposed sale, and allowing such other party a time of not less than 180 days from the date of such written offer within which to accept same.

2. In exercising any voting rights to which either party may be entitled by virtue of ownership of stock or voting trust certificates held by them in either of said corporation, each party will consult and confer with the other and the parties will act jointly in exercising such voting rights in accordance with such agreement as they may reach with respect to any matter calling for the exercise of such voting rights.

3. In the event the parties fail to agree with respect to any matter covered by paragraph 2 above, the question in disagreement shall be submitted for arbitration to Karl D. Loos, of Washington, D.C. as arbitrator and his decision thereon shall be binding upon the parties hereto. Such arbitration shall be exercised to the end of assuring for the respective corporations good management and such participation therein by the members of the Ringling family as the experience, capacity and ability of each may warrant. The parties may at any time by written agreement designate any other individual to act as arbitrator in lieu of said Loos.

4. Each of the parties hereto will enter into and execute such voting trust agreement or agreements and such other instruments as, from time to time they may deem advisable and as they may be advised by counsel are appropriate to effectuate the purposes and objects of this agreement.

5. This agreement shall be in effect from the date hereof and shall continue in effect for a period of ten years unless sooner terminated by mutual agreement in writing by the parties hereto.

6. The agreement of April 1934 is hereby terminated.

7. This agreement shall be binding upon and inure to the benefit of the heirs, executors, administrators and assigns of the parties hereto respectively.

The Mr. Loos mentioned in the agreement is an attorney and has represented both parties since 1937, and, before and after the voting trust was terminated in late 1942, advised them with respect to the exercise of their voting rights. At the annual meetings in 1943 and the two following years, the parties voted their shares in accordance with mutual understandings arrived at as a result of discussions. In each of these years, they elected five of the seven directors. Mrs. Ringling and Mrs. Haley each had sufficient votes, independently of the other, to elect two of the seven directors. By both voting for an additional candidate, they could be sure of his election regardless of how Mr. North, the remaining stockholder, might vote.[10]

Some weeks before the 1946 meeting, they discussed with Mr. Loos the matter of voting for directors. They were in accord that Mrs. Ringling should cast sufficient votes to elect herself and her son; and that Mrs. Haley should elect herself and her husband; but they did not agree upon a fifth director. The day before the meeting, the discussions were continued, Mrs. Haley being

10. [By the Court] Each lady was entitled to cast 2205 votes (since each had the cumulative voting rights of 315 shares, and there were 7 vacancies in the directorate). The sum of the votes of both is 4410, which is sufficient to allow 882 votes for each of 5 persons. Mr. North, holding 370 shares, was entitled to cast 2590 votes, which obviously cannot be divided so as to give to more than two candidates as many as 882 votes each. It will be observed that in order for Mrs. Ringling and Mrs. Haley to be sure to elect five directors (regardless of how Mr. North might vote) they must act together in the sense that their combined votes must be divided among five different candidates and at least one of the five must be voted for by both Mrs. Ringling and Mrs. Haley.

represented by her husband since she could not be present because of illness. In a conversation with Mr. Loos, Mr. Haley indicated that he would make a motion for an adjournment of the meeting for sixty days, in order to give the ladies additional time to come to an agreement about their voting. On the morning of the meeting, however, he stated that because of something Mrs. Ringling had done, he would not consent to a postponement. Mrs. Ringling then made a demand upon Mr. Loos to act under the third paragraph of the agreement "to arbitrate the disagreement" between her and Mrs. Haley in connection with the manner in which the stock of the two ladies should be voted. At the opening of the meeting, Mr. Loos read the written demand and stated that he determined and directed that the stock of both ladies be voted for an adjournment of sixty days. Mrs. Ringling then made a motion for adjournment and voted for it. Mr. Haley, as proxy for his wife, and Mr. North voted against the motion. Mrs. Ringling (herself or through her attorney, it is immaterial which,) objected to the voting of Mrs. Haley's stock in any manner other than in accordance with Mr. Loos' direction. The chairman ruled that the stock could not be voted contrary to such direction, and declared the motion for adjournment had carried. Nevertheless, the meeting proceeded to the election of directors. Mrs. Ringling stated that she would continue in the meeting "but without prejudice to her position with respect to the voting of the stock and the fact that adjournment had not been taken." Mr. Loos directed Mrs. Ringling to cast her votes.

> 882 for Mrs. Ringling,
>
> 882 for her son, Robert, and
>
> 441 for a Mr. Dunn, who had been a member of the board for several years. She complied. Mr. Loos directed that Mrs. Haley's votes be cast
>
> 882 for Mrs. Haley,
>
> 882 for Mr. Haley, and
>
> 441 for Mr. Dunn.

Instead of complying, Mr. Haley attempted to vote his wife's shares

> 1103 for Mrs. Haley, and
>
> 1102 for Mr. Haley.

Mr. North voted his shares

> 864 for a Mr. Woods,
>
> 863 for a Mr. Griffin, and
>
> 863 for Mr. North.

The chairman ruled that the five candidates proposed by Mr. Loos, together with Messrs. Woods and North, were elected. The Haley–North group disputed this ruling insofar as it declared the election of Mr. Dunn; and insisted that Mr. Griffin, instead, had been elected. A directors' meeting followed in which Mrs. Ringling participated after stating that she would do so "without prejudice to her position that the stockholders' meeting had been adjourned and that the directors' meeting was not properly held." Mr. Dunn and Mr. Griffin, although each was challenged by an opposing faction, attempted to join in voting as directors for different slates of officers. Soon after the meeting, Mrs. Ringling instituted this proceeding.

The Vice Chancellor determined that the agreement to vote in accordance with the direction of Mr. Loos was valid as a "stock pooling agreement" with lawful objects and purposes, and that it was not in violation of any public policy of this state. He held that where the arbitrator acts under the agreement and one party refuses to comply with his direction, "the Agreement constitutes the willing party * * * an implied agent possessing the irrevocable proxy of the recalcitrant party for the purpose of casting the particular vote". It was ordered that a new election be held before a master, with the direction that the master should recognize and give effect to the agreement if its terms were properly invoked.

Before taking up defendants' objections to the agreement, let us analyze particularly what it attempts to provide with respect to voting, including what functions and powers it attempts to repose in Mr. Loos, the "arbitrator". The agreement recites that the parties desired "to continue to act jointly in all matters relating to their stock ownership or interest in" the corporation. The parties agreed to consult and confer with each other in exercising their voting rights and to act jointly—that is, concertedly; unitedly; towards unified courses of action—in accordance with such agreement as they might reach. Thus, so long as the parties agree for whom or for what their shares shall be voted, the agreement provides no function for the arbitrator. His role is limited to situations where the parties fail to agree upon a course of action. In such cases, the agreement directs that "the question in disagreement shall be submitted for arbitration" to Mr. Loos "as arbitrator and his decision thereon shall be binding upon the parties". These provisions are designed to operate in aid of what appears to be a primary purpose of the parties, "to act jointly" in exercising their voting rights, by providing a means for fixing a course of action whenever they themselves might reach a stalemate.

Should the agreement be interpreted as attempting to empower the arbitrator to carry his directions into effect? Certainly there is no express delegation or grant of power to do so, either by authorizing him to vote the shares or to compel either party to vote them in accordance with his directions. The agreement expresses no other function of the arbitrator than that of deciding questions in disagreement which prevent the effectuation of the purpose "to act jointly". The power to enforce a decision does not seem a necessary or usual incident of such a function. Mr. Loos is not a party to the agreement. It does not contemplate the transfer of any shares or interest in shares to him, or that he should undertake any duties which the parties might compel him to perform. They provided that they might designate any other individual to act instead of Mr. Loos. The agreement does not attempt to make the arbitrator a trustee of an express trust. What the arbitrator is to do is for the benefit of the parties, not for his own benefit. Whether the parties accept or reject his decision is no concern of his, so far as the agreement or the surrounding circumstances reveal. We think the parties sought to bind each other, but to be bound only to each other, and not to empower the arbitrator to enforce decisions he might make.

From this conclusion, it follows necessarily that no decision of the arbitrator could ever be enforced if both parties to the agreement were unwilling that it be enforced, for the obvious reason that there would be no one to enforce it. Under the agreement, something more is required after the arbitrator has given his decision in order that it should become compulsory: at least one of the parties must determine that such decision shall be carried into effect. Thus, any "control" of the voting of the shares, which is reposed in the arbitrator, is substantially limited in action under the agreement in that it is subject to the overriding power of the parties themselves.

The agreement does not describe the undertaking of each party with respect to a decision of the arbitrator other than to provide that it "shall be binding upon the parties". It seems to us that this language, considered with relation to its context and the situations to which it is applicable, means that each party promised the other to exercise her own voting rights in accordance with the arbitrator's decision. The agreement is silent about any exercise of the voting rights of one party by the other. The language with reference to situations where the parties arrive at an understanding as to voting plainly suggests "action" by each, and "exercising" voting rights by each, rather than by one for the other. There is no intimation that this method should be different where the arbitrator's decision is to be carried into effect. Assuming that a power in each party to exercise the voting rights of the other might be a relatively more effective or convenient means of enforcing a decision of the arbitrator than would be available without the power, this would not justify implying a delegation of the power in the absence of some indication that the parties bargained for that means. The method of voting actually employed by the parties tends to show that they did not construe the agreement as creating powers to vote each other's shares; for at meetings prior to 1946 each party apparently exercised her own voting rights, and at the 1946 meeting, Mrs. Ringling, who wished to enforce the agreement, did not attempt to cast a ballot in exercise of any voting rights of Mrs. Haley. We do not find enough in the agreement or in the circumstances to justify a construction that either party was empowered to exercise voting rights of the other.

Having examined what the parties sought to provide by the agreement, we come now to defendants' contention that the voting provisions are illegal and revocable. They say that the courts of this state have definitely established the doctrine "that there can be no agreement, or any device whatsoever, by which the voting power of stock of a Delaware corporation may be irrevocably separated from the ownership of the stock, except by an agreement which complies with Section 18" of the Corporation Law, Rev.Code 1935, § 2050, and except by a proxy coupled with an interest. They rely on Perry v. Missouri–Kansas P.L. Co., 22 Del.Ch. 33, 191 A. 823; In re Public Industrial Corporation, 19 Del.Ch. 398, reported as In re Chilson, 168 A. 82; Aldridge v. Franco Wyoming Oil Co., 24 Del.Ch. 126, 7 A.2d 753, affirmed in 24 Del.Ch. 349, 14 A.2d 380; Belle Isle Corporation v. Corcoran, Del.Sup., 49 A.2d 1; and contend that the doctrine is derived from Section 18 itself, Rev.Code of Del.1935, § 2050. The statute reads, in part, as follows:

"Sec. 18. Voting Trusts: * * *—One or more stockholders may by agreement in writing deposit capital stock of an original issue with or transfer capital stock to any person or persons, or corporation or corporations authorized to act as trustee, for the purpose of vesting in said person or persons, corporation or corporations, who may be designated Voting Trustee or Voting Trustees, the right to vote thereon for any period of time determined by such agreement, not exceeding ten years, upon the terms and conditions stated in such agreement. Such agreement may contain any other lawful provisions not inconsistent with said purpose.

* * * Said Voting Trustees may vote upon the stock so issued or transferred during the period in such agreement specified; stock standing in the names of such Voting Trustees may be voted either in person or by proxy, and in voting said stock, such Voting Trustees shall incur no responsibility as stockholder, trustee or otherwise, except for their own individual malfeasance."[11]

In our view, neither the cases nor the statute sustain the rule for which the defendants contend. Their sweeping formulation would impugn well-recognized means by which a shareholder may effectively confer his voting rights upon others while retaining various other rights. For example, defendants' rule would apparently not permit holders of voting stock to confer upon stockholders of another class, by the device of an amendment of the certificate of incorporation, the exclusive right to vote during periods when dividends are not paid on stock of the latter class. The broad prohibitory meaning which defendants find in Section 18 seems inconsistent with their concession that proxies coupled with an interest may be irrevocable, for the statute contains nothing about such proxies. The statute authorizes, among other things, the deposit or transfer of stock in trust for a specified purpose, namely, "vesting" in the transferee "the right to vote thereon" for a limited period; and prescribes numerous requirements in this connection. Accordingly, it seems reasonable to infer that to establish the relationship and accomplish the purpose which the statute authorizes, its requirements must be complied with. But the statute does not purport to deal with agreements whereby shareholders attempt to bind each other as to how they shall vote their shares. Various forms of such pooling agreements, as they are sometimes called, have been held valid and have been distinguished from voting trusts. We think the particular agreement before us does not violate Section 18 or constitute an attempted evasion of its requirements, and is not illegal for any other reason. Generally speaking, a shareholder may exercise wide liberality of judgment in the matter of voting, and it is not objectionable, that his motives may be for personal profit, or determined by whims or caprice, so long as he violates no duty owed his fellow shareholders. Heil v. Standard G. & E. Co., 17 Del.Ch. 214, 151 A. 303. The ownership of voting stock imposes no legal duty to vote at all. A group of shareholders may, without impropriety, vote their respective shares so as to obtain advantages of concerted action. They may lawfully contract with each other to vote in the future in such way as they, or a majority of their group, from time to time determine. Reasonable provisions for cases of failure of the group to reach a determination because of an even division in their ranks seem unobjectionable. The provision here for submission to the arbitrator is plainly designed as a deadlock-breaking measure, and the arbitrator's decision cannot be enforced unless at least one of the parties (entitled to cast one-half of their combined votes) is willing that it be enforced. We find the provision reasonable. It does not appear that the agreement enables the parties to take any unlawful advantage of the outside

---

11. [By the Editor] Omitted portions of the section provide requirements for the filing of a copy of the agreement in the principal Delaware office of the corporation for the issuance of certificates of stock to the voting trustees, for the voting of stock where there are more than one voting trustee, and for the extension of the agreement for additional periods, not exceeding ten years each. The current Delaware voting trust statute, Del. G.C.L. § 218, was amended in 1994 to eliminate the ten-year limitation on the life of a voting trust but retained the requirement that a copy be filed with the corporation.

shareholder, or of any other person. It offends no rule of law or public policy of this state of which we are aware.

Legal consideration for the promises of each party is supplied by the mutual promises of the other party. The undertaking to vote in accordance with the arbitrator's decision is a valid contract. The good faith of the arbitrator's action has not been challenged and, indeed, the record indicates that no such challenge could be supported. Accordingly, the failure of Mrs. Haley to exercise her voting rights in accordance with his decision was a breach of her contract. It is no extenuation of the breach that her votes were cast for two of the three candidates directed by the arbitrator. His directions to her were part of a single plan or course of action for the voting of the shares of both parties to the agreement, calculated to utilize an advantage of joint action by them which would bring about the election of an additional director. The actual voting of Mrs. Haley's shares frustrates that plan to such an extent that it should not be treated as a partial performance of her contract.

Throughout their argument, defendants make much of the fact that all votes cast at the meeting were by the registered shareholders. The Court of Chancery may, in a review of an election, reject votes of a registered shareholder where his voting of them is found to be in violation of rights of another person. Compare: In re Giant Portland Cement Co., Del.Ch., 21 A.2d 697. It seems to us that upon the application of Mrs. Ringling, the injured party, the votes representing Mrs. Haley's shares should not be counted. Since no infirmity in Mr. North's voting has been demonstrated, his right to recognition of what he did at the meeting should be considered in granting any relief to Mrs. Ringling; for her rights arose under a contract to which Mr. North was not a party. With this in mind, we have concluded that the election should not be declared invalid, but that effect should be given to a rejection of the votes representing Mrs. Haley's shares. No other relief seems appropriate in this proceeding. Mr. North's vote against the motion for adjournment was sufficient to defeat it. With respect to the election of directors, the return of the inspectors should be corrected to show a rejection of Mrs. Haley's votes, and to declare the election of the six persons for whom Mr. North and Mrs. Ringling voted.

This leaves one vacancy in the directorate. The question of what to do about such a vacancy was not considered by the court below and has not been argued here. For this reason, and because an election of directors at the 1947 annual meeting (which presumably will be held in the near future) may make a determination of the question unimportant, we shall not decide it on this appeal. If a decision of the point appears important to the parties, any of them may apply to raise it in the Court of Chancery, after the mandate of this court is received there.

An order should be entered, directing a modification of the order of the Court of Chancery in accordance with this opinion.

Notes

(1) Does the remedy adopted by the Court uphold the purpose of the agreement? What is the net effect of depriving Mrs. Haley of the right to vote?

(2) Is the decision upholding the agreement consistent with the Court's action in McQuade v. Stoneham, p. 401, supra?

(3) The Chancellor held that "the Agreement constitutes the willing party to the Agreement an implied agent possessing the irrevocable proxy of the recalcitrant party for the purpose of casting the particular vote." 29 Del.Ch. 318, 335, 49 A.2d 603, 611 (1946). Do you see any practical problem this might create?

(4) Consider MBCA § 7.31. The Official Comment states that section 7.31(b) "avoids the result reached in the Ringling case." Does it?

(5) State ex rel. Babione v. Martin, 97 Ohio App.3d 539, 647 N.E.2d 169 (1994) holds that a written agreement entered into by eight shareholders in 1976 that they "would stick together until we get control of the company" does not create a common law pooling arrangement since it did not refer expressly to the voting of shares. If not that, then what did the agreement contemplate?

NEW YORK—McKINNEY'S BUS.CORP.LAW

§ 609. Proxies.

(a) Every shareholder entitled to vote at a meeting of shareholders or to express consent or dissent without a meeting may authorize another person or persons to act for him by proxy.

(b) Every proxy must be signed by the shareholder or his attorney-in-fact. No proxy shall be valid after the expiration of eleven months from the date thereof unless otherwise provided in the proxy. Every proxy shall be revocable at the pleasure of the shareholder executing it, except as otherwise provided in this section.

(c) The authority of the holder of a proxy to act shall not be revoked by the incompetence or death of the shareholder who executed the proxy unless, before the authority is exercised, written notice of an adjudication of such incompetence or of such death is received by the corporate officer responsible for maintaining the list of shareholders.

(d) Except when other provision shall have been made by written agreement between the parties, the record holder of shares which he holds as pledgee or otherwise as security or which belong to another, shall issue to the pledgor or to such owner of such shares, upon demand therefor and payment of necessary expenses thereof, a proxy to vote or take other action thereon.

(e) A shareholder shall not sell his vote or issue a proxy to vote to any person for any sum of money or anything of value, except as authorized in this section and section 620 (Agreements as to voting; provision in certificate of incorporation as to control of directors).

(f) A proxy which is entitled "irrevocable proxy" and which states that it is irrevocable, is irrevocable when it is held by any of the following or a nominee of any of the following:

   (1) A pledgee;

   (2) A person who has purchased or agreed to purchase the shares;

   (3) A creditor or creditors of the corporation who extend or continue credit to the corporation in consideration of the proxy if the proxy states that it was given in consideration of such extension or continuation of

credit, the amount thereof, and the name of the person extending or continuing credit;

(4) A person who has contracted to perform services as an officer of the corporation, if a proxy is required by the contract of employment, if the proxy states that it was given in consideration of such contract of employment, the name of the employee and the period of employment contracted for;

(5) A person designated by or under an agreement under paragraph (a) of section 620.

(g) Notwithstanding a provision in a proxy, stating that it is irrevocable, the proxy becomes revocable after the pledge is redeemed or the debt of the corporation is paid, or the period of employment provided for in the contract of employment has terminated, or the agreement under paragraph (a) of section 620 has terminated; and in a case provided for in subparagraphs (f)(3) or (4), becomes revocable three years after the date of the proxy or at the end of the period, if any, specified therein, whichever period is less, unless the period of irrevocability is renewed from time to time by the execution of a new irrevocable proxy as provided in this section. This paragraph does not affect the duration of a proxy under paragraph (b).

(h) A proxy may be revoked, notwithstanding a provision making it irrevocable, by a purchaser of shares without knowledge of the existence of the provision unless the existence of the proxy and its irrevocability is noted conspicuously on the face or back of the certificate representing such shares.

§ 620. Agreements as to Voting; Provision in Certificate of Incorporation as to Control of Directors

(a) An agreement between two or more shareholders, if in writing and signed by the parties thereto, may provide that in exercising any voting rights, the shares held by them shall be voted as therein provided, or as they may agree, or as determined in accordance with a procedure agreed upon by them. * * *

Notes

(1) A proxy appointment, like other grants of authority to an agent, is usually revocable whether or not it is stated to be irrevocable. Several situations exist, however, where the common law courts felt it necessary to recognize irrevocable proxies. These situations were usually analyzed as those involving a "proxy coupled with an interest," a notion roughly analogous to a "power coupled with an interest" in the law of agency. The leading case is Hunt v. Rousmanier's Adm'rs, 21 U.S. (8 Wheat.) 174, 5 L.Ed. 589 (1823). Of course, the phrase "proxy coupled with an interest" does not help to decide anything, and at common law the whole area was one of confusion. See Proctor L. Thomas, Irrevocable Proxies, 43 Tex.L.Rev. 733 (1965). In New York, the vagueness of this test is eliminated by McKinney's Bus.Corp.Law § 609(f), which covers the most common kinds of "interests" that a proxy may be "coupled" with, thereby becoming irrevocable. Do you see any underlying principle or theory by which these types of interests were selected? Do you see any risk or danger in compiling such a list and making it exclusive? Compare the language of MBCA § 7.22(d) with § 609 of the New York statute in this regard.

(2) In Haft v. Haft, 671 A.2d 413, 419–423 (Del.Ch.1995), Chancellor Allen addressed a contention that an irrevocable proxy granted to the chief executive officer of the corporation was enforceable because of the CEO's interest in the corporation:

> The Delaware General Corporation Law states that a proxy may be made irrevocable "if, and only as long as, it is coupled with an interest * * * in the stock itself or an interest in the corporation generally." 8 Del.C. § 212(e) (1991). Do Herbert Haft's interests, other than as a secured creditor, qualify under the statute? As I now explain, in my opinion they do.

> * * * The language * * * ("an interest in the corporation generally") was introduced * * * to erase the implication arising from dicta in a 1933 Master's Report, which had been confirmed by this court. The report was in the case of In re Chilson, Del.Ch., 168 A. 82 (1933). The Chilson dicta was to the effect that in order to support irrevocability of a proxy, the holder had to have an interest in the stock itself. * * * [T]he enactment of new § 212(e) in 1967, * * * made it very clear that other interests (interests other than in the stock itself) could legitimately be contractually protected by the grant of an irrevocable proxy. * * *

> No Delaware court has been required to address this question under the language of amended Section 212. In now doing so, it is appropriate to acknowledge that the corporate law has tended to distrust and discourage the separation of the shareholder claim as equity investor (i.e., the right to enjoy distributions on stock if, as, and when declared) from the right to vote stock. For example there was for many years a rather clear rule against the sale of a corporate vote unattached to the sale of the underlying stock. A powerful argument can be advanced that generally the congruence of the right to vote and the residual rights of ownership will tend towards efficient wealth production.

> A proxy is, of course, a means temporarily to split the power to vote from the residual ownership claim of the stockholder. In the vast number of instances in which proxies to vote stock are used, however, this split occasions no significant divergence between the interests of the proxy holder and the holder of the residual corporate interest because the proxy is of relatively short duration and in all events is revocable unilaterally. Thus, in effect, the grant of the proxy represented a judgment (which may be enforced through revocation) that the holder of the proxy will exercise it in the economic interest of the residual owner. A potentially inefficient split between the interests of the voter and the interests of the residual owners may, however, develop when the proxy is irrevocable. Such a holder is free from the unilateral control of the grantor and may be expected to be inclined to exercise voting rights in a way that benefits himself. There is of course, as a general matter, nothing legally suspect in contracting parties exercising contracted-for rights in a self-interested manner.[12] Yet the exercise of voting control over corporations by persons whose interest in them is not chiefly or

---

12. [By the Judge] I note that this statement is subject to qualification in at least three circumstances: (1) a contract between a fiduciary and the person or entity for whom she acts (the "trust" or "corporation" etc.); (2) a contract between a fiduciary and a person who is an express beneficiary of the "trust" etc., if the contract relates to the business of the "trust" and (3) an implied obligation of good faith and fair dealing, which under certain circumstances will be found to impose a limitation on a arm's-length contracting party's ability to exercise legal rights in a way that deprives the other contracting party of the substance of the express bargain that the parties had reached.

solely as a residual owner will create circumstances in which the corporation will be less than optimally efficient in the selection of risky investment projects. (A simple, if gross, example: the holder of an irrevocable proxy with voting control might simply refuse to elect a board that will accept the best investment projects (those with the highest risk adjusted rate of return) unless some side payment to him is arranged). The special additional costs associated with such a divorce between ownership and voting (the costs being expressed either as an otherwise unnecessary expense or as the selection of non-optimizing investment projects) will of course tend to diminish as the voter's interest becomes aligned with the residual owners interest.

In this light, the dicta of In re Chilson may be thought to offer a means of limiting the agency costs that irrevocable proxies occasion. By recognizing only an interest in the stock itself as an interest that will support the irrevocability of a proxy, the rule of Chilson would eliminate a class of cases in which the incentives of the proxy holder to exploit the corporation would be greatest, that is, those in which she simply has no economic interest at all in the residual equity of the firm. Of course the Chilson rule does not entirely eliminate the inefficient incentive structure that the divorce of voting power and benefit occasions; the proxy voter/secured lender still is a creditor and thus may not be inclined to accept high-risk/high-reward projects, even if they have a positive risk-adjusted net present value. But the Chilson rule would moderate the effect. * * *

In the field of corporation law, courts have for centuries played and do still play an enormously important role in creating that law interstitially through the accretionary process of case by case rulings. * * * When, in the absence of authoritative text or precedent, courts are modernly called upon to fashion corporate law rules interstitially, it is appropriate for the court, among other considerations, to consider the future effects generally of alternative rules and, in doing so, to consider especially the efficiency effects of those alternatives, to the extent they can reliably be detected. Thus, reasoning of the foregoing kind is not inappropriate to the institutional role of courts. But while not inappropriate, rarely will such reasoning directly produce an applicable rule or a ruling. To state what I would suppose is obvious, the corporate law, as applied in specific cases by courts, is institutionally a rich stew; the corporation law's underlying efficiency concerns are mediated through a body of authoritative rules, principles and practices to which courts owe loyalty. In this instance I confess to the view that a corporation law rule allowing for the specific enforceability of an irrevocable proxy that is coupled only with the holder's interest in maintaining a salaried office seems mischievous in terms of its possible efficiency effects. But in light of the 1967 amendment to the Delaware statutory law * * * and the absence of contrary precedent, I am required to express the opinion that such an interest—the interest that Herbert Haft had and retains as the senior executive officer of Dart—is sufficient under our law to render specifically enforceable the express contract for an irrevocable proxy. * * *

(3) Consider § 609(e) of the New York statute, a provision which has no analogue in the MBCA. Does this mean that all sales of votes are per se invalid no matter what the circumstances? In Schreiber v. Carney, 447 A.2d 17 (Del.Ch. 1982), the Court was faced with a situation where a major shareholder committed itself to withdraw its opposition to a merger in exchange for a favorable loan from a participant in the merger. There was full disclosure of the arrangement to the

independent shareholders, who overwhelmingly approved the proposed transaction. The Court stated:

It is clear that the loan constituted vote-buying as that term has been defined by the courts. Vote-buying, despite its negative connotation, is simply a voting agreement supported by consideration personal to the stockholder, whereby the stockholder divorces his discretionary voting power and votes as directed by the offeror. The record clearly indicates that Texas International purchased or "removed" the obstacle of Jet Capital's opposition. Indeed, this is tacitly conceded by the defendants. However, defendants contend that the analysis of the transaction should not end here because the legality of vote-buying depends on whether its object or purpose is to defraud or in some manner disenfranchise the other stockholders. Defendants contend that because the loan did not defraud or disfranchise any group of shareholders, but rather enfranchised the other shareholders by giving them a determinative vote in the proposed merger, it is not illegal *per se*. Defendants, in effect, contend that vote-buying is not void *per se* because the end justified the means. * * *

The present case presents a peculiar factual setting in that the proposed vote-buying consideration was conditional upon the approval of a majority of the disinterested stockholders after a full disclosure to them of all pertinent facts and was purportedly for the best interests of all Texas International stockholders. It is therefore necessary to do more than merely consider the fact that Jet Capital saw fit to vote for the transaction after a loan was made to it by Texas International. As stated in Oceanic Exploration Co. v. Grynberg, Del.Supr., 428 A.2d 1 (1981), a case involving an analogous situation, to do otherwise would be tantamount to "[d]eciding the case on * * * an abstraction divorced from the facts of the case and the intent of the law." 428 A.2d 5. * * *

There are essentially two principles which appear in [the traditional vote-buying] cases. The first is that vote-buying is illegal *per se* if its object or purpose is to defraud or disenfranchise the other stockholders. A fraudulent purpose is as defined at common law, as a deceit which operates prejudicially upon the property rights of another.

The second principle which appears in these old cases is that vote-buying is illegal *per se* as a matter of public policy, the reason being that each stockholder should be entitled to rely upon the independent judgment of his fellow stockholders. Thus, the underlying basis for this latter principle is again fraud but as viewed from a sense of duty owed by all stockholders to one another. The apparent rationale is that by requiring each stockholder to exercise his individual judgment as to all matters presented, "[t]he security of the small stockholders is found in the natural disposition of each stockholder to promote the best interests of all, in order to promote his individual interests." Cone v. Russell, 48 N.J.Eq. 208, 21 A. 847, 849 (1891). In essence, while self interest motivates a stockholder's vote, theoretically, it is also advancing the interests of the other stockholders. Thus, any agreement entered into for personal gain, whereby a stockholder separates his voting right from his property right was considered a fraud upon this community of interests. * * *

An automatic application of this rationale to the facts in the present case, however, would be to ignore an essential element of the transaction. The agreement in question was entered into primarily to further the interests of

Texas International's other shareholders. Indeed, the shareholders, after reviewing a detailed proxy statement, voted overwhelmingly in favor of the loan agreement. Thus, the underlying rationale for the argument that vote-buying is illegal *per se,* as a matter of public policy, ceases to exist when measured against the undisputed reason for the transaction.

Moreover, the rationale that vote-buying is, as a matter of public policy, illegal *per se* is founded upon considerations of policy which are now outmoded as a necessary result of an evolving corporate environment. According to 5 Fletcher *Cyclopedia Corporation* (Perm.Ed.) § 2066:

> The theory that each stockholder is entitled to the personal judgment of each other stockholder expressed in his vote, and that any agreement among stockholders frustrating it was invalid, is obsolete because it is both impracticable and impossible of application to modern corporations with many widely scattered stockholders, and the courts have gradually abandoned it. * * *

This is not to say, however, that vote-buying accomplished for some laudable purpose is automatically free from challenge. Because vote-buying is so easily susceptible of abuse it must be viewed as a voidable transaction subject to a test for intrinsic fairness.

447 A.2d at 23–26. The Court refused to grant summary judgment invalidating the transaction on the ground that it constituted vote-buying.

(4) Del.Gen.Corp.Law § 228 permits action by shareholders without a meeting if written consent, setting forth the action taken "shall be signed by the holders of outstanding stock having not less than the minimum number of votes that would be necessary to authorize or take such action at a meeting at which all shares entitled to vote thereon were present and voted." Contrast MBCA § 7.04. In a publicly held corporation, unanimity as a practical matter is impossible to attain; as a result, the MBCA provision can only be used by corporations with relatively few shareholders. Not so for § 228 of the Delaware statute, which allows decisions by majority action to be effected in publicly held corporations without holding a meeting. Indeed, the power of shareholders to act by majority consent without a meeting is a potentially fearsome weapon in the hands of aggressors in contested takeover bids. Through this device, an aggressor who is able to obtain a majority of the outstanding voting shares may act immediately to replace the board of directors, oust incumbent management, amend bylaws, and defuse anti-takeover defenses. As noted by the Delaware Supreme Court, the "broad use [of § 228] in takeover battles, which we now observe, was not contemplated" in 1967 when this section was added to the Delaware General Corporation Law. Allen v. Prime Computer, Inc., 540 A.2d 417, 419 (Del.1988). But is not such a provision simply basic shareholder democracy in action? If a majority of the shareholders desire to do X, why should they have to wait until a meeting to do so? Is there an advantage in having a discussion at a meeting as a prerequisite to action? On the other hand, how realistic is that argument when the corporation is publicly held and virtually all shareholders vote by proxy long before the meeting?

(5) Once the powerful force of the majority consent provision was recognized, corporations quickly attempted to defuse that aggressive weapon. In Datapoint Corp. v. Plaza Securities Co., 496 A.2d 1031 (Del.1985), the Delaware Supreme Court held that a corporation could not impose procedural restrictions on § 228 by adopting a bylaw[13] that significantly delayed the effective date of an action

---

13. [By the Editor] Section 228 permits the articles of incorporation to limit or qualify the effect of that section. Such an amendment, however, requires action by the shareholders taken by majority consent under that section. The Court nevertheless recognized that consummation of shareholder action by consent might be deferred "until a ministerial-type review of the sufficiency of the consents has been performed." 496 A.2d at 1036. In Allen v. Prime Computer, Inc., supra, the Court held that a mandatory 20 day delay, ostensibly to enable the corporation to determine whether the consents were lawfully obtained, was more than "ministerial-type" review and was invalid.

(6) Del.Gen.Corp.Law § 213(b) provides that the "record date for determining stockholders entitled to consent to corporate action in writing without a meeting * * * shall be the first date on which a signed written consent setting forth the action taken or proposed to be taken is delivered to the corporation * * *." Why is this provision necessary? What if notice that consents are being solicited is received by the corporation but no actual written consent has been received; may the board of directors establish a record date for that purpose, say, 45 days later? See Empire of Carolina, Inc. v. Deltona Corp., 514 A.2d 1091 (Del.1985).

(7) Should consents be subject to the same rules of revocability as an ordinary proxy? Or should consents be deemed to be "self executing" so that once a majority has executed consents, the corporation has irrevocably acted? Or should they be analogized to voting agreements which are not revocable because they constitute contracts? In Calumet Indus., Inc. v. MacClure, 464 F.Supp. 19 (N.D.Ill. 1978), the Court accepted the proxy analogy, a view that was also accepted in dictum in Allen v. Prime Computer, Inc., supra, at 420. See also Pabst Brewing Co. v. Jacobs, 549 F.Supp. 1068 (D.Del.1982). Accepting that result, how long should a consent remain effective? In 1987, the Delaware legislature amended § 228 by adding a new subsection (c) that requires all consents to be dated and provides that consents are effective only if they are dated within 60 days after the earliest dated consent is delivered to the corporation.

(8) Election of directors through a consent procedure does not satisfy the statutory requirement that an annual meeting be held. Hoschett v. TSI International Software, Ltd.,, 683 A.2d 43 (Del.Ch.1996). This case involved a corporation with less than 40 shareholders of record. In 1997, § 211 of the Delaware GCL was amended in several respects in response to this decision, including the addition of a provision that *unanimous* written consent may serve as a substitute for a meeting.

BROWN v. McLANAHAN

United States Court of Appeals, Fourth Circuit, 1945.
148 F.2d 703.

Before PARKER, SOPER, and DOBIE, CIRCUIT JUDGES.

DOBIE, CIRCUIT JUDGE.

This appeal from an order granting a motion to dismiss, involves the equitable rights attaching to certain voting trust certificates representing shares of preferred stock of the Baltimore Transit Company (hereinafter called the Company).

The appellant, Dorothy K. Brown (hereinafter referred to as plaintiff), as the holder of voting trust certificates representing 500 shares of the preferred

while the bylaw amendment effected in *Data-point* was implemented by the directors acting alone.

stock of the Company, brought a class action against the voting trustees, the directors of the Company, the Company itself, the indenture trustee for the holders of the Company's debentures, and the debenture holders as a class (herein collectively referred to as defendants), seeking to set aside as unlawful an amendment of the Company's charter which purports to vest voting rights in the debenture holders. On oral argument before this Court, it was stated that the holders of 45,000 shares of preferred stock have indicated their approval of this suit.

The securities involved in this litigation were issued under a plan of reorganization of the United Railways and Electric Company of Baltimore, and The Maryland Electric Railways Company and Subsidiary Companies, under Section 77B of the Bankruptcy Act, 11 U.S.C.A. § 207. The plan was approved by the United States District Court for the District of Maryland. In re United Railways & Electric Co. of Baltimore's Reorganization, 11 F.Supp. 717.

That part of the reorganization plan relevant to the question before us may be briefly summarized.

The plan provided for the issuance of three types of securities. Debentures in the amount of $22,083,381 and 233,427 shares of preferred stock were issued to the holders of all first lien bonds on the basis of $500 principal amount of debentures, and five shares of preferred stock, par value $100 per share for each $1,000 principal amount of the bonds; 169,112 shares of new common stock, without par value, were issued to the old common stockholders and to unsecured creditors.

Under the plan of reorganization, voting rights were vested exclusively in the preferred and common stock. Each share of preferred entitled the holder to one vote on all corporate matters (except that the power to elect one director was exclusively vested in the common stock) and further, so long as any six months' installment of dividends on the preferred remained in arrears, the holders of the preferred stock held the *exclusive right* to vote for the election of all but one director. Three shares of common stock entitled the holder to one vote.

The plan also provided for the establishment of a voting trust of all the preferred and common stock of the reorganized company for a period of ten years, the maximum period permitted by Maryland law. In accordance with this provision, all the stock was issued to eight voting trustees under a voting trust agreement which was to terminate on July 1, 1945. The trustees in turn issued voting trust certificates to those entitled to distribution under the plan. Under the plan, the voting rights were to revert, on termination of the trust, to the certificate holders in proportion to the number of shares represented.

No dividends have ever been paid on the preferred stock, and pursuant to the charter provision, at all times since dividends have been in arrears, the exclusive right to elect all but one director has been vested in the preferred stock.

The eight voting trustees are also a majority of the directors of the Company, elected as such by their own vote as trustees. On June 21, 1944, *without notice of any kind to the certificate holders,* the directors passed a resolution recommending, and the voting trustees as stockholders voted to adopt, an amendment to the Company's charter.

Article VII of the Voting Trust Agreement, by authority of which the trustees purportedly acted, provides in part as follows:

(1) Until the termination of the trusts of this instrument the entire right to vote upon or with respect to all shares of Preferred and/or Common Stock deposited, or at any time held hereunder, and the right to otherwise authorize, approve or oppose on behalf of said shares of stock any corporate action of The Baltimore Transit Company shall be vested exclusively in said Trustees; without limiting the generality or scope of the foregoing provisions such rights shall include the right to vote or act with respect to any amendment of the certificate of incorporation of the Company, the increase, reduction, classification, reclassification of its capital stock, change in the par value, preference and restrictions and qualifications of all shares, the creation of any debts or liens, any amendment to the By–Laws, the election or removal of directors, the acceptance of stock in payment of dividends as well as every other right of an absolute owner of said shares, * * *

Briefly, the amendment effected several changes in voting rights. It eliminated the arrearage clause which had provided for exclusive voting rights in the preferred stock. It also granted voting rights to the holders of debentures, one vote for each $100 principal amount of the debentures, thus creating approximately 221,000 new votes eligible to be cast in all corporate matters. And, further, as of the date of termination of the voting trust agreement on July 1, 1945, the common stockholders would be deprived of their exclusive right to elect one director.

These facts are all substantially set forth in plaintiff's complaint. The complaint alleges, and for purposes of the motion to dismiss these allegations must be accepted as true, that the creation of 221,000 new votes in the debentures will dilute the voting power of the stock; that the amendment will deprive the voting trust certificate holders of their right to control the management of the Company, and the election of its directors after the expiration of the voting trust; that these voting trustees are holders of substantial amounts of debentures, either in their own right, or as officers of various banks.

Plaintiff contends that the action of the voting trustees in adopting the amendment was a breach of the fiduciary duty owed to the certificate holders and seeks fourfold relief that: (1) The amendment of June 21, 1944, be declared null and void; (2) the voting trustees be removed; (3) the voting trust be terminated; and (4) damages be allowed in the alternative.

The crux of the complaint is that the voting trustees, faced with the fact that the voting trust would shortly expire and that they would no longer be able to control the corporation, proceeded to amend its charter so that they would be able to hold on to the control by giving voting rights to the debentures (thereby enhancing the value of these debentures) which were largely owned or controlled by them or by corporations in which they were interested and to take away from the preferred stock the power of control which resided in it when dividends were in arrears. * * *

Plaintiff contends that such action on the part of the trustees was invalid for three reasons: (1) Because it was beyond the powers vested in the trustees to diminish the voting power, which they held in trust for the holders of preferred stock as well as for other stockholders and debenture holders, so that upon the termination of the trust they would not be able to return it to those from whom they had received it in the same condition in which it was received; (2) because it was an abuse of trust to use the voting power which the trustees held in trust for the benefit of preferred stockholders as well as of the debenture holders to the advantage of the latter and the detriment of the former; and (3) that it was an abuse of trust to use the voting power for their own benefit and the benefit of corporations in which they were interested and to the detriment of preferred stockholders who were beneficiaries of the trust. We think the action of the trustees was invalid for all three reasons. As to the third reason, it could well be that the evidence at the trial may show the facts to be different from the facts as alleged. There seems to be no dispute as to the facts to which the first and second reasons apply.

As to the first and second reasons, we think it perfectly clear that it was not intended by the voting trust agreement to vest the trustees with power either to impair the voting power of the preferred stock which they held in trust or to use the power for the benefit of the debenture holders and to the detriment of the holders of preferred stock. It is true that the power to amend the charter for proper purposes was conferred upon them; but at the time of the creation of the voting trust it was not permissible under the law to vest voting power in the debenture holders. An amendment of the law made it legal to do this; but it could not have been intended at the time of the creation of the voting trust that the trustees should exercise the voting power in a way which the law did not then recognize and which would result in taking from the holders of stock a part of the very power which they had conferred upon the trustees to be held in trust for their benefit. It is elementary that a trustee may not exercise powers granted in a way that is detrimental to the cestuis que trustent; nor may one who is trustee for different classes favor one class at the expense of another. Such an exercise of power is in derogation of the trust and may not be upheld, even though the thing done be within the scope of powers granted to the trustees in general terms. It is well settled that the depositaries of the power to vote stock are trustees in the equitable sense, Henry L. Doherty & Co. v. Rice, C.C., 186 F. 204, 214, and a voting trust is a trust in the accepted equitable view. * * *

Defendants strongly urge that the real beneficiaries here and now are the debenture holders and not the certificate holders. Such cases as Mackin v. Nicollet Hotel, 8 Cir., 25 F.2d 783, and Clark v. Foster, 98 Wash. 241, 167 P. 908, are cited for the proposition that it is the existence of a voting trust, in many cases restricting the powers of the stockholder, that attracts lending by bondholders. Assuming the correctness of this contention, we still find no such situation here. This plan of reorganization was an attempt to salvage utility companies sinking in the quagmire of bankruptcy. These debenture holders accepted, in lieu of their old obligations, two kinds of property, ownership of the company and a creditor's lien. Ownership control, for purposes of judicious management, was placed in the hands of trustees. When the debenture holders sold their ultimate rights to stock ownership with its attendant control of the Company's affairs, they retained only their creditor's lien. We are not at liberty here to distort the established rules of property and to find that by some process of corporate alchemy the legal ownership of the Company has been transmuted into evidence of debt.

The sale of the voting trust certificates by the original holders vested all equitable rights in their transferees and we cannot say that one might sell the equitable rights in preferred stock to a bona fide purchaser, and subsequently by indirection, impair or destroy the inherent equitable property in those certificates, to the benefit of the original seller. Meinhard v. Salmon, 249 N.Y. 458, 464, 164 N.E. 545, 62 A.L.R. 1. * * *

We are of the opinion, and so hold, that the action taken by these trustees was beyond the limit of their authority. The motion to dismiss should therefore have been denied.

The judgment of the District Court will be reversed and the cause remanded for further proceedings in accordance with the views herein expressed. The amendment to the charter of June 21, 1944 should be declared void, but what further relief should be granted upon the complaint is a matter resting in the sound discretion of the District Court.

Reversed and remanded.

Notes

(1) Consider MBCA § 7.30. An earlier version of the Delaware voting trust statute, Del.Gen.Corp.Law § 218 is set forth in *Ringling Bros.*, page 448–9, supra. It is important to recognize that the procedural requirements with respect to the creation of a voting trust—particularly the filing of a copy of the voting trust agreement with the corporation—is essential for the validity of a voting trust. This rule is a reflection of the fact that the early attitude of courts to voting trusts was unfavorable, and mistrust may still continue to some extent in some states. The comment of Mr. Justice Douglas (in a nonjudicial context) that a voting trust is "little more than a vehicle for corporate kidnapping," William O. Douglas, Democracy and Finance 43 (1940), is a clear reflection of this early attitude. The Securities and Exchange Commission has historically opposed the use of voting trusts, and the New York Stock Exchange refuses to list voting stock where there exists "a voting trust, irrevocable proxy, or any similar arrangement to which the company or any of its officers or directors is a party, either directly or indirectly."

(2) There has been some recognition that a voting trust should be viewed as simply another control mechanism that may in certain situations be the subject of abuse but generally is no more subject to criticism than other control devices. This perspective is most clearly set forth in Oceanic Exploration Co. v. Grynberg, 428 A.2d 1, 7–8 (Del.1981):

> It is important to recognize that there has been a significant change from the days of our original 1925 statute. Voting trusts were viewed with "disfavor" or "looked upon with indulgence" by the courts. Other contractual arrangements interfering with stock ownership, such as irrevocable proxies, were viewed with suspicion. The desire for flexibility in modern society has altered such restrictive thinking. The trend of liberalization was markedly apparent in the 1967 changes to our own § 218. Voting or other agreements and irrevocable proxies were given favorable treatment and restrictive judicial interpretations as to the absolute voiding of voting trusts for terms beyond the statutory limit were changed by statute. The trend was not to extend the

voting trust restrictions beyond the class of trust being regulated and beyond the reasons for statutory regulation.

Most voting trust statutes, like § 7.30 of the MBCA mandates a ten year life span for voting trusts. Compare this section with § 7.29, which has no maximum period for the existence of a voting trust. In 1994, Delaware amended its voting trust statute to eliminate the 10–year provision, perhaps a further recognition that the early attitude towards voting trusts was misplaced.

(3) Brown v. McLanahan involves the use of a voting trust in a newly reorganized corporation where the old debenture holders and others in control of the reorganized corporation presumably have no prior management experience. Could a pooling agreement have worked in that situation? What other situations dictate the use of a voting trust rather than the more informal pooling agreement?

(a) A voting trust may be used, of course, as a control device. For example, the oldest child of the sole shareholder of a business who has recently died leaving several heirs may wish to try to run the business for a period of time free of sibling rivalry or criticism. The other children may be willing to give such a person an opportunity to try, and may place their shares in a voting trust for a temporary period. Of course, the sole shareholder before his death may create a voting trust in order to effectuate exactly the same purpose.

(b) Creditors may insist that controlling shares be placed in a voting trust as a condition to the extension of credit. The most spectacular illustration of this was the voting trust in which creditors of Trans World Airlines, Inc. required Howard Hughes to place his 75 percent of TWA stock in 1966 as a condition to making loans of over $80 million to finance the purchase of jumbo jets. After the trust was created, Hughes had no voice in TWA management, and that corporation brought suit against Hughes Tool Company and Hughes individually for damages under the antitrust laws for conduct occurring prior to the voting trust. Who was the *cestui* of that voting trust under Brown v. McLanahan? Hughes later agreed to sell the shares of TWA in the voting trust, and this sale took place when TWA was near its historic high in price. Mr. Hughes received a check for $546,549,771 from this sale. See John McDonald, Howard Hughes's Biggest Surprise, Fortune, July 1, 1966, at 119–20. Despite the sale, the antitrust suit continued. Major stopping points include Trans World Airlines, Inc. v. Hughes, 332 F.2d 602 (2d Cir.1964), cert. dismissed as improvidently granted 380 U.S. 248, 85 S.Ct. 934, 13 L.Ed.2d 817 (1965), upholding the entry of a default judgment for the refusal of Hughes Tool Company to submit to discovery and, particularly, the refusal of Howard Hughes to submit to a deposition, and Trans World Airlines, Inc. v. Hughes, 449 F.2d 51 (2d Cir.1971) affirming the entry of a judgment for $137,611,435.95 and the ultimate reversal of the case by the United States Supreme Court on a ground that had been repeatedly argued but never accepted during approximately 10 years of litigation. Hughes Tool Co. v. Trans World Airlines, Inc., 409 U.S. 363, 93 S.Ct. 647, 34 L.Ed.2d 577 (1973), rehearing denied 410 U.S. 975, 93 S.Ct. 1435, 35 L.Ed.2d 707 (1973).

(c) Regulatory agencies may insist that voting control of a regulated corporation be placed in a voting trust as a condition for permitting private parties to acquire the regulated corporation or, more commonly, the parent corporation of a regulated corporation when the corporation is a relatively small portion of the parent's business. For example, § 102(a) of the Interstate Transportation Act, 49 U.S.C.A. § 11323(a), provides that certain acquisitions of rail carriers may only be carried out with the approval and authorization of the Surface Transportation Board. For an example of the use of the voting trust under a predecessor section, see Chicago West Pullman Corporation and Chicago West Pullman Transportation Corporation, Finance Docket No. 31390, 1989 WL 237934 (I.C.C. Feb. 21, 1989). The Federal Communications Commission follows a somewhat similar practice with respect to transfers of holders of radio or television licenses. Some state insurance commissions permit transfers of control of regulated insurance companies if the shares are placed in an irrevocable voting trust with acceptable trustees.

(4) In Hall v. Staha, 303 Ark. 673, 800 S.W.2d 396 (1990), Hatfield and Staha formed a Delaware limited partnership, MED–MAX Associates Limited Partnership, and transferred their stock in Dunhall Pharmaceuticals, Inc., a profitable seller of pharmaceuticals, to the limited partnership. The limited partnership also obtained Dunhall shares from a number of other shareholders in exchange for limited partnership interests; Hatfield and Staha also transferred some shares in exchange for limited partnership interests. MED–MAX ultimately acquired 50.5 percent of the Dunhall stock. While Hatfield and Staha were the general partners, there was no disclosure of the identity of the limited partners. The Court held that MED–MAX was an illegal voting trust since it was a "secret, uncontrolled, combination[] of stockholders formed to acquire voting control of a corporation to the possible detriment of the nonparticipating stockholders." 800 S.W.2d at 402. The votes cast by MED–MAX at a shareholders' meeting were invalidated. Is there any reason why a limited partnership cannot be a voting trust?

LEHRMAN v. COHEN

Supreme Court of Delaware, 1966.
43 Del.Ch. 222, 222 A.2d 800.

HERRMANN, JUSTICE.

The primary problem presented on this appeal involves the applicability of the Delaware Voting Trust Statute. Other questions involve the legality of stock having voting power but no dividend or liquidation rights except repayment of par value, and an alleged unlawful delegation of directorial duties and powers.

These are the material facts:

Giant Food Inc. (hereinafter the "Company") was incorporated in Delaware in 1935 by the defendant N.M. Cohen and Samuel Lehrman, deceased father of the plaintiff Jacob Lehrman. From its inception, the Company was controlled by the Cohen and Lehrman families, each of which owned equal quantities of the voting stock, designated Class AC (held by the Cohen family) and Class AL (held by the Lehrman family) common stock. The two classes of stock have cumulative voting rights and each is entitled to elect two members of the Company's four-member board of directors.

Over the years, as may have been expected, there were differences of opinion between the Cohen and Lehrman families as to operating policies of the Company. Samuel Lehrman died in 1949; each of his children inherited part of his stock in the Company; but a dispute arose among the children regarding an *inter vivos* gift of certain shares made to the plaintiff by his father shortly before his death. To eliminate the Lehrman family dispute and its possible disruption of the affairs of the Company, an arrangement was made which settled the dispute and permitted the plaintiff to acquire all of the outstanding Class AL stock, thereby vesting in him voting power equal to that held by the Cohen family. The arrangement involved repurchase by the Company of the stock held by the plaintiff's brothers and sister, their relinquishment of any claim to the stock gift, and an equalizing surrender of certain stock by the Cohens to the Company for retirement. An essential part of the arrangement, upon the insistence of the Cohens, was the establishment of a fifth directorship to obviate the risk of deadlock which would have continued if the equal division of voting power between AL and AC stock were continued.

To implement the arrangement, on December 31, 1949, the Company's certificate of incorporation was amended, *inter alia,* to create a third class of voting stock, designated Class AD common stock, entitled to elect the fifth director. Article Fourth of the amendment to the certificate of incorporation provided for the issuance of one share of Class AD stock, having a par value of $10. and the following rights and powers:

> The holder of Class AD common stock shall be entitled to all of the rights and privileges pertaining to common stock without any limitations, prohibitions, restrictions or qualifications except that the holder of said Class AD stock shall not be entitled to receive any dividends declared and paid by the corporation, shall not be entitled to share in the distribution of assets of the corporation upon liquidation or dissolution either partial or final, except to the extent of the par value of said Class AD common stock, and in the election of Directors shall have the right to vote for and elect one of the five Directors hereinafter provided for.

> The corporation shall have the right, at any time, to redeem and call in the Class AD stock by paying to the holder thereof the par value of said stock, provided however, that such redemption or call shall be authorized and directed by the affirmative vote of four of the five Directors hereinafter provided for.[14]

By resolution of the board of directors, the share of Class AD stock was issued forthwith to the defendant Joseph B. Danzansky, who had served as counsel to the Company since 1944. All corporate action regarding the creation and the issuance of the Class AD stock was accomplished by the unanimous vote of the AC and AL stockholders and of the board of directors. In April 1950, pursuant to the arrangement, Danzansky voted his share of AD stock to elect himself as the Company's fifth director; and he served as such until the institution of this action in 1964. During that entire period, the AC and AL stock have been voted to elect two directors each. From 1950 through 1964, Danzansky regularly attended board meetings, raised and discussed general items of business, and voted on all issues as they came before the board. He

---

14. [By the Court] Article Fourth of the amendment also co-related the Class AL and the Class AC common stock as follows:

"The holders of Class AL common stock shall be entitled to all of the rights and privileges pertaining to common stock without any limitations, prohibitions, restrictions, or qualifications except that the holder or holders of said Class AL common stock, in the election of Directors, shall have the right to vote for and elect two of the five Directors hereinafter provided for.

The holders of Class AC common stock shall be entitled to all of the rights and privileges pertaining to common stock without any limitations, prohibitions, restrictions, or qualifications except that the holder or holders of said Class AC common stock, in the election of Directors, shall have the right to vote for and elect two of the five Directors hereinafter provided for."

was not obliged to break any deadlock among the directors prior to October 1, 1964 because no such deadlock arose before that date.

Beginning in December 1959, 200,000 shares of non-voting common stock of the Company were sold in a public issue for over $3,000,000. Each prospectus published in connection with the public issue contained the following statement:

> "Common Stock AD is not a participating stock, and the only purpose for the provision and issuance of such stock is to prevent a deadlock in case the Directors elected by the Common Stock AC and the Directors elected by the Common Stock AL cannot reach an agreement."

Similarly, a letter on behalf of the Company to the Commissioner of Internal Revenue, dated July 15, 1959, contained the following statement:

> As can be seen from the enclosed certified copy of the stock provisions of the certificate of Incorporation, as amended, the Class AD common stock is not a participating stock, the only purpose for the provision and issuance of such a stock being to prevent a deadlock in case the AC and AL Directors cannot reach an agreement.

From the outset and until October 1, 1964, the defendant N.M. Cohen was president of the Company. On that date, a resolution was adopted at the Company's annual stockholders' meeting to give Danzansky a fifteen year executive employment contract at an annual salary of $67,600, and options for 25,000 shares of the non-voting common stock of the Company. The AC and AD stock were voted in favor and the AL stock was voted against the resolution. At a directors meeting held the same day, Danzansky was elected president of the Company by a 3–2 vote, the two AL directors voting in opposition. On December 11, 1964, Danzansky resigned as director and voted his share of AD stock to elect as the fifth director Millard F. West, Jr., a former AL director and investment banker whose firm was one of the underwriters of the public issue of the Company's stock. The newly constituted board ratified the election of Danzansky as president; and, on January 27, 1965, after the commencement of this action and after a review and report by a committee consisting of the new AD director and one AL director, Danzansky's employment contract was approved and adopted with certain modifications.

The plaintiff brought this action on December 11, 1964, basing it upon two claims: The First Claim charges that the creation, issuance, and voting of the one share of Class AD stock resulted in an arrangement illegal under the law of this State for the reasons hereinafter set forth. The Second Claim, addressed to the events of October 1, 1964, charges that the election of Danzansky as president of the Company and his employment contract violated the terms of the 1959 deadlock-breaking arrangement, as made between the holders of the AC and AL stock, and constituted breaches of contract and fiduciary duty. The plaintiff and the defendants filed cross-motions for summary judgment as to the First Claim. The Court of Chancery, after considering the contentions now before us and discussed infra, granted summary judgment in favor of the defendants and denied the plaintiff's motion for summary judgment. The plaintiff appeals.

I.

The plaintiff's primary contention is that the Class AD stock arrangement is, in substance and effect, a voting trust; that, as such, it is illegal because not limited to a ten year period as required by the Voting Trust Statute. The defendants deny that the AD stock arrangement constitutes a disguised voting trust; but they concede that if it is, the arrangement is illegal for violation of the Statute. Thus, issue is clearly joined on the point.

The criteria of a voting trust under our decisions have been summarized by this Court in Abercrombie v. Davies, 36 Del.Ch. 371, 130 A.2d 338 (1957). The tests there set forth, accepted by both sides of this cause as being applicable,[15] are as follows: (1) the voting rights of the stock are separated from the other attributes of ownership; (2) the voting rights granted are intended to be irrevocable for a definite period of time; and (3) the principal purpose[16] of the grant of voting rights is to acquire voting control of the corporation.

Adopting and applying these tests, the plaintiff says, as to the first element, that the AD arrangement provides for a divorcement of voting rights from beneficial ownership of the AC and AL stock; that the creation and issuance of the share of AD stock is tantamount to a pooling by the AC and AL stockholders of a portion of their voting stock and giving it to a trustee, in the person of the AD stockholder, to vote for the election of the fifth director; that after the creation of the AD stock, the AC and AL stockholders each hold but 40% of the voting power, and the AD stockholder holds the controlling balance of 20%; that the AD stock has no property rights except the right to a return of the $10. paid as the par value; and that, therefore, there has been a transfer of the voting rights devoid of any participating property rights. So runs the argument of the plaintiff in support of his contention that the first of the *Abercrombie* criteria for a voting trust is met.

The contention is unacceptable. The AD arrangement did not separate the voting rights of the AC or the AL stock from the other attributes of ownership of those classes of stock. Each AC and AL stockholder retains complete control over the voting of his stock; each can vote his stock directly; no AL or AC stockholder is divested of his right to vote his stock as he sees fit; no AL or AC stock can be voted against the shareholder's wishes; and the AL and AC stock continue to elect two directors each.

The AD stock arrangement, as we view it, became a part of the capitalization of the Company. The fact that there is but a single share, or that the par value is nominal, is of no legal significance; the one share and the $10. par value might have been multiplied many times over, with the same consequence. It is true that the creation of the separate class of AD stock may have

15. [By the Court] While the tests and criteria set forth in the *Abercrombie* case prevail, its facts are entirely different. There, several stockholders, each representing a minority interest, agreed to place their stock in escrow for a period of ten years, in exchange for stock receipts, for the purpose of acquiring voting control of the corporation. Agents were appointed and, by irrevocable proxies, the agents were given joint and several voting rights and sole power of decision; no stockholder retained the right to vote his own stock. On those facts, an attempt having been thus made to separate the vote from the stock, this Court held that the stockholders had created a voting trust subject to the controls and limitations of § 218.

16. [By the Court] It is noteworthy, in this connection, that in Abercrombie, this Court distinguished between purpose and motive, stating that it considered only purpose to be material (130 A.2d 338, 341).

diluted the voting *power* which had previously existed in the AC and AL stock—the usual consequence when additional voting stock is created—but the creation of the new class did not divest and separate the voting *rights* which remain vested in each AC and AL shareholder, together with the other attributes of the ownership of that stock. The fallacy of the plaintiff's position lies in his premise that since the voting power of the AC and AL stock was reduced by the creation of the AD stock, the percentage of reduction became the *res* of a voting trust. In any recapitalization involving the creation of additional voting stock, the voting power of the previously existing stock is diminished; but a voting trust is not necessarily the result.

Since the holders of the Class AC and Class AL stock of the Company did not separate the voting rights from the other attributes of ownership of those classes when they created the Class AD stock, the first *Abercrombie* test of a voting trust is not met.

This conclusion disposes of the second and third *Abercrombie* tests, i.e., that the voting rights granted are irrevocable for a definite period of time, and that the principal object of the grant of voting rights is voting control of the corporation. Having held that the AC and AL stockholders have not divested themselves of their voting rights, although they may have diluted their voting powers, we do not reach the remaining *Abercrombie* tests, both of which assume the divestiture of voting rights.

In the final analysis, the essence of the question raised by the plaintiff in this connection is this: Is the substance and purpose of the AD stock arrangement sufficiently close to the substance and purpose of § 218 to warrant its being subjected to the restrictions and conditions imposed by that Statute? The answer is negative not only for the reasons above stated, but also because § 218 regulates trusts and pooling agreements amounting to trusts, not other and different types of arrangements and undertakings possible among stockholders. Compare Ringling Bros.–Barnum & Bailey Combined Shows Inc. v. Ringling, 29 Del.Ch. 610, 53 A.2d 441 (1947); Abercrombie v. Davies, supra. The AD stock arrangement is neither a trust nor a pooling agreement.

We hold, therefore, that the Class AD stock arrangement is not controlled by the Voting Trust Statute.

II.

The plaintiff's second point is that even if the Class AD stock arrangement is not a voting trust in substance and effect, the AD stock is illegal, nevertheless, because the creation of a class of stock having voting rights only, and lacking any substantial participating proprietary interest in the corporation, violates the public policy of this State as declared in § 218.

The fallacy of this argument is twofold: First, it is more accurate to say that what the law has disfavored, and what the public policy underlying the Voting Trust Statute means to control, is the separation of the vote from the stock—not from the stock ownership. Clearly, the AD stock arrangement is not violative of that public policy. Secondly, there is nothing in § 218, either expressed or implied, which requires that all stock of a Delaware corporation must have both voting rights and proprietary interests. Indeed, public policy to the contrary seems clearly expressed by 8 Del.C. § 151(a) which authorizes, in very broad terms, such voting powers and participating rights as may be stated in the certificate of incorporation. Non-voting stock is specifically authorized by § 151(a); and in the light thereof, consistency does not permit the conclusion, urged by the plaintiff, that the present public policy of this State condemns the separation of voting rights from beneficial stock ownership.

We conclude that the plaintiff's contention in this regard cannot withstand the force and effect of § 151(a). In our view, that Statute permits the creation of stock having voting rights only, as well as stock having property rights only. The voting powers and the participating rights of the Class AD stock being specified in the Company's certificate of incorporation, we are of the opinion that the Class AD stock is legal by virtue of § 151(a). * * *

We are told that if the AD stock arrangement is allowed thus to stand, our Voting Trust Statute will become a "dead letter" because it will be possible to evade and circumvent its purpose simply by issuing a class of non-participating voting stock, as was done here. We have three negative reactions to this argument:

First, it presupposes a divestiture of the voting rights of the AC and AL stock—an untenable supposition as has been stated. Secondly, it fails to take into account the main purpose of a Voting Trust Statute: to avoid secret, uncontrolled combinations of stockholders formed to acquire voting control of the corporation to the possible detriment of non-participating shareholders. It may not be said that the AD stock arrangement contravenes that purpose. Finally on this point, if we misconceive the legislative intent, and if the AD stock arrangement in this case reveals a loophole in § 218 which should be plugged, it is for the General Assembly to accomplish—not for us to attempt by interstitial judicial legislation.

III.

The plaintiff advances yet another reason for invalidating the AD stock. The essence of this argument is that the only function of that class of stock is to break directorial deadlocks; that the issuance of the AD stock is merely a technical device to permit that result; that, as such, it is illegal because it permits the AC and AL directors of the Company to delegate their statutory duties to the AD director as an arbitrator.

We see nothing inherently wrong or contrary to the public policy of this State, as plaintiff seems to suggest, about a device, otherwise lawful, designed by the stockholders of a corporation to break deadlocks of directors. The plaintiff says in this connection, that if public policy sanctioned such device, our General Corporation Law would provide for it. The fallacy of this argument lies in the assumption that legislative silence is a dependable indicator of public policy. We know of no reason, either under our statutes or our decisions, which would prevent the stockholders of a Delaware corporation from protecting themselves and their corporation, by a plan otherwise lawful, against the paralyzing and often fatal consequences of a stalemate in the directorate of the corporation. We hold, therefore, that the AD stock arrangement had a proper purpose.

As to the means adopted for the accomplishment of that purpose, we find the AD stock arrangement valid by virtue of § 141(a) of the Delaware Corporation Law which provides:

> "The business of every corporation organized under the provisions of this chapter shall be managed by a board of directors, except as hereinafter or in its certificate of incorporation otherwise provided."

The AD stock arrangement was created by the unanimous action of the stockholders of the Company by amendment to the certificate of incorporation. The stockholders thereby provided how the business of the corporation is to be managed, as is their privilege and right under § 141(a). It was this stockholder action which delegated to the AD director whatever powers and duties he possesses; they were not delegated to him by his fellow directors, either out of their own powers and duties, or otherwise.

It is settled, of course, as a general principle, that directors may not delegate their duty to manage the corporate enterprise. But there is no conflict with that principle where, as here, the delegation of duty, if any, is made not by the directors but by stockholder action under § 141(a), via the certificate of incorporation.

In our judgment, therefore, the AD stock arrangement is not invalid on the ground that it permits the AC and AL directors of the Company to delegate their statutory duties to the AD director.

On this point, the plaintiff relies mainly upon the Chancery Court decision in Abercrombie v. Davies, 35 Del.Ch. 599, 611, 123 A.2d 893 (1956). There, in considering an agreement requiring all eight directors to submit a disputed question to an arbitrator if seven were unable to agree, the Chancery Court stated that legal sanction may not be accorded to an agreement, at least when made by less than all the stockholders, which takes from the board of directors the power of determining substantial management policy. The plaintiff's reliance is misplaced, because, *inter alia,* the *Abercrombie* arrangement was not created by the certificate of incorporation, within the authority of § 141(a). * * *

Our conclusions upon these questions make it unnecessary to discuss the defendants' contentions that the plaintiff's action is barred by the principles of estoppel, laches, acquiescence and ratification.

Finding no error in the judgment below, it is affirmed.

Notes

(1) In accord is Stroh v. Blackhawk Holding Corp., 48 Ill.2d 471, 272 N.E.2d 1 (1971), where a corporation, before selling Class A shares to the public at $4.00 per share, created 500,000 shares of voting Class B stock which had no right to dividends and no rights on dissolution. These shares, constituting 28.78 percent of the voting stock, were sold to the promoters for ¼ cent per share. The Court upheld the validity of the Class B shares over the dissent of Justice Schaefer, who accused the majority of stating "that the ownership incidents of ownership may be eliminated. What remains, then, is a disembodied right to manage the assets of a corporation, divorced from any financial interest in those assets except such as may accrue from the power to manage them. In my opinion, what is left after the economic rights are 'removed and eliminated' is not a share of corporate stock under the law of Illinois." 272 N.E.2d at 8.

(2) Is not the decision in the principal case correct since it is not possible to draw a line between the permissible and the impermissible?

(3) Other cases support the ability of Delaware corporations to create unusual share voting patterns:

(a) Providence and Worcester Co. v. Baker, 378 A.2d 121 (Del.1977). The corporation's certificate of incorporation provided that a shareholder was entitled to (i) one vote per share for each share he owned up to fifty shares and (ii) one vote for every twenty shares he owned in excess of fifty, but (iii) no shareholder might vote more than one fourth of all the outstanding shares. The Court upheld this voting arrangement under the Delaware statute. These voting restrictions, it should be noted, did not limit the power of persons to cast large numbers of votes by proxy but rather limited the voting power of individual owners of shares. Would this voting arrangement be upheld under the last sentence of MBCA § 6.01(a)?

(b) Williams v. Geier, 671 A.2d 1368 (Del.1996) upheld a "tenure voting" plan by a 3–2 vote. Under this plan each share of common stock of Cincinnati Milacron, Inc. on the date the plan was implemented became entitled to 10 votes. However, if a share was sold or transferred thereafter, its voting power was immediately reduced to one vote per share; if the new holder retained the share for three years, it resumed being entitled to 10 votes per share. A family group owned more than 50 percent of Milacron, a publicly held corporation, but only three of the ten directors were associated with the family group. The stated reasons for recommending this plan was (a) provide current and longer-term shareholders with a greater voice in the company, (b) permit the issuance of additional shares of common stock with minimal dilution of voting rights, and (c) discourage takeovers. Tenure voting clearly benefits a controlling family group in this situation, since it not only discourages takeovers but also deters transfers of shares by individual members of that group.

LING AND CO. v. TRINITY SAV. AND LOAN ASS'N

Supreme Court of Texas, 1972.
482 S.W.2d 841.

REAVLEY, JUSTICE.

Trinity Savings and Loan Association sued Bruce W. Bowman for the balance owed on a promissory note and also to foreclose on a certificate for 1500 shares of Class A Common Stock in Ling & Company, Inc. pledged by Bowman to secure payment of the note. Ling & Company was made a party to the suit by Trinity Savings and Loan because of Ling & Company's insistence that the transfer of its stock was subject to restrictions that were unfulfilled. Bowman did not appear and has not appealed from the judgment against him. The trial court entered summary judgment in favor of Trinity Savings and Loan, against the contentions of Ling & Company, foreclosing the security interest in the stock and ordering it sold. The court of civil appeals affirmed. 470 S.W.2d 441. We reverse the judgments and remand the case to the trial court.

The objection to the foreclosure and public sale of this stock is based upon restrictions imposed upon the transfer of the stock by the articles of incorporation of Ling & Company. It is conceded that no offer of sale has been made to the other holders of this class of stock and that the approval of the pledge of the stock has not been obtained from the New York Stock Exchange. It is the position of Trinity Savings and Loan that all of the restrictions upon the transfer of any interest in this stock are invalid and of no effect. This has been the holding of the courts below.

The face and back of the stock certificate are reproduced and attached to this opinion.

The restrictions appear in Article Four of the Ling & Company articles of incorporation, as amended and filed with the Secretary of State in 1968. Section D requires the holder to obtain written approval of the New York Stock Exchange prior to the sale or encumbrance of the stock if, at the time, Ling & Company is a member corporation of the Exchange. Then Section E(4) prevents the sale of the stock without first affording the corporation the opportunity to buy and, if it fails to purchase, giving that opportunity to all holders of the same class of stock. The method of computation of the price, based upon the corporate books, is provided in this section of the articles.

The court of civil appeals struck down the restrictions for [two] reasons: the lack of conspicuous notice thereof on the stock certificate, [and] the unreasonableness of the restrictions, * * *.

CONSPICUOUSNESS

The Texas Business Corporation Act as amended in 1957, V.A.T.S.Bus. Corp.Act, art. 2.22, subd. A, provides that a corporation may impose restrictions on the transfer of its stock if they are "expressly set forth in the articles of incorporation * * * and * * * copied at length or in summary form on the face or so copied on the back and referred to on the face of each certificate * * *" Article 2.19, subd. F, enacted by the Legislature at the same time, permits the incorporation by reference on the face or back of the certificate of the provision of the articles of incorporation which restricts the transfer of the stock. The court of civil appeals objected to the general reference to the articles of incorporation and the failure to print the full conditions imposed upon the transfer of the shares. However, reference is made on the face of the certificate to the restrictions described on the reverse side; the notice on the reverse side refers to the particular article of the articles of incorporation as restricting the transfer or encumbrance and requiring "the holder hereof to grant options to purchase the shares represented hereby first to the Corporation and then pro rata to the other holders of the Class A Common Stock * * *" We hold that the content of the certificate complies with the requirements of the Texas Business Corporation Act.

There remains the requirement of the Texas [Uniform Commercial] Code that the restriction or reference thereto on the certificate must be conspicuous. Sec. [8–204] requires that a restriction on transferability be "noted conspicuously on the security." Sec. [1–201(10)] defines "conspicuous" and makes the determination a question of law for the court to decide. It is provided that a conspicuous term is so written as to be noticed by a reasonable person. Examples of conspicuous matter are given there as a "printed heading in capitals * * * [or] larger or other contrasting type or color." This means that something must appear on the face of the certificate to attract the attention of a reasonable person when he looks at it. 1 Anderson, Uniform Commercial Code 87 (2nd ed. 1970). The line of print on the face of the Ling & Company certificate does not stand out and cannot be considered conspicuous.

Our holding that the restriction is not noted conspicuously on the certificate does not entitle Trinity Savings and Loan to a summary judgment under this record. Sec. [8–204] provides that the restriction is effective against a person with actual knowledge of it. The record does not establish conclusively that Trinity Savings and Loan lacked knowledge of the restriction on January 28, 1969, the date the record indicates when Bowman executed an assignment of this stock to Trinity Savings and Loan.

Reasonableness

Art. 2.22, subd. A of the Texas Business Corporation Act provides that a corporation may impose restrictions on disposition of its stock if the restrictions "do not unreasonably restrain or prohibit transferability." The court of civil appeals has held that the restrictions on the transferability of this stock are unreasonable for two reasons: because of the required approval of the New York Stock Exchange and because of successive options to purchase given the corporation and the other holders of the same class of stock.

Ling & Company in its brief states that it was a brokerage house member of the New York Stock Exchange at an earlier time and that Rule 315 of the Exchange required approval of any sale or pledge of the stock. Under these circumstances we must disagree with the court of civil appeals holding that this provision of article 4D of the articles of incorporation is "arbitrary, capricious, and unreasonable." Nothing appears in the summary judgment proof on this matter, and the mere provision in the article is no cause for vitiating the restrictions as a matter of law.

It was also held by the intermediate court that it is unreasonable to require a shareholder to notify all other record holders of Class A Common Stock of his intent to sell and to give the other holders a ten day option to buy. The record does not reveal the number of holders of this class of stock; we only know that there are more than twenty. We find nothing unusual or oppressive in these first option provisions. See 2 O'Neal, Close Corporations, § 7.13 (1971). Conceivably the number of stockholders might be so great as to make the burden too heavy upon the stockholder who wishes to sell and, at the same time, dispel any justification for contending that there exists a reasonable corporate purpose in restricting the ownership. But there is no showing of that nature in this summary judgment record. * * *

The summary judgment proof does not justify the holding that restrictions on the transfer of this stock were ineffective as to Trinity Savings and Loan Association. The judgment below is reversed and the cause is remanded to the trial court.

Daniel, J., concurs in result.

Incorporated Under the Laws of The State of Texas

NUMBER A 62   SHARES 1,500

LING & COMPANY, INC.

CLASS A COMMON STOCK PAR VALUE $0.10 PER SHARE

This Certifies That   BRUCE W. BOWMAN   *is the owner of*

One Thousand Five Hundred (1,500)--

fully paid and non-assessable shares of the Class A Common Stock of Ling & Company, Inc., a Texas corporation (the "Corporation"), such shares being of the par value of ten cents ($0.10) each, transferable only on the books of the Corporation by the holder hereof in person or by duly authorized attorney upon surrender of this certificate properly endorsed.

The shares represented by this certificate are subject to all the terms, conditions and provisions of the Articles of Incorporation of the Corporation, as the same may be amended from time to time, which Articles are incorporated herein by reference as though fully set forth herein. Copies of the Articles of Incorporation may be obtained from the Secretary of State of the State of Texas or upon written request therefor from the Secretary of the Corporation.

See reverse side hereof for specific reference to provisions setting forth preferences, limitations and restrictions.

IN WITNESS WHEREOF, the Corporation has caused this certificate to be signed by its duly authorized officers and to be sealed with the seal of the Corporation this 28th day of January 19 69.

Ray Pearce SECRETARY   *Arthur S. Mills* PRESIDENT

For Value Received_____ hereby sell, assign, and transfer unto_____

_____ *Shares*

of the Capital Stock represented by the within Certificate, and do hereby irrevocably constitute and appoint

_____ *Attorney*

to transfer the said Stock on the books of the within named Corporation with full power of substitution in the premises.

Dated_____ 19___

In presence of

NOTICE: The shares represented by this certificate are subject to all the terms, conditions and provisions of the Articles of Incorporation of the Corporation, as the same may be amended from time to time, which Articles are incorporated herein by reference as though fully set forth herein. Copies of the Articles of Incorporation may be obtained from the Secretary of State of the State of Texas or upon written request therefor from the Secretary of the Corporation. Reference is specifically made to the provisions of Article Four of the Articles of Incorporation which set forth the designations, preferences, limitations and relative rights of the shares of each class of capital stock authorized to be issued, which deny pre-emptive rights, prohibit cumulative voting, restrict the transfer, sale, assignment, pledge, hypothecation or encumbrance of any of the shares represented hereby under certain conditions, and which under certain conditions require the holder hereof to grant options to purchase the shares represented hereby first to the Corporation and then pro rata to the other holders of the Class A Common Stock, all as set forth in said Article Four. Reference is also specifically made to the provisions of Article Nine which vests the power to adopt, alter, amend or repeal the by-laws in the Board of Directors except to the extent such power may be modified or divested by action of shareholders representing a majority of the holders of the Class A Common Stock.

(A5715)

Notes

(1) Consider MBCA §§ 6.27, 1.40(3).

(2) Share transfer restrictions essentially constitute contractual obligations that limit the power of owners to freely transfer their shares. There are several different justifications for imposing share transfer restrictions, and the type of restriction imposed may depend on the objective. Consider MBCA § 6.27(c). What kinds of "status" are referred to in subsection (c)(1)? The Official Comment refers to election of close corporation status under an integrated close corporation statute, subchapter S, and "entitlement to a program or eligibility for a privilege administered by governmental agencies or national securities exchanges." Pre-

sumably, the share transfer restriction involved in *Ling* was of the latter type, designed to allow the New York Stock Exchange to police ownership interests in member firms. MBCA § 6.27(c)(3) also refers to "other reasonable purpose[s]"which presumably includes provisions in closely held corporations, designed to enable the owners to remain close, i.e., to select the persons with whom they will be associated in business, and to permit withdrawing participants to liquidate their investments on some reasonable basis. See the Waldbaum excerpt that follows.

(3) A variety of possible share transfer restrictions are described in MBCA § 6.27(d). In closely held corporations, the two most common types of restrictions are buy-sell agreements (see subsection (d)(1)) and option agreements (see subsection (d)(2)). An option does not guarantee the shareholder a specified price, whereas a buy-sell agreement does. The restrictions described in subsections (d)(3) and (d)(4) are potentially more onerous since they may prohibit all transfers to anyone at any price; it will be noted that they are valid only if the prohibition "is not manifestly unreasonable." Does it follow that (d)(1) and (d)(2) restrictions are valid even if they are "manifestly unreasonable"?

(4) Some share transfer restrictions in closely held corporations are phrased as rights of first refusal, giving the corporation or the shareholders an opportunity to meet the best price the shareholder has been able to obtain from outsiders. Do you think that this kind of restraint might "chill" the interest of outsiders in making offers for shares? Does such a provision give any real protection to a minority shareholder?

(5) Fender v. Prescott, 101 A.D.2d 418, 476 N.Y.S.2d 128 (1984) involved a buy-sell agreement under which "either party could offer to buy out the other, and, thereupon, the offeree had the option to elect to be either the purchaser or the seller in accordance with the terms of the offer." 476 N.Y.S.2d at 130. Is there any reason not to enforce this type of restraint?

(6) The traditional view is that share transfer restrictions constitute a restraint on alienation, and therefore are strictly construed. This attitude is changing. One case, for example, has described this attitude as "anachronistic." Bruns v. Rennebohm Drug Stores, Inc., 151 Wis.2d 88, 442 N.W.2d 591, 596 (App.1989). Nevertheless, because of this historic approach, it is important to specify clearly and unambiguously the essential attributes of the restrictions. This should include such matters as whether the purchase is optional or mandatory, the persons who may or must purchase the shares and the sequence in which they may purchase, the manner in which the price is to be determined, the time periods during which persons may decide whether or not to purchase (if an option), and the events (e.g., proposed sale, death, bankruptcy, family gift, etc.) which triggered the restriction. It has been held, for example, that a restriction against sales "to the public" does not prohibit a sale to another shareholder, or that a prohibition against an "officer-stockholder" does not cover a corporation owned by an officer-stockholder.

(7) Despite their wide use, there is not a great deal of recent litigation over the validity and enforceability of share transfer restrictions. In Joslin v. Shareholder Services Group, 948 F.Supp. 627 (S.D.Tex.1996), a written restriction on alienation printed on a stock certificates stated "NONE OF THE SHARES EVIDENCED BY THIS CERTIFICATE SHALL BE SOLD, TRANSFERRED, PLEDGED OR ASSIGNED WITHOUT THE PRIOR WRITTEN CONSENT OF THE COMPANY * * * ." Despite this language, John Pass, in whose name the certificate was registered, pledged the stock to a bank to secure a loan without the

consent of the Company. The loan was never paid, Pass went bankrupt, and the pledged certificate was later transferred (again apparently without the consent of the Company) to the FDIC and subsequently purchased by the plaintiff. Pass, the record owner of the shares, presented the Company with an apparently fraudulent affidavit that the certificate had been lost or stolen, and the issuer paid Pass $97,000 to reacquire and retire the shares. The plaintiff brought suit against the Company and Pass for a declaratory judgment that he was the owner of the shares in question, but lost when the court held that the legend on the certificate prevented the Bank, the FDIC, and the plaintiff from ever acquiring any interest in the shares. The court held that the legend made all unauthorized transfers "void" and therefore each holder had actual notice that the transfer was prohibited.

RODNEY J. WALDBAUM, BUY–SELL AGREEMENTS

The Practical Accountant, May/June 1972, at pp. 17–25.

One of the legal characteristics of a corporation is that it has perpetual existence. Yet, the death or withdrawal of a share-holder-officer in a small corporation is often followed by the demise of the business. *In many cases, this termination is due to the lack of an effective and fair buy-sell agreement.*

Take a fairly common situation: Tom, Dick and Harry are equal shareholders of a small corporation. They have no buy-sell agreement. But they do have a common interest in taking substantial risks and plowing as much of the earnings back into the business as they can afford in order to build for the future.

Tom dies and the interests of Tom's family become almost immediately antagonistic to those of Dick and Harry. While Dick and Harry still remain interested in the growth of the corporation, Tom's family needs security and a return from the business.

Almost without exception, closely held corporations do not pay dividends. So, unless Tom's family can provide some services to the corporation and thereby get on the payroll, the prospects for their receiving any return from Tom's shares are very poor indeed. Even if there were no unfavorable tax consequences, the surviving shareholders would be disinclined to pay dividends. The funds could be better used for corporate growth and a payout might require a reduction of their salaries.

The problem of what are fair salaries and what is a fair return on invested capital is a thorny one. It is a problem not likely to be satisfactorily solved by Tom's widow and the surviving shareholders.

Tom's widow, as a minority shareholder, now finds herself the proud owner of shares of stock from which she receives no return.

Would Tom's widow be in a secure position if she had inherited a controlling interest? Not necessarily. This fact offers no assurance that the business will continue, for Dick and Harry may well be unwilling to continue under such circumstances. Worse yet, they may well be capable of starting a competing business on their own.

If the corporation had elected Subchapter S treatment, then Dick and Harry may be justifiably concerned that the election will be terminated. If any of the transferees of Tom's shares refuse to consent to the election, or if

Tom's shares are transferred to several beneficiaries so that the number of shareholders is increased to more than [seventy-five], or if one of the transferees is a corporation, trust, partnership, or non-resident alien, then the Subchapter S status will be lost.

Frequently the only solution is for Tom's estate to sell his shares to the surviving shareholders. But there is an obvious conflict of interest between the survivors and Tom's family in establishing the price to be paid for the shares.

What are the magic ingredients in buy-sell agreements which solve these problems? There are two: First, bargaining positions are usually equal since none of the shareholders knows whether he will be on the buying end or the selling end of the agreement. Secondly, once there is an agreement everybody knows where he stands and can plan accordingly.

Finding a Fair Price. The key to any buy-sell agreement is, of course, the fairness of the price to be paid to the deceased shareholder's estate for his shares. Usually this price is determined in one of four ways:

(1) Use book value of the shares as of the date of death or the end of the preceding accounting period. The desirability of this method depends upon the extent market value corresponds to book value.

(2) Use a fixed price set out in the agreement, arrived at between the shareholders. This method works only if it is periodically reviewed and updated.

(3) Have the price fixed by appraisal after death. Two difficulties with this method are *uncertainty* and *delay*.

(4) Use a self-adjusting formula. There is no end to the formulas which can be used. * * *

Two Basic Agreements. There are two basic types of buy-sell agreements and there are substantial differences between them.

The first type is a cross-purchase agreement between the shareholders. Each shareholder agrees to personally purchase his proportionate share of the stock of the other shareholders in the event of their death, and binds his estate to sell the shares he owns to the surviving shareholders in proportion to their respective holdings. The capitalization of the corporation remains unchanged.

The second type is a stock-redemption agreement. The corporation becomes a party to the agreement as well as the shareholders. The corporation would agree to redeem or purchase the shares of the first shareholder to die, and each of the two shareholders would bind his estate to sell or tender for redemption the shares he owns. Upon the death of the first shareholder, the corporation buys his shares using corporate funds.

Both types of buy-sell agreements fix the price to be paid for the shares and specify the terms for payment. In addition to the two basic types of agreements, there are hybrid agreements which consist of both a cross-purchase agreement and a redemption agreement. For instance, if a corporation has two shareholders, each owning 100 shares of stock, there could be cross-purchase agreement with respect to 50 shares of stock and a stock-redemption agreement with respect to the remaining 50 shares.

In community property states buy-sell agreements always include the wife's community interest. Therefore, the wives of all the shareholders should be signatories to the agreement.

Which type of agreement is used usually depends upon where the money is. Where neither the corporation nor the shareholders have sufficient funds, the agreements are usually funded by insurance.

Whichever type of agreement is used, it should set forth the method of payment and the interest which will accrue on any deferred portion of the purchase price. As security for such deferred portion, a pledge of all the shares of the corporation, including those being purchased, may be required.

Cross-purchase agreements are deceptively simple. However, they have several practical disadvantages and are sometimes difficult to fund by insurance.

Their obvious disadvantage is that the shares of a deceased shareholder must be paid for with after-tax dollars of the surviving shareholders. Another disadvantage is that the obligation to purchase usually falls most heavily upon the shareholders least able to bear it.

Also although cross-purchase agreements are reasonably satisfactory where there are only a few shareholders, they become increasingly cumbersome as the number of shareholders increase. Consequently, many cross-purchase agreements are drafted to terminate upon the first death. * * *

In *stock-redemption agreements* the corporation itself buys back the deceased shareholder's shares using corporate funds. In some instances, the corporation may hold the shares as treasury stock rather than canceling them. For practical purposes, however, the results are the same.

[T]he stock-redemption agreement has several advantages. The most obvious is that corporate earnings and profits are being used for the benefit of shareholders without the usual dividend or tax cost result. Such agreements are also easier to handle where there are a number of shareholders.

However, there are some practical problems even in a simple unfunded redemption agreement.

One is whether the corporation will have sufficient surplus, as required by the laws of most states, to redeem the shares tendered by the estate of a deceased shareholder.

If not, there are several possible solutions: (1) the stockholders could agree to a change in the corporate capitalization so as to create the required surplus; (2) the shareholder could agree to contribute sufficient additional capital to allow redemptions; (3) the shareholders could agree to purchase such shares as the corporation is unable to redeem.

A more common problem is that the corporation cannot spare the necessary funds and still continue to operate efficiently.

One solution is for the corporation to fund its obligations by the purchase of insurance. Or, the corporation could distribute some of its assets, such as real estate, to the estate of the deceased shareholder and then lease them back. A third arrangement is to provide for the payments to the estate of the deceased shareholder to be spread over a period of years in the hope that the required funds can be provided out of future earnings. * * *

Notes

(1) The Prudential Life Insurance Company has prepared a set of sample forms for "Model Business Insurance Agreements" that it distributes free to attorneys. The Forward states:

> We deem it a Privilege to address these prefatory remarks to our friends in the legal profession, for whom this booklet is primarily intended. There is a growing awareness on the part of attorneys of the serious financial problems created by the untimely death of a successful businessman. Prudence demands that proper measures on sound legal advise be taken to formulate a plan that will effectively prevent disastrous economic results and provide for orderly disposition of business interests at death. In many cases, a carefully drawn Buy-and-Sell Agreement will prove to be an essential element of such a plan. Given a Buy-and-Sell Agreement it is apparent that life insurance is the ideal method of funding it.

(2) Consider the restrictions on corporate repurchases of stock set forth in MBCA § 6.40, discussed in Chapter 7, Section I, supra. Might they permit a corporation to refuse to redeem shares pursuant to a buy-sell agreement? If so, a carefully prepared estate plan may go awry. Is there any way to avoid these restrictions? Should the other shareholders be asked to bind themselves in advance to cause the corporation to meet the requirements of § 6.40 if possible? Should they be asked to guarantee the performance of the buy-sell agreement by the corporation? If so, how should such provisions be phrased? Would such an obligation have unfavorable tax consequences?

(3) Buy-sell agreements that are triggered by the death of a shareholder may raise serious estate tax problems for the decedent's estate. The stock is likely to be the principal asset in the estate and have considerable (but uncertain) value. The critical question is whether the amount received pursuant to the buy-sell agreement determines the value of the stock for estate tax purposes. Prior to 1990 this issue was largely governed by case law, but today is addressed by § 2703(b) of the Internal Revenue Code. In order for the buy-sell price to establish the value of the shares for estate tax purposes (1) the price must be either fixed or determinable and must have been reasonable when made; (2) the estate must be obligated to offer to sell the shares at the agreed price; (3) the obligation must have been binding on the decedent during his lifetime; (4) the agreement must be a bona fide business arrangement; (5) the agreement must not be a device to pass the decedent's share to the natural objects of his or her bounty for less than adequate and full consideration in money or money's worth (determined as of the date of the agreement), and (6) at the time the agreement was entered into it must be comparable to those of similar agreements entered into by persons in an arm's length transaction. If these requirements are not met it is quite possible that the Internal Revenue Service may seek a valuation for estate tax purposes considerably higher than the amount actually received by the estate as payment for the shares.

(4) Many close corporation situations continue to arise in which no buy-sell agreement exists despite the obvious advantages of such agreements. Should the legislature create a mandatory buy-out obligation in an integrated close corporation statute? In other words, what about including provisions in a close corporation statute analogous to the provisions of UPA (1914) that permit the estate of a deceased partner to have the value of the interest of the estate ascertained and paid to it? See page 00 supra. A few states have experimented with such provisions but they seem more controversial than in the partnership setting. How should the

price be set? A liquidation or book value may be inappropriate since minority shareholders usually cannot compel a dissolution; since there is no market for the shares, a statute will presumably have to provide a judicially determined fair price with the attendant costs and uncertainties. A judicial determination of fair price may lead to a price that is quite a bit higher than the maximum price the corporation might have been willing to pay for the shares on a voluntary basis or a price quite a bit lower than the shareholder would have accepted voluntarily. Is it reasonable to impose a mandatory buy-out obligation on a small business? If so, the threat of invoking a mandatory buy-out remedy at an inconvenient time may carry considerable weight. Might that not be one reason the corporate form, with its greater permanence, was originally chosen?

(5) Presumably, a mandatory dissolution upon demand of a single shareholder, analogous to a partnership, could be created by an appropriately drafted agreement. How might such an agreement be drafted to ensure that the required number of shareholders in fact vote for dissolution? A pooling agreement? A voting trust? An irrevocable proxy? A simple contractual agreement signed by all the shareholders that does not designate what voting device is to be employed to assure that there is an affirmative vote to dissolve? See Wilcox v. Stiles, 127 Or.App. 671, 873 P.2d 1102 (1994)[contractual agreement in two-person corporation (each owning 50 percent of the shares) required both parties to vote for dissolution in the event of a deadlock; one party refused to cooperate or participate in vote and questioned whether deadlock existed; other party then made offer to buy the non-cooperating partner's shares which the court viewed as reasonable and ordered specifically enforced].

(6) The Georgia integrated close corporation statute, Ga. Bus. Corp. Code § 14–2–933(a), provides: "The articles of incorporation, bylaws adopted by the shareholders, or an agreement among all the shareholders of a statutory close corporation may authorize one or more shareholders, or the holders of a specified number or percentage of shares of any class or series, to dissolve the corporation at will or upon the occurrence of a specified event or contingency." Would you recommend an electing close corporation take advantage of this section? If so, in what circumstances?

(7) Share transfer restrictions obviously may provide considerable protection to minority shareholders who may otherwise be frozen out of corporate affairs, to shareholders who retire, and to the heirs or devisees of deceased shareholders. Share transfer restrictions may also be designed, however, for the benefit of the corporation and its controlling shareholders who may wish to be able to eliminate undesired shareholders at attractive prices. Some restrictions appear to be designed to ensure that shares of highly profitable corporations owned by a relatively few family members remain in the hands of the family over one or more generations. A share transfer restriction with this goal in mind is drafted so as to cover gifts and bequests of shares as well as sales to third persons. The option to trigger the buy-sell obligation is vested in the corporation rather than the shareholder. And the price is likely to be set at a low and fixed level with no provision for adjustment based on the success of the corporation. Grandon v. Amcore Trust Co., 225 Ill.App.3d 630, 167 Ill.Dec. 670, 588 N.E.2d 311 (1992), cert. denied 146 Ill.2d 627, 176 Ill.Dec. 797, 602 N.E.2d 451 (1992), for example, involved the Sterling Gazette Company, a corporation owned by the Grandon family that had published the "Sterling Daily Gazette," a daily newspaper, since 1903. Thirty-three shares of the Sterling Gazette Company had left the Grandon family in the 1960s, when Preston Grandon, the majority shareholder at the time, gave them to his third wife, Marie, who in turn placed them in two trusts for the

benefit of her children from an earlier marriage. The share certificates received by Marie, those issued in her name, and the shares issued in the names of the trusts, all contained a restrictive legend that provided that the purchaser of the stock agreed to resell the stock to Sterling Gazette Company for $250 per share upon the shareholder's death or severance of his connection with the company. This legend setting a $250 price had been in effect since before 1964 (when Marie acquired the shares). In 1986, the company sought to acquire the shares from the trusts for $250 per share since manifestly the trusts and their beneficiaries had no connection with the company. The Court concluded that the restriction was unenforceable since there was no reference to a buy-sell agreement in the articles of incorporation or the bylaws, and the gift of the shares to Marie did not constitute acceptance by her of a buy-sell agreement. Presumably, $250 represented only a tiny fraction of the value of the shares in the Sterling Gazette Company in 1986. Cases such as this raise at least two basic questions. First, is there any reason to refuse to enforce a buy-sell agreement at a price that is so low that it bears no relationship to the potential value of shares? Second, may a corporation enforce such a buy-sell agreement selectively, applying it in the case of shares owned by persons other than family members and waiving it in the case of shares owned by family members?

(8) Many cases hold that a share transfer restriction is valid even though it compels a shareholder to sell shares at an arbitrary price that may not reflect the real value of the shares. See, e.g., Unigroup, Inc. v. O'Rourke Storage & Transfer Co., 980 F.2d 1217 (8th Cir.1992)(book value); In re Estate of Mather, 410 Pa. 361, 189 A.2d 586 (1963)(price of $1 per share upheld despite contention that shares were worth $1,060 per share); Allen v. Biltmore Tissue Corp., 2 N.Y.2d 534, 161 N.Y.S.2d 418, 141 N.E.2d 812 (1957)(repurchase at original price issued).

C. DEADLOCKS

GEARING v. KELLY

Court of Appeals of New York, 1962.
11 N.Y.2d 201, 227 N.Y.S.2d 897, 182 N.E.2d 391.

PER CURIAM.

Appellants, who own 50% of the stock of the Radium Chemical Company, Inc., seek, within the provisions of section 25 of the General Corporation Law, Consol.Laws, c. 23, to set aside the election of a director.

In a proceeding under that section, the court sits as a court of equity which may order a new election " as justice may require". We have concluded, as did the majority of the Appellate Division, that appellants have failed to show that justice requires a new election, in that they may not now complain of an irregularity which they themselves have caused.

Mrs. Meacham stayed away from the meeting of March 6, 1961 for the sole purpose of preventing a quorum from assembling, and intended, in that manner, to paralyze the board. There can be no doubt, and indeed it is not even suggested, that she lacked notice or any manner found it temporarily inconvenient to present herself at that particular time and place. It is certain, then, that Mrs. Meacham's absence from the noticed meeting of the board was intentional and deliberate. Much is said by appellants about a desire to protect their equal ownership of stock through equal representation on the board. It is, however, clear that such balance was voluntarily surrendered in 1955. Whether this was done in reliance on representations of Kelly, Sr., as alleged in the plenary suit, is properly a matter for that litigation, rather than the summary type of action here.

The relief sought by appellants, the ordering of a new election, would, furthermore, be of no avail to them, for Mrs. Meacham would then be required, as evidence of her good faith, to attend. Such a futile act will not be ordered.

The identity of interests of the appellants is readily apparent. Mrs. Gearing has fully indorsed and supported all of the demands and actions of her daughter, and has associated herself with the refusal to attend the directors' meeting. A court of equity need not permit Mrs. Gearing to attach actions of the board of directors which were marred through conduct of the director whom she has actively encouraged. To do so would allow a director to refuse to attend meetings, knowing that thereafter an associated stockholder could frustrate corporate action until all of their joint demands were met.

The failure of Mrs. Meacham to attend the directors' meeting, under the present circumstances, bars appellants from invoking an exercise of the equitable powers lodged in the courts under the statute.

The order appealed from should be affirmed, with costs.

FROESSEL, JUDGE (dissenting).

The bylaws of Radium Chemical Company, Inc., provided for a board of four directors, a majority of whom "shall constitute a quorum for the transaction of business". Prior to 1955 the board consisted of appellant Meacham, who had succeeded her father (appellant Gearing's late husband), respondent Kelly, Sr., and Margaret E. Lee. In 1955 Kelly, Jr., was elected to the then vacant directorship. The board continued thus until Margaret Lee offered her resignation in 1961 and, on March 6 of that year, at a meeting of the board of directors at which she and the two Kellys were present, her resignation was accepted. Thereupon the two Kellys elected Julian Hemphill, a son-in-law of Kelly, Sr., to replace Margaret Lee.

I agree with Justice Eager, who dissented in the Appellate Division, that two members of the board were insufficient to constitute a quorum in this case for the purpose of electing the new director. It necessarily follows that the election of Julian Hemphill is not merely irregular, as the majority hold, but is wholly void and must be set aside.

Section 25 of the General Corporation Law grants to the court two alternatives in a case such as this: (1) to confirm the election, or (2) to order a new election as justice may require (Matter of Faehndrich, 2 N.Y.2d 468, 474, 161 N.Y.S.2d 99, 104, 141 N.E.2d 597, 600). As we held in the case just cited, the clause "as justice may require" does not enlarge the court's power nor authorize it to grant different relief from that specified in the statute. There is no basis whatever here for the application of the doctrine of estoppel, and in no event could it reasonably be applied to the nondirector, appellant Gearing, a substantial stockholder in this corporation. The purported election is, therefore, a nullity.

This is a mere contest for control, and the court should not assist either side, each of which holds an equal interest in the corporation, particularly where, as here, petitioners were willing that director Meacham attend meetings for the purpose of transacting all the necessary business of the board, but were unwilling that she attend a meeting, the purpose of which was to strip them of every vestige of control. Appellant Meacham had surrendered nothing in 1955 when she permitted Kelly, Jr., to become a director as well as his father, for Margaret Lee was then a third director.

The statute mandates a new election and that should be ordered. It is no answer to say that the results will probably be the same. If the parties are deadlocked, whether as directors or stockholders, and choose to remain that way, they have other remedies, and I see no reason why we should help one side or the other by disregarding a bylaw that follows the statute (General Corporation Law, § 27), particularly when it results in giving the Kellys complete control of the corporation.

I would, therefore, reverse the order appealed from, and modify the order of Special Term by ordering a special election and affirming it in all other respects.

DESMOND, C.J., and FULD, VAN VOORHIS, BURKE and FOSTER, JJ., concur in Per Curiam opinion.

FROESSEL, J., dissents in an opinion in which DYE, J., concurs.

Notes

(1) Many state statutes relating to the filling of vacancies on the board of directors are based on the first sentence of MBCA (1969) § 38: "[a]ny vacancy occurring in the board of directors may be filled by the affirmative vote of a majority of the remaining directors though less than a quorum of the board of directors." If this statute had been in effect in New York at the time Gearing v. Kelly arose, would the Kellys need the presence of Mrs. Meacham in order to elect Hemphill? What does the clause "though less than a quorum" in § 38 modify? Compare MBCA § 8.10(a)(3). Does the language of that section resolve all possible ambiguity?

(2) Consider also the possible application of MBCA § 8.05(e) to the facts of this case. Judge Eager, dissenting in the Court below, commented:

> It is obvious that the assembling of a quorum of the directors for the purpose of the filling of the vacancy in the board would tend to perpetuate in the Kelly family the control of this corporation. The vacancy would be filled by a Kelly nominee. Thereupon, the Kelly family with their fifty percent stock holdings could deadlock the vote at future stockholders' meetings and effectively block an election of new or other directors by stockholders. Thus, their controlled board would continue in office. All this would tend to relegate the petitioners to the status of mere minority stockholders and defeat their rights as holders of fifty percent of the stock. This would give the Kelly family an undue and unconscionable advantage and thus, clearly, estoppel as a doctrine applicable for the promotion of justice, should not be applied here.

Gearing v. Kelly, 15 A.D.2d 219, 222–23, 222 N.Y.S.2d 474, 478 (1961). Is he correct or does it depend on the manner in which directors are to be elected? Compare, for example, the election strategies that should have been followed in the Stancil case (page 436) where an odd number of directors were being elected by cumulative voting in a corporation also owned equally by two factions.

IN RE RADOM & NEIDORFF, INC.

Court of Appeals of New York, 1954.
307 N.Y. 1, 119 N.E.2d 563.

DESMOND, JUDGE.

Radom & Neidorff, Inc., the proposed dissolution of which is before us here, is a domestic corporation which has for many years, conducted, with great success, the business of lithographing or printing musical compositions. For some thirty years prior to February 18, 1950, Henry Neidorff, now deceased, husband of respondent Anna Neidorff, and David Radom, brother-in-law of Neidorff and brother of Mrs. Neidorff, were the sole stockholders, each holding eighty shares. Henry Neidorff's will made his wife his executrix and bequeathed her the stock, so that, ever since his death, petitioner-appellant David Radom and Anna Neidorff, brother and sister, have been the sole and equal stockholders. Although brother and sister, they were unfriendly before Neidorff's death and their estrangement continues. On July 17, 1950, five months after Neidorff's death, Radom brought this proceeding, praying that the corporation be dissolved under section 103 of the General Corporation Law, Consol.Laws, c. 23, the applicable part of which is as follows:

§ 103. *Petition in Case of Deadlock*

Unless otherwise provided in the certificate of incorporation, if a corporation has an even number of directors who are equally divided respecting the management of its affairs, or if the votes of its stockholders are so divided that they cannot elect a board of directors, the holders of one-half of the stock entitled to vote at an election of directors may present a verified petition for dissolution of the corporation as prescribed in this article.

That statute, like others in article 9 of the General Corporation Law, describes the situations in which dissolution may be petitioned for, but, as we shall show later, it does not mandate the granting of the relief in every such case.

The petition here stated to the court that the corporation is solvent and its operations successful, but that, since Henry Neidorff's death, his widow (respondent here) has refused to co-operate with petitioner as president, and that she refuses to sign his salary checks, leaving him without salary, although he has the sole burden of running the business. It was alleged, too, that, because of "unresolved disagreements" between petitioner and respondent, election of any directors, at a stockholders' meeting held for that purpose in June, 1950, had proved impossible. A schedule attached to the petition showed corporate assets consisting of machinery and supplies worth about $9,500, cash about $82,000, and no indebtedness except about $17,000 owed to petitioner (plus his salary claim). Mrs. Neidorff's answering papers alleged that, while her husband was alive, the two owners had each drawn about $25,000 per year from the corporation, that, shortly after her husband's death, petitioner had asked her to allow him alone to sign all checks, which request she refused, that he had then offered her $75,000 for her stock, and, on her rejection thereof, had threatened to have the corporation dissolved and to buy it in at a low price or, if she should be the purchaser, that he would start a competing business. She further alleged that she has not, since her husband's death, interfered with Radom's conduct of the business and has signed all corporate checks sent her by him except checks for his own salary which, she says, she declined to sign because of a stockholder's derivative suit brought by her against Radom, and still pending, charging him with enriching himself at this corporation's expense.

Because of other litigation now concluded, see Matter of Radom's Estate, 305 N.Y. 679, 112 N.E.2d 768, to which Mrs. Neidorff was not a party, but which had to do with a contest as to the ownership of the Radom stock, respondent's answering papers in this dissolution proceeding were not filed until three years after the petition was entered. From the answering papers it appears, without dispute, that for those three years, the corporation's profits before taxes had totaled about $242,000, or an annual average of about $71,000, on a gross annual business of about $250,000, and that the corporation had, in 1953, about $300,000 on deposit in banks. There are many other accusations and counteraccusations in these wordy papers, but the only material facts are undisputed: first, that these two equal stockholders dislike and distrust each other; second, that, despite the feuding and backbiting, there is no stalemate or impasse as to corporate policies; third, that the corporation is not sick but flourishing; fourth, that dissolution is not necessary for the corporation or for either stockholders; and, fifth, that petitioner, though he is in an uncomfortable and disagreeable situation for which he may or may not be at fault, has no grievance cognizable by a court except as to the nonpayment of his salary, hardly a ground for dissolving the corporation.

Special Term held that these papers showed a basic and irreconcilable conflict between the two stockholders requiring dissolution, for the protection of both of them, if the petition's allegations should be proven. An order for a reference was, accordingly, made, but respondent appealed therefrom, and no hearings were held by the Referee. The Appellate Division reversed the order and dismissed the petition, pointing out, among other things, that not only have the corporation's activities not been paralyzed but that its profits have increased and its assets trebled during the pendency of this proceeding, that the failure of petitioner to receive his salary did not frustrate the corporate business and was remediable by means other than dissolution. The dismissal of the proceeding was "without prejudice, however, to the bringing of another proceeding should deadlock in fact arise in the selection of a board of directors, at a meeting of stockholders to be duly called, or if other deadlock should occur threatening impairment or in fact impairing the economic operations of the corporation." 282 App.Div. 854, 124 N.Y.S.2d 424, 425. Petitioner then appealed to this court.

It is worthy of passing mention, at least, that respondent has, in her papers, formally offered, and repeated the offer on the argument of the appeal before us, "to have the third director named by the American Arbitration Association, any Bar Association or any recognized and respected public body."

Clearly, the dismissal of this petition was within the discretion of the Appellate Division. General Corporation Law, § 106. There is no absolute right to dissolution under such circumstances. Even when majority stockholders file a petition because of internal corporate conflicts, the order is granted only when the competing interests "are so discordant as to prevent efficient management" and the "object of its corporate existence cannot be attained." Hitch v. Hawley, 132 N.Y. 212, 221, 30 N.E. 401, 404. The prime inquiry is, always, as to necessity for dissolution, that is, whether judicially-imposed death "will be beneficial to the stockholders or members and not injurious to the public," General Corporation Law, § 117; Hitch v. Hawley, supra. * * * Taking everything in the petition as true, this was not such a case, and so there was no need for a reference, or for the taking of proof, under sections 106 and 113 of the General Corporation Law.

The order should be affirmed, with costs.

FULD, JUDGE (dissenting).

Section 103 of the General Corporation Law, insofar as here relevant, permits a petition for dissolution of a corporation by the holders of one half of the shares of stock entitled to vote for directors "if the votes of its stockholders are so divided that they cannot elect a board of directors". That is the precise situation in the case before us, for the petition explicitly recites that petitioner Radom and respondent Neidorff "are hopelessly deadlocked with respect to the management and operation of the corporation" and that serious disputes have developed between them with the result that "the votes of the two stockholders are so divided that they cannot elect a Board of Directors." * * *

For upwards of thirty years, petitioner Radom and Henry Neidorff, respondent's husband, shared equally in the ownership and management of Radom & Neidorff, Inc. Through all that time, their relationship was harmonious as well as profitable. Neidorff died in 1950, at which time respondent, through inheritance, acquired her present 50% stock interest in the business. Since then, all has been discord and conflict. The parties, brother and sister, are at complete loggerheads; they have been unable to elect a board of directors; dividends have neither been declared nor distributed, although the corporation has earned profits; debts of the corporation have gone unpaid, although the corporation is solvent; petitioner, who since Neidorff's death has been the sole manager of the business, has not received a penny of his salary—amounting to $25,000 a year—because respondent has refused to sign any corporate check to his order. More, petitioner's business judgment and integrity, never before questioned, have been directly attacked in the stockholder's derivative suit, instituted by respondent, charging that he has falsified the corporation's records, converted its assets and otherwise enriched himself at its expense. Negotiations looking to the purchase by one stockholder of the other's interest were begun—in an effort to end the impasse—but they, too, have failed.

In very truth, as petitioner states in his papers, "a corporation of this type, with only two stockholders in it cannot continue to operate with incessant litigation and feuding between the two stockholders, and with differences as fundamental and wholly irreconcilable as are those of Mrs. Neidorff and myself. * * * [S]ettlement of these differences cannot be effected, while continuance on the present basis is impossible, so that there is no alternative to judicial dissolution." Indeed, petitioner avers, in view of the unceasing discord and the fact that he has had to work without salary and advance his own money to the corporation, he does not, whether or not dissolution be granted, "propose to continue to labor in and operate this business."

It is, then, undisputed and indisputable that the stockholders are not able to elect a board of directors. In addition, it is manifest, on the facts alleged, that the Supreme Court could find that the stockholders are hopelessly deadlocked vis-à-vis the management of the corporation; that the corporation cannot long continue to function effectively or profitably under such condition; that petitioner's resignation as president and manager—which he contemplates—will be highly detrimental to the interests of both corporation and stockholders and cannot help but result in substantial loss; and that petitioner is not responsible for the deadlock that exists. In such circumstances, the requisite statutory hearing may well establish that dissolution is indispensable, the only remedy available. As the high court of New Jersey recently declared in applying to somewhat comparable facts a statute similar to section 103 of our General Corporation Law, Matter of Collins–Doan Co., 3 N.J. 382, 396, 70 A.2d 159, 166, 13 A.L.R.2d 1250, "In the case at hand, *there is a want of that community of interest essential to corporate operation.* Dissolution will serve the interests of the shareholders as well as public policy. * * * And, if the statutory authority be deemed discretionary in essence, there is no ground for withholding its affirmative exercise here, *for there is no alternative corrective remedy.* * * * The dissension is such as to defeat the end for which the corporation was organized." (Emphasis supplied.)

Here, too, the asserted dissension, the court could find, permits of no real or effective remedy but a section 103 dissolution. And that is confirmed by a consideration of the alternatives seemingly open to petitioner. He could remain as president and manager of the corporation, without compensation, completely at odds with his embittered sister—certainly neither a natural nor a satisfying way in which to conduct a business. Or he could carry out his present plan to quit the enterprise—and thereby risk a loss, to corporation and stockholders, far greater than that involved in terminating the business. Or he could, without quitting, set up a competing enterprise and thereby expose himself to suit for breach of fiduciary duty to the corporation. Cf. Duane Jones Co. v. Burke, 306 N.Y. 172, 117 N.E.2d 237. It is difficult to believe that the legislature could have intended to put one in petitioner's position to such a choice. Reason plainly indicates, and the law allows, the reasonable course of orderly dissolution pursuant to section 103.

Respondent, however, suggests that, in view of the fact that petitioner is managing the business profitably, he should continue to do so, defend against the stockholder's suit which she brought attacking his honor and integrity and himself start an action for the compensation denied him for more than three years. But, it seems self-evident, more and further litigation would only aggravate, not cure, the underlying deadlock of which petitioner complains. And, if he were to bring the suggested suit for salary due him, the question arises, whom should he sue, and who is to defend? The mere proposal that petitioner embark on a series of actions against the corporation, of which he is president and half owner, indicates the extent of the present impasse, as well as the futility of perpetuating it. The same is true of the other alternative suggested by respondent, namely, that the third of the three directors, required by section 5 of the Stock Corporation Law, Consol.Laws, c. 59, be appointed by an impartial party. The deadlock of which petitioner complains is between the stockholders, not the directors, and when stockholders are deadlocked, section 103 calls for dissolution, not arbitration. Beyond that, and even if the offer to elect an impartial director were relevant, it would still be necessary to inquire when it was made and under what circumstances. It does not justify, alone or in conjunction with the other facts, a summary dismissal of the proceeding without a hearing.

Although respondent relies on the fact that the corporation is now solvent and operating at a profit, it is manifest that, if petitioner carries out his plan to resign as president and quits the business, there may be irreparable loss, not alone to him and respondent, as the owners of the corporation, but also to the corporation's creditors. Quite apart from that, however, the sole issue under section 103 is whether there is a deadlock as to the management of the corporation, not whether business is being conducted at a profit or loss. Whether the petition should or should not be entertained surely cannot be made to turn on proof that the corporation is on the verge of ruin or insolvency.

Insolvency may be a predicate for dissolution, but not under section 103. By virtue of other provisions of Article 9 of the General Corporation Law— sections 101 and 102—directors and stockholders may seek dissolution, when the corporation is insolvent, in order to prevent further loss to the owners and creditors. Section 103, however—which bears the title, *"Petition in case of deadlock"*—was designed to serve a far different purpose. As amended in 1944, upon the recommendation of the Law Revision Commission, that section provides for dissolution "if the votes of its stockholders are so divided that they cannot elect a board of directors." Nothing in the statute itself or in its legislative history suggests that a "Petition in case of deadlock" must wait until the corporation's profits have dried up and financial reverses set in. Had the commission or the legislature intended to incorporate such a qualification into section 103, it could readily have done so. The only test envisaged by the commission, however, was that which the legislature enacted, and a court may not import any other. * * *

The order of the Appellate Division should be reversed and that at Special Term affirmed.

CONWAY, DYE and VAN VOORHIS, JJ., concur with DESMOND, J.

FULD, J., dissents in opinion in which LEWIS, C.J., and FROESSEL, J., concur.

Notes

(1) See MBCA § 14.30(2), a statute that is typical of many state involuntary dissolution statutes. The Official Comment to this section makes it clear that the use of the word "may" in the preambular material preserves the Court's discretion (applied in *Radom*) "as to whether dissolution is appropriate even though grounds exist under the specific circumstances." Why should not the remedy of involuntary dissolution be generally available to minority shareholders in closely held corporations to the same extent that remedy is available to partners in a general partnership?

(2) Compare MBCA §§ 14.01, 14.02, 14.20. Might a dissatisfied shareholder in a closely held corporation be able to use these alternative dissolution provisions to avoid the limitations of § 14.30(2)?

(3) For an interesting evaluation of the dynamics of the interaction between Mrs. Neidorff and her brother, see Abram Chayes, Madame Wagner and the Close Corporation, 73 Harv.L.Rev. 1532, 1545–47 (1960).

(4) In re Hedberg–Freidheim & Co., 233 Minn. 534, 535–37, 47 N.W.2d 424, 426–27 (1951), the Court was faced with a request for involuntary dissolution of a corporation equally owned by the Hedberg and Freidheim families under the following circumstances:

> The allegations of the petition * * * show that since the year 1935 there has been continuous dissension, which has become more pronounced in recent years, between the two families with respect to the operation of the business of the corporation. * * *

> Fred Hedberg has been in charge of production for the corporation, and Charles Freidheim has had charge of collections, credits, financial details, the supervision and construction of new buildings, purchasing of equipment, and arranging for the possible expansion and further development of the business. However, for the last two or three years Hedberg has practically taken over the operation of the corporation's business without consultation with the other directors.

> Since 1947, Hedberg has refused to speak to or converse with Freidheim in connection with the business and affairs of the corporation except at formal meetings of its board of directors and shareholders. In order for Freidheim to communicate with Hedberg, Freidheim has been compelled to send messages to Hedberg through Hedberg's son. Recently, Hedberg caused a partition to be built in the office of the corporation between their respective desks so as to remove himself from personal contact with Freidheim. He has openly expressed himself to the corporation's employees of his bitterness toward Freidheim to such an extent that the employees have become fearful and dissatisfied. Suggestions made by Freidheim with respect to operation of the business, business policies, bonuses to employees, and various public relations are always vetoed by Hedberg without regard to the consideration of the merits thereof. Differences exist between them on a number of basic questions of corporate policy and management. They need not be enumerated here. It is sufficient to state that because of the lack of cooperation, exchange of ideas, and refusal on Hedberg's part to permit proposals made by Freidheim to be put into effect, even those relating to the departments of the business over which Freidheim is supposed to have charge, a stalemate has been reached, * * *

The Court ordered dissolution even though the business of the corporation had prospered in the past. In reaching this conclusion, the Court relied in part on the language of the applicable Minnesota statute that allows dissolution when the shareholders "are so deadlocked that [the corporation's] *business cannot longer be conducted with advantage to its shareholders.*" 47 N.W.2d at 427. The last clause of MBCA § 14.30(2)(i) was drawn from this 1933 Minnesota statute.

[handwritten: doesn't say "shareholders generally"]

D. MODERN REMEDIES FOR OPPRESSION, DISSENSION OR DEADLOCK

Involuntary dissolution was the original statutory remedy developed for deadlock situations where the corporation was on dead center and the participants had no way to resolve the situation. As early as 1933, a few states broadened their involuntary dissolution statutes to include oppression, significant misconduct by the directors or by those in control of the corporation, and the misapplication or wasting of assets. Earlier versions of the Model Act adopted this pattern, which gradually found its way into most corporation statutes. MBCA § 14.30(2) is thus typical of most state statutes dealing with involuntary dissolution.

Recent developments have broadened available remedies in the closely held corporation in two directions. First, the kinds of conduct within a closely held corporation that are viewed as oppressive have been broadened both by statute and by judicial decisions analogizing the closely held corporation to a partnership. Conduct that was viewed as entirely appropriate in the 1950s is now quite routinely viewed as oppressive. Second, remedies available to minority shareholders in closely held corporations have been broadened both by specific statutory provisions (including, but by no means limited to, the integrated close corporation statutes discussed in Zion v. Kurtz and the following notes) and by judicial decisions in states whose statutes still state that dissolution is the remedy for such conduct. See Robert B. Thompson, The Shareholder's Cause of Action for Oppression, 48 Bus. Law. 699 (1993).

DAVIS v. SHEERIN

Court of Appeals of Texas, 1988.
754 S.W.2d 375, error denied.

Before EVANS, C.J., and SAM BASS and DUNN, JJ.

DUNN, JUSTICE.

This is an appeal from portions of a trial court's judgment, in which James L. Sheerin ("appellee") was declared to own a 45% share in a corporation * * *. The major challenges are against an ordered buy-out of appellee's stock in the corporation * * *. William H. Davis ("appellant") is the owner of the remaining 55% interest in * * * [the corporation].

In May of 1985, appellee brought suit individually in his own right, and as a shareholder on behalf of W.H. Davis Co., Inc., a Texas corporation ("the corporation"), against William H. Davis and Catherine L. Davis ("appellants") based on allegations of appellants' oppressive conduct toward appellee as a minority shareholder, and their breaches of fiduciary duties owed to appellee and the corporation. * * *

In 1955, William Davis and appellee incorporated a business, initially started by William Davis, in which appellant Davis owned 55% and appellee owned 45% of the corporation's stock. Appellants and appellee all served as directors and officers, with William Davis serving as president and running the day-to-day operations of the business. Appellee, unlike appellants, was not employed by the corporation. In 1960, appellee and appellant William Davis formed a partnership for the purpose of acquiring real estate.

The precipitating cause of appellee's lawsuit in 1985 was appellants' denial of appellee's right to inspect the corporate books, unless appellee produced his stock certificate. Appellants claimed that appellee had made a gift to them, in the late 1960's, of his 45% interest. * * *

Following a six-week trial to a jury, the trial court, in addition to declaring that appellee owned a 45% interest in the corporation, * * * ordered [a] "buy-out" by appellants of appellee's 45% of the stock in the corporation for $550,000, the fair value determined by the jury * * *.

In points of error one through seven, appellants challenge the court's order that they buy-out appellee's 45% interest in the corporation. Appellants' basic argument is two fold: (1) the remedy of a "buy-out" is not available to a minority shareholder under Texas law, and (2) if such a remedy were available, the facts of this case are not appropriate for, nor do the jury's findings support, the application of this remedy based on the court's determination of oppressive conduct.

The Texas Business Corporation Act does not expressly provide for the remedy of a "buy-out" for an aggrieved minority shareholder. Tex.Bus.Corp. Act. art. 7.05 (Vernon 1980) does provide for the appointment of a receiver, with the eventual possibility of liquidation, for aggrieved shareholders who can establish the existence of one of five situations, including illegal, oppressive, or fraudulent conduct by those in control.

Nor do we find any Texas cases where the particular remedy of a "buy-out" has been ordered, unless provided for in a contract between the parties. But courts of other jurisdictions have recognized a "buy-out" as an appropriate remedy, even in the absence of express statutory or contractual authority. *See Alaska Plastics, Inc. v. Coppock,* 621 P.2d 270 (Alaska 1980); *Sauer v. Moffitt,* 363 N.W.2d 269 (Iowa.Ct.App.1984); *McCauley v. Tom McCauley & Son, Inc.,* 104 N.M. 523, 724 P.2d 232 (Ct.App.1986) (granting the option of liquidation or "buy-out"); *In re Wiedy's Furniture Clearance Center Co.,* 108 A.D.2d 81, 487 N.Y.S.2d 901 (1985); *Delaney v. Georgia–Pacific Corp.,* 278 Or. 305, 564 P.2d 277 (1977). Alaska, Iowa, New Mexico, New York, and Oregon all have statutes that provide for liquidation as the remedy for oppressive acts, and, in the above cited cases, the courts allowed a "buy-out" as a less harsh remedy. Other states' statutes specifically provide for a "buy-out," either as a remedy for an aggrieved minority shareholder, * * * [citing the statutes of five states], or as an option available to a majority shareholder to avoid a liquidation order, * * * [citing the statutes of two states].

Both parties rely on *Patton v. Nicholas,* 154 Tex. 385, 279 S.W.2d 848 (1955), to support their respective arguments in favor of or against a court's authority in Texas to order a "buy-out." In that case, the court reversed an order of liquidation in a suit brought by an aggrieved minority shareholder, although it found that liquidation might be an appropriate remedy in some instances. * * * [A discussion of earlier Texas law is omitted.]

We conclude that Texas courts, under their general equity power, may decree a "buy-out" in an appropriate case where less harsh remedies are inadequate to protect the rights of the parties.

Having decided that a "buy-out" is an available remedy under the court's general equity powers, we must decide whether it was appropriate in this case. The trial court's judgment reflects that its "buy-out" order was based on the jury's finding of conspiracy to deprive appellee of his stock, on the evidence and arguments, and on its conclusion that appellants acted oppressively against appellee and would continue to do so. * * *

Oppressive conduct is the most common violation for which a "buy-out" was found to be an appropriate remedy in other jurisdictions. *See, e.g. Alaska Plastics,* 621 P.2d 270, *Wiedy's,* 487 N.Y.S.2d 901; *McCauley,* 724 P.2d 232; *Baker v. Commercial Body Builders, Inc.,* 264 Or. 614, 507 P.2d 387 (1973). Courts take an especially broad view of the application of oppressive conduct to a closely-held corporation, where oppression may more easily be found. *Skierka v. Skierka Bros. Inc.,* 629 P.2d 214 (Mont.1981). An ordered "buy-out" of stock at its fair value is an especially appropriate remedy in a closely-held corporation, where the oppressive acts of the majority are an attempt to "squeeze out" the minority, who do not have a ready market for the corporation's shares, but are at the mercy of the majority.

The Texas Business Corporation Act, which provides a cause of action based on oppressive conduct, does not define oppressive conduct. *See* art. 7.05. Nor do we find any Texas decision providing a definition. We therefore turn again to decisions of other jurisdictions to consider what constitutes oppressive conduct.

Oppressive conduct has been described as an expansive term that is used to cover a multitude of situations dealing with improper conduct, and a narrow definition would be inappropriate. *McCauley,* 724 P.2d at 236. Courts may determine, according to the facts of the particular case, whether the acts complained of serve to frustrate the legitimate expectations of minority shareholders, or whether the acts are of such severity as to warrant the requested relief.

The New York court in *Wiedy's* held that oppression should be deemed to arise only when the majority's conduct substantially defeats the expectations that objectively viewed were both reasonable under the circumstances and were central to the minority shareholder's decision to join the venture. *Wiedy's,* 487 N.Y.2d at 903.

Courts in states with statutes containing situations establishing causes of action for minority shareholders, similar to those allowed in the Texas statute, have held that oppressive conduct is an independent ground for relief not requiring a showing of fraud, illegality, mismanagement, wasting of assets, nor deadlock, the other grounds available for shareholders, though these factors are frequently present. *Fix v. Fix Material Co., Inc.,* 538 S.W.2d 351, 358 (Mo.Ct.App.1976) (citing *Gidwitz v. Lanzit Corrugated Box Co.,* 20 Ill.2d 208, 170 N.E.2d 131, 135[1] (1960)).

While noting that general definitions are of little value for application in a specific case, the Oregon supreme court in *Baker* cited the most quoted definitions of oppressive conduct as:

"burdensome, harsh and wrongful conduct," "a lack of probity and fair dealing in the affairs of a company to the prejudice of some of its members," or "a visible departure from the standards of fair dealing, and a violation of fair play on which every shareholder who entrusts his money to a company is entitled to rely."

Baker, 507 P.2d at 393. * * *

Our review of the record shows that the jury made the following findings in regards to appellants' conduct:

(1) appellants conspired to deprive appellee of his stock ownership in the corporation;

(2) appellants received informal dividends by making profit sharing contributions for their benefit and to the exclusion of appellee, and that this was a willful breach of fiduciary duty;

(3) appellants wasted corporate funds by using them for their legal fees, and that this was a willful breach of fiduciary duty;

(4) appellants did not convert appellee's stock;

(5) appellants were not paid excessive compensation;

(6) there was no malicious suppression of dividends;

(7) various purchases or investments did not constitute a breach of fiduciary duty; and

(8) appellants did not conspire to breach their fiduciary duty.

The jury also found that appellee did not make a gift of his stock to appellants, represent that he would, nor agree to do so in the future. We note that appellants do not challenge any of the jury findings favorable to appellee, except the finding on conspiracy, a challenge that we have already overruled.

Some of the undisputed evidence that the trial court could have also considered in its conclusion of oppressive conduct includes the following:

(1) appellants claimed that appellee had gifted them his stock in the late 1960's even though the records of the corporation and income tax returns through 1986 clearly show appellee as a 45% stockholder, and appellants and/or their son had made several attempts to purchase appellee's stock in the 1970's and 1980's;

(2) a letter from the corporation's attorney, dated May 16, 1979, referred to appellant Davis' "wish to avoid declaring dividends and disburse the surplus in the form of bonuses to the officers of the corporation" and the fact that such action may result in an allegation by appellee of "fraudulent intent to deny a shareholder his right to dividends" and "would probably be characterized as a direct effort to deny a shareholder his dividends;" and

(3) appellants approved the minutes of a special meeting of the Board of Director on February 7, 1986, after the filing of this lawsuit, that stated that "Mr. Sheerin's opinions or actions would have no effect on the Board's deliberations."

Even though there were findings of the absence of some of the typical "squeeze out" techniques used in closely held corporations, e.g., no malicious suppression of dividends or excessive salaries, we find that conspiring to deprive one of his ownership of stock in a corporation, especially when the corporate records clearly indicate such ownership, is more oppressive than either of those techniques. Appellant's conduct not only would substantially defeat any reasonable expectations appellee may have had, as required by the New York Court in *Wiedy's,* but would totally extinguish any such expectations. * * *

Appellee's complaints of appellants' conduct go far beyond "dissatisfaction with corporate management," nor does appellants' conduct fall under the protection of the business judgment rule, two instances found to be inappropriate for causes of action under article 7.05. in a Texas case cited by appellants. *See Texarkana College Bowl, Inc. v. Phillips*, 408 S.W.2d 537, 539 (Tex.Civ.App.—Texarkana 1966, no writ).

We therefore hold that the jury's finding of conspiracy to deprive appellee of his interest in the corporation, together with the acts of willful breach of a fiduciary duty as found by the jury, and the undisputed evidence indicating that appellee would be denied any future voice in the corporation, are sufficient to support the trial court's conclusion of oppressive conduct and the likelihood that it would continue in the future.

Under the analysis set out by the *Patton* court in its determination of whether liquidation was appropriate, we must determine whether lesser remedies than a "buy-out" could adequately protect appellee's interests. In *Patton,* the court found sufficient evidence to support only the malicious suppression of dividends claim, and thus concluded that a mandatory injunction to pay reasonable dividends then and in the future was adequate, with the additional protection of the court retaining jurisdiction.

In this case, the award of damages and certain injunctions might be sufficient to remedy the willful breaches of fiduciary duty found by the jury, i.e., informal dividends to appellants by making contributions to the profit sharing plan and waste of corporate funds for legal fees. However, based on appellants' conduct denying appellee any interest or voice in the corporation, we find that these remedies are inadequate to protect appellee's interest and his rights in the corporation.

Appellants' oppressive conduct, along with their attempts to purchase appellee's stock, are indications of their desire to gain total control of the corporation. That is exactly what a "buy-out" will achieve. We disagree with appellants' suggestion that a "buy-out" is a more drastic remedy than liquidation. *See Stefano v. Coppock,* 705 P.2d 443, 446 (Alaska 1985). This is especially true in light of the fact that appellants do not challenge the jury's finding of $550,000 as the fair value of appellee's stock, which is the amount set by the trial court for the "buy-out." * * *

Based on the facts of this case, we find that a "buy-out" was an appropriate remedy, and that the trial court did not abuse its discretion.

Notes

(1) Cases hold that a court may order a buyout even where the statute, like MBCA § 14.30(2), only refers to dissolution as the appropriate remedy may not be as radical as they first appear. Consider Harry J. Haynsworth, The Effectiveness of Involuntary Dissolution Suits as a Remedy for Close Corporation Dissension, 35 Clev.St.L.Rev. 25, 50–55 (1987):

> What results actually occur in close corporation involuntary dissolution suits? One way to answer this question is to examine existing published opinions. For the purposes of this article, the opinions published in 1984 and 1985 in which involuntary dissolution was one of the major causes of action were analyzed. These two years were chosen simply because they were the two most recent years for which decisions were available. Given the number

and variety of cases during 1984 and 1985, it is doubtful that increasing the number of years in the sample would have yielded any significantly different or additional conclusions.

The 1984 and 1985 involuntary dissolution cases present an interesting statistical profile. There were a total of forty-seven cases that qualified for the sample. Forty-five of the cases came from twenty different states * * *.

Ten of the cases in the sample involved technical legal issues in which no decision on the type of relief, if any, had been made at the time the opinion was issued. * * *

Of the remaining thirty-seven cases, a buy-out was the most frequent relief ordered by the court or elected by the defendants. This result occurred in twenty of the decisions (fifty-four percent). Dissolution was ordered in ten of the cases (twenty-seven percent). In four of the cases (eleven percent), no substantial relief was granted to the plaintiff on the merits. Finally, in the three other cases (eight percent) relief other than either dissolution or a buy-out was the exclusive remedy ordered; and in eleven of the dissolution and buy-out cases (thirty percent of the total and thirty-seven percent of the dissolution and buy-out cases), additional relief was also granted. This additional relief included compensatory damages, punitive damages, an accounting, cancellation of issued stock, partial liquidation and other innovative orders * * *.

That a court-supervised buy-out was the predominant form of ultimate relief and that a buy-out occurred twice as frequently as a court-ordered liquidation is not surprising. A buy-out, assuming fair value is received for the shares, gives the plaintiff a cash-out right that he or she would not otherwise have, and in many cases, this is undoubtedly the principal motivation behind the lawsuit. Getting rid of a dissatisfied shareholder permanently is also advantageous to the corporation and remaining shareholders. Moreover, * * * judges have consistently stated that dissolution should be ordered only as a last resort when no alternative remedy is feasible; and the dissolution cases in the sample used in this article illustrate that in this instance, judges are practicing what they preach.

What is somewhat surprising is the number of cases in which a court-supervised buy-out is the result of the involuntary dissolution suit. In a previous study of the fifty-four involuntary dissolution opinions decided between 1960–1976 conducted by Professors J.A.C. Hetherington and Michael P. Dooley of the University of Virginia,[17] a court-ordered or court supervised buy-out was involved in only three of the cases, whereas dissolution was ordered in sixteen of the twenty-seven cases in which some affirmative relief was granted.

Professors Hetherington and Dooley not only analyzed the judicial opinions issued between 1960 and the end of 1976, but they also followed up on each case to determine the ultimate outcome. Interestingly, out of all the cases, including those for which relief had been denied, fifty-four percent actually ended up with one side buying out the other. This is exactly the same percentage as the buy-out cases in the 1984–1985 decisions. This parallelism suggests that recent decisions more accurately mirror the results ultimately negotiated by the parties than the decisions rendered a decade or more ago.

---

17. [By the Author] Hetherington & Dooley, Illiquidity And Exploitation: A Proposed Statutory Solution to the Remaining Close Corporation Problem, 63 Va.L.Rev. 1 (1976).

(2) In 1991, the Committee on Corporate Laws added MBCA § 14.34. In describing the background of this new section, the Official Comment[18] states:

> The proceeding for judicial dissolution has become an increasingly important remedy for minority shareholders of closely-held corporations who believe that the value of their investment is threatened by reason of circumstances or conduct described in section 14.30(2). If the petitioning shareholder proves one or more grounds under section 14.30(2), he is entitled to some form of relief but many courts have hesitated to award dissolution, the only form of relief explicitly provided, because of its adverse effects on shareholders, employees, and others who may have an interest in the continuation of the business.

> Commentators have observed that it is rarely necessary to dissolve the corporation and liquidate its assets in order to provide relief: the rights of the petitioning shareholder are fully protected by liquidating only his interest and paying the fair value of his shares while permitting the remaining shareholders to continue the business.

Under MBCA § 14.34, does the petitioning shareholder have any say in whether his shares are purchased? Might that not "chill" the filing of petitions under MBCA § 14.30? The Official Comment to § 14.34 notes that that section "makes strategic use of section 14.30(2) a high-risk proposition for the petitioning shareholder." May a nonpetitioning shareholder elect to purchase the shares of a petitioning shareholder? See MBCA § 14.34(b).

(3) Closely held shares by definition have no market value. How is "fair value" to be determined under § 14.34? A somewhat analogous determination of "fair value" is required in the appraisal procedure under MBCA § 13.30, but the Official Comment to § 14.34 points out that the "two proceedings are not wholly analogous, * * * and the court should consider all relevant facts and circumstances of the particular case in determining fair value." The Official Comment then continues:

> For example, liquidating value may be relevant in cases of deadlock but an inappropriate measure in other cases. If the court finds that the value of the corporation has been diminished by the wrongful conduct of controlling shareholders, it would be appropriate to include as an element of fair value the petitioner's proportional claim for any compensable corporate injury. In cases where there is dissension but no evidence of wrongful conduct, "fair value" should be determined with reference to what the petitioner would likely receive in a voluntary sale of shares to a third party, taking into account his minority status. If the parties have previously entered into a shareholders' agreement that defines or provides a method for determining the fair value of shares to be sold, the court should look to such definition or method unless the court decides it would be unjust or inequitable to do so in light of the facts and circumstances of the particular case.

(4) Virginia cases take the position that a court, in an involuntary dissolution proceeding, does not have power to impose remedies such as requiring the payment of a dividend, disallowing a claim for rent, or requiring the restoration of funds oppressively removed from the corporation by the controlling shareholders. Giannotti v. Hamway, 239 Va. 14, 387 S.E.2d 725 (1990); White v. Perkins, 213

---

18. Reprinted from *Model Business Corporation Act Annotated* with the permission of the American Bar Association.

Va. 129, 189 S.E.2d 315 (1972). Rather, the court is limited to the statutory remedies of involuntary dissolution and appointment of a custodian, remedies set forth explicitly in Virginia's involuntary dissolution statute. In *Giannotti*, the dissenting judge objected to the decision to liquidate a profitable corporation that had acted oppressively by refusing to pay dividends and paying out the bulk of its earnings to its majority shareholders in the form of salaries, bonuses, and directors' fees: "To liquidate the corporation is to kill the goose that laid the golden egg." 387 S.E.2d, at 734.

(5) An increasing number of state statutes expressly recognize a mandatory buyout as an available remedy. In considering these statutes, one should distinguish between statutes applicable to corporations generally and those applicable only to corporations that have elected special close corporation treatment, though decisions such as Zion v. Kurtz (p. 417, supra) and the principal case may make that distinction less important than might first appear.

(6) The word "oppressive" does not carry "an essential inference of imminent disaster; it can contemplate a continued course of conduct." Gidwitz v. Lanzit Corrugated Box Co., 20 Ill.2d 208, 214, 170 N.E.2d 131, 135 (1960). See also Giannotti v. Hamway, 239 Va. 14, 387 S.E.2d 725 (1990). The *Gidwitz* and *Giannotti* courts stated that "oppressive" is not synonymous with "illegal" or "fraudulent" and its application does not necessarily involve a finding of mismanagement or misapplication of assets. Other courts have referred to general concepts of "a lack of probity and fair dealing" or departure from standards of "fair play." White v. Perkins, 213 Va. 129, 134, 189 S.E.2d 315, 319–20 (1972); Giannotti v. Hamway, 239 Va. 14, 387 S.E.2d 725 (1990). Still other courts have associated "oppressive" with violations of the fiduciary duty of good faith and fair dealing imposed by Donahue v. Rodd Electrotype, page 378, supra, and similar cases. Exadaktilos v. Cinnaminson Realty Co., Inc., 167 N.J.Super. 141, 154–56, 400 A.2d 554, 561–62 (1979), involved § 14A:12–7(1)(c) of New Jersey Stat.Ann., which authorizes, in the case of a corporation with less than 25 shareholders, the appointment of a custodian if the persons in control of the corporation "have acted oppressively or unfairly toward one or more minority shareholders in their capacities as shareholders, directors, officers, or employees." The Court stated:

> To implement the intent of the Legislature, a method must be developed whereby it can be decided when a particular course of corporate conduct has resulted in the oppression of a minority shareholder.

> The special circumstances, arrangements and personal relationships that frequently underlie the formation of close corporations generate certain expectations among the shareholders concerning their respective roles in corporate affairs, including management and earnings. These expectations preclude the drawing of any conclusions about the impact of a particular course of corporate conduct on a shareholder without taking into consideration the role that he is expected to play. Accordingly, a court must determine initially the understanding of the parties in this regard. Armed with this information, the court can then decide whether the controlling shareholders have acted in a fashion that is contrary to this understanding or in the language of the statute, "have acted oppressively * * * toward one or more minority shareholders."

> The expectations of the parties in the instant suit with regard to their participation in corporate affairs are not established by any agreement; they must be gleaned from the evidence presented. Here, the corporation is close and small and operates a single restaurant. Three of its shareholders had

lengthy experience in the restaurant business prior to the corporation's formation. Although the corporation operates, technically, with one director who is not the largest stockholder, its business decisions actually have been made informally by these three shareholders. Except for its organizational meeting, no director or shareholder meetings have been held since the corporation's inception in 1972. Plaintiff, the fourth shareholder, had no restaurant experience at the time he received his stock as a gift from his father-in-law. By giving him the stock, Skordas sought to provide him with an opportunity to learn the restaurant business and eventually take part in its management.

There is some indication that plaintiff's opportunity was extended over the objections of the other two shareholders and it is clear that they never welcomed him as a fellow participant in the enterprise. The evidence shows that plaintiff failed to get along with employees, causing the loss of key personnel, that he quit on more than one occasion, without reason or notice, and that he was not compatible with the other principals. Plaintiff's discharge from employment with the corporation, therefore, was because of his unsatisfactory performance.

The circumstances under which the parties' expectations in these areas were disappointed do not establish oppressive action toward plaintiff by the controlling shareholders. The promise of employment was honored, the opportunity being lost to plaintiff through no fault of defendants. The parties' expectation that plaintiff would at some time participate in management was likewise thwarted by plaintiff's failure to satisfy the condition precedent to participation, i.e., that he learn the business.

See also Robert B. Thompson, The Shareholder's Cause of Action for Oppression, 48 Bus.Law. 699 (1993).

(7) Most oppression cases involve actions by majority shareholders that injure minority shareholders. However, minority shareholders also owe duties to the majority and breach of these duties may be viewed as oppressive in some instances. In Rexford Rand Corp. v. Ancel, 58 F.3d 1215 (7th Cir.1995), a minority shareholder was fired as an employee of the corporation for reasons that were in dispute. The corporation subsequently failed to file its annual report with the state of Illinois, and was administratively dissolved, thereby making its name generally available. The minority shareholder, learning of this, reserved the name "Rexford Rand Corporation" for his own use and began conducting business under that name in competition with the corporation. The court, relying on concepts developed in *Donahue*, held this conduct violated a duty owed to the corporation and required the name to be transferred back to the original corporation:

Next, we turn to the merits. Under Illinois law, a shareholder in a close corporation owes a duty of loyalty to the corporation and to the other shareholders. Shareholders must "deal with the utmost good faith, fairly, honestly, and openly with their fellow stockholders." This duty is necessary * * * because while a closely held corporation embodies the corporate form, it in many ways resembles a partnership. Thus, "the mere fact that a business is run as a corporation rather than a partnership does not shield the business venturers from a fiduciary duty similar to that of true partners." Hagshenas [v. Gaylord], 145 Ill.Dec. at 552, [557 N.E.2d 316, at 322 (1990)].

Generally, imposing a fiduciary duty on shareholders in a close corporation shields minority shareholders from oppressive conduct by the majority.

Shareholders in close corporations have often invested a "substantial percentage" of their assets in the corporation, see Donahue v. Rodd Electrotype Co., 367 Mass. 578, 328 N.E.2d 505, 514 (1975), and their position in the corporation may provide them with their only source of income. * * *

In addition, minority shareholders owe a duty of loyalty to a close corporation in certain circumstances. Minority shareholders have an obligation as de facto partners in the joint venture not to do damage to the corporate interests. * * * Rexford Rand contends that Gregory acted unscrupulously and thus breached his duty of loyalty by reserving the Rexford Rand name for himself rather than informing Selwyn and Albert that Illinois was preparing to administratively dissolve the corporation.

Gregory acknowledges that, under normal circumstances, he would have owed a duty of loyalty to Rexford Rand. He argues, however, that his duty terminated after the alleged freeze-out, which deprived him of his position in the corporation as well as the benefits of his stock ownership. The Illinois courts have never decided whether a freeze-out terminates a minority shareholder's duty of loyalty to a close corporation. * * * Our research indicates that only one court has addressed the question of whether a freeze-out terminates a shareholder's fiduciary duty to a close corporation. In J Bar H, Inc. v. Johnson, 822 P.2d 849 (Wyo.1991), the Supreme Court of Wyoming stated that "where a shareholder/director/employee of a close corporation has been wrongfully terminated from employment with the corporation and has been unjustly prevented from fulfilling her function as a director or officer, she can no longer be considered to act in a fiduciary capacity for the corporation." Id. at 861. The court reasoned that "the fiduciary duty not to compete depends on the ability to exercise the status which creates it." A minority shareholder who has been frozen out no longer exercises the influence over corporate affairs that gives rise to a fiduciary duty. Consequently, no fiduciary duty should remain after a freeze-out. * * *

While we understand the reluctance of the J Bar H court to place a fiduciary duty on a shareholder who has been frozen out, we do not believe that J Bar H achieves the optimal result. Gregory may have been the victim of oppressive activity, and he may have believed that reserving the Rexford Rand name for his own use would induce Albert and Selwyn to buy out his stock at a fair price. Gregory's desire to obtain a fair buyout is not itself objectionable * * *. The method by which he sought to induce a settlement, however, is troubling. By appropriating the corporate name, Gregory threatened to cause serious damage to the well-being of the corporation and to imperil Selwyn and Albert's investment as well as his own. The freeze-out did not deprive Gregory of his status as a shareholder, and as a shareholder in a close corporation, Gregory should have placed the interests of the corporation above his personal interests. * * *. If shareholders take it upon themselves to retaliate any time they believe they have been frozen out, disputes in close corporations will only increase. Rather, if unable to resolve matters amicably, aggrieved parties should take their claims to court and seek judicial resolution. Thus, the decision of the district court returning the name to the corporation * * * is affirmed.

(8) In Muellenberg v. Bikon Corp., 669 A.2d 1382, 1388–89 (N.J.1996), majority and minority shareholders sharply disputed who was primarily at fault in oppressing the other; the court, after carefully weighing the equities, concluded that it was appropriate to require the majority shareholders to sell

their shares to the minority shareholder. The court stated "while a minority buy-out of the majority is an uncommon remedy, it was the appropriate one here."

NDUS. SALES, INC.

of Illinois, 1991.
Dec. 703, 586 N.E.2d 661.

n of the court:

decision in a shareholder's derivative
ndants had breached fiduciary obli-
ities and repeatedly attempting to
l court awarded plaintiff monetary
ppointed a provisional director to
to break any deadlock between

(1) whether the appointment of
f Operations of the company, as
horizing such appointment; (2)
er the statute, whether the trial
nal director for allegedly failing
follow statutory guidelines; (3)
rney fees to plaintiff separate
court's injunction protecting
d; and (5) whether damages

p
pl
ev
co
to
whe
fron
the
were

F
found
develo
preside
husban
Ralph a
the only

("Manny") Abreau was co-
("Ebro"), a company that
y ran the company as its
Plaintiff succeeded to her
lent of Ebro. Defendants
and "William") are co-owners and
uant La Preferida, Inc., the other 50% shareholder

in Ebro and a company that distributed Ebro's products.

In a thoughtful 42-page opinion, the trial judge carefully and explicitly set out his findings. The trial court found that Ralph created Ebro Industrial Sales, Inc., as a minority-owned business (later renamed Unica Industrial Sales, Inc.) to directly compete with Ebro Foods, Inc. in securing the business of Kraft Foods and awarded damages of $211,269 to Ebro for the lost Kraft business. The trial court also found that defendants repeatedly tried to obtain the master formulas for Ebro's products so that they might have the product made elsewhere and sell it themselves without going through Ebro. The court determined that ownership of the formulas is exclusive to Ebro and that all shareholders are enjoined from disclosing the formulas or data from which the formulas may be ascertained. The court also removed Ralph as director and five other people from employment at Ebro, finding that there had been oppressive and fraudulent self-dealing conduct that threatened the viability of Ebro as a solvent corporation.

Since Ebro was left with only two directors, plaintiff and La Preferida's candidate, Emil Smider, the trial court appointed a provisional director to stabilize the two hostile factions in the best interest of Ebro, pursuant to section 12.55(b) of the Illinois Business Corporation Act ("IBCA").

[Editor: IBCA § 12.55 reads in part as follows:

ALTERNATIVE REMEDIES TO JUDICIAL DISSOLUTION.—(a) In either an action for dissolution pursuant to Section 12.50 or in an action which alleges the grounds for dissolution set fourth in Section 12.50 but which does not seek dissolution, the Circuit Court, in lieu of dismissing the action or ordering dissolution, may retain jurisdiction and:

(1) Appoint a provisional director;

(2) Appoint a custodian; or

(3) In an action by a shareholder, order a purchase of the complaining shareholder's shares * * *.

(b) A provisional director may be appointed in the discretion of the court if it appears that such action by the court will remedy the grounds alleged by the complaining shareholder to support the jurisdiction of the court under Section 12.50. A provisional director may be appointed notwithstanding the fact that there is no vacancy on the board of directors and shall have all the rights and powers of a duly elected director, including the right to notice of and to vote at meetings of directors, until such time as the provisional director is removed by order of court or, unless otherwise ordered by court, removed by a vote of the shareholders sufficient either to elect a majority of the board of directors or if greater than majority voting is required by the articles of incorporation or the by-laws, to elect the requisite number of directors needed to take action. * * *]

Defendants first contend the trial court erred in appointing Silvio Vega ("Vega"), General Manager of Operations at Ebro and plaintiff's son-in-law, to serve as provisional director because the IBCA implicitly requires the provisional director to be an impartial third party. While the statute does not explicitly require the provisional director be impartial, defendants argue that because 11 of 16 state statutes enacting the remedy of provisional directors expressly require impartiality, the rest of the statutes assume impartiality. Defendant also relies on the fact that the trial court acknowledged that Vega could not be characterized as impartial in the "traditional" sense, and, in oral arguments, defendants observed that there is "no such thing as an impartial son-in-law."

We disagree that there is a strict requirement of impartiality in appointing a provisional director. Defendant's presumptive reading of legislative intent overlooks the fact that when the legislature enacted the IBCA in 1983, it was well aware of other states' statutes expressly requiring some degree of impartiality and chose to bypass that language and place reliance on the trial court's discretion. * * *

A provisional director is appointed as an alternative remedy to judicial dissolution in times of corporate strife to help guide the company through crisis toward the goal of stabilization and prosperity. When appointing a provisional director, the trial court considers only the best interests of the corporation, and not those of any warring factions. If the trial court, based upon the particular situation, finds that there is no traditionally independent third party with the skills and abilities necessary to fulfill the position within an urgent time frame, it may use its discretion to appoint a provisional director in the best interest of the corporation, whether or not that person has been aligned or appears to have been aligned with a particular group of shareholders.

To impose a strict requirement that the court find and appoint a traditionally impartial independent third party, and allow that person time to familiarize himself with the history and goals of the company and its current crisis situation, regardless of the urgency of the situation or the availability of highly competent people who may not be traditionally impartial, is to ignore the mission of section 12.55.

In this case, we find the appointment of Vega was made in the best interest of the corporation and that even though he could not be described as traditionally impartial, the trial court properly exercised discretion, given the circumstances of the case and Vega's background.

We reject the trial judge's reasoning that his right to appoint Vega is founded in the misdeeds of the defendants. The statute imposes upon the court a more goal-oriented approach.

Factors that a trial court may balance in evaluating candidates for provisional director include: degree and quality of past involvement in the corporation; an understanding of the corporation's history and current situation; experience and abilities in providing a cooperative and unifying element; need for immediate appointment; degree of impartiality; and above all, a true interest in the viability and advancement of the corporation as an entity and not allegiance to one of the deadlocked factions.

Defendants argue that Vega is merely a parrot or handmaiden of plaintiff, voting with plaintiff on matters simply because he is her son-in-law. We uphold the trial court's finding that this is an inaccurate and unfair description of Vega, given his experience, knowledge and involvement in the corporation.

Vega has worked for Ebro for over 17 years and is familiar with every aspect of the corporation; he holds a CPA degree that enables him to understand the financial complexities of the business; he has complete knowledge of the history of Ebro's relationship with La Preferida and the Steinbarths, and the symbiosis between the two companies.

While defendants recognize that the remedy is for the benefit of the corporation whose viability is threatened by the intershareholder dispute, they state that the intent of the statute is not to create an imbalance on the board in favor of the complaining shareholder. Defendants are correct in this interpretation, but overlook the fact that they have retained all of the shareholder rights that they had prior to the appointment of the provisional director.

Defendants cite *Gidwitz v. Lanzit Corrugated Box Co.* (1960), 20 Ill.2d 208, 170 N.E.2d 131, to support its argument that Vega should be removed because defendants are effectively prohibited from participating in major corporate decisions because Vega creates a *de facto* majority in favor of plaintiff. In *Gidwitz*, dissident factions arose among shareholders of a corporation and the court dissolved the corporation because it found that the president, with the support of other family members owning one-half of the shares, ran the company oppressively. The court stated that the business was run by the president almost as a sole proprietorship with no regard for the views of the other one-half of the shareholders and directors.

We find this case differs from *Gidwitz* in that the trial court made no findings that any of Vega's actions were "oppressive," nor did it find that La Preferida was excluded from participating in the management of Ebro.

We agree with the trial court's findings in this case that a simple split in votes, however consistent, does not create a *de facto* majority, nor does it disenfranchise a shareholder. Corporation law does not guarantee shareholders the outcome of a vote, merely a right to vote. Given the trial court's findings in the underlying derivative suit, it is to be expected that a provisional director, bound by duty to act in the best interests of the corporation, might be wary of votes cast by the offending shareholder in the suit. Simply because the provisional director does not agree with a voting shareholder does not automatically evidence improper impartiality.

We find Vega's appointment was properly within the discretion of the trial court and posed no infringement on defendants' shareholder rights.

Defendants next contend that even if the appointment of Vega is valid, he should be removed from office because he performed certain acts that are inconsistent with his statutory and court-imposed duties and responsibilities. Defendants argue that Vega failed his responsibilities as provisional director when he:

(1) submitted a proposal to Kraft for the sale of jalapeno peppers which entailed additional expenses for Ebro of approximately $300,000 without prior review by or approval of the Board of Directors;

(2) terminated La Preferida's 25–year role as the exclusive distributor of the "El Ebro" line of food products without presenting a cost-benefit analysis to or seeking the approval of the Board of Directors;

(3) hired a new auditor to prepare a certified audit for 1990 without the approval of the Board of Directors;

(4) voted against a proposal limiting management's ability to make financial and operational commitments on behalf of the corporation;

(5) voted in favor of reimbursing plaintiff for attorneys' fees and costs and to pay directly the attorneys' fees and costs on appeal even though there was no deadlock on the issue and even though defendant's director asked that the vote be postponed so he could further consider the issue;

(6) failed to attempt to reach any compromise prior to voting on disputed proposals;

(7) failed to ensure the preparation of complete and accurate minutes of board meetings; and

(8) failed to provide defendant's director an agenda for a meeting until the start of the meeting.

Because a provisional director is an officer of the court, it is the trial court's duty to oversee the provisional director's actions. Upon reviewing the evidence and the parties' arguments, the trial court found that even though technical inaccuracies may have occurred regarding board procedure, none of the oversights, either separate or cumulative, were enough to justify removal of Vega. The court found that the provisional director breached no duty to the corporation and remains committed to the best interests of Ebro.

We find the record upholds the trial court's determinations, and we affirm, with the exception of the charges involving the unilateral management decision to hire a new certified auditor and the mode of approval of attorney fees for Zenaida, which we reverse as inconsistent with the duties of a provisional director. * * *

It is generally accepted, unless corporate bylaws provide otherwise, that it is improper for management of a corporation to directly hire the auditors whose mission it is to evaluate management's performance. Auditors are often selected by a committee of independent non-management directors or by a full board of directors. (R. Knepper, *Liability of Corporate Officers and Directors*, sec. 1.03, at 5–6 (4th Ed.1988); Brodsky & Adamski, Corporate Officers & Directors, sec. 8.05, at 8 (1984); Farrell, *The Audit Committee–A Lawyer's View*, 28 Bus.Law. 1089, 1091 (1973).) While there is no Illinois law directly addressing this issue, we find that in the instant case, any decision regarding the selection of a new auditor should have been reserved for the full Board of Directors and not made unilaterally by management, absent any contrary corporate bylaws. We find invalid Vega's unilateral appointment of an auditor and order the full Board of Directors to vote on selection of an auditor.

We also hold invalid the Board of Directors' vote to reimburse plaintiff and order that the proposal be put to a vote that incorporates proper procedure. In that decision, plaintiff and Vega voted in favor of reimbursing plaintiff for attorney fees while Smider abstained, stating he needed more time to study the proposal. The trial court determined that all relief for plaintiff's attorney fees be considered by the corporation directly and that the board must find a way to "filter" it down to plaintiff. From the record it appears that the process used to reach the outcome of the vote was deficient in that Vega and plaintiff improperly voted.

Provisional directors appointed under section 12.55 are officers of the court and serve at the discretion and direction of the court. The trial court specifically instructed Vega to vote only upon deadlocked matters. We do not find Smider's abstention on the vote created a deadlock. Smider stated that he abstained from the vote because he had received the proposal only a short while before the meeting. Smider requested that the decision be postponed so he could vote on the matter cognizant of all relevant information. The trial court had instructed Vega, as provisional director, to ensure that the board of Directors operated in a "very formal fashion—the board of directors meetings would be set meetings; people would know when they would be; agendas would be kept; that a record of the board of directors meeting would be kept * * * that there be some record so that people can validate what was said."

We do not find it unreasonable under the circumstances for Smider to ask that the vote be postponed until he could thoroughly review the proposal for reimbursement; to vote without doing so would be an abdication of his duty as director to vote only when fully informed. Because there was no deadlock, we find Vega improperly voted on this issue. * * *

[W]e reiterate the trial court's admonition that in a uniquely structured corporate situation such as this, it is highly prudent to retain outside counsel to avoid further complications in the decision-making process. Complex issues regarding legality of votes and the division of corporate responsibility between management and the board need to be examined carefully in order to adhere to corporate bylaws and corporation law. * * *

For all of the foregoing reasons, we affirm in part and reverse and remand in part in accordance with this opinion.

Affirmed in part; affirmed as modified in part; vacated in part and remanded.

Notes

The Georgia integrated close corporation statute defines "extraordinary relief" for oppression or deadlock in close corporations to be involuntary dissolution or share buyouts. Ga. Bus. Corp. Code, §§ 14–2–942, 14–2–943. In addition, § 14–2–941 authorizes the following types of "ordinary relief":

(1) The performance, prohibition, alternation, or setting aside of any action of the corporation or of its shareholders, directors, or officers or of any other party to the proceeding;

(2) The cancellation or alteration of any provision in the corporation's articles of incorporation, bylaws, or agreement among the shareholders;

(3) The removal from office of any director or officer;

(4) The appointment of any individual as a director or officer;

(5) An accounting with respect to any matter in dispute;

(6) The appointment of a custodian to manage the business and affairs of the corporation;

(7) The appointment of a provisional director (who has all the rights, powers, and duties of a duly elected director) to serve for the term and under conditions prescribed by the court;

(8) The payment of dividends;

(9) The award of damages to any aggrieved party.

E. ACTION BY DIRECTORS

BALDWIN v. CANFIELD

Supreme Court of Minnesota, 1879.
26 Minn. 43, 1 N.W. 261.

[Editor: A corporation, The Minneapolis Agricultural and Mechanical Association, owned valuable real estate. All the shares of stock were owned by William S. King. In late 1872, King borrowed $10,000 from Baldwin, the cashier of the State National Bank. The loan was secured by a pledge of the stock of the association, and King stated to Baldwin that the stock represented the land. In August 1873, King entered into a contract with Canfield to sell the real estate owned by the association for $65,000 in bonds issued by the

Northern Pacific Railroad Corporation. Originally King agreed to convey the real estate personally, but Canfield learned that it was held by the association, and King agreed that he would have the association convey the real estate to Canfield and, in addition, would redeem the pledged shares and deliver them to Canfield.

King caused the directors of the association to execute a deed as described by the Court below and delivered it to Canfield. Canfield delivered the bonds to King but "through inadvertence" did not demand a delivery of the stock. King did not redeem the pledged shares but converted the bonds to his own use.]

Berry, J.

After the agreement of August 14, 1873, between King and Canfield, King, in pursuance thereof and in order to carry it out, caused a deed to be executed by the several persons heretofore named as the directors of said association. This deed, which is in form one of bargain and sale without covenants, purports to be a conveyance of the fair ground property by the Minneapolis Agricultural and Mechanical Association to Thomas H. Canfield, and is signed as follows, viz.:

The Minneapolis Agricultural and Mechanical Association

[Seal]

By R.J. Mendenhall, Thomas Lowry, W.D. Washburn, C.G. Goodrich, G.F. Stevens, Wm. S. King, Levi Butler, W.W. Eastman, W.P. Westfall, Dorilus Morrison, Geo. A. Brackett, directors of said corporation.

The execution of this deed was never authorized or directed at or by any meeting of said directors of said association, nor was any resolution ever passed by said board of directors in reference to the execution of said deed by said last-named parties, or any of them, or authorizing the seal of said corporation to be attached to any such deed, or authorizing the sale or conveyance of said property in any way to said Canfield. The deed was executed by the parties above named separately and at different times, wherever they happened to be, at the request of King or his attorney, for the purpose of enabling King to convey said property to Canfield. The deed was executed by Stevens at Utica, in the state of New York, by Morrison and Brackett in the city of New York, and by the other signers thereof in Hennepin county. * * *

This action was brought by Baldwin and the State National Bank of Minneapolis, as plaintiffs, against the Minneapolis Agricultural and Mechanical Association, and King and Canfield, as defendants. Canfield appeared and answered. Neither of the other defendants was served with process or appeared in the action. * * *

The fourth conclusion is called in question by the counsel for defendant Canfield, but we have no doubt of its correctness. As we have already seen, the court below finds that, by its articles of incorporation, the government of the Minneapolis Agricultural and Mechanical Association, and the management of its affairs, was vested in the board of directors. The legal effect of this was to invest the directors with such government and management *as a board,* and not otherwise. This is in accordance with the general rule that the governing body of a corporation, as such, are agents of the corporation only as a board, and not individually. Hence it follows that they have no authority to act, save when assembled at a board meeting. The separate action, individually, of the persons composing such governing body, is not the action of the constituted body of men clothed with corporate powers. In Vermont a somewhat different rule is allowed, as in the Bank of Middlebury v. Rutland & Washington R. Co., 30 Vt. 159. In that case, and perhaps others in that state, it is held that directors may bind their corporation by acting separately, if this is their usual practice in transacting the corporate business. But we think that the general rule before mentioned is the more rational one, and it is supported by the great weight of authority. From the application of this rule to the facts of this case, it follows that the fourth conclusion of law, viz., that the deed purporting to be made by the association was not the act and deed of such association, and therefore did not convey the title to the premises in question to Canfield, is correct. The directors took no action as a board with reference to the sale of the premises or the execution of any deed thereof. So far as in any way binding the corporation is concerned, their action in executing the deed was a nullity. They could not bind it by their separate and individual action. Hence it follows that the so-called deed is not only ineffectual as a conveyance of real property, but equally so as a contract to convey.

[An order canceling Canfield's deed as a cloud upon the title of the real estate was affirmed.]

MICKSHAW v. COCA COLA BOTTLING CO.

Superior Court of Pennsylvania, 1950.
166 Pa.Super. 148, 70 A.2d 467.

DITHRICH, JUDGE.

This is an action in assumpsit brought to recover the difference in pay between what plaintiff received for his military service in World War II and what he would have received had he continued to work for defendant.

On October 1, 1940, the following article appeared in the Sharon Herald:

"Coca–Cola Firm to Pay All Draftees

The Coca–Cola Bottling Co., Inc. of Sharon to-day took a place among the outstanding patriotic firms of the Shenango Valley.

William Feinberg, Manager, announced that any employee called to the colors through the conscription law will not lose a cent in wages. The company is prepared to pay the difference between the government wages and the amount the employee received before he went to camp.

Feinberg said this ruling will protect every man employed by the company and the 'pay while away' plan will be continued as long as the man is in service.

The announcement, made to employees today, gives them a more optimistic view on the approaching draft. If called, they will be able to leave with knowledge that dependents will continue to receive customary income as long as they are away."

Plaintiff testified that Feinberg, manager and secretary of the defendant, showed the article to him and two of the three other employees liable to be conscripted, stating " * * * that he was going to take care of us when he went into the service, that he would pay the difference between what we made at the Coca Cola Company and what the government paid us."

Plaintiff continued in defendant's employ for two years. Then in October 1942, having received notice to report for his Selective Service physical examination, he enlisted in the Coast Guard and served with that branch some 37 months. He returned from the service and resumed working for defendant in December 1945. In May 1947 he left the employ of defendant, and in September of that year first made demand for payment for those years during which he was in service. He said the reason for the delay was that since he had returned to the employ of defendant he was afraid that demand for the difference in pay during his absence in the service would imperil his job. His claim was for $3,588. Upon trial the jury awarded him $1,000. From the denial of motions for a new trial and for judgment n.o.v. defendant appeals. * * *

The remaining three questions are answered in the following excerpts from the opinion of President Judge Rowley, which we adopt:

" 'If the statement was made, did William Feinberg have the authority to bind the Coca Cola Bottling Company, a corporation?' * * *

"The control of the business of a private corporation is vested in its board of directors. There were three directors of the defendant corporation, William Feinberg, Myer Ackerman, and his father, Samuel Ackerman.

"Director Feinberg testified that he authorized the publication which stated that announcement of the proposal had been made to the employees that day. Director Myer Ackerman testified that he knew of the published announcement on the day it appeared. Upon direct examination, Myer Ackerman was asked

" 'Q. Did the directors take any action, approving the payment, making up the difference between what employees of your company would receive, if they were drafted, and what they would have received if they had remained in your employ? A. It was not discussed until after we saw it in the paper.

" 'Q. Did you have anything to do with putting in the paper that particular article? A. I didn't object to it.'

"It therefore appears that the directors of the corporation did discuss the proposal; that director Feinberg authorized the proposal, and director Myer Ackerman acquiesced in it.

"Feinberg, secretary and director, Myer Ackerman, vice-president and director, Arnold Hyman, assistant manager and all the employees, Mickshaw, Zoldan, Rossi and Gray, knew of the published proposal on or about the date of its appearance. It would not be a violent assumption to infer that the third director, Samuel Ackerman, then president of the company, also knew of it. However that may be, Feinberg and Myer Ackerman constituted a majority of the board and we think that their conduct was a sufficient ratification of the proposal.

"It would be grossly unjust to require a claimant against a corporation to prove his case by formal corporate records. It is well known that corporations which include few stockholders do not often act with as much formality as larger companies. This is especially so where the members of the board, actually and directly, personally conduct the business. * * *

"Plaintiff's suit is based upon an oral proposal alleged to have been made to him by Feinberg. The substance of the proposal was embodied in the newspaper item published at the direction of Feinberg. This publication was, tacitly at least, approved by Myer Ackerman. There was no disavowal by Samuel Ackerman, the third director, or by the corporation, of Feinberg's authority to make the published proposal. If the circumstances warranted the inference that the corporation, by previous authorization, or by subsequent ratification, or by acquiescence with knowledge of the facts, approved Feinberg's published offer, we think it may be assumed that he could bind his company by an oral proposal of substantially the same terms to the same persons.

"It was undisputed that the proposal was published, that the publication was directed by Feinberg; that Myer Ackerman approved it; and that Samuel Ackerman did not disavow it; that no officer of the company had disavowed it to the date of trial. * * *

"It seems to us that the trial revolved about two points: first whether Feinberg could bind the corporation without a resolution of the board of directors, and second, whether Feinberg made the proposal as claimed by plaintiff. The first question was answered by the Court, the second by the jury. * * *"

COOKE v. LYNN SAND & STONE COMPANY

Appeals Court of Massachusetts, 1994.
37 Mass.App.Ct. 490, 640 N.E.2d 786.

Before IRELAND, KAPLAN and LAURENCE, JJ.

KAPLAN, JUSTICE.

The plaintiff, [James H. Cooke,] who was a director, officer, and shareholder of a closely held corporation, sued to enforce an employment contract naming the corporation as employer and himself as employee. We hold that the contract * * * is invalid and should be denied enforcement. The plaintiff's claim for alleged misrepresentation also fails.

 HOLDING:

* * * Lynn Sand & Stone Company (Lynn Sand) was a family owned company in the business described as crushed stone and ready mixed concrete manufacturing. It was founded in 1918 by the plaintiff's grandfather, upon whose death in 1930 the plaintiff's father, Theodore Cooke, took over. He retired in 1968 but served thereafter as chairman of the board of directors.

The plaintiff, after taking a postcollege degree of bachelor of science at the University of Colorado, joined the company with the title of chief engineer in 1955. He worked continuously there, first under his father, Theodore, then under Raymond F. Pybus, who was president in the years 1968–1975. In 1975, the plaintiff became president and assumed active management of the company. Robert Prosperi (not a member of the Cooke family) joined the company in the fall of 1975, later became a vice president, and undertook duties as the plaintiff's subordinate. The two men ran the day-to-day business, consulting from time to time with Theodore. The board of directors met annually to receive reports, but it took little action by way of guiding the progress of the business.

In 1981–1982 the board of directors consisted of Theodore, the plaintiff (son), Nancy Latta (daughter), Phillips Cooke (son), and Prosperi. Officers included: the plaintiff, president; Prosperi, Phillips, and Latta, vice presidents. Theodore owned about thirty-three percent of the company (and controlled more); the plaintiff and Phillips (with spouses) about twenty-two percent each; the rest was also substantially in family hands.

The plaintiff fixed his own salary largely in accordance with a formula described in the record and also set Prosperi's salary. They served at will without written contracts. In 1979, however, Prosperi asked for a contract, evidently to stabilize his position in the company, and company counsel wrote a five-year contract for him * * *. Theodore was told in advance about the contract; it was not presented to the board of directors for approval or ratification, but the members knew about it.

At this time there was in force a resolution of the board adopted at its annual meeting on April 30, 1979: "It was voted unanimously to authorize the president and vice presidents to sign contracts and documents in the name of the corporation when they believe such action to be in its best interest." The same resolution was adopted at the annual meetings held on May 13, 1980, May 5, 1981, and April 22, 1982, but in the last case the authorization was only to the plaintiff and Prosperi by name.[19]

On June 10, 1981, the 1979 contract with Prosperi was superseded by a five-year contract written by him dating from January 1, 1981. It was signed for the company by the plaintiff, as president, and by Prosperi, as employee. The contract was not referred to the board. Prosperi may have had a rising impression that the company would be sold and felt that he needed solid protection against dismissal by the new owners.[20]

Similar considerations were at work in the plaintiff's mind on his own account. While Prosperi was in the course of preparing his 1981 contract, the plaintiff asked him to prepare a like five-year draft naming the plaintiff as employee (alike except for the salary and related terms); he intended to show the draft to Theodore to get his approval. Although retired, Theodore was still a power in the company by reason of family status and major stock ownership, besides his chairmanship of the board. In May, 1981, the plaintiff showed the draft to Theodore and discussed with him the advisability of the plaintiff's securing this contract for a term of years. Theodore's response was that the plaintiff should see what the others thought of it. Following the conversation, the plaintiff on May 26, 1981, circulated the draft contract to the board members. The draft left room for signature by Theodore, board chairman, for the company, as employer, and by the plaintiff, as employee. The plaintiff wrote that he was circulating the draft "at Dad's request in his capacity as Chairman of the Board of Directors. Please communicate your comments,

19. [By the Court] It is not made clear how the change came to be made.

20. [By the Court] The plaintiff mentioned that in practice Prosperi was receiving more salary than noted on the 1979 contract, and so adjustment of the contract was called for.

approval or disapproval to him since this is a Board of Directors matter."[21] Nothing came of this. The plaintiff did not speak to the board members nor the members to him. A couple of weeks after May 26, Theodore, on a visit to the company office, bringing the draft with him, told the plaintiff that he was a member of the family and didn't need a contract. (It appears that no family member had ever had a written contract with the company.) The plaintiff said he threw the draft into the waste paper basket.

On July 2, 1982, a new employment contract for Prosperi to run afresh for five years from July 1, 1982, was drawn up by him and executed in the same form as the 1981 Prosperi contract. It was not referred to the board of directors.

Shortly after the making of the 1982 Prosperi contract, the plaintiff instructed Prosperi to write a contract for him similar to the Prosperi contract (except for salary and related provisions). The plaintiff says that this was at Prosperi's suggestion; it was surely with a view to the possible takeover of the company. Prosperi complied, and the parties signed on September 3, 1982. Now the roles were reversed: Prosperi now signed as vice president on the part of the company, and the plaintiff signed as employee.

This September, 1982, contract was not referred to the board, nor did the members know at the time that it existed. Neither the plaintiff's contract nor Prosperi's was mentioned in the notes to the year-end financial statements sent to board members and stockholders.

In early 1983, a number of possible purchasers of the business were heard from. The plaintiff proposed himself as a buyer (apparently on a stock purchase basis). Trimount Bituminous Products Co. (Trimount) had long been in touch with Theodore and Phillips Cooke, and on April 14, 1983, at a meeting attended among others by the plaintiff, Trimount presented, in the form of an unsigned letter, a tentative offer to acquire the substantial assets of Lynn Sand. On April 25, 1983, Milton Heffron and John Benevento made an offer to purchase the shares of Lynn Sand. This, unlike the assets offer, would involve the takeover by the purchaser of contracts to which Lynn Sand was a party. So also it seemed possible that the Trimount company might change to an offer for shares. At this point the plaintiff decided to disclose his contract (and Prosperi's). The plaintiff had to be wary of letting a sale go through with important information withheld by him. Thus the plaintiff, probably on April 25, sent to the prospective buyers, including, as he said, Trimount and Stuart M. Lamb, Jr., its president, a "To Whom It May Concern" memorandum informing them of the contracts and setting out a bare sketch of the terms (the text was not supplied). On April 29 the plaintiff sent a memorandum to the members of the board of directors of Lynn Sand, enclosing the memorandum previously sent to the prospective buyers.[22]

---

21. [By the Court] The memorandum continued: "In the past I have waived having a contract although I would have been more comfortable with one. Since we are now actively engaged in exploring a 'taxes deferred' merger with Lonestar Industries (and perhaps some others in the future) I feel some urgency to have one. I have patterned the draft from the agreement the Company has with Bob Prosperi. The text of his is almost identical."

22. [By the Court] About the contracts, the memorandum said: "These were made for the benefit of the company to keep our resumes 'off the street.' "

Phillips Cooke testified that he spoke with Theodore promptly after April 29. Both believed the plaintiff's purported contract was invalid. They communicated their opinion to Lamb.

Perhaps a few days before May 4, Lamb met with the plaintiff and they discussed the plaintiff's possible future in case of a takeover. The plaintiff did not mention his contract. Nor did Lamb refer to the contract. Lamb says he did not know of it at the time, but this sometimes translates as a reflection of his understanding that the contract was simply void. Following the meeting with the plaintiff, Lamb sent the plaintiff a letter dated May 4 inviting him to work in effect for Trimount in the event of a "marriage" between the two companies, but at a salary of $60,000 (no term beyond a year mentioned), which was substantially less than the annual salary set in the plaintiff's contract. Lamb wrote to Theodore on May 9, saying that he had had a long talk with the plaintiff regarding his responsibilities if a marriage should take place and enclosing a copy of the May 4 letter. The letter to Theodore is in line with Phillips' testimony that from an early point in the negotiations with Lamb, which were conducted on the side of Lynn Sand by Theodore and Phillips, Theodore had impressed on Lamb that any buyer must find a place for the plaintiff in the new organization—the buyer to do this as a good faith or business understanding, not as a legal obligation.

Trimount on May 18, 1983, made a definite written offer for the purchase of the shares of Lynn Sand that might be tendered by the shareholders, provided the shares of Theodore and Phillips Cooke, amounting to a majority, were tendered. The plaintiff learned of the offer that day. Theodore had his attorney, Mr. Richard Wyman, review the offer. Wyman drew up an "Addendum"[23] which became part of the offer on May 19 and was seen the same day by the plaintiff. The Addendum contained the following two items (other terms will be mentioned below):

    1. Notwithstanding the provisions of paragraph 2, the parties agree as follows:

    (a) Undisclosed liabilities which do not materially affect the net worth of Lynn shall not be deemed a breach of the stockholders warranties, representations and agreements under paragraph 2.

    (b) The outstanding employment contracts between (1) Lynn and Robert Prosperi and (2) Lynn and James Cooke shall not be deemed undisclosed liabilities of Lynn, and Trimount recognizes that this agreement is subject to said contracts.

All shares of the company were tendered. The plaintiff tendered his shares on May 27 at the stated offering price per share, a total of about $1.1 million.[24]

The plaintiff went to work under Trimount auspices after the takeover but refused to accept a monthly salary check based on an annual salary of $60,000 and insisted on performance of the 1982 contract. The impasse ended

23. [By the Court] Initialed by Lamb and Phillips Cooke.

24. [By the Court] On May 29, the plaintiff circulated a memorandum to the staff of Lynn

Sand stating that he was extremely disappointed in members of his family; he had tried to purchase the company by a leveraged buyout

with a letter from Lamb terminating the relationship as of July 8, 1983.[25] (The Prosperi contract raised no problem as he was put to work immediately at an advanced salary without regard to the contract.) * * *

[The Court held that Cooke's employment contract was executed in violation of fiduciary duties and the duty of candor he owed to the corporation. The Court also questioned whether the contract met a standard of fairness.]

The secret 1982 contract cannot be validated by reference to the resolution of the board of directors, adopted annually, to authorize the president and a vice president to sign contracts in the name of the corporation. The resolution was boilerplate. Quite naturally it looks to contracts by the corporation with third parties, not with an insider. This was the view taken by the plaintiff's fellow directors who considered the contract to be void (the view communicated to Trimount's president). The plaintiff himself acquiesced in the limited scope of the resolution; when he submitted the 1981 draft contract to board members for their "approval or disapproval" he said, "this is a Board of Directors matter"—not a matter for decision by the plaintiff and Prosperi.[26]

There has been argument that the Addendum to the letter offer of May 18, 1983, initialed by Lamb and Phillips Cooke, might serve to make the contract enforceable. There is nothing in the Addendum that represents a ratification by Lynn Sand of the contract and no such action was ever taken by the board of directors or the shareholders—the votes, of course, would not have been there. Nor did the Addendum represent any adoption or assumption of the contract by Trimount. As noted above, paragraph 1(b) speaks of the contract as "outstanding" and states that the agreement is "subject" to it. There is no language of adoption or assumption, and the paragraph is readily understood as acknowledging that a claim may be asserted under the contract and that Trimount has been made aware of it (so Lynn Sand's selling shareholders may not be charged later with concealment). * * * A contrary interpretation, that Trimount was accepting the plaintiff's five-year contract, is lexically possible in the abstract but in the circumstances of this case is unlikely to the point of being incongruous. There is no basis for a belief that

but was "precluded" from doing so mainly by his father.

25. [By the Court] In a letter of July 7, 1983, to the plaintiff, Lamb wrote that he had recently been furnished with a copy of the purported contract of 1982 between Lynn Sand and the plaintiff. Lynn Sand (now a subsidiary of Trimount) did not recognize the validity of the contract as its execution was not authorized by the board of directors. When Lamb met with Theodore in the latter part of 1982 to discuss the purchase of the company, he was told there was no such employment agreement. In meetings with the plaintiff in the latter part of 1982 and early in 1983 the plaintiff never mentioned the contract. After the plaintiff's April 29, 1983, memorandum to the board, Theodore and Phillips each stated to Lamb that the board had never been shown the contract, had never authorized it, and did not recognize its validity. At the time of the purchase of the shares owned by Theodore and

Phillips, they and Jim Porath, the company's former accountant, requested that Lamb acknowledge his awareness of the plaintiff's claim to employment so that no charge could be made against the selling shareholders for failing to disclose a liability not shown on the year-end financial statement of the company. Lamb acknowledged the disclosure of the plaintiff's claim but not the validity of the claim. Lamb was still willing to continue the plaintiff's employment under the terms of the letter of May 4, 1983, but not under the alleged contract.

26. [By the Court] If, as we suggest, the resolution did not empower president/vice president to make a contract with an insider, then the 1982 contract appears invalid unless ratified by the board of directors, and a separate showing of breach of fiduciary duty may be considered redundant although strongly supportive of the result.

Trimount (Lamb) would intend any such interpretation or result. Nor would the plaintiff have understood the paragraph in such a sense. Theodore disapproved of a company contract with the plaintiff and had been kept in ignorance of the purported contract; in fact he repudiated it. The plaintiff could hardly suppose that Theodore or Phillips would have prevailed on Lamb to embrace the contract liability as part of the takeover. (We note, by the way, that the Addendum was written by Theodore's attorney who presumably knew and would respect Theodore's views.)[27] * * *

Judgment for the defendants.

Notes

(1) Consider particularly MBCA § 8.21. To what extent does this section supplant various common law doctrines such as ratification, estoppel, acquiescence, and unjust enrichment that might lead a court to hold a corporation bound on an obligation even though it was not formally approved by the board of directors acting at a meeting?

(2) Since a majority of the board acting at a meeting can bind the corporation, why should not a majority acting informally pursuant to MBCA § 8.21 also bind the corporation? Some states authorize a majority of shareholders to act informally without a meeting. See p. 456, supra. Why not directors as well?

(3) Directors may be subject to personal liability for failing to exercise due care in making decisions (and for failing to make decisions or paying attention to corporate affairs). See MBCA § 8.30. This liability, however, is limited by the so-called "business judgment rule" and possibly by specific exonerating provisions in the articles of incorporation. See MBCA § 2.02(b)(4). These duties and limitations on duties largely evolved in cases involving publicly held corporations and are discussed in that context. See Chapter 10.

(4) Directors may also be subject to personal liability for violating a duty of loyalty to the corporation, specifically self-dealing transactions and usurpation of corporate opportunities. See MBCA §§ 8.60–8.63. These duties are discussed in Chapter 11.

(5) The various mechanics and requirements for directors and directors meetings are set forth in MBCA §§ 8.20–8.25.

F. AUTHORITY OF OFFICERS

BLACK v. HARRISON HOME CO.

Supreme Court of California, 1909.
155 Cal. 121, 99 P. 494.

ANGELLOTTI, J.

This action is one originally brought by plaintiffs to compel specific performance of an alleged contract for the sale by defendant corporation to plaintiffs of lots 1 and 2 in block J of the Morris Vineyard tract, in the city of Los Angeles. * * *

[Editor: The Harrison Home Co. originally issued 1,000 shares of stock. In 1895, Mrs. Sarah Harrison apparently owned 502 shares and her daughter,

---

27. [By the Court] The plaintiff claimed that the Addendum was in effect a false statement on which he relied in selling his shares. This misrepresentation count falls with the other.

Sarah = 502
Olive = 498

Olive M Harrison, owned 498 shares. On May 31, 1905, Olive M. Harrison died "intestate, never having been married and being without issue. She was then a woman of about 35 years of age." On June 15, 1905, Mrs. Harrison entered into a contract to sell a piece of real estate owned by the corporation. Twelve days later her lawyer notified the buyer that the corporation declined to comply with the contract "on account of misunderstanding and seeming misrepresentations" by which they were obtained, and also "by reason of the fact that Mrs. Harrison has not the requisite authority to enter into such a contract or to fulfill it on behalf of the Harrison Home Company." This refusal was duly communicated to the parties, and this action followed.]

It is an elementary principle of corporation law that the president of a corporation has no power, merely because he is president, to bind the corporation by contract. The management of the affairs of a corporation is ordinarily in the hands of its board of directors, and the president has only such power as has been given him by the by-laws and by the board of directors, and such other power as may arise from his having assumed and exercised the power in the past with the apparent consent and acquiescence of the corporation. The general rule in this regard is stated in 2 Cook on Corporations § 716, as follows: "The president of a corporation has no power to buy, sell, or contract for the corporation, nor to control its property, funds, or management. This is a rule which prevails everywhere, excepting possibly in the state of Illinois. * * * It is true that the board of directors may expressly authorize the president to contract; or his authority to contract may arise from his having assumed and exercised that power in the past; or the corporation may ratify his contract or accept the benefits of it, and thereby be bound. But the general rule is that the president cannot act or contract for the corporation any more than any other one director." * * *

The principal claim of plaintiffs and interveners is that defendant corporation is estopped to deny the binding effect of the acts of Mrs. Harrison. In the discussion of this branch of the case, much is made by appellants of the asserted fact that Mrs. Harrison is the owner of all the stock of the defendant corporation and is really the only person interested therein, and that she is here using the corporation simply to protect herself against her contract for the conveyance of what is practically her own property. If we assume that her ownership of all the stock would be a material factor, the trouble with appellants' position is that the record does not warrant the conclusion that the stock is so owned. Olive M. Harrison, the daughter, upon the record before us, must be held to have been the absolute owner, at the time of her death, only two weeks before the transactions in question, of 498 shares, practically one-half of the entire stock of the corporation. Giving the utmost force to the stipulation of the parties as to her dying intestate, never having been married and without issue, the property left by her is subject to administration and the payment of her debts, and Mrs. Harrison will have only what is left after administration. It cannot be assumed that Olive M. Harrison did not leave creditors, or that it will not be necessary to sell in due course of administration all or some portion of her stock to pay debts and expenses of the administration. Under these circumstances, Mrs. Harrison did not have absolute control of such stock at the time of the transactions in question, or at any time prior to the trial of this action, and cannot be held to have been such an owner thereof that her acts could affect the stock owned by her daughter at the time of her death.

There is nothing in the record warranting the assumption of learned counsel for plaintiffs and interveners that prior to the transaction in question the president of defendant corporation had ever assumed and exercised any power to bind the corporation by his own contract for the disposition of its real estate. * * * The authorities cited by counsel in support of the well-settled rule that a corporation may be so estopped cannot be held applicable. * * * They simply affirm what are well-settled rules, viz., that a corporation will be bound so far as third persons are concerned by the acts of its agent which are within the apparent scope of his authority, and that the authority of an officer to make certain contracts on behalf of the corporation may arise as to third persons from his having assumed and exercised that authority in the past with the acquiescence of the corporation, and that a corporation may ratify and render binding a contract entered into by one of its officers in excess of his authority. None of these rules has, in our judgment, any application upon the record before us.

There was no acceptance by defendant of any benefit of either of these transactions, and consequently no estoppel on that ground. * * *

The judgment and orders denying a new trial are affirmed.

Notes

(1) The comments in the principal case about the relative roles of the board of directors and the president of a corporation are not only representative of early judicial thinking but also seem firmly grounded in the language of many corporation statutes. Compare MBCA §§ 8.01, 8.41, last paragraph.

(2) Most corporation statutes specify that every corporation must have designated officers, usually a president, a secretary, and a treasurer. Earlier versions of the MBCA also specified these officers, but the Model Act generally does not. Compare MBCA § 8.40(a); see, however, §§ 8.40(c), 1.40(20). Why not require designated officers? The Official Comment to § 8.40 suggests that "[e]xperience has shown * * * that little purpose is served by a statutory requirement that there be certain officers, and statutory requirements may sometimes create problems of implied or apparent authority or confusion with nonstatutory offices the corporation desires to create."

(3) Presumably, the chief executive officer of a small corporation, no matter what his or her formal title, will be required to take a number of actions on his or her own authority. For example, who is to hire secretaries, order needed equipment and supplies and the like? Where does one go to find the basis of authority? One possible source is the bylaws of the corporation, which usually describe the roles and responsibilities of the principal officers. James R. Burkhard, Proposed Model Bylaws To Be Used With The Revised Model Business Corporation Act (1984), 46 Bus.Law. 189, 225–26 (1990),[28] suggests the following descriptions of the roles of the president, secretary, and treasurer:

§ 4.4 President.

The president shall be the principal executive officer of the corporation and, subject to the control of the board of directors, shall in general supervise and control all of the business and affairs of the corporation. He shall, when present, preside at all meetings of the shareholders and of the board of directors. He may sign, with the secretary or any other proper officer of the corporation thereunto authorized by the board of directors, certificates for shares of the corporation and deeds, mortgages, bonds, contracts, or other instruments which the board of directors has authorized to be executed, except in cases where the signing and execution thereof shall be expressly delegated by the board of directors or by these bylaws to some other officer or agent of the corporation, or shall be required by law to be otherwise signed or executed; and in general shall perform all duties incident to the office of president and such other duties as may be prescribed by the board of directors from time to time. * * *

§ 4.6 The Secretary.

The secretary shall: (a) keep the minutes of the proceedings of the shareholders and of the board of directors in one or more books provided for that purpose; (b) see that all notices are duly given in accordance with the provisions of these bylaws or as required by law; (c) be custodian of the corporate records and of any seal of the corporation and if there is a seal of the corporation, see that it is affixed to all documents the execution of which on behalf of the corporation under its seal is duly authorized; (d) when requested or required, authenticate any records of the corporation; (e) keep a register of the post office address of each shareholder which shall be furnished to the secretary by such shareholder; (f) sign with the president, or a vice-president, certificates for shares of the corporation, the issuance of which shall have been authorized by resolution of the board of directors; (g) have general charge of the stock transfer books of the corporation; and (h) in general perform all duties incident to the office of secretary and such other duties as from time to time may be assigned to him by the president or by the board of directors. * * *

§ 4.7 The Treasurer.

The treasurer shall: (a) have charge and custody of and be responsible for all funds and securities of the corporation; (b) receive and give receipts for moneys due and payable to the corporation from any source whatsoever, and deposit all such moneys in the name of the corporation in such banks, trust companies, or other depositories as shall be selected by the board of directors; and (c) in general perform all of the duties incident to the office of treasurer and such other duties as from time to time may be assigned to him by the president or by the board of directors. If required by the board of directors, the treasurer shall give a bond for the faithful discharge of his duties in such sum and with such surety or sureties as the board of directors shall determine. * * *

Burkhard notes that these bylaws "grant very little express authority to the officers," and that it may be desirable to set specific limits on authority, e.g., in a closely held corporation, "all checks in excess of $5,000 must bear the signature of the president and secretary." Id. at 225.

(4) Where else might one look for authority? What should be the dividing line between the proper and the improper, i.e., between things the operating officer can do on his own and the things that should be approved by the board of directors?

LEE v. JENKINS BROS.

United States Court of Appeals, Second Circuit, 1959.
268 F.2d 357.

MEDINA, CIRCUIT JUDGE. * * *

[Editor: In 1919, the Crane Company agreed to sell its Bridgeport, Connecticut, plant to a New Jersey Corporation, Jenkins Brothers. Jenkins Brothers felt it needed to employ competent personnel, and sought to employ Lee, the business manager of Crane Company. Yardley, the President of Jenkins Brothers and a substantial stockholder, met with Lee at a hotel on June 1, 1920, and sought to entice him to join Jenkins Brothers. Also present was a vice president and his wife, though at the time of the trial in October 1957 only Lee was alive to describe the conversation.]

First, Lee testified:

As far as the pension that I had earned with Crane Company he said the company [Jenkins Brothers] would pay that pension (and) if they didn't or, if anything came up, he would assume the liability himself, he would guarantee payment of the pension; and in consideration of that promise I agreed to go to work for Jenkins Bros. on June 1, 1920.

The amount of the pension referred to by Mr. Yardley was a maximum of $1500 a year and that would be paid me when I reached the age of 60 years; regardless of what happened in the meantime, if I were with the company or not, I would be given a credit for those 13 years of service with the maximum pension of $1500.

Later Lee put it this way:

Mr. Farnham Yardley said that Jenkins would assume the obligation for my credit pension record with Crane Company and, if anything happened and they did not pay it, he would guarantee it himself.

Mr. Yardley's words were 'regardless of what happens, you will get that pension if you join our company.'

Finally, Lee summarized his position:

My claim is that the company through the chairman of the board of directors and the president, promised me credit for my 13 years of service with Crane Company, regardless of what happened I would receive a pension at the age of 60, not to exceed $1,500 a year. If I was discharged in 1921 or 1922 or left I would still get that pension. That is what I am asking for.

This agreement was never reduced to writing.

Lee's prospects with Jenkins turned out to be just about as bright as he had hoped. He subsequently became vice president and general manager in charge of manufacturing and a director of the company. At that time he was receiving a salary of $25,000 from Jenkins, $8,000 more from an affiliate, plus an annual 10 percent bonus. In 1945, however, after 25 years with Jenkins, Lee was discharged at the age of 55 * * *.

In the discussion which follows we assume *arguendo*, that there was evidence sufficient to support a finding that Yardley orally agreed on behalf of the corporation that Lee would be paid at the age of 60 a pension not to exceed $1500, and that Yardley's words "regardless of what happens" were, as Lee contends, to be interpreted as meaning that Lee would receive this pension even if he were not working for Jenkins at the time the pension became payable. Jenkins asserts that Yardley had no authority to bind it to such an "extraordinary" contract, express, implied, or apparent and the trial court so found. There is nothing in the proofs submitted by Lee to warrant any finding of actual authority in Yardley. The Certificate of Incorporation and By–Laws of Jenkins are not in evidence nor was any course of conduct shown as between the corporation and Yardley. Accordingly, on the phase of the case now under discussion, we are dealing only with apparent authority. See 2 Fletcher, Cyclopedia Corporations, Section 449 (Perm.Ed.1954). * * *

The ascertainment of the Connecticut law on this critical question of Yardley's apparent authority is a far from simple task. The Connecticut cases have not yet quite come to grips with the question. Hence, it is necessary to consult the "general" law on the subject, on the assumption that, if a general rule can be found, Connecticut would follow it. * * *

Our question on this phase of the case then boils itself down to the following: can it be said as a matter of law that Yardley as president, chairman of the board, substantial stockholder and trustee and son-in-law of the estate of the major stockholder, had no power in the presence of the company's most interested vice president to secure for a "reasonable" length of time badly needed key personnel by promising an experienced local executive a life pension to commence in 30 years at the age of 60, even if Lee were not then working for the corporation, when the maximum liability to Jenkins under such a pension was $1500 per year.

A survey of the law on the authority of corporate officers does not reveal a completely consistent pattern. For the most part the courts perhaps have taken a rather restrictive view on the extent of powers of corporate officials, but the dissatisfaction with such an approach has been manifested in a variety of exceptions such as ratification, estoppel, and promissory estoppel. * * *

The rule most widely cited is that the president only has authority to bind his company by acts arising in the usual and regular course of business but not for contracts of an "extraordinary" nature. The substance of such a rule lies in the content of the term "extraordinary" which is subject to a broad range of interpretation.

The growth and development of this rule occurred during the late nineteenth and early twentieth centuries when the potentialities of the corporate form of enterprise were just being realized. As the corporation became a more common vehicle for the conduct of business it became increasingly evident that many corporations, particularly small closely held ones, did not normally function in the formal ritualistic manner hitherto envisaged. While the boards of directors still nominally controlled corporate affairs, in reality officers and managers frequently ran the business with little, if any, board supervision. The natural consequence of such a development was that third parties commonly relied on the authority of such officials in almost all the multifarious transactions in which corporations engaged. The pace of modern business life was too swift to insist on the approval by the board of directors of every transaction that was in any way "unusual."

The judicial recognition given to these developments has varied considerably. Whether termed "apparent authority" or an "estoppel" to deny authority, many courts have noted the injustice caused by the practice of permitting corporations to act commonly through their executives and then allowing them to disclaim an agreement as beyond the authority of the contracting officer, when the contract no longer suited its convenience. Other courts, however, continued to cling to the past with little attempt to discuss the unconscionable results obtained or the doctrine of apparent authority. Such restrictive views have been generally condemned by the commentators.

The summary of holdings pro and con in general on the subject of what are and what are not "extraordinary" agreements is inconclusive at best * * *. But the pattern becomes more distinct when we turn to the more limited area of employment contracts.

It is generally settled that the president as part of the regular course of business has authority to hire and discharge employees and fix their compensation. In so doing he may agree to hire them for a specific number of years if the term selected is deemed reasonable. But employment contracts for life or on a "permanent" basis are generally regarded as "extraordinary" and beyond the authority of any corporate executive if the only consideration for the promise is the employee's promise to work for that period. Jenkins would have us analogize the pension agreement involved herein to these generally condemned lifetime employment contracts because it extends over a long period of time, is of indefinite duration, and involves an indefinite liability on the part of the corporation.

It is not surprising that lifetime employment contracts have met with substantial hostility in the courts, for these contracts are often oral, uncorroborated, vague in important details and highly improbable. Accordingly, the courts have erected a veritable array of obstacles to their enforcement. They have been construed as terminable at will, too indefinite to enforce, *ultra vires,* lacking in mutuality or consideration, abandoned or breached by subsequent acts, and the supporting evidence deemed insufficient to go to the jury, as well as made without proper authority.

Where reasons have been given to support the conclusion that lifetime employments are "extraordinary," and hence made without authority, a scrutiny of these reasons may be helpful for their bearing on the analogous field of pension agreements. It is said that: they unduly restrict the power of the shareholders and future boards of directors on questions of managerial policy; they subject the corporation to an inordinately substantial amount of liability; they run for long and indefinite periods of time. Of these reasons the only one applicable to pension agreements is that they run for long and indefinite periods of time. There the likeness stops. Future director or shareholder control is in no way impeded; the amount of liability is not disproportionate; the agreement was not only not unreasonable but beneficial and necessary to the corporation; and pension contracts are commonly used fringe benefits in employment contracts. Moreover, unlike the case with life employment contracts, courts have often gone out of their way to find pension promises binding and definite even when labeled gratuitous by the employer. The consideration given to the employee involved is not at all dependent on profits or sales, nor does it involve some other variable suggesting director discretion.

In this case Lee was hired at a starting salary of $4,000 per year plus a contemplated pension of $1500 per year in thirty years. Had Lee been hired at a starting salary of $10,000 per year the cost to the corporation over the long run would have been substantially greater, yet no one could plausibly contend that such an employment contract was beyond Yardley's authority.

The cases on executive authority to make pension agreements are few. In West v. Hunt Foods, Inc., 1951, 101 Cal.App.2d 597, 225 P.2d 978, the most recent case on the subject, a nonsuit was reversed on the theory that the jury might have decided in plaintiff's favor either upon the basis of authority in the president and vice-president to make the promise of a pension or on the basis of a promissory estoppel. In Langer v. Superior Steel Corp., 1935, 318 Pa. 490, 178 A. 490, authority was found lacking in the president, who acted in direct violation of a directors' resolution, to promise a pension for life in return for past services. His apparent authority was not discussed. In Plowman v. Indian Refining Co., D.C.E.D.Ill.1937, 20 F.Supp. 1, the vice president was found to lack authority gratuitously to promise 18 employees life pensions at half wages. * * *

Apparent authority is essentially a question of fact. It depends not only on the nature of the contract involved, but the officer negotiating it, the corporation's usual manner of conducting business, the size of the corporation and the number of its stockholders, the circumstances that give rise to the contract, the reasonableness of the contract, the amounts involved, and who the contracting third party is, to list a few but not all of the relevant factors. In certain instances a given contract may be so important to the welfare of the corporation that outsiders would naturally suppose that only the board of directors (or even the shareholders) could properly handle it. It is in this light that the "ordinary course of business" rule should be given its content. Beyond such "extraordinary" acts, whether or not apparent authority exists is simply a matter of fact.

Accordingly, we hold that, assuming there was sufficient proof of the making of the pension agreement, Connecticut, in the particular circumstances of this case, would probably take the view that reasonable men could differ on the subject of whether or not Yardley had apparent authority to make the contract, and that the trial court erred in deciding the question as a matter of law. We do not think Connecticut would adopt any hard and fast rule against apparent authority to make pension agreements generally, on the theory that they were in the same category as lifetime employment contracts. * * *

Notes

(1) Consider MBCA § 8.01(b). Does this grant of authority to directors have a negative implication with respect to the actual or apparent authority of corporate officers? Assume that all corporate powers are being exercised "under the direction of" (rather than "by") the board of directors, as is almost always the case in large, publicly held corporations. Should that give the senior officers of the corporation greater authority than a senior executive with the same title might have in a corporation where corporate powers are being exercised "by" the board?

Consider The American Law Institute, Principles of Corporate Governance: Analysis and Recommendations 84–86:[29]

In general, questions concerning the authority of senior executives are normally special issues of agency law, and, as in agency law, the major relevant concepts are those of actual and apparent authority. When an agent is an executive of a corporation, the application of both these concepts often rests on the executive's formal position. * * *

* * * Although the rules on this issue have varied in the past, the accepted modern rule is that (unless restricted by a corporate standard that the third person has reason to know) the president has apparent authority by virtue of that position to take actions in the ordinary course of business, but not extraordinary actions.

The difficulty, of course, lies in drawing a line between what is ordinary and what is extraordinary. Any attempt at precision in drawing this line would almost certainly be futile, because the issue is highly dependent on the context in which it arises, and the types of business transactions that may arise are endlessly variable. Nevertheless, certain boundaries can be identified. To begin with, some matters, such as the declaration of dividends, are required by statute to be decided by the board. Typically, the statutes also enumerate certain matters that the board cannot delegate to a committee. By parity of reasoning, it would normally not be within the authority of the president or other senior executives to take binding action on these matters.

Beyond these boundaries, among the elements to be taken into account for purposes of determining what constitutes an "extraordinary" action, which would normally be outside the apparent authority of senior executives, are the economic magnitude of the action in relation to corporate assets and earnings, the extent of risk involved, the time span of the action's effect, and the cost of reversing the action. Examples of the kinds of actions that would normally be "extraordinary" include the creation or retirement of long-term or other significant debt, the reacquisition of significant amounts of equity, significant capital investments, business combinations including those effected for cash, the disposition of significant businesses, entry into important new lines of business, significant acquisitions of stock in other corporations, and actions that would foreseeably expose the corporation to significant litigation or significant new regulatory problems. A useful generalization is that decisions that would make a significant change in the structure of the business enterprise, or the structure of control over the enterprise, are extraordinary corporate actions, and therefore are normally outside the apparent authority of senior executives.

Until recently, the courts have often tended to be somewhat restrictive in determining the apparent authority of a president, perhaps influenced by statutory language that the business of the corporation shall be managed by the board. Some of the recent cases tend to interpret the president's apparent authority in a more expansive manner, perhaps influenced by the growing realization that in practice the management of the business of the corporation is normally conducted by or under the supervision of its executives. See, e.g., Lee v. Jenkins Bros., 268 F.2d 357 (2d Cir.), cert. denied, 361 U.S. 913 (1959). But see, e.g., Lucey v. Hero Int'l Corp., 361 Mass. 569, 281 N.E.2d 266 (1972);

Parks v. Midland Ford Tractor, 416 S.W.2d 22 (Mo.App.1967); Nelms v. A & A Liquor Stores, Inc., 445 S.W.2d 256 (Tex.Civ.App.1969). * * * Section 3.01 [similar to MBCA § 8.01(b)] does not directly alter the basic rules in this area, but it should reinforce the judicial tendency to give the authority of senior executives an expansive interpretation in cases involving third persons—a tendency built on a sound understanding of the normal expectations of third persons dealing with such executives. * * *

(2) Another issue that has given rise to litigation is whether a corporate president has power to commence a lawsuit without the prior authorization of the board of directors? What about a lawsuit that is in the ordinary course of business of the corporation, e.g. a collection suit to recover money owed by a customer of the corporation? What about a lawsuit that involves the relative rights of shareholders among themselves? What about litigation that the Court determines to be "extraordinary"? For recent examples of such litigation, see Keogh Corp. v. Howard, Weil, Labouisse, Friedrichs Inc., 827 F.Supp. 269 (S.D.N.Y.1993)(suit instituted by corporate president alleged that Howard, Weil obtained control of Keogh's board of directors through extortion, bribery, and fraud in violation of the Racketeer Influenced and Corrupt Organizations Act; suit dismissed because only the board of directors had authority to "initiate litigation out of the ordinary course of business"); Anmaco, Inc. v. Bohlken, 13 Cal.App.4th 891, 16 Cal.Rptr.2d 675 (1993)(there is no "presumptive or implied authority in the president to institute litigation in the name of the corporation against a co-director and equal shareholder. Pressing the corporation into litigation as a plaintiff is inappropriate where the other shareholder-director could claim equal authority to bring suit in the corporate name. This is particularly obvious in the instant case where Bohlken is not only an equal director and shareholder, but is also Chief Executive Officer of the company. The proper vehicle for such a suit, when the gravamen of the complaint is injury to the corporation, is a shareholder's derivative action.") 16 Cal.Rptr.2d at 679.

IN THE MATTER OF DRIVE–IN DEV. CORP.

United States Court of Appeals, Seventh Circuit, 1966.
371 F.2d 215.

SWYGERT, CIRCUIT JUDGE.

The principal question in this appeal relates to the circumstances which may bind a corporation to a guaranty of the obligations of a related corporation when it is contended that the corporate officer who executed the guaranty had no authority to do so. The facts giving rise to the question underlie a claim filed by the National Boulevard Bank of Chicago in an arrangement proceeding under chapter XI of the Bankruptcy Act, 11 U.S.C.A. §§ 701–799, in which the Drive In Development Corporation was the debtor. National Boulevard's claim was disallowed by the referee, whose decision was confirmed by the district court.

Drive In was one of four subsidiary companies controlled by Tastee Freez Industries, Inc., a holding company that conducted no business of its own. * * *

[Editor: The officers of Drive In executed a guarantee of payment to induce National Boulevard Bank to make a loan to Drive In's parent corporation. The guarantee was executed by one Maranz on behalf of Drive In as

"Chairman" and one Dick attested to its execution as secretary. National Boulevard requested a copy of the authorizing resolution of the board of directors of Drive In. A copy, certified by Dick with the corporate seal affixed, was duly delivered. No such resolution, however, was contained in Drive In's corporate minute book, and the directors' testimony left it uncertain as to whether any such resolution had ever been considered or approved at a directors meeting. National Boulevard advanced substantial sums under the guaranty.]

Turning to the merits of the objections to National Boulevard's claim, the referee found that Drive In's minute book did not show that a resolution authorizing Maranz to sign the guaranty was adopted by the directors and that Dick could not recall a specific directors' meeting at which such a resolution was approved. From these findings, the referee concluded that Maranz, who signed the guaranty on behalf of Drive In, had no authority, "either actual or implied or apparent," to bind Drive In. This conclusion was erroneous. Drive In was estopped to deny Maranz' express authority to sign the guaranty because of the certified copy of a resolution of Drive In's board of directors purporting to grant such authority furnished to the bank by Dick, whether or not such a resolution was in fact formally adopted. Dick was the secretary of the corporation. Generally, it is the duty of the secretary to keep the corporate records and to make proper entries of the actions and resolutions of the directors. Therefore it was within the authority of Dick to certify that a resolution such as challenged here was adopted. Statements made by an officer or agent in the course of a transaction in which the corporation is engaged and which are within the scope of his authority are binding upon the corporation. Consequently Drive In was estopped to deny the representation made by Dick in the certificate forwarded to National Boulevard, in the absence of actual or constructive knowledge on the part of the bank that the representation was untrue. * * *

The objectors argue that since William Schneider, a vice president of National Boulevard, requested Dick to furnish the certified copy of a resolution granting authority to execute the guaranty, and since Hugh Driscoll, another vice president of National Boulevard, was also a director of Tastee Freez and was familiar with the organization of the subsidiaries, the bank was somehow in a position to know that no resolution had in fact been adopted by Drive In's board of directors. These facts, however, fall far short of proving such knowledge on the part of National Boulevard.

* * * Although intercorporate contracts of guaranty do not usually occur in the regular course of commercial business, here the interrelationship of Tastee Freez and its subsidiaries presented a situation in which the guaranty was not so unusual as would ordinarily obtain. Furthermore, the realities of modern corporate business practices do not contemplate that those who deal with officers or agents acting for a corporation should be required to go behind the representations of those who have authority to speak for the corporation and who verify the authority of those who presume to act for the corporation. * * *

The order of the district court confirming the referee's order is reversed in part and affirmed in part.

Notes

Essentially in accord is American Union Financial Corp. v. University Nat'l Bank of Peoria, 44 Ill.App.3d 566, 3 Ill.Dec. 248, 358 N.E.2d 646 (1976). What if the third person should know that the directors could not have possibly adopted the resolution being certified to by the secretary on the date specified? In Keystone Leasing Corp. v. Peoples Protective Life Ins. Co., 514 F.Supp. 841 (E.D.N.Y.1981), the Court refused to grant the third person the benefit of the estoppel principle set forth in *In the Matter of Drive In Dev. Corp.* where the third person "must have been aware" that the transaction had not been authorized by the board of directors.

Chapter Nine

CONTROL AND MANAGEMENT IN THE PUBLICLY HELD CORPORATION

A. "SOCIAL RESPONSIBILITY" OR THE LACK THEREOF

THE ROLE OF GIANT CORPORATIONS IN THE AMERICAN AND WORLD ECONOMIES: CORPORATE SECRECY: OVERVIEWS

Hearings before the Subcommittee on Monopoly of the Select
Committee on Small Business, United States Senate,
92nd Cong. 1st Sess., November 9 and 12, 1971.

SENATOR NELSON. * * *

The subject matter of these hearings—corporate giantism and corporate secrecy—is as broad and complex as world commerce itself. But the basic issue may be expressed in one word.

The word is power. The issue is power: economic, political, social, cultural power.

Power to decide what kind of jobs will be created and what kind will be terminated.

Power to determine whether new jobs that are made and old jobs that are wiped out will be located in New York, San Francisco, Hong Kong or Frankfurt.

Power strongly to influence, if not finally settle, whether Americans will travel about their cities in vehicles that are polluting, expensive, and dangerous or clean, cheap and safe.

Power to overload every sanitary landfill in the country by substituting throwaway bottles for returnable pop and beer bottles.

Power to determine—and here we come down to the very particular interest and jurisdiction of this committee and subcommittee—whether small, independent entrepreneurs will or will not have opportunities left open to them to enter and strive and compete in particular lines of commerce.

It is now many years since small business was forced out of most types of manufacturing, including almost all those of major economic importance. Today, retailing and farming are being made, by giant corporations, increasingly precarious occupations for entrepreneurs who are not also millionaires. * * *

Corporate giantism is a shorthand way of describing an economic and social development that is still quite new in American and world history.

The corporation is a human invention to serve human, social needs. In theory, it is subservient both to the State that creates it and the market in which it competes. If the corporation does not fulfill its social obligations, under the theory, the State can amend or even revoke its charter. If it lapses in economic efficiency, its market competitors will force it to improve—or force it out.

For most of the approximately 2 million American corporations, this theory is also close to fact. But for a very few corporations—less than 1 percent of the total—the theory no longer seems to fit the facts. These few corporations have become much larger in economic size and power than either the States that chartered them or the markets in which they buy and sell.

Compare, for example, Standard Oil Co. (New Jersey) with the State that granted its charter and whose name the company bears (in parentheses). Jersey Standard had 1967 sales of almost $13.3 billion. The combined general revenues of the State and all local governments of the State of New Jersey that year were under $3 billion. * * *

RICHARD J. BARBER, THE AMERICAN CORPORATION: ITS POWER, ITS MONEY, ITS POLITICS[1]

Pp. 19–20 (1970).

General Motors' yearly operating revenues exceed those of all but a dozen or so countries. Its sales receipts are greater than the *combined* general revenues of New York, New Jersey, Pennsylvania, Ohio, Delaware, and the six New England states. Its 1,300,000 stockholders are equal to the population of Washington, Baltimore, or Houston. GM employees number well over 700,000 and work in 127 plants in the United States and forty-five in countries spanning Europe, South Africa, North America, and Australasia. Their total cash wages are more than twice the personal income of Ireland. GM's Federal corporate tax payments approach $2 billion, or enough to pay for all Federal grants in fiscal year 1970 in the field of health research. The enormity of General Motors, seen from whatever angle, is stupefying, but it should not be thought of as unique. Some 175 other manufacturing, merchandising, and transportation companies now have annual sales of at least a billion dollars. * * *

To gain a better impression of the scale of the bigger U.S. companies one has to view them against a larger industrial backdrop. Looked at this way, we find that a mere 100 firms—less than a tenth of 1 percent of a total 300,000 firms—account for fully a third of the value added by manufacturing (sales less the cost of materials and services purchased), employ 25 percent of manufacturing employees (and make a third of all wages payments), make nearly 40 percent of new capital expenditures, and own about half of all assets used in manufacturing. What this means is that the presidents of a hundred companies—a group sufficiently small to be seated comfortably in the reading room of the Union League Club in Philadelphia—represent almost as much wealth and control as large a share of the nation's economic activity as the next largest 300,000 manufacturers—a group that would completely fill four Yankee Stadiums.

WILLIAM ALLEN,[2] OUR SCHIZOPHRENIC CONCEPTION OF THE BUSINESS CORPORATION
14 Cardozo L.Rev. 261, 264-76 (1992).

Two inconsistent conceptions have dominated our thinking about corporations since the evolution of the large integrated business corporation in the late nineteenth century. Each conception could claim dominance for a particular period, or among one group or another, but neither has so commanded agreement as to exclude the other from the discourses of law or the thinking of business people.

In the first conception, the corporation is seen as the private property of its stockholder-owners. The corporation's purpose is to advance the purposes of these owners (predominantly to increase their wealth), and the function of directors, as agents of the owners, is faithfully to advance the financial interests of the owners. I call this the property conception of the corporation * * *.

The second conception sees the corporation not as the private property of stockholders, but as a social institution. According to this view, the corporation is not strictly private; it is tinged with a public purpose. The corporation comes into being and continues as a legal entity only with governmental concurrence. The legal institutions of government grant a corporation its juridical personality, its characteristic limited liability, and its perpetual life. This conception sees this public facilitation as justified by the state's interest in promoting the general welfare. Thus, corporate purpose can be seen as including the advancement of the general welfare. The board of directors' duties extend beyond assuring investors a fair return, to include a duty of loyalty, in some sense, to all those interested in or affected by the corporation. * * * The corporation itself is, in this view, capable of bearing legal *and* moral obligations. To law and economics scholars, who have been so influential in academic corporate law, this model is barely coherent and dangerously wrong.

These two, apparently inconsistent, conceptions have coexisted in our thinking over the last century. For most of the century the lack of agreement on the ultimate nature and purpose of the business corporation has not generated intense conflict. * * * By the 1980s however, emerging global

2. [By the Editor] William T. Allen was   until 1997.
Chancellor of the Delaware Chancery Court

competition, capital market innovation, and the growth and evolution of institutional investors, among other factors, made possible the takeover movement, which glaringly exposed our inconsistent thinking about the nature of the business corporation. * * *

Dodge v. Ford Motor Co. reflects as pure an example as exists of the property conception of the corporation. In this conception, the corporation is seen as it is in its nineteenth century roots, as essentially a sort of limited liability partnership. The rights of creditors, employees and others are strictly limited to statutory, contractual, and common law rights. Once the directors have satisfied those legal obligations, they have fully satisfied all claims of these "constituencies." This property view of the nature of corporations, and of the duties owed by directors, equates the duty of directors with the duty to maximize profits of the firm for the benefit of shareholders.

This model of the public corporation is highly coherent and offers several alternative arguments to support the legitimacy of corporate power in our democracy. The first argument in favor of the property concept is political and normative. It is premised on the conclusionary notion that shareholders "own" the corporation, and asserts that to admit the propriety of non-profit maximizing behavior is to approve agents spending other people's money in pursuit of their own, perhaps eccentric, views of the public good. * * *

The second rationale for the property model is that the model, and action consistent with it, maximize wealth creation. This rationale asserts that the purpose of business corporations is the creation of wealth, nothing else. It asserts that business corporations are not formed to assist in self-realization through social interaction; they are not formed to create jobs or to provide tax revenues, they are not formed to endow university departments or to pursue knowledge. All of these other things—job creation, tax payments, research, and social interaction—desirable as they may be, are said to be side effects of the pursuit of profit for the residual owners of the firm.

This argument asserts that the creation of more wealth should always be the corporation's objective, regardless of who benefits. The sovereign's taxing and regulatory power can then address questions of social costs and re-distribution of wealth. * * *

[T]he last quarter of the nineteenth century saw the emergence of social forces that would oppose the conception of business corporations as simply the property of contracting stockholders. The scale and scope of the modern integrated business enterprise that emerged in the late nineteenth century required distinctive professional management skills and huge capital invest-ments that often necessitated risk sharing through dispersed stock ownership. National securities markets emerged and stockholders gradually came to look less like flesh and blood owners and more like investors who could slip in or out of a particular stock almost costlessly. These new giant business corpora-tions came to seem to some people like independent entities, with purposes, duties, and loyalties of their own; purposes that might diverge in some respect from shareholder wealth maximization.

Henry Ford's losing position in *Dodge v. Ford Motor Co.* reflected an idea that was in the air. Others saw these new corporate social actors as different. * * *

This social entity conception sees the purpose of the corporation as not individual but social. Surely contributors of capital (stockholders and bondholders) must be assured a rate of return sufficient to induce them to contribute their capital to the enterprise. But the corporation has other purposes of perhaps equal dignity: the satisfaction of consumer wants, the provision of meaningful employment opportunities, and the making of a contribution to the public life of its communities. Resolving the often conflicting claims of these various corporate constituencies calls for judgment, indeed calls for wisdom, by the board of directors of the corporation. But in this view no single constituency's interest may significantly exclude others from fair consideration by the board. This view appears to have been the dominant view among business leaders for at least the last fifty years. * * *

One would think that whether the corporation law endorses the property conception or the social entity conception would have important consequences. * * *[But] for the fifty years preceding that contentious decade [the 1980s], we did not share agreement on the legal nature of the public business corporation and that failure did not seem especially problematic.

The law "papered over" the conflict in our conception of the corporation by invoking a murky distinction between long-term profit maximization and short-term profit maximization. Corporate expenditures which at first blush did not seem to be profit maximizing, could be squared with the property conception of the corporation by recognizing that they might redound to the long-term benefit of the corporation and its shareholders. Thus, without purporting to abandon the idea that directors ultimately owe loyalty only to stockholders and their financial interests, the law was able to approve reasonable corporate expenditures for charitable or social welfare purposes or other actions that did not maximize current profit. * * *

PLAYBOY INTERVIEW: MILTON FRIEDMAN[3]

Playboy Magazine, Feb. 1973, at 59.

PLAYBOY: Quite apart from emission standards and effluent taxes, shouldn't corporate officials take action to stop pollution out of a sense of social responsibility?

FRIEDMAN: I wouldn't buy stock in a company that hired that kind of leadership. A corporate executive's responsibility is to make as much money for the stockholders as possible, as long as he operates within the rules of the game. When an executive decides to take action for reasons of social responsibility, he is taking money from someone else—from the stockholders, in the form of lower dividends; from the employees, in the form of lower wages; or from the consumer, in the form of higher prices. The responsibility of a corporate executive is to fulfill the terms of his contract. If he can't do that in good conscience, then he should quit his job and find another way to do good. He has the right to promote what he regards as desirable moral objectives only with his own money. If, on the other hand, the executives of U.S. Steel undertake to reduce pollution in Gary for the purpose of making the town

---

3. From the "PLAYBOY Interview: Milton Friedman." PLAYBOY Magazine, (February 1973); copyright © 1973 by PLAYBOY. Used with permission. Interview conducted by Geoffrey Norman.

attractive to employees and thus lowering labor costs, then they are doing the stockholders' bidding. And everybody benefits: The stockholders get higher dividends; the customer gets cheaper steel; the workers get more in return for their labor. That's the beauty of free enterprise.

RICHARD A. RODEWALD, THE CORPORATE SOCIAL RESPONSIBILITY DEBATE: UNANSWERED QUESTIONS ABOUT THE CONSEQUENCES OF MORAL REFORM

25 Am.Bus.L.J. 443, 444–47, 450–53, 455–56, 460–63 (1987).

Consider a hypothetical case that represents the kind of corporate decisionmaking problem that moral reformers believe requires a new conception of the moral responsibilities of corporate managers. In this case, the top management of "ACE Manufacturing Inc.," headquartered in "North City," a city in the northeastern United States, has to decide whether or not to relocate to the Sunbelt.[4]

For the purposes of our present discussion, assume that the managers of ACE have only two viable options: (1) they can decide to stay in North City and remodel ACE's present facilities, or (2) they can sell these facilities and build new ones on a new site in a semirural area of the Sunbelt. From the point of view of maximizing long-range corporate profits, moving to the Sunbelt is the better alternative. However, this option will likely have seriously harmful consequences for North City and many of ACE's present workers. ACE's departure would significantly damage North City's tax base. Moreover, this damage is likely to become devastating if ACE's move provides a signal to other corporations that it is time for them to get out also.

In addition, most of ACE's lower-level employees will be unable to make the move to the Sunbelt. Two-thirds of the skilled workers will lose their jobs and 25% of these will not find new ones. All the unskilled workers will lose their jobs and most of these will have to go on welfare. These displaced workers may lose even more than their jobs and economic security, however. They also face an increased risk of losing their homes, their families, their self-respect, and sometimes their physical health or even their lives.

Given these facts, what should the managers of ACE decide to do?

Initially, it might seem that so long as ACE will not go broke in North City, top management ought to decide to continue doing business there in order to avoid the harm that relocating would cause others. Simply by being individual "moral agents," the managers of ACE have "natural moral duties" to tell the truth and be honest, keep their promises, pay their debts, treat others fairly, do no harm, do good, help others in need, and benefit those who have benefited them in the past (the duty of gratitude). It seems that a strong argument can be built for claiming that it would be morally wrong for the managers of ACE to move to the Sunbelt solely on the premise that they have a natural moral duty not to impose on others the kind of suffering this move would cause just for the sake of some economic gain.

---

4. [By the Author] The essentials of this case description have been borrowed from a simulation exercise that AT & T has used in its management training programs: Relocation: A Corporate Decision (Del Mar, Ca.: Simile II, 1977).

This argument is invalid, however. Even if the premise is true, the conclusion does not necessarily follow. What persons morally ought to do in any particular case is not determined solely by their natural moral duties. Our natural moral duties are only "prima facie" duties which, while generally binding on conduct, can sometimes be overridden by other considerations that are morally superior in particular cases. * * *

The Traditional View: Managers as the Agents of Capital

The traditional theory of the role of corporate managers in democratic capitalist societies holds that managers are supposed to be agents of the owners of capital. * * * [Under this] view of corporate responsibility, the managers of ACE are not morally obligated to stay in North City just because moving to the Sunbelt would impose significant hardships on many of those who remain behind. What this view implies is that if moving to the Sunbelt will maximize ACE's long-run profits and violate no laws or requirements of market morality, then this is what the managers of ACE are morally obligated to do. Of course, it also follows that they should not lie to their workers or misrepresent their plans to relocate in order to forestall any falloff of productivity that is likely to follow once workers discover that they are going to lose their jobs. * * *

From the traditional point of view, the suffering that ACE's move to the Sunbelt would impose on North City and many of its workers is an unintended side-effect of a sound business decision. The suffering is a "negative externality" of ACE's business activities much like pollution is sometimes a negative externality of production. In the traditional view, it is the function of government to protect noninvestors from these sorts of externalities. * * *

The Moral Reform View: Managers as Agents of Society

Moral reformers * * * claim that we need to adopt a new conception of corporate social responsibility. They put forth what we may call *agent-of-society* views of corporate responsibility. On these views corporate managers should go beyond considerations of profits, legality and market morality and take into account all of the human, social and environmental consequences of their business decisions. They should pursue profits within the law and the requirements of market morality, but they should also try to do whatever they can to use the resources at their command in nonharmful and socially useful ways. * * *

Consider our relocation case again. In any agent-of-society view of corporate responsibility, the managers of ACE should give serious weight to all of the economic and noneconomic human costs that moving to the Sunbelt would likely impose upon their displaced workers and the citizens of North City. Take a narrow version that only requires managers to do no harm and to come to the aid of others in need when they can do so at a reasonable cost to their firms. Initially, this view seems to require that the managers of ACE should be prepared to stay in North City and make a reasonable sacrifice of profits in order to avoid these costs. However, if staying would be unreasonably costly to ACE, they should inform those who will be affected about their intentions to move as soon as reasonably possible. Moreover, they should be prepared to provide reasonable aid and compensation to North City and those workers who would lose their jobs in order to ameliorate their suffering during the transition between ACE's departure and the time when new industries take its place and its displaced workers find new jobs. In this way, ACE can internalize some of the costs of the negative externalities its move would produce.

However, management's moral responsibilities in this case are even more complicated. Given that workers in the Sunbelt need jobs and Sunbelt cities need new industries, ACE's failure to move might violate the obligation to come to their aid. Moreover, whether they stay and take the less profitable alternative or move and expend economic resources compensating North City and those workers who lose their jobs, the managers of ACE will have fewer resources available to expend on supplies, price cuts, higher wages, new jobs, new investments to fend off competition, dividends and the like. Thus, whatever they decide to do, they will impose financial costs on their stockholders, suppliers and customers, as well as their present and future workers.

Consequently, even in a narrow agent-of-society view, ACE's managers must attempt to estimate not only the costs that will be imposed upon their present workers and the citizens of North City if they decide to relocate, but also the harm that others will suffer if they do not. If it is reasonable to expect that relatively greater harm will be imposed by moving than by staying, then they would have to weigh the balance of harm against the rights of stockholders whose interests are served by moving. In light of all this, they would have to try to determine what would count as a reasonable sacrifice of profits to either avoid or ameliorate this harm.

Wider agent-of-society views only complicate matters further by expanding the range of nonmarket considerations that the managers of ACE would be morally required to take into account and the number of social and moral goals they ought to pursue. Take just one example: If it turns out that the work force they would end up with in the Sunbelt would be comprised of far fewer women and minorities, ACE's management might have to weigh the claims of justice that require working toward greater race and sex equality against the economic benefits of a more profitable ACE doing business in the Sunbelt. * * *

LARRY R. FISCHEL, THE CORPORATE GOVERNANCE MOVEMENT
35 Vand.L.Rev. 1259, 1268–70 (1982).

It has become fashionable to argue that the pursuit of profit maximization by corporations is at variance with the public interest. Proponents of this argument, however, face the insuperable problem of defining what the public interest is, and when the pursuit of profit maximization should be sacrificed for these ends. As Harold Demsetz has remarked, centuries of philosophers and economists have tried and failed to provide any workable definition of "the fair price," "the just wage," or "fair competition," let alone what constitutes "the good society."[5] * * *

Although potential conflict exists between profit maximization and pursuit of other goals, far more consistency is present between the two than

---

5. [By the Author] Demsetz, Social Responsibility in the Enterprise Economy, 10 Sw. U.L.Rev. 1, 1 (1978).

generally assumed. A successful business venture provides jobs to workers and goods and services that consumers want to buy. While these benefits may not appear to be particularly dramatic, they should not be underestimated, as the tens of thousands of workers in distressed industries who have had to give back concessions previously won or have lost their jobs outright will readily attest. Much the same is true is other areas. * * * Frequently this harmony of interests exists, but is difficult to perceive. Firms that close plants to move to different geographical areas commonly are accused, for example, of lacking a sense of responsibility to affected workers and the community as a whole. The difficulty with this argument is that it ignores the presumably greater benefits that will accrue to workers and the community in the new locale where the firm can operate more profitably. A firm that causes dislocations by moving a plant is behaving no more "unethically" than a firm that causes dislocations by, say, inventing a new technology that causes competitors to go out of business.

I do not mean to suggest that profit maximization will always lead to the socially optimal result. In those situations in which externalities are present—pollution is the most common example—a firm may impose costs on others without providing compensation. But even this situation is misunderstood. If a firm dumps pollutants in a stream, the firm imposes costs on the users of the stream that may exceed the benefits to the firm. It does not follow, however, that pollution is immoral behavior which should be halted. Consider the reciprocal case in which the firm does not pollute because of concern for users of the stream and instead relies on a more expensive method of disposing wastes. In this situation the users of the stream impose costs on the firm's investors, employees, and consumers that may exceed the benefits to users of the stream. Neither polluting nor failing to pollute is *a priori* the "ethically" or "morally" correct course of action. * * *

Notes

(1) Frank H. Easterbrook & Larry R. Fischel, The Economic Structure of Corporate Law 38 (1991):[6]

> [A] manager told to serve two masters (a little for the equity holders, a little for the community) has been freed of both and is answerable to neither. Faced with a demand from either group, the manager can appeal to the interests of the other. Agency costs rise and social wealth falls. Far better to alter incentives by establishing rules that attach prices to acts (such as pollution and layoffs) while leaving managers free to maximize the wealth of the residual claimants subject to the social constraints.

(2) Jay W. Lorsch, Pawns or Potentates: The Reality of America's Corporate Boards 37–8 (1989):[7]

> The directors of a large company are gathered around the boardroom table, discussing management's proposal to adopt a "southern strategy" for the manufacturing facilities of its major division. The proposal involves

---

6. Reprinted by permission of the publishers from *The Economic Structure of Corporate Law* by Frank H. Easterbrook and Daniel R. Fischel, Cambridge, Mass.: Harvard University Press, Copyright © 1991 by the President and Fellows of Harvard College.

7. Jay W. Lorsch with Elizabeth MacIver, *Pawns or Potentates: The Reality of America's Corporate Boards.*

gradually closing older, unionized plants in three northern urban areas, and building new facilities in the South, which would be nonunion, at least initially, thereby lowering labor costs. As the discussion continues, various directors ask questions or offer opinions about the proposal's merits.

But most striking to an objective observer would be the confusion about what criteria should be used to judge the proposal. Some directors are concerned about the proposal's impact on the present northern work force. Others question whether the nonunionized southern workers could produce a quality product, how long it might take, and what impact there might be on customers. Interspersed are references to "doing what is best for the shareholders," but no clear statement defines how to judge the shareholders' interests. Nor is mention made of the importance of the proposal for the company's long-term position in an increasingly competitive global marketplace.

Such discussions are typical in many boardrooms because directors usually don't share a strong consensus about accountabilities to various constituencies and, therefore, about their purposes in serving. Further, the norm in most boardrooms is to avoid discussing such matters. * * *

The confusion about accountabilities seems surprising in light of the widely accepted belief that directors are legally accountable to the shareholders alone. Directors *do* believe the shareholders are their most important constituents when reaching decisions, but concern for the corporation's long-term future ranked a close second. Other considerations varied among individuals, but in general were less important. * * *

(3) Chancellor Allen suggests that the event that caused the Delaware courts to confront the difficult choice between the property and social entity conceptions of the corporation was the takeover movement of the 1980s described in chapter 14 of this casebook. In his words:

* * * Two things made the takeover phenomenon very problematic for the legal theory of the corporation.

The first is that the takeover movement put so much at stake. The issue in the takeover cases was not whether a donation of corporate funds could be made to a museum or college * * *. The issue was frequently whether all of the shareholders would be permitted to sell their shares, whether a change in corporate control would occur; and often whether a radical restructuring of the enterprise would go forward, with dramatic effects on creditors, employees, management, suppliers, and communities. As the junk bond market grew in size, larger and larger enterprises were faced with these prospects. * * *

A second difference between the issues of the takeover era and those of the prior sixty years was that the short-term/long-term distinction was really of little analytical or rhetorical use in resolving the takeover issues. The most pressing of these issues involved the question whether a board of directors could take action that precluded shareholders from accepting a non-coercive, all cash tender offer.[8] That question obviously raised the further question: Whose interests is the board of directors suppose to foster or protect when substantially all of the shareholders want to sell control of the corporation?

---

8. [By the Author] *See* Lucian A. Bebchuk, *The Pressure to Tender: An Analysis and a Proposed Remedy,* 12 Del.J.Corp.L. 911 (1987); *see also* John C. Coffee, Jr., *The Uncertain Case for Takeover Reforms: An Essay on Stock-* *holders, Stakeholders and Bust–Ups,* 1988 Wis. L.Rev. 435, 439 ("[T]he problem of coercion in takeovers * * * represents the hobgoblin of the law professors.").

The long-term/short-term distinction could not persuasively be used to answer or evade that question when it arose in this context. It is one thing to say that an expenditure of corporate funds that benefits the community—an education grant or the installation of an unmandated pollution control device—is really for the long-term financial benefit of shareholders. * * * It is, however, rather a different thing to justify precluding the shareholders from selling their stock at a large immediate profit on the ground that in the long run that will be good for them. While one might of course say that, many people would find it disturbing to put such a result on the basis that directors know what is better for shareholder then they themselves do. * * *

Courts were not anxious to grapple with this question. To resolve the matter seemed plainly to call for the making of policy in an environment that was warmly contested by powerful interests and in which no widely accepted doctrine offered a clear guide. * * *

Nevertheless, ultimately both our courts and, more importantly, our legislatures have, in effect, endorsed the entity view. In *Paramount Communications, Inc. v. Time, Inc. ("Time Warner")*,[9] the Delaware Supreme Court seems to have expressed the view that corporate directors, if they act in pursuit of some vision of the *corporation's* long-term welfare, may take action that precludes shareholders from accepting an immediate high-premium offer for their shares. This important case might be interpreted as constituting implicit judicial acknowledgment of the social entity conception, as clearly as *Dodge v. Ford Motor Co.* reflects the alternative property conception of the corporation.

THE AMERICAN LAW INSTITUTE, PRINCIPLES OF CORPORATE GOVERNANCE: ANALYSIS & RECOMMENDATIONS[10]

§ 2.01. The Objective and Conduct of the Corporation

(a) Subject to the provisions of Subsection (b) and § 6.02 (Action of Directors That Has the Foreseeable Effect of Blocking Unsolicited Tender Offers), a corporation should have as its objective the conduct of business activities with a view to enhancing corporate profit and shareholder gain.

(b) Even if corporate profit and shareholder gain are not thereby enhanced, the corporation, in the conduct of its business:

(1) Is obliged, to the same extent as a natural person, to act within the boundaries set by law;

(2) May take into account ethical considerations that are reasonably regarded as appropriate to the responsible conduct of business; and

(3) May devote a reasonable amount of resources to public welfare, humanitarian, educational, and philanthropic purposes.

Notes

Many transactions (such as charitable contributions) that provide no direct benefit to the corporation may be justified on the theory that the directors are

9. [By the Author] 571 A.2d 1140 (Del. 1989).

10. Copyright (1994) by The American Law Institute. Reprinted with the permission of the American Law Institute.

maximizing the "long term" profits of the business. While doubtless many such actions do in fact benefit the corporation on a long term basis, the problem is that practically any expenditure can be justified by this argument, and its acceptance virtually means that "anything goes" so far as the use of corporate assets is concerned. Does § 2.01(b) adequately channel the power to enter into non-profit-maximizing transactions?

ILLINOIS BUSINESS CORPORATION ACT
Illinois–Smith–Hurd Ann. 805 ILCS 5/8.85.

5/8.85 Discharge of Duties—Considerations

In discharging the duties of their respective positions, the board of directors, committees of the board, individual directors and individual officers may, in considering the best long term and short term interests of the corporation, consider the effects of any action (including without limitation, action which may involve or relate to a change or potential change in control of the corporation) upon employees, suppliers and customers of the corporation or its subsidiaries, communities in which offices or other establishments of the corporation or its subsidiaries are located, and all other pertinent factors.

PENNSYLVANIA BUSINESS CORPORATION LAW
15 Penn. Stat. § 1715.

§ 1715 Exercise of Powers Generally

(a) General rule.—In discharging the duties of their respective positions, the board of directors, committees of the board and individual directors of a business corporation may, in considering the best interests of the corporation, consider to the extent they deem appropriate:

(1) The effects of any action upon any or all groups affected by such action, including shareholders, employees, suppliers, customers and creditors of the corporation, and upon communities in which offices or other establishments of the corporation are located.

(2) The short-term and long-term interests of the corporation, including benefits that may accrue to the corporation from its long-term plans and the possibility that these interests may be best served by the continued independence of the corporation.

(3) The resources, intent and conduct (past, stated and potential) of any person seeking to acquire control of the corporation.

(4) All other pertinent factors.

(b) Consideration of interests and factors.—The board of directors, committees of the board and individual directors shall not be required, in considering the best interests of the corporation or the effects of any action, to regard any corporate interest or the interests of any particular group affected by such action as a dominant or controlling interest or factor. * * *

Notes

(1) These statutes, generally known as "other constituency" or "alternative constituency" statutes, have been extremely popular. At least 28 states have

adopted similar statutes, which vary considerably in language. This phenomenon is "[o]ne of the most remarkable but least remarked developments in corporation law in many years." James J. Hanks, Non–Stockholder Constituency Statutes: An Idea Whose Time Should Never Have Come, Insights, Vol. 3, No. 12, at 20 (Dec. 1989). While considerable law review commentary has been devoted to these statutes, they have not been particularly controversial at the state level; indeed, they have been enacted almost routinely with little or no attention paid to the fact that they apparently dramatically change the basic ground rules of corporate governance. Their genesis, however, is clear: they were enacted in response to the fear of takeovers during the 1980s. As described by Hanks, "Opponents of hostile takeovers apparently felt that by giving directors a wider range of factors upon which to base a rejection of a takeover offer, they would help protect the directors from liability and thus encourage them to resist takeover offers." Id.

(2) Committee on Corporate Laws, Other Constituencies Statutes: Potential for Confusion, 45 Bus. Law. 2253, 2268–70 (1990):[11]

The proponents of other constituencies statutes correctly recognize that many groups in addition to shareholders have a continuing and important economic stake in the welfare of corporations with which they have relationships. Often the shareholder's interest in the corporation is transitory, frequently a matter of days or weeks, while that of a manager or other employee may embrace a career and that of a community far longer. Similarly, a supplier may be almost wholly dependent upon one corporate customer for its economic viability, and a corporate customer may also have a measure of dependence upon its supplier. A community and its desirability as a corporate home and a residence for its citizens may depend upon one or a handful of corporations. A friendly or unfriendly change of control of a corporation can create severe hardships for many of these constituencies.

The issue [is] whether state corporation laws, and, in particular, a broadening of the interests that directors may consider, constitute an efficient and desirable way to provide protections for non-shareholder groups. The Committee has concluded that permitting—much less requiring—directors to consider these interests without relating such consideration in an appropriate fashion to shareholder welfare * * * would conflict with directors' responsibility to shareholders and could undermine the effectiveness of the system that has made the corporation an efficient device for the creation of jobs and wealth.

The Committee believes that the better interpretation of these statutes, and one that avoids such consequences, is that they confirm what the common law has been: directors may take into account the interests of other constituencies but only as and to the extent that the directors are acting in the best interests, long as well as short term, of the shareholders and the corporation. * * *

While legislatures may not have intended it, adding other constituencies provisions to state corporation laws may have ramifications that go far beyond a simple enumeration of the other interests directors *may* recognize in discharging their duties. Directors might have a duty to oppose a transaction with whatever means are available because it would have a demonstrably adverse impact upon one or more of the constituencies (e.g., the acquirer plans to move the headquarters from the small town in which the company had been rooted for decades resulting in community disruption and loss of jobs). * * *

The confusion of directors in trying to comply with such statutes, if interpreted to require directors to balance the interests of various constituencies without according primacy to shareholder interests, would be profoundly troubling. Even under existing law, particularly where directors must act quickly, it is often difficult for directors acting in good faith to divine what is in the best interests of shareholders and the corporation. If directors are required to consider other interests as well, the decision-making process will become a balancing act or search for compromise. When directors must not only decide what their duty of loyalty mandates, but also to whom their duty of loyalty runs (and in what proportions), poorer decisions can be expected.

* * * [T]he reallocation of wealth is a function for which directors are not especially suited and one beyond the general pale of their perceived mandate from society. Such allocations of wealth (which essentially a balancing of the interests of various constituencies would be) are *political* decisions. Absent the vesting of enforceable rights in those whose interests would have to be acknowledged, directors would not be accountable for their conduct in preferring the interests of one constituency over others.

(3) Can § 1715 of the Pennsylvania statute be construed in the manner suggested by the Committee on Corporate Laws? Section 1715 was enacted by Pennsylvania in 1990; prior to that time, the Pennsylvania statute was similar to the Illinois statute quoted above. However, § 1715 departed so far from traditional corporate norms that corporate officers and directors expressed concern about its desirability; the state found it necessary to amend the Pennsylvania Business Corporation Law to permit corporations to "opt out" of § 1715 and instead become subject to § 1716, which is similar to the Illinois statute.

(4) For a discussion of the first direct application of § 1715 of the Pennsylvania statutes to a takeover controversy, see Vincent F. Garrity, Jr., and Mark A. Morton, Would the CSX/Conrail Express Have Derailed in Delaware? A Comparative Analysis of Lock–Up Provisions Under Delaware and Pennsylvania Law, 51 U.Miami L.Rev. 677 (1997). In the "Epilogue," 51 U. Miami L.Rev., at 711–12, the authors conclude, "in what may be viewed as ironic, the Pennsylvania statute, which was clearly designed to provide a board of directors with an expanded arsenal of weapons to resist a hostile takeover by, among other things, permitting consideration of other, non-shareholder constituencies, may have contributed to the eventual outcome * * * of obtaining the best value reasonably available to all the shareholders."

B. SHAREHOLDERS

1. IN GENERAL

UNITED STATES TEMPORARY NATIONAL ECONOMIC COMMITTEE [BUREAUCRACY AND TRUSTEESHIP IN LARGE CORPORATIONS]

Monograph No. 11, pp. 19–23 (1940).

THE SEPARATION OF OWNERSHIP AND CONTROL

Another result of industrial concentration and the diffusion of ownership is so important that it deserves special consideration. It is the separation of ownership from control. Theoretically, of course, the holders of a majority of the voting stock control a corporation. But "the assumption that the owners of common or voting stock control a company is for the most part a fiction so far as the large corporations listed on exchanges are concerned."

Three general types or sources of control may be differentiated: control by the holders of a majority of the voting stock, control by an active minority, and control by management. * * * The most common form of control among the large corporations may be termed management control. When stockholding is sufficiently diffuse the position of management becomes almost impregnable.

Management does not need to own stock; the strategic advantages of its location are quite sufficient. A presumption of worth is in its favor and, more concretely, the proxy machinery is at its disposal. Management chooses the proxy committee and by making appointments from among the members of management assures its own continuance. The effectiveness of this machinery is too formidable for small stockholders to overcome. The Financial Editor of the Chicago Daily News, for example, describes the situation thus:

> Taking industry as a whole, the methods of using proxies gives the average stockholder [no] * * * chance to express an opinion * * *. He can agree or keep still. The proxy which is sent out lets him vote for the management: if he objects he can come to the meeting and register a kick. When he gets there he will be in the minority.
>
> The management usually enters the meeting with enough votes to carry any measure, regardless of those present.

Only the cataclysmic uprising of an indignant majority of the stockholders is sufficient to overthrow the management. And before such a crucial stage is reached even a not too astute management will usually have made concessions, sometimes of a quite minor nature, which are adequate to prevent the revolt. In business as in politics, taking the enemy into camp often works admirably in extending peace between groups.

The relatively helpless position of the dispersed stockholders makes it imperative that those in command of the large corporations consider the rights of these disfranchised citizens of the economic community. In other words, the dispersion of stock ownership requires, in the interests of justice, that the control group act not only in its own interests, but also as a trustee for the interests of those who are unable to make their demands effective. A 1928 statement by a subsequent chairman of Marshall Field and Company and chairman of the board of the American Management Association may be appropriately repeated. James O. McKinsey commented that the dispersion of stock ownership

> has brought about the situation in which the board of directors acts in a fiduciary capacity. If they fully realize their responsibility, this naturally leads them to exercise closer supervision over the activities of the business than if they were not representing a large group who were not familiar with the activities of the business and who were not exercising any responsibility for the management of the business other than selecting the directors to represent them.

It must be recognized, on the other hand, that it is not easy for the control group to give consideration to the interests of the scattered stockholders. One important reason for this is that their interests may be divergent. The concern of management with high salaries may result in lower dividends to the stockholders than would otherwise be possible. Or again, since those in control of a corporation are the first to gain information which will have an effect upon the value of the stock, the insiders may be able to buy or sell in such a way as to make substantial profits at the expense of those who are induced to sell or of new stockholders who are induced to buy without having inside information. * * *

JOSEPH A. LIVINGSTON, THE AMERICAN STOCKHOLDER[12]

Pp. 60–61, 67 (1958).

Here's a natural question: If a stockholder is not satisfied with a company's management, why should he start a proxy fight, why should he sue, why shouldn't he just sell his stock and be done with it?

Answer: That is what most stockholders do.

It is the easiest, cheapest, and, from many points of view, the most practical way to express stockholder dissatisfaction with a management, a company, or an industry.

The right to sell is a vote. And the stock market—Wall Street—is the polling booth. If the price of a stock goes up, it registers stockholder-investor-satisfaction. If it goes down, it registers dissatisfaction in the market place. * * *

This right to sell stock—to vote for or against a management in the market place—is different from a vote at a stockholders' meeting. When a stockholder votes against a slate of directors, he is exercising his right as a stockholder, as an owner. He hopes to change the management and improve the company. But a stockholder who sells says to hell with it. He is not going to reform the company. He is not an owner trying to increase the value of his property. He says, in effect, "Include me out." * * *

Thus, the market-place vote has power. It is a positive warning, a financial warning, to an incumbent management, of stockholder dissatisfaction. It lets the officers know that dissatisfaction has got beyond the discussion stage. The "big boys" are selling. So, the management might bestir itself—make changes—to strengthen the company's position. For that reason, selling stock is not an entirely empty gesture. True, the big investors do not fight for a change; they do not stay with the company that is retrogressing. But their leave-taking has an effect.

DANIEL R. FISCHEL, EFFICIENT CAPITAL MARKET THEORY, THE MARKET FOR CORPORATE CONTROL, AND THE REGULATION OF CASH TENDER OFFERS

57 Tex.L.Rev. 1, 3–5, 8–9 (1978).

An efficient capital market[13] is one in which a trader cannot improve his overall chances of speculative gain by obtaining public information about the companies whose securities are in the market and evaluating that information intelligently in determining which stocks to buy and sell. Paradoxically, the efficiency of the market results from the competitive efforts of securities analysts and investors who strive to earn superior returns by identifying mispriced securities—securities that are either overvalued or undervalued. The goal of securities analysis is to discover information that suggests differences between current market prices and what these prices "should" be, the securities' intrinsic values. The securities analyst acts on this information by buying, selling, or recommending securities. The process ensures that market prices reflect all available information. * * * [I]n an efficient capital

---

13. [By the Author] Two major implications of efficient capital market theory are that (1) security prices adjust rapidly and in an unbiased manner to any new information, and (2) price changes behave in a random manner. B. Lev, Financial Statement Analysis: A New Approach 212 (1974). If prices of securities did not adjust rapidly and without bias, investors could profit by trading during the time during which securities did not reflect all available information or during periods when the market either overcompensated or undercompensated for new information. Similarly, if security prices did not move randomly, investors could capitalize on systematic price movements to earn above average returns.

The empirical support for efficient capital market theory exists in three forms—weak, semi-strong, and strong. The weak form has focused on the significance of securities' past price movements. Repeated studies have demonstrated that historic patterns of past prices are of no value in predicting future price movements. The semi-strong form asserts that security prices reflect all publicly available information about that security. Empirical tests of the semi-strong form have tested the speed of adjustment of security prices to such events as stock splits, annual earnings announcements and large secondary offerings of common stock. These tests indicate a quick price adjustment process in which the information revealed by specific events is anticipated by the market. The strong form of efficient capital market theory is that even nonpublic information is quickly reflected in security prices. Tests of the strong form have proven inconclusive. Several studies of professionally managed mutual funds have concluded that these funds, despite huge expenditures to identify mispriced securities, were unable to consistently outperform the market. Other studies have found, however, that corporate insiders can profit by trading on inside information not available to other investors.

For a survey of the literature on the empirical support for efficient capital market theory, see Note, The Efficient Capital Market Hypothesis, Economic Theory and the Regulation of the Securities Industry, 29 Stan.L.Rev. 1031, 1041–54 (1977).

market in which a large number of buyers and sellers react through a market mechanism such as the New York Stock Exchange to cause market prices to reflect fully and instantly all available information about a company's securities, investors should not be able to "beat the market" systematically by identifying undervalued or overvalued securities. * * *

Efficient capital market theory implies that if a publicly traded company is poorly or less than optimally managed, the price of its securities will reflect this fact accurately and promptly. That a capital market is efficient, however, does not imply that there is a similarly efficient mechanism whereby control shifts from less capable managers to others who can manage corporate assets more profitably. The market for corporate control, so called by Henry Manne in his ground-breaking work on the subject,[14] must perform that function in our economic system.

Poor performance of a company's securities in the capital market is a common indication of poor management. The lower the market price of the securities compared to what it would be with better management, the more attractive the firm is to outsiders with the ability to take the firm over. The most common takeover device is the merger. This takeover device is not available, however, when incumbent management opposes the shift in control because merger statutes uniformly require approval by the directors of the two corporations. The two techniques that can be used to shift control when there is opposition are the direct purchase of shares and the proxy contest. * * *

One of the basic themes of corporation law is the significance for shareholders of the modern corporation's separation of ownership and control. In their famous work on this subject, Professors Berle and Means assumed that managers do not seek to maximize what is most important to shareholders—appreciation of the shareholders' underlying investment.

Berle and Means failed to recognize, however, that unity of ownership and control is not a necessary condition of efficient performance of a firm. If the owner of a wholly owned firm is its manager, he will make operating decisions that maximize his utility.[15] After the owner-manager sells equity in the firm to raise capital, however, his incentive to search out new profitable ventures diminishes because he now bears only a fraction of the losses resulting from less profitable investments.[16] The agency relationship between shareholders and managers inevitably calls into question the identity of the agent's decisions with decisions that would maximize the welfare of shareholders.[17]

Various market mechanisms exist, however, to minimize this divergence of interests between managers and shareholders. As Alchian has illustrated,

14. [By the Author] E.g., Manne, Cash Tender Offers for Shares—A Reply to Chairman Cohen, 1967 Duke L.J. 231; Manne, Mergers and the Market for Corporate Control, 73 J.Pol.Econ. 110 (1965).

15. [By the Author] Jensen & Meckling, Theory of the Firm: Managerial Behavior: Agency Costs and Ownership Structure, 3 J.Fin.Econ. 305, 312 (1976).

16. [By the Author] Similarly, as the owner-manager's share of the equity falls and his fractional claim on the outcome falls, he will have greater incentives to appropriate larger amounts of corporate resources in the form of perquisites. Id. at 313.

17. [By the Author] In addition to this inevitable residual loss, other costs of the agency relationship are monitoring expenditures by the principal and bonding expenditures by the agent. Id. at 308.

an architect or builder does not share in its profits or losses (as only the owners do) absent contractual arrangement. Yet the architect or builder is vitally interested in the success of the building. The greater the profits generated by his efforts, the greater the demand for his services. Corporate managers are in precisely the same situation. While they do not directly share in the profits of an enterprise, successful performance increases the demand for their services as managers. Managers have a further incentive to maximize profit if their compensation is in some way linked to performance—stock options are a common example of this type of arrangement. Intensity of competition in the firm's product market also provides an incentive for managerial efficiency.

The market for corporate control and the threat of cash tender offers in particular are of great importance in creating incentives for management to maximize the welfare of shareholders. Theoretically, shareholders may oust poor management on their own initiative, but the costs to individual shareholders of monitoring management performance and campaigning for its defeat in shareholder elections when performance is poor are prohibitive. On the other hand, inefficient performance by management is reflected in share price thus making the corporation a likely candidate for a takeover bid. Since a successful takeover bid often results in the displacement of current management, managers have a strong incentive to operate efficiently and keep share prices high.

Notes

Robert W. Hamilton and Richard A. Booth, Business Basics for Law Students: Essential Terms and Concepts, § 15.2 (1998):*

There is no doubt that many market professionals do not agree with the efficient capital market hypothesis in all of its implications. To be sure, one often hears about mutual fund managers or large investors who have beaten the market five or ten years in a row. Economic theorists tend to reject such anecdotal evidence on the ground that it merely reflects the laws of chance. After all, someone may be able to guess the outcome of ten coin flips once in a while. There are, however, some anomalies that cannot be explained by the theory. For example, the market tends to go up in January. * * * Another example was the sharp market break that occurred in October, 1987: There appears to have been nothing during the period of that decline that can account for a decline of nearly one-third in the value of many stocks. Nevertheless, the evidence supporting the efficient capital market theory at least during periods of normal market activity is great, and it is clear that the theory provides a valuable insight as to how the market operates. * * *

Several theories have been advanced to explain 'anomalies' in market pricing. They look to **noise** or **chaos** inherent in active trading markets. In other words, although the interaction of many traders has the effect of ultimately driving market prices to a close to proper level, market prices by their very nature tend to fluctuate as certain theories, opinions, and even fads gain favor among investors. The theory has intuitive appeal given that anecdotal evidence suggests that investors often copy each other's trades. * * *

* Reprinted with the permission of Aspen Law & Business/Panel Publishers, a division of   Aspen Publishers, Inc. The text set forth above is subject to further revision.

In any event, the essential idea behind alternative theories of how the market works is that although a trader may not be able consistently to beat the market, it does not necessarily follow that the market consistently establishes (say) the highest price that a bidder for control would be willing to pay. * * *

In addition to market anomalies and the takeover phenomenon, there are several large investors, perhaps most notably Warren Buffett, the CEO of Berkshire Hathaway, who have consistently made large gains as a result of large investments in publicly held companies. * * * While such examples are not explainable by a simplistic view of market efficiency, they are consistent with a limited view of what efficiency means, namely, that it is very difficult for passive investors to beat the market through a strategy of active trading.

2. THE GROWTH OF INSTITUTIONAL INVESTORS

RICHARD H. KOPPES, CORPORATE GOVERNANCE: IN-STITUTIONAL INVESTORS, NOW IN CONTROL OF MORE THAN HALF THE SHARES OF U.S. CORPORA-TIONS, DEMAND MORE ACCOUNTABILITY
The National Law Journal, April 14, 1997, p. B5.*

Nothing has so defined the revolution of corporate governance over the last 20 years as the rise of institutional investors. This key group has become a powerful force in corporate America. As activists, institutional investors have set the standards and terms for the corporate governance reform movement and are changing the face of American business.

Aging baby boomers have fueled the increase in public and private funds from approximately $2 trillion in 1986 to more than $5 trillion today—accounting for a sizable portion of all institutional investments.

While patterns of share ownership in the United States are almost always changing in one way or another, the 1990s marked a watershed: For the first time on record, institutional investors controlled more than half the shares in American corporations. By contrast, as recently as 40 years ago, these institutions together held less than 10 percent of the outstanding shares. Progressive institutionalization has been the dominant ongoing change in U.S. share ownership.

This change in ownership structure has had a number of important consequences over time. Many institutional investors have such large holdings that they have become permanent, long-term shareowners of major corporations. As buy-and-hold players, institutional investors have become the patient capital of companies. As a result they have an economic interest in using corporate governance to improve performance.

And as the size of their holdings has grown, institutional investors have discovered ownership rights. The practice of simply selling shares in disgust has given way to the realization that taking an active role as an owner makes economic sense.

Notes

(1) The principal kinds of institutional investors are (a) pension funds created by corporate employers, by states and cities for their employees, and by universi-

* Reprinted with permission from April 14, 1997 issue of The National Law Journal.

ties, churches, and foundations; (b) mutual funds (and other types of investment companies) that offer opportunities to invest in broad portfolios of securities; (c) insurance companies, both life and casualty; (d) foundations; (e) university and charitable endowments; (f) banks investing trust funds; (g) brokerage firms; and (h) a variety of investment vehicles for sophisticated investors, many in the form of limited partnerships.

(2) The growth of institutional investors described by Mr. Koppes is graphically revealed by statistics. In 1953, individual investors held 90 percent of all outstanding shares listed on the New York Stock Exchange, while institutional investors held less than 10 percent. By 1992, more than 50 percent of all NYSE shares were held by institutional investors. Just over one percent of U.S. households own two-thirds of all publicly traded equity securities directly held by individuals. Of course, many additional individuals own stock indirectly through institutional investors such as mutual funds, annuities, and retirement or profit-sharing plans. The Wharton School & The New York Stock Exchange, Inc., The Policy Implications of Stockownership Patterns 3–5 (1993). In terms of dollars, "[I]t took a decade for all institutions to see their assets nearly triple, from $672.6 billion in 1970 to $1.9 trillion in 1980. The next decade brought more than a tripling in assets, to $6.3 trillion in 1990, and then a staggering increase of slightly more than 75 percent in five-and-one-half years, to $11.1 trillion at the end of the second quarter of 1996." The Conference Board, Institutional Investment Report: Patterns of institutional investment and control in the United States, No. 1, vol. 1, January 1997, at 4.

(3) Even more graphic are the statistics relating to ownership of shares in specific large corporations. In 1995, the market value of the 1,000 largest domestic corporations constituted 74.5 percent of the value of all domestic corporations. Institutional investors owned over 50 percent of the shares of 650 of these 1,000 companies; they owned over 90 percent of the shares of 42 of these companies and 80 percent or more of 158 of them. The Conference Board, The Brancato Report on Institutional Investment, Concentration of Ownership and Foreign Equity Holdings, vol. 3, ed. 3 (Sept., 1996), pp.10–15.

(4) Another indication of institutional investor activity is the growth of larger securities transactions. The New York Stock Exchange collects data on "block transactions" involving single trades of 10,000 shares or more. In 1970, there were 17,217 such transactions, representing 13 percent of the total value of all shares traded on the NYSE. In 1995, the number of such transactions had risen to 1,963,889, representing 53.6 percent of the value of all shares traded on the NYSE. The Conference Board, The Brancato Report on Institutional Investment: Equity Turnover and Investment Strategies, vol. 3, Ed. 2, at 16 (May 1996). And these figures understate the trading activities of institutional investors, since there exist several proprietary computerized trading systems open only to institutional investors that do not report transactions in NYSE-listed shares.

(5) Even though the collective holdings of institutional investors may carry with them potential control over individual companies, it is unusual for any single institutional investor to own more than 3 percent of the voting shares of a major company. For example, the 7th largest corporation in mid–1996 was IBM Corporation; 50.4 percent of its shares were owned by institutional investors. Five institutional investors alone owned 11.6 percent of its shares; ten owned 16.8 percent, 20 owned 20.5 percent, and 25 owned 26.1 percent. Ibid., at 33. Of course even a 1 percent investment in IBM (nearly 5.5 million shares) represents a huge dollar investment. There are, of course, thousands of institutional investors, and

most large companies have hundreds of separate institutional investors as shareholders. IBM shares, for example, were held by 703 different institutions in 1990. Columbia Institutional Investor Project; Columbia University School of Law, Oct. 1991 at 5.

(6) Institutional investors almost always have fiduciary duties to persons other than the issuers of the portfolio securities in which they invest. For example, pension funds have a duty to the employees covered by the fund to maximize the funds available for retirement benefits. These duties to third parties are construed by some institutional investors as requiring that they strive to maximize the gain to the institutional investor even though the gain is on a short term basis. This short-horizon investment philosophy, when being applied by a relatively small number of shareholders which collectively may own more than 50 percent of the outstanding securities issued by the largest domestic corporations is itself a source of concern. However, as suggested by Mr. Koppes, many institutional investors, particularly employee retirement plans, do not adopt a policy of short-term maximization of gains but view themselves as permanent investors in individual companies.

(7) Institutional investors generally vote shares as they think best without seeking to ascertain the wishes of the beneficiaries as to how shares should be voted (indeed, an investigation of beneficiary desires probably is impractical in most situations). However, some pension, retirement and employee savings plans provide for "pass through" voting in which beneficial owners determine how shares are to be voted.

ALFRED CONARD, BEYOND MANAGERIALISM: INVESTOR CAPITALISM?

22 U.Mich.J.L.Ref. 117, 139, 144–45 (1988).

Whether institutional investors will exert their latent power to enhance the profitability of enterprises will depend, in large part, on the motivation of institutional managers. They are presumably no more and no less faithful than enterprise managers to their fiduciary duties. Like enterprise managers, institutional managers can be expected to maximize the financial returns of their funds, so long as the effort to do so contributes to their own rewards and job security. When their rewards are threatened and, even more, when their job security is imperiled, some of them are likely, like enterprise managers, to put their personal rewards and job security ahead of the interests of their constituents. * * *

According to a broad current of conventional wisdom, investors of all kinds are wise to forgo active participation in corporate governance, because they can protect their interests at less expense by selling their shares in enterprises that are inefficiently managed and switching their resources to better-managed companies. This principle of investor behavior has been called the "Wall Street rule." Its validity is said to be corroborated by the infrequency of investor opposition to management proposals and the even greater infrequency of investor nominations of directorial candidates to oppose the managers' nominations.

Although the Wall Street rule fits a typical individual investor, there are reasons to doubt that it fits a typical institutional investor in the 1980s.

Selling out is a good alternative only for the holder of a small block of shares who gets the news before it is public or before others have time to act on it. The holding of a large fund or a large family of funds may be too large to liquidate without pushing down the price. * * *

BERNARD BLACK, SHAREHOLDER PASSIVITY REEXAMINED

89 Mich.L.Rev. 520, 521–24 (1990).

The problem of who watches the watchers is as old as government, and not much more tractable for corporate than for government organizations. In theory, the shareholders of public companies elect directors, who watch corporate officers, who manage/watch the company on the shareholders' behalf. But since Berle and Means, we have understood that this theory is a fiction. The managers—the current officers and directors—pick the directors, and the shareholder rubberstamp the manager's choices. Perhaps thrice in a thousand cases, unhappy shareholders mount a proxy fight. About one fourth of the time, they win.

Most modern corporate scholars, especially those with a law-and-economics bent, accept shareholder passivity as inevitable. They rely on market forces, especially takeovers, to limit managerial discretion. The critics' claim, stripped to its essentials, is that shareholders don't care much about voting except in extreme cases and never will. Collective action problems, which arise because each shareholder owns a small fraction of a company's stock, explain why shareholders can't be expected to care. I will call this view the "passivity story." * * *

I argue that the critics' legal analysis is misdirected; their factual assumptions about shareholder size are obsolete; and their collective action explanation for passivity is superficial. Shareholder voting, historically only a minor nuisance to corporate managers, can become an important part of the multi-strand web of imperfect constraints on managers, *if* legal rules permit. My emphasis is on the formal act of voting. Much actual oversight undoubtedly will be informal, but meaningful informal oversight will take place only if the formal power is available should it be needed. * * *

The passivity story also assumes a company with thousands of anonymous shareholders, each owning a tiny fraction of the company's voting stock. That assumption, never wholly true, is increasingly obsolete. Institutional investors have grown large enough so that a limited number of institutions own a sizeable percentage of the shares of most public companies. Moreover, the fastest growing institutions are public pension funds and mutual funds, which face fewer direct conflicts of interest in monitoring corporate managers than the corporate pension funds and bank trust departments who were formerly the principal institutional shareholders. Large institutions can combine forces, form trade groups to represent their collective interest, and one way or another act as monitors of corporate managers, if they see profit in doing so. Legal obstacles notwithstanding, some institutions are trying to do just that.

GERALD T. GARVEY AND PETER L. SWAN, THE ECONOMICS OF CORPORATE GOVERNANCE: BEYOND THE MARSHALLIAN FIRM[18]

1 J.Corp.Fin. 139, 146, 150 (1994).*

* * * [M]any sizeable institutional shareholders such as CalPERS have attempted, sometimes successfully, to affect corporate decisions. But those who would mount a challenge are at a severe disadvantage relative to management, not only in terms of their own knowledge of the corporation's real situation but also in terms of their ability to communicate with their fellow shareholders and to finance a campaign. Class action suits brought by shareholders are even less rewarding for the participants.

At present, large shareholders face enormous costs in influencing the behavior of executives. While some commentators claim that this will change with the appearance of large pension funds and other potential 'relationship investors' able to exert a major influence over corporate policies, to date there is little systematic evidence of such a trend. While institutional investors have come to hold a substantial fraction of many firms' shares, the institutions are themselves large organizations and it is not at all clear that the managers of institutional funds will push corporate managers to maximize the wealth of the fund's beneficiaries. Lakonishok, Shleifer and Vishny (1990)[19] argue that large pension funds tend to underperform the market, and Murphy and Van Nuys (1992)[20] provide evidence that pension fund managers have little incentive to actively monitor the firms in which they invest. This suggests that the highly publicized incidents of institutional activism by shareholders such as CalPERS may by the exception rather than the rule.

* * * The implicit theoretical lens used in most studies is the legal and economic model that assumes efficiency is monotonically increasing in the degree to which actions are made in shareholder interests. That is, shareholders are the only constituency that *should* matter. * * * The main argument here is that it is far easier to interpret the evidence as reflecting a world where managers have substantial leeway, at least ex post, to depart from maximizing shareholder wealth. Moreover, *other* claimants appear to exert substantial influence over corporate policy choices. * * *

Notes

(1) The organization referred to as CalPERS in this excerpt is the California Public Employees Retirement System, perhaps the most activist institutional investor in the corporate governance area. Other active institutional investors include TIAA/CREF, an organization that provides retirement plans for public and private university and college teachers, pension plans maintained by labor unions

---

18. [By the Editor] Numerous references to both the legal and economics literature in this excerpt have been eliminated. The conclusions reached are based largely on a survey of this literature.

* Reprinted with kind permission from Elsevier Science-NL, Sara Burgerhartstraat 25, 1055 KV Amsterdam, The Netherlands.

19. [By the Editor] The Structure and Performance of the Money Management Industry, Brookings Papers in Economic Activity: Microeconomics, 339–92.

20. [By the Editor] Murphy, K.J. and K. Van Nuys, 1993, Public Pension Funds: Ark of the Lost Raiders?, Working paper, Harvard Business School, Cambridge MA.

for their members, and Wisconsin and other state public employees retirement systems.

(2) The development of activism by institutional investors has gone through several distinct phases.

(a) Prior to the 1980s, institutional investors tended to view themselves purely as investors who should support rather than confront management. During this period investments by individual institutional investors were much smaller than they are today, and it may have been possible for them to dispose of holdings on the open market if they were dissatisfied with management. In other words, institutional investors could act in much the same way as individual shareholders and exercise the "Wall Street option" if they were not satisfied with management.

(b) Institutional investor involvement in the oversight or monitoring of portfolio companies began during the takeover movement of the 1980s. With the development of poison pills (often called "shareholder rights plans" by management) and other defensive tactics in the mid–1980s, management of target companies were able to block cash offers for target company shares at premiums that were often 50 percent or more above the prior market price. (For a discussion of poison pills and other defensive tactics, see chapter 14, part H.) Faced with the significant loss of profitable resale opportunities, a few large institutional investors introduced shareholder proposals in 1985 and 1986 seeking the withdrawal of poison pills. (The rather arcane law of shareholder proposals under the SEC proxy regulations is discussed in Part 4 of Section D of this Chapter.) In the spring of 1987, shareholder proposals on this topic were introduced by institutional investors in more than 60 companies.[21] However, efforts to organize institutional investors were limited because of concern that direct communication among investors might be viewed as solicitation of proxies in violation of the SEC proxy regulations. As described in part 1 of Section D of this Chapter, these restrictions were not significantly relaxed until 1992.

Shareholder proposals to revoke poison pills in the 1980s had only a few instances of spectacular success—for example, in 1988, a 51.9 percent favorable vote of shareholders of USAir Group and a 61.2 percent favorable vote of shareholders of Santa Fe/Southern Pacific. In the aggregate, during the 1989 "proxy season," support for these proposals averaged 27.9 percent of the shares voting, up only slightly from the 26.4 percent during the 1988 season. While this might be viewed as an impressive showing, clearly a significant number of institutional investors did not vote with the petitioning institutional investors in favor of these proposals. James E. Heard, Shareholder Activism, Pension Fund Proxy Campaigns Highlight 1989 Annual Meeting Season, Insights, Vol. 3, No. 6, at 20–21 (June 1989)[22] tried to put a favorable "spin" on these results:

> More significant than the voting results, however, was the number of companies that agreed to the actions requested. In exchange for withdrawal of a proposal sponsored by CalPERS, Great Northern Nekoosa agreed either to redeem its poison pill or to submit it for shareholder approval within three

21. [By the Editor] A CREF administrator justified the shareholder proposals relating to defensive tactics introduced by CREF as follows in 1987: About 25 percent of CREF's portfolio of $30 billion was invested in companies that appeared to be subject to takeover bids. Surveys showed that poison pills reduced the value of shares by about one percent on the average. Poison pills therefore affected $7.5 billion of CREF's portfolio, reducing its value by $75 million. CREF's anti pill crusade in 1987 cost only about $10,000, clearly cost justifiable. See Alfred F. Conard, Beyond Managerialism: Investor Capitalism? 22 U.Mich.J.L.Ref. 117, 145 n. 94 (1988).

22. Insights: The Corporate & Securities Law Advisor. Copyright Prentice Hall Law & Business.

years. Dayton Hudson reached a similar understanding with CREF, and CREF withdrew its proposal. * * * Six companies—American Home Products, Continental, First Interstate Bancorp, J.C. Penney, TRW and Unocal—agreed to adopt confidential voting in exchange for withdrawal of secret ballot proposals.

The willingness of these companies to consider the merits of the shareholder proposals offers evidence that, even though activist institutions are still losing the votes, the shareholder campaigns of the past three years are beginning to have an effect. The willingness of both institutional activists and corporate management to discuss the issues, and their ability to reach compromise, suggests that constructive dialogue may be possible on a wide range of issues. * * *

One [new] approach is the establishment of shareholder advisory committees to advise companies on corporate governance issues and other significant matters. * * *

(c) As described in chapter 14, the takeover movement of the 1980s ended rather unexpectedly in about 1990 following the collapse of the brokerage firm of Drexel Burnham, Lambert, Inc., the criminal conviction of Michael Milkin, and changes in economic and political conditions generally. Attention turned from poison pills and other defensive tactics to the more traditional issues of managerial efficiency, profitability of the enterprise, and executive compensation. The early 1990s were a recessionary period which occurred at the same time many industries were facing unexpected technological and structural change. Many respected and well-known corporations announced massive losses, huge layoffs, and major changes in product lines. At the same time, unfavorable publicity was directed at high levels of executive compensation, which appeared to be little affected by poor performance of the enterprise. During this period, a surprisingly large number of Chief Executive Officers lost their jobs. Corporations removing their CEOs during this period included American Express, IBM, General Motors, First Boston, Eli Lilly, Sunbeam Oster, Westinghouse, Eastman Kodak, and Compaq Computer. While the extent of the involvement of institutional investors in these developments is impossible to document, it is generally believed that their influence was substantial. Articles describing these events commonly refer to the influence of "activist shareholders" and "pressure" from shareholders. E.g., Judith H. Dobrzynski, A GM Postmortem: Lessons for Corporate America, Bus. Wk., Nov. 9, 1992, at 87; John A. Byrne, Requiem for Yesterday's CEO: Old–Style Execs Who Can't Adapt Are Losing Their Hold, Bus. Wk., Feb. 15, 1993, at 32, 33. Judith H. Dobrzynski, Activist Boards, Yes. Panicky Boards, No, Bus. Wk., Dec. 28, 1992, at 40, describes events occurring at Westinghouse in November, 1992:

[R]epresentatives of the California Public Employees' Retirement System aired their complaints to Westinghouse CEO Paul E. Lego. They also told Lego they wanted to meet with outside directors, including Frank C. Carlucci III, vice-chairman of Caryle Group. Within days, Carlucci "offered, through an intermediary, to resign from the board," says Richard H. Koppes, CalPERS' general counsel. "Our request to meet him was interpreted as we were targeting him." CalPERS merely wanted to talk to Carlucci, who couldn't be reached for comment.

Other stories refer to specific institutional investors "targeting" a specific underperforming company or "notifying" the company that it planned to withhold its vote in the election of directors as a "message."

(3) In October, 1992, the SEC amended its proxy regulations to permit much freer communication among institutional investors without fear of being charged with violation of the regulations so long as there was no solicitation of proxies. See Section D, part 1 of this chapter. Anecdotal evidence indicates that corporate executives of corporations in which institutional investors had substantial holdings almost immediately displayed increased sensitivity to the concerns of major shareholders. For example, in July 1993, IBM announced the formation of a new "corporate governance" committee of the board of directors composed entirely of outside directors. This followed a decision by the same board in January 1993 to appoint a similar committee solely to consider executive compensation matters within IBM. About the same time, TIAA/CREF announced that it planned to open discussion with directors at a number of underperforming portfolio companies. In 1994, General Motors released corporate governance guidelines that showed considerable sensitivity to concerns of institutional investors. In 1996, "Chrysler directors met with 40 of the auto maker's institutional shareholders. Senior managers were present at the beginning of many of these sessions, but then excused themselves so shareholders could have a frank discussion of governance issues with directors. 'With few exceptions, corporate boards are much more responsive to our concerns today than even three years ago,' says Kurt N. Schacht, general counsel for Wisconsin's Investment Board." John A. Byrne, The Best and & Worst Boards: Our New Report Card on Corporate Governance, Business Week, November 25, 1996, 82, 94.

(4) Economic conditions began to improve in the early 1990s, accompanied by a revival of the takeover movement and a return of unsolicited takeover bids (though most mergers in the 1990s have involved negotiated transactions). The attention of institutional investors returned to proposals to eliminate poison pills, with much greater success than in the earlier period. Joann S. Lublin, 'Poison Pills' Are Giving Shareholders a Big Headache, Union Proposals Assert, Wall St. J., May 23, 1997, p. c1, col. 3, states that in 1997 14 measures to eliminate poison pills had been voted on and had garnered an average of 53.7 percent of the ballots cast, and that between 1988 and 1996, 52 non-binding resolutions to curb poison pills had won a majority of the votes cast; thereafter, half of the companies involved had abandoned their poison pills. An example involves May Department Stores, a publicly owned corporation, 70 percent of the stock of which is owned by institutional investors. The proposal to eliminate May's poison pill was presented by the pension fund of the Union of Needletrades, Industrial and Textile Industries and Textile Employees (UNITE), which owned 53,418 of May's 250.6 million shares. Both May and UNITE lobbied the large shareholders extensively, and the proposal to remove the poison pill appears to have been approved by a narrow vote.

(5) Some institutional investors have created monitoring programs for portfolio corporations. Perhaps the most extensive program is by TIAA/CREF, which owns approximately one percent of all equities issued by large publicly held publicly corporations; it directly monitors 25 governance issues (including board independence and conflicts of interest) for 1,500 companies. The New York State Retirement Fund screens the economic performance of about 900 companies. Specific governance proposals put forth by institutional investors include "destaggering" boards of directors in order to give shareholders greater voting power (Reebok Corporation), executive compensation [Walt Disney, and others], and the elimination of ineffective chief executive officers and individual directors. See Joann S. Lublin, Irate Shareholders Target Ineffective Board Members, Wall St. J., November 6, 1995, Section B, p. 1, col. 5 [reporting a strong negative vote by

institutional investors in Archer–Daniels–Midland Company before the management reorganization that occurred in that company]. Some institutional investors show their displeasure at corporate governance policies in specific corporations by withholding their vote for management nominated directors. See Richard H. Koppes, Corporate Governance, Institutional investors, now in control of more than half the shares of U.S. corporations, demand more accountability, The National Law Journal, April 14, 1997, p. b5, reporting that following a $90 million payout by Walt Disney to former President Michael Ovitz, the holders of 12.5 percent of Disney shares withheld their votes for five directors in protest. These holders included CalPERS, Barclays Global Investors, CREF, and the State of Wisconsin Investment Board. A similar protest occurred in W.R. Grace & Co. in May 1995 over the award of a $20 million severance payment to former CEO J.P. Bolduc. It is not a coincidence that the most active institutional investors generally have been pension and retirement funds, since they have long-term interests that require substantial payments in the future to employees; their portfolios are so large that they are unlikely to try to sell shares on a wide scale in protest of corporate governance issues. They are, in short, the epitome of the long term investor.

(6) Anecdotal evidence aside, it is difficult to assess the impact of this involvement of institutional investors on corporate performance. For one thing, there is the matter of coverage. The broad scale monitoring programs described in the previous note are relatively new. In the late 1980s and early 1990s most of the attention was focused on a relatively small number of large and highly visible companies. Many substantial companies with relatively poor track records did not become the subject of attention by institutional investors. This point was strongly made in an aptly entitled article, Stuart Misher, Weak Force: Shareholder Activism, Despite Hoopla, Leaves Most CEOs Unscathed, Wall St.J., May 24, 1993, at 1, col. 6. But see Leslie Scism, Midsize Companies No Longer Escape Activists' Ire, Wall St.J., Nov. 3, 1993, at c1, col. 3. A 1996 study of the 1990–1993 period by researchers at Purdue University concluded that activism by institutional investors with respect to specific companies had no "appreciable effect" on performance, as gauged by return on equity, return on investment, and market performance. For a similarly negative view of institutional investor activity based on a detailed study of one incident, see D. Gordon Smith, Corporate Governance and Managerial Incompetence: Lessons from Kmart, 74 N.C.L.Rev. 1037 (1996).

(7) A study by Professors John Core, Robert Holthausen and David Larcker of the Wharton School concluded that corporations with the following characteristics tend to pay their CEOs more than other corporations and their returns on assets and stock performance are weaker than other corporations: the same person serving as CEO and chairman, a large board of directors, outside directors directly appointed by the CEO, outside directors who receive income from an association with the company, and directors who sit on several outside boards or who are aged 70 or more,. This study was based on data on 205 large corporations collected in 1982, 1983, and 1984. E.S. Browning, Heard on the Street: Wharton Study Connects Strengths and Flaws of Directors to Companies' Financial Returns, Wall Street Journal, April 25, 1987, p. C2, col. 4.

(8) There has also been extensive theoretical law review analysis of the current and possible future roles of institutional investors, including issues such as how effective were investor managers at this new job, how were the managers selected, and whose interests they attempting to further? At least eight major articles were published on these topics in the early 1990s, during the hiatus in the takeover movement. Another basic question is, Who oversees the overseers? For a

rather negative assessment of this question, see Roberta Romano, Public Pension Fund Activism in Corporate Governance Reconsidered, 93 Colum.L.Rev. 795, 796 (1993) ("Public fund managers must navigate carefully around the shoals of considerable political pressure to temper investment policies with local considerations, such as fostering in-state employment, which are not aimed at maximizing the value of their portfolios' assets"). See also Mark J. Roe, Strong Managers, Weak Owners: The Political Roots of American Corporate Finance (1994).

3. NOMINEES, BOOK ENTRY, AND "STREET NAMES"

ROLE OF GIANT CORPORATIONS

HEARINGS BEFORE THE SUBCOMMITTEE ON MONOPOLY
OF THE SELECT COMMITTEE ON SMALL BUSINESS

United States Senate, 92nd Cong., 2d Sess., Pt. 4, at 5322–24
(1972) (Correspondence of W.S. Mitchell, President, Safeway Stores, Inc.)

Safeway Stores, Inc., Top 30 Shareholders, Mar. 3, 1972

[Record, beneficial owner]	[Number of shares]
Kane & Co., Chase Manhattan Bank[23]	2,206,363
Cede & Co., NYSE	1,372,062
Merrill Lynch Pierce Fenner	646,752
Ince & Co., Morgan Guaranty Trust	594,224
Myers & Co., Windsor Fund	512,000
Cudd & Co., Chase Manhattan	305,828
King & Co., First National City Bank	259,326
Food & Co., Bank of California	233,000
Sigler & Co., Manu. Hanover Trust	202,225
Egger & Co., Chase Manhattan Bank	188,664
Brown Brothers Harriman & Co.	182,229
Eddy & Co., Bankers Trust Co.	167,325
Finman & Co., Bankers Trust Co.	166,400
Sabat Co., Savings Banks Trust Co.	162,700
Salkeld & Co., Bankers Trust Co.	151,705
O'Neill & Co., Bank of New York	150,000
Lynn & Co., Morgan Guaranty Trust	125,000
Seafirst & Co., Seattle Nat. Bank	123,439
Ferro & Co., Nat. Shawmut Bank of Boston	114,100
Gmster & Co., Bank of America	93,000
Loeb Rhoades & Co.	80,919
Gunther & Co., Swiss Bank Corp.	74,138
Bid & Co., New England Merchants National Bank	72,000
Seatel & Co., Seattle First National Bank	70,000
Dicot & Co., Bank of America	65,000
Spinnaker & Co., State Street Bank and Trust	57,000
Nay & Co., Security Pacific National Bank	56,058
Safinsco	55,000
Trund & Co., United California Bank	54,500
Gavin & Co., Morgan Guaranty Trust	52,800
Total	8,593,757

Total outstanding shares, 25,620,931

23. [By the Editor] The registered holder of the shares in this list is the nominee whose name appears on the left (e.g., "Kane & Co."). The name of the institution was added by the person preparing the list for presentation to the Senate Subcommittee. Of course, in the records of Safeway Stores only the name of the nominee appears.

Notes

(1) Other material presented to the Select Committee indicate that Kane & Co. was the nominee for the employees' Profit Sharing Plan, and King & Co. and Food & Company for the Safeway Retirement Plan.

(2) In 1986, Safeway Stores was acquired in a leveraged buyout by Kohlberg, Kravis, Roberts, for a purchase price of $4.25 billion, and ceased to be a listed publicly held company. The corporation thereafter again went public with KKR in control of its operations.

FINAL REPORT OF THE SECURITIES AND EXCHANGE COMMISSION ON THE PRACTICE OF RECORDING THE OWNERSHIP OF SECURITIES IN THE RECORDS OF THE ISSUER IN OTHER THAN THE NAME OF THE BENEFICIAL OWNER OF SUCH SECURITIES[24]

A. Background

The practice of registering securities in the records of issuers in other than the name of the beneficial owner is commonly referred to as "nominee" and "street" name registration. Nominee name registration refers to arrangements used by institutional investors (insurance companies and investment companies among others) and financial intermediaries (brokers, banks and trust companies) for the registration of securities held by them for their own account or for the account of their customers who are the beneficial owners of the securities.[25] Street name registration, a specialized type of nominee name registration, refers to the practice of a broker registering in its name, or in the name of its nominee, securities left with it by customers or held by it for its own account.

American institutions first began extensively to register securities in nominee name in the 1930's[26] in an effort to escape onerous transfer requirements placed on corporations and fiduciaries by issuers seeking to protect themselves from judicially imposed liability for improper transfers.[27] Custom-

---

24. (December 3, 1976) Pp. 1–6. This report is usually called "The Street Name Study."

25. [By the Commission] A nominee is, typically, a partnership formed exclusively to act as the recordholder of securities. Each of the nominee's general partners is an employee of the professional fiduciary or corporate institutional investor and legally is empowered to make transfers of nominee stock. As employees depart or assume other duties, they retire from the partnership, and new partners are admitted so that the partnership continues as a creature of the parent entity. Often, the partnership name is short, is derived from the name of a partner or former partner, and includes at the end " & Co.," the traditional indication of a partnership. The name may have no relation to the name of the fiduciary or institution for which the nominee acts.

26. [By the Commission] Brokers at that time employed street name registration primarily as a convenient method of holding secu-

rities pledged by customers in connection with margin transactions and as a means of avoiding transfer taxes.

27. [By the Commission] An issuer transferring record ownership of its securities was obligated to protect equitable, or beneficial, interests, as well as legal, or record, interests. If the character of a transfer made in breach of trust were discoverable on reasonable inquiry, failure to make that inquiry rendered the issuer liable to the beneficial owner. This doctrine was established in Lowry v. Commercial and Farmers' Bank, 15 F.Cas. 1040 (No. 8581) (C.C.Md.1848), which held that corporations were responsible for the propriety of transfers of their stock by fiduciaries. A corporation was: " * * * the custodian of the shares of stock, and clothed with power sufficient to protect the rights of everyone interested, from unauthorized transfers; it is a trust placed in the hands of the corporation for the protection of individual interests, and like every other trustee it is bound to execute the trust with proper

arily, issuers required the submission of all supporting documents[28] before transferring stock held by fiduciaries and required corporate investors to demonstrate the authority and incumbency of the individual officer or employee acting on their behalf. The use of the nominee as the registered holder of stock eliminated from the issuer's records any evidence of a fiduciary relationship and made the recordholder a non-corporate entity. Thus nominees could transfer securities without meeting the requirements placed on corporate or fiduciary shareholders.

Nominee registration still serves to facilitate transfers, but today it provides other important benefits to the securities industry as well. The widespread use of nominee registration, however, has collateral effects which may be disadvantageous. First, it makes communications between issuers and their shareowners more circuitous due to the interpositioning of intermediaries. Second, it tends to complicate regulation by masking beneficial owners of securities. Third, since the jurisdiction of certain sections of the Securities Exchange Act of 1934 (the "Act") is based upon a shareholder-of-record standard, the concentration of securities ownership in nominees may have the effect of inappropriately removing or excluding issuers from the jurisdiction of the Act.

Because of concern regarding these consequences, Congress, in June 1975, enacted Section 12(m) of the Act. Section 12(m) authorized and directed the Commission to undertake a study and investigation of the practice of recording the ownership of securities in the records of the issuer in other than the name of the beneficial owner of such securities and to determine (1) whether the practice is consistent with the purposes of the Act * * * and (2) whether steps can be taken to facilitate communications between issuers and the beneficial owners of their securities while at the same time retaining the benefits of such practice. * * *

D. SUMMARY OF CONCLUSIONS AND RECOMMENDATIONS

The Commission has concluded that the practice of registering securities in the records of the issuer in other than the name of the beneficial owner of such securities is consistent with the purposes of the Act * * * The practice benefits investors and the securities industry by facilitating the transfer of record ownership and the clearance and settlement of securities transactions. In addition, it is integral to the operation of securities depositories. At the same time, the widespread use of nominee and street name registration causes certain problems. The Commission has found, however, that established procedures have overcome many of these problems, and the Commission believes that the problems which remain can be mitigated within the framework of the current system.

The Commission, therefore, recommends that no steps be taken which would discourage the use of nominee and street name registration or diminish the benefits which the practice provides. * * *

---

diligence and care, and is responsible for any injury sustained by its negligence or misconduct." Id. at 1047.

28. [By the Commission] For example, a certified copy of the will, trust instrument, or court order of sale.

Most publicly traded shares owned by individual investors today are held in a form of ownership that is best described as "book entry." One unique consequence of book entry ownership is that a single nominee, Cede & Co. (Cede), has become the record owner of an astonishingly high percentage of all publicly traded shares. Cede and Company is the nominee for the Depository Trust Company (DTC), the central clearing facility for the New York Stock Exchange.[29] In order to understand book entry ownership, some history is required.[30]

From time immemorial, securities transactions involving publicly traded shares have been settled five days after the transaction date by the delivery of certificates, recorded either in street name[31] or in the name of the selling shareholders and suitably indorsed. Wall Street maintained a small army of messengers whose duties were to deliver packages containing indorsed or street name certificates to the offices of various brokerage firms to permit individual transactions to be settled. This system worked adequately until the volume of trading increased dramatically in the late 1960s—volume doubled and even tripled in a relatively short period—and the traditional method of handling securities transfers simply broke down. The back offices of the major New York brokerage firms became awash in uncompleted transactions and share certificates of uncertain ownership; more than 150 brokerage firms failed or were forcibly merged before these problems were straightened out in the early 1970s.[32]

The back office crisis was solved by the creation of book entry share ownership, which has permitted the volume of trading on the New York Stock Exchange to grow from a range of five to ten million shares a day in the early 1960s to more than 600 million shares a day in the 1990s. The basic concept is the "immobilization" of share certificates in a clearing house and the recordation of all transfers thereafter to the maximum possible extent through entries on the books of the clearing house and the brokerage firms rather than by transfer of certificates. Brokerage firms that are participants in the clearing house deposit shares owned for their own account as well as for the accounts of their customers with the clearing house, all to be recorded in the name of the nominee, Cede, on the books of each issuing corporation. Certificates are actually deposited at DTC's offices in New York or elsewhere. The ownership of securities by individual shareholders is thereafter reflected solely by direct book entries in the records of the brokerage firm, and indirect book entries in the records of the central depository under the name of the brokerage firm. Once this system is set up, most transactions in shares are

---

29. [By the Editor] The other two clearing houses in the United States are the Mid–West Securities Depository Company and the Philadelphia Depository Trust Company.

30. [By the Editor] Much of the information set forth in this text and the following notes is drawn from the Report of Thomas H. Jackson, Special Master dated January 28, 1992, in State of Delaware v. State of New York, No. 111 Original, (Oct. Term, 1991) United States Supreme Court.

31. [By the Editor] "Street name" here refers to certificates recorded in the name of a Wall Street brokerage firm and indorsed in blank. Street name certificates were routinely

used in New York to close securities transactions since they were essentially bearer securities and could be delivered with a minimum of paperwork.

32. [By the Editor] For a general description of the back office crisis, see Joel Seligman, The Transformation of Wall Street: A History of the Securities and Exchange Commission and Modern Corporate Finance 340–56 (1982); Study of Unsafe and Unsound Practices of Brokers and Dealers, Report and Recommendations of the SEC, H.R. Doc. No. 92–231, 92nd Cong., 1st Sess. (1971).

settled simply by changes in book entries either within the central depository or in the records of brokerage firms, or both, with no movement of certificates at all.

An essential aspect of this plan was the enactment of the Securities Investor Protection Act of 1970,[33] which insures investors against losses from the insolvency of brokerage firms, thereby allowing investors to rely with confidence on monthly statements from brokerage firms showing specified securities in the investors' accounts.

DTC is the principal clearing house in the United States. In 1989, it was estimated that DTC held approximately 72 percent of the shares of companies represented in the Dow Jones Industrial Average, 65 percent of the shares of all U.S. companies listed on the New York Stock Exchange, and 85 percent of the principal amount of all municipal bonds. The "participants" in DTC—the organizations that have securities held by DTC—consist of the major brokerage firms, banks, and other clearing agencies in the United States and Canada. As of 1989, DTC had about 600 participants.

DTC's primary mission (as is the mission of all clearing houses) is the reduction of costs for securities transactions offered to the public by its participants. Each participant has a book entry position in securities it has deposited with DTC. When a participant deposits physical certificates with DTC or receives securities via transfer by book entry from other participants, its account balance is credited. As a practical matter, offsetting transactions by each participant are netted each day, and only net changes are reflected by book entry changes at DTC. Thus, in substantial part, settlement of transactions between participants is handled by adjustments to book accounts rather than the movement of certificates.[34]

Today, when a person makes a routine purchase of publicly traded shares through a broker, the purchaser will not receive a certificate for those shares unless special arrangements are made. Rather, his or her ownership will be

---

33. [By the Editor] 15 U.S.C.A. §§ 78aaa-lll. The Act insures against broker insolvency up to $500,000 for each account, except that the maximum is $100,000 to the extent that a claim is for cash rather than securities. This insurance is provided by the Securities Investor Protection Corporation, which is funded by assessments against its members composed of brokers and dealers registered under the Securities Exchange Act of 1934.

34. [By the Editor] Some movement of securities nevertheless occurs in book entry transactions. Members of the security industry regularly process demands for physical transmission of certificates to be registered in the name of a beneficial owner or a nominee. Such a demand usually arises because a retail customer desires a certificate rather than a book entry. In some instances, an extra charge may be imposed for this service. Presumably, individual investors who make this election to become registered owners recall the traditional form of registering securities transactions before 1970. Some may not trust the book entry system. In addition, institutional investors may also decide to place book entry investments in

the name of their own nominees, and request the delivery of certificates. Typically, where a demand for a certificate is made, DTC locates a certificate in an appropriate denomination in its vault and forwards that certificate directly to the issuer's transfer agent for registration pursuant to instructions from the participant who has ordered the certificate. The transfer agent may register the transfer and deliver the certificate directly to the designee specified by the participant. This process may take as long as two weeks, depending on the location and workload of the transfer agent.

DTC also has arrangements with many transfer agents by which certificates registered in the name of Cede are placed in the custody of the transfer agent for the benefit of DTC. A single "balance" certificate is then issued by the transfer agent to reflect DTC's ownership interest; when a demand for a certificate is received, the transfer agent may simply issue the certificate as ordered and reduce the balance of shares shown in DTC's "balance" account. This service is not available from all transfer agents and for all registered securities.

reflected simply by monthly statements of account from the brokerage firm that show the investor is the owner of a specified number of shares. The brokerage firm, in turn, is normally either a participant in DTC or affiliated with such a participant. As a result, in the modern securities world of book entry, no specific share certificates anywhere can be attributed to any single beneficial owner. There is simply a huge common pool of certificates or master certificates held in the name of Cede and a very large number of beneficial owners who rely entirely on the bookkeeping records of DTC and the brokerage firm to establish ownership.

An investor may specify, of course, that he wishes to receive physical certificates registered in his name, though some brokers may charge a fee for doing so. A subsequent transfer of certificated shares is more complicated than the sale of book entry shares, requiring the physical delivery of the certificate on the settlement date, appropriately indorsed, which may require a trip to a bank or brokerage firm to obtain a guarantee of the signature of the registered owner.

Notes

(1) Because of (a) the historic use of "street names" to facilitate securities transactions, (b) nominee ownership by institutional investors, and (c) the widespread use of the book entry system by all participants in securities trading, the records of share ownership maintained by publicly held issuers shed almost no light on beneficial ownership. Cede & Co. is by far the largest record owner of shares in most publicly held corporations, but there is no way to discover the beneficial ownership of those shares except by examining records of DTC and its members. The ownership of the great bulk of modern American industry is thus hidden today below one or more layers of nominee ownership.

(2) In the book entry system, there are always at least two intermediaries between an individual beneficial owner of shares and the issuer or its transfer agent. This system is largely invisible to the ordinary investor who usually receives both his dividends and voting information on time.

(a) Distributions are handled today by wire transfers directly to the accounts of participants in DTC. Each participant allocates the payments to individual investors entitled thereto on the records of the brokerage firm on the same day. The brokerage firm then either credits the appropriate account with the payment, or prepares a check which is mailed or delivered to the owner of the account.

(b) The book entry system creates obvious problems in connection with voting by proxy and the distribution of information in the form of annual reports, proxy statements, and interim financials. The SEC first attacked this problem in 1965 by requiring issuers to deliver to banks, securities dealers, brokers or voting trustees, upon their request, sufficient copies of annual reports and other materials to provide beneficial owners with copies. However, many record owners did not in fact receive such material. One study in 1973, for example, revealed that of the 17 percent of corporate stock then held in street name, as many as 68 percent of the beneficial owners were not receiving annual reports. The Silence Imposed by Street Names, Bus. Wk., Dec. 8, 1973, at 40. In 1974, the SEC significantly revised the rules to improve the transmission of materials to beneficial owners; the rules of securities exchanges and the National Association of Securities Dealers were also amended to require brokers and dealers to obtain and forward such materials to beneficial owners in a timely manner. These rules now primarily appear in 17 C.F.R. §§ 240.14a–3, 240.14b–1, 240.14b–2, and to a lesser extent, 240.14c–7

(1997). Apparently, the system for distribution of documents under these rules and procedures works efficiently and seamlessly in most circumstances.

(c) The book entry system has long created problems for issuers in connection with holding meetings, assuring the presence of quorums and so forth. Stephen P. Norman, Shareholder Communications: Direct Registration of Beneficial Shareholders, Insights, Vol. 3, No. 6, at 10, 10–12 (June 1989):

> Corporate Secretaries of large and small companies alike generally agree that the proxy system, insofar as it pertains to beneficial as opposed to record shareholders, has become increasingly complex. It has become more difficult for publicly-owned companies to obtain voting instructions from their institutionally-held shares on a timely basis. Overall voting totals remain at or near previous levels, but there is a growing sense that the vote is somewhat hastily assembled at the last-minute and a fair number of voting instructions are not received until after the meetings have been held.

> Several factors have contributed to the strains on the existing proxy system. The chief factor is layered ownership patterns whereby voting instructions are relayed from the person with voting authority to one or more intermediary custodians, who pass them on to an independent service bureau which in turn passes them on to the issuer's tabulator. * * * [T]he need to pass voting instructions along a chain of intermediaries before they reach the tabulator creates the potential for clerical error. The concept of passing voting instructions between different entities is akin to that of a relay in which runners exchange a baton under the pressures of a race. Even Olympians occasionally drop the baton, and errors have occurred along the chain of intermediaries in reporting votes. * * *

> Lateness is another nervous-making aspect of the proxy system. Companies frequently lack a quorum less than five business days prior to their shareholder meetings. When Corporate Secretaries or their solicitors seek to obtain the missing votes by calling the fund manager or person with voting authority, the caller is frequently told that the fund manager's voting instructions have already been passed to the fund manager's custodian bank who in turn should have passed them to the independent service bureau whose procedures call for them to tabulate the instructions before forwarding them to the issuer's solicitor or tabulator. Thus, there is much needless chasing of votes that have already been sent and the occasional re-sending of voting instructions that sometimes overtake the original, with the increased pressure on the tabulator to avoid double counting. * * *

(d) For a more current evaluation, see John C. Wilcox, Shareholder Communications: Electronic Communication and Proxy Voting, Insights, vol. 11, No. 3, March 1997, 8:*

> America's proxy system has always invited controversy. Measured in terms of results, it performs extremely well. U.S. companies achieve quorums averaging more than 80 percent of outstanding shares * * *. But to know the proxy system well is not to love it. * * * Those who deal frequently with the proxy process, while praising its neutrality, will often use less than flattering terms to describe its mechanics and inner works. "Cumbersome," "confusing," "inefficient," "costly," "slow," "outdated," "overregulated," "of Byzantine

complexity," and "inhibiting" are among the complaints voiced by critics. * * * They see it as an impenetrable thicket of state, federal, and stock exchange regulations governing a highly complex infrastructure of depositories, nominees, custodians, agents, and service providers, all working on behalf of a shareholder population whose diversity is itself a source of confusion.

(3) In 1983, the SEC developed a more direct means of communication between registrants and their beneficial owners. 17 C.F.R. § 240.14b–1(b)(3) (1997) sets forth the basic concept. It requires each broker/dealer to:

Provide the registrant, upon the registrant's request, with the names, addresses and securities positions, compiled as of a date specified in the registrant's request which is no earlier than five business days after the date the registrant's request is received, of its customers who are beneficial owners of the registrant's securities and who have not objected to disclosure of such information; * * *

(a) The reaction of the brokerage community to the nonobjecting beneficial owner (NOBO) approach has been strongly negative. David M. Doret, et al., Carey v. PEI: Voting Shortcuts Cut Short, Insights, Vol. 3, No. 12, at 3, 7 (Dec. 1989):

[B]rokerage firms in particular, as well as many fiduciary institutions, strongly disfavor the adoption of procedures which will disclose the identity of underlying beneficial holders. They fear it creates a shopping list of clients on which their competitors may prey. In addition, institutional holders often wish that their positions remain confidential. While participation in direct registration is optional at the shareholder level, an institution may fear pressure toward directly registering its position if that opportunity becomes available. On the other hand, many beneficial owners may want to be directly, not indirectly, involved in the solicitation process and not have communications pass through an intermediate layer.

(b) Sadler v. NCR Corp., 928 F.2d 48 (2d Cir.1991) holds that a corporation may be required to produce a NOBO list as well as a shareholders list under state law. See also Parsons v. Jefferson–Pilot Corp., 333 N.C. 420, 426 S.E.2d 685 (1993) (common law inspection right includes NOBO list if it is in the corporation's possession, but the corporation cannot be required to compile such a list if it does not use the list in making its own solicitations); Cenergy Corp. v. Bryson Oil & Gas P.L.C., 662 F.Supp. 1144 (D.Nev.1987) (right to inspect corporate records includes right to inspect NOBO list); Nu Med Home Health Care, Inc. v. Hospital Staffing Services, 664 So.2d 353 (Fla.App.1995)(corporation cannot be compelled to obtain a NOBO list; one judge dissented); Luxottica Group v. United Shoe Corp., 919 F.Supp. 1091 (S.D.Ohio 1995)(disclosure of NOBO list not required at all under Ohio statute).

(4) The "settlement" of a securities transaction involves the payment of the purchase price by the buyer and the delivery of the securities by the seller. After a transaction has been entered into, even though settlement has not occurred, a purchaser of securities carries the economic risk that the securities may decline in value and the economic benefit that the securities may increase in value. Settlement historically occurred five business days after the transaction, colloquially called T + 5. Effective as of June 7, 1995, the SEC reduced the period between the transaction and the settlement from five days to three, from T + 5 to T + 3. At the same time, the SEC proposed a major change in the method of recording share ownership directly by issuers or their transfer agents. BNA Securities Law Daily,

Letters Show Direct Registration System is Welcomed by Most Individual Investors, April 24, 1995, 4/24/95 SLD d4 (Westlaw)[35]:

Late last year, * * * in anticipation of the securities industry's move to T+3 * * * the SEC issued a concept release soliciting comments on * * * a direct registration system (DRS) that would allow [individual investors] to hold securities in book-entry form directly with the issuer. * * * By shortening the settlement cycle, T+3 is intended to reduce the risks of nonpayment from customer to broker and from broker to clearing corporation.

The DRS described in the SEC's concept release would be a transfer agent-operated book-entry DRS. The participation of issuers and transfer agents would not be required; rather, the DRS would be operated at their election. * * *

Currently, individual investors have two options for holding their securities. They either can hold stock certificates or place their shares in "street name" with a broker.[36] An investor's shares are held in street name when a broker-dealer or bank physically controls the stock certificate as custodian or in nominee name.

Under the * * * [SEC proposal] investors could exercise a third option for holding their securities by having their securities registered directly on the issuer's books, while retaining the right to receive a certificate. Thus, the SEC's DRS concept is crafted to give investors three options: they could "instruct the broker-dealer at the time of purchase to register the securities directly on the books of the issuer, to leave the securities with (their) broker in street name, or to request a certificate," the SEC release stated.

When an investor does not choose any option, the securities would be registered on the books of the issuer in book-entry form as the default form of registration, according to the concept release. An investor also could establish a DRS account with a specific company by submitting physical stock certificates or cash payments to the company's transfer agent. The shareholder would retain the right to obtain a certificate on demand. In addition, a DRS shareholder could designate a broker-dealer to which his or her stock could be transferred.

Under the DRS concept, an issuer's shareholder communications would be sent directly to the investor from the transfer agent, and the transfer agent would vote the securities according to the investor's instructions. The investors who participate in the DRS could either receive their cash dividends, or, if the issuer offers a dividend reinvestment and stock purchase plans (DRSPP), reinvest their cash dividends in the purchase of new securities.

Book-entry registration already is offered to dividend reinvestment plans and shares of registered investment companies. Indeed, the DRS is modeled on DRSPPs. About 1,000 corporations and closed-end mutual funds offer DRSPPs, which allow investors to purchase shares directly from the issuer by reinvesting their dividends, and in many cases, by making optional cash payments. In general, under new SEC policy (26 SRLR 1599), DRSPPs may allow persons other than shareholders or employees of the issuer or its subsidiaries to participate in the DRSPPs.

35. Reprinted with permission from *BNA Securities Law Daily,* April 24, 1995. Copyright 1995 by the Bureau of National Affairs, Inc. [By the Editor] The sequence of paragraphs and comments in this excerpt have been reorganized to simplify the discussion and eliminate repetition.

36. [By the Editor] Throughout this excerpt, references to "street name" are references to the book entry system of ownership.

However, the Securities Industry Association—which represents the business interests of about 700 securities firms, including investment banks, brokers, dealers, and mutual funds—is opposed to any DRS. In a March comment letter, the SIA called any type of DRS "completely unnecessary" to achieving the SEC's objective of a three-business-day settlement cycle for the securities industry—T + 3. There are alternatives to the SEC's DRS concept that more adequately would meet the SEC's goals, the SIA argued. * * * The SIA also expressed a concern about "whether issuers and transfer agents involved in the proposed DRS would be acting as unregistered broker-dealers" under the 1934 Securities Exchange Act in their offering and selling of securities. * * *. In its critical letter in early April, the SIA argued that the application of the '34 Act broker-dealer registration provisions to the proposed DRS is a "seminal issue that must be addressed before any type of such a system is considered for approval." Another issue raised by the SIA relates to protections afforded investors who participate in the DRS. "(T)hey will not have the benefit of the many regulatory protections that exist for investors that purchase or sell via, or hold their securities in 'street name' at, a broker-dealer," the association stated. In sum, the SIA urged that "(t)ransfer agents are capitalized to a much smaller extent than broker-dealers, and are not subject to the SEC's broker-dealers' net capital, customer protection, financial reporting, and disclosure requirements, as well as brokers' blanket bonding minimums and SIPC insurance."

The SIA went on to argue that street name securities ownership is "much more advantageous than directly registered securities ownership" on the basis of convenience and the degree of control an investor exercises over his securities holdings. * * * Moreover, the SIA explored alternatives that it believes would "more adequately" meet the SEC's goals of "safety, soundness, and reduced risk in marketplace operation, as well as the needs and rights of investors." Under one alternative, apparently favored by the SIA, customers' securities would be registered at a centralized depository, instead of with an issuer or transfer agent.

* * * [The] National Association of Investors Corp.—a Madison Heights, Mich., group representing 270,000 individual investors and investment clubs—commented that its members are "overwhelmingly in favor of direct registration with the provision that a stock certificate may be requested."

NAIC elaborated on one of the disadvantages of holding securities in street name, as follows: "When the stock is held in street name, [investors] are virtually locked-in to dealing with only one broker when a sell decision is made by the investor. There would be little incentive for the broker to negotiate commissions for the sale when the investor is captive." However, the group continued, "(i)f the investor were to 'shop' other brokers for a better commission, the stock would have to be transferred from the existing account to that of another broker. In many cases, brokers have initiated a charge for that to be accomplished," the letter stated. "In addition," NAIC remarked, "there can be a time lag in which the price of the stock can decline, thus costing the investor funds he/she might otherwise realized. Since the SEC has mandated negotiated commissions, this puts the individual who registers stock in street name at a disadvantage," it concluded.

On the other hand, NAIC members prefer to avoid the "expense of a safety deposit box" which is required to safeguard a stock certificate, the letter disclosed. In fact, the "only reason that certificates are being requested on the initial purchase is to be able to participate in dividend reinvestment plans," according to NAIC.

An electronic communication system between transfer agents and depositories would comprise an integral part of the DRS contemplated by the SEC * * *. Robert L. D. Colby, Deputy Director, Division of Market Regulation at the SEC, told a public SEC meeting April 4 that "there isn't (an electronic) system built currently that could handle the volume (of transactions in a DRS)." * * *

(5) On December 5, 1996, the SEC approved an amendment to New York Stock Exchange Rule 501.1 to permit "account statements" rather than stock certificates to be used to record ownership of shares. This amendment was in response to a filing by the Depository Trust Company to create a DRS with electronic linkage between transfer agents, broker/dealers and DTC to accommodate the spin-off of National Cash Register shares by AT & T. The new NCR shares were issued in electronically registered form, with stock certificates being issued only if specifically requested by a shareholder. John C. Wilcox, Shareholder Communications: Electronic Communication and Proxy Voting, Insights, Vol. 11, No. 3 March 1997, p. 8, 9.

(6) While the book entry system is the predominant form of securities ownership today, a significant number of shares continue to be held outside of this system. Publicly traded securities issued by many smaller corporations may not qualify for book entry ownership at all. Many institutional investors hold portfolio securities in the names of their own nominees and do not participate in the book entry system. Finally, a significant number of individual investors continue to hold physical certificates to represent their ownership of shares, though these shareholders are a minority.

(7) The book entry system has been superimposed upon state statutes that continue to require action by record owners. It should not be surprising that this combination sometimes creates problems. Examples include Tabbi v. Pollution Control Indus., Inc., 508 A.2d 867 (Del.Ch.1986) (in order to perfect the right of appraisal following a merger, state law requires that a demand letter must be received from the record owner before the vote is taken on the merger [compare MBCA § 13.21]; "a demand filed by Cede on behalf of Shearson Lehman/American Express, Inc. * * * with respect to 44,500 shares held beneficially" was untimely even though Shearson had prepared the demand letter two days before the meeting and sent it by overnight courier to Cede; for some reason it was delivered one day late and Cede's demand letter to the issuer was received by the issuer one hour and five minutes after the polls were closed); Enstar Corp. v. Senouf, 535 A.2d 1351 (Del.1987) (right to stock appraisal not validly perfected when demand for appraisal was made in the name of the beneficial owner and signed by an employee of the brokerage firm but not in the name of Cede); Alabama By–Product Corp. v. Cede & Co., 657 A.2d 254 (Del.1995)(inadvertent withdrawals of shares from appraisal proceeding by agents for record owners not binding on beneficial owners under language of Del. GCL § 262; one Justice dissented); and Allison v. Preston, 651 A.2d 772 (Del.Ch.1994) (the manager of an employee's saving plan that also provided for a "pass through" of voting rights to beneficial owners solicited members with respect to a disputed proxy contest; the manager received proxy forms from both factions in the contest and followed the members' wishes by voting 80,386 shares favorably on one proxy form and 80,386 shares unfavorably on the other; since negative votes are not allowed, the inspector of elections proposed to disallow both proxies but the court held that the

obvious intent of the shareholders should be respected and only the favorable proxy should be considered).

(8) The Independent Election Corporation of America (IECA) contracts with banks and brokerage houses to disseminate proxy material directly to the beneficial owners of securities. In a contested election situation, IECA tabulates the proxies on behalf of the beneficial shareholders and then executes a "contest voting form" which indicates the beneficial shareholders' votes for each of IECA's clients. See Concord Fin. Group, Inc. v. Tri–State Motor Transit Co. of Delaware, 567 A.2d 1, 7 n. 12 (Del.Ch.1989). This opinion also discusses the problem of "overvotes":

> Q & R Clearing Corp. ("Q & R Clearing") holds 5,329 shares of stock of Tri–State for certain beneficial holders. The record holder of these shares is Cede & Co. ("Cede"). Cede gave an "omnibus" proxy to Q & R Clearing entitling Q & R Clearing to vote 5,329 shares of the total number of shares of Tri–State held of record by Cede. Q & R Clearing, in turn, authorized the IECA to vote the 5,329 shares of Tri–State which Q & R Clearing was entitled to vote under the proxy from Cede.

> Pursuant to its authority to vote shares held by customers of Q & R Clearing, IECA issued proxies to vote 100 shares for Management and 6,200 shares for the Committee. Added together, the proxies submitted by IECA on behalf of Q & R Clearing exceeded, by almost 1,000 votes, the number of shares which Q & R Clearing was entitled to vote under the omnibus proxy from Cede.

> As was its usual practice when it discovered a broker had voted more shares than it was allotted, the Inspector called IECA in order to determine the correct amount of votes that should be cast by Q & R Clearing. The Inspector talked to Charles Pasfield, Vice President of Corporate Client Services at IECA, who in turn spoke to Q & R Clearing. Mr. Pasfield, in accordance with IECA's usual practice, called the contact person at Q & R Clearing who was previously known to IECA and who is specifically assigned the task of rectifying overvotes. Q & R Clearing instructed IECA to reduce the shares voted in favor of the Committee by 1,524 shares. This oral instruction was later confirmed in writing. Thus, Q & R Clearing, through IECA, cast, and the Inspector counted, 4,676 votes for the Committee and 100 votes for Management. Q & R Clearing did not vote the remaining 553 shares.

567 A.2d at 14–15. This procedure was held to be improper, the Court concluding that Q & R Clearing proxies should not have been voted at all:

> In this case, the Committee, its proxy solicitor, and the beneficial owners who declined to avail themselves of the advantages of record ownership must bear a responsibility for the brokerage overvotes that occurred in the Tri–State election. The Inspector erred as a matter of law in the present case by receiving extrinsic evidence concerning the proxy submitted by IECA to vote the Q & R Clearing proxy. Since that proxy overvoted the stock it represented, and since that error could not be corrected by looking at the face of the proxy or the books and records of Tri–State, the proxy should have been disregarded with no votes attributable to that proxy being cast for either Management or the Committee.

567 A.2d, at 16–17. Following this decision, Delaware amended its General Corporation Law, § 231, to permit inspectors of election to consider "other reliable information for the limited purpose of reconciling proxies and ballots

submitted by or on behalf of banks, brokers, their nominees or similar persons which represent more votes than the holder of a proxy is authorized by the record owner to cast or more votes than the stockholder holds of record."

(9) See MBCA § 7.23. The Official Comment states that a "corporation may limit or qualify the procedure as it deems appropriate," and that "[i]t is expected that experimentation with various devices under this section may reveal other areas which the corporation's plan should address." Do not the cases summarized in the previous note indicate that a system of voting of the type contemplated by this section should be made compulsory?

C. DIRECTORS

ROBERT W. HAMILTON, RELIANCE AND LIABILITY STANDARDS FOR OUTSIDE DIRECTORS

24 Wake Forest L.Rev. 5, 9–12 (1989).

Modern boards of directors have practically nothing to do with the day-to-day business of the corporation. Publicly held corporations are immense economic entities. They may have hundreds of plants, tens or hundreds of thousands of employees, billions of dollars in sales, and hundreds of thousands of shareholders. They may have operations in foreign countries that rival in size their American operations. The internal organization of such large economic entities necessarily involves complex hierarchical structures in which successively higher levels of management are given increasingly broad discretion and responsibility. Indeed, starting at the lowest level of corporate management, such as shop foreman or a similar position, successive layers of broader responsibility can be traced up through several levels of management. By following this process through to its logical conclusion, the highest level reached still would be below the level of the board of directors.

Even this description does not adequately describe the complexity of the internal structure of many publicly held corporations. Many corporations today are so large and are involved in so many diverse lines of business that business decision-making is diversified and diffused. Several largely independent internal hierarchical structures may exist within the lower levels of the corporate bureaucracy, each culminating in a single person or, in rare instances, a small committee that has responsibility for one or more areas of operations.[37] A person may be "President of the Plastics Division" or "Head of the Chemicals Sector" of a large corporation with responsibility for the profitability of a multi-plant business with sales of billions of dollars per year and yet be several hierarchical levels below the highest management level within the corporation itself.

Above these lower level internal hierarchies there is an "umbrella organization," the "corporate headquarters" or "home office" of the publicly held corporation, of which the board of directors loosely forms a part. The "Plastics Division" or "Chemical Sector" in this situation may be structured

---

37. [By the Author] For example, Johnson & Johnson has 165 autonomous units worldwide. General Electric is considerably more centralized; it has "only" 14 key businesses along with four additional support businesses that report directly to corporate headquarters. John A. Byrne & Laurie Baum, *The Limits of Power*, Bus.Wk., October 23, 1987, at 34 (special ed.).

as a wholly owned subsidiary of the publicly held corporation, or it may be a department or division of the corporation with no separate legal structure. In either event, it may have its own "board of directors," consisting usually of management personnel drawn from the operating components and from corporate headquarters staff, to advise and assist its managers. It may function as a largely autonomous business having wide discretion over research, product development, advertising, sales policies, and other matters. These semi-autonomous businesses within a single corporate structure often are described as "profit centers."

There are centralized levels of bureaucracy in corporate headquarters above these profit centers that have general oversight of the management of each profit center. Corporate headquarters imposes constraints on autonomy by setting profit goals or objectives for each center that are expected to be met—or sought—each year in terms of net profit, return on invested capital, or other similar measures. The operating head of the profit center has the responsibility for meeting these goals and may lose his or her job if the goals are not met. In addition, corporate headquarters usually handles certain core functions for all branches of the business. These functions relate to the processes of evaluation of performance and control over funds, specifically auditing, legal services, management compensation policies, fringe benefits, and accounting. Others are handled centrally because of perceived efficiency. It is not uncommon, for example, for corporate headquarters to handle the investment of excess funds. Under such a system, each profit center is required to turn over all excess funds on a daily basis to headquarters for investment, with the profit center having the privilege of withdrawing funds as needed for operations. Typically, corporate headquarters also has the sole responsibility of raising capital and allocating it among the profit centers. These functions require centralized review and approval of proposed capital investments by profit centers to assure that the corporation divides its limited resources among competing proposals put forth by autonomous profit centers in order to maximize overall return. Despite these restraints by corporate headquarters, many profit centers are sufficiently discrete and independent that they may be sold off by the corporation or be spun off as entirely separate entities without major changes in operating procedures.

Corporate headquarters itself has a hierarchical structure. At the highest levels are a series of executive managers, usually organized on a functional rather than a product basis, who have ultimate authority over broad areas of corporate activities. They have titles, such as "chief legal officer," "chief operations officer," "chief financial officer," and "chief accounting officer," that bear no relationship to the traditional corporate officers of "President," "Secretary," or "Treasurer" referred to in older state corporation statutes. At the ultimate apex is an individual referred to almost universally as the chief executive officer (the "CEO") who has responsibility for the enterprise as a whole. The CEO may have additional titles and roles, such as "President" or "Chairman of the Board of Directors," but many CEOs do not. The CEO has responsibility for the management team that directs the enterprise. If, for example, he loses confidence in the chief financial officer, the CEO must replace him and find a more satisfactory one. In theory, the CEO has power to call the shots in the corporate bureaucracy on narrow issues as well as broad ones, where and when he wishes. Of course, the CEO, as the head of a large bureaucratic organization, cannot hope to run details of the business operations; if he is to be effective, authority over details must be delegated to subordinates, and the CEO must concentrate on the broadest issues relating to the corporation.[38]

Because the CEO has ultimate responsibility for the success or failure of the business, he—and quite possibly he alone—will make the final decision on whether to embark upon a radical change in business strategy that may lead to the loss of his or her job if the change turns out to be disastrous. He may decide, for example, to close fifteen plants in order to redirect the primary emphasis of the corporation, or to develop a new product such as a state-of-the-art airplane or modern computer that will strain the economic resources of the entire entity and may well be unsuccessful; "betting the company" is the slang phrase that describes such fundamental and risky decisions. Such decisions may or may not be reviewed by the board of directors before they are implemented, but it is almost certain that if the CEO wishes to embark on such a course of action, the board of directors will acquiesce in that decision despite the reservations of many, or even all, members.[39]

Where then does the board of directors fit in? It does not have a place in the clearly demarcated hierarchy that leads from shop foreman or steward to CEO. The board is also not part of a direct chain of command above the CEO, since many or most important business decisions do not come before the board at all. Rather, it is somewhere above the CEO, and floating off to one side. Its principal source of power is a cataclysmic one: If it loses confidence in the CEO, it can compel his resignation and the installation of a successor. Obviously, such a power is an extreme one with wide-reaching implications upon the management of the business and is used only rarely and in extreme circumstances. Furthermore, it is not exercised easily. Because of the manner of their selection and the nature of their working relationships with the CEO, directors tend to give the CEO the benefit of the doubt. Even a discussion among directors about the possibility of replacing the CEO is a serious matter fraught with danger and uncertainty.

H.R. LAND, BUILDING A MORE EFFECTIVE BOARD OF DIRECTORS

[An undated promotional brochure published in about 1972 by H.R. Land & Company, Management Consultants, Los Angeles, California.]

The corporate Board of Directors is a topic of increasing concern to Chief Executive Officers. Directors, now keenly aware of their legal liabilities, are

---

38. [By the Author] The effect of this delegation of details has been characterized as follows:

[P]ower—having great influence, force, and authority—is slipping through the chief executive's hands, and has been for some time. * * * Now a chief executive hardly ever "runs" anything. * * * Chief executives, many management gurus agree, are less powerful today than they were 10 or 15 years ago. The most significant reason is that their task is much bigger. It's one thing to manage a single operation well. It's another thing to decide that you're no longer in a certain business, to change, cut back, deal with foreign competition. The agenda has been greatly expanded. * * *

John A. Byrne and Laurie Baum, The Limits of Power, Bus. Wk., October 23, 1987, 33–34.

39. [By the Author] A vote on an issue of the nature described in the text is, in effect, a vote of confidence on the stewardship of the CEO. For example, the CEO of United Airlines in 1985 proposed that the corporation branch out into related areas such as hotel management and car rental. He also proposed that the name of the corporation be changed to Allegis Corporation to reflect the broader area of operations. When this proposal was presented to the board of directors, a majority concluded that the proposed diversification was unwise and voted against the proposal. The CEO promptly resigned, as everyone understood that the vote was a vote of lack of confidence in the CEO's stewardship. * * *

pressing for greater participation in corporate affairs and new forms of compensation. In response to this greater interest on the part of their directors, a number of Chief Executives are rethinking the use of their boards and adopting new policies intended to strengthen the director/management relationship.

This report is designed to assist the Chief Executive Officer in dealing with his board. It is based upon independent interviews conducted by H.R. Land & Company with Chief Executives and Directors representing more than 60 corporations active in all segments of the economy. The survey sample purposely included small privately held firms and medium sized regionally traded companies as well as widely traded Fortune 500 corporations.

No attempt has been made to develop statistical tabulations of the findings. Rather, *the emphasis is on policies and techniques which could be of practical value to large numbers of Chief Executive Officers.* Because of the many types of corporations included in the study, not all of the ideas presented are suitable for use in any one firm. Our intent has been to present a number of ideas from which a Chief Executive might select and adopt those which are appropriate for use in his own firm.

The CEO Determines the Board's Effectiveness

The Principal Determinant of the Effectiveness of a Board of Directors is the Chief Executive Officer. His personal convictions on what a board should be will do more to shape the role of his directors than any other single factor. In most instances we found the board to be a mirror image of the CEO's desires and intentions. Exceptions tended to occur only where the board was made up of individuals representing major equity interests or financial institutions who were not necessarily of the CEO's choosing.

The attitude of the CEO is critical; he creates the atmosphere—hopefully one of candor and frankness in which the directors feel their participation is of real value. The ideal CEO/director relationship is one of professional respect and admiration. Friendship is a part of the relationship, but it must remain a "business" friendship rather than a "personal" relationship if the directors' "check and balance" function is to remain intact. The most effective boards seem to share a philosophy in which both the CEO and each director consider themselves as donors and recipients in a mutually beneficial relationship.

Obviously the CEO's actions have a major impact on the board. What he does to select, attract, involve, motivate, compensate and protect his directors is the subject of the remainder of this booklet. Equally important are the personal touches—periodically inviting a director to lunch, remembering his individual likes and dislikes, being cognizant of his other business and personal obligations, letting him know you are thinking of him on special occasions. * * *

How a Potential Director Views Board Membership

* * * In asking directors what motivated them to accept membership on individual boards the most frequent responses centered on (1) existing or

potential *personal relationships* with management and the other directors, (2) the *experience and satisfaction* accompanying board membership, and (3) *status and prestige* attached to being a corporate director. Annual retainers and meeting fees were rarely cited as a reason for accepting, although the opportunity for a *capital gain* is obviously a strong motivating factor. In this regard, one professional director told us that he looks for companies whose stock is depressed, whose management has an equity position strong enough to provide him with a "fair" block of stock, and whose circumstances are such that outside help is clearly needed.

GETTING DIRECTORS INVOLVED

The Key to Making a Director Effective is to Involve Him Personally. A good way to establish the feeling of "our company" is with financial participation. Some publicly traded firms make attractive investment financing available for their directors; in a privately held business financial involvement can be achieved by allowing a director to buy in at book and, when he resigns, to sell at book. * * *

Notes

(1) The author of the foregoing brochure presumably never dreamed that it would find its way into a law school casebook or a set of readings as to the role of directors in corporations. As a result, his point of view is revealing in terms of the relative roles of the CEO and individual directors. In Land's view, who selects the individuals who are invited to join the board of directors? Does he envision the CEO to be subservient to the board or the board subservient to the CEO? The relationship between CEO and board envisioned by Land was probably reasonably accurate for most corporations of the era: not only did the CEO personally select and approve each director but most boards consisted primarily (or, in some cases, entirely) of inside directors—persons who held lucrative positions with the corporation that were terminable at the will of the CEO. The CEO was almost always the chair of the board of directors, he presided at all meetings, and controlled the agenda. Furthermore, a retiring CEO usually selected his successor. One commentator has described boards of this era as "[l]ittle more than a claque of the CEO's cronies, [who] would quietly nod and smile at their buddy's flip charts and rubber-stamp his agenda for the corporation." John A. Byrne, The Best and Worst Boards: Our New Report Card on Corporate Governance, Business Week, November 25, 1996, 82. As described below, there have been massive changes in corporate governance since then and the typical modern board bears little resemblance to the board of the 1960s. Changes, however, occurred slowly, and are continuing today.

(2) The beginning of these changes can be traced to the Watergate scandals of the early 1970s. As part of the general disclosures of misconduct during the Nixon era, it was revealed that a large number of publicly held corporations had engaged in a significant amount of illegal or questionable conduct: paying bribes or "commissions" to high-placed officials in friendly countries, making illegal campaign contributions to American politicians, and the like. About four hundred corporations voluntarily admitted such conduct, including such well-known names as Lockheed Aircraft Corporation, Gulf Oil Corporation, Northrop Corporation, and G.D. Searle and Company. A. A. Sommer, the Impact of the SEC on Corporate Governance, reprinted in Deborah A. DeMott, Corporations at the Crossroads, Governance and Reform 200 (1980). Some of this conduct might be explainable on the basis of the arguments, "it is not illegal over there" or "everyone does it."

Some of the conduct, however, constituted clear and knowing violations of criminal law: for example, an officer of Northrop Corporation personally delivered a suitcase containing $50,000 in cash to President Nixon as a campaign contribution, knowing that it came from corporate funds and was therefore illegal. A number of individuals and corporations pleaded guilty or nolo contendere to criminal charges based on similar conduct. In some instances, the SEC brought suit to compel changes in the governance of specific corporations, and in other instances, it negotiated plans for impartial investigations of responsibility for misconduct.

(3) Throughout this period of widespread disclosures, it was apparent that many directors were unaware of the existence of illegal or inappropriate conduct within their own corporations. Indeed, in some instances it was also doubtful that top management knew of the illegal use of fairly large sums of money. The magnitude and volume of these disclosures prompted the most massive review of corporate governance since the 1930s and led indirectly to the development of the modern theory of corporate governance described below.

(4) Perhaps the high point of director noninvolvement is the widely told story that the directors of Penn Central were not advised that the corporation was filing for reorganization under the bankruptcy laws until after the filing was made.

(5) In 1972, Arthur Goldberg, the former Supreme Court Justice, resigned his various corporate directorships on the ground that the board "is relegated to an advisory and legitimizing function that is substantially different from the role of policy maker and guardian of shareholder and public interest contemplated by the law of corporations." Arthur J. Goldberg, Debate on Outside Directors, N.Y. Times, Oct. 29, 1972, Sec. 3, at 1, col. 3. He proposed a "committee of overseers" composed of outside directors with general responsibility for supervising company operations and making periodic reports to the board of directors. Id. at 3, col. 2. He further proposed that the committee have authority to hire "a small staff of experts" who would be responsible only to the board and would be totally independent of management control. Id. Do you believe that such an independent staff is a good idea? Such proposals have been strongly opposed by persons within corporate management, and have apparently never been fully tested. Arguments against this proposal are that it would be divisive, that it would create a "we-against-they" attitude, and that it would not be conducive to the mutual trust required for the smooth functioning of the board and of the corporation. Are these legitimate concerns? Does the need for such an independent staff justify its costs? How much oversight can one really expect from a "small" staff in a multibillion dollar corporation?

(6) In 1978, then Chairman Harold Williams of the SEC suggested there should be only one management representative on the board, that that person should be the corporation's chief executive officer, and that he should be barred from also acting as chairman of the board. See Management Should Fill Only One Seat On a Firm's Board, SEC Chairman Urges, Wall St. J., Jan. 19, 1978, at 4, col. 2. These suggestions were met with total silence; Chairman Williams' views were so far ahead of then current practice that they did not even merit serious discussion.

(7) What do boards of directors actually do? They do not manage the business of the corporation—everyone agrees that the CEO and other officers—"the management" of the corporation—do that. MBCA § 8.01(b) provides an unsatisfactory and incomplete answer when it states that the business and affairs of a corporation may be "managed under the direction of" the board of directors. More

light is shed by studies based on what outside directors say they actually do. One such study, completed in 1971, is Myles L. Mace, Directors: Myth and Reality (1971); a more recent study is Jay W. Lorsch, Pawns or Potentates: The Reality of America's Corporate Boards (1989). Both studies are based on interviews with a large number of persons who serve as directors in publicly held corporations, and a comparison of the two studies' conclusions shows clearly that the role of directors has continued to evolve since the 1970s. See also Paul H. Zalecki, The Corporate Governance Role of The Inside and Outside Directors, 24 U.Toledo L.Rev. 831 (1993).

(8) According to Mace, directors at regular meetings where there is no crisis demanding immediate action performed only two basic functions:

(a) They provide advice and counsel to management. They may be a sounding board from which a variety of views on board or difficult questions may be obtained. The views of a director with expertise in an area such as law or finance may be given greater weight with respect to questions arising within his or her area of expertise. Nevertheless, Professor Mace concluded that "sometimes, but not too frequently" the views of outside directors will provoke reconsideration or modification, and that "occasionally, but only very rarely" does it lead to a reversal of a decision. Myles L. Mace, The President and the Board of Directors, 50 Harv.Bus.Rev. 37 (March–April 1972).

(b) They provide discipline to management, who must appear before them and present information and defend business decisions. Even though the board may not question the management's conclusion, the mere fact that it is a possibility requires an organization of thoughts and points of view and a careful review of work of subordinates. The mere fact that a difficult question *might* be asked ensures that the chief executive officer will prepare carefully for his appearance before the board.

Mace, Directors: Myth and Reality, at 178–81. Among the things a board of directors generally did *not* do, according to Mace, are: a) establish basic objectives, corporate strategies and broad policies of the company, b) ask discerning questions at meetings, or c) select a new chief executive officer to succeed a retiring CEO. The selection of a new CEO, according to Mace, was usually made by the outgoing CEO. Mace, supra, at 184–90. Directors interviewed by Mace recognized a responsibility to monitor the CEO and replace him if he become ineffective or incompetent. However, directors who owed considerable allegiance to the CEO (as was true in the 1960s and 1970s) found this task extremely unpleasant: Directors preferred to resign, to have a management study performed by outsiders, or to appoint a committee to meet with the CEO and request that he resign, rather than formally vote to remove the CEO.

(9) Writing nearly twenty years later, Lorsch identified two additional roles of directors in "normalcy" situations: consideration of long-term strategic planning, and efforts to make sure that the corporation "does the right thing," that is, assuring that the corporation's affairs are conducted in ethical, legal, and socially responsible ways. Lorsch recognized that many CEOs felt that board involvement in strategic planning could infringe on the CEO's "prerogatives" (as it clearly would have at the time of Mace's interviews) but participation in that area had become accepted. Concern with "doing the right thing" was largely reflected in the work of the audit committee of the board of directors and the development of compliance programs in various areas by committees of the board. Lorsch also pointed out that the CEO dominance over the board of directors by way of control

of the selection process, the agenda, and corporate information in general had waned significantly since Mace's era. Lorsch, Pawns or Potentates, at 75–80.

BAYLESS MANNING, THE BUSINESS JUDGMENT RULE AND THE DIRECTOR'S DUTY OF ATTENTION: TIME FOR REALITY[40]
39 Bus.Law 1477, 1481–92 (August 1984).

Practically all the current debate centers upon "outside" directors. In the real world, what do such directors—"good" directors—actually do in the discharge of their responsibilities? What is generally expected of them in the market place.[41]

TIME DEVOTED

The outside directors of a corporation are part-time people with respect to the amount of working time that is allocated to the affairs of the company. The most recent survey (1982) shows that the average director of a publicly held company devotes a total of about 123 hours per year to his board and committee work, including travel.[42] That averages less than 3 hours a week, or about 1.5 working days a month.

Directors of companies in crisis conditions often find themselves compelled to devote much greater amounts of time. Also, in some companies, special agreements (with or without special compensation) between the company and a particular director may obligate him to devote more time to his directorship than the rest of the members of the board. * * *

No human being can stay on top of all [the problems] in a major company on a one-and-a-half-day-a-month basis.

PACE AND DELIBERATION

Much of the routine housekeeping work of a board of directors does not demand or warrant significant deliberation. Some important matters that come to the board can be and are dealt with in a deliberate manner over several meetings. A few matters, like the choice of a new CEO from among several in-house candidates, can often be pondered and observed carefully over a period of years, but most significant matters cannot be dealt with in that way by a board. The pace of commercial events often demands quick response or even, as in takeover situations, almost instant response. Even issues that are fully recognized to be vitally important can often not be considered extensively by a board because its agenda is at the time crammed with other exigent items or with matters which, though less significant, are mandated as compulsory agenda items under applicable laws or regulations.

UNCERTAINTY AND RISK-TAKING

Businessmen make business decisions. They are not courts, able and willing to pursue a matter to the last argument in the search of the "right"

---

40. Copyright 1984 by the American Bar Association. All rights reserved. Reprinted with permission of the American Bar Association and its Section of Corporation, Banking and Business Law.

41. [By the Author] While an effort will be made here to keep in mind the great diversity of the nation's tens of thousands of corpora-

tions, most of our available data relates to larger companies, and the descriptions offered here may be correspondingly skewed.

42. [By the Author] Korn Ferry International Board of Directors, Tenth Annual Study, Feb. 1983, at 9.

answer. They are not researchers meticulously seeking truth. They are not scientists striving for ever more refined solutions in a field of narrow specialization. And when an issue comes to a board of directors, the process of discussion and decision is nothing like the lawyer's world of briefs and adversary argumentation. The decisions the businessman must make are fraught with risk, and he is quite accustomed to making these decisions in a hurry on the basis of hunch and manifestly sparse data. The businessman and the board of directors thrive or die in a sea of uncertainty. * * *

DIVERSITY OF DIRECTORS

CEOs understandably prefer other CEOs and corporate officers as directors because of their familiarity with the boardroom process and with the realities of business management,[43] but today, increasing numbers of outside directors are persons who fall into other categories. Academics and persons with political backgrounds are often members of the modern board, while the percentage of lawyers and bankers has declined. A changing society has brought more women and persons of minority ethnic background into the boardroom. Moreover, it is increasingly common to include on boards some persons who have specialized skills that are invaluable to the work of the board, such as the musician on the board of the record company or the physicist board member of Silicon Valley, Inc. These increasingly diverse members can and do contribute significantly to the total work product of the board, but, at the same time, these members of diverse nonbusiness backgrounds are often not knowledgeable about many matters that come up on the board's agenda. They are even less aware of many aspects of the normal business life of the enterprise that do not customarily rise to the level of board attention.

DECISIONAL PROCESS

To judge by their statements, many lawyers without personal boardroom experience have a total misconception of the decisional process as it actually functions in the boardroom. The lawyer's professional experience in courts, legislatures, and semi-political bodies tends to lead him to assume that all decisional process is inevitably made up of a series of discrete, separate issues presented one at a time, debated by both or all sides, and voted on. In fact boards of directors typically do not operate that way at all, except, perhaps, in conditions of internal warfare or mortal crisis. Actions are usually by consensus. If a significant sentiment of disagreement is sensed by the chairman, the matter is usually put over for later action, and sources of compromise and persuasion are pursued in the interim. Advice from individual directors is most often volunteered to, or solicited by, the CEO informally on a one-on-one basis, rather than pursued in group debate at a board meeting.

CHARACTER OF THE AGENDA

A transcript of a typical board meeting will reflect four kinds of items on the agenda. Fully three quarters of the board's time will be devoted to reports by the management and board committees, routine housekeeping resolutions passed unanimously with little or no discussion, and information responding

43. [By the Author] Korn Ferry International Board of Directors, Tenth Annual Study, Feb. 1983, at 5.

to specific questions that had earlier been put to the management by directors about a wide range of topics sometimes accompanied by suggestions from the board members, usually procedural in character. Perhaps the remaining one quarter of the meeting time will be addressed to a decision, typically unanimous, on one or two specific different business items, such as the sale of a subsidiary or the establishment of a compensation plan. If, as is the average, a board meets eight times a year, the arithmetic would indicate that a full year of the board's work would contain only ten or fifteen discrete transactional decisions of the type that are generally assumed to make up the main work of the board, and of those discrete transactional matters, many will be neither very important nor controversial, such as a decision to terminate a long-standing banking relationship in favor of a new one that provides better service.

Contrariwise, some issues that have little economic significance may, because of their delicacy, consume great amounts of the board's time—such as the awkward matter of imposing mandatory retirement on the aging founder, builder, and principal owner of the company.

AGENDA-SETTING—INITIATIVES BY THE BOARD

Agenda-setting and the scope of board initiative together comprise the single most important, and least understood, aspect of the board's work life.

With the two very important exceptions noted below, the question of what the board will discuss and act on is typically determined by the management or by the corporation's automatic built-in secular equivalent of an ecclesiastical calendar, that is, shareholders' meeting date, fiscal year, cycle of audit committee meetings, and similar matters. The board can, and a good board will, from time to time suggest topics for exploration or discussion, or request the management to report in the near future on this or that matter of interest to the board. The board can press management to get on with a necessary undertaking or desired program, such as the establishment of a job classification system, and to report back to the board about the action taken. But the board itself has little capacity to generate significant proposals, other than generalized suggestions looking toward the establishment of procedures or systems. Almost all of what a board does is made up of matters that are brought to it; matters generated by the board itself are very rare. Typically, boards cannot take, and are not expected to take, initiatives.

There are two major exceptions to this generalization about agenda-setting. Both are of extreme importance, and both are fully understood by normal, healthily functioning boards and managements.

First, no board can deny the existence of a built-in paramount responsibility with regard to what may be called the organic or structural integrity of the company. This organic integrity is essentially made up of two elements. A company must have a *functioning management* in place and operating at all times. A board can itself see that this is done. And a company must have an *internal information system* in place that is generally suitable for an enterprise of the company's character to keep the management informed about what is going on and particularly to provide the accounting data on which to base financial statements. The board cannot design, install, operate, or monitor the operation of such systems; but the board can press for the installation and call for periodic assurances that they are in place. As to these two organic elements of the enterprise, the directors may not wait for the management to bring issues to their attention. The responsibility of the board in these two key regards is inherent and ongoing; it is up to the board to take the initiative to keep itself informed about them and to take such periodic action as its business judgment dictates.

Second, no director or group of directors may choose to ignore credible signals of serious trouble in the company. If a director is informed through a credible source that there is reason to believe that the chief financial officer is a compulsive gambler, the director must take an initiative; he may not sit back and wait for the management to bring the matter to the board's attention. There will usually be a wide range of possible actions which a director could reasonably take to pursue such a matter and thereby fulfill his obligation as a director; but he cannot simply do nothing. Execution of this responsibility of a director will be episodic and, typically, infrequent, but the responsibility itself is ongoing and present every day.

ACTIONS NOT TAKEN

All these realities of directional life add up to a deeper one. From among an infinite number of useful things that a board of directors *might* reasonably have done or looked into in a given time period, the number that will *not* have been done by the most qualified, best-run, and most diligent board in the world will always be far greater than the number that *were* done. If a corporate transaction goes sour, or a company fails, any plaintiff's lawyer of even the most modest talent and imagination will always be able to find a subject matter X as to which he can denounce its directors, declaiming: "Surely any reasonable prudent person in these circumstances would have explored subject X, but this board sat back, did nothing, and did not even inquire into it." That argument in hindsight will always sound plausible. It may appeal to some juries, or even some courts, inexperienced in the reality of business life. But it is most often just hokum and rhetoric.

No court confronted with this retrospective argument about directional delinquency should ever allow itself to forget the reality that at any given time the roster of possible candidates for a place on the agenda of the board is infinite and that agenda items are mutually exclusive, that is, hours spent on one agenda item are hours not spent on an infinity of other possible agenda items. The number of items considered will always be vastly exceeded by the number not considered. And the plaintiff's retrospective indictment, though apparently plausible, is in fact hollow, because it can be as easily designed to hurl against the best-performing board as against the worst.[44] * * *

HOMEWORK AND SCOPE OF INQUIRY

Assume that a particular item has in ordinary course come onto the board's agenda and that it is one of that limited number that specifically calls for affirmative decisional action. No one disputes that the board should look into the matter before acting, but in a particular situation, what does that mean? How much time should be devoted to the item (to the exclusion of

---

44. [By the Author] Indeed, the argument can be framed to be even more applicable to the best of boards than to the worst, by the contention that the outstanding board had to have been sloppy in not exploring subject X, since a board composed of such experienced men and women was bound to be more aware than an average board that subject X was a problem.

others)? Is it enough for the directors to read the papers sent by the management? The appendices? A summary cover letter? With what degree of concentration? And what degree of comprehension by the individual director? Regardless of the topic's technical character, what of the director's specialized experience or absence of qualification in the subject? In what degree, if any, should the director carry out research going beyond the documentation provided to him by the company or draw on recollection of data (or rumors) acquired elsewhere? Should the director insist that he be provided an opinion of outside consultants in support of the information and recommendations made by the management?

One does not have to reflect very long about such questions to come to two realizations. The first is that there is no conceivable way to lay down *a priori* answers to such questions. The second is that the point made earlier about agenda-setting in general context has even greater application in the specific. At all times and in all circumstances, the scope of investigation actually undertaken on a matter, whatever it is, will always be less than the possible scope and depth of investigation that could have been undertaken. In every instance of corporate misfortune, it will therefore be an easy cheap shot to fling at the director on the witness stand, "You mean you voted to proceed with this birdcage transaction without even consulting the definitive manual on birdcages put out by the U.S. Department of Commerce?" * * *

ATTENDANCE

* * * How important is attendance, taken alone? In the real world, the answer will depend on the decisional process actually utilized by the CEO and his board. If the CEO is in continuous consultation with his directors, and if decisions of substance are worked out through prior soundings so that the meeting is only a formality (a very common pattern), or if the CEO arranges the agenda so that big issues do not come up unless his key qualified directors are present to participate, then the whole issue of frequency of attendance may be peripheral at best. A judge who does not regularly show up in his courtroom can be safely concluded not to be doing his job and to be either ill or delinquent, but that image cannot be automatically transferred to the wholly different processes of boards of directors. In most circumstances it will be very hard for a plaintiff to demonstrate that a director's sporadic attendance was causally linked to later difficulties of the company.

RELIANCE

The Model Act and the ALI drafts are quite realistic in their recognition that directors may safely rely upon officers and employees of the corporation, accountants, engineers, lawyers, and other expert consultants who they have reason to believe are competent. Expert consultation inspired by a perceived need to know on the part of the board is obviously constructive and indispensable. An inoculation of expert outside opinion is also of help in preventing an epidemic of liability in the boardroom. The law has also become more realistic in recognizing that much of a board's work is, and must be, done in committee, and in according to the board the privilege of reliance upon the work product of its committees.

It is less widely understood, and not explicitly recognized in the law, that the dynamics of the boardroom are also deeply dependent upon a matrix of other reliances among individual officers and directors. Director X, at a meeting asks in respect of particular transaction A, "Will we have any trouble with our auditors if we do A?" Director Y, who is recognized by his colleagues to be the board's most knowledgeable member in matters of accounting (who may, or may not, be a member of the audit committee) says, "Don't worry, X, I don't think we'll have any problem there." Thereupon the conversation moves on to another topic, the group deferring in an informal way to the expertise and judgment of one of its members in whom it has confidence. (The same interchange could, of course, have involved the company's chief financial officer rather than Y.) Does this kind of interchange among businessmen comply with legally articulated standards like "duty to inquire," or "duty to inform itself"? If the answer is "no" (as at least some commentators would undoubtedly say), then the tension between the law and reality is in a crisis condition. To operate at all, any group decisional process must be built on a substrate of such interconnected informal delegation and deference. A board is free to ask any question, but a board that does not have confidence in and rejects the answer it receives is at a point of pathological collapse as a decisional apparatus.

A correlative of the board's reliance must be a special informal obligation on the part of the person or committee relied upon to do his or its homework well or to be willing to answer to a board member's question, "I do not know." The expectations of the rest of the board are that they will receive a specially informed opinion, and they are entitled to get it.

So, once again, the normal decisional process in the boardroom is quite different from the piece-by-piece, person-by-person, issue-by-issue, question-by-question, adversary interrogational and debate process which a lawyer or judge tends to perceive as the normal way to arrive at professional conclusions. (That is one of the major reasons why businessmen think lawyers make poor directors until they learn, if they learn, that corporate decision-making requires other ways of doing.)

DEPTH OF INQUIRY

The point about deference and reliance as an element of "inquiry" has another aspect with which the lawyer will more readily empathize because it matches part of his own working experience. Assuming that the director specifically undertakes to "inquire" into a matter, how deeply should he go? Wherever the questioning stops, it would always be possible to question still further, as every lawyer knows. * * *

JUDGMENT

Finally, we come to the matter of judgment itself. Assume, again, that a board is going through one of those episodes of discrete transactional decision which lawyers' discourse assumes to be normal but is in fact rare. Assume that questions have been asked and inquiry made to a satisfactory extent, whatever that may mean. Now, as perceived by the legal writing, the board weighs the matter and makes a judgment, and it is that judgment that is protected by the business judgment rule.

Boardroom reality is far different from this lawyer-oriented model, not only in the respects discussed earlier but usually in the character of "judgment" itself. The differences are fundamental and warrant comment. * * * Problems come in galaxies. Responsive actions are multiple aggregates. The actions taken are the result of dozens of different tradeoffs including, importantly, tradeoffs of different degrees of certainty and uncertainty and short-term payoffs in exchange for hoped-for long-term payoffs—and vice versa. No issue is free-standing, and no action taken can be evaluated as though it were an isolated thing. * * * As a result, seeking in retrospect to revisit and evaluate a single "judgment on an issue" by a board of directors will almost always be a distortion of reality, because no such free-standing single judgment ever happened. * * *

Second, * * * judgments of boards of directors are mainly in the nature of decisions whether to hurl a veto.

A chief executive who generally enjoys the confidence of his board will usually be able to carry any proposal he makes if he does his homework, prepares his supporting arguments, is backed up by his other officers, and—of key importance—personally throws his full weight behind the proposal. Courts and the public must understand that quite commonly a director will go along with a business proposal that he does not really like. He may well think, and will sometimes say aloud in the board meeting, "I do not like this proposal. It seems risky and I believe other uses for the same resources would be more promising. But I may be wrong; I respect the contrary views of my colleagues; and I have to accord great weight to the CEO's strong support for this project. *After all, he is the one who will have the primary responsibility for seeing to it that it works out successfully.* So I will not vote no." When that happens, everyone in the corporate world knows the meaning of the italicized words. The director is saying that he will go along this time, but the CEO is on notice that if he proves to be wrong and the project fails, he may well have lost that director's confidence.

To cite another illustration. Even if a director is strongly opposed to a project, he may still go along because the CEO is determined to proceed and, in the director's best judgment, the disruption that would be caused by firing the CEO at this time would be more injurious to the interests of the company and its shareholders than the negative risks of the project proposed. In such a case, the real business judgment the director makes is not to throw his javelin today. That kind of aggregative judgment is not, in the lawyer's sense, "on the merits" of the narrow particular issue at hand, but it is very much on the issue of the director's perception of the best interests of the company. How can a court later evaluate such a nonjudgment judgment?

Thus, the decisional process of a board of directors only occasionally involves a go or no-go issue at all; often involves a cost-benefit mix of tradeoffs on multiple issues, in search of the least bad result; and is continuously obscured by the weight given by directors to the injury that will likely be visited upon the interests of the company and shareholders if the board splinters or if it suddenly dumps its CEO. * * *

Companies * * * differ from each other markedly in personality and in operating style. Contemporary literature has hit upon the term "corporate culture" to refer to the evident fact that each company is a distinctive social organization with its own viewpoints, management style, attitudes, self-image, and ways of doing. Every board of directors also has its own personality and manner of working with the management. * * *

SPASMODIC INTENSITY OF ATTENTION

Not only is company A different from company B. An additional clearly observable phenomenon in the sociology of boardroom life is that the board of company A behaves differently at different times. The intensity and quantity of all forms of the board's attention rises and falls as the company passes through calm or stormy seas. When matters are going well, the board tends to settle into watchful but quiet routine, confident in the management's performance and willing to be led. If the wind begins to rise, the board will stir and come to life, ask many questions, occasionally exercise its veto, and perhaps oust the CEO. If the hurricane comes, the board members will typically respond energetically out of their sense of responsibility, pouring time, energy, study, attention, and initiative into the company's affairs, sometimes to the point of temporarily assuming full executive control. When the storm is weathered, perhaps with a new captain installed, the board will resume a less active but watchful mode. Thus, a degree of attention that would be normal in usual circumstances could be considered as insufficient when the going gets rough. * * *

CORPORATE DIRECTOR'S GUIDEBOOK

Second Edition (1994).
Committee on Corporate Laws, Section of Business Law, American Bar Association
Pages 4–5, 15–16, 24–44[45]

SECTION 2. RESPONSIBILITIES OF A CORPORATE DIRECTOR

A. *Oversight Responsibilities*

* * * [The] language [of MBCA § 8.01(b)] is used to emphasize the responsibilities of directors, especially directors of publicly held corporations to oversee the management of the corporation—not to manage, but to oversee. This responsibility includes;

- approving fundamental operating, financial, and other corporate plans, strategies, and objectives;

- evaluating the performance of the corporation and its senior management and taking appropriate action, including removal, when warranted

- selecting, regularly evaluating, and fixing the compensation of senior executives;

- requiring, approving, and implementing senior executive succession plans;

- adopting policies of corporate conduct, including compliance with applicable laws and regulations, and maintenance of accounting, financial and other controls;

- reviewing the process of providing appropriate financial and operational information to decisionmakers (including board members); and

- evaluating the overall effectiveness of the board.

Stated broadly, the principal responsibility of a corporate director is to promote the best interests of the corporation and its shareholders in directing the corporation's business and affairs.

In so doing, the director should give primary consideration to long-term economic objectives. However, a director should also be concerned that the corporation conducts its affairs with due appreciation of public expectations, taking into consideration trends in the law and ethical standards. Furthermore, pursuit of the corporation's economic objectives may include consideration of the effect of corporate policies and operations upon the corporation's employees, the public, and the environment. Many states have adopted legislation expressly recognizing that corporate directors may consider the effect of corporate action on constituencies other than shareholders, such as employees, local communities, suppliers and customers. Nevertheless, the law normally does not hold a corporate director directly responsible to constituencies other than shareholders in the formulation of corporate policy. * * *

SECTION 4. BOARD STRUCTURE AND OPERATIONS

Boards of directors should be structured and their proceedings conducted in a way calculated to encourage, reinforce, and demonstrate the board's role as an independent and informed monitor of the conduct of the corporation's affairs and the performance of its management. * * * It is also important that the board not only exercise independent judgment, but also be perceived by shareholders and other corporate constituencies to be doing so. To encourage an environment likely to nurture independence in fact and to communicate that appearance of independence, at least a majority of members of the boards of publicly held corporations should be independent of management.

A director who is an executive officer of the corporation or who is an employee devoting substantially full time and attention to the affairs of the corporation, one of its subsidiaries, or any other corporation controlling or controlled by the corporation, will be viewed as a management director. A director who has not been active in the management of the corporation and who is therefore otherwise properly described as a nonmanagement director may nonetheless have some relationship with the corporation or its management that could be viewed as interfering with the exercise of independent judgment. As a general rule a director will be viewed as independent only if he or she is a nonmanagement director free of any material business or professional relationship with the corporation or its management. The circumstances and various relationships that have been often identified as presumptively inconsistent with independence include:

- a close family or similar relationship with a member of key management;

- any business or professional relationship with the corporation that is material to the corporation or the director; and

- any ongoing business or professional relationship with the corporation, whether or not material in an economic sense, that involves continued dealings with management, such as the relationship between a corporation and investment bankers or corporate counsel. * * *

The question of what will be discussed and acted on by the board is typically initially determined by management. Directors should be given an opportunity to place items on the agenda. Further, the board should satisfy itself that there is an overall annual agenda of matters that require recurring and focused attention, such as achievement of principal operational or financial objectives and review of the performance of the CEO and other members of executive management. * * *

SECTION 7. COMMITTEES OF THE BOARD

Much of the work of the typical board of directors is performed in committee. This is recognized by regulatory bodies, institutional investors, and others urging more effective governance. * * *

This Guidebook focuses only on board oversight committees and does not address such committees as executive, finance, and strategic planning. * * *

SECTION 8. THE AUDIT COMMITTEE

Since first recommended by the NYSE in 1939, the Audit Committee has become a common component of the corporate governance structure of public companies. It typically functions as an overseer of the corporation's financial reporting process and internal controls. * * *

The Audit Committee should be composed solely of independent directors. * * * Directors who are employed by the corporation do not qualify as independent directors. In addition, directors who are engaged in material business transactions with the corporation and directors who serve on a regular basis as professional advisers, legal counsel, or consultants for the corporation would normally not qualify as independent.

B. Principal Functions

* * * The following list of recommended duties of Audit Committees is drawn in substantial part from the ALI's *Principles of Corporate Governance*:

- Recommend which firm to engage as the corporation's external auditor and whether to terminate that relationship.
- Review the external auditor's compensation, the proposed terms of its engagement, and its independence.
- Review the appointment and replacement of the senior internal auditing executive, if any.
- Serve as a channel of communication between the external auditor and the board and between the senior internal auditing executive, if any, and the board.
- Review the results of each external audit, including any qualifications in the external auditor's opinion, any related management letter, management's responses to recommendations made by the external auditor in connection with the audit, reports submitted to the Audit Committee by the internal auditing department that are material to the corporation as a whole, and management's responses to those reports.
- Review the corporation's annual financial statements and any significant disputes between management and the external auditor that arose in connection with the preparation of those financial statements.
- Consider, in consultation with the external auditor and the senior internal auditing executive, if any, the adequacy of the corporation's

internal financial controls. Among other things, these controls must be designed to provide reasonable assurance that the corporation's publicly reported financial statements are presented fairly in conformity with generally accepted accounting principles.

● Consider major changes and other major questions of choice regarding the appropriate auditing and accounting principles and practices to be followed when preparing the corporation's financial statements.

● Review the procedures employed by the corporation in preparing published financial statements and related management commentaries.

● Meet periodically with management to review the corporation's major financial exposures. * * *

SECTION 9. THE COMPENSATION COMMITTEE

The 1978 edition of the *Corporate Director's Guidebook* stated that the existence and function of the Compensation Committee have been largely overshadowed by the widespread attention given to the Audit Committee. Times have changed. Executive compensation as become *the* issue of discussion in today's corporate governance debate.

The executive compensation debate revolves around four questions:

● Are the CEO and the other senior executives paid too much?

● Is their compensation reasonably related to personal and corporate performance?

● Are their post-employment benefits properly related to the overall benefit of the corporation and reasonable in amount?

● Is there effective oversight of management's compensation?

The Compensation Committee is at the center of that debate. When functioning responsibly, it not only addresses the first three questions but also provides credibility and substance to the concept of independent and effective oversight.

* * * The Compensation Committee should be composed solely of non-management directors. Insider relationships and interlocking Compensation Committee membership (with CEO-directors sitting on each other's Compensation Committees) are strongly discouraged * * *. [T]he committee should not be composed solely of highly paid executives.

The CEO will often wish to meet with the Compensation Committee, but the CEO should neither be on the Committee nor participate in all of its meetings. * * * To provide both the reality and the appearance of independent oversight, it is necessary to have Committee meetings without members of management present, particularly when the compensation of the CEO and other senior executives is determined.

A. *Principal Functions*

The functions of the Compensation Committee are well summarized in the ALI's *Principles of Corporate Governance*:

1) Review and recommend to the board, or determine, the annual salary, bonus, stock options, and other benefits, direct and indirect of the senior executives.

2) Review new executive compensation programs; review on a periodic basis the operation of the corporation's executive compensation programs to determine whether they are properly coordinated; establish and periodically review policies for the administration of executive compensation programs; and take steps to modify any executive compensation programs that yield payments and benefits that are not reasonably related to executive performance.

3) Establish and periodically review policies in the area of management perquisites. * * *

The Committee should also review the benefits and perquisites provided to company executives. Important among these are benefits provided upon retirement or other termination of employment. There is significant concern that these benefits are often not sufficiently related to job performance.

B.　*Other Responsibilities*

Other responsibilities that may appropriately be taken on by the Compensation Committee are:

- planning for executive development and succession; in that capacity, some Compensation Committees take on a broader role, actually planning for management development and evaluation of key personnel;

- considering indemnification issues, although these are often handled by the Audit Committee;

- reviewing expense accounts of senior executives;

- reviewing "fringe" benefits, such as loans made or guaranteed by the corporation; and

- reviewing and recommending to the board, or determining the compensation of directors.

SECTION 10.　THE NOMINATING COMMITTEE

In the last quarter-century, there has been a dramatic change in thinking in the business and legal communities regarding the need for and purposes of a Nominating Committee. For example, the 1979 Corporate Laws Committee report on Overview Committees noted that "only a minority of publicly-held corporations have as yet established a Nominating Committee." By 1990, The Business Roundtable was advocating that each corporation have a Nominating Committee, with membership limited to nonmanagement directors, undertaking an expanded role. Today, the vast majority of large publicly held corporations have Nominating Committees and, if they are not already composed solely of outside directors, shareholder activist organizations are pressing for that change.

A.　*Membership*

The Nominating Committee should be composed of directors who are not officers or employees of the corporation. That does not mean there is no role for the CEO. The CEO, although not a member of the Nominating Committee, will nonetheless be expected to have a significant role in recommending candidates and recruiting them for the board. The Nominating Committee Chair should have prominent involvement in the recruiting process in order to reinforce the perception as well as the reality that the invitee's selection is being made by the Committee and the board, and not by the CEO.

B. Principal Functions

The two principal functions of most Nominating Committees are to recommend to the board:

- the slate of nominees of directors to be elected by the shareholders (and any directors to be elected by the board to fill vacancies); and

- the directors to be selected for membership on the various board committee.

The Committee may also be authorized to recommend that individual directors be designated as chairs of board committees, particularly committees that perform oversight functions, such as the Audit, Nominating, and Compensation Committees. * * *

C. Selecting Directors

The basic responsibility of the Nominating Committee is to recommend to the board or to the shareholders nominees for election to the board. In many situations this entails review by the Nominating Committee of the performance and contribution of their fellow directors as well as the qualifications of any proposed new directors. This review is a key element of good corporate governance because the board is likely to adopt the Committee's recommended choices. The majority of shareholders are likely to vote for the nominees selected by the board. In the absence of malfeasance, it is not likely that a director will be removed during his or her term of office. * * *

One of the criticisms often directed against corporate boards is that initial election (often by the board to fill a vacancy) is tantamount to being awarded tenure until retirement age. A thoughtful review by the Nominating Committee of a director coming to the end of his or her term is the most effective mechanism to address this criticism. * * *

D. Management Directors

The CEO may recommend to the Nominating Committee that other senior officers of the company be appointed to the board. As noted in the ALI's *Principles of Corporate Governance*, "recommendations as to nominees made by the chief executive officer for directorships to be filled by other senior executives should normally carry very substantial weight." However, any such recommendations should also be considered in view of the size and structure of the board, given the current trend toward having fewer, and certainly less than a majority of, management directors on the board.

Senior officers who are also directors may be reluctant to take a position contrary to that espoused by the CEO. Accordingly, some argue that the attendance at board meetings of such senior officers in a nondirector, nonvoting capacity is sufficient to ensure that directors have ready access to all necessary information regarding the business and operations of the corporation, without compromising the independence of judgment that an effective director must enjoy. However, the nonmanagement directors may wish to utilize one or more board positions to evaluate the succession prospects of certain individuals and to ensure that they themselves develop a peer relationship and firsthand contact with senior executives who have detailed knowledge of the corporation's business.

E. Management Succession

The Nominating Committee is increasingly vested with the responsibility for recommending to the full board a successor to the CEO when a vacancy occurs through retirement or otherwise. The Nominating Committee often also reviews and approves proposed changes involving other senior management positions, with the understanding that the CEO is given considerable discretion in selecting and retaining members of the management team. In order to carry out these functions, Nominating Committee members should actively and directly review the performance of the CEO and members of senior management. The Nominating Committee may also wish to consider establishing emergency procedures for management succession in the event of unexpected death, disability, or departure of the CEO and to review management planning for the replacement of other members of the senior management team.

SECTION 11. OTHER OVERSIGHT RESPONSIBILITIES

Directors have various other oversight responsibilities. These include the following:

A. Philanthropic Activities

A corporation may devote a reasonable amount of its resources to public welfare or charitable, scientific, or educational purposes. It is appropriate that a program of charitable giving have a philosophy, purpose, budget, and realistic management.

B. Political Activity

Corporate officers and employees frequently participate actively in the governmental process by seeking to influence legislative activities, shaping regulations, or encouraging or preventing government action. The actions and political positions taken are often highly visible and may affect the reputation of the corporation. * * *

Notes

(1) This Guidebook is the product of a group composed primarily of corporation attorneys, many of whom regularly represent corporate management. As a result it has received considerable attention. More than 20,000 copies of the 1978 edition were sold and it is likely that the 1994 edition will be equally popular. Comments in this Guidebook should indicate how far the system of corporate governance has moved since Land's survey of boards of directors and Mace's examination of what roles directors played.

(2) Many corporations have created additional committees of various types in addition to the basic committees described in the *Guidebook*. The proliferation of these new types of committees also reveals the extent of increased participation by directors in corporate planning. These committees include:

a) *Strategic Planning Committee.* For a "healthy" business, this committee works with management to examine long-term strategic issues, validate planning assumptions, integrate short-term decisions with long-term planning, and consider business acquisitions or asset dispositions. An "unhealthy" corporation may use this committee to review asset dispositions or consider restructuring or recapitalization possibilities to improve the condition of the corporation. Close cooperation between management and this committee is obviously necessary if the committee is to have value to the corporation.

b) *Public Policy Committee.* This committee makes recommendations to the board with respect to matters of public and social policy affecting the corporation, including charitable and political contributions, employment practices, shareholder proposals that relate to matters of public concern, and community and consumer relationships.

c) *Finance Committee.* This committee reviews and monitors the overall financial position of the corporation, including the long-and short-term financing requirements of the corporation, foreign exchange exposure, insurance coverage, and related matters. At one time, these matters may have been considered by the audit committee or the board of directors as a whole to the extent they were considered by the board at all.

d) *Environmental Compliance Committee.* This committee's role is to assist management in identifying and monitoring potential environmental problems and compliance requirements. It may also review major litigation involving environmental issues facing the corporation. Some institutional investors have urged the naming of a director specifically to represent environmental and related interests. Corporations, however, have generally refused to do this on the ground that appointment of "constituency directors" is undesirable.

e) *Management Development Committee.* This committee considers matters of management succession both at the CEO level and at the levels of executive officers and heads of divisions and subsidiaries. In many corporations this function is performed by the compensation committee.

f) *Technology Committee.* In corporations in high technology industries, this committee may review technological developments which may have an impact on competitiveness of the company. "Hi Tech" corporations may have management information systems designed to ensure that executives are aware of technological developments; the technology committee may oversee and review the performance of such systems.

g) *Employee Benefits Committee.* This committee reviews the administration of employee benefit plans, including the management of investments, the creation of investment guidelines, and the allocation of pension funds into various categories of investments.

(3) The Corporate Directors Guidebook offers the following suggestions with respect to committees of the board:

Each corporation needs to tailor the functions of these committees to its own needs. In doing so, particular care should be taken that their membership reflects the makeup of the full board. Thus, an Executive Committee that frequently acts on important matters (as opposed to being a standby resource acting only in emergency or administrative situations) should reflect the composition of the full board. It should not be composed solely of management directors. Furthermore, the Executive Committee should not be so powerful that the board is seen as having first-and second-class citizens.

If a director or officer is alleged to have engaged in conduct damaging to the corporation or violating some law, the corporate response and the extent to which the individual should be supported, terminated, or otherwise sanctioned should be based on reviews by officers and directors who have no interest in the matter. This may be handled by a committee specifically appointed for the purpose or by an appropriately organized existing committee.

There are special situations—tender offers, alleged misconduct by a director or officer, major criminal investigations, management buyouts—that may require special committee handling. These unique, sometimes life-threatening events are not treated here; neither are the difficult issues faced by special litigation committees appointed when derivative litigation is brought against directors.

Guidebook, at 26.

(4) The backbone of the modern view of corporate governance is based on basic concepts embodied in this *Guidebook*: "at least a majority of members" of a board of directors should be "independent of management," and the critical oversight committees—audit, compensation, and nominating—should be staffed entirely by "independent" or "nonmanagement" directors. Most publicly held corporations accept these basic principles today either wholly or in part.

(a) Virtually all publicly held corporations today have boards composed primarily of nonmanagement directors. A survey of 100 large corporations made in 1989 by SpencerStuart Executive Search Consultants (a "head hunter" that recruits high level executives and directors) showed that the ratio of outside directors to inside directors was 3/1. In 1991, another study showed the same ratio continued though board sizes had been reduced; on the average a board of directors consisted of nine outside directors and three inside directors. Korn/Ferry, Board of Directors 5, 15 (1991). In 1997 the trend toward smaller boards of directors has continued and it is not uncommon today to have a board composed entirely of nonmanagement directors (except for the CEO who is also the chairman of the board) or at most one or two inside directors.

(b) Audit and compensation committees are typically staffed entirely by nonmanagement directors, but the pattern is more mixed with respect to nominating committees. See Stuart Misher, Firms Restrict CEOs in Picking Board Members, Wall St. J., Mar. 15, 1993, at B1, col. 6 (a survey of 809 large corporations in 1992 shows that 30 percent of these corporations bar inside directors from sitting on the committee that nominates candidates for directors; a similar survey in 1990 showed that only 16 percent of corporations limited such participation). Where the committee consists solely of outside directors, it is customary for the CEO and members of the management team to attend at least a portion of most meetings and to offer recommendations about prospective candidates for board service. The CEO thus continues to have a voice in the selection of outside directors since he is expected to have a good working relationship with each director.

(5) The unprecedented spate of dismissals of CEOs in the early 1990s (see note 2(c) page 550) itself reflected a significant change in relationship between the CEO and the board of directors since the 1970s. Rather than the CEO leading and the board of directors concurring, the independence of the board of directors had increased to the point that "the CEO is viewed more as a key employee rather than as the ultimate boss of the enterprise." Gilbert Fischsberg, Chief Executives See Their Power Shrink, Wall St.J., March 15, 1993, at B1, col. 3. See John A. Byrne, Requiem for Yesterday's CEO, Bus. Wk., Feb. 15, 1993, at 32. Many corporations have separated the roles of chairman of the board of directors and CEO or, where the CEO is also the chairman, have appointed a "lead director" to run the board in a time of crisis. Boards also provide institutionally for the periodic review of the performance of the CEO by outside directors. Joann S.

Lublin, CEOs Give Up More Clout to Boards: Chiefs Endorse Lead Directors, Performance Reviews, Wall St.J., July 26, 1996, at A10A. As this title indicates, most CEOs have accepted these innovations. Despite these changes, however, criticism is still made that directors wait too long before concluding that changes at the top are necessary. Judith H. Dobrzynski, Those Board Revolts Prove the System Works, Right? Wrong, Bus. Wk., Feb. 15, 1993, at 35. Directors have also taken an active role in providing for transfers of leadership (sometimes by providing financial inducements to CEOs to agree to retire at a specific age or to identify potential future CEOs within the corporation) and in determining the identity of the new CEO. Joann S. Lublin, CEOs Have Less Say in Designating Successors, Wall St.J., June 24, 1997, at B1, col. 3.

(6) Since 1989 there has been an outpouring of principles of corporate governance from a variety of sources, including: Corporate Governance and American Competitiveness, Business Roundtable, 46 Bus.Law. 241 (1990); The Working Group on Corporate Governance, A New Compact for Owners and Directors, Harv. Bus. Rev., July–Aug. 1991, at 141 (prepared by "a working group of distinguished lawyers representing large public companies and leading institutional investors"); Principles for Global Corporate Responsibility: Bench Marks for Measuring Business Performance (1995) (prepared by three church-related committees on corporate responsibility); The Business Charter for Sustainable Development (1990), proposed by the International Chamber of Commerce; The Ceres Principles (1992) proposed by the Coalition for Environmentally Responsible Economics (in response to the Exxon Valdez disaster); the GM Board Guidelines on Corporate Governance Issues; The Code of Best Practice (1992) prepared by the English Cadbury Committee on the Financial Aspects of Corporate Governance; and Guidelines for Enhancing Professionalism of Board Members, prepared by the National Association of Corporate Directors (1996). These principles may deal in part with subjects other than corporate governance; however, they also propose aspects of corporate governance not discussed in the *Guidebook*. For example, paragraph 11 of the "GM Board Guidelines on Corporate Governance Issues" states that "[t]he outside directors of the board will meet in executive session three times each year. The format of these meetings will include a discussion with the CEO on each occasion." In 1997, CalPERS' staff proposed a new set of guidelines, including a proposal that outside directors serving more than ten years should no longer be viewed as independent directors and that mandatory retirement ages be set for directors; these proposals turned out to be controversial and were not approved by the organization, but are a source of continuing discussion.

(7) Several industry-wide organizations involve themselves primarily with issues of corporate governance. The National Association of Corporate Directors (NACD) is a not-for-profit organization that focuses on the needs of individuals serving on boards of directors; its membership includes more than 1,500 chairmen, CEOs, CFOs, presidents, directors and other persons who serve on or deal with boards of directors. The Council of Institutional Investors, the Institutional Shareholder Service, Inc., and the Investor Responsibility Research Center all provide, on a shared cost basis, mechanisms for the collection, evaluation, and dissemination of information relevant to corporate governance issues. Many institutional investors are members of and support these organizations.

(8) Data collected by Directorship, a consulting firm, reported that in 1995, 68 directors of Fortune 1,000 companies sat on nine or more corporate boards. The CEO of BellSouth sat on the board of nine Fortune 1,000 companies, including his own. Directors sitting on multiple boards are sometimes referred to

as "trophy" directors since they are persons with high visibility and, often, periods of public service prior to becoming directors. Names include Joseph Califano, Jr., and Vernon E. Jordan. A study by Graef Crystal found no statistically significant difference in the performance of corporations with trophy directors and those without, except that the pay of CEOs tended to be higher in corporations with trophy directors than others. Judith H. Dobrzinski, When Directors Play Musical Chairs, New York Times, November 17, 1996, sec. 3, p. 1, col. 4. These multiple directorships, and cross directorships (CEO of Corporation A serving on the board of Corporation B while the CEO of Corporation B serves on the board of Corporation A), have been criticized. Elizabeth Lesly, Are These 10 Stretched Too Thin? Business Week, November 13, 1995, at 78; America's Least Valuable Directors: A Study of Corporate Board Directors, A Report by the Internal Brotherhood of Teamsters, Office of Corporate Affairs (Spring 1996). The Guidelines proposed by the National Association of Corporate Directors urge directors to become active participants and decision makers, not merely passive advisers, budget at least four full 40–hour weeks of service for every board on which serve, limit their number of board memberships (2 for an active CEO, 3 for active senior executives, 6 for retired executives or professional directors), and limit the length of service to 10 or 15 years (to allow room for new and younger directors). John A. Byrne, Listen Up: The National Association of Corporate Directors' new guidelines won't tolerate inattentive, passive, uninformed board members, Business Week, November 25, 1996, 100.

(9) Nonmanagement directors are well-paid. In 1995, one "trophy" director on 10 boards received reported fees of $785,200 in 1995. Robert A.G. Monks and Nell Minow, Power and Accountability 174–75, (1991) state that the average compensation for an outside director of one of the 100 largest corporations was $45,650 per year. By 1994 this figure had reached $50,000 per year, but compensation in excess of $100,000 was common. Report of the NACD Blue Ribbon Commission on Director Compensation 29 (1995). Many corporations also offer directors fringe and retirement benefits, as well as extra compensation for serving on committees of the board of directors. Compensation may be on a per meeting basis or an annual lump sum—$3,000 to $5,000 per year for committee service. Chairmen of committees may receive additional compensation. Retirement benefits provided substantial benefits in future years but no immediate out-of-pocket costs. However, in the middle 1990s a major development in compensation for nonmanagement directors occurred. See Report of the NACD Blue Ribbon Commission on Director Professionalism, 5 (1996): "Boards should set a substantial target for stock ownership by each director and a time period during which this target is to be met. * * * Boards should pay directors solely in the form of equity and cash—with equity representing a substantial portion of the total up to 100 percent; boards should dismantle existing benefit programs and avoid creating new ones." The justification is that "[a] significant ownership stake leads to a stronger alignment of interests between directors and shareholders, and between executives and shareholders." More than 100 publicly held corporations implemented these proposals in whole or in part within the first year after they were announced.[46] See Charles M. Elson, Director Compensation and the Management–

---

46. [By the Editor] The Corporate Director's Guidebook offers the following suggestion with respect to director compensation: "The board should be alert to avoid compensation policies or the use of corporate perquisites that might tend to subvert the independence of its outside directors or divert their focus from proper long-range corporate objectives. In this respect, some believe that stock options and restricted stock grants to directors strengthen directors' interest in the overall success of the corporation, while others believe that these forms of compensation tend to align directors'

Captured Board—The History of a Symptom and a Cure, 50 SMU L.Rev. 127 (1996); Charles M. Elson, The Duty of Care, Compensation, and Stock Ownership, 63 U.Cin.L.Rev. 649 (1995); Charles M. Elson, Executive Overcompensation—A Board–Based Solution, 34 B.C.L.Rev. 937 (1993). Professor Elson was a member of the NACD Commission.

(10) Historically, it has been very common for lawyers for a corporation also to serve on its board of directors. This practice has been the subject of some concern both from an ethical standpoint and from its possible effect on the objectivity of the legal advice thereby obtained. A comparison of proxy statement filings with the SEC between 1979 and 1981 revealed a 25 percent decline in the number of lawyer/directors during this period. Over 43 percent of the reporting companies, however, had at least one attorney on their board of directors in 1981. Analysis of Results of 1981 Proxy Statement Disclosure Monitoring Program, SEC Rel. No. 34–18532, 47 Fed.Reg. 10792, 10793 (1982). During the 1980s and 1990s, the number of lawyers serving on boards of directors of their clients—or indeed on the board of directors of any public corporation—almost certainly continued to decline, though empirical data appears to be lacking. To some extent, corporations find the lawyer/director less necessary: "The view of most chairmen I've worked with is that if he needs solid legal advice he can go buy it." Comments of Thomas J. Neff, president of SpencerStuart, quoted in George Melloan, A Good Director is Getting Harder to Find, Wall St.J., Feb. 9, 1988, at 29, col. 3. Another factor undoubtedly of increasing importance is the fear of personal liability or exposure to litigation for failing to fulfill the various duties and obligations of directors. Lawyers who are themselves in corporate practice and well aware of the law on the subject of director liabilities are particularly reluctant to serve. Nevertheless, many lawyers continue to appear on boards of directors. Vernon E. Jordan, a "trophy" director who serves on eight boards of directors, is a senior partner in a major Washington, D.C. law firm. A 1993 survey of the 100 largest banks, 50 largest savings institutions and 50 largest diversified financial services companies, for example, showed that 94 of them had attorneys on their boards; many had more than one attorney. Margaret C. Fisk, Law Department Numbers Rise at U.S. Banks, Nat'l L.J., Oct. 4, 1993, at S2. This survey also listed the major law firms used by the financial institution during 1992–1993; the affiliation of about half of the lawyer/directors listed were different from the major law firms listed. Rule 1.7 of the Model Rules of Professional Conduct requires the professional judgment of a lawyer to be independent and uninfluenced by conflicting interests. The lawyer who is a director and who also provides outside legal advice has a potential problem under this rule. See Robert E. O'Malley and Harry H. Schneider, Jr., Danger: Lawyer on Board, ABA J., July 1993, at 102.

(11) Should the composition of boards of directors be broadened to include representatives of various constituencies or "stakeholders"? Should the composition also be broadened to include representatives of groups that historically have never been represented on boards of directors. Perhaps the following persons or organizations might deserve representation:

    (a) The general public;

    (b) Customers;

    (c) The Internal Revenue Service;

    (d) The Department of Justice or Federal Trade Commission;

interests too closely with those of management." Guidebook, at 19.

(e) Employees (The continental European board of directors contains employee representatives, and there is experience with this suggestion in the United States; See Hoerr, Blue Collars in the Boardroom: Putting Business First, Bus. Wk., Dec. 14, 1987 at 126, listing "employee designated board members" in eight corporations, including Chrysler, three steel companies, Pan American Airlines, and Kaiser Aluminum);

(f) Institutional investors;

(g) Small shareholders;

(h) The mayor of the city in which the corporation's home office is located;

(i) The governor of the state in which that city is located;

(j) Women and minority groups. Women currently make up about ten percent of directors in Fortune 500 companies, a number that has increased steadily since the 1960s. See Judith H. Dobrzynski, Women Pass Milestone in the Board Room, New York Times, December 12, 1996, p. D4, col. 3. Corporations also have attempted to increase the number of minority directors, though in 1996, racial minorities occupied only 4 percent of board seats at the 878 largest publicly held corporations. This percentage was up from 2.4 percent in 1992. Joann S. Lublin, Competition for Minority Directors Heats Up, Wall Street Journal, February 18, 1997, p. B1, col. 3.

(12) What about the creation of a cadre of professional directors who devote their full time and activity to serving as directors on a limited number of boards? There has long existed an unorganized group of individuals who serve as professional directors as their principal or sole occupation. At current levels of directoral compensation, service on a few boards would provide a comfortable income. Many retired CEOs serve on the boards of several corporations and might be viewed as professional directors since essentially all of their earned income is from director-related compensation.

(13) With respect to constituency representation generally, consider the following comments of Professor Ben M. Enis, a professor of marketing at the University of Southern California, in a Letter to the Editor of the Wall Street Journal, July 25, 1989 at A19, col. 2:

> This is a recipe for disaster. Directors would represent competing interest groups, e.g., those wanting maximum short-term dividends, those advancing various political agendas * * *, those favoring increased investments in basic research, or whatever. These director blocs would cause stockholder meetings to resemble U.N. debates: lots of rhetoric, little action. The only ones to gain would be the activists (presumably not business people) elected to such directorships, and lawyers (including perhaps those contemplating a career shift from public to private sector) who represent those activists in stockholder suits against management.

Professor Enis was responding to a suggestion that directors should be selected from slates of outside candidates that reflect categories of shareholders.

(14) there is also a basic question whether the addition of outside directors results in improved corporate performance:

(a) Laura Lin, The Effectiveness of Outside Directors as A Corporate Governance Mechanism: Theories and Evidence, 90 Nw.L.Rev. 898, 961–62 (1996):*

---

* Reprinted by special permission of Northwestern University School of Law. North-western University Law Review, Vol. 90, Issue 3, pp. 898, 961–62 (1996).

Since the board of directors has been the focal point of the corporate governance debate, this Article sought to answer one of the most fundamental questions underlying this debate. Namely, does board composition make any difference at all in the overall firm performance and outcomes of specific corporate transactions? Although currently empirical results do not conclusively resolve the debate about effectiveness of outside directors as monitors of management, and much work remains to be done in this area, these studies do cast doubt on the two extreme positions on board effectiveness. More specifically, the empirical data do not support either of the following propositions: (1) that regardless of its composition, the board is ineffective because it is co-opted by management, or (2) that a board composed of a majority of outside directors who are independent from management, can always be relied on as an effective monitor of managerial decisions.

Professor Lin states that "there is some support for the proposition that outside directors make a difference in specific transactions involving potential conflicts of interest between management and shareholders—for example, turnover due to poor firm performance, the level and structure of executive compensation, corporate acquisitions, adoption of poison pills, and management buy-outs." Id., at 962.

(b) In an earlier study commissioned by the Business Roundtable, Professor MacAvoy concluded that independent persons on boards of directors have no discernible effect on compliance with the law by corporations. Paul MacAvoy, ALI Proposals for Increased Control of the Corporation By the Board of Directors: An Economic Analysis, in Statement of The Business Roundtable on the American Law Institute's Proposed "Principles of Corporate Governance and Structure: Restatement and Recommendations, Appendix C" (1983). In a second study in the same period, Barry D. Baysinger and Henry N. Butler concluded that the presence of a few independent directors appeared to improve corporate profit performance, but that the effect of the number of independent directors was subject to diminishing marginal increases—and indeed absolute declines in relative performance as their number increased. Baysinger and Butler concluded that the number of independent directors should not exceed 30 percent of the board for maximum effectiveness. Barry D. Baysinger and Henry N. Butler, Revolution Versus Evolution in Corporation Law: The ALI's Project and the Independent Director, 52 Geo.Wash.L.Rev. 557 (1984). For criticisms of the methodologies of these two studies, see Comments of Melvin A. Eisenberg, Conference Panel Discussion: Federalism Issues in Corporate Governance, 45 Ohio St.L.J. 591, 596–597; Melvin A. Eisenberg, New Modes of Discourse in the Corporate Law Literature, 52 Geo.Wash.L.Rev. 582, 598–603 (Baysinger and Butler), 603–608 (MacAvoy).

(c) A report, Answer to Better Corporate Governance Isn't More Outside Directors, Panelists Say, BNA USA Law Week, vol. 6, No. 8, pp. 2123–4, Aug. 26, 1997, quotes Professor Bernard Black as stating that an April, 1997 study shows "no empirical support for the current push for firms to establish 'supermajority independent' boards by severely limiting the number of inside directors—often to only one or two inside directors."

(15) In November, 1996, Business Week introduced a "Report Card" of the "best" and "worst" boards of directors. John A. Byrne, The Best and Worst Boards: Our New Report Card for Corporate Governance, p. 82. This "Report Card" listed the 25 "best" and "worst" boards as ranked by Business Week after a "survey of 295 of the nation's largest pension funds and money managers," and a ranking of 212 companies singled out by poll respondents in accordance with

"guidelines or best practices articulated by corporate-governance experts. Points were awarded to boards that met the criteria. Points were subtracted for failing the tests." Id., at 85–86. For example, points were awarded if a company had no more than two inside directors, no insiders on audit, nominating or compensation committees, no interlocking directorships with other companies, and no outside directors who drew consulting, legal or other fees from the company. Points were also awarded if all directors owned at least $100,000 in stock (to better align their interests with those of investors) and if the corporation did not offer pensions to its directors. Among the "best" boards were Campbell Soups, General Electric, Compaq, Colgate Palmolive, and Chrysler; among the "worst," Archer Daniels Midland, Champion International, Rollins Environmental, Nationsbank, and AT & T. Not surprisingly, these rankings, subjective as they may be, appear to have had an immediate effect, particularly on corporations that ranked on the list of 25 worst boards. See Anthony Bianco and others, Corporate Governance: The Rush to Quality on Corporate Boards, Business Week, March 3, 1997, 34. See also, Joann S. Lublin, Competition for Minority Directors Heats Up, Wall Street Journal, February 18, 1997, B1, col. 3.

(15) One interesting aspect of the Business Week "Report Card" was the recognition that some corporations that ranked relatively low in terms of corporate governance had enviable economic records over a long period. The clearest example was Coca Cola, which has been "one of the world's most rewarding investments" but ranked 20th on the list of best managed boards. Some institutional investors put the dollars first but others give more weight to strong governance: " 'We're looking at governance first and then performance,' says Richard M. Schlefer, an assistant vice president at * * *[TIAA/CREF]. 'If a company has a governance structure that doesn't withstand scrutiny, we don't want to wait until there is a problem to get involved.' " Business Week, supra, at 85. In contrast, Linda Scott, director of investor affairs for the New York State Retirement Fund, is quoted as saying "It's all bottom line. * * * It's 'How much money did you make for us this past year?' We're not here to make sure that boards are composed of good directors. We're here to make sure boards make money for us." Business Week, supra, at 106.

D. PROXY REGULATION

1. SCOPE OF REGULATION

SECURITIES EXCHANGE ACT OF 1934
§§ 14(A), 12(A), 12(G)
15 U.S.C.A. §§ 78n, 78l.

PROXIES

Section 14. (a) It shall be unlawful for any person, by the use of the mails or by any means or instrumentality of interstate commerce or of any facility of a national securities exchange or otherwise, in contravention of such rules and regulations as the Commission may prescribe as necessary or appropriate in the public interest or for the protection of investors, to solicit or to permit the use of his name to solicit any proxy or consent or authorization in respect of any security (other than an exempted security) registered pursuant to section 12 of this title.

REGISTRATION REQUIREMENTS FOR SECURITIES

Section 12. (a) It shall be unlawful for any member, broker, or dealer to effect any transaction in any security (other than an exempted security) on a national securities exchange unless a registration is effective as to such security for such exchange in accordance with the provisions of this title and the rules and regulations thereunder. * * *

(g)(1) Every issuer which is engaged in interstate commerce, or in a business affecting interstate commerce, or whose securities are traded by use of the mails or any means or instrumentality of interstate commerce shall—

(A) within one hundred and twenty days after the last day of its first fiscal year ended after the effective date of this subsection on which the issuer has total assets exceeding $1,000,000 and a class of equity security (other than an exempted security) held of record by seven hundred and fifty or more persons; and

(B) within one hundred and twenty days after the last day of its first fiscal year ended after two years from the effective date of this subsection on which the issuer has total assets exceeding $1,000,000 and a class of equity security (other than an exempted security) held of record by five hundred or more but less than seven hundred and fifty persons, register such security by filing with the Commission a registration statement * * *.

(4) Registration of any class of security pursuant to this subsection shall be terminated ninety days, or such shorter period as the Commission may determine, after the issuer files a certification with the Commission that the number of holders of record of such class of security is reduced to less than three hundred persons. * * *

(5) For the purposes of this subsection the term "class" shall include all securities of an issuer which are of substantially similar character and the holders of which enjoy substantially similar rights and privileges. * * *

Notes

(1) The "effective date" referred to in § 12(g)(1) is July 1, 1964. Pub.Law 88–467 § 13(1), 78 Stat. 565.

(2) The SEC has adopted the following regulations under § 12(g):

§ 240.12g–1 Exemption from section 12(g).

An issuer shall be exempt from the requirement to register any class of equity securities pursuant to section 12(g)(1) if on the last day of its most recent fiscal year the issuer had total assets not exceeding $10 million * * *

§ 240.12g–4 Certifications of termination of registration under section 12(g).

(a) Termination of registration of a class of securities shall take effect 90 days * * * after the issuer certifies to the Commission * * * that:

(1) Such class of securities is held of record by: (i) Less than 300 persons; or (ii) by less than 500 persons, where the total assets of the issuer have not exceeded $10 million on the last day of each of the issuer's most recent three fiscal years. * * *

17 C.F.R. §§ 240.12g–1, 240.12g–4 (1997). The statutory provision, of course, requires registration of corporations with more than $1 million of assets if they

meet the number of shareholders requirement. In 1982, the SEC increased the asset requirement from $1 million to $3 million primarily as an "inflation adjustment" to the original statutory criterion established in 1964. The increase from $3 million to $5 million was promulgated in 1986. The SEC estimated that about 700 issuers were likely to be affected by the increase in the asset requirement from $3 million to $5 million. SEC Rel. No. 34–22483, 50 Fed.Reg. 41162 (1985).

(3) Under § 12(g) and rules 12g–1 and 12g–4, how should the following problems be resolved:

(a) Company A sells securities under § 4(2) of the Securities Act of 1933 every year for three years. It eventually has total assets of $10 million and 450 shareholders. Does Company A have to register under § 12?

(b) Company B sells securities under § 4(2) every year for three years. Eventually it has total assets of $4.8 million and 700 shareholders. Does Company B have to register under § 12?

(c) Company C has been registered under § 12(g) for four years, and has consistently had $4.8 million in total assets and 450 shareholders. May its registration under § 12 be terminated?

(4) A corporation that is required to register a securities issue under § 12 is subject to a significant degree of regulation under various sections of the Securities Exchange Act of 1934 in addition to the regulation of proxy solicitations. Many of these sections are discussed below and in the following chapters. When considering federally imposed requirements under the 1934 Act it is important to ascertain whether the requirements are applicable only to corporations required to register under § 12, or whether they are more broadly applicable to all corporations using the mails or the facilities of interstate commerce.

(5) Registration of the publicly held securities of an issuer under § 12 of the 1934 Act should be distinguished from the registration of an issue for its public distribution under the 1933 Act described in Chapter 7. Registration under § 12 of the 1934 Act involves the submission of information about the issuer, its organization, its finances, its securities, and similar matters. There is also a requirement for the periodic revision of information; these periodic reports are colloquially referred to as 8–K and 10–K reports. Historically, registration of an issue under the 1933 Act for sale to the public was considered more onerous and difficult than supplying information for registration under § 12. The emphasis on full disclosure at the time an issue is sold publicly under the 1933 Act is partly an historical accident, and a more rational system would doubtless emphasize issuer registration and periodic full disclosure rather than full disclosure only when the issuer wishes to sell securities. In 1982, the SEC achieved essentially this result by regulation through its integrated disclosure program, SEC Rel. No. 33–6383, AS Rel. No. 306, 47 Fed.Reg. 11380 (1982). The general effect of this program is to permit issuers that have filed reports under the 1934 Act for more than three years to incorporate by reference this information in its 1933 Act filing, thereby greatly simplifying the registration process under that Act.

(6) Why should proxy regulation be a federal matter? The MBCA and most state business corporation acts are essentially silent on proxy rules and requirements. Also, when most publicly held corporations solicit proxies, they in fact are soliciting shareholders in every state.

(7) Accepting the notion of federal regulation, is it nevertheless desirable for Congress to give an administrative agency, such as the SEC, such a blank check as

§ 14(a) appears to grant? The conditions giving rise to this broad grant of power have been described as follows:

> At the time of the enactment of the Securities Exchange Act of 1934, the proxy had become a device for continuing management in corporate office and for ratifying its policies. The control of corporations by insiders had been perpetuated through the solicitation of proxies by management, which simply requested that stockholders execute and return proxies without disclosing the purposes for which the proxies were to be used.
>
> The legislative history of the Securities Exchange Act of 1934 indicates, however, that the Congress was concerned also with the abuse of proxies by seekers of corporate power. A congressional report (Sen.Rep. No. 1455, 73d Cong., 2d Sess., 77 (1934)) states that "the rules and regulations promulgated by the Commission will protect investors from promiscuous solicitation of their proxies, on the one hand by irresponsible outsiders seeking to wrest control of a corporation away from honest and conscientious corporate officials; and on the other hand by unscrupulous corporate officials seeking to retain control of the management by concealing or distorting facts."

Andrew D. Orrick, The Revised Proxy Rules of the Securities and Exchange Commission, 11 Bus.Law. (No. 3) 32–33 (April 1956).[47]

(8) In 1988, the SEC promulgated Rule 19c–4, which prohibited national securities exchanges from listing for trading the securities of corporations that created weighted or unequal voting classifications for classes of common shares, the so-called "one share/one vote" principle. In Business Roundtable v. S.E.C., 905 F.2d 406, 410–411 (D.C.Cir., 1990), the Court invalidated this rule on the ground that it exceeded the power granted to the Commission by § 14 of the Securities Exchange Act:

> * * * [A]lthough § 14(a) broadly bars use of the mails (and other means) "to solicit * * * any proxy" in contravention of Commission rules and regulations, it is not seriously disputed that Congress's central concern was with disclosure. See J.I. Case Co. v. Borak, 377 U.S. 426, 431, 84 S.Ct. 1555, 1559, 12 L.Ed.2d 423 (1964) ("The purpose of § 14(a) is to prevent management or others from obtaining authorization for corporate action by means of deceptive or inadequate disclosure in proxy solicitation"); see also Santa Fe Industries, Inc. v. Green, 430 U.S. 462, 477–78, 97 S.Ct. 1292, 1302–04, 51 L.Ed.2d 480 (1977) (emphasizing Exchange Act's philosophy of full disclosure and dismissing the fairness of the terms of the transaction as "at most a tangential concern of the statute" once full and fair disclosure has occurred).
>
> While the House Report indeed speaks of fair corporate suffrage, it also plainly identifies Congress's target—the solicitation of proxies by well informed insiders "without fairly informing the stockholders of the purposes for which the proxies are to be used." 1934 House Report at 14. The Senate Report contains no vague language about "corporate suffrage," but rather explains the purpose of the proxy protections as ensuring that stockholders have "adequate knowledge" about the "financial condition of the corporation * * * [and] the major questions of policy, which are decided at stockholders' meetings." S.Rep. No. 792, 73d Cong., 2d Sess. 12 (1934) ("1934 Senate Report"). Finally, both reports agree on the power that the proxy sections

---

47. Copyright 1956 by the American Bar Association. All rights reserved. Reprinted with the permission of the American Bar Association and its Section of Corporation, Banking and Business Law.

gave the Commission—"power to control the conditions under which proxies may be solicited." 1934 House Report at 14. See also 1934 Senate Report at 12 (similar language).

That proxy regulation bears almost exclusively on disclosure stems as a matter of necessity from the nature of proxies. Proxy solicitations are, after all, only communications with potential absentee voters. The goal of federal proxy regulation was to improve those communications and thereby to enable proxy voters to control the corporation as effectively as they might have by attending a shareholder meeting. Id. See also S.Rep. No. 1455, 73d Cong., 2d Sess. 74 (1934); Sheldon E. Bernstein and Henry G. Fischer, The Regulation of the Solicitation of Proxies: Some Reflections on Corporate Democracy, 7 U.Chi.L.Rev. 226, 227–28 (1940).

We do not mean to be taken as saying that disclosure is necessarily the sole subject of § 14. See Louis Loss, Fundamentals of Securities Regulation 452–53 (1988) (asserting that § 14 is not limited to ensuring disclosure), quoted in Final Rule, 53 Fed.Reg. at 26,391 n. 163; * * * For example, the Commission's Rule 14a–4(b)(2) requires a proxy to provide some mechanism for a security holder to withhold authority to vote for each nominee individually. * * * It thus bars a kind of electoral tying arrangement, and may be supportable as a control over management's power to set the voting agenda, or, slightly more broadly, voting procedures. * * * But while Rule 14a–4(b)(2) may lie in a murky area between substance and procedure, Rule 19c–4 much more directly interferes with the substance of what the shareholders may enact. It prohibits certain reallocations of voting power and certain capital structures, even if approved by a shareholder vote subject to full disclosure and the most exacting procedural rules.

905 F.2d, at 410. See also Eckstein v. Balcor Film Investors, 8 F.3d 1121, 1130 (7th Cir.1993), where Judge Easterbrook encapsulates the holding of *Business Roundtable* by stating that § 14 does not include "merit regulation." The legislative history of the 1934 Act is fragmentary and the court's reading, at best, is open to serious question. See Jill E. Fisch, From Legitimacy to Logic: Reconstructing Proxy Regulation, 46 Vand.L.Rev. 1129, 1173–1189 (1993). However, a judicial opinion carries more weight than a law review article.

STUDEBAKER CORP. v. GITTLIN

United States Court of Appeals, Second Circuit, 1966.
360 F.2d 692.

FRIENDLY, CIRCUIT JUDGE:

Richard Gittlin, a stockholder of Studebaker Corporation, a Michigan corporation, appeals from an order of the District Court for the Southern District of New York, in an action brought against him by the corporation. The order enjoined the use of other stockholders' authorizations in a New York state court proceeding to obtain inspection of Studebaker's shareholders list, N.Y. Business Corporation Law, McKinney's Consol.Laws, c. 4, § 1315, save after compliance with the Proxy Rules of the Securities and Exchange Commission issued under § 14(a) of the Securities Exchange Act. * * *

Studebaker's resort to the district court was occasioned by the service upon it on March 21 of papers in a proceeding begun by Gittlin in the Supreme Court of New York to inspect the record of the company's shareholders. Gittlin's application to the New York court recited that he was the record owner of 5,000 shares of Studebaker stock and that he was acting on behalf of himself and on written authorization from 42 other shareholders owning in excess of 145,000 shares which constituted more than 5% of the company's stock; that he and his associates had been endeavoring to get the Studebaker management to agree to certain changes in its board of directors and had announced their intention to solicit proxies for the forthcoming annual meeting if the request was not met; and that when these talks had broken down, he had requested access to the stockholders list and had been refused.

Studebaker's affidavit and subsequent complaint allege that Gittlin obtained the authorization from the 42 other stockholders in violation of the Proxy Rules issued by the SEC under § 14(a) of the Securities Exchange Act. Specifically the company contends that Gittlin claimed to be holding the authorizations as early as March 14, and that at that time he had made no filing of proxy material with the SEC. * * *

The contention most heavily pressed is that § 14(a) of the Securities Exchange Act does not include authorizations for the limited purpose of qualifying under a state statute permitting the holders of a given percentage of shares to obtain inspection of a stockholders list. The statute is worded about as broadly as possible, forbidding any person "to solicit any proxy or consent or authorization" in respect of any security therein specified "in contravention of such rules and regulations as the Commission may prescribe as necessary or appropriate in the public interest or for the protection of investors"; the definitions in the Proxy Rules, 14a–1, exhaust the sweep of the power thus conferred. The assistant general counsel of the SEC, which responded to our request for its views with promptness and definitude, stated at the argument that the Commission believes § 14(a) should be construed, in all its literal breadth, to include authorizations to inspect stockholders lists, even in cases where obtaining the authorizations was not a step in a planned solicitation of proxies.[48]

We need not go that far to uphold the order of the district court. In SEC v. Okin, 132 F.2d 784 (2d Cir.1943), this court ruled that a letter which did not request the giving of any authorization was subject to the Proxy Rules if it was part of "a continuous plan" intended to end in solicitation and to prepare the way for success. This was the avowed purpose of Gittlin's demand for inspection of the stockholders list and, necessarily, for his soliciting authorizations sufficient to aggregate the 5% of the stock required by § 1315 of New York's Business Corporation Law. Presumably the stockholders who gave authorizations were told something and, as Judge L. Hand said in *Okin*, "one need only spread the misinformation adequately before beginning to solicit, and the Commission would be powerless to protect shareholders." 132 F.2d at 786. Moreover, the very fact that a copy of the stockholders list is a valuable

48. [By the Court] The Commission states in a letter to the court:

"Section 14(a) of the Securities Exchange Act of 1934 and the Commission's rules thereunder apply to any proxy, consent, authorization and are not limited to proxies, consents, and authorizations in situations involving elections to office. There is no reason to suppose that Congress intended that

the protective provisions of the proxy rules should not reach other situations in which a stockholder is requested to permit another to act for him, whatever may be the purpose of the authorization."

The Proxy Rules [14a–2(b)], exempt solicitation otherwise than on behalf of management where the total number of persons solicited is less than ten.

instrument to a person seeking to gain control, is a good reason for insuring that shareholders have full information before they aid its procurement. We see no reason why, in such a case, the words of the Act should be denied their literal meaning. * * *

This brings us to Gittlin's claim that Studebaker made no adequate showing of need for injunctive relief in failing to demonstrate "irreparable injury." Recitation of this term generally produces more dust than light. A plaintiff asking an injunction because of the defendant's violation of a statute is not required to show that otherwise rigor mortis will set in forthwith; all that "irreparable injury" means in this context is that unless an injunction is granted, the plaintiff will suffer harm which cannot be repaired. At least that is enough where, as here, the only consequence of an injunction is that the defendant must effect a compliance with the statute which he ought to have done before. To be sure, time is of the essence in proxy contests—at least the participants generally think it to be. But the district court could properly have considered that the public interest in enforcing the Proxy Rules outweighed any inconvenience to Gittlin in having to start again. In this aspect decision rested in the judge's sound discretion; we find no abuse.

Affirmed.

Notes

(1) The question of what constitutes a "solicitation" has also arisen in other contexts, particularly in connection with proxy fights and other struggles for control discussed in Chapter 14. See, e.g., Brown v. Chicago, Rock Island & Pac. R.R. Co., 328 F.2d 122 (7th Cir.1964)[an advertisement directed to "Rock Island Stockholders, Employees, Shippers, and Midwest Communities" is not a "solicitation"]; Allen v. Lloyd's of London, 94 F.3d 923 (4th Cir.1996)[settlement offer by Lloyd's to American "Names" that provided each Name the choice of waiving claim against Lloyd's in exchange for partial funding by Lloyd's of Name's liability to Lloyd's is not a solicitation subject to section 14(a)].

(2) The broad definition of "solicitation" approved in the Studebaker Corp. case obviously chilled the ability of institutional investors to communicate with each other and present a common front when approaching management of corporations with respect to matters of corporate governance of interest to investors generally. The cost of preparing and filing a proxy statement for this purpose was estimated to exceed $50,000, and the problems of timing might make such an approach impractical in any event. In October 1992, the SEC amended rule 14a–1 to add a "safe harbor":

(2) The terms ["solicit" and "solicitation"] do not apply, however, to: * * *

(iv) A communication by a security holder who does not otherwise engage in a proxy solicitation (other than a solicitation exempt under § 240.14a–2) stating how the security holder intends to vote and the reasons therefor, provided that the communication:

(A) Is made by means of speeches in public forums, press releases, published or broadcast opinions, statements, or advertisements appearing in a broadcast media, or newspaper, magazine or other bona fide publication disseminated on a regular basis,

(B) Is directed to persons to whom the security holder owes a fiduciary duty in connection with the voting of securities of a registrant held by the security holder, or

(C) Is made in response to unsolicited requests for additional information with respect to a prior communication by the security holder made pursuant to this paragraph (1)(2)(iv).

17 C.F.R. § 240.14a–1(2)(1997). In addition, the SEC exempted from the costly proxy statement creation process "[a]ny solicitation by or on behalf of any person who does not, at any time during such solicitation, seek directly or indirectly, either on its own or another's behalf, the power to act as proxy for a security holder and does not furnish or otherwise request, or act on behalf of a person who furnishes or requests, a form of revocation, abstention, consent or authorization." There are ten exceptions to this provision to prevent candidates and others directly involved with the proxy solicitation from using these "free" communications. 17 C.F.R. § 240.14a–2(b)(1)(1997). The SEC must be provided copies of the communication within three business days after it is distributed. 17 C.F.R. § 240.14a–6(g)(1997). See Comment, The Recent Revisions to Federal Proxy Regulations: Lifting the Ban on Shareholders Communications, 68 Tulane L.Rev. 69 (1993); Carol Goforth, Proxy Reform as a Means of Increasing Shareholder Participation in Corporate Governance: Too Little But Not Too Late, 43 Am. U.L.Rev. 379 (1994).

(3) 17 C.F.R. § 240.14a–2(b)(2) (1997) exempts a solicitation "made otherwise than on behalf of the registrant where the total number of persons solicited is not more than 10."

(4) 17 C.F.R. § 240.14a–3(f) (1997) permits communications by means of "speeches in public forums, press releases, published or broadcast opinions, statements, or advertisements appearing in a broadcast media, newspaper, magazine or other bona fide publication disseminated on a regular basis" if there is a definitive proxy statement on file with the SEC and no form of proxy or consent is provided to a security holder in connection with the communication.

(5) These modified regulations (excluding § 240.14a–2(b)(2)) became effective in October 1992. See Bernard Black, Next Steps in Proxy Reform, 18 J. Corp. L. 1, 3 (1992) (efforts by Business Roundtable to defeat proposed proxy regulations described). During the "proxy season" in the Spring of 1993, numerous institutional investors took advantage of them. For example, Leslie Scism, Midsize Companies No Longer Escape Activists' Ire, Wall St.J., Nov. 3, 1993, at C1, reports that "two top New York City fund executives used computerized databases to identify the largest shareholders [of Cracker Barrel Old Country Store, Inc.], dispatched 300 letters and now are following up with calls" in an effort to persuade Cracker Barrel to adopt a policy prohibiting discrimination against homosexuals.

2. PROXY FORMS, PROXY STATEMENTS, AND ANNUAL REPORTS

The comprehensive federal proxy regulations provide the basic structure for whatever corporate democracy that exists in the modern public corporation. The import of these rather lengthy and detailed regulations is difficult to summarize. Further, the sequence in which they are set forth by the SEC is not very logical. It is simpler to discuss them by subject matter rather than numerically even though the result is skipping around the numbers. Portions of these regulations are discussed in this Chapter, and in Chapter 14, and together all the significant areas are covered. The mere listing of the principal areas should give an introductory notion of their scope:

(a) The regulations relating to the form of proxy, the proxy statement, and annual reports are discussed immediately below;

(b) The regulation prohibiting false and misleading statements in connection with proxies is discussed in Part (3) of this Section of this Chapter;

(c) The regulation requiring the inclusion of certain shareholder proposals in the proxy solicitation is discussed in Part (4) of this Section of this Chapter.

(d) The regulation requiring communications to be mailed to securities holders in certain circumstances is discussed in Section E of this Chapter; and

(e) The regulations relating to proxy fights are discussed in Chapter 14.

a. Form of Proxy. Rule 14a–4 of the proxy regulations contains specific requirements as to the form of proxy documents. The purpose of this rule is to ensure that shareholders have the option to vote to approve or disapprove issues submitted to them, and to vote for or against the directors proposed by the persons soliciting the proxy, usually management. Broad grants of discretionary power to the nominee are prohibited subject to certain exceptions; for example, generally a proxy may not confer power to vote for a person as a director unless he is named in the proxy statement as a nominee. However, a proxy may confer discretion to vote for a person not named to replace a bona fide nominee who is unable to serve or for good cause will not serve. Similarly, a proxy must be for a specified meeting, and undated or post-dated proxies are prohibited (Rule 14a–10).

b. Proxy Statements. Rule 14a–3 requires that a proxy solicitation be accompanied by a proxy statement containing the information set forth in Schedule 14A, 17 C.F.R. § 240.14a–101 (1997). However, for several items, Schedule 14A in turn refers to two more general regulations applicable to public disclosures: Regulation S–X (relating to financial data) and Regulation S–K (relating to non financial data). The type of information required depends of course to some extent on the type of issue to be presented to the shareholders for their vote. The following is the disclosure requirements relating to the annual selection of an independent public accountant:

Item 9. Independent public accountants. If the solicitation is made on behalf of the registrant and relates to: (1) The annual (or special meeting in lieu of annual) meeting of security holders at which directors are to be elected, or a solicitation of consents or authorizations in lieu of such meeting or (2) the election, approval or ratification of the registrant's accountant, furnish the following information describing the registrant's relationship with its independent public accountant:

(a) The name of the principal accountant selected or being recommended to security holders for election, approval or ratification for the current year. If no accountant has been selected or recommended, so state and briefly describe the reasons therefor.

(b) The name of the principal accountant for the fiscal year most recently completed if different from the accountant selected or recommended for the current year or if no accountant has yet been selected or recommended for the current year.

(c) The proxy statement shall indicate: (1) Whether or not representatives of the principal accountant for the current year and for the most recently completed fiscal year are expected to be present at the security holders' meeting, (2) whether or not they will have the opportunity to make a statement if they desire to do so, and (3) whether or not such representatives are expected to be available to respond to appropriate questions.

(d) If during the registrant's two most recent fiscal years or any subsequent interim period, (1) an independent accountant who was previously engaged as the principal accountant to audit the registrant's financial statements, or an independent accountant on whom the principal accountant expressed reliance in its report regarding a significant subsidiary, has resigned (or indicated it has declined to stand for re-election after the completion of the current audit) or was dismissed, or (2) a new independent accountant has been engaged as either the principal accountant to audit the registrant's financial statements or as an independent accountant on whom the principal accountant has expressed or is expected to express reliance in its report regarding a significant subsidiary, then, notwithstanding any previous disclosure, provide the information required by Item 304(a) of Regulation S–K (§ 229.304 of this chapter).[49]

Schedule 14A, Item 9, 17 C.F.R. § 240.14a–101 (1997). The information in the proxy statement must be "clearly presented." Rule 14a–5. Furthermore, there is a procedure by which preliminary copies of certain proxy statements and soliciting material must be submitted to the SEC for review. Prior to 1992, preliminary review was required of virtually all such material, but the October 22, 1992 amendments narrowed sharply the SEC's program of making preliminary reviews of proxy documents. Proxy statements must be submitted for preliminary review only if out-of-the-ordinary matters are to be considered. Rule 14a–6. Copies of the definitive documents must be filed with the SEC when they are distributed to shareholders.

Generally, it is difficult to given an accurate description of these disclosure documents. The following is an example of a routine proxy that meets SEC requirements. The notice of annual meeting and proxy statement that accompanied this routine proxy are set forth in Appendix Two, p. 1111 infra.

---

49. [By the Editor] Item 304 of Regulation S–K applies only when there has been a change in or disagreement with the independent public accountant within the prior two most recent fiscal years. Item 304 is composed of four densely packed pages of instructions relating to various aspects of the reasons for the change and the nature of the disagreement.

BARNES & NOBLE, INC.
ANNUAL MEETING JUNE 04, 1997

Nominees for Director:

Irene R. Miller, William Dillard, II, Michael N. Rosen.

Proxy Services
4 Corporate Plaza
Corporate Park 287
Piscataway, NJ 08855

To Our Clients:

We have recently received the enclosed proxy material which relates to shares carried by us in your account but not registered in your name. We urge you to return your proxy so that we may vote your shares in accordance with your instructions. It is understood, that if you sign without marking each item on the card, you wish us to vote your shares on each such unmarked item as recommended by the party making the solicitation.

New York Stock Exchange Rule 451 states, if instructions are not received by the tenth day before the meeting, the proxy may be given at discretion by the owner of record of the stock; provided the proxy soliciting material is transmitted to the beneficial owner of the stock at least fifteen days before the meeting. When the proxy soliciting material is transmitted to the beneficial owner of the stock twenty-five days or more before the meeting, the proxy may be given fifteen days before the meeting at the discretion of the owner of record of the stock.

If you are unable to communicate with us by such date, we will nevertheless follow your instructions, even if our discretionary vote has already been given provided your instructions are received prior to the meeting.

If you wish to attend the meeting and vote in person, please contact your Financial Consultant so that a proxy can be issued for that purpose.

We would appreciate your executing the enclosed proxy and returning it to us in the self-addressed envelope also enclosed.

Please return your voting instructions promptly.
CODE 1160L (Rev 10/91)   Proxy 1/2

↓   PLEASE TEAR OFF AT PERFORATION AND RETURN SIGNED PORTION AS SOON AS POSSIBLE.   ↓

PROXY VOTING INSTRUCTIONS   Please mark choices ☒ in blue or black ink.
BARNES & NOBLE, INC. - ANNUAL MEETING JUNE 04, 1997
If no specification is made, this proxy will be voted FOR each item.   **E**

1. Election of Directors.
(see list above)

To withhold authority for an individual
nominee, check this box and use back of
form.

2. Ratification of the appointment of BDO Seidman, LLP as the independent
certified public accountants of the company for the fiscal year ending
January 31, 1998.

      FOR   WITHHOLD

      FOR ALL EXCEPT

      FOR   AGAINST   ABSTAIN

To withhold vote for an individual nominee, mark the appropriate box on the reverse side and write the nominee's name in the following space

If you have comments, mark appropriate box on the reverse side and use the following space:

INSTRUCTIONS:
1. Use the reverse side to specify your voting instructions for each proposal.
2. Sign and date the form.
3. Tear off at perforation and return this portion of the form only.

Your shares will be voted as directed herein. If signed and no direction is given for any item, it will be voted as recommended above.

```
                    000000021300      2101  1
                    07083  06777410   51266551
                    L  97106          100.0000
```

Signature   Date

Signature (if jointly owned)   Date

Check this box only if you have comments and use back of form. ☐

Check this box only if you wish to attend and vote at the meeting. ☐

PLEASE NOTE: WHEN PLACING THIS FORM IN THE BUSINESS REPLY ENVELOPE PLEASE BE SURE THE ADDRESS BELOW APPEARS THROUGH THE WINDOW.

> PROXY SERVICES
> P.O. BOX 44300
>
> NEW BRUNSWICK NJ 08944-4300

YOUR VOTE IS IMPORTANT REGARDLESS OF THE NUMBER OF SHARES YOU OWN. BY RETURNING YOUR VOTING INSTRUCTIONS PROMPTLY, YOU CAN AVOID THE INCONVENIENCE OF RECEIVING FOLLOW-UP MAILINGS PLUS HELP TO AVOID THE EXPENSES ASSOCIATED WITH SUCH ADDITIONAL MAILINGS.

c. Annual Reports. Rule 14a–3 provides that if a solicitation is by management and relates to an annual meeting at which directors are to be elected, the solicitation must be accompanied by preceded by an annual report containing the financial information and other material described in the rule. 17 C.F.R. § 240.14a–3(b)(1997). Many state incorporation statutes do not require the distribution of even such minimal information to shareholders; see, however, MBCA §§ 16.20–16.22. The SEC has long recognized that the annual report is an effective means of communication between management and security holders. In part this was because annual reports are generally readable and avoid legalistic and technical terminology. In its integration of filings under the various securities acts, the SEC broadened the information required to be included in annual reports but added a postscript:

> The Commission is aware that increasing the amount of required disclosure in annual security holder reports involves a risk that readability may be impaired. Although it is difficult to predict with certainty what the effect may be, the Commission does not believe that the changes implemented today should or will have general adverse consequences. The Commission staff, however, will continue to monitor the situation and, if

adverse effects do occur, the new disclosure requirements will be revisited promptly.

SEC Rel. No. 33–6231, 34–17114, 45 Fed.Reg. 63630, 63631 (1980). It is not practical to provide an example of an annual report, but they are widely available; indeed many issuers treat the annual report as a modest advertising device, using flashy covers and high quality paper and printing, and offering to mail copies free to any person who asks.

    d. Management's Discussion of Financial Condition and Results of Operations. 2 Loss & Seligman, Securities Regulation 668 (3d ed. 1989) states that "[o]ften the most important textual disclosure item" in the annual report is formally known as "Management's Discussion and Analysis of Financial Condition and Results of Operations," usually shortened to "MD & A." Codified as Item 303 of Regulation S–K, it is to consist of a discussion of the registrant's "financial condition, changes in financial condition and results of operations," specifically with respect to liquidity and capital resources. It "also shall provide such other information that the registrant believes to be necessary to an understanding of its financial condition, changes in financial condition and results of operations." 17 C.F.R. § 229.303(a) (1997). In the promulgating release, the purpose of the MD & A is somewhat fancifully stated to be "to give the investor an opportunity to look at the company through the eyes of management by providing both a short-and long-term analysis of the business of the company." Concept Release on Management's Discussion and Analysis of Financial Condition and Operations, Sec.Act Rel. 33–6711 (April 17, 1987), at 3. Item 303 must be responded to not only in the annual report, but also whenever financial information must be made public.

    In order to appreciate the MD & A, and the problems it creates for issuers, a brief discussion of the SEC's approach toward the disclosure of forward-looking information is helpful. See generally Edmund W. Kitch, The Theory and Practice of Securities Disclosure, 61 Brook.L.Rev. 763 (1995). Historically, the SEC insisted that financial disclosures be limited to historical facts. "Conjecture and speculations as to the future are left by the Act to the investor on the theory that he is as competent as anyone to predict the future from the given facts." Harry Heller, Disclosure Requirements Under Federal Securities Regulation, 16 Bus.Law. 300, 307, n. 31 (1961). This position that full disclosure should be limited to "hard"—that is readily verifiable—historical data and that projections or predictions were "soft"—that is, unverifiable—and therefore inherently misleading—permitted easy administration by the SEC but was unrealistic: investors generally are interested in future predictions rather than past events, investors are certainly less able to make reliable predictions about the future from past data than knowledgeable management, and undue emphasis on historical data leads to long and unreadable prospectuses and proxy statements. Consult Homer Kripke, The SEC and Corporate Disclosure: Regulation in Search of a Purpose (1979).

The SEC decided to permit projections of financial data, discussion of management objectives and goals for future performance, and the assumptions underlying such statements, ("forward looking statements") only after considerable soul-searching and a study by an advisory committee, SEC Rel. No. 33–

5993, 43 Fed.Reg. 53251 (1978). In 1979, the SEC adopted a "safe harbor" rule that provided that such statements would not be deemed false or misleading unless they were "made or reaffirmed without a reasonable basis or [were] disclosed other than in good faith." 17 C.F.R. §§ 230.175, 240.3b–6 (1997). The Private Securities Litigation Reform Act of 1995 (discussed in chapter 12) enacted a new section 21E to the Securities Exchange Act of 1934 providing a much broader and more secure "safe harbor" provision while preserving Rule 3b–6. See Edward A. Fallone, Section 10(b) and the Vagaries of Federal Common Law: The Merits of Codifying the Private Cause of Action Under a Structuralist Approach, 1997 U.Ill.L.Rev. 71, 86.

One of the most significant provisions of the Act creates a statutory safe harbor for the disclosure of forward-looking information. Congress acted to create this safe harbor out of fear that the prospect of abusive litigation has discouraged corporate managers from disclosing internal projections and similar forecasts to the marketplace. The Act's safe harbor applies to forward-looking statements made by a reporting company, its management or employees, or by auditors and underwriters engaged in its behalf.

Statements that qualify for the safe harbor cannot give rise to private liability if either of two tests is met. First, no private liability may be imposed for forward-looking statements made without actual knowledge that the statements were false or misleading. Second, no private liability may be imposed if the forward-looking statement is identified as such when made and is accompanied by meaningful cautionary language identifying important factors that could prevent the statement from becoming accurate. (Footnotes omitted)

See Jeanne Calderon and Rachel Kowal, Safe Harbors: Historical and Current Approaches to Future Forecasting, 22 J.Corp.L. 661 (1997). Rather paradoxically, this new section does not appear to have the intended effect in the relatively brief period since its enactment. Item 10(b) of Regulation S–K encourages but does not require the use of "management's projections of future economic performance" in other financial information filed with the SEC and sets forth extensive guidelines for the use and presentation of projections. 17 C.F.R. § 229.10(b) (1997).

The MD & A requirements in effect often mandate a discussion of forward-looking information in annual reports and other financial documents filed with the SEC. As discussed in 17 C.F.R. § 229.303 (Item 303), Instruction 7, "forward looking information is to be distinguished from presently known data which will impact upon future operating results, such as known future increases in costs of labor or materials. This latter data may be required to be disclosed. Any forward-looking information supplied is expressly covered by the safe harbor rules for projections. See Rule 175 under the Securities Act, 17 C.F.R. 230.175, Rule 3b–6 under the Exchange Act, 17 C.F.R. 240.3b–6, and Securities Act Release, No. 6084."

The following administrative proceeding deals with compliance with Item 303 in two SEC periodic disclosure documents, Forms 10–K and 10–Q, but is "the" SEC statement as to the interpretation of Rule 175 and the MD & A requirement.

IN THE MATTER OF CATERPILLAR, INC.

Administrative Proceeding File No. 3–7692.
SEC Rel. No. 34–30532 (1992).

The Commission deems it appropriate and in the public interest that public administrative proceedings be instituted pursuant to Section 21C of the Securities Exchange Act of 1934 ("Exchange Act") to determine whether Caterpillar Inc. ("Caterpillar") has failed to comply with Section 13(a) of the Exchange Act and Rules 13a–1 and 13a–13 promulgated under the Exchange Act in connection with reports on Form 10–K and Form 10–Q filed with the Commission. Accordingly, such proceedings are hereby instituted.

In anticipation of the institution of these administrative proceedings, Caterpillar has submitted an Offer of Settlement for the purpose of disposing of the issued raised in these proceedings. * * *

On the basis of this Order and the Respondent's Offer of Settlement, the Commission finds the following: * * *

This matter involves Caterpillar's failure in its Form 10–K for the year ended December 31, 1989, and it Form 10–Q for the first quarter of 1990 to comply with Item 303 of Regulation S–K, Management's Discussion and Analysis of Financial Conditions and Results of Operations ("MD & A"). Specifically, the MD & A rules required Caterpillar to disclose information about the 1989 earnings of Caterpillar Brasil, S.A. ("CBSA"), its wholly owned Brazilian subsidiary, and uncertainties about CBSA's 1990 earnings.

1. CBSA's 1989 Results

Caterpillar has had a Brazilian subsidiary since the 1950's. Nineteen eighty-nine was an exceptionally profitable year for CBSA. That year, without accounting for the effect of integration, CBSA accounted for some 23 percent of Caterpillar's net profits of $497 million, although its revenues represented only 5 percent of the parent company's revenues. In 1989, CBSA's operating profit was in line with prior years but a number or nonoperating items contributed to greater than usual overall profit. Those items included currency translation gains, export subsidies, interest income, and Brazilian tax loss carryforwards. Many of these gains were caused by the hyperinflation in Brazil in 1989 and the fact that the dollar-cruzado exchange rate lagged behind inflation.

CBSA's financial results were presented on a consolidated basis with the remainder of Caterpillar's operations. Thus, the impact of DBSA's operations on Caterpillar's overall results was not apparent from the face of Caterpillar's financial statements or the notes thereto.

2. Management's View of CBSA

Caterpillar was and is a highly integrated organization. Its various divisions and subsidiaries were, and are, very interdependent. As a consequence, Caterpillar typically viewed and managed the organization on a consolidated basis. While unadjusted profit numbers for subsidiaries and divisions were available to management, they were not viewed by management as reliable indicators of that subsidiary's or division's contribution to the consolidated enterprise. The various divisions and subsidiaries were not viewed as profit centers but rather as cost centers. Profit and results of operations were managed on a consolidated basis. Because of that management perspective, the profit contribution of each subsidiary or division has not historically been used as a basis for personnel, product sourcing or disclosure decisions.

In January of 1990, accounting department personnel began to separately analyze CBSA's 1989 results compared with its 1990 forecast. In the process of that analysis, the various components of CBSA's results were aggregated. The result of that analysis was conveyed to top management and then to the board. By the middle of February 1990—i.e., at least two weeks before Caterpillar filed its 1989 Form 10-K—Caterpillar's top management had recognized that, to adequately understand Caterpillar's 1990 forecast, it was necessary to understand CBSA's 1990 forecast. Management also recognized that CBSA's future performance was exceptionally difficult to predict—particularly in light of anticipated sweeping economic reforms to be instituted by a new administration in Brazil—and that there were substantial uncertainties whether CBSA would repeat its exceptional 1989 earnings in 1990.

The board of directors was told in February 1990 that Brazil was "volatile" and that "the impact of Brazil is so significant to reduced 1990 projected results, [management] felt it was necessary to explain it [to the directors] in some detail."

Minutes of the February 1990 board meeting include the following about Brazil:

> [Management] commented on results of operations in Brazil because of the significant [negative] impact they will have on overall results for 1990. Beginning in February 1990 and continuing through the rest of the year management departed from this usual practice of viewing the company as a whole and provided projections to the board of directors which separated out the impact of Brazil.

During the interim between the February board meeting and the next board meeting, held on April 11, 1990, a new administration took office in Brazil. Fernando Collor de Mello, who had been elected president of Brazil in December 1989, was inaugurated on March 15, 1990, "putting an end," as one Brazilian business journal put it, "to weeks of intense speculation as to what economic measures he will actually announce." Collor immediately instituted sweeping economic and monetary changes in an effort to bring Brazil's hyperinflation under control. * * *

When the Caterpillar board met on April 11, management gave presentations in which it discussed, among other things, the likely negative effects the Collor plan would have on CBSA's sales and profits:

> At our last meeting, we reviewed the impact that [CBSA] is expected to have on our 1990 results * * *. Brazil is volatile and difficult to predict. Their recently announced economic reforms have made the situation even more uncertain.

> The impact of these reforms is not at all clear, so we have made no attempt to change the forecast. However, it's difficult to see any short-term positives, so there is considerable risk that Brazil's new economic plan could bring additional pressure on our 1990 profit.

[Management] * * * also noted * * * that the profit in Brazil will be substantially lower than in 1989.

Throughout April and May of 1990 Caterpillar continued to monitor the events in Brazil and their effects on CBSA, including the consequences of the Collor plan on Caterpillar. * * * However, after a review of April and May results, the company concluded the new economic policies would cause CBSA to suffer significant losses in 1990. It also concluded that those losses would not likely be balanced by gains in other parts of the world and consolidated results would be lower than originally anticipated.

At 8:00 a.m. on Monday, June 25, 1990, before the beginning of trading, the company voluntarily issued a press release explaining that the anticipated results for 1990 would be substantially lower than previously projected. * * *

3. PREPARATION AND REVIEW OF CATERPILLAR'S PERIODIC REPORTS

The MD & A sections of the 1989 10–K and 10–Q for the first quarter of 1990 were drafted by employees in Caterpillar's accounting department.[50] Prior to the issuance of those reports, the language of the MD & A was reviewed by the Controller, Financial Vice President, Treasurer, and the company's legal, economic, and public affairs departments. After that, the language of the MD & A was reviewed by the top officers of the Company.

The board of directors reviewed the final draft of the 1989 Form 10–K, including the MD & A, at the February 1990 board meeting. At that time, the board, including top management, who were members of the board, received a written opinion of the company's independent auditor that the financial statements complied with the rules and regulations of the Commission,[51] and also an opinion of the company's General Counsel that the Form 10–K complied with all the rules and regulations of the Commission.

In rendering their opinion on the financial statements contained in Caterpillar's 1989 Form 10–K, the auditor had reviewed the disclosure set forth in the MD & A for inconsistencies with the financial statements but did not opine on the MD & A. The General Counsel was aware of management's concerns regarding Brazil, however, he disregarded management's statements about Brazil when reviewing and opining upon the MD & A disclosure regarding Brazil.

---

50. [By the Commission] The same employees also drafted portions of management's presentations regarding Brazil to the February and April 1990 meetings of the board of directors.

51. [By the Commission] The Auditor's opinion stated:

We have audited the consolidated financial statements of Caterpillar, Inc. and subsidiaries as of December 31, 1989, 1988 and 1987 and for each of the three years then ended. In our report appearing on Page A–3 of the Appendix to the 1990 Annual Meeting Proxy Statement, we expressed our opinion that the Company's consolidated financial statements present fairly, in all material respects, financial position, results of operations and cash flows for these periods, in conformity with generally accepted accounting principles.

In connection with our 1989 audit, we have also read the full text of the 1989 Form 10–K and have provided our consent to the application of our report to the consolidated financial statements and schedules to be included in the 1989 Form 10–K to be filed with the Securities and Exchange Commission. In our opinion these comply in all material respects with the accounting requirements of the Securities Exchange Act of 1934 and the published rules and regulations of the Commission thereunder.

4. CATERPILLAR'S DISCLOSURE REGARDING CBSA

Neither the 1989 Form 10–K nor the first quarter 1990 Form 10–Q indicated the extent to which CBSA had affected Caterpillar's bottom line in 1989, nor did they indicate that a decline in CBSA's future results could have a material adverse effect on Caterpillar's bottom line in 1990.[52] * * *

Nothing in the MD & A section of the 1989 Form 10–K suggested the disproportionate impact of CBSA's profits on Caterpillar's 1989 overall profitability. Similarly, the 1989 Form 10–K and the Form 10–Q for the first quarter of 1990 did not adequately mention management's uncertainty about CBSA's 1990 performance.

II. *Applicable Law*

*** A. *Management's Discussion and Analysis as Required by Item 303 of Regulation S–K*

For reports on Form 10–K, Item 303(a) requires the registrant to discuss the liquidity, capital resources, and results of operations of the registrant and to "provide such other information that the registrant believes to be necessary to an understanding of its financial condition, changes in financial condition and results of operations." Item 303(a) also specifically requires

> [W]here in the registrant's judgment a discussion of segment information or of other subdivisions of the registrant's business would be appropriate to an understanding of such business, the discussion shall focus on each relevant, reportable segment or other subdivision of the business and on the registrant as a whole.

Test

In discussing results of operations the registrant is to "[d]escribe any unusual or infrequent events or transactions * * * that materially affected the amount of reported income from continuing operations and in each case, indicate the extent to which income was so affected." Item 303(a)(3)(i). Furthermore, the registrant is to describe other significant components of revenues or expenses

---

52. [By the Commission] The 1989 Form 10–K contained the following statements about Brazil:

Sales Outside the United States

Dealer machine sales rose in most selling areas, with demand especially strong in Europe, Brazil, Australia, and the Far East.

Latin America

Sales rose 14% in 1989, the sixth consecutive year of improvement. The biggest gain was in Brazil, where very high inflation rates increased demand for hard goods, including earth moving equipment. (Given the extraordinarily high rate of inflation in Brazil, many contractors preferred to own hard assets, such as equipment, rather than depreciating cruzados.) Toward year-end, however, sales growth in Brazil moderated as interest rates rose.

Outlook

Latin American countries continue to be plagued with debt problems. However, debt rescheduling; stable profitable commodity prices; and increased privatization should help business in some countries. Sales in Brazil, however, could be hurt by post-election policies which will likely aim at curbing inflation.

The Form 10–Q for the first quarter of 1990 contained the following statements about Brazil:

Demand also rose in a number of Latin American countries. In Brazil, demand increased over one year ago despite the uncertainty of the Brazilian economy.

The company hasn't changed its outlook from what was stated in its 1989 annual report.

Caterpillar Chairman George Schaefer said:

First-quarter sales were somewhat stronger than anticipated. Nevertheless, the company continues to be concerned about tight monetary policies in major industrial countries; the recent weakening of the Japanese yen; and the uncertainty of the economic situation in Brazil.

that should be described to allow a reader of the company's financial statements to understand the registrant's results of operations. Id.

As a separate component of the discussion of results of operations, the registrant is to discuss "any known trends or uncertainties that have had or that the registrant reasonably expects will have a material favorable or unfavorable impact on net sales or revenues or income from continuing operations." Item 303(a)(3)(ii). "The discussion and analysis shall focus specifically on material events and uncertainties known to management that would cause reported financial information not to be necessarily indicative of future operating results." Instruction 3 to Item 303(a). Registrants are instructed to discuss both new matters which will have an impact on future results, and matters which have previously had an impact on reported operations but which are not expected to have an impact on future operations. Id.

For interim reports such as a Form 10–Q, Item 303(b) requires a discussion and analysis of the results of operations to enable the reader to assess material changes in financial condition and results of operations that have occurred since the end of the preceding fiscal year. Item 303(b). Discussions of material changes in results of operations must identify any significant elements of the registrant's income or loss from continuing operations which do not arise from or are not necessarily representative of the registrant's business. Instruction 4 to Item 303(b).

B. The MD & A Release

In 1989, the Commission determined that additional interpretive guidance was needed regarding a number of areas of MD & A disclosure and published an interpretive release. Release Nos. 33–6835, 34–26831, IC–16961, FR–36 (May 18, 1989) (hereafter "MD & A Release"). Drawing on earlier releases, the MD & A Release noted the underlying rationale for requiring MD & A disclosure and management's core responsibility in providing that disclosure: The MD & A is needed because, without such a narrative explanation, a company's financial statements and accompanying footnotes

> may be insufficient for an investor to judge the quality of earnings and the likelihood that past performance is indicative of future performance. MD & A is intended to give the investor an opportunity to look at the company through the eyes of management by providing both a short and long-term analysis of the business of the company.

MD & A Release Par. III.A (quoting Securities Act Release No. 6771 (April 24, 1987)). It is management's responsibility in the MD & A

> to identify and address those key variables and other qualitative and quantitative factors which are peculiar to and necessary for an understanding and evaluation of the company.[53]

MD & A Release Par. III.A (quoting Securities Act Release No. 6349 (September 28, 1981)). The MD & A Release further notes,

---

53. [By the Commission] Although an auditor or other third party may review the MD & A section of a periodic report, the substance of the S–K Item 303 disclosure is the responsibility of management.

The MD & A requirements are intentionally flexible and general. Because no two registrants are identical, good MD & A disclosure for one registrant is not necessarily good * * * for another. The same is true for MD & A disclosure of the same registrant in different years.

MD & A Release Par. IV.

As to prospective information, the MD & A Release sets forth the following test for determining when disclosure is required:

Where a trend, demand, commitment, event or uncertainty is known, management must make two assessments:

(1) Is the known trend, demand, commitment, event or uncertainty likely to come to fruition? If management determines that it is not reasonably likely to occur, no disclosure is required.

(2) If management cannot make that determination, it must evaluate objectively the consequences of the known trend, demand, commitment, event or uncertainty, on the assumption that it will come to fruition.

Disclosure is then required unless management determines that a material effect on the registrant's financial condition or results of operations is not reasonably likely to occur.

MD & A Release Par. III.B. Where the test for disclosure is met, "MD & A disclosure of the effects [of the uncertainty,] quantified to the extent reasonably practicable, [is] required."[54] Id. * * *

C. Analysis

Regulation S–K requires disclosure of information necessary to understand the registrant's financial statements. Item 303(a); MD & A Release Par. III.A. Caterpillar's failure to include required information about CBSA in the MD & A left investors with an incomplete picture of Caterpillar's financial condition and results of operations and denied them the opportunity to see the company "through the eyes of management." MD & A Release Par. IV.

Specifically, by failing (i) in its Annual Report on Form 10–K for the year ended December 31, 1989 to provide an adequate discussion and analysis of the impact of CBSA on its 1989 results of operations as contained in its financial statements, and (ii) to adequately disclose in its 1989 Form 10–K and in its Quarterly Report on Form 10–Q for the first quarter of 1990 known uncertainties reasonably likely to have a material effect on Caterpillar's future results of operations, due to CBSA's questionable ability to repeat its 1989 performance, Caterpillar violated Section 13(a) of the Exchange Act and Rules 13a–1 and 13a–13 thereunder.[55] * * *

---

54. [By the Commission] The Commission has noted:

Both required disclosure regarding the future impact of presently known trends, events or uncertainties and optional forward-looking information may involve some prediction or projection. The distinction between the two rests with the nature of the prediction required. Required disclosure is based on currently known trends, events, and uncertainties that are reasonably expected to have material effects * * *. In contrast, optional forward-looking disclosure involves anticipating a future trend or event or anticipating a less predictable impact of a known event, trend or uncertainty.

Securities Act Release No. 6711 (April 24, 1987) (final paragraph of Part III); MD & A Release P III.B. (text at n. 21).

55. [By the Commission] During the time period in question, Caterpillar did not have adequate procedures in place designed to en-

Given the magnitude of CBSA's contribution to Caterpillar's overall earnings, disclosure of the extent of that contribution was required under the MD & A provisions of Regulation S–K since CBSA's earnings materially affected Caterpillar's reported income from continuing operations. See, Item 303(a)(3)(i). Furthermore, the MD & A should have discussed various factors which contributed to CBSA's earnings including currency translation gains, export subsidies, interest income, and Brazilian tax loss carryforwards since such items were significant components of CBSA's revenues that should have been identified and addressed in order for a reader of the company's financial statements to understand Caterpillar's results of operations. * * *

By the time of the February 14, 1990, board meeting—two weeks before Caterpillar's Form 10–K for 1989 was filed—management could not conclude that lower earnings from CBSA were not reasonably likely to occur, nor could management conclude that a material effect on Caterpillar's results of operations was not reasonably likely to occur due to CBSA's lower earnings. It was at that meeting that management told the company's directors "the impact of Brazil is so significant to reduced 1990 projected results, * * * it was necessary to explain it [to the directors] in some detail."

By the end of the first quarter of 1990, before Caterpillar's Form 10–Q for the first quarter of 1990 was filed, management had concluded that "the profit in Brazil will be substantially lower than in 1989." Therefore, it became even more apparent that management could not conclude that lower earnings from CBSA were not reasonably likely to occur, nor could management conclude that a material effect on Caterpillar's results of operations was not reasonably likely to occur due to CBSA's lower earnings. Thus, discussion of the uncertainties surrounding CBSA's earnings, and possible material future impact on Caterpillar's overall financial condition and results of operations was required. * * *

Caterpillar's MD & A disclosure was deficient in two respects. First, Caterpillar's Annual Report on Form 10–K for the year ended December 31, 1989 should have discussed the impact of CBSA on Caterpillar's overall results of operations. Second, both the Annual Report on Form 10–K for 1989 and the Quarterly Report on Form 10–Q for the first quarter of 1990 should have discussed the future uncertainties regarding CBSA's operations, the possible risk of Caterpillar having materially lower earnings as a result of that risk and, to the extent reasonably practicable, quantified the impact of such risk. MD & A Release Par.III.B. The MD & A disclosure in the 1989 Form 10–K and the Form 10–Q for the first quarter of 1990 failed to adequately disclose the risk of lower earnings and did not attempt to quantify the impact of lower earnings from CBSA on Caterpillar. * * *

Notes

(1) Edmund W. Kitch, The Theory and Practice of Securities Disclosure, 61 Brook.L.Rev. 763, 807–19 (1995):

The Commission has not been pleased with issuer compliance with Item 303. In Release 33–6835, issued in May 1989, the Commission reported that the staff had undertaken "a special review of the MD & A disclosures to assess the adequacy of disclosure practices and to identify any common areas of

sure compliance with the MD & A requirements.

deficiencies." Of the 218 registrants reviewed, 206 received letters of comment, many of which related to more than one report. * * * The Commission treated this high level of deficiency as a problem of lack of understanding by registrants, and proceeded to discuss what disclosure was required and to give examples of adequate disclosure. * * * As it turned out the Commission had had enough of preaching. It was time for a test case, and the object of the test case turned out to be the Caterpillar Corporation. * * *

(2) Professor Kitch also pointed out that the SEC's analysis of the economic importance of the Brazil operations to Caterpillar was less than complete, that the issue was not the profitability of the operations of Caterpillar in Brazil had declined, but whether the overall profitability of Caterpillar had declined as a result. It was quite possible, he suggests, that the company could have made the forecast of 1990 earnings it did in good faith and did not learn until later that its other operations would not offset the negative events in Brazil. His strongest criticism, however, was directed at the reliance by the SEC on management's communications with the board of directors:

> The most troubling aspect of Caterpillar is the use of the management's communications with the board of directors as a measure of what is known by management, and what is material. After Caterpillar, registrants are wise to review management's communications with the board of directors to insure that they correspond to the company's SEC filings. If the information fits within Item 303, it will also have to be disclosed to shareholders. One way to prevent communications with the board from flowing immediately to the public-disclosure documents would be for management to adopt a guarded and obscure style with the board: "Management thought the Board might be interested to learn about the unusual developments in Brazil, which have been hard on the Brazilian economy. Caterpillar, of course, has an operation in Brazil, and these developments are hard on the members of the Caterpillar family in Brazil. Management is sure that the Board joins us in extending expressions of sympathy and concern to all Brazilians. Just in passing, you might also be interested to learn that some of the many analyses of our operating results show Brazil as having made an important contribution to our profits last year, so you know that Caterpillareans in Brazil are important members of our family. It looks like they won't be able to help us as much this year, but of course we know that the other worldwide members of the Caterpillar family will be striving to make up the difference. By the way, did you guys see that show on television last night with the talking parrot?" Such a style of communication would address the concern that direct and forceful communication would require disclosure of the information so communicated, but it would not serve the needs of effective board governance. Even more troubling, some managements may be tempted not to communicate with the board at all in order to avoid the public disclosure requirement of Item 303.

> Caterpillar made two mistakes. First of all, its communications to the market resulted in a sharp drop in the stock price, an event likely to bring trouble from either the Commission or private litigants. Second, in its conference call to analysts after the press release, Caterpillar mentioned the importance of Brazil to the company's 1989 earnings. No doubt the thought was to downplay the significance of the earnings decline, but when it had reported the 1989 earnings, it had not downplayed their significance by noting that the earnings had been significantly boosted by odd developments in Brazil that were unlikely to continue. In other words, Caterpillar was happy to take advantage of the Brazilian explanation when it suited its

purpose, but had ignored it when it did not. If Caterpillar's legal position was to be that the Brazilian factor was unimportant, then it needed to adhere to that position for better and for worse.

Caterpillar agreed as part of its settlement to "implement and maintain procedures designed to ensure compliance with Item 303 of Regulation S–K." What these procedures might be the opinion does not say. The opinion does say, however, that the procedures which Caterpillar had been following were insufficient * * * [but does] not say what more Caterpillar was to do. Perhaps it is to form an interdepartmental oversight committee for Item 303, or hire another lawyer specifically to advise on Item 303 compliance. Caterpillar received a slap on the wrist;[56] still, serious questions were raised: Will the SEC continue to engage in a low-level wrestling match with issuers, or will it escalate its campaign to ensure that securities holders are able to "look at the company through the eyes of management?" What further consequence might be in store for an issuer that fails to identify the known trends required by item 303? The SEC could proceed directly against the issuer and the responsible officers and directors or recommend the matter for criminal prosecution.

(3) See Quinton F. Seamons, et al., Requirements and Pitfalls of MD & A Disclosure, 11 Insights, No. 8 (Aug. 1997), at 9.

3. FALSE OR MISLEADING STATEMENTS IN CONNECTION WITH PROXY SOLICITATIONS

REGULATION 14A. SOLICITATION OF PROXIES
17 C.F.R. § 240.14a–9 (1997).

§ 240.14a–9 FALSE OR MISLEADING STATEMENTS

(a) No solicitation subject to this regulation shall be made by means of any proxy statement, form of proxy, notice of meeting or other communication, written or oral, containing any statement which, at the time and in the light of the circumstances under which it is made, is false or misleading with respect to any material fact, or which omits to state any material fact necessary in order to make the statements therein not false or misleading or necessary to correct any statement in any earlier communication with respect to the solicitation of a proxy for the same meeting or subject matter which has become false or misleading.

---

56. [By the Author] Caterpillar and certain of its officers and directors were sued in July 1990 in two class actions filed in the United States District Court for the Central District of Illinois "on behalf of all persons (other than the defendants) who purchased or otherwise acquired common stock of Caterpillar and certain options relating to common stock of Caterpillar, between Jan. 19, 1990 and June 26, 1990.... The complaints allege that the defendants fraudulently issued public statements and reports during the class period which were misleading in that they failed to disclose material adverse information relating to Caterpillar's Brazilian operations, its factory modernization program and its reorganization plan." Form 10–K for the Caterpillar Corporation for the Year Ending Dec. 31, 1992, at 7, Item 3,

filed March 3, 1993. The class actions are pending. * * * The impact of the SEC action on the class action (which may result in the payment of substantial sums by or on behalf of Caterpillar) is unclear. * * * The SEC settlement order is based only on a violation of the reporting requirements contained in Securities and Exchange Act § 13(a), 15 U.S.C. § 78m(a) (1995). The class plaintiffs, on the other hand, will have to show a violation of Securities and Exchange Act § 10(b), 15 U.S.C. S 78j(b) (1995), and a resulting loss from the violation. At the very least, the fact that Caterpillar has agreed that its disclosures were in violation of the Act will assist the "atmosphere" of the lawsuit in a manner favorable to plaintiffs. * * *

(b) The fact that a proxy statement, form of proxy or other soliciting material has been filed with or examined by the Commission shall not be deemed a finding by the Commission that such material is accurate or complete or not false or misleading, or that the Commission has passed upon the merits of or approved any statement contained therein or any matter to be acted upon by security holders. No representation contrary to the foregoing shall be made.

Note: The following are some examples of what, depending upon particular facts and circumstances, may be misleading within the meaning of this section.

(a) Predictions as to specific future market values.

(b) Material which directly or indirectly impugns character, integrity or personal reputation, or directly or indirectly makes charges concerning improper, illegal or immoral conduct or associations, without factual foundation.

(c) Failure to so identify a proxy statement, form of proxy and other soliciting material as to clearly distinguish it from the soliciting material of any other person or persons soliciting for the same meeting or subject matter.

(d) Claims made prior to a meeting regarding the results of a solicitation.

Notes

(1) Is this provision a restatement of common law principles or is it broader? In a pre–1964 case, Bresnick v. Home Title Guar. Co., 175 F.Supp. 723 (S.D.N.Y. 1959), the Court stated that the test at common law "is not compliance with the technical rules, but rather whether the proxy soliciting material was so tainted with fraud that an inequitable result was accomplished." 175 F.Supp. at 725.

(2) The note to rule 14a–9 formerly included, as examples of potentially misleading statements, "predictions as to specific future market values, earnings, or dividends," and was changed to its present form in July 1979 to reflect the SEC policy with respect to forward looking statements described briefly in the prior section. SEC Rel. No. 34–15944, 44 Fed.Reg. 38810 (1979).

J.I. CASE CO. v. BORAK

Supreme Court of the United States, 1964.
377 U.S. 426, 84 S.Ct. 1555, 12 L.Ed.2d 423.

Mr. Justice Clark delivered the opinion of the Court.

This is a civil action brought by respondent, a stockholder of petitioner J.I. Case Company, charging deprivation of the preemptive rights of respondent and other shareholders by reason of a merger between Case and the American Tractor Corporation. It is alleged that the merger was effected through the circulation of a false and misleading proxy statement by those proposing the merger. The complaint was in two counts, the first based on diversity and claiming a breach of the directors' fiduciary duty to the stockholders. The second count alleged a violation of § 14(a) of the Securities Exchange Act of 1934 with reference to the proxy solicitation material. The trial court held that as to this count it had no power to redress the alleged violations of the Act but was limited solely to the granting of declaratory relief thereon under § 27 of the Act.[57] The court held Wis.Stat., 1961, § 180.405(4), which requires posting security for expenses in derivative actions,[58] applicable to both counts, except that portion of Count 2 requesting declaratory relief. It ordered the respondent to furnish a bond in the amount of $75,000 thereunder and upon his failure to do so, dismissed the complaint, save that part of Count 2 seeking a declaratory judgment. On interlocutory appeal the Court of Appeals reversed on both counts, holding that the District Court had the power to grant remedial relief and that the Wisconsin statute was not applicable. 317 F.2d 838. We granted certiorari. 375 U.S. 901, 84 S.Ct. 195, 11 L.Ed.2d 143. We consider only the question of whether § 27 of the Act authorizes a federal cause of action for rescission or damages to a corporate stockholder with respect to a consummated merger which was authorized pursuant to the use of a proxy statement alleged to contain false and misleading statements violative of § 14(a) of the Act. This being the sole

57. [By the Court] Section 27 of the Act, provides in part: "The district courts of the United States, the Supreme Court of the District of Columbia, and the United States courts of any Territory or other place subject to the jurisdiction of the United States shall have exclusive jurisdiction of violations of this title or the rules and regulations thereunder, and of all suits in equity and actions at law brought to enforce any liability or duty created by this title or the rules and regulations thereunder. Any criminal proceeding may be brought in the district wherein any act or transaction constituting the violation occurred. Any suit or action to enforce any liability or duty created by this title or rules and regulations thereunder, or to enjoin any violation of such title or rules and regulations, may be brought in any such district or in the district wherein the defendant is found or is an inhabitant or transacts business, and process in such cases may be served in any other district of which the defendant is an inhabitant or wherever the defendant may be found."

58. [By the Editor] Deborah A. DeMott, Shareholder Derivative Actions: Law and Practice § 3:01 (1987) describes "security for expenses" statutes as follows:

Nineteen states have statutes permitting the corporation, and in some instances other defendants, to demand that the plaintiff in a derivative suit provide security for the expenses, including attorney fees, that may be incurred in the defense of the suit. The amount of security is determined by the court. With few exceptions, these statutes apply *only* to plaintiffs whose stockholdings fall beneath a percentage amount stated in the statute, typically five percent of a class of outstanding stock or $25,000 in market value. Defendants may have recourse to the security if they prevail in the litigation, although some statutes limit recourse to those cases which the court determines were brought without reasonable cause. * * *

Plaintiffs may be able to avoid the security requirements by purchasing more shares themselves or by seeking the intervention as plaintiffs of additional stockholders, so that the aggregate holdings of the plaintiffs and intervenors exceed the amount or percentage provided by the statute. The potential impact of security for expense statutes is also limited by the fact that Congress has never enacted a general security statute applicable to all derivative actions raising federal claims. * * *

The significance of security for expense statutes is that, in the cases to which they apply, the plaintiff confronts a substantial economic risk should the defendants prevail in the action. This risk is one that is not typically imposed on the plaintiff in the United States; the "American" rule generally is that, with a few exceptions, both parties bear their own litigation expenses, including, most importantly, attorney fees, and that the court does not shift the prevailing party's attorney fees to the nonprevailing party at the termination of the litigation. When applicable, security for expense statutes obviously depart from this basic rule; further, the statutes, by permitting defendants to demand that security be posted well in advance of a final outcome to the litigation, may impose a greater economic risk on the plaintiff than would a rule which simply shifted the successful defendant's expenses to the plaintiff after the final resolution of the litigation. It was originally believed that these statutes would deter baseless derivative suits, or suits brought solely to extract a settlement through the "annoyance value" of the suit. The present trend appears to be away from reposing great confidence in the ability of security requirements to deter strike suits.

Reprinted with permission. Published by Callaghan & Co.

question raised by petitioners in their petition for certiorari, we will not consider other questions subsequently presented.

I.

Respondent, the owner of 2,000 shares of common stock of Case acquired prior to the merger, brought this suit based on diversity jurisdiction seeking to enjoin a proposed merger between Case and the American Tractor Corporation (ATC) on various grounds, including breach of the fiduciary duties of the Case directors, self-dealing among the management of Case and ATC and misrepresentations contained in the material circulated to obtain proxies. The injunction was denied and the merger was thereafter consummated. Subsequently successive amended complaints were filed and the case was heard on the aforesaid two-count complaint. The claims pertinent to the asserted violation of the Securities Exchange Act were predicated on diversity jurisdiction as well as on § 27 of the Act. They alleged: that petitioners, or their predecessors, solicited or permitted their names to be used in the solicitation of proxies of Case stockholders for use at a special stockholders' meeting at which the proposed merger with ATC was to be voted upon; that the proxy solicitation material so circulated was false and misleading in violation of § 14(a) of the Act and Rule 14a–9 which the Commission had promulgated thereunder; that the merger was approved at the meeting by a small margin of votes and was thereafter consummated; that the merger would not have been approved but for the false and misleading statements in the proxy solicitation material; and that Case stockholders were damaged thereby. The respondent sought judgment holding the merger void and damages for himself and all other stockholders similarly situated, as well as such further relief "as equity shall require." The District Court ruled that the Wisconsin security for expenses statute did not apply to Count 2 since it arose under federal law. However, the court found that its jurisdiction was limited to declaratory relief in a private, as opposed to a government, suit alleging violation of § 14(a) of the Act. Since the additional equitable relief and damages prayed for by the respondent would, therefore, be available only under state law, it ruled those claims subject to the security for expenses statute. After setting the amount of security at $75,000 and upon the representation of counsel that the security would not be posted, the court dismissed the complaint, save that portion of Count 2 seeking a declaration that the proxy solicitation material was false and misleading and that the proxies and, hence, the merger were void.

II.

It appears clear that private parties have a right under § 27 to bring suit for violation of § 14(a) of the Act. Indeed, this section specifically grants the appropriate District Courts jurisdiction over "all suits in equity and actions at law brought to enforce any liability or duty created" under the Act. The petitioners make no concessions, however, emphasizing that Congress made no specific reference to a private right of action in § 14(a); that, in any event, the right would not extend to derivative suits and should be limited to prospective relief only. In addition, some of the petitioners argue that the merger can be dissolved only if it was fraudulent or non-beneficial, issues upon which the proxy material would not bear. But the causal relationship of the proxy material and the merger are questions of fact to be resolved at trial, not here. We therefore do not discuss this point further.

III.

While the respondent contends that his Count 2 claim is not a derivative one, we need not embrace that view, for we believe that a right of action exists as to both derivative and direct causes.

The purpose of § 14(a) is to prevent management or others from obtaining authorization for corporate action by means of deceptive or inadequate disclosure in proxy solicitation. The section stemmed from the congressional belief that "[f]air corporate suffrage is an important right that should attach to every equity security bought on a public exchange." H.R.Rep. No. 1383, 73d Cong., 2d Sess., 13. It was intended to "control the conditions under which proxies may be solicited with a view to preventing the recurrence of abuses which * * * [had] frustrated the free exercise of the voting rights of stockholders." Id., at 14. "Too often proxies are solicited without explanation to the stockholder of the real nature of the questions for which authority to cast his vote is sought." S.Rep. No. 792, 73d Cong., 2d Sess., 12. These broad remedial purposes are evidenced in the language of the section which makes it "unlawful for any person * * * to solicit or to permit the use of his name to solicit any proxy or consent or authorization in respect of any security * * * registered on any national securities exchange in contravention of such rules and regulations as the Commission may prescribe as necessary or appropriate in the public interest *or for the protection of investors.*" (Italics supplied.) While this language makes no specific reference to a private right of action, among its chief purposes is "the protection of investors," which certainly implies the availability of judicial relief where necessary to achieve that result.

The injury which a stockholder suffers from corporate action pursuant to a deceptive proxy solicitation ordinarily flows from the damage done the corporation, rather than from the damage inflicted directly upon the stockholder. The damage suffered results not from the deceit practiced on him alone but rather from the deceit practiced on the stockholders as a group. To hold that derivative actions are not within the sweep of the section would therefore be tantamount to a denial of private relief. Private enforcement of the proxy rules provides a necessary supplement to Commission action. As in antitrust treble damage litigation, the possibility of civil damages or injunctive relief serves as a most effective weapon in the enforcement of the proxy requirements. The Commission advises that it examines over 2,000 proxy statements annually and each of them must necessarily be expedited. Time does not permit an independent examination of the facts set out in the proxy material and this results in the Commission's acceptance of the representations contained therein at their face value, unless contrary to other material on file with it. Indeed, on the allegations of respondent's complaint, the proxy material failed to disclose alleged unlawful market manipulation of the stock of ATC, and this unlawful manipulation would not have been apparent to the Commission until after the merger.

We, therefore, believe that under the circumstances here it is the duty of the courts to be alert to provide such remedies as are necessary to make effective the congressional purpose. As was said in Sola Electric Co. v. Jefferson Electric Co., 317 U.S. 173, 176, 63 S.Ct. 172, 174, 87 L.Ed. 165 (1942):

When a federal statute condemns an act as unlawful, the extent and nature of the legal consequences of the condemnation, though left by the statute to judicial determination, are nevertheless federal questions, the answers to which are to be derived from the statute and the federal policy which it has adopted.

It is for the federal courts "to adjust their remedies so as to grant the necessary relief" where federally secured rights are invaded. "And it is also well settled that where legal rights have been invaded, and a federal statute provides for a general right to sue for such invasion, federal courts may use any available remedy to make good the wrong done." Bell v. Hood, 327 U.S. 678, 684, 66 S.Ct. 773, 777, 90 L.Ed. 939 (1946). Section 27 grants the District Courts jurisdiction "of all suits in equity and actions at law brought to enforce any liability or duty created by this title * * *." In passing on almost identical language found in the Securities Act of 1933, the Court found the words entirely sufficient to fashion a remedy to rescind a fraudulent sale, secure restitution and even to enforce the right to restitution against a third party holding assets of the vendor. Deckert v. Independence Shares Corp., 311 U.S. 282, 61 S.Ct. 229, 85 L.Ed. 189 (1940). This significant language was used:

> "The power to *enforce* implies the power to make effective the right of recovery afforded by the Act. And the power to make the right of recovery effective implies the power to utilize any of the procedures or actions normally available to the litigant according to the exigencies of the particular case." At 288 of 311 U.S., at 233 of 61 S.Ct.

Nor do we find merit in the contention that such remedies are limited to prospective relief. This was the position taken in Dann v. Studebaker–Packard Corp., 6 Cir., 288 F.2d 201, where it was held that the "preponderance of questions of state law which would have to be interpreted and applied in order to grant the relief sought. * * * is so great that the federal question involved * * * is really negligible in comparison." At 214. But we believe that the overriding federal law applicable here would, where the facts required, control the appropriateness of redress despite the provisions of state corporation law, for it "is not uncommon for federal courts to fashion federal law where federal rights are concerned." Textile Workers Union of America v. Lincoln Mills, 353 U.S. 448, 457, 77 S.Ct. 912, 918, 1 L.Ed.2d 972 (1957). In addition, the fact that questions of state law must be decided does not change the character of the right; it remains federal. As Chief Justice Marshall said in Osborn v. Bank of United States, 9 Wheat. 738, 6 L.Ed. 204 (1824):

> If this were sufficient to withdraw a case from the jurisdiction of the federal Courts, almost every case, although involving the construction of a law, would be withdrawn * * *. At 819–820 of 9 Wheat.

Moreover, if federal jurisdiction were limited to the granting of declaratory relief, victims of deceptive proxy statements would be obliged to go into state courts for remedial relief. And if the law of the State happened to attach no responsibility to the use of misleading proxy statements, the whole purpose of the section might be frustrated. Furthermore, the hurdles that the victim might face (such as separate suits, as contemplated by Dann v. Studebaker–Packard Corp., supra, security for expenses statutes, bringing in all parties necessary for complete relief, etc.) might well prove insuperable to effective relief.

IV.

Our finding that federal courts have the power to grant all necessary remedial relief is not to be construed as any indication of what we believe to be the necessary and appropriate relief in this case. We are concerned here only with a determination that federal jurisdiction for this purpose does exist. Whatever remedy is necessary must await the trial on the merits.

The other contentions of the petitioners are denied.

Affirmed.

Notes

(1) The significant issue in the Borak case, discussed by the Court rather summarily, was whether a private cause of action existed for violations of rule 14a–9. The same question has arisen under a number of statutes and regulations since 1964, several involving other provisions of the securities acts. It is clear that the Supreme Court no longer follows the rather free-wheeling and broad brush approach used by Justice Clark in *Borak*.[59] In Touche Ross & Co. v. Redington, 442 U.S. 560, 575–78, 99 S.Ct. 2479, 2489–90, 61 L.Ed.2d 82, 95–97 (1979), Justice Rehnquist writing for the court dismissed an argument based on *Borak* by stating "in a series of cases since *Borak* we have adhered to a stricter standard for the implication of private causes of action, and we follow that stricter standard today." Despite the change in attitude about the implication of private causes of action under federal statutes and regulations, the holding in *Borak* itself, that a private cause of action exists under rule 14a–9, has not been seriously questioned.

(2) The private cause of action recognized in the principal case was materially strengthened by the Supreme Court's decision in Mills v. Electric Auto–Lite Co., 396 U.S. 375, 90 S.Ct. 616, 24 L.Ed.2d 593 (1970). This case involved a proxy statement relating to a proposed merger where the misstatement did not go to the value of the transaction itself but to the manner of its approval. The proxy statement had prominently disclosed that Electric Auto–Lite's board of directors had recommended approval of the merger but did not disclose that Auto–Lite's board had in fact been selected by the other party to the merger, Merganthaler Linotype Company, which had owned or controlled about 54 percent of Auto–Lite's shares for several years. Would the failure to disclose this additional information have influenced the decisions of shareholders as to whether or not to vote in favor of the merger? The principal issue before the Supreme Court, however, was not whether the statements made in the proxy statement were materially misleading but rather, assuming that they were, what standard of causation should exist between the materially misleading statement and the transaction in order to set forth a claim under rule 14a–9. Mr. Justice Harlan's opinion set forth a rule that is easily applied:

---

59. [By the Editor] Indeed, it would be difficult to find a federal statute or regulation that did not meet Justice Clark's test for implying a private cause of action. Justice Powell sharply criticized *Borak* in his dissent in Cannon v. University of Chicago, 441 U.S. 677, 735–36, 99 S.Ct. 1946, 1977–78, 60 L.Ed.2d 560, 599 (1979): "I find this decision both unprecedented and incomprehensible as a matter of public policy. The decision's rationale, which lies ultimately in the judgment that '[p]rivate enforcement of the proxy rules pro-vides a necessary supplement to Commission action,' ignores the fact that Congress, in determining the degree of regulation to be imposed on companies covered by the Securities Exchange Act, already had decided that private enforcement was unnecessary. More significant for present purposes, however, is the fact that *Borak*, rather than signaling the start of a trend in this Court, constitutes a singular and, I believe, aberrant interpretation of a federal regulatory statute."

[T]he Court of Appeals for the Seventh Circuit * * * affirmed the District Court's conclusion that the proxy statement was materially deficient, but reversed on the question of causation. The court acknowledged that, if an injunction had been sought a sufficient time before the stockholders' meeting, "corrective measures would have been appropriate." 403 F.2d 429, 435 (1968). However, since this suit was brought too late for preventive action, the courts had to determine "whether the misleading statement and omission caused the submission of sufficient proxies," as a prerequisite to a determination of liability under the Act. If the respondents could show, "by a preponderance of probabilities, that the merger would have received a sufficient vote even if the proxy statement had not been misleading in the respect found," petitioners would be entitled to no relief of any kind. Id., at 436.

The Court of Appeals acknowledged that this test corresponds to the common-law fraud test of whether the injured party relied on the misrepresentation. However, rightly concluding that "[r]eliance by thousands of individuals, as here, can scarcely be inquired into" (id., at 436 n. 10), the court ruled that the issue was to be determined by proof of the fairness of the terms of the merger. If respondents could show that the merger had merit and was fair to the minority shareholders, the trial court would be justified in concluding that a sufficient number of shareholders would have approved the merger had there been no deficiency in the proxy statement. In that case respondents would be entitled to a judgment in their favor. * * *

The decision below, by permitting all liability to be foreclosed on the basis of a finding that the merger was fair, would allow the stockholders to be bypassed, at least where the only legal challenge to the merger is a suit for retrospective relief after the meeting has been held. A judicial appraisal of the merger's merits could be substituted for the actual and informed vote of the stockholders. The result would be to insulate from private redress an entire category of proxy violations—those relating to matters other than the terms of the merger. Even outrageous misrepresentations in a proxy solicitation, if they did not relate to the terms of the transaction, would give rise to no cause of action under § 14(a). Particularly if carried over to enforcement actions by the Securities and Exchange Commission itself, such a result would subvert the congressional purpose of ensuring full and fair disclosure to shareholders.

Further, recognition of the fairness of the merger as a complete defense would confront small shareholders with an additional obstacle to making a successful challenge to a proposal recommended through a defective proxy statement. The risk that they would be unable to rebut the corporation's evidence of the fairness of the proposal, and thus to establish their cause of action, would be bound to discourage such shareholders from the private enforcement of the proxy rules that "provides a necessary supplement to Commission action." J.I. Case Co. v. Borak, 377 U.S., at 432, 84 S.Ct. at 1560.[60] * * *

60. [By the Court] The Court of Appeals' ruling that "causation" may be negated by proof of the fairness of the merger also rests on a dubious behavioral assumption. There is no justification for presuming that the shareholders of every corporation are willing to accept any and every fair merger offer put before them; yet such a presumption is implicit in the opinion of the Court of Appeals. That court gave no indication of what evidence petitioners might adduce, once respondents had established that the merger proposal was equitable, in order to show that the shareholders would nevertheless have rejected it if the solicitation had not been misleading. Proof of actual reliance by thousands of individuals would, as the court acknowledged, not be feasible, see R. Jennings & H. Marsh, Securities Regulation,

Where the misstatement or omission in a proxy statement has been shown to be "material," as it was found to be here, that determination itself indubitably embodies a conclusion that the defect was of such a character that it might have been considered important by a reasonable shareholder who was in the process of deciding how to vote.[61] This requirement that the defect have a significant *propensity* to affect the voting process is found in the express terms of Rule 14a–9, and it adequately serves the purpose of ensuring that a cause of action cannot be established by proof of a defect so trivial, or so unrelated to the transaction for which approval is sought, that correction of the defect or imposition of liability would not further the interests protected by § 14(a).

There is no need to supplement this requirement, as did the Court of Appeals, with a requirement of proof of whether the defect actually had a decisive effect on the voting. Where there has been a finding of materiality, a shareholder has made a sufficient showing of causal relationship between the violation and the injury for which he seeks redress if, as here, he proves that the proxy solicitation itself, rather than the particular defect in the solicitation materials, was an essential link in the accomplishment of the transaction. This objective test will avoid the impracticalities of determining how many votes were affected, and, by resolving doubts in favor of those the statute is designed to protect, will effectuate the congressional policy of ensuring that the shareholders are able to make an informed choice when they are consulted on corporate transactions.

396 U.S. at 379–85, 90 S.Ct. at 619–22, 24 L.Ed.2d at 599–602.

(3) Why didn't the plaintiffs in *Mills* seek a temporary restraining order? Not having done so, and the merger having been completed, what remedy can the Court provide? Mr. Justice Harlan also considered this question:

Our conclusion that petitioners have established their case by showing that proxies necessary to approval of the merger were obtained by means of a materially misleading solicitation implies nothing about the form of relief to which they may be entitled. We held in *Borak* that upon finding a violation the courts were "to be alert to provide such remedies as are necessary to make effective the congressional purpose," noting specifically that such remedies are not to be limited to prospective relief. 377 U.S., at 433, 434, 84 S.Ct. at 1560. In devising retrospective relief for violation of the proxy rules, the federal courts should consider the same factors that would govern the relief granted for any similar illegality or fraud. One important factor may be the

---

Cases and Materials 1001 (2d ed. 1968); and reliance on the *nondisclosure* of a fact is a particularly difficult matter to define or prove, see 3 L. Loss, Securities Regulation 1766 (2d ed. 1961). In practice, therefore, the objective fairness of the proposal would seemingly be determinative of liability. But, in view of the many other factors that might lead shareholders to prefer their current position to that of owners of a larger, combined enterprise, it is pure conjecture to assume that the fairness of the proposal will always be determinative of their vote.

61. [By the Court] In this case, where the misleading aspect of the solicitation involved failure to reveal a serious conflict of interest on the part of the directors, the Court of Appeals concluded that the crucial question in deter-

mining materiality was "whether the minority shareholders were sufficiently alerted to the board's relationship to their adversary to be on their guard." 403 F.2d, at 434. An adequate disclosure of this relationship would have warned the stockholders to give more careful scrutiny to the terms of the merger than they might to one recommended by an entirely disinterested board. Thus, the failure to make such a disclosure was found to be a material defect "as a matter of law," thwarting the informed decision at which the statute aims, regardless of whether the terms of the merger were such that a reasonable stockholder would have approved the transaction after more careful analysis.

fairness of the terms of the merger. Possible forms of relief will include setting aside the merger or granting other equitable relief, but, as the Court of Appeals below noted, nothing in the statutory policy "requires the court to unscramble a corporate transaction merely because a violation occurred." 403 F.2d, at 436. In selecting a remedy the lower courts should exercise " 'the sound discretion which guides the determinations of courts of equity,' " keeping in mind the role of equity as "the instrument for nice adjustment and reconciliation between the public interest and private needs as well as between competing private claims." Hecht Co. v. Bowles, 321 U.S. 321, 329–330, 64 S.Ct. 587, 591–592, 88 L.Ed. 754 (1944), quoting from Meredith v. Winter Haven, 320 U.S. 228, 235, 64 S.Ct. 7, 11, 88 L.Ed. 9 (1943). * * *

Monetary relief will, of course, also be a possibility. Where the defect in the proxy solicitation relates to the specific terms of the merger, the district court might appropriately order an accounting to ensure that the shareholders receive the value that was represented as coming to them. On the other hand, where, as here, the misleading aspect of the solicitation did not relate to terms of the merger, monetary relief might be afforded to the shareholders only if the merger resulted in a reduction of the earnings or earnings potential of their holdings. In short, damages should be recoverable only to the extent that they can be shown. If commingling of the assets and operations of the merged companies makes it impossible to establish direct injury from the merger, relief might be predicated on a determination of the fairness of the terms of the merger at the time it was approved. These questions, of course, are for decision in the first instance by the District Court on remand, and our singling out of some of the possibilities is not intended to exclude others.

396 U.S. at 386–89, 90 S.Ct. at 622–24, 24 L.Ed.2d at 603–04. Are damages really an appropriate remedy for a violation such as that involved in *Mills*?

(4) In *Mills*, Mr. Justice Harlan also concluded that the minority shareholders' attorneys should be entitled to an interim award of attorneys' fees from Auto–Lite (actually from Merganthaler, its successor, since the merger had been completed) on the basis of a partial summary judgment on the issue of liability:

Although the question of relief must await further proceedings in the District Court, our conclusion that petitioners have established their cause of action indicates that the Court of Appeals should have affirmed the partial summary judgment on the issue of liability. The result would have been not only that respondents, rather than petitioners, would have borne the costs of the appeal, but also, we think, that petitioners would have been entitled to an interim award of litigation expenses and reasonable attorneys' fees. We agree with the position taken by petitioners, and by the United States as *amicus,* that petitioners, who have established a violation of the securities laws by their corporation and its officials, should be reimbursed by the corporation or its survivor for the costs of establishing the violation.

The absence of express statutory authorization for an award of attorneys' fees in a suit under § 14(a) does not preclude such an award in cases of this type. * * *

While the general American rule is that attorneys' fees are not ordinarily recoverable as costs, both the courts and Congress have developed exceptions to this rule for situations in which overriding considerations indicate the need for such a recovery. A primary judge-created exception has been to award expenses where a plaintiff has successfully maintained a suit, usually on behalf of a class, that benefits a group of others in the same manner as himself. To allow the others to obtain full benefit from the plaintiff's efforts without contributing equally to the litigation expenses would be to enrich the others unjustly at the plaintiff's expense. This suit presents such a situation. The dissemination of misleading proxy solicitations was a "deceit practiced on the stockholders as a group," J.I. Case Co. v. Borak, 377 U.S., at 432, 84 S.Ct., at 1560, and the expenses of petitioners' lawsuit have been incurred for the benefit of the corporation and the other shareholders.

The fact that this suit has not yet produced, and may never produce, a monetary recovery from which the fees could be paid does not preclude an award based on this rationale. * * *

In many suits under § 14(a), particularly where the violation does not relate to the terms of the transaction for which proxies are solicited, it may be impossible to assign monetary value to the benefit. Nevertheless, the stress placed by Congress on the importance of fair and informed corporate suffrage leads to the conclusion that, in vindicating the statutory policy, petitioners have rendered a substantial service to the corporation and its shareholders. Whether petitioners are successful in showing a need for significant relief may be a factor in determining whether a further award should later be made. But regardless of the relief granted, private stockholders' actions of this sort "involve corporate therapeutics," and furnish a benefit to all shareholders by providing an important means of enforcement of the proxy statute. To award attorneys' fees in such a suit to a plaintiff who has succeeded in establishing a cause of action is not to saddle the unsuccessful party with the expenses but to impose them on the class that has benefited from them and that would have had to pay them had it brought the suit.

396 U.S. at 389–92, 396–97, 90 S.Ct. at 624–25, 627–28, 24 L.Ed.2d, at 605–06, 608–09. This last holding was too much for Mr. Justice Black, who commented that he did not agree with the holding "that stockholders who hire lawyers to prosecute their claims in such a case can recover attorneys' fees in the absence of a valid contractual agreement so providing or an explicit statute creating such a right of recovery." He added, "The courts are interpreters, not creators, of legal rights to recover and if there is a need for recovery of attorneys' fees to effectuate the policies of the Act here involved, that need should in my judgment be met by Congress, not by this Court." 396 U.S. at 397, 90 S.Ct. at 628, 24 L.Ed.2d, at 609. The leading post-*Mills* case involving the shifting of attorneys' fees is Alyeska Pipeline Serv. Co. v. Wilderness Soc'y, 421 U.S. 240, 95 S.Ct. 1612, 44 L.Ed.2d 141 (1975), where the Court held that it was improper to award attorneys' fees to several environmental organizations on the theory that they were acting as a "private attorney general." *Mills* was cited as an example of the "historic power of equity to permit the trustee of a fund or property, or a party preserving or recovering a fund for the benefit of others in addition to himself, to recover his costs, including his attorneys' fees, from the fund or property itself or directly from the other parties enjoying the benefit." 421 U.S. at 257–58, 95 S.Ct. at 1621–22, 44 L.Ed.2d at 153. The dissent argued that *Mills* and other cases simply cannot be reconciled with the majority's argument. Does *Alyeska* significantly limit the recovery of attorneys' fees for proxy violations?

(5) Both the causation holding and the interim award of attorneys' fees in *Mills* undoubtedly encouraged the development of entrepreneurial litigation by plaintiffs' attorneys in the securities area. Mr. Justice Black's dissent in *Mills* apparently assumed that the individual shareholders who served as plaintiffs in

this litigation determined who their lawyers should be. The reality, however, is often far different. Consult John C. Coffee, Jr. Understanding the Plaintiff's Attorney: The Implications of Economic Theory for Private Enforcement of Law Through Class and Derivative Actions, 86 Colum.L.Rev. 669, 677–79, 681–84 (1986):[62]

In theory, a fundamental premise of American legal ethics is that clients, not their attorneys, should define litigation objectives. Yet, in the context of class and derivative actions, it is well understood that the actual client generally has only a nominal stake in the outcome of the litigation. Empirical studies have shown this, and courts, when dissatisfied with the performance of plaintiff's attorneys, are prone to emphasize that the plaintiff's attorney has no "true" identifiable client. Despite these grumblings, our legal system has long accepted, if somewhat uneasily, the concept of the plaintiff's attorney as an entrepreneur who performs the socially useful function of deterring undesirable conduct. This acceptance is manifested in a variety of ways: by permitting the attorney to advance the expenses of the litigation and receive reimbursement only if successful; by sometimes permitting the attorney to settle a class or derivative action over the objections of the actual client who is serving as representative of the class; and by allowing the use of fee formulas that view "the lawyer as a calculating entrepreneur regulated by calculating judges." Thus, although our law publicly expresses homage to individual clients, it privately recognizes their limited relevance in this context.

Although this legal structure is largely unparalleled in other common law systems, it has its obvious advantages. First, it enables clients who are dispersed or have suffered relatively small injuries to receive legal representation without incurring the substantial transaction costs of coordination. Absent such a system, a classic "free rider" problem would arise because litigation is a form of "public good" in which the benefits of an action accrue to persons who are not required to bear their share of the action's costs. * * * Second, because the attorney as private enforcer looks to the court, not the client, to award him a fee if successful, the attorney can find the legal violation first and the client second. In principle, this system should encourage the attorney to invest in search costs and seek out violations of the law that are profitable for him to challenge, rather than wait passively for an aggrieved client to arrive at his door. Thus, the attorney becomes a "bounty hunter"—or, less pejoratively, an independent monitoring force—motivated to prosecute legal violations still unknown to prospective clients. * * *

What happens when client control is so weak as to make the attorney virtually an independent entrepreneur? In some areas of contemporary litigation, the pattern is typically one of the lawyer finding the client, rather than vice versa. A principal characteristic of these areas is that plaintiff's attorneys typically have low search costs. That is, plaintiff's attorneys can discover the existence of potentially meritorious legal claims at low cost to themselves. * * *

For example, a dramatic market decline in a corporation's stock value may lead the plaintiff's attorney to infer the existence of previously undisclosed and material adverse information. The plaintiff's attorney will thus be motivated to search for a securities law violation. The mass tort, such as an

---

62. Copyright © 1986 by the Directors of the Columbia Law Review Association, Inc. All rights reserved. This article originally appeared at 86 Colum.L.Rev. 669 (1986). Reprinted by permission.

airplane crash or a toxic disaster, provides another obvious example. Similarly, a publicized takeover attempt may lead to a "greenmail" transaction, the adoption of a "poison pill," or some other defensive measure by the board of directors of a target corporation, thereby indicating the potential for a derivative suit.

Empirical evidence suggests that such dramatic, highly visible events underlie most securities class actions and derivative suits. * * *

Once the plaintiff's attorney has decided to bring suit, identifying and securing a nominal client is often only a necessary procedural step that seldom poses a substantial barrier for the experienced professional. In the securities and derivative suit areas, there are well-known individuals who possess broad (but thin) securities portfolios and have served as the lead plaintiff in numerous previous class actions.[63] Formerly, some plaintiff's law firms even invested their own firm's profit-sharing plan broadly in the stocks of numerous corporations in order to have an in-house plaintiff at hand.[64] Although the payment of a forwarding fee is generally forbidden by legal ethics, there is reason to believe in some fields that nonspecialist attorneys often direct a client who has legal standing to a plaintiff's attorney in return for such a fee (or for a nominal role in the case that will entitle the nonspecialist attorney to a share of any court awarded attorney's fees). * * *

As a normative matter, such a description of the attorney-client relationship may seem offensive to those accustomed to viewing the relationship as a fiduciary one. Yet for analytical purposes, one better understands the behavior of the plaintiff's attorney in class and derivative actions if one views him not as an agent, but more as an entrepreneur who regards a litigation as a risky asset that requires continuing investment decisions. Furthermore, a purely fiduciary perspective is misleading because it assumes that the client's preferences with respect to when an action should be settled are exogenously determined, when, in fact, they are largely influenced by the fee award formula adopted by the court. * * *

The dynamics with respect to section 14(a) litigation were dramatically changed in 1995 by the enactment of the Private Securities Litigation Reform Act of 1995, Pub. Law 104–67, 109 Stat. 737. The background and impact of this legislation is discussed in Chapter 12, section D.

---

63. [By the Author] A near legendary example is a Mr. Harry Lewis, who by his own account in sworn depositions has served as the named plaintiff in "several hundred" filed cases and at least 52 reported corporate and securities law decisions in federal courts. See Branson, The American Law Institute Principles of Corporate Governance and the Derivative Action: A View from the Other Side, [43 Wash. & Lee L.Rev. 399, 400 n. 8 (1986)]. What motivates such a client? Some suspect there are secret fee-splitting arrangements in such cases, but it is also possible that professional plaintiffs simply enjoy litigation and can engage in it relatively costlessly.

64. [By the Author] See, e.g., Lowenschuss v. Kane, 520 F.2d 255, 259 n. 2 (2d Cir.1975) (plaintiff was attorney whose firm's pension plan invested in takeover target). In fact, any "cooperative" pension or profit-sharing plan can provide the plaintiff's attorney with a client that can obtain standing to sue many companies in the stock market. Recent interpretations of legal ethics have indicated that a law firm cannot represent itself or its affiliates. See Kramer v. Scientific Control Corp., 534 F.2d 1085 (3d Cir.1976); cf. Lorber v. Beebe, 407 F.Supp. 279, 293 (S.D.N.Y.1975) (partner of attorney-class representative disqualified from serving as counsel for the class). There is no apparent basis for distinguishing between the disqualification of a lawyer's spouse and other affiliates, such as a controlled corporation or a trust. Frequently, however, one plaintiff's attorney will serve as a client for another. See, e.g., Weiss v. Temporary Inv. Fund, Inc., 692 F.2d 928 (3d Cir.1982) (Mr. Melvyn Weiss is a well-known securities plaintiff's attorney.).

(6) In Mills v. Elec. Auto–Lite Co., 552 F.2d 1239 (7th Cir.1977), cert. denied, 434 U.S. 922, 98 S.Ct. 398, 54 L.Ed.2d 279, the Court reversed the lower court's award of damages of $1,233,918.35 plus interest and, concluding that the merger terms were fair, held that the plaintiffs should recover nothing. The Court further held that the plaintiffs were not entitled to compensation for fees and expenses incurred after their initial victory in the United States Supreme Court, citing *Alyeska*.

TSC INDUS., INC. v. NORTHWAY, INC.

Supreme Court of the United States, 1976.
426 U.S. 438, 96 S.Ct. 2126, 48 L.Ed.2d 757.

Mr. Justice Marshall delivered the opinion of the Court.

The proxy rules promulgated by the Securities and Exchange Commission under the Securities Exchange Act of 1934 bar the use of proxy statements that are false or misleading with respect to the presentation or omission of material facts. We are called upon to consider the definition of a material fact under those rules, and the appropriateness of resolving the question of materiality by summary judgment in this case.

I

The dispute in this case centers on the acquisition of petitioner TSC Industries, Inc., by petitioner National Industries, Inc. In February 1969 National acquired 34% of TSC's voting securities by purchase from Charles E. Schmidt and his family. Schmidt, who had been TSC's founder and principal shareholder, promptly resigned along with his son from TSC's board of directors. Thereafter, five National nominees were placed on TSC's board; and Stanley R. Yarmuth, National's president and chief executive officer, became chairman of the TSC board, and Charles F. Simonelli, National's executive vice president, became chairman of the TSC executive committee. On October 16, 1969, the TSC board, with the attending National nominees abstaining, approved a proposal to liquidate and sell all of TSC's assets to National. * * * On November 12, 1969, TSC and National issued a joint proxy statement to their shareholders, recommending approval of the proposal. The proxy solicitation was successful, * * * and the exchange of shares was effected.

This is an action brought by respondent Northway, a TSC shareholder, against TSC and National, claiming that their joint proxy statement was incomplete and materially misleading in violation of § 14(a) of the Securities Exchange Act of 1934, and Rules 14a–3 and 14a–9, promulgated thereunder. The basis of Northway's claim under Rule 14a–3 is that TSC and National failed to state in the proxy statement that the transfer of the Schmidt interests in TSC to National had given National control of TSC. The Rule 14a–9 claim, insofar as it concerns us, is that TSC and National omitted from the proxy statement material facts relating to the degree of National's control over TSC and the favorability of the terms of the proposal to TSC shareholders.

* * * [T]he Court of Appeals reversed the District Court's denial of summary judgment to Northway on its Rule 14a–9 claims, holding that certain omissions of fact were material as a matter of law. 512 F.2d 324 (1975).

We granted certiorari because the standard applied by the Court of Appeals in resolving the question of materiality appeared to conflict with the standard applied by other Courts of Appeals. 423 U.S. 820, 96 S.Ct. 33, 46 L.Ed.2d 37 (1975). We now hold that the Court of Appeals erred in ordering that partial summary judgment be granted to Northway.

II

A

As we have noted on more than one occasion, § 14(a) of the Securities Exchange Act "was intended to promote 'the free exercise of the voting rights of stockholders' by ensuring that proxies would be solicited with 'explanation to the stockholder of the real nature of the questions for which authority to cast his vote is sought.' " Mills v. Electric Auto–Lite Co., 396 U.S. 375, 381, 90 S.Ct. 616, 620, 24 L.Ed.2d 593 (1970). See also J.I. Case Co. v. Borak, 377 U.S. 426, 431, 84 S.Ct. 1555, 1559, 12 L.Ed.2d 423 (1964). In *Borak,* the Court held that § 14(a)'s broad remedial purposes required recognition under § 27 of the Securities Exchange Act, of an implied private right of action for violations of the provision. And in *Mills,* we attempted to clarify to some extent the elements of a private cause of action for violation of § 14(a). In a suit challenging the sufficiency under § 14(a) and Rule 14a–9 of a proxy statement soliciting votes in favor of a merger, we held that there was no need to demonstrate that the alleged defect in the proxy statement actually had a decisive effect on the voting. So long as the misstatement or omission was material, the causal relation between violation and injury is sufficiently established, we concluded, if "the proxy solicitation itself * * * was an essential link in the accomplishment of the transaction." 396 U.S., at 385, 90 S.Ct., at 622. After *Mills,* then, the content given to the notion of materiality assumes heightened significance.[65]

B

The question of materiality, it is universally agreed, is an objective one, involving the significance of an omitted or misrepresented fact to a reasonable investor. Variations in the formulation of a general test of materiality occur in the articulation of just how significant a fact must be or, put another way, how certain it must be that the fact would affect a reasonable investor's judgment.

The Court of Appeals in this case concluded that material facts include "all facts which a reasonable shareholder *might* consider important." 512 F.2d, at 330 (emphasis added). This formulation of the test of materiality has been explicitly rejected by at least two courts as setting too low a threshold for the imposition of liability under Rule 14a–9. * * *

C

In formulating a standard of materiality under Rule 14a–9, we are guided, of course, by the recognition in *Borak* and *Mills* of the Rule's broad remedial purpose. That purpose is not merely to ensure by judicial means that the transaction, when judged by its real terms, is fair and otherwise adequate, but

65. [By the Court] Our cases have not considered, and we have no occasion in this case to consider, what showing of culpability is required to establish the liability under § 14(a) of a corporation issuing a materially mislead- ing proxy statement, or of a person involved in the preparation of a materially misleading proxy statement. See Ernst & Ernst v. Hochfelder, 425 U.S. 185, 209 n. 28, 96 S.Ct. 1375, 1388, 47 L.Ed.2d 668 (1976).

to ensure disclosures by corporate management in order to enable the shareholders to make an informed choice. As an abstract proposition, the most desirable role for a court in a suit of this sort, coming after the consummation of the proposed transaction, would perhaps be to determine whether in fact the proposal would have been favored by the shareholders and consummated in the absence of any misstatement or omission. But as we recognized in *Mills,* supra, at 382 n. 5, 90 S.Ct., at 620, such matters are not subject to determination with certainty. Doubts as to the critical nature of information misstated or omitted will be commonplace. And particularly in view of the prophylactic purpose of the Rule and the fact that the content of the proxy statement is within management's control, it is appropriate that these doubts be resolved in favor of those the statute is designed to protect.

We are aware, however, that the disclosure policy embodied in the proxy regulations is not without limit. Some information is of such dubious significance that insistence on its disclosure may accomplish more harm than good. The potential liability for a Rule 14a–9 violation can be great indeed, and if the standard of materiality is unnecessarily low, not only may the corporation and its management be subjected to liability for insignificant omissions or misstatements, but also management's fear of exposing itself to substantial liability may cause it simply to bury the shareholders in an avalanche of trivial information—a result that is hardly conducive to informed decision-making. Precisely these dangers are presented, we think, by the definition of a material fact adopted by the Court of Appeals in this case—a fact which a reasonable shareholder *might* consider important. We agree with Judge Friendly, speaking for the Court of Appeals in *Gerstle,* that the "might" formulation is "too suggestive of mere possibility, however unlikely." 478 F.2d, at 1302.

The general standard of materiality that we think best comports with the policies of Rule 14a–9 is as follows: An omitted fact is material if there is a substantial likelihood that a reasonable shareholder would consider it important in deciding how to vote. This standard is fully consistent with *Mills* general description of materiality as a requirement that "the defect have a significant *propensity* to affect the voting process." It does not require proof of a substantial likelihood that disclosure of the omitted fact would have caused the reasonable investor to change his vote. What the standard does contemplate is a showing of a substantial likelihood that, under all the circumstances, the omitted fact would have assumed actual significance in the deliberations of the reasonable shareholder. Put another way, there must be a substantial likelihood that the disclosure of the omitted fact would have been viewed by the reasonable investor as having significantly altered the "total mix" of information made available.[66]

D

The issue of materiality may be characterized as a mixed question of law and fact, involving as it does the application of a legal standard to a particular

66. [By the Court] In defining materiality under Rule 14a–9, we are, of course, giving content to a rule promulgated by the SEC pursuant to broad statutory authority to promote "the public interest" and "the protection of investors." Cf. Ernst & Ernst v. Hochfelder, 425 U.S., at 212–214, 96 S.Ct., at 1390–1391. Under these circumstances, the SEC's view of the proper balance between the need to insure adequate disclosure and the need to avoid the adverse consequences of setting too low a threshold for civil liability is entitled to consideration. The standard we adopt is supported by the SEC.

set of facts. In considering whether summary judgment on the issue is appropriate, we must bear in mind that the underlying objective facts, which will often be free from dispute, are merely the starting point for the ultimate determination of materiality. The determination requires delicate assessments of the inferences a "reasonable shareholder" would draw from a given set of facts and the significance of those inferences to him, and these assessments are peculiarly ones for the trier of fact. Only if the established omissions are "so obviously important to an investor, that reasonable minds cannot differ on the question of materiality" is the ultimate issue of materiality appropriately resolved "as a matter of law" by summary judgment. * * *

[In Part III of its opinion the Court conducts a careful reexamination of the facts and concludes that none of the claimed omissions were material.]

IV

In summary, none of the omissions claimed to have been in violation of Rule 14a–9 were, so far as the record reveals, materially misleading as a matter of law, and Northway was not entitled to partial summary judgment. The judgment of the Court of Appeals is reversed, and the case is remanded for further proceedings consistent with this opinion.

It is so ordered.

Mr. Justice Stevens took no part in the consideration or decision of this case.

Notes

(1) What are the implications of this decision for the interim recovery of plaintiffs' fees and expenses under *Mills*?

(2) Shidler v. All American Life & Fin. Corp., 775 F.2d 917 (8th Cir.1985) involved a proxy statement for a merger that included a statement that under Iowa law the transaction required the approval of two-thirds of all classes of shares, common and preferred, voting together in a single election. This statement turned out to be incorrect since the Iowa Supreme Court later concluded that Iowa law required a two-thirds vote of each class of shares, voting separately. Shidler v. All American Life & Fin. Corp., 298 N.W.2d 318 (Iowa 1980). This result, however, could hardly have been predicted with certainty since the issue was a novel one under Iowa law. In holding that no claim for relief under rule 14a–9 was stated, the Court concluded that rule 14a–9 did not impose strict liability, and that the lower court's conclusion that the corporation and its directors were not negligent in including the incorrect statement was not "clearly erroneous." The Court held, however, that a claim might be stated under Iowa law for damages for conversion or breach of contract. Consult also Nelson v. All American Life & Fin. Corp., 889 F.2d 141 (8th Cir.1989).

(3) If a person drafting a proxy statement includes a material statement that he knows to be false a violation of 14a–9 has clearly occurred. What if the person drafting the statement is careless and fails to verify the accuracy of the statement?. What if the person is "reckless" or "grossly" negligent? This issue is specifically reserved by the Court in footnote 65 of its opinion.

VIRGINIA BANKSHARES, INC. v. SANDBERG

Supreme Court of the United States, 1991.
501 U.S. 1083, 111 S.Ct. 2749, 115 L.Ed.2d 929.

JUSTICE SOUTER delivered the opinion of the Court.

* * * The questions before us are whether a statement couched in conclusory or qualitative terms purporting to explain directors' reasons for recommending certain corporate action can be materially misleading within the meaning of Rule 14a–9, and whether causation of damages compensable under § 14(a) can be shown by a member of a class of minority shareholders whose votes are not required by law or corporate bylaw to authorize the corporate action subject to the proxy solicitation. We hold that knowingly false statements of reasons may be actionable even though conclusory in form, but that respondents have failed to demonstrate the equitable basis required to extend the § 14(a) private action to such shareholders when any indication of congressional intent to do so is lacking.

I

In December 1986, First American Bankshares, Inc., (FABI), a bank holding company, began a "freeze-out" merger,[67] in which the First American Bank of Virginia (Bank) eventually merged into Virginia Bankshares, Inc., (VBI), a wholly owned subsidiary of FABI. VBI owned 85% of the Bank's shares, the remaining 15% being in the hands of some 2,000 minority shareholders. FABI hired the investment banking firm of Keefe, Bruyette & Woods (KBW) to give an opinion on the appropriate price for shares of the minority holders, who would lose their interests in the Bank as a result of the merger. Based on market quotations and unverified information from FABI, KBW gave the Bank's executive committee an opinion that $42 a share would be a fair price for the minority stock. The executive committee approved the merger proposal at that price, and the full board followed suit.

Although Virginia law required only that such a merger proposal be submitted to a vote at a shareholders' meeting, and that the meeting be preceded by circulation of a statement of information to the shareholders, the directors nevertheless solicited proxies for voting on the proposal at the annual meeting set for April 21, 1987.[68] In their solicitation, the directors urged the proposal's adoption and stated they had approved the plan because of its opportunity for the minority shareholders to achieve a "high" value, which they elsewhere described as a "fair" price, for their stock.

Although most minority shareholders gave the proxies requested, respondent Sandberg did not, and after approval of the merger she sought damages in the United States District Court for the Eastern District of Virginia from

---

67. [By the Editor] In a "freeze-out" merger, minority shareholders (who do not have the power to block the merger with their votes) are required to accept cash in a specified amount for their shares and have no right to a continuing ownership interest in the combined entity. However, if dissatisfied with the offered price, they also have a statutory right of dissent-and-appraisal that permits them, if they follow the prescribed procedures, to have a judicial ap-

praisal of the value of their shares and be paid that appraised value. Freeze-out mergers are discussed in chapters 11 and 16.

68. [By the Court] Had the directors chosen to issue a statement instead of a proxy solicitation, they would have been subject to an SEC antifraud provision analogous to Rule 14a–9. See 17 CFR 240.14c–6 (1990).

VBI, FABI, and the directors of the Bank. She pleaded two counts, one for soliciting proxies in violation of § 14(a) and Rule 14a–9, and the other for breaching fiduciary duties owed to the minority shareholders under state law. Under the first count, Sandberg alleged, among other things, that the directors had not believed that the price offered was high or that the terms of the merger were fair, but had recommended the merger only because they believed they had no alternative if they wished to remain on the board. At trial, Sandberg invoked language from this Court's opinion in *Mills v. Electric Auto–Lite Co.*, 396 U.S. 375, 385, 90 S.Ct. 616, 622, 24 L.Ed.2d 593 (1970), to obtain an instruction that the jury could find for her without a showing of her own reliance on the alleged misstatements, so long as they were material and the proxy solicitation was an "essential link" in the merger process.

The jury's verdicts were for Sandberg on both counts, after finding violations of Rule 14a–9 by all defendants and a breach of fiduciary duties by the Bank's directors. The jury awarded Sandberg $18 a share, having found that she would have received $60 if her stock had been valued adequately. * * *

On appeal, the United States Court of Appeals for the Fourth Circuit affirmed * * *, holding that certain statements in the proxy solicitation were materially misleading for purposes of the Rule, and that respondents could maintain their action even though their votes had not been needed to effectuate the merger. 891 F.2d 1112 (1989).[69] We granted certiorari because of the importance of the issues presented. 495 U.S. 903, 110 S.Ct. 1921, 109 L.Ed.2d 285 (1990).

II

The Court of Appeals affirmed petitioners' liability for two statements found to have been materially misleading in violation of § 14(a) of the Act, one of which was that "The Plan of Merger has been approved by the Board of Directors because it provides an opportunity for the Bank's public shareholders to achieve a high value for their shares." Petitioners argue that statements of opinion or belief incorporating indefinite and unverifiable expressions cannot be actionable as misstatements of material fact within the meaning of Rule 14a–9, and that such a declaration of opinion or belief should never be actionable when placed in a proxy solicitation incorporating statements of fact sufficient to enable readers to draw their own, independent conclusions.

A

We consider first the actionability per se of statements of reasons, opinion or belief. Because such a statement by definition purports to express what is consciously on the speaker's mind, we interpret the jury verdict as finding that the directors' statements of belief and opinion were made with knowledge that the directors did not hold the beliefs or opinions expressed, and we confine our discussion to statements so made. That such statements may be materially significant raises no serious question. * * *

69. [By the Court] The Court of Appeals reversed the District Court, however, on its refusal to certify a class of all minority shareholders in Sandberg's action. Consequently, it ruled that petitioners were liable to all of the Bank's former minority shareholders for $18 per share. 891 F.2d, at 1119.

B

1

But, assuming materiality, the question remains whether statements of reasons, opinions, or beliefs are statements "with respect to * * * material fact[s]" so as to fall within the strictures of the Rule. * * *

* * * [D]irectors' statements of reasons or belief * * * are factual in two senses: as statements that the directors do act for the reasons given or hold the belief stated and as statements about the subject matter of the reason or belief expressed. In neither sense does the proof or disproof of such statements * * * [permit the plaintiff] to manufacture claims of hypothetical action, unconstrained by independent evidence. Reasons for directors' recommendations or statements of belief are * * * characteristically matters of corporate record subject to documentation, to be supported or attacked by evidence of historical fact outside a plaintiff's control. Such evidence would include not only corporate minutes and other statements of the directors themselves, but circumstantial evidence bearing on the facts that would reasonably underlie the reasons claimed and the honesty of any statement that those reasons are the basis for a recommendation or other action, a point that becomes especially clear when the reasons or beliefs go to valuations in dollars and cents.

It is no answer to argue, as petitioners do, that the quoted statement on which liability was predicated did not express a reason in dollars and cents, but focused instead on the "indefinite and unverifiable" term, "high" value, much like the similar claim that the merger's terms were "fair" to shareholders.[70] The objection ignores the fact that such conclusory terms in a commercial context are reasonably understood to rest on a factual basis that justifies them as accurate, the absence of which renders them misleading. Provable facts either furnish good reasons to make a conclusory commercial judgment, or they count against it, and expressions of such judgments can be uttered with knowledge of truth or falsity just like more definite statements, and defended or attacked through the orthodox evidentiary process that either substantiates their underlying justifications or tends to disprove their existence. In addressing the analogous issue in an action for misrepresentation, the court in *Day v. Avery*, 179 U.S.App.D.C. 63, 548 F.2d 1018 (1976), for example, held that a statement by the executive committee of a law firm that no partner would be any "worse off" solely because of an impending merger could be found to be a material misrepresentation. Id., at 70–72, 548 F.2d at 1025–1027. Cf. *Vulcan Metals Co. v. Simmons Mfg. Co.*, 248 F. 853, 856 (C.A.2 1918) (L. Hand, J.) ("An opinion is a fact.... When the parties are so

---

70. [By the Court] Petitioners are also wrong to argue that construing the statute to allow recovery for a misleading statement that the merger was "fair" to the minority shareholders is tantamount to assuming federal authority to bar corporate transactions thought to be unfair to some group of shareholders. It is, of course, true that we said in *Santa Fe Industries, Inc. v. Green*, 430 U.S. 462, 479, 97 S.Ct. 1292, 1304, 51 L.Ed.2d 480 (1977), that " '[c]orporations are creatures of state law, and investors commit their funds to corporate directors on the understanding that, except where federal law *expressly* requires certain responsibilities of directors with respect to stockholders, state law will govern the internal affairs of the corporation,' " quoting *Cort v. Ash*, 422 U.S. 66, 84, 95 S.Ct. 2080, 2091, 45 L.Ed.2d 26 (1975). But § 14(a) does impose responsibility for false and misleading proxy statements. Although a corporate transaction's "fairness" is not, as such, a federal concern, a proxy statement's claim of fairness presupposes a factual integrity that federal law is expressly concerned to preserve.

situated that the buyer may reasonably rely upon the expression of the seller's opinion, it is no excuse to give a false one"). In this case, whether $42 was "high," and the proposal "fair" to the minority shareholders depended on whether provable facts about the Bank's assets, and about actual and potential levels of operation, substantiated a value that was above, below, or more or less at the $42 figure, when assessed in accordance with recognized methods of valuation.

Respondents adduced evidence for just such facts in proving that the statement was misleading about its subject matter and a false expression of the directors' reasons. Whereas the proxy statement described the $42 price as offering a premium above both book value and market price, the evidence indicated that a calculation of the book figure based on the appreciated value of the Bank's real estate holdings eliminated any such premium. The evidence on the significance of market price showed that KBW had conceded that the market was closed, thin and dominated by FABI, facts omitted from the statement. There was, indeed, evidence of a "going concern" value for the Bank in excess of $60 per share of common stock, another fact never disclosed. However conclusory the directors' statement may have been, then, it was open to attack by garden-variety evidence, subject neither to a plaintiff's control nor ready manufacture, and there was no undue risk of open-ended liability or uncontrollable litigation in allowing respondents the opportunity for recovery on the allegation that it was misleading to call $42 "high."
* * *

2

Under § 14(a), then, a plaintiff is permitted to prove a specific statement of reason knowingly false or misleadingly incomplete, even when stated in conclusory terms. In reaching this conclusion we have considered statements of reasons of the sort exemplified here, which misstate the speaker's reasons and also mislead about the stated subject matter (e.g., the value of the shares). A statement of belief may be open to objection only in the former respect, however, solely as a misstatement of the psychological fact of the speaker's belief in what he says. In this case, for example, the Court of Appeals alluded to just such limited falsity in observing that "the jury was certainly justified in believing that the directors did not believe a merger at $42 per share was in the minority stockholders' interest but, rather, that they voted as they did for other reasons, e.g., retaining their seats on the board." 891 F.2d, at 1121.

The question arises, then, whether disbelief, or undisclosed belief or motivation, standing alone, should be a sufficient basis to sustain an action under § 14(a), absent proof by the sort of objective evidence described above that the statement also expressly or impliedly asserted something false or misleading about its subject matter. We think that proof of mere disbelief or belief undisclosed should not suffice for liability under § 14(a), and if nothing more had been required or proven in this case we would reverse for that reason. * * *

C

Petitioners' fall-back position assumes the same relationship between a conclusory judgment and its underlying facts that we described in Part II–B–1, supra. Thus, citing *Radol v. Thomas*, 534 F.Supp. 1302, 1315, 1316

(S.D.Ohio 1982), petitioners argue that even if conclusory statements of reason or belief can be actionable under § 14(a), we should confine liability to instances where the proxy material fails to disclose the offending statement's factual basis. There would be no justification for holding the shareholders entitled to judicial relief, that is, when they were given evidence that a stated reason for a proxy recommendation was misleading, and an opportunity to draw that conclusion themselves.

The answer to this argument rests on the difference between a merely misleading statement and one that is materially so. While a misleading statement will not always lose its deceptive edge simply by joinder with others that are true, the true statements may discredit the other one so obviously that the risk of real deception drops to nil. Since liability under § 14(a) must rest not only on deceptiveness but materiality as well (i.e., it has to be significant enough to be important to a reasonable investor deciding how to vote), petitioners are on perfectly firm ground insofar as they argue that publishing accurate facts in a proxy statement can render a misleading proposition too unimportant to ground liability.

But not every mixture with the true will neutralize the deceptive. If it would take a financial analyst to spot the tension between the one and the other, whatever is misleading will remain materially so, and liability should follow. *Gerstle v. Gamble–Skogmo, Inc.*, 478 F.2d 1281, 1297 (C.A.2 1973) ("[I]t is not sufficient that overtones might have been picked up by the sensitive antennae of investment analysts"). * * * The point of a proxy statement, after all, should be to inform, not to challenge the reader's critical wits. Only when the inconsistency would exhaust the misleading conclusion's capacity to influence the reasonable shareholder would a § 14(a) action fail on the element of materiality.

Suffice it to say that the evidence invoked by petitioners in the instant case fell short of compelling the jury to find the facial materiality of the misleading statement neutralized. The directors claim, for example, to have made an explanatory disclosure of further reasons for their recommendation when they said they would keep their seats following the merger, but they failed to mention what at least one of them admitted in testimony, that they would have had no expectation of doing so without supporting the proposal.[71] And although the proxy statement did speak factually about the merger price in describing it as higher than share prices in recent sales, it failed even to mention the closed market dominated by FABI. None of these disclosures that the directors point to was, then, anything more than a half-truth, and the record shows that another fact statement they invoke was arguably even worse. The claim that the merger price exceeded book value was controverted, as we have seen already, by evidence of a higher book value than the directors conceded, reflecting appreciation in the Bank's real estate portfolio. Finally,

---

71. [By the Court] Petitioners fail to dissuade us from recognizing the significance of omissions such as this by arguing that we effectively require them to accuse themselves of breach of fiduciary duty. Subjection to liability for misleading others does not raise a duty of self-accusation; it enforces a duty to refrain from misleading. We have no occasion to decide whether the directors were obligated to state the reasons for their support of the merger proposal here, but there can be no question that the statement they did make carried with it no option to deceive. Cf. *Berg v. First American Bankshares, Inc.*, 254 U.S.App.D.C. 198, 205, 796 F.2d 489, 496 (1986) ("Once the proxy statement purported to disclose the factors considered * * *, there was an obligation to portray them accurately").

the solicitation omitted any mention of the Bank's value as a going concern at more than $60 a share, as against the merger price of $42. There was, in sum, no more of a compelling case for the statement's immateriality than for its accuracy.

III

The second issue before us, left open in *Mills v. Electric Auto–Lite Co.,* is whether causation of damages compensable through the implied private right of action under § 14(a) can be demonstrated by a member of a class of minority shareholders whose votes are not required by law or corporate bylaw to authorize the transaction giving rise to the claim. *J.I. Case Co. v. Borak,* 377 U.S. 426, 84 S.Ct. 1555, 12 L.Ed.2d 423 (1964), did not itself address the requisites of causation, as such, or define the class of plaintiffs eligible to sue under § 14(a). But its general holding, that a private cause of action was available to some shareholder class, acquired greater clarity with a more definite concept of causation in *Mills,* where we addressed the sufficiency of proof that misstatements in a proxy solicitation were responsible for damages claimed from the merger subject to complaint.

* * * The *Mills* Court avoided the evidentiary morass that would have followed from requiring individualized proof that enough minority shareholders had relied upon the misstatements to swing the vote [by holding] that causation of damages by a material proxy misstatement could be established by showing that minority proxies necessary and sufficient to authorize the corporate acts had been given in accordance with the tenor of the solicitation[. The] Court described such a causal relationship by calling the proxy solicitation an "essential link in the accomplishment of the transaction." In the case before it, the Court found the solicitation essential, as contrasted with one addressed to a class of minority shareholders without votes required by law or by-law to authorize the action proposed, and left it for another day to decide whether such a minority shareholder could demonstrate causation.

In this case, respondents address *Mills'* open question by proffering two theories that the proxy solicitation addressed to them was an "essential link" under the *Mills* causation test.[72] They argue, first, that a link existed and was essential simply because VBI and FABI would have been unwilling to proceed with the merger without the approval manifested by the minority shareholders' proxies, which would not have been obtained without the solicitation's express misstatements and misleading omissions. On this reasoning, the causal connection would depend on a desire to avoid bad shareholder or public relations, and the essential character of the causal link would stem not from

---

72. [By the Court] Citing the decision in *Schlick v. Penn–Dixie Cement Corp.,* 507 F.2d 374, 382–383 (C.A.2 1974), petitioners characterize respondents' proffered theories as examples of so-called "sue facts" and "shame facts" theories. "A 'sue fact' is, in general, a fact which is material to a sue decision. A 'sue decision' is a decision by a shareholder whether or not to institute a representative or derivative suit alleging a state-law cause of action." Gelb, Rule 10b–5 and *Santa Fe*—Herein of Sue Facts, Shame Facts, and Other Matters, 87 W.Va.L.Rev. 189, 198, and n. 52 (1985), quoting Borden, "Sue Fact" Rule Mandates Disclosure to Avoid Litigation in State Courts, 10 SEC '82, pp. 201, 204–205 (1982). See also Note, Causation and Liability in Private Actions for Proxy Violations, 80 Yale L.J. 107, 116 (1970) (discussing theories of causation). "Shame facts" are said to be facts which, had they been disclosed, would have "shamed" management into abandoning a proposed transaction.

the enforceable terms of the parties' corporate relationship, but from one party's apprehension of the ill will of the other.

In the alternative, respondents argue that the proxy statement was an essential link between the directors' proposal and the merger because it was the means to satisfy a state statutory requirement of minority shareholder approval, as a condition for saving the merger from voidability resulting from a conflict of interest on the part of one of the Bank's directors, Jack Beddow, who voted in favor of the merger while also serving as a director of FABI. Under the terms of [MBCA § 8.31(a)], minority approval after disclosure of the material facts about the transaction and the director's interest was one of three avenues to insulate the merger from later attack for conflict, the two others being ratification by the Bank's directors after like disclosure, and proof that the merger was fair to the corporation. On this theory, causation would depend on the use of the proxy statement for the purpose of obtaining votes sufficient to bar a minority shareholder from commencing proceedings to declare the merger void.[73]

Although respondents have proffered each of these theories as establishing a chain of causal connection in which the proxy statement is claimed to have been an "essential link," neither theory presents the proxy solicitation as essential in the sense of *Mills'* causal sequence, in which the solicitation links a directors' proposal with the votes legally required to authorize the action proposed. As a consequence, each theory would, if adopted, extend the scope of *Borak* actions beyond the ambit of *Mills*, and expand the class of plaintiffs entitled to bring *Borak* actions to include shareholders whose initial authorization of the transaction prompting the proxy solicitation is unnecessary.

Assessing the legitimacy of any such extension or expansion calls for the application of some fundamental principles governing recognition of a right of action implied by a federal statute, the first of which was not, in fact, the considered focus of the *Borak* opinion. The rule that has emerged in the years since *Borak* and *Mills* came down is that recognition of any private right of action for violating a federal statute must ultimately rest on congressional intent to provide a private remedy, *Touche Ross & Co. v. Redington*, 442 U.S. 560, 575, 99 S.Ct. 2479, 2488–2489, 61 L.Ed.2d 82 (1979). From this the corollary follows that the breadth of the right once recognized should not, as a general matter, grow beyond the scope congressionally intended.

This rule and corollary present respondents with a serious obstacle, for we can find no manifestation of intent to recognize a cause of action (or class of plaintiffs) as broad as respondents' theory of causation would entail. At first blush, it might seem otherwise, for the *Borak* Court certainly did not

---

73. [By the Court] The district court and court of appeals have grounded causation on a further theory, that Virginia law required a solicitation of proxies even from minority shareholders as a condition of consummating the merger. While the provisions of [MBCA §§ 11.03(a),(d),(e)] are said to have required the Bank to solicit minority proxies, they actually compelled no more than submission of the merger to a vote at a shareholders' meeting, [MBCA § 11.03(e)], preceded by issuance of an informational statement, [MBCA § 11.03(d)]. There was thus no need under this statute to solicit proxies, although it is undisputed that the proxy solicitation sufficed to satisfy the statutory obligation to provide a statement of relevant information. On this theory causation would depend on the use of the proxy statement to satisfy a statutory obligation, even though a proxy solicitation was not, as such, required. In this Court, respondents have disclaimed reliance on any such theory.

ignore the matter of intent. Its opinion adverted to the statutory object of "protection of investors" as animating Congress' intent to provide judicial relief where "necessary," *Borak*, 377 U.S., at 432, 84 S.Ct., at 1559–1560, and it quoted evidence for that intent from House and Senate Committee Reports, id., at 431–32, 84 S.Ct., at 1559–1560. *Borak*'s probe of the congressional mind, however, never focused squarely on private rights of action, as distinct from the substantive objects of the legislation, and one member of the *Borak* Court later characterized the "implication" of the private right of action as resting modestly on the Act's "exclusively procedural provision affording access to a federal forum." *Bivens v. Six Unknown Fed. Narcotics Agents*, 403 U.S. 388, 403, n. 4, 91 S.Ct. 1999, 2008, n. 4, 29 L.Ed.2d 619 (1971) (Harlan, J., concurring in judgment) (internal quotation marks omitted). In fact, the importance of enquiring specifically into intent to authorize a private cause of action became clear only later, see *Cort v. Ash*, 422 U.S., at 78, 95 S.Ct., at 2087–2088, and only later still, in *Touche Ross*, was this intent accorded primacy among the considerations that might be thought to bear on any decision to recognize a private remedy. There, in dealing with a claimed private right under § 17(a) of the Act, we explained that the "central inquiry remains whether Congress intended to create, either expressly or by implication, a private cause of action." 442 U.S., at 575–576, 99 S.Ct., at 2489.

Looking to the Act's text and legislative history mindful of this heightened concern reveals little that would help toward understanding the intended scope of any private right. According to the House report, Congress meant to promote the "free exercise" of stockholders' voting rights, H.R.Rep. No. 1383, 73d Cong., 2d Sess., 14 (1934), and protect "[f]air corporate suffrage," id., at 13, from abuses exemplified by proxy solicitations that concealed what the Senate report called the "real nature" of the issues to be settled by the subsequent votes, S.Rep. No. 792, 73d Cong., 2d Sess., 12 (1934). While it is true that these reports, like the language of the Act itself, carry the clear message that Congress meant to protect investors from misinformation that rendered them unwitting agents of self-inflicted damage, it is just as true that Congress was reticent with indications of how far this protection might depend on self-help by private action. The response to this reticence may be, of course, to claim that § 14(a) cannot be enforced effectively for the sake of its intended beneficiaries without their participation as private litigants. *Borak*, supra, 377 U.S., at 432, 84 S.Ct., at 1559–1560. But the force of this argument for inferred congressional intent depends on the degree of need perceived by Congress, and we would have trouble inferring any congressional urgency to depend on implied private actions to deter violations of § 14(a), when Congress expressly provided private rights of action in §§ 9(e), 16(b) and 18(a) of the same Act.[74]

The congressional silence that is thus a serious obstacle to the expansion of cognizable *Borak* causation is not, however, a necessarily insurmountable barrier. This is not the first effort in recent years to expand the scope of an

---

74. [By the Court] The object of our enquiry does not extend further to question the holding of either *J.I. Case Co. v. Borak*, 377 U.S. 426, 84 S.Ct. 1555, 12 L.Ed.2d 423 (1964), or *Mills v. Electric Auto–Lite Co.*, 396 U.S. 375, 90 S.Ct. 616, 24 L.Ed.2d 593 (1970) at this date, any more than we have done so in the past, see *Touche Ross & Co. v. Redington*, 442 U.S. 560, 577, 99 S.Ct. 2479, 2489–2490, 61 L.Ed.2d 82 (1979). Our point is simply to recognize the hurdle facing any litigant who urges us to enlarge the scope of the action beyond the point reached in *Mills*.

action originally inferred from the Act without "conclusive guidance" from Congress, and we may look to that earlier case for the proper response to such a plea for expansion. There, we accepted the proposition that where a legal structure of private statutory rights has developed without clear indications of congressional intent, the contours of that structure need not be frozen absolutely when the result would be demonstrably inequitable to a class of would-be plaintiffs with claims comparable to those previously recognized. Faced in that case with such a claim for equality in rounding out the scope of an implied private statutory right of action, we looked to policy reasons for deciding where the outer limits of the right should lie. We may do no less here, in the face of respondents' pleas for a private remedy to place them on the same footing as shareholders with votes necessary for initial corporate action.

A

[We reject] respondents' first theory, that a desire to avoid minority shareholders' ill will should suffice to justify recognizing the requisite causality of a proxy statement needed to garner that minority support.

* * * [If this were accepted, c]ausation would turn on inferences about what the corporate directors would have thought and done without the minority shareholder approval unneeded to authorize action. A subsequently dissatisfied minority shareholder would have virtual license to allege that managerial timidity would have doomed corporate action but for the ostensible approval induced by a misleading statement, and opposing claims of hypothetical diffidence and hypothetical boldness on the part of directors would probably provide enough depositions in the usual case to preclude any judicial resolution short of the credibility judgments that can only come after trial. Reliable evidence would seldom exist. Directors would understand the prudence of making a few statements about plans to proceed even without minority endorsement, and discovery would be a quest for recollections of oral conversations at odds with the official pronouncements, in hopes of finding support for ex post facto guesses about how much heat the directors would have stood in the absence of minority approval. The issues would be hazy, their litigation protracted, and their resolution unreliable. Given a choice, we would reject any theory of causation that raised such prospects, and we reject this one.[75]

B

The theory of causal necessity derived from the requirements of Virginia law dealing with postmerger ratification seeks to identify the essential character of the proxy solicitation from its function in obtaining the minority

---

75. [By the Court] In parting company from us on this point, Justice Kennedy emphasizes that respondents in this particular case substantiated a plausible claim that petitioners would not have proceeded without minority approval. FABI's attempted freeze-out merger of a Maryland subsidiary had failed a year before the events in question when the subsidiary's directors rejected the proposal because of inadequate share price, and there was evidence of FABI's desire to avoid any renewal of adverse comment. The issue before us, however, is whether to recognize a theory of causation generally, and our decision against doing so rests on our apprehension that the ensuing litigation would be exemplified by cases far less tractable than this. Respondents' burden to justify recognition of causation beyond the scope of *Mills* must be addressed not by emphasizing the instant case but by confronting the risk inherent in the cases that could be expected to be characteristic if the causal theory were adopted.

approval that would preclude a minority suit attacking the merger. Since the link is said to be a step in the process of barring a class of shareholders from resort to a state remedy otherwise available, this theory of causation rests upon the proposition of policy that § 14(a) should provide a federal remedy whenever a false or misleading proxy statement results in the loss under state law of a shareholder plaintiff's state remedy for the enforcement of a state right. Respondents agree with the suggestions of counsel for the SEC and FDIC that causation be recognized, for example, when a minority shareholder has been induced by a misleading proxy statement to forfeit a state-law right to an appraisal remedy by voting to approve a transaction, cf. *Swanson v. American Consumers Industries, Inc.*, 475 F.2d 516, 520–521 (C.A.7 1973), or when such a shareholder has been deterred from obtaining an order enjoining a damaging transaction by a proxy solicitation that misrepresents the facts on which an injunction could properly have been issued. Respondents claim that in this case a predicate for recognizing just such a causal link exists in [MBCA § 8.31(a)(2)], which sets the conditions under which the merger may be insulated from suit by a minority shareholder seeking to void it on account of Beddow's conflict.

This case does not, however, require us to decide whether § 14(a) provides a cause of action for lost state remedies, since there is no indication in the law or facts before us that the proxy solicitation resulted in any such loss. The contrary appears to be the case. Assuming the soundness of respondents' characterization of the proxy statement as materially misleading, the very terms of the Virginia statute indicate that a favorable minority vote induced by the solicitation would not suffice to render the merger invulnerable to later attack on the ground of the conflict. The statute bars a shareholder from seeking to avoid a transaction tainted by a director's conflict if, inter alia, the minority shareholders ratified the transaction following disclosure of the material facts of the transaction and the conflict. [MBCA § 8.31(a)(2)]. Assuming that the material facts about the merger and Beddow's interests were not accurately disclosed, the minority votes were inadequate to ratify the merger under state law, and there was no loss of state remedy to connect the proxy solicitation with harm to minority shareholders irredressable under state law.[76] Nor is there a claim here that the statement misled respondents into entertaining a false belief that they had no chance to upset the merger, until the time for bringing suit had run out.

The judgment of the Court of Appeals is reversed.

It is so ordered.

JUSTICE SCALIA, concurring in part and concurring in the judgment.

I

As I understand the Court's opinion, the statement "In the opinion of the Directors, this is a high value for the shares" would produce liability if in fact it was not a high value and the Directors knew that. It would not produce liability if in fact it was not a high value but the Directors honestly believed

---

76. [By the Court] In his opinion dissenting on this point, Justice KENNEDY suggests that materiality under Virginia law might be defined differently from the materiality standard of our own cases, resulting in a denial of state remedy even when a solicitation was materially misleading under federal law. Respondents, however, present nothing to suggest that this might be so.

otherwise. The statement "The Directors voted to accept the proposal because they believe it offers a high value" would not produce liability if in fact the Directors' genuine motive was quite different—except that it would produce liability if the proposal in fact did not offer a high value and the Directors knew that.

I agree with all of this. However, not every sentence that has the word "opinion" in it, or that refers to motivation for Directors' actions, leads us into this psychic thicket. Sometimes such a sentence actually represents facts as facts rather than opinions—and in that event no more need be done than apply the normal rules for § 14(a) liability. I think that is the situation here. In my view, the statement at issue in this case is most fairly read as affirming *separately* both the fact of the Directors' opinion *and* the accuracy of the facts upon which the opinion was assertedly based. It reads as follows:

> The Plan of Merger has been approved by the Board of Directors because it provides an opportunity for the Bank's public shareholders to achieve a high value for their shares. App. to Pet. for Cert. 53a.

Had it read "because *in their estimation* it provides an opportunity, etc." it would have set forth nothing but an opinion. As written, however, it asserts both that the Board of Directors acted for a particular reason *and* that that reason is correct. * * *

If the present case were to proceed, therefore, I think the normal § 14(a) principles governing misrepresentation of fact would apply.

II

I recognize that the Court's disallowance (in Part II–B–2) of an action for misrepresentation of belief is entirely contrary to the modern law of torts, as authorities cited by the Court make plain. I have no problem with departing from modern tort law in this regard, because I think the federal cause of action at issue here was never enacted by Congress, and hence the more narrow we make it (within the bounds of rationality) the more faithful we are to our task. * * *

JUSTICE STEVENS, with whom JUSTICE MARSHALL joins, concurring in part and dissenting in part.

While I agree in substance with Parts I and II of the Court's opinion, I do not agree with the reasoning in Part III. * * *

The case before us today involves a merger that has been found by a jury to be unfair, not fair. The interest in providing a remedy to the injured minority shareholders therefore is stronger, not weaker, than in *Mills*. The interest in avoiding speculative controversy about the actual importance of the proxy solicitation is the same as in *Mills*. Moreover, as in *Mills*, these matters can be taken into account at the remedy stage in appropriate cases. Accordingly, I do not believe that it constitutes an unwarranted extension of the rationale of *Mills* to conclude that because management found it necessary—whether for "legal or practical reasons"—to solicit proxies from minority shareholders to obtain their approval of the merger, that solicitation "was an essential link in the accomplishment of the transaction." In my opinion, shareholders may bring an action for damages under § 14(a) of the Securities Exchange Act of 1934, whenever materially false or misleading statements are made in proxy statements. That the solicitation of proxies is not required by law or by the bylaws of a corporation does not authorize corporate officers, once they have decided for whatever reason to solicit proxies, to avoid the constraints of the statute. I would therefore affirm the judgment of the Court of Appeals.

JUSTICE KENNEDY, with whom JUSTICE MARSHALL, JUSTICE BLACKMUN, and JUSTICE STEVENS join, concurring in part and dissenting in part.

I am in general agreement with Parts I and II of the majority opinion, but do not agree with the views expressed in Part III regarding the proof of causation required to establish a violation of § 14(a). With respect, I dissent from Part III of the Court's opinion. * * *

I

The severe limits the Court places upon possible proof of nonvoting causation in a § 14(a) private action are justified neither by our precedents nor any case in the courts of appeals. These limits are said to flow from a shift in our approach to implied causes of action that has occurred since we recognized the § 14(a) implied private action in J.I. Case Co. v. *Borak*, 377 U.S. 426, 84 S.Ct. 1555, 12 L.Ed.2d 423 (1964).

I acknowledge that we should exercise caution in creating implied private rights of action and that we must respect the primacy of congressional intent in that inquiry. Where an implied cause of action is well accepted by our own cases and has become an established part of the securities laws, however, we should enforce it as a meaningful remedy unless we are to eliminate it altogether. As the Court phrases it, we must consider the causation question in light of the underlying "policy reasons for deciding where the outer limits of the right should lie."

According to the Court, acceptance of non-voting causation theories would "extend the scope of *Borak* actions beyond the ambit of *Mills*." But *Mills* did not purport to limit the scope of *Borak* actions, and some courts have applied nonvoting causation theories to *Borak* actions for at least the past 25 years.

To the extent the Court's analysis considers the purposes underlying § 14(a), it does so with the avowed aim to limit the cause of action and with undue emphasis upon fears of "speculative claims and procedural intractability." The result is a sort of guerrilla warfare to restrict a well-established implied right of action. If the analysis adopted by the Court today is any guide, Congress and those charged with enforcement of the securities laws stand forewarned that unresolved questions concerning the scope of those causes of action are likely to be answered by the Court in favor of defendants.

B

The Court seems to assume, based upon the footnote in *Mills* reserving the question, that Sandberg bears a special burden to demonstrate causation because the public shareholders held only 15 percent of the Bank's stock. Justice Stevens is right to reject this theory. Here, First American Bankshares, Inc. (FABI) and Virginia Bankshares, Inc. (VBI) retained the option to back out of the transaction if dissatisfied with the reaction of the minority shareholders, or if concerned that the merger would result in liability for violation of duties to the minority shareholders. The merger agreement was conditioned upon approval by two-thirds of the shareholders, App. 463, and

VBI could have voted its shares against the merger if it so decided. To this extent, the Court's distinction between cases where the "minority" shareholders could have voted down the transaction and those where causation must be proved by nonvoting theories is suspect. Minority shareholders are identified only by a post hoc inquiry. The real question ought to be whether an injury was shown by the effect the nondisclosure had on the entire merger process, including the period before votes are cast.

The Court's distinction presumes that a majority shareholder will vote in favor of management's proposal even if proxy disclosure suggests that the transaction is unfair to minority shareholders or that the board of directors or majority shareholder are in breach of fiduciary duties to the minority. If the majority shareholder votes against the transaction in order to comply with its state law duties, or out of fear of liability, or upon concluding that the transaction will injure the reputation of the business, this ought not to be characterized as nonvoting causation. Of course, when the majority shareholder dominates the voting process, as was the case here, it may prefer to avoid the embarrassment of voting against its own proposal and so may cancel the meeting of shareholders at which the vote was to have been taken. For practical purposes, the result is the same: because of full disclosure the transaction does not go forward and the resulting injury to minority shareholders is avoided. The Court's distinction between voting and nonvoting causation does not create clear legal categories. * * *

There is no authority whatsoever for limiting § 14(a) to protecting those minority shareholders whose numerical strength could permit them to vote down a proposal. One of Section 14(a)'s "chief purposes is 'the protection of investors.'" *J.I. Case Co., v. Borak*, 377 U.S., at 432, 1559–1560. Those who lack the strength to vote down a proposal have all the more need of disclosure. The voting process involves not only casting ballots but also the formulation and withdrawal of proposals, the minority's right to block a vote through court action or the threat of adverse consequences, or the negotiation of an increase in price. The proxy rules support this deliberative process. These practicalities can result in causation sufficient to support recovery.

The facts in the case before us prove this point. Sandberg argues that had all the material facts been disclosed, FABI or the Bank likely would have withdrawn or revised the merger proposal. The evidence in the record, and more that might be available upon remand, meets any reasonable requirement of specific and nonspeculative proof.

FABI wanted a "friendly transaction" with a price viewed as "so high that any reasonable shareholder will accept it." Management expressed concern that the transaction result in "no loss of support for the bank out in the community, which was important." Although FABI had the votes to push through any proposal, it wanted a favorable response from the minority shareholders. Because of the "human element involved in a transaction of this nature," FABI attempted to "show those minority shareholders that [it was] being fair."

The theory that FABI would not have pursued the transaction if full disclosure had been provided and the shareholders had realized the inadequacy of the price is supported not only by the trial testimony but also by notes of the meeting of the Bank's board which approved the merger. The inquiry into causation can proceed not by "opposing claims of hypothetical diffidence and hypothetical boldness," but through an examination of evidence of the same type the Court finds acceptable in its determination that directors' statements of reasons can lead to liability. Discussion at the board meeting focused upon matters such as "how to keep PR afloat" and "how to prevent adverse reac[tion]/perception," demonstrating the directors' concern that an unpopular merger proposal could injure the Bank.

Only a year or so before the Virginia merger, FABI had failed in an almost identical transaction, an attempt to freeze out the minority shareholders of its Maryland subsidiary. FABI retained Keefe, Bruyette & Woods (KBW) for that transaction as well, and KBW had given an opinion that FABI's price was fair. The subsidiary's board of directors then retained its own adviser and concluded that the price offered by FABI was inadequate. The Maryland transaction failed when the directors of the Maryland bank refused to proceed; and this was despite the minority's inability to outvote FABI if it had pressed on with the deal.

In the Virginia transaction, FABI again decided to retain KBW. Beddow, who sat on the boards of both FABI and the Bank, discouraged the Bank from hiring its own financial adviser, out of fear that the Maryland experience would be repeated if the Bank received independent advice. Directors of the Bank testified they would not have voted to approve the transaction if the price had been demonstrated unfair to the minority. Further, approval by the Bank's board of directors was facilitated by FABI's representation that the transaction also would be approved by the minority shareholders.

These facts alone suffice to support a finding of causation, but here Sandberg might have had yet more evidence to link the nondisclosure with completion of the merger. FABI executive Robert Altman and Bank Chairman Drewer met on the day before the shareholders meeting when the vote was taken. Notes produced by petitioners suggested that Drewer, who had received some shareholder objections to the $42 price, considered postponing the meeting and obtaining independent advice on valuation. Altman persuaded him to go forward without any of these cautionary measures. This information, which was produced in the course of discovery, was kept from the jury on grounds of privilege. Sandberg attacked the privilege ruling on five grounds in the Court of Appeals. In light of its ruling in favor of Sandberg, however, the panel had no occasion to consider the admissibility of this evidence.

Though I would not require a shareholder to present such evidence of causation, this case itself demonstrates that nonvoting causation theories are quite plausible where the misstatement or omission is material and the damage sustained by minority shareholders is serious. As Professor Loss summarized the holdings of a "substantial number of cases," even if the minority cannot alone vote down a transaction,

> minority stockholders will be in a better position to protect their interests with full disclosure and ... an unfavorable minority vote might influence the majority to modify or reconsider the transaction in question. In [*Schlick v. Penn–Dixie Cement Corp.*, 507 F.2d 374, 384 (C.A.2 1974),] where the stockholders had no appraisal rights under state law because the stock was listed on the New York Stock Exchange, the court advanced two additional considerations: (1) the *market* would be informed; and (2)

even 'a rapacious controlling management' might modify the terms of a merger because it would not want to 'hang its dirty linen out on the line and thereby expose itself to suit or Securities Commission or other action—in terms of reputation and future takeovers.'

L. Loss, Fundamentals of Securities Regulation at 1119–1120 (footnote omitted).

I conclude that causation is more than plausible; it is likely, even where the public shareholders cannot vote down management's proposal. Causation is established where the proxy statement is an essential link in completing the transaction, even if the minority lacks sufficient votes to defeat a proposal of management. * * *

Notes

(1) Do you agree that a statement that an offer price is higher than "book value" is misleading because the statement would not be true if a recalculated book value—based on current market values for real estate rather than historical cost—was used? Would it be misleading if the disclosure made clear that the comparison was being made with book value "calculated in the traditional manner and without regard to current real estate values"? Would an average investor understand that distinction? Or would the proxy statement have to say what the recalculated book value was if "book value" is referred to at all?

(2) After this decision, could the SEC amend rule 14a–9 to make it applicable to proxy solicitations that are not "essential" to the transaction in the sense used by Justice Souter? Or does that require an amendment to § 14(a) of the Securities Exchange Act of 1934?

(3) What do you think of Justice Scalia's approach toward cases involving implied causes of action that because "the federal cause of action at issue here was never enacted by Congress, * * * the more narrow we make it (within the bounds of rationality) the more faithful we are to our task"? What is "the task" that Justice Scalia refers to?

(4) If the protection of rule 14a–9 is removed from minority shareholders by *Virginia Bankshares*, can any statement, no matter how outrageously wrong, be made by management? Should the common law rule (see page 616, supra) remain applicable to a proxy statement that is knowingly false?

(5) One question left open in Justice Souter's opinion is whether a different rule should be applicable if minority shareholders induced to vote in favor of a proposal because of false statements thereby lose state remedies, such as the right of dissent and appraisal (see Chapter 16) or the right to serve as a derivative plaintiff (see Chapter 10). Two decisions holding that *Virginia Bankshares* does not extend that far are Howing Co. v. Nationwide Corp., 972 F.2d 700 (6th Cir.1992), cert. denied 507 U.S. 1004, 113 S.Ct. 1645, 123 L.Ed.2d 266 (1993), and Wilson v. Great American Indus., Inc. 979 F.2d 924 (2d Cir.1992). But see Roosevelt v. E.I. Du Pont de Nemours & Co., 958 F.2d 416 (D.C.Cir.1992); Scattergood v. Perelman, 945 F.2d 618 (3d Cir.1991). For an analysis of these issues, see Scott Jordan, Loss of State Claims as a Basis for Rule 10b–5 and 14a–9 Actions: The Impact of *Virginia Bankshares*, 49 Bus.Law. 295 (1993); Note, Virginia Bankshares v. Sandberg: Should Minority Approval be Required by Law or Corporate Bylaw? 37 Ariz.L.Rev.913 (1995).

4. SHAREHOLDER PROPOSALS

REGULATION 14A. SOLICITATION OF PROXIES
17 C.F.R. § 240.14a–8 (1997).

§ 240.14a–8 PROPOSALS OF SECURITY HOLDERS

(a) If any security holder of a registrant notifies the registrant of his intention to present a proposal for action at a forthcoming meeting of the registrant's security holders, the registrant shall set forth the proposal in its proxy statement and identify it in its form of proxy and provide means by which security holders can make the specification required by Rule 14a–4(b).[77] Notwithstanding the foregoing, the registrant shall not be required to include the proposal in its proxy statement or form of proxy unless the security holder (hereinafter, the "proponent") has complied with the requirements of this paragraph and paragraphs (b) and (c) of this section:

(1) *Eligibility.* At the time he submits the proposal, the proponent shall be a record or beneficial owner of at least 1% or $1000 in market value of securities entitled to be voted on the proposal at the meeting and have held such securities for at least one year, and he shall continue to own such securities through the date on which the meeting is held. * * * In the event the registrant includes the proponent's proposal in its proxy soliciting material for the meeting and the proponent fails to comply with the requirement that he continuously hold such securities through the meeting date, the registrant shall not be required to include any proposals submitted by the proponent in its proxy material for any meeting held in the following two calendar years.

(2) *Notice and Attendance at the Meeting.* At the time he submits a proposal, a proponent shall provide the registrant in writing with his name, address, the number of the registrant's voting securities that he holds of record or beneficially, the dates upon which he acquired such securities, and documentary support for a claim of beneficial ownership. A proposal may be presented at the meeting either by the proponent or his representative who is qualified under state law to present the proposal on the proponent's behalf at the meeting. In the event that the proponent or his representative fails, without good cause, to present the proposal for action at the meeting, the registrant shall not be required to include any proposals submitted by the proponent in its proxy soliciting material for any meeting held in the following two calendar years.

(3) *Timeliness.* The proponent shall submit his proposal sufficiently far in advance of the meeting so that it is received by the issuer within the following time periods: * * *

---

77. [By the Editor] The provision referred to reads as follows:

(b)(1) Means shall be provided in the form of proxy whereby the person solicited is afforded an opportunity to specify by boxes a choice between approval or disapproval of, or abstention with respect to each separate matter referred to therein as intended to be acted upon, other than elections to office. A proxy may confer discretionary authority with respect to matters as to which a choice is not specified by the security holder provided that the form of proxy states in bold-face type how it is intended to vote the shares represented by the proxy in each such case.

(4) *Number of Proposals.* The proponent may submit no more than one proposal and an accompanying supporting statement for inclusion in the registrant's proxy materials for a meeting of security holders. If the proponent submits more than one proposal, or if he fails to comply with the 500 word limit mentioned in paragraph (b)(1) of this section, he shall be provided the opportunity to reduce the items submitted by him to the limits required by this rule, within 14 calendar days of notification of such limitations by the registrant.

(b)(1) *Supporting Statement.* The registrant, at the request of the proponent, shall include in its proxy statement a statement of the proponent in support of the proposal, which statement shall not include the name and address of the proponent. A proposal and its supporting statement in the aggregate shall not exceed 500 words. The supporting statement shall be furnished to the registrant at the time that the proposal is furnished, and the registrant shall not be responsible for such statement and the proposal to which it relates.

(2) *Identification of Proponent.* The proxy statement shall also include either the name and address of the proponent and the number of shares of the voting security held by the proponent or a statement that such information will be furnished by the registrant to any person, orally or in writing as requested, promptly upon the receipt of any oral or written request therefor.

(c) The registrant may omit a proposal and any statement in support thereof from its proxy statement and form of proxy under any of the following circumstances:

(1) If the proposal is, under the laws of the registrant's domicile, not a proper subject for action by security holders.

NOTE. Whether a proposal is a proper subject for action by security holders will depend on the applicable state law. Under certain states' laws, a proposal that mandates certain action by the registrant's board of directors may not be a proper subject matter for shareholder action, while a proposal recommending or requesting such action of the board may be proper under such state laws.

(2) If the proposal, if implemented, would require the registrant to violate any state law or Federal law of the United States, or any law of any foreign jurisdiction to which the registrant is subject, except that this provision shall not apply with respect to any foreign law compliance with which would be violative of any state law or Federal law of the United States;

(3) If the proposal or the supporting statement is contrary to any of the Commission's proxy rules and regulations, including Rule 14a–9 * * *;

(4) If the proposal relates to the redress of a personal claim or grievance against the registrant or any other person, or if it is designed to result in a benefit to the proponent or to further a personal interest, which benefit or interest is not shared with the other security holders at large;

(5) If the proposal relates to operations which account for less than 5 percent of the registrant's total assets at the end of its most recent fiscal year, and for less than 5 percent of its net earnings and gross sales for its most recent fiscal year, and is not otherwise significantly related to the registrant's business;

(6) If the proposal deals with a matter beyond the registrant's power to effectuate;

(7) If the proposal deals with a matter relating to the conduct of the ordinary business operations of the registrant;   *Lot of litigation about this one*

(8) If the proposal relates to an election to office;

(9) If the proposal is counter to a proposal to be submitted by the registrant at the meeting;

(10) If the proposal has been rendered moot;

(11) If the proposal is substantially duplicative of a proposal previously submitted to the registrant by another proponent, which proposal will be included in the registrant's proxy material for the meeting;

(12) If the proposal deals with substantially the same subject matter as a prior proposal submitted to security holders in the registrant's proxy statement and form of proxy relating to any annual or special meeting of security holders held within the preceding five calendar years, it may be omitted from the registrant's proxy materials relating to any meeting of security holders held within three calendar years after the latest such previous submission: *Provided, That*

    (i) If the proposal was submitted at only one meeting during such preceding period, it received less than three percent of the total number of votes cast in regard thereto; or

    (ii) If the proposal was submitted at only two meetings during such preceding period, it received at the time of its second submission less than six percent of the total number of votes cast in regard thereto; or

    (iii) If the prior proposal was submitted at three or more meetings during such preceding period, it received at the time of its latest submission less than 10 percent of the total number of votes cast in regard thereto; or

(13) If the proposal relates to specific amounts of cash or stock dividends.

(d) Whenever the registrant asserts, for any reason, that a proposal and any statement in support thereof received from a proponent may properly be omitted from its proxy statement and form of proxy, it shall file with the Commission * * * the following items:

(1) the proposal;

(2) any statement in support thereof as received from the proponent;

(3) a statement of the reasons why the registrant deems such omission to be proper in the particular case; and

(4) where such reasons are based on matters of law, a supporting opinion of counsel. The registrant shall at the same time, if it has not already done so notify the proponent of its intention to omit the proposal from its proxy statement and form of proxy and shall forward to him a copy of the statement of reasons why the registrant deems the omission of the proposal to be proper and a copy of such supporting opinion of counsel.

(e) If the registrant intends to include in the proxy statement a statement in opposition to a proposal received from a proponent, it shall * * * promptly forward to the proponent a copy of the statement in opposition to the proposal. In the event the proponent believes that the statement in opposition contains materially false or misleading statements within the meaning of Rule 14a–9 and the proponent wishes to bring this matter to the attention of the Commission, the proponent promptly should provide the staff with a letter setting forth the reasons for this view and at the same time promptly provide the registrant with a copy of his letter.

Notes

(1) Rule 14a–8 has long been viewed by the SEC as a potentially important element of corporate democracy since it in effect permits individual shareholders to place proposals before the body of shareholders through the corporation's proxy statement. Is this right of ballot access based on state law or is it federally created? See Jill E. Fisch, From Legitimacy to Logic: Reconstructing Proxy Regulation, 46 Vand.L.Rev. 1129, 1143–1148 (1993):

Many of the restrictions in Rule 14a–8 appear both sensible and within the SEC's power to impose. Few commentators would argue with the propriety of permitting management to exclude proposals that are false and misleading or that call for the corporation to violate state or federal law. Only the first basis for exclusion, however, which requires that the proposal deal with a matter that is a proper subject for shareholder action under state law, is strictly true to the SEC's original premise that proper subject is determined by state law.

Moreover, many of the bases for exclusion are not grounded directly in state law. * * * Rule 14a–8(a)(1) imposes minimum ownership requirements and holding period qualifications upon shareholders who seek inclusion of a proposal under Rule 14a–8. No uniform state or common-law principle requires that a shareholder hold one percent or one thousand dollars worth of a corporation's stock for a minimum of one year before making a motion at a shareholders' meeting. No state law bars a shareholder from making the same motion or proposal in successive years, yet Rule 14a–8(c)(12) limits a shareholder's ability to do so. Additionally, state law does not restrict shareholders to dealing with issues concerning more than five percent of the corporation's total assets or extraordinary business matters. The SEC, however, has imposed these limits on shareholder democracy.

Many of the restrictions imposed by the proxy rules can be attributed to a pragmatic effort by the SEC to limit the number of shareholder proposals and to restrict use of the proxy statement to issues of general importance to shareholders. Although such limits may be desirable, they have no foundation in state or common-law restrictions regarding proper subjects to be raised at a shareholders' meeting. The SEC's authority to impose these restrictions on the use of the proxy mechanism is therefore unclear.

Apart from pragmatic concerns, the SEC's restrictions appear to stem primarily from the general principle that state law vests management, rather than shareholders, with the authority to run the corporation. State corporation statutes generally provide that the corporation shall be managed by or under the direction of the board of directors. This common provision suggests that a shareholder proposal affecting the management of the corporation's affairs may improperly interfere with the board's authority.

The absence of modern judicial decisions voiding shareholder action on the basis of these statutes suggests that their limitation on shareholder activity is, at best, minimal. Additionally, it would seem that framing the proposal as a shareholder recommendation rather than an attempt to bind the board would address any limitation the statutes impose. * * *

Accordingly, both in determining appropriate criteria for excluding shareholder proposals and in applying those criteria, the SEC does not replicate passively the annual meeting process by applying state law principles, but creates a federal common law as to what constitutes a proper subject for shareholder action.

(2) The major sources of shareholder proposals today are the members of the Interfaith Center on Corporate Responsibility, a loose organization of nearly 250 Protestant and Roman Catholic denominations, religious communities, agencies, pension funds,[78] healthcare systems, dioceses, and a few individuals. In 1997 nearly one hundred ICCR-member religious investors sponsored 191 resolutions to 137 companies. Examples include: requesting RJR Nabisco "to adopt a policy ending Joe Camel ads anywhere in the world by the end of 1997;" requesting Anheuser Busch to "revise existing company educational materials and develop all future materials to include in a prominent fashion the definition of moderate drinking found in the Dietary Guidelines * * *;" to General Electric to "no longer seek new nuclear fuel sales abroad, and instead, promote the sale of safer, lower-risk, energy-efficient alternate generating systems to foreign markets;" and to more than 40 companies to endorse the CERES Principles for Public Environmental Accountability. However, many proposals also relate to traditional corporate governance concerns, for example: proposals to Coca–Cola and four other companies to create a Nominating Committee of the board of directors consisting entirely of independent directors; to Texaco and four other companies to declassify the election of directors so that all directors are elected annually; and to more than a dozen companies to make formal review of executive compensation policies. The Corporate Examiner, Vol. 25, No. 7–8, at 8–10, 14 (1997).

(3) Are resolutions raising social policy issues such as those described in note (2) appropriate matters for inclusion under rule 14a–8? Should not they be excludable under rule 14a–8(c)(7)? There is obviously some connection between Anheuser Busch's operations and the shareholders' proposal to warn customers to drink only moderately. It is equally obvious that proposals of this nature also could be viewed as relating to the "ordinary business operations" of the issuer. The construction of this clause in the context of social responsibility issues has a considerable history. The original attitude of the SEC was to permit proposals of this nature to be excluded, but the courts disagreed. The leading case involved an attempt in 1968 by an organization called the Medical Committee for Human Rights, to require Dow Chemical Company to include the following "resolution" in its proxy statement:

> RESOLVED, that the shareholders of the Dow Chemical Company request the Board of Directors, in accordance with the laws of the State of Delaware, and the Composite Certificate of Incorporation of the Dow Chemical Company, to adopt a resolution setting forth an amendment to the Composite Certificate of Incorporation of the Dow Chemical Company that napalm shall not be sold to any buyer unless that buyer gives reasonable assurance that the substance will not be used on or against human beings.

78. [By the Editor] Before 1992, rule 14a–8 was widely used by institutional investors to raise economic issues with individual corporations, often with a considerable degree of suc-cess. Today, most of these issues are raised directly with the targeted issuer. See pages 551–53, supra.

The letter concluded with the following statement:

> Finally, we wish to note that our objections to the sale of this product [are] primarily based on the concerns for human life inherent in our organization's credo. However, we are further informed by our investment advisers that this product is also bad for our company's business as it is being used in the Vietnamese War. It is now clear from company statements and press reports that it is increasingly hard to recruit the highly intelligent, well-motivated, young college men so important for company growth. There is, as well, an adverse impact on our global business, which our advisers indicate, suffers as a result of the public reaction to this product.

In Medical Comm. for Human Rights v. SEC, 432 F.2d 659 (D.C.Cir.1970), vacated as moot 404 U.S. 403, 92 S.Ct. 577, 30 L.Ed.2d 560 (1972), the Court did not hold that this proposal was includable, but strongly intimated that it was, and that rule 14a–8 was an important mechanism for shareholder democracy and control of management:

> The management of Dow Chemical Company is repeatedly quoted in sources which include the company's own publications as proclaiming that the decision to continue manufacturing and marketing napalm was made not *because* of business considerations, but *in spite of* them; that management in essence decided to pursue a course of activity which generated little profit for the shareholders and actively impaired the company's public relations and recruitment activities because management considered this action morally and politically desirable. The proper political and social role of modern corporations is, of course, a matter of philosophical argument extending far beyond the scope of our present concern; the substantive wisdom or propriety of particular corporate political decisions is also completely irrelevant to the resolution of the present controversy. What *is* of immediate concern, however, is the question of whether the corporate proxy rules can be employed as a shield to isolate such managerial decisions from shareholder control. After all, it must be remembered that "[t]he control of great corporations by a very few persons was the abuse at which Congress struck in enacting Section 14(a)." SEC v. Transamerica Corp., * * * 163 F.2d at 518. We think that there is a clear and compelling distinction between management's legitimate need for freedom to apply its expertise in matters of day-to-day business judgment, and management's patently illegitimate claim of power to treat modern corporations with their vast resources as personal satrapies implementing personal political or moral predilections. It could scarcely be argued that management is more qualified or more entitled to make these kinds of decisions than the shareholders who are the true beneficial owners of the corporation; and it seems equally implausible that an application of the proxy rules which permitted such a result could be harmonized with the philosophy of corporate democracy which Congress embodies in section 14(a) of the Securities Exchange Act of 1934.

432 F.2d at 681. The Supreme Court appeal, incidentally, became moot after the corporation voluntarily submitted the Medical Committee proposal to its shareholders, where it received the support of less than three percent of the shares voting on the issue.

(4) In SEC Rel. No. 34–12999, 41 Fed. Reg. 52,994, 52,998 (1976), the SEC announced a major change in policy:

> [T]he term "ordinary business operations" has been deemed on occasion to include certain matters which have significant policy, economic or other

implications inherent in them. For instance, a proposal that a utility company not construct a proposed nuclear power plant has in the past been considered excludable * * *. In retrospect, however, it seems apparent that the economic and safety considerations attendant to nuclear power plants are of such magnitude that a determination whether to construct one is not an "ordinary" business matter. Accordingly proposals of that nature, as well as others that have major implications, will in the future be considered beyond the realm of an issuer's ordinary business operations, and future interpretive letters of the Commission's staff will reflect that view.

* * * [W]here proposals involve business matters that are mundane in nature and do not involve any substantial policy or other considerations, the subparagraph may be relied upon to omit them.

Following the 1976 release, the SEC required a number of corporations to include proposals reporting on their compliance with the requirements of equal opportunity and affirmative action. Generally, the SEC considered whether the subject of the reporting related to "day-to-day" employment matters (in which event the proposal was excludable as relating to "ordinary business matters") or whether it raised significant policy considerations. To what extent do the examples set forth in note (2) involve "matters that are mundane in nature"?

(5) In March 1991, the SEC's position with respect to employment matters changed significantly. This new policy was set forth most explicitly in a "no action letter"[79] addressed to Cracker Barrel Old Country Store, Inc. relating to a proposal that Cracker Barrel be required to establish a policy not to discriminate against homosexuals. 1992 WL 289095 (Oct. 13, 1992):

As a general rule, the staff views proposals directed at a company's employment policies and practices with respect to its non-executive workforce to be uniquely matters relating to the conduct of the company's ordinary business operations. Examples of the categories of proposals that have been deemed to be excludable on this basis are: employee health benefits, general compensation issues not focused on senior executives, management of the workplace, employee supervision, labor-management relations, employee hiring and firing, conditions of employment and employee training and motivation.

Notwithstanding the general view that employment matters concerning the workforce of the company are excludable as matters involving the conduct of day-to-day business, exceptions have been made in some cases where a proponent based an employment-related proposal on "social policy" concerns. In recent years, however, the line between includable and excludable employment-related proposals based on social policy considerations has become increasingly difficult to draw. The distinctions recognized by the staff are characterized by many as tenuous, without substance and effectively nullifying the application of the ordinary business exclusion to employment related proposals.

The Division has reconsidered the application of Rule 14a–8(c)(7) to employment-related proposals in light of these concerns and the staff's experience with these proposals in recent years. As a result, the Division has determined that the fact that a shareholder proposal concerning a company's employment policies and practices for the general workforce is tied to a social

---

79. [By the Editor] A "no action" letter is a letter sent by SEC staff to a corporation stating that "it will not recommend any enforcement action to the Commission if the proposal is omitted." The legal status of such a letter is discussed in the following text.

issue will no longer be viewed as removing the proposal from the realm of ordinary business operations of the registrant. Rather, determinations with respect to any such proposals are properly governed by the employment-based nature of the proposal.

This is to be distinguished from proposals relating to the compensation of senior executives and directors. The Commission continues to regard issues affecting CEO and other senior executive and director compensation as unique decisions affecting the nature of the relationships among shareholders, those who run the corporation on their behalf and the directors who are responsible for overseeing management performance. Consequently, unlike proposals relating to the rank and file workforce, proposals concerning senior executive and director compensation are viewed by the Commission as inherently outside the scope of normal or routine practices in the running of the company's operations.

Efforts by labor unions to enjoin the implementation of this revised policy relating to employment-related proposals failed essentially on procedural grounds. However, in 1997, the SEC proposed to reverse the *Cracker Barrel* interpretation:

The Cracker Barrel interpretation has been controversial since it was announced. While the reasons for adopting the Cracker Barrel interpretation continue to have some validity, as well as significant support in the corporate community,* we believe that reversal of the position is warranted in light of the broader package of reforms proposed today. Reversal will require companies to include proposals in their proxy materials that some shareholders believe are important to companies and fellow shareholders. In place of the 1992 position, the Division would return to its approach to such proposals prevailing before it adopted the position. That is, employment-related proposals focusing on significant social policy issues could not automatically be excluded under the "ordinary business" exclusion.

Under this proposal, the "bright line" approach for employment-related proposals established by the Cracker Barrel position would be replaced by the case-by-case analysis that prevailed previously. Return to a case-by-case approach should redress the concerns of shareholders interested in submitting for a vote by fellow shareholders employment-related proposals raising significant social issues. While this would be a change in the Commission's interpretation of the rule, we nonetheless request your comments on whether we should reverse the Cracker Barrel interpretation. * * *

Proposed Rule: Amendments to Rules on Shareholder Proposals, SEC Rel. No. 34–39093 (September 25, 1997), at 9–10.

(6) In Roosevelt v. E.I. Du Pont de Nemours & Co., 958 F.2d 416 (D.C.Cir. 1992), the Court held the the "ordinary business operations" exception applied to a proposal that Du Pont present a report to shareholders detailing the timing of Du Pont's phasing out of the production of chlorofluorocarbons ("CFCs") on the ground that Du Pont was committed to a phase-out of CFCs and the only point of contention—the rapidity with which the near-term phase should occur—was a matter of ordinary business operations.

---

* [By the SEC] In response to the Questionnaire, 91% of companies favored excluding employment-related shareholder proposals raising significant social policy issues under the Cracker Barrel interpretation. Eighty-six percent of shareholders thought such proposals should be included.

(7) What about a proposal that an importer of various food products make a study of the methods by which its French supplier of paté de foie gras force-feeds its geese to determine whether these methods cause undue pain or suffering to these animals? See Lovenheim v. Iroquois Brands, Ltd., 618 F.Supp. 554 (D.D.C. 1985), requiring the inclusion of the proposal. Would it make any difference under rule 14a–8 if the defendant's sale of paté produced only $79,000 of its annual gross revenues of about $141,000,000? (It didn't.)

RAUCHMAN v. MOBIL CORP.

United States Court of Appeals, Sixth Circuit, 1984.
739 F.2d 205.

Before ENGEL and KEITH, CIRCUIT JUDGES, and WEICK, SENIOR CIRCUIT JUDGE.

ENGEL, CIRCUIT JUDGE.

The principal issue in this appeal is whether defendant Mobil Corporation properly refused to include in its proxy statement a proposal which would amend Mobil's bylaws to prevent a citizen of an OPEC country from sitting on Mobil's board of directors. The plaintiff's claim is premised upon the existence of an implied private cause of action under section 14(a) of the Securities Exchange Act, and upon rule 14a–8 promulgated thereunder. Rauchman asserts that Mobil was required to include the proposal in the corporation's proxy statement for the 1982 annual meeting.

I.

The plaintiff, Irvin Rauchman, owns sixty-four voting shares of Mobil stock. In 1981, pursuant to Securities Exchange Commission (SEC or Commission) rule 14a–8(a), Rauchman submitted a proposed amendment to Mobil's bylaws for inclusion in Mobil's proxy statement for the company's 1982 annual meeting.

The proposal read as follows:

Proposal: It is resolved that the bylaws of the Corporation are amended to read as follows: Citizens of countries belonging to OPEC are not qualified for election to, or membership on, the Corporation's Board of Directors.

Supporting Statement: On October 31, 1980, Mobil's directors appointed a Saudi Arabian citizen to its Board of Directors. This individual reportedly has ties to members of the present Saudi Arabian government. Saudi Arabia, of course, makes harmful political use of its oil supply. Mobil, by appointing a Saudi Arabian to its Board of Directors, is, in effect, also approving of Saudi Arabia's activities.

Other corporations successfully transact business with OPEC countries without appointing citizens of those countries to their boards. Other means are available to obtain a working relationship with OPEC. Mobil has erred by associating with a country that has, for example, provided an abundance of cash and weapons to the Palestine Liberation Organization. A provision in Mobil's bylaws excluding citizens of OPEC countries from its Board of Directors will be a step in the right direction.

The[r]e are qualified American citizens who can contribute to the continued success of Mobil. It is unnecessary for Mobil to prostitute itself to the power of OPEC and become a silent partner to OPEC's destructive activities.

Evidently, Mr. Rauchman's concern with the presence of an OPEC citizen on the Mobil board was caused by the appointment to the board of Suliman S. Olayan, a Saudi Arabian citizen.

After receiving Rauchman's proposal, Mobil wrote to the SEC staff requesting that the staff recommend to the Commission that no action be taken if Mobil did not include Rauchman's proposal in the proxy statement. Mobil maintained in its letter to the SEC that under rule 14a–8(c)(8), which allows a company to exclude a proposal if it relates to an election to office of the company's board of directors, the proposal need not be included. Mobil took this position because Olayan was eligible for reelection at Mobil's 1982 annual meeting. The SEC staff responded with a letter indicating that it would not recommend any enforcement action to the Commission if Mobil omitted the proposal. In its letter the staff noted that

> [t]here appears to be some basis for your opinion that the proposal may be omitted from the Company's proxy material under Rule 14a–8(c)(8), since it relates to the election to office of the Company's Board of Directors. In the staff's view, the proposal and supporting statement call into question the qualifications of Mr. Olayan for reelection and thus the proposal may be deemed an effort to oppose management's solicitation on behalf of the reelection of this person. Under the circumstances, this Division will not recommend any enforcement action to the Commission if the Company omits the proposal from its proxy material.

Following the staff's determination, Rauchman brought suit in the United States District Court for the Southern District of Ohio to force Mobil to include the proposal in the Company's proxy statement. The district court assumed that Rauchman had a private right of action under section 14(a) of the Securities Exchange Act and rule 14a–8 promulgated thereunder. The court then found that Mobil properly excluded Rauchman's proposal from its proxy statement because the proposal related to an election to office. The court found that the proposal was related to the reelection of Olayan to Mobil's board of directors because, had the proposal been adopted, Mr. Olayan would have been ineligible to sit on Mobil's board. Thus, the court concluded: "Rauchman's proposal * * * is clearly intended to render Mr. Olayan ineligible to serve as a Mobil director." Based on these findings the district court granted Mobil's motion for summary judgment.

II.

* * * [The Court concludes with "substantial reservations" that a private cause of action exists for violation of rule 14a–8.]

III.

Turning therefore to the merits of the appeal, we conclude that the district judge did not err in granting Mobil's motion for summary judgment. It was undisputed that Suliman S. Olayan, a Saudi Arabian citizen, was running for reelection to Mobil's board of directors. The election of Olayan to the board would have been forbidden by the proposed bylaw amendment, since the amendment would have made him ineligible to sit on the board. Paragraph one of the proposed comment submitted by Rauchman unmistakably and expressly referred to Olayan, although not by name. In our view, this circumstance sufficiently supports the trial judge's holding that the proposal relates to an election to office and, under the rules of the Commission, was not required to be included.

It is suggested on appeal that the proposal would have only an incidental impact upon Olayan's reelection. We disagree. As the district court noted, "Mobile [sic] stockholders could not vote for Rauchman's proposal and at the same time ratify the nomination of Mr. Olayan." By forcing the shareholders to choose between ratifying the proposal and reelecting Olayan, Rauchman's proposal could clearly be viewed as an "effort to oppose management's solicitation on behalf of" Olayan's reelection. It is a form of electioneering which Mobil was not required to include in its proxy statement.

Plaintiff suggests in his brief that if we conclude that Mr. Olayan's presence on the Mobil board of directors invalidates Rauchman's "otherwise proper proposal," the remedy would be to insert a "grandfather clause" rendering the bylaw inapplicable to Olayan. We are not aware that this suggestion was ever made to the district court or to Mobil until this appeal. We are not disposed to act on that suggestion at this late date and at this level.

Mobil argued that the proposed bylaw would transgress the laws of the state of Mobil's incorporation (Delaware) and of the state of its principal place of business (New York). Mobil also argued that Rauchman's proposal conflicts with the executive agreement of November 7, 1983, 48 Stat. 1826, between the United States and Saudi Arabia. In view of our decision that the proposal relates to an election to office, it is unnecessary for us to consider Mobil's contention that the proposal could be excluded under rule 14a–8(c)(2) which permits a company to omit any proposal which, if implemented, would "require the issuer to violate any state law or federal law of the United States."

We believe that Mobil was fully within its rights in declining to submit the proposed proxy material, at least in the form proposed by Mr. Rauchman. Affirmed.

Notes

(1) The election of directors is probably the most significant power that shareholders possess. Shouldn't the shareholders therefore be able to vote on Rauchman's proposal as a matter both of common sense and (presumably) of state law? Even if the proposal is an indirect attack on Mr. Olayan's candidacy, what is wrong with that? Shouldn't shareholders, as a matter of common sense and (presumably) of state law, also have the power to vote against a candidate proposed by management?

(2) Does not the SEC's rules with respect to the nomination of directors and to voting tend to ensure the election of management candidates and to reduce shareholder effectiveness? See Jill E. Fisch, From Legitimacy to Logic: Reconstructing Proxy Regulation, 46 Vand.L.Rev. 1129, 1162–64 (1993):

> * * * In spite of congressional concern in 1934 that corporate insiders controlled the election process, a concern to which the proxy regulations appear to be addressed, insider domination of the election process remains pervasive today. * * * The continued ability of corporate insiders to control

director elections can be attributed, in part, to deficiencies in the federal proxy rules. The proxy rules both have failed to provide affirmative access for shareholders to participate in the nomination process and have thwarted shareholder attempts at participation.

The most obvious omission from the federal proxy rules is a mechanism for shareholders to access the nomination process. * * * In 1942, the SEC proposed a rule that would have required corporations to include shareholder nominated director candidates in the corporation's proxy statement.[80] Corporate management criticized the rule on the grounds that it was unworkable; shareholders might nominate unqualified candidates or create ballot confusion by nominating too many candidates. These interferences with effective corporate management could prove costly in connection with the wartime effort. Ultimately the SEC abandoned its efforts to pass the rule. Ironically, the exclusion [of Rule 14a–8] originated with * * * [this] proposal * * *. The unfavorable public response to that proposal led to a staff interpretation that Rule 14a–8 did not permit shareholder proposals in support of a slate of challengers. Subsequently, the SEC amended the text of the Rule to exclude proposals relating to director elections explicitly. * * *

Although the SEC has not interpreted the exclusion to bar general proposals relating to election procedures, such as cumulative voting rights and general qualifications for directors, the provision prevents a shareholder from using Rule 14a–8 to nominate or advocate the election of a particular director. Furthermore, the SEC has allowed management to rely on the exclusion to bar any proposal that could be viewed as interfering with election of existing directors or director slates. * * *

(3) In United Paperworkers Int'l Union v. Int'l Paper Co., 985 F.2d 1190, (2d Cir.1993), the Union filed a rule 14a–8 request that the company sign and actively implement the "Valdez principles" relating to reducing waste, marketing safe products, and providing redress for environmental damage. The company included the proposal in its proxy statement, and recommended a vote against it, stating that "International Paper is dedicated to safe and environmentally sound products, packaging and operations"; that the Valdez principles are consistent with the company's "long-standing policies on environment, health and safety", and that the company had a "strong environmental compliance program." It turns out that these statements were false: the company had been accused of numerous environmental offenses, had pleaded guilty to felonies, had agreed to pay large fines, and had been the target of numerous administrative complaints. The District Court refused to enjoin the meeting and the Valdez proposal was defeated, receiving 5.937 percent of the votes cast. What should be done about false opposition statements? The District Court ordered the corporation to resubmit the Valdez proposal at the next annual meeting, and the Court of Appeals directed that a statement "such as the following" should be included:

(i) that the district court declared the board of directors' March 31, 1992 proxy statement, in responding to the Valdez Proposal, to be materially misleading in violation of federal securities law; (ii) that the district court declared the shareholder vote held May 12, 1992, on the Valdez Resolution null and void; and (iii) that the district court ordered the Company to resubmit the proposal for a new vote of the shareholders.

80. [By the Author] Exchange Act Release No. 3347, 1942 SEC LEXIS 44 (Dec. 18, 1942).

Id. at 1202. Is that sufficient? Should a court get in the business of writing corrective language for a proxy statement?

(4) Most shareholder proposals are phrased as recommendations or requests for director action and thus fall comfortably within the note to rule 14a–8(c)(1). However, not all proposals are so phrased. In 1992, a shareholder of Exxon proposed the creation of a three member shareholder advisory committee to review the management of Exxon's business affairs and to advise the board of directors both of its own views and the views of other shareholders; the advisory committee was to have the power to employ outside advisers and also to include a 2,500 word report and evaluation in the Exxon proxy statement. Large shareholders were entitled to nominate advisory committee members who would be elected by the shareholders along with the directors. The critical state law issue raised by this proposal was that it was cast in the form of a proposed amendment to the Exxon bylaws, a matter on which shareholders are entitled to vote under New Jersey law. The SEC staff required the proposal to be included over the arguments (i) that it was excludable under rule 14a–8(c)(7) as relating to "ordinary business operations" and (ii) that it was not a "proper subject" of shareholder action under New Jersey law since it was inconsistent with the general prescription that the business affairs of the corporation was to be managed by or under the direction of a board of directors. The proposal received the affirmative vote of about 8 percent of Exxon shareholders. Consider also Grimes v. Ohio Edison Co., 992 F.2d 455 (2d Cir.1993), in which a shareholder attempted to propose an amendment to the articles of incorporation that would have required shareholder approval for loans in excess of a certain amount. The Court affirmed the District Court's decision not to require that this proposal be included on the ground that it related to "ordinary business operations." Under the MBCA, a shareholder proposal to amend the articles of incorporation should be excludable on the ground that it is not a proper subject for shareholder action in the absence of initial consideration and favorable recommendation by the board of directors. MBCA § 10.03(b).

(5) The Exxon decision, however, was not followed in early 1993 when a similar mandatory bylaw proposal was advanced for inclusion in the Pennzoil proxy statement. Pennzoil submitted an opinion by its Delaware counsel that the proposal was contrary to Delaware statutory and case law since it interfered with the discretion of directors. After the staff indicated that it intended to issue a no action letter permitting the proposal to be excluded, the applicant amended the proposal to make it a request addressed to the board of directors. The staff, however, concluded that this proposal need not be included since it provided that the proposed bylaw could be amended only by shareholders and that was not proper under state law. The history of the Exxon/Pennzoil proposals is discussed in John C. Coffee, Jr., The SEC and the Institutional Investor: a Halftime Report, 15 Cardozo L.Rev. 837, 882–891 (1994); see also Charles F. Richards & Anne C. Foster, Exxon Revisited: The SEC Allows Pennzoil To Exclude Both Mandatory and Precatory Proposals Seeking to Create a Shareholder Advisory Committee, 48 Bus. Law. 1509 (1993); John C. Coffee, Jr., The Bylaw Battlefield: Can Institutions Change the Outcome of Corporate Control Contests, 51 U. Miami L. Rev. 605 (1997).

(6) Rule 14a–4 provides that an issuer's proxy materials must disclose matters that it believes will be presented at the meeting, "whether raised by management or shareholders." In 1996, two labor unions targeted ten companies for shareholder proposals and, in an effort to avoid rule 14a–8 limitations, submitted proposals directly under rule 14a–4 with a statement that they will be raised by individual shareholders at the meeting and requesting that information

about them be included in the company's proxy statement. The Company refused. This "backdoor" approach to avoiding the limitations of Rule 14a–8 was short-circuited when the SEC informally accepted the Company's position on the specific facts presented, but there is obvious tension between Rule 14a–8 and Rule 14a–4.

(7) General Motors Proxy Statement for annual meeting of May 20, 1988, at ii:

> Occasionally, inquiries have been made as to why the Board of Directors opposes these proposals [by shareholders] in the Proxy Statement. The Board of Directors does not disagree with all stockholder proposals submitted to the Corporation. When the Board finds that a stockholder proposal is consistent with the best interests of the Corporation and the stockholders, it normally can be implemented without need for a stockholder vote. The Corporation, over the years, has adopted a number of stockholder proposals and other suggestions. Thus, the stockholder proposals that appear in the Proxy Statement are those with which the Board of Directors disagrees and believes it must oppose in fulfilling its obligations to represent and safeguard the best interest of stockholders as a whole.

In September, 1997, the SEC published proposed amendments to Rule 14a–8. Proposed Amendments to Rules on Shareholder Proposals, SEC Rel. No. 34–39093, September 25, 1997. The Executive Summary, pages 1–2, describes the principal changes as follows:

> The proposals today would make it easier for shareholders to include a broader range of proposals in companies' proxy materials, and provide companies with clearer ground rules and more flexibility to exclude proposals that failed to attract significant shareholder support in prior years. We are proposing a "package" of reforms that we believe best accommodates the concerns of most participants in the shareholder proposal process, including proposals to accomplish the following:

> ● recast the rule into a more understandable Question & Answer format;[81] * * *

> ● make it more difficult to present proposals again that received an insignificant percentage of the votes cast on earlier submissions, enhancing shareholders' ability to decide for themselves which proposals are important to the company;[82]

> ● introduce an "override" mechanism permitting 3% of the share ownership to override a company's decision to exclude a proposal under certain of the bases for exclusion;[83]

---

81. [By the Editor] The proposed rule consists of 14 questions and answers. In addition, the SEC has made an effort to use "plain English," e.g. substituting "substantially implemented" for "moot" in rule 14a–8(c)(10) and "specific business decisions normally left to the discretion of management" for "ordinary business operations" in Rule 14a–8(7).

82. [By the Editor] The proposed revision would increase the threshold percentages in Rule 14a–8(c)(12) from 3% to 6% for proposals submitted once previously, from 6% to 15% if the proposal was submitted twice previously, and from 10% to 30% if the proposal was submitted three or more times previously.

83. [By the Editor] The override provision would apply to exclusions under paragraphs

- adopt a new qualified exemption from the proxy rules under Section 14(a) of the Exchange Act, and a safe harbor under Section 13(d) of the Exchange Act and rule 13d–5, to make it easier for shareholders to use the new "override;"[84]

- streamline the exclusion for matters considered irrelevant to corporate business, to permit companies to exclude proposals that relate to economically insignificant portions of their businesses;[85]

- streamline our administration of the rule whereby companies are permitted to exclude proposals furthering personal grievances or special interests;[86] and

- provide clearer ground rules for management's exercise of discretionary voting authority when a shareholder notifies the company that it intends to present a proposal outside the mechanism of rule 14a–8.[87]

Several of these proposed changes have proved to be highly controversial, and it is likely that they will not be implemented in the form proposed.

5. COMMUNICATING WITH SHAREHOLDERS

REGULATION 14A. SOLICITATION OF PROXIES
17 C.F.R. § 240.14a–7 (1997).

§ 2.40.14a–7 OBLIGATIONS OF REGISTRANTS TO PROVIDE A LIST
OF, OR MAIL SOLICITING MATERIAL TO, SECURITY HOLDERS

(a) If the registrant has made or intends to make a proxy solicitation in connection with a security holder meeting or action by consent or authorization, upon the written request by any record or beneficial holder of securities of the class entitled to vote at the meeting or to execute a consent or authorization to provide a list of security holders or to mail the requesting security holder's materials, regardless of whether the request references this section, the registrant shall:

(1) Perform the acts set forth in either paragraphs (a)(2)(i) or (a)(2)(ii) of this section, at the registrant's * * * option * * *.

(c)(3) and (c)(5). In most publicly held corporations, a few institutional investors could join together to make the necessary 3% override.

84. [By the Editor] Schedule 13D and 13G would be amended to relieve shareholders from any proxy statement delivery requirement and beneficial ownership reporting requirement arising solely as a result of joining together to exercise the 3% override.

85. [By the Editor] Rule 14a–8(c)(5) would be amended to reduce the *de minimis* test from 5% of gross revenue or total assets to the lesser of $10 million or 3% of gross revenue or total assets. The phrase "and is not otherwise significantly related to the registrant's business" would be deleted and the exclusion limited to "proposals relating to the purchase or sale of products or services."

86. [By the Editor] Rule 14a–8(c)(4) would be amended to essentially exclude the SEC from review of personal grievance objections unless the personal claim, grievance or interest of the proponent is apparent on the face of the proposal. The SEC staff would express "no view" on all other objections and the parties would be free to litigate the applicability of the exclusion.

87. [By the Editor] See notes (5) and (6) above. Rule 14a–4(c) would be revised to allow management voting discretion in all cases where management did not have notice of the matter more than 45 days before the date on which the company mailed its proxy materials. If management had notice before that date, it would be able to exercise voting discretion only if the proxy card permits shareholders to withhold such discretionary authority to the extent that item is not checked.

(i) Mail copies of any proxy statement, form of proxy or other soliciting material furnished by the security holder to the record holders, including banks, brokers, and similar entities, designated by the security holder. * * * The registrant shall mail the security holder material with reasonable promptness after tender of the material to be mailed, envelopes or other containers therefor, postage or payment for postage and other reasonable expenses of effecting such mailing. The registrant shall not be responsible for the content of the material; or

(ii) Deliver the following information to the requesting security holder within five business days of receipt of the request: a reasonably current list of the names, addresses and security positions of the record holders, including banks, brokers and similar entities, holding securities in the same class or classes as holders which have been or are to be solicited on management's behalf, or any more limited group of such holders designated by the security holder if available or retrievable under the registrant's or its transfer agent's security holder data systems; the most recent list of names, addresses and security positions of [nonobjecting] beneficial owners * * * in the possession, or which subsequently comes into the possession, of the registrant. All security holder list information shall be in the form requested by the security holder to the extent that such form is available to the registrant without undue burden or expense. The registrant shall furnish the security holder with updated record holder information on a daily basis or, if not available on a daily basis, at the shortest reasonable intervals, *provided, however*, the registrant need not provide beneficial or record holder information more current than the record date for the meeting or action.

* * * [T]he registrant shall have the option to either mail the security holder's material or furnish the security holder list as set forth in paragraph (a)(2) of this section.

(c) The security holder shall reimburse the reasonable expenses incurred by the registrant in performing the acts requested pursuant to paragraph (a) of this section.

Notes

(1) Omitted portions of this rule provide that the requesting security holder (and not the registrant) has the basic option provided by rule 14a–7 in two narrow classes of cases: limited partnership rollup transactions, and "going private" transactions subject to rule 13e–3.

(2) If you were representing an issuer that has received a request under rule 14a–7, would you recommend that the issuer offer to mail the requesting shareholder's soliciting material or supply the information required under rule 14a–7(a)(2)(ii)?

(3) Many institutional investors routinely publish detailed information about their portfolios, and it may be possible to learn the identities of the major beneficial owners of a large, publicly held corporation through this route more simply (and without alerting the registrant) than by invoking rule 14a–7 or seeking to inspect the shareholders list under state law.

Chapter Ten

DUTY OF CARE AND THE BUSINESS JUDGMENT RULE

LITWIN v. ALLEN

Supreme Court of New York, 1940.
25 N.Y.S.2d 667.

SHIENTAG, JUSTICE.

[Editor: This was a derivative suit brought on behalf of persons owning 36 shares of the stock of Guaranty Trust Company ("Trust Company") out of 900,000 outstanding against the directors of Guaranty Trust, members of the banking firm of J.P. Morgan & Co., and directors of a subsidiary of the Trust Company called Guaranty Company of New York ("Guaranty Company."). The complaint sought to impose liability on the defendants for losses incurred as a result of four transactions. The Court concluded that no liability existed for three of the transactions. The portions of the opinion set forth below relate to the Justice's general discussion and the fourth transaction on which liability was imposed. The sequence of the paragraphs set forth below has been rearranged.] * * *

II.

THE MISSOURI PACIFIC BOND TRANSACTION

This transaction involves the participation by the Trust Company or Guaranty Company or both, to the extent of $3,000,000, in a purchase of Missouri Pacific convertible debentures on October 16, 1930, through the firm of J.P. Morgan & Co. at par, with an option to the seller, Alleghany Corporation to repurchase them at the same price at any time within six months.

In the fall of 1930, the question of putting Alleghany Corporation in funds to the extent of $10,500,000 was first broached. Alleghany had purchased certain terminal properties in Kansas City and St. Joseph, Missouri, and the balance of the purchase price, amounting to slightly in excess of $10,000,000 and interest, had to be paid by October 16. Alleghany needed money to make this payment. Because of the borrowing limitation in Alleghany's charter (which limitation had been reached or exceeded in October 1930) Alleghany was unable to borrow the money. To overcome this borrowing limitation and solely to enable Alleghany to consummate the purchase of the terminal properties, discussions were commenced concerning the means whereby the necessary money could be raised. It is important that this circumstance be constantly kept in mind, in order that the purpose and pattern of the transaction as it did take place be fully understood.

Not being able to make a loan, the way that Alleghany could raise the necessary funds was by sale of some of the securities that it held. Among them was a large block of about $23,500,000 of Missouri Pacific convertible 5½ debentures. These were unsecured and subordinate to other Missouri Pacific bond issues. They were convertible into common stock at the rate of ten shares for each $1,000 bond. In 1929, Guaranty Company had participated to the extent of $1,500,000 in the underwriting of these bonds at 97½. At one time in 1929 the bonds had sold as high as 124 and had never gone below par except in November 1929 when they sold at 97. Between October 1 and October 10, 1930 Missouri Pacific common stock had dropped from 53 to 44. There was a decline in the bonds from 113 in April 1930 to 107 on October 1, 1930, and thereafter a decline of about two more points to 105½ by the date of the consummation of the transaction we are considering on October 16, 1930.

The Van Sweringens suggested that $10,000,000 of these bonds be sold to J.P. Morgan & Co. for cash at par, the latter to give an option to Alleghany to buy them back within six months for the price paid. If the transaction were carried through on that basis, namely, a sale by Alleghany with an option to them to repurchase at the same price, the same purpose would be accomplished, for Alleghany at any rate, as if a loan had been made.

The defendants testified that they were informed that the Van Sweringens insisted upon the option to repurchase within six months in order that there might be no possibility of their loss of control of Missouri Pacific through Alleghany, since these bonds were convertible and the privilege to do so might be exercised by third parties in the event of a distribution of these bonds in the market; this, despite the fact that the common stock of Missouri Pacific was then quoted in the neighborhood of 44, while the conversion price was 100.

The fact is that the only purpose served by the option was to make the transaction conform as closely as possible to a loan without the usual incidents of a loan transaction. * * *

At or shortly before the time that the Trust Company made its written commitment to J.P. Morgan & Co. to participate in the bond purchase, the Guaranty Company committed itself to the Trust Company to take up the bonds from the Trust Company at the end of the six-months' period, on April 16, 1931, for the same price that the Trust Company paid, that is, par and interest, if Alleghany failed to exercise its option to repurchase. * * *

The decline in the market continued. On October 23, 1930, when the Executive Committee of the Trust Company approved the transaction the Missouri Pacific bonds were at 103⅞. On November 5, 1930, when the Board of Directors of the Trust Company gave its approval, the bonds sold for 102⅞, and on November 18, 1930, when the board of the Guaranty Company approved its commitment, the bonds had dropped to 98⅝. At the end of the six months' period, on April 16, 1931, the bonds sold at 86 high and 81 low (the quotations being for the week ending April 18), and Guaranty Company took them over from the Trust Company at par and accrued interest and carried them on its books as an investment. * * *

[T]he main transactions attacked in this case * * * took place in October, 1930. There had been a crash in the stock market in October, 1929. In April, 1930, there was an upswing in the market. Shortly thereafter there began a slow but steady decline until October, 1930, when there was another severe break. The real significance of what was taking place was, generally speaking, missed at the time, but is plain in retrospect. Forces were at work which for the most part were unforeseeable. Men who were judging conditions in October, 1930, by what had been the course and the experience of past panics thought that the bottom had been reached and that the worst of the depression was over; that any change would be for the better and that recovery might reasonably be envisaged for the near future. Experience turned out to be fallacious and judgment proved to be erroneous; but that did not become apparent until some time in 1931. In order to judge the transactions complained of, therefore, we must not only hold an inquest on the past but, what is much more difficult, we must attempt to take ourselves back to the time when the events here questioned occurred and try to put ourselves in the position of those who engaged in them. * * *

There is no evidence in this case of any improper influence or domination of the directors or officers of the Trust Company or of the Guaranty Company by J.P. Morgan & Co. When J.P. Morgan & Co. were advised by Shriver that there would be a participation in the purchase to the extent of $5,000,000 the latter was told that such a commitment would be accepted only to the extent of $3,000,000 because the First National Bank of New York would be given a similar amount while Morgan & Co. themselves would participate to the extent of the balance amounting to $4,500,000. Moreover, there is no evidence to indicate that any of the defendants' officers or directors acted in bad faith or profited or attempted to profit or gain personally by reason of any phase of this transaction. * * *

I shall now proceed to consider generally the rules to be applied in determining the liability of directors. It has sometimes been said that directors are trustees. If this means that directors in the performance of their duties stand in a fiduciary relationship to the company, that statement is essentially correct. Bosworth v. Allen, 168 N.Y. 157, 61 N.E. 163, 55 L.R.A. 751, 85 Am.St.Rep. 667. "The directors are bound by all those rules of conscientious fairness, morality, and honesty in purpose which the law imposes as the guides for those who are under the fiduciary obligations and responsibilities. They are held, in official action, to the extreme measure of candor, unselfishness, and good faith. Those principles are rigid, essential, and salutary." Kavanaugh v. Kavanaugh Knitting Co., 226 N.Y. 185, 193, 123 N.E. 148, 151.

It is clear that a director owes loyalty and allegiance to the company—a loyalty that is undivided and an allegiance that is influenced in action by no consideration other than the welfare of the corporation. Any adverse interest of a director will be subjected to a scrutiny rigid and uncompromising. He may not profit at the expense of his corporation and in conflict with its rights; he may not for personal gain divert unto himself the opportunities which in equity and fairness belong to his corporation. He is required to use his independent judgment. In the discharge of his duties a director must, of course, act honestly and in good faith, but that is not enough. He must also exercise some degree of skill and prudence and diligence.

In a leading case the Court of Appeals, in referring to the duties of directors, said: "They should know of and give direction to the general affairs of the institution and its business policy, and have a general knowledge of the manner in which the business is conducted, the character of the investments, and the employment of the resources. No custom or practice can make a directorship a mere position of honor void of responsibility, or cause a name to become a substitute for care and attention. The personnel of a directorate may give confidence and attract custom; it must also afford protection." Kavanaugh v. Gould, 223 N.Y. 103, 106, 119 N.E. 237, 238.

In other words, directors are liable for negligence in the performance of their duties. Not being insurers, directors are not liable for errors of judgment or for mistakes while acting with reasonable skill and prudence. It has been said that a director is required to conduct the business of the corporation with the same degree of fidelity and care as an ordinarily prudent man would exercise in the management of his own affairs of like magnitude and importance. General rules, however, are not altogether helpful. In the last analysis, whether or not a director has discharged his duty, whether or not he has been negligent, depends upon the facts and circumstances of a particular case, the kind of corporation involved, its size and financial resources, the magnitude of the transaction, and the immediacy of the problem presented. A director is called upon "to bestow the care and skill" which the situation demands. New York Cent. Railroad Company v. Lockwood, 17 Wall. 357, 382, 383, 21 L.Ed. 627.

Undoubtedly, a director of a bank is held to stricter accountability than the director of an ordinary business corporation. A director of a bank is entrusted with the funds of depositors, and the stockholders look to him for protection from the imposition of personal liability. Gause v. Commonwealth Trust Co., 196 N.Y. 134, 153–155, 89 N.E. 476, 24 L.R.A., N.S., 967. But clairvoyance is not required even of a bank director. The law recognizes that the most conservative director is not infallible, and that he will make mistakes, but if he uses that degree of care ordinarily exercised by prudent bankers he will be absolved from liability although his opinion may turn out to have been mistaken and his judgment faulty.

Finally, in order to determine whether transactions approved by a director subject him to liability for negligence, we must "look at the facts as they exist at the time of their occurrence, not aided or enlightened by those which subsequently take place". Purdy v. Lynch, 145 N.Y. 462, 475, 40 N.E. 232, 236. "A wisdom developed after an event, and having it and its consequences as a source, is a standard no man should be judged by." Costello v. Costello, 209 N.Y. 252, 262, 103 N.E. 148, 152. * * *

Although * * * there is no case precisely in point, it would seem that if it is against public policy for a bank, anxious to dispose of some of its securities, to agree to buy them back at the same price, it is even more so where a bank purchases securities and gives the seller the option to buy them back at the same price, thereby incurring the entire risk of loss with no possibility of gain other than the interest derived from the securities during the period that the bank holds them. Here, if the market price of the securities should rise, the holder of the repurchase option would exercise it in order to recover his securities from the bank at the lower price at which he sold them to the bank.

If the market price should fall, the seller holding the option will not exercise it and the bank will sustain the loss. Thus, any benefit of a sharp rise in the price of the securities is assured the seller and any risk of heavy loss is inevitably assumed by the bank. If such an option agreement as is here involved were sustained, it would force the bank to set aside for six months whatever securities it had purchased. A bank certainly could not free itself from this obligation by engaging in a "short sale". In other words, while a resale option would force a bank to freeze an amount of cash equal to the selling price of the securities sold by it, a repurchase option would force a bank to freeze the securities themselves for the period of the option. In both situations the true financial condition of the bank could not be determined wholly from its books. It would depend upon the fluctuations of the market. In both cases there is a contingent liability which the balance sheet does not show. * * *

Directors are not in the position of trustees of an express trust who, regardless of good faith, are personally liable for losses arising from an infraction of their trust deed. Matter of Smith, 279 N.Y. 479, 489, 18 N.E.2d 666; see Fletcher Cyc. Corp., Perm.Ed., § 847. If liability is to be imposed on these directors it should rest on a more solid foundation. I find liability in this transaction because the entire arrangement was so improvident, so risky, so unusual and unnecessary as to be contrary to fundamental conceptions of prudent banking practice. A bank director when appointed or elected takes oath that he will, so far as the duty devolves on him "diligently and honestly administer the affairs of the bank or trust company." Banking Law, § 117. The oath merely adds solemnity to the obligation which the law itself imposes. Honesty alone does not suffice; the honesty of the directors in this case is unquestioned. But there must be more than honesty—there must be diligence, and that means care and prudence, as well. This transaction, it has been said, was unusual; it was unique, yet there is nothing in the record to indicate that the advice of counsel was sought. It is not surprising that a precedent cannot be found dealing with such a situation.

What sound reason is there for a bank, desiring to make an investment, short term or otherwise, to buy securities under an arrangement whereby any appreciation will inure to the benefit of the seller and any loss will be borne by the bank? The five and one-half point differential is no answer. It does not meet the fundamental objection that whatever loss there is would have to be borne by the Bank and whatever gain would go to the customer. There is more here than a question of business judgment as to which men might well differ. The directors plainly failed in this instance to bestow the care which the situation demanded. Unless we are to do away entirely with the doctrine that directors of a bank are liable for negligence in administering its affairs liability should be imposed in connection with this transaction.

The same result would be reached if we adopted the defendants' version of this transaction, namely, that it was initially a purchase by the Guaranty Company, with an option to the Alleghany Corporation to rebuy at the same price, and that the transaction was financed by the Bank, so that the immediate interest that the Bank had in it was a short term 5½% investment. * * *

Whichever way we look at this transaction, therefore, it was so improvident, so dangerous, so unusual and so contrary to ordinary prudent banking practice as to subject the directors who approved it to liability in a derivative stockholders' action.

The real issue as to damages is whether the directors should be liable for the total loss suffered when the bonds were ultimately sold, approximately an 81% loss, or only for that portion of the loss which accrued within the six months option period, making allowance for a period thereafter during which defendants could make reasonable and diligent efforts to sell the bonds. The record discloses that none of the bonds were sold until October 8, 1931, about six months after the Alleghany option had expired, and that they were not completely disposed of until December 28, 1937. The Missouri Pacific Railroad went into receivership in April, 1933, and between August 2 and September 25, 1933, $126,000 more of the bonds were purchased by the Company in an attempt to reduce the loss. A total loss was sustained on the bonds of approximately $2,250,000.

I believe that as to the decline of the bonds after April 16, 1931, there is no causal connection with the option which had expired on that date. A director is not liable for loss or damage other than what was proximately caused by his own acts or omissions in breach of his duty. The portion of the present transaction which is tainted with improvidence and negligence is the repurchase option. Once the option had expired, there was nothing to prevent the directors of the Company, which had taken over the bonds in accordance with its agreement, from selling them. Any loss on the bonds which was incurred after the option had expired on April 16, 1931, was occasioned as a result of the directors' independent business judgment in holding them thereafter. The further loss should not be laid at the door of the improper but already expired repurchase option.

Therefore, defendants are only liable for the loss attributable to the improper repurchase option itself, and this option ceased to be the motivating cause of the loss within a reasonable time after April 16, 1931. The price of the bonds for the week ending April 18, 1931, was 86 high and 81 low and closing. The matter will be referred to a Referee for assessment of damages to determine what price could have been obtained for these bonds if defendants had proceeded to sell them after April 16, 1931.

DEFENDANTS CHARGED WITH LIABILITY

The next question to consider is: Against what defendants has liability been established?

1. All of the directors who were present and voted at the meetings of the Executive Committee of the Trust Company on October 23, 1930, and the meeting of the Board of Directors of the Trust Company on November 5, 1930, are liable. * * * [R]atification by directors of a transaction already consummated by the officers or by themselves acting as officers imposes liability upon the directors, since the ratification is equivalent to prior acquiescence. Fletcher, Cyc.Corp., Perm.Ed., § 782, and cases there collected. Ratification of the officer's acts was essential in order completely to bind the Bank and the Company, and in any case such ratification vitiated a possible later rescission on the ground that it was not authorized by the directors.

2. Mr. Swan is liable even though he did not actually vote on the transaction as a director. His active participation and acquiescence are sufficient.

3. The defendants Kimball, Shriver and Stephenson while not directors are liable as officers who actively participated in the transaction.

4. No director of the Guaranty Company, as such, except Walker, is liable. He admittedly knew of the transaction, but there is nothing in the record to show that the repurchase option was brought to the attention of the directors at the meeting of the Executive Committee or of the Board of Directors of Guaranty Company. * * *

Notes

(1) Patricia A. McCoy, The Notional Business Judgment Rule in Banking, 44 Cath.U.L.Rev. 1031, 1038–40 (1995):

The one aspect of judicial substantive bank regulation that the corporate law literature has probed consists of a handful of cases, notably Hun v. Cary[1] and Litwin v. Allen, that struck down bank decisions for lack of "minimum rationality." These cases earned the sobriquet "minimum rationality" because they sought to stamp out transactions that were patently irrational from the bank's or depositors' point of view: i.e., transactions with no apparent profit potential on their face. * * *

In the half century since Litwin, its soundness on the facts has been rightly challenged. True, the directors signed away the right to potential market appreciation for six months while retaining the risk of loss. But the matter did not end there. Even without a put, the transaction might have been potentially profitable if the directors had bargained for some other consideration, such as higher interest or a collateral financial benefit. And in fact, they did: after all, Guaranty Trust was entitled to 5% interest. Whether the Litwin court failed to grasp this fact or purposely imposed a stiffer duty of care out of conflict-of-interest concerns[2] remains unclear.

These uncertainties are testament to the fact that it is no easy thing to pinpoint lack of profit potential from the bench, even with the benefit of hindsight. For this reason, later courts shied away from this type of financial analysis in banking cases, leaving Hun and Litwin in splendid isolation. One sign of the "minimum rationality" doctrine's demise is the fact that another class of bank transactions with no direct profit potential—interest-free check overdrafts to outside customers—almost never is penalized by the bench. Arguably, such overdrafts flunk a potential profitability test because they are loans without interest or formal terms for repayment. Nonetheless, most courts have treated disinterested overdrafts leniently, preferring to view them as a low-risk, "tied" product that could attract a potentially profitable upswing in deposits.[3] The fact that courts do not even ask if overdrafts are

---

1. [By the Author] 82 N.Y. 65 (N.Y. 1880).

2. [By the Author] * * * Those concerns inhered in the fact that the buyback arrangements served other financial interests of Guaranty Trust's affiliates. Guaranty Trust was a bank affiliate of J.P. Morgan & Company, while Alleghany was the principal holding company for the tottering Van Sweringen railroad system. J.P. Morgan & Company had invested heavily in the Van Sweringen businesses and obviously had an interest in preserving its investment by staving off the financial collapse of the Van Sweringen empire.

3. [By the Author] See, e.g., Wynn v. Tallapoosa County Bank, 168 Ala. 469, 53 So. 228, 240 (Ala. 1910) (recognizing a "uniform and long-continued acquiescence of the officers and committees of a bank" in allowing cashiers to

potentially profitable shows how moribund the "minimum rationality" test has become.

(2) Another early case involving a somewhat different factual pattern is Bates v. Dresser, 251 U.S. 524, 40 S.Ct. 247, 64 L.Ed. 388 (1920). In this case, a bank president who was also a director was held liable for the amount stolen by one Coleman, a young bookkeeper at the bank. Mr. Justice Holmes explains:

> The position of the president is different. Practically he was the master of the situation. He was daily at the bank for hours, he had the deposit ledger in his hands at times and might have had it at any time. He had had hints and warnings in addition to those that we have mentioned, warnings that should not be magnified unduly, but still that taken with the auditor's report of 1903, the unexplained shortages, the suggestion of the teller, Cutting, in 1905, and the final seeming rapid decline in deposits, would have induced scrutiny but for an invincible repose upon the *status quo*. In 1908 one Fillmore learned that a package containing $150 left with the bank for safe keeping was not to be found, told Dresser of the loss, wrote to him that he could but conclude that the package had been destroyed or removed by someone connected with the bank, and in later conversation said that it was evident that there was a thief in the bank. He added that he would advise the president to look after Coleman, that he believed he was living at a pretty fast pace, and that he had pretty good authority for thinking that he was supporting a woman. In the same year or the year before, Coleman, whose pay was never more than twelve dollars a week, set up an automobile, as was known to Dresser and commented on unfavorably, to him. There was also some evidence of notice to Dresser that Coleman was dealing in copper stocks. In 1909 came the great and inadequately explained seeming shrinkage in the deposits. No doubt plausible explanations of his conduct came from Coleman and the notice as to speculations may have been slight, but taking the whole story of the relations of the parties, we are not ready to say that the two courts below erred in finding that Dresser had been put upon his guard. However little the warnings may have pointed to the specific facts, had they been accepted they would have led to an examination of the depositors' ledger, a discovery of past and a prevention of future thefts.

251 U.S. at 530–31, 40 S.Ct. at 249–50, 64 L.Ed. at 395. The other directors were held not liable, since they reasonably relied on bank examinations and the president. The thefts in this case were reasonably well hidden by the simple expedient of charging them against inactive accounts, including the account of the defendant President.

act alone in allowing check overdrafts); * * * But see Campbell v. Watson, 62 N.J. Eq. 396, 50 A. 120, 142 (N.J.Ch.1901) (refusing to apply the business judgment rule to shelter the approval of worthless loans that were meant to cover a bank president's sizable overdrafts and that obviously involved self-dealing).

Check overdrafts are one of the few lending topics that federal regulators (with the notable exception of the Office of Thrift Supervision) have declined to supervise except insofar as such overdrafts violate restrictions on loans to one borrower and insider loans. The Office of Thrift Supervision specifically permits check account overdrafts up to stated aggregate lim-

its per thrift. See 12 C.F.R. §§ 545.46–545.47 (1995). For restrictions on check overdraft privileges for insiders and loans to one borrower, see 12 U.S.C. § 375b(6) (1994); 12 C.F.R. §§ 32.105, 215.3–215.5 & app. (1995). The new FDIC audit guidelines recommend that check overdrafts by insiders be disclosed. 12 C.F.R. pt. 363, app. A (1995). Thus, federal policy on this subject continues to mirror the traditional attitude of the judiciary, which regarded interest-free overdrafts to outside customers as a low-risk necessity of business. Alternatively, the treatment of check overdrafts can be viewed as a type of de minimis rule.

SHLENSKY v. WRIGLEY

Appellate Court of Illinois, 1968.
95 Ill.App.2d 173, 237 N.E.2d 776.

SULLIVAN, JUSTICE.

This is an appeal from a dismissal of plaintiff's amended complaint on motion of the defendants. The action was a stockholders' derivative suit against the directors for negligence and mismanagement. The corporation was also made a defendant. Plaintiff sought damages and an order that defendants cause the installation of lights in Wrigley Field and the scheduling of night baseball games.

Plaintiff is a minority stockholder of defendant corporation, Chicago National League Ball Club (Inc.), a Delaware corporation with its principal place of business in Chicago, Illinois. Defendant corporation owns and operates the major league professional baseball team known as the Chicago Cubs. The corporation also engages in the operation of Wrigley Field, the Cubs' home park, the concessionaire sales during Cubs' home games, television and radio broadcasts of Cubs' home games, the leasing of the field for football games and other events and receives its share, as visiting team, of admission moneys from games played in other National League stadia. The individual defendants are directors of the Cubs and have served for varying periods of years. Defendant Philip K. Wrigley is also president of the corporation and owner of approximately 80% of the stock therein.

Plaintiff alleges that since night baseball was first played in 1935 nineteen of the twenty major league teams have scheduled night games. In 1966, out of a total of 1620 games in the major leagues, 932 were played at night. Plaintiff alleges that every member of the major leagues, other than the Cubs, scheduled substantially all of its home games in 1966 at night, exclusive of opening days, Saturdays, Sundays, holidays and days prohibited by league rules. Allegedly this has been done for the specific purpose of maximizing attendance and thereby maximizing revenue and income.

The Cubs, in the years 1961–65, sustained operating losses from its direct baseball operations. Plaintiff attributes those losses to inadequate attendance at Cubs' home games. He concludes that if the directors continue to refuse to install lights at Wrigley Field and schedule night baseball games, the Cubs will continue to sustain comparable losses and its financial condition will continue to deteriorate.

Plaintiff alleges that, except for the year 1963, attendance at Cubs' home games has been substantially below that at their road games, many of which were played at night.

Plaintiff compares attendance at Cubs' games with that of the Chicago White Sox, an American League club, whose weekday games were generally played at night. The weekend attendance figures for the two teams was similar; however, the White Sox week-night games drew many more patrons than did the Cubs' weekday games.

Plaintiff alleges that the funds for the installation of lights can be readily obtained through financing and the cost of installation would be far more than offset and recaptured by increased revenues and incomes resulting from the increased attendance.

Plaintiff further alleges that defendant Wrigley has refused to install lights, not because of interest in the welfare of the corporation but because of his personal opinions "that baseball is a 'daytime sport' and that the installation of lights and night baseball games will have a deteriorating effect upon the surrounding neighborhood." It is alleged that he has admitted that he is not interested in whether the Cubs would benefit financially from such action because of his concern for the neighborhood, and that he would be willing for the team to play night games if a new stadium were built in Chicago.

Plaintiff alleges that the other defendant directors, with full knowledge of the foregoing matters, have acquiesced in the policy laid down by Wrigley and have permitted him to dominate the board of directors in matters involving the installation of lights and scheduling of night games, even though they knew he was not motivated by a good faith concern as to the best interests of defendant corporation, but solely by his personal views set forth above. It is charged that the directors are acting for a reason or reasons contrary and wholly unrelated to the business interests of the corporation; that such arbitrary and capricious acts constitute mismanagement and waste of corporate assets, and that the directors have been negligent in failing to exercise reasonable care and prudence in the management of the corporate affairs.

The question on appeal is whether plaintiff's amended complaint states a cause of action. It is plaintiff's position that fraud, illegality and conflict of interest are not the only bases for a stockholder's derivative action against the directors. Contrariwise, defendants argue that the courts will not step in and interfere with honest business judgment of the directors unless there is a showing of fraud, illegality or conflict of interest.

The cases in this area are numerous and each differs from the others on a factual basis. However, the courts have pronounced certain ground rules which appear in all cases and which are then applied to the given factual situation. The court in Wheeler v. Pullman Iron and Steel Company, 143 Ill. 197, 207, 32 N.E. 420, 423, said:

> It is, however, fundamental in the law of corporations, that the majority of its stockholders shall control the policy of the corporation, and regulate and govern the lawful exercise of its franchise and business. * * * Every one purchasing or subscribing for stock in a corporation impliedly agrees that he will be bound by the acts and proceedings done or sanctioned by a majority of the shareholders, or by the agents of the corporation duly chosen by such majority, within the scope of the powers conferred by the charter, and courts of equity will not undertake to control the policy or business methods of a corporation, although it may be seen that a wiser policy might be adopted and the business more successful if other methods were pursued. The majority of shares of its stock, or the agents by the holders thereof lawfully chosen, must be permitted to control the business of the corporation in their discretion, when not in violation of its charter or some public law, or corruptly and fraudulently subversive of the rights and interests of the corporation or of a shareholder.

The standards set in Delaware are also clearly stated in the cases. In Davis v. Louisville Gas & Electric Co., 16 Del.Ch. 157, 142 A. 654, a minority shareholder sought to have the directors enjoined from amending the certificate of incorporation. The court said on page 659:

> We have then a conflict in view between the responsible managers of a corporation and an overwhelming majority of its stockholders on the one hand and a dissenting minority on the other—a conflict touching matters of business policy, such as has occasioned innumerable applications to courts to intervene and determine which of the two conflicting views should prevail. The response which courts make to such applications is that it is not their function to resolve for corporations questions of policy and business management. The directors are chosen to pass upon such questions and their judgment *unless shown to be tainted with fraud* is accepted as final. The judgment of the directors of corporations enjoys the benefit of a presumption that it was formed in good faith and was designed to promote the best interests of the corporation they serve. (Emphasis supplied) * * *

Plaintiff argues that the allegations of his amended complaint are sufficient to set forth a cause of action under the principles set out in Dodge v. Ford Motor Co., 204 Mich. 459, 170 N.W. 668. In that case plaintiff, owner of about 10% of the outstanding stock, brought suit against the directors seeking payment of additional dividends and the enjoining of further business expansion. In ruling on the request for dividends the court indicated that the motives of Ford in keeping so much money in the corporation for expansion and security were to benefit the public generally and spread the profits out by means of more jobs, etc. The court felt that these were not only far from related to the good of the stockholders, but amounted to a change in the ends of the corporation and that this was not a purpose contemplated or allowed by the corporate charter. The court relied on language found in Hunter v. Roberts, Throp & Co., 83 Mich. 63, 47 N.W. 131, 134, wherein it was said:

> Courts of equity will not interfere in the management of the directors unless it is clearly made to appear that they are guilty of fraud or misappropriation of the corporate funds, or refuse to declare a dividend when the corporation has a surplus of net profits which it can, without detriment to its business, divide among its stockholders, and when a refusal to do so would amount to such an abuse of discretion as would constitute a fraud or breach of that good faith which they are bound to exercise toward the stockholders.

From the authority relied upon in that case it is clear that the court felt that there must be fraud or a breach of that good faith which directors are bound to exercise toward the stockholders in order to justify the courts entering into the internal affairs of corporations. This is made clear when the court refused to interfere with the directors' decision to expand the business. The following appears on page 684 of 170 N.W.:

> We are not, however, persuaded that we should interfere with the proposed expansion of the business of the Ford Motor Company. In view of the fact that the selling price of products may be increased at any time, the ultimate results of the larger business cannot be certainly estimated. *The judges are not business experts.* It is recognized that plans must often be made for a long future, for expected competition, for a continuing as well as an immediately profitable venture. * * * We are not satisfied that

the alleged motives of the directors, in so far as they are reflected in the conduct of business, menace the interests of the shareholders. (Emphasis supplied)

Plaintiff in the instant case argues that the directors are acting for reasons unrelated to the financial interest and welfare of the Cubs. However, we are not satisfied that the motives assigned to Philip K. Wrigley, and through him to the other directors, are contrary to the best interests of the corporation and the stockholders. For example, it appears to us that the effect on the surrounding neighborhood might well be considered by a director who was considering the patrons who would or would not attend the games if the park were in a poor neighborhood. Furthermore, the long run interest of the corporation in its property value at Wrigley Field might demand all efforts to keep the neighborhood from deteriorating. By these thoughts we do not mean to say that we have decided that the decision of the directors was a correct one. That is beyond our jurisdiction and ability. We are merely saying that the decision is one properly before directors and the motives alleged in the amended complaint showed no fraud, illegality or conflict of interest in their making of that decision.

While all the courts do not insist that one or more of the three elements must be present for a stockholder's derivative action to lie, nevertheless we feel that unless the conduct of the defendants at least borders on one of the elements, the courts should not interfere. The trial court in the instant case acted properly in dismissing plaintiff's amended complaint.

We feel that plaintiff's amended complaint was also defective in failing to allege damage to the corporation. * * *

There is no allegation that the night games played by the other nineteen teams enhanced their financial position or that the profits, if any, of those teams were directly related to the number of night games scheduled. There is an allegation that the installation of lights and scheduling of night games in Wrigley Field would have resulted in large amounts of additional revenues and incomes from increased attendance and related sources of income. Further, the cost of installation of lights, funds for which are allegedly readily available by financing, would be more than offset and recaptured by increased revenues. However, no allegation is made that there will be a net benefit to the corporation from such action, considering all increased costs.

Plaintiff claims that the losses of defendant corporation are due to poor attendance at home games. However, it appears from the amended complaint, taken as a whole, that factors other than attendance affect the net earnings or losses. For example, in 1962, attendance at home and road games decreased appreciably as compared with 1961, and yet the loss from direct baseball operation and of the whole corporation was considerably less.

The record shows that plaintiff did not feel he could allege that the increased revenues would be sufficient to cure the corporate deficit. The only cost plaintiff was at all concerned with was that of installation of lights. No mention was made of operation and maintenance of the lights or other possible increases in operating costs of night games and we cannot speculate as to what other factors might influence the increase or decrease of profits if the Cubs were to play night home games. * * *

Finally, we do not agree with plaintiff's contention that failure to follow the example of the other major league clubs in scheduling night games constituted negligence. Plaintiff made no allegation that these teams' night schedules were profitable or that the purpose for which night baseball had been undertaken was fulfilled. Furthermore, it cannot be said that directors, even those of corporations that are losing money, must follow the lead of the other corporations in the field. Directors are elected for their business capabilities and judgment and the courts cannot require them to forego their judgment because of the decisions of directors of other companies. Courts may not decide these questions in the absence of a clear showing of dereliction of duty on the part of the specific directors and mere failure to "follow the crowd" is not such a dereliction.

For the foregoing reasons the order of dismissal entered by the trial court is affirmed.

Affirmed.

Notes

1. In Francis v. United Jersey Bank, 87 N.J. 15, 432 A.2d 814 (1981), the sons of the founder of a corporation, an "insurance reinsurance" business, siphoned large sums of money from the corporation in the form of "shareholder loans" and other improper payments to family members. These distributions were reflected on the financial statements of the corporation as "shareholders loans." As a result of these transactions, the corporation became insolvent; the bankruptcy trustee brought suit against the widow of the founder for more than $10,000,000, representing funds transferred unlawfully from the firm to the family members while she was a director of the company. The Court described the conduct of the defendant as follows:

> Mrs. Pritchard was not active in the business of Pritchard & Baird and knew virtually nothing of its corporate affairs. She briefly visited the corporate offices in Morristown on only one occasion, and she never read or obtained the annual financial statements. She was unfamiliar with the rudiments of reinsurance and made no effort to assure that the policies and practices of the corporation, particularly pertaining to the withdrawal of funds, complied with industry custom or relevant law. Although her husband had warned her that Charles, Jr. would "take the shirt off my back," Mrs. Pritchard did not pay any attention to her duties as a director or to the affairs of the corporation.

> After her husband died in December 1973, Mrs. Pritchard became incapacitated and was bedridden for a six-month period. She became listless at this time and started to drink rather heavily. Her physical condition deteriorated, and in 1978 she died. The trial court rejected testimony seeking to exonerate her because she "was old, was grief-stricken at the loss of her husband, sometimes consumed too much alcohol and was psychologically overborne by her sons." 162 N.J.Super. at 371, 392 A.2d 1233. That court found that she was competent to act and that the reason Mrs. Pritchard never knew what her sons "were doing was because she never made the slightest effort to discharge any of her responsibilities as a director of Pritchard & Baird." 162 N.J.Super. at 372, 392 A.2d 1233.

432 A.2d at 819–20. The Court stated that "directors are under a continuing obligation to keep informed about the activities of the corporation," that "while

directors are not required to audit corporate books, they should maintain familiarity with the financial status of the corporation by a regular review of financial statements," and that "a director is not an ornament, but an essential component of corporate governance, * * * [and] cannot protect himself behind a paper shield bearing the motto, 'dummy director'." 432 A.2d at 822–23. A judgment against the estate of the director was affirmed:

As a director of a substantial reinsurance brokerage corporation, she should have known that it received annually millions of dollars of loss and premium funds which it held in trust for ceding and reinsurance companies. Mrs. Pritchard should have obtained and read the annual statements of financial condition of Pritchard & Baird. Although she had a right to rely upon financial statements prepared in accordance with N.J.S.A. 14A:6–14, such reliance would not excuse her conduct. The reason is that those statements disclosed on their face the misappropriation of trust funds.

From those statements, she should have realized that, as of January 31, 1970, her sons were withdrawing substantial trust funds under the guise of "Shareholders' Loans." The financial statements for each fiscal year commencing with that of January 31, 1970, disclosed that the working capital deficits and the "loans" were escalating in tandem. Detecting a misappropriation of funds would not have required special expertise or extraordinary diligence; a cursory reading of the financial statements would have revealed the pillage. Thus, if Mrs. Pritchard had read the financial statements, she would have known that her sons were converting trust funds. When financial statements demonstrate that insiders are bleeding a corporation to death, a director should notice and try to stanch the flow of blood.

In summary, Mrs. Pritchard was charged with the obligation of basic knowledge and supervision of the business of Pritchard & Baird. Under the circumstances, this obligation included reading and understanding financial statements, and making reasonable attempts at detection and prevention of the illegal conduct of other officers and directors. She had a duty to protect the clients of Pritchard & Baird against policies and practices that would result in the misappropriation of money they had entrusted to the corporation. She breached that duty. * * *

Nonetheless, the negligence of Mrs. Pritchard does not result in liability unless it is a proximate cause of the loss. * * *

Within Pritchard & Baird, several factors contributed to the loss of the funds: commingling of corporate and client monies, conversion of funds by Charles, Jr. and William and dereliction of her duties by Mrs. Pritchard. The wrongdoing of her sons, although the immediate cause of the loss, should not excuse Mrs. Pritchard from her negligence which also was a substantial factor contributing to the loss. Her sons knew that she, the only other director, was not reviewing their conduct; they spawned their fraud in the backwater of her neglect. Her neglect of duty contributed to the climate of corruption; her failure to act contributed to the continuation of that corruption. Consequently, her conduct was a substantial factor contributing to the loss.

Analysis of proximate cause is especially difficult in a corporate context where the allegation is that nonfeasance of a director is a proximate cause of damage to a third party. Where a case involves nonfeasance, no one can say "with absolute certainty what would have occurred if the defendant had acted otherwise." [W. Prosser, Law of Torts,] § 41 [(4th Ed.1971)] at 242. Nonetheless, where it is reasonable to conclude that the failure to act would produce a particular result and that result has followed, causation may be inferred. Ibid. We conclude that even if Mrs. Pritchard's mere objection had not stopped the depredations of her sons, her consultation with an attorney and the threat of suit would have deterred them. That conclusion flows as a matter of common sense and logic from the record. Whether in other situations a director has a duty to do more than protest and resign is best left to case-by-case determinations. In this case, we are satisfied that there was a duty to do more than object and resign. Consequently, we find that Mrs. Pritchard's negligence was a proximate cause of the misappropriations.

(2) Consider MBCA § 8.30(a). This is obviously traditional language of "due care." Is it appropriate language to define the duty of care in connection with duties of directors? One can usefully talk about "the care an ordinarily prudent person in a like position would exercise under similar circumstances" in a variety of ordinary life situations, such as driving an automobile, felling trees, and the like. One can also conclude that Mrs. Pritchard's behavior did not constitute "due care" no matter how narrowly that phrase is defined. But does the same standard have meaning in the more rarified world of directors of large publicly held corporations, acting in the milieu described by Manning (p. 572, supra)? Do the "similar circumstances" involve persons acting on other boards of directors? Is the "ordinarily prudent person" an "average Joe" in the United States, with an average IQ and whose formal education ended at high school?

Section 8.30(a) was taken directly from MBCA (1969) § 35, added in 1974, after an extended discussion. This language is a distillate of the statutes of several states, including New York and New Jersey. The Official Comment to § 8.30(a) expands somewhat on the meaning of these words:

> Several of the phrases chosen to define the general standard of care in section 8.30(a) deserve specific mention:
>
> (1) The reference to "ordinarily prudent person" embodies long traditions of the common law, in contrast to suggested standards that might call for some undefined degree of expertise, like "ordinarily prudent businessman." The phrase recognizes the need for innovation, essential to profit orientation, and focuses on the basic director attributes of common sense, practical wisdom, and informed judgment.
>
> (2) The phrase "in a like position" recognizes that the "care" under consideration is that which would be used by the "ordinarily prudent person" if he were a director of the particular corporation.
>
> (3) The combined phrase "in a like position * * * under similar circumstances" is intended to recognize that (a) the nature and extent of responsibilities will vary, depending upon such factors as the size, complexity, urgency, and location of activities carried on by the particular corporation, (b) decisions must be made on the basis of the information known to the directors without the benefit of hindsight, and (c) the special background, qualifications, and management responsibilities of a particular director may be relevant in evaluating his compliance with the standard of care. Even though the quoted phrase takes into account the special background, qualifications and management responsibilities of a particular director, it does not excuse a director lacking business experience or particular expertise from exercising the common sense, practical wisdom, and informed judgment of an "ordinarily prudent person."

(3) The American Law Institute, Principles of Corporate Governance: Analysis and Recommendations, § 4.01:[4]

(a) A director or officer has a duty to the corporation to perform the director's or officer's functions in good faith, in a manner that he or she reasonably believes to be in the best interests of the corporation, and with the care that an ordinarily prudent person would reasonably be expected to exercise in a like position and under similar circumstances. This Subsection (a) is subject to the provisions of Subsection (c) (the business judgment rule) where applicable.

(1) The duty in Subsection (a) includes the obligation to make, or cause to be made, an inquiry when, but only when, the circumstances would alert a reasonable director or officer to the need therefor. The extent of such inquiry shall be such as the director or officer reasonably believes to be necessary.

(2) In performing any of his or her functions (including oversight functions), a director or officer is entitled to rely on materials and persons in accordance with §§ 4.02 and 4.03 (reliance on directors, officers, employees, experts, other persons, and committees of the board).

(b) Except as otherwise provided by statute or by a standard of the corporation and subject to the board's ultimate responsibility for oversight, in performing its functions (including oversight functions), the board may delegate, formally or informally by course of conduct, any function (including the function of identifying matters requiring the attention of the board) to committees of the board or to directors, officers, employees, experts, or other persons; a director may rely on such committees and persons in fulfilling the duty under this Section with respect to any delegated function if the reliance is in accordance with §§ 4.02 and 4.03.

(c) A director or officer who makes a business judgment in good faith fulfills the duty under this Section if the director or officer:

(1) is not interested in the subject of the business judgment;

(2) is informed with respect to the subject of the business judgment to the extent the director or officer reasonably believes to be appropriate under the circumstances; and

(3) rationally believes that the business judgment is in the best interests of the corporation.

(d) A person challenging the conduct of a director or officer under this Section has the burden of proving a breach of the duty of care, including the inapplicability of the provisions as to the fulfillment of duty under Subsection (b) or (c), and, in a damage action, the burden of proving that the breach was the legal cause of damage suffered by the corporation.[5]

---

4. Copyright (1994) by The American Law Institute. Reprinted with the permission of The American Law Institute.

5. [By the Editor] Section 7.18 states that "legal cause" of loss exists where the plaintiff proves "that (i) satisfaction of the applicable standard would have been a substantial factor in averting the loss, and (ii) the likelihood of injury would have been foreseeable to an ordi-

narily prudent person in like position to that of the defendant and in similar circumstances. It is not a defense to liability in such cases that damage to the corporation would not have resulted but for the acts or omissions of other individuals." The American Law Institute, Principles of Corporate Governance: Analysis and Recommendations § 7.18.

(5) Does not paragraph (c) of § 4.01 set forth a quite different and broader test for liability than that set forth in paragraph (a) and in MBCA § 8.30? This principle is called the "business judgment rule." Charles Hansen, The ALI Corporate Governance Project: Of the Duty of Due Care and the Business Judgment Rule, 41 Bus.Law. 1237, 1238–42, 1247 (1986):[6]

[T]he Model Business Corporation Act, adopted by a number of states, contains an important section on directors' duties that, while supportable by dicta, does not reflect case holdings. * * *

The foundation stone of the American law of corporate governance is currently enunciated in the holdings (not the dicta) of the leading corporate law states: there must be a minimum of interference by the courts in internal corporate affairs. Except in the egregious case of bad judgment or when there is evidence of bad faith, courts have made no attempt to second-guess directors on the substantive soundness of decisions reached. The courts have assiduously sought to keep hands off the powerful yet delicate mechanism of corporate wealth production at the core of our economic well-being. * * *

The applicable duty as applied by the courts to a director's decision is intimately linked to, and limited by, the "business judgment rule," a doctrine limiting the liability of a director in the good faith pursuit of one's duties. Under that rule, as long as a director acts in good faith and with due care in the process sense, the director will not be found liable even though the decision itself was not that of the "ordinarily prudent person." The process due care test will be met if the director takes appropriate steps to become informed. Thus, the description of the duty in section 4.01(a) [of the ALI Corporate Governance Project] as "the care that an ordinarily prudent person would reasonably be expected to exercise in a like position and under similar circumstances" is misleading.

To focus the problem, can it be argued seriously that the director's decisions are to be judged against the standard of section 4.01(a)? If it can be established that the director's decision was not the decision of "an ordinarily prudent person ... in a like position ... under similar circumstances," will that director be liable for failure to use "due care"? The answer is obviously no, since the cases are legion, holding that under the business judgment rule a director's conduct is not to be so measured. *Cramer v. General Telephone & Electronics Corp.*, for example, states the appropriate principle of law: "Absent bad faith or some other corrupt motive, directors are normally not liable to the corporation for mistakes of judgment. . . ."[7] * * *

A careful reading of the cases illustrates the substantial difference between applying the due care test in tort law and the standard actually employed by the courts in reaching decisions under corporate law. In tort law, the due care standard is results oriented; that is, whether or not the acts of the director measure up to the behavior of the so-called reasonable person under the same or similar circumstances, in effect the test of section 4.01(a).

In contrast, under corporate law, the standard of due care is met if two tests are satisfied: (i) due care must be used in "ascertaining relevant facts and law before making the decision," and (ii) the decision must be made after

---

6. Copyright 1986 by the American Bar Association. All rights reserved. Reprinted with the permission of the American Bar Association and its Section of Corporation, Banking and Business Law.

7. [By the Author] 582 F.2d 259, 274 (3d Cir.1978).

reasonable deliberation. * * * Thus, the due care standard in corporate law is applied to the decision-making process and not to its result. Even though a decision made or a result reached is not that of the hypothetical ordinarily prudent person, no liability will attach as long as the decision-making process meets the standard. * * *

The one possible exception to applying the standard of due care to process, rather than to content or result, concerns egregious conduct. In a few outrageous cases, the objective reasonableness of a particular business judgment may be important. Thus, if the court finds the judgment itself "grossly unsound," "a gross abuse of discretion," one which would have been reached by "no person of sound ordinary business judgment," "so unwise or unreasonable as to fall outside the permissible bounds of the directors' sound discretion," or "an abuse of discretion," and "egregious," the directors will not meet the standards of the business judgment rule. * * *

In the non-decision-making context, or when the director is not exercising business judgment, an ordinarily prudent person due care formulation is closer to reality. Absent the affirmative exercise of business judgment, the business judgment rule and the necessary limitations it imposes on the duty of care do not apply.

Even in a non-decision-making context, however, the required due care standard would appear to be less stringent than that which "an ordinarily prudent person would reasonably be expected to exercise in a like position under similar circumstances." While it is true that this so-called traditional language appears in the cases, a careful examination of the facts of the cases and the holdings based thereon yields a different result. Using such an analysis, it would appear that directors have been found liable only in the non-decision-making context upon obvious and prolonged failure to exercise oversight or supervision.

A typical case is *Francis v. United Jersey Bank.* * * *

Does Hansen's analysis explain Litwin v. Allen? Bates v. Dresser? Shlensky v. Wrigley? Francis v. United Jersey Bank?

(6) In 1996 Chancellor Allen reflected on the scope of the business judgment rule in In re Caremark International Inc. Derivative Litigation, 1996 WL 549894 (Del.Ch.1996):

Director liability for a breach of the duty to exercise appropriate attention may * * * follow from a board decision that results in a loss because that decision was ill advised or "negligent". * * * [This] class of cases will typically be subject to review under the director-protective business judgment rule, assuming the decision made was the product of a process that was either deliberately considered in good faith or was otherwise rational. What should be understood, but may not widely be understood by courts or commentators who are not often required to face such questions,[8] is that compliance with a director's duty of care can never appropriately be judicially determined by reference to the content of the board decision that leads to a corporate loss, apart from consideration of the good faith or rationality of the process employed. That is, whether a judge or jury considering the matter after the fact, believes a decision substantively wrong, or degrees of wrong extending

---

8. [By the Chancellor] See American Law Institute, Principles of Corporate Governance § 4.01(c)(to qualify for business judgment treatment a director must "rationally" believe that the decision is in the best interest of the corporation).

through "stupid" to "egregious" or "irrational", provides no ground for director liability, so long as the court determines that the process employed was either rational or employed in a good faith effort to advance corporate interests. To employ a different rule—one that permitted an "objective" evaluation of the decision—would expose directors to substantive second guessing by ill-equipped judges or juries, which would, in the long-run, be injurious to investor interests.[9] Thus, the business judgment rule is process oriented and informed by a deep respect for all good faith board decisions.

Indeed, one wonders on what moral basis might shareholders attack a good faith business decision of a director as "unreasonable" or "irrational". Where a director in fact exercises a good faith effort to be informed and to exercise appropriate judgment, he or she should be deemed to satisfy fully the duty of attention. If the shareholders thought themselves entitled to some other quality of judgment than such a director produces in the good faith exercise of the powers of office, then the shareholders should have elected other directors.* * *

Is there no conceivable case where a conscious decision is "so far out" that it should lead to liability even though the decision-making process was impeccable?

(7) All modern authorities recognize that the "business judgment rule" summarized briefly by Hansen (and the subject of the following principal case) is a major qualification to the sparse language of due care in § 8.30 of the MBCA. Accepting this, shouldn't the text of § 8.30 give at least some minimal legislative recognition to the existence of such a major qualification? The Official Comment to § 8.30 explains:

In determining whether to impose liability, the courts recognize that boards of directors and corporate managers continuously make decisions that involve the balancing of risks and benefits for the enterprise. Although some decisions turn out to be unwise or the result of a mistake of judgment, it is unreasonable to reexamine these decisions with the benefit of hindsight. Therefore, a director is not liable for injury or damage caused by his decision, no matter how unwise or mistaken it may turn out to be, if in performing his duties he met the requirements of section 8.30.

Even before statutory formulations of directors' duty of care, courts sometimes invoked the business judgment rule in determining whether to impose liability in a particular case. In doing so, courts have sometimes used language similar to the standards set forth in section 8.30(a). The elements of the business judgment rule and the circumstances for its application are continuing to be developed by the courts. In view of that continuing judicial development, section 8.30 does not try to codify the business judgment rule or to delineate the differences, if any, between that rule and the standards of

---

9. [By the Chancellor] The vocabulary of negligence while often employed, is not well-suited to judicial review of board attentiveness, especially if one attempts to look to the substance of the decision as any evidence of possible "negligence." Where review of board functioning is involved, courts leave behind as a relevant point of reference the decisions of the hypothetical "reasonable person", who typically supplies the test for negligence liability. It is doubtful that we want business men and women to be encouraged to make decisions as hypothetical persons of ordinary judgment and pru-

dence might. The corporate form gets its utility in large part from its ability to allow diversified investors to accept greater investment risk. If those in charge of the corporation are to be adjudged personally liable for losses on the basis of a substantive judgment based upon what an persons of ordinary or average judgment and average risk assessment talent regard as "prudent" "sensible" or even "rational", such persons will have a strong incentive at the margin to authorize less risky investment projects.

director conduct set forth in this section. That is a task left to the courts and possibly to later revisions of this Model Act.

This somewhat ambiguous formulation of very basic concepts about directoral liability was a compromise position taken by the Committee on Corporate Laws only after extended and extremely time-consuming efforts to codify the business judgment rule within the context of § 8.30; these efforts did not lead to anything nearly approaching consensus. The compromise set forth in the Official Comment was informally capsulated by one committee member who commented in effect, "we are saying that there is a business judgment rule, that we know what it is and when it should be applied, but we can't define it." In 1997, the Committee on Corporate Laws has under consideration a reformulation of § 8.30 that would give express statutory recognition to the business judgment rule.

(8) Justice Shientag comments in *Litwin* that a higher standard of care is required of bank directors than of general business corporations. Is that suggested distinction justifiable? Is banking different from other industries, such as pharmaceuticals or the manufacture of airplanes? Certainly the legal development has been different. Patricia A. McCoy, A Political Economy of the Business Judgment Rule In Banking: Implications for Corporate Law, 47 Case Wes.Res.L.Rev. 1 (1996), traces the history of the standard of care in banking from the Nineteenth Century to the present and concludes that the liability issue for bank directors has been influenced by factors such as the development of savings banks and federal insurance programs, and has undergone wide variations depending on the number of bank failures. The 1980s and 1990s saw hundreds of lawsuits filed by federal bank regulatory authorities (predominantly the Federal Deposit Insurance Corporation (FDIC) and the Resolution Trust Company (RTC)) against thousands of officers and directors of failed banks and savings and loan associations.[10] Many of these suits involved claims of self-dealing as well as claims of negligence or gross negligence—self-dealing involves personal involvement in and personal benefit from transactions with the financial institution and is discussed in the following chapter. The negligence or gross negligence claims against directors were largely based on decisions to make specific loans: disastrous loans for the development of real estate or new businesses, loans that sometimes failed before a single payment was made, loans that were extended or "rolled over" two or three times, usually with accrued interest being added to the principal as the probability of repayment steadily diminished, and so forth. Often, records of failed banks or thrifts were in chaotic condition (particularly after being summarily seized and stored in warehouses): lost boxes of internal records, files in which critical documents such as appraisals were missing, partial files in different boxes, incomplete or skeletal minutes of meetings of loan committees or boards of directors, and the like. Memories of directors who had reviewed hundreds or thousands of transactions were often sketchy or faulty. The RTC and FDIC argued strongly that actions by directors and officers should be judged by the duty of care set forth in the old bank cases while the defendants argued strenuously that their actions should be evaluated under the more lenient business judgment rule, since the Federal Government had encouraged them to branch out from traditional banking functions.

---

10. [By the Editor] During that period more than 700 S & Ls and 300 banks failed at a cost to American taxpayers of hundreds of billions of dollars. Some 1,300 persons were indicted, and over 1,000 convicted of criminal conduct in connection with these failures. Harris Weinstein, Advising Corporate Directors After the Savings and Loan Disaster, 48 Bus. Law. 1499, 1500 (1993).

(9) About one-half of modern S & Ls and banks are state chartered and the other half federal-chartered. Pre-*Erie* federal court decisions created a federal standard of due care for bank directors of federally chartered corporations, while numerous early state court decisions established varying standards for state-created institutions. The result was a cacophony of decisions, some of which applied a pure due care standard while others recognized the business judgment rule. In F.D.I.C. v. Bierman, 2 F.3d 1424, 1432 (7th Cir.1993), for example, the Court held directors personally liable on numerous loans, applying the standard of the old bank cases that directors must "exercise ordinary care and prudence in the administration of the affairs of a bank" which includes being "something more than officiating as figureheads." The Court mentioned but did not consider the possible application of the business judgment rule. By the late 1990s, these cases appear to have pretty much ended with scant recoveries by the federal regulatory agencies.

(10) In the Financial Institutions Reform, Recovery, and Enforcement Act of 1989 (FIRREA), 12 U.S.C.A. § 1821(k), Congress attempted to clarify the standard of care for directors of financial institutions:

> A director or officer of an insured depository institution may be held personally liable for monetary damages in any civil action by, on behalf of, or at the request or direction of the [RTC] * * * for gross negligence, including any similar conduct or conduct that demonstrates a greater disregard of a duty of care (than gross negligence) including intentional tortious conduct, as such terms are defined and determined under applicable State law. Nothing in this paragraph shall impair or affect any right of the [RTC] under other applicable law.

In Atherton v. F.D.I.C, ___ U.S. ___, 117 S.Ct. 666, 136 L.Ed.2d 656 (1997), the Supreme Court held that the early federal law of bank director liability had disappeared with Erie R. Co. v. Tompkins, 304 U.S. 64, 58 S.Ct. 817, 82 L.Ed. 1188 (1938) and that state law defined the duty of directors of both federal- and state-chartered institutions, subject to § 1821(k), which the court construed to mean "the statute's 'gross negligence' standard provides only a floor—a guarantee that officers and directors must meet at least a gross negligence standard. It does not stand in the way of a stricter standard that the laws of some States provide." 117 S.Ct., at 674.

Directors and former directors of financial institutions are not without political clout at the state level. Prior to *Atherton*, the legislatures of at least seven states attempted to ameliorate the duty of care placed on bank and thrift directors by the early bank cases. The Texas statute, H.B. 1076 (73d Leg. Reg. Sess.), enacted in 1993 provides:

> SECTION 1. * * * C. For the purpose of applying this article to the Financial Institutions Reform, Recovery, and Enforcement Act of 1989, a disinterested director or officer of an insured depository institution may not be held personally liable in an action seeking monetary damages brought by the Federal Deposit Insurance Corporation, the Resolution Trust Corporation, or any other federal banking regulatory agency * * * unless the damages arise from the gross negligence or willful or intentional misconduct of the officer or director during the officer's or director's term of office with the insured depository institution. * * *

> SECTION 2. This Act is not intended to change existing law regarding the personal liability of a director or officer of an insured depository institution but is a clarification of the law in effect immediately before the effective

date of this Act regarding those matters. This Act applies to an action brought by a federal regulatory agency under 12 U.S.C. Section 1821(k) against a director or officer of an insured depository institution, regardless of whether the action was filed before, on, or after the effective date of this Act, unless the action was finally adjudicated by a court of competent jurisdiction before the effective date of this Act.

SMITH v. VAN GORKOM

Supreme Court of Delaware, 1985.
488 A.2d 858.

Before HERRMANN, C.J., and McNEILLY, HORSEY, MOORE and CHRISTIE, JJ., constituting the Court en banc.

HORSEY, JUSTICE (for the majority):

This appeal from the Court of Chancery involves a class action brought by shareholders of the defendant Trans Union Corporation ("Trans Union" or "the Company"), originally seeking rescission of a cash-out merger of Trans Union into the defendant New T Company ("New T"), a wholly-owned subsidiary of the defendant, Marmon Group, Inc. ("Marmon"). Alternate relief in the form of damages is sought against the defendant members of the Board of Directors of Trans Union * * *.

Following trial, the former Chancellor granted judgment for the defendant directors by unreported letter opinion dated July 6, 1982. Judgment was based on [the finding that] that the Board of Directors had acted in an informed manner so as to be entitled to protection of the business judgment rule in approving the cash-out merger * * *. The plaintiffs appeal.

Speaking for the majority of the Court, we conclude that [the ruling] of the Court of Chancery [is] clearly erroneous. Therefore, we reverse and direct that judgment be entered in favor of the plaintiffs and against the defendant directors for the fair value of the plaintiffs' stockholdings in Trans Union, in accordance with Weinberger v. UOP, Inc., Del.Supr., 457 A.2d 701 (1983).[11]

We hold * * * that the Board's decision, reached September 20, 1980, to approve the proposed cash-out merger was not the product of an informed business judgment * * *.

I.

The nature of this case requires a detailed factual statement. The following facts are essentially uncontradicted:

–A–

Trans Union was a publicly-traded, diversified holding company, the principal earnings of which were generated by its railcar leasing business. During the period here involved, the Company had a cash flow of hundreds of millions of dollars annually. However, the Company had difficulty in generating sufficient taxable income to offset increasingly large investment tax credits (ITCs). Accelerated depreciation deductions had decreased available taxable income against which to offset accumulating ITCs. The Company took

11. [By the Court] It has been stipulated that plaintiffs sue on behalf of a class consisting of 10,537 shareholders (out of a total of 12,844) and that the class owned 12,734,404 out of 13,357,758 shares of Trans Union outstanding.

these deductions, despite their effect on usable ITCs, because the rental price in the railcar leasing market had already impounded the purported tax savings.

In the late 1970's, together with other capital-intensive firms, Trans Union lobbied in Congress to have ITCs refundable in cash to firms which could not fully utilize the credit. During the summer of 1980, defendant Jerome W. Van Gorkom, Trans Union's Chairman and Chief Executive Officer, testified and lobbied in Congress for refundability of ITCs and against further accelerated depreciation. By the end of August, Van Gorkom was convinced that Congress would neither accept the refundability concept nor curtail further accelerated depreciation.

Beginning in the late 1960's, and continuing through the 1970's, Trans Union pursued a program of acquiring small companies in order to increase available taxable income. In July 1980, Trans Union Management prepared the annual revision of the Company's Five Year Forecast. This report was presented to the Board of Directors at its July, 1980 meeting. The report projected an annual income growth of about 20%. The report also concluded that Trans Union would have about $195 million in spare cash between 1980 and 1985, "with the surplus growing rapidly from 1982 onward." The report referred to the ITC situation as a "nagging problem" and, given that problem, the leasing company "would still appear to be constrained to a tax breakeven." The report then listed four alternative uses of the projected 1982–1985 equity surplus: (1) stock repurchase; (2) dividend increases; (3) a major acquisition program; and (4) combinations of the above. The sale of Trans Union was not among the alternatives. The report emphasized that, despite the overall surplus, the operation of the Company would consume all available equity for the next several years, and concluded: "As a result, we have sufficient time to fully develop our course of action."

–B–

On August 27, 1980, Van Gorkom met with Senior Management of Trans Union. Van Gorkom reported on his lobbying efforts in Washington and his desire to find a solution to the tax credit problem more permanent than a continued program of acquisitions. Various alternatives were suggested and discussed preliminarily, including the sale of Trans Union to a company with a large amount of taxable income.

Donald Romans, Chief Financial Officer of Trans Union, stated that his department had done a "very brief bit of work on the possibility of a leveraged buy-out." This work had been prompted by a media article which Romans had seen regarding a leveraged buy-out by management. The work consisted of a "preliminary study" of the cash which could be generated by the Company if it participated in a leveraged buy-out. As Romans stated, this analysis "was very first and rough cut at seeing whether a cash flow would support what might be considered a high price for this type of transaction."

On September 5, at another Senior Management meeting which Van Gorkom attended, Romans again brought up the idea of a leveraged buy-out as a "possible strategic alternative" to the Company's acquisition program. Romans and Bruce S. Chelberg, President and Chief Operating Officer of Trans Union, had been working on the matter in preparation for the meeting. According to Romans: They did not "come up" with a price for the Company.

They merely "ran the numbers" at $50 a share and at $60 a share with the "rough form" of their cash figures at the time. Their "figures indicated that $50 would be very easy to do but $60 would be very difficult to do under those figures." This work did not purport to establish a fair price for either the Company or 100% of the stock. It was intended to determine the cash flow needed to service the debt that would "probably" be incurred in a leveraged buyout, based on "rough calculations" without "any benefit of experts to identify what the limits were to that, and so forth." These computations were not considered extensive and no conclusion was reached.

At this meeting, Van Gorkom stated that he would be willing to take $55 per share for his own 75,000 shares. He vetoed the suggestion of a leveraged buy-out by Management, however, as involving a potential conflict of interest for Management. Van Gorkom, a certified public accountant and lawyer, had been an officer of Trans Union for 24 years, its Chief Executive Officer for more than 17 years, and Chairman of its Board for 2 years. It is noteworthy in this connection that he was then approaching 65 years of age and mandatory retirement.

For several days following the September 5 meeting, Van Gorkom pondered the idea of a sale. He had participated in many acquisitions as a manager and director of Trans Union and as a director of other companies. He was familiar with acquisition procedures, valuation methods, and negotiations; and he privately considered the pros and cons of whether Trans Union should seek a privately or publicly-held purchaser.

Van Gorkom decided to meet with Jay A. Pritzker, a well-known corporate takeover specialist and a social acquaintance. However, rather than approaching Pritzker simply to determine his interest in acquiring Trans Union, Van Gorkom assembled a proposed per share price for sale of the Company and a financing structure by which to accomplish the sale. Van Gorkom did so without consulting either his Board or any members of Senior Management except one: Carl Peterson, Trans Union's Controller. Telling Peterson that he wanted no other person on his staff to know what he was doing, but without telling him why, Van Gorkom directed Peterson to calculate the feasibility of a leveraged buy-out at an assumed price per share of $55. Apart from the Company's historic stock market price,[12] and Van Gorkom's long association with Trans Union, the record is devoid of any competent evidence that $55 represented the per share intrinsic value of the Company.

Having thus chosen the $55 figure, based solely on the availability of a leveraged buy-out, Van Gorkom multiplied the price per share by the number of shares outstanding to reach a total value of the Company of $690 million. Van Gorkom told Peterson to use this $690 million figure and to assume a $200 million equity contribution by the buyer. Based on these assumptions, Van Gorkom directed Peterson to determine whether the debt portion of the purchase price could be paid off in five years or less if financed by Trans Union's cash flow as projected in the Five Year Forecast, and by the sale of

---

12. [By the Court] The common stock of Trans Union was traded on the New York Stock Exchange. Over the five year period from 1975 through 1979, Trans Union's stock had traded within a range of a high of $39½ and a low of $24¼. Its high and low range for 1980 through September 19 (the last trading day before announcement of the merger) was $38¼ –$29½.

certain weaker divisions identified in a study done for Trans Union by the Boston Consulting Group ("BCG study"). Peterson reported that, of the purchase price, approximately $50–80 million would remain outstanding after five years. Van Gorkom was disappointed, but decided to meet with Pritzker nevertheless.

Van Gorkom arranged a meeting with Pritzker at the latter's home on Saturday, September 13, 1980. Van Gorkom prefaced his presentation by stating to Pritzker: "Now as far as you are concerned, I can, I think, show how you can pay a substantial premium over the present stock price and pay off most of the loan in the first five years. * * * If you could pay $55 for this Company, here is a way in which I think it can be financed."

Van Gorkom then reviewed with Pritzker his calculations based upon his proposed price of $55 per share. Although Pritzker mentioned $50 as a more attractive figure, no other price was mentioned. However, Van Gorkom stated that to be sure that $55 was the best price obtainable, Trans Union should be free to accept any better offer. Pritzker demurred, stating that his organization would serve as a "stalking horse" for an "auction contest" only if Trans Union would permit Pritzker to buy 1,750,000 shares of Trans Union stock at market price which Pritzker could then sell to any higher bidder. After further discussion on this point, Pritzker told Van Gorkom that he would give him a more definite reaction soon.

On Monday, September 15, Pritzker advised Van Gorkom that he was interested in the $55 cash-out merger proposal and requested more information on Trans Union. Van Gorkom agreed to meet privately with Pritzker, accompanied by Peterson, Chelberg, and Michael Carpenter, Trans Union's consultant from the Boston Consulting Group. The meetings took place on September 16 and 17. Van Gorkom was "astounded that events were moving with such amazing rapidity."

On Thursday, September 18, Van Gorkom met again with Pritzker. At that time, Van Gorkom knew that Pritzker intended to make a cash-out merger offer at Van Gorkom's proposed $55 per share. Pritzker instructed his attorney, a merger and acquisition specialist, to begin drafting merger documents. There was no further discussion of the $55 price. However, the number of shares of Trans Union's treasury stock to be offered to Pritzker was negotiated down to one million shares; the price was set at $38—75 cents above the per share price at the close of the market on September 19. At this point, Pritzker insisted that the Trans Union Board act on his merger proposal within the next three days, stating to Van Gorkom: "We have to have a decision by no later than Sunday [evening, September 21] before the opening of the English stock exchange on Monday morning." Pritzker's lawyer was then instructed to draft the merger documents, to be reviewed by Van Gorkom's lawyer, "sometimes with discussion and sometimes not, in the haste to get it finished."

On Friday, September 19, Van Gorkom, Chelberg, and Pritzker consulted with Trans Union's lead bank regarding the financing of Pritzker's purchase of Trans Union. The bank indicated that it could form a syndicate of banks that would finance the transaction. On the same day, Van Gorkom retained James Brennan, Esquire, to advise Trans Union on the legal aspects of the merger. Van Gorkom did not consult with William Browder, a Vice–President and director of Trans Union and former head of its legal department, or with William Moore, then the head of Trans Union's legal staff.

On Friday, September 19, Van Gorkom called a special meeting of the Trans Union Board for noon the following day. He also called a meeting of the Company's Senior Management to convene at 11:00 a.m., prior to the meeting of the Board. No one, except Chelberg and Peterson, was told the purpose of the meetings. Van Gorkom did not invite Trans Union's investment banker, Salomon Brothers or its Chicago-based partner, to attend.

Of those present at the Senior Management meeting on September 20, only Chelberg and Peterson had prior knowledge of Pritzker's offer. Van Gorkom disclosed the offer and described its terms, but he furnished no copies of the proposed Merger Agreement. Romans announced that his department had done a second study which showed that, for a leveraged buy-out, the price range for Trans Union stock was between $55 and $65 per share. Van Gorkom neither saw the study nor asked Romans to make it available for the Board meeting.

Senior Management's reaction to the Pritzker proposal was completely negative. No member of Management, except Chelberg and Peterson, supported the proposal. Romans objected to the price as being too low;[13] he was critical of the timing and suggested that consideration should be given to the adverse tax consequences of an all-cash deal for low-basis shareholders; and he took the position that the agreement to sell Pritzker one million newly-issued shares at market price would inhibit other offers, as would the prohibitions against soliciting bids and furnishing inside information to other bidders. Romans argued that the Pritzker proposal was a "lock up" and amounted to "an agreed merger as opposed to an offer." Nevertheless, Van Gorkom proceeded to the Board meeting as scheduled without further delay.

Ten directors served on the Trans Union Board, five inside (defendants Bonser, O'Boyle, Browder, Chelberg, and Van Gorkom) and five outside (defendants Wallis, Johnson, Lanterman, Morgan and Reneker). All directors were present at the meeting, except O'Boyle who was ill. Of the outside directors, four were corporate chief executive officers and one was the former Dean of the University of Chicago Business School. None was an investment banker or trained financial analyst. All members of the Board were well informed about the Company and its operations as a going concern. They were familiar with the current financial condition of the Company, as well as operating and earnings projections reported in the recent Five Year Forecast. The Board generally received regular and detailed reports and was kept abreast of the accumulated investment tax credit and accelerated depreciation problem.

Van Gorkom began the Special Meeting of the Board with a twenty-minute oral presentation. Copies of the proposed Merger Agreement were delivered too late for study before or during the meeting.[14] He reviewed the

13. [By the Court] Van Gorkom asked Romans to express his opinion as to the $55 price. Romans stated that he "thought the price was too low in relation to what he could derive for the company in a cash sale, particularly one

which enabled us to realize the values of certain subsidiaries and independent entities."

14. [By the Court] The record is not clear as to the terms of the Merger Agreement. The Agreement, as originally presented to the Board on September 20, was never produced

Company's ITC and depreciation problems and the efforts theretofore made to solve them. He discussed his initial meeting with Pritzker and his motivation in arranging that meeting. Van Gorkom did not disclose to the Board, however, the methodology by which he alone had arrived at the $55 figure, or the fact that he first proposed the $55 price in his negotiations with Pritzker.

Van Gorkom outlined the terms of the Pritzker offer as follows: Pritzker would pay $55 in cash for all outstanding shares of Trans Union stock upon completion of which Trans Union would be merged into New T Company, a subsidiary wholly-owned by Pritzker and formed to implement the merger; for a period of 90 days, Trans Union could receive, but could not actively solicit, competing offers; the offer had to be acted on by the next evening, Sunday, September 21; Trans Union could only furnish to competing bidders published information, and not proprietary information; the offer was subject to Pritzker obtaining the necessary financing by October 10, 1980; if the financing contingency were met or waived by Pritzker, Trans Union was required to sell to Pritzker one million newly-issued shares of Trans Union at $38 per share.

Van Gorkom took the position that putting Trans Union "up for auction" through a 90-day market test would validate a decision by the Board that $55 was a fair price. He told the Board that the "free market will have an opportunity to judge whether $55 is a fair price." Van Gorkom framed the decision before the Board not as whether $55 per share was the highest price that could be obtained, but as whether the $55 price was a fair price that the stockholders should be given the opportunity to accept or reject.[15]

Attorney Brennan advised the members of the Board that they might be sued if they failed to accept the offer and that a fairness opinion was not required as a matter of law.

Romans attended the meeting as chief financial officer of the Company. He told the Board that he had not been involved in the negotiations with Pritzker and knew nothing about the merger proposal until the morning of the meeting; that his studies did not indicate either a fair price for the stock or a valuation of the Company; that he did not see his role as directly addressing the fairness issue; and that he and his people "were trying to search for ways to justify a price in connection with such a [leveraged buy-out] transaction, rather than to say what the shares are worth." Romans testified:

> I told the Board that the study ran the numbers at 50 and 60, and then the subsequent study at 55 and 65, and that was not the same thing as saying that I have a valuation of the company at X dollars. But it was a way—a first step towards reaching that conclusion.

Romans told the Board that, in his opinion, $55 was "in the range of a fair price," but "at the beginning of the range."

Chelberg, Trans Union's President, supported Van Gorkom's presentation and representations. He testified that he "participated to make sure that

by defendants despite demands by the plaintiffs. Nor is it clear that the directors were given an opportunity to study the Merger Agreement before voting on it. All that can be said is that Brennan had the Agreement before him during the meeting.

15. [By the Court] In Van Gorkom's words: The "real decision" is whether to "let the stockholders decide it" which is "all you are being asked to decide today."

the Board members collectively were clear on the details of the agreement or offer from Pritzker;" that he "participated in the discussion with Mr. Brennan, inquiring of him about the necessity for valuation opinions in spite of the way in which this particular offer was couched;" and that he was otherwise actively involved in supporting the positions being taken by Van Gorkom before the Board about "the necessity to act immediately on this offer," and about "the adequacy of the $55 and the question of how that would be tested."

The Board meeting of September 20 lasted about two hours. Based solely upon Van Gorkom's oral presentation, Chelberg's supporting representations, Romans' oral statement, Brennan's legal advice, and their knowledge of the market history of the Company's stock,[16] the directors approved the proposed Merger Agreement. * * *.

The Merger Agreement was executed by Van Gorkom during the evening of September 20 at a formal social event that he hosted for the opening of the Chicago Lyric Opera. Neither he nor any other director read the agreement prior to its signing and delivery to Pritzker. * * *

[Following the approval of the Pritzker proposal, Trans Union retained Salomon Brothers to actively seek other possible offers. This search produced two other possible purchasers, one at $60 per share and the other at $2 to $5 above the $55 price. However, one potential bidder withdrew when Pritzker refused to rescind its merger agreement with Trans Union and the other withdrew when an executive in an important Trans Union subsidiary declined to join the buying group. Van Gorkom made no effort to assist either of these potential offerors and may have affirmatively discouraged them.]

On December 19, this litigation was commenced and, within four weeks, the plaintiffs had deposed eight of the ten directors of Trans Union, including Van Gorkom, Chelberg and Romans, its Chief Financial Officer. On January 21, Management's Proxy Statement for the February 10 shareholder meeting was mailed to Trans Union's stockholders. On January 26, Trans Union's Board met and, after a lengthy meeting, voted to proceed with the Pritzker merger. The Board also approved for mailing, "on or about January 27," a Supplement to its Proxy Statement. The Supplement purportedly set forth all information relevant to the Pritzker Merger Agreement, which had not been divulged in the first Proxy Statement. * * *

On February 10, the stockholders of Trans Union approved the Pritzker merger proposal. Of the outstanding shares, 69.9% were voted in favor of the merger; 7.25% were voted against the merger; and 22.85% were not voted.

II.

We turn to the issue of the application of the business judgment rule to the September 20 meeting of the Board.

---

16. [By the Court] The Trial Court stated the premium relationship of the $55 price to the market history of the Company's stock as follows:

    * * * the merger price offered to the stockholders of Trans Union represented a premium of 62% over the average of the high and low prices at which Trans Union stock had traded in 1980, a premium of 48% over the last closing price, and a premium of 39% over the highest price at which the stock of Trans Union had traded any time during the prior six years.

The Court of Chancery concluded from the evidence that the Board of Directors' approval of the Pritzker merger proposal fell within the protection of the business judgment rule. The Court found that the Board had given sufficient time and attention to the transaction, since the directors had considered the Pritzker proposal on three different occasions, on September 20, and on October 8, 1980 and finally on January 26, 1981. On that basis, the Court reasoned that the Board had acquired, over the four-month period, sufficient information to reach an informed business judgment on the cash-out merger proposal. The Court ruled:

> * * * that given the market value of Trans Union's stock, the business acumen of the members of the board of Trans Union, the substantial premium over market offered by the Pritzkers and the ultimate effect on the merger price provided by the prospect of other bids for the stock in question, that the board of directors of Trans Union did not act recklessly or improvidently in determining on a course of action which they believed to be in the best interest of the stockholders of Trans Union.

[W]e conclude that the Court's ultimate finding that the Board's conduct was not "reckless or imprudent" is contrary to the record and not the product of a logical and deductive reasoning process.

* * * [The Court reviews the Delaware law relating to the duty of care and the business judgment rule and concludes that in Delaware director liability "is predicated upon concepts of gross negligence."]

III.

* * * The issue of whether the directors reached an informed decision to "sell" the Company on September 20, 1980 must be determined only upon the basis of the information then reasonably available to the directors and relevant to their decision to accept the Pritzker merger proposal. This is not to say that the directors were precluded from altering their original plan of action, had they done so in an informed manner. What we do say is that the question of whether the directors reached an informed business judgment in agreeing to sell the Company, pursuant to the terms of the September 20 Agreement presents, in reality, two questions: (A) whether the directors reached an informed business judgment on September 20, 1980; and (B) if they did not, whether the directors' actions taken subsequent to September 20 were adequate to cure any infirmity in their action taken on September 20. We first consider the directors' September 20 action in terms of their reaching an informed business judgment.

–A–

On the record before us, we must conclude that the Board of Directors did not reach an informed business judgment on September 20, 1980 in voting to "sell" the Company for $55 per share pursuant to the Pritzker cash-out merger proposal. * * *

(1)

A substantial premium may provide one reason to recommend a merger, but in the absence of other sound valuation information, the fact of a premium alone does not provide an adequate basis upon which to assess the fairness of an offering price. Here, the judgment reached as to the adequacy of the premium was based on a comparison between the historically depressed Trans Union market price and the amount of the Pritzker offer. Using market price as a basis for concluding that the premium adequately reflected the true value of the Company was a clearly faulty, indeed fallacious, premise, as the defendants' own evidence demonstrates. * * *

The parties do not dispute that a publicly-traded stock price is solely a measure of the value of a minority position and, thus, market price represents only the value of a single share. Nevertheless, on September 20, the Board assessed the adequacy of the premium over market, offered by Pritzker, solely by comparing it with Trans Union's current and historical stock price.

Indeed, as of September 20, the Board had no other information on which to base a determination of the intrinsic value of Trans Union as a going concern. As of September 20, the Board had made no evaluation of the Company designed to value the entire enterprise, nor had the Board ever previously considered selling the Company or consenting to a buy-out merger. Thus, the adequacy of a premium is indeterminate unless it is assessed in terms of other competent and sound valuation information that reflects the value of the particular business.

Despite the foregoing facts and circumstances, there was no call by the Board, either on September 20 or thereafter, for any valuation study or documentation of the $55 price per share as a measure of the fair value of the Company in a cash-out context. It is undisputed that the major asset of Trans Union was its cash flow. Yet, at no time did the Board call for a valuation study taking into account that highly significant element of the Company's assets.

We do not imply that an outside valuation study is essential to support an informed business judgment; nor do we state that fairness opinions by independent investment bankers are required as a matter of law. Often insiders familiar with the business of a going concern are in a better position than are outsiders to gather relevant information; and under appropriate circumstances, such directors may be fully protected in relying in good faith upon the valuation reports of their management. See 8 Del.C. § 141(e).

Here, the record establishes that the Board did not request its Chief Financial Officer, Romans, to make any valuation study or review of the proposal to determine the adequacy of $55 per share for sale of the Company. On the record before us: The Board rested on Romans' elicited response that the $55 figure was within a "fair price range" within the context of a leveraged buy-out. No director sought any further information from Romans. No director asked him why he put $55 at the bottom of his range. No director asked Romans for any details as to his study, the reason why it had been undertaken or its depth. No director asked to see the study; and no director asked Romans whether Trans Union's finance department could do a fairness study within the remaining 36–hour period available under the Pritzker offer.

Had the Board, or any member, made an inquiry of Romans, he presumably would have responded as he testified: that his calculations were rough and preliminary; and, that the study was not designed to determine the fair value of the Company, but rather to assess the feasibility of a leveraged buy-out financed by the Company's projected cash flow, making certain assumptions as to the purchaser's borrowing needs. Romans would have presumably also informed the Board of his view, and the widespread view of Senior Management, that the timing of the offer was wrong and the offer inadequate.

The record also establishes that the Board accepted without scrutiny Van Gorkom's representation as to the fairness of the $55 price per share for sale of the Company—a subject that the Board had never previously considered. The Board thereby failed to discover that Van Gorkom had suggested the $55 price to Pritzker and, most crucially, that Van Gorkom had arrived at the $55 figure based on calculations designed solely to determine the feasibility of a leveraged buy-out.[17] No questions were raised either as to the tax implications of a cash-out merger or how the price for the one million share option granted Pritzker was calculated.

We do not say that the Board of Directors was not entitled to give some credence to Van Gorkom's representation that $55 was an adequate or fair price. Under § 141(e), the directors were entitled to rely upon their chairman's opinion of value and adequacy, provided that such opinion was reached on a sound basis. Here, the issue is whether the directors informed themselves as to all information that was reasonably available to them. Had they done so, they would have learned of the source and derivation of the $55 price and could not reasonably have relied thereupon in good faith.

None of the directors, Management or outside, were investment bankers or financial analysts. Yet the Board did not consider recessing the meeting until a later hour that day (or requesting an extension of Pritzker's Sunday evening deadline) to give it time to elicit more information as to the sufficiency of the offer, either from inside Management (in particular Romans) or from Trans Union's own investment banker, Salomon Brothers, whose Chicago specialist in merger and acquisitions was known to the Board and familiar with Trans Union's affairs.

Thus, the record compels the conclusion that on September 20 the Board lacked valuation information adequate to reach an informed business judgment as to the fairness of $55 per share for sale of the Company. * * *

(2)

* * * [The court concludes in this portion of the opinion that there was not a "post-September 20 market test" of the $55 price sufficient to confirm the reasonableness of the board's decision.]

(3)

The directors' unfounded reliance on both the premium and the market test as the basis for accepting the Pritzker proposal undermines the defendants' remaining contention that the Board's collective experience and sophistication was a sufficient basis for finding that it reached its September 20

---

17. [By the Court] As of September 20 the directors did not know: that Van Gorkom had arrived at the $55 figure alone, and subjectively, as the figure to be used by Controller Peterson in creating a feasible structure for a leveraged buy-out by a prospective purchaser; that Van Gorkom had not sought advice, information or assistance from either inside or outside Trans Union directors as to the value of the Company as an entity or the fair price per Company as an entity or the fair price per share for 100% of its stock; that Van Gorkom had not consulted with the Company's investment bankers or other financial analysts; that Van Gorkom had not consulted with or confided in any officer or director of the Company except Chelberg; and that Van Gorkom had deliberately chosen to ignore the advice and opinion of the members of his Senior Management group regarding the adequacy of the $55 price.

decision with informed, reasonable deliberation.[18] Compare Gimbel v. Signal Companies, Inc., Del.Ch., 316 A.2d 599 (1974), aff'd per curiam, Del.Supr., 316 A.2d 619 (1974). There, the Court of Chancery preliminary enjoined a board's sale of stock of its wholly-owned subsidiary for an alleged grossly inadequate price. It did so based on a finding that the business judgment rule had been pierced for failure of management to give its board "the opportunity to make a reasonable and reasoned decision." 316 A.2d at 615. The Court there reached this result notwithstanding the board's sophistication and experience; the company's need of immediate cash; and the board's need to act promptly due to the impact of an energy crisis on the value of the underlying assets being sold—all of its subsidiary's oil and gas interests. The Court found those factors denoting competence to be outweighed by evidence of gross negligence; that management in effect sprang the deal on the board by negotiating the asset sale without informing the board; that the buyer intended to "force a quick decision" by the board; that the board meeting was called on only one-and-a-half days' notice; that its outside directors were not notified of the meeting's purpose; that during a meeting spanning "a couple of hours" a sale of assets worth $480 million was approved; and that the Board failed to obtain a *current* appraisal of its oil and gas interests. The analogy of *Signal* to the case at bar is significant.

(4)

Part of the defense is based on a claim that the directors relied on legal advice rendered at the September 20 meeting by James Brennan, Esquire, who was present at Van Gorkom's request. Unfortunately, Brennan did not appear and testify at trial even though his firm participated in the defense of this action. There is no contemporaneous evidence of the advice given by Brennan on September 20, only the later deposition and trial testimony of certain directors as to their recollections or understanding of what was said at the meeting. Since counsel did not testify, and the advice attributed to Brennan is hearsay received by the Trial Court over the plaintiffs' objections, we consider it only in the context of the directors' present claims. In fairness to counsel, we make no findings that the advice attributed to him was in fact given. We focus solely on the efficacy of the defendants' claims, made months and years later, in an effort to extricate themselves from liability.

Several defendants testified that Brennan advised them that Delaware law did not require a fairness opinion or an outside valuation of the Company before the Board could act on the Pritzker proposal. If given, the advice was correct. However, that did not end the matter. Unless the directors had before them adequate information regarding the intrinsic value of the Company, upon which a proper exercise of business judgment could be made, mere

---

18. [By the Court] Trans Union's five "inside" directors had backgrounds in law and accounting, 116 years of collective employment by the Company and 68 years of combined experience on its Board. Trans Union's five "outside" directors included four chief executives of major corporations and an economist who was a former dean of a major school of business and chancellor of a university. The "outside" directors had 78 years of combined experience as chief executive officers of major corporations and 50 years of cumulative experience as directors of Trans Union. Thus, defendants argue that the Board was eminently qualified to reach an informed judgment on the proposed "sale" of Trans Union notwithstanding their lack of any advance notice of the proposal, the shortness of their deliberation, and their determination not to consult with their investment banker or to obtain a fairness opinion.

advice of this type is meaningless; and, given this record of the defendants' failures, it constitutes no defense here.[19] * * *

We conclude that Trans Union's Board was grossly negligent in that it failed to act with informed reasonable deliberation in agreeing to the Pritzker merger proposal on September 20; and we further conclude that the Trial Court erred as a matter of law in failing to address that question before determining whether the directors' later conduct was sufficient to cure its initial error.

A second claim is that counsel advised the Board it would be subject to lawsuits if it rejected the $55 per share offer. It is, of course, a fact of corporate life that today when faced with difficult or sensitive issues, directors often are subject to suit, irrespective of the decisions they make. However, counsel's mere acknowledgement of this circumstance cannot be rationally translated into a justification for a board permitting itself to be stampeded into a patently unadvised act. While suit might result from the rejection of a merger or tender offer, Delaware law makes clear that a board acting within the ambit of the business judgment rule faces no ultimate liability. Pogostin v. Rice, supra. Thus, we cannot conclude that the mere threat of litigation, acknowledged by counsel, constitutes either legal advice or any valid basis upon which to pursue an uninformed course.

Since we conclude that Brennan's purported advice is of no consequence to the defense of this case, it is unnecessary for us to invoke the adverse inferences which may be attributable to one failing to appear at trial and testify. * * *

IV.

Whether the directors of Trans Union should be treated as one or individually in terms of invoking the protection of the business judgment rule and the applicability of 8 Del.C. § 141(c) are questions which were not originally addressed by the parties in their briefing of this case. This resulted in a supplemental briefing and a second rehearing en banc on two basic questions: (a) whether one or more of the directors were deprived of the protection of the business judgment rule by evidence of an absence of good faith; and (b) whether one or more of the outside directors were entitled to invoke the protection of 8 Del.C. § 141(e) by evidence of a reasonable, good faith reliance on "reports," including legal advice, rendered the Board by certain inside directors and the Board's special counsel, Brennan.

The parties' response, including reargument, has led the majority of the Court to conclude: (1) that since all of the defendant directors, outside as well as inside, take a unified position, we are required to treat all of the directors as one as to whether they are entitled to the protection of the business judgment rule; and (2) that considerations of good faith, including the presumption that the directors acted in good faith, are irrelevant in determining the threshold issue of whether the directors as a Board exercised an informed business judgment. For the same reason, we must reject defense

---

19. [By the Court] Nonetheless, we are satisfied that in an appropriate factual context a proper exercise of business judgment may include, as one of its aspects, reasonable reliance upon the advice of counsel. This is wholly outside the statutory protections of 8 Del.C. § 141(e) involving reliance upon reports of officers, certain experts and books and records of the company.

counsel's *ad hominem* argument for affirmance: that reversal may result in a multi-million dollar class award against the defendants for having made an allegedly uninformed business judgment in a transaction not involving any personal gain, self-dealing or claim of bad faith.[20]

In their brief, the defendants similarly mistake the business judgment rule's application to this case by erroneously invoking presumptions of good faith and "wide discretion":

> This is a case in which plaintiff challenged the exercise of business judgment by an independent Board of Directors. There were no allegations and no proof of fraud, bad faith, or self-dealing by the directors. * * *

> The business judgment rule, which was properly applied by the Chancellor, allows directors wide discretion in the matter of valuation and affords room for honest differences of opinion. In order to prevail, plaintiffs had the heavy burden of proving that the merger price was so grossly inadequate as to display itself as a badge of fraud. That is a burden which plaintiffs have not met.

However, plaintiffs have not claimed, nor did the Trial Court decide, that $55 was a grossly inadequate price per share for sale of the Company. That being so, the presumption that a board's judgment as to adequacy of price represents an honest exercise of business judgment (absent proof that the sale price was grossly inadequate) is irrelevant to the threshold question of whether an informed judgment was reached.

* * * We hold, therefore, that the Trial Court committed reversible error in applying the business judgment rule in favor of the director defendants in this case.

On remand, the Court of Chancery shall conduct an evidentiary hearing to determine the fair value of the shares represented by the plaintiffs' class, based on the intrinsic value of Trans Union on September 20, 1980. Such valuation shall be made in accordance with Weinberger v. UOP, Inc., supra. Thereafter, an award of damages may be entered to the extent that the fair value of Trans Union exceeds $55 per share. * * *

REVERSED and REMANDED for proceedings consistent herewith.

McNEILLY, JUSTICE, dissenting:

The majority opinion reads like an advocate's closing address to a hostile jury. And I say that not lightly. Throughout the opinion great emphasis is directed only to the negative, with nothing more than lip service granted the positive aspects of this case. In my opinion Chancellor Marvel (retired) should have been affirmed. The Chancellor's opinion was the product of well reasoned conclusions, based upon a sound deductive process, clearly supported by

---

20. [By the Editor] In the petition for rehearing that was ultimately denied in this case, the Court quotes the beginning of the oral argument made by counsel for the individual defendants as follows:

COUNSEL: I'll make the argument on behalf of the nine individual defendants against whom the plaintiffs seek more than $100,000,000 in damages. That is the ultimate issue in this case, whether or not nine honest, experienced businessmen should be subject to damages in a case where—

At this point counsel was interrupted by the Court with a question and never returned to the beginning point.

the evidence and entitled to deference in this appeal. Because of my diametrical opposition to all evidentiary conclusions of the majority, I respectfully dissent.

It would serve no useful purpose, particularly at this late date, for me to dissent at great length. I restrain myself from doing so, but feel compelled to at least point out what I consider to be the most glaring deficiencies in the majority opinion. The majority has spoken and has effectively said that Trans Union's Directors have been the victims of a "fast shuffle" by Van Gorkom and Pritzker. That is the beginning of the majority's comedy of errors. The first and most important error made is the majority's assessment of the directors' knowledge of the affairs of Trans Union and their combined ability to act in this situation under the protection of the business judgment rule.

Trans Union's Board of Directors consisted of ten men, five of whom were "inside" directors and five of whom were "outside" directors. The "inside" directors were Van Gorkom, Chelberg, Bonser, William B. Browder, Senior Vice–President–Law, and Thomas P. O'Boyle, Senior Vice–President–Administration. At the time the merger was proposed the inside five directors had collectively been employed by the Company for 116 years and had 68 years of combined experience as directors. The "outside" directors were A.W. Wallis, William B. Johnson, Joseph B. Lanterman, Graham J. Morgan and Robert W. Reneker. With the exception of Wallis, these were all chief executive officers of Chicago based corporations that were at least as large as Trans Union. The five "outside" directors had 78 years of combined experience as chief executive officers, and 53 years cumulative service as Trans Union directors.

The inside directors wear their badge of expertise in the corporate affairs of Trans Union on their sleeves. But what about the outsiders? Dr. Wallis is or was an economist and math statistician, a professor of economics at Yale University, dean of the graduate school of business at the University of Chicago, and Chancellor of the University of Rochester. Dr. Wallis had been on the Board of Trans Union since 1962. He also was on the Board of Bausch & Lomb, Kodak, Metropolitan Life Insurance Company, Standard Oil and others.

William B. Johnson is a University of Pennsylvania law graduate, President of Railway Express until 1966, Chairman and Chief Executive of I.C. Industries Holding Company, and member of Trans Union's Board since 1968.

Joseph Lanterman, a Certified Public Accountant, is or was President and Chief Executive of American Steel, on the Board of International Harvester, Peoples Energy, Illinois Bell Telephone, Harris Bank and Trust Company, Kemper Insurance Company and a director of Trans Union for four years.

Graham Morgan is a chemist, was Chairman and Chief Executive Officer of U.S. Gypsum, and in the 17 and 18 years prior to the Trans Union transaction had been involved in 31 or 32 corporate takeovers.

Robert Reneker attended University of Chicago and Harvard Business Schools. He was President and Chief Executive of Swift and Company, director of Trans Union since 1971, and member of the Boards of seven other corporations including U.S. Gypsum and the Chicago Tribune.

Directors of this caliber are not ordinarily taken in by a "fast shuffle". I submit they were not taken into this multi-million dollar corporate transaction without being fully informed and aware of the state of the art as it pertained to the entire corporate panorama of Trans Union. True, even directors such as these, with their business acumen, interest and expertise, can go astray. I do not believe that to be the case here. These men knew Trans Union like the back of their hands and were more than well qualified to make on the spot informed business judgments concerning the affairs of Trans Union including a 100% sale of the corporation. Lest we forget, the corporate world of then and now operates on what is so aptly referred to as "the fast track". These men were at the time an integral part of that world, all professional business men, not intellectual figureheads. * * *

Notes

(1) Why did the defendants' lawyers in *Van Gorkom* adopt a "one for all and all for one" approach? Assuming there was gross negligence, is it not clear that some of the directors might have had a defense that would not have been available to Van Gorkom himself and possibly other inside directors?

(2) Following the Delaware Supreme Court opinion in *Van Gorkom*, the case was settled with the approval of the Delaware Chancery Court. The settlement involved the payment by the defendants of $23,500,000, $10,000,000 of which was provided through the defendants' directors' and officers' (D & O) liability insurance policy. The plaintiffs' attorneys are reputed to have received $18 million of this recovery and the shareholders $5.5 million. Some time after the sale of Trans Union, Van Gorkom was appointed Undersecretary for Management in the Department of State. Secretary of State Schultz was reported to have selected Van Gorkom personally because he wanted a "trusted confidant" in that position. So far as Trans Union itself is concerned, the Pritzker buyout was apparently not as successful as Pritzker had expected. These miscellaneous facts are taken from Arthur Fleischer, et al., Board Games (1988), Chapter 1.

(3) The response of the corporate bar to *Van Gorkom* was one of shocked incredulity. "The Delaware Supreme Court * * * exploded a bomb. Stated minimally, the Court * * * pierced the Business Judgment Rule and imposed liability on independent (even eminent) outside directors of Trans Union Corporation * * * because (roughly) the Court thought they had not been careful enough, and had not enquired enough, before deciding to accept and recommend to Transunion's shareholders a cash-out merger at a per share price that was less than the 'intrinsic value' of the shares. * * * The corporate bar generally views the decision as atrocious and predicts the most dire consequences as directors come to realize how exposed they have become." Bayless Manning, in an unpublished newsletter for his clients. Professor Richard Buxbaum, in a CLE newsletter for California Bar subscribers, headlined his analysis of the case "Summer Lightning Out of Delaware."

(4) Leo Herzel & Leo Katz, Smith v. Van Gorkom: The Business of Judging Business Judgment, 41 Bus.Law. 1187, 1188–89, 1191 (1986):[21]

> To most (including the authors) the court's decision seems misguided and Trans Union's actions entirely proper. Van Gorkom was a seasoned chief executive officer and substantial stockholder. He was well placed and motivated to strike a good deal, even when acting by himself. The other directors were also experienced and sophisticated. There was no reason why they

---

21. Copyright 1986 by the American Bar Association. All rights reserved. Reprinted with the permission of the American Bar Association and its Section of Corporation, Banking and Business Law.

shouldn't have been able to recognize and approve a good deal at the drop of a hat. Investment bankers are expensive and surely not indispensable. When a good offer is in hand, they may well be superfluous. Merger documents are written by lawyers for lawyers, and typically no one else scrutinizes them. Admittedly, the board was a bit slapdash in its compliance with corporate formalities—did Van Gorkom really have to sign at a social affair for the opera? But that's not a breach of the duty of care. * * *

The other effect of *Smith v. Van Gorkom* will be greater formalism on the part of the board, as it goes about the business of cultivating an aura of care, diligence, thoroughness, and circumspection. (As one director put it: "Prudence and diligence are no longer assumed but require a certain amount of posturing.")

Such formalism has a lot of costs. Most obviously, it will mean more reliance on and more fees for lawyers, investment bankers, accountants, management consultants, and economists, and who knows, maybe sociologists, statisticians, psychologists, demographers, and population geneticists. In short, experts of every stripe, whose advice might shed some light on some aspect of the board's decision. After all, every decision has untold consequences and ramifications.

(5) Robert W. Hamilton, Reliance and Liability Standards for Outside Directors, 24 Wake Forest L.Rev. 5, 28–29 (1989):

Whether the result reached by the Delaware Supreme Court in *Van Gorkom* was correct or incorrect, the immediate consequences of the decision on the business community were deeply disturbing. Many outside directors began to reassess their willingness to serve as directors at all, and isolated instances of resignations were reported.[22] The number of lawyers serving on boards of directors of their clients declined. Even some inside directors began to have qualms about the desirability of their service on the board of directors of the company that employed them. The prestige and financial rewards of serving on boards of directors of publicly held corporations had to be weighed against the remote risk of a crushing liability being imposed on the board members. Many potential outside directors, in particular, decided that this risk outweighed the benefits. It became considerably more difficult to find desirable persons who were willing to become outside directors. On another level, general counsels made recommendations to boards of directors that they hire expensive financial advisers, commission extensive studies, and otherwise improve the paper record of their decisional process in order to reduce the risk of liability in situations similar to *Van Gorkom*. It was a widely held

22. [By the Author] See Baum & Byrne, *The Job Nobody Wants*, Bus. Wk., Sept. 8, 1986, at 56 (reporting ten instances of mass resignations of outside directors). The decision in *Van Gorkom* was handed down during a "liability insurance crisis" in the United States. During this period insurance companies writing liability insurance in a variety of areas were reducing their exposure by reducing coverage limits, increasing premiums, and declining entirely to insure specific risks. Directors' and officers' liability insurance was involved in this process, and some of the activities described in the text may have been the consequence of the difficulties some companies were experiencing in obtaining or maintaining acceptable levels of liability insurance for their directors. See Lewin, *Director Insurance Drying Up*, N.Y. Times, March 7, 1986, at D1, col. 3 ("[b]ecause of increased litigation, large court awards and a rapidly shrinking pool of available insurance, many companies can no longer find, or afford, insurance for their directors and officers"). Anecdotal evidence indicates that this crisis thereafter eased. Glaberson, *Liability Rates Flattening Out as Crisis Eases*, N.Y. Times, Feb. 9, 1987, at A1, col. 5 ("companies that could not buy [insurance] coverage at any price are [now] finding it").

belief that the cost of this exercise exceeded the benefits to the decisional process.

(6) In David B. Hilder, Risky Business: Liability Insurance Is Difficult to Find Now For Directors, Officers, Wall St.J. (July 10, 1985), at 1, col. 6, Walter B. Wriston, a member of the board of directors of nine corporations and the former chief executive officer of a major bank, is reported as stating, "I don't know of anybody who would join a board without D & O insurance." Such insurance is usually augmented by a corporate policy of indemnifying directors against costs of litigation to the maximum extent permissible under public policy. Indemnification and insurance are discussed in Chapter 13. It seems clear that the availability of D & O insurance was limited during the period of the middle 1980s. For a speculative assessment of the causes, see Roberta Romano, What Went Wrong with Directors' and Officers' Liability Insurance?, 14 Del. J.Corp.L. 1 (1989). Arguably, the decision in *Van Gorkom* contributed to this drying up of insurance; Professor Romano, however, comments:

> The court [in *Van Gorkom*] further indicated that if specific procedures had been followed, such as obtaining an investment banker's fairness opinion, there would have been no liability. Given * * * standard business practice, the opinion is not a scandalous harbinger of increased exposure. Quite to the contrary, the decision arguably lowered the standard of conduct by defining breaches of the duty of care in terms of "gross" rather than "ordinary" negligence.

14 Del.J.Corp.L. at 24. Of course, the sheer magnitude of the potential liability in cases like *Van Gorkom* makes it difficult to satisfy any risk averse potential director that the insurance being provided, no matter how large, is adequate.

(7) Cede & Co., Cinerama, Inc. v. Technicolor, Inc., 634 A.2d 345 (Del.1993) involved a merger negotiated in 1982 (two years before Smith v. Van Gorkom was decided) under circumstances roughly comparable to those that occurred in *Van Gorkom*. In a suit brought by an individual shareholder, the Court of Chancery, however, refused to impose personal liability on the directors, despite a finding of gross negligence, unless the plaintiff could establish not only that it suffered a loss but also that the loss was caused by the grossly negligent conduct of the directors. The rule of *Van Gorkom* would lead to "draconian results," Chancellor Allen stated, unless modified to require this proof of causation. The Delaware Supreme Court reversed, holding that to require the plaintiff to show a causal connection between the defendants' gross negligence and the damage or loss suffered by the plaintiff "would lead to most unfortunate results, detrimental to goals of heightened and enlightened standards for corporate governance of Delaware corporations." Once the controlling principles of *Van Gorkom* become applicable and the requirements of the business judgment rule are not met, the defendants may avoid liability only if they can establish the entire fairness of the transaction. Tort principles of causation or proximate cause "have no place in a business judgment rule standard of review analysis." Subsequently, Chancellor Allen concluded that no liability existed because the transaction was in all respects fair to shareholders opinions in this case. 663 A.2d 1134 (Del.Ch.1994), aff'd 663 A.2d 1156 (Del.1995).

(8) Should it not be an absolute defense that a director sought the advice of counsel for the corporation and acted only after receiving an informal opinion that the conduct was lawful? Consider MBCA § 8.30(b)(2). Compare Tillman v. Wheaton–Haven Recreation Ass'n, Inc., 517 F.2d 1141 (4th Cir.1975), where directors of a nonprofit corporation were held personally liable under 42 U.S.C.A. § 1983 for unlawfully discriminating against black plaintiffs despite the fact that they had

been assured by counsel that the exclusion of blacks from the neighborhood swimming pool association was lawful. The Court stated:

> The flaw in the directors' argument is their failure to place the defense of due diligence in its proper context. Due diligence is a defense for corporate directors who are charged with failing to exercise reasonable care. Its genesis is the law of negligence. None of the cases on which the directors rely applies the doctrine to an intentionally tortious act against a third person. An analysis of the cases cited as supporting the directors exposes the fallacy of their position.

517 F.2d at 1144. Judge Boreman dissented, arguing that at the time the discrimination took place it was not possible to know whether or not the conduct was legal, and that "[t]o hold the directors to a standard of legal acumen greater than that possessed by the federal judiciary would be unconscionable." Id. at 1151.

(9) Chancellor Allen reflected on the *Van Gorkom* decision in Gagliardi v. TriFoods Int'l Inc., 683 A.2d 1049 (Del.Ch.1996). He stated, "I start with what I take to be an elementary precept of corporation law: in the absence of facts showing self-dealing or improper motive, a corporate officer or director is not legally responsible to the corporation for losses that may be suffered as a result of a decision that an officer made or that directors authorized in good faith." To this statement he appended the following footnote:

> I * * * note that in making this simple statement, I count Smith v. Van Gorkom, Del.Supr., 488 A.2d 858 (1985), not as a "negligence" or due care case involving no loyalty issues, but as an early and, as of its date, not yet fully rationalized, "Revlon" or "change in control" case. See Jonathan Macey and Geoffrey Miller, TransUnion Reconsidered, 98 YALE L.J. 127. As such I see it as reflecting a concern with the TransUnion board's independence and loyalty to the company's shareholders in a critical "sale of the company" context.

Do you think this is a plausible reading of *Van Gorkom*?

(10) In In re Caremark International Inc. Derivative Litigation, 1996 WL 549894 (Del.Ch.1996) Chancellor Allen considered a "claim that the directors allowed a situation to develop and continue which exposed the corporation to enormous legal liability" and that in so doing they violated a duty to be active monitors of corporate performance. He stated:

> The complaint thus does not charge either director [with] self-dealing or the more difficult loyalty-type problems arising from cases of suspect director motivation, such as entrenchment or sale of control contexts. The theory here advanced is possibly the most difficult theory in corporation law upon which a plaintiff might hope to win a judgment. * * *

> The * * * cases in which director liability for inattention is theoretically possible entail circumstances in which a loss eventuates not from a decision but, from unconsidered inaction. Most of the decisions that a corporation, acting through its human agents, makes are, of course, not the subject of director attention. Legally, the board itself will be required only to authorize the most significant corporate acts or transactions: mergers, changes in capital structure, fundamental changes in business, appointment and compensation of the CEO, etc. As the facts of this case graphically demonstrate, ordinary business decisions that are made by officers and employees deeper in the interior of the organization can, however, vitally affect the welfare of the corporation and its ability to achieve its various strategic and financial goals.

* * * Financial and organizational disasters such as * * * [what occurred here] raise the question, what is the board's responsibility with respect to the organization and monitoring of the enterprise to assure that the corporation functions within the law to achieve its purposes? * * *

In 1963, the Delaware Supreme Court in Graham v. Allis–Chalmers Mfg. Co.,[23] addressed the question of potential liability of board members for losses experienced by the corporation as a result of the corporation having violated the anti-trust laws of the United States. There was no claim in that case that the directors knew about the behavior of subordinate employees of the corporation that had resulted in the liability. Rather, as in this case, the claim asserted was that the directors ought to have known of it and if they had known they would have been under a duty to bring the corporation into compliance with the law and thus save the corporation from the loss. The Delaware Supreme Court concluded that, under the facts as they appeared, there was no basis to find that the directors had breached a duty to be informed of the ongoing operations of the firm. In notably colorful terms, the court stated that "absent cause for suspicion there is no duty upon the directors to install and operate a corporate system of espionage to ferret out wrongdoing which they have no reason to suspect exists." The Court found that there were no grounds for suspicion in that case and, thus, concluded that the directors were blamelessly unaware of the conduct leading to the corporate liability.

How does one generalize this holding today? Can it be said today that, absent some ground giving rise to suspicion of violation of law, that corporate directors have no duty to assure that a corporate information gathering and reporting systems exists which represents a good faith attempt to provide senior management and the Board with information respecting material acts, events or conditions within the corporation, including compliance with applicable statutes and regulations? I certainly do not believe so. I doubt that such a broad generalization of the Graham holding would have been accepted by the Supreme Court in 1963. The case can be more narrowly interpreted as standing for the proposition that, absent grounds to suspect deception, neither corporate boards nor senior officers can be charged with wrongdoing simply for assuming the integrity of employees and the honesty of their dealings on the company's behalf. See 188 A.2d at 130–31.

A broader interpretation of Graham v. Allis Chalmers—that it means that a corporate board has no responsibility to assure that appropriate information and reporting systems are established by management—would not, in any event, be accepted by the Delaware Supreme Court in 1996, in my opinion. In stating the basis for this view, I start with the recognition that in recent years the Delaware Supreme Court has made it clear—especially in its jurisprudence concerning takeovers, from Smith v. Van Gorkom through QVC v. Paramount Communications[24]—the seriousness with which the corporation law views the role of the corporate board. Secondly, I note the elementary fact that relevant and timely information is an essential predicate for satisfaction of the board's supervisory and monitoring role under Section 141 of the Delaware General Corporation Law. Thirdly, I note the potential impact of the federal organizational sentencing guidelines on any business organization. Any rational person attempting in good faith to meet an organizational

23. [By the Chancellor] Del.Supr., 188 A.2d 125 (1963).

24. [By the Chancellor] Del.Supr., 637 A.2d 34 (1994).

governance responsibility would be bound to take into account this development and the enhanced penalties and the opportunities for reduced sanctions that it offers.

In light of these developments, it would, in my opinion, be a mistake to conclude that our Supreme Court's statement in Graham concerning "espionage" means that corporate boards may satisfy their obligation to be reasonably informed concerning the corporation, without assuring themselves that information and reporting systems exist in the organization that are reasonably designed to provide to senior management and to the board itself timely, accurate information sufficient to allow management and the board, each within its scope, to reach informed judgments concerning both the corporation's compliance with law and its business performance.

DEL. GEN. CORP. LAW
§ 102(b)(7).

§ 102 CONTENTS OF CERTIFICATE OF INCORPORATION

* * * (b) In addition to the matters required to be set forth in the certificate of incorporation by subsection (a) of this section, the certificate of incorporation may also contain any or all of the following matters: * * *

(7) A provision eliminating or limiting the personal liability of a director to the corporation or its stockholders for monetary damages for breach of fiduciary duty as a director, provided that such provision shall not eliminate or limit the liability of a director (i) for any breach of the director's duty of loyalty to the corporation or its stockholders, (ii) for acts or omissions not in good faith or which involve intentional misconduct or a knowing violation of law, (iii) under section 174 of this Title,[25] or (iv) for any transaction from which the director derived an improper personal benefit. No such provision shall eliminate or limit the liability of a director for any act or omission occurring prior to the date when such provision becomes effective. * * *

JAMES J. HANKS, RECENT STATE LEGISLATION ON DIRECTOR AND OFFICER LIABILITY LIMITATION AND INDEMNIFICATION[26]
43 Bus.Law. 1207, 1209–13, 1216–17, 1219–20, 1231–36 (1988).

The first state to respond to the developments of the mid–1980s was Indiana, in April 1986, followed by Delaware in June. Since then, forty other states have adopted some form of legislation designed to reduce the risk of directors' personal liability for money damages. * * *

CHARTER OPTION STATUTES

The most popular form of director liability statute has been the so-called "charter option" statute, first enacted by Delaware, effective July 1, 1986. Since then, charter option statutes have been adopted by thirty other states.

---

25. [By the Editor] Section 174 refers to the liability of directors for unlawful dividends and stock repurchases or redemptions.

26. Copyright 1988 by the American Bar Association. All rights reserved. Reprinted with the permission of the American Bar Association and its Section of Corporation, Banking and Business Law.

* * * [The Delaware statute] authorizes restricting liability for money damages, but not expanding it as, for example, making directors liable for simple negligence.

The statutory language also means that, while the stockholders may decide for themselves whether to eliminate or limit the liability of directors, they may not delegate this power to the directors. * * *

In the two years since the Delaware statute became effective, stockholders of hundreds—probably thousands—of American corporations have approved, generally by substantial majorities, liability-limitation charter amendments. Many charter amendments simply repeat the language of the statute, including its exceptions. Other amendments provide for elimination of liability to the maximum extent permitted by law from time to time. * * *

The potentially most troublesome of the Delaware exceptions is the one for breach of the duty of loyalty. The phrase "duty of loyalty" appears nowhere else in the Delaware General Corporation Law or, so far as is known, anywhere else in the corporation statute of any other state that has adopted this exception in a charter option statute. Even Delaware lawyers concede that the Delaware courts are unclear as to the parameters of the duty of loyalty. The Delaware Supreme Court itself has had difficulty in distinguishing the duty of care from the duty of loyalty. The fact that one of the other exceptions to the Delaware statute is for "improper personal benefit" suggests that breach of the duty of loyalty means something more than just self-dealing. Moreover, case law development of the duty of loyalty in Delaware has been based in substantial part on the duties of trustees under trust law. Delaware trust law includes concepts (e.g., the "exclusive benefit" rule) not necessarily appropriate to corporate directors and officers. Finally, many states have adopted a statutory standard of conduct for directors patterned after section 8.30(a) of the Revised Model Business Corporation Act, * * * Prohibiting liability limitation in language different from a statutory standard of care may lead to confusion in interpretation.

It will not be surprising, therefore, if stockholders of Delaware corporations that have adopted exculpatory charter provisions begin alleging violations of the duty of loyalty for acts or omissions that until now would have supported a claim for breach of the duty of care. * * *

The improper personal benefit exception could also be exploited, especially because it is not limited to the actual receipt of money, property, or services and therefore might be interpreted to include less easily measurable considerations, such as business goodwill, personal friendship, or social ingratiation. In voting against a takeover proposal, for example, a director might be charged with having received an improper personal benefit in the form of continued tenure on the board. * * *

Perhaps because Delaware was the first state to adopt a charter option statute and because changes in Delaware's corporate statute always attract attention, many corporations have reincorporated to Delaware. Meanwhile, hundreds of other corporations already incorporated in Delaware have amended or proposed amending their charters in order to add exculpatory provisions. * * *

RISK ALLOCATION

The principal public policy issue in director and officer liability legislation is the allocation of the economic cost of the directors' exculpated conduct. Under every director liability statute * * * liability is (under the self-executing statutes) or may be (under the charter option statutes) limited for at least simple negligence and gross negligence. * * *

Charter option statutes simply permit the stockholders to decide for themselves whether to assume this risk or to leave it with the directors. By contrast, the other director liability statutes enacted to date are direct or indirect determinations by the legislatures to shift the risk from the directors to the stockholders. * * * Generally, the legislatures that have enacted these statutes have done so with very little discussion of the benefits and costs of shifting from the directors to the stockholders the costs of the directors' misconduct. Most of these statutes have been enacted in the context of sharply increased premiums for D & O insurance (or its unavailability at any price) and the consequent loss or prospective loss of outside directors. The lobbying and editorial comments surrounding many of these statutes have often been accompanied by emphasis on economic development, including comparisons with statutes in other (especially neighboring) states. Little attention has been paid to the issue of whether limiting the liability of directors and officers is wise in the absence of an insurance "crisis" or after it recedes. * * *

Supporters of legislated (as opposed to stockholder-determined) exculpation for directors would probably * * * claim that it is more in society's interests to encourage competent, qualified individuals to serve as directors than to provide for recovery of the occasional loss to corporations caused by directors' acts or omissions. Indeed, good directors are probably less likely to cause injury to the corporation. As Judge Learned Hand declared: "The law ought not make trusteeship so hazardous that responsible individuals * * * will shy away from it."[27] Certainly, it is well within the power of state legislatures, not to mention the stockholders themselves, to make this choice. * * *

Notes

Zirn v. VLI Corporation, 621 A.2d 773, 783 (Del.1993) was a suit by shareholders of an acquired corporation against its directors claiming "equitable fraud" arising from a breach of duty to disclose the real factors that motivated the board of directors to approve the acquisition transaction. The directors argued that in any event they were shielded from liability by Article Ninth of VLI's Certificate which apparently tracked the language of Delaware GCL § 102(b)(7). The Court rejected this argument:

> * * * This provision, which purports to protect directors from monetary liability for breaches of fiduciary duty, does not shield directors from liability for equitable fraud. Moreover, the legislative history of the statute authorizing this provision, 8 Del.C. § 102(b)(7), indicates that corporations are empowered to shield directors from breaches of the duty of care, not the duty of loyalty, which also embraces the duty of loyalty, which also embraces the duty

---

27. [By the Author] Dabney v. Chase Nat'l Bank, 196 F.2d 668, 675 (2d Cir.1952).

of disclosure that is at issue here. Even defendants' own proxy materials note that the provision's applicability is limited to the duty of care.

On a subsequent appeal, Zirn v. VLI Corporation, 681 A.2d 1050, 1061–2 (Del. 1996), the Court concluded that while the directors had made misleading partial disclosures, their actions were taken in good faith and therefore protected by § 102(b)(7):

> We agree with the Defendants and hold that the VLI directors are shielded from liability by 8 Del.C. § 102(b)(7) and the amendment to VLI's Certificate of Incorporation giving effect to that statutory provision. The record reveals that any misstatements or omissions that occurred were made in good faith. The VLI directors lacked any pecuniary motive to mislead the VLI stockholders intentionally and no other plausible motive for deceiving the stockholders has been advanced. A good faith erroneous judgment as to the proper scope or content of required disclosure implicates the duty of care rather than the duty of loyalty. Thus, the disclosure violations at issue here fall within the ambit of the protection of section 102(b)(7).[28]

> Had the stockholders of VLI acted at the appropriate time and demonstrated the disclosure violation found herein, they could have sought an injunctive remedy. Unfortunately, the time for such action has passed. We recognize that our decision will leave the former stockholders of VLI without any redress. This, however, is the result envisaged by section 102(b)(7). VLI's stockholders approved the amendment to the VLI Certificate of Incorporation with full knowledge of its import.

This conclusion was based on a similar holding in Arnold v. Society for Savings Bancorp, Inc., 650 A.2d 1270, 1289 (Del.1994), subsequent appeal, 678 A.2d 533 (Del.1996).

GALL v. EXXON CORP.

United States District Court, Southern District of New York, 1976.
418 F.Supp. 508.

ROBERT L. CARTER, DISTRICT JUDGE.

Defendants have moved, pursuant to Rule 56, F.R.Civ.P., for summary judgment dismissing plaintiff's complaint on the grounds that the Special Committee on Litigation ("Special Committee"), acting as the Board of Directors of Exxon Corporation ("Exxon"), has determined in the good faith exercise of its sound business judgment that it is contrary to the interests of Exxon to institute suit on the basis of any matters raised in plaintiff's complaint. Defendants' motion is hereby denied without prejudice to its renewal after plaintiff has conducted relevant discovery.

---

28. [By the Court] The Court is cognizant of its statement in Zirn I pertaining to this issue. * * * That statement was made before the record here had been fully developed * * *. Moreover, this statement was not necessary to the holding in Zirn I, and therefore is dictum. "[T]he doctrine of the law of the case normally requires that matters previously ruled upon by the same court be put to rest." * * * The doctrine is not inflexible, however. It applies only to those matters necessary to a given decision and those matters which were decided on the basis of a fully developed record. Where, as here, this Court could not have envisioned the full factual posture of a particular claim, the prior ruling cannot be considered to be the law of the case.

I

FACTS

Plaintiff's complaint arises out of the alleged payment by Exxon Corporation of some $59 million in corporate funds as bribes or political payments, which were improperly contributed to Italian political parties and others during the period 1963–1974, in order to secure special political favors as well as other allegedly illegal commitments.

II

On September 24, 1975, Exxon's Board of Directors unanimously resolved, pursuant to Article III, Section 1, of Exxon's By–Laws to establish a Special Committee on Litigation, composed of Exxon directors Jack F. Bennett, Richard P. Dobson and Edward G. Harness,[29] and refer to the Special Committee for the determination of Exxon's action the matters raised in this and several other pending actions relating to the Italian expenditures. * * *

On January 23, 1976, after an investigation of approximately four months, including interviews with over 100 witnesses, the Special Committee issued the "Determination and Report of the Special Committee on Litigation" ("Report"), an 82–page document summarizing the Committee's findings and recommendations. The facts as uncovered by the Special Committee may be briefly summarized as follows. * * *

[Editor: The Committee report described a pattern of secret payments made for various purposes between 1963 and 1972 and political contributions to Italian political parties during the same period. The secret payments, totaling about 39 million dollars, were made through secret bank accounts not reflected on the books of Exxon's Italian subsidiary, Esso Italiana. The political contributions, totaling about 20 million dollars, were channeled through newspaper and public relations firms connected with Italian political parties; these payments were reflected by fictitious invoices purportedly for services rendered. Several of the Exxon directors named as defendants in this suit were aware of the existence of at least the political payments in Italy prior to their termination in 1972. Some of the defendants had simply been advised of the existence of the payments; others, in positions of responsibility within corporate management urged that the contributions be phased out as promptly as possible. Some of the defendant-directors were also aware of the payments made through the secret bank accounts, but apparently the knowledge of these payments was more limited than the knowledge about the political contributions.]

III

After careful review, analysis and investigation, and with the advice and concurrence of Special Counsel,[30] the Special Committee unanimously deter-

---

29. [By the Court] * * * According to the affidavits submitted, each of the members of the Special Committee has confirmed that he has not been in any way connected or involved with the matters relating to the Italian expenditures referred to in this action or in the other related actions and none has been named as a defendant in any of the pending actions. Indeed, none of the members of the Committee was elected to the Exxon Board until long after the Italian expenditures complained of were terminated and Exxon had taken steps to ensure that such expenditures would not be resumed.

30. [By the Court] At its second meeting on October 29, 1975, the Special Committee appointed Justice Joseph Weintraub, former

mined on January 23, 1976, that it would be contrary to the interests of Exxon and its shareholders for Exxon, or anyone on its behalf, to institute or maintain a legal action against any present or former Exxon director or officer.[31] The Committee further resolved to direct and authorize the proper officers of Exxon and its General Counsel to oppose and seek dismissal of all shareholder derivative actions relating to payments made by or on behalf of Esso Italiana S.p.A., which had been filed against any present or former Exxon director or officer.

IV

Discussion

There is no question that the rights sought to be vindicated in this lawsuit are those of Exxon and not those of the plaintiff suing derivatively on the corporation's behalf. Since it is the interests of the corporation which are at stake, it is the responsibility of the directors of the corporation to determine, in the first instance, whether an action should be brought on the corporation's behalf. It follows that the decision of corporate directors whether or not to assert a cause of action held by the corporation rests within the sound business judgment of the management. See, e.g., United Copper Securities Co. v. Amalgamated Copper Co., 244 U.S. 261, 263–4, 37 S.Ct. 509, 61 L.Ed. 1119 (1917).

This principle, which has come to be known as the business judgment rule, was articulated by Mr. Justice Brandeis speaking for a unanimous Court in United Copper Securities Co. v. Amalgamated Copper Co., supra, 244 U.S. at 263–64, 37 S.Ct. at 510. In that case the directors of a corporation chose not to bring an antitrust action against a third party. Mr. Justice Brandeis said:

> Whether or not a corporation shall seek to enforce in the courts a cause of action for damages is, like other business questions, ordinarily a matter of internal management, and is left to the discretion of the directors, in the absence of instruction by vote of the stockholders. Courts interfere seldom to control such discretion intra vires the corporation, except where the directors are guilty of misconduct equivalent to a breach of trust, or where they stand in a dual relation which prevents an unprejudiced exercise of judgment. * * *

It is clear that absent allegations of fraud, collusion, self-interest, dishonesty or other misconduct of a breach of trust nature, and absent allegations that the business judgment exercised was grossly unsound, the court should not at the instigation of a single shareholder interfere with the judgment of the corporate officers. * * *

In recent months, the legality and morality of foreign political contributions, bribes and other payments by American corporations has been widely debated. The issue before me for decision, however, is not whether the payments made by Esso Italiana to Italian political parties and other unauthorized payments were proper or improper. Were the court to frame the issue in

Chief Justice of the New Jersey Supreme Court, as its Special Counsel.

31. [By the Court] Among the factors cited by the Special Committee in reaching its decision were the unfavorable prospects for success of the litigation, the cost of conducting the litigation, interruption of corporate business affairs and the undermining of personnel morale.

this way, it would necessarily involve itself in the business decisions of every corporation, and be required to mediate between the judgment of the directors and the judgment of the shareholders with regard to particular corporate actions. As Mr. Justice Brandeis said in his concurring opinion in Ashwander v. Tennessee Valley Authority, 297 U.S. [288,] at 343, 56 S.Ct. [466,] at 481, "[i]f a stockholder could compel the officers to enforce every legal right, courts instead of chosen officers, would be the arbiters of the corporation's fate." Rather, the issue is whether the Special Committee, acting as Exxon's Board of Directors and in the sound exercise of their business judgment, may determine that a suit against any present or former director or officer would be contrary to the best interests of the corporation. * * *

V

Plaintiff also calls into question the disinterestedness and bona fides of the Special Committee, suggesting that the members of the Special Committee may have been personally involved in the transactions in question, or, at the least, interested in the alleged wrongdoing "in a way calculated to impair their exercise of business judgment on behalf of the corporation." Klotz v. Consolidated Edison of New York, Inc., supra, 386 F.Supp. at 581.[32]

With the foregoing in mind, I am constrained to conclude that it is premature at this stage of the lawsuit to grant summary judgment. Plaintiff must be given an opportunity to test the bona fides and independence of the Special Committee through discovery and, if necessary, at a plenary hearing. Issues of intent, motivation, and good faith are particularly inappropriate for summary disposition.

Accordingly, defendants' motion for summary judgment is hereby denied without prejudice to its renewal after plaintiff has conducted relevant discovery. * * *

Notes

(1) *Gall* involved a decision by presumably independent directors not to pursue a derivative suit in which other directors were the ultimate target. In invoking the business judgment rule, Judge Carter relied on *United Copper Securities Co.*, a case involving a decision by directors not to sue an unrelated third party. Are these situations really comparable?

(2) The litigation committee device adopted by Exxon to seek dismissal of the Gall suit has become the standard response of publicly held corporations to derivative suits brought or threatened by shareholders which the corporation does not desire to have pursued. In effect it transmutes a discussion of the merits of the plaintiffs' suit into a discussion of the *bona fides* of the business judgment of a special committee of the board to discontinue inconvenient litigation. Should plaintiffs be entitled at least to a judicial hearing on their complaints? If a

32. [By the Court] * * * At a hearing held on February 27, 1976, plaintiff, for the first time, questioned the independence and bona fides of the members of the Special Committee. Subsequently, on March 2, 1976, plaintiff submitted to the court a statement * * * challenging defendants' assertion that the resolution of the Special Committee was made in the independent, disinterested and good faith exercise of their business judgment. Rule 56, F.R.Civ. P., requires that the moving party demonstrate, on the basis of admissible evidence adduced from persons with personal knowledge of the facts, that "there is no genuine issue as to any material fact." Where this initial showing is not made, summary judgment will be denied, even though the party opposing the motion has submitted no probative evidence to support its position or to establish that there is a genuine issue for trial.

litigation committee decides that a meritorious suit should be dismissed does not wrongful conduct go unpunished? Is this problem really as simple as that? Should not directors who are really independent and disinterested be able to determine what litigation should be pursued?

(3) The development of the independent litigation committee has produced a torrent of law review commentary. Consider the policy arguments in the following excerpts:

(a) Michael P. Dooley and E. Norman Veasey, The Role of the Board in Derivative Litigation: Delaware Law and the Current ALI Proposals Compared, 44 Bus.Law. 503, 521–22 (1989):*

> There is a very simple explanation for the limitation on judicial review inherent in the business judgment rule. As Arrow points out, "If every decision of A is to be reviewed by B, then all we have really is a shift in the locus of authority from A to B and hence no solution to the original problem." The power to hold to account is the power to interfere and, ultimately, the power to decide. If stockholders are given too easy access to courts, the effect is to transfer decisionmaking power from the board to the stockholders or, more realistically, to one or a few stockholders whose interests may not coincide with those of the larger body of stockholders. By limiting judicial review of board decisions, the business judgment rule preserves the statutory scheme of centralizing authority in the board of directors. In doing so, it also preserves the value of centralized decisionmaking for the stockholders and protects them against unwarranted interference in that process by one of their number. Although it is customary to think of the business judgment rule as protecting directors from stockholders, it ultimately serves the more important function of protecting stockholders from themselves.

(b) James D. Cox, Searching for the Corporation's Voice in Derivative Suit Litigation: A Critique of *Zapata* and the ALI Project, 1982 Duke L.J. 959, 960 (1982):

> As a starting point, * * * [I assume,] that the corporation has a legitimate interest in raising at any stage in the litigation its concern that a derivative suit does it more harm than good. A derivative suit against managers or directors may ultimately lead to charges against the corporation for the defendant's litigation costs, the corporation's own litigation costs incident to its participation as a nominal defendant, and the more indefinite costs associated with any litigation, such as loss of morale, deflection of employee time, and injury to the corporate reputation. Even if the defendant's fault is conceded, the recoverable amount after deduction of the attorney's fees of the plaintiff may be insufficient to cover the costs of the suit; if the complaint is less well-founded, the cost-benefit ratio is even higher.

> The derivative suit plaintiff is self-selected; without election or appointment he presents himself as spokesman for the corporate interest. Because the plaintiff usually has no significant financial interest in the corporation, the possibly harmful economic effects of prosecuting the suit cannot be expected to guide his decision to litigate.

(b) Comment, The Propriety of Judicial Deference to Corporate Boards of Directors, 96 Harv.L.Rev. 1894, 1896, 1906–1908 (1983):[33]

The corporate board is a group, and as such it is likely to exhibit certain behavioral tendencies identified by researchers in the field of social psychology known as group dynamics. * * *

[A]ny constructive influence that the board's collective decision-making might have on solutions to particular problems is likely to be outweighed by the destructive effect, known as "conformity" or "groupthink," that group dynamics demonstrably and inevitably produce. This conformity may simply be outward: individuals may publicly agree with the group's judgment while privately believing that judgment to be incorrect. Yet the group may well also shape the individual's inward view of the correct judgment: the individual may rely on the group's perceptions and evaluations in assessing the alternatives and reaching a conclusion.

The occurrence of either outward or inward conformity in a boardroom would lead one to doubt the meaningfulness of board approval. In fact, both outward and inward conformity are likely: as will be shown, boards of directors are characterized by the sorts of factors that, social psychologists assert, increase the degree of conformity within a group. * * *

When it is the board that decides to seek dismissal or not to sue, the implications of group dynamics clearly make questionable a legal rule according the decision any weight in the disposition of the motion to dismiss. * * * [T]he directors will be aware that a vote to proceed with the suit could greatly harm management, with whom the directors must associate both professionally and socially and to whom the directors owe their prestigious positions. In an ongoing, cohesive group like a board, these factors will encourage at least outward conformity. The directors are thus apt to vote as management would obviously want them to: they will routinely decide to seek dismissal. Judicial deference to the board's decision amounts to deference to the challenged decision by management and hence seriously impairs the shareholders' ability to protect their interests.

When the decision not to pursue the suit is made by a specially appointed, disinterested committee, the argument that approval by board members ought to be legally irrelevant might seem less persuasive. * * * Management defendants are absent when the committee reviews the facts and reaches its decision about the suit; moreover, the committee often consists of new directors appointed for the primary purpose of staffing the committee. The committee is therefore not subject to pressure arising from preexisting ties with board members and managers. Nevertheless, the committee members know that they will continue to associate—both professionally and socially— with the defendant directors after they make their determination about the suit. In addition, newly appointed directors probably feel a considerable affinity with those who appointed them. Thus, the pressures on the committee members to conform their judgment to the wishes of management defendants may not be significantly less weighty than the pressures on the board. Like a decision by the board, a decision by a special committee is essentially made by challenged management and ought to be of no legal consequence.

For an even stronger statement that directors have a "structural bias" in favor of dismissing all derivative litigation, see James D. Cox & Henry C. Munsinger, Bias in the Boardroom: Psychological Foundations and Legal Implications of Corporation Cohesion, 48 Law & Contem.Probs. 83 (Summer 1985). Many corporate lawyers reject the underlying premise of this argument, which is also not accepted by some commentators familiar with the underlying social science research. See Robert J. Haft, Business Decisions by the New Board: Behavioral Science and Corporate Law, 80 Mich.L.Rev. 1 (1981); Charles W. Murdock, Corporate Governance: The Role of Special Litigation Committees, 68 Wash. L.Rev. 79, 101–20 (1993); Renier Kraakman, Hyun Park, and Steven Shavell, When Are Shareholder Suits in Shareholder Interests?, 82 Geo.L.J. 1733 (1994)(attempts to evaluate the fundamental relationship between shareholder suits and shareholder welfare).

(4) Several pre–1981 cases accept apparently without reservation the reasoning set forth in *Gall.* (The year 1981 is important because of the Delaware decisions discussed directly below.) Auerbach v. Bennett, 47 N.Y.2d 619, 419 N.Y.S.2d 920, 393 N.E.2d 994 (1979) (New York law definitively construed by the New York Court of Appeals); Abbey v. Control Data Corp., 603 F.2d 724 (8th Cir.1979) (Delaware law); Lewis v. Anderson, 615 F.2d 778 (9th Cir.1979) (California law). Burks v. Lasker, 441 U.S. 471, 99 S.Ct. 1831, 60 L.Ed.2d 404 (1979), involved the dismissal of a suit against a registered investment company; the major issue was whether state or federal law (represented by the Investment Company Act of 1940) controlled. The Court held that state law controlled, but in passing commented that "[t]here may well be situations in which the independent directors could reasonably believe that the best interests of the shareholders call for a decision not to sue * * *" and that in certain cases "it would certainly be consistent with the Act to allow the independent directors to terminate a suit, even though not frivolous." 441 U.S. at 485, 99 S.Ct. at 1841, 60 L.Ed.2d at 417. A concurring opinion referred to "this generally accepted principle" and stated that a decision not to sue a wrongdoer "is no different" from other collective "directoral decisions." 441 U.S. at 487, 99 S.Ct. at 1842, 60 L.Ed.2d at 418–19. Galef v. Alexander, 615 F.2d 51 (2d Cir.1980), on the other hand, held the business judgment rule approach of *Gall* inapplicable to suits based on § 14(a) of the Securities Exchange Act of 1934. The court argued that the goal of § 14(a) is "that communications from management be accurate and complete as to all material facts," and the achievement of that goal "would quite clearly be frustrated if a director who was made a defendant in a derivative action for providing inadequate information in connection with a proxy solicitation were permitted to cause the dismissal of that action simply on the basis of his judgment that its pursuit was not in the best interests of the corporation." 615 F.2d at 63.

(5) In Kamen v. Kemper Fin. Serv., Inc., 500 U.S. 90, 111 S.Ct. 1711, 114 L.Ed.2d 152 (1991), the Court held that even in a suit clearly brought under federal law state law should be applied to "fill the interstices of federal remedial schemes" unless the particular state law in question is inconsistent with the policies underlying the federal statute. The Court of Appeals had adopted a rule requiring that a demand be made on directors before commencing a derivative suit under the Investment Company Act of 1940 (as proposed by the ALI's Corporate Governance Project, quoted at p. 738 below); this decision was reversed, the Supreme Court holding that state law that permits a demand to be dispensed with if it is "futile" should be applied in suits based on federal law.

(6) One practical question involving the procedure followed in *Gall* is how independent must a "litigation committee" be? If you were attorney for a plaintiff faced with the prospect of a *Gall*-type defense, might you consider naming all the directors as defendants? Could a director without direct involvement in a transaction be sufficiently independent to satisfy the *Gall* principle, if named a nominal defendant? Assume the corporation appoints or elects two new directors and names them as the litigation committee. Do you have any basis for naming them as defendants? What about bringing or threatening a derivative suit claiming that

a decision by an independent committee was itself a violation of fiduciary duty? Even if the prospects for success of such a suit are slim, could it be used to disqualify directors from serving on the "litigation committee?" Could the corporation appoint yet another litigation committee in order to consider dismissing that suit?

ZAPATA CORP. v. MALDONADO

Supreme Court of Delaware, 1981.
430 A.2d 779.

[Editor: The Delaware Chancery Court described the underlying controversy involved in this case as follows:

The relevant facts, construed most favorably to Maldonado, show that in 1970 Zapata's board of directors adopted a stock option plan under which certain of Zapata's officers and directors were granted options to purchase Zapata common stock at $12.15 per share. The plan provided for the exercise of the options in five separate installments, the last of which was to occur on July 14, 1974. In 1971 this plan was ratified by Zapata's stockholders. As the date for the exercise of the final options grew near, however, Zapata was planning a tender offer for 2,300,000 of its own shares. Announcement of the tender offer was expected to be made just prior to July 14, 1974, and it was predicted that the effect of the announcement would be to increase the then market price of Zapata stock from $18–$19 per share to near the tender offer price of $25 per share.

Zapata's directors, most of whom were optionees under the 1970 plan, were aware that the optionees would incur substantial additional federal income tax liability if the options were exercised after the date of the tender offer announcement and that this additional liability could be avoided if the options were exercised prior to the announcement. This was so because the amount of capital gain for federal income tax purposes to the optionees would have been an amount equal to the difference between the $12.15 option price and the price on the date of the exercise of the option: $18–$19 if the options were exercised prior to the tender offer announcement, or nearly $25 if the options were exercised immediately after the announcement.

In order to reduce the amount of federal income tax liability the optionees would incur in exercising their options, Zapata's directors accelerated the date on which the options could be exercised to July 2, 1974. On that day the optionees exercised their options and the directors requested the New York Stock Exchange to suspend trading in Zapata shares pending "an important announcement". On July 8, 1974 Zapata announced the tender offer. The market price of Zapata stock promptly rose to $24.50.

413 A.2d 1251, 1254–5.]

Before DUFFY, QUILLEN and HORSEY, JJ.

Quillen, Justice:

This is an interlocutory appeal from an order entered on April 9, 1980, by the Court of Chancery denying appellant-defendant Zapata Corporation's

(Zapata) alternative motions to dismiss the complaint or for summary judgment. The issue to be addressed has reached this Court by way of a rather convoluted path.

In June, 1975, William Maldonado, a stockholder of Zapata, instituted a derivative action in the Court of Chancery on behalf of Zapata against ten officers and/or directors of Zapata, alleging, essentially, breaches of fiduciary duty. Maldonado did not first demand that the board bring this action, stating instead such demand's futility because all directors were named as defendants and allegedly participated in the acts specified.[34] * * *

By June, 1979, four of the defendant-directors were no longer on the board, and the remaining directors appointed two new outside directors to the board. The board then created an "Independent Investigation Committee" (Committee), composed solely of the two new directors, to investigate Maldonado's actions, as well as a similar derivative action then pending in Texas, and to determine whether the corporation should continue any or all of the litigation. The Committee's determination was stated to be "final, * * * not * * * subject to review by the Board of Directors and * * * in all respects * * * binding upon the Corporation."

Following an investigation, the Committee concluded, in September, 1979, that each action should "be dismissed forthwith as their continued maintenance is inimical to the Company's best interests * * *." Consequently, Zapata moved for dismissal or summary judgment * * *.

On March 18, 1980, the Court of Chancery, in a reported opinion, the basis for the order of April 9, 1980, denied Zapata's motions, holding that Delaware law does not sanction this means of dismissal. More specifically, it held that the "business judgment" rule is not a grant of authority to dismiss derivative actions and that a stockholder has an individual right to maintain derivative actions in certain instances. Maldonado v. Flynn, Del.Ch., 413 A.2d 1251 (1980). * * * We limit our review in this interlocutory appeal to whether the Committee has the power to cause the present action to be dismissed.

We begin with an examination of the carefully considered opinion of the Vice Chancellor which states, in part, that the "business judgment" rule does not confer power "to a corporate board of directors to terminate a derivative suit", 413 A.2d at 1257. His conclusion is particularly pertinent because several federal courts, applying Delaware law, have held that the business judgment rule enables boards (or their committees) to terminate derivative suits * * *.

As the term is most commonly used, and given the disposition below, we can understand the Vice Chancellor's comment that "the business judgment rule is irrelevant to the question of whether the Committee has the authority to compel the dismissal of this suit". 413 A.2d at 1257. Corporations, existing because of legislative grace, possess authority as granted by the legislature. Directors of Delaware corporations derive their managerial decision making power, which encompasses decisions whether to initiate, or refrain from

---

34. [By the Court] Court of Chancery Rule 23.1 states in part: "The complaint shall also allege with particularity the efforts, if any, made by the plaintiff to obtain the action he desires from the directors or comparable authority and the reasons for his failure to obtain the action or for not making the effort."

entering, litigation,[35] from 8 Del.C. § 141(a).[36] This statute is the fount of directorial powers. The "business judgment" rule is a judicial creation that presumes propriety, under certain circumstances, in a board's decision.[37] Viewed defensively, it does not create authority. In this sense the "business judgment" rule is not relevant in corporate decision making until after a decision is made. It is generally used as a defense to an attack on the decision's soundness. The board's managerial decision making power, however, comes from § 141(a). The judicial creation and legislative grant are related because the "business judgment" rule evolved to give recognition and deference to directors' business expertise when exercising their managerial power under § 141(a).

In the case before us, although the corporation's decision to move to dismiss or for summary judgment was, literally, a decision resulting from an exercise of the directors' (as delegated to the Committee) business judgment, the question of "business judgment", in a defensive sense, would not become relevant until and unless the decision to seek termination of the derivative lawsuit was attacked as improper. This question was not reached by the Vice Chancellor because he determined that the stockholder had an individual right to maintain this derivative action.

Thus, the focus in this case is on the power to speak for the corporation as to whether the lawsuit should be continued or terminated. As we see it, this issue in the current appellate posture of this case has three aspects: the conclusions of the Court below concerning the continuing right of a stockholder to maintain a derivative action; the corporate power under Delaware law of an authorized board committee to cause dismissal of litigation instituted for the benefit of the corporation; and the role of the Court of Chancery in resolving conflicts between the stockholder and the committee.

Accordingly, we turn first to the Court of Chancery's conclusions concerning the right of a plaintiff stockholder in a derivative action. We find that its determination that a stockholder, once demand is made and refused, possesses an independent, individual right to continue a derivative suit for breaches of fiduciary duty over objection by the corporation, as an absolute rule, is erroneous. * * * McKee v. Rogers, Del.Ch. 156 A. 191 (1931), stated "as a general rule" that "a stockholder cannot be permitted * * * to invade the discretionary field committed to the judgment of the directors and sue in the corporation's behalf when the managing body refuses. This rule is a well settled one." 156 A. at 193.

The *McKee* rule, of course, should not be read so broadly that the board's refusal will be determinative in every instance. Board members, owing a well-established fiduciary duty to the corporation, will not be allowed to cause a derivative suit to be dismissed when it would be a breach of their fiduciary duty. Generally disputes pertaining to control of the suit arise in two contexts.

35. [By the Court] See Dent, The Power of Directors to Terminate Shareholder Litigation: The Death of the Derivative Suit? 75 Nw. U.L.Rev. 96, 98 & n. 14 (1980); Comment, The Demand and Standing Requirements in Stockholder Derivative Actions, 44 U.Chi.L.Rev. 168, 192 & nn. 153–54 (1976) (herein Stockholder Derivative Actions).

36. [By the Court] 8 Del.C. § 141(a) states:

The business and affairs of every corporation organized under this chapter shall be managed by or under the direction of a board of directors.

37. [By the Court] See Arsht, The Business Judgment Rule Revisited, 8 Hofstra L.Rev. 93, 97, 130–33 (1979).

Consistent with the purpose of requiring a demand, a board decision to cause a derivative suit to be dismissed as detrimental to the company, after demand has been made and refused, will be respected unless it was wrongful.[38] See, e.g., United Copper Securities Co. v. Amalgamated Copper Co., 244 U.S. 261, 263–64, 37 S.Ct. 509, 510, 61 L.Ed. 1119, 1124 (1917). A claim of a wrongful decision not to sue is thus the first exception and the first context of dispute. Absent a wrongful refusal, the stockholder in such a situation simply lacks legal managerial power.

But it cannot be implied that, absent a wrongful board refusal, a stockholder can never have an individual right to initiate an action. For, as is stated in *McKee,* a "well settled" exception exists to the general rule.

> [A] stockholder may sue in equity in his derivative right to assert a cause of action in behalf of the corporation, *without prior demand* upon the directors to sue, when it is apparent that a demand would be futile, that the officers are under an influence that sterilizes discretion and could not be proper persons to conduct the litigation.

156 A. at 193 (emphasis added). This exception, the second context for dispute, is consistent with the Court of Chancery's statement below, that "[t]he stockholders' individual right to bring the action does not ripen, however, * * * unless he can show a demand to be futile."

These comments in *McKee* and in the opinion below make obvious sense. A demand, when required and refused (if not wrongful), terminates a stockholder's legal ability to initiate a derivative action.[39] But where demand is properly excused, the stockholder does possess the ability to initiate the action on his corporation's behalf.

These conclusions, however, do not determine the question before us. Rather, they merely bring us to the question to be decided. It is here that we part company with the Court below. Derivative suits enforce corporate rights and any recovery obtained goes to the corporation. "The right of a stockholder to file a bill to litigate corporate rights is, therefore, solely for the purpose of preventing injustice where it is apparent that material corporate rights would not otherwise be protected." We see no inherent reason why the "two phases" of a derivative suit, the stockholder's suit to compel the corporation to sue and the corporation's suit should automatically result in the placement in the hands of the litigating stockholder sole control of the corporate right throughout the litigation. To the contrary, it seems to us that such an inflexible rule would recognize the interest of one person or group to the exclusion of all others within the corporate entity. Thus, we reject the view of the Vice Chancellor as to the first aspect of the issue on appeal.

38. [By the Court] In other words, when stockholders, after making demand and having their suit rejected, attack the board's decision as improper, the board's decision falls under the "business judgment" rule and will be respected if the requirements of the rule are met. See Dent, * * * 75 Nw.U.L.Rev. at 100–01 & nn. 24–25. That situation should be distinguished from the instant case, where demand was not made, and the power of the board to seek a dismissal, due to disqualification, presents a threshold issue. For examples of what has been held to be a wrongful decision not to sue, see Stockholder Derivative Actions, supra note 23, 44 U.Chi.L.Rev. at 193–98. We recognize that the two contexts can overlap in practice.

39. [By the Court] Even in this situation it may take litigation to determine the stockholder's lack of power, i.e., standing.

The question to be decided becomes: When, if at all, should an authorized board committee be permitted to cause litigation, properly initiated by a derivative stockholder in his own right, to be dismissed? As noted above, a board has the power to choose not to pursue litigation when demand is made upon it, so long as the decision is not wrongful. If the board determines that a suit would be detrimental to the company, the board's determination prevails. Even when demand is excusable, circumstances may arise when continuation of the litigation would not be in the corporation's best interests. Our inquiry is whether, under such circumstances, there is a permissible procedure under § 141(a) by which a corporation can rid itself of detrimental litigation. If there is not, a single stockholder in an extreme case might control the destiny of the entire corporation. This concern was bluntly expressed by the Ninth Circuit in Lewis v. Anderson, 615 F.2d 778, 783 (9th Cir.1979), cert. denied, 449 U.S. 869, 101 S.Ct. 206, 66 L.Ed.2d 89 (1980): "To allow one shareholder to incapacitate an entire board of directors merely by leveling charges against them gives too much leverage to dissident shareholders." But, when examining the means, including the committee mechanism examined in this case, potentials for abuse must be recognized. This takes us to the second and third aspects of the issue on appeal.

Before we pass to equitable considerations as to the mechanism at issue here, it must be clear that an independent committee possesses the corporate power to seek the termination of a derivative suit. Section 141(c) allows a board to delegate all of its authority to a committee. Accordingly, a committee with properly delegated authority would have the power to move for dismissal or summary judgment if the entire board did.

Even though demand was not made in this case and the initial decision of whether to litigate was not placed before the board, Zapata's board, it seems to us, retained all of its corporate power concerning litigation decisions. If Maldonado had made demand on the board in this case, it could have refused to bring suit. Maldonado could then have asserted that the decision not to sue was wrongful and, if correct, would have been allowed to maintain the suit. The board, however, never would have lost its statutory managerial authority. The demand requirement itself evidences that the managerial power is retained by the board. When a derivative plaintiff is allowed to bring suit after a wrongful refusal, the board's authority to choose whether to pursue the litigation is not challenged although its conclusion—reached through the exercise of that authority—is not respected since it is wrongful. Similarly, Rule 23.1, by excusing demand in certain instances, does not strip the board of its corporate power. It merely saves the plaintiff the expense and delay of making a futile demand resulting in a probable tainted exercise of that authority in a refusal by the board or in giving control of litigation to the opposing side. But the board entity remains empowered under § 141(a) to make decisions regarding corporate litigation. The problem is one of member disqualification, not the absence of power in the board.

The corporate power inquiry then focuses on whether the board, tainted by the self-interest of a majority of its members, can legally delegate its authority to a committee of two disinterested directors. We find our statute clearly requires an affirmative answer to this question. As has been noted, under an express provision of the statute, § 141(c), a committee can exercise all of the authority of the board to the extent provided in the resolution of the board. Moreover, at [least] by analogy to our statutory section on interested directors, 8 Del.C. § 141, it seems clear that the Delaware statute is designed to permit disinterested directors to act for the board.[40]

We do not think that the interest taint of the board majority is per se a legal bar to the delegation of the board's power to an independent committee composed of disinterested board members. The committee can properly act for the corporation to move to dismiss derivative litigation that is believed to be detrimental to the corporation's best interest.

Our focus now switches to the Court of Chancery which is faced with a stockholder assertion that a derivative suit, properly instituted, should continue for the benefit of the corporation and a corporate assertion, properly made by a board committee acting with board authority, that the same derivative suit should be dismissed as inimical to the best interests of the corporation.

At the risk of stating the obvious, the problem is relatively simple. If, on the one hand, corporations can consistently wrest bona fide derivative actions away from well-meaning derivative plaintiffs through the use of the committee mechanism, the derivative suit will lose much, if not all, of its generally-recognized effectiveness as an intra-corporate means of policing boards of directors. If, on the other hand, corporations are unable to rid themselves of meritless or harmful litigation and strike suits, the derivative action, created to benefit the corporation, will produce the opposite, unintended result. * * * It thus appears desirable to us to find a balancing point where bona fide stockholder power to bring corporate causes of action cannot be unfairly trampled on by the board of directors, but the corporation can rid itself of detrimental litigation.

As we noted, the question has been treated by other courts as one of the "business judgment" of the board committee. If a "committee, composed of independent and disinterested directors, conducted a proper review of the matters before it, considered a variety of factors and reached, in good faith, a business judgment that [the] action was not in the best interest of [the corporation]", the action must be dismissed. The issues become solely inde-

---

40. [By the Court] 8 Del.C. § 144 [Interested directors; quorum] states:

(a) No contract or transaction between a corporation and 1 or more of its directors or officers, or between a corporation and any other corporation, partnership, association, or other organization in which 1 or more of its directors or officers are directors or officers, or have a financial interest, shall be void or voidable solely for this reason, or solely because the director or officer is present at or participates in the meeting of the board or committee which authorizes the contract or transaction, or solely because his or their votes are counted for such purpose, if:

(1) The material facts as to his relationship or interest and as to the contract or transaction are disclosed or are known to the board of directors or the committee, and the board or committee in good faith authorizes the contract or transaction by the affirmative votes of a majority of the disinterested directors, even though the disinterested directors be less than a quorum; or

(2) The material facts as to his relationship or interest and as to the contract or transaction are disclosed or are known to the shareholders entitled to vote thereon, and the contract or transaction is specifically approved in good faith by vote of the shareholders; or

(3) The contract or transaction is fair to the corporation as of the time it is authorized, approved or ratified, by the board of directors, a committee, or the shareholders.

(b) Common or interested directors may be counted in determining the presence of a quorum at a meeting of the board of directors or of a committee which authorizes the contract or transaction.

pendence, good faith, and reasonable investigation. The ultimate conclusion of the committee, under that view, is not subject to judicial review.

We are not satisfied, however, that acceptance of the "business judgment" rationale at this stage of derivative litigation is a proper balancing point. While we admit an analogy with a normal case respecting board judgment, it seems to us that there is sufficient risk in the realities of a situation like the one presented in this case to justify caution beyond adherence to the theory of business judgment.

The context here is a suit against directors where demand on the board is excused. We think some tribute must be paid to the fact that the lawsuit was properly initiated. It is not a board refusal case. Moreover, this complaint was filed in June of 1975 and, while the parties undoubtedly would take differing views on the degree of litigation activity, we have to be concerned about the creation of an "Independent Investigation Committee" four years later, after the election of two new outside directors. Situations could develop where such motions could be filed after years of vigorous litigation for reasons unconnected with the merits of the lawsuit.

Moreover, notwithstanding our conviction that Delaware law entrusts the corporate power to a properly authorized committee, we must be mindful that directors are passing judgment on fellow directors in the same corporation and fellow directors, in this instance, who designated them to serve both as directors and committee members. The question naturally arises whether a "there but for the grace of God go I" empathy might not play a role. And the further question arises whether inquiry as to independence, good faith and reasonable investigation is sufficient safeguard against abuse, perhaps subconscious abuse.

There is another line of exploration besides the factual context of this litigation which we find helpful. The nature of this motion finds no ready pigeonhole, as perhaps illustrated by its being set forth in the alternative. It is perhaps best considered as a hybrid summary judgment motion for dismissal because the stockholder plaintiff's standing to maintain the suit has been lost. But it does not fit neatly into a category described in Rule 12(b) of the Court of Chancery Rules nor does it correspond directly with Rule 56 since the question of genuine issues of fact on the merits of the stockholder's claim are not reached. * * *

Whether the Court of Chancery will be persuaded by the exercise of a committee power resulting in a summary motion for dismissal of a derivative action, where a demand has not been initially made, should rest, in our judgment, in the independent discretion of the Court of Chancery. We thus steer a middle course between those cases which yield to the independent business judgment of a board committee and this case as determined below which would yield to unbridled plaintiff stockholder control. In pursuit of the course, we recognize that "[t]he final substantive judgment whether a particular lawsuit should be maintained requires a balance of many factors— ethical, commercial, promotional, public relations, employee relations, fiscal as well as legal." But we are content that such factors are not "beyond the judicial reach" of the Court of Chancery which regularly and competently deals with fiduciary relationships, disposition of trust property, approval of settlements and scores of similar problems. We recognize the danger of judicial overreaching but the alternatives seem to us to be outweighed by the fresh view of a judicial outsider. Moreover, if we failed to balance all the interests involved, we would in the name of practicality and judicial economy foreclose a judicial decision on the merits. At this point, we are not convinced that is necessary or desirable.

After an objective and thorough investigation of a derivative suit, an independent committee may cause its corporation to file a pretrial motion to dismiss in the Court of Chancery. The basis of the motion is the best interests of the corporation, as determined by the committee. The motion should include a thorough written record of the investigation and its findings and recommendations. Under appropriate Court supervision, akin to proceedings on summary judgment, each side should have an opportunity to make a record on the motion. As to the limited issues presented by the motion noted below, the moving party should be prepared to meet the normal burden under Rule 56 that there is no genuine issue as to any material fact and that the moving party is entitled to dismiss as a matter of law.[41] The Court should apply a two-step test to the motion.

First, the Court should inquire into the independence and good faith of the committee and the bases supporting its conclusions. Limited discovery may be ordered to facilitate such inquiries. The corporation should have the burden of proving independence, good faith and a reasonable investigation, rather than presuming independence, good faith and reasonableness.[42] If the Court determines either that the committee is not independent or has not shown reasonable bases for its conclusions, or, if the Court is not satisfied for other reasons relating to the process, including but not limited to the good faith of the committee, the Court shall deny the corporation's motion. If, however, the Court is satisfied under Rule 56 standards that the committee was independent and showed reasonable bases for good faith findings and recommendations, the Court may proceed, in its discretion, to the next step.

The second step provides, we believe, the essential key in striking the balance between legitimate corporate claims as expressed in a derivative stockholder suit and a corporation's best interests as expressed by an independent investigating committee. The Court should determine, applying its own independent business judgment, whether the motion should be granted.[43] This means, of course, that instances could arise where a committee can establish its independence and sound bases for its good faith decisions and still have the corporation's motion denied. The second step is intended to thwart instances where corporate actions meet the criteria of step one, but the result does not appear to satisfy its spirit, or where corporate actions would simply prema-

[handwritten: Two step process]

41. [By the Court] We do not foreclose a discretionary trial of factual issues but that issue is not presented in this appeal. See Lewis v. Anderson, supra, 615 F.2d at 780. Nor do we foreclose the possibility that other motions may proceed or be joined with such a pretrial summary judgment motion to dismiss, e.g., a partial motion for summary judgment on the merits.

42. [By the Court] Compare Auerbach v. Bennett, 47 N.Y.2d 619, 419 N.Y.S.2d 920, 928–29, 393 N.E.2d 994 (1979). Our approach here is analogous to and consistent with the Delaware approach to "interested director" transactions, where the directors, once the transaction is attacked, have the burden of establishing its "intrinsic fairness" to a court's careful scrutiny. See, e.g., Sterling v. Mayflower Hotel Corp., Del.Supr., 93 A.2d 107 (1952).

43. [By the Court] This step shares some of the same spirit and philosophy of the statement by the Vice Chancellor: "Under our system of law, courts and not litigants should decide the merits of litigation." 413 A.2d at 1263.

turely terminate a stockholder grievance deserving of further consideration in the corporation's interest. The Court of Chancery of course must carefully consider and weigh how compelling the corporate interest in dismissal is when faced with a non-frivolous lawsuit. The Court of Chancery should, when appropriate, give special consideration to matters of law and public policy in addition to the corporation's best interests.

If the Court's independent business judgment is satisfied, the Court may proceed to grant the motion, subject, of course, to any equitable terms or conditions the Court finds necessary or desirable.

The interlocutory order of the Court of Chancery is reversed and the cause is remanded for further proceedings consistent with this opinion.

Notes

Following this decision, several courts refused to grant decisions by litigation committees the finality that appeared to be required under pre-Zapata decisions. Among these cases are Joy v. North, 692 F.2d 880 (2d Cir.1982), cert. denied sub nom. Citytrust v. Joy, 460 U.S. 1051, 103 S.Ct. 1498, 75 L.Ed.2d 930 (1983) (nominally decided under Connecticut law); Hasan v. CleveTrust Realty Investors, 729 F.2d 372 (6th Cir.1984) (no presumption of regularity or good faith to support litigation committee decision); In Matter of Continental Illinois Sec. Litig., 732 F.2d 1302 (7th Cir.1984). While there were dissents in some of these cases, the majority opinions generally reflect skepticism about the wisdom of uncritical acceptance of the principle that plaintiffs attacking a corporate transaction should be remitted only to an attack on the independence and good faith of a litigation committee. However, the development of Delaware law was not complete.

ARONSON v. LEWIS

Supreme Court of Delaware, 1984.
473 A.2d 805.

Before McNEILLY, MOORE and CHRISTIE, JJ.

MOORE, JUSTICE:

In the wake of Zapata Corp. v. Maldonado, Del.Supr., 430 A.2d 779 (1981), this Court left a crucial issue unanswered: when is a stockholder's demand upon a board of directors, to redress an alleged wrong to the corporation, excused as futile prior to the filing of a derivative suit? We granted this interlocutory appeal to the defendants, Meyers Parking System, Inc. (Meyers), a Delaware corporation, and its directors, to review the Court of Chancery's denial of their motion to dismiss this action, pursuant to Chancery Rule 23.1, for the plaintiff's failure to make such a demand or otherwise demonstrate its futility. The Vice Chancellor ruled that plaintiff's allegations raised a "reasonable inference" that the directors' action was unprotected by the business judgment rule. Thus, the board could not have impartially considered and acted upon the demand. See Lewis v. Aronson, Del.Ch., 466 A.2d 375, 381 (1983).

We cannot agree with this formulation of the concept of demand futility. In our view demand can only be excused where facts are alleged with particularity which create a reasonable doubt that the directors' action was entitled to the protections of the business judgment rule. Because the plaintiff failed to make a demand, and to allege facts with particularity indicating that such demand would be futile, we reverse the Court of Chancery and remand with instructions that plaintiff be granted leave to amend the complaint.

I.

The issues of demand futility rest upon the allegations of the complaint. The plaintiff, Harry Lewis, is a stockholder of Meyers. The defendants are Meyers and its ten directors, some of whom are also company officers.

In 1979, Prudential Building Maintenance Corp. (Prudential) spun off its shares of Meyers to Prudential's stockholders. Prior thereto Meyers was a wholly owned subsidiary of Prudential. Meyers provides parking lot facilities and related services throughout the country. Its stock is actively traded over-the-counter.

This suit challenges certain transactions between Meyers and one of its directors, Leo Fink, who owns 47% of its outstanding stock. Plaintiff claims that these transactions were approved only because Fink personally selected each director and officer of Meyers.[44]

Prior to January 1, 1981, Fink had an employment agreement with Prudential which provided that upon retirement he was to become a consultant to that company for ten years. This provision became operable when Fink retired in April 1980. Thereafter, Meyers agreed with Prudential to share Fink's consulting services and reimburse Prudential for 25% of the fees paid Fink. Under this arrangement Meyers paid Prudential $48,332 in 1980 and $45,832 in 1981.

On January 1, 1981, the defendants approved an employment agreement between Meyers and Fink for a five year term with provision for automatic renewal each year thereafter, indefinitely. Meyers agreed to pay Fink $150,000 per year, plus a bonus of 5% of its pre-tax profits over $2,400,000. Fink could terminate the contract at any time, but Meyers could do so only upon six months' notice. At termination, Fink was to become a consultant to Meyers and be paid $150,000 per year for the first three years, $125,000 for the next three years, and $100,000 thereafter for life. Death benefits were also included. Fink agreed to devote his best efforts and substantially his entire business time to advancing Meyers' interests. The agreement also provided that Fink's compensation was not to be affected by any inability to perform services on Meyers' behalf. Fink was 75 years old when his employment agreement with Meyers was approved by the directors. There is no claim that he was, or is, in poor health.

Additionally, the Meyers board approved and made interest-free loans to Fink totalling $225,000. These loans were unpaid and outstanding as of August 1982 when the complaint was filed. At oral argument defendants' counsel represented that these loans had been repaid in full.

The complaint charges that these transactions had "no valid business purpose", and were a "waste of corporate assets" because the amounts to be paid are "grossly excessive", that Fink performs "no or little services", and because of his "advanced age" cannot be "expected to perform any such services". The plaintiff also charges that the existence of the Prudential

---

44. [By the Court] The Court of Chancery stated that Fink had been chief executive offi- cer of Prudential prior to the spinoff and thereafter became chairman of Meyers' board.

consulting agreement with Fink prevents him from providing his "best efforts" on Meyers' behalf. Finally, it is alleged that the loans to Fink were in reality "additional compensation" without any "consideration" or "benefit" to Meyers.

The complaint alleged that no demand had been made on the Meyers board because:

13. * * * such attempt would be futile for the following reasons:

(a) All of the directors in office are named as defendants herein and they have participated in, expressly approved and/or acquiesced in, and are personally liable for, the wrongs complained of herein.

(b) Defendant Fink, having selected each director, controls and dominates every member of the Board and every officer of Meyers.

(c) Institution of this action by present directors would require the defendant-directors to sue themselves, thereby placing the conduct of this action in hostile hands and preventing its effective prosecution.

The relief sought included the cancellation of the Meyers–Fink employment contract and an accounting by the directors, including Fink, for all damage sustained by Meyers and for all profits derived by the directors and Fink. * * *

IV.

A.

A cardinal precept of the General Corporation Law of the State of Delaware is that directors, rather than shareholders, manage the business and affairs of the corporation. 8 Del.C. § 141(a). * * * The existence and exercise of this power carries with it certain fundamental fiduciary obligations to the corporation and its shareholders.[45] Loft, Inc. v. Guth, Del.Ch., 2 A.2d 225 (1938), aff'd, Del.Supr., 5 A.2d 503 (1939). Moreover, a stockholder is not powerless to challenge director action which results in harm to the corporation. The machinery of corporate democracy and the derivative suit are potent tools to redress the conduct of a torpid or unfaithful management. The derivative action developed in equity to enable shareholders to sue in the corporation's name where those in control of the company refused to assert a claim belonging to it. The nature of the action is two-fold. First, it is the equivalent of a suit by the shareholders to compel the corporation to sue. Second, it is a suit by the corporation, asserted by the shareholders on its behalf, against those liable to it.

45. [By the Court] The broad question of structuring the modern corporation in order to satisfy the twin objectives of managerial freedom of action and responsibility to shareholders has been extensively debated by commentators. See, e.g., Fischel, The Corporate Governance Movement, 35 Vand.L.Rev. 1259 (1982); Dickstein, Corporate Governance and the Shareholders' Derivative Action: Rules and Remedies for Implementing the Monitoring Model, 3 Cardozo L.Rev. 627 (1982); Haft, Business Decisions by the New Board: Behavioral Science and Corporate Law, 80 Mich. L.Rev. 1 (1981); Dent, The Revolution in Corporate Governance, The Monitoring Board, and The Director's Duty of Care, 61 B.U.L.Rev. 623 (1981); Moore, Corporate Officer & Director Liability: Is Corporate Behavior Beyond the Control of Our Legal System? 16 Capital U.L.Rev. 69 (1980); Jones, Corporate Governance: Who Controls the Large Corporation? 30 Hastings L.J. 1261 (1979); Small, The Evolving Role of the Director in Corporate Governance, 30 Hastings L.J. 1353 (1979).

By its very nature the derivative action impinges on the managerial freedom of directors.[46] Hence, the demand requirement of Chancery Rule 23.1 exists at the threshold, first to ensure that a stockholder exhausts his intracorporate remedies, and then to provide a safeguard against strike suits. Thus, by promoting this form of alternate dispute resolution, rather than immediate recourse to litigation, the demand requirement is a recognition of the fundamental precept that directors manage the business and affairs of corporations.

In our view the entire question of demand futility is inextricably bound to issues of business judgment and the standards of that doctrine's applicability. The business judgment rule is an acknowledgment of the managerial prerogatives of Delaware directors under Section 141(a). See Zapata Corp. v. Maldonado, 430 A.2d at 782. It is a presumption that in making a business decision the directors of a corporation acted on an informed basis, in good faith and in the honest belief that the action taken was in the best interests of the company. Kaplan v. Centex Corp., Del.Ch., 284 A.2d 119, 124 (1971); Robinson v. Pittsburgh Oil Refinery Corp., Del.Ch., 126 A. 46 (1924). Absent an abuse of discretion, that judgment will be respected by the courts. The burden is on the party challenging the decision to establish facts rebutting the presumption. See Puma v. Marriott, Del.Ch., 283 A.2d 693, 695 (1971).

The function of the business judgment rule is of paramount significance in the context of a derivative action. It comes into play in several ways—in addressing a demand, in the determination of demand futility, in efforts by independent disinterested directors to dismiss the action as inimical to the corporation's best interests, and generally, as a defense to the merits of the suit. However, in each of these circumstances there are certain common principles governing the application and operation of the rule.

First, its protections can only be claimed by disinterested directors whose conduct otherwise meets the tests of business judgment. From the standpoint of interest, this means that directors can neither appear on both sides of a transaction nor expect to derive any personal financial benefit from it in the sense of self-dealing, as opposed to a benefit which devolves upon the corporation or all stockholders generally. Sinclair Oil Corp. v. Levien, Del. Supr., 280 A.2d 717, 720 (1971); Cheff v. Mathes, Del.Supr., 199 A.2d 548, 554 (1964). See also 8 Del.C. § 144. Thus, if such director interest is present, and the transaction is not approved by a majority consisting of the disinterested directors, then the business judgment rule has no application whatever in determining demand futility.

---

46. [By the Court] Like the broader question of corporate governance, the derivative suit, its value, and the methods employed by corporate boards to deal with it have received much attention by commentators. See, e.g., Brown, Shareholder Derivative Litigation and the Special Litigation Committee, 43 U.Pitt.L.Rev. 601 (1982); Coffee and Schwartz, The Survival of the Derivative Suit: An Evaluation and a Proposal for Legislative Reform, 81 Colum.L.Rev. 261 (1981); Shnell, A Procedural Treatment of Derivative Suit Dismissals by Minority Directors, 69 Calif.L.Rev. 885 (1981);

Dent, The Power of Directors to Terminate Shareholder Litigation: The Death of the Derivative Suit? 75 N.W.U.L.Rev. 96 (1980); Jones, An Empirical Examination of the Incidence of Shareholder Derivative and Class Action Lawsuits, 1971–1978, 60 B.U.L.Rev. 306 (1980); Comment, The Demand and Standing Requirements in Stockholder Derivative Actions, 44 U.Chi.L.Rev. 168 (1976); Dykstra, The Revival of the Derivative Suit, 116 U.Pa. L.Rev. 74 (1967); Note, Demand on Directors and Shareholders as a Prerequisite to a Derivative Suit, 73 Harv.L.Rev. 729 (1960).

Second, to invoke the rule's protection directors have a duty to inform themselves, prior to making a business decision, of all material information reasonably available to them. Having become so informed, they must then act with requisite care in the discharge of their duties. While the Delaware cases use a variety of terms to describe the applicable standard of care, our analysis satisfies us that under the business judgment rule director liability is predicated upon concepts of gross negligence.[47] See Veasey & Manning, Codified Standard—Safe Harbor or Uncharted Reef? 35 Bus.Law. 919, 928 (1980).

However, it should be noted that the business judgment rule operates only in the context of director action. Technically speaking, it has no role where directors have either abdicated their functions, or absent a conscious decision, failed to act.[48] But it also follows that under applicable principles, a conscious decision to refrain from acting may nonetheless be a valid exercise of business judgment and enjoy the protections of the rule.

The gap in our law, which we address today, arises from this Court's decision in *Zapata Corp. v. Maldonado*. There, the Court defined the limits of a board's managerial power granted by Section 141(a) and restricted application of the business judgment rule in a factual context similar to this action. Zapata Corp. v. Maldonado, 430 A.2d at 782–86, rev'g, Maldonado v. Flynn, Del.Ch., 413 A.2d 1251 (1980).

By way of background, this Court's review in *Zapata* was limited to whether an independent investigation committee of disinterested directors had the *power* to cause the derivative action to be dismissed. Preliminarily, it was noted in *Zapata* that "[d]irectors of Delaware corporations derive their managerial decision making power, which encompasses decisions whether to initiate, or refrain from entering, litigation, from 8 Del.C. § 141(a)". In that context, this Court observed that the business judgment rule has no relevance to corporate decision making until *after a decision has been made*. In *Zapata*, we stated that a shareholder does not possess an independent individual right to continue a derivative action. Moreover, where demand on a board has been made and refused, we apply the business judgment rule in reviewing the board's refusal to act pursuant to a stockholder's demand. Unless the business judgment rule does not protect the refusal to sue, the shareholder lacks the legal managerial power to continue the derivative action, since that power is terminated by the refusal. We also concluded that where demand is excused a shareholder possesses the ability to initiate a derivative action, but the right

47. [By the Court] While the Delaware cases have not been precise in articulating the standard by which the exercise of business judgment is governed, a long line of Delaware cases holds that director liability is predicated on a standard which is less exacting than simple negligence. Sinclair Oil Corp. v. Levien, Del.Supr., 280 A.2d 717, 722 (1971), rev'g, Del. Ch., 261 A.2d 911 (1969) ("fraud or gross overreaching"); Getty Oil Co. v. Skelly Oil Co., Del.Supr., 267 A.2d 883, 887 (1970), rev'g, Del. Ch., 255 A.2d 717 (1969) ("gross and palpable overreaching"); Warshaw v. Calhoun, Del. Supr., 221 A.2d 487, 492–93 (1966) ("bad faith * * * or a gross abuse of discretion"); Moskowitz v. Bantrell, Del.Supr., 190 A.2d 749, 750 (1963) ("fraud or gross abuse of discretion");

Penn Mart Realty Co. v. Becker, Del.Ch., 298 A.2d 349, 351 (1972) ("directors may breach their fiduciary duty * * * by being grossly negligent"); Kors v. Carey, Del.Ch., 158 A.2d 136, 140 (1960) ("fraud, misconduct or abuse of discretion"); Allaun v. Consolidated Oil Co., Del.Ch., 147 A. 257, 261 (1929) ("reckless indifference to or a deliberate disregard of the stockholders").

48. [By the Court] Although questions of director liability in such cases have been adjudicated upon concepts of business judgment, they do not in actuality present issues of business judgment. See Arsht, Fiduciary Responsibilities of Directors, Officers & Key Employees, 4 Del.J.Corp.L. 652, 659 (1979).

to prosecute it may be terminated upon the exercise of applicable standards of business judgment. The thrust of *Zapata* is that in either the demand-refused or the demand-excused case, the board still retains its Section 141(a) managerial authority to make decisions regarding corporate litigation. Moreover, the board may delegate its managerial authority to a committee of independent disinterested directors. See 8 Del.C. § 141(c). Thus, even in a demand-excused case, a board has the power to appoint a committee of one or more independent disinterested directors to determine whether the derivative action should be pursued or dismissal sought. Under *Zapata,* the Court of Chancery, in passing on a committee's motion to dismiss a derivative action in a demand excused case, must apply a two-step test. First, the court must inquire into the independence and good faith of the committee and review the reasonableness and good faith of the committee's investigation. Second, the court must apply its own independent business judgment to decide whether the motion to dismiss should be granted.

After *Zapata* numerous derivative suits were filed without prior demand upon boards of directors. The complaints in such actions all alleged that demand was excused because of board interest, approval or acquiescence in the wrongdoing. In any event, the *Zapata* demand-excused/demand-refused bifurcation, has left a crucial issue unanswered: when is demand futile and, therefore, excused? * * *

The trial court correctly recognized that demand futility is inextricably bound to issues of business judgment, but stated the test to be based on allegations of fact, which, if true, "show that there is a reasonable inference" the business judgment rule is not applicable for purposes of a pre-suit demand.

The problem with this formulation is the concept of reasonable inferences to be drawn against a board of directors based on allegations in a complaint. As is clear from this case, and the conclusory allegations upon which the Vice Chancellor relied, demand futility becomes virtually automatic under such a test. Bearing in mind the presumptions with which director action is cloaked, we believe that the matter must be approached in a more balanced way.

Our view is that in determining demand futility the Court of Chancery in the proper exercise of its discretion must decide whether, under the particularized facts alleged, a reasonable doubt is created that: (1) the directors are disinterested and independent and (2) the challenged transaction was otherwise the product of a valid exercise of business judgment. Hence, the Court of Chancery must make two inquiries, one into the independence and disinterestedness of the directors and the other into the substantive nature of the challenged transaction and the board's approval thereof. As to the latter inquiry the court does not assume that the transaction is a wrong to the corporation requiring corrective steps by the board. Rather, the alleged wrong is substantively reviewed against the factual background alleged in the complaint. As to the former inquiry, directorial independence and disinterestedness, the court reviews the factual allegations to decide whether they raise a reasonable doubt, as a threshold matter, that the protections of the business judgment rule are available to the board. Certainly, if this is an "interested" director transaction, such that the business judgment rule is inapplicable to the board majority approving the transaction, then the inquiry ceases. In that event futility of demand has been established by any objective or subjective standard.[49] See, e.g., Bergstein v. Texas Internat'l Co., Del.Ch., 453 A.2d 467, 471 (1982) (because five of nine directors approved stock appreciation rights plan likely to benefit them, board was interested for demand purposes and demand held futile). This includes situations involving self-dealing directors. See Sinclair Oil Corp. v. Levien, Del.Supr., 280 A.2d 717 (1971).

However, the mere threat of personal liability for approving a questioned transaction, standing alone, is insufficient to challenge either the independence or disinterestedness of directors, although in rare cases a transaction may be so egregious on its face that board approval cannot meet the test of business judgment, and a substantial likelihood of director liability therefore exists. See Gimbel v. Signal Cos., Inc., Del.Ch., 316 A.2d 599, aff'd, Del.Supr., 316 A.2d 619 (1974). In sum the entire review is factual in nature. The Court of Chancery in the exercise of its sound discretion must be satisfied that a plaintiff has alleged facts with particularity which, taken as true, support a reasonable doubt that the challenged transaction was the product of a valid exercise of business judgment. Only in that context is demand excused.

B.

Having outlined the legal framework within which these issues are to be determined, we consider plaintiff's claims of futility here: Fink's domination and control of the directors, board approval of the Fink–Meyers employment agreement, and board hostility to the plaintiff's derivative action due to the directors' status as defendants.

Plaintiff's claim that Fink dominates and controls the Meyers' board is based on: (1) Fink's 47% ownership of Meyers' outstanding stock, and (2) that he "personally selected" each Meyers director. Plaintiff also alleges that mere approval of the employment agreement illustrates Fink's domination and control of the board. In addition, plaintiff argued on appeal that 47% stock ownership, though less than a majority, constituted control given the large number of shares outstanding, 1,245,745.

Such contentions do not support any claim under Delaware law that these directors lack independence. In Kaplan v. Centex Corp., Del.Ch., 284 A.2d 119 (1971), the Court of Chancery stated that "[s]tock ownership alone, at least when it amounts to less than a majority, is not sufficient proof of domination or control". Id. at 123. Moreover, in the demand context even proof of majority ownership of a company does not strip the directors of the presumptions of independence, and that their acts have been taken in good faith and in the best interests of the corporation. There must be coupled with the allegation of control such facts as would demonstrate that through personal or other relationships the directors are beholden to the controlling person. See Mayer v. Adams, Del.Ch., 167 A.2d 729, 732, aff'd, Del.Supr., 174 A.2d 313 (1961). To date the principal decisions dealing with the issue of control or

---

49. [By the Court] We recognize that drawing the line at a majority of the board may be an arguably arbitrary dividing point. Critics will charge that we are ignoring the structural bias common to corporate boards throughout America, as well as the other unseen socialization processes cutting against independent discussion and decisionmaking in the boardroom. The difficulty with structural bias in a demand futile case is simply one of establishing it in the complaint for purposes of Rule 23.1. We are satisfied that discretionary review by the Court of Chancery of complaints alleging specific facts pointing to bias on a particular board will be sufficient for determining demand futility.

domination arose only after a full trial on the merits. Thus, they are distinguishable in the demand context unless similar particularized facts are alleged to meet the test of Chancery Rule 23.1.

The requirement of director independence inheres in the conception and rationale of the business judgment rule. The presumption of propriety that flows from an exercise of business judgment is based in part on this unyielding precept. Independence means that a director's decision is based on the corporate merits of the subject before the board rather than extraneous considerations or influences. While directors may confer, debate, and resolve their differences through compromise, or by reasonable reliance upon the expertise of their colleagues and other qualified persons, the end result, nonetheless, must be that each director has brought his or her own informed business judgment to bear with specificity upon the corporate merits of the issues without regard for or succumbing to influences which convert an otherwise valid business decision into a faithless act.

Thus, it is not enough to charge that a director was nominated by or elected at the behest of those controlling the outcome of a corporate election. That is the usual way a person becomes a corporate director. It is the care, attention and sense of individual responsibility to the performance of one's duties, not the method of election, that generally touches on independence.

We conclude that in the demand-futile context a plaintiff charging domination and control of one or more directors must allege particularized facts manifesting "a direction of corporate conduct in such a way as to comport with the wishes or interests of the corporation (or persons) doing the controlling". Kaplan, 284 A.2d at 123. The shorthand shibboleth of "dominated and controlled directors" is insufficient. In recognizing that *Kaplan* was decided after trial and full discovery, we stress that the plaintiff need only allege specific facts; he need not plead evidence. * * *

Here, plaintiff has not alleged any facts sufficient to support a claim of control. The personal-selection-of-directors allegation stands alone, unsupported. At best it is a conclusion devoid of factual support. The causal link between Fink's control and approval of the employment agreement is alluded to, but nowhere specified. The director's approval, alone, does not establish control, even in the face of Fink's 47% stock ownership. See Kaplan v. Centex Corp., 284 A.2d at 122, 123. The claim that Fink is unlikely to perform any services under the agreement, because of his age, and his conflicting consultant work with Prudential, adds nothing to the control claim. Therefore, we cannot conclude that the complaint factually particularizes any circumstances of control and domination to overcome the presumption of board independence, and thus render the demand futile.

C.

Turning to the board's approval of the Meyers–Fink employment agreement, plaintiff's argument is simple: all of the Meyers directors are named defendants, because they approved the wasteful agreement; if plaintiff prevails on the merits all the directors will be jointly and severally liable; therefore, the directors' interests in avoiding personal liability automatically and absolutely disqualifies them from passing on a shareholder's demand.

Such allegations are conclusory at best. * * * The complaint does not allege particularized facts indicating that the agreement is a waste of corporate assets. Indeed, the complaint as now drafted may not even state a cause of action, given the directors' broad corporate power to fix the compensation of officers.

In essence, the plaintiff alleged a lack of consideration flowing from Fink to Meyers, since the employment agreement provided that compensation was not contingent on Fink's ability to perform any services. The bare assertion that Fink performed "little or no services" was plaintiff's conclusion based solely on Fink's age and the existence of the Fink–Prudential employment agreement. As for Meyers' loans to Fink, beyond the bare allegation that they were made, the complaint does not allege facts indicating the wastefulness of such arrangements. Again, the mere existence of such loans, given the broad corporate powers conferred by Delaware law, does not even state a claim.[50]

In sustaining plaintiff's claim of demand futility the trial court relied on Fidanque v. American Maracaibo Co., Del.Ch., 92 A.2d 311, 321 (1952), which held that a contract providing for payment of consulting fees to a retired president/director was a waste of corporate assets. In *Fidanque,* the court found after trial that the contract and payments were in reality compensation for past services. This was based upon facts not present here: the former president/director was a 70 year old stroke victim, neither the agreement nor the record spelled out his consulting duties at all, the consulting salary equalled the individual's salary when he was president and general manager of the corporation, and the contract was silent as to continued employment in the event that the retired president/director again became incapacitated and unable to perform his duties. Contrasting the facts of *Fidanque* with the complaint here, it is apparent that plaintiff has not alleged facts sufficient to render demand futile on a charge of corporate waste, and thus create a reasonable doubt that the board's action is protected by the business judgment rule.

D.

Plaintiff's final argument is the incantation that demand is excused because the directors otherwise would have to sue themselves, thereby placing the conduct of the litigation in hostile hands and preventing its effective prosecution. This bootstrap argument has been made to and dismissed by other courts. See, e.g., Lewis v. Graves, 701 F.2d 245, 248–49 (2d Cir.1983). Its acceptance would effectively abrogate Rule 23.1 and weaken the managerial power of directors. Unless facts are alleged with particularity to overcome the presumptions of independence and a proper exercise of business judgment, in which case the directors could not be expected to sue themselves, a bare claim of this sort raises no legally cognizable issue under Delaware corporate law.

V.

In sum, we conclude that the plaintiff has failed to allege facts with particularity indicating that the Meyers directors were tainted by interest,

---

50. [By the Court] Plaintiff's allegation ignores 8 Del.C. § 143 which expressly authorizes interest-free loans to "any officer or employee of the corporation * * * whenever, in the judgment of the directors, such loan * * * may reasonably be expected to benefit the corporation." 8 Del.C. § 143.

lacked independence, or took action contrary to Meyers' best interests in order to create a reasonable doubt as to the applicability of the business judgment rule. Only in the presence of such a reasonable doubt may a demand be deemed futile. Hence, we reverse the Court of Chancery's denial of the motion to dismiss, and remand with instructions that plaintiff be granted leave to amend his complaint to bring it into compliance with Rule 23.1 based on the principles we have announced today. * * *

Reversed and Remanded.

Notes

(1) Dennis J. Block & Prussin, Termination of Derivative Suits Against Directors on Business Judgment Grounds: From *Zapata* to *Aronson*, 39 Bus.Law. 1503, 1505–1506 (Aug. 1984):[51]

> In *Zapata* the court held that the two-step test is to apply only in "demand-excused" cases, that is, cases where the shareholder was not required to make a demand upon the directors prior to commencing suit. In cases where demand is required and is refused, under *Zapata* the two-step test does not apply, and the directors' decision not to bring an action will be respected so long as it satisfies the standards of the business judgment rule.

> *Aronson* makes it clear that demand will almost always be required unless a majority of the Board is so directly self-interested in the challenged transaction that there is serious doubt that the business judgment rule would protect that transaction. Self-interest, for these purposes, is defined in terms of direct financial interest in the challenged transaction: the fact that a majority of directors voted to approve the transaction—and are therefore named as defendants in the action—does *not* constitute the requisite self-interest and will not excuse demand. After *Aronson* there should be relatively few demand-excused cases, and therefore relatively few cases where the *Zapata* two-step test will be applied. Thus, in run-of-the-mill cases the test actually applied will be the same under Delaware and New York law, the business judgment rule.

(2) The practical and tactical problems faced by a plaintiff under the complex Delaware structure of rules set forth in *Zapata* and *Aronson* were further complicated by two additional holdings.

(a) Spiegel v. Buntrock, 571 A.2d 767, 775 (Del.1990), holds that where a shareholder makes a demand, he thereby "tacitly acknowledges the absence of facts to support a finding of futility," thus placing his case in the hands of the board of directors under the business judgment rule. As a result of this "waiver" rule, plaintiffs today seldom make demand in Delaware, but instead litigate the issue whether demand was excused. See John C. Coffee, Jr., New Myths and Old Realities: The American Law Institute Faces the Derivative Action, 48 Bus. Law. 1407, 1414 (1993).

(b) In Levine v. Smith, 591 A.2d 194 (Del.1991), a case involving General Motors' buy-out of Ross Perot (discussed in the following note), Levine made a demand on the directors, which demand was refused by the unanimous decision of the board of directors exclusive of Perot. Levine then filed an amended complaint arguing that the refusal of the demand by the board of directors was not a proper exercise of business judgment. He sought the right to institute limited discovery in an effort to establish that the refusal was wrongful. The Court held that discovery should not be permitted following a refused demand, and to obtain judicial review of the claim of wrongful refusal, the plaintiff must allege particularized facts that create reasonable doubt that the refusal was a proper exercise of business judgment. In other words judicial review of a decision rejecting a demand was subject to the same pleading standard established in *Aronson* to determine whether demand was excused.

(c) In Scattered Corporation v. Chicago Stock Exchange, 701 A.2d 70 (Del. 1997), the court stated that in determining whether a demand was wrongfully refused, the plaintiff may use the "tools at hand" to obtain information about the basis of the decision. These "tools" include the statutory right of inspection of books, records, and minutes of meetings, but not discovery or production of records through a writ of mandamus.

(3) The Delaware Supreme Court has considered the application of the "demand excused" standard of Aronson in several cases with mixed results. Grobow v. Perot, 539 A.2d 180 (Del.1988), involved the decision by the board of directors of General Motors to have the corporation repurchase Ross Perot's shares in GM at a substantial premium in order to obtain Perot's resignation from the GM board. Perot had become a director of GM when GM purchased Perot's company, Electronic Data Systems, but as a director, Perot had harshly and publicly criticized GM management. The terms of the repurchase included not only a substantial premium over market price (the total buyout price was $745 million and the value of the shares and notes purchased, while in dispute, could not have exceeded $680 million) but also a so-called "hush mail" provision, under which Perot agreed to make no further public criticisms of GM subject to a $7.5 million liquidated damage clause. The complaint alleged that these transactions lacked any valid business purpose, constituted waste, and were motivated by a desire to entrench the board and save it from further public embarrassment. The suit was filed without making a demand on the board of directors; General Motors moved to dismiss the case for failing to make a demand. The Delaware Supreme Court concluded that there were no well pleaded claims of fraud, bad faith, or self-dealing "in the usual sense of personal profit or betterment" and therefore demand was required. In Heineman v. Datapoint Corp., 611 A.2d 950 (Del.1992), on the other hand, the Delaware Supreme Court held that demand was excused where it concluded that the complaint set forth particularized facts alleging that (a) following a successful contest for corporate control, the victors used their newly acquired positions to cause the corporation to reimburse them for the costs of waging that contest, and (b) the new directors caused the corporation to enter into a contract by which a substantial amount of the corporation's assets were diverted to an arbitrage pool whose participants include entities in which a majority of the new directors held an interest.

(4) In virtually every case in which derivative litigation has been considered by a litigation committee or by the board of directors since 1984, the determination has been that pursuit of the litigation is not in the best interest of the corporation. Does this not lend credence to the objection that there is in fact "structural bias" in this decisional process? Or should this datum be explained on the basis that virtually all derivative litigation filed today is without merit? For such a thesis, see Roberta Romano, The Shareholder Suit: Litigation without Foundation?, 7 J.L. Econ. & Org. 56 (1991); Larry R. Fischel & Michael Bradley, The Role of Liability Rules and the Derivative Suit in Corporate Law: A Theoretical and Empirical Analysis, 71 Cornell L.Rev. 261 (1986); Richard W. Duesenberg,

The Business Judgment Rule and Shareholder Derivative Suits: A View From the Inside, 60 Wash. U. L.Q. 311 (1982). Whatever the explanation, certainly one consequence of the use of litigation committees during this period is that control of derivative litigation has largely passed to the board of directors.

(5) The rules established in Delaware are complex and interconnected. They have been criticized on the ground that they prolong litigation by encouraging sparring over the preliminary question whether a demand was required. Judge Easterbrook, in a concurring opinion in Starrels v. First Nat'l Bank of Chicago, 870 F.2d 1168, 1172–76 (7th Cir.1989), offers a negative assessment of the Delaware rules:

> Why must shareholders demand that corporations act before filing suit? The rule could reflect a hope that the dispute will go away without litigation, that the board of directors will "do something" (or persuade the putative plaintiff that suit is pointless). Demand then initiates a form of alternative dispute resolution, much like mediation. Steps to control the volume of litigation are welcome, and courts give this as a justification for the demand rule. It is not, however, a powerful one, because on balance the rule creates more litigation than it prevents. It is difficult to identify cases in which the board's response to a demand satisfied the shareholder and thus prevented litigation; even if the board acts the shareholder may believe the board did too little. It is easy to point to hundreds of cases * * * in which the demand requirement was itself the centerpiece of the litigation.

> An approach uncertain in scope and discretionary in operation—that is, any rule except one invariably requiring or excusing demand—promotes litigation. When the stakes are high (as they frequently are in cases of this character), even a small disagreement between the parties about the application of a legal rule makes it difficult to resolve disagreements peaceably. It will be especially hard to resolve disputes out of court when, as in Delaware, making a demand affects the merits. A demand may be understood to concede that the board of directors possesses the discretion not to pursue the claim—and to block the investor's pursuit of it too. See Zapata Corp. v. Maldonado, 430 A.2d 779 (Del.1981). The case reports overflow with decisions concerning the demand requirement, and under *Aronson*'s approach litigation to determine whether a demand should have been made entails questions closely associated with "the merits". As a way to curtail litigation, the demand rule is a flop.[52]

> The persuasive rationale for the demand requirement is that it allows directors to make a business decision about a business question: whether to invest the time and resources of the corporation in litigation. Firms must make operational decisions; if these misfire, they must decide what to do next. Each decision must be made with the interests of the corporation at heart. Whether to fire a negligent employee, or to extend another chance, is no less a "business decision" than the choice to hire him initially or approve his strategy. So too the decision to file a lawsuit or choose something simpler—discharge, demotion, dressing-down, ratification—in the wake of questionable conduct. Even doing nothing is justified when the resources of top managers required to act exceed the injury to the firm; when "something must be done", acts short of litigation could have net benefits exceeding those of

---

52. [By the Judge] Even without the link between demand and the board's ability to squelch the suit, there is a steady flow of litigation about the demand requirement. Why this should occur is something of a mystery. * * *

litigation. If the directors run the show, then they must control litigation (versus other remedies) to the same extent as they make the initial business decision. They may conclude that internal remedies such as discharge or a reduction in compensation are more cost-effective for the firm. A lawsuit that seems to have good prospects and a positive value (net of attorneys' fees) still may be an unwise business decision because of the value of managerial time that would have to be invested, time unavailable to pursue the principal business of the corporation. Similarly, a lawsuit that appears to have a negative net value may be useful to the firm if it deters future misconduct.

Choosing between litigation and some other response may be difficult, depending on information unavailable to courts and a sense of the situation in which business executives are trained. Managers who make such judgment calls poorly ultimately give way to superior executives; no such mechanism "selects out" judges who try to make business decisions. In the long run firms are better off when business decisions are made by business specialists, even granting the inevitable errors. If principles such as the "business judgment rule" preserve room for managers to err in making an operational decision, so too they preserve room to err in deciding what remedies to pursue.

This rationale need not, however, imply universal demand. If courts would not respect the directors' decision not to file suit, then demand would be an empty formality. Perhaps the directors are interested in the transaction, so that they have a financial stake in the transaction and bear the burden of establishing its propriety. In such duty-of-loyalty cases courts frequently say that demand would be "futile". Or perhaps all of the directors are so ensnarled in the transaction that even when only the duty of care is at stake, their judgment could not be respected. Again demand would be an empty gesture. Delaware attempts to identify these cases and excuse demand in them.[53]

Aronson surveys these justifications and limits. The court observes that a decision not to sue is a business judgment. * * * Yet the rule of law devised in *Aronson* does not track the court's own remarks. * * *

A final oddment in the *Aronson* approach. Rule 23.1 and its parallel in Delaware practice require the court to determine at the pleading stage whether demand was necessary. This requires courts to adjudicate the merits on the pleadings, for a decision that the business judgment rule shelters the challenged conduct *is* "the merits" in derivative litigation, and under *Aronson* also shows that demand was necessary. It is a bobtailed adjudication, without evidence. If facts suggesting (at the one-in-ten level) that the business judgment rule will not prevent recovery have come to light, the investor may plead them and litigate further, setting the stage for still another decision about the scope of the business judgment rule. If facts of this character would come to light only with discovery, then demand is necessary and plaintiff may

---

53. [By the Judge] Whether the game is worth the candle is a different question. Difficulties in sorting cases into demand–required and demand–excused bins might justify a universal requirement, with the understanding that requiring demand does not always give the corporation authority to block litigation. There is much to recommend the American Law Institute's proposal to require universal demand and decouple that requirement from doctrines concerning the board's ability to pre-vent or dismiss derivative litigation. Principles of Corporate Governance: Analysis and Recommendations §§ 7.03, 7.08, and commentary at 64–71 (Tent. Draft No. 8, 1988). (Section 7.03(b) of Tentative Draft No. 8 would excuse demand when "irreparable injury to the corporation would otherwise result", but the Institute voted to require the shareholder to serve demand even after commencing a suit in advance of demand in reliance on feared "irreparable injury".)

not litigate at all—for in Delaware a demand-required case is one the board may elect to prevent or dismiss under *Zapata*. The amount of information in the public domain is unrelated to the ability of the board to make a business judgment concerning litigation, is unrelated indeed to any function of the demand requirement. Why should the board acquire the power to dismiss under *Zapata* just because the plaintiff needs discovery and so cannot make the required showing "with particularity" in the complaint? *Aronson* and its successors do not discuss the point.

A rule of universal demand, as the American Law Institute has proposed, would avoid these difficulties. If Delaware thinks it wise to distinguish demand-required and demand-excused cases, then a rule requiring demand unless the board is so wrapped up in the transaction that it cannot be relied on to make a business decision about the wisdom of litigation would do nicely. It would reflect the functions of having a demand rule in the first place. A rule excusing demand when there is a serious question about the status of the "challenged transaction" does not respond to the reasons for thinking demand useful, and one wonders whether it might be better to have no demand requirement at all than to excuse demand when the board might want to sue and compel demand when the board could not responsibly litigate.

See also John C. Coffee, Jr., New Myths and Old Realities: The American Law Institute Faces the Derivative Action, 48 Bus. Law. 1407, 1414 (1993):[54]

Delaware's demand rule also results in a substantial amount of collateral litigation and sometimes can be a trap for the unwary. For example, issues arise as to (i) whether a skeptical or protesting letter from a shareholder constitutes a demand (thereby waiving the issue of board independence) or only a request for information; (ii) whether a non-specific letter from a shareholder is too indefinite to constitute a demand (and thus requires no board response); (iii) how long after demand the plaintiff must wait for a response before filing its action; (iv) how broadly a demand letter relates when there are multiple issues; and (v) what effect does demand have when there is a subsequent change in the composition of the board. Nonetheless, the shareholder plaintiff usually faces an unattractive choice: either (i) not make a demand and thereby accept the burden of convincing the court that seemingly respectable directors should be deemed too biased even to deserve an opportunity to respond to demand, or (ii) make demand and thereby acknowledge the applicability of the business judgment rule to the directors' decision whether or not to reject demand (and, for most practical purposes, concede the outcome of the case).

(6) Given these criticisms, it is not surprising that mandatory demand in all cases has become the corner-stone of alternative systems for resolving derivative litigation in the corporate context.

CUKER v. MIKALAUSKAS

Supreme Court of Pennsylvania, 1997.
547 Pa. 600, 692 A.2d 1042.

Before FLAHERTY, C.J., and ZAPPALA, CAPPY, CASTILLE, NIGRO, and NEWMAN, JJ.

---

54. Copyright (1993) by the American Bar Association. All rights reserved. Reprinted with permission of the American Bar Association and its Section of Corporation, Banking and Business Law.

FLAHERTY, C.J.

PECO Energy Company filed a motion for summary judgment seeking termination of minority shareholder derivative actions. When the motion was denied by the court of common pleas, PECO sought extraordinary relief in this court pursuant to Pa.R.A.P. 3309. We granted the petition, limited to the issue of "whether the 'business judgment rule' permits the board of directors of a Pennsylvania corporation to terminate derivative lawsuits brought by minority shareholders."

PECO is a publicly regulated utility incorporated in Pennsylvania which sells electricity and gas to residential, commercial, and industrial customers in Philadelphia and four surrounding counties. PECO is required to conform to PUC regulations which govern the provision of service to residential customers, including opening, billing, and terminating accounts. PECO is required to report regularly to the PUC on a wide variety of statistical and performance information regarding its compliance with the regulations as interpreted by the PUC. Like other utilities, PECO is required to undergo a comprehensive management audit at the direction of the PUC approximately every ten years. The most recent audit was conducted by Ernst & Young. The report issued in 1991 recommended changes in twenty-two areas, including criticisms and recommendations regarding PECO's credit and collection function.

* * * [Following the PUC report, one set of minority shareholders filed a demand on PECO (the Katzman demand)], alleging wrongdoing by some PECO directors and officers. This Katzman demand, made in May, 1993, asserted that the delinquent officers had damaged PECO by mismanaging the credit and collection function, particularly as to the collection of overdue accounts. The shareholders demanded that PECO authorize litigation against the wrongdoers to recover monetary damages sustained by PECO. At its meeting of June 28, 1993, PECO's board responded by creating a special litigation committee to investigate the Katzman allegations.

Less than a month later, a second group of minority shareholders filed a complaint against PECO officers and directors. Cuker v. Mikalauskas, July Term, 1993, No. 3470 (C.P.Phila.). The Cuker complaint * * * made the same allegations as those in the Katzman demand * * *. The Cuker complaint was filed before the special litigation committee had begun its substantive work of investigating and evaluating the Katzman demand, so the committee's work encompassed both the Katzman and Cuker matters. Only the twelve nondefendant members of the PECO board acted to create the special committee, which consisted of three outside directors who had never been employed by PECO and who were not named in the Katzman demand or the Cuker complaint.

The work of the special committee was aided by the law firm of Dilworth, Paxson, Kalish & Kauffman, as well as PECO's regular outside auditor, Coopers & Lybrand, selected to assist in accounting matters because Coopers was knowledgeable about the utility industry and was familiar with PECO's accounting practices. The special committee conducted an extensive investigation over many months while maintaining a separate existence from PECO and its board of directors and keeping its deliberations confidential. The special committee held its final meeting on January 26, 1994, whereupon it reached its conclusions and prepared its report.

The report of the special committee concluded that there was no evidence of bad faith, self-dealing, concealment, or other breaches of the duty of loyalty by any of the defendant officers. It also concluded that the defendant officers "exercised sound business judgment in managing the affairs of the company" and that their actions "were reasonably calculated to further the best interests of the company." The three-hundred-page report identified numerous factors underlying the conclusions of the special committee. Significant considerations included the utility's efforts before the PUC to raise electricity rates in consequence of the expense of new nuclear generating plants. Other factors were the impact of PUC regulations limiting wintertime termination of residential service and other limitations on the use of collection techniques such as terminations of overdue customers, particularly with a large population of poverty level users among PECO's customer base. These considerations were supported by PUC documents which criticized PECO for aggressive and excessive terminations in recent years. The report of the special litigation committee also described how PECO's management had been attentive to the credit and collection function, with constant efforts to improve performance in that area. According to the report, limiting the use of terminations as a collection technique was a sound business judgment, reducing antagonism between the PUC and PECO and resulting in rate increases which produced revenue far in excess of the losses attributed to nonaggressive collection tactics. The report concluded that proceeding with a derivative suit based largely on findings of the Ernst & Young audit would not be in the best interests of PECO.

When it received the report of the special litigation committee with appendices containing the documents and interviews underlying the report, the board debated the recommendations at two meetings early in 1994. The twelve nondefendant members of the PECO board voted unanimously on March 14, 1994 to reject the Katzman demand and to terminate the Cuker action.

In the Cuker action, the court of common pleas rejected PECO's motion for summary judgment. The court stated that "the 'business judgment rule' [has been] adopted in some states but never previously employed in Pennsylvania." The court held that as a matter of Pennsylvania public policy, a corporation lacks power to terminate pending derivative litigation. * * * PECO sought extraordinary relief in this court under our King's Bench powers, which we granted.

* * * [The Court concludes that the business judgment rule permits the board of directors of a Pennsylvania corporation to terminate derivative lawsuits brought by minority shareholders.] Ironically, this court has never used the term "business judgment rule" in a corporate context nor has it explicitly adopted the business judgment rule. Nevertheless a review of Pennsylvania decisions establishes that the business judgment doctrine or rule is the law of Pennsylvania. * * *

The * * * practical effect of [our] holding needs elaboration. Assuming that an independent board of directors may terminate shareholder derivative actions, what is needed is a procedural mechanism for implementation and judicial review of the board's decision. Without considering the merits of the action, a court should determine the validity of the board's decision to terminate the litigation; if that decision was made in accordance with the appropriate standards, then the court should dismiss the derivative action prior to litigation on the merits.

The business judgment rule should insulate officers and directors from judicial intervention in the absence of fraud or self-dealing, if challenged decisions were within the scope of the directors' authority, if they exercised reasonable diligence, and if they honestly and rationally believed their decisions were in the best interests of the company. It is obvious that a court must examine the circumstances surrounding the decisions in order to determine if the conditions warrant application of the business judgment rule. If they do, the court will never proceed to an examination of the merits of the challenged decisions, for that is precisely what the business judgment rule prohibits. In order to make the business judgment rule meaningful, the preliminary examination should be limited and precise so as to minimize judicial involvement when application of the business judgment rule is warranted.

To achieve these goals, a court might stay the derivative action while it determines the propriety of the board's decision. The court might order limited discovery or an evidentiary hearing to resolve issues respecting the board's decision. Factors bearing on the board's decision will include whether the board or its special litigation committee was disinterested, whether it was assisted by counsel, whether it prepared a written report, whether it was independent, whether it conducted an adequate investigation, and whether it rationally believed its decision was in the best interests of the corporation (i.e., acted in good faith). If all of these criteria are satisfied,[55] the business judgment rule applies and the court should dismiss the action.

These considerations and procedures are all encompassed in Part VII, chapter 1 of the ALI Principles (relating to the derivative action), which provides a comprehensive mechanism to address shareholder derivative actions. A number of its provisions are implicated in the action at bar. Sections 7.02 (standing), 7.03 (the demand rule), 7.04 (procedure in derivative action), 7.05 (board authority in derivative action), 7.06 (judicial stay of derivative action), 7.07, 7.08, and 7.09 (dismissal of derivative action), 7.10 (standard of judicial review), and 7.13 (judicial procedures) are specifically applicable to this case.[56] These sections set forth guidance which is consistent with Pennsylvania law and precedent, which furthers the policies inherent in the business judgment rule, and which provides an appropriate degree of specificity to guide the trial court in controlling the proceedings in this litigation.

We specifically adopt §§ 7.02–7.10, and § 7.13 of the ALI Principles.[57] In doing so we have weighed many considerations. First, the opinion of the trial

55. [By the Court] It should be noted that respondents contest all of these criteria * * *. Until factual determinations are made in regard to these disputed issues, a trial court cannot conclude whether or not the business judgment rule requires dismissal of the action.

56. [By the Court] ALI Principles §§ 4.01, 4.02, and 4.03 (duties of directors and officers; the business judgment rule; reliance on committees and other persons) are similar but not

identical to the statutory standards found in 15 Pa.C.S. §§ 512, 513, 515, 1712, 1713, and 1715. The statutory standards, of course, control the duties of directors and the application of the business judgment rule in Pennsylvania.

57. [By the Court] The full text of these sections is set forth in the appendix to this opinion. * * * Our adoption of these sections is not a rejection of other sections not cited. We have identified and studied the sections which

court, the questions certified to the Superior Court, and the inability of PECO to obtain a definitive ruling from the lower courts all demonstrate the need for specific guidance from this court on how such litigation should be managed; the ALI principles provide such guidance in specific terms which will simplify this litigation. Second, we have often found ALI guidance helpful in the past, most frequently in adopting or citing sections of various Restatements; the scholarship reflected in work of the American Law Institute has been consistently reliable and useful. Third, the principles set forth by the ALI are generally consistent with Pennsylvania precedent. Fourth, although the ALI Principles incorporate much of the law of New York and Delaware, other states with extensive corporate jurisprudence, the ALI Principles better serve the needs of Pennsylvania. Although New York law parallels Pennsylvania law in many respects, it does not set forth any procedures to govern the review of corporate decisions relating to derivative litigation, and this omission would fail to satisfy the needs evident in this case. Delaware law permits a court in some cases ("demand excused" cases) to apply its own business judgment in the review process when deciding to honor the directors' decision to terminate derivative litigation. In our view, this is a defect which could eviscerate the business judgment rule and contradict a long line of Pennsylvania precedents. Delaware law also fails to provide a procedural framework for judicial review of corporate decisions under the business judgment rule.

Accordingly, we adopt the specified sections of the ALI Principles, reverse the orders of the court of common pleas, and remand the matter for further proceedings consistent with this opinion.

Orders reversed and case remanded.

APPENDIX

2 ALI, Principles of Corporate Governance: Analysis and Recommendations (1994).

§ 7.02 Standing to Commence and Maintain a Derivative Action

(a) A holder of an equity security has standing to commence and maintain a derivative action if the holder:

(1) Acquired the equity security either (A) before the material facts relating to the alleged wrong were publicly disclosed or were known by, or specifically communicated to, the holder, or (B) by devolution of law, directly or indirectly, from a prior holder who acquired the security as described in the preceding clause (A);

(2) Continues to hold the equity security until the time of judgment, unless the failure to do so is the result of corporate action in which the holder did not acquiesce, and either (A) the derivative action was commenced prior to the corporate action terminating the holder's status, or (B) the court finds that the holder is better able to represent the interests of the shareholders than any other holder who has brought suit;

apply to this case and have adopted those which appear most relevant. The entire publication, all seven parts, is a comprehensive, cohesive work more than a decade in preparation. Additional sections of the publication, particularly procedural ones due to their interlocking character, may be adopted in the future. Issues in future cases or, perhaps, further proceedings in this case might implicate additional sections of the ALI Principles. Courts of the Commonwealth are free to consider other parts of the work and utilize them if they are helpful and appear to be consistent with Pennsylvania law.

(3) Has complied with the demand requirement of § 7.03 (Exhaustion of Intracorporate Remedies; The Demand Rule) or was excused by its terms; and

(4) Is able to represent fairly and adequately the interests of the shareholders.

(b) On a timely motion, a holder of an equity security should be permitted to intervene in a derivative action, unless the court finds that the interests to be represented by the intervenor are already fairly and adequately represented or that the intervenor is unable to represent fairly and adequately the interests of the shareholders.

(c) A director of a corporation has standing to commence and maintain a derivative action unless the court finds that the director is unable to represent fairly and adequately the interest of the shareholders.

§ 7.03 Exhaustion of Intracorporate Remedies: The Demand Rule

(a) Before commencing a derivative action, a holder or a director should be required to make a written demand upon the board of directors of the corporation, requesting it to prosecute the action or take suitable corrective measures, unless demand is excused under § 7.03(b). The demand should give notice to the board, with reasonable specificity, of the essential facts relied upon to support each of the claims made therein.

(b) Demand on the board should be excused only if the plaintiff makes a specific showing that irreparable injury to the corporation would otherwise result, and in such instances demand should be made promptly after commencement of the action.

(c) Demand on shareholders should not be required.

(d) Except as provided in § 7.03(b), the court should dismiss a derivative action that is commenced prior to the response of the board or a committee thereof to the demand required by § 7.03(a), unless the board or committee fails to respond within a reasonable time.

§ 7.04 Pleading, Demand Rejection, Procedure, and Costs in a Derivative Action

The legal standards applicable to a derivative action should provide that:

(a) Particularity; Demand Rejection.

(1) In General. The complaint shall plead with particularity facts that, if true, raise a significant prospect that the transaction or conduct complained of did not meet the applicable requirements of Parts IV (Duty of Care and the Business Judgment Rule), V (Duty of Fair Dealing), or VI (Role of Directors and Shareholders in Transactions in Control and Tender Offers), in light of any approvals of the transaction or conduct communicated to the plaintiff by the corporation.

(2) Demand Rejection. If the corporation rejects the demand made on the board pursuant to § 7.03, and if, at or following the rejection, the corporation delivers to the plaintiff a written reply to the demand which states that the demand was rejected by directors who were not interested in the transaction or conduct described in and forming the basis for the demand and that those directors constituted a majority of the entire

board and were capable as a group of objective judgment in the circumstances, and which provides specific reasons for those statements, then the complaint shall also plead with particularity facts that, if true, raise a significant prospect that either:

    (A) The statements in the reply are not correct;

    (B) If Part IV, V, or VI provides that the underlying transaction or conduct would be reviewed under a standard other than the business judgment rule, either (i) that the disinterested directors who rejected the demand did not satisfy the good faith and informational requirements (§ 4.01(c)(2)) of the business judgment rule or (ii) that disinterested directors could not reasonably have determined that rejection of the demand was in the best interests of the corporation.

If the complaint fails to set forth sufficiently such particularized facts, defendants shall be entitled to dismissal of the complaint prior to discovery.

    (b) **Attorney's Certification.** Each party's attorney of record shall sign every pleading, motion, and other paper filed on behalf of the party, and such signature shall constitute the attorney's certification that (i) to the best of the attorney's knowledge, information, and belief, formed after reasonable inquiry, the pleading, motion, or other paper is well grounded in fact and is warranted by existing law or by a good faith argument for the extension, modification, or reversal of existing law, and (ii) the pleading, motion, or other paper is not interposed for any improper purpose, such as to harass or to cause unnecessary delay or needless increase in the cost of litigation.

    (c) **Security for Expenses.** Except as authorized by statute or judicial rule applicable to civil actions generally, no bond, undertaking, or other security for expenses shall be required.

    (d) **Award of Costs.** The court may award applicable costs, including reasonable attorney's fees and expenses, against a party, or a party's counsel:

    (1) At any time, if the court finds that any specific claim for relief or defense was asserted or any pleading, motion, request for discovery, or other action was made or taken in bad faith or without reasonable cause; or

    (2) Upon final judgment, if the court finds, in light of all the evidence, and considering both the state and trend of the substantive law, that the action taken as a whole was brought, prosecuted, or defended in bad faith or in an unreasonable manner.

§ 7.05 Board of Committee Authority in Regard to a Derivative Action

    (a) The board of a corporation in whose name or right a derivative action is brought has standing on behalf of the corporation to:

    (1) Move to dismiss the action on account of the plaintiff's lack of standing under § 7.02 (Standing to Commence and Maintain a Derivative Action) or the plaintiff's failure to comply with § 7.03 (Exhaustion of Intracorporate Remedies: The Demand Rule) or § 7.04(a) or (b) (Pleading, Demand Rejection, Procedure, and Costs in a Derivative Action) or move for dismissal of the complaint or for summary judgment;

(2) Move for a stay of the action, including discovery, as provided by § 7.06 (Authority of Court to Stay a Derivative Action);

(3) Move to dismiss the action as contrary to the best interests of the corporation, as provided in §§ 7.07–7.12 (dismissal of a derivative action based on a motion requesting dismissal by the board, a board committee, the shareholders, or a special panel);

(4) Oppose injunctive or other relief materially affecting the corporation's interests;

(5) Adopt or pursue the action in the corporation's right;

(6) Comment on, object to, or recommend any proposed settlement, discontinuance, compromise, or voluntary dismissal by agreement between the plaintiff and any defendant under § 7.14 (Settlement of a Derivative Action by Agreement Between the Plaintiff and a Defendant), or any award of attorney's fees and other expenses under § 7.17 (Plaintiff's attorney's Fees and Expenses); and

(7) Seek to settle the action without agreement of the plaintiff under § 7.15 (Settlement of a Derivative Action Without the Agreement of the Plaintiff).

Except as provided above, the corporation may not otherwise defend the action in the place of, or raise defenses on behalf of, other defendants.

(b) The board of a corporation in whose name or right a derivative action is brought may:

(1) Delegate its authority to take any action specified in § 7.05(a) to a committee of directors; or

(2) Request the court to appoint a special panel in lieu of a committee of directors, or a special member of a committee, under § 7.12 (Special Panel or Special Committee Members).

§ 7.06 Authority of Court to Stay a Derivative Action

In the absence of special circumstances, the court should stay discovery and all further proceedings by the plaintiff in a derivative action on the motion of the corporation and upon such conditions as the court deems appropriate pending the court's determination of any motion made by the corporation under § 7.04(a)(2) and the completion within a reasonable period of any review and evaluation undertaken and diligently pursued pursuant to § 7.09 (Procedures for Requesting Dismissal of a Derivative Action). On the same basis the court may stay discovery and further proceedings pending (a) the resolution of a related action or (b) such other event or development as the interests of justice may require.

§ 7.07 Dismissal of a Derivative Action Based on a Motion Requesting Dismissal by the Board or a Committee: General Statement

(a) The court having jurisdiction over a derivative action should dismiss the action as against one or more of the defendants based on a motion by the board or a properly delegated committee requesting dismissal of the action as in the best interests of the corporation, if:

(1) In the case of an action against a person other than a director, senior executive, or person in control of the corporation, or an associate of any such person, the determinations of the board or committee underlying the motion satisfy the requirements of the business judgment rule as specified in § 4.01;

(2) In the case of an action against a director, senior executive, or person in control of the corporation, or an associate of any such person, the conditions specified in § 7.08 (Dismissal of a Derivative Action Against Directors, Senior Executives, Controlling Persons, or Associates Based on a Motion Requesting Dismissal by the Board or a Committee) are satisfied; or

(3) In any case, the shareholders approve a resolution requesting dismissal of the action in the manner provided in § 7.11 (Dismissal of a Derivative Action Based Upon Action by the Shareholders).

(b) Regardless of whether a corporation chooses to proceed under § 7.08 or § 7.11, it is free to make any other motion available to it under the law, including a motion to dismiss the complaint or for summary judgment.

§ 7.08 Dismissal of a Derivative Action Against Directors, Senior Executives, Controlling Persons, or Associates Based on a Motion Requesting Dismissal by the Board or a Committee

The court should, subject to the provisions of § 7.10(b) (retention of significant improper benefit), dismiss a derivative action against a defendant who is a director, a senior executive, or a person in control of the corporation, or an associate of any such person, if:

(a) The board of directors or a properly delegated committee thereof (either in response to a demand or following commencement of the action) has determined that the action is contrary to the best interests of the corporation and has requested dismissal of the action;

(b) The procedures specified in § 7.09 (Procedures for Requesting Dismissal of a Derivative Action) for the conduct of a review and evaluation of the action were substantially complied with (either in response to a demand or following commencement of the action), or any material departures therefrom were justified under the circumstances; and

(c) The determinations of the board or committee satisfy the applicable standard of review set forth in § 7.10(a) (Standard of Judicial Review with Regard to a Board of Committee Motion Requesting Dismissal of a Derivative Action Under § 7.08).

§ 7.09 Procedures for Requesting Dismissal of a Derivative Action

(a) The following procedural standards should apply to the review and evaluation of a derivative action by the board or committee under § 7.08 (Dismissal of a Derivative Action Against Directors, Senior Executives, Controlling Persons, or Associates Based on a Motion Requesting Dismissal by the Board or a Committee) or § 7.11 (Dismissal of a Derivative Action Based Upon Action by the Shareholders):

(1) The board or a committee should be composed of two or more persons, no participating member of which was interested in the action, and should as a group be capable of objective judgment in the circumstances;

(2) The board or committee should be assisted by counsel of its choice and such other agents as it reasonably considers necessary;

(3) The determinations of the board or committee should be based upon a review and evaluation that was sufficiently informed to satisfy the standards applicable under § 7.10(a); and

(4) If the board or committee determines to request dismissal of the derivative action, it shall prepare and file with the court a report or other written submission setting forth its determinations in a manner sufficient to enable the court to conduct the review required under § 7.10 (Standard of Judicial Review with Regard to a Board or Committee Motion Requesting Dismissal of a Derivative Action Under § 7.08).

(b) If the court is unwilling to grant a motion to dismiss under § 7.08 or § 7.11 because the procedures followed by the board or committee departed materially from the standards specified in § 7.09(a), the court should permit the board or committee to supplement its procedures, and make such further reports or other written submissions, as will satisfy the standards specified in § 7.09(a), unless the court decides that (i) the board or committee did not act on the basis of a good faith belief that its procedures and report were justified in the circumstances; (ii) unreasonable delay or prejudice would result; or (iii) there is no reasonable prospect that such further steps would support dismissal of the action.

§ 7.10   Standard of Judicial Review with Regard to a Board or Committee Motion Requesting Dismissal of a Derivative Action Under § 7.08

(a) Standard of Review. In deciding whether an action should be dismissed under § 7.08 (Dismissal of a Derivative Action Against Directors, Senior Executives, Controlling Persons, or Associates Based on a Motion Requesting Dismissal by the Board or a Committee), the court should apply the following standards of review:

(1) If the gravamen of the claim is that the defendant violated a duty set forth in Part IV (Duty of Care and the Business Judgment Rule), other than by committing a knowing and culpable violation of law that is alleged with particularity, or if the underlying transaction or conduct would be reviewed under the business judgment rule under § 5.03, § 5.04, § 5.05, § 5.06, § 5.08, or § 6.02, the court should dismiss the claim unless it finds that the board's or committee's determinations fail to satisfy the requirements of the business judgment rule as specified in § 4.01(c).

(2) In other cases governed by Part V (Duty of Fair Dealing) or Part VI (Role of Directors and Shareholders in Transactions in Control and Tender Offers), or to which the business judgment rule is not applicable, including cases in which the gravamen of the claim is that defendant committed a knowing and culpable violation of law in breach of Part IV, the court should dismiss the action if the court finds, in light of the

applicable standards under Part IV, V, or VI that the board or committee was adequately informed under the circumstances and reasonably determined that dismissal was in the best interests of the corporation, based on grounds that the court deems to warrant reliance.

(3) In cases arising under either Subsection (a)(1) or (a)(2), the court may substantively review and determine any issue of law.

(b) Retention of Significant Improper Benefit. The court shall not dismiss an action if the plaintiff establishes that dismissal would permit a defendant, or an associate, to retain a significant improper benefit where:

(1) The defendant, either alone or collectively with others who are also found to have received a significant improper benefit arising out of the same transaction, possesses control of the corporation; or

(2) Such benefit was obtained:

(A) As the result of a knowing and material misrepresentation or omission or other fraudulent act; or

(B) Without advance authorization or the requisite ratification of such benefit by disinterested directors (or, in the case of a nondirector senior executive, advance authorization by a disinterested superior), or authorization or ratification by disinterested shareholders, and in breach of § 5.02 (Transactions with the Corporation) or § 5.04 (Use by a Director or Senior Executive of Corporate Property, Material Non–Public Corporate Information, or Corporate Position); unless the court determines, in light of specific reasons advanced by the board or committee, that the likely injury to the corporation from continuation of the action convincingly outweighs any adverse impact on the public interest from dismissal of the action.

(c) Subsequent Developments. In determining whether the standards of § 7.10(a) are satisfied or whether § 7.10(b) or any of the exceptions set forth therein are applicable, the court may take into account considerations set forth by the board or committee (or otherwise brought to the court's attention) that reflect material developments subsequent to the time of the underlying transaction or conduct or to the time of the motion by the board or committee requesting dismissal.

§ 7.13 Judicial Procedures on Motions to Dismiss a Derivative Action Under § 7.08 or § 7.11

(a) Filing of Report or Other Written Submission. Upon a motion to dismiss an action under § 7.08 (Dismissal of a Derivative Action Against Directors, Senior Executives, Controlling Persons, or Associates Based on a Motion Requesting Dismissal by the Board or a Committee) or § 7.11 (Dismissal of a Derivative Action Based Upon Action by the Shareholders), the corporation shall file with the court a report or other written submission setting forth the procedures and determinations of the board or committee, or the resolution of the shareholders. A copy of the report or other written submission, including any supporting documentation filed by the corporation, shall be given to the plaintiff's counsel.

(b) Protective Order. The court may issue a protective order concerning such materials, where appropriate.

(c) Discovery. Subject to § 7.06 (Authority of Court to Stay a Derivative Action), if the plaintiff has demonstrated that a substantial issue exists whether the applicable standards of § 7.08, § 7.09, § 7.10, § 7.11, or § 7.12 have been satisfied and if the plaintiff is unable without undue hardship to obtain the information by other means, the court may order such limited discovery or limited evidentiary hearing, as to issues specified by the court, as the court finds to be (i) necessary to enable it to render a decision on the motion under the applicable standards of § 7.08, § 7.09, § 7.10, § 7.11, or § 7.12, and (ii) consistent with an expedited resolution of the motion. In the absence of special circumstances, the court should limit on a similar basis any discovery that is sought by the plaintiff in response to a motion for summary judgment by the corporation or any defendant to those facts likely to be in dispute. The results of any such discovery may be made subject to a protective order on the same basis as under § 7.13(b).

(d) Burdens of Proof. The plaintiff has the burden of proof in the case of a motion (1) under § 7.08 where the standard of judicial review is determined under § 7.10(a)(1) because the basis of the claim involves a breach of a duty set forth in Part IV (Duty of Care and the Business Judgment Rule) or because the underlying transaction would be reviewed under the business judgment rule, or (2) under § 7.07(a)(1) (suits against third parties and lesser corporate officials). The corporation has the burden of proof in the case of a motion under § 7.08 where the standard of judicial review is determined under § 7.10(a)(2) because the underlying transaction would be reviewed under a standard other than the business judgment rule, except that the plaintiff retains the burden of proof in all cases to show (i) that a defendant's conduct involved a knowing and culpable violation of law, (ii) that the board or committee as a group was not capable of objective judgment in the circumstances as required by § 7.09(a)(a), and (iii) that dismissal of the action would permit a defendant or an associate thereof to retain a significant improper benefit under § 7.10(b). The corporation shall also have the burden of proving under § 7.10(b) that the likely injury to the corporation from continuation of the action convincingly outweighs any adverse impact on the public interest from dismissal of the action. In the case of a motion under § 7.11 (Dismissal of a Derivative Action Based Upon Action by the Shareholders), the plaintiff has the burden of proof with respect to § 7.11(b), (c), and (d), and the corporation has the burden of proof with respect to § 7.11(a).

(e) Privilege. The plaintiff's counsel should be furnished a copy of related legal opinions received by the board or committee if any opinion is tendered to the court under § 7.13(a). Subject to that requirement, communications, both oral and written, between the board or committee and its counsel with respect to the subject matter of the action do not forfeit their privileged character, and documents, memoranda, or other material qualifying as attorney's work product do not become subject to discovery, on the grounds that the action is derivative or that the privilege was waived by the production to the plaintiff or the filing with the court of a report, other written submission, or supporting documents pursuant to § 7.13.

Notes

(1) The ALI's Principles of Corporate Governance is not a statute intended for adoption by individual states. Rather, it is a statement of "black letter" principles (several of which are quoted by the Court in its appendix) followed by a plain text explanation of the operation of the "black letter" principles. In this respect it is similar to the various Restatements with which all law students are familiar. Of the various sections quoted by the Court in *Cuker*, by far the most controversial is § 7.10, which was developed and approved only after exhaustive discussion and negotiation. This section was explained as "a mechanism for judicial review of the board's power to dismiss a derivative action [which] is necessary if fiduciary duties are to remain meaningful legal obligations." Comment to § 7.10, The American Law Institute, Principles of Corporate Governance: Analysis and Recommendations.[58] However, much of the controversy arose because of the Reporters' plain text explanation of the operation of this section:

> [I]n a simple due care case alleging, for example, a failure of business judgment because a major corporate project or investment proved unsuccessful, only a relatively simple inquiry should typically be necessary to demonstrate that the requirements of the business judgment rule were satisfied. In such a case, the reviewing court need not conclude that the determinations "warrant reliance," but only that they meet the standard of the business judgment rule. Often, a brief inquiry by the board or committee may demonstrate that the corporate decisionmaker had been adequately informed at the time it acted with respect to the project or investment and that it rationally believed that its decision was in the best interests of the corporation. No more than a short report or other written submission setting forth the board's or committee's conclusions would be necessary. In general, discovery by the plaintiff should be strictly controlled in such a case or not permitted at all.
> * * *
> At the other end of the spectrum from the due care case is the case involving a substantial duty of loyalty issue, such as one, for example, when a majority of the board personally benefited from the transaction and then expanded the board's size to appoint new directors to staff a litigation committee, which later recommended dismissal of the action. Here, close judicial scrutiny of the justifications offered for dismissal is obviously appropriate. Under *Zapata*, if a majority received a pecuniary benefit, the Delaware courts would excuse demand and permit the trial court to use its own "independent business judgment." Section 7.10 avoids the use of the potentially misleading phrase "independent business judgment." Rather, § 7.10 contemplates that heightened judicial scrutiny should be reserved for a limited number of instances and that, overall, the degree of judicial scrutiny should relate to the legal standards [applicable to the conduct in question]. Thus, for example, if * * * the transaction was one in which the burden of proving fairness remained on the director or senior executive, the reviewing court should be mindful that in this instance Part V invites close judicial scrutiny. Therefore, less deference to the justifications asserted for dismissal by the board or committee would be warranted.
> Put simply, the court should review the board's or committee's determinations in a manner that is consistent with the standards of review and

burdens of proof established by [other parts of these principles]. This does not mean, however, that § 7.10 specifies a uniform standard of review for all duty of loyalty cases. The closest review will be in those cases in which the defendant has the burden of proving fairness. For example, such a standard would apply in the case of a corporate opportunity when the corporate rejection of the opportunity was not by a disinterested majority of the board, with the result that * * * the defendant must prove the fairness of the defendant's conduct. Conversely, if a disinterested board had earlier rejected the corporate opportunity after appropriate disclosure, then the board's decision is protected by the business judgment rule * * * and correspondingly a motion to dismiss is to be reviewed under the similar standard * * *. An intermediate case [occurs when] a self interested transaction is approved in advance by disinterested directors or a disinterested superior, the court should determine whether the directors or senior executive "could reasonably have concluded that the transaction was fair to the corporation," even when there has been full disclosure and disinterested approval. In such a case, the standard of review * * * should be less exacting than in a case in which the defendant is required to prove the fairness of the transaction, but more searching than in a case in which the business judgment rule is applicable. * * *

Procedurally, the plaintiff is not limited to rebutting the determinations made in the board's or committee's report or other written submissions, but may produce probative evidence as to any matter relating to the action or its impact on the corporation, even if not addressed in the board's or committee's report or other written submission. * * * [T]he court may also consider developments occurring subsequent to the date of the board's or committee's report in determining whether the findings warrant reliance. After the court has fairly evaluated plaintiff's evidence and arguments, it may, if it deems it appropriate, adopt the board's or committee's report or other written submission as its own decision or adopt such portions thereof as it finds sufficiently persuasive to satisfy the relevant standard * * *.

Cases may arise in which the court is unable to find that the determinations set forth in the report or other written submission tendered by the board or committee "warrant reliance," but in which the court is also unpersuaded as to the action's merit. In such instances, the court may in its discretion request additional determinations, information, or data from any party. The intent underlying § 7.10 is never to limit the court's discretion through narrow pleading rules.

In some circumstances, disputed factual issues may make it necessary for the court to hold a limited evidentiary hearing, or to delay its decision for additional discovery, before it rules on the motion. However, the importance of an expedited decision should normally lead the court to constrain discovery * * * and seek an early resolution of the motion.

This formulation was bitterly attacked, particularly by members who were familiar with the Delaware structure for resolving derivative litigation, as "departing dramatically from well settled principles" established in many cases and as accepting a "litigation model" of corporate governance. Michael Dooley & E. Norman Veasey, The Role of the Board in Derivative Litigation Delaware Law and the Current ALI Proposals Compared, 44 Bus. Law. 503 (1989); Dennis J. Block, et al., Derivative Litigation: Current Law Versus the American Law Institute, 48 Bus. Law. 1443 (1993). Every suggestion of even superficial judicial review of the merits of a litigation committee decision in the "demand required" context is systematically referred to by Dooley and Veasey as "judicially intrusive review." The Block article also accuses the reporters of seeking to undermine a compromise negotiated at an earlier plenary session of the Institute. Id. at 1470, 1474. For a spirited defense, see John C. Coffee, Jr., New Myths and Old Realities: The American Law Institute Faces the Derivative Action, 48 Bus. Law. 1407 (1993). See also Carol B. Swanson, Juggling Shareholder Rights and Strike Suits in Derivative Litigation: The ALI Drops the Ball, 77 Minn. L.Rev. 1339 (1993)

(2) The Committee on Corporate Laws created its own solution to the derivative litigation issue in 1989 when it approved Subchapter D of chapter 7 of the MBCA, §§ 7.40 et seq. The critical sections are § 7.42, relating to demand, and § 7.44 relating to the dismissal of derivative suits. The Official Comment to § 7.42 explains the demand requirement:[59]

> Section 7.42 requires a written demand on the corporation in all cases. The demand must be made at least 90 days before commencement of suit unless irreparable injury to the corporation would result. This approach has been adopted for two reasons. First, even though no director may be independent, the demand will give the board of directors the opportunity to reexamine the act complained of in the light of a potential lawsuit and take corrective action. Secondly, the provision eliminates the time and expense of the litigants and the court involved in litigating the question whether demand is required. It is believed that requiring a demand in all cases does not impose an onerous burden since a relatively short waiting period of 90 days is provided and this period may be shortened if irreparable injury to the corporation would result by waiting for the expiration of the 90 day period. Moreover, the cases in which demand is excused are relatively rare. Many plaintiffs' counsel as a matter of practice make a demand in all cases rather than litigate the issue whether demand is excused. * * *
>
> There is no obligation on the part of the corporation to respond to the demand. However, if the corporation, after receiving the demand, decides to institute litigation or, after a derivative proceeding has commenced, decides to assume control of the litigation, the shareholder's right to commence or control the proceeding ends unless it can be shown that the corporation will not adequately pursue the matter. As stated in *Lewis v. Graves*, 701 F.2d 245, 247–48 (2d Cir.1983):
>
> > The [demand] rule is intended "to give the derivative corporation itself the opportunity to take over a suit which was brought on its behalf in the first place, and thus to allow the directors the chance to occupy their normal status as conductors of the corporation's affairs." Permitting corporations to assume control over shareholder derivative suits also has numerous practical advantages. Corporate management may be in a better position to pursue alternative remedies, resolving grievances without burdensome and expensive litigation. Deference to directors' judgments may also result in the termination of meritless actions brought solely for their settlement or harassment value. Moreover, where litigation is appropriate, the derivative corporation will often be in a better position to bring or assume the suit because of superior financial re-

---

59. Reprinted from *Model Business Corporation Act Annotated* with the permission of   Prentice Hall Law & Business.

sources and knowledge of the challenged transactions. [Citations omitted.]

The more critical and controversial section is § 7.44, dealing with the finality of committee and/or board of directors determinations. The Official Comment elaborates upon the language of § 7.44(a):[60]

> Section 7.44(a) requires that the determination be made by the appropriate persons in good faith after conducting a reasonable inquiry upon which their conclusions are based. The word "inquiry" rather than "investigation" has been used to make it clear that the scope of the inquiry will depend upon the issues raised and the knowledge of the group making the determination with respect to the issues. In some cases, the issues may be so simple or the knowledge of the group so extensive that little additional inquiry is required. In other cases, the group may need to engage counsel and other professionals to make an investigation and assist the group in its evaluation of the issues.

> The phrase "in good faith" modifies both the determination and the inquiry. The test, which is also included in sections 8.30 (general standards of conduct for directors) and 8.51 (authority to indemnify), is a subjective one, meaning "honestly or in an honest manner." "The Corporate Director's Guidebook," 33 Bus.Law. 1595, 1601 (1978). As stated in *Abella v. Universal Leaf Tobacco Co.*, 546 F.Supp. 795, 800 (E.D.Va.1982), "the inquiry intended by this phrase goes to the spirit and sincerity with which the investigation was conducted, rather than the reasonableness of its procedures or basis for conclusions."

> The phrase "upon which its conclusions are based" requires that the inquiry and the conclusions follow logically. This provision authorizes the court to examine the determination to ensure that it has some support in the findings of the inquiry. * * * This phrase does not require the persons making the determination to prepare a written report that sets forth their determination and the bases therefor, since circumstances will vary as to the need for such a report. There may, however, be many instances where good corporate practice will commend such a procedure.

> Section 7.44 is not intended to modify the general standards of conduct for directors set forth in section 8.30 of the Model Act, but rather to make those standards somewhat more explicit in the derivative proceeding context.

As of 1996, eleven states had in substance adopted Subchapter D. Marx v. Akers, 88 N.Y.2d 189, 644 N.Y.S.2d 1034, 666 N.E.2d 1034, 1040 (1996)(noting that New York is not one of those states). Is § 7.44 a reasonable accommodation between the interests of the plaintiff shareholders and the corporation? Is there any "wiggle room" in the language of § 7.44(a), "A derivative proceeding *shall be dismissed* by the court on motion if * * * "? Does not this language prevent the kind of evaluation recommended by the ALI formulation?

(3) The Delaware litigation committee procedures are of course of central importance primarily because of the very large number of publicly held corporations incorporated in that state. The two alternative solutions—one put forth by the ALI, the other by the Committee on Corporate Laws—also deal with the core issue whether a court should simply defer to the business judgment of a litigation committee or board of directors, without more, or whether it should make some

---

60. Reprinted from *Model Business Corporation Act Annotated* with the permission of Prentice Hall Law & Business.

kind of substantive review of the apparent merits of that decision. Several state courts have had an opportunity to consider this aspect of the litigation committee device in the absence of statute with mixed results.

(a) A number of states appear to give the committee decision at least the same degree of deference that it is given in Delaware. Dennis J. Block et al., Derivative Litigation: Current Law Versus The American Law Institute, 48 Bus. Law. 1443, 1443–44, 1447 (1993) states that since 1984, "the courts both in and out of Delaware have ruled with near unanimity" that the business judgment rule is the appropriate standard of judicial review. The authors of this article also state (apparently somewhat optimistically) that this "rule has * * * been stated as a presumption by courts applying the laws of at least twenty-one other jurisdictions during the last decade." For an example of cases in this category, see Skoglund v. Brady, 541 N.W.2d 17 (Minn.App.1995)[Judicial review is limited to "determining whether committee was independent and conducted its investigation in good faith."]

(b) Basically accepting the "structural bias" argument, the Court in Miller v. Register & Tribune Syndicate, Inc., 336 N.W.2d 709 (Iowa 1983), held that the board of directors was unable to delegate the power to bind the corporation to an independent litigation committee if the board of directors was itself unable to act because a majority was interested in the transaction; the Court suggested that a committee might be appointed by judicial order in this situation.

(c) In Alford v. Shaw, 318 N.C. 289, 349 S.E.2d 41 (1986), the North Carolina Supreme Court uncritically adopted the *Gall* approach in a case involving charges of fraud and self-dealing by a majority of the board of directors; defendant directors participated in the selection of new directors to serve as the special litigation committee. See Deborah DeMott, the Corporate Fox and the Shareholders' Hen House: Reflections on Alford v. Shaw, 65 N.C.L.Rev. 569 (1987). The North Carolina Court then granted a petition for rehearing, and significantly modified—indeed, virtually rejected the underlying premises of—its earlier opinion. 320 N.C. 465, 358 S.E.2d 323 (1987). Relying largely on section 55–55 of the North Carolina statutes [similar to § 7.45 of the MBCA (1984)] the Court stated:

> To make the required assessment under section 55–55, the court must of necessity evaluate the adequacy of materials prepared by the corporation which support the corporation's decision to settle or dismiss a derivative suit along with the plaintiff's forecast of evidence. If it appears likely that plaintiff could prevail on the merits, but that the amount of the recovery would not be sufficient to outweigh the detriment to the corporation, the court could still allow discontinuance, dismissal, compromise, or settlement.
>
> Although the recommendations of the special litigation committee is not binding on the court, in making this determination the court may choose to rely on such recommendation. To rely blindly on the report of a corporation-appointed committee which assembled such materials on behalf of the corporation is to abdicate the judicial duty to consider the interests of shareholders imposed by the statute. This abdication is particularly inappropriate in a case such as this one, where shareholders allege serious breaches of fiduciary duties owed to them by the directors controlling the corporation.

Section 55–55(c) is a broadening of the *Zapata* approach. * * *

The *Zapata* Court limited its two-step judicial inquiry to cases in which demand upon the corporation was futile and therefore excused. However, we find no justification for such limitation in our statutes. The language of section 55–55(c) is inclusive and draws no distinctions between demand-excused and other types of cases. Cf. ALI Principles of Corporate Governance: Analysis and Recommendations § 7.08 & Reporter's Notes 2 & 4 at 135–139 (Council Draft No. 6, Oct. 10, 1986) (issue of demand of minimal importance in determining scope of review; demand-excused/demand-required distinction not determinative). Thus, court approval is required for disposition of *all* derivative suits, even where the directors are not charged with fraud or self-dealing, or where the plaintiff and the board agree to discontinue, dismiss, compromise, or settle the lawsuit.

320 N.C. at 471–72, 358 S.E.2d at 327. consult James D. Cox, Heroes in the Law: Alford v. Shaw, 66 N.C.L.Rev. 565 (1988).

(d) In Houle v. Low, 407 Mass. 810, 824, 556 N.E.2d 51, 59 (1990), the Court states that a reviewing court should determine whether the committee (i) was independent and disinterested and (ii) "reached a reasonable and principled decision." Lewis v. Boyd, 838 S.W.2d 215, 224 (Tenn.App.1992), adopts the same test.

(e) Michigan amended its corporation statute in 1989 to authorize a court to appoint one or more "disinterested persons" at the request of the corporation to make findings with respect to a derivative suit; if this route is followed, a determination by such persons will be accepted unless the plaintiff establishes that the determination was not made in good faith or that the investigation was not reasonable. Mich. B.C.A. § 450.1495(1). See Joel Seligman, The Disinterested Person: An Alternative Approach to Shareholder Derivative Litigation, 55 Law & Contemp. Probs. 357 (Autumn 1992). If the determination is made by incumbent directors, the burden shifts to the corporation to establish that the determination was made in good faith and the investigation was reasonable unless all independent disinterested directors agree with the determination.

(f) North Carolina has a similar statute, which provides that upon motion by the corporation, a court may appoint a committee composed of two or more disinterested directors or other disinterested persons acceptable to the corporation; after considering the report and other relevant evidence, "the Court shall determine whether the proceeding should be continued or not." N.C. Bus. Corp. Act § 55–7–40(c). See Crown Crafts, Inc. v. Aldrich, 148 F.R.D. 547 (E.D.N.C.1993)(federal court declines to appoint a committee under this section). Other states have enacted similar statutes. See also MBCA § 7.44(f).

(4) Most of the concern about derivative suits, litigation committees and the like relate to publicly held corporations. The elaborate procedures of the ALI Principles of Corporate Governance are not suitable for closely held corporations with relatively few shareholders. Section 7.01(d) of the Principles sets forth a simple and practical solution for derivative litigation within such corporations:

> In the case of a closely held corporation, the court in its discretion may treat an action raising derivative claims as a direct action, exempt it from those restrictions and defenses applicable only to derivative actions, and order an individual recovery, if it finds that to do so will not (i) unfairly expose the corporation or the defendants to a multiplicity of actions, (ii) materially prejudice the interests of creditors of the corporation, or (iii) interfere with a fair distribution of the recovery among all interested persons.

For a case adopting this approach, see Barth v. Barth, 659 N.E.2d 559, 562–63 (Ind.1995), where the court commented:

In determining that a trial court has discretion to decide whether a plaintiff must proceed by direct or by derivative action, we make the following observations, drawn largely from the Comment to § 7.01(d). First, permitting such litigation to proceed as a direct action will exempt the plaintiff from the requirements of Ind.Code § 23–1–32–1 et seq., including the provisions that permit a special committee of the board of directors to recommend dismissal of the lawsuit. Ind.Code § 23–1–32–4. As such, the court in making its decision should consider whether the corporation has a disinterested board that should be permitted to consider the lawsuit's impact on the corporation. A.L.I., Corporate Governance Project § 7.01 comment e. Second, in some situations it may actually be to the benefit of the corporation to permit the plaintiff to proceed by direct action. This will permit the defendant to file a counterclaim against the plaintiff, whereas counterclaims are generally prohibited in derivative actions. Also, in a direct action each side will normally be responsible for its own legal expenses; the plaintiff, even if successful, cannot ordinarily look to the corporation for attorney's fees.

Chapter Eleven

DUTY OF LOYALTY AND CONFLICT OF INTEREST

A. SELF–DEALING

MARCIANO v. NAKASH

Supreme Court of Delaware, 1987.
535 A.2d 400.

Before HORSEY, MOORE and WALSH, JJ.

WALSH, JUSTICE.

This is an appeal from a decision of the Court of Chancery which validated a claim in liquidation of Gasoline, Ltd. ("Gasoline"), a Delaware corporation, placed in custodial status pursuant to 8 *Del.C.* § 226 by reason of a deadlock among its board of directors. Fifty percent of Gasoline is owned by Ari, Joe, and Ralph Nakash (the "Nakashes") and fifty percent by Georges, Maurice, Armand and Paul Marciano (the "Marcianos"). The Vice Chancellor ruled that $2.5 million in loans made by the Nakashes faction to Gasoline were valid and enforceable debts of the corporation, notwithstanding their origin in self-dealing transactions. The Marcianos argue that the disputed debt is voidable as a matter of law but, in any event, the Nakashes failed to meet their burden of establishing full fairness. We conclude that the Vice Chancellor applied the proper standard for review of self-dealing transactions and the finding of full fairness is supported by the record. Accordingly, we affirm. * * *

The parties agree that the loans made by the Nakashes to Gasoline were interested transactions. The Nakashes as officers of Gasoline executed the various documents which supported the loans and at the same time guaranteed those loans extended through their wholly owned entities. It is also not disputed that, given the control deadlock, the questioned transactions did not receive majority approval of Gasoline's directors or shareholders. The Marcianos argue that the loan transaction is voidable at the option of the corporation notwithstanding its fairness or the good faith of its participants. A review of this contention, rejected by the Court of Chancery, requires analysis of the concept of director self-dealing under Delaware law.

It is a long-established principle of Delaware corporate law that the fiduciary relationship between directors and the corporation imposes fundamental limitations on the extent to which a director may benefit from dealings with the corporation he serves. *Guth v. Loft, Inc.,* Del.Supr., 5 A.2d 503 (1939). Thus, the "voting [for] and taking" of compensation may be deemed "constructively fraudulent" in the absence of shareholder ratification, or statutory or bylaw authorization. *Cahall v. Lofland,* Del.Ch., 114 A. 224, 232 (1921). Perhaps the strongest condemnation of interested director conduct appears in *Potter v. Sanitary Co. of America,* Del.Ch., 194 A. 87 (1937), a decision which the Marcianos advance as definitive of the rule of per se voidability. In *Potter* the Court of Chancery characterized transactions between corporations having common directors and officers "constructively fraudulent," absent shareholder ratification.

Support can also be found for the per se rule of voidability in this Court's decision in *Kerbs v. California Eastern Airways Inc.,* Del.Supr., 90 A.2d 652 (1952). The *Kerbs* court, in considering the validity of a profit sharing plan, ruled that the self-interest of the directors who voted on the plan caused the transaction to be voidable. The court concluded that the profit sharing plan was voidable based on the common law rule that the vote of an interested director will not be counted in determining whether the challenged action received the affirmative vote of a majority of the board of directors. *Id.* at 658 (*citing Bovay v. H.M. Byllesby & Co.,* Del.Supr., 38 A.2d 808 (1944)).

The principle of per se voidability for interested transactions, which is sometimes characterized as the common law rule, was significantly ameliorated by the 1967 enactment of Section 144 of the Delaware General Corporation Law.[1] The Marcianos argue that section 144(a) provides the only basis for immunizing self-interested transactions and since none of the statute's component tests are satisfied the stricture of the common law per se rule applies. The Vice Chancellor agreed that the disputed loans did not withstand a section 144(a) analysis but ruled that the common law rule did not invalidate transactions determined to be intrinsically fair. We agree that section 144(a) does not provide the only validation standard for interested transactions.

It overstates the common law rule to conclude that relationship, alone, is the controlling factor in interested transactions. Although the application of the per se voidability rule in early Delaware cases resulted in the invalidation of interested transactions, the result was not dictated simply by a tainted relationship. Thus in *Potter,* the Court, while adopting the rule of voidability, emphasized that interested transactions should be subject to close scrutiny. Where the undisputed evidence tended to show that the transaction would advance the personal interests of the directors at the expense of stockholders, the stockholders, upon discovery, are entitled to disavow the transaction.

Further, the court examined the motives of the defendant directors and the effect the transaction had on the corporation and its shareholders.

In other Delaware cases, decided before the enactment of section 144, interested director transactions were deemed voidable only after an examination of the fairness of a particular transaction *vis-a-vis* the nonparticipating shareholders and a determination of whether the disputed conduct received the approval of a noninterested majority of directors or shareholders. *Keenan v. Eshleman,* Del.Supr., 2 A.2d 904, 908 (1938); *Blish v. Thompson Automatic*

---

1. [By the Editor] Section 144 of Title 8 Del.C. *is set forth in footnote 40, p. 718 supra.*

Arms Corp., Del.Supr., 64 A.2d 581, 602 (1948). The latter test is now crystallized in the ratification criteria of section 144(a), although the nonquorum restriction of *Kerbs* has been superceded by the language of subparagraph (b) of section 144.

The Marcianos view compliance with section 144 as the sole basis for avoiding the per se rule of voidability. The Court of Chancery rejected this contention and we agree that it is not consonant with Delaware corporate law. This Court in *Fliegler v. Lawrence,* Del.Supr., 361 A.2d 218 (1976), a post-section 144 decision, refused to view section 144 as either completely preemptive of the common law duty of director fidelity or as constituting a grant of broad immunity. As we stated in *Fliegler:* "It merely removes an 'interested director' cloud when its terms are met and provides against invalidation of an agreement 'solely' because such a director or officer is involved." *Id.* at 222. In *Fliegler* this Court applied a two-tiered analysis: application of section 144 coupled with an intrinsic fairness test.

If section 144 validation of interested director transactions is not deemed exclusive, as *Fliegler* clearly holds, the continued viability of the intrinsic fairness test is mandated not only by fact situations, such as here present, where shareholder deadlock prevents ratification but also where shareholder control by interested directors precludes independent review. Indeed, if an independent committee of the board, contemplated by section 144(a)(1) is unavailable, the sole forum for demonstrating intrinsic fairness may be a judicial one. In such situations the intrinsic fairness test furnishes the substantive standard against which the evidential burden of the interested directors is applied. * * *

This case illustrates the limitation inherent in viewing section 144 as the touchstone for testing interested director transactions. Because of the shareholder deadlock, even if the Nakashes had attempted to invoke section 144, it was realistically unavailable. The ratification process contemplated by section 144 presupposes the functioning of corporate constituencies capable of providing assents. Just as the statute cannot "sanction unfairness" neither can it invalidate fairness if, upon judicial review, the transaction withstands close scrutiny of its intrinsic elements.[2]

[The Marcianos claimed that the Nakashes had not proved that the costs of the loans were fair to the corporation and also that some of the proceeds of the loans had been used to pay invoices from companies controlled by the Nakashes. The Court held, however, that the Chancellor's conclusion that the terms of the loans met the "intrinsic fairness standard" was supported by the record and was the product of a logical deductive process. The Court concluded that the possible misuse of the proceeds of the loans should be litigated in a derivative proceeding brought by the Marcianos which was then pending.]

---

2. [By the Court] Although in this case none of the curative steps afforded under section 144(a) were available because of the director-shareholder deadlock, a non-disclosing director seeking to remove the cloud of interestedness would appear to have the same burden under section 144(a)(3), as under prior case law, of proving the intrinsic fairness of a questioned transaction which had been approved or ratified by the directors or shareholders. Folk, *The Delaware General Corp. Law: A Commentary and Analysis,* 86 (1972). On the other hand, approval by fully-informed disinterested directors under section 144(a)(1), or disinterested stockholders under section 144(a)(2), permits invocation of the business judgment rule and limits judicial review to issues of gift or waste with the burden of proof upon the party attacking the transaction.

We hold, therefore, that the Court of Chancery properly applied the intrinsic fairness test in determining the validity of the interested director transactions and its finding of full fairness is clearly supported by the record. Accordingly, the decision is Affirmed.

Notes

(1) Consider the general problem of a director who enters into a business transaction with the corporation—for example, the purchase of property from, or the sale of property to the corporation. Such transactions can take many forms but they have one element in common. There is an obvious risk that the transaction will be skewed in favor of the director and as a result will be harmful to the corporation. Such a risk, of course, is increased if the interested director owns sufficient shares so that he or she can elect or remove a majority of the directors. What position should the law take with respect to such transactions? The position taken during the last part of the nineteenth century was that all such transactions were voidable at the instance of the corporation or its shareholders without regard to the fairness or unfairness of the transaction. This absolute position now appears to be totally rejected, in part because it is clear that many such transactions are beneficial to the corporation and are entered into by the director to assist rather than to harm the corporation. However, consider the structure of § 144 of the Delaware GCL. It provides that "no contract or transaction * * * shall be void or voidable *solely* * * * [for specified reasons] *if"* one of three circumstances exist. Read literally this provision seems to assume a general principle of automatic voidability and then carves out three exceptions. The Nakash loans do not fit within any of these three specified circumstances and therefore would appear to be voidable. [If the loans were fair, as the court concludes, why didn't they fall with § 144(a)(3)?] The reason the court did not follow this reasoning lies in the narrow way § 144(a)(3) is drafted and the court's earlier decision in *Fliegler*, cited in the courts opinion. *Fliegler* involved an apparently unfair transaction between a corporation and its majority shareholder who was also a director; the transaction was submitted to the shareholders and approved, with the interested majority shareholder voting in favor to approve his own transaction. The court rejected the literal language of § 144 (which did not prevent interested shareholders from voting) with the statement, "[n]othing in the statute sanctions unfairness to Agau or removes the transaction from judicial scrutiny." Id., at 222. As a result, in Delaware the language of § 144 has never been held to be controlling and the court has proceeded to develop the non-statutory tests for self dealing transactions set forth in note 2 of the opinion. It is not clear under these standards whether ratification by disinterested and fully informed shareholders validates the transaction entirely or simply removes the taint created by the conflict, leaving the transaction subject to review, presumably under the business judgment rule. See In re Wheelabrator Technologies Shareholders Litigation, 663 A.2d 1194 (Del.Ch.1995).

(2) The problem with self dealing transactions is deciding what tests should be applied to sort out the harmful transaction from the harmless or desirable one. Several possible tests have received some degree of modern judicial approval in the absence of statute:

(a) Such a transaction is voidable if it is not approved or ratified by a disinterested majority of the directors or by the shareholders without regard to its fairness;

(b) Such a transaction is *not* voidable if the interested director can show that the transaction is fair to the corporation;

(c) Such a transaction is voidable if the plaintiff shows that the transaction is unfair to the corporation;

(d) Such a transaction is voidable only if the plaintiff shows that the transaction constitutes fraud, waste, or serious overreaching;

(e) Such a transaction is *not* voidable if it has been approved or ratified by a disinterested majority of the directors, and no further inquiry need be made into its fairness;

(f) Such a transaction is *not* voidable if it has been approved or ratified by a majority of the disinterested shareholders and no further inquiry need be made into its fairness;

(g) Such a transaction is always voidable if the vote of the interested director is necessary to approve the transaction or his presence is necessary to form a quorum;

(h) Such a transaction is always voidable if the interested director participates in the decision-making process, urging approval of the transaction, but does not vote.

Thought will reveal that these alternatives (and there may be others not mentioned) are not mutually exclusive, since some relate to the *procedures* by which the transaction was approved while others (particularly (b), (c), and (d)) relate to the *substance*—the effect of the transaction on the corporation—and it is possible to combine them. For example, one might establish a rule that such a transaction is voidable if it is unfair (alternative (c)) or constitutes waste (alternative (d)) but the disinterested shareholders may ratify the transaction (alternative (f)). Would such a rule be desirable? Or, one might establish the rule that a transaction that is voidable under alternative (a) may be made not voidable if the director can establish fairness (alternative (b)). Would that rule be desirable? Of course, at the extreme, there probably is no reason to consider setting aside a transaction approved by *all* the shareholders, no matter how damaging to the corporation, though one can imagine situations involving injury to creditors or senior interests.

To the extent the procedures followed in approving a transaction are made determinative, difficult issues arise relating to who has the burden of proof, the identification of what types of interest should disqualify a person from being "disinterested," and what degree of participation by an "interested" director or shareholder should be viewed as tainting the outcome, and how voting by interested and disinterested directors mesh with the quorum and voting rules for boards of directors. See Kenneth B. Davis, Jr., Approval by Disinterested Directors, 20 J. Corp. L. 215 (1995). Many of these issues are addressed ambiguously, if at all, by statute.

(3) While many transactions between directors and their corporation have been held to be valid in the absence of a controlling statute, considerable confusion exists in the case law as to the circumstances which may validate such transactions. If one examines the results of cases (as contrasted with statements in the opinions), the following comments accurately reflect most of the decisions:

(a) If the Court feels the transaction to be fair to the corporation, it will be upheld;

(b) If the Court feels that the transaction involves fraud, undue over-reaching or waste of corporate assets (e.g., a director using corporate assets for personal purposes without paying for them), the transaction will be set aside; and

(c) If the Court feels that the transaction does not involve fraud, undue overreaching or waste of corporate assets, but is not convinced that the transaction is fair, the transaction will be upheld only where the interested director can convincingly show that the transaction was approved (or ratified) by a truly disinterested majority of the board of directors without participation by the interested director or by a majority of the disinterested shareholders, after full disclosure of all relevant facts.

(4) Consider carefully the suggestion by the Delaware Supreme Court in n. 2 that where "fully-informed disinterested directors" or "disinterested stockholders" approve a conflict of interest transaction under § 144, the business judgment rule may be invoked to limit judicial review to "issues of gift or waste." Is that consistent with the language of § 144? Is that consistent with the rules relating to special litigation committees discussed in the preceding chapter?

(5) Today, the treatment of conflict of interest transactions is largely controlled by statute. As of December 1, 1995, 48 states had statutes dealing with such transactions. Most of these statutes are similar in structure to Del. GCL § 144 though there are significant variations in language. Most of these statutes were enacted after 1975, and there is little or no case law under most of them.

(6) The 1984 Model Business Corporation Act included § 8.31 that was modeled after many of these state statutes. Like these statutes, the Official Comment to this section stated that its purpose was to eliminate the "automatic rule of voidability" under the early case law, and "does not mean that all transactions that meet one or more of the tests set forth in Section 8.31(a) are automatically valid." Section 8.31, as originally promulgated, is set forth in a footnote in the Statutory Supplement. However, several Committee members expressed dissatisfaction with this very traditional provision.

(7) In December 1988, the Committee on Corporate Laws withdrew § 8.31 and approved a new treatment of conflict-of-interest transactions, now codified as §§ 8.60–8.63 of the MBCA. The new subchapter F, as it is usually called, is a much more ambitious undertaking than earlier conflict-of-interest statutes or § 8.31. Subchapter F is structured similarly to § 8.31: a conflict of interest transaction is not voidable by the corporation if (a) it has been approved by disinterested directors or shareholders, or (b) the interested director establishes the fairness of the transaction. Unlike § 8.31, however, subchapter F is designed to create a series of "bright line" principles that increase predictability and enhance practical administrability. Does the conflict-of-interest area lend itself to "bright line" treatment?

(a) Subchapter F deals only with "transactions" between a director and the corporation. It does not deal with issues such as whether an opportunity is or is not a corporate opportunity,[3] or nontransactional policy decisions, e.g., whether the corporation should establish a divisional headquarters in the director's home town. Whatever rules are applicable to judge the validity and propriety of such transactions are unaffected by subchapter F.

(b) One important "bright line" is that the definition of "conflicting interest" in § 8.60(1) is exclusive—an interest of a director is a conflicting interest *if and only if* it meets the requirements of this definition. As an example of an interest of a director that may influence his or her decision but does not constitute a

---

3. [By the Editor] See part B of this Chapter. It might be pointed out that the early Delaware case of Fliegler v. Lawrence, discussed in *Nakash*, did involve the usurpation of a corporate opportunity.

statutory "conflicting interest," the Official Comment uses this hypothetical: if D (a director of X Co.) is a major creditor of Y Co., and the issue is some transaction between X Co. and Y Co., D's creditor interest in Y Co. may possibly influence D's vote as a director of X Co. on a contemplated transaction between X Co. and Y Co. D's creditor interest in Y Co., however, does not create a "conflicting interest" when D votes as a director of X Co. on the transaction, since D's creditor interest in Y Co. does not fit any subcategory of the definition of "conflicting interest" in § 8.60(1)(ii) or of "related person" in § 8.60(3). However, if that interest is so large that it would reasonably be expected to affect his judgment, it would fall within § 8.60(1)(i).

(c) The definition of "director's conflicting interest transaction" in § 8.60(2) is similarly preclusive: it not only designates the exclusive area within which the rules of subchapter F are to be applied under § 8.61(b), but also prohibits a court from applying conflict of interest provisions to circumstances that lie outside that definition. This preclusive effect is described by the following two illustrations drawn from the Official Comment to § 8.61(a):[4]

> (i) "If a plaintiff charges that a director had a conflict of interest with respect to a transaction of the corporation because the other party was his cousin, the answer of the court should be: 'No. A cousin, as such and without more, is not included in section 8.60(3) as a related person—and under section 8.61(a), I have no authority to reach out further.'"

> (ii) "If a plaintiff contends that the director had a conflict of interest in a corporate transaction because the other party is president of the golf club the director wants desperately to join, the court should respond: 'No. The only director's conflicting interest on the basis of which I can set aside a corporate transaction or impose other sanctions is a financial interest as defined in section 8.60.'"

(d) Section 8.62(d) creates a new defined term, "qualified director," to describe the directors who may vote to approve a director's conflicting interest transaction and thus "sanitize" the transaction. Such approval means that the transaction "may not be enjoined, set aside, or give rise to an award of damages or other sanctions, in a proceeding by a shareholder" because of the director's interest in the transaction. See § 8.61(b). In other words, it is "sanitized" for all purposes. Would it be desirable to provide for at least some degree of judicial oversight of all conflict of interest transactions? If so, isn't subchapter F a well-meaning but flawed exercise?

(7) Abstractly, self-dealing transactions have two attributes that make a substantial degree of judicial oversight desirable: (1) they are voluntary transactions on the part of the self-dealing director and (2) they provide an opportunity for direct pecuniary enrichment at the expense of the corporation by the self-dealing director. Indeed, most commentary on directors' duties recognize that breaches of the duty of loyalty raise serious problems that merit continuing judicial scrutiny. For example, in Kenneth E. Scott, Corporation Law and the American Law Institute Corporate Governance Project, 35 Stan.L.Rev. 927 (1983), the author urged (long before the Trans Union case) that liability for violations of the duty of care should be entirely eliminated but that judicial vigilance over violations of the duty of loyalty should be vigorously encouraged. Does subchapter F go against the grain of this analysis by withdrawing (or appearing to withdraw)

---

4. Reprinted from *Model Business Corporation Act Annotated* with the permission of Prentice Hall Law & Business.

all judicial scrutiny from conflict of interest cases, relying instead on the vote of "qualified directors" to protect the corporation and minority shareholders against overreaching transactions?

(8) Many modern self-dealing cases involve small, closely held corporations, and in most of these cases, the self-dealing individual is a significant shareholder in the corporation. How useful is subchapter F in this context since most such corporations probably will not have "qualified directors" to review the transaction?

(9) The Official Comment to § 8.61(b) also includes the following commentary:[5]

Clause (1) of subsection (b) * * * [is] subject to one critically important predicate condition. The condition—an obvious one—is that the board's action must comply with the care, best interest, and good faith criteria prescribed in section 8.30(a) for all directors' actions. If the directors who voted for the conflicting interest transaction were qualified directors under subchapter F, but approved the transaction merely as an accommodation to the director with the conflicting interest, going through the motions of board action without complying with the requirements of section 8.30(a), the action of the board would not be given effect for purposes of section 8.61(b)(1).

Board action on a director's conflicting interest transaction provides a context in which the function of the 'best interests of the corporation' language in section 8.30(a) is brought into clear focus. Consider, for example, a situation in which it is established that the board of a manufacturing corporation approved a cash loan to a director where the duration, security, and interest terms of the loan were at prevailing commercial rates, but (i) the loan was not made in the course of the corporation's ordinary business and (ii) the loan required a commitment of limited working capital that would otherwise have been used in furtherance of the corporation's business activities. Such a loan transaction would not be afforded safe-harbor protection by section 8.62(b)(1) since the board did not comply with the requirement in section 8.30(a) that the board's action be, in its reasonable judgment, in the best interests of the corporation—that is that the action will, as the board judges the circumstances at hand, yield favorable results (or reduce detrimental results) as judged from the perspective of furthering the corporation's business activities.

If a determination is made that the terms of a director's conflicting interest transaction, judged according to the circumstances at the time of commitment, were manifestly unfavorable to the corporation, that determination would be relevant to an allegation that the director's action was not taken in good faith and therefore did not comply with section 8.30(a).

Despite the apparent conclusive nature of any decision by qualified directors, isn't this an invitation for courts to examine the terms of the transaction to determine whether the terms are "manifestly unfavorable" and therefore constitute evidence that the approval was an "accommodation" rather than a "business judgment?" If a court should review a transaction to determine whether terms are "manifestly unfavorable" as a basis for deciding whether an appropriate business judgment was made by the qualified directors, why shouldn't it review the transaction

---

5. Reprinted from *Model Business Corporation Act Annotated* with the permission of Prentice Hall Law & Business.

directly for unfairness? Why should it have to go through the circumlocution of finding that the transaction was "manifestly unfavorable" and then concluding that § 8.30 was not complied with? If this standard of review was intended, should the quoted statements from the commentary have been included in the text of § 8.61 since they are, in effect, a major qualification upon a statute that on its face is unqualified?

(10) Most state statutes contain provisions restricting or prohibiting loans to employees or directors. For example, § 42 of the 1960 Model Act provided, "No loans shall be made by a corporation to its officers or directors, and no loans shall be made by a corporation secured by its shares." For a description of the background of such legislation and a plea for its retention, see Jayne W. Barnard, Corporate Loans to Directors and Officers: Every Business Now a Bank, 1988 Wis.L.Rev. 237 (1988). Why should loans to a director be any different from any other self-dealing transaction? Why should loans by a corporation "secured by its shares" be subject to a special prohibition? Section 8.32 of the MBCA (set forth in a footnote in the Statutory Supplement) was based on these loan restriction statutes, though it liberalized the rules with respect to director loans to the point that only an unusual loan might fall subject to its prohibitions. However, when subchapter F was adopted, the Committee on Corporate Laws also withdrew § 8.32 in its entirety without discussing the justification for doing so. Of course, the hypothetical situation described in the Official Comment to subchapter F (see note (10)) itself involves a corporate loan to a director.

HELLER v. BOYLAN

Supreme Court of New York, 1941.
29 N.Y.S.2d 653.

[Editor: Only the portions of this opinion dealing with the incentive compensation plan are included.]

COLLINS, JUSTICE.

In this derivative action 7 out of a total of 62,000 stockholders—holding under 1,000 out of a total of 5,074,076 shares—of the American Tobacco Company, seek recovery for the corporation from the Company's directors for alleged improper payments to certain of the Company's officers.

The suit derives from an incentive compensation by-law of the Company, known as Article XII, virtually unanimously adopted by the stockholders in March, 1912. Thereunder 10 percent of the annual profits over the earnings of the corresponding properties in 1910 are to be distributed, 2½ percent to the president and 1½ percent to each of the five vice-presidents "in addition to the fixed salary of each of said officers."

The profits, and consequently the bonuses, undulated with the years; but at all times they were quite lush. By virtue of this by-law, the officers have received from and including 1929 to and including 1939—in addition to $3,784,999.69 in salaries—bonuses aggregating $11,672,920.27, or total compensation during that eleven-year period of $15,457,919.69. The president alone, George W. Hill, Sr., received $592,370 in 1929; $1,010,508 in 1930; $1,051,570 in 1931; $825,537.49 in 1932. The other payments to him during such period were obese, the thinnest being $137,042.65, in 1938, and the average around $400,000. The other officers likewise received handsome compensation though not as huge.

The plaintiffs maintain that these large bonus payments bore no relation to the value of the services for which they were given, that, consequently, they were in reality a gift in part, and that the majority stockholders committed waste and spoliation in thus giving away corporate property against the protest of the minority. Rogers v. Hill, 289 U.S. 582, 590–592, 53 S.Ct. 731, 77 L.Ed. 1385, 88 A.L.R. 744.

The validity of the by-law is not challenged. Indeed, its legality has been sustained. Rogers v. Hill, supra. Nor do plaintiffs impugn the principle of incentive compensation. Rather, they regard it "a legitimate means of accomplishing a desired result," and do not question "that the extra effort, spurred by the promise of extra compensation, may have been an important factor in the prosperity of the Company." That the Company has been singularly prosperous is indubitable. Its growth has been prodigious, its record for earnings is an enviable one, the management has been extraordinarily efficient, and the stockholders, as well as the officers, have been the beneficiaries of this immensely capable organization. The Company has made money even in direful times. Its capital investment is $265,000,000. It produces more than 200,000,000 cigarettes a day. In 1939 the Company's sales amounted to $262,416,000, its most popular brand—"Lucky Strike"—yielding $218,542,-749. The Company is one of the world's giant industrial enterprises. Its activities are farflung, if not worldwide. Nevertheless, charge the plaintiffs, the payments to the officers have become "so large as in substance and effect to amount to spoliation or waste of corporate property." Rogers v. Hill, supra.

This is not the first time some of these payments have been attacked. An earlier assault was made by another stockholder, Richard Reid Rogers, and from that litigation stems several of the issues involved in the present suit. It is the principle evoked by the Rogers case which mainly supplies the pattern for this one. * * *

[In] Rogers v. Hill, 289 U.S. 582, 53 S.Ct. 731, 735, 77 L.Ed. 1385, 88 A.L.R. 744, Butler, J., for the unanimous Court, enunciated the principle * * * thus:

> It follows from what has been shown that when adopted the by-law was valid. But plaintiff alleges that the measure of compensation fixed by it is not now equitable or fair. And he prays that the court fix and determine the fair and reasonable compensation of the individual defendants, respectively, for each of the years in question. The allegations of the complaint are not sufficient to permit consideration by the court of the validity or reasonableness of any of the payments on account of fixed salaries or of special credits or of the allotments of stock therein mentioned. Indeed, plaintiff alleges that other proceedings have been instituted for the restoration of special credits, and his suits to invalidate the stock allotments were recently considered here. Rogers v. Guaranty Trust Co., 288 U.S. 123, 53 S.Ct. 295, 77 L.Ed. 652 [89 A.L.R. 720]. The only payments that plaintiff by this suit seeks to have restored to the company are the payments made to the individual defendants under the by-law.
>
> We come to consider whether these amounts are subject to examination and revision in the District Court. As the amounts payable depend upon the gains of the business, the specified percentages are not per se unreasonable. The by-law was adopted in 1912 by an almost unanimous

vote of the shares represented at the annual meeting and presumably the stockholders supporting the measure acted in good faith and according to their best judgment. The tabular statement in the margin shows the payments to individual defendants under the by-law. Plaintiff does not complain of any made prior to 1921. Regard is to be had to the enormous increase of the company's profits in recent years. The 2½ percent yielded President Hill $447,870.30 in 1929 and $842,507.72 in 1930. The 1½ percent yielded to each of the vice presidents, Neiley and Riggio, $115,-141.86 in 1929 and $409,495.25 in 1930 and for these years payments under the by-law were in addition to the cash credits and fixed salaries shown in the statement.

While the amounts produced by the application of the prescribed percentages give rise to no inference of actual or constructive fraud, the payments under the by-law have by reason of increase of profits become so large as to warrant investigation in equity in the interest of the company. Much weight is to be given to the action of the stockholders, and the by-law is supported by the presumption of regularity and continuity. But the rule prescribed by it cannot, against the protest of a shareholder, be used to justify payments of sums as salaries so large as in substance and effect to amount to spoliation or waste of corporate property. The dissenting opinion of Judge Swan indicates the applicable rule: 'If a bonus payment has no relation to the value of services for which it is given, it is in reality a gift in part, and the majority stockholders have no power to give away corporate property against the protest of the minority.' 60 F.2d 109, 113. The facts alleged by plaintiff are sufficient to require that the District Court, upon a consideration of all the relevant facts brought forward by the parties, determine whether and to what extent payments to the individual defendants under the by-laws constitute misuse and waste of the money of the corporation [citing cases].

Following Rogers' victory in the Supreme Court, and before the "investigation in equity" was launched, negotiations for adjustment were started. These eventuated in a settlement, from which the Company benefited—at the time of the settlement in July, 1933—by $6,200,000 and a further saving of about $2,250,000 by March, 1940. Many more millions were saved—inasmuch as the settlement reduced the bonus base and the employee's stock subscription plan was revised. In addition, Rogers was paid a fee of $525,000, the net being $263,000, and the income tax thereon exhausting the remaining $262,-000. Thus ended the Rogers campaign.

But the echoes therefrom persisted. Seven stockholders, including three of the plaintiffs in this action (Heller, Wile and Mandelkor), and represented by most of the attorneys who appear for the plaintiffs here, assailed the settlement and sought to have it cancelled on the ground that the huge fee to Rogers was in the nature of a bribe. * * *

THE PERPLEXITIES OF THE CASE

Quite obviously, this case carries a number of perplexities. A few of them will be noted:

1. The general reluctance of the Courts to interfere with the internal management of a corporation. Pragmatism by the Courts—interference or

meddling with free and lawful enterprise honestly conducted–is repugnant to our concept of government. Of course the hesitancy is overcome if fraud or bad faith or over-reaching appears—if the fiduciaries have been faithless to their trust.

2.　Though this is a derivative stockholders' action, only 7 out of 62,000 stockholders have joined the onslaught; these 7 holding less than 1,000 out of a total of 5,074,076 shares of the Company. This factor, though significant, bears only on the equities; it is by no means decisive. Tyranny over the minority by the majority is abhorrent and will not be tolerated. The majority cannot, save by due legal process, make that which is illegal, legal, nor can it confiscate the company's assets or dispense them as unearned bounties. Majority rule does not license subjugation or immunize spoliation. The possession of power does not authorize or excuse its abuse. Power is not a franchise to do wrong. The majority cannot any more than the minority violate the law with impunity.

3.　This case differs from most stockholders suits in that in those cases it is the conduct of directors which forms the basis of the complaint, whereas here not only is the by-law a creature of the stockholders, but on at least two other occasions, one in April, 1933, and again in April, 1940, the stockholders, by almost unanimous vote, ratified many of the payments involved in this suit. To be sure, "the majority stockholders have no power to give away corporate property against the protest of the minority." Rogers v. Hill, supra [60 F. 114].

4.　The fact that the by-law has been in existence since 1912 and has been held valid.

5.　The embarrassment which some of the defendants might experience in refunding even a part of what they received, especially since taxes were paid thereon.

6.　The language of finality contained in paragraph 4 of the by-law.[6]

7.　The paucity of apposite precedents.

Let it be emphasized, however, that the above are alluded to only as difficulties; they enter into the equities, but do not constitute a bar. * * *

Now, even a high-bracketer would deem [the stipends involved in this case] munificent. To the person of moderate income they would be princely—perhaps as something unattainable; to the wage-earner ekeing out an existence, they would be fabulous, and the unemployed might regard them as fantastic, if not criminal. To others they would seem immoral, inexcusably unequal, and an indictment of our economic system. The opinion of Judge Swan has been unfairly paraphrased as announcing that "no man can be worth $1,000,000 a year". But see George T. Washington, of the Cornell Law School, The Corporation Executive's living wage, Harvard Law Review,

---

6. [By the Editor] Section 4 reads as follows:

The declaration of the Treasurer as to the amount of net profits for the year and the sum due anyone hereunder shall be binding and conclusive on all parties, and no one claiming hereunder shall have the right to question the said declaration, or to any examination of the books or accounts of the Company, and nothing herein contained shall give any incumbent of any office any right to claim to continue therein, or any other right except as herein specifically expressed.

March, 1941, Vol. LIV. 759. Many economists advocate a ceiling for compensation.

At the stockholders meeting on April 3, 1941, a holder of 80 shares of common stock—who thought the compensation grandiose—offered a resolution to restrict the president's bonus to a maximum of $100,000 and to impose other limitations. But the resolution was defeated by 2,193,418 votes to 74,571. Harvard Law Review, supra 747.

Let it be boldly marked that the particular business before this Court is not the revamping of the social or economic order—*justiciable* disputes confront it. * * *

Here, the plaintiffs proffered no testimony whatever in support of their charge of waste. The figures, they reason, speak for themselves, and the defendants must justify them. The figures do speak, but just what do they say as a matter of equity? They are immense, staggeringly so. Even so, is that enough to compel the substitution of the Court's judgment for that of the stockholders? Larger compensation has been judicially approved. * * *

Assuming, arguendo, that the compensation should be revised, what yardstick is to be employed? Who or what is to supply the measuring-rod? The conscience of equity? Equity is but another name for human being temporarily judicially robed. He is not omnipotent or omniscient. Can equity be so arrogant as to hold that it knows more about managing this corporation than its stockholders?

Yes, the Court possesses the *power* to prune these payments, but openness forces the confession that the pruning would be synthetic and artificial rather than analytic or scientific. Whether or not it would be fair and just, is highly dubious. Yet, merely because the problem is perplexing is no reason for eschewing it. It is not timidity, however, which perturbs me. It is finding a rational or just gauge for revising these figures were I inclined to do so. No blueprints are furnished. The elements to be weighed are incalculable; the imponderables, manifold. To act out of whimsy or caprice or arbitrariness would be more than inexact—it would be the precise antithesis of justice; it would be a farce.

If comparisons are to be made, with whose compensation are they to be made—executives? Those connected with the motion picture industry? Radio artists? Justices of the Supreme Court of the United States? The President of the United States? Manifestly, the material at hand is not of adequate plasticity for fashioning into a pattern or standard. Many instances of positive underpayment will come to mind, just as instances of apparent rank overpayment abound. Haplessly, intrinsic worth is not always the criterion. A classic might perhaps produce trifling compensation for its author, whereas a popular novel might yield a titanic fortune. Merit is not always commensurately rewarded, whilst mediocrity sometimes unjustly brings incredibly lavish returns. Nothing is so divergent and contentious and inexplicable as values.

Courts are ill-equipped to solve or even to grapple with these entangled economic problems. Indeed, their solution is not within the juridical province. Courts are concerned that corporations be honestly and fairly operated by its directors, with the observance of the formal requirements of the law; but what is reasonable compensation for its officers is primarily for the stockholders. This does not mean that fiduciaries are to commit waste, or misuse or abuse trust property, with impunity. A just cause will find the Courts at guard and implemented to grant redress. But the stockholder must project a less amorphous plaint than is here presented.

On this branch of the case, I find for the defendants. Yet it does not follow that I affirmatively approve these huge payments. It means that I cannot by any reliable standard find them to be waste or spoliation; it means that I find no valid ground for disapproving what the great majority of stockholders have approved. In the circumstances, if a ceiling for these bonuses is to be erected, the stockholders who built and are responsible for the present structure must be the architects. Finally, it is not amiss to accent the antiseptic policy stressed by Judge Liebell in Winkelman et al. v. General Motors Corporation, D.C.S.D.N.Y. decided August 14, 1940, 39 F.Supp. 826, that: "The duty of the director executives participating in the bonus seems plain—they should be the first to consider unselfishly whether under all the circumstances their bonus allowances are fair and reasonable".

Notes

(1) Why is there reluctance to set aside "huge," "staggering," "munificent," or "quite lush" payments of salary to corporate officers?

(2) The 1990s have seen an unprecedented furor over levels of executive compensation. "When twelve chief executives of major U.S. corporations accompanied President Bush to Japan early in 1992, complaints about their compensation surfaced in advance of the trip, and the ensuing publicity equalled or surpassed that given to the planned negotiation of trade agreements." Douglas C. Michael, The Corporate Officer's Independent Duty as A Tonic for the Anemic Law of Executive Compensation, 17 J. Corp. L. 785, 788 (Summer 1992). "As the 1997 proxy season draws to a close, CEO pay again has hit unprecedented levels. According to * * * [a *Business Week* survey] average total compensation for the top execs at big companies rose 54% in 1996 to $5.8 million, outstripping most corporate profit and stock growth. Unsurprisingly, such sums have stirred outrage among ordinary Americans—most of whom are seeing pay raises in the 3% to 5% range. The big shocker: Top Executives agree. A * * * [*Business Week* poll] shows that top executives at America's largest companies, like most of the public, think the current compensation system is out of whack." Jennifer Reingold, Corporate Governance, Even Executives Are Wincing at Executive Pay, Business Week May 12, 1997, at 40. This furor is also evidenced by headlines in normally staid business journals. For example, the *Wall Street Journal* placed the following statement in large type on the front page of its 1995 report on CEO compensation: "Raking It In: CEO pay is soaring again thanks to rising profits, directors' pursuit of outside talent and reduced public criticism." Joann S. Lublin, Executive Pay, Wall St. J., Apr. 12, 1995, at R1. Other examples include, John A. Byrne, "Gross Compensation? New CEO pay figures make top brass look positively piggy," Business Week, March 18, 1996, at 34, and the cover of *Business Week* for April 21, 1997: "Executive Pay, It's Out of Control, By relying heavily on stock options, many companies make exorbitant payouts for so-so performances, dilute real shareholder return, and glorify CEOs at the expense of other employees. The bottom line: Don't Confuse a bull market with managerial genius."

(3) *Business Week* assembled the following information about the relationship between average CEO compensation as compared with average incomes in other occupations for the period 1960–1992:

Year	Worker	Teacher	Engineer	CEO
1960	$ 4,665	$ 4,995	$ 9,828	$ 190,383
1970	$ 6,933	$ 8,626	$14,695	$ 548,787
1980	$15,008	$15,970	$28,486	$ 624,996
1992	$24,411	$34,098	$58,240	$3,842,247

John A. Byrne, Executive Pay: The Party Ain't Over Yet; Reform May Be In the Works * * * But So Far, You Wouldn't Know It, Business Week, April 23, 1993 at 56–57. Between 1960 and 1992, average CEO compensation grew from about 50 times the average worker's salary to 150 times that salary. By 1996, CEO compensation had grown to 209 times the average worker's compensation. In contrast, comparable ratios in Europe and Japan have remained stable during this period between 15:1 to 25:1. James E. Heard, Executive Compensation: Shareholders Focus Concerns On Executive Compensation At 1992 Annual Meetings, Insights, Vol. 6, No. 6 at 20 (June 1992). The 1996 figure appears in Jennifer Reingold, Executive Pay, Business Week, April 21, 1997, at 58, 59. See also John A. Byrne, How High Can CEO Pay Go? Business Week, April 22, 1996, at 100–101:

Year	Executive Pay	Worker Pay	Layoffs
1990	$1.95 million	$176 billion	316,047
1995	$3.75 million	$308 billion	439,882
—	+75%	+16%	+39%

(4) Lawrence Rout, Editor's Note, Executive Pay, Wall Street Journal, April 10, 1997, at R2:

In 1990, when we first started doing this report, I recall being amazed at the number of calls and letters we received about CEO compensation. "Obscene," "unfair," "ridiculous,"—people were really angry.

What surprised me even more, though, was that in subsequent years, the number of angry readers went steadily down. People still wrote, but increasingly it was to complain about those who might want to *limit* how much a CEO could make, Last year, I don't think we got more than a half-dozen of the old-fashioned, how-dare-they-earn-so-much-when-I-earn-so-little responses.

So what's so fascinating about * * * [this year's cover story] is that it suggests the pendulum may be starting to swing back. People are once again beginning to ask, How much is *too* much? More important, at least some of the noise seems to be coming from the boardrooms, where directors are questioning whether pay-for-performance plans really amount to pay-for-showing-up plans.

(5) The average CEO compensation figures set forth above hide some very high compensation levels for individual CEOs. To take some 1996 examples: Lawrence Goss, CEO of Green Tree Financial received $102,449,000 in the form of salary and bonus; Andrew Grove, CEO of Intel received salary and bonus of $3,003,000 plus long term compensation of $94,587,000, Sanford Weill, CEO of Travelers Group received salary and bonus of $6,330,000 plus long term compensation of $87,828,000. The CEO who was listed as twentieth in terms of compensation in 1996 was Drew Lewis, CEO of Union Pacific, whose salary and bonus was $3,131,000 plus long term compensation of $18,320,000, for a total of $21,452,000. Jennifer Reingold, Executive Pay, supra, at 58–59. And, it should be emphasized, these are *annual* salaries; many CEOs appear on the list of highest paid year-

after-year. Douglas C. Michael, The Corporate Officer's Independent Duty as A Tonic for the Anemic Law of Executive Compensation, 17 J. Corp. L. 785, 792 (1993):

> Why does all this arouse the public's outrage? It is not the financial impact; no one has suggested that lavish spending on executive compensation is a severe or even material drain on the earnings of these corporations. Rather, it is the effect on morals and morale, magnified by the current political and economic climate, that is the problem.

(6) Four observations might be made about the very high levels of executive compensation described in the previous notes:

First, they are roughly comparable with compensation levels for the highest paid professional athletes, entertainers and the like. They are considerably higher than the salaries of high-level government officials with roughly comparable (or greater) responsibilities. Mark J. Lowenstein, Reflections on Executive Compensation and a Modest Proposal for (Further) Reform, 50 SMU Law Rev. 201 (1996) points out that "[l]ittle controversy follows a disclosure that a movie star will receive $10 million for his or her next motion picture, but criticism abounds when the media reports that the average compensation for the country's highest paid CEOs exceed $2 million. People feel, instinctively, that if a movie studio pays a star $10 million * * * the star must be worth that much, but the public is skeptical that the studio's CEO is worth $10 million * * *." Why is that? Professor Lowenstein suggests it is because the studio and the star seem to be dealing at arm's length while "the CEO and the board at least seem to sit on the same side of the table when the CEO's compensation is determined."

Second, the amount of compensation paid to specific CEOs does not appear to be directly related either to the size of the business or its long-term profitability. Accidents of history, the supply and demand for corporate executives in specific lines of business, and industry tradition all affect income patterns for specific corporations and specific industries. This is dramatically illustrated by the 1997 Executive Compensation Special Report by Business Week which, for the first time, sought to measure CEO "overachievers" and "underperformers"—those who gave shareholders and companies the most for their pay, and those who gave them the least. Among those who gave shareholders the most for their pay are familiar names: William Gates and Warren Buffett, for example. Those who gave the least include leaders in the race for maximum compensation, Sanford Weill and Lawrence Coss, among others.

Third, despite Professor Michael's comment quoted in note (5), the steady increase in CEO compensation has begun to have an effect on the corporate bottom line and on shareholder wealth. The compensation of Lawrence Coss is unusual in that it is pursuant to a contract (he is paid 2.5 percent of pretax income) so that his 1996 pay directly reduced Green Tree's bottom line by 16 percent. Most long term compensation today is in the form of stock options (discussed below) and are not treated as expenses that reduce the company's reported earnings (but dilute shareholders' interests). If this dilution were treated as an expense, earnings in many companies would have been reduced from 5 to 20 percent. The compensation of many CEOs, in other words, is rising more rapidly than the earnings of these companies. Jennifer Reingold, Corporate Governance, Even Executives Are Wincing at Executive Pay, Business Week, May 12, 1997, at 62.

Fourth, there is some limited empirical work that attempts to study whether CEOs are really overcompensated. There are obvious problems with determining what should be the standard for measuring "how much is too much." Professor Lowenstein reviews this literature and suggests "that no clear answer emerges from this work." 50 SMU L.Rev., supra, at 201.

(7) The principal reason for the growth in compensation levels in the 1990s has been the general acceptance of the idea that it is desirable to tie executive compensation to improvement in shareholder wealth. The most popular way to do this is by granting CEOs options to purchase shares at a fixed price which is set somewhat below the current market price of the stock. The theory is that these options create an incentive for the CEO to increase the market price of the company's shares and thereby benefit all shareholders. And until recently, shareholders generally did not complain about high levels of compensation if that was the consequence of significant increases in the value of the shares. If share values overall increased by billions of dollars, stock option compensation in the tens of millions of dollars to the CEO may seem well worth it to many shareholders. However, share prices are affected by things other than CEO competence: First, the long-term bull market in stocks; second, the wide-spread use of stock options that have an exercise price *below* the current market price—instant value creation, so to speak; and, third, share repurchase plans under which companies in effect support their stock price by making open-market repurchases of their shares. Where stock prices do not go up, some corporations have revised management stock options by reducing the exercise price, thus guaranteeing senior executives a profit even their efforts may have led to a reduction in the value of the company's stock.

(8) CEOs of corporations that are not doing well also receive substantial compensation. For example, Stephen M. Case, CEO of American Online, Inc., received compensation totaling $33.5 million from 1993 through 1996 even though the company had a return on equity of minus 413 percent during this period.

(9) Is there any chance of attacking high-levels of executive compensation as "self-dealing" or as "spoilation or waste"? Presumably if a CEO actually "writes his own ticket," without review by independent directors or shareholders, a test of "fairness" or "intrinsic fairness" might be applicable. Nevertheless it is not at all clear whether such a test would effectively limit CEO compensation. How could a court apply a fairness test except by comparing a CEO's income with the incomes of other CEOs? Might this not lead to putting the label of "fair" on compensation levels in the millions or tens of millions of dollars? In any event, however, the "spoilation or waste" standards of Rogers v. Hill apparently have not been invoked to attack modern levels of executive compensation.

(10) In most publicly held corporations today, of course, the CEO does not "write his own ticket." Rather, there is a compensation committee that is composed of outside directors to pass on levels of executive compensation; presumably if this committee approves the level of compensation for the CEO the test will shift from "fairness" to "lack of business judgment." Traditionally, compensation committees acted in a reactive role, screening management proposals rather than implementing their own policies, but with the furor over executive compensation levels and the additional legal requirements being imposed on compensation committees discussed below, those committees are taking a more active role in establishing policies and goals. However, compensation committees usually strive to to assure comparability with compensation paid to executives with similar responsibilities in other publicly held corporations. Comparability is usually based on surveys conducted by compensation-consulting firms. Committees may simply "slot" an executive within the range of compensation levels for executives with

similar responsibilities using, for example, the 75th percentile as a reference point for the compensation level for a satisfactory employee, or the 85th percentile for one who has shown superior performance. While committees thus obviously consider job-related performance as well as comparability in setting compensation levels, the use of comparability as a factor probably assures that salary levels continue to rise even with an independent compensation committee. See Joseph Hinsey, The Buck Starts Here: The Who, What & How of a Compensation Committee, Bus. Law Today, Mar./Apr. 1993, at 32.

(11) Professor Lowenstein suggests that the current furor over executive compensation can be traced to deficiencies in corporate governance. Mark J. Lowenstein, Reflections on Executive Compensation and a Modest Proposal for (Further) Reform, 50 SMU Law Rev. 201, 221–22 (1996). Do you agree? His "modest proposal" for further reform is to require that shareholders vote annually to approve or disapprove the CEO's annual compensation package. The vote would be advisory but a negative vote should have major repercussions. A positive vote presumably would be viewed as a ratification of the compensation plan. Do you think this is a good idea? Consider also the suggestion of Charles M. Elson, Executive Overcompensation—A Board–Based Solution, 34 Boston Coll.L.Rev. 937 (1993), to increase the holdings of shares by disinterested directors by paying their compensation in restricted stock. He states that an apparent relationship exists between fairness of executive compensation and the number of outside directors with significant equity holdings. This suggestion is, of course, consistent with the proposal that directors should generally be paid in stock rather than in cash or retirement benefits.

(12) Executive compensation has been the target of regulatory actions in the 1990s that have the potential of increasing scrutiny of that sensitive subject.

(a) *Shareholder Proposals.* For many years, the SEC staff took the position that shareholder proposals relating to executive compensation under rule 14a–8 of the Securities Exchange Act of 1934 (see Chapter 9, Section D, p. 647 supra) were excludable from proxy statements on the ground that they related to the "ordinary business operations" of the issuer. In February 1992, the SEC announced that it was reversing this policy. Shortly thereafter, the staff released letters stating that the following proposals, among others, must be included in proxy statements:

     i) Capping total compensation at no more than 20 times the pay of the average employee;

     ii) Eliminating a retirement plan for directors;

     iii) Prohibiting management bonuses until dividends reach a specified level;

     iv) Adopting a policy that for future stock option grants, the exercise price cannot be adjusted downward; and

     v) Cutting management salaries and stock options until the company becomes profitable.

Regulation of Communications Among Securityholders, S.E.C. Rel. 34–30849, 57 Fed.Reg. 29,564 (1992). Compensation proposals, however, are still excludable if they purport to be self-executing (on the theory that they interfere with the board's management discretion), if they relate to employees other than senior management, or if they relate to pension plans and the like.

(b) *Disclosure of Executive Compensation*. In October 1992, the SEC adopted major amendments to its rules governing disclosure of executive compensation. SEC Rel. No. 33–6962, 57 Fed. Reg. 48,126 (Oct. 16, 1992). These rules have four basic components: (i) they require disclosure in a single table of the specific amounts of compensation awarded, earned, or paid to the chief executive officer and the four most highly compensated executives during the three most recent fiscal years, presented in seven categories; (ii) they require detailed disclosure of specific forms of compensation granted or awarded during the year to the designated executives—awards of stock options or stock appreciation rights, disclosure of exercised and unexercised stock options or stock appreciation rights, awards of long-term incentive plan awards, employment contracts of all types, and pension plans; (iii) they require a line graph comparing total shareholder return on a class of stock with market and industry indicators for five years; and (iv) they require a report on compensation of the designated executives by the Compensation Committee of the board of directors (or if there is no such committee, by the board of directors itself). The report must discuss the bases for awarding compensation, including factors and criteria, and also contain a "specific discussion" of the relationship between the company's performance and the CEO's compensation. In SEC Rel. No. 33–7009, 58 Fed. Reg. 42,882, 42,888 (Aug. 6, 1993), the SEC staff announced the results of a review of over 1,000 proxy statements dealing with the Compensation Committee report. This release states that the quality of the reports ranged from superlative to abysmal with most reports somewhere in between, and that the principal recurring problem was "a lack of specificity." It is difficult to summarize these executive disclosure requirements. The proxy statement set forth in Appendix Two, pages 1111–1128, infra, is an example of their operations. Do you think this approach is desirable, or is it "too much disclosure"?

(c) *Revenue Reconciliation Act of 1993*. This Act added a new § 162(m) to the Internal Revenue Code, disallowing corporate deductions for executive compensation for 1994 and later years to the extent that the compensation for an executive exceeds $1 million per year. This provision applies only to publicly held corporations and only to "covered" employees—the CEO and the four highest paid executives. However, an exception—and it is unquestionably a major exception—is that compensation based "on performance goals" is not subject to disallowance. In a classic example of a tax statute that imposes substantive legal requirements, § 162(m)(4)(C) provides that performance goals (i) must be "determined by a compensation committee of the board of directors of the taxpayer which is comprised solely of 2 or more outside directors," (ii) the material terms under which the remuneration is to be paid must be disclosed to the shareholders and approved by a majority vote before the compensation is awarded, and (iii) the compensation committee must certify that the performance goals and other material terms have been satisfied. Complex and detailed final regulations were issued under this section in 1995. Treas.Reg. § 1.62–27, 60 Fed.Reg. 65534 (1995). Is it appropriate to use the Internal Revenue Code to police the area of executive compensation? Section 162(m) applies only to publicly held corporations; if § 162(m) is a desirable rule, shouldn't it apply to the deductibility of compensation by all corporations? Is one million dollars an appropriate cap? It obviously is an arbitrary round number, which may either be "too high" or "too low," depending on the circumstances. Also, why should it be limited to the CEO and the next three highest paid employees? If the limitation is desirable, shouldn't it apply to all employees with compensation in excess of $1,000,000?

Certainly § 162(m) has had an effect on current compensation practices: Long-term compensation plans have been modified so that they are based on "performance goals" that comply with § 162(m) and the regulations; compensation arrangements have been shifted toward deferred compensation plans; and the membership of compensation committees have been revised to make sure that the members are all "outside" directors as defined in the regulations. However, not all companies have made these adjustments. Since the only effect of noncompliance with § 162(m) is the disallowance of a portion of a corporate deduction, many corporations have simply continued to pay executives in excess of $1.0 million per year and foregone the tax deduction, even though that increases somewhat their total tax bills.

(13) Executive compensation may take many forms. A checklist for the required reporting of various types of compensation under the SEC disclosure program listed 24 different kinds or types of compensation arrangements. See Alan Kailer, Preparing the Executive Compensation Tables, Insights, Vol. 6, No. 12, at 10 (Dec. 1992). Other types of popular compensation plans include:

(a) A *restricted stock plan* involves the issuance of shares to an executive subject to substantial restrictions on transfer or substantial risks of forfeiture which affect its value and which provide incentive to remain with the corporation.

(b) A *phantom stock plan* does not involve the issuance of shares. Rather the executive is credited with "units" on the books of the corporation. The value of a unit is equal to the market value of a share of the corporation's stock when the unit is created, and is increased by the amount of dividends paid on a share of stock plus the increase in value of a share as of a date specified by the participant. Units may be paid on death or retirement, or with the consent of a committee if the participant voluntarily terminates his employment. The plan permits deferral of some income which is based on the market performance of the corporation's stock but no particular tax advantage. See Lieberman v. Koppers Co., 38 Del.Ch. 239, 149 A.2d 756 (1959), affirmed sub nom. Lieberman v. Becker, 38 Del.Ch. 540, 155 A.2d 596 (1959).

(c) *Stock appreciation rights* (SARs) are bonus payments to executives computed on the basis of the growth in value of a predetermined number of hypothetical shares computable and payable at a time partially within the control of the recipient. SARs obviously provide benefits similar to stock options or phantom stock plans. *Performance unit payments* (PUPs) are bonus payments set on a predetermined formula for achieving long-term company goals (e.g., a ten percent compound earnings growth per year over five years). Why are phantom stock plans, SARs, PUPs, and similar arrangements so attractive?

(d) *"Rabbi" and "Secular" Trusts*. Many corporations have nonqualified retirement plans for executives. These plans are usually not funded; the only assurance that nonqualified benefits will actually be forthcoming in the future is the employer's unsecured promise to pay the benefits. Unfunded plans include many deferred compensation arrangements, severance compensation agreements, and retiree life and medical insurance plans. For many executives today unfunded plans represent the majority of the retirement benefits promised to them. It is increasingly accepted that no corporation is too large to be taken over by some other corporation, or so successful as to be immune from all risk of insolvency. As a result, highly compensated employees may be uneasy about the reliability of unsecured promises; they demand some additional assurance or security that the promised benefits will actually be forthcoming. Such assurance is usually provided in the form of "rabbi trusts" or "secular trusts," or by the purchase of commercial insurance or annuity contracts. A "rabbi trust" is a revocable trust created with a bank or trust company as trustee to hold funds for the executive's retirement. The trust becomes irrevocable if a change in control occurs; the assets of such a trust become available to the corporation's creditors in the event of insolvency but the employee is assured of benefits in the absence of that unlikely event. A "secular trust" is similar to a rabbi trust except that in addition to protection against changes in control, the assets of the trust are unavailable to the creditors of the corporation in the event of insolvency. In a secular trust, the employee is taxed on contributions to the trust in the year made; in a rabbi trust (if properly created), the employee is not taxed until the year in which specific benefits are paid or made available to the employee, obviously a desirable tax attribute from the standpoint of the employee.

SINCLAIR OIL CORP. v. LEVIEN

Supreme Court of Delaware, 1971.
280 A.2d 717.

WOLCOTT, CHIEF JUSTICE.

This is an appeal by the defendant, Sinclair Oil Corporation (hereafter Sinclair), from an order of the Court of Chancery, 261 A.2d 911 in a derivative action requiring Sinclair to account for damages sustained by its subsidiary, Sinclair Venezuelan Oil Company (hereafter Sinven), organized by Sinclair for the purpose of operating in Venezuela, as a result of dividends paid by Sinven, the denial to Sinven of industrial development, and a breach of contract between Sinclair's wholly-owned subsidiary, Sinclair International Oil Company, and Sinven.

Sinclair, operating primarily as a holding company, is in the business of exploring for oil and of producing and marketing crude oil and oil products. At all times relevant to this litigation, it owned about 97% of Sinven's stock. The plaintiff owns about 3000 of 120,000 publicly held shares of Sinven. Sinven, incorporated in 1922, has been engaged in petroleum operations primarily in Venezuela and since 1959 has operated exclusively in Venezuela.

Sinclair nominates all members of Sinven's board of directors. The Chancellor found as a fact that the directors were not independent of Sinclair. Almost without exception, they were officers, directors, or employees of corporations in the Sinclair complex. By reason of Sinclair's domination, it is clear that Sinclair owed Sinven a fiduciary duty. Sinclair concedes this.

The Chancellor held that because of Sinclair's fiduciary duty and its control over Sinven, its relationship with Sinven must meet the test of intrinsic fairness. The standard of intrinsic fairness involves both a high degree of fairness and a shift in the burden of proof. Under this standard the burden is on Sinclair to prove, subject to careful judicial scrutiny, that its transactions with Sinven were objectively fair. Guth v. Loft, Inc., 23 Del.Ch. 255, 5 A.2d 503 (1939).

Sinclair argues that the transactions between it and Sinven should be tested, not by the test of intrinsic fairness with the accompanying shift of the burden of proof, but by the business judgment rule under which a court will not interfere with the judgment of a board of directors unless there is a showing of gross and palpable overreaching. Meyerson v. El Paso Natural Gas

Co., 246 A.2d 789 (Del.Ch.1967). A board of directors enjoys a presumption of sound business judgment, and its decisions will not be disturbed if they can be attributed to any rational business purpose. A court under such circumstances will not substitute its own notions of what is or is not sound business judgment.

We think, however, that Sinclair's argument in this respect is misconceived. When the situation involves a parent and a subsidiary, with the parent controlling the transaction and fixing the terms, the test of intrinsic fairness, with its resulting shifting of the burden of proof, is applied. The basic situation for the application of the rule is the one in which the parent has received a benefit to the exclusion and at the expense of the subsidiary.

Recently, this court dealt with the question of fairness in parent-subsidiary dealings in Getty Oil Co. v. Skelly Oil Co., [267 A.2d 833 (Del.Sup.) 1970]. In that case, both parent and subsidiary were in the business of refining and marketing crude oil and crude oil products. The Oil Import Board ruled that the subsidiary, because it was controlled by the parent, was no longer entitled to a separate allocation of imported crude oil. The subsidiary then contended that it had a right to share the quota of crude oil allotted to the parent. We ruled that the business judgment standard should be applied to determine this contention. Although the subsidiary suffered a loss through the administration of the oil import quotas, the parent gained nothing. The parent's quota was derived solely from its own past use. The past use of the subsidiary did not cause an increase in the parent's quota. Nor did the parent usurp a quota of the subsidiary. Since the parent received nothing from the subsidiary to the exclusion of the minority stockholders of the subsidiary, there was no self-dealing. Therefore, the business judgment standard was properly applied.

A parent does indeed owe a fiduciary duty to its subsidiary when there are parent-subsidiary dealings. However, this alone will not evoke the intrinsic fairness standard. This standard will be applied only when the fiduciary duty is accompanied by self-dealing—the situation when a parent is on both sides of a transaction with its subsidiary. Self-dealing occurs when the parent, by virtue of its domination of the subsidiary, causes the subsidiary to act in such a way that the parent receives something from the subsidiary to the exclusion of, and detriment to, the minority stockholders of the subsidiary.

We turn now to the facts. The plaintiff argues that, from 1960 through 1966, Sinclair caused Sinven to pay out such excessive dividends that the industrial development of Sinven was effectively prevented, and it became in reality a corporation in dissolution.

From 1960 through 1966, Sinven paid out $108,000,000 in dividends ($38,000,000 in excess of Sinven's earnings during the same period). The Chancellor held that Sinclair caused these dividends to be paid during a period when it had a need for large amounts of cash. Although the dividends paid exceeded earnings, the plaintiff concedes that the payments were made in compliance with 8 Del.C. § 170, authorizing payment of dividends out of surplus or net profits. However, the plaintiff attacks these dividends on the ground that they resulted from an improper motive—Sinclair's need for cash. The Chancellor, applying the intrinsic fairness standard, held that Sinclair did not sustain its burden of proving that these dividends were intrinsically fair to the minority stockholders of Sinven.

Since it is admitted that the dividends were paid in strict compliance with 8 Del.C. § 170, the alleged excessiveness of the payments alone would not state a cause of action. Nevertheless, compliance with the applicable statute may not, under all circumstances, justify all dividend payments. If a plaintiff can meet his burden of proving that a dividend cannot be grounded on any reasonable business objective, then the courts can and will interfere with the board's decision to pay the dividend.

Sinclair contends that it is improper to apply the intrinsic fairness standard to dividend payments even when the board which voted for the dividends is completely dominated. In support of this contention, Sinclair relies heavily on American District Telegraph Co. [ADT] v. Grinnell Corp., (N.Y.Sup.Ct.1969) aff'd. 33 A.D.2d 769, 306 N.Y.S.2d 209 (1969). Plaintiffs were minority stockholders of ADT, a subsidiary of Grinnell. The plaintiffs alleged that Grinnell, realizing that it would soon have to sell its ADT stock because of a pending anti-trust action, caused ADT to pay excessive dividends. Because the dividend payments conformed with applicable statutory law, and the plaintiffs could not prove an abuse of discretion, the court ruled that the complaint did not state a cause of action. Other decisions seem to support Sinclair's contention. In Metropolitan Casualty Ins. Co. v. First State Bank of Temple, 54 S.W.2d 358 (Tex.Civ.App.1932), rev'd. on other grounds, 79 S.W.2d 835 (Sup.Ct.1935), the court held that a majority of interested directors does not void a declaration of dividends because all directors, by necessity, are interested in and benefited by a dividend declaration.

We do not accept the argument that the intrinsic fairness test can never be applied to a dividend declaration by a dominated board, although a dividend declaration by a dominated board will not inevitably demand the application of the intrinsic fairness standard. Moskowitz v. Bantrell, 41 Del.Ch. 177, 190 A.2d 749 (Del.Supr.1963). If such a dividend is in essence self-dealing by the parent, then the intrinsic fairness standard is the proper standard. For example, suppose a parent dominates a subsidiary and its board of directors. The subsidiary has outstanding two classes of stock, X and Y. Class X is owned by the parent and Class Y is owned by minority stockholders of the subsidiary. If the subsidiary, at the direction of the parent, declares a dividend on its Class X stock only, this might well be self-dealing by the parent. It would be receiving something from the subsidiary to the exclusion of and detrimental to its minority stockholders. This self-dealing, coupled with the parent's fiduciary duty, would make intrinsic fairness the proper standard by which to evaluate the dividend payments.

Consequently it must be determined whether the dividend payments by Sinven were, in essence, self-dealing by Sinclair. The dividends resulted in great sums of money being transferred from Sinven to Sinclair. However, a proportionate share of this money was received by the minority shareholders of Sinven. Sinclair received nothing from Sinven to the exclusion of its minority stockholders. As such, these dividends were not self-dealing. We hold therefore that the Chancellor erred in applying the intrinsic fairness test as to these dividend payments. The business judgment standard should have been applied.

We conclude that the facts demonstrate that the dividend payments complied with the business judgment standard and with 8 Del.C. § 170. The motives for causing the declaration of dividends are immaterial unless the plaintiff can show that the dividend payments resulted from improper motives and amounted to waste. The plaintiff contends only that the dividend payments drained Sinven of cash to such an extent that it was prevented from expanding.

The plaintiff proved no business opportunities which came to Sinven independently and which Sinclair either took to itself or denied to Sinven. As a matter of fact, with two minor exceptions which resulted in losses, all of Sinven's operations have been conducted in Venezuela, and Sinclair had a policy of exploiting its oil properties located in different countries by subsidiaries located in the particular countries.

From 1960 to 1966 Sinclair purchased or developed oil fields in Alaska, Canada, Paraguay, and other places around the world. The plaintiff contends that these were all opportunities which could have been taken by Sinven. The Chancellor concluded that Sinclair had not proved that its denial of expansion opportunities to Sinven was intrinsically fair. He based this conclusion on the following findings of fact. Sinclair made no real effort to expand Sinven. The excessive dividends paid by Sinven resulted in so great a cash drain as to effectively deny to Sinven any ability to expand. During this same period Sinclair actively pursued a company-wide policy of developing through its subsidiaries new sources of revenue, but Sinven was not permitted to participate and was confined in its activities to Venezuela.

However, the plaintiff could point to no opportunities which came to Sinven. Therefore, Sinclair usurped no business opportunity belonging to Sinven. Since Sinclair received nothing from Sinven to the exclusion of and detriment to Sinven's minority stockholders, there was no self-dealing. Therefore, business judgment is the proper standard by which to evaluate Sinclair's expansion policies.

Since there is no proof of self-dealing on the part of Sinclair, it follows that the expansion policy of Sinclair and the methods used to achieve the desired result must, as far as Sinclair's treatment of Sinven is concerned, be tested by the standards of the business judgment rule. Accordingly, Sinclair's decision, absent fraud or gross overreaching, to achieve expansion through the medium of its subsidiaries, other than Sinven, must be upheld.

Even if Sinclair was wrong in developing these opportunities as it did, the question arises, with which subsidiaries should these opportunities have been shared? No evidence indicates a unique need or ability of Sinven to develop these opportunities. The decision of which subsidiaries would be used to implement Sinclair's expansion policy was one of business judgment with which a court will not interfere absent a showing of gross and palpable overreaching. No such showing has been made here.

Next, Sinclair argues that the Chancellor committed error when he held it liable to Sinven for breach of contract.

In 1961 Sinclair created Sinclair International Oil Company (hereafter International), a wholly owned subsidiary used for the purpose of coordinating all of Sinclair's foreign operations. All crude purchases by Sinclair were made thereafter through International.

On September 28, 1961, Sinclair caused Sinven to contract with International whereby Sinven agreed to sell all of its crude oil and refined products to International at specified prices. The contract provided for minimum and maximum quantities and prices. The plaintiff contends that Sinclair caused this contract to be breached in two respects. Although the contract called for payment on receipt, International's payments lagged as much as 30 days after receipt. Also, the contract required International to purchase at least a fixed minimum amount of crude and refined products from Sinven. International did not comply with this requirement.

Clearly, Sinclair's act of contracting with its dominated subsidiary was self-dealing. Under the contract Sinclair received the products produced by Sinven, and of course the minority shareholders of Sinven were not able to share in the receipt of these products. If the contract was breached, then Sinclair received these products to the detriment of Sinven's minority shareholders. We agree with the Chancellor's finding that the contract was breached by Sinclair, both as to the time of payments and the amounts purchased.

Although a parent need not bind itself by a contract with its dominated subsidiary, Sinclair chose to operate in this manner. As Sinclair has received the benefits of this contract, so must it comply with the contractual duties.

Under the intrinsic fairness standard, Sinclair must prove that its causing Sinven not to enforce the contract was intrinsically fair to the minority shareholders of Sinven. Sinclair has failed to meet this burden. Late payments were clearly breaches for which Sinven should have sought and received adequate damages. As to the quantities purchased, Sinclair argues that it purchased all the products produced by Sinven. This, however, does not satisfy the standard of intrinsic fairness. Sinclair has failed to prove that Sinven could not possibly have produced or some way have obtained the contract minimums. As such, Sinclair must account on this claim.

Finally, Sinclair argues that the Chancellor committed error in refusing to allow it a credit or setoff of all benefits provided by it to Sinven with respect to all the alleged damages. The Chancellor held that setoff should be allowed on specific transactions, e.g., benefits to Sinven under the contract with International, but denied an overall setoff against all damages claimed. We agree with the Chancellor, although the point may well be moot in view of our holding that Sinclair is not required to account for the alleged excessiveness of the dividend payments.

We will therefore reverse that part of the Chancellor's order that requires Sinclair to account to Sinven for damages sustained as a result of dividends paid between 1960 and 1966, and by reason of the denial to Sinven of expansion during that period. We will affirm the remaining portion of that order and remand the cause for further proceedings.

Notes

(1) Serious problems can arise in a number of areas whenever there are minority shareholders in a corporate subsidiary. For example, the Internal Revenue Code permits a corporation to file a "consolidated return" with subsidiaries that are at least 80 percent owned. The effect of consolidation is that a single return is filed covering the income or loss of all the corporations as a group, and the result may be that a valuable tax loss owned by a subsidiary may be utilized to

offset income of the parent or of other subsidiaries within the group. Today, problems created by consolidated returns within parent/subsidiary groups are usually handled by formal written agreements, known as tax allocation or tax sharing agreements. These agreements typically provide that the parent corporation will compensate the subsidiary in cash for the net tax benefits actually obtained by the parent as a result of the consolidation. For a case involving such an agreement (after the subsidiary was sold by the parent to an outside third party), see Summit Nat'l Life Ins. Co. v. Cargill, Inc., 807 F.Supp. 363 (E.D.Pa. 1992), affirmed 981 F.2d 1248 (3d Cir.1992).

(2) Given such problems, does it help to include a clause in the subsidiary's articles of incorporation that attempts to validate all transactions between subsidiary and parent, and in effect warns shareholders that such transactions may take place? While such a clause will not provide total protection, it may be given some effect by shifting the burden of proving unfairness or "exonerating" the arrangement from "adverse inferences." See Spiegel v. Beacon Participations, Inc., 297 Mass. 398, 417, 8 N.E.2d 895, 907 (1937). Such clauses also usually cover transactions between corporations with common directors (interlocking directors) but with no ownership of securities of one corporation by the other.

(3) Problems such as those involved in the principal case can be avoided by the elimination of the minority shareholders. How can this be done? A negotiated buy-out? What if the minority is unwilling to sell at a reasonable price? Could Sinclair create a wholly owned subsidiary, "X Corporation," transfer its holdings of Sinven to it, and then merge Sinven into X Corporation, requiring the minority shareholders to accept cash rather than X Corporation stock? Compare MBCA §§ 11.01(b)(3) particularly the phrase "or into cash or other property in whole or in part," 11.03(b), 11.04; see also *Virginia Bankshares,* page 632, supra. What protection does the minority have? See MBCA § 13.02(a) and, generally, MBCA ch. 13. Should there be any judicial review of the motives of the controlling shareholders proposing such mergers?

WEINBERGER v. UOP, INC.

Supreme Court of Delaware, 1983.
457 A.2d 701.

Before HERRMANN, C.J., McNEILLY, QUILLEN, HORSEY and MOORE, JJ., constituting the Court en Banc.

MOORE, JUSTICE:

This post-trial appeal was reheard en banc from a decision of the Court of Chancery. It was brought by the class action plaintiff below, a former shareholder of UOP, Inc., who challenged the elimination of UOP's minority shareholders by a cash-out merger between UOP and its majority owner, The Signal Companies, Inc. * * * [T]he defendants in this action were Signal, UOP, [and] certain officers and directors of those companies * * *. The present Chancellor held that the terms of the merger were fair to the plaintiff and the other minority shareholders of UOP. Accordingly, he entered judgment in favor of the defendants.

Numerous points were raised by the parties, but we address only the following questions presented by the trial court's opinion:

(1) The plaintiff's duty to plead sufficient facts demonstrating the unfairness of the challenged merger;

(2) The burden of proof upon the parties where the merger has been approved by the purportedly informed vote of a majority of the minority shareholders;

(3) The fairness of the merger in terms of adequacy of the defendants' disclosures to the minority shareholders;

(4) The fairness of the merger in terms of adequacy of the price paid for the minority shares and the remedy appropriate to that issue; and

(5) The continued force and effect of Singer v. Magnavox Co., Del.Supr., 380 A.2d 969, 980 (1977), and its progeny. * * *

I.

The facts found by the trial court, pertinent to the issues before us, are supported by the record, and we draw from them as set out in the Chancellor's opinion.

Signal is a diversified, technically based company operating through various subsidiaries. Its stock is publicly traded on the New York, Philadelphia and Pacific Stock Exchanges. UOP, formerly known as Universal Oil Products Company, was a diversified industrial company engaged in various lines of business, including petroleum and petrochemical services and related products, construction, fabricated metal products, transportation equipment products, chemicals and plastics, and other products and services including land development, lumber products and waste disposal. Its stock was publicly held and listed on the New York Stock Exchange.

In 1974 Signal sold one of its wholly-owned subsidiaries for $420,000,000 in cash. See Gimbel v. Signal Companies, Inc., Del.Ch., 316 A.2d 599, aff'd, Del.Supr., 316 A.2d 619 (1974). While looking to invest this cash surplus, Signal became interested in UOP as a possible acquisition. Friendly negotiations ensued, and Signal proposed to acquire a controlling interest in UOP at a price of $19 per share. UOP's representatives sought $25 per share. In the arm's length bargaining that followed, an understanding was reached whereby Signal agreed to purchase from UOP 1,500,000 shares of UOP's authorized but unissued stock at $21 per share.

This purchase was contingent upon Signal making a successful cash tender offer for 4,300,000 publicly held shares of UOP, also at a price of $21 per share. This combined method of acquisition permitted Signal to acquire 5,800,000 shares of stock, representing 50.5% of UOP's outstanding shares. The UOP board of directors advised the company's shareholders that it had no objection to Signal's tender offer at that price. Immediately before the announcement of the tender offer, UOP's common stock had been trading on the New York Stock Exchange at a fraction under $14 per share.

The negotiations between Signal and UOP occurred during April 1975, and the resulting tender offer was greatly oversubscribed. However, Signal limited its total purchase of the tendered shares so that, when coupled with the stock bought from UOP, it had achieved its goal of becoming a 50.5% shareholder of UOP.

Although UOP's board consisted of thirteen directors, Signal nominated and elected only six. Of these, five were either directors or employees of Signal. The sixth, a partner in the banking firm of Lazard Freres & Co., had been one of Signal's representatives in the negotiations and bargaining with UOP concerning the tender offer and purchase price of the UOP shares.

However, the president and chief executive officer of UOP retired during 1975, and Signal caused him to be replaced by James V. Crawford, a long-time employee and senior executive vice president of one of Signal's wholly-owned subsidiaries. Crawford succeeded his predecessor on UOP's board of directors and also was made a director of Signal.

By the end of 1977 Signal basically was unsuccessful in finding other suitable investment candidates for its excess cash, and by February 1978 considered that it had no other realistic acquisitions available to it on a friendly basis. Once again its attention turned to UOP.

The trial court found that at the instigation of certain Signal management personnel, including William W. Walkup, its board chairman, and Forrest N. Shumway, its president, a feasibility study was made concerning the possible acquisition of the balance of UOP's outstanding shares. This study was performed by two Signal officers, Charles S. Arledge, vice president (director of planning), and Andrew J. Chitiea, senior vice president (chief financial officer). Messrs. Walkup, Shumway, Arledge and Chitiea were all directors of UOP in addition to their membership on the Signal board.

Arledge and Chitiea concluded that it would be a good investment for Signal to acquire the remaining 49.5% of UOP shares at any price up to $24 each. Their report was discussed between Walkup and Shumway who, along with Arledge, Chitiea and Brewster L. Arms, internal counsel for Signal, constituted Signal's senior management. In particular, they talked about the proper price to be paid if the acquisition was pursued, purportedly keeping in mind that as UOP's majority shareholder, Signal owed a fiduciary responsibility to both its own stockholders as well as to UOP's minority. It was ultimately agreed that a meeting of Signal's executive committee would be called to propose that Signal acquire the remaining outstanding stock of UOP through a cash-out merger in the range of $20 to $21 per share.

The executive committee meeting was set for February 28, 1978. As a courtesy, UOP's president, Crawford, was invited to attend, although he was not a member of Signal's executive committee. On his arrival, and prior to the meeting, Crawford was asked to meet privately with Walkup and Shumway. He was then told of Signal's plan to acquire full ownership of UOP and was asked for his reaction to the proposed price range of $20 to $21 per share. Crawford said he thought such a price would be "generous", and that it was certainly one which should be submitted to UOP's minority shareholders for their ultimate consideration. He stated, however, that Signal's 100% ownership could cause internal problems at UOP. He believed that employees would have to be given some assurance of their future place in a fully-owned Signal subsidiary. Otherwise, he feared the departure of essential personnel. Also, many of UOP's key employees had stock option incentive programs which would be wiped out by a merger. Crawford therefore urged that some adjustment would have to be made, such as providing a comparable incentive in Signal's shares, if after the merger he was to maintain his quality of personnel and efficiency at UOP.

Thus, Crawford voiced no objection to the $20 to $21 price range, nor did he suggest that Signal should consider paying more than $21 per share for the minority interests. Later, at the executive committee meeting the same factors were discussed, with Crawford repeating the position he earlier took with Walkup and Shumway. Also considered was the 1975 tender offer and the fact that it had been greatly oversubscribed at $21 per share. For many reasons, Signal's management concluded that the acquisition of UOP's minority shares provided the solution to a number of its business problems.

Thus, it was the consensus that a price of $20 to $21 per share would be fair to both Signal and the minority shareholders of UOP. Signal's executive committee authorized its management "to negotiate" with UOP "for a cash acquisition of the minority ownership in UOP, Inc., with the intention of presenting a proposal to [Signal's] board of directors * * * on March 6, 1978". Immediately after this February 28, 1978 meeting, Signal issued a press release stating:

> The Signal Companies, Inc. and UOP, Inc. are conducting negotiations for the acquisition for cash by Signal of the 49.5 percent of UOP which it does not presently own, announced Forrest N. Shumway, president and chief executive officer of Signal, and James V. Crawford, UOP president.

> Price and other terms of the proposed transaction have not yet been finalized and would be subject to approval of the boards of directors of Signal and UOP, scheduled to meet early next week, the stockholders of UOP and certain federal agencies.

The announcement also referred to the fact that the closing price of UOP's common stock on that day was $14.50 per share.

Two days later, on March 2, 1978, Signal issued a second press release stating that its management would recommend a price in the range of $20 to $21 per share for UOP's 49.5% minority interest. This announcement referred to Signal's earlier statement that "negotiations" were being conducted for the acquisition of the minority shares.

Between Tuesday, February 28, 1978 and Monday, March 6, 1978, a total of four business days, Crawford spoke by telephone with all of UOP's non-Signal, i.e., outside, directors. Also during that period, Crawford retained Lehman Brothers to render a fairness opinion as to the price offered the minority for its stock. He gave two reasons for this choice. First, the time schedule between the announcement and the board meetings was short (by then only three business days) and since Lehman Brothers had been acting as UOP's investment banker for many years, Crawford felt that it would be in the best position to respond on such brief notice. Second, James W. Glanville, a long-time director of UOP and a partner in Lehman Brothers, had acted as a financial advisor to UOP for many years. Crawford believed that Glanville's familiarity with UOP, as a member of its board, would also be of assistance in enabling Lehman Brothers to render a fairness opinion within the existing time constraints.

Crawford telephoned Glanville, who gave his assurance that Lehman Brothers had no conflicts that would prevent it from accepting the task. Glanville's immediate personal reaction was that a price of $20 to $21 would certainly be fair, since it represented almost a 50% premium over UOP's market price. Glanville sought a $250,000 fee for Lehman Brothers' services, but Crawford thought this too much. After further discussions Glanville finally agreed that Lehman Brothers would render its fairness opinion for $150,000.

During this period Crawford also had several telephone contacts with Signal officials. In only one of them, however, was the price of the shares discussed. In a conversation with Walkup, Crawford advised that as a result of his communications with UOP's non-Signal directors, it was his feeling that the price would have to be the top of the proposed range, or $21 per share, if the approval of UOP's outside directors was to be obtained. But again, he did not seek any price higher than $21.

Glanville assembled a three-man Lehman Brothers team to do the work on the fairness opinion. These persons examined relevant documents and information concerning UOP, including its annual reports and its Securities and Exchange Commission filings from 1973 through 1976, as well as its audited financial statements for 1977, its interim reports to shareholders, and its recent and historical market prices and trading volumes. In addition, on Friday, March 3, 1978, two members of the Lehman Brothers team flew to UOP's headquarters in Des Plaines, Illinois, to perform a "due diligence" visit, during the course of which they interviewed Crawford as well as UOP's general counsel, its chief financial officer, and other key executives and personnel.

As a result, the Lehman Brothers team concluded that "the price of either $20 or $21 would be a fair price for the remaining shares of UOP". They telephoned this impression to Glanville, who was spending the weekend in Vermont.

On Monday morning, March 6, 1978, Glanville and the senior member of the Lehman Brothers team flew to Des Plaines to attend the scheduled UOP directors meeting. Glanville looked over the assembled information during the flight. The two had with them the draft of a "fairness opinion letter" in which the price had been left blank. Either during or immediately prior to the directors' meeting, the two-page "fairness opinion letter" was typed in final form and the price of $21 per share was inserted.

On March 6, 1978, both the Signal and UOP boards were convened to consider the proposed merger. Telephone communications were maintained between the two meetings. Walkup, Signal's board chairman, and also a UOP director, attended UOP's meeting with Crawford in order to present Signal's position and answer any questions that UOP's non-Signal directors might have. Arledge and Chitiea, along with Signal's other designees on UOP's board, participated by conference telephone. All of UOP's outside directors attended the meeting either in person or by conference telephone.

First, Signal's board unanimously adopted a resolution authorizing Signal to propose to UOP a cash merger of $21 per share as outlined in a certain merger agreement and other supporting documents. This proposal required that the merger be approved by a majority of UOP's outstanding minority shares voting at the stockholders meeting at which the merger would be considered, and that the minority shares voting in favor of the merger, when coupled with Signal's 50.5% interest would have to comprise at least two-thirds of all UOP shares. Otherwise the proposed merger would be deemed disapproved.

UOP's board then considered the proposal. Copies of the agreement were delivered to the directors in attendance, and other copies had been forwarded earlier to the directors participating by telephone. They also had before them UOP financial data for 1974–1977, UOP's most recent financial statements, market price information, and budget projections for 1978. In addition they had Lehman Brothers' hurriedly prepared fairness opinion letter finding the price of $21 to be fair. Glanville, the Lehman Brothers partner, and UOP director, commented on the information that had gone into preparation of the letter.

Signal also suggests that the Arledge–Chitiea feasibility study, indicating that a price of up to $24 per share would be a "good investment" for Signal, was discussed at the UOP directors' meeting. The Chancellor made no such finding, and our independent review of the record, detailed infra, satisfies us by a preponderance of the evidence that there was no discussion of this document at UOP's board meeting. Furthermore, it is clear beyond peradventure that nothing in that report was ever disclosed to UOP's minority shareholders prior to their approval of the merger.

After consideration of Signal's proposal, Walkup and Crawford left the meeting to permit a free and uninhibited exchange between UOP's non-Signal directors. Upon their return a resolution to accept Signal's offer was then proposed and adopted. While Signal's men on UOP's board participated in various aspects of the meeting, they abstained from voting. However, the minutes show that each of them "if voting would have voted yes".

On March 7, 1978, UOP sent a letter to its shareholders advising them of the action taken by UOP's board with respect to Signal's offer. This document pointed out, among other things, that on February 28, 1978 "both companies had announced negotiations were being conducted".

Despite the swift board action of the two companies, the merger was not submitted to UOP's shareholders until their annual meeting on May 26, 1978. In the notice of that meeting and proxy statement sent to shareholders in May, UOP's management and board urged that the merger be approved. The proxy statement also advised:

> The price was determined after *discussions* between James V. Crawford, a director of Signal and Chief Executive Officer of UOP, and officers of Signal which took place during meetings on February 28, 1978, and in the course of several subsequent telephone conversations. (Emphasis added.)

In the original draft of the proxy statement the word "negotiations" had been used rather than "discussions". However, when the Securities and Exchange Commission sought details of the "negotiations" as part of its review of these materials, the term was deleted and the word "discussions" was substituted. The proxy statement indicated that the vote of UOP's board in approving the merger had been unanimous. It also advised the shareholders that Lehman Brothers had given its opinion that the merger price of $21 per share was fair to UOP's minority. However, it did not disclose the hurried method by which this conclusion was reached.

As of the record date of UOP's annual meeting, there were 11,488,302 shares of UOP common stock outstanding, 5,688,302 of which were owned by the minority. At the meeting only 56%, or 3,208,652, of the minority shares were voted. Of these, 2,953,812, or 51.9% of the total minority, voted for the merger, and 254,840 voted against it. When Signal's stock was added to the minority shares voting in favor, a total of 76.2% of UOP's outstanding shares approved the merger while only 2.2% opposed it.

By its terms the merger became effective on May 26, 1978, and each share of UOP's stock held by the minority was automatically converted into a right to receive $21 cash.

II.

A.

A primary issue mandating reversal is the preparation by two UOP directors, Arledge and Chitiea, of their feasibility study for the exclusive use and benefit of Signal. This document was of obvious significance to both Signal and UOP. Using UOP data, it described the advantages to Signal of ousting the minority at a price range of $21–$24 per share. Mr. Arledge, one of the authors, outlined the benefits to Signal:[7]

Purpose of the Merger

(1) Provides an outstanding investment opportunity for Signal—(Better than any recent acquisition we have seen).

(2) Increases Signal's earnings.

(3) Facilitates the flow of resources between Signal and its subsidiaries—(Big factor—works both ways).

(4) Provides cost savings potential for Signal and UOP.

(5) Improves the percentage of Signal's 'operating earnings' as opposed to 'holding company earnings'.

(6) Simplifies the understanding of Signal.

(7) Facilitates technological exchange among Signal's subsidiaries.

(8) Eliminates potential conflicts of interest.

Having written those words, solely for the use of Signal, it is clear from the record that neither Arledge nor Chitiea shared this report with their fellow directors of UOP. We are satisfied that no one else did either. This conduct hardly meets the fiduciary standards applicable to such a transaction.
* * *

The Arledge–Chitiea report speaks for itself in supporting the Chancellor's finding that a price of up to $24 was a "good investment" for Signal. It shows that a return on the investment at $21 would be 15.7% versus 15.5% at $24 per share. This was a difference of only two-tenths of one percent, while it meant over $17,000,000 to the minority. Under such circumstances, paying UOP's minority shareholders $24 would have had relatively little long-term effect on Signal, and the Chancellor's findings concerning the benefit to Signal, even at a price of $24, were obviously correct.

Certainly, this was a matter of material significance to UOP and its shareholders. Since the study was prepared by two UOP directors, using UOP information for the exclusive benefit of Signal, and nothing whatever was done to disclose it to the outside UOP directors or the minority shareholders,

---

7. [By the Court] The parentheses indicate certain handwritten comments of Mr. Arledge.

a question of breach of fiduciary duty arises. This problem occurs because there were common Signal–UOP directors participating, at least to some extent, in the UOP board's decision-making processes without full disclosure of the conflicts they faced.[8]

B.

In assessing this situation, the Court of Chancery was required to:

> [E]xamine what information defendants had and to measure it against what they gave to the minority stockholders, in a context in which 'complete candor' is required. In other words, the limited function of the Court was to determine whether defendants had disclosed all information in their possession germane to the transaction in issue. And by 'germane' we mean, for present purposes, information such as a reasonable shareholder would consider important in deciding whether to sell or retain stock.

> * * * Completeness, not adequacy, is both the norm and the mandate under present circumstances.

Lynch v. Vickers Energy Corp., Del.Supr., 383 A.2d 278, 281 (1977) (*Lynch I*). This is merely stating in another way the long-existing principle of Delaware law that these Signal designated directors on UOP's board still owed UOP and its shareholders an uncompromising duty of loyalty. The classic language of Guth v. Loft, Inc., Del.Supr., 5 A.2d 503, 510 (1939), requires no embellishment:

> A public policy, existing through the years, and derived from a profound knowledge of human characteristics and motives, has established a rule that demands of a corporate officer or director, peremptorily and inexorably, the most scrupulous observance of his duty, not only affirmatively to protect the interests of the corporation committed to his charge, but also to refrain from doing anything that would work injury to the corporation, or to deprive it of profit or advantage which his skill and ability might properly bring to it, or to enable it to make in the reasonable and lawful exercise of its powers. The rule that requires an undivided and unselfish loyalty to the corporation demands that there shall be no conflict between duty and self-interest."

Given the absence of any attempt to structure this transaction on an arm's length basis, Signal cannot escape the effects of the conflicts it faced, particularly when its designees on UOP's board did not totally abstain from participation in the matter. There is no "safe harbor" for such divided loyalties in Delaware. When directors of a Delaware corporation are on both sides of a transaction, they are required to demonstrate their utmost good

---

8. [By the Court] Although perfection is not possible, or expected, the result here could have been entirely different if UOP had appointed an independent negotiating committee of its outside directors to deal with Signal at arm's length. See, e.g., Harriman v. E.I. Du Pont de Nemours & Co., 411 F.Supp. 133 (D.Del.1975). Since fairness in this context can be equated to conduct by a theoretical, wholly independent, board of directors acting upon the matter before them, it is unfortunate that this course apparently was neither considered nor pursued. Johnston v. Greene, Del.Supr., 121 A.2d 919, 925 (1956). Particularly in a parent-subsidiary context, a showing that the action taken was as though each of the contending parties had in fact exerted its bargaining power against the other at arm's length is strong evidence that the transaction meets the test of fairness. Getty Oil Co. v. Skelly Oil Co., Del.Supr., 267 A.2d 883, 886 (1970).

faith and the most scrupulous inherent fairness of the bargain. Gottlieb v. Heyden Chemical Corp., Del.Supr., 91 A.2d 57, 57–58 (1952). The requirement of fairness is unflinching in its demand that where one stands on both sides of a transaction, he has the burden of establishing its entire fairness, sufficient to pass the test of careful scrutiny by the courts. Sterling v. Mayflower Hotel Corp., Del.Super., 93 A.2d 107, 110 (1952).

There is no dilution of this obligation where one holds dual or multiple directorships, as in a parent-subsidiary context. Levien v. Sinclair Oil Corp., Del.Ch., 261 A.2d 911, 915 (1969). Thus, individuals who act in a dual capacity as directors of two corporations, one of whom is parent and the other subsidiary, owe the same duty of good management to both corporations, and in the absence of an independent negotiating structure (see note [5], supra), or the directors' total abstention from any participation in the matter, this duty is to be exercised in light of what is best for both companies. Warshaw v. Calhoun, Del.Supr., 221 A.2d 487, 492 (1966). The record demonstrates that Signal has not met this obligation.

C.

The concept of fairness has two basic aspects: fair dealing and fair price. The former embraces questions of when the transaction was timed, how it was initiated, structured, negotiated, disclosed to the directors, and how the approvals of the directors and the stockholders were obtained. The latter aspect of fairness relates to the economic and financial considerations of the proposed merger, including all relevant factors: assets, market value, earnings, future prospects, and any other elements that affect the intrinsic or inherent value of a company's stock. Moore, The "Interested" Director or Officer Transaction, 4 Del.J.Corp.L. 674, 676 (1979). See Tri–Continental Corp. v. Battye, Del.Supr., 74 A.2d 71, 72 (1950); 8 Del.C. § 262(h). However, the test for fairness is not a bifurcated one as between fair dealing and price. All aspects of the issue must be examined as a whole since the question is one of entire fairness. However, in a non-fraudulent transaction we recognize that price may be the preponderant consideration outweighing other features of the merger. Here, we address the two basic aspects of fairness separately because we find reversible error as to both.

D.

Part of fair dealing is the obvious duty of candor required by Lynch I, supra. Moreover, one possessing superior knowledge may not mislead any stockholder by use of corporate information to which the latter is not privy. Lank v. Steiner, Del.Supr., 224 A.2d 242, 244 (1966). Delaware has long imposed this duty even upon persons who are not corporate officers or directors, but who nonetheless are privy to matters of interest or significance to their company. Brophy v. Cities Service Co., Del.Ch., 70 A.2d 5, 7 (1949). With the well-established Delaware law on the subject, and the Court of Chancery's findings of fact here, it is inevitable that the obvious conflicts posed by Arledge and Chitiea's preparation of their "feasibility study", derived from UOP information, for the sole use and benefit of Signal, cannot pass muster.

The Arledge–Chitiea report is but one aspect of the element of fair dealing. How did this merger evolve? It is clear that it was entirely initiated by Signal. The serious time constraints under which the principals acted were all set by Signal. It had not found a suitable outlet for its excess cash and considered UOP a desirable investment, particularly since it was now in a position to acquire the whole company for itself. For whatever reasons, and they were only Signal's, the entire transaction was presented to and approved by UOP's board within four business days. Standing alone, this is not necessarily indicative of any lack of fairness by a majority shareholder. It was what occurred, or more properly, what did not occur, during this brief period that makes the time constraints imposed by Signal relevant to the issue of fairness.

The structure of the transaction, again, was Signal's doing. So far as negotiations were concerned, it is clear that they were modest at best. Crawford, Signal's man at UOP, never really talked price with Signal, except to accede to its management's statements on the subject, and to convey to Signal the UOP outside directors' view that as between the $20–$21 range under consideration, it would have to be $21. The latter is not a surprising outcome, but hardly arm's length negotiations. Only the protection of benefits for UOP's key employees and the issue of Lehman Brothers' fee approached any concept of bargaining.

As we have noted, the matter of disclosure to the UOP directors was wholly flawed by the conflicts of interest raised by the Arledge–Chitiea report. All of those conflicts were resolved by Signal in its own favor without divulging any aspect of them to UOP.

This cannot but undermine a conclusion that this merger meets any reasonable test of fairness. The outside UOP directors lacked one material piece of information generated by two of their colleagues, but shared only with Signal. True, the UOP board had the Lehman Brothers' fairness opinion, but that firm has been blamed by the plaintiff for the hurried task it performed, when more properly the responsibility for this lies with Signal. There was no disclosure of the circumstances surrounding the rather cursory preparation of the Lehman Brothers' fairness opinion. Instead, the impression was given UOP's minority that a careful study had been made, when in fact speed was the hallmark, and Mr. Glanville, Lehman's partner in charge of the matter, and also a UOP director, having spent the weekend in Vermont, brought a draft of the "fairness opinion letter" to the UOP directors' meeting on March 6, 1978 with the price left blank. We can only conclude from the record that the rush imposed on Lehman Brothers by Signal's timetable contributed to the difficulties under which this investment banking firm attempted to perform its responsibilities. Yet, none of this was disclosed to UOP's minority.

Finally, the minority stockholders were denied the critical information that Signal considered a price of $24 to be a good investment. Since this would have meant over $17,000,000 more to the minority, we cannot conclude that the shareholder vote was an informed one. Under the circumstances, an approval by a majority of the minority was meaningless. Lynch I, 383 A.2d at 279, 281.

Given these particulars and the Delaware law on the subject, the record does not establish that this transaction satisfies any reasonable concept of fair dealing, and the Chancellor's findings in that regard must be reversed.

E.

Turning to the matter of price, plaintiff also challenges its fairness. His evidence was that on the date the merger was approved the stock was worth at least $26 per share. In support, he offered the testimony of a chartered investment analyst who used two basic approaches to valuation: a comparative analysis of the premium paid over market in ten other tender offer-merger combinations, and a discounted cash flow analysis.

In this breach of fiduciary duty case, the Chancellor perceived that the approach to valuation was the same as that in an appraisal proceeding. Consistent with precedent, he rejected plaintiff's method of proof and accepted defendants' evidence of value as being in accord with practice under prior case law. This means that the so-called "Delaware block" or weighted average method was employed wherein the elements of value, i.e., assets, market price, earnings, etc., were assigned a particular weight and the resulting amounts added to determine the value per share. This procedure has been in use for decades. See In re General Realty & Utilities Corp., Del.Ch., 52 A.2d 6, 14–15 (1947). However, to the extent it excludes other generally accepted techniques used in the financial community and the courts, it is now clearly outmoded. It is time we recognize this in appraisal and other stock valuation proceedings and bring our law current on the subject.

While the Chancellor rejected plaintiff's discounted cash flow method of valuing UOP's stock, as not corresponding with "either logic or the existing law," it is significant that this was essentially the focus, i.e., earnings potential of UOP, of Messrs. Arledge and Chitiea in their evaluation of the merger. Accordingly, the standard "Delaware block" or weighted average method of valuation, formerly employed in appraisal and other stock valuation cases, shall no longer exclusively control such proceedings. We believe that a more liberal approach must include proof of value by any techniques or methods which are generally considered acceptable in the financial community and otherwise admissible in court, subject only to our interpretation of 8 Del.C. § 262(h), infra. This will obviate the very structured and mechanistic procedure that has heretofore governed such matters. See Jacques Coe & Co. v. Minneapolis–Moline Co., Del.Ch., 75 A.2d 244, 247 (1950); Tri–Continental Corp. v. Battye, Del.Ch., 66 A.2d 910, 917–18 (1949).

Fair price obviously requires consideration of all relevant factors involving the value of a company. * * *

Although the Chancellor received the plaintiff's evidence, his opinion indicates that the use of it was precluded because of past Delaware practice. While we do not suggest a monetary result one way or the other, we do think the plaintiff's evidence should be part of the factual mix and weighed as such. Until the $21 price is measured on remand by the valuation standards mandated by Delaware law, there can be no finding at the present stage of these proceedings that the price is fair. Given the lack of any candid disclosure of the material facts surrounding establishment of the $21 price, the majority of the minority vote, approving the merger, is meaningless.

The plaintiff has not sought an appraisal, but rescissory damages of the type contemplated by Lynch v. Vickers Energy Corp., Del., 429 A.2d 497, 505–

06 (1981) (*Lynch II*).[9] In view of the approach to valuation that we announce today, we see no basis in our law for *Lynch II* 's exclusive monetary formula for relief. On remand the plaintiff will be permitted to test the fairness of the $21 price by the standards we herein establish, in conformity with the principle applicable to an appraisal—that fair value be determined by taking "into account all relevant factors" [see 8 Del.C. § 262(h), supra]. In our view this includes the elements of rescissory damages if the Chancellor considers them susceptible of proof and a remedy appropriate to all the issues of fairness before him. To the extent that Lynch II, 429 A.2d at 505–06, purports to limit the Chancellor's discretion to a single remedial formula for monetary damages in a cash-out merger, it is overruled.

RULE

While a plaintiff's monetary remedy ordinarily should be confined to the more liberalized appraisal proceeding herein established, we do not intend any limitation on the historic powers of the Chancellor to grant such other relief as the facts of a particular case may dictate. The appraisal remedy we approve may not be adequate in certain cases, particularly where fraud, misrepresentation, self-dealing, deliberate waste of corporate assets, or gross and palpable overreaching are involved. Cole v. National Cash Credit Association, Del.Ch., 156 A. 183, 187 (1931). Under such circumstances, the Chancellor's powers are complete to fashion any form of equitable and monetary relief as may be appropriate, including rescissory damages. Since it is apparent that this long completed transaction is too involved to undo, and in view of the Chancellor's discretion, the award, if any, should be in the form of monetary damages based upon entire fairness standards, i.e., fair dealing and fair price.

Obviously, there are other litigants, like the plaintiff, who abjured an appraisal and whose rights to challenge the element of fair value must be preserved.[10] Accordingly, the quasi-appraisal remedy we grant the plaintiff here will apply only to: (1) this case; (2) any case now pending on appeal to this Court; (3) any case now pending in the Court of Chancery which has not yet been appealed but which may be eligible for direct appeal to this Court; (4) any case challenging a cash-out merger, the effective date of which is on or before February 1, 1983; and (5) any proposed merger to be presented at a shareholders' meeting, the notification of which is mailed to the stockholders on or before February 23, 1983. Thereafter, the provisions of 8 Del.C. § 262, as herein construed, respecting the scope of an appraisal and the means for perfecting the same, shall govern the financial remedy available to minority shareholders in a cash-out merger. Thus, we return to the well established principles of Stauffer v. Standard Brands, Inc., Del.Supr., 187 A.2d 78 (1962) and David J. Greene & Co. v. Schenley Industries, Inc., Del.Ch., 281 A.2d 30

---

9. [By the Editor] Rescissory damages are defined in *Lynch* as "damages which are the monetary equivalent of rescission and which will, in effect, equal the increment in value that [the defendant] enjoyed as a result of acquiring and holding the * * * stock in issue. That is consistent with the basis for liability which is the law of the case, and it is a norm applied when the equitable remedy of rescission is impractical." 429 A.2d at 501. When calculating rescissory damages, the principle of mitigation of damages is inapplicable, i.e., dam-

ages are not reduced by amounts the plaintiff could have saved by making an investment in the security in question at some later time. However, damages are reduced by any amount received by the plaintiff in connection with the wrongful transaction that gave rise to the right to rescissory damages. Id. at 505–06.

10. [By the Court] Under 8 Del.C. § 262(a), (d) & (e), a stockholder is required to act within certain time periods to perfect the right to an appraisal.

(1971), mandating a stockholder's recourse to the basic remedy of an appraisal.

III.

Finally, we address the matter of business purpose. The defendants contend that the purpose of this merger was not a proper subject of inquiry by the trial court. The plaintiff says that no valid purpose existed—the entire transaction was a mere subterfuge designed to eliminate the minority. The Chancellor ruled otherwise, but in so doing he clearly circumscribed the thrust and effect of *Singer*. This has led to the thoroughly sound observation that the business purpose test "may be * * * virtually interpreted out of existence, as it was in *Weinberger* ".

The requirement of a business purpose is new to our law of mergers and was a departure from prior case law. In view of the fairness test which has long been applicable to parent-subsidiary mergers, Sterling v. Mayflower Hotel Corp., Del.Supr., 93 A.2d 107, 109–10 (1952), the expanded appraisal remedy now available to shareholders, and the broad discretion of the Chancellor to fashion such relief as the facts of a given case may dictate, we do not believe that any additional meaningful protection is afforded minority shareholders by the business purpose requirement of the trilogy of *Singer, Tanzer* [v. International General Industries, Inc., 379 A.2d 1121 (Del.1977)], [Roland International Corp. v.] *Najjar* [407 A.2d 1032 (Del.1979)], and their progeny. Accordingly, such requirement shall no longer be of any force or effect.

 RULE

The judgment of the Court of Chancery, finding both the circumstances of the merger and the price paid the minority shareholders to be fair, is reversed. The matter is remanded for further proceedings consistent herewith. Upon remand the plaintiff's post-trial motion to enlarge the class should be granted. * * *

Reversed and Remanded.

Notes

(1) In a "cash out" merger a parent corporation owning more than 50 percent of the stock of a subsidiary corporation may compel the minority shareholders of the subsidiary to accept cash for their shares in an amount determined by the parent, subject, however, to the appraisal rights provided in Chapter 13 of the MBCA. The process by which this is accomplished is a merger in which minority shareholders in the subsidiary corporation is required to accept cash rather than shares in the continuing corporation, as permitted by § 11.01(a)(3) of the MBCA. In the modern law of corporations it is important to recognize that a "merger" is not limited to the intuitive notion of two independent corporations agreeing to fuse together with shareholders of both corporations having a continuing interest in the fused enterprise.

(2) Why is not the appraisal remedy an acceptable solution for all "cash out" merger problems? If the minority shareholder is dissatisfied with the amount offered by the corporation, a right to obtain the fair value of the shares as judicially determined seems reasonable. What can be wrong with that? While this remedy has superficial plausibility, in many states the traditional appraisal remedy is not attractive since it usually does not lead to an adequate payment to dissenting shareholders. There are at least five problems with this remedy, at least in its traditional form: (1) the shareholders must litigate with the corpora-

tion as to the fair value issue; the corporation usually has extensive resources and intimate knowledge of where the skeletons are while the shareholder does not; (2) the shareholder receives nothing until the litigation establishing fair value, including appeals, is exhausted; as a result he or she may receive nothing for five years or so (while a person accepting the transaction receives immediate payment), and an ultimate award of statutory interest is not likely to be viewed as adequate compensation for the loss of the use of the proceeds for a long period; (3) the shareholder must bear his or her own litigation expenses, which may be substantial, particularly if asset valuations are involved; (4) the method of valuation routinely used in most states, the "Delaware block" approach discussed in *Weinberger,* may not yield a valuation that is realistic; and (5) the payment of interest on the award is discretionary with the Court, so that no interest at all may be awarded, or interest may be calculated on a simple interest basis rather than on a compound interest basis, as occurred, for example, in In the Matter of the Appraisal of Shell Oil Co., 607 A.2d 1213 (Del.1992). These inadequacies, in part, were of course recognized in the Court's opinion in *Weinberger*; they are also addressed in part in Chapter 13 of the MBCA, which, among other things, gives the dissenter some immediate payment before the appraisal suit is filed. In addition, Cede & Co. v. Technicolor, Inc., 684 A.2d 289 (Del.1996) adopts a loss measurement standard in a two-step acquisition that is quite favorable to dissenting shareholders.

(3) For an examination of the appraisal remedy which arguably understates the problems of this traditional remedy and overstates the reliability of market values in "thinly traded" markets, see Joel Seligman, Reappraising the Appraisal Remedy, 52 Geo.Wash.L.Rev. 829 (1984). For more sympathetic evaluations (from the standpoint of dissenters) see Robert B. Thompson, Exit, Liquidity, and Majority Rule: Appraisal's Role in Corporate Law, 84 Geo.L.J. 1 (1995); Samuel C. Thompson, A Lawyer's Guide to Modern Valuation Techniques in Mergers and Acquisitions, 21 J.Corp.L. 457 (1996).

(4) Singer v. Magnavox, 380 A.2d 969 (Del.1977), overruled by the principal case, applied a double test to "cash out" mergers: the transaction must meet a test of "entire fairness" and there must be a "business purpose" other than a purpose of eliminating the minority shareholders. Actual experience in Delaware with the "business purpose" test revealed that it apparently did not help to separate abusive transactions from proper ones. In Tanzer v. International Gen. Indus., Inc., 379 A.2d 1121 (Del.1977), for example, the Court held that the parent corporation's actions should be measured by reference to its status and interest as a shareholder, including its own corporate concerns, and therefore a purpose "to facilitate long term debt financing" of the parent was a proper business purpose. Id. at 1124–25. Some courts, however, have required a business purpose (as well as meeting the *Wineberger* standards). In Alpert v. 28 Williams St. Corp. 63 N.Y.2d 557, 483 N.Y.S.2d 667, 473 N.E.2d 19 (1984), for example, the New York Court of Appeals stated that in addition to fair dealing and fair price, the directors must justify the variant treatment between the majority and the minority by showing some business purpose for the transaction:

> In the context of a freeze-out merger, variant treatment of the minority shareholders—i.e., causing their removal—will be justified when related to the advancement of a general corporate interest. The benefit need not be great, but it must be for the corporation. For example, if the sole purpose of the merger is reduction of the number of profit sharers—in contrast to increasing the corporation's capital or profits, or improving its management structure—there will exist no "independent corporate interest". All of these

purposes ultimately seek to increase the individual wealth of the remaining shareholders. What distinguishes a proper corporate purpose from an improper one is that, with the former, removal of the minority shareholders furthers the objective of conferring some general gain upon the corporation. Only then will the fiduciary duty of good and prudent management of the corporation serve to override the concurrent duty to treat all shareholders fairly. We further note that a finding that there was an independent corporate purpose for the action taken by the majority will not be defeated merely by the fact that the corporate objective could have been accomplished in another way, or by the fact that the action chosen was not the best way to achieve the bona fide business objective.

In sum, in entertaining an equitable action to review a freeze-out merger, a court should view the transaction as a whole to determine whether it was tainted with fraud, illegality, or self-dealing, whether the minority shareholders were dealt with fairly, and whether there exists any independent corporate purpose for the merger.

63 N.Y.2d at 573, 483 N.Y.S.2d at 676–77, 473 N.E.2d at 28. See also Coggins v. New England Patriots Football Club, 397 Mass. 525, 531, 492 N.E.2d 1112, 1117 (1986), where the Court said that "[u]nlike the Delaware court * * * we believe the 'business-purpose' test is an additional useful means under our statutes and case law for examining a transaction in which a controlling stockholder eliminates the minority interest in a corporation." On the other hand, several courts have accepted the *Weinberger* conclusion: Fleming v. International Pizza Supply Corp., 676 N.E.2d 1051 (Ind.1997)[appraisal is exclusive remedy and dissenting shareholders may litigate claims of breach of fiduciary duty or fraud within the appraisal remedy]; Persinger v. Carmazzi, 190 W.Va. 683, 690, 441 S.E.2d 646, 653 (1994)["attempting to infer the motivations behind a majority shareholder's buyout of shares is like trying to catch the wind in a net"].

(5) Because of the large number of publicly held corporations incorporated in Delaware and the high level of merger activity during the 1980s and mid–1990s, the Delaware courts have had numerous opportunities to consider and apply the *Weinberger* principles in various contexts. This outpouring of post-*Weinberger* litigation has influenced developments in other states. Many courts find attractive the flexibility and open-endedness of the *Weinberger* tests of intrinsic fairness both in procedure and price.

(6) It has become customary in Delaware cash-out transactions to structure the procedure so that "independent" directors of the subsidiary negotiate the terms of the transaction with representatives of the parent, and that approval of the transaction is conditional upon an affirmative vote of a majority of the minority shareholders. One consequence is that it has become standard practice to place outside persons on the board of directors of subsidiaries that have publicly-held minority shares. Cases discussing these procedural requirements include Rosenblatt v. Getty Oil Co., 493 A.2d 929 (Del.1985), where the negotiation over price seems clearly to have been at arms length; *Rosenblatt*, incidentally, adopts the test of "materiality" established by Justice Marshall in TSC Indus., Inc. v. Northway, Inc. (page 628, supra) as the appropriate test under the "fair dealing" branch of *Weinberger*, and Citron v. E.I. DuPont de Nemours & Co., 584 A.2d 490 (Del.Ch.1990), involving a cash-out merger by which DuPont increased its 69.54 percent ownership of the common stock of Remington Arms Company to 100 percent. Negotiation of the terms of the transaction on behalf of Remington was placed exclusively in the hands of three directors of Remington that had no

connection with DuPont and were not Remington executives. As described by the Court, the negotiations were at arms' length and adversarial; ultimate approval of the transaction was conditioned on acceptance by a majority of the minority shareholders. The Court held in *Citron* that the test of intrinsic fairness remained applicable to cash out transactions but that the arms' length procedures adopted by DuPont and Remington placed the burden on the plaintiff to show the unfairness of the transaction, which the plaintiff was unable to do.

(7) Normally an interested director or shareholder under *Weinberger* has the burden of proving that a challenged transaction is entirely fair to the corporation and its shareholders. The reason to have an independent committee, of course, is to replicate arm's length bargaining and thereby shift this burden of proof in a shareholder suit to the plaintiff. In many cases this allocation of the burden of proof is outcome determinative. In Kahn v. Lynch Communication Systems, Inc., 638 A.2d 1110 (Del.1994), a properly constituted and appropriately functioning special committee was created, but the defendants were not able to show that the bargaining process replicated a truly arms-length bargaining process. Hence the burden of proof did not shift to the plaintiff. On remand, the defendants were able to persuade the court that there had been full disclosure and the price was entirely fair so that the transaction was upheld. The Supreme Court accepted this conclusion. Kahn v. Lynch Communication Systems, Inc., 669 A.2d 79 (Del.1995). In Kahn v. Tremont Corporation, 694 A.2d 422 (Del.1997), the Court held (in an unusual 2–1–2 decision) that the burden did not shift where the chairman of the independent committee had close associations with the corporation and in fact dominated the negotiation process while the other two members of the committee were passive. As a result, arms length bargaining was not replicated.

(8) In all of these cases, the Delaware courts, have emphasized the importance of full disclosure to the minority shareholders, and have not hesitated to enjoin cash out transactions when such disclosure was lacking (e.g., Joseph v. Shell Oil Co., 482 A.2d 335 (Del.Ch.1984), holding affirmed in connected case, Selfe v. Joseph, 501 A.2d 409 (Del.1985)). Similarly, the Delaware courts have set aside transactions where there appears to have been manipulation of the transaction to minimize the financial rights of minority shareholders (e.g., Rabkin v. Philip A. Hunt Chem. Corp., 498 A.2d 1099 (Del.1985)), or the use of unfair or abusive tactics (e.g., Sealy Mattress Co. of N.J. v. Sealy, Inc., 532 A.2d 1324, 1335 (Del.Ch.1987)). In the Sealy case, the Court stated:

> Indeed, if one were setting out to write a textbook study on how one might violate as many fiduciary precepts as possible in the course of a single merger transaction, this case would be a good model.

In these cases involving particularly egregious misconduct, "rescissory damages" may be available if the transaction in question has been consummated and cannot readily be unwound.

(9) "Fairness opinions," such as the one provided by Lehman Brothers in connection with the UOP buyout, are virtually standard operating procedures in transactions involving corporate control and cash out transactions. They state that the price is "fair from a financial point of view," and thereby provide assurance to the directors. Valuation of a minority interest in a large corporation is subjective to some extent in many circumstances, and there is a good chance that independent valuations of the same business might vary considerably. Hence, it is certainly not a coincidence that the overwhelming bulk of fairness opinions come in very close to the figure desired by the board of directors authorizing the opinion. There apparently has been no recent example of liability being imposed

on an investment banker for an inaccurate fairness letter. Should liability be imposed on the preparers of fairness opinions for negligence? For bad faith? Should procedures be established to ensure that the preparer of a fairness opinion is not beholden in some sense to the board of directors arranging for the fairness opinion and authorizing payment of the writer's fee? Is it appropriate for the writer of a fairness opinion to negotiate a fee that is in part based on the success of the transaction? There is a substantial literature on fairness opinions and their role in a variety of transactions. A good description of these and other problems from three different points of view appear in Ted J. Fiflis, Responsibility of Investment Bankers to Shareholders, 70 Wash. U.L.Q. 497 (1992), and two shorter articles commenting on the Fiflis article: William J. Carney, Fairness Opinions: How Fair Are They and Why We Should Do Nothing About It, 70 Wash. U. L.Q. 523 (1992), and Dale A. Oesterle, Fairness Opinions as Magic Pieces of Paper, 70 Wash. U. L.Q. 541 (1992). See also Lucian Arye Bebchuk & Marcel Kahan, Fairness Opinions: How Fair Are They and What Can Be Done About It? 1989 Duke L.J. 27 (1989); Charles M. Elson, Fairness Opinions: Are They Fair or Should We Care? 53 Ohio St. L.J. 951 (1992).

(10) Rule 13e–3, 17 C.F.R. § 240.13e–3 (1997), promulgated under the Securities Exchange Act of 1934, is applicable to "going private" transactions which involve the solicitation of public shareholders in cash-out transactions. This rule and the accompanying schedule requires the issuer or affiliate to state whether it "believes that the Rule 13e–3 transaction is fair or unfair to unaffiliated security holders" and discuss "in reasonable detail the material factors upon which the belief * * * is based and, to the extent practicable, the weight assigned to each such factor." 17 C.F.R. § 240.13e–100, Item 8(a), (b)(1997). If the issuer receives an outside opinion or appraisal, it must be disclosed along with a description of the relationship between the preparer of the opinion or appraisal and the issuer. Id. at Item 9(b). The SEC staff also requires disclosure of the analyses underlying the opinion in considerable detail, including specific values or ranges of values derived from such analyses. These disclosure requirements probably result in considerably greater care being taken in the preparation of a fairness opinion. The SEC staff also requires similar disclosures in connection with outside opinions or appraisals obtained in connection with control transactions that do not involve the elimination of public shareholders and which therefore are not subject to rule 13e–3.

B. CORPORATE OPPORTUNITY

NORTHEAST HARBOR GOLF CLUB, INC. v. HARRIS

Supreme Judicial Court of Maine, 1995.
661 A.2d 1146.

Before Wathen, C.J., and Roberts, Glassman, Dana, and Lipez, JJ.

Roberts, Justice.

Northeast Harbor Golf Club, Inc., appeals from a judgment entered in the Superior Court (Hancock County, Atwood, J.) following a nonjury trial. The Club maintains that the trial court erred in finding that Nancy Harris did not breach her fiduciary duty as president of the Club by purchasing and developing property abutting the golf course. Because we today adopt principles different from those applied by the trial court in determining that Harris's activities did not constitute a breach of the corporate opportunity doctrine, we vacate the judgment.

HOLDING

I.

THE FACTS

Nancy Harris was the president of the Northeast Harbor Golf Club, a Maine corporation, from 1971 until she was asked to resign in 1990. The Club also had a board of directors that was responsible for making or approving significant policy decisions. The Club's only major asset was a golf course in Mount Desert. During Harris's tenure as president, the board occasionally discussed the possibility of developing some of the Club's real estate in order to raise money. Although Harris was generally in favor of tasteful development, the board always "shied away" from that type of activity.

In 1979, Robert Suminsby informed Harris that he was the listing broker for the Gilpin property, which comprised three noncontiguous parcels located among the fairways of the golf course. The property included an unused right-of-way on which the Club's parking lot and clubhouse were located. It was also encumbered by an easement in favor of the Club allowing foot traffic from the green of one hole to the next tee. Suminsby testified that he contacted Harris because she was the president of the Club and he believed that the Club would be interested in buying the property in order to prevent development.

Harris immediately agreed to purchase the Gilpin property in her own name for the asking price of $45,000. She did not disclose her plans to purchase the property to the Club's board prior to the purchase. She informed the board at its annual August meeting that she had purchased the property, that she intended to hold it in her own name, and that the Club would be "protected." The board took no action in response to the Harris purchase. She testified that at the time of the purchase she had no plans to develop the property and that no such plans took shape until 1988.

1979

In 1984, while playing golf with the postmaster of Northeast Harbor, Harris learned that a parcel of land owned by the heirs of the Smallidge family might be available for purchase. The Smallidge parcel was surrounded on three sides by the golf course and on the fourth side by a house lot. It had no access to the road. With the ultimate goal of acquiring the property, Harris instructed her lawyer to locate the Smallidge heirs. Harris testified that she told a number of individual board members about her attempt to acquire the Smallidge parcel. At a board meeting in August 1985, Harris formally disclosed to the board that she had purchased the Smallidge property.[11] The minutes of that meeting show that she told the board she had no present plans to develop the Smallidge parcel. Harris testified that at the time of the purchase of the Smallidge property she nonetheless thought it might be nice to have some houses there. Again, the board took no formal action as a result of Harris's purchase. Harris acquired the Smallidge property from ten heirs, paying a total of $60,000. In 1990, Harris paid $275,000 for the lot and building separating the Smallidge parcel from the road in order to gain access to the otherwise landlocked parcel.

1985

---

11. [By the Court] In fact, it appears that Harris did not take title to the property until October 26, 1985. She had only signed a pur-chase and sale agreement at the time of the August board meeting.

The trial court expressly found that the Club would have been unable to purchase either the Gilpin or Smallidge properties for itself, relying on testimony that the Club continually experienced financial difficulties, operated annually at a deficit, and depended on contributions from the directors to pay its bills. On the other hand, there was evidence that the Club had occasionally engaged in successful fund-raising, including a two-year period shortly after the Gilpin purchase during which the Club raised $115,000. The Club had $90,000 in a capital investment fund at the time of the Smallidge purchase.

In 1987 or 1988, Harris divided the real estate into 41 small lots, 14 on the Smallidge property and 27 on the Gilpin property. Apparently as part of her estate plan, Harris conveyed noncontiguous lots among the 41 to her children and retained others for herself. In 1991, Harris and her children exchanged deeds to reassemble the small lots into larger parcels. At the time the Club filed this suit, the property was divided into 11 lots, some owned by Harris and others by her children who are also defendants in this case. Harris estimated the value of all the real estate at the time of the trial to be $1,550,000.

In 1988, Harris, who was still president of the Club, and her children began the process of obtaining approval for a five-lot subdivision known as Bushwood on the lower Gilpin property. Even when the board learned of the proposed subdivision, a majority failed to take any action. A group of directors formed a separate organization in order to oppose the subdivision on the basis that it violated the local zoning ordinance. After Harris's resignation as president, the Club also sought unsuccessfully to challenge the subdivision. See Northeast Harbor Golf Club, Inc. v. Town of Mount Desert, 618 A.2d 225 (Me.1992). Plans of Harris and her family for development of the other parcels are unclear, but the local zoning ordinance would permit construction of up to 11 houses on the land as currently divided.

After Harris's plans to develop Bushwood became apparent, the board grew increasingly divided concerning the propriety of development near the golf course. At least two directors, Henri Agnese and Nick Ludington, testified that they trusted Harris to act in the best interests of the Club and that they had no problem with the development plans for Bushwood. Other directors disagreed.

In particular, John Schafer, a Washington, D.C., lawyer and long-time member of the board, took issue with Harris's conduct. He testified that he had relied on Harris's representations at the time she acquired the properties that she would not develop them. According to Schafer, matters came to a head in August 1990 when a number of directors concluded that Harris's development plans irreconcilably conflicted with the Club's interests. As a result, Schafer and two other directors asked Harris to resign as president. In April 1991, after a substantial change in the board's membership, the board authorized the instant lawsuit against Harris for the breach of her fiduciary duty to act in the best interests of the corporation. The board simultaneously resolved that the proposed housing development was contrary to the best interests of the corporation.

The Club filed a complaint against Harris, her sons John and Shepard, and her daughter-in-law Melissa Harris. As amended, the complaint alleged

II. claims

that during her term as president Harris breached her fiduciary duty by purchasing the lots without providing notice and an opportunity for the Club to purchase the property and by subdividing the lots for future development. The Club sought an injunction to prevent development and also sought to impose a constructive trust on the property in question for the benefit of the Club.

The trial court found that Harris had not usurped a corporate opportunity because the acquisition of real estate was not in the Club's line of business. Moreover, it found that the corporation lacked the financial ability to purchase the real estate at issue. Finally, the court placed great emphasis on Harris's good faith. It noted her long and dedicated history of service to the Club, her personal oversight of the Club's growth, and her frequent financial contributions to the Club. The court found that her development activities were "generally * * * compatible with the corporation's business." This appeal followed.

Trial ct holding

II.

THE CORPORATE OPPORTUNITY DOCTRINE

Corporate officers and directors bear a duty of loyalty to the corporations they serve. As Justice Cardozo explained the fiduciary duty in Meinhard v. Salmon, 249 N.Y. 458, 164 N.E. 545, 546 (1928): * * * Maine has embraced this "unbending and inveterate" tradition. Corporate fiduciaries in Maine must discharge their duties in good faith with a view toward furthering the interests of the corporation. They must disclose and not withhold relevant information concerning any potential conflict of interest with the corporation, and they must refrain from using their position, influence, or knowledge of the affairs of the corporation to gain personal advantage. See Rosenthal v. Rosenthal, 543 A.2d 348, 352 (Me.1988); 13–A M.R.S.A. § 716 (Supp.1994).

RULE

Despite the general acceptance of the proposition that corporate fiduciaries owe a duty of loyalty to their corporations, there has been much confusion about the specific extent of that duty when, as here, it is contended that a fiduciary takes for herself a corporate opportunity. See, e.g., Victor Brudney & Robert C. Clark, A New Look at Corporate Opportunities, 94 Harv.L.Rev. 998, 998 (1981) ("Not only are the common formulations vague, but the courts have articulated no theory that would serve as a blueprint for constructing meaningful rules."). This case requires us for the first time to define the scope of the corporate opportunity doctrine in Maine.

Various courts have embraced different versions of the corporate opportunity doctrine. The test applied by the trial court and embraced by Harris is generally known as the "line of business" test. The seminal case applying the line of business test is Guth v. Loft, Inc., 5 A.2d 503 (Del.1939). In Guth, the Delaware Supreme Court adopted an intensely factual test stated in general terms as follows:

Line of business test

[I]f there is presented to a corporate officer or director a business opportunity which the corporation is financially able to undertake, is, from its nature, in the line of the corporation's business and is of practical advantage to it, is one in which the corporation has an interest or a reasonable expectancy, and, by embracing the opportunity, the self-interest of the officer or director will be brought into conflict with that of

① Corp financially able to undertake   ④ corp has interest
② In line of corp's business
③ of Practical advantage to corp   ⑤ self interest or officer conflicts w/

his corporation, the law will not permit him to seize the opportunity for himself.

Id. at 511. The "real issue" under this test is whether the opportunity "was so closely associated with the existing business activities * * * as to bring the transaction within that class of cases where the acquisition of the property would throw the corporate officer purchasing it into competition with his company." Id. at 513. The Delaware court described that inquiry as "a factual question to be decided by reasonable inferences from objective facts." Id.

The line of business test suffers from some significant weaknesses. First, the question whether a particular activity is within a corporation's line of business is conceptually difficult to answer. The facts of the instant case demonstrate that difficulty. The Club is in the business of running a golf course. It is not in the business of developing real estate. In the traditional sense, therefore, the trial court correctly observed that the opportunity in this case was not a corporate opportunity within the meaning of the Guth test. Nevertheless, the record would support a finding that the Club had made the policy judgment that development of surrounding real estate was detrimental to the best interests of the Club. The acquisition of land adjacent to the golf course for the purpose of preventing future development would have enhanced the ability of the Club to implement that policy. The record also shows that the Club had occasionally considered reversing that policy and expanding its operations to include the development of surrounding real estate. Harris's activities effectively foreclosed the Club from pursuing that option with respect to prime locations adjacent to the golf course.

Second, the Guth test includes as an element the financial ability of the corporation to take advantage of the opportunity. The court in this case relied on the Club's supposed financial incapacity as a basis for excusing Harris's conduct. Often, the injection of financial ability into the equation will unduly favor the inside director or executive who has command of the facts relating to the finances of the corporation. Reliance on financial ability will also act as a disincentive to corporate executives to solve corporate financing and other problems. In addition, the Club could have prevented development without spending $275,000 to acquire the property Harris needed to obtain access to the road.

The Massachusetts Supreme Judicial Court adopted a different test in Durfee v. Durfee & Canning, Inc., 323 Mass. 187, 80 N.E.2d 522 (1948). The Durfee test has since come to be known as the "fairness test." According to Durfee, the

true basis of governing doctrine rests on the unfairness in the particular circumstances of a director, whose relation to the corporation is fiduciary, taking advantage of an opportunity [for her personal profit] when the interest of the corporation justly call[s] for protection. This calls for application of ethical standards of what is fair and equitable * * * in particular sets of facts.

Id. at 529 (quoting Ballantine on Corporations 204–05 (rev. ed. 1946)). As with the Guth test, the Durfee test calls for a broad-ranging, intensely factual inquiry. The Durfee test suffers even more than the Guth test from a lack of principled content. It provides little or no practical guidance to the corporate officer or director seeking to measure her obligations.

The Minnesota Supreme Court elected "to combine the 'line of business' test with the 'fairness' test." Miller v. Miller, 301 Minn. 207, 222 N.W.2d 71, 81 (1974). It engaged in a two-step analysis, first determining whether a particular opportunity was within the corporation's line of business, then scrutinizing "the equitable considerations existing prior to, at the time of, and following the officer's acquisition." Id. The Miller court hoped by adopting this approach "to ameliorate the often-expressed criticism that the [corporate opportunity] doctrine is vague and subjects today's corporate management to the danger of unpredictable liability." Id. In fact, the test adopted in Miller merely piles the uncertainty and vagueness of the fairness test on top of the weaknesses in the line of business test.

Despite the weaknesses of each of these approaches to the corporate opportunity doctrine, they nonetheless rest on a single fundamental policy. At bottom, the corporate opportunity doctrine recognizes that a corporate fiduciary should not serve both corporate and personal interests at the same time. As we observed in Camden Land Co. v. Lewis, 101 Me. 78, 97, 63 A. 523, 531 (1905), corporate fiduciaries "owe their whole duty to the corporation, and they are not to be permitted to act when duty conflicts with interest. They cannot serve themselves and the corporation at the same time." The various formulations of the test are merely attempts to moderate the potentially harsh consequences of strict adherence to that policy. It is important to preserve some ability for corporate fiduciaries to pursue personal business interests that present no real threat to their duty of loyalty.

III.

THE AMERICAN LAW INSTITUTE APPROACH

In an attempt to protect the duty of loyalty while at the same time providing long-needed clarity and guidance for corporate decisionmakers, the American Law Institute has offered the most recently developed version of the corporate opportunity doctrine. PRINCIPLES OF CORPORATE GOVERNANCE § 5.05 (May 13, 1992), provides as follows:

> § 505   Taking of Corporate Opportunities by Directors or Senior Executives
>
> (a) General Rule. A director [§ 1.13] or senior executive [§ 1.33] may not take advantage of a corporate opportunity unless:
>
> > (1) The director or senior executive first offers the corporate opportunity to the corporation and makes disclosure concerning the conflict of interest [§ 1.14(a)] and the corporate opportunity [§ 1.14(b)];
> >
> > (2) The corporate opportunity is rejected by the corporation; and
> >
> > (3) Either:
> >
> > > (A) The rejection of the opportunity is fair to the corporation;
> > >
> > > (B) The opportunity is rejected in advance, following such disclosure, by disinterested directors [§ 1.15], or, in the case of a senior executive who is not a director, by a disinterested superi-

or, in a manner that satisfies the standards of the business judgment rule [§ 4.01(c)]; or

　　　(C) The rejection is authorized in advance or ratified, following such disclosure, by disinterested shareholders [§ 1.16], and the rejection is not equivalent to a waste of corporate assets [§ 1.42].

　(b) Definition of a Corporate Opportunity. For purposes of this Section, a corporate opportunity means:

　　(1) Any opportunity to engage in a business activity of which a director or senior executive becomes aware, either:

　　　(A) In connection with the performance of functions as a director or senior executive, or under circumstances that should reasonably lead the director or senior executive to believe that the person offering the opportunity expects it to be offered to the corporation; or

　　　(B) Through the use of corporate information or property, if the resulting opportunity is one that the director or senior executive should reasonably be expected to believe would be of interest to the corporation; or

　　(2) Any opportunity to engage in a business activity of which a senior executive becomes aware and knows is closely related to a business in which the corporation is engaged or expects to engage.

　(c) Burden of Proof. A party who challenges the taking of a corporate opportunity has the burden of proof, except that if such party establishes that the requirements of Subsection (a)(3)(B) or (C) are not met, the director or the senior executive has the burden of proving that the rejection and the taking of the opportunity were fair to the corporation.

　(d) Ratification of Defective Disclosure. A good faith but defective disclosure of the facts concerning the corporate opportunity may be cured if at any time (but no later than a reasonable time after suit is filed challenging the taking of the corporate opportunity) the original rejection of the corporate opportunity is ratified, following the required disclosure, by the board, the shareholders, or the corporate decisionmaker who initially approved the rejection of the corporate opportunity, or such decisionmaker's successor.

　(e) Special Rule Concerning Delayed Offering of Corporate Opportunities. Relief based solely on failure to first offer an opportunity to the corporation under Subsection (a)(1) is not available if: (1) such failure resulted from a good faith belief that the business activity did not constitute a corporate opportunity, and (2) not later than a reasonable time after suit is filed challenging the taking of the corporate opportunity, the corporate opportunity is to the extent possible offered to the corporation and rejected in a manner that satisfies the standards of Subsection (a).

The central feature of the ALI test is the strict requirement of full disclosure prior to taking advantage of any corporate opportunity. Id., § 5.05(a)(1). "If the opportunity is not offered to the corporation, the director or senior executive will not have satisfied § 5.05(a)." Id., cmt. to § 5.05(a). The corporation must then formally reject the opportunity. Id., § 505(a)(2). The ALI test is discussed at length and ultimately applied by the Oregon Supreme Court in Klinicki v. Lundgren, 298 Or. 662, 695 P.2d 906 (1985). As Klinicki describes the test, "full disclosure to the appropriate corporate body is * * * an absolute condition precedent to the validity of any forthcoming rejection as well as to the availability to the director or principal senior executive of the defense of fairness." Id. at 920. A "good faith but defective disclosure" by the corporate officer may be ratified after the fact only by an affirmative vote of the disinterested directors or shareholders. Principles of Corporate Governance § 5.05(d).

The ALI test defines "corporate opportunity" broadly. It includes opportunities "closely related to a business in which the corporation is engaged." Id., § 5.05(b). It also encompasses any opportunities that accrue to the fiduciary as a result of her position within the corporation. Id. This concept is most clearly illustrated by the testimony of Suminsby, the listing broker for the Gilpin property, which, if believed by the factfinder, would support a finding that the Gilpin property was offered to Harris specifically in her capacity as president of the Club. If the factfinder reached that conclusion, then at least the opportunity to acquire the Gilpin property would be a corporate opportunity. The state of the record concerning the Smallidge purchase precludes us from intimating any opinion whether that too would be a corporate opportunity.

Under the ALI standard, once the Club shows that the opportunity is a corporate opportunity, it must show either that Harris did not offer the opportunity to the Club or that the Club did not reject it properly. If the Club shows that the board did not reject the opportunity by a vote of the disinterested directors after full disclosure, then Harris may defend her actions on the basis that the taking of the opportunity was fair to the corporation. Id., § 5.05(c). If Harris failed to offer the opportunity at all, however, then she may not defend on the basis that the failure to offer the opportunity was fair. Id., cmt. to § 5.05(c).

The Klinicki court viewed the ALI test as an opportunity to bring some clarity to a murky area of the law. Klinicki, 695 P.2d at 915. We agree, and today we follow the ALI test. The disclosure-oriented approach provides a clear procedure whereby a corporate officer may insulate herself through prompt and complete disclosure from the possibility of a legal challenge. The requirement of disclosure recognizes the paramount importance of the corporate fiduciary's duty of loyalty. At the same time it protects the fiduciary's ability pursuant to the proper procedure to pursue her own business ventures free from the possibility of a lawsuit.

The importance of disclosure is familiar to the law of corporations in Maine. Pursuant to 13–A M.R.S.A. § 717 (1981), a corporate officer or director may enter into a transaction with the corporation in which she has a personal or adverse interest only if she discloses her interest in the transaction and secures ratification by a majority of the disinterested directors or shareholders.[12] * * * Like the ALI rule, section 717 was designed to "elimi-

12.   [By the Court] Unlike the ALI rule, 13–A M.R.S.A. § 717(1)(C) permits the director to defend on the ground of fairness even in the absence of disclosure. We are not troubled by

nate the inequities and uncertainties caused by the existing rules." Model Business Corp. Act § 41, ¶ 2, at 844 (1971).

IV.

Conclusion

The question remains how our adoption of the rule affects the result in the instant case. The trial court made a number of factual findings based on an extensive record.[13] The court made those findings, however, in the light of legal principles that are different from the principles that we today announce. Similarly, the parties did not have the opportunity to develop the record in this case with knowledge of the applicable legal standard. In these circumstances, fairness requires that we remand the case for further proceedings. Those further proceedings may include, at the trial court's discretion, the taking of further evidence. * * *

Judgment vacated [and remanded] for further proceedings consistent with the opinion herein.

All concurring.

Notes

(1) A moment's reflection should reveal, first, that the corporate opportunity doctrine is of central importance in assuring the integrity of a business, second, that issues about its application arise frequently in American economic life (in many instances not in litigation but in decision-making and advising corporate directors and officers about what they may and may not do), third, that its application cannot be determined by simple hard and fast rules but by a particularized analysis of the circumstances, and finally, courts may readily disagree whether a specific opportunity should be viewed as a corporate opportunity. Section 5.05 seems to be a reasonable effort to encapsulate tests for this difficult, fact-sensitive area.

(2) The earliest test for corporate opportunities has been described as the "interest or expectancy" test. Professor Richard A. Epstein analyzes this test in the context of a contractual approach toward corporation law:

> (In) Lagarde v. Anniston Lime & Stone Co.,[14] a corporation had a one-third interest in a limestone quarry, an option to acquire a second third, and the possibility that it just might purchase the last third. Certain directors and shareholders, however, purchased the last two pieces of the mine. Their actions were held to violate the corporate opportunity rule with respect to the second piece but not the third piece. The first part of the decision seems correct. Indeed, one does not need an explicit doctrine of corporate law to

this difference because the nature of the transactions covered by section 717 is such that the board will necessarily be aware of the transaction. It may therefore act to protect the interests of the corporation even if it is not aware of the interest of the fiduciary. In the case of a usurpation of a corporate opportunity, the corporation is defenseless unless the director discloses.

13. [By the Court] Harris raised the defense of laches and the statute of limitations

but the court made no findings on those issues. We do not intimate what result the application of either doctrine would produce in this case. Similarly, it was not necessary for the court to address the issue of remedy in the first trial. The court has broad discretion to fashion an equitable remedy based on the facts and circumstances of the case. We decline to invade its province by commenting prematurely on what remedy, if any, may be appropriate.

14. [By the Editor] 126 Ala. 496, 28 So. 199 (1900).

respond to what appears to be an interference with a preexisting contract. But, the court held that the mere expectation for the last piece did not count because it was not borne of contract.

That result seems wrong as a matter of first principle. Here, there is not simply competition for resources between the corporation and the directors, but competition for resources that have clear synergies with properties already owned and possessed by the corporation. Stated simply, the operation of the mine can surely take place far more effectively under a single owner. Perhaps an outsider could frustrate that plan by seeking to acquire the third piece, but it is highly unlikely that a corporate director should be given that slack.

Once a director completes such a purchase, he then occupies a position that is, at least in part, adverse to that of the corporation. As he seeks to gain a larger share of the common venture, he will be armed in any negotiations with knowledge that he has about the internal operations of the corporation. That knowledge could prove of immense assistance in negotiating over the operation of the mine or the divisions of the spoils. Within a contractual framework, the total gains for the corporation and the directors seem smaller with that divided authority than without it. * * *

In similar fashion, it seems virtually automatic to say that a corporate director could not acquire, for example, the landlord's interest in any lease where the corporation is a tenant. It is too much to require the corporation to negotiate with one of its own. Whether one thinks of corporate opportunity as a doctrine of contract or trust law, the outcome in this class of cases seems to be pretty much the same. It would take a powerful contractual agreement to reverse this understanding.

Richard A. Epstein, Contract and Trust in Corporate Law: The Case of Corporate Opportunity, 21 Del.J.Corp.L. 5, 14–15 (1996).

(2) The most widely cited test is the "seminal" holding in Guth v. Loft, discussed in the principal case. In addition to the criticisms of this test in the principal opinion, Professor Pat K. Chew complains that it is much too favorable to the corporation:

Although the court described the line of business test as one that would preclude the fiduciaries from pursuing an opportunity that would compete with the corporation, the court's application of the test precludes fiduciaries from taking any opportunity to which the corporation can adapt its resources. The court determined that Pepsi–Cola and Loft were in the same line of business because Loft's plant, equipment, executives, personnel, and finances could have been adequately adapted to develop the Pepsi–Cola opportunity. The wholesale and retail operations for soft drinks utilize different outputs and inputs, production facilities, and distribution channels. Despite these differences, with sufficient financial resources Loft could have adapted to this or virtually any other diversification. Thus, under the Guth court's adaptability test, virtually all opportunities presumptively belong to the corporation.

If courts interpret the line of business test to preclude only immediately competitive opportunities, then the test in theory is less expansive than if it is interpreted to preclude opportunities that may be feasible after corporate adaption. Many contested opportunities, however, are competitive to the corporation. Hence, in practice, either the adaptability test or the competitiveness test would reach the same result. Courts will find the fiduciaries breached their duties, and the cumulative effect will be that fiduciaries will routinely lose corporate opportunity cases.

This result affects societal and individual interests. Next to an absolute prohibition against fiduciaries' pursuant of any opportunities, the test's prohibition against fiduciaries' pursuant of any competing opportunities is the most likely to restrain competition in the marketplace and to infringe upon individuals' freedom to start their own businesses. Despite these consequences, the line of business test neither acknowledges any noncorporate interests nor considers the reasonable expectations of the parties. * * *

Pat K. Chew, Competing Interests in the Corporate Opportunity Doctrine, 67 N.C.L.Rev. 435, 456–58 (1989). Not surprisingly, a significant number of corporate opportunity cases arise in Delaware. While *Guth* is always cited as the controlling case, Delaware courts have in fact moved toward the fairness test both in holding and in dicta. In Johnston v. Greene, 121 A.2d 919, 923 (Del.Ch.1956), for example, the court stated that the test in every corporate opportunity case was "whether or not the director had appropriated something to himself *that in all fairness should belong to his corporation.*" (Emphasis added) This language was quoted approvingly in the most recent Delaware corporate opportunity case, Broz v. Cellular Information Systems, Inc., 673 A.2d 148 (Del.1996), which added that *Guth* provided "guidelines * * * in balancing the equities."

(3) Michael Begert, The Corporate Opportunity Doctrine and Outside Business Interests, 56 U.Chi.L.Rev. 827, 829–32 (1989):

At common law, courts developed a host of factors for determining whether a participant's fiduciary duty requires her to pass up a business opportunity, or whether, instead, she is free to take it for herself. Though the application of these factors has varied from state to state, certain considerations have proved dominant: whether the corporation has a previous connection to the opportunity; whether the opportunity is essential to the corporation; whether the corporation has the ability to undertake the opportunity; and whether the corporation has consented to the transaction.

Although these factors can be extracted from the case law, the corporate participant will find it difficult to use them as a guide to behavior under the current regime, since in any given case a factor may be ignored or given unpredicted weight. * * *

1. Feasibility of corporate action.

* * * Corporate inability may take two forms: financial inability or refusal of third parties to deal with the corporation. * * * For good reasons, courts have refused to allow financial inability alone to justify a participant's appropriation of an opportunity otherwise available to the corporation. * * * If directors are permitted to justify their conduct on such a theory, there will be a temptation to refrain from exerting their best efforts on behalf of the corporation since, if it does not meet the obligations, an opportunity of profit will be open to them personally. * * *

2. Corporate waiver of the opportunity.

Under the common law, certain actions by the corporation, such as consent, implied rejection, and ratification, are deemed to waive the corporation's right to object to a participant's individual use of a corporate opportunity. First, the corporation may consent to a pattern of outside investment by participants. * * * [It] it may also consent by explicitly or implicitly rejecting the opportunity. The "evil" necessitating the corporate opportunity doctrine is "a fiduciary diverting or usurping a corporate opportunity without the corporation having the opportunity to first act." Therefore, if the director first offers the opportunity to the corporation with full disclosure and the disinterested board members reject the opportunity, then the director may take it. Such a formal rejection always constitutes a defense.

In some cases a formal rejection is unnecessary. If the participant can show that other participants knew about the opportunity, yet failed to act upon it, then the court might find that the other participants rejected the opportunity by implication. * * * [Another] instance of waiver occurs if the corporation "ratifies" the participant's actions. If a corporation fails to act immediately after learning of a participant's use of an opportunity, that inaction might constitute implicit ratification. Provided such a ratification is by disinterested directors of an undominated board, or by disinterested shareholders, it might estop the corporation from bringing a claim for usurpation of corporate opportunity. However, ratification requires that the company and disinterested management be aware of all the material facts. Hence full and formal disclosure may be necessary in any event.

(4) Pat K. Chew argues strongly that the corporate opportunity doctrine is warped in favor of the corporation and that as a result, it is a serious "restraint on individuals' freedom to compete [which] is contrary to society's long-standing goal of promoting competition." She argues:

> * * * [T]he right to start a new business based on an innovative product, a new management approach, or an unmet market niche is an integral part of our capitalist system. The promotion of entrepreneurship is justified considering the contributions it has made to this country. Over the last two decades, small and medium sized companies created more new jobs than any other sector in the economy, serving as the largest source of economic growth. While many new businesses are not based on a technological innovation, much technological innovation has come from new firms. Furthermore, the importance of entrepreneurship promises to increase in the future. Both academia and government recognize the role of entrepreneurship in enhancing American competitiveness in the global economy.

> Despite the importance of entrepreneurship, the corporate opportunity doctrine does not explicitly take it into account. This omission is explained in part by a lack of understanding of how the results in corporate opportunity cases and entrepreneurship are related. * * * These results may (1) decrease the number of business opportunities that are successfully developed and (2) systematically discourage fiduciaries' entrepreneurial instincts.

67 N.C.L.Rev., at 451–2. Do you agree? If so, does § 5.05 of the Corporate Governance Project give adequate weight to these values?

(5) For a review of recent cases, see Harvey Gelb, The Corporate Opportunity Doctrine—Recent Cases and the Elusive Goal of Clarity, 31 Richmond L. Rev. 371 (1997).

C. DUTIES TO OTHER CONSTITUENCIES

The foregoing materials make clear that the principal duties owed by corporate officers and directors run to holders of the common stock. However, limited duties also exist with respect to preferred shareholders and to creditors.

(1) *Preferred shareholders.* In Jedwab v. MGM Grand Hotels, Inc., 509 A.2d 584, 594 (Del.Ch.1986), the Court stated:

> [W]ith respect to matters relating to preferences or limitations that distinguish preferred stock from common, the duty of the corporation and its directors is essentially contractual and the scope of the duty is appropriately defined by reference to the specific words evidencing that contract; where however the right asserted is not to a preference as against the common stock but rather a right shared equally with the common, the existence of such right and the scope of the correlative duty may be measured by equitable [i.e. fiduciary] as well as legal standards.

Whatever the merits of the *Jedwab* distinction, Delaware courts have also recognized fiduciary duties running to preferred shareholders on questions such as whether the proceeds of a merger were being fairly divided between preferred and common shareholders. In re FLS Holdings, Inc. Shareholders Litigation, 1993 WL 104562 (Del.Ch.1993). However, in HB Korenvaes Inv., L.P. v. Marriott Corp., 1993 WL 205040, Fed.Sec.L.Rep. ¶ 97,728 (Del.Ch. 1993), the Court refused to consider a plausible fiduciary duty claim that a special dividend of stock to the common shareholders was designed to reorganize Marriott into two corporations in order to permit the resumption of dividends on the common shares without honoring the preferreds' priority right. The Court accepted the argument that since the certificate of incorporation contained a provision relating to the payment of special dividends, that provision was necessarily controlling. See Robert B. Robbins & Barton Clark, The Board's Fiduciary Duty to Preferred Stockholders, Insights, Vol. 7, No. 11 at 18 (Nov. 1993).

(2) *Holders of Convertible Securities.* Where convertible securities are called, the corporation has a duty to provide the holders of those securities with accurate information about the value of the alternatives, i.e. to convert into common or to allow the securities to be called for redemption. Zahn v. Transamerica Corporation, 162 F.2d 36 (3d Cir.1947); Speed v. Transamerica Corporation, 235 F.2d 369 (3d Cir.1956)[Transamerica violated its fiduciary duty by calling the preferred for redemption without advising preferred shareholders that an unrealized appreciation in tobacco inventory made the conversion option more attractive than redemption]. Since this leading case, the usual practice of corporations is to give notice and precise information as to which course is most desirable for preferred shareholders under the circumstances. Van Gemert v. Boeing Co., 520 F.2d 1373 (2d Cir.1975), cert. denied 423 U.S. 947, 96 S.Ct. 364, 46 L.Ed.2d 282 (1975), held inadequate such a notice. The facts of this case were summarized as follows in a subsequent Supreme Court decision affirming the allowance of plaintiffs' counsel fees:

> In March 1966, The Boeing Company called for the redemption of certain convertible debentures. Boeing announced the call through newspaper notices and mailings to investors who had registered their debentures. The notices, given in accordance with the indenture agreement, recited that each $100 amount of principal could be redeemed for $103.25 or converted into two shares of the Company's common stock. They set March 29 as the deadline for the exercise of conversion rights. Two shares of the Company's common stock on that date were worth $316.25. When

the deadline expired, the holders of debentures with a face value of $1,544,300 had not answered the call. These investors were left with the right to redeem their debentures for slightly more than face value. Boeing Co. v. Van Gemert, 444 U.S. 472, 474, 100 S.Ct. 745, 747, 62 L.Ed.2d 676 (1980). Boeing literally complied with the notice requirements of the indenture and the requirements of the New York Stock Exchange. But that was not enough under the circumstances:

> The duty of reasonable notice arises out of the contract between Boeing and the debenture holders, pursuant to which Boeing was exercising its right to redeem the debentures. An issuer of debentures has a duty to give adequate notice either on the face of the debentures, Abramson v. Burroughs Corp., (S.D.N.Y.1972) (Lumbard, C.J., sitting by designation), or in some other way, of the notice to be provided in the event the company decides to redeem the debentures. Absent such advice as to the specific notice agreed upon by the issuer and the trustee for the debenture holders, the debenture holders' reasonable expectations as to notice should be protected.

> For less sophisticated investors * * * putting the notice provisions only in the 113–page Indenture Agreement was effectively no notice at all. It was not reasonable for Boeing to expect these investors to send off for, and then to read understandingly, the 113–page Indenture Agreement referred to in both the prospectus and the debentures themselves in order to find out what notice would be provided in the event of redemption.

> Boeing could very easily have run more than two advertisements in a single paper prior to the eleventh hour (March 28), at which time it issued its belated news release and advertised for the third time in the Wall Street Journal and for the first time in the New York Times. * * * Had Boeing attempted * * * mail notice to original subscribers, and also given further newspaper publicity either by appropriate news releases or advertising earlier in the redemption period, we would have a different case and reasonable and sufficient notice might well be found.

520 F.2d at 1383. "[A]lmost all" of the newspaper notices actually published "were in fine print, buried in the multitude of information and data published about the financial markets and scarcely of a kind to attract the eye of the average lay investor or debenture holder." Id. at 1379. For an essentially inconsistent decision, see Meckel v. Continental Resources Co., 758 F.2d 811 (2d Cir.1985).

(3) *Creditors.* As a general rule, directors do not owe fiduciary duties to creditors—whether they be short-term trade creditors, long-term bondholders, or holders of debt securities convertible into common shares. Simons v. Cogan, 549 A.2d 300 (Del.1988); Geyer v. Ingersoll Publications Co., 621 A.2d 784 (Del.Ch.1992). This is because the rights of holders of debt securities are defined exclusively by the contractual terms of their obligations, not by an open-ended fiduciary duty. There are, of course, noncontractual doctrines that protect creditors to some extent, such as fraud, deceit, fraudulent conveyance principles, and rules against illegal distributions, but there is no general fiduciary duty owed to creditors. During the 1980s and early 1990s, a number of leveraged buyouts involved the addition of large amounts of debt to the

balance sheets of target corporations, thereby reducing outstanding investment-quality bonds or debentures previously issued by the corporation to the category of "junk bonds." When these transactions occurred, the holders of outstanding debt securities suffered very substantial capital losses. Since the specific transactions were not prohibited by the trust indentures, however, courts refused to intervene. See generally Morey W. McDaniel, Stockholders and Stakeholders, 21 Stetson L.Rev. 121 (1991); David M.W. Harvey, Bondholders' Rights and the Case for a Fiduciary Duty, 65 St. John's L.Rev. 1023 (1991); George S. Corey et al., Are Bondholders Owed a Fiduciary Duty? 18 Fla. St. U. L.Rev. 971 (1991); Morey W. McDaniel, Bondholders and Stockholders, 13 J. Corp. L. 205 (1988); W. Morey McDaniel, Bondholders and Corporate Governance, 41 Bus. Law. 413 (1986).

When a corporation is insolvent and the shareholders have no viable economic interest in the enterprise but the corporation is not in federal bankruptcy proceedings, the directors' primary duties shift from the shareholders to the creditors to preserve the value of the corporate assets for eventual distribution to creditors. Clarkson Co. Ltd. v. Shaheen, 660 F.2d 506 (2d Cir.1981). In Credit Lyonnais Bank Nederland, N.V. v. Pathe Communications Corp., 1991 WL 277613, 17 Del.J.Corp.L. 1099 (Del.Ch.1991), Chancellor Allen suggested that this duty should shift once the corporation enters "the vicinity of insolvency." Directors then owe their duty to "the corporate enterprise," predominantly the interests of creditors and employees. Footnote 55 explains his reasoning as follows:

> The possibility of insolvency can do curious things to incentives, exposing creditors to risks of opportunistic behavior and creating complexities for directors. Consider, for example, a solvent corporation having a single asset, a judgment for $51 million against a solvent debtor. The judgment is on appeal and thus subject to modification or reversal. Assume that the only liabilities of the company are to bondholders in the amount of $12 million. Assume that the array of probable outcomes of the appeal is as follows:

		Expected Value
25% chance of affirmance	($51mm)	$12.75
70% chance of modification	($ 4mm)	2.80
5% chance of reversal	($ 0)	–0–
Expected Value of Judgment on Appeal		$15.55

Thus, the best evaluation is that the current value of the equity is $3.55 million. ($15.55 million expected value of judgment on appeal − $12 million liability to bondholders). Now assume an offer to settle at $12.5 million (also consider one at $17.5 million). By what standard do the directors of the company evaluate the fairness of these offers? The creditors of this solvent company would be in favor of accepting either a $12.5 million offer or a $17.5 million offer. In either event they will avoid the 75% risk of insolvency and default. The stockholders, however, will plainly be opposed to acceptance of a $12.5 million settlement (under which they get practically nothing). More importantly, they very well may be opposed to acceptance of the $17.5

million offer under which the residual value of the corporation would increase from \$3.5 to \$5.5 million. This is so because the litigation alternative, with its 25% probability of a \$39 million outcome to them (\$51 million − \$12 million = \$39 million) has an expected value to the residual risk bearer of \$9.75 million (\$39 million × 25% chance of affirmance), substantially greater than the \$5.5 million available to them in the settlement. While in fact the stockholders' preference would reflect their appetite for risk, it is possible (and with diversified shareholders likely) that shareholders would prefer rejection of both settlement offers.

But if we consider the community of interests that the corporation represents it seems apparent that one should in this hypothetical accept the best settlement offer available providing it is greater than \$15.55 million, and one below that amount should be rejected. But that result will not be reached by a director who thinks he owes duties directly to shareholders only. It will be reached by directors who are capable of conceiving of the corporation as a legal and economic entity. Such directors will recognize that in managing the business affairs of a solvent corporation in the vicinity of insolvency, circumstances may arise when the right (both the efficient and the fair) course to follow for the corporation may diverge from the choice that the stockholders (or the creditors, or the employees, or any single group interested in the corporation) would make if given the opportunity to act.

The suggestion made in this note has been the subject of a significant amount of academic commentary. Is this a practical standard? Insolvency itself is not always a clear concept; is "the vicinity of insolvency" a practicable standard to mark the time this major shift in the focus of the duties of directors occurs? Is there anything wrong if a board of directors of a corporation in "the vicinity of insolvency" takes aggressive and risky steps to save the corporation, even though the unsecured creditors carry most of the risk and receive little of the benefit?

Notes

For an interesting analysis of the taxonomy of fiduciary duties in the modern era, see Deborah A. DeMott, Fiduciary Obligation Under Intellectual Siege: Contemporary Challenges to the Duty to Be Loyal, 30 Osgoode Hall L.J. 472 (1992).

Chapter Twelve

TRANSACTIONS IN SHARES: RULE 10B–5, INSIDER TRADING AND SECURITIES FRAUD

A. THE DEVELOPMENT OF A FEDERAL REMEDY: RULE 10B–5

SECURITIES EXCHANGE ACT OF 1934
15 U.S.C.A. § 78j (1981).

Section 10. It shall be unlawful for any person, directly or indirectly, by the use of any means or instrumentality, of interstate commerce or of the mails, or of any facility of any national securities exchange—* * *

(b) To use or employ, in connection with the purchase or sale of any security registered on a national securities exchange or any security not so registered, any manipulative or deceptive device or contrivance in contravention of such rules and regulations as the Commission may prescribe as necessary or appropriate in the public interest or for the protection of investors.

RULE 10B–5: EMPLOYMENT OF MANIPULATIVE AND DECEPTIVE DEVICES
17 C.F.R. § 240.10b–5 (1997).

It shall be unlawful for any person, directly or indirectly, by the use of any means or instrumentality of interstate commerce, or of the mails or of any facility of any national securities exchange,

(a) to employ any device, scheme, or artifice to defraud,

(b) to make any untrue statement of a material fact or to omit to state a material fact necessary in order to make the statements made, in the light of the circumstances under which they were made, not misleading, or

(c) to engage in any act, practice, or course of business which operates or would operate as a fraud or deceit upon any person,

in connection with the purchase or sale of any security.

Notes

(1) Comments of Milton Freeman, Conference on Codification of the Federal Securities Laws, 22 Bus.Law. 793, 922 (1967):[1]

* * * I think it would be appropriate for me now to make a brief statement of what actually happened when 10b–5 was adopted, where it would be written down and be available to everybody, not just the people who are willing to listen to me.

It was one day in the year 1943, I believe. I was sitting in my office in the SEC building in Philadelphia and I received a call from Jim Treanor who was then the Director of the Trading and Exchange Division. He said, "I have just been on the telephone with Paul Rowen," who was then the SEC Regional Administrator in Boston, "and he has told me about the president of some company in Boston who is going around buying up the stock of his company from his own shareholders at $4.00 a share, and he has been telling them that the company is doing very badly, whereas, in fact, the earnings are going to be quadrupled and will be $2.00 a share for this coming year. Is there anything we can do about it?" So he came upstairs and I called in my secretary and I looked at Section 10(b) and I looked at Section 17, and I put them together, and the only discussion we had there was where "in connection with the purchase or sale" should be, and we decided it should be at the end.

We called the Commission and we got on the calendar, and I don't remember whether we got there that morning or after lunch. We passed a piece of paper around to all the commissioners. All the commissioners read the rule and they tossed it on the table, indicating approval. Nobody said anything except Sumner Pike who said, "Well," he said, "we are against fraud, aren't we?" That is how it happened.

Louis[2] is absolutely right that I never thought that twenty odd years later it would be the biggest thing that had ever happened. It was intended to give the Commission power to deal with this problem. It had no relation in the Commission's contemplation to private proceedings. * * *

(2) A variety of factors contributed to the original growth of Rule 10b–5. A major factor was that the state law of securities fraud was embryonic. There was little question that if A sold shares of stock to B on the basis of a misrepresentation, B could sue A for fraud under state law. Some state blue sky laws also provided a limited remedy against fraud in the sale of registered securities by issuers, but there appeared to be no practical state remedy against many perceived abuses in the markets for publicly traded securities. An early effort to bring a private action against a corporate officer who had engaged in insider trading—he had purchased shares from the plaintiff in an anonymous transaction on the Boston Stock Exchange prior to the release of good news that raised the price of the stock—was unsuccessful because of the lack of an affirmative misstatement by the defendant, and no duty was owed by a corporate officer to an individual shareholder.[3] Goodwin v. Agassiz, 283 Mass. 358, 186 N.E. 659 (Mass. 1933).

1. Copyright 1967 by the American Bar Association. All rights reserved. Reprinted with the permission of the American Bar Association and its Section of Corporation, Banking and Business Law.

2. [By the Editor] The reference is to Professor Louis Loss of the Harvard Law School,

co-author of the major treatise on Securities Regulation.

3. [By the Editor] The court also suggested that since the "good news" was a theory about the existence of copper deposits, a premature affirmative disclosure might have injured the corporation.

Where, however, the managers dealt personally with the shareholders or hid their identities by the use of intermediaries, concepts of fraud, misrepresentation and reliance were developed that form part of the basis of the modern state law of securities fraud and influenced developments under Rule 10b–5. This is well-illustrated by two famous cases:

(a) In Strong v. Repide, 213 U.S. 419, 29 S.Ct. 521, 53 L.Ed. 853 (1909), the majority shareholder was conducting negotiations to sell certain real estate owned by the corporation to the Philippine government. A formal offer to purchase had been made, but the shareholder was holding out for more money. While negotiations were pending, he purchased the plaintiff's stock in the following manner:

> While this state of things existed, and before the final offer had been made by the governor, the defendant, although still holding out for a higher price for the lands, took steps, about the middle or latter part of September, 1903, to purchase the 800 shares of stock in his company owned by Mrs. Strong, which he knew were in the possession of F. Stuart Jones, as her agent. The defendant, having decided to obtain these shares, instead of seeing Jones, who had an office next door, employed one Kauffman, a connection of his by marriage, and Kauffman employed a Mr. Sloan, a broker, who had an office some distance away, to purchase the stock for him, and told Sloan that the stock was for a member of his wife's family. Sloan communicated with the husband of Mrs. Strong and asked if she desired to sell her stock. The husband referred him to Mr. Jones for consultation, who had the stock in his possession. Sloan did not know who wanted to buy the shares, nor did Jones when he was spoken to. Jones would not have sold at the price he did had he known it was the defendant who was purchasing, because, as he said, it would show increased value, as the defendant would not be likely to purchase more stock unless the price was going up. As the articles of incorporation, by subdivision 20, required a resolution of the general meeting of stockholders for the purpose of selling more than one hacienda, and as no such general meeting had been called at the time of the sale of the stock, Mr. Jones might well have supposed there was no immediate prospect of a sale of the lands being made, while at the same time defendant had knowledge of the probabilities thereof, which he had acquired by his conduct of the negotiations for their sale, as agent of all the shareholders, and while acting specially for them and himself.

213 U.S. at 425, 29 S.Ct. at 523, 53 L.Ed. at 858. The price for the purchased shares was approximately one-tenth what they were worth three months later after the real estate was sold to the government.

The Court concluded that the complaint stated a cause of action. Even if it were conceded that the ordinary relationship between director and shareholder was not of such a fiduciary nature as to require disclosure of "the general knowledge which [a director] may possess" regarding the value of shares, the Court stated, "yet there are cases where, by reason of the special facts, such duty exists." 213 U.S. at 431, 29 S.Ct. at 525, 53 L.Ed. at 860. The "special facts" pointed to by the Court included the role of the defendant as director, principal

State law may permit the corporation (either directly or through a derivative suit) to recover profits from trading on non-public corporate information by an officer or director of the corporation. Brophy v. Cities Service Co., 70 A.2d 5 (Del.Ch.1949); Diamond v. Oreamuno, 24 N.Y.2d 494, 301 N.Y.S.2d 78, 248 N.E.2d 910 (1969); In re ORFA Securities Litigation, 654 F.Supp. 1449 (D.N.J.1987); Safecard Services, Inc. v. Halmos, 912 P.2d 1132 (Wyo. 1996). While not all courts have recognized this theory, it may readily be justified as involving the use of corporate property—proprietary information—for non-corporate purposes.

shareholder and sole negotiator for the corporation with full power to accept or reject the government's offer as well as the affirmative steps taken to conceal the identity of the defendant as the purchaser of the shares.

(b) In Hotchkiss v. Fischer, 136 Kans. 530, 16 P.2d 531 (1932), the plaintiff, a widow in need of funds, had inherited 2,300 shares of The Elmhurst Company. Shortly before the annual meeting of the company, she traveled from her home in Burr Oak, Kansas, to Topeka to talk with defendant, the president of the company. Her plan was to retain the shares if a dividend were declared, but to sell them, at a sacrifice if necessary, if there was to be no dividend. She talked with the defendant on January 12 and 13, 1926. When asked whether a dividend would be declared, defendant replied that he could not inform plaintiff on that subject and would have no information until he conferred with directors coming from New York. He showed her financial statements, and stated that the company was in a sound financial position and had improved its position under his management, but painted a rather dark picture about specific matters. When asked what her stock was worth, he replied that he could supply information, but the worth of the stock "is a matter you have to determine yourself."

On January 15, the defendant purchased the plaintiff's shares for $1.25 per share; on January 16, he met with the New York directors and ascertained that they were in favor of paying a dividend. On January 18, the directors declared a dividend of $1 per share.

In the course of finding for the plaintiff, the Court defined the duty of the defendant to the plaintiff in the following terms:

> It is commonly said that directors of a corporation are "trustees" for stockholders. Accuracy of nomenclature need not be discussed. Directors act in a fiduciary capacity in management of corporate affairs, and a director negotiating with a shareholder for purchase of shares acts in a relation of scrupulous trust and confidence. The court deems it proper to withhold application of its rule relating to purchase of trust property by trustees proper, to purchase by a director of corporate shares, but such transactions must be subjected to the closest scrutiny, and, unless conducted with the utmost fairness, the wronged shareholder may invoke proper remedy.

136 Kans., at 538, 16 P.2d at 535.

(c) Later cases involving closely held corporations in state courts treat the Kansas view as a "minority rule" and a rule of "strict accountability." See Blazer v. Black, 196 F.2d 139 (10th Cir.1952); Amen v. Black, 234 F.2d 12 (10th Cir.1956); Delano v. Kitch, 542 F.2d 550 (10th Cir.1976), cert. denied, 456 U.S. 946, 102 S.Ct. 2012, 72 L.Ed.2d 468 (1982). On the other hand, the language of *Strong* that "special facts" create an affirmative duty to disclose appears in a number of opinions, and there is a tendency to relax the requirement that the facts be "special." See, e.g. Van Schaack Holdings, Ltd. v. Van Schaack, 867 P.2d 892 (Colo.1994), where the court found rather generalized information about the future of a piece of real estate to be "special facts." Further, the line between "special facts" and the rule of "strict accountability" tends to blur in practice, as many state courts have found that a general fiduciary duty exists in closely held corporations with respect to dealings between controlling and minority shareholders. See chapter 7, Section H. As a result, the early common law position that there is no liability in the absence of actual fraud or deception appears to have largely disappeared in recent state securities fraud cases. Bailey v. Vaughan, 178 W.Va. 371, 375–77, 359 S.E.2d 599, 603–05 (1987) summarizes these state law developments:

Some confusion exists in this area of a director's liability for purchasing stock from shareholders by virtue of the propensity of textwriters to segregate the cases into what are termed "majority" and "minority" rules and a third category termed the "special facts or circumstances" rule. Under this methodology, the majority rule is stated in terms that a director or officer of a corporation has no duty, in purchasing shares of a stockholder, to disclose information that he has gained in his position which is unknown to the shareholder and which would increase the value of the shares to be purchased. The minority rule is cast as holding that the director or officer has a duty to disclose all information which he may possess which may increase the value of the shares to be purchased. The special facts or circumstances rule holds that the director or officer is required to disclose those facts or circumstances of which he is aware that would increase the value of the shares he intends to purchase.

When we turn to the majority rule, we find that the cases cited for this rule often involve situations where there has been no inside or special information obtained which would influence the value of the shares purchased. Consequently, the court finds no impediment to the purchase, but it is difficult to conclude that the court intends to create a per se rule of no liability as there is often some limiting language. Included in this group are cases which have apparently been moderated by later decisions. We come to the conclusion that there is presently no majority rule that enables a director to utilize insider information which points to substantial undervaluation of the corporate shares and then to purchase shares from an uninformed shareholder without any liability.

Furthermore, it appears that the distinction between the minority rule and the special circumstances rule is shadowy at best. In order for the director to be liable under either rule, it must be shown that he possessed some special knowledge not available to the shareholder which enabled him to purchase the stock at a price that was lower than its actual value. Thus, it is the enhanced knowledge of the increased value which he has failed to disclose that underlies both theories of liability. We are aware of no minority view case that erects a per se rule against the purchase by a director or officer of another stockholder's shares. * * *

From the foregoing law, we are drawn to the conclusion that a director, who solicits a shareholder to purchase his stock and fails to disclose information not known to the shareholder that bears upon the potential increase in value of the shares, shall be liable to the shareholder either to have the sale rescinded or to respond in damages.[4]

(3) The first step in the development of Rule 10b–5—and in retrospect most certainly a significant one—was the holding by Judge Kirkpatrick in 1947 that rule 10b–5 could be the basis of a private suit to rescind a securities transaction. Kardon v. National Gypsum Co., 73 F.Supp. 798 (E.D.Pa.1947). The facts of this case, as set forth by Judge Kirkpatrick, were as follows:

---

4. [By the Editor] [By the Editor] Most of the cases dealing with "special facts" and discussed in Bailey v. Vaughan, supra, antedate World War II. In contrast, there are thousands of cases brought under rule 10b–5 in the federal courts involving facts similar to those cases. A number of states have old statutes that deal with fraud in connection with sales of stock. Texas, for example, has a statute, originally enacted in 1919, that defines fraud in connection with "a transaction involving * * * stock of a corporation" and provides a measure of damages that may include attorney's fees and the cost of expert witnesses in some situations. Vernon's Tex. Code Ann. Bus. & Com. § 27.01. There is no reported litigation under this section involving corporate stock since World War II.

The plaintiffs, Morris and Eugene B. Kardon (father and son), and the defendants, Leon A. Slavin and William Slavin (brothers), owned all the capital stock of Western Board and Paper Co. and Michigan Paper Stock Co., its affiliate, each of the four holding one fourth. Western was engaged in manufacturing paper board and other paper products, having its plant located at Kalamazoo, and Michigan was a purchasing agent dealing chiefly in waste paper and similar materials for Western. All four were officers and together constituted the entire board of directors, the two Slavins and Eugene Kardon living in Kalamazoo and being actively engaged in operating the plant and Morris Kardon living in Philadelphia. All four were familiar with the plant, assets and business of the corporation.

Prior to March 18, 1946, Leon Slavin had agreed for the corporation, by written instrument, considered by the parties to it to be binding, to sell to National Gypsum, the plant and equipment of Western for the sum of $1,500,000. * * * The agreement was signed by Leon Slavin in his capacity as Executive Vice President of Western.

On March 18, 1946, the Slavins purchased all the stock of the Kardons in the two corporations, Western and Michigan, for $504,000. At that time the Kardons knew nothing whatever about the negotiations with National Gypsum, and the Slavins did not disclose any of the facts relating to them although admittedly, at the meeting at which the sale of the stock was consummated, Leon Slavin, in answer to a preliminary question by the Kardons' attorney, whether he had made any agreement for the sale of the stock, answered No.[5]

Having acquired the plaintiffs' stock, the Slavins proceeded to consummate the transaction with National Gypsum. * * *

73 F.Supp. at 800. On the critical question whether rule 10b–5 might be used as the basis for a private cause of action in federal court, the judge simply stated that while the statute and rule "does not even provide in express terms for a remedy, * * * the existence of a remedy is implicit under general principles of the law." Id. at 802. Is this not a simple, garden-variety fraud case of little national or federal interest? Why should such litigation be in the federal courts in the absence of diversity? Rather surprisingly, various limiting doctrines for rule 10b–5 later developed by the Supreme Court do not affect at all the availability of that rule for plaintiffs in *Kardon*-type cases, and such cases may continue to be freely brought in federal courts under the federal cause of action provided by rule 10b–5. See, e.g., Glick v. Campagna, 613 F.2d 31 (3d Cir.1979). Indeed, one possible doctrine that might deflect many of these garden-variety fraud cases back to state court— the so-called "sale of business" doctrine—was expressly rejected by the United States Supreme Court in Landreth Timber Co. v. Landreth, 471 U.S. 681, 105 S.Ct. 2297, 85 L.Ed.2d 692 (1985).

(4) Rule 10b–5 quickly became the provision routinely relied upon in all cases involving claims of securities fraud, deception, or trading in securities on the basis of undisclosed information in both publicly held and closely held corporations. The language of the rule was broad, flexible, and not hedged with qualifications or limiting doctrine. Hence it was relatively easy to rely on this Rule in cases

---

5. [By the Court] At this point there is the only substantial dispute of fact in the case. I accept the plaintiffs' version to the effect that the question expressly mentioned the assets as well as the stock. However, it makes very little difference because even if the version given by the defendants is accepted it is perfectly clear that, in the light of the circumstances under which Leon Slavin's answer was made, he omitted to state a material fact necessary to make his answer not misleading, Rule X–10B–5(2).

involving misleading public statements by issuers and others that adversely affected the market price of shares, and securities transactions by corporate officers and directors based on non-public information. Further, the early Rule 10b–5 case law, as it developed, was almost uniformly favorable to plaintiffs. Much of it arose on motions to dismiss in which the allegations in the complaint were accepted as true for purposes of the motion. Judicial unwillingness to dispose of plausible allegations summarily on the pleadings led to the development of precedents generally favorable to plaintiffs, and such precedents in turn began to feed on themselves; liberal decisions under rule 10b–5 served as precedents for even broader developments. Even though complaints under rule 10b–5 often described conduct that also arguably constituted breach of state-created fiduciary duties plaintiffs naturally preferred the federal forum with its rule 10b–5 precedents rather than the limited or nonexistent case law in the state courts. Rule 10b–5 flourished, and the state law tended to atrophy.

(5) The decisions of the United States Supreme Court relating to rule 10b–5 before 1975, while not numerous, undoubtedly contributed to this trend. The first case reaching the Supreme Court, Securities and Exch. Comm'n v. National Sec., Inc., 393 U.S. 453, 89 S.Ct. 564, 21 L.Ed.2d 668 (1969), well illustrates the initial attitude of the Court to this rule. The basic claim by the SEC in this case was that two insurance companies had been merged by the use of a proxy statement that contained false and misleading statements; § 14 did not apply because the case arose before the 1964 amendments to § 12 of the Securities Exchange Act of 1934. The Court, through Justice Marshall, stated:

> Although § 10(b) and rule 10b–5 may well be the most litigated provisions in the federal securities laws, this is the first time this Court has found it necessary to interpret them. We enter this virgin territory cautiously. The questions presented are narrow ones. They arise in an area where glib generalizations and unthinking abstractions are major occupational hazards. Accordingly, in deciding this particular case, remembering what is not involved is as important as determining what is. With this in mind, we turn to respondents' particular contentions. * * *

> According to the amended complaint, Producers' shareholders were misled in various material respects prior to their approval of a merger. The deception furthered a scheme which resulted in their losing their status as shareholders in Producers and becoming shareholders in a new company. Moreover, by voting in favor of the merger, each approving shareholder individually lost any right under Arizona law to obtain an appraisal of his stock and payment for it in cash. Ariz.Rev.Stat.Ann. § 10–347 (1956). Whatever the terms "purchase" and "sale" may mean in other contexts, here an alleged deception has affected individual shareholders' decisions in a way not at all unlike that involved in a typical cash sale or share exchange. The broad antifraud purposes of the statute and the rule would clearly be furthered by their application to this type of situation. Therefore we conclude that Producers' shareholders "purchased" shares in the new company by exchanging them for their old stock. * * *

> Respondents' alternative argument that rule 10b–5 does not cover misrepresentations which occur in connection with proxy solicitations can be dismissed rather quickly. Section 14 of the 1934 Act, and the rules adopted pursuant to that section, set up a complex regulatory scheme covering proxy solicitations. * * * The two sections of the Act apply to different sets of situations. Section 10(b) applies to all proscribed conduct in connection with a

purchase or sale of any security; § 14 applies to all proxy solicitations, whether or not in connection with a purchase or sale. The fact that there may well be some overlap is neither unusual nor unfortunate. * * *

393 U.S. at 465–68, 89 S.Ct. at 571–73, 21 L.Ed.2d at 679–81. This rather free-wheeling approach toward rule 10b–5 moved Mr. Justice Harlan, with whom Mr. Justice Stewart joined, to dissent:

> I am at a loss to understand why the Court finds it necessary to * * * construe Rule 10b–5 promulgated under § 10(b) of the Securities Exchange Act of 1934. The Court of Appeals did not reach this question * * *. The Government's petition for certiorari is similarly limited. * * * When the respondents' brief on the merits argued that Rule 10b–5 did not apply to the present case, the Solicitor General did not even attempt to present the Government's position on that score because he quite properly believed that "the question is not appropriately before this Court for decision."

> Despite the fact that we have not heard the views of the Securities and Exchange Commission, the Court chooses this case as a vehicle to construe for the first time one of the most important and elusive provisions of the securities laws. Moreover, the decision has far-reaching radiations, despite the fact that the precise issue presented is a narrow one. Courts and commentators have long debated whether Rule 10b–5 should be read as a sweeping prohibition against fraud in the securities industry when this results in rendering nullities of the other antifraud provisions of more limited scope which can be found in the statute books. * * * Even those who take an extremely broad view of the scope of the Rule have recognized that it could well be argued that the courts should not rush in to apply § 10(b) to regulate proxy solicitations where Congress has refused to permit the Commission to intervene under § 14. * * * Nevertheless, the majority believes it can answer this question "rather quickly," without any real recognition of the basic principles which hang in the balance. * * *

> I am unwilling to decide these fundamental matters without full-dress argument. Indeed, if the courts of appeals are not to be permitted to develop the law in this area on a case-by-case basis, I think it much wiser for us to consider the basic issues in a case which squarely raises them rather than in one which is of marginal importance.

393 U.S. at 469–72, 89 S.Ct. at 573–74, 21 L.Ed.2d at 681–83. Two other Supreme Court decisions that reflect expansive readings of rule 10b–5 are Superintendent of Insurance of New York v. Bankers Life and Casualty Co., 404 U.S. 6, 92 S.Ct. 165, 30 L.Ed.2d 128 (1971), and Affiliated Ute Citizens of Utah v. United States, 406 U.S. 128, 92 S.Ct. 1456, 31 L.Ed.2d 741 (1972). In these opinions, the Supreme Court gave every indication of following the development of rule 10b–5 by the lower federal courts, particularly the Second Circuit, and no indication that a dramatic turn was about to occur. In many respects, *Superintendent of Insurance*, decided in 1971, reflects the high point in the growth of rule 10b–5.

(6) In addition to this fertile soil (from the plaintiff's standpoint), procedural advantages also encouraged the use of rule 10b–5. The federal forum was viewed as superior for several reasons: nationwide service of process under § 27 of the Securities Exchange Act of 1934, liberal venue provisions, and generous discovery rules. The doctrine of pendent jurisdiction permits a federal court to hear both the rule 10b–5 claim and the state claim in a single proceeding, while a state court cannot hear the rule 10b–5 claim. Further, the state security-for-expenses statutes for derivative suits were inapplicable to rule 10b–5 suits, and hence, where they

were potentially applicable, a plaintiff could avoid posting an expensive bond simply by framing his complaint under Rule 10b–5. Finally, there may have been a belief that federal judges tended to be more sympathetic to plaintiffs than state judges.

(6) Is there likely to be a problem meeting the jurisdictional requirements of rule 10b–5 and § 10(b)? What about the use of an *intra*-state telephone? What about using a private mail system such as Federal Express or Airborne? What about computer networks or telefax? Section 3(a)(17) of the Securities Exchange Act of 1934, as amended in 1975, states that the term "interstate commerce" includes "intrastate use of (A) any facility of a national securities exchange or of a telephone or other interstate means of communication or (B) any other interstate instrumentality." 15 U.S.C.A. § 78c(a)(17) (1981). Does that solve all possible problems? What about hand-carrying cash or checks across a city? In an office elevator? What about a bank transmitting a check for collection?

(7) Even though the private cause of action for violations of rule 10b–5 was judicially created in Kardon v. National Gypsum Co., supra n. (3), it has received legislative recognition in at least two federal statutes. In Musick, Peeler & Garrett v. Employers Ins. of Wausau, 508 U.S. 286, 292, 113 S.Ct. 2085, 2089, 124 L.Ed.2d 194, 202 (1993), the Court referred to these two instances and commented that "[w]e infer from these references an acknowledgment of the 10b–5 action without any further expression of legislative intent to define it. Indeed, [one] statute not only treats the 10b–5 action as an accepted feature of our securities laws, but avoids entangling Congress in its formulation. That task, it would appear, Congress has left to us."

———

Beginning in 1975, changes in personnel on the United States Supreme Court resulted in a significant change in approach toward Rule 10b–5. In a word, the period of unlimited growth and the use of Rule 10b–5 as a sort of universal solvent to resolve all securities problems was over. Three decisions define the modern scope of Rule 10b–5.

(1) *Blue Chip Stamps v. Manor Drug Stores,* 421 U.S. 723, 95 S.Ct. 1917, 44 L.Ed.2d 539 (1975). In this case, the Court was faced with a claim by a person who was offered an opportunity to purchase securities but failed to do so because of materially misleading and overly pessimistic statements in the prospectus. An earlier decision by the Second Circuit, Birnbaum v. Newport Steel Corp., 193 F.2d 461 (2d Cir.), certiorari denied,, 343 U.S. 956, 72 S.Ct. 1051, 96 L.Ed. 1356 (1952), had held that private plaintiffs in Rule 10b–5 suits should be limited to actual purchasers or sellers of securities. Over the dissent of the then liberal wing of the Court—Justices Blackmun, Douglas and Brennan—Justice Rehnquist approved of the *Birnbaum* rule in an opinion that reflected profound skepticism about the growth of Rule 10b–5. The opinion starts with a brief outline of the provisions of the Securities Act of 1933, the Securities Exchange Act of 1934, and Rule 10b–5. The Court then launched into a discussion of the scope of Rule 10b–5:

> Having said all this, we would by no means be understood as suggesting that we are able to divine from the language of § 10(b) the express "intent of Congress" as to the contours of a private cause of action under Rule 10b–5. When we deal with private actions under Rule

10b–5, we deal with a judicial oak which has grown from little more than a legislative acorn. Such growth may be quite consistent with the congressional enactment and with the role of the federal judiciary in interpreting it, see J.I. Case v. Borak, supra, but it would be disingenuous to suggest that either Congress in 1934 or the Securities and Exchange Commission in 1942 foreordained the present state of the law with respect to Rule 10b–5. It is therefore proper that we consider, in addition to the factors already discussed, what may be described as policy considerations when we come to flesh out the portions of the law with respect to which neither the congressional enactment nor the administrative regulations offer conclusive guidance. * * *

A great majority of the many commentators on the issue before us have taken the view that the *Birnbaum* limitation on the plaintiff class in a Rule 10b–5 action for damages is an arbitrary restriction which unreasonably prevents some deserving plaintiffs from recovering damages which have in fact been caused by violations of Rule 10b–5. See, e.g., Lowenfels, The Demise of the *Birnbaum* Doctrine: A New Era for Rule 10b–5, 54 Va.L.Rev. 268 (1968). The Securities and Exchange Commission has filed an *amicus* brief in this case espousing that same view. We have no doubt that this is indeed a disadvantage of the *Birnbaum* rule,[6] and if it had no countervailing advantages it would be undesirable as a matter of policy, however much it might be supported by precedent and legislative history. But we are of the opinion that there are countervailing advantages to the *Birnbaum* rule, purely as a matter of policy, although those advantages are more difficult to articulate than is the disadvantage.

There has been widespread recognition that litigation under Rule 10b–5 presents a danger of vexatiousness different in degree and in kind from that which accompanies litigation in general. * * * We believe that the concern expressed for the danger of vexatious litigation which could result from a widely expanded class of plaintiffs under Rule 10b–5 is founded in something more substantial than the common complaint of the many defendants who would prefer avoiding lawsuits entirely to either settling them or trying them. These concerns have two largely separate grounds.

The first of these concerns is that in the field of federal securities laws governing disclosure of information even a complaint which by objective standards may have very little chance of success at trial has a settlement value to the plaintiff out of any proportion to its prospect of success at trial so long as he may prevent the suit from being resolved against him by dismissal or summary judgment. The very pendency of the lawsuit may frustrate or delay normal business activity of the defendant which is totally unrelated to the lawsuit. * * *

The potential for possible abuse of the liberal discovery provisions of the Federal Rules of Civil Procedure may likewise exist in this type of

6. [By the Court] Obviously this disadvantage is attenuated to the extent that remedies are available to nonpurchasers and nonsellers under state law. Thus for example in *Birnbaum* itself, while the plaintiffs found themselves without federal remedies, the conduct alleged as the gravamen of the federal complaint later provided the basis for recovery in a cause of action based on state law. And in the immediate case, respondent has filed a state court class action held in abeyance pending the outcome of this suit.

case to a greater extent than they do in other litigation. The prospect of extensive deposition of the defendant's officers and associates and the concomitant opportunity for extensive discovery of business documents, is a common occurrence in this and similar types of litigation. To the extent that this process eventually produces relevant evidence which is useful in determining the merits of the claims asserted by the parties, it bears the imprimatur of the Federal Rules of Civil Procedure and of the many cases liberally interpreting them. But to the extent that it permits a plaintiff with a largely groundless claim to simply take up the time of a number of other people, with the right to do so representing an *in terrorem* increment of the settlement value, rather than a reasonably founded hope that the process will reveal relevant evidence, it is a social cost rather than a benefit. Yet to broadly expand the class of plaintiffs who may sue under Rule 10b–5 would appear to encourage the least appealing aspect of the use of the discovery rules.

Without the *Birnbaum* rule, an action under Rule 10b–5 will turn largely on which oral version of a series of occurrences the jury may decide to credit, and therefore no matter how improbable the allegations of the plaintiff, the case will be virtually impossible to dispose of prior to trial other than by settlement. * * *

The *Birnbaum* rule, on the other hand, permits exclusion prior to trial of those plaintiffs who were not themselves purchasers or sellers of the stock in question. The fact of purchase of stock and the fact of sale of stock are generally matters which are verifiable by documentation, and do not depend upon oral recollection, so that failure to qualify under the *Birnbaum* rule is a matter that can normally be established by the defendant either on a motion to dismiss or on a motion for summary judgment.

Obviously there is no general legal principle that courts in fashioning substantive law should do so in a manner which makes it easier, rather than more difficult, for a defendant to obtain a summary judgment. But in this type of litigation, where the mere existence of an unresolved lawsuit has settlement value to the plaintiff not only because of the possibility that he may prevail on the merits, an entirely legitimate component of settlement value, but because of the threat of extensive discovery and disruption of normal business activities which may accompany a lawsuit which is groundless in any event, but cannot be proved so before trial, such a factor is not to be totally dismissed. The *Birnbaum* rule undoubtedly excludes plaintiffs who have in fact been damaged by violations of Rule 10b–5, and to that extent it is undesirable. But it also separates in a readily demonstrable manner the group of plaintiffs who actually purchased or actually sold, and whose version of the facts is therefore more likely to be believed by the trier of fact, from the vastly larger world of potential plaintiffs who might successfully allege a claim but could seldom succeed in proving it. And this fact is one of its advantages.

The second ground for fear of vexatious litigation is based on the concern that, given the generalized contours of liability, the abolition of the *Birnbaum* rule would throw open to the trier of fact many rather hazy issues of historical fact the proof of which depended almost entirely on oral testimony. We in no way disparage the worth and frequent high value of oral testimony when we say that dangers of its abuse appear to exist in this type of action to a peculiarly high degree. The Securities and Exchange Commission, while opposing the adoption of the *Birnbaum* rule by this Court, states that it agrees with petitioners "that the effect, if any, of a deceptive practice on someone who has neither purchased nor sold securities may be more difficult to demonstrate than is the effect on a purchaser or seller." The brief also points out that frivolous suits can be brought whatever the rules of standing, and reminds us of this Court's recognition "in a different context" that "the expense and annoyance of litigation is 'part of the social burden of living under government.' "Petroleum Exploration, Inc. v. Public Service Comm'n, 304 U.S. 209, 222, 58 S.Ct. 834, 841, 82 L.Ed. 1294. The Commission suggests that in particular cases additional requirements of corroboration of testimony and more limited measure of damages would correct the dangers of an expanded class of plaintiffs.

But the very necessity, or at least the desirability, of fashioning unique rules of corroboration and damages as a correlative to the abolition of the *Birnbaum* rule suggests that the rule itself may have something to be said for it. * * *

In today's universe of transactions governed by the 1934 Act, privity of dealing or even personal contact between potential defendant and potential plaintiff is the exception and not the rule. The stock of issuers is listed on financial exchanges utilized by tens of millions of investors and corporate representations reach a potential audience, encompassing not only the diligent few who peruse filed corporate reports or the sizeable number of subscribers to financial journals, but the readership of the Nation's daily newspapers. Obviously neither the fact that issuers or other potential defendants under Rule 10b–5 reach a large number of potential investors, or the fact that they are required by law to make their disclosures conform to certain standards, should in any way absolve them from liability for misconduct which is proscribed by Rule 10b–5.

But in the absence of the *Birnbaum* rule, it would be sufficient for a plaintiff to prove that he had failed to purchase or sell stock by reason of a defendant's violation of Rule 10b–5. The manner in which the defendant's violation caused the plaintiff to fail to act could be as a result of the reading of a prospectus, as respondent claims here, but it could just as easily come as a result of a claimed reading of information contained in the financial pages of a local newspaper. Plaintiff's proof would not be that he purchased or sold stock, a fact which would be capable of documentary verification in most situations, but instead that he decided *not* to purchase or sell stock. Plaintiff's entire testimony could be dependent upon uncorroborated oral evidence of many of the crucial elements of his claim, and still be sufficient to go to the jury. The jury would not even have the benefit of weighing the plaintiff's version against the defendant's version, since the elements to which the plaintiff would testify would be in many cases totally unknown and unknowable to the defendant. The very real risk in permitting those in respondent's position to sue under Rule 10b–5 is that the door will be open to recovery of substantial damages on the part of one who offers only his own testimony to prove that he ever consulted a prospectus of the issuer, that he paid any attention to it, or that the representations contained in it damaged him.[7] The virtue of the *Birnbaum* rule, simply stated, in this situation, is that it limits the class of plaintiffs to those who have at least dealt in the security to which the prospectus, representation, or omission relates. And their dealing in the security, whether by way of purchase or sale, will generally be an objectively demonstrable fact in an area of the law otherwise very much dependent upon oral testimony. In the absence of the *Birnbaum* doctrine, bystanders to the securities marketing process could await developments on the sidelines without risk, claiming that inaccuracies in disclosure caused nonselling in a falling market and that unduly pessimistic predictions by the issuer followed by a rising market caused them to allow retrospectively golden opportunities to pass. * * *

We quite agree that if Congress had legislated the elements of a private cause of action for damages, the duty of the Judicial Branch would be to administer the law which Congress enacted; the Judiciary may not circumscribe a right which Congress has conferred because of any disagreement it might have with Congress about the wisdom of creating so expansive a liability. But as we have pointed out, we are not dealing here with any private right created by the express language of § 10(b) or of Rule 10b–5. No language in either of those provisions speaks at all to the contours of a private cause of action for their violation. However flexibly we may construe the language of both provisions, nothing in such construction militates against the *Birnbaum* rule. We are dealing with a private cause of action which has been judicially found to exist, and which will have to be judicially delimited one way or another unless and until Congress addresses the question. Given the peculiar blend of legislative, administrative, and judicial history which now surrounds Rule 10b–5, we believe that practical factors to which we have adverted, and to which other courts have referred, are entitled to a good deal of weight.

Thus we conclude that what may be called considerations of policy, which we are free to weigh in deciding this case, are by no means entirely on one side of the scale. Taken together with the precedential support for the *Birnbaum* rule over a period of more than 20 years, and the consistency of that rule with what we can glean from the intent of

---

7. [By the Court] The SEC, recognizing the necessity for limitations on nonpurchaser, nonseller plaintiffs in the absence of the *Birnbaum* rule, suggests two such limitations to mitigate the practical adverse effects flowing from abolition of the rule. First it suggests requiring some corroborative evidence in addition to oral testimony tending to show that the investment decision of a plaintiff was affected by an omission or misrepresentation. Apparently ownership of stock or receipt of a prospectus or press release would be sufficient corroborative evidence in the view of the SEC to reach the jury. We do not believe that such a requirement would adequately respond to the concerns in part underlying the *Birnbaum* rule. Ownership of stock or receipt of a prospectus says little about whether a plaintiff's investment decision was affected by a violation of Rule 10b–5 or whether a decision was even made. Second, the SEC would limit the vicarious liability of corporate issuers to nonpurchasers and nonsellers to situations where the corporate issuer has been unjustly enriched by a violation. We have no occasion to pass upon the compatibility of this limitation with § 20(a) of the 1934 Act. We do not believe that this proposed limitation is relevant to the concerns underlying in part the *Birnbaum* rule as we have expressed them. * * *

Congress, they lead us to conclude that it is a sound rule and should be followed. * * *

Notes

(1) One issue discussed in *Blue Chip* was whether rule 10b–5 might apply to transactions that also fall within express liability provisions of other federal securities laws. This issue was definitively answered in Herman & MacLean v. Huddleston, 459 U.S. 375, 103 S.Ct. 683, 74 L.Ed.2d 548 (1983), where the Court unanimously held that a cause of action may be maintained under rule 10b–5 for fraudulent misrepresentations and omissions in a 1933 Act prospectus even though that conduct might also be actionable under § 11 of the 1933 Act. The Court stated that the two statutes covered different conduct and liability of different persons, and that "[i]t would be anomalous indeed if the special protection afforded to purchasers in a registered offering by the 1933 Act were deemed to deprive such purchasers of the protections against manipulation and deception that § 10(b) makes available to all persons who deal in securities." 459 U.S. at 383, 103 S.Ct. at 687, 74 L.Ed.2d at 556. The Court also concluded that liability may be established under rule 10b–5 by "a preponderance of the evidence" rather than by "clear and convincing evidence," the standard of proof required in civil fraud actions at common law. 459 U.S. at 390, 103 S.Ct. at 691, 74 L.Ed.2d at 561.

(2) The *Birnbaum* principle involves a qualifying test for *plaintiffs* in rule 10b–5 suits. As will appear below, a *defendant* may readily violate rule 10b–5 even though it is not a purchaser or seller of securities, e.g., by influencing the market by a false press release or preparing a prospectus that contains false statements. Further, the issuer itself may be a nonselling defendant in rule 10b–5 cases.

---

(2) *Ernst & Ernst v. Hochfelder*, 425 U.S. 185, 96 S.Ct. 1375, 47 L.Ed.2d 668 (1976). This case involved a claim against an accounting firm for failing to have discovered a major fraud in a securities firm under the following circumstances:

> Petitioner, Ernst & Ernst, is an accounting firm. From 1946 through 1967 it was retained by First Securities Company of Chicago (First Securities), a small brokerage firm and member of the Midwest Stock Exchange and of the National Association of Securities Dealers, to perform periodic audits of the firm's books and records. In connection with these audits Ernst & Ernst prepared for filing with the Securities and Exchange Commission (Commission) the annual reports required of First Securities under § 17(a) of the 1934 Act.[8] It also prepared for First

8. [By the Court] Section 17(a) requires that securities brokers or dealers "make * * * and preserve * * * such accounts * * * books, and other records, and make such reports, as the Commission by its rules and regulations may prescribe as necessary or appropriate in the public interest or for the protection of investors." During the period relevant here, Commission Rule 17a–5, 17 CFR § 240.17a–5 (1975), required that First Securities file an annual report of its financial condition that included a certificate stating "clearly the opin-ion of the accountant with respect to the financial statement covered by the certificate and the accounting principles and practices reflected therein." The rule required Ernst & Ernst to state in its certificate, *inter alia,* "whether the audit was made in accordance with generally accepted auditing standards applicable in the circumstances" and provided that nothing in the rule should "be construed to imply authority for the omission of any procedure which independent accountants

Securities responses to the financial questionnaires of the Midwest Stock Exchange (Exchange).

Respondents were customers of First Securities who invested in a fraudulent securities scheme perpetrated by Leston B. Nay, president of the firm and owner of 92% of its stock. Nay induced the respondents to invest funds in "escrow" accounts that he represented would yield a high rate of return. Respondents did so from 1942 through 1966, with the majority of the transactions occurring in the 1950's. In fact, there were no escrow accounts as Nay converted respondents' funds to his own use immediately upon receipt. These transactions were not in the customary form of dealings between First Securities and its customers. The respondents drew their personal checks payable to Nay or a designated bank for his account. No such escrow accounts were reflected on the books and records of First Securities, and none was shown on its periodic accounting to respondents in connection with their other investments. Nor were they included in First Securities' filings with the Commission or the Exchange.

This fraud came to light in 1968 when Nay committed suicide, leaving a note that described First Securities as bankrupt and the escrow accounts as "spurious." Respondents subsequently filed this action for damages against Ernst & Ernst in the United States District Court for the Northern District of Illinois under § 10(b) of the 1934 Act. The complaint charged that Nay's escrow scheme violated § 10(b) and Commission Rule 10b–5,[9] and that Ernst & Ernst had "aided and abetted" Nay's violations by its "failure" to conduct proper audits of First Securities. As revealed through discovery, respondents' cause of action rested on a theory of negligent nonfeasance. The premise was that Ernst & Ernst had failed to utilize "appropriate auditing procedures" in its audits of First Securities, thereby failing to discover internal practices of the firm said to prevent an effective audit. The practice principally relied on was Nay's rule that only he could open mail addressed to him at First Securities or addressed to First Securities to his attention, even if it arrived in his absence. Respondents contended that if Ernst & Ernst had conducted a proper audit, it would have discovered this "mail rule." The existence of the rule then would have been disclosed in reports to the Exchange and to the Commission by Ernst & Ernst as an irregular procedure that prevented an effective audit. This would have led to an investigation of Nay that would have revealed the fraudulent scheme. Respondents specifically disclaimed the existence of fraud or intentional misconduct on the part of Ernst & Ernst.[10] * * *

would ordinarily employ in the course of an audit for the purpose of expressing the opinions required" by the rule.

9. [By the Court] Immediately after Nay's suicide the Commission commenced receivership proceedings against First Securities. In those proceedings all of the respondents except two asserted claims based on the fraudulent escrow accounts. These claims ultimately were allowed in SEC v. First Securities Co., 463 F.2d 981, 986 (CA7), cert. denied, 409 U.S. 880, 93 S.Ct. 85, 34 L.Ed.2d 134 (1972), where the court held that Nay's conduct violated § 10(b) and Rule 10b–5, and that First Securities was liable for Nay's fraud as an aider and abettor. The question of Ernst & Ernst's liability was not considered in that case.

10. [By the Court] In their response to interrogatories in the District Court respondents conceded that they did "not accuse Ernst & Ernst of deliberate, intentional fraud," merely with "inexcusable negligence."

As in *Blue Chip*, the court approached the issue of whether scienter was required as an element of a Rule 10b–5 violation in a narrow fashion:

* * * During the 30–year period since a private cause of action was first implied under § 10(b) and Rule 10b–5, a substantial body of case law and commentary has developed as to its elements. Courts and commentators long have differed with regard to whether scienter is a necessary element of such a cause of action, or whether negligent conduct alone is sufficient. In addressing this question, we turn first to the language of § 10(b), for "[t]he starting point in every case involving construction of a statute is the language itself."[11]

Section 10(b) makes unlawful the use or employment of "any manipulative or deceptive device or contrivance" in contravention of Commission rules. The words "manipulative or deceptive" used in conjunction with "device or contrivance" strongly suggest that § 10(b) was intended to proscribe knowing or intentional misconduct. * * * [Their use makes] unmistakable a congressional intent to proscribe a type of conduct quite different from negligence.[12] Use of the word "manipulative" is especially significant. It is and was virtually a term of art when used in connection with securities markets. It connotes intentional or willful conduct designed to deceive or defraud investors by controlling or artificially affecting the price of securities.[13] * * *

* * * The Commission contends * * * that subsections (b) and (c) of Rule 10b–5 are cast in language which—if standing alone—could encompass both intentional and negligent behavior. * * * Viewed in isolation the language of subsection (b), and arguably that of subsection (c), could be read as proscribing, respectively, any type of material misstatement or omission, and any course of conduct, that has the effect of defrauding investors, whether the wrongdoing was intentional or not.

We note first that such a reading cannot be harmonized with the administrative history of the rule, a history making clear that when the Commission adopted the rule it was intended to apply only to activities that involved scienter.[14] More importantly, Rule 10b–5 was adopted

---

11. [By the Editor] The court cites for this proposition the opinion of Justice Powell, concurring in *Blue Chip*.

12. [By the Court] Webster's International Dictionary (2d ed. 1934) defines "device" as "[t]hat which is devised, or formed by design; a contrivance; an invention; project; scheme; often, a scheme to deceive; a stratagem; an artifice," and "contrivance" in pertinent part as "[a] thing contrived or used in contriving; a scheme, plan, or artifice." In turn, "contrive" in pertinent part is defined as "[t]o devise; to plan; to plot * * * [t]o fabricate * * * design; invent * * * to scheme * * *." The Commission also ignores the use of the terms "[t]o use or employ," language that is supportive of the view that Congress did not intend § 10(b) to embrace negligent conduct.

13. [By the Court] Webster's International Dictionary, supra, defines "manipulate" as "to manage or treat artfully or fraudulently; as to

manipulate accounts * * * 4. *Exchanges.* To force (prices) up or down, as by matched orders, wash sales, fictitious reports * * *; to rig."

14. [By the Court] Apparently the rule was a hastily drafted response to a situation clearly involving intentional misconduct. * * * See Conference on Codification of the Federal Securities Laws, 22 Bus.Law. 793, 922 (1967) (remarks of Milton Freeman, one of the rule's co-drafters). * * * There is no indication in the administrative history of the Rule that any of the subsections was intended to proscribe conduct not involving scienter. Indeed the Commission's release issued contemporaneously with the rule explained:

"The Securities and Exchange Commission today announced the adoption of a rule prohibiting fraud by any person in connection with the purchase of securities. The previously existing rules against fraud in the

pursuant to authority granted the Commission under § 10(b). The rule-making power granted to an administrative agency charged with the administration of a federal statute is not the power to make law. Rather, it is " 'the power to adopt regulations to carry into effect the will of Congress as expressed by the statute.' " Dixon v. United States, 381 U.S. 68, 74, 85 S.Ct. 1301, 1305, 14 L.Ed.2d 223, 228 (1965). Thus, despite the broad view of the Rule advanced by the Commission in this case, its scope cannot exceed the power granted the Commission by Congress under § 10(b). * * * When a statute speaks so specifically in terms of manipulation and deception, and of implementing devices and contrivances—the commonly understood terminology of intentional wrongdoing—and when its history reflects no more expansive intent, we are quite unwilling to extend the scope of the statute to negligent conduct.[15] * * *

Notes

(1) In footnote 17 of his opinion in *Hochfelder* Justice Powell stated:

In this opinion the term "scienter" refers to a mental state embracing intent to deceive, manipulate, or defraud. In certain areas of the law recklessness is considered to be a form of intentional conduct for purposes of imposing liability for some act. We need not address here the question whether, in some circumstances, reckless behavior is sufficient for civil liability under § 10(b) and Rule 10b–5.

Since this case concerns action for damages we also need not consider the question whether scienter is a necessary element in an action for injunctive relief under § 10(b) and Rule 10b–5.

The question whether scienter should be required in SEC enforcement actions seeking injunctive relief was definitely resolved in Aaron v. Securities and Exch. Comm'n, 446 U.S. 680, 100 S.Ct. 1945, 64 L.Ed.2d 611 (1980), where the Court held that scienter was a critical ingredient of all rule 10b–5 cases. Justice Blackmun, with whom Justices Brennan and Marshall joined, dissented, disagree-

purchase of securities applied only to brokers and dealers. The new rule closes a loophole in the protections against fraud administered by the Commission by prohibiting individuals or companies from buying securities if they engage in fraud in their purchase." SEC Release No. 3230 (May 21, 1942).

That same year, in its Annual Report, the Commission again stated that the purpose of the rule was to protect investors against "fraud":

"During the fiscal year the Commission adopted Rule X–10B–5 as an additional protection to investors. The new rule prohibits fraud by any person in connection with the purchase of securities, while the previously existing rules against fraud in the purchase of securities applied only to brokers and dealers." 1942 Annual Report of the Securities Exchange Commission 10.

15. [By the Court] As we find the language and history of § 10(b) dispositive of the appropriate standard of liability, there is no occasion to examine the additional considerations of "policy," set forth by the parties, that may

have influenced the lawmakers in their formulation of the statute. We do note that the standard urged by respondents would significantly broaden the class of plaintiffs who may seek to impose liability upon accountants and other experts who perform services or express opinions with respect to matters under the Acts * * * :

This case, on its facts, illustrates the extreme reach of the standard urged by respondents. As investors in transactions initiated by Nay, not First Securities, they were not foreseeable users of the financial statements prepared by Ernst & Ernst. Respondents conceded that they did not rely on either these financial statements or Ernst & Ernst's certificates of opinion. The class of persons eligible to benefit from such a standard, though small in this case, could be numbered in the thousands in other cases. Acceptance of respondents' view would extend to new frontiers the "hazards" of rendering expert advice under the Acts, raising serious policy questions not yet addressed by Congress.

ing with the Court's "textual exegesis and its assessment of history, [and particularly its] failure to appreciate the structural interrelationship among equitable remedies in the 1933 and 1934 Acts." 446 U.S. at 713, 100 S.Ct. at 1964, 64 L.Ed.2d at 636.

(2) Virtually all lower courts addressing the question whether "reckless disregard" might constitute "scienter" since *Hochfelder* have concluded that a rule 10b–5 violation may be grounded on "recklessness" or "reckless disregard of the truth" and that knowing, intentional misconduct is not a necessary ingredient of establishing liability. See, e.g., First Interstate Bank of Denver, N.A. v. Pring, 969 F.2d 891, 901 (10th Cir.1992), stating that "[t]he established rule is that recklessness is sufficient scienter for a primary violation of § 10(b) and Rule 10b–5." The Supreme Court granted certiorari in this case and reversed it on the ground that rule 10b–5 does not contemplate claims based on aiding and abetting. See page 831, infra.

———

(3) *Santa Fe Indus., Inc. v. Green*, 430 U.S. 462, 97 S.Ct. 1292, 51 L.Ed.2d 480 (1977). This case involved the question whether rule 10b–5 could be applied to a Delaware short-form cash-out merger when the transaction was unfair to the minority shareholders but the effect of the transaction was fully disclosed.[16] Court of Appeals held that although Rule 10b–5 clearly reaches material misrepresentations and nondisclosures in connection with the purchase or sale of securities, neither misrepresentation nor nondisclosure was an essential element of a rule 10b–5 action; rather, the rule also reached "breaches of fiduciary duty by a majority against minority shareholders without any charge of misrepresentation or lack of disclosure."[17] The Court of Appeals held:

> "We hold that a complaint alleges a claim under Rule 10b–5 when it charges, in connection with a Delaware short-form merger, that the majority has committed a breach of its fiduciary duty to deal fairly with minority shareholders by effecting the merger without any justifiable business purpose. The minority shareholders are given no prior notice of the merger, thus having no opportunity to apply for injunctive relief, and the proposed price to be paid is substantially lower than the appraised value reflected in the Information Statement." Id., at 1291.

The Supreme Court reversed:

> *Ernst & Ernst* makes clear that in deciding whether a complaint states a cause of action for "fraud" under rule 10b–5, "we turn first to the language of § 10(b), for '[t]he starting point in every case involving construction of a statute is the language itself.' " * * *

16. [By the Editor] The Delaware appraisal procedure was available to dissenting shareholders on the facts of this case, but that remedy was unattractive because the case antedated by several years the *Weinberger* liberalization of the rules surrounding this state-created remedy.

17. [By the Court] Id., at 1287. The court concluded its discussion thus:

"Whether full disclosure has been made is not the crucial inquiry since it is the merger and the undervaluation which constituted the fraud, and not whether or not the majority determines to lay bare their real motives. If there is no valid corporate purpose for the merger, then even the most brazen disclosure of that fact to the minority shareholders in no way mitigates the fraudulent conduct." 533 F.2d, at 1292.

To the extent that the Court of Appeals would rely on the use of the term "fraud" in rule 10b–5 to bring within the ambit of the rule all breaches of fiduciary duty in connection with a securities transaction, its interpretation would, like the interpretation rejected by the Court in *Ernst & Ernst,* "add a gloss to the operative language of the statute quite different from its commonly accepted meaning." Id., at 199. But as the Court there held, the language of the statute must control the interpretation of the rule.[18] * * * Thus the claim of fraud and fiduciary breach in this complaint states a cause of action under any part of rule 10b–5 only if the conduct alleged can be fairly viewed as "manipulative or deceptive" within the meaning of the statute.

It is our judgment that the transaction, if carried out as alleged in the complaint, was neither deceptive nor manipulative and therefore did not violate either § 10(b) of the Act or rule 10b–5. * * * [T]he cases do not support the proposition, adopted by the Court of Appeals below and urged by respondents here, that a breach of fiduciary duty by majority stockholders, without any deception, misrepresentation, or nondisclosure, violates the statute and the Rule.

It is also readily apparent that the conduct alleged in the complaint was not "manipulative" within the meaning of the statute. "Manipulation" is "virtually a term of art when used in connection with securities markets." Ernst & Ernst, 425 U.S., at 199, 96 S.Ct., at 1384. The term refers generally to practices, such as wash sales, matched orders, or rigged prices, that are intended to mislead investors by artificially affecting market activity. * * * Section 10(b)'s general prohibition of practices deemed by the SEC to be "manipulative"—in this technical sense of artificially affecting market activity in order to mislead investors—is fully consistent with the fundamental purpose of the 1934 Act "to substitute a philosophy of full disclosure for the philosophy of caveat emptor. * * *" Affiliated Ute Citizens v. United States, 406 U.S. 128, 151, 92 S.Ct. 1456, 1471, 31 L.Ed.2d 741 (1972). Indeed, nondisclosure is usually essential to the success of a manipulative scheme. No doubt Congress meant to prohibit the full range of ingenious devices that might be used to manipulate securities prices. But we do not think it would have chosen this "term of art" if it had meant to bring within the scope of § 10(b) instances of corporate mismanagement such as this, in which the essence of the complaint is that shareholders were treated unfairly by a fiduciary. * * *

The language of the statute is, we think, "sufficiently clear in its context" to be dispositive here, Ernst & Ernst, 425 U.S., at 201, 96 S.Ct., at 1385; but even if it were not, there are additional considerations that weigh heavily against permitting a cause of action under Rule 10b–5 for the breach of corporate fiduciary duty alleged in this complaint. Congress did not expressly provide a private cause of action for violations of

---

18. [By the Court] The case for adhering to the language of the statute is even stronger here than in *Ernst & Ernst,* where the interpretation of Rule 10b–5 rejected by the Court was strongly urged by the Commission. See also Piper v. Chris–Craft Industries, Inc., 430 U.S. 1, 97 S.Ct. 926, 51 L.Ed.2d 124 (1977), and Blue Chip Stamps v. Manor Drug Stores, 421 U.S. 723, 95 S.Ct. 1917, 44 L.Ed.2d 539 (1975) (rejecting interpretations of Rule 10b–5 urged by the SEC as *amicus curiae*). * * *

§ 10(b). Although we have recognized an implied cause of action under that section in some circumstances, Superintendent of Insurance v. Bankers Life & Cas. Co., supra, we have also recognized that a private cause of action under the antifraud provisions of the Securities Exchange Act should not be implied where it is "unnecessary to ensure the fulfillment of Congress' purposes" in adopting the Act. Piper v. Chris–Craft Industries, 430 U.S., at 41, 97 S.Ct., at 949 (1977). As we noted earlier, the Court repeatedly has described the "fundamental purpose" of the Act as implementing a "philosophy of full disclosure"; once full and fair disclosure has occurred, the fairness of the terms of the transaction is at most a tangential concern of the statute. As in Cort v. Ash, 422 U.S. 66, 78, 80, 95 S.Ct. 2080, 2087, 2090, 45 L.Ed.2d 26 (1975), we are reluctant to recognize a cause of action here to serve what is "at best a subsidiary purpose" of the federal legislation.

A second factor in determining whether Congress intended to create a federal cause of action in these circumstances is "whether 'the cause of action [is] one traditionally relegated to state law. * * * ' "Piper v. Chris–Craft Industries, Inc., 430 U.S., at 40, 97 S.Ct., at 949, quoting Cort v. Ash, 422 U.S., at 78, 95 S.Ct., at 2087. The Delaware Legislature has supplied minority shareholders with a cause of action in the Delaware Court of Chancery to recover the fair value of shares allegedly undervalued in a short-form merger. Of course, the existence of a particular state law remedy is not dispositive of the question whether Congress meant to provide a similar federal remedy, but as in *Cort* and *Piper,* we conclude that "it is entirely appropriate in this instance to relegate respondent and others in his situation to whatever remedy is created by state law." 422 U.S., at 84, 95 S.Ct., at 2091; 430 U.S., at 41, 97 S.Ct., at 949.

The reasoning behind a holding that the complaint in this case alleged fraud under Rule 10b–5 could not be easily contained. It is difficult to imagine how a court could distinguish, for purposes of Rule 10b–5 fraud, between a majority stockholder's use of a short-form merger to eliminate the minority at an unfair price and the use of some other device, such as a long-form merger, tender offer, or liquidation, to achieve the same result; or indeed how a court could distinguish the alleged abuses in these going private transactions from other types of fiduciary self-dealing involving transactions in securities. The result would be to bring within the Rule a wide variety of corporate conduct traditionally left to state regulation. In addition to posing a "danger of vexatious litigation which could result from a widely expanded class of plaintiffs under Rule 10b–5," Blue Chip Stamps v. Manor Drug Stores, 421 U.S., at 740, 95 S.Ct., at 1927 (1975), this extension of the federal securities laws would overlap and quite possibly interfere with state corporate law.[19]

---

19. [By the Court] For example, some States apparently require a "valid corporate purpose" for the elimination of the minority interest through a short-form merger, whereas other States do not. Compare Bryan v. Brock & Blevins Co., 490 F.2d 563 (CA5), cert. denied, 419 U.S. 844, 95 S.Ct. 77, 42 L.Ed.2d 72 (1974) (merger arranged by controlling stockholder for no business purpose except to eliminate 15% minority stockholder violated Georgia short-form merger statute) with Stauffer v. Standard Brands, Inc., 41 Del.Ch. 7, 187 A.2d 78 (Sup.Ct.1962) (Delaware short-form merger statute allows majority stockholder to eliminate the minority interest without any corporate purpose and subject only to an appraisal remedy). Thus to the extent that Rule 10b–5 is interpreted to require a valid corporate pur-

* * * Absent a clear indication of congressional intent, we are reluctant to federalize the substantial portion of the law of corporations that deals with transactions in securities, particularly where established state policies of corporate regulation would be overridden. As the Court stated in Cort v. Ash, supra, "Corporations are creatures of state law, and investors commit their funds to corporate directors on the understanding that, except where federal law *expressly* requires certain responsibilities of directors with respect to stockholders, state law will govern the internal affairs of the corporation." 422 U.S., at 84, 95 S.Ct., at 2091 (emphasis added).

Notes

At the time *Santa Fe Industries v. Green* was decided, there was virtually no state law or precedent dealing with the propriety of "cash mergers," "going private," or similar transactions so long as the transactions met the procedural requirements of the relevant merger provisions of the corporation act. The practical effect of the Supreme Court's decision in this case was to focus attention on state law as the regulator of transactions that literally followed state statute but were or might be unfair to defenseless interests. Six years following the decision in *Santa Fe,* the Delaware Supreme Court imposed duties of "intrinsic fairness" or "fiduciary duties" as a matter of state law to protect such interests. See Weinberger v. UOP, Inc., supra page 778 and the cases cited in the notes following that case.

The United States Supreme Court has resolved significant Rule 10b–5 issues in the 1990s, involving the relevant statute of limitations, the doctrine of aiding and abetting, and the right to contribution among defendants. They reveal the continuing controversial nature of the private cause of action under Rule 10b–5 and the continuing intent of the Supreme Court to contain or limit the scope of the Rule 10b–5 implied cause of action.

(1) *The Statute of Limitations.* A recurring issue in rule 10b–5 litigation has been what statute of limitations should be applicable in these cases. Since there is no statute of limitations expressly applicable to an implied cause of action, for nearly four decades courts struggled with this question. The generally accepted view was that a statute of limitations should be "borrowed" from the applicable state law. Fischman v. Raytheon Mfg. Co., 188 F.2d 783 (2d Cir.1951). However, this was more complex than might first appear, states have several different statutes of limitations that arguably might be "borrowed." Some courts of appeals selected the statute set forth in the state securities law or blue sky statute while others applied the statute applicable to common law fraud or misrepresentation. Time periods for specific types of litigation also vary from state to state within each circuit so that the time period for one case might be different than for another. There was also the question whether state law doctrines relating to discovery periods, equitable tolling doctrines, or delayed accrual dates due to fraudulent concealment should also be borrowed. Finally, in cases involving national or

pose for elimination of minority shareholders as well as a fair price for their shares, it would impose a stricter standard of fiduciary duty than that required by the law of some States.

multiple-state frauds, a choice of law issue had to be addressed. In practice, the borrowing doctrine gave plaintiffs a field day for forum shopping for the most beneficial statute of limitations since the venue and service of process provisions of the Securities Exchange Act usually permitted suit to be brought in virtually any district.

On June 20, 1991, the United States Supreme Court massively roiled the waters of rule 10b–5 litigation when it handed down Lampf, Pleva, Lipkind, Prupis & Petigrow v. Gilbertson, 501 U.S. 350, 111 S.Ct. 2773, 115 L.Ed.2d 321 (1991). Rather than borrowing a state statute of limitations, the majority concluded that courts should look to the statute from which the federal cause of action was implied to determine whether a uniform period of limitations was imposed in similar suits. The majority also concluded that the appropriate statute for application to all rule 10b–5 cases was that suits must be "brought within one year after the discovery of the facts constituting the cause of action and within three years after such cause of action accrued." 15 U.S.C.A. § 78r(c) (1981). Under this statute there is no tolling or delayed accrual dates. See generally Alan R. Bromberg and Lewis D. Lowenfels, SEC Rule 10b–5 and Its New Statute of Limitations: The Circuits Defy the Supreme Court, 51 Bus. Law. 1 (1996).

The one year/three year period was much shorter than the state statutes of limitations previously applied in rule 10b–5 cases as augmented by equitable tolling principles. The issue whether this statute should be applied retroactively to pending Rule 10b–5 cases unexpectedly led to Congressional action and further Supreme Court litigation.[20]

(2) *"Aiding and Abetting."* Prior to 1993, many Federal District Courts and Courts of Appeal had recognized that claims against aiders and abettors could be pursued under Rule 10b–5. Indeed, the issue seemed so clearly to be settled that the original petition for writ of certiorari in Central Bank of, N.A.

---

20. [By the Editor] *Lampf, Pleva* did not explicitly address the retroactivity issue, but another case decided the same day, James B. Beam Distilling Co. v. Georgia, 501 U.S. 529, 111 S.Ct. 2439, 115 L.Ed.2d 481 (1991), did. The Court there stated that a rule of selective prospectivity was inappropriate, and that "when the Court has applied a rule of law to the litigants in one case it must do so with respect to all others not barred by procedural requirements or res judicata." 501 U.S. at 543, 111 S.Ct. at 2448, 115 L.Ed.2d at 493. Following this unambiguous direction, lower federal courts concluded that retroactive application of the *Lampf, Pleva* rule was required, and cases that failed to comply with the one year/three year periods were dismissed even though they were timely filed under the rules in effect when they were filed. See, e.g., Welch v. Cadre Capital, 946 F.2d 185 (2d Cir.1991). Defendants in scores of pending rule 10b–5 fraud cases gleefully obtained dismissal on this ground. Among these cases were highly publicized prosecutions against Ivan Boesky and Michael Milken. The case against Milken alone involved more than a billion dollars. At this time, the publicity over the savings and loan scandals was at its peak, and there was shock and dismay that many defendants appeared to have been granted immunity on a quixotic and unthinking basis. Congress quickly moved to overrule the retrospective application of *Lampf, Pleva*. Codified as § 27A of the Securities Exchange Act, Congress provided that "[a]ny private civil action implied under section [10(b)] of this title that was commenced on or before June 19, 1991—(1) which was dismissed as time barred subsequent to June 19, 1991, and (2) which would have been timely filed under the limitation period provided by the laws applicable in the jurisdiction, including principles of retroactivity, as such laws existed on June 19, 1991, shall be reinstated on motion by the plaintiff" within 60 days after the enactment of § 27A. 15 U.S.C.A. § 78aa–1(b) (1993). Defendants immediately attacked this provision as being unconstitutional under various theories, particularly that it interfered with the judicial role and violated the separation of powers doctrine of the United States Constitution. In Plaut v. Spendthrift Farm, Inc., 514 U.S. 211, 115 S.Ct. 1447, 131 L.Ed.2d 328 (1995), a majority of the Supreme Court agreed, Justices Stevens and Ginsburg dissenting.

v. First Interstate Bank of Denver, 508 U.S. 959, 113 S.Ct. 2927, 124 L.Ed.2d 678 (1993) (a suit against an aider or abettor) did not present the question as one for review.[21] However, the Supreme Court on its own motion directed the parties to brief and argue the issue, and then, in a sharply divided 5–4 set of opinions, adopted a literalistic interpretation of § 10(b) and Rule 10b–5 and concluded that claims based on aiding and abetting were not authorized under that Rule. The majority opinion attempted to rationalize its varying decisions under Rule 10b–5 by distinguishing between two recurring issues: what was "the scope of conduct prohibited by § 10(b)" and, second, "where the defendant has committed a violation of § 10(b), * * * the elements of the 10b–5 private liability scheme: for example, whether there is a right to contribution, what the statute of limitations is, whether there is a reliance requirement, and whether there is an in pari delicto defense." 511 U.S., at 172, 114 S.Ct. at 1439. The "scope of prohibited conduct," the majority stated, is controlled by the text of the statute, while "the elements of the 10b–5 private liability scheme" has required the court "to infer how the 1934 Congress would have addressed the issue" if Rule 10b–5 were created by statute. And the presence or absence of an implied private right of action for aiding and abetting violations of § 10(b) and rule 10b–5 involved, the majority felt, "the scope of conduct prohibited by § 10(b)" and such conduct is not covered by that section. The majority also pointed out that some express liability provisions in the securities acts apparently did not provide for aiding and abetting liability. While the language of the statute controlled, the Court added, the practical concerns first voiced by Justice Rehnquist in *Blue Chip* were particularly likely in aiding and abetting cases. Finally, the Court made clear that its holding was limited to aiding and abetting:

> The absence of § 10(b) aiding and abetting liability does not mean that secondary actors in the securities markets are always free from liability under the securities acts. Any person or entity, including a lawyer, accountant, or bank, who employs a manipulative device or makes a material misstatement (or omission) on which a purchaser or seller of securities relies may be liable as a primary violator under 10b–5, assuming all of the requirements for primary liability under Rule 10b–5 are met.

511 U.S., at 191, 114 S.Ct., at 1455.

In the Private Securities Litigation Reform Act of 1995, Congress restored the remedy against aiders or abettors but only in connection with suits brought by the SEC. Securities Exchange Act of 1934, § 20, as amended by Pub. Law 104–67, 109 Stat. 737, § 104. See generally Robert S. De Leon, The Fault Lines Between Primary Liability and Aiding and Abetting Claims Under Rule 10b–5, 22 J.Corp.L. 723 (1997).

(3) *Right of Contribution.* In Musick, Peeler & Garrett, v. Employers Ins. of Wausau, 508 U.S. 286, 113 S.Ct. 2085, 124 L.Ed.2d 194 (1993), the Supreme Court held that there is an implied right of contribution among defendants in § 10 and rule 10b–5 cases, Justices Scalia and Thomas dissenting. The court relied on analogous express liability provisions in the securities

---

21. [By the Editor] However, the aiding and abetting issue had been specifically question reserved in both *Hochfelder* and Herman & MacLean v. Huddleston, 459 U.S. 375, 103 S.Ct. 683, 74 L.Ed.2d 548 (1983).

acts, and on the nearly uniform acceptance of the right of contribution by lower federal courts. On the surface, this opinion seems inconsistent in principle with the holding in *Central Bank*. In the Private Securities Litigation Reform Act of 1995, Congress substituted a complex scheme of proportionate liability for the joint and several liability among defendants that previously existed under Rule 10b–5 (and that gave rise to the right of contribution). Securities Exchange Act of 1934, § 21D(g), added by Pub. Law 104–67, 109 Stat. 737, § 201. Section 21D(g)(8) preserves the right of contribution among persons who are found liable for the same damages, but in proportion to their relative responsibility.

B. INSIDER TRADING

The first statement that trading on the basis of inside information in the anonymous securities markets might violate Rule 10b–5 appeared in In the Matter of Cady, Roberts & Co., 40 SEC 907 (1961). This was an administrative proceeding by the SEC to discipline a broker who learned from a director of Curtiss–Wright Corporation that Curtiss–Wright planned to reduce its dividend and who then sold Curtiss–Wright common stock (and entered into several short sales of that stock) before the announcement of the dividend cut was made. Chairman Cary's opinion for the Commission broadly stated that insider trading violated rule 10b–5:

> We have already noted that the anti-fraud provisions are phrased in terms of "any person" and that a special obligation has been traditionally required of corporate insiders, e.g., officers, directors and controlling stockholders. These three groups, however, do not exhaust the classes of persons upon whom there is such an obligation. Analytically, the obligation rests on two principal elements; first, the existence of a relationship giving access, directly or indirectly, to information intended to be available only for a corporate purpose and not for the personal benefit of anyone; and second, the inherent unfairness involved where a party takes advantage of such information knowing it is unavailable to those with whom he is dealing. In considering these elements under the broad language of the anti-fraud provisions we are not to be circumscribed by fine distinctions and rigid classifications. Thus our task here is to identify those persons who are in a special relationship with a company and privy to its internal affairs, and thereby suffer correlative duties in trading in its securities. Intimacy demands restraint lest the uninformed be exploited.

40 SEC at 912. Chairman Cary also rejected arguments that an insider's responsibility was limited to existing shareholders, that there was no prohibition against selling shares to members of the general public, and that Rule 10b–5 was only applicable to face-to-face transactions or cases of misrepresentation or manipulation. "If purchasers on an exchange had available material information known by a selling insider, we may assume that their investment judgment would be affected and their decision whether to buy might accordingly be modified. Consequently, any sales by the insider must await disclosure of the information." 40 SEC at 914.

DENNIS W. CARLTON & LARRY R. FISCHEL, THE REGULATION OF INSIDER TRADING
35 Stan.L.Rev. 857, 857–58, 866, 868 (1983).

Imagine two firms, A and B, which are identical in all respects except that, in its charter, firm A prohibits the trading of its shares based on inside (nonpublic) information. The firm requires insiders (employees) to report their trades, which a special committee or an independent accounting firm then checks to ensure compliance with the charter provision. Firm B, by contrast, neither prohibits insider trading nor requires reporting. Insiders openly trade shares of firm B and regularly earn positive abnormal returns. In competitive capital markets, which charter provision will survive?

Despite the deceptive simplicity of this question, it has no obvious answer. The consensus, to the extent that any exists, appears to be that firm A's charter will survive because it eliminates various perceived harmful effects of insider trading. Thus, investors would pay less for shares in B. The managers of B, in order to maximize the value of B shares, would have to adopt a similar charter provision.

As for these harmful effects, many believe that insider trading is "unfair" and undermines public confidence in capital markets. Other critics have argued that insider trading creates perverse incentives by allowing corporate managers to profit on bad news as well as good, encourages managers to invest in risky projects, impedes corporate decisionmaking, and tempts managers to delay public disclosure of valuable information. Some also have argued that insider trading is an inefficient compensation scheme because, in effect, it compensates risk-averse managers with a benefit akin to lottery tickets. Still others have claimed that insider trading allows insiders to divert part of the firm's earnings that would otherwise go to shareholders and therefore raises the firm's cost of capital. Under this "insider trading is harmful to investors" hypothesis, competitive capital markets would force firm B to prohibit insider trading.

The difficulty with this hypothesis is that it appears to be contradicted by the actions of firms. Although no one has conducted rigorous empirical research in this area, it is generally believed that firms have made little, if any, attempt to prohibit insider trading, at least until very recently and then perhaps only as a response to regulation. * * * Because unambiguous welfare statements can be very difficult to make even in simple economic models involving uncertainty, to expect any analysis to prove that insider trading is solely harmful or solely beneficial is unrealistic. The desirability of insider trading is ultimately an empirical question. Nevertheless, analyzing how insider trading affects information transmission and shapes incentives will enable us to understand better the consequences of different allocations of the property rights in valuable information.

A. Information Effects

The social gains from efficient capital markets are well known. The more accurately prices reflect information, the better prices guide capital investment in the economy. * * *

Since the firm's shareholders value the ability to control information that flows to the stock market, they may also value insider trading because it gives the firm an additional method of communicating and controlling information. If insiders trade, the share price will move closer to what it would have been had the information been disclosed. How close will depend on the amount of "noise" surrounding the trade. The greater the ability of market participants to identify insider trading, the more information such trading will convey.
* * *

Several reasons explain why communicating information through insider trading may be of value to the firm. Through insider trading, a firm can convey information it could not feasibly announce publicly because an announcement would destroy the value of the information, would be too expensive, not believable, or—owing to the uncertainty of the information—would subject the firm to massive damage liability if it turned out ex post to be incorrect. Conversely, firms also could use insider trading to limit the amount of information to be reflected in price. Controlling the number of traders who have access to information may be easier than controlling how much information gets announced over time. In other words, announcement of information need not be continuous, while trading on inside information can be. Thus, insider trading gives firms a tool either to increase or to decrease the amount of information that is contained in share prices.

Notes

(1) Following similar economic reasoning, the authors also suggest that corporations may prefer to permit insiders to trade on inside information because it "allows a manager to alter his compensation package in light of new knowledge, thereby avoiding continual renegotiation," and it "provides firms with valuable information concerning prospective managers." Id. at 870, 871.

(2) A somewhat earlier study of insider trading, primarily using economic analysis (but also examining the extent of the enforcement effort against such trading during the 1970s), concludes that "the harm caused by insider trading can be objectively measured and that so measured it does not cause any detectable injury to investors." Michael P. Dooley, Enforcement of Insider Trading Restrictions, 66 Va.L.Rev. 1, 55 (1980). For an argument that some anonymous investor is inevitably harmed by such trading see William K.S. Wang, Trading on Material Nonpublic Information on Impersonal Stock Markets: Who is Harmed, and Who Can Sue Whom Under SEC Rule 10b–5? 54 S.Cal.L.Rev. 1217 (1981). For a further articulation of this argument, see William K.S. Wang and Marc I. Steinberg, Insider Trading, Chs. 2–3 (1996).

(3) Is not all this simply beside the point because trading on inside information—a sure thing—is simply unfair and immoral? Professors Carleton and Fischel respond to this argument as follows:

> We have left for last the most common argument against insider trading—that it is unfair or immoral. The prevalence of this intuition is so powerful that many commentators have argued that insider trading should be prohibited even if it is efficient. What is commonly left unsaid is how and why insider trading is unfair.
>
> Kenneth Scott has pointed out that if the existence of insider trading is known, as it surely is, outsiders will not be disadvantaged because the price they pay will reflect the risk of insider trading. This is a useful insight and in

some sense is a complete response to the claim that investors are exploited by insider trading. * * *

A more powerful response to the argument that insiders profit at the expense of outsiders is that if insider trading is a desirable compensation scheme, it benefits insiders and outsiders alike. Nobody would argue seriously that salaries, options, bonuses, and other compensation devices allow insiders to profit at the expense of outsiders because these sums otherwise would have gone to shareholders. Compensating managers in this fashion increases the size of the pie, and thus outsiders as well as insiders profit from the incentives managers are given to increase the value of the firm. Insider trading does not come "at the expense of" outsiders for precisely the same reason.

Contrary to popular sentiment with respect to insider trading, therefore, there is no tension between considerations of fairness and of efficiency. To say that insider trading is a desirable method of compensating corporate managers is to say that shareholders would voluntarily enter into contractual arrangements with insiders giving them property rights in valuable information. If insider trading is efficient, no independent notions of fairness suggest that it should be prohibited.

Dennis W. Carlton & Larry R. Fischel, The Regulation of Insider Trading, 35 Stan.L.Rev. 857, 880–82 (1983).

(4) The first real attack on the wisdom of a broad prohibition against insider trading appeared in a provocative little book by Professor Henry G. Manne entitled "Insider Trading and the Stock Market" (1966). (Professors Carlton & Fischel, incidentally, refer to this book as "brilliant" and state that it is the "starting point for anyone interested in the subject." Dennis W. Carlton & Larry R. Fischel, The Regulation of Insider Trading, 35 Stan.L.Rev. 857 n. 1 (1983).) Professor Manne also questioned the wisdom of a broad prohibition against insider trading on the basis of economic analysis by considering the theoretical market adjustment mechanisms where insiders were prohibited from trading on inside information and where they were permitted to do so. He concluded that "the odds against any long-term investor's being hurt by an insider trading on undisclosed information is almost infinitesimally small" but that a "rule *allowing* insiders to trade freely may be fundamental to the survival of our corporate system." Henry G. Manne, supra at 110 (emphasis added). His argument favoring such trading essentially was that it was a useful device to compensate true innovators within the corporation ("entrepreneurs") for their innovations, and that other, more traditional forms of compensation might not adequately do so.

This analysis was attacked (often caustically but not very successfully) in about fifteen book reviews published in various law reviews. Professor Manne's riposte appears in Henry G. Manne, Insider Trading and the Law Professors, 23 Vand.L.Rev. 547 (1970). The final words in this debate appear in Daniel Ferber, The Case Against Insider Trading: A Response to Professor Manne, 23 Vand. L.Rev. 621 (1970) and Henry G. Manne, A Rejoinder to Mr. Ferber, 23 Vand. L.Rev. 627 (1970).

(5) For a harsh attack on Dean Manne's economics, see Mark Klock, Mainstream Economics and the Case for Prohibiting Inside Trading, 10 Ga.St.L.J. 297 (1994). Professor Klock is an economist but not a lawyer. He also criticizes the economics of other "law and economics" scholars who have written on the insider trading issue. Klock concludes that allocational economic analysis justifies a ban on inside trading, with a possible exception based on the cost of enforcing such a

ban. See also, Boyd Kimball Dyer, Economic Analysis, Insider Trading, and Game Markets, 1992 Utah L.Rev. 1, 6 (1992), who argues that the prohibition against insider trading may be justified on economic grounds: "[My article] challenges the critics [of the insider trading prohibition] not for using economic principles, but for using them badly. * * * The critics have confused economic efficiency (the allocation of resources to uses) with economic fairness (the distribution of wealth)."

SECURITIES AND EXCHANGE COMM'N v. TEXAS GULF SULPHUR CO.

United States Court of Appeals, Second Circuit, 1968.
401 F.2d 833, cert. denied, 394 U.S. 976, 89 S.Ct. 1454, 22 L.Ed.2d 756 (1969).

Before LUMBARD, CHIEF JUDGE, and WATERMAN, MOORE, FRIENDLY, SMITH, KAUFMAN, HAYS, ANDERSON and FEINBERG, CIRCUIT JUDGES.

WATERMAN, CIRCUIT JUDGE:

This action was commenced in the United States District Court for the Southern District of New York by the Securities and Exchange Commission (the SEC) pursuant to Sec. 21(e) of the Securities Exchange Act of 1934 (the Act), against Texas Gulf Sulphur Company (TGS) and several of its officers, directors and employees, to enjoin certain conduct by TGS and the individual defendants said to violate Section 10(b) of the Act, and Rule 10b–5 (the Rule) promulgated thereunder, and to compel the rescission by the individual defendants of securities transactions assertedly conducted contrary to law * * *.

THE FACTUAL SETTING

This action derives from the exploratory activities of TGS begun in 1957 on the Canadian Shield in eastern Canada. In March of 1959, aerial geophysical surveys were conducted over more than 15,000 square miles of this area by a group led by defendant Mollison, a mining engineer and a Vice President of TGS. The group included defendant Holyk, TGS's chief geologist, defendant Clayton, an electrical engineer and geophysicist, and defendant Darke, a geologist. These operations resulted in the detection of numerous anomalies, i.e., extraordinary variations in the conductivity of rocks, one of which was on the Kidd 55 segment of land located near Timmins, Ontario.

On October 29 and 30, 1963, Clayton conducted a ground geophysical survey on the northeast portion of the Kidd 55 segment which confirmed the presence of an anomaly and indicated the necessity of diamond core drilling for further evaluation. Drilling of the initial hole, K–55–1, at the strongest part of the anomaly was commenced on November 8, and terminated on November 12 at a depth of 655 feet. Visual estimates by Holyk of the core of K–55–1 indicated an average copper content of 1.15% and an average zinc content of 8.64% over a length of 599 feet. This visual estimate convinced TGS that it was desirable to acquire the remainder of the Kidd 55 segment, and in order to facilitate this acquisition TGS President Stephens instructed the exploration group to keep the results of K–55–1 confidential and undisclosed even as to other officers, directors, and employees of TGS. The hole was concealed and a barren core was intentionally drilled off the anomaly. Meanwhile, the core of K–55–1 had been shipped to Utah for chemical assay which, when received in early December, revealed an average mineral content of 1.18% copper, 8.26% zinc, and 3.94% ounces of silver per ton over a length of 602 feet. These results were so remarkable that neither Clayton, an experienced geophysicist, nor four other TGS expert witnesses, had ever seen or heard of a comparable initial exploratory drill hole in a base metal deposit. So, the trial court concluded, "There is no doubt that the drill core of K–55–1 was unusually good and that it excited the interest and speculation of those who knew about it." [258 F.Supp.,] at 282. By March 27, 1964, TGS decided that the land acquisition program had advanced to such a point that the company might well resume drilling, and drilling was resumed on March 31.

During this period, from November 12, 1963 when K–55–1 was completed, to March 31, 1964 when drilling was resumed, certain of the individual defendants[22] and persons[23] said to have received "tips" from them, purchased

22. [By the Court] The purchases by the parties during this period were:

Purchase Date		Purchaser	Shares Number	Shares Price	Calls Number	Calls Price
1964						
Nov.	12	Fogarty	300	17¾–18		
	15	Clayton	200	17¾		
	15	Fogarty	700	17⅝–17⅞		
	15	Mollison	100	17⅞		
	19	Fogarty	500	18⅛		
	26	Fogarty	200	17¾		
	29	Holyk (Mrs.)	50	18		
Chemical Assays of Drill Core of K–55–1 Received December 9–13, 1963						
1963						
Dec.	10	Holyk (Mrs.)	100	20⅜		
	12	Holyk (or wife)			200	21
	13	Mollison	100	21⅛		
	30	Fogarty	200	22		
	31	Fogarty	100	23¼		
1964						
Jan.		Holyk (or wife)			100	23⅝
		Murray			400	23¼
	24	Holyk (or wife)			200	22¼–22⅜
Feb.	10	Fogarty	300	22⅛–22¼		
	20	Darke	300	24⅛		
	24	Clayton	400	23⅞		
	24	Holyk (or wife)			200	24⅛
	26	Holyk (or wife)			200	23⅜
	26	Huntington	50	23¼		
Feb.	27	Darke (Moran as nominee)			1000	22⅝–22¾
Mar.		Holyk (Mrs.)	200	22⅜		
	3	Clayton	100	22¼		
	16	Huntington			100	22⅜
	16	Holyk (or wife)			300	23¼
	17	Holyk (Mrs.)	100	23⅞		
	23	Darke			1000	24¾
	26	Clayton	200	25		
Land Acquisition Completed March 27, 1964						
Mar.	30	Darke			1000	25½
	30	Holyk (Mrs.)	100	25⅞		
Core Drilling of Kidd Segment Resumed March 31, 1964						
April	1	Clayton	60	26½		
	1	Fogarty	400	26½		
	2	Clayton	100	26⅞		
	6	Fogarty	400	28⅛–28⅞		
	8	Mollison (Mrs.)	100	28⅛		

23. See note 23 on page 839.

TGS stock or calls[24] thereon. Prior to these transactions these persons had owned 1135 shares of TGS stock and possessed no calls; thereafter they owned a total of 8235 shares and possessed 12,300 calls.

On February 20, 1964, also during this period, TGS issued stock options to 26 of its officers and employees whose salaries exceeded a specified amount, five of whom were the individual defendants Stephens, Fogarty, Mollison, Holyk, and Kline. Of these, only Kline was unaware of the detailed results of K–55–1, but he, too, knew that a hole containing favorable bodies of copper and zinc ore had been drilled in Timmins. At this time, neither the TGS Stock Option Committee nor its Board of Directors had been informed of the results of K–55–1, presumably because of the pending land acquisition program which required confidentiality. All of the foregoing defendants accepted the options granted them. * * *

First Press Release Issued April 12, 1964				
April	15	Clayton	200	29⅜
	16	Crawford (and wife)	600	30⅛–30¼
Second Press Release Issued 10:00–10:10 or 10:15 A.M., April 16, 1964				
April 16 (app. 10:20 A.M.)				
Coates (for family trusts)			2000	31–31⅝

23. [By the Court]. The purchases made by "tippees" during this period were:

Purchase Date		Purchaser	Shares Number	Shares Price	Calls Number	Calls Price
Chemical Assays of K–55–1 Received Dec. 9–13, 1963						
1963						
Dec.	30	Caskey (Darke)			300	22¼
1964						
Jan.	16	Westreich (Darke)	2000	21¼–21¾		
Feb.	17	Atkinson (Darke)	50	23¼	200	23⅛
	17	Westreich (Darke)	50	23¼	1000	23¼–23⅜
	24	Miller (Darke)			200	23¾
	25	Miller (Darke)			300	23⅜–23½
Mar.		E.W. Darke (Darke)			500	22½–22⅝
	17	E.W. Darke (Darke)			200	23⅜
	30	Atkinson (Darke)			400	25¾–25⅞
		Caskey (Darke)	100	25⅞		
		E.W. Darke (Darke)			1000	25¾–25⅞
		Miller (Darke)			200	25½
		Westreich (Darke)	500	25¾		
	30–31	Klotz (Darke)	2000	25½–26⅛		
Second Press Release Issued April 16, 1964 (Reported over Dow Jones tape at 10:54 A.M.)						
April 16 (from 10:31 A.M.)						
		Haemisegger (Coates)	1500	31¼–35		

In this connection, we point out that, though several of the Holyk purchases of shares and calls made between November 29, 1963 and March 30, 1964 were in the name of Mrs. Holyk or were in the names of both spouses, we have treated these purchases as if made in the name of defendant Holyk alone.

Defendant Mollison purchased 100 shares on November 15 in his name only and on April 8 100 shares were purchased in the name of Mrs. Mollison. We have made no distinction between those purchases.

Defendant Crawford ordered 300 shares about midnight on April 15 and 300 more shares the following morning, to be purchased for himself, and his wife, and these purchases are treated as having been made by the defendant Crawford.

In these particulars we have followed the lead of the court below. * * * It would be unrealistic to include any of these purchases as having been made by other than the defendants, and unrealistic to include them as having been made by members of the general public receiving "tips" from insiders.

24. [By the Court] A "call" is a negotiable option contract by which the bearer has the right to buy from the writer of the contract a

[Editor: Texas Gulf had discovered one of the largest copper/zinc deposits in North America. As drilling explorations continued at the site to determine the size of the deposit, Texas Gulf also sought to acquire land or mineral rights in the area. Rumors leaked out that Texas Gulf had made a major mineral discovery. On April 12, Texas Gulf issued a press release downplaying the importance of the exploration activity, but issued a corrective release four days later confirming the scope of the discovery.]

During the period of drilling in Timmins, the market price of TGS stock fluctuated but steadily gained overall. On Friday, November 8, when the drilling began, the stock closed at 17⅜; on Friday, November 15, after K–55–1 had been completed, it closed at 18. After a slight decline to 16⅜ by Friday, November 22, the price rose to 20⅞ by December 13, when the chemical assay results of K–55–1 were received, and closed at a high of 24⅛ on February 21, the day after the stock options had been issued. It had reached a price of 26 by March 31, after the land acquisition program had been completed and drilling had been resumed, and continued to ascend to 30⅛ by the close of trading on April 10, at which time the drilling progress up to then was evaluated for the April 12th press release. On April 13, the day on which the April 12 release was disseminated, TGS opened at 30⅛, rose immediately to a high of 32 and gradually tapered off to close at 30⅞. It closed at 30¼ the next day, and at 29⅜ on April 15. On April 16, the day of the official announcement of the Timmins discovery, the price climbed to a high of 37 and closed at 36⅜. By May 15, TGS stock was selling at 58¼.

I. The Individual Defendants

A. *Introductory*

Rule 10b–5, on which this action is predicated, * * * was promulgated * * * to prevent inequitable and unfair practices and to insure fairness in securities transactions generally, whether conducted face-to-face, over the counter, or on exchanges, see 3 Loss, Securities Regulation 1455–56 (2d ed. 1961). The Act and the Rule apply to the transactions here, all of which were consummated on exchanges. Whether predicated on traditional fiduciary concepts, see, e.g., Hotchkiss v. Fischer, 136 Kan. 530, 16 P.2d 531 (Kan. 1932), or on the "special facts" doctrine, see, e.g., Strong v. Repide, 213 U.S. 419, 29 S.Ct. 521, 53 L.Ed. 853 (1909), the Rule is based in policy on the justifiable expectation of the securities marketplace that all investors trading on impersonal exchanges have relatively equal access to material information. The essence of the Rule is that anyone who, trading for his own account in the securities of a corporation has "access, directly or indirectly, to information intended to be available only for a corporate purpose and not for the personal benefit of anyone" may not take "advantage of such information knowing it is unavailable to those with whom he is dealing," i.e., the investing public. Matter of Cady, Roberts & Co., 40 SEC 907, 912 (1961). Insiders, as directors or management officers are, of course, by this Rule, precluded from so unfairly dealing, but the Rule is also applicable to one possessing the information who may not be strictly termed an "insider" within the meaning of Sec. 16(b) of the Act. Thus, anyone in possession of material inside

certain number of shares of a particular stock at a fixed price on or before a certain agreed-upon date.

information must either disclose it to the investing public, or if he is disabled from disclosing it in order to protect a corporate confidence, or he chooses not to do so, must abstain from trading in or recommending the securities concerned while such inside information remains undisclosed. So, it is here no justification for insider activity that disclosure was forbidden by the legitimate corporate objective of acquiring options to purchase the land surrounding the exploration site; if the information was, as the SEC contends, material,[25] its possessors should have kept out of the market until disclosure was accomplished. Cady, Roberts, supra at 911.

B. Material Inside Information

[Editor: The Court concludes that K–55–1 constituted "material" information, an issue now controlled by the test of TSC Industries v. Northway, supra. In the course of this discussion, the Court included observations about insider trading that are relevant today:]

An insider is not, of course, always foreclosed from investing in his own company merely because he may be more familiar with company operations than are outside investors. An insider's duty to disclose information or his duty to abstain from dealing in his company's securities arises only in "those situations which are essentially extraordinary in nature and which are reasonably certain to have a substantial effect on the market price of the security if [the extraordinary situation is] disclosed." Fleischer, Securities Trading and Corporate Information Practices: The Implications of the Texas Gulf Sulphur Proceeding, 51 Va.L.Rev. 1271, 1289.

Nor is an insider obligated to confer upon outside investors the benefit of his superior financial or other expert analysis by disclosing his educated guesses or predictions. 3 Loss, op. cit. supra at 1463. The only regulatory objective is that access to material information be enjoyed equally, but this objective requires nothing more than the disclosure of basic facts so that outsiders may draw upon their own evaluative expertise in reaching their own investment decisions with knowledge equal to that of the insiders. * * *

The speculators and chartists of Wall and Bay Streets are also "reasonable" investors entitled to the same legal protection afforded conservative traders. * * *

Our survey of the facts found below conclusively establishes that knowledge of the results of the discovery hole, K–55–1, would have been important to a reasonable investor and might have affected the price of the stock.[26] * * *

[A] major factor in determining whether the K–55–1 discovery was a material fact is the importance attached to the drilling results by those who

---

25. [By the Court] Congress intended by the Exchange Act to eliminate the idea that the use of inside information for personal advantage was a normal emolument of corporate office. See Sections 2 and 16 of the Act.

26. [By the Court] We do not suggest that material facts must be disclosed immediately; the timing of disclosure is a matter for the business judgment of the corporate officers entrusted with the management of the corporation within the affirmative disclosure requirements promulgated by the exchanges and by the SEC. Here, a valuable corporate purpose was served by delaying the publication of the K–55–1 discovery. We do intend to convey, however, that where a corporate purpose is thus served by withholding the news of a material fact, those persons who are thus quite properly true to their corporate trust must not during the period of non-disclosure deal personally in the corporation's securities or give to outsiders confidential information not generally available to all the corporations' stockholders and to the public at large.

knew about it. In view of other unrelated recent developments favorably affecting TGS, participation by an informed person in a regular stock-purchase program, or even sporadic trading by an informed person, might lend only nominal support to the inference of the materiality of the K–55–1 discovery; nevertheless, the timing by those who knew [of their stock purchases] and their purchases of *short-term calls*—purchases in some cases by individuals who had never before purchased calls or even TGS stock— virtually compels the inference that the insiders were influenced by the drilling results. This insider trading activity, * * * surely constitutes highly pertinent evidence and the only truly objective evidence of the materiality of the K–55–1 discovery. * * *

Our decision to expand the limited protection afforded outside investors * * * is not at all shaken by fears that the elimination of insider trading benefits will deplete the ranks of capable corporate managers by taking away an incentive to accept such employment. Such benefits, in essence, are forms of secret corporate compensation, see Cary, Corporate Standards and Legal Rules, 50 Calif.L.Rev. 408, 409–10 (1962), derived at the expense of the uninformed investing public and not at the expense of the corporation which receives the sole benefit from insider incentives. Moreover, adequate incentives for corporate officers may be provided by properly administered stock options and employee purchase plans of which there are many in existence. In any event, the normal motivation induced by stock ownership, i.e., the identification of an individual with corporate progress, is ill-promoted by condoning the sort of speculative insider activity which occurred here; for example, some of the corporation's stock was sold at market in order to purchase short-term calls upon that stock, calls which would never be exercised to increase a stockholder equity in TGS unless the market price of that stock rose sharply.

The core of Rule 10b–5 is the implementation of the Congressional purpose that all investors should have equal access to the rewards of participation in securities transactions. It was the intent of Congress that all members of the investing public should be subject to identical market risks— which market risks include, of course, the risk that one's evaluative capacity or one's capital available to put at risk may exceed another's capacity or capital. The insiders here were not trading on an equal footing with the outside investors. They alone were in a position to evaluate the probability and magnitude of what seemed from the outset to be a major ore strike; they alone could invest safely, secure in the expectation that the price of TGS stock would rise substantially in the event such a major strike should materialize, but would decline little, if at all, in the event of failure, for the public, ignorant at the outset of the favorable probabilities would likewise be unaware of the unproductive exploration, and the additional exploration costs would not significantly affect TGS market prices. Such inequities based upon unequal access to knowledge should not be shrugged off as inevitable in our way of life, or in view of the congressional concern in the area, remain uncorrected.

We hold, therefore, that all transactions in TGS stock or calls by individuals apprised of the drilling results of K–55–1 were made in violation of Rule 10b–5. Inasmuch as the visual evaluation of that drill core (a generally reliable estimate though less accurate than a chemical assay) constituted material information, those advised of the results of the visual evaluation as well as those informed of the chemical assay traded in violation of law. The geologist Darke possessed undisclosed material information and traded in TGS securities. Therefore we reverse the dismissal of the action as to him and his personal transactions. The trial court also found that Darke, after the drilling of K–55–1 had been completed and with detailed knowledge of the results thereof, told certain outside individuals that TGS "was a good buy." These individuals thereafter acquired TGS stock and calls. The trial court also found that later, as of March 30, 1964, Darke not only used his material knowledge for his own purchases but that the substantial amounts of TGS stock and calls purchased by these outside individuals on that day, was "strong circumstantial evidence that Darke must have passed the word to one or more of his 'tippees' that drilling on the Kidd 55 segment was about to be resumed." 258 F.Supp. at 284. Obviously if such a resumption were to have any meaning to such "tippees," they must have previously been told of K–55–1.

Unfortunately, however, there was no definitive resolution below of Darke's liability in these premises for the trial court held as to him, as it held as to all the other individual defendants, that this "undisclosed information" never became material until April 9. As it is our holding that the information acquired after the drilling of K–55–1 was material, we, on the basis of the findings of direct and circumstantial evidence on the issue that the trial court has already expressed, hold that Darke violated Rule 10b–5(3) and Section 10(b) by "tipping" and we remand, pursuant to the agreement of the parties, for a determination of the appropriate remedy. As Darke's "tippees" are not defendants in this action, we need not decide whether, if they acted with actual or constructive knowledge that the material information was undisclosed, their conduct is as equally violative of the Rule as the conduct of their insider source, though we note that it certainly could be equally reprehensible. * * *

C. When May Insiders Act?

Appellant Crawford, who ordered[27] the purchase of TGS stock shortly before the TGS April 16 official announcement, and defendant Coates, who placed orders with and communicated the news to his broker immediately after the official announcement was read at the TGS-called press conference, concede that they were in possession of material information. They contend, however, that their purchases were not proscribed purchases for the news had already been effectively disclosed. We disagree.

Crawford telephoned his orders to his Chicago broker about midnight on April 15 and again at 8:30 in the morning of the 16th, with instructions to buy at the opening of the Midwest Stock Exchange that morning. The trial

---

27. [By the Court] The effective protection of the public from insider exploitation of advance notice of material information requires that the time that an insider places an order, rather than the time of its ultimate execution, be determinative for Rule 10b–5 purposes. Otherwise, insiders would be able to "beat the news," cf. Fleischer, supra, 51 Va.L.Rev. at 1291, by requesting in advance that their orders be executed immediately after the dissem- ination of a major news release but before outsiders could act on the release. Thus it is immaterial whether Crawford's orders were executed before or after the announcement was made in Canada (9:40 A.M., April 16) or in the United States (10:00 A.M.) or whether Coates's order was executed before or after the news appeared over the Merrill Lynch (10:29 A.M.) or Dow Jones (10:54 A.M.) wires.

court's finding that "he sought to, and did, 'beat the news,' "258 F.Supp. at 287, is well documented by the record. The rumors of a major ore strike which had been circulated in Canada and, to a lesser extent, in New York, had been disclaimed by the TGS press release of April 12, which significantly promised the public an official detailed announcement when possibilities had ripened into actualities. The abbreviated announcement to the Canadian press at 9:40 A.M. on the 16th by the Ontario Minister of Mines and the report carried by The Northern Miner, parts of which had sporadically reached New York on the morning of the 16th through reports from Canadian affiliates to a few New York investment firms, are assuredly not the equivalent of the official 10–15 minute announcement which was not released to the American financial press until after 10:00 A.M. Crawford's orders had been placed before that. Before insiders may act upon material information, such information must have been effectively disclosed in a manner sufficient to insure its availability to the investing public. Particularly here, where a formal announcement to the entire financial news media had been promised in a prior official release known to the media, all insider activity must await dissemination of the promised official announcement.

Coates was absolved by the court below because his telephone order was placed shortly before 10:20 A.M. on April 16, which was after the announcement had been made even though the news could not be considered already a matter of public information. This result seems to have been predicated upon a misinterpretation of dicta in *Cady, Roberts,* where the SEC instructed insiders to "keep out of the market until the established procedures for public release of the information are *carried out* instead of hastening to execute transactions in advance of, and in frustration of, the objectives of the release," 40 SEC at 915 (emphasis supplied). This reading of a news release, which prompted Coates into action, is merely the first step in the process of dissemination required for compliance with the regulatory objective of providing all investors with an equal opportunity to make informed investment judgments. Assuming that the contents of the official release could instantaneously be acted upon,[28] at the minimum Coates should have waited until the news could reasonably have been expected to appear over the media of widest circulation, the Dow Jones broad tape, rather than hastening to insure an advantage to himself and his broker son-in-law.[29] * * *

---

28. [By the Court] Although the only insider who acted after the news appeared over the Dow Jones broad tape is not an appellant and therefore we need not discuss the necessity of considering the advisability of a "reasonable waiting period" during which outsiders may absorb and evaluate disclosures, we note in passing that, where the news is of a sort which is not readily translatable into investment action, insiders may not take advantage of their advance opportunity to evaluate the information by acting immediately upon dissemination. In any event, the permissible timing of insider transactions after disclosures of various sorts is one of the many areas of expertise for appropriate exercise of the SEC's rulemaking power, which we hope will be utilized in the future to

provide some predictability of certainty for the business community.

29. [By the Court] The record reveals that news usually appears on the Dow Jones broad tape 2–3 minutes after the reporter completes dictation.

Here, assuming that the Dow Jones reporter left the press conference as early as possible, 10:10 A.M., the 10–15 minute release (which took at least that long to dictate) could not have appeared on the wire before 10:22, and for other reasons unknown to us did not appear until 10:54. Indeed, even the abbreviated version of the release reported by Merrill Lynch over its private wire did not appear until 10:29. Coates, however, placed his call no later than 10:20.

E. *May Insiders Accept Stock Options Without Disclosing Material Information To The Issuer?*

On February 20, 1964, defendants Stephens, Fogarty, Mollison, Holyk and Kline accepted stock options issued to them and a number of other top officers of TGS, although not one of them had informed the Stock Option Committee of the Board of Directors or the Board of the results of K–55–1, which information we have held was then material. The SEC sought rescission of these options. The trial court, in addition to finding the knowledge of the results of the K–55 discovery to be immaterial, held that Kline had no detailed knowledge of the drilling progress and that Holyk and Mollison could reasonably assume that their superiors, Stephens and Fogarty, who were directors of the corporation, would report the results if that was advisable; indeed all employees had been instructed not to divulge this information pending completion of the land acquisition program. Therefore, the court below concluded that only directors Stephens and Fogarty, of the top management, would have violated the Rule by accepting stock options without disclosure, but it also found that they had not acted improperly as the information in their possession was not material. In view of our conclusion as to materiality we hold that Stephens and Fogarty violated the Rule by accepting them. However, as they have surrendered the options and the corporation has canceled them, we find it unnecessary to order that the injunctions prayed for be actually issued. We point out, nevertheless, that the surrender of these options after the SEC commenced the case is not a satisfaction of the SEC claim, and a determination as to whether the issuance of injunctions against Stephens and Fogarty is advisable in order to prevent or deter future violations of regulatory provisions is remanded for the exercise of discretion by the trial court.

Contrary to the belief of the trial court that Kline had no duty to disclose his knowledge of the Kidd project before accepting the stock option offered him, we believe that he, a vice president, who had become the general counsel of TGS in January 1964, but who had been secretary of the corporation since January 1961, and was present in that capacity when the options were granted, and who was in charge of the mechanics of issuance and acceptance of the options, was a member of top management and under a duty before accepting his option to disclose any material information he may have possessed, and, as he did not disclose such information to the Option Committee we direct rescission of the option he received.[30] As to Holyk and Mollison,

---

30. [By the Court] The options granted on February 20, 1964 to Mollison, Holyk, and Kline were ratified by the Texas Gulf directors on July 15, 1965 after there had been, of course, a full disclosure and after this action had been commenced. However, the ratification is irrelevant here, for we would hold with the district court that a member of top management, as was Kline, is required, before accepting a stock option, to disclose material inside information which, if disclosed, might affect the price of the stock during the period when the accepted option could be exercised. Kline had known since November 1962 that K–55–1 had been drilled, that the drilling had intersected a sulphide body containing copper and zinc, and that TGS desired to acquire adjacent property.

Of course, if any of the five knowledgeable defendants had rejected his option there might well have been speculation as to the reason for the rejection. Therefore, in a case where disclosure to the grantors of an option would seriously jeopardize corporate security, it could well be desirable, in order to protect a corporation from selling securities to insiders who are in a position to appreciate their true worth at a price which may not accurately reflect the true value of the securities and at the same time to preserve when necessary the secrecy of corporate activity, not to require that an insider

the SEC has not appealed the holding below that they, not being then members of top management (although Mollison was a vice president) had no duty to disclose their knowledge of the drilling before accepting their options. Therefore, the issue of whether, by accepting, they violated the Act, is not before us, and the holding below is undisturbed. * * *

CONCLUSION

In summary, therefore, we affirm the finding of the court below that appellants Richard H. Clayton and David M. Crawford have violated [§ 10b] and Rule 10b–5; we reverse the judgment order entered below dismissing the complaint against appellees Charles F. Fogarty, Richard H. Clayton, Richard D. Mollison, Walter Holyk, Kenneth H. Darke, Earl L. Huntington, and Francis G. Coates, as we find that they have violated [§ 10b] and Rule 10b–5. As to these eight individuals we remand so that in accordance with the agreement between the parties the Commission may notice a hearing before the court below to determine the remedies to be applied against them. We reverse the judgment order dismissing the complaint against Claude O. Stephens, Charles F. Fogarty, and Harold B. Kline as recipients of stock options, direct the district court to consider in its discretion whether to issue injunction orders against Stephens and Fogarty, and direct that an order issue rescinding the option granted Kline and that such further remedy be applied against him as may be proper by way of an order of restitution. * * *

FRIENDLY, CIRCUIT JUDGE (concurring):

Agreeing with the result reached by the majority and with most of Judge Waterman's searching opinion, I take a rather different approach to * * * a situation that will not often arise, involving as it does the acceptance of stock options during a period when inside information likely to produce a rapid and substantial increase in the price of the stock was known to some of the grantees but unknown to those in charge of the granting. I suppose it would be clear, under Ruckle v. Roto American Corp., 339 F.2d 24 (2 Cir.1964),[31] that if a corporate officer having such knowledge persuaded an unknowing board of directors to grant him an option at a price approximating the current market, the option would be rescindable in an action under Rule 10b–5. It would seem, by the same token, that if, to make the pill easier to swallow, he urged the directors to include others lacking the knowledge he possessed, he would be liable for all the resulting damage. The novel problem in the instant case is to define the responsibility of officers when a directors' committee administering a stock option plan proposes of its own initiative to make options available to them and others at a time when they know that the option price, geared to the market value of the stock, did not reflect a substantial increment likely to be realized in short order and was therefore unfair to the corporation.

possessed of undisclosed material information reject the offer of a stock option, but only to require that he abstain from exercising it until such time as there shall have been a full disclosure and, after the full disclosure, a ratification such as was voted here. However, as this suggestion was not presented to us, we do not consider it or make any determination with reference to it.

31. [By the Judge] * * * If we were writing on a clean slate, I would have some doubt whether the framers of the Securities Exchange Act intended § 10b to provide a remedy for an evil that had long been effectively handled by derivative actions for waste of corporate assets under state law simply because in a particular case the waste took the form of a sale of securities. * * *

A rule requiring a minor officer to reject an option so tendered would not comport with the realities either of human nature or of corporate life. If the SEC had appealed the ruling dismissing this portion of the complaint as to Holyk and Mollison, I would have upheld the dismissal quite apart from the special circumstance that a refusal on their part could well have broken the wall of secrecy it was important for TGS to preserve. Whatever they knew or didn't know about Timmins, they were entitled to believe their superiors had reported the facts to the Option Committee unless they had information to the contrary. Stephens, Fogarty and Kline stand on an altogether different basis; as senior officers they had an obligation to inform the Committee that this was not the right time to grant options at 95% of the current price. Silence, when there is a duty to speak, can itself be a fraud. I am unimpressed with the argument that Stephens, Fogarty and Kline could not perform this duty on the peculiar facts of this case, because of the corporate need for secrecy during the land acquisition program. Non-management directors would not normally challenge a recommendation for postponement of an option plan from the President, the Executive Vice President, and the Vice President and General Counsel. Moreover, it should be possible for officers to communicate with directors, of all people, without fearing a breach of confidence. Hence, as one of the foregoing hypotheticals suggests, I am not at all sure that a company in the position of TGS might not have a claim against top officers who breached their duty of disclosure for the entire damage suffered as a result of the untimely issuance of options, rather than merely one for rescission of the options issued to them.[32] Since that issue is not before us, I merely make the reservation of my position clear. * * *

[Concurring opinions of JUDGES IRVING R. KAUFMAN, HAYS, and ANDERSON, and dissenting opinion of JUDGE MOORE (with whom CHIEF JUDGE LUMBARD concurs) are omitted.]

Notes

(1) On remand, the District Court required Darke to pay to TGS the profits which he and his tippees made on TGS stock prior to April 17, 1964, and required Holyk, Huntington, and Clayton to pay to TGS the profits which each of them made on the TGS stock prior to April 17, 1964. The order stated that the payments were to be held in escrow in an interest-bearing account for a period of five years, subject to disposition in such manner as the Court might direct upon application by the SEC or other interested person, or on the Court's own motion. At the end of the five years, any money remaining undisposed of would become the property of TGS. To protect these defendants against double liability, any private judgments against them arising out of the events of this case were to be paid from this fund. This order was affirmed in its entirety by a panel consisting of Judges Friendly, Waterman, and Hays. 446 F.2d 1301 (2d Cir.1971), cert.

---

32. [By the Judge] Though the Board of Directors of TGS ratified the issuance of the options after the Timmins discovery had been fully publicized, it obviously was of the belief that Kline had committed no serious wrong in remaining silent. Throughout this litigation TGS has supported the legality of the actions of all the defendants—the company's counsel having represented, among others, Stephens, Fogarty and Kline. Consequently, I agree with the majority in giving the Board's action no weight here. If a fraud of this kind may ever be cured by ratification, compare Continental Securities Co. v. Belmont, 206 N.Y. 7, 99 N.E. 138, 51 L.R.A., N.S., 112 (1912), with Claman v. Robertson, 164 Ohio St. 61, 128 N.E.2d 429 (1955); that cannot be done without an appreciation of the illegality of the conduct proposed to be excused.

denied, 404 U.S. 1005, 92 S.Ct. 561, 30 L.Ed.2d 558 (1971). The Court specifically rejected the argument that the required restitution constituted a penalty:

> Restitution of the profits on these transactions merely deprives the appellants of the gains of their wrongful conduct. Nor does restitution impose a hardship in this case. The lowest purchase price of any of the transactions here was $17.75 per share paid by Clayton on November 15, 1963. The mean average price of the stock on April 17, 1964, has been stipulated by the parties to be $40.375 per share. By May 15, 1964, the stock was selling at $58.25 per share. The court's order requires only restitution of the profits made by the violators prior to general knowledge of the ore strike on April 17, 1964, and, in effect, leaves the appellants all the profits accrued after that date. It would severely defeat the purposes of the Act if a violator of Rule 10b–5 were allowed to retain the profits from his violation. The district court's order corrects this by effectively moving the purchase dates of the violators' purchases up to April 17, 1964.

> As to the requirement that Darke make restitution for the profits derived by his tippees, admittedly more of a hardship is imposed. However, without such a remedy, insiders could easily evade their duty to refrain from trading on the basis of inside information. Either the transactions so traded could be concluded by a relative or an acquaintance of the insider, or implied understandings could arise under which reciprocal tips between insiders in different corporations could be given.

446 F.2d at 1308.

Later cases recognize that full "disgorgement" or restitution may be sought from tippees as well as from insiders themselves. See, e.g., SEC v. Lund, 570 F.Supp. 1397 (C.D.Cal.1983). Presumably, Darke's tippees could have been required to restore the profits they made if they had been named as parties in the original suit by the SEC.

(2) What kind of trading strategy should an officer or director adopt to eliminate or minimize exposure under Rule 10b–5? The New York Stock Exchange Listed Company Manual § 309.00, discusses this problem and offers the following analysis:

> Shareholders have indicated however that they want directors and officers to have a meaningful investment in the companies they manage. So, in the interest of promoting better shareholder relationships, some general rules under which corporate officials may properly buy or sell stock in their company may be helpful. One appropriate method of purchase might be a periodic investment program where the directors or officers make regular purchases under an established program administered by a broker and where the timing of purchases is outside the control of the individual. It would also seem appropriate for officials to buy or sell stock in their companies for a 30–day period commencing one week after the annual report has been mailed to shareholders and otherwise broadly circulated (provided, of course, that the annual report has adequately covered important corporate developments and that no new major undisclosed developments occur within that period).

> Transactions may also be appropriate under the following circumstances, provided that prior to making a purchase or sale a director or officer contacts the chief executive officer of the company to be sure there are no important developments pending which need to be made public before an insider could properly participate in the market:

- Following a release of quarterly results, which includes adequate comment on new developments during the period. This timing of transactions might be even more appropriate where the report has been mailed to shareholders.

- Following the wide dissemination of information on the status of the company and current results. For example, transactions may be appropriate after a proxy statement or prospectus which gives such information in connection with a merger or new financing.

- At those times when there is relative stability in the company's operations and the market for its securities. Under these circumstances, timing of transactions may be relatively less important. Of course such periods of relative stability will vary greatly from time to time and will also depend to a large extent on the nature of the industry or the company.

Where a development of major importance is expected to reach the appropriate time for announcement within the next few months, transactions by directors and officers should be avoided.

Corporate officials should wait until after the release of earnings, dividends, or other important developments have appeared in the press before making a purchase or sale. This permits the news to be widely disseminated and negates the inference that officials had an inside advantage. Similarly, transactions just prior to important press releases should be avoided.

In granting stock options to directors and key officers, the same philosophy that relates to purchases and sales may well apply. Where an established pattern or formula is part of a plan specifically approved by shareholders, the question of timing may not arise. In taking up an option, the timing of a purchase is not usually critical as the price is set at the time the option is granted. The reasoning relating to stock options might also apply to employee stock purchase plans in which directors and officers may be entitled to participate.

The considerations that affect director and officer transactions in stock of their own company may be pertinent to transactions in the shares of other companies with which discussions of merger, acquisition, important contracts, etc., are being considered or carried on. The same considerations apply to the families or close associates of directors and officers who are often presumed to have preferential access to information. As far as the public is concerned, they also are insiders. While this assumption may be unjustified in many cases, it is a fact of life which those in positions of leadership and responsibility cannot ignore.

Some companies have adopted policies for the guidance of their personnel relating to transactions in the company's stock, as well as other areas where conflicts of interest could arise. Such policies can be very helpful to employees who have access to important confidential information, as well as to the directors and officers.

In the final analysis, directors and officers must be guided by a sense of fairness to all segments of the investing public. * * *

CHIARELLA v. UNITED STATES

Supreme Court of the United States, 1980.
445 U.S. 222, 100 S.Ct. 1108, 63 L.Ed.2d 348.

MR. JUSTICE POWELL delivered the opinion of the Court.

The question in this case is whether a person who learns from the confidential documents of one corporation that it is planning an attempt to secure control of a second corporation violates § 10(b) of the Securities Exchange Act of 1934 if he fails to disclose the impending takeover before trading in the target company's securities.

I

Petitioner is a printer by trade. In 1975 and 1976, he worked as a "markup man" in the New York composing room of Pandick Press, a financial printer. Among documents that petitioner handled were five announcements of corporate takeover bids. When these documents were delivered to the printer, the identities of the acquiring and target corporations were concealed by blank spaces or false names. The true names were sent to the printer on the night of the final printing.

The petitioner, however, was able to deduce the names of the target companies before the final printing from other information contained in the documents. Without disclosing his knowledge, petitioner purchased stock in the target companies and sold the shares immediately after the takeover attempts were made public. By this method, petitioner realized a gain of slightly more than $30,000 in the course of 14 months. Subsequently, the Securities and Exchange Commission (Commission or SEC) began an investigation of his trading activities. In May 1977, petitioner entered into a consent decree with the Commission in which he agreed to return his profits to the sellers of the shares. On the same day, he was discharged by Pandick Press.

In January 1978, petitioner was indicted on 17 counts of violating § 10(b) of the Securities Exchange Act of 1934 (1934 Act) and SEC Rule 10b–5.[33] After petitioner unsuccessfully moved to dismiss the indictment, he was brought to trial and convicted on all counts.

The Court of Appeals for the Second Circuit affirmed petitioner's conviction. 588 F.2d 1358 (1978). We granted certiorari, 441 U.S. 942, 99 S.Ct. 2158, 60 L.Ed.2d 1043 (1979), and we now reverse.

II

* * * This case concerns the legal effect of the petitioner's silence. The District Court's charge permitted the jury to convict the petitioner if it found that he willfully failed to inform sellers of target company securities that he knew of a forthcoming takeover bid that would make their shares more valuable. In order to decide whether silence in such circumstances violates

---

33. [By the Court] Only Rules 10b–5(a) and (c) are at issue here. Rule 10b–5(b) provides that it shall be unlawful "[t]o make any untrue statement of a material fact or to omit to state a material fact necessary in order to make the statements made, in the light of the circum-stances under which they were made, not misleading." The portion of the indictment based on this provision was dismissed because the petitioner made no statements at all in connection with the purchase of stock.

§ 10(b), it is necessary to review the language and legislative history of that statute as well as its interpretation by the Commission and the federal courts.

Although the starting point of our inquiry is the language of the statute, Ernst & Ernst v. Hochfelder, 425 U.S. 185, 197, 96 S.Ct. 1375, 1382, 47 L.Ed.2d 668 (1976), § 10(b) does not state whether silence may constitute a manipulative or deceptive device. Section 10(b) was designed as a catch-all clause to prevent fraudulent practices. But neither the legislative history nor the statute itself affords specific guidance for the resolution of this case. When Rule 10b–5 was promulgated in 1942, the SEC did not discuss the possibility that failure to provide information might run afoul of § 10(b).

The SEC took an important step in the development of § 10(b) when it held that a broker-dealer and his firm violated that section by selling securities on the basis of undisclosed information obtained from a director of the issuer corporation who was also a registered representative of the brokerage firm. In Cady, Roberts & Co., 40 SEC 907 (1961), the Commission decided that a corporate insider must abstain from trading in the shares of his corporation unless he has first disclosed all material inside information known to him. The obligation to disclose or abstain derives from

> [a]n affirmative duty to disclose material information[,] [which] has been traditionally imposed on corporate 'insiders,' particular officers, directors, or controlling stockholders. We, and the courts have consistently held that insiders must disclose material facts which are known to them by virtue of their position but which are not known to persons with whom they deal and which, if known, would affect their investment judgment. Id., at 911.

The Commission emphasized that the duty arose from (i) the existence of a relationship affording access to inside information intended to be available only for a corporate purpose, and (ii) the unfairness of allowing a corporate insider to take advantage of that information by trading without disclosure.[34]

That the relationship between a corporate insider and the stockholders of his corporation gives rise to a disclosure obligation is not a novel twist of the law. At common law, misrepresentation made for the purpose of inducing reliance upon the false statement is fraudulent. But one who fails to disclose material information prior to the consummation of a transaction commits fraud only when he is under a duty to do so. And the duty to disclose arises when one party has information "that the other [party] is entitled to know because of a fiduciary or other similar relation of trust and confidence between them." In its *Cady, Roberts* decision, the Commission recognized a relationship of trust and confidence between the shareholders of a corporation and those insiders who have obtained confidential information by reason of

---

34. [By the Court] In *Cady, Roberts*, the broker-dealer was liable under § 10(b) because it received nonpublic information from a corporate insider of the issuer. Since the insider could not use the information, neither could the partners in the brokerage firm with which he was associated. The transaction of *Cady, Roberts* involved sale of stock to persons who previously may not have been shareholders in the corporation. The Commission embraced the reasoning of Judge Learned Hand that "the director or officer assumed a fiduciary relation to the buyer by the very sale; for it would be a sorry distinction to allow him to use the advantage of his position to induce the buyer into the position of a beneficiary although he was forbidden to do so once the buyer had become one." Id., at 914, n. 23, quoting *Gratz v. Claughton*, 187 F.2d 46, 49 (CA2), cert. denied, 341 U.S. 920, 71 S.Ct. 741, 95 L.Ed. 1353 (1951).

their position with that corporation.[35] This relationship gives rise to a duty to disclose because of the "necessity of preventing a corporate insider from * * * [taking] unfair advantage of the uninformed minority stockholders." Speed v. Transamerica Corp., 99 F.Supp. 808, 829 (D.Del.1951).

The federal courts have found violations of § 10(b) where corporate insiders used undisclosed information for their own benefit. E.g., SEC v. Texas Gulf Sulphur Co., 401 F.2d 833 (C.A.2 1968), cert. denied, 404 U.S. 1005, 92 S.Ct. 561, 30 L.Ed.2d 558 (1971). The cases also have emphasized, in accordance with the common-law rule, that "[t]he party charged with failing to disclose market information must be under a duty to disclose it." Frigitemp Corp. v. Financial Dynamics Fund, Inc., 524 F.2d 275, 282 (C.A.2 1975). Accordingly, a purchaser of stock who has no duty to a prospective seller because he is neither an insider nor a fiduciary has been held to have no obligation to reveal material facts. * * *

Thus, administrative and judicial interpretations have established that silence in connection with the purchase or sale of securities may operate as a fraud actionable under § 10(b) despite the absence of statutory language or legislative history specifically addressing the legality of nondisclosure. But such liability is premised upon a duty to disclose arising from a relationship of trust and confidence between parties to a transaction. Application of a duty to disclose prior to trading guarantees that corporate insiders, who have an obligation to place the shareholder's welfare before their own, will not benefit personally through fraudulent use of material nonpublic information.[36]

III

In this case, the petitioner was convicted of violating § 10(b) although he was not a corporate insider and he received no confidential information from the target company. Moreover, the "market information" upon which he relied did not concern the earning power or operations of the target company, but only the plans of the acquiring company. Petitioner's use of that information was not a fraud under § 10(b) unless he was subject to an affirmative duty to disclose it before trading. In this case, the jury instructions failed to specify any such duty. In effect, the trial court instructed the jury that petitioner owed a duty to everyone; to all sellers, indeed, to the market as a whole. The jury simply was told to decide whether petitioner used material,

---

35. [By the Court] The dissent of Mr. Justice Blackmun suggests that the "special facts" doctrine may be applied to find that silence constitutes fraud where one party has superior information to another. This Court has never so held. In Strong v. Repide, 213 U.S. 419, 431–434, 29 S.Ct. 521, 525, 526, 53 L.Ed. 853 (1909), this Court applied the special facts doctrine to conclude that a corporate insider had a duty to disclose to a shareholder. In that case, the majority shareholder of a corporation secretly purchased the stock of another shareholder without revealing that the corporation, under the insider's direction, was about to sell corporate assets at a price that would greatly enhance the value of the stock. The decision in Strong v. Repide was premised upon the fiduciary duty between the corporate insider and the shareholder. See Pepper v. Litton, 308 U.S.

295, 307, n. 15, 60 S.Ct. 238, 245, n. 15, 84 L.Ed. 281 (1939).

36. [By the Court] "Tippees" of corporate insiders have been held liable under § 10(b) because they have a duty not to profit from the use of inside information that they know is confidential and know or should know came from a corporate insider, Shapiro v. Merrill Lynch, Pierce, Fenner & Smith, 495 F.2d 228, 237–238 (C.A.2 1974). The tippee's obligation has been viewed as arising from his role as a participant after the fact in the insider's breach of a fiduciary duty. Subcommittees of American Bar Association Section of Corporation, Banking, and Business Law, Comment Letter on Material, Non-Public Information (Oct. 15, 1973) reprinted in BNA, Securities Regulation & Law Report No. 233, at D–1, D–2 (Jan. 2, 1974).

nonpublic information at a time when "he knew other people trading in the securities market did not have access to the same information."

The Court of Appeals affirmed the conviction by holding that "[a]nyone— corporate insider or not—who regularly receives material nonpublic information may not use that information to trade in securities without incurring an affirmative duty to disclose." Although the court said that its test would include only persons who regularly receive material nonpublic information, its rationale for that limitation is unrelated to the existence of a duty to disclose.[37] The Court of Appeals, like the trial court, failed to identify a relationship between petitioner and the sellers that could give rise to a duty. Its decision thus rested solely upon its belief that the federal securities laws have "created a system providing equal access to information necessary for reasoned and intelligent investment decisions." The use by anyone of material information not generally available is fraudulent, this theory suggests, because such information gives certain buyers or sellers an unfair advantage over less informed buyers and sellers.

This reasoning suffers from two defects. First not every instance of financial unfairness constitutes fraudulent activity under § 10(b). See Santa Fe Industries Inc. v. Green, 430 U.S. 462, 474–477, 97 S.Ct. 1292, 1301–1303, 51 L.Ed.2d 480 (1977). Second, the element required to make silence fraudulent—a duty to disclose—is absent in this case. No duty could arise from petitioner's relationship with the sellers of the target company's securities, for petitioner had no prior dealings with them. He was not their agent, he was not a fiduciary, he was not a person in whom the sellers had placed their trust and confidence. He was, in fact, a complete stranger who dealt with the sellers only through impersonal market transactions.

We cannot affirm petitioner's conviction without recognizing a general duty between all participants in market transactions to forgo actions based on material, nonpublic information. Formulation of such a broad duty, which departs radically from the established doctrine that duty arises from a specific relationship between two parties, should not be undertaken absent some explicit evidence of congressional intent.

As we have seen, no such evidence emerges from the language or legislative history of § 10(b). Moreover, neither the Congress nor the Commission ever has adopted a parity-of-information rule. * * *

---

37. [By the Court] The Court of Appeals said that its "regular access to market information" test would create a workable rule embracing "those who occupy * * * strategic places in the market mechanism." 588 F.2d, at 1365. These considerations are insufficient to support a duty to disclose. A duty arises from the relationship between parties, and not merely from one's ability to acquire information because of his position in the market.

The Court of Appeals also suggested that the acquiring corporation itself would not be a "market insider" because a tender offeror creates, rather than receives, information and takes a substantial economic risk that its offer will be unsuccessful. Again, the Court of Appeals departed from the analysis appropriate to recognition of a duty. The Court of Appeals for the Second Circuit previously held, in a manner consistent with our analysis here, that a tender offeror does not violate § 10(b) when it makes preannouncement purchases precisely because there is no relationship between the offeror and the seller: "We know of no rule of law * * * that a purchaser of stock, who was not an 'insider' and had no fiduciary relation to a prospective seller, had any obligation to reveal circumstances that might raise a seller's demands and thus abort the sale." General Time Corp. v. Talley Industries, 403 F.2d 159, 164 (1968), cert. denied, 393 U.S. 1026, 89 S.Ct. 631, 21 L.Ed.2d 570 (1969).

We see no basis for applying such a new and different theory of liability in this case. As we have emphasized before, the 1934 Act cannot be read " 'more broadly than its language and the statutory scheme reasonably permit.' " Touche Ross & Co. v. Redington, 442 U.S. 560, 578, 99 S.Ct. 2479, 2490, 61 L.Ed.2d 82 (1979). Section 10(b) is aptly described as a catch-all provision, but what it catches must be fraud. When an allegation of fraud is based upon nondisclosure, there can be no fraud absent a duty to speak. We hold that a duty to disclose under § 10(b) does not arise from the mere possession of nonpublic market information. The contrary result is without support in the legislative history of § 10(b) and would be inconsistent with the careful plan that Congress has enacted for regulation of the securities markets. Cf. Santa Fe Industries Inc. v. Green, 430 U.S., at 479, 97 S.Ct., at 1304.[38]

IV

In its brief to this Court, the United States offers an alternative theory to support petitioner's conviction. It argues that petitioner breached a duty to the acquiring corporation when he acted upon information that he obtained by virtue of his position as an employee of a printer employed by the corporation. The breach of this duty is said to support a conviction under § 10(b) for fraud perpetrated upon both the acquiring corporation and the sellers.

We need not decide whether this theory has merit for it was not submitted to the jury. * * *

The jury instructions demonstrate that petitioner was convicted merely because of his failure to disclose material, nonpublic information to sellers from whom he bought the stock of target corporations. The jury was not instructed on the nature or elements of a duty owed by petitioner to anyone other than the sellers. Because we cannot affirm a criminal conviction on the basis of a theory not presented to the jury, we will not speculate upon whether such a duty exists, whether it has been breached, or whether such a breach constitutes a violation of § 10(b).

The judgment of the Court of Appeals is reversed.

[The separate opinions of Mr. Justice Stevens, concurring in the majority opinion and judgment, and Mr. Justice Brennan, concurring in the judgment, are omitted.]

---

38. [By the Court] Mr. Justice Blackmun's dissent would establish the following standard for imposing criminal and civil liability under § 10(b) and Rule 10b–5:

"[P]ersons having access to confidential material information that is not legally available to others generally are prohibited * * * from engaging in schemes to exploit their structural information advantage through trading in affected securities."

This view is not substantially different from the Court of Appeals theory that anyone "who regularly receives material nonpublic information may not use that information to trade in securities without incurring an affirmative duty to disclose," and must be rejected for the reasons stated in Part III. Additionally, a judicial holding that certain undefined activities "generally are prohibited" by § 10(b) would raise questions whether either criminal or civil defendants would be given fair notice that they have engaged in illegal activity.

It is worth noting that this is apparently the first case in which criminal liability has been imposed upon a purchaser for § 10(b) nondisclosure. Petitioner was sentenced to a year in prison, suspended except for one month, and a five-year term of probation.

MR. CHIEF JUSTICE BURGER, dissenting.

I believe that the jury instructions in this case properly charged a violation of § 10(b) and Rule 10b–5, and I would affirm the conviction.

I

As a general rule, neither party to an arm's length business transaction has an obligation to disclose information to the other unless the parties stand in some confidential or fiduciary relation. See Prosser, Law of Torts § 106 (2d ed.1955). This rule permits a businessman to capitalize on his experience and skill in securing and evaluating relevant information; it provides incentive for hard work, careful analysis, and astute forecasting. But the policies that underlie the rule also should limit its scope. In particular, the rule should give way when an informational advantage is obtained, not by superior experience, foresight, or industry, but by some unlawful means. * * * I would read § 10(b) and Rule 10b–5 to encompass and build on this principle: to mean that a person who has misappropriated nonpublic information has an absolute duty to disclose that information or to refrain from trading.

The language of § 10(b) and of Rule 10b–5 plainly support such a reading. By their terms, these provisions reach *any* person engaged in *any* fraudulent scheme. This broad language negates the suggestion that congressional concern was limited to trading by "corporate insiders" or to deceptive practices related to "corporate information."[39] Just as surely Congress cannot have intended one standard of fair dealing for "white collar" insiders and another for the "blue collar" level. The very language of § 10(b) and Rule 10b–5 "by repeated use of the word 'any' [was] obviously meant to be inclusive." Affiliated Ute Citizens v. United States, 406 U.S. 128, 151, 92 S.Ct. 1456, 1471, 31 L.Ed.2d 741 (1972).

The history of the statute and of the rule also supports this reading * * *.

II

The Court's opinion, as I read it, leaves open the question whether § 10(b) and Rule 10b–5 prohibit trading on misappropriated nonpublic information.[40] Instead, the Court apparently concludes that this theory of the case was not submitted to the jury. In the Court's view, the instructions given the jury were premised on the erroneous notion that the mere failure to disclose nonpublic information, however acquired, is a deceptive practice. And because of this premise, the jury was not instructed that the means by which Chiarella acquired his informational advantage—by violating a duty owed to the acquiring companies—was an element of the offense.

39. [By the Chief Justice] Academic writing in recent years has distinguished between "corporate information"—information which comes from within the corporation and reflects on expected earnings or assets—and "market information." See, e.g., Fleischer, Mundheim & Murphy, An Initial Inquiry into the Responsibility to Disclose Market Information, 121 U.Pa.L.Rev. 798, 799 (1973). It is clear that the § 10(b) and Rule 10b–5 by their terms and by their history make no such distinction. See Brudney, Insiders, Outsiders, and Informational Advantages Under the Federal Securities Laws, 93 Harv.L.Rev. 322, 329–333 (1979).

40. [By the Chief Justice] There is some language in the Court's opinion to suggest that only "a relationship between petitioner and the sellers * * * could give rise to a duty [to disclose]." The Court's holding, however, is much more limited, namely that mere possession of material nonpublic information is insufficient to create a duty to disclose or to refrain from trading. Accordingly, it is my understanding that the Court has not rejected the view, advanced above, that an absolute duty to disclose or refrain arises from the very act of misappropriating nonpublic information.

The Court's reading of the District Court's charge is unduly restrictive. * * * In sum, the evidence shows beyond all doubt that Chiarella, working literally in the shadows of the warning signs in the printshop, misappropriated—stole to put it bluntly—valuable nonpublic information entrusted to him in the utmost confidence. He then exploited his ill-gotten informational advantage by purchasing securities in the market. In my view, such conduct plainly violates § 10(b) and Rule 10b–5. Accordingly, I would affirm the judgment of the Court of Appeals.

MR. JUSTICE BLACKMUN, with whom MR. JUSTICE MARSHALL joins, dissenting.

Although I agree with much of what is said in Part I of the dissenting opinion of The Chief Justice, I write separately because, in my view, it is unnecessary to rest petitioner's conviction on a "misappropriation" theory. The fact that petitioner Chiarella purloined, or, to use The Chief Justice's word, "stole," information concerning pending tender offers certainly is the most dramatic evidence that petitioner was guilty of fraud. He has conceded that he knew it was wrong, and he and his co-workers in the print shop were specifically warned by their employer that actions of this kind were improper and forbidden. But I also would find petitioner's conduct fraudulent within the meaning of § 10(b) [and] Rule 10b–5, even if he had obtained the blessing of his employer's principals before embarking on his profiteering scheme. Indeed, I think petitioner's brand of manipulative trading, with or without such approval, lies close to the heart of what the securities laws are intended to prohibit.

The Court continues to pursue a course, charted in certain recent decisions, designed to transform § 10(b) from an intentionally elastic "catch-all" provision to one that catches relatively little of the misbehavior that all too often makes investment in securities a needlessly risky business for the uninitiated investor. See, e.g., Ernst & Ernst v. Hochfelder, 425 U.S. 185, 96 S.Ct. 1375, 47 L.Ed.2d 668 (1976); Blue Chip Stamps v. Manor Drug Stores, 421 U.S. 723, 95 S.Ct. 1917, 44 L.Ed.2d 539 (1975). Such confinement in this case is now achieved by imposition of a requirement of a "special relationship" akin to fiduciary duty before the statute gives rise to a duty to disclose or to abstain from trading upon material nonpublic information.[41] The Court admits that this conclusion finds no mandate in the language of the statute or its legislative history. Yet the Court fails even to attempt a justification of its ruling in terms of the purposes of the securities laws, or to square that ruling with the long-standing but now much abused principle that the federal securities laws are to be construed flexibly rather than with narrow technicality. * * *

Whatever the outer limits of the Rule, petitioner Chiarella's case fits neatly near the center of its analytical framework. He occupied a relationship to the takeover companies giving him intimate access to concededly material information that was sedulously guarded from public access. The information, in the words of Cady, Roberts & Co., 40 SEC, at 912, was "intended to be available only for a corporate purpose and not for the personal benefit of

---

41. [By the Justice] The Court fails to specify whether the obligations of a special relationship must fall directly upon the person engaging in an allegedly fraudulent transaction, or whether the derivative obligations of "tippees" that lower courts long have recognized, are encompassed by its rule.

anyone." Petitioner, moreover, knew that the information was unavailable to those with whom he dealt. And he took full, virtually riskless advantage of this artificial information gap by selling the stocks shortly after each takeover bid was announced. By any reasonable definition, his trading was "inherent[ly] unfai[r]." This misuse of confidential information was clearly placed before the jury. Petitioner's conviction, therefore, should be upheld and I dissent from the Court's upsetting that conviction.

Notes

(1) Would the Court's construction of rule 10b–5 reach the following persons:

(a) The secretary or messenger who overhears snippets of conversations from his superiors, infers that a favorable development is about to occur, and buys shares of his employer?

(b) The person sitting in a restaurant who overhears conversations at the next table from which she infers that a favorable development is about to occur with respect to XX Company, and buys shares in XX Company?

(c) The reporter who attends a press conference at which a favorable development is announced, and then, immediately after the conference and before the news appears on the ticker services, telephones his broker and places an order to purchase?

(d) A subtippee who believes his tippee has "connections" with employees of the corporation but is not himself employed by the corporation?

(2) Vincent Chiarella was apparently the first person against whom criminal charges were filed for violation of rule 10b–5. The press noted at the time that he was a "blue collar" worker and commented that it seemed unfair to apply the criminal process only against persons in lower economic classes.

(3) The criminalization of insider trading reached a new level in Carpenter v. United States, 484 U.S. 19, 108 S.Ct. 316, 98 L.Ed.2d 275 (1987), where the court upheld a conviction under the mail and wire fraud statute, 18 U.S.C.A. §§ 1341, 1343,[42] of Kenneth Felis and R. Foster Winans under the following circumstances:

> In 1981, Winans became a reporter for the Wall Street Journal (the Journal) and in the summer of 1982 became one of the two writers of a daily column, "Heard on the Street." That column discussed selected stocks or groups of stocks, giving positive and negative information about those stocks

---

42. [By the Editor] Section 1341 provides:

Whoever, having devised or intending to devise any scheme or artifice to defraud, or for obtaining money or property by means of false or fraudulent pretenses, representations, or promises, or to sell, dispose of, loan, exchange, alter, give away, distribute, supply, or furnish or procure for unlawful use any counterfeit or spurious coin, obligation, security, or other article, or anything represented to be or intimated or held out to be such counterfeit or spurious article, for the purpose of executing such scheme or artifice or attempting so to do, places in any post office or authorized depository for mail matter, any matter or thing whatever to be sent or delivered by the Postal Service, or takes or receives therefrom, any such matter or thing, or knowingly causes to be delivered by

mail according to the direction thereon, or at the place at which it is directed to be delivered by the person to whom it is addressed, any such matter or thing, shall be fined not more than $1,000 or imprisoned not more than five years, or both.

Section 1343 provides:

Whoever, having devised or intending to devise any scheme or artifice to defraud, or for obtaining money or property by means of false or fraudulent pretenses, representations, or promises, transmits or causes to be transmitted by means of wire, radio, or television communication in interstate or foreign commerce, any writings, signs, signals, pictures, or sounds for the purpose of executing such scheme or artifice, shall be fined not more than $1,000 or imprisoned not more than five years, or both.

and taking "a point of view with respect to investment in the stocks that it reviews." Winans regularly interviewed corporate executives to put together interesting perspectives on the stocks that would be highlighted in upcoming columns, but, at least for the columns at issue here, none contained corporate inside information or any "hold for release" information. Because of the "Heard" column's perceived quality and integrity, it had the potential of affecting the price of the stocks which it examined. The District Court concluded on the basis of testimony presented at trial that the "Heard" column "does have an impact on the market, difficult though it may be to quantify in any particular case."

The official policy and practice at the Journal was that prior to publication, the contents of the column were the Journal's confidential information. Despite the rule, with which Winans was familiar, he entered into a scheme in October 1983 with Peter Brant and petitioner Felis, both connected with the Kidder Peabody brokerage firm in New York City, to give them advance information as to the timing and contents of the "Heard" column. This permitted Brant and Felis and another conspirator, David Clark, a client of Brant, to buy or sell based on the probable impact of the column on the market. Profits were to be shared. The conspirators agreed that the scheme would not affect the journalistic purity of the "Heard" column, and the District Court did not find that the contents of any of the articles were altered to further the profit potential of petitioners' stock-trading scheme. Over a four-month period, the brokers made prepublication trades on the basis of information given them by Winans about the contents of some 27 Heard columns. The net profits from these trades were about $690,000.

In November 1983, correlations between the "Heard" articles and trading in the Clark and Felis accounts were noted at Kidder Peabody and inquiries began. Brant and Felis denied knowing anyone at the Journal and took steps to conceal the trades. Later, the Securities and Exchange Commission began an investigation. Questions were met by denials both by the brokers at Kidder Peabody and by Winans at the Journal. As the investigation progressed, the conspirators quarreled, and on March 29, 1984, Winans and Carpenter went to the SEC and revealed the entire scheme. This indictment and a bench trial followed. Brant, who had pled guilty under a plea agreement, was a witness for the Government.

In addition, Felis and Winans were convicted for conspiracy under 18 U.S.C.A. § 371,[43] and David Carpenter, Winans' roommate, was convicted for aiding and abetting. The defendants were also charged for criminal violations of § 10(b) and Rule 10b–5 under the theory set forth in Chief Justice Burger's dissent, an issue on which the Justices were evenly divided and therefore did not address. The convictions under the mail and wire fraud statutes, however, were unanimously affirmed:

> We have little trouble in holding that the conspiracy here to trade on the Journal's confidential information is not outside the reach of the mail and wire fraud statutes, provided the other elements of the offenses are satisfied. The Journal's business information that it intended to be kept confidential

---

43. [By the Editor] Section 371 provides:

If two or more persons conspire either to commit any offense against the United States, or to defraud the United States, or any agency thereof in any manner or for any purpose, and one or more of such persons do any act to effect the object of the conspiracy, each shall be fined not more than $10,000 or imprisoned not more than five years, or both.

was its property; the declaration to that effect in the employee manual merely removed any doubts on that score and made the finding of specific intent to defraud that much easier. Winans continued in the employ of the Journal, appropriating its confidential business information for his own use, all the while pretending to perform his duty of safeguarding it. In fact, he told his editors twice about leaks of confidential information not related to the stock-trading scheme, demonstrating both his knowledge that the Journal viewed information concerning the "Heard" column as confidential and his deceit as he played the role of a loyal employee. Furthermore, the District Court's conclusion that each of the petitioners acted with the required specific intent to defraud is strongly supported by the evidence.

Lastly, we reject the submission that using the wires and the mail to print and send the Journal to its customers did not satisfy the requirement that those mediums be used to execute the scheme at issue. The courts below were quite right in observing that circulation of the "Heard" column was not only anticipated but an essential part of the scheme. Had the column not been made available to Journal customers, there would have been no effect on stock prices and no likelihood of profiting from the information leaked by Winans.

The federal mail and wire fraud statute, 18 U.S.C.A. § 1341, is widely used by federal prosecutors in white collar crime cases. A U.S. attorney has written that it is "our Stradivarius, our Colt 45, our Louisville Slugger, our Cuinsinart—and our true love." Jed S. Rakoff, The Federal Mail Fraud Statute (Part 1), 18 Duq. L.Rev. 771 (1980). Rakoff adds, "We may flirt with RICO, show off with 10b–5, and call the conspiracy law 'darling,' but we always come home to the virtues of 18 U.S.C. § 1341 * * *." Prison sentences are quite routinely imposed upon convictions under this statute, and the decision in the principal case therefore significantly "raised the ante" for persons considering knowing use of material inside information for securities trading.

(4) The theory of liability set forth in Chief Justice Burger's dissenting opinion in *Chiarella* (and which evenly divided the Justices in *Carpenter*), is called the misappropriation theory. Basically, it provides that an insider trading violation may be based on a breach of fiduciary duty by the trader, regardless of whether that duty runs to the issuer of the securities involved or to other parties. Following *Chiarella* and *Carpenter*, the Second, Third, Seventh and Ninth Circuits endorsed the misappropriation theory but the Fourth and Eighth Circuits rejected it. This conflict was ultimately resolved by the United States Supreme Court in *O'Hagan* in 1997. See page 861, infra.

(5) If Chiarella is guilty under rule 10b–5 under the misappropriation theory, have we not simply criminalized violations by employees of employer work rules? Is there any public harm to the securities markets or securities trading if Chiarella disobeys the signs posted by his employer? For a negative evaluation of *Carpenter* on the grounds that it "overcriminalizes" what should essentially be a matter for the civil law and that it tends to "trivialize" the mail and wire fraud case of *McNally,* see John C. Coffee, Jr., Hush!: The Criminal Status of Confidential Information after *McNally* and *Carpenter* and the Enduring Problem of Overcriminalization, 26 Am.Crim.L.Rev. 121 (1988). For the perspective of an official of the Department of Justice on the *Carpenter* decision and background on the mail and wire fraud statute, see Michael R. Dreeben, Insider Trading and Intangible Rights: The Redefinition of the Mail Fraud Statute, 26 Am.Crim.L.Rev. 181 (1988). See generally, Charles C. Cox & Kevin S. Fogarty, Bases of Insider

Trading Law, 49 Ohio St.L.Rev. 353 (1988); Lawrence E. Mitchell, The Jurisprudence of the Misappropriation Theory and the New Insider Trading Legislation: From Fairness to Efficiency and Back, 52 Alb.L.Rev. 775 (1988).

(6) Approximately four months after *Chiarella* was decided, the SEC adopted rule 14e–3 pursuant to §§ 14(e) and 23 of the Securities Exchange Act. SEC Rel. No. 34–17120, 45 Fed.Reg. 60410 (1980). These sections of the Exchange Act are part of the Williams Act (described in chapter 14), relating to takeover bids and cash tender offers. The SEC release describes the purpose and scope of this rule as follows:

> The rule pertains to trading by persons in securities which may be the subject of a tender offer as well as tipping of material, nonpublic information relating to a contemplated tender offer. It should be noted that the rule applies only in the context of tender offers. * * *

II. Synopsis of Rule

> * * * Rule 14e–3(a) imposes a duty of disclosure under Section 14(e) on any person who trades in securities which will be sought or are being sought in a tender offer while that person is in possession of material information which he knows or has reason to know is nonpublic and has been acquired directly or indirectly from the offering person, from the issuer or from an officer, director, partner or employee or any other person acting on behalf of the offering person or the issuer. Since no duty to disclose would arise if a person subject to the rule does not purchase or sell or cause the purchase or sale of such securities while in possession of such information, the rule establishes a specific duty to "disclose or abstain from trading" under Section 14(e). The "disclose or abstain from trading" framework of Rule 14e–3(a) is similar to the approach taken in *Texas Gulf* and *Cady, Roberts* which the *Chiarella* Court cited with approval. In the Commission's view this framework is the least restrictive method of regulating this abusive practice. * * *

> The operation of Rule 14e–3(a) may be illustrated by examples. It should be emphasized that these examples are not exclusive and do not constitute the only situations in which the duty under Rule 14e–3(a) would arise:

> > (1) If an offering person tells another person that the offering person will make a tender offer which information is nonpublic, the other person has acquired material, nonpublic information directly from the offering person and has a duty under Rule 14e–3(a). * * *

> > (3) If the offering person sends a nonpublic letter to a subject company notifying the subject company of a proposed tender offer at a specified price and upon specified terms and the management of the subject company learns the contents of the letter, the management of the subject company has acquired material, nonpublic information directly from the offering person. An individual member of such management will violate Rule 14e–3(a) if he purchases or sells or causes the purchase or sale of the securities to be sought in the tender offer.

> > (4) If, under the facts in the preceding example, the management of the subject company also tells other persons not affiliated with management of the letter, then those other persons have acquired material, nonpublic information indirectly from the offering person and are under a duty to disclose or abstain from trading under Rule 14e–3(a). * * *

(6) If a person steals, converts or otherwise misappropriates material, nonpublic information relating to a tender offer from an offering person, such person will have acquired the information directly from the offering person and has a duty under Rule 14e–3(a).

(7) If an offering person tells another person of his intention to make a tender offer, and such other person subsequently tells a third person that a tender offer will be made and this third person knows or has reason to know that this non-public information came indirectly from the offering person, then this third person has a duty under Rule 14e–3(a).

45 Fed.Reg. 60410–60414. The validity of Rule 14e–3 remained in some doubt until the Supreme Court's decision in *O'Hagan* in 1997, set forth infra.

UNITED STATES v. O'HAGAN

Supreme Court of the United States, 1997.
— U.S. —, 117 S.Ct. 2199, 138 L.Ed.2d 724.

JUSTICE GINSBURG delivered the opinion of the Court.

This case concerns the interpretation and enforcement of § 10(b) and § 14(e) of the Securities Exchange Act of 1934, and rules made by the Securities and Exchange Commission pursuant to these provisions, Rule 10b–5 and Rule 14e-3(a). Two prime questions are presented. The first relates to the misappropriation of material, nonpublic information for securities trading; the second concerns fraudulent practices in the tender offer setting. In particular, we address and resolve these issues: (1) Is a person who trades in securities for personal profit, using confidential information misappropriated in breach of a fiduciary duty to the source of the information, guilty of violating § 10(b) and Rule 10b–5? (2) Did the Commission exceed its rulemaking authority by adopting Rule 14e–3(a), which proscribes trading on undisclosed information in the tender offer setting, even in the absence of a duty to disclose? Our answer to the first question is yes, and to the second question, viewed in the context of this case, no.

I

Respondent James Herman O'Hagan was a partner in the law firm of Dorsey & Whitney in Minneapolis, Minnesota. In July 1988, Grand Metropolitan PLC (Grand Met), a company based in London, England, retained Dorsey & Whitney as local counsel to represent Grand Met regarding a potential tender offer for the common stock of the Pillsbury Company, headquartered in Minneapolis. Both Grand Met and Dorsey & Whitney took precautions to protect the confidentiality of Grand Met's tender offer plans. O'Hagan did no work on the Grand Met representation. Dorsey & Whitney withdrew from representing Grand Met on September 9, 1988. Less than a month later, on October 4, 1988, Grand Met publicly announced its tender offer for Pillsbury stock.

On August 18, 1988, while Dorsey & Whitney was still representing Grand Met, O'Hagan began purchasing call options for Pillsbury stock. Each option gave him the right to purchase 100 shares of Pillsbury stock by a specified date in September 1988. Later in August and in September, O'Hagan made additional purchases of Pillsbury call options. By the end of September, he owned 2,500 unexpired Pillsbury options, apparently more than any other individual investor. O'Hagan also purchased, in September 1988, some 5,000 shares of Pillsbury common stock, at a price just under $39 per share. When Grand Met announced its tender offer in October, the price of Pillsbury stock rose to nearly $60 per share. O'Hagan then sold his Pillsbury call options and common stock, making a profit of more than $4.3 million.

The Securities and Exchange Commission (SEC or Commission) initiated an investigation into O'Hagan's transactions, culminating in a 57–count indictment. The indictment alleged that O'Hagan defrauded his law firm and its client, Grand Met, by using for his own trading purposes material, nonpublic information regarding Grand Met's planned tender offer.[44] According to the indictment, O'Hagan used the profits he gained through this trading to conceal his previous embezzlement and conversion of unrelated client trust funds.[45] O'Hagan was charged with 20 counts of mail fraud, in violation of 18 U.S.C. § 1341; 17 counts of securities fraud, in violation of § 10(b) of the Securities Exchange Act of 1934, and SEC Rule 10b–5; 17 counts of fraudulent trading in connection with a tender offer, in violation of § 14(e) of the Exchange Act and SEC Rule 14e–3(a); and 3 counts of violating federal money laundering statutes, 18 U.S.C. §§ 1956(a)(1)(B)(i), 1957. A jury convicted O'Hagan on all 57 counts, and he was sentenced to a 41–month term of imprisonment.

A divided panel of the Court of Appeals for the Eighth Circuit reversed all of O'Hagan's convictions. 92 F.3d 612 (1996). Liability under § 10(b) and Rule 10b–5, the Eighth Circuit held, may not be grounded on the "misappropriation theory" of securities fraud on which the prosecution relied. The Court of Appeals also held that Rule 14e–3(a)—which prohibits trading while in possession of material, nonpublic information relating to a tender offer— exceeds the SEC's § 14(e) rulemaking authority because the rule contains no breach of fiduciary duty requirement. The Eighth Circuit further concluded that O'Hagan's mail fraud and money laundering convictions rested on violations of the securities laws, and therefore could not stand once the securities fraud convictions were reversed. Judge Fagg, dissenting, stated that he would recognize and enforce the misappropriation theory, and would hold that the SEC did not exceed its rulemaking authority when it adopted Rule 14e–3(a) without requiring proof of a breach of fiduciary duty.

Decisions of the Courts of Appeals are in conflict on the propriety of the misappropriation theory under § 10(b) and Rule 10b–5, and on the legitimacy of Rule 14e–3(a) under § 14(e). We granted certiorari, 519 U.S. ___, 117 S.Ct. 759, 136 L.Ed.2d 695 (1997), and now reverse the Eighth Circuit's judgment.

---

44. [By the Court] As evidence that O'Hagan traded on the basis of nonpublic information misappropriated from his law firm, the Government relied on a conversation between O'Hagan and the Dorsey & Whitney partner heading the firm's Grand Met representation. That conversation allegedly took place shortly before August 26, 1988. O'Hagan urges that the Government's evidence does not show he traded on the basis of nonpublic information. O'Hagan points to news reports on August 18 and 22, 1988, that Grand Met was interested in acquiring Pillsbury, and to an earlier, August 12, 1988, news report that Grand Met had put up its hotel chain for auction to raise funds for an acquisition. O'Hagan's challenge to the sufficiency of the evidence remains open for consideration on remand.

45. [By the Court] O'Hagan was convicted of theft in state court, sentenced to 30 months' imprisonment, and fined. See State v. O'Hagan, 474 N.W.2d 613, 615, 623 (Minn.App. 1991). The Supreme Court of Minnesota disbarred O'Hagan from the practice of law. See In re O'Hagan, 450 N.W.2d 571 (Minn.1990).

II

We address first the Court of Appeals' reversal of O'Hagan's convictions under § 10(b) and Rule 10b–5. Following the Fourth Circuit's lead, see United States v. Bryan, 58 F.3d 933, 943–959 (1995), the Eighth Circuit rejected the misappropriation theory as a basis for § 10(b) liability. We hold, in accord with several other Courts of Appeals, that criminal liability under § 10(b) may be predicated on the misappropriation theory.[46] * * *

A

* * * [Section] 10(b) of the Exchange Act * * * proscribes (1) using any deceptive device (2) in connection with the purchase or sale of securities, in contravention of rules prescribed by the Commission. The provision, as written, does not confine its coverage to deception of a purchaser or seller of securities, see United States v. Newman, 664 F.2d 12, 17 (C.A.2 1981); rather, the statute reaches any deceptive device used "in connection with the purchase or sale of any security."

Pursuant to its § 10(b) rulemaking authority, the Commission has adopted Rule 10b–5 * * *. Liability under Rule 10b–5, our precedent indicates, does not extend beyond conduct encompassed by § 10(b)'s prohibition. See Ernst & Ernst v. Hochfelder, 425 U.S. 185, 214, 96 S.Ct. 1375, 1391, 47 L.Ed.2d 668 (1976) (scope of Rule 10b–5 cannot exceed power Congress granted Commission under § 10(b)); see also Central Bank of Denver, N.A. v. First Interstate Bank of Denver, N. A., 511 U.S. 164, 173, 114 S.Ct. 1439, 1446, 128 L.Ed.2d 119 (1994) ("We have refused to allow [private] 10b–5 challenges to conduct not prohibited by the text of the statute.").

Under the "traditional" or "classical theory" of insider trading liability, § 10(b) and Rule 10b–5 are violated when a corporate insider trades in the securities of his corporation on the basis of material, nonpublic information. Trading on such information qualifies as a "deceptive device" under § 10(b), we have affirmed, because "a relationship of trust and confidence [exists] between the shareholders of a corporation and those insiders who have obtained confidential information by reason of their position with that corporation." Chiarella v. United States, 445 U.S. 222, 228, 100 S.Ct. 1108, 1114, 63 L.Ed.2d 348 (1980). That relationship, we recognized, "gives rise to a duty to disclose [or to abstain from trading] because of the 'necessity of preventing a corporate insider from * * * tak[ing] unfair advantage of * * * uninformed * * * stockholders.' " Id., at 228–229, 100 S.Ct., at 1115 (citation omitted). The classical theory applies not only to officers, directors, and other permanent insiders of a corporation, but also to attorneys, accountants, consultants, and others who temporarily become fiduciaries of a corporation. See Dirks v. SEC, 463 U.S. 646, 655, n. 14, 103 S.Ct. 3255, 3262, 77 L.Ed.2d 911 (1983).

---

46. [By the Court] Twice before we have been presented with the question whether criminal liability for violation of § 10(b) may be based on a misappropriation theory. In Chiarella v. United States * * * the jury had received no misappropriation theory instructions, so we declined to address the question. In Carpenter v. United States, * * * the Court divided evenly on whether, under the circumstances of that case, convictions resting on the misappropriation theory should be affirmed. See Barbara B. Aldave, The Misappropriation Theory: Carpenter and Its Aftermath, 49 Ohio St. L.J. 373, 375 (1988) (observing that "Carpenter was, by any reckoning, an unusual case," for the information there misappropriated belonged not to a company preparing to engage in securities transactions, e.g., a bidder in a corporate acquisition, but to the Wall Street Journal).

The "misappropriation theory" holds that a person commits fraud "in connection with" a securities transaction, and thereby violates § 10(b) and Rule 10b–5, when he misappropriates confidential information for securities trading purposes, in breach of a duty owed to the source of the information. Under this theory, a fiduciary's undisclosed, self-serving use of a principal's information to purchase or sell securities, in breach of a duty of loyalty and confidentiality, defrauds the principal of the exclusive use of that information. In lieu of premising liability on a fiduciary relationship between company insider and purchaser or seller of the company's stock, the misappropriation theory premises liability on a fiduciary-turned-trader's deception of those who entrusted him with access to confidential information.

The two theories are complementary, each addressing efforts to capitalize on nonpublic information through the purchase or sale of securities. The classical theory targets a corporate insider's breach of duty to shareholders with whom the insider transacts; the misappropriation theory outlaws trading on the basis of nonpublic information by a corporate "outsider" in breach of a duty owed not to a trading party, but to the source of the information. The misappropriation theory is thus designed to "protec[t] the integrity of the securities markets against abuses by 'outsiders' to a corporation who have access to confidential information that will affect th[e] corporation's security price when revealed, but who owe no fiduciary or other duty to that corporation's shareholders." Ibid.

In this case, the indictment alleged that O'Hagan, in breach of a duty of trust and confidence he owed to his law firm, Dorsey & Whitney, and to its client, Grand Met, traded on the basis of nonpublic information regarding Grand Met's planned tender offer for Pillsbury common stock. App. 16. This conduct, the Government charged, constituted a fraudulent device in connection with the purchase and sale of securities.[47]

B

We agree with the Government that misappropriation, as just defined, satisfies § 10(b)'s requirement that chargeable conduct involve a "deceptive device or contrivance" used "in connection with" the purchase or sale of securities. We observe, first, that misappropriators, as the Government describes them, deal in deception. A fiduciary who "[pretends] loyalty to the principal while secretly converting the principal's information for personal gain," Brief for United States 17, "dupes" or defrauds the principal. See Aldave, Misappropriation: A General Theory of Liability for Trading on Nonpublic Information, 13 Hofstra L.Rev. 101, 119 (1984).

We addressed fraud of the same species in Carpenter v. United States, 484 U.S. 19, 108 S.Ct. 316, 98 L.Ed.2d 275 (1987), which involved the mail fraud statute's proscription of "any scheme or artifice to defraud," 18 U.S.C. § 1341. Affirming convictions under that statute, we said in *Carpenter* that an

47. [By the Court] The Government could not have prosecuted O'Hagan under the classical theory, for O'Hagan was not an "insider" of Pillsbury, the corporation in whose stock he traded. Although an "outsider" with respect to Pillsbury, O'Hagan had an intimate association with, and was found to have traded on confidential information from, Dorsey & Whitney, counsel to tender offeror Grand Met. Under the misappropriation theory, O'Hagan's securities trading does not escape Exchange Act sanction, as it would under the dissent's reasoning, simply because he was associated with, and gained nonpublic information from, the bidder, rather than the target.

employee's undertaking not to reveal his employer's confidential information "became a sham" when the employee provided the information to his co-conspirators in a scheme to obtain trading profits. 484 U.S., at 27, 108 S.Ct., at 321. A company's confidential information, we recognized in *Carpenter*, qualifies as property to which the company has a right of exclusive use. The undisclosed misappropriation of such information, in violation of a fiduciary duty, the Court said in *Carpenter*, constitutes fraud akin to embezzlement " 'the fraudulent appropriation to one's own use of the money or goods entrusted to one's care by another.' " Id., at 27, 108 S.Ct., at 317 (quoting Grin v. Shine, 187 U.S. 181, 189, 23 S.Ct. 98, 101–102, 47 L.Ed. 130 (1902)); see Aldave, 13 Hofstra L.Rev., at 119. Carpenter's discussion of the fraudulent misuse of confidential information, the Government notes, "is a particularly apt source of guidance here, because [the mail fraud statute] (like Section 10(b)) has long been held to require deception, not merely the breach of a fiduciary duty."

Deception through nondisclosure is central to the theory of liability for which the Government seeks recognition. As counsel for the Government stated in explanation of the theory at oral argument: "To satisfy the common law rule that a trustee may not use the property that [has] been entrusted [to] him, there would have to be consent. To satisfy the requirement of the Securities Act that there be no deception, there would only have to be disclosure." [S]ee generally Restatement (Second) of Agency §§ 390, 395 (1958) (agent's disclosure obligation regarding use of confidential information).[48]

The misappropriation theory advanced by the Government is consistent with Santa Fe Industries, Inc. v. Green, 430 U.S. 462, 97 S.Ct. 1292, 51 L.Ed.2d 480 (1977), a decision underscoring that § 10(b) is not an all-purpose breach of fiduciary duty ban; rather, it trains on conduct involving manipulation or deception. In contrast to the Government's allegations in this case, in *Santa Fe Industries*, all pertinent facts were disclosed by the persons charged with violating § 10(b) and Rule 10b–5; therefore, there was no deception through nondisclosure to which liability under those provisions could attach. Similarly, full disclosure forecloses liability under the misappropriation theory: Because the deception essential to the misappropriation theory involves feigning fidelity to the source of information, if the fiduciary discloses to the source that he plans to trade on the nonpublic information, there is no "deceptive device" and thus no § 10(b) violation—although the fiduciary-turned-trader may remain liable under state law for breach of a duty of loyalty.[49]

---

48. [By the Court] Under the misappropriation theory urged in this case, the disclosure obligation runs to the source of the information, here, Dorsey & Whitney and Grand Met. Chief Justice Burger, dissenting in Chiarella, advanced a broader reading of § 10(b) and Rule 10b–5; the disclosure obligation, as he envisioned it, ran to those with whom the misappropriator trades ("a person who has misappropriated nonpublic information has an absolute duty to disclose that information or to refrain from trading") * * *. The Government does not propose that we adopt a misappropriation theory of that breadth.

49. [By the Court] Where, however, a person trading on the basis of material, nonpublic information owes a duty of loyalty and confidentiality to two entities or persons—for example, a law firm and its client—but makes disclosure to only one, the trader may still be liable under the misappropriation theory.

We turn next to the § 10(b) requirement that the misappropriator's deceptive use of information be "in connection with the purchase or sale of [a] security." This element is satisfied because the fiduciary's fraud is consummated, not when the fiduciary gains the confidential information, but when, without disclosure to his principal, he uses the information to purchase or sell securities. The securities transaction and the breach of duty thus coincide. This is so even though the person or entity defrauded is not the other party to the trade, but is, instead, the source of the nonpublic information. See Aldave, 13 Hofstra L.Rev., at 120 ("a fraud or deceit can be practiced on one person, with resultant harm to another person or group of persons"). A misappropriator who trades on the basis of material, nonpublic information, in short, gains his advantageous market position through deception; he deceives the source of the information and simultaneously harms members of the investing public.

The misappropriation theory targets information of a sort that misappropriators ordinarily capitalize upon to gain no-risk profits through the purchase or sale of securities. Should a misappropriator put such information to other use, the statute's prohibition would not be implicated. The theory does not catch all conceivable forms of fraud involving confidential information; rather, it catches fraudulent means of capitalizing on such information through securities transactions.

The Government notes another limitation on the forms of fraud § 10(b) reaches: "The misappropriation theory would not * * * apply to a case in which a person defrauded a bank into giving him a loan or embezzled cash from another, and then used the proceeds of the misdeed to purchase securities." In such a case, the Government states, "the proceeds would have value to the malefactor apart from their use in a securities transaction, and the fraud would be complete as soon as the money was obtained." In other words, money can buy, if not anything, then at least many things; its misappropriation may thus be viewed as sufficiently detached from a subsequent securities transaction that § 10(b)'s "in connection with" requirement would not be met.

The dissent's charge that the misappropriation theory is incoherent because information, like funds, can be put to multiple uses misses the point. The Exchange Act was enacted in part "to insure the maintenance of fair and honest markets," and there is no question that fraudulent uses of confidential information fall within § 10(b)'s prohibition if the fraud is "in connection with" a securities transaction. It is hardly remarkable that a rule suitably applied to the fraudulent uses of certain kinds of information would be stretched beyond reason were it applied to the fraudulent use of money.

The dissent does catch the Government in overstatement. Observing that money can be used for all manner of purposes and purchases, the Government urges that confidential information of the kind at issue derives its value *only* from its utility in securities trading. See Brief for United States 10, 21 (several times emphasizing the word "only"). Substitute "ordinarily" for "only," and the Government is on the mark.[50] * * *

---

50. [By the Court] The dissent's evident struggle to invent other uses to which O'Hagan plausibly might have put the nonpublic information is telling. It is imaginative to suggest that a trade journal would have paid O'Hagan dollars in the millions to publish his information. Counsel for O'Hagan hypothesized, as a nontrading use, that O'Hagan could have

The misappropriation theory comports with § 10(b)'s language, which requires deception "in connection with the purchase or sale of any security," not deception of an identifiable purchaser or seller. The theory is also well-tuned to an animating purpose of the Exchange Act: to insure honest securities markets and thereby promote investor confidence. See 45 Fed.Reg. 60412 (1980) (trading on misappropriated information "undermines the integrity of, and investor confidence in, the securities markets"). Although informational disparity is inevitable in the securities markets, investors likely would hesitate to venture their capital in a market where trading based on misappropriated nonpublic information is unchecked by law. An investor's informational disadvantage vis-a-vis a misappropriator with material, nonpublic information stems from contrivance, not luck; it is a disadvantage that cannot be overcome with research or skill. See Brudney, Insiders, Outsiders, and Informational Advantages Under the Federal Securities Laws, 93 Harv. L.Rev. 322, 356 (1979) ("If the market is thought to be systematically populated with * * * transactors [trading on the basis of misappropriated information] some investors will refrain from dealing altogether, and others will incur costs to avoid dealing with such transactors or corruptly to overcome their unerodable informational advantages."); Aldave, 13 Hofstra L.Rev., at 122–123.

In sum, considering the inhibiting impact on market participation of trading on misappropriated information, and the congressional purposes underlying § 10(b), it makes scant sense to hold a lawyer like O'Hagan a § 10(b) violator if he works for a law firm representing the target of a tender offer, but not if he works for a law firm representing the bidder. The text of the statute requires no such result.[51] The misappropriation at issue here was properly made the subject of a § 10(b) charge because it meets the statutory requirement that there be "deceptive" conduct "in connection with" securities transactions.

C

The Court of Appeals rejected the misappropriation theory primarily on two grounds. First, as the Eighth Circuit comprehended the theory, it requires neither misrepresentation nor nondisclosure. * * * Second and "more obvious," the Court of Appeals said, the misappropriation theory is not moored to § 10(b)'s requirement that "the fraud be 'in connection with the

"misappropriat[ed] this information of [his] law firm and its client, deliver[ed] it to [Pillsbury], and suggest[ed] that [Pillsbury] in the future * * * might find it very desirable to use [O'Hagan] for legal work." But Pillsbury might well have had large doubts about engaging for its legal work a lawyer who so stunningly displayed his readiness to betray a client's confidence. Nor is the Commission's theory "incoherent" or "inconsistent," for failing to inhibit use of confidential information for "personal amusement * * * in a fantasy stock trading game."

51. [By the Court] As noted earlier, however, the textual requirement of deception precludes § 10(b) liability when a person trading on the basis of nonpublic information has disclosed his trading plans to, or obtained authorization from, the principal—even though such conduct may affect the securities markets in the same manner as the conduct reached by the misappropriation theory. Contrary to the dissent's suggestion, the fact that § 10(b) is only a partial antidote to the problems it was designed to alleviate does not call into question its prohibition of conduct that falls within its textual proscription. Moreover, once a disloyal agent discloses his imminent breach of duty, his principal may seek appropriate equitable relief under state law. Furthermore, in the context of a tender offer, the principal who authorizes an agent's trading on confidential information may, in the Commission's view, incur liability for an Exchange Act violation under Rule 14e–3(a).

purchase or sale of any security.' " * * * "[O]nly a breach of a duty to parties to the securities transaction," the Court of Appeals concluded, "or, at the most, to other market participants such as investors, will be sufficient to give rise to § 10(b) liability." 92 F.3d, at 618. We read the statute and our precedent differently, and note again that § 10(b) refers to "the purchase or sale of any security," not to identifiable purchasers or sellers of securities. * * * [A discussion of earlier Supreme Court decisions is omitted.]

In sum, the misappropriation theory, as we have examined and explained it in this opinion, is both consistent with the statute and with our precedent. Vital to our decision that criminal liability may be sustained under the misappropriation theory, we emphasize, are two sturdy safeguards Congress has provided regarding scienter. To establish a criminal violation of Rule 10b–5, the Government must prove that a person "willfully" violated the provision. Furthermore, a defendant may not be imprisoned for violating Rule 10b–5 if he proves that he had no knowledge of the rule.[52] O'Hagan's charge that the misappropriation theory is too indefinite to permit the imposition of criminal liability, thus fails not only because the theory is limited to those who breach a recognized duty. In addition, the statute's "requirement of the presence of culpable intent as a necessary element of the offense does much to destroy any force in the argument that application of the [statute]" in circumstances such as O'Hagan's is unjust.

III

We consider next the ground on which the Court of Appeals reversed O'Hagan's convictions for fraudulent trading in connection with a tender offer, in violation of § 14(e) of the Exchange Act and SEC Rule 14e–3(a). A sole question is before us as to these convictions: Did the Commission, as the Court of Appeals held, exceed its rulemaking authority under § 14(e) when it adopted Rule 14e–3(a) without requiring a showing that the trading at issue entailed a breach of fiduciary duty? We hold that the Commission, in this regard and to the extent relevant to this case, did not exceed its authority.

The governing statutory provision, § 14(e) of the Exchange Act, reads in relevant part:

> It shall be unlawful for any person * * * to engage in any fraudulent, deceptive, or manipulative acts or practices, in connection with any tender offer.* * * The [SEC] shall, for the purposes of this subsection, by rules and regulations define, and prescribe means reasonably designed to prevent, such acts and practices as are fraudulent, deceptive, or manipulative.

Section 14(e)'s first sentence prohibits fraudulent acts in connection with a tender offer. This self-operating proscription was one of several provisions added to the Exchange Act in 1968 by the Williams Act. The section's second sentence delegates definitional and prophylactic rulemaking authority to the Commission. Congress added this rulemaking delegation to § 14(e) in 1970 amendments to the Williams Act.

Through § 14(e) and other provisions on disclosure in the Williams Act, Congress sought to ensure that shareholders "confronted by a cash tender offer for their stock [would] not be required to respond without adequate

---

52. [By the Court] The statute provides no such defense to imposition of monetary fines.

information." Rondeau v. Mosinee Paper Corp., 422 U.S. 49, 58, 95 S.Ct. 2069, 2076, 45 L.Ed.2d 12 (1975). As we recognized in Schreiber v. Burlington Northern, Inc., 472 U.S. 1, 105 S.Ct. 2458, 86 L.Ed.2d 1 (1985), Congress designed the Williams Act to make "disclosure, rather than court imposed principles of 'fairness' or 'artificiality,' * * * the preferred method of market regulation." we explained, "supplements the more precise disclosure provisions found elsewhere in the Williams Act, while requiring disclosure more explicitly addressed to the tender offer context than that required by § 10(b)." [472 U.S.], at 10–11, 105 S.Ct., at 2464.

Relying on § 14(e)'s rulemaking authorization, the Commission, in 1980, promulgated Rule 14e–3(a). * * * As characterized by the Commission, Rule 14e–3(a) is a "disclose or abstain from trading" requirement. 45 Fed.Reg. 60410 (1980).[53] The Second Circuit concisely described the rule's thrust:

> "One violates Rule 14e–3(a) if he trades on the basis of material nonpublic information concerning a pending tender offer that he knows or has reason to know has been acquired 'directly or indirectly' from an insider of the offeror or issuer, or someone working on their behalf. Rule 14e–3(a) is a disclosure provision. It creates a duty in those traders who fall within its ambit to abstain or disclose, *without regard to whether the trader owes a pre-existing fiduciary duty* to respect the confidentiality of the information." United States v. Chestman, 947 F.2d 551, 557 (1991) (en banc) (emphasis added), cert. denied, 503 U.S. 1004, 112 S.Ct. 1759, 118 L.Ed.2d 422 (1992).

* * * [The Court holds that this Rule does not exceed the SEC's powers under § 14(e) of the Securities Exchange Act.]

We need not resolve in this case whether the Commission's authority under § 14(e) to "define * * * such acts and practices as are fraudulent" is broader than the Commission's fraud-defining authority under § 10(b), for we agree with the United States that Rule 14e–3(a), as applied to cases of this genre, qualifies under § 14(e) as a "means reasonably designed to prevent" fraudulent trading on material, nonpublic information in the tender offer context. * * * We hold * * * that under § 14(e), the Commission may prohibit acts, not themselves fraudulent under the common law or § 10(b), if the prohibition is "reasonably designed to prevent * * * acts and practices [that] are fraudulent."[54]

Because Congress has authorized the Commission, in § 14(e), to prescribe legislative rules, we owe the Commission's judgment "more than mere deference or weight." Batterton v. Francis, 432 U.S. 416, 424–426, 97 S.Ct. 2399, 2406, 53 L.Ed.2d 448 (1977). Therefore, in determining whether Rule 14e–3(a)'s "disclose or abstain from trading" requirement is reasonably designed to prevent fraudulent acts, we must accord the Commission's assessment "controlling weight unless [it is] arbitrary, capricious, or manifestly contrary to the statute." Chevron U.S.A. Inc. v. Natural Resources Defense Council,

---

53. [By the Court] The rule thus adopts for the tender offer context a requirement resembling the one Chief Justice Burger would have adopted in Chiarella for misappropriators under § 10(b).

54. [By the Court] The Commission's power under § 10(b) is more limited. * * * Rule 10b–5 may proscribe only conduct that § 10(b) prohibits.

Inc., 467 U.S. 837, 844, 104 S.Ct. 2778, 2782, 81 L.Ed.2d 694 (1984). In this case, we conclude, the Commission's assessment is none of these. * * *

IV

Based on its dispositions of the securities fraud convictions, the Court of Appeals also reversed O'Hagan's convictions, under 18 U.S.C. § 1341, for mail fraud. Reversal of the securities convictions, the Court of Appeals recognized, "d[id] not as a matter of law require that the mail fraud convictions likewise be reversed." (citing Carpenter * * *). But in this case, the Court of Appeals said, the indictment was so structured that the mail fraud charges could not be disassociated from the securities fraud charges, and absent any securities fraud, "there was no fraud upon which to base the mail fraud charges." 92 F.3d, at 627–628.

The United States urges that the Court of Appeals' position is irreconcilable with Carpenter: Just as in Carpenter, so here, the "mail fraud charges are independent of [the] securities fraud charges, even [though] both rest on the same set of facts." We need not linger over this matter, for our rulings on the securities fraud issues require that we reverse the Court of Appeals judgment on the mail fraud counts as well.[55]

O'Hagan, we note, attacked the mail fraud convictions in the Court of Appeals on alternate grounds; his other arguments, not yet addressed by the Eighth Circuit, remain open for consideration on remand.

The judgment of the Court of Appeals for the Eighth Circuit is reversed, and the case is remanded for further proceedings consistent with this opinion.

It is so ordered.

JUSTICE SCALIA, concurring in part and dissenting in part.

I join Parts I, III, and IV of the Court's opinion. I do not agree, however, with Part II of the Court's opinion, containing its analysis of respondent's convictions under § 10(b) and Rule 10b–5.

I do not entirely agree with Justice Thomas's analysis of those convictions either, principally because it seems to me irrelevant whether the Government's theory of why respondent's acts were covered is "coherent and consistent." It is true that with respect to matters over which an agency has been accorded adjudicative authority or policymaking discretion, the agency's action must be supported by the reasons that the agency sets forth, SEC v. Chenery Corp., 318 U.S. 80, 94, 63 S.Ct. 454, 462, 87 L.Ed. 626 (1943); see also SEC v. Chenery Corp., 332 U.S. 194, 196, 67 S.Ct. 1575, 91 L.Ed. 1995 (1947), but I do not think an agency's unadorned application of the law need be, at least where (as here) no Chevron deference is being given to the agency's interpretation. In point of fact, respondent's actions either violated

---

55. [By the Court] The dissent finds O'Hagan's convictions on the mail fraud counts, but not on the securities fraud counts, sustainable. Under the dissent's view, securities traders like O'Hagan would escape SEC civil actions and federal prosecutions under legislation targeting securities fraud, only to be caught for their trading activities in the broad mail fraud net. If misappropriation theory cases could proceed only under the federal mail and wire fraud statutes, practical consequences for individual defendants might not be large; however, "proportionally more persons accused of insider trading [might] be pursued by a U.S. Attorney, and proportionally fewer by the SEC," Our decision, of course, does not rest on such enforcement policy considerations.

§ 10(b) and Rule 10b–5, or they did not—regardless of the reasons the Government gave. And it is for us to decide.

While the Court's explanation of the scope of § 10(b) and Rule 10b–5 would be entirely reasonable in some other context, it does not seem to accord with the principle of lenity we apply to criminal statutes (which cannot be mitigated here by the Rule, which is no less ambiguous than the statute). * * * In light of that principle, it seems to me that the unelaborated statutory language: "[t]o use or employ in connection with the purchase or sale of any security * * * any manipulative or deceptive device or contrivance," § 10(b), must be construed to require the manipulation or deception of a party to a securities transaction.

JUSTICE THOMAS, with whom THE CHIEF JUSTICE joins, concurring in the judgment in part and dissenting in part.

Today the majority upholds respondent's convictions for violating § 10(b) of the Securities Exchange Act of 1934, and Rule 10b–5 promulgated thereunder, based upon the Securities and Exchange Commission's "misappropriation theory." Central to the majority's holding is the need to interpret § 10(b)'s requirement that a deceptive device be "use[d] or employ[ed], in connection with the purchase or sale of any security." Because the Commission's misappropriation theory fails to provide a coherent and consistent interpretation of this essential requirement for liability under § 10(b), I dissent.

The majority also sustains respondent's convictions under § 14(e) of the Securities Exchange Act, and Rule 14e–3(a) promulgated thereunder, regardless of whether respondent violated a fiduciary duty to anybody. I dissent too from that holding because, while § 14(e) does allow regulations prohibiting nonfraudulent acts as a prophylactic against certain fraudulent acts, neither the majority nor the Commission identifies any relevant underlying fraud against which Rule 14e–3(a) reasonably provides prophylaxis. With regard to the respondent's mail fraud convictions, however, I concur in the judgment of the Court.

I

I do not take issue with the majority's determination that the undisclosed misappropriation of confidential information by a fiduciary can constitute a "deceptive device" within the meaning of § 10(b). Nondisclosure where there is a pre-existing duty to disclose satisfies our definitions of fraud and deceit for purposes of the securities laws.

Unlike the majority, however, I cannot accept the Commission's interpretation of when a deceptive device is "use[d] ... in connection with" a securities transaction. Although the Commission and the majority at points seem to suggest that any relation to a securities transaction satisfies the "in connection with" requirement of § 10(b), both ultimately reject such an overly expansive construction and require a more integral connection between the fraud and the securities transaction. The majority states, for example, that the misappropriation theory applies to undisclosed misappropriation of confidential information "for securities trading purposes," thus seeming to require a particular intent by the misappropriator in order to satisfy the "in connection with" language. * * * The Commission goes further, and argues that the misappropriation theory satisfies the "in connection with" requirement because it "depends on an inherent connection between the deceptive conduct and the purchase or sale of a security." * * *

The Commission's construction of the relevant language in § 10(b), and the incoherence of that construction, become evident as the majority attempts to describe why the fraudulent theft of information falls under the Commission's misappropriation theory, but the fraudulent theft of money does not. * * * And when the majority seeks to distinguish the embezzlement of funds from the embezzlement of information, it becomes clear that neither the Commission nor the majority has a coherent theory regarding § 10(b)'s "in connection with" requirement. * * *

Notes

(1) Justice Thomas' dissent (only a small portion of which is reprinted above) points out logical problems in the position of the majority (and the SEC) with respect to the "in connection with" requirement. Accepting that it is illogical for purposes of argument, is that a justification for rejecting the misappropriation doctrine? Consider the consequences. If an attorney represents the aggressor in a takeover attempt, he does not violate Rule 10b–5 if he capitalizes on that information and buys stock (or options on stock) of the target. However, if he had represented the target, he would have committed a serious crime if he made the same purchases. Isn't that even more illogical? Perhaps the answer is that Rule 14e–3 should have been upheld and the misappropriation doctrine rejected? Might there be other situations in a non-takeover context in which similar irrational results would arise?

(2) During the course of the oral argument in O'Hagan, the Government conceded that on the facts of Carpenter v. United States, if Winans had gone to the Wall Street Journal and said, "look, you know , you're not paying me very much; I'd like to make a little bit more money by buying stock, the stocks that are going to appear in my Heard on the Street column," and the Wall Street Journal had said, "that's fine," there would have been no deception of the Wall Street Journal, and no violation of Rule 10b–5. Do you agree? If not, what possible theory is available, given the language of § 10(b) and Rule 10b–5?

(3) *O'Hagan* was, of course, a major victory for the SEC. However, it did not resolve all problems. For one thing, Justice Ginsburg's opinion consistently refers to O'Hagan trading "on the basis of" insider information. The phrase preferred by the SEC is "trading while in possession of" insider information. Does Justice Ginsburg's formulation mean that a person may possess insider information but trade "on the basis of" other factors (such as the mistaken belief that the information has been released publicly) without violating Rule 10b–5? See United States v. Teicher, 987 F.2d 112, 120–1 (2d Cir.1993), where the Court held that the appropriate standard of causation was "knowing possession" of insider information at the time of the trade ("As a matter of policy then, a requirement of a causal connection between the information and the trade could frustrate attempts to distinguish between legitimate trades and those conducted in connection with inside information. * * * Unlike a loaded weapon which may stand ready but unused, material information can not lay idle in the human brain").

(4) In SEC v. Mayhew, 121 F.3d 44 (2d Cir. 1997), decided shortly after *O'Hagan*, the Court held that an indirect tippee of an insider violated Rule 14e–3 when he traded upon non-public information about a proposed merger.

DIRKS v. SEC

Supreme Court of the United States, 1983.
463 U.S. 646, 103 S.Ct. 3255, 77 L.Ed.2d 911.

JUSTICE POWELL delivered the opinion of the Court.

Petitioner Raymond Dirks received material nonpublic information from "insiders" of a corporation with which he had no connection. He disclosed this information to investors who relied on it in trading in the shares of the corporation. The question is whether Dirks violated the antifraud provisions of the federal securities laws by this disclosure.

I.

In 1973, Dirks was an officer of a New York broker-dealer firm who specialized in providing investment analysis of insurance company securities to institutional investors. On March 6, Dirks received information from Ronald Secrist, a former officer of Equity Funding of America. Secrist alleged that the assets of Equity Funding, a diversified corporation primarily engaged in selling life insurance and mutual funds, were vastly overstated as the result of fraudulent corporate practices. Secrist also stated that various regulatory agencies had failed to act on similar charges made by Equity Funding employees. He urged Dirks to verify the fraud and disclose it publicly.

Dirks decided to investigate the allegations. He visited Equity Funding's headquarters in Los Angeles and interviewed several officers and employees of the corporation. The senior management denied any wrongdoing, but certain corporation employees corroborated the charges of fraud. Neither Dirks nor his firm owned or traded any Equity Funding stock, but throughout his investigation he openly discussed the information he had obtained with a number of clients and investors. Some of these persons sold their holdings of Equity Funding securities, including five investment advisers who liquidated holdings of more than $16 million.[56]

While Dirks was in Los Angeles, he was in touch regularly with William Blundell, The *Wall Street Journal's* Los Angeles bureau chief. Dirks urged Blundell to write a story on the fraud allegations. Blundell did not believe, however, that such a massive fraud could go undetected and declined to write the story. He feared that publishing such damaging hearsay might be libelous.

During the two-week period in which Dirks pursued his investigation and spread word of Secrist's charges, the price of Equity Funding stock fell from $26 per share to less than $15 per share. This led the New York Stock Exchange to halt trading on March 27. Shortly thereafter California insurance authorities impounded Equity Funding's records and uncovered evidence of the fraud. Only then did the Securities and Exchange Commission (SEC) file a complaint against Equity Funding[57] and only then, on April 2, did the *Wall*

56. [By the Court] Dirks received from his firm a salary plus a commission for securities transactions above a certain amount that his clients directed through his firm. But "[i]t is not clear how many of those with whom Dirks spoke promised to direct some brokerage business through [Dirks' firm] to compensate Dirks, or how many actually did so." The Boston Company Institutional Investors, Inc., promised Dirks about $25,000 in commissions, but it is unclear whether Boston actually generated any brokerage business for his firm.

57. [By the Court] As early as 1971, the SEC had received allegations of fraudulent ac-

Street Journal publish a front-page story based largely on information assembled by Dirks. Equity Funding immediately went into receivership.[58]

The SEC began an investigation into Dirks' role in the exposure of the fraud. After a hearing by an administrative law judge, the SEC found that Dirks had aided and abetted violations of § 17(a) of the Securities Act of 1933,[59] § 10(b) of the Securities Exchange Act of 1934, and SEC Rule 10b–5, by repeating the allegations of fraud to members of the investment community who later sold their Equity Funding stock. The SEC concluded: "Where 'tippees'—regardless of their motivation or occupation—come into possession of material 'information that they know is confidential and know or should know came from a corporate insider,' they must either publicly disclose that information or refrain from trading." Recognizing, however, that Dirks "played an important role in bringing [Equity Funding's] massive fraud to light," the SEC only censured him.

Dirks sought review in the Court of Appeals for the District of Columbia Circuit. The court entered judgment against Dirks "for the reasons stated by the Commission in its opinion." * * *

In view of the importance to the SEC and to the securities industry of the question presented by this case, we granted a writ of certiorari. 459 U.S. 1014, 103 S.Ct. 371, 74 L.Ed.2d 506 (1982). We now reverse. * * *

III.

We were explicit in *Chiarella* in saying that there can be no duty to disclose where the person who has traded on inside information "was not [the corporation's] agent, * * * was not a fiduciary, [or] was not a person in whom the sellers [of the securities] had placed their trust and confidence." 445 U.S., at 232, 100 S.Ct., at 1116. Not to require such a fiduciary relationship, we recognized, would "depar[t] radically from the established doctrine that duty arises from a specific relationship between two parties" and would amount to "recognizing a general duty between all participants in market transactions to forgo actions based on material, nonpublic information." Id., at 232, 233, 100 S.Ct., at 1116, 1117. This requirement of a specific relationship between the shareholders and the individual trading on inside information has created analytical difficulties for the SEC and courts in policing tippees who trade on

---

counting practices at Equity Funding. Moreover, on March 9, 1973, an official of the California Insurance Department informed the SEC's regional office in Los Angeles of Secrist's charges of fraud. Dirks himself voluntarily presented his information at the SEC's regional office beginning on March 27.

58. [By the Court] A federal grand jury in Los Angeles subsequently returned a 105–count indictment against 22 persons, including many of Equity Funding's officers and directors. All defendants were found guilty of one or more counts, either by a plea of guilty or a conviction after trial.

59. [By the Editor] Section 17(a) of the Securities Act of 1933, 15 U.S.C.A. § 77q(a) (1981), provides:

It shall be unlawful for any person in the offer or sale of any securities by the use of any means or instruments of transportation or communication in interstate commerce or by the use of the mails, directly or indirectly—

(1) to employ any device, scheme, or artifice to defraud, or

(2) to obtain money or property by means of any untrue statement of a material fact or any omission to state a material fact necessary in order to make the statements made, in the light of the circumstances under which they were made, not misleading, or

(3) to engage in any transaction, practice, or course of business which operates or would operate as a fraud or deceit upon the purchaser.

inside information. Unlike insiders who have independent fiduciary duties to both the corporation and its shareholders, the typical tippee has no such relationships.[60] In view of this absence, it has been unclear how a tippee acquires the *Cady, Roberts* duty to refrain from trading on inside information.

A.

The SEC's position, as stated in its opinion in this case, is that a tippee "inherits" the *Cady, Roberts* obligation to shareholders whenever he receives inside information from an insider:

"In tipping potential traders, Dirks breached a duty which he had assumed as a result of knowingly receiving confidential information from [Equity Funding] insiders. Tippees such as Dirks who receive non-public material information from insiders become 'subject to the same duty as [the] insiders.' Shapiro v. Merrill Lynch, Pierce, Fenner & Smith, Inc. [495 F.2d 228, 237 (C.A.2 1974) (quoting Ross v. Licht, 263 F.Supp. 395, 410 (S.D.N.Y.1967))]. Such a tippee breaches the fiduciary duty which he assumes from the insider when the tippee knowingly transmits the information to someone who will probably trade on the basis thereof. * * * Presumably, Dirks' informants were entitled to disclose the [Equity Funding] fraud in order to bring it to light and its perpetrators to justice. However, Dirks—standing in their shoes—committed a breach of the fiduciary duty which he had assumed in dealing with them, when he passed the information on to traders." 21 SEC Docket, at 1410, n. 42.

This view differs little from the view that we rejected as inconsistent with congressional intent in *Chiarella*. In that case, the Court of Appeals agreed with the SEC and affirmed Chiarella's conviction, holding that " '[a]nyone—corporate insider or not—who regularly receives material nonpublic information may not use that information to trade in securities without incurring an affirmative duty to disclose.' " United States v. Chiarella, 588 F.2d 1358, 1365 (C.A.2 1978) (emphasis in original). Here, the SEC maintains that anyone who knowingly receives nonpublic material information from an insider has a fiduciary duty to disclose before trading.[61]

---

60. [By the Court. This famous footnote is number 14 in the original opinion.] Under certain circumstances, such as where corporate information is revealed legitimately to an underwriter, accountant, lawyer, or consultant working for the corporation, these outsiders may become fiduciaries of the shareholders. The basis for recognizing this fiduciary duty is not simply that such persons acquire nonpublic corporate information, but rather that they have entered into a special confidential relationship in the conduct of the business of the enterprise and are given access to information solely for corporate purposes. When such a person breaches his fiduciary relationship, he may be treated more properly as a tipper than a tippee. See Shapiro v. Merrill Lynch, Pierce, Fenner & Smith, Inc., 495 F.2d 228, 237 (C.A.2 1974) (investment banker had access to material information when working on a proposed public offering for the corporation). For such a duty to be imposed, however, the corporation must expect the outsider to keep the disclosed

nonpublic information confidential, and the relationship at least must imply such a duty.

61. [By the Court] Apparently, the SEC believes this case differs from *Chiarella* in that Dirks' receipt of inside information from Secrist, an insider, carried Secrist's duties with it, while Chiarella received the information without the direct involvement of an insider and thus inherited no duty to disclose or abstain. The SEC fails to explain, however, why the receipt of nonpublic information from an insider automatically carries with it the fiduciary duty of the insider. As we emphasized in *Chiarella*, mere possession of nonpublic information does not give rise to a duty to disclose or abstain; only a specific relationship does that. And we do not believe that the mere receipt of information from an insider creates such a special relationship between the tippee and the corporation's shareholders.

Apparently recognizing the weakness of its argument in light of *Chiarella*, the SEC at-

In effect, the SEC's theory of tippee liability in both cases appears rooted in the idea that the antifraud provisions require equal information among all traders. This conflicts with the principle set forth in *Chiarella* that only some persons, under some circumstances, will be barred from trading while in possession of material nonpublic information. * * * We reaffirm today that "[a] duty [to disclose] arises from the relationship between parties * * * and not merely from one's ability to acquire information because of his position in the market." 445 U.S., at 232–233, n. 14, 100 S.Ct., at 1116–17, n. 14.

Imposing a duty to disclose or abstain solely because a person knowingly receives material nonpublic information from an insider and trades on it could have an inhibiting influence on the role of market analysts, which the SEC itself recognizes is necessary to the preservation of a healthy market.[62] It is commonplace for analysts to "ferret out and analyze information," 21 SEC, at 1406,[63] and this often is done by meeting with and questioning corporate officers and others who are insiders. And information that the analysts obtain normally may be the basis for judgments as to the market worth of a corporation's securities. The analyst's judgment in this respect is made available in market letters or otherwise to clients of the firm. It is the nature of this type of information, and indeed of the markets themselves, that such information cannot be made simultaneously available to all of the corporation's stockholders or the public generally.

B.

The conclusion that recipients of inside information do not invariably acquire a duty to disclose or abstain does not mean that such tippees always are free to trade on the information. The need for a ban on some tippee trading is clear. Not only are insiders forbidden by their fiduciary relationship from personally using undisclosed corporate information to their advantage, but they may not give such information to an outsider for the same improper purpose of exploiting the information for their personal gain. * * * Similarly,

---

tempts to distinguish that case factually as involving not "inside" information, but rather "market" information, i.e., "information generated within the company relating to its assets or earnings." This Court drew no such distinction in *Chiarella* and, as The Chief Justice noted, "[i]t is clear that § 10(b) and Rule 10b–5 by their terms and by their history make no such distinction." 445 U.S., at 241, n. 1, 100 S.Ct., at 1121, n. 1 (dissenting opinion).

62. [By the Court] The SEC expressly recognized that "[t]he value to the entire market of [analysts'] efforts cannot be gainsaid; market efficiency in pricing is significantly enhanced by [their] initiatives to ferret out and analyze information, and thus the analyst's work redounds to the benefit of all investors." 21 S.E.C., at 1406. The SEC asserts that analysts remain free to obtain from management corporate information for purposes of "filling in the 'interstices in analysis'. * * * " But this rule is inherently imprecise, and imprecision prevents parties from ordering their actions in accord with legal requirements. Unless the parties have some guidance as to where the line is between permissible and impermissible disclo-

sures and uses, neither corporate insiders nor analysts can be sure when the line is crossed.

63. [By the Court] On its facts, this case is the unusual one. Dirks is an analyst in a broker-dealer firm, and he did interview management in the course of his investigation. He uncovered, however, startling information that required no analysis or exercise of judgment as to its market relevance. Nonetheless, the principle at issue here extends beyond these facts. The SEC's rule—applicable without regard to any breach by an insider—could have serious ramifications on reporting by analysts of investment views.

Despite the unusualness of Dirks' "find," the central role that he played in uncovering the fraud at Equity Funding, and that analysts in general can play in revealing information that corporations may have reason to withhold from the public, is an important one. Dirks' careful investigation brought to light a massive fraud at the corporation. And until the Equity Funding fraud was exposed, the information in the trading market was grossly inaccurate. But for Dirks' efforts, the fraud might well have gone undetected longer.

the transactions of those who knowingly participate with the fiduciary in such a breach are "as forbidden" as transactions "on behalf of the trustee himself." Mosser v. Darrow, 341 U.S. 267, 272, 71 S.Ct. 680, 682 (1951). As the Court explained in *Mosser,* a contrary rule "would open up opportunities for devious dealings in the name of the others that the trustee could not conduct in his own." 341 U.S., at 271, 71 S.Ct., at 682. See SEC v. Texas Gulf Sulphur Co., 446 F.2d 1301, 1308 (CA2), cert. denied, 404 U.S. 1005, 92 S.Ct. 561, (1971). Thus, the tippee's duty to disclose or abstain is derivative from that of the insider's duty. As we noted in *Chiarella,* "[t]he tippee's obligation has been viewed as arising from his role as a participant after the fact in the insider's breach of a fiduciary duty." 445 U.S., at 230, n. 12, 100 S.Ct., at 1115, n. 12.

Thus, some tippees must assume an insider's duty to the shareholders not because they receive inside information, but rather because it has been made available to them *improperly.* And for rule 10b–5 purposes, the insider's disclosure is improper only where it would violate his *Cady, Roberts* duty. Thus, a tippee assumes a fiduciary duty to the shareholders of a corporation not to trade on material nonpublic information only when the insider has breached his fiduciary duty to the shareholders by disclosing the information to the tippee and the tippee knows or should know that there has been a breach. As Commissioner Smith perceptively observed in *Investors Management Co.:* "[T]ippee responsibility must be related back to insider responsibility by a necessary finding that the tippee knew the information was given to him in breach of a duty by a person having a special relationship to the issuer not to disclose the information * * *." 44 SEC, at 651 (concurring in the result). Tipping thus properly is viewed only as a means of indirectly violating the *Cady, Roberts* disclose-or-abstain rule.[64]

C.

In determining whether a tippee is under an obligation to disclose or abstain, it thus is necessary to determine whether the insider's "tip" constituted a breach of the insider's fiduciary duty. All disclosures of confidential corporate information are not inconsistent with the duty insiders owe to shareholders. In contrast to the extraordinary facts of this case, the more typical situation in which there will be a question whether disclosure violates the insider's *Cady, Roberts* duty is when insiders disclose information to

---

64. [By the Court] We do not suggest that knowingly trading on inside information is ever "socially desirable or even that it is devoid of moral considerations." Dooley, Enforcement of Insider Trading Restrictions, 66 Va.L.Rev. 1, 55 (1980). Nor do we imply an absence of responsibility to disclose promptly indications of illegal actions by a corporation to the proper authorities—typically the SEC and exchange authorities in cases involving securities. Depending on the circumstances, and even where permitted by law, one's trading on material nonpublic information is behavior that may fall below ethical standards of conduct. But in a statutory area of the law such as securities regulation, where legal principles of general application must be applied, there may be "significant distinctions between actual legal obligations and ethical ideals." SEC, Report of the

Special Study of Securities Markets, H.R.Doc. No. 95, 88th Cong., 1st Sess., pt. 1, pp. 237–238 (1963). The SEC recognizes this. At oral argument, the following exchange took place:

"QUESTION: So, it would not have satisfied his obligation under the law to go to the SEC first?

"[SEC's counsel]: That is correct. That an insider has to observe what has come to be known as the abstain or disclosure rule. Either the information has to be disclosed to the market if it is inside information * * * or the insider must abstain."

Thus, it is clear that Rule 10b–5 does not impose any obligations simply to tell the SEC about the fraud before trading.

analysts. In some situations the insider will act consistently with his fiduciary duty to shareholders, and yet release of the information may affect the market. For example, it may not be clear—either to the corporate insider or to the recipient analyst—whether the information will be viewed as material nonpublic information. Corporate officials may mistakenly think the information already has been disclosed or that it is not material enough to affect the market. Whether disclosure is a breach of duty therefore depends in large part on the purpose of the disclosure. This standard was identified by the SEC itself in *Cady, Roberts:* a purpose of the securities laws was to eliminate "use of inside information for personal advantage." 40 SEC, at 912, n. 15. Thus, the test is whether the insider personally will benefit, directly or indirectly, from his disclosure. Absent some personal gain, there has been no breach of duty to stockholders. And absent a breach by the insider, there is no derivative breach. As Commissioner Smith stated in *Investors Management Co.:* "It is important in this type of case to focus on policing insiders and what they do * * * rather than on policing information *per se* and its possession. * * *" 44 SEC, at 648 (concurring in the result).

The SEC argues that, if inside-trading liability does not exist when the information is transmitted for a proper purpose but is used for trading, it would be a rare situation when the parties could not fabricate some ostensibly legitimate business justification for transmitting the information. We think the SEC is unduly concerned. In determining whether the insider's purpose in making a particular disclosure is fraudulent, the SEC and the courts are not required to read the parties' minds. Scienter in some cases is relevant in determining whether the tipper has violated his *Cady, Roberts* duty.[65] But to determine whether the disclosure itself "deceive[s], manipulate[s], or defraud[s]" shareholders, Aaron v. SEC, 446 U.S. 680, 686, 100 S.Ct. 1945, 1950 (1980), the initial inquiry is whether there has been a breach of duty by the insider. This requires courts to focus on objective criteria, i.e., whether the insider receives a direct or indirect personal benefit from the disclosure, such as a pecuniary gain or a reputational benefit that will translate into future earnings. Cf. 40 SEC, at 912, n. 15; Brudney, Insiders, Outsiders, and Informational Advantages Under the Federal Securities Laws, 93 Harv.L.Rev. 324, 348 (1979) ("The theory * * * is that the insider, by giving the information out selectively, is in effect selling the information to its recipient for cash, reciprocal information, or other things of value for himself. * * *"). There are objective facts and circumstances that often justify such an inference. For example, there may be a relationship between the insider and the recipient that suggests a *quid pro quo* from the latter, or an intention to benefit the particular recipient. The elements of fiduciary duty and exploitation of nonpublic information also exist when an insider makes a gift of confidential

---

65. [By the Court] *Scienter*—"a mental state embracing intent to deceive, manipulate, or defraud," Ernst & Ernst v. Hochfelder, 425 U.S. 185, 193, n. 12, 96 S.Ct. 1375, 1381, n. 12 (1976)—is an independent element of a Rule 10b–5 violation. See Aaron v. SEC, 446 U.S. 680, 695, 100 S.Ct. 1945, 1955, (1980). * * * It is not enough that an insider's conduct results in harm to investors; rather, a violation may be found only where there is "intentional or willful conduct designed to deceive or defraud in-

vestors by controlling or artificially affecting the price of securities." Ernst & Ernst v. Hochfelder, supra, at 199, 96 S.Ct., at 1383. The issue in this case, however, is not whether Secrist or Dirks acted with *scienter,* but rather whether there was any deceptive or fraudulent conduct at all, i.e., whether Secrist's disclosure constituted a breach of his fiduciary duty and thereby caused injury to shareholders. Only if there was such a breach did Dirks, a tippee, acquire a fiduciary duty to disclose or abstain.

information to a trading relative or friend. The tip and trade resemble trading by the insider himself followed by a gift of the profits to the recipient.

Determining whether an insider personally benefits from a particular disclosure, a question of fact, will not always be easy for courts. But it is essential, we think, to have a guiding principle for those whose daily activities must be limited and instructed by the SEC's inside-trading rules, and we believe that there must be a breach of the insider's fiduciary duty before the tippee inherits the duty to disclose or abstain. In contrast, the rule adopted by the SEC in this case would have no limiting principle.[66]

IV.

Under the inside-trading and tipping rules set forth above, we find that there was no actionable violation by Dirks. It is undisputed that Dirks himself was a stranger to Equity Funding, with no pre-existing fiduciary duty to its shareholders. He took no action, directly or indirectly, that induced the shareholders or officers of Equity Funding to repose trust or confidence in him. There was no expectation by Dirks' sources that he would keep their information in confidence. Nor did Dirks misappropriate or illegally obtain the information about Equity Funding. Unless the insiders breached their *Cady, Roberts* duty to shareholders in disclosing the nonpublic information to Dirks, he breached no duty when he passed it on to investors as well as to the *Wall Street Journal.*

It is clear that neither Secrist nor the other Equity Funding employees violated their *Cady, Roberts* duty to the corporation's shareholders by providing information to Dirks.[67] The tippers received no monetary or personal benefit for revealing Equity Funding's secrets, nor was their purpose to make a gift of valuable information to Dirks. As the facts of this case clearly indicate, the tippers were motivated by a desire to expose the fraud. In the absence of a breach of duty to shareholders by the insiders, there was no

---

66. [By the Court] Without legal limitations, market participants are forced to rely on the reasonableness of the SEC's litigation strategy, but that can be hazardous, as the facts of this case make plain. * * *

67. [By the Court] In this Court, the SEC appears to contend that an insider invariably violates a fiduciary duty to the corporation's shareholders by transmitting nonpublic corporate information to an outsider when he has reason to believe that the outsider may use it to the disadvantage of the shareholders. "Thus, regardless of any ultimate motive to bring to public attention the derelictions at Equity Funding, Secrist breached his duty to Equity Funding shareholders." Brief for Respondent 31. This perceived "duty" differs markedly from the one that the SEC identified in *Cady, Roberts* and that has been the basis for federal tippee-trading rules to date. In fact, the SEC did not charge Secrist with any wrongdoing, and we do not understand the SEC to have relied on any theory of a breach of duty by Secrist in finding that Dirks breached his duty to Equity Funding's shareholders. * * *

Chiarella made it explicitly clear there is no general duty to forgo market transactions "based on material, nonpublic information." 455 U.S., at 233, 100 S.Ct., at 1117. Such a duty would "depar[t] radically from the established doctrine that duty arises from a specific relationship between two parties."

Moreover, to constitute a violation of Rule 10b–5, there must be fraud. See Ernst & Ernst v. Hochfelder, 425 U.S. 185, 199, 96 S.Ct. 1375, 1383, 47 L.Ed.2d 668 (1976) (statutory words "manipulative," "device," and "contrivance * * * connot[e] intentional or willful conduct designed to *deceive or defraud* investors by controlling or artificially affecting the price of securities") (emphasis added). There is no evidence that Secrist's disclosure was intended to or did in fact "deceive or defraud" anyone. Secrist certainly intended to convey relevant information that management was unlawfully concealing, and—so far as the record shows—he believed that persuading Dirks to investigate was the best way to disclose the fraud. Other efforts had proved fruitless. Under any objective standard, Secrist received no direct or indirect personal benefit from the disclosure.

derivative breach by Dirks. Dirks therefore could not have been "a participant after the fact in [an] insider's breach of a fiduciary duty." Chiarella, 445 U.S., at 230, n. 12, 100 S.Ct., at 1115, n. 12.

V.

We conclude that Dirks, in the circumstances of this case, had no duty to abstain from use of the inside information that he obtained. The judgment of the Court of Appeals therefore is

Reversed.

JUSTICE BLACKMUN, with whom JUSTICE BRENNAN and JUSTICE MARSHALL join, dissenting. * * * [The dissenting opinion is omitted.]

Notes

(1) Academic commentary on the "benefit" requirement imposed by *Dirks* has been generally negative: "This benefit requirement is a curious and largely unnecessary wrinkle; if there is one clear understanding in the common law of fiduciary responsibility, it is that an intent to benefit is not a necessary element." Donald Langevoort, Commentary—The Insider Trading Sanctions Act of 1984 and its Effect on Existing Law, 37 Vand.L.Rev. 1273, 1292 (1984). On the other hand, the SEC appears to have little problem in finding a "benefit" in order to meet this requirement. When Paul Thayer, then Deputy Secretary of Defense and former CEO of LTV, Inc., was charged with passing information to a group of eight friends, including a young woman who was a former LTV employee, for example, the SEC charged that Mr. Thayer received a personal benefit because of his "close personal relationship" with the woman. Kenneth B. Noble, Thayer Quits as Defense Deputy Over Expected Charges by SEC, N.Y. Times, Jan. 5, 1984, at A1, col. 3–4; Kenneth B. Noble, SEC Says Thayer Gave Stock Data on "Insider" Basis, N.Y. Times, Jan. 6, 1984, at A1, col. 2. In United States v. Reed, 601 F.Supp. 685 (S.D.N.Y.1985), the Court refused to dismiss an indictment of a tippee who was the son of the tipper, even though there was no evidence that the father intended to benefit his son by the disclosure. See also SEC v. Gaspar, 1985 WL 521 (CBM) (S.D.N.Y.1985) (tipper received an "enhanced professional relationship" from tippee).

(2) In SEC v. Switzer, 590 F.Supp. 756 (W.D.Okl.1984), Barry Switzer, then coach of the University of Oklahoma football team, was attending a high school track meet in which his son was competing. He decided to take a sun bath on a row of bleachers; while lying there unobtrusively he happened to overhear an acquaintance, Mr. Platt, talking with Mrs. Platt about problems facing his business. Switzer traded profitably on the information he thereby learned, but was absolved of liability under the Dirks standard since Switzer was basically an eavesdropper and the information was not disclosed by Mr. Platt for his own benefit.

(3) Courts have also readily accepted the idea set forth in footnote 60 (footnote number 14 in Justice Powell's opinion) that a person may become a "temporary insider." See SEC v. Lund, 570 F.Supp. 1397 (C.D.Cal.1983) (a confidant of a corporate officer); SEC v. Musella, 578 F.Supp. 425 (S.D.N.Y.1984) (the manager of office services of Sullivan and Cromwell); SEC v. Tome, 638 F.Supp. 596 (S.D.N.Y.1986) (social friend and adviser to CEO). Following the original decision in *Musella* (relating to the manager of office services of Sullivan and Cromwell), the SEC proceeded against two New York City police officers who were "third tier tippees" utilizing the same information (but who did not know

the original source of the information on which they were trading). SEC v. Musella, 678 F.Supp. 1060 (S.D.N.Y.1988). The police officers nevertheless were required to disgorge the rather modest profits they made since they had "made a conscious and deliberate choice not to ask [the second tier tippee] any questions about the confidential source whose existence they suspected." The Court concluded that the police officers had reason to know that the "first tier tippee" (the office manager at Sullivan and Cromwell and a "temporary insider") had breached a fiduciary duty by misappropriating confidential information. In yet another Musella opinion, the Court held that a friend of Musella who also knew the information being supplied to him came from an inside source violated rule 10b–5. SEC v. Musella, 748 F.Supp. 1028 (S.D.N.Y.1989).

UNITED STATES v. CHESTMAN

United States Court of Appeals, Second Circuit, 1991.
947 F.2d 551, cert. denied, 503 U.S. 1004, 112 S.Ct. 1759, 118 L.Ed.2d 422 (1992).

Before OAKES, CHIEF JUDGE, FEINBERG,[68] MESKILL, NEWMAN, KEARSE, CARDAMONE, WINTER, PRATT, MINER, ALTIMARI, MAHONEY and McLAUGHLIN, CIRCUIT JUDGES.

ON REHEARING IN BANC

MESKILL, CIRCUIT JUDGE, joined by CARDAMONE, PRATT, MINER and ALTIMARI, CIRCUIT JUDGES: * * *

[Ira Waldbaum was the controlling shareholder of Waldbaum, Inc., a corporation that owned a large supermarket chain. In 1986, Ira agreed to sell the corporation to A & P. Ira told his sister, Shirley Witkin, three of his children, and a nephew, about the pending sale, admonished them to keep the news quiet and confidential until after a public announcement, and offered to tender their shares, along with his controlling block, to enable them to avoid the administrative difficulties of tendering after the public announcement. Shirley nevertheless told her daughter, Susan Loeb, who in turn told her husband, Keith Loeb. The circumstances under which these disclosures occurred are described at some length in the dissenting opinion below. Keith Loeb then telephoned Robert Chestman, a broker used by the junior members of the family, and told him that Waldbaum, Inc. was going to be sold at a "substantially higher" price than the market price. Chestman knew that Susan Loeb was a granddaughter of the Waldbaums. That morning Chestman executed several purchases of Waldbaum stock both for his own account and for the discretionary accounts of several customers, including Keith Loeb. After the SEC investigation began, Keith agreed to cooperate with the government, disgorging a profit of $25,000 and paying a $25,000 fine. Chestman was indicted and convicted on 31 counts of violation of rule 10b–5, mail fraud, violation of rule 14e–3(a), and one count of perjury. A panel of the Second Circuit set aside this conviction in its entirety, 903 F.2d 75 (2d Cir.1990).]

[The first portion of Judge Meskill's majority opinion upholds Chestman's conviction on the rule 14e–3(a) counts. See pages 860, 872, supra.]

---

68. [By the Court] Judge Feinberg participated in the decision to rehear the appeal *in banc* and heard oral argument. He subsequently retired from regular active service, however, and thus did not vote in the *in banc* decision. *See* 28 U.S.C. § 46(c); *United States v. American-Foreign S.S. Corp.*, 363 U.S. 685, 80 S.Ct. 1336, 4 L.Ed.2d 1491 (1960).

B. RULE 10B–5

Chestman's Rule 10b–5 convictions were based on the misappropriation theory, which provides that "one who misappropriates nonpublic information in breach of a fiduciary duty and trades on that information to his own advantage violates Section 10(b) and Rule 10b–5." *SEC v. Materia*, 745 F.2d 197, 203 (2d Cir.1984), *cert. denied*, 471 U.S. 1053, 105 S.Ct. 2112, 85 L.Ed.2d 477 (1985). With respect to the shares Chestman purchased on behalf of Keith Loeb, Chestman was convicted of aiding and abetting Loeb's misappropriation of nonpublic information in breach of a duty Loeb owed to the Waldbaum family and to his wife Susan. As to the shares Chestman purchased for himself and his other clients, Chestman was convicted as a "tippee" of that same misappropriated information. Thus, while Chestman is the defendant in this case, the alleged misappropriator was Keith Loeb. The government agrees that Chestman's convictions cannot be sustained unless there was sufficient evidence to show that (1) Keith Loeb breached a duty owed to the Waldbaum family or Susan Loeb based on a fiduciary or similar relationship of trust and confidence, and (2) Chestman knew that Loeb had done so. We have heretofore never applied the misappropriation theory—and its predicate requirement of a fiduciary breach—in the context of family relationships. * * *

3. *Fiduciary Duties and Their Functional Equivalent*

* * * [W]e turn to our central inquiry—what constitutes a fiduciary or similar relationship of trust and confidence in the context of Rule 10b–5 criminal liability? We begin by noting two factors that do not themselves create the necessary relationship.

First, a fiduciary duty cannot be imposed unilaterally by entrusting a person with confidential information. *Walton v. Morgan Stanley & Co.*, 623 F.2d 796, 799 (2d Cir.1980) (applying Delaware law). *Walton* concerned the conduct of an investment bank, Morgan Stanley. While investigating possible takeover targets for one of its clients, Morgan Stanley obtained unpublished material information (internal earnings reports) on a confidential basis from a prospective target, Olinkraft. After its client abandoned the planned takeover, Morgan Stanley was charged with trading in Olinkraft's stock on the basis of the confidential information. Observing that the parties had bargained at "arm's length" and that there had not been a pre-existing agreement of confidentiality between Morgan Stanley and Olinkraft, we rejected the argument that

> Morgan Stanley became a fiduciary of Olinkraft by virtue of the receipt of the confidential information * * *. [T]he fact that the information was confidential did nothing, in and of itself, to change the relationship between Morgan Stanley and Olinkraft's management. Put bluntly, although, according to the complaint, Olinkraft's management placed its confidence in Morgan Stanley not to disclose the information, Morgan Stanley owed no duty to observe that confidence.

Walton, 623 F.2d at 799. *See also Dirks*, 463 U.S. at 662 n. 22, 103 S.Ct. at 3265 n. 22 (citing *Walton* approvingly as "a case turning on the court's determination that the disclosure did not impose any fiduciary duties on the recipient of the inside information"). Reposing confidential information in another, then, does not by itself create a fiduciary relationship.

Second, marriage does not, without more, create a fiduciary relationship. " '[M]ere kinship does not of itself establish a confidential relation.' * * * Rather, the existence of a confidential relationship must be determined independently of a preexisting family relationship." *Reed*, 601 F.Supp. at 706. Although spouses certainly may by their conduct become fiduciaries, the marriage relationship alone does not impose fiduciary status. In sum, more than the gratuitous reposal of a secret to another who happens to be a family member is required to establish a fiduciary or similar relationship of trust and confidence.

We take our cues as to what *is* required to create the requisite relationship from the securities fraud precedents and the common law. *See Chiarella*, 445 U.S. at 227–30, 100 S.Ct. at 1114–16. * * * [I]t is clear that the relationships involved in this case—those between Keith and Susan Loeb and between Keith Loeb and the Waldbaum family—were not traditional fiduciary relationships.

That does not end our inquiry, however. The misappropriation theory requires us to consider not only whether there exists a fiduciary relationship but also whether there exists a "similar relationship of trust and confidence." * * *

A fiduciary relationship involves discretionary authority and dependency: One person depends on another—the fiduciary—to serve his interests. In relying on a fiduciary to act for his benefit, the beneficiary of the relation may entrust the fiduciary with custody over property of one sort or another. Because the fiduciary obtains access to this property to serve the ends of the fiduciary relationship, he becomes duty-bound not to appropriate the property for his own use. What has been said of an agent's duty of confidentiality applies with equal force to other fiduciary relations: "an agent is subject to a duty to the principal not to use or to communicate information confidentially given him by the principal or acquired by him during the course of or on account of his agency." Restatement (Second) of Agency § 395 (1958). These characteristics represent the measure of the paradigmatic fiduciary relationship. A similar relationship of trust and confidence consequently must share these qualities.

In *Reed*, 601 F.Supp. 685, the district court confronted the question whether these principal characteristics of a fiduciary relationship—dependency and influence—were necessary factual prerequisites to a similar relationship of trust and confidence. There a member of the board of directors of Amax, Gordon Reed, disclosed to his son on several occasions confidential information concerning a proposed tender offer for Amax. Allegedly relying on this information, the son purchased Amax stock call options. The son was subsequently indicted for violating, among other things, Rule 10b–5 based on breach of a fiduciary duty arising between the father and son. The son then moved to dismiss the indictment, contending that he did not breach a fiduciary duty to his father. The district court sustained the indictment.

Both the government and Chestman rely on *Reed*. The government draws on *Reed*'s application of the misappropriation theory in the family context and its expansive construction of relationships of trust and confidence. Chestman, without challenging the holding in *Reed*, argues that *Reed* cannot sustain his Rule 10b–5 convictions because, unlike *Reed* senior and junior, Keith and

Susan Loeb did not customarily repose confidential business information in one another. Neither party challenges the holding of *Reed*. And we decline to do so *sua sponte*. To remain consistent with our interpretation of a "similar relationship of trust and confidence," however, we limit *Reed* to its essential holding: the repeated disclosure of business secrets between family members may substitute for a factual finding of dependence and influence and thereby sustain a finding of the functional equivalent of a fiduciary relationship. We note, in this regard, that *Reed* repeatedly emphasized that the father and son "frequently discussed business affairs." * * *

We have little trouble finding the evidence insufficient to establish a fiduciary relationship or its functional equivalent between Keith Loeb and the Waldbaum family. The government presented only two pieces of evidence on this point. The first was that Keith was an extended member of the Waldbaum family, specifically the family patriarch's (Ira Waldbaum's) "nephew-in-law." The second piece of evidence concerned Ira's discussions of the business with family members. "My children," Ira Waldbaum testified, "have always been involved with me and my family and they know we never speak about business outside of the family." His earlier testimony indicates that the "family" to which he referred were his "three children who were involved in the business."

Lending this evidence the reasonable inferences to which it is entitled, it falls short of establishing the relationship necessary for fiduciary obligations. Kinship alone does not create the necessary relationship. The government proffered nothing more to establish a fiduciary-like association. It did not show that Keith Loeb had been brought into the family's inner circle, whose members, it appears, discussed confidential business information either because they were kin or because they worked together with Ira Waldbaum. Keith was not an employee of Waldbaum and there was no showing that he participated in confidential communications regarding the business. The critical information was gratuitously communicated to him. The disclosure did not serve the interests of Ira Waldbaum, his children or the Waldbaum company. Nor was there any evidence that the alleged relationship was characterized by influence or reliance of any sort. Measured against the principles of fiduciary relations, the evidence does not support a finding that Keith Loeb and the Waldbaum family shared either a fiduciary relation or its functional equivalent.

The government's theory that Keith breached a fiduciary duty of confidentiality to Susan suffers from similar defects. The evidence showed: Keith and Susan were married; Susan admonished Keith not to disclose that Waldbaum was the target of a tender offer; and the two had shared and maintained confidences in the past.

Keith's status as Susan's husband could not itself establish fiduciary status. Nor, absent a pre-existing fiduciary relation or an express agreement of confidentiality, could the coda—"Don't tell." That leaves the unremarkable testimony that Keith and Susan had shared and maintained generic confidences before. The jury was not told the nature of these past disclosures and therefore it could not reasonably find a relationship that inspired fiduciary, rather than normal marital, obligations.

In the absence of evidence of an explicit acceptance by Keith of a duty of confidentiality, the context of the disclosure takes on special import. While acceptance may be implied, it must be implied from a pre-existing fiduciary-like relationship between the parties. Here the government presented the jury with insufficient evidence from which to draw a rational inference of implied acceptance. Susan's disclosure of the information to Keith served no purpose, business or otherwise. The disclosure also was unprompted. Keith did not induce her to convey the information through misrepresentation or subterfuge. Superiority and reliance, moreover, did not mark this relationship either before or after the disclosure of the confidential information. Nor did Susan's dependence on Keith to act in her interests for some purpose inspire the disclosure. The government failed even to establish a pattern of sharing business confidences between the couple. The government, therefore, failed to offer sufficient evidence to establish the functional equivalent of a fiduciary relation.

In sum, because Keith owed neither Susan nor the Waldbaum family a fiduciary duty or its functional equivalent, he did not defraud them by disclosing news of the pending tender offer to Chestman. Absent a predicate act of fraud by Keith Loeb, the alleged misappropriator, Chestman could not be derivatively liable as Loeb's tippee or as an aider and abettor. Therefore, Chestman's Rule 10b–5 convictions must be reversed. * * *

C. MAIL FRAUD

[The court held that "whatever ethical obligation Loeb may have owed the Waldbaum family or Susan Loeb, it was too ethereal to be protected by either the securities or mail fraud statutes."]

Accordingly, we affirm the Rule 14e–3(a) convictions and reverse the Rule 10b–5 and mail fraud convictions. The reversal of these convictions does not warrant reconsideration of the sentence since the sentences on the Rule 10b–5 and mail fraud convictions are concurrent with the sentences in the Rule 14(e)–3(a) counts. The panel's reversal of the perjury conviction remains intact.

WINTER, CIRCUIT JUDGE (joined by OAKES, CHIEF JUDGE, NEWMAN, KEARSE, and McLAUGHLIN, CIRCUIT JUDGES), concurring in part and dissenting in part:

I concur in the decision to affirm Chestman's convictions under Section 14(e) of the Securities Exchange Act of 1934, and under Rule 14e–3. I respectfully dissent, however, from the reversals of his convictions under Section 10(b) and under the mail fraud statute.

1) Insider Trading

The difficulty this court finds in resolving the issues raised by this appeal stems largely from the history of the development of the law concerning insider trading. * * *

Notwithstanding the ambiguities surrounding Section 10(b)'s impact on insider trading—including its very definition—Congress has increased the penalties for violations of that prohibition. The SEC in turn has failed to promulgate rules outside the area of tender offers but its decisions have continued to march, in the eyes of one commentator, to the beat of its own drummer.

It is hardly surprising that disagreement exists within an *in banc* court of appeals as to the import of present caselaw. Nor is it surprising that the lower courts have added to the *Dirks* breach of duty doctrine a misappropriation of information doctrine, which prohibits trading in securities based on material, nonpublic information acquired in violation of a duty to any owner of such information, whether or not the owner is the corporation whose shares are traded.

b) Property Rights in Inside Information

One commentator has attempted to explain the Supreme Court decisions in terms of the business-property rationale for banning insider trading mentioned in *Cady, Roberts & Co. See* Easterbrook, *[Insider Trading, Secret Agents, Evidentiary Privileges and the Production of Information*, 1981 Sup. Ct.Rev. 309], at 309–39. That rationale may be summarized as follows. Information is perhaps the most precious commodity in commercial markets. It is expensive to produce, and, because it involves facts and ideas that can be easily photocopied or carried in one's head, there is a ubiquitous risk that those who pay to produce information will see others reap the profit from it. Where the profit from an activity is likely to be diverted, investment in that activity will decline. If the law fails to protect property rights in commercial information, therefore, less will be invested in generating such information.

For example, mining companies whose investments in geological surveys have revealed valuable deposits do not want word of the strike to get out until they have secured rights to the land. If word does get out, the price of the land not only will go up, but other mining companies may also secure the rights. In either case, the mining company that invested in geological surveys (including the inevitably sizeable number of unsuccessful drillings) will see profits from that investment enjoyed by others. If mining companies are unable to keep the results of such surveys confidential, less will be invested in them.

Similarly, firms that invest money in generating information about other companies with a view to some form of combination will maintain secrecy about their efforts, and if secrecy cannot be maintained, less will be invested in acquiring such information. Hostile acquirers will want to keep such information secret lest the target mount defensive actions or speculators purchase the target's stock. Even when friendly negotiations with the other company are undertaken, the acquirer will often require the target corporation to maintain secrecy about negotiations, lest the very fact of negotiation tip off others on the important fact that the two firms think a combination might be valuable. *See, e.g., Staffin v. Greenberg*, 672 F.2d 1196, 1207 n. 12 (3d Cir.1982) ("If, as is often the case, a merger will benefit both the acquired company and its shareholders, an insider may be obliged to maintain strict confidentiality to avoid ruining the corporate opportunity through premature disclosure. Indeed, the record is clear in this case that [the buyer] very nearly withdrew from merger discussions upon hearing of [the seller's] * * * press release."). * * * In the instant matter, A & P made secrecy a condition of its acquisition of Waldbaum's.

Insider trading may reduce the return on information in two ways. First, it creates incentives for insiders to generate or disclose information that may disregard the welfare of the corporation. That risk is not implicated by the facts in the present case, and no further discussion is presently required.

Second, insider trading creates a risk that information will be prematurely disclosed by such trading, and the corporation will lose part or all of its property in that information. Although trades by an insider may rarely affect market price, others who know of the insider's trading may notice that a trader is unusually successful, or simply perceive unusual activity in a stock and guess the information and/or make piggyback trades.[69] A broker who executes a trade for a geologist or for a financial printer may well draw relevant conclusions. Or, as in the instant matter, the trader, Loeb, may tell his or her broker about the inside information, who may then trade on his or her account, on clients' accounts, or may tell friends and relatives. One inside trader has publicly attributed his exposure in part to the fact that the bank through which he made trades piggybacked on the trades, as did the broker who made the trades for the bank. *See* Levine, *The Inside Story of An Inside Trader*, Fortune, May 21, 1990, at 80. Once activity in a stock reaches an unusual stage, others may guess the reason for the trading—the corporate secret. Insider trading thus increases the risk that confidential information acquired at a cost may be disclosed. If so, the owner of the information may lose its investment.

This analysis provides a policy rationale for prohibiting insider trading when the property rights of a corporation in information are violated by traders. However, the rationale stops well short of prohibiting all trading on material nonpublic information. Efficient capital markets depend on the protection of property rights in information. However, they also require that persons who acquire and act on information about companies be able to profit from the information they generate so long as the method by which the information is acquired does not amount to a form of theft. A rule commanding equal access would result in a securities market governed by relative degrees of ignorance because the profit motive for independently generating information about companies would be substantially diminished. Easterbrook, *supra*, at 313–14. Under such circumstances, the pricing of securities would be less accurate than in circumstances in which the production of information is encouraged by legal protection.

One may speculate that it was for these reasons that the Supreme Court declined in *Chiarella* to adopt a broad ban on trading on material nonpublic information[70] and then imposed in *Dirks* a breach of fiduciary duty require-

---

69. [By the Judge] Section 16(a) of the '34 Act requires insiders to report trades in a corporation's stock (i) at the time of a new issue, (ii) when they become an insider, and (iii) each month thereafter in which trades occur. Where insiders are able to avoid "profits" as defined in Section 16(b) and trade heavily—e.g., a series of purchases that cannot be matched with sales during the six months at either end of the activity—other traders may well draw accurate inferences. In that respect, federal law causes the information on which insiders are trading to become known.

70. [By the Judge] Comprehensive protection of those who trade with insiders is unat-

tainable because the most common form of insider trading by far is failing to trade. An insider possessing nonpublic information may purchase or sell other securities or borrow instead of trading in the corporation's stock. Such trading seems virtually undiscoverable and unregulable, however, although it is functionally indistinguishable from insider trading so far as those who deal with the trader are concerned.

Under the business property rationale, not-trading because of inside information is not the functional equivalent of trading because not-trading creates at most a negligible risk of disclosure of corporate secrets. Unlike trading,

ment—not running to those with whom the trader buys or sells. Under the *Dirks* rule, insider trading is illegal only where the trader has received the information as a result of the trader's or tipper's breach of a duty to keep information confidential.

The misappropriation theory * * * fits within this rationale. Misappropriation also involves the misuse of confidential information in a way that risks making information public in a fashion similar to trading by corporate insiders. In *U.S. v. Carpenter*, for example, where the information belonged to the *Wall Street Journal* rather than to the corporations whose shares were traded, the misuse of information created an incentive on the part of the traders to create false information that might affect the efficiency of the market's pricing of the corporations' stock. Moreover, the potential for piggy-backing would add to that inefficiency. * * *

c) The Instant Case

When this analysis is applied to a family-controlled corporation such as that involved in the instant case, I believe that family members who have benefitted from the family's control of the corporation are under a duty not to disclose confidential corporate information that comes to them in the ordinary course of family affairs. In the case of family-controlled corporations, family and business affairs are necessarily intertwined, and it is inevitable that from time to time normal familial interactions will lead to the revelation of confidential corporate matters to various family members. Indeed, the very nature of familial relationships may cause the disclosure of corporate matters to avoid misunderstandings among family members or suggestions that a family member is unworthy of trust.

Keith Loeb learned of the pending acquisition of Waldbaum's by A & P through precisely such interactions. His wife Susan was asked one day by her sister to take carpool responsibilities for their children. When Susan inquired as to why this was necessary, the sister was vague and said that she had to take their mother somewhere. After further inquiry, the sister flatly declined to tell Susan what was going on. Susan did not say, "Gee, confidential corporate information must be involved, and I have no right to such information." Instead, concerned about her mother's ongoing health problems, Susan made direct inquiry of her mother, who revealed that Susan's sister took her to get stock certificates to give to Ira Waldbaum for the initial phase of the A & P acquisition. The mother swore Susan to secrecy, telling Susan that the acquisition would be very profitable to the family and premature disclosure could ruin the deal. Susan then asked whether she could tell her husband Keith. Instead of saying, "No, Keith may be your husband but you are to button your lips in his presence," her mother assented but warned against disclosure to anyone else.

Susan and Keith Loeb jointly owned a large number of Waldbaum shares at that time, all of which had been a gift from her mother. The Loebs' children also owned shares received as a gift from their grandmother. Susan told Keith about the A & P acquisition in the course of discussing the financial benefits they and their children would receive as a result of that

---

not-trading does not involve persons other than the trader, such as brokers, and does not create an unusual volume. *But see* Easter-

brook, *supra*, at 336–37 (discussing signals sent to such parties by *not* trading).

transaction. She stressed the need for absolute secrecy. Susan testified that she and her husband had shared confidences in the past and that on each such occasion they had indicated to each other that the confidences would be respected. Thereafter, Keith Loeb informed Chestman about the A & P acquisition in the hope of making a profit.

I have little difficulty in concluding that Chestman's convictions can be affirmed on either the *Dirks* rule or on a misappropriation theory. The disclosure of information concerning the A & P acquisition among Ira Wald-baum's extended family was the result of ordinary familial interactions that can be expected in the case of family-controlled corporations. Members of a family who receive such information are placed in a position in which their trading on the information risks financial injury to the corporation, its public shareholders and other family members. When members of a family have benefitted from the family's control of a corporation and are in a position to acquire such information in the ordinary course of family interactions, that position carries with it a duty not to disclose. * * * Such a duty is of course based on mutual understandings among family members—quite explicit in this case—and owed to the family. However, the duty originates in the corporation and is ultimately intended to protect the corporation and its public shareholders. The duty is thus also owed to the corporation, to a degree sufficient in my view to trigger the *Dirks* rule. Because trading on inside information so acquired by family members amounts to theft, the misappropriation theory also applies.

Under my colleagues' theory, the disclosure of family corporate information can be avoided only by family members extracting formal, express promises of confidentiality or by elderly mothers in poor health refusing to tell their daughters about mysterious travels. If disclosure is made, daughters may not disclose their mother's doings or potential financial benefits to the daughters' husbands without a formal, express promise of confidentiality. If, for example, Susan had earlier shared with Keith her concerns about her mother's mysterious travels before learning of their purpose, she would not have been able to tell him what she later learned about those travels no matter how persistently he asked. For my colleagues in the majority, the critical gap in the government's case was that Susan did not testify either that on this occasion Keith agreed not to disclose the pending acquisition by A & P or that prior confidential communications between her and her husband had involved the Waldbaum's corporation.

I have no lack of sympathy with my colleagues' concern about the difficulty of drawing lines in this area. Nevertheless, the line they draw seems very unrealistic in that it expects family members to behave like strangers toward each other. It also leads to the perverse and circular result that where family business interests are concerned, family members must act as if there are no mutual obligations of trust and confidence because the law does not recognize such obligations. Under such a regime, parents and children must conceal their comings and goings, family members must cease to speak when a son-in-law enters a room, and offended members of the family must understand that such conduct is always related only to business.

I thus believe that a family member (i) who has received or expects (e.g., through inheritance) benefits from family control of a corporation, here gifts of stock, (ii) who is in a position to learn confidential corporate information through ordinary family interactions, and (iii) who knows that under the circumstances both the corporation and the family desire confidentiality, has a duty not to use information so obtained for personal profit where the use risks disclosure. The receipt or expectation of benefits increases the interest of such family members in corporate affairs and thus increases the chance that they will learn confidential information. Disclosure in the present case occurred in the course of a discussion that included, *inter alia*, an examination of the benefits of the A & P acquisition to Susan, Keith and their children. Susan's warning to Keith about secrecy was clearly intended to protect the corporation as well as the family and clearly had originated with Ira Waldbaum. In such circumstances, Susan's saying "Don't tell" is enough for me. Not to have such a rule means that a family-controlled corporation with public shareholders is subject to greater risk of disclosure of confidential information than is a corporation that is entirely publicly owned.

I see no room for argument over whether there was sufficient evidence for the jury to find that Chestman knew Keith Loeb was violating an obligation. The record fairly brims with Chestman's consciousness that Keith Loeb was behaving improperly. * * *

MINER, CIRCUIT JUDGE, concurring:

I concur in the comprehensive opinion of Judge Meskill * * *. I write only to comment upon the "familial relationship" rule of insider trading proposed by Judge Winter in his partially dissenting opinion.

The rule urged upon us would impose a duty of nondisclosure upon "a family member (i) who has received or expects (e.g., through inheritance) benefits from family control of a corporation, here gifts of stock, (ii) who is in a position to learn confidential corporate information through ordinary family interactions, and (iii) who knows that under the circumstances both the corporation and the family desire confidentiality." The duty is said to consist of an obligation "not to use information so obtained for personal profit where the use risks disclosure." *Id.*

The rationale for the proposed rule apparently is rooted in the notion that family members would be encouraged to speak freely on all matters pertaining to the family, knowing that the lips of those who receive confidential corporate information in the course of ongoing family interchanges would be sealed. Thus, in this case, so the argument goes, Ira Waldbaum could reveal the pending stock sale to his sister, Shirley Witkin, who could reveal it to her daughter, Susan Loeb, who could reveal it to her husband, Keith Loeb, all with the understanding that a duty imposed by law on each family member would protect against use of the confidential information for profit. Without the rule, it is maintained, family members in this case would have been inhibited from discussing such matters as the reason for Shirley Witkin's unusual absence from her home, because such a discussion inevitably would lead to disclosure of the confidential information regarding the sale of Waldbaum stock to A & P.

It seems to me, however, that family discourse would be inhibited, rather than promoted, by a rule that would automatically assure confidentiality on the part of a family member receiving non-public corporate information. What speaker, secure in the knowledge that a relative could be prosecuted for insider trading, would reveal to that relative anything remotely connected with corporate dealings? Given the uncertainties surrounding the definition of insider trading, a term as yet unclarified by Congress, what family members would want to receive any information whatsoever that might bear on the family business? How could family news be disseminated freely in an atmosphere where the members must be ultra-sensitive to whether "both the corporation and the family" are seeking some measure of confidentiality "under the circumstances."

The difficulty of identifying those who would be covered by the proposed familial rule adds an additional element of uncertainty to what already are uncertain crimes. It is not clear just who would be subject to the duty of confidentiality: family members "who ha[ve] received or expect[] * * * benefits from family control of a corporation" belong to a very broad category indeed. Here, those who have received gifts of stock are included. But does the category include those who have received only small amounts of stock? Does it matter what proportion the stock bears to the total issued and outstanding shares? Does the category include one who expects to receive stock through inheritance but never receives any? Does it include grandchildren who expect ultimately to inherit assets purchased with the proceeds of the sale of the family-controlled corporation? The net would be spread wider than appropriate in a criminal context. * * *

In the same vein, it is conceivable that minor children could find themselves "in a position to learn confidential corporate information through ordinary family interactions." If they came into the possession of such information and somehow acquired the knowledge "that under the circumstances both the corporation and the family desire[d] confidentiality," would they become tippers who would expose other family members to criminal liability as tippees when they passed the information along?

It is important to note that in the case at bar we deal with an attenuated trail of family confidences in which information was received without any assurance of confidentiality by the receiver and without any prior sharing of business information within the family. Neither Shirley Witkin nor her daughter nor her son-in-law were involved in any way in the operation of the Waldbaum business or privy to any of its past secrets. Family relationships being what they are, it makes little sense under the circumstances to imply assurances that confidentiality would be maintained. Of course, a different situation obtains where the giver of business confidences, in addition to having a family relationship with the receiver, also has a history of reposing such confidences in the receiver. *See United States v. Reed*, 601 F.Supp. 685, 712, 717 (S.D.N.Y.), *rev'd on other grounds*, 773 F.2d 477 (2d Cir.1985) (son of corporate director as receiver of non-public corporate information). Under those circumstances, the duty of confidentiality is implied from the business relationship coupled with the family one.

Finally, to further extend the concept of confidential duty would be to take the courts into an area of securities regulation not yet entered by Congress. It would give the wrong signal to prosecutors in their continuing efforts to push against existing boundaries in the prosecution of securities fraud cases. "[P]rosecutors can often claim that some confidential relationship was abused—whether between lovers, family members, longtime friends, or simply that well-known confidential relationship between bartender and drunk. Such a test inherently creates legal uncertainty and invites selective prosecutions." Coffee, *Outsider Trading, That New Crime*, Wall St.J., Nov. 14, 1990, at 16, col. 4. I would await further instructions from Congress before sailing into this unchartered area.

[The opinion of MAHONEY, CIRCUIT JUDGE, concurring in part and dissenting in part, is omitted.]

SECURITIES EXCHANGE ACT OF 1934
15 U.S.C.A. § 78u–1 (1997).

Section 21A. Civil Penalties for Insider Trading

(a) AUTHORITY TO IMPOSE CIVIL PENALTIES

(1) *Judicial actions by commission authorized.* Whenever it shall appear to the Commission that any person has violated any provision of this chapter or the rules or regulations thereunder by purchasing or selling a security while in possession of material, nonpublic information in, or has violated any such provision by communicating such information in connection with, a transaction on or through the facilities of a national securities exchange or from or through a broker or dealer, and which is not part of a public offering by an issuer of securities other than standardized options, the Commission—

(A) may bring an action in a United States district court to seek, and the court shall have jurisdiction to impose, a civil penalty to be paid by the person who committed such violation; and

(B) may, subject to subsection (b)(1) of this Section, bring an action in a United States district court to seek, and the court shall have jurisdiction to impose, a civil penalty to be paid by a person who, at the time of the violation, directly or indirectly controlled the person who committed such violation.

(2) *Amount of penalty for person who committed violation.* The amount of the penalty which may be imposed on the person who committed such violation shall be determined by the court in light of the facts and circumstances, but shall not exceed three times the profit gained or loss avoided as a result of such unlawful purchase, sale, or communication.

(3) *Amount of penalty for controlling person.* The amount of the penalty which may be imposed on any person who, at the time of the violation, directly or indirectly controlled the person who committed such violation, shall be determined by the court in light of the facts and circumstances, but shall not exceed the greater of $1,000,000, or three times the amount of the profit gained or loss avoided as a result of such controlled person's violation. If such controlled person's violation was a violation by communication, the profit gained or loss avoided as a result of the violation shall, for purposes of this paragraph only, be deemed to be limited to the profit gained or loss avoided by the person or persons to whom the controlled person directed such communication.

(b) LIMITATIONS ON LIABILITY

(1) *Liability of controlling persons.* No controlling person shall be subject to a penalty under subsection (a)(1)(B) of this section unless the Commission establishes that—

(A) such controlling person knew or recklessly disregarded the fact that such controlled person was likely to engage in the act or acts constituting the violation and failed to take appropriate steps to prevent such act or acts before they occurred; or

(B) such controlling person knowingly or recklessly failed to establish, maintain, or enforce any policy or procedure required under section 15(f) of this title[71] or section 204A of the Investment Advisers Act of 1940 and such failure substantially contributed to or permitted the occurrence of the act or acts constituting the violation.

(2) *Additional restrictions on liability.* No person shall be subject to a penalty under subsection (a) of this section solely by reason of employing another person who is subject to a penalty under such subsection, unless such employing person is liable as a controlling person under paragraph (1) of this subsection. Section 20(a) of this title[72] shall not apply to actions under subsection (a) of this section.

(c) AUTHORITY OF COMMISSION

The Commission, by such rules, regulations, and orders as it considers necessary or appropriate in the public interest or for the protection of investors, may exempt, in whole or in part, either unconditionally or upon specific terms and conditions, any person or transaction or class of persons or transactions from this section.

(d) PROCEDURES FOR COLLECTION

(1) *Payment of penalty to treasury.* A penalty imposed under this section shall (subject to subsection (e) of this section) be payable into the Treasury of the United States. * * *

(e) AUTHORITY TO AWARD BOUNTIES TO INFORMANTS

Notwithstanding the provisions of subsection (d)(1) of this section, there shall be paid from amounts imposed as a penalty under this section and recovered by the Commission or the Attorney General, such sums, not to exceed 10 percent of such amounts, as the Commission deems appropriate, to the person or persons who provide information leading to the imposition of such penalty. Any determinations under this subsection, including whether, to whom, or in what amount to make payments, shall be in the sole discretion of the Commission, except that no such payment shall be made to any member, officer, or employee of any appropriate regulatory agency, the Department of

---

71. [By the Editor] The referenced section reads as follows:

Sec. 15(f) Every registered broker or dealer shall establish, maintain and enforce written policies and procedures reasonably designed, taking into consideration the nature of such broker's or dealer's business, to prevent the misuse in violation of this title, or the rules or regulations thereunder, of material, nonpublic information by such broker or dealer or any person associated with such broker or dealer. The Commission, as it deems necessary or appropriate in the public interest or for the protection of investors, shall adopt rules or regulations to require specific policies or procedures reasonably de-

signed to prevent misuse in violation of this title (or the rules or regulations thereunder) of material, nonpublic information.

72. [By the Editor] Section 20(a) provides:

Every person who, directly or indirectly, controls any person liable under any provision of this title or of any rule or regulation thereunder shall also be liable jointly and severally with and to the same extent as such controlled person to any person to whom such controlled person is liable, unless the controlling person acted in good faith and did not directly or indirectly induce the act or acts constituting the violation or cause of action.

Justice, or a self-regulatory organization. Any such determination shall be final and not subject to judicial review.

(F) Definition

For purposes of this section, "profit gained" or "loss avoided" is the difference between the purchase or sale price of the security and the value of that security as measured by the trading price of the security a reasonable period after public dissemination of the nonpublic information.

Notes

(1) Section 21A was enacted as part of the Insider Trading Sanctions Act of 1984, Pub.L.No. 98–376, 98 Stat. 1264 (ITSA). The power to impose civil penalties greatly increases the risk of insider trading, since the penalty is added to the disgorgement of profit, and the inside trader ends up much worse off than if he had never traded at all. Courts have consistently added substantial civil penalties to the disgorgement of insider trading profits. In one case involving trading on confidential information in shares of Motel 6, for example, one defendant was ordered to disgorge illegal profits of $717,233, pay prejudgment interest of $519,634, and a civil penalty of $2.15 million. 1997 WL 48039 (SEC).

(2) A second statute, the Insider Trading and Securities Fraud Enforcement Act of 1988, Pub.L.No. 100–704, 102 Stat. 4677 (codified in scattered sections of 15 U.S.C.)(ITSFEA) increased the criminal penalties for willful violation of the Securities Acts or regulations issued thereunder from $100,000 and five years to $1,000,000 and ten years for individuals, and a fine of up to $2,500,000 when the defendant is a "person other than a natural person." ITSFEA, § 4.

(3) Given these penalties, it is surprising that cases continue to arise involving lawyers or sophisticated persons "who should have known better." These usually are high profile cases involving lawyers or corporate executives. Cases involving the transfer of information within families also continue to arise with some regularity. Examples of people who should have known better: In SEC v. Norgren, Anstalt, Garvey, Gleeman & Gleeman, 52 SEC Docket 1956, 89 Civ. 7667 (JMC), 1992 WL 298041 (SEC)(1992), the S.E.C filed charges against Garvey, a paralegal for the takeover law firm of Skadden, Arps, Slate, Meagher & Flom and against Gleeman, a childhood friend and Wharton school graduate; Gleeman had been the mastermind of a scheme to trade on information provided by Garvey through bank accounts in the Cayman Islands. Gleeman's father actually set up the accounts and did the trading, but the plan was quickly detected. Civil and criminal charges were filed against all three; both Garvey and Gleeman settled the civil charges and pleaded guilty to the criminal counts; Garvey received a probationary sentence. In SEC v. Downe, 51 SEC Docket 995, 92 Civ. 4092 (MP), 1992 WL 117216 (SEC) (1992), the SEC charged that seven prominent socialites exchanged inside information about transactions over poker games, during parties, and on yachting excursions over a two-year period during the 1980s. Among the defendants were a brother of the founder of Revlon, Inc., a son-in-law of Henry Ford II, a former CEO of Kidde, Inc., a former board chairman of Anametrics, Inc., and a former senior broker with Oppenheimer & Co. Several settlements were negotiated, essentially requiring disgorgement of profits based on such information. One defendant alone agreed to disgorge $1.6 million in profits. See Junda Woo, Martin Revson Settles SEC Claims Of Insider Trading, Wall St. J., Nov. 4, 1993, at B16, col. 3. Mr. Downe's attorney was quoted as saying that in order to settle the SEC suits, "Mr. Downe was prepared to sell a prized contemporary-art and photography collection, homes in Ireland and South-

ampton, N.Y., a Florida condominium, securities and his interest in various partnerships and business ventures.''

(4) In 1995, the SEC filed 45 new insider trading cases; in addition, at the end of that year the SEC had about 265 active cases pending that involved insider trading. Many of these defendants might be categorized as "ordinary Joes" rather than sophisticated insiders. Harvey Pitt, a leading defense lawyer commented in 1995 that of the 15 cases he was currently handling, "90 percent fall in the Main Street category." The mix of cases he handles has changed, he said, since "Wall Street professionals have really learned a lesson." Karen Donovan, Insider Trading is Still Big, But Traders 'Average Joes,' Nat'l L.J., October 16, 1995, B1, at B2, col. 3. Many of these 'Average Joe' cases are settled. The following anecdotal sampling of cases indicates the willingness of the SEC and the Department of Justice to invest prosecutorial resources in order to pursue these persons with modest means:

(a) In 1996, Cameron, a "close friend" of Donald Tyson, a former chairman of Tyson Foods Inc. settled charges that he had purchased Tyson stock based on a possible merger that he had heard about from his friend. Cameron agreed to disgorge $46,125 in unlawful profits, pay $18,153.43 in prejudgment interest, and a $46,125 civil penalty. Tyson also agreed to pay a $46,125 civil penalty to dismiss the suit.

(b) A typesetting supervisor for Applied Graphics Technology, Inc., a printing company where *Business Week* is published, agreed to pay $46,000 (about the amount that he, his girlfriend, and his girlfriend's family made on 43 securities transactions over six months), based on advance knowledge of stories that later appeared in *Business Week*.

(c) In 1997, a general counsel of a small Atlanta-based medical services company agreed to disgorge $8,450, plus $1,183.27 in prejudgment interest, and a civil penalty of $8,450, in order to settle claims brought by the SEC that she gave non-public information to other individuals.

(d) A former employee of Household International Inc., her husband, and a family friend settled charges that they traded on information about Household's plans to acquire a Texas company. The employee resigned from Household and agreed to disgorge $1,383 in profits plus a civil penalty of $2,320; the family friend, a broker at A.G. Edwards Co., agreed to disgorge $2,950, representing profits he and two of his clients made on the information, plus a civil penalty of $937 and a one-year suspension from the securities business.

(e) A "second tier tippee" settled SEC charges that he traded on nonpublic information involving a tender offer for two trucking companies; he agreed to disgorge profits of $29,250 and pay a penalty of $21,343.75. The tippee learned of the information from a business associate and his "live-in companion" while vacationing in the British West Indies.

(5) The SEC has also not hesitated to pursue law firm partners, associates, paralegals, and others who engage in insider trading on the basis of information obtained through law firms. One cannot assume that even modest profits will not be discovered and vigorously pursued. It is unlikely that a law firm would provide any assistance to, or retain, a partner, associate, or staff employee charged with insider trading—rather, the most likely response is immediate dismissal. The prohibitions against insider trading are therefore of particular concern to partners and employees of law firms. The temptation to engage in even a discreet amount

of trading on inside information obtained from one's work should be sternly resisted.

(6) Consider section 21A(a)(1)(B)(page 892 supra) which was added by ITS-FEA in 1988. Under these provisions, would Texas Gulf Sulphur, Inc. have been liable for the insider trading transactions of Darke (the geologist)? Would Pandick Press have been liable for Chiarella's transactions? As a result of this provision, a wide variety of employers whose employees may have access to valuable inside information have found it necessary to "establish, maintain, [and] enforce" policies or procedures designed to prevent the misuse of such information: issuers, accounting firms, financial printing companies, and the like. Furthermore, the policies or procedures must go much deeper down into the organization than merely the officers, directors, partners, and top-level personnel. It is likely that most readers of this note will have firsthand experience with these procedures, either by being subject to them personally or by creating and applying such policies on behalf of clients, or both.

(7) Might the law firm of Sullivan and Cromwell be held liable as a controlling person of the office manager who engaged in inside trading? The same question might be asked of Skadden, Arps, Slate, Meagher and Flom for the actions of Garvey, a paralegal. See ABA Subcommittee on Civil Litigation and SEC Enforcement Matters, Law Firm Policies Regarding Insider Trading and Confidentiality, 47 Bus. Law. 235 (1991)[73]:

> Notwithstanding the Commission's hortatory urgings, considerable differences of view exist whether, and to what extent, and under what circumstances, law firms can be vicariously liable for the trading activities of firm members and/or employees. In this context, although a large number of law firms have resorted to formal, written, statements of policy regarding insider trading and client confidentiality, it must be borne in mind that no court has held that law firms must have in place a formal statement of policy or procedures in order to avoid vicarious liability for the errant acts of misguided employees or members. Indeed, as then SEC Commissioner Philip R. Lochner, Jr., recently wrote, "[i]n some cases, depending on the size of the firm and the nature of its practice, the best procedure [for a law firm to adopt] may be no procedure."

> Nonetheless, because so many law firms appear to have decided, on their own, to adopt these policies, the Subcommittee on Civil Litigation and Enforcement Matters (the "Subcommittee") of the American Bar Association's Section of Business Law Federal Securities Law Committee undertook a survey of existing law firm confidentiality and/or securities trading policies, in the hope that, by setting forth a variety of examples, those firms that deemed it appropriate to adopt such policies might have some guidance on the types of provisions that might be included.[74]

73. Copyright (1991) by the American Bar Association. All rights reserved. Reprinted with permission of the American Bar Association and its Section of Corporation, Banking and Business Law.

74. [By the Subcommittee] Upon reviewing a draft of this report, SEC Chairman Richard C. Breeden noted his concern that attorneys are still being implicated in insider trading cases. Although Chairman Breeden declined to provide specific comments on the draft or the kinds of procedures he believes a particular law firm should consider adopting, he did state that law firms would be "well-advised to revisit the issue or protecting client confidences and to consider what measures may be required to prevent violations of the federal securities laws." *See* Letter from Richard C. Breeden to Harvey L. Pitt (May 20, 1991), on file with *The Business Lawyer*.

See also Peter M.O. Wong, Insider Trading Regulation of Law Firms: Expanding ITSFEA's Policy and Procedures Requirement, 44 Hastings L.J. 1159 (1993).

(8) Assume that you overhear a colleague talking about or appearing to execute a transaction that sounds suspiciously like insider trading. May you turn him or her in and claim a ''bounty'' for doing so? See § 21A(e) (page 893, supra). Senator D'Amato described the objective of this provision as follows on the floor of the United States Senate:

> To those who oppose bounty I ask that they put themselves in the place of an employee or coworker of an insider trader. What incentive is there to blow the whistle that can counteract the clear risk to profession and livelihood? They may answer that civic duty is enough, and one would hope they were right. But I disagree. Bounty is a positive incentive we can offer and I see no real cost in doing so. ·

134 Cong.Rec. S17219 (Oct. 21, 1988). The SEC has issued regulations describing the procedures for applying for, and obtaining, bounties under this section. 17 C.F.R. § 201.61 (1997).

SECURITIES EXCHANGE ACT OF 1934
15 U.S.C.A. § 78t–1 (1997).

Section 20A. Liability to contemporaneous traders for insider trading

(a) Private rights of action based on contemporaneous trading

Any person who violates any provision of this chapter or the rules or regulations thereunder by purchasing or selling a security while in possession of material, nonpublic information shall be liable in an action in any court of competent jurisdiction to any person who, contemporaneously with the purchase or sale of securities that is the subject of such violation, has purchased (where such violation is based on a sale of securities) or sold (where such violation is based on a purchase of securities) securities of the same class.

(b) Limitations on liability

(1) *Contemporaneous trading actions limited to profit gained or loss avoided.* The total amount of damages imposed under subsection (a) of this section shall not exceed the profit gained or loss avoided in the transaction or transactions that are the subject of the violation.

(2) *Offsetting disgorgements against liability.* The total amount of damages imposed against any person under subsection (a)of this section shall be diminished by the amounts, if any, that such person may be required to disgorge, pursuant to a court order obtained at the instance of the Commission, in a proceeding brought * * * relating to the same transaction or transactions.

(3) *Controlling person liability.* No person shall be liable under this section solely by reason of employing another person who is liable under this section, but the liability of a controlling person under this section shall be subject to section 78t(a) of this title.

(4) *Statute of limitations.* No action may be brought under this section more than 5 years after the date of the last transaction that is the subject of the violation.

(c) JOINT AND SEVERAL LIABILITY FOR COMMUNICATING

Any person who violates any provision of this title or the rules or regulations thereunder by communicating material, nonpublic information shall be jointly and severally liable under subsection (a) of this section with, and to the same extent as, any person or persons liable under subsection (a)of this section to whom the communication was directed.

(d) AUTHORITY NOT TO RESTRICT OTHER EXPRESS OR IMPLIED RIGHTS OF ACTION

Nothing in this section shall be construed to limit or condition the right of any person to bring an action to enforce a requirement of this title or the availability of any cause of action implied from a provision of this chapter.

(e) PROVISIONS NOT TO AFFECT PUBLIC PROSECUTIONS

This section shall not be construed to bar or limit in any manner any action by the Commission or the Attorney General under any other provision of this chapter, nor shall it bar or limit in any manner any action to recover penalties, or to seek any other order regarding penalties.

Notes

(1) Prior to enactment of this section, the question whether private actions may be maintained against persons trading on inside information had arisen in a number of cases; the leading cases in which such suits were permitted are Elkind v. Liggett & Myers, Inc., 635 F.2d 156 (2d Cir.1980), and Shapiro v. Merrill Lynch, Pierce, Fenner & Smith, Inc., 495 F.2d 228 (2d Cir.1974). A majority of courts, however, did not permit such suits, in part dismayed by the complex and erratic consequences of such litigation, particularly in the computation of damages. See Fridrich v. Bradford, 542 F.2d 307 (6th Cir.1976), cert. denied 429 U.S. 1053, 97 S.Ct. 767, 50 L.Ed.2d 769 (1977) (defendants did not purchase shares from plaintiffs and their trading in no way affected the plaintiffs' decision to sell; private civil liability does not need to be coextensive with the reach of the SEC); Moss v. Morgan Stanley Inc., 719 F.2d 5 (2d Cir.1983), cert. denied sub nom. Moss v. Newman, 465 U.S. 1025, 104 S.Ct. 1280, 79 L.Ed.2d 684 (1984)(defendants were tippees of aggressor in proposed tender offer and traded in the target's stock; the Court held that the tippees owed no duty to the plaintiffs on an impersonal market).

(2) Plaintiffs have not had much greater success under § 20A, which was added by ITSFEA in 1988. Most (though not all) complaints have been dismissed or summary judgments for defendants have been entered before trial. Major issues have been how contemporaneous must "contemporaneous trading" be and how particularized allegations must be that the defendants in fact possessed material nonpublic information at the time of trading. Simon v. American Power Conversion Corp., 945 F.Supp. 416 (D.R.I.1996) held that trading that occurred during the same week was "contemporaneous" and refused to grant a motion to dismiss, while In re AST Research Securities Litigation, 887 F.Supp. 231 (C.D.Cal.1995) took the position that trading must occur on the same day if it is to meet the "contemporaneous trading" requirement. Other cases have suggested that a five- or six-day period is "contemporaneous." Other § 20A cases in which defendants obtained dismissal of complaints or summary judgments include In re VeriFone Securities Litigation, 11 F.3d 865 (9th Cir.1993)(plaintiffs traded before any trades by insiders); Fujisawa Pharmaceutical Co., Ltd. v. Kapoor, 932 F.Supp. 208 (N.D.Ill.1996)(§ 20A does not apply to direct face-to-face transactions between insiders); Clay v. Riverwood Int'l Corp., 964 F.Supp. 1559 (N.D.Ga.1997)(exercise

of stock appreciation right cannot be matched with open market purchase of stock). Obviously, the broader the period that is deemed to be "contemporaneous" the greater the exposure of the defendant, though abstractly it is difficult to explain why a person who traded on an impersonal stock exchange four days after the defendant's trade should have a cause of action while one who traded one month later does not. In neither case is the confluence of the two trades based on more than chance. See William K.S. Wang, Trading on Material Nonpublic Information on Impersonal Stock Markets: Who is Harmed, and Who Can Sue Whom Under SEC Rule 10b–5? 1217, 54 S.Cal.L.Rev. 1274–84 (1981).

(3) Should a person receiving a false tip have a claim against his tipper? Of course, if the information had been accurate, the tippee would have himself violated rule 10b–5, and a plausible argument may be made that he has unclean hands and should not be permitted to maintain a suit against his tipper. Several lower courts split on the issue whether the *in pari delicto* defense should be applied in such a case, but the United States Supreme Court firmly resolved the disagreement in Bateman Eichler, Hill Richards, Inc. v. Berner, 472 U.S. 299, 105 S.Ct. 2622, 86 L.Ed.2d 215 (1985). The Court stated that a plaintiff should be barred in these circumstances only where "(1) as a direct result of his own actions, the plaintiff bears at least substantially equal responsibility for the violations he seeks to redress, and (2) preclusion of suit would not significantly interfere with the effective enforcement of the securities laws and protection of the investing public." 472 U.S. at 310–11, 105 S.Ct. at 2629, 86 L.Ed.2d at 224.

SECURITIES EXCHANGE ACT OF 1934
48 Stat. 896 (1934), 15 U.S.C.A. § 78p (1997).

Section 16.   Directors, officers, and principal stockholders

(a) Every person who is directly or indirectly the beneficial owner of more than 10 percent of any class of any equity security (other than an exempted security) which is registered pursuant to section 12 of this title, or who is a director or an officer of the issuer of such security, shall file, at the time of the registration of such security on a national securities exchange or by the effective date of a registration statement filed pursuant to section 12(g) of this title, or within ten days after he becomes such beneficial owner, director, or officer, a statement with the Commission (and, if such security is registered on a national securities exchange, also with the exchange) of the amount of all equity securities of such issuer of which he is the beneficial owner, and within ten days after the close of each calendar month thereafter, if there has been a change in such ownership during such month, shall file with the Commission (and if such security is registered on a national securities exchange, shall also file with the exchange), a statement indicating his ownership at the close of the calendar month and such changes in his ownership as have occurred during such calendar month.

(b) For the purpose of preventing the unfair use of information which may have been obtained by such beneficial owner, director, or officer by reason of his relationship to the issuer, any profit realized by him from any purchase and sale, or any sale and purchase, of any equity security of such issuer (other than an exempted security) within any period of less than six months, unless such security was acquired in good faith in connection with a debt previously contracted, shall inure to and be recoverable by the issuer, irrespective of any intention on the part of such beneficial owner, director, or officer in entering into such transaction of holding the security purchased or of not repurchasing the security sold for a period exceeding six months. Suit to recover such profit may be instituted at law or in equity in any court of competent jurisdiction by the issuer, or by the owner of any security of the issuer in the name and in behalf of the issuer if the issuer shall fail or refuse to bring such suit within sixty days after request or shall fail diligently to prosecute the same thereafter; but no such suit shall be brought more than two years after the date such profit was realized. This subsection shall not be construed to cover any transaction where such beneficial owner was not such both at the time of the purchase and sale, or the sale and purchase, of the security involved, or any transaction or transactions which the Commission by rules and regulations may exempt as not comprehended within the purpose of this subsection.

Notes

(1) Section 16(b), enacted as part of the original 1934 Exchange Act, is probably the most quirky provision of the federal securities law. Read § 16(b) again, carefully. From the first, the courts have held that this section establishes a "crude rule of thumb" and that it is no defense to argue that the offsetting transactions were entered into for innocent reasons unconnected with inside information about the corporation's affairs. If a purchase and sale (or sale and purchase) by an officer, director, or 10% shareholder takes place within a six-month period, the "profit" is automatically recoverable by the corporation. Section 16(b) states that its purpose is to prevent "the unfair use of information which may have been obtained by [the] beneficial owner, director, or officer by reason of his relationship to the issuer." The conventional reading of this statement of purpose is rather literal, that it prevents an insider from trading on nonpublic information and then restoring his or her securities position after that information has become public. However, section 16(b) is almost completely ineffective to achieve this purpose since most persons trading on nonpublic information are willing to hold securities for more than six months in order to capitalize on that information. A more rational explanation of § 16(b) is that its true purpose is to prevent manipulation of market prices by insiders. Dennis W. Carlton & Larry R. Fischel, The Regulation of Insider Trading, 35 Stan. L.Rev. 857, 892 (1983); Frank H. Easterbrook & Larry R. Fischel, The Economic Structure of Corporate Law 273–74 (1991). Based on original research into the background and origins of § 16(b), other alternative explanations have been put forth. Steve Thel, The Genius of Section 16: Regulating the Management of Publicly Held Companies, 42 Hastings L.J. 391 (1991) (purpose was to discourage manipulation of corporate affairs to create opportunities to trade corporate stock profitably since insiders must invest for the long term); Karl Shumpei Okamoto, Rereading Section 16(b) of the Securities Exchange Act, 27 Ga. L.Rev. 183 (1992) (purpose was to deter insiders from sending false signals that artificially affect prices when in fact there was no inside information at all).

(2) How are violations discovered? Nothing could be easier, since the reports required by § 16(a) are promptly made publicly available by the SEC. It is simply a matter of comparing transactions.

(3) Is there any incentive to find violations given the fact that the recovery inures to the corporation? Again from the first, the courts recognized that attorneys for plaintiff shareholders who locate § 16(b) violations, bring them to the attention of the corporation, and if necessary, bring suit on them (as

contemplated by § 16(b)) are entitled to attorneys' fees. Further, "[s]ince in many cases such as this the possibility of recovering attorney's fees will provide the sole stimulus for the enforcement of § 16(b), the allowance must not be too niggardly." Smolowe v. Delendo Corp., 136 F.2d 231, 241 (2d Cir.1943), cert. denied, 320 U.S. 751, 64 S.Ct. 56, 88 L.Ed. 446 (1943). Finally, it is not necessary to actually resort to litigation in order to earn the fee. Gilson v. Chock Full O'Nuts Corp., 326 F.2d 246 (2d Cir.1964). It is enough to find violations and report them to the corporation if they lead to payment to the corporation.

(4) How difficult is it to find a plaintiff in whose name a suit may be brought to recover for a § 16(b) violation? Not difficult at all, since there is no requirement that the plaintiff be a shareholder at the time of either the purchase or sale, and the ownership of a single share purchased specifically for bringing the suit is sufficient. See generally 9 Louis Loss & Joel Seligman, Securities Regulation 4286–89 (3d ed. 1992). In a word, it is legalized champerty. See also Robert W. Hamilton, Convertible Securities and Section 16(b): The End of an Era, 44 Tex.L.Rev. 1447, 1450 n. 18 (1966):

> In Magida v. Continental Can Co., 231 F.2d 843 (2d Cir.), cert. denied, 351 U.S. 972, 76 S.Ct. 1031, 100 L.Ed. 1490 (1956), the court refused to allow the assertion of the defense of champerty even though the plaintiff's pro rata share of recovery could amount to only $1.10 and costs and expenses would reach many times that amount. Plaintiff's original counsel of record testified that plaintiff, "under the terms of an oral retainer, had agreed to pay such costs and expenses," but the court commented that "the true facts of the arrangements between them were * * * heavily obscured by numerous invocations of the attorney-client privilege by the attorney of record." Id. at 847–48. Counsel of record in this case was Morris J. Levy, who has represented a large number of § 16(b) stockholder-plaintiffs.

> The stockholder-plaintiff in a number of the § 16(b) cases is one Isadore Blau. In Blau v. Lamb, 314 F.2d 618 (2d Cir.), cert. denied, 375 U.S. 813, 84 S.Ct. 44, 11 L.Ed.2d 49 (1963), the district court "sought to determine the beneficial ownership" of one hundred shares of stock in Blau's name which formed the basis of his entitlement to act as plaintiff. The district court had "held unbelievable Blau's own testimony that he had cash funds adequate to pay the account, noting the lack of any bank accounts or signs of wealth beyond Blau's own statement" and had concluded that he was holding the stock as nominee for some undisclosed person and was not the real party in interest so that he was not a proper party plaintiff. Id. at 619. The court of appeals reversed on the ground that the corporation was the real party in interest and the stockholder did not have to be a beneficial owner of the stock to be a § 16(b) plaintiff. The court of appeals commented that "Blau obviously had sufficient indicia of ownership to protect his right under the statute * * *." Id. at 620.

(5) How are profits computed if there is a series of transactions? In a word, punitively. "The only rule whereby all possible profits can surely be recovered is that of lowest price in, highest price out within six months." Smolowe v. Delendo Corp., supra note (3), at 239, Gratz v. Claughton, 187 F.2d 46 (2d Cir.1951), cert. denied, 341 U.S. 920, 71 S.Ct. 741, 95 L.Ed. 1353 (1951). To illustrate:

Assume that an insider enters into the following transactions, which are grouped together for simplicity of analysis:

(1)	7/1/75	Buys 100 shares	@	115
(2)	5/15/76	Sells 100 shares	@	93
(3)	5/18/76	Buys 100 shares	@	90
(4)	5/21/76	Buys 100 shares	@	95
(5)	5/23/76	Sells 100 shares	@	97
(6)	5/26/76	Buys 100 shares	@	105
(7)	5/29/76	Sells 100 shares	@	108
(8)	8/10/76	Sells 100 shares	@	115

A businessman examining this sequence of transactions would probably conclude that the insider made a profit of $300 on transactions (2) and (3), $200 on (4) and (5), $300 on (6) and (7), and $0 on (1) and (8), closing the account, for a total trading profit of $800. However, by matching lowest price in with highest price out, the following tabulation is made:

Purchases	Sales	Profit
100 @ 90 (trans. (3))	100 @ 115 (trans. (8))	2500
100 @ 95 (trans. (4))	100 @ 108 (trans. (7))	1300
100 @ 105 (trans. (6))	100 @ 97 (trans. (5))	0

Thus there is a total § 16(b) profit of $3,800. In this computation, all transactions which yield losses are to be ignored. The Supreme Court has not had occasion to consider specifically the propriety of this method of calculating "profits."

(6) An officer, director or ten percent shareholder, subject to § 16(b), must accommodate his or her securities transactions to the requirements of that section, whether or not the transactions are motivated by nonpublic information. In order to avoid application of that section, a covered person who purchases or sells securities of the corporation must avoid entering into an offsetting transaction—a sale if the other transaction was a purchase, or a purchase if the other transaction was a sale—for a period that begins six months before the transaction in question and ends six months after the transaction. In effect, in-and-out trading is proscribed for a one-year period surrounding every transaction. Of course, § 16(b) is not violated if there are either a succession of purchase transactions or a succession of sale transactions without any offsetting transactions, no matter how much nonpublic information is used. Further, there is no "profit" to return to the corporation if the highest sale price during every possible six-month period is below the lowest purchase price during every possible six-month period surrounding the transaction; however, as illustrated in note (5) above, transactions are matched in such a way that a single purchase at a lower price than any sale price will generate § 16(b) profits no matter what the net profit or loss in the account was over the same or a different period.

(7) Section 16(b), in short, is an *in terrorem* provision that appears to combine an effective enforcement system with virtually no loopholes for a violator. Since avoidance of the section is relatively easy—spacing offsetting transaction six months and one day apart provides complete protection—one might assume that violations are rather rare, the product of ignorance, carelessness or inattention. The reality is far different. The federal reports—particularly those before about 1980—fairly bristle with cases in which § 16(b) has been applied. In addition to these reported cases, there are numerous, uncountable instances in which officers and directors voluntarily repaid § 16(b) profits to the issuer because they had no plausible defense; certainly, in many of these transaction nonpublic information was not involved. In a few instances, these voluntary repayments involved very

large sums that must have had devastating consequences for the long-term or retirement planning of the unfortunate officer or director. Why have there been so many inadvertent violations? In a few instances, persons clearly covered by § 16(b) violated the section because they were unaware of the section's existence, careless in calculating the six month period, or because they relied on uninformed or erroneous advice. Much more common are cases involving uncertainty as to the applicability of § 16(b): Should a conversion of convertible preferred into common be viewed as a "sale" of the convertible or a "purchase" of the common, or both? Is a receipt of an option to purchase a "purchase?" Or is the "purchase" the time the option is exercised? Or are there two purchases in an option situation? Is a person who was not an officer or director at the time of the first transaction but was at the time of the second transaction covered by the section? What about a person who was an officer or director at the time of the first transaction but not at the time of the second? What about a person who has the title of "vice president" but has almost no discretionary authority? It is fair to say that in most of the reported cases in which liability for § 16(b) profits was imposed, the transactions did not in fact appear to involve the use of nonpublic information but liability was imposed because § 16(b) is an automatic liability section. Karl Shumpei Okamoto, Oversimplification and the SEC's Treatment of Derivative Securities Trading by Corporate Insiders, 1993 Wisc.L.Rev. 1287, 1289–90* accurately summarized the law of § 16(b) when he wrote:

> It is difficult to accommodate the broad goal of deterring insider trading within this narrow prohibition of short-swing trading. There is no necessary correlation between the simple fact of a purchase and sale or a sale and purchase within six months and the abuse of inside information. Inside information can be abused with but one trade, and matched trades are not ineluctably motivated by inside information. Therefore, courts have been forced to struggle with the innocent insider whose activity fits within the literal prohibition, as well as with the clearly culpable insider whose antics do not. Cohesive rules of application have evaded the courts as they seek to apply the basic statute to a purpose it was not well suited to achieve.

(8) Today, general counsel of issuers of registered securities regularly distribute cautionary memoranda to directors, officers, large shareholders, and employees who may have access to nonpublic material information. Since 1988, these memoranda have been virtually required by ITSFEA, but even before the enactment of that statute, they were widely used. They universally described the possible application of section 16(b), cautioning the reader of the dangers of inadvertent violations from innocent transactions and recommending that officers, directors, and ten percent shareholders obtain legal advice before purchasing or writing puts and calls, exercising employee stock options, making gifts of securities, exercising conversion privileges, or generally acquiring or disposing of interests in equity securities when any possible offsetting transactions exist. Persons subject to § 16(b) are also in effect rewarned periodically of the pitfalls of this section when information relating to possible filings under § 16(a) is solicited. In part as a result of this informational effort, it does appear that the number of inadvertent § 16(b) cases has declined significantly in recent years, though that may be as much a result of the exemptive regulations issued by the SEC in 1991 and 1996 that went a long way toward rationalizing the coverage of § 16(b).

(9) The last sentence of § 16(b) grants the SEC power to exempt transactions from that section if they are "not comprehended within the purpose of this subsection." Prior to 1991, the SEC exercised this power of exemption sparingly and unsystematically. Perhaps the most important exemptions were § 240.16b–3 (relating to employee benefit plans and stock appreciation rights), and § 240.16b–6 (relating to the exercise of long-term options). In 1991, however, the SEC adopted new regulations that significantly reduce areas of uncertainty about the application of § 16(b) and modify to some extent policies previously adopted by the SEC; in 1996 the SEC returned to the task and smoothed out additional "rough edges," particularly in the director and officer compensation area. 17 C.F.R. § 240.16a–1 (1997), et seq.; Rel.No. 34–28869, 56 Fed. Reg. 7241 (Feb. 8, 1991), Rel.No. 34–37260 (June 14, 1996). These regulations constitute more than 15 densely packed pages of the Code of Federal Regulations. They deal with the following significant issues:

(a) The definition of "officers" is narrowed to include only the issuer's president, principal financial officer, principal accounting officer, any vice president in charge of a principal business unit, division, or function, and other persons performing policy-making functions for the issuer. Any executive officer identified as such in an issuer's 10–K Annual Report is presumed to be an "officer" for purposes of § 16.

(b) The definitions of "beneficial owner" and "equity security" are made more objective, defining direct and indirect pecuniary interests, but excluding ownership of derivatives such as options or warrants.

(c) The treatment of derivative securities—warrants, options, puts, and calls—are treated quite differently than before. Previously, acquiring an option or a call to purchase securities was not a § 16(b) purchase; the purchase occurred when the option or call was exercised. Under the new regulations, the acquisition of an option is a § 16(b) purchase and the exercise is not. 16 C.F.R. §§ 240.16a–4, 240.16b–6 (1997). Previously, a covered person might speculate on inside information by matching the acquisition of a derivative with the purchase or sale of the underlying security without incurring § 16(b) liability. This is now prevented, but a covered person may now exercise a stock option and immediately sell the acquired shares without incurring § 16(b) liability. Whether this is a step forward or backward may be debated. See Marc I. Steinberg & Daryl L. Landsdale, The Judicial and Regulatory Constriction of Section 16(b) of the Securities Exchange Act of 1934, 68 Notre Dame L. Rev. 33, 60–69 (1992); Karl Shumpei Okamoto, Oversimplification and the SEC's Treatment of Derivative Securities Trading by Corporate Insiders, 1993 Wisc.L.Rev. 1287.

(d) Purchases or sales made before a person becomes an officer or director need not be reported and therefore may not be matched with sales or purchases after the person becomes an officer or director. 17 C.F.R. § 240.16a–2(a) (1997). Steinberg & Landsdale criticize this change as giving away a "crown jewel" of the prohibitions against insider trading. Steinberg & Landsdale, supra at 69–78.

(e) The rules with respect to employee benefit plans were substantially reorganized and supplemented in 1991 and then completely revised in 1996 to meet criticisms and complaints about the complexity of the 1991 regulations. 17 C.F.R. § 240.16b–3 (1997). Basically, the 1996 regulations work from the premise that transactions between an issuer and its officers and directors who owe state law fiduciary duties to the issuer and its shareholders do not present the possibility of insider trading. The revised regulations completely exempt compensation and stock purchase plans that are qualified for favorable tax treatment.

They also provide guidelines for the application of § 16(b) to "discretionary decisions" by participants in these plans. See Ronald O. Mueller, SEC Adopts Final, Section 16 Rule Revisions, Insights, Vol. 10, No. 8, at 2 (August 1996).

(f) The 1996 regulations also make numerous changes designed to simplify the reporting requirements for specific transactions under § 16(a).

(10) The 10 percent shareholder provision of § 16(b) obviously makes the section potentially applicable in takeover situations wherever an aggressor acquires more than 10 percent of the target's shares but fails to acquire control of the target and thereafter disposes of the purchased shares within six months. That disposition may be to the target by private sale at a premium (greenmail), to a successful competitor for control, or on the open market by a series of sales, usually to risk arbitrageurs or conceivably to a long-term investor who is not seeking control of the target. Since takeover disputes rarely extend for long periods, the probability is relatively high that the sale will occur within six months of some or all of the purchases. The United States Supreme Court addressed this issue in a series of opinions during the 1970s, and like the lower federal courts, became trapped by the irreconcilable tensions between § 16(b) as an objective crude rule of thumb, on the one hand, and the unjust or irrational results often reached when that objective standard is literally applied on the other. The Court reached plausible results through a process of interpretation:

(a) In Reliance Elect. Co. v. Emerson Elect. Co., 404 U.S. 418, 92 S.Ct. 596, 30 L.Ed.2d 575 (1972), an aggressor purchased 13.2 percent of the target's stock in an unsuccessful takeover attempt; when it was clear the battle was lost, the aggressor sold its shares to the successful purchaser in two sales, the first that reduced its holding to 9.6 percent, and the second the balance of its holding. In a 4–3 decision, the Supreme Court held that § 16(b) applied to the first sale but not to the second, since the seller was no longer a 10 percent shareholder.

(b) In Kern County Land Co. v. Occidental Petroleum Corp., 411 U.S. 582, 93 S.Ct. 1736, 36 L.Ed.2d 503 (1973), Occidental purchased more than 10 percent of Kern County shares in a takeover attempt, but was blocked by a defensive merger between Kern County and Tenneco. As a result of the merger Occidental received Tenneco preferred shares. Occidental requested the SEC to exempt the exchange, but the SEC refused. Occidental thereafter granted Tenneco the option to purchase its preference shares exercisable exactly six months and one-day after the the Tenneco tender offer expired. In a 6–3 decision, the Supreme Court held that the exchange transaction and the grant of the option was not within § 16(b) because they did not lend themselves to the evil against which § 16(b) was directed—the utilization of confidential information.

(c) In Foremost–McKesson, Inc. v. Provident Sec. Co., 423 U.S. 232, 96 S.Ct. 508, 46 L.Ed.2d 464 (1976) it finally solved most § 16(b) problems in the takeover context by holding that the transaction by which a person becomes a 10 percent shareholder is not itself a purchase that may be matched with subsequent sales. On the perhaps debatable assumption that the aggressor who accepts cash tenders from tens or hundreds of thousands of shareholders does so in a single transaction, most of the problems of applying § 16(b) to takeover situations disappeared. Of course, all purchases after the one that increases the holding to above ten percent continued to be subject to § 16(b).

(11) Do you think that with the growth of rule 10b–5, and particularly with the enactment by Congress of ITSA and ITSFEA during the 1980s, that § 16(b) is now obsolete and should be repealed? Section 16(b) still prevents in-and-out trading by officers, directors, and large shareholders within a six month period. Is

that a sufficient justification to retain this section, despite the inequities and champertous litigation that it generates from time to time? The SEC has considered proposals to recommend the repeal of this section, but has never actually supported such a proposal.

C. SECURITIES FRAUD

BASIC INC. v. LEVINSON

Supreme Court of the United States, 1988.
485 U.S. 224, 108 S.Ct. 978, 99 L.Ed.2d 194.

JUSTICE BLACKMUN delivered the opinion of the Court.

This case requires us to apply the materiality requirement of § 10(b) of the Securities Exchange Act of 1934, and the Securities and Exchange Commission's Rule 10b–5, in the context of preliminary corporate merger discussions. We must also determine whether a person who traded a corporation's shares on a securities exchange after the issuance of a materially misleading statement by the corporation may invoke a rebuttable presumption that, in trading, he relied on the integrity of the price set by the market.

I

Prior to December 20, 1978, Basic Incorporated was a publicly traded company primarily engaged in the business of manufacturing chemical refractories for the steel industry. As early as 1965 or 1966, Combustion Engineering, Inc., a company producing mostly alumina-based refractories, expressed some interest in acquiring Basic, but was deterred from pursuing this inclination seriously because of antitrust concerns it then entertained. In 1976, however, regulatory action opened the way to a renewal of Combustion's interest. The "Strategic Plan," dated October 25, 1976, for Combustion's Industrial Products Group included the objective: "Acquire Basic Inc. $30 million."

Beginning in September 1976, Combustion representatives had meetings and telephone conversations with Basic officers and directors,[75] * * * concerning the possibility of a merger.[76] During 1977 and 1978, Basic made three public statements denying that it was engaged in merger negotiations.[77] On

---

75. [By the Court] In addition to Basic itself, petitioners are individuals who had been members of its board of directors prior to 1979 * * *

76. [By the Court] In light of our disposition of this case, any further characterization of these discussions must await application, on remand, of the materiality standard adopted today.

77. [By the Court] On October 21, 1977, after heavy trading and a new high in Basic stock, the following news item appeared in the Cleveland Plain Dealer:

[Basic] President Max Muller said the company knew no reason for the stock's activity and that no negotiations were under way with any company for a merger. He said Flintkote recently denied Wall Street rumors that it would make a tender offer of $25 a

share for control of the Cleveland-based maker of refractories for the steel industry.

On September 25, 1978, in reply to an inquiry from the New York Stock Exchange, Basic issued a release concerning increased activity in its stock and stated that

management is unaware of any present or pending company development that would result in the abnormally heavy trading activity and price fluctuation in company shares that have been experienced in the past few days.

On November 6, 1978, Basic issued to its shareholders a "Nine Months Report 1978." This Report stated:

With regard to the stock market activity in the Company's shares we remain unaware of any present or pending developments which

December 18, 1978, Basic asked the New York Stock Exchange to suspend trading in its shares and issued a release stating that it had been "approached" by another company concerning a merger. On December 19, Basic's board endorsed Combustion's offer of $46 per share for its common stock, and on the following day publicly announced its approval of Combustion's tender offer for all outstanding shares.

Respondents are former Basic shareholders who sold their stock after Basic's first public statement of October 21, 1977, and before the suspension of trading in December 1978. Respondents brought a class action against Basic and its directors, asserting that the defendants issued three false or misleading public statements and thereby were in violation of § 10(b) of the 1934 Act and of Rule 10b–5. Respondents alleged that they were injured by selling Basic shares at artificially depressed prices in a market affected by petitioners' misleading statements and in reliance thereon.

The District Court adopted a presumption of reliance by members of the plaintiff class upon petitioners' public statements that enabled the court to conclude that common questions of fact or law predominated over particular questions pertaining to individual plaintiffs. See Fed.Rule Civ.Proc. 23(b)(3). The District Court therefore certified respondents' class. On the merits, however, the District Court granted summary judgment for the defendants. It held that, as a matter of law, any misstatements were immaterial: there were no negotiations ongoing at the time of the first statement, and although negotiations were taking place when the second and third statements were issued, those negotiations were not "destined, with reasonable certainty, to become a merger agreement in principle."

The United States Court of Appeals for the Sixth Circuit affirmed the class certification, but reversed the District Court's summary judgment, and remanded the case. 786 F.2d 741 (1986). The court reasoned that while petitioners were under no general duty to disclose their discussions with Combustion, any statement the company voluntarily released could not be " 'so incomplete as to mislead.' " *Id.*, at 746, quoting *SEC v. Texas Gulf Sulphur Co.*, 401 F.2d 833, 862 (C.A.2 1968) (en banc), cert. denied *sub nom. Coates v. SEC*, 394 U.S. 976, 89 S.Ct. 1454, 22 L.Ed.2d 756 (1969). In the Court of Appeals' view, Basic's statements that no negotiations were taking place, and that it knew of no corporate developments to account for the heavy trading activity, were misleading. With respect to materiality, the court rejected the argument that preliminary merger discussions are immaterial as a matter of law, and held that "once a statement is made denying the existence of any discussions, even discussions that might not have been material in absence of the denial are material because they make the statement made untrue." 786 F.2d, at 749.

The Court of Appeals joined a number of other circuits in accepting the "fraud-on-the-market theory" to create a rebuttable presumption that respondents relied on petitioners' material misrepresentations, noting that without the presumption it would be impractical to certify a class under Fed.Rule Civ.Proc. 23(b)(3).

would account for the high volume of trading
and price fluctuations in recent months.

We granted certiorari, 479 U.S. 1083, 107 S.Ct. 1284, 94 L.Ed.2d 142 (1987), to resolve the split, among the Courts of Appeals as to the standard of materiality applicable to preliminary merger discussions, and to determine whether the courts below properly applied a presumption of reliance in certifying the class, rather than requiring each class member to show direct reliance on Basic's statements.

II

The 1934 Act was designed to protect investors against manipulation of stock prices. Underlying the adoption of extensive disclosure requirements was a legislative philosophy: "There cannot be honest markets without honest publicity. Manipulation and dishonest practices of the market place thrive upon mystery and secrecy." H.R.Rep. No. 1383, 73d Cong., 2d Sess., 11 (1934). This Court "repeatedly has described the 'fundamental purpose' of the Act as implementing a 'philosophy of full disclosure.'" *Santa Fe Industries, Inc. v. Green,* 430 U.S. 462, 477–478, 97 S.Ct. 1292, 1303, 51 L.Ed.2d 480 (1977), quoting *SEC v. Capital Gains Research Bureau, Inc.,* 375 U.S. 180, 186, 84 S.Ct. 275, 280, 11 L.Ed.2d 237 (1963).

Pursuant to its authority under § 10(b) of the 1934 Act, the Securities and Exchange Commission promulgated Rule 10b–5. Judicial interpretation and application, legislative acquiescence, and the passage of time have removed any doubt that a private cause of action exists for a violation of § 10(b) and Rule 10b–5, and constitutes an essential tool for enforcement of the 1934 Act's requirements.

The Court previously has addressed various positive and common-law requirements for a violation of § 10(b) or of Rule 10b–5. The Court also explicitly has defined a standard of materiality under the securities law, see *TSC Industries, Inc. v. Northway, Inc.,* 426 U.S. 438, 96 S.Ct. 2126, 48 L.Ed.2d 757 (1976), concluding in the proxy-solicitation context that "[a]n omitted fact is material if there is a substantial likelihood that a reasonable shareholder would consider it important in deciding how to vote." *Id.,* at 449, 96 S.Ct., at 2132. Acknowledging that certain information concerning corporate developments could well be of "dubious significance," *id.,* at 448, 96 S.Ct., at 2132, the Court was careful not to set too low a standard of materiality; it was concerned that a minimal standard might bring an overabundance of information within its reach, and lead management "simply to bury the shareholders in an avalanche of trivial information—a result that is hardly conducive to informed decisionmaking." *Id.,* at 448–449, 96 S.Ct., at 2132. It further explained that to fulfill the materiality requirement "there must be a substantial likelihood that the disclosure of the omitted fact would have been viewed by the reasonable investor as having significantly altered the 'total mix' of information made available." We now expressly adopt the *TSC Industries* standard of materiality for the § 10(b) and Rule 10b–5 context.

III

The application of this materiality standard to preliminary merger discussions is not self-evident. Where the impact of the corporate development on the target's fortune is certain and clear, the *TSC Industries* materiality definition admits straightforward application. Where, on the other hand, the event is contingent or speculative in nature, it is difficult to ascertain whether the "reasonable investor" would have considered the omitted information significant at the time. Merger negotiations, because of the ever-present possibility that the contemplated transaction will not be effectuated, fall into the latter category.

A

Petitioners urge upon us a Third Circuit test for resolving this difficulty. Under this approach, preliminary merger discussions do not become material until "agreement-in-principle" as to the price and structure of the transaction has been reached between the would-be merger partners. See *Greenfield v. Heublein, Inc.,* 742 F.2d 751, 757 (C.A.3 1984), cert. denied, 469 U.S. 1215 (1985). By definition, then, information concerning any negotiations not yet at the agreement-in-principle stage could be withheld or even misrepresented without a violation of Rule 10b–5.

Three rationales have been offered in support of the "agreement-in-principle" test. The first derives from the concern expressed in *TSC Industries* that an investor not be overwhelmed by excessively detailed and trivial information, and focuses on the substantial risk that preliminary merger discussions may collapse: because such discussions are inherently tentative, disclosure of their existence itself could mislead investors and foster false optimism. The other two justifications for the agreement-in-principle standard are based on management concerns: because the requirement of "agreement-in-principle" limits the scope of disclosure obligations, it helps preserve the confidentiality of merger discussions where earlier disclosure might prejudice the negotiations; and the test also provides a usable, brightline rule for determining when disclosure must be made.

None of these policy-based rationales, however, purports to explain why drawing the line at agreement-in-principle reflects the significance of the information upon the investor's decision. The first rationale, and the only one connected to the concerns expressed in *TSC Industries,* stands soundly rejected, even by a Court of Appeals that otherwise has accepted the wisdom of the agreement-in-principle test. "It assumes that investors are nitwits, unable to appreciate—even when told—that mergers are risky propositions up until the closing." *Flamm v. Eberstadt,* 814 F.2d [1169], at 1175, [(7th Cir.) cert. denied 484 U.S. 853 (1987)]. Disclosure, and not paternalistic withholding of accurate information, is the policy chosen and expressed by Congress. * * *

The second rationale, the importance of secrecy during the early stages of merger discussions, also seems irrelevant to an assessment whether their existence is significant to the trading decision of a reasonable investor. To avoid a "bidding war" over its target, an acquiring firm often will insist that negotiations remain confidential, and at least one Court of Appeals has stated that "silence pending settlement of the price and structure of a deal is beneficial to most investors, most of the time." *Flamm v. Eberstadt,* 814 F.2d, at 1177.[78]

---

78. [By the Court] Reasoning backwards from a goal of economic efficiency, that Court of Appeals stated: "Rule 10b–5 is about *fraud,* after all, and it is not fraudulent to conduct business in a way that makes investors better off...." *Flamm v. Eberstadt,* 814 F.2d, at 1177.

We need not ascertain, however, whether secrecy necessarily maximizes shareholder wealth—although we note that the proposition is at least disputed as a matter of theory and empirical research[79]—for this case does not concern the *timing* of a disclosure; it concerns only its accuracy and completeness. * * *

The final justification offered in support of the agreement-in-principle test seems to be directed solely at the comfort of corporate managers. A bright-line rule indeed is easier to follow than a standard that requires the exercise of judgment in the light of all the circumstances. But ease of application alone is not an excuse for ignoring the purposes of the securities acts and Congress' policy decisions. Any approach that designates a single fact or occurrence as always determinative of an inherently fact-specific finding such as materiality, must necessarily be over-inclusive or underinclusive. In *TSC Industries* this Court explained: "The determination [of materiality] requires delicate assessments of the inferences a 'reasonable shareholder' would draw from a given set of facts and the significance of those inferences to him * * *." 426 U.S., at 450. After much study, the Advisory Committee on Corporate Disclosure cautioned the SEC against administratively confining materiality to a rigid formula.[80] Courts also would do well to heed this advice.

We therefore find no valid justification for artificially excluding from the definition of materiality information concerning merger discussions, which would otherwise be considered significant to the trading decision of a reasonable investor, merely because agreement-in-principle as to price and structure has not yet been reached by the parties or their representatives. * * *

C

Even before this Court's decision in *TSC Industries,* the Second Circuit had explained the role of the materiality requirement of Rule 10b–5, with respect to contingent or speculative information or events, in a manner that gave that term meaning that is independent of the other provisions of the Rule. Under such circumstances, materiality "will depend at any given time upon a balancing of both the indicated probability that the event will occur and the anticipated magnitude of the event in light of the totality of the company activity." *SEC v. Texas Gulf Sulphur Co.,* 401 F.2d [833, 849 (2d Cir.1968)]. Interestingly, neither the Third Circuit decision adopting the agreement-in-principle test nor petitioners here take issue with this general standard. Rather, they suggest that with respect to preliminary merger

---

79. [By the Court] See *Flamm v. Eberstadt,* 814 F.2d, at 1177, n. 2 (citing scholarly debate). See also *In re Carnation Co.,* Exchange Act Release No. 22214, 33 S.E.C. Docket 1025, 1030 (1985) ("The importance of accurate and complete issuer disclosure to the integrity of the securities markets cannot be overemphasized. To the extent that investors cannot rely upon the accuracy and completeness of issuer statements, they will be less likely to invest, thereby reducing the liquidity of the securities markets to the detriment of investors and issuers alike").

80. [By the Court] "Although the Committee believes that ideally it would be desirable to have absolute certainty in the application of the materiality concept, it is its view that such a goal is illusory and unrealistic. The materiality concept is judgmental in nature and it is not possible to translate this into a numerical formula. The Committee's advice to the [SEC] is to avoid this quest for certainty and to continue consideration of materiality on a case-by-case basis as problems are identified." Report of the Advisory Committee on Corporate Disclosure to the Securities and Exchange Commission 327 (House Committee on Interstate and Foreign Commerce, 95th Cong., 1st Sess.) (Comm. Print) (1977).

discussions, there are good reasons to draw a line at agreement on price and structure.

In a subsequent decision, the late Judge Friendly, writing for a Second Circuit panel, applied the *Texas Gulf Sulphur* probability/magnitude approach in the specific context of preliminary merger negotiations. After acknowledging that materiality is something to be determined on the basis of the particular facts of each case, he stated:

> Since a merger in which it is bought out is the most important event that can occur in a small corporation's life, to wit, its death, we think that inside information, as regards a merger of this sort, can become material at an earlier stage than would be the case as regards lesser transactions—and this even though the mortality rate of mergers in such formative stages is doubtless high. *SEC v. Geon Industries, Inc.,* 531 F.2d 39, 47–48 (1976).

We agree with that analysis.[81]

Whether merger discussions in any particular case are material therefore depends on the facts. Generally, in order to assess the probability that the event will occur, a factfinder will need to look to indicia of interest in the transaction at the highest corporate levels. Without attempting to catalog all such possible factors, we note by way of example that board resolutions, instructions to investment bankers, and actual negotiations between principals or their intermediaries may serve as indicia of interest. To assess the magnitude of the transaction to the issuer of the securities allegedly manipulated, a factfinder will need to consider such facts as the size of the two corporate entities and of the potential premiums over market value. No particular event or factor short of closing the transaction need be either necessary or sufficient by itself to render merger discussions material.[82]

As we clarify today, materiality depends on the significance the reasonable investor would place on the withheld or misrepresented information.[83]

---

81. [By the Court] The SEC in the present case endorses the highly fact-dependent probability/magnitude balancing approach of *Texas Gulf Sulphur.* It explains: "The *possibility* of a merger may have an immediate importance to investors in the company's securities even if no merger ultimately takes place." The SEC's insights are helpful, and we accord them due deference.

82. [By the Court] To be actionable, of course, a statement must also be misleading. Silence, absent a duty to disclose, is not misleading under Rule 10b–5. "No comment" statements are generally the functional equivalent of silence. * * * See New York Stock Exchange Listed Company Manual § 202.01 (premature public announcement may properly be delayed for valid business purpose and where adequate security can be maintained). It has been suggested that given current market practices, a "no comment" statement is tantamount to an admission that merger discussions are underway. See *Flamm v. Eberstadt,* 814 F.2d, at 1178. That may well hold true to the extent that issuers adopt a policy of truthfully

denying merger rumors when no discussions are underway, and of issuing "no comment" statements when they are in the midst of negotiations. There are, of course, other statement policies firms could adopt; we need not now advise issuers as to what kind of practice to follow, within the range permitted by law. Perhaps more importantly, we think that creating an exception to a regulatory scheme founded on a prodisclosure legislative philosophy, because complying with the regulation might be "bad for business," is a role for Congress, not this Court.

83. [By the Court] We find no authority in the statute, the legislative history, or our previous decisions for varying the standard of materiality depending on who brings the action or whether insiders are alleged to have profited. See, *e.g., Pavlidis v. New England Patriots Football Club, Inc.,* 737 F.2d 1227, 1231 (C.A.1 1984) ("A fact does not become more material to the shareholder's decision because it is withheld by an insider, or because the insider might profit by withholding it").

The fact-specific inquiry we endorse here is consistent with the approach a number of courts have taken in assessing the materiality of merger negotiations.[84] Because the standard of materiality we have adopted differs from that used by both courts below, we remand the case for reconsideration of the question whether a grant of summary judgment is appropriate on this record.

IV

A

We turn to the question of reliance and the fraud-on-the-market theory. Succinctly put:

> The fraud on the market theory is based on the hypothesis that, in an open and developed securities market, the price of a company's stock is determined by the available material information regarding the company and its business.* * * Misleading statements will therefore defraud purchasers of stock even if the purchasers do not directly rely on the misstatements.* * * The causal connection between the defendants' fraud and the plaintiffs' purchase of stock in such a case is no less significant than in a case of direct reliance on misrepresentations. *Peil v. Speiser,* 806 F.2d 1154, 1160–1161 (C.A.3 1986).

Our task, of course, is not to assess the general validity of the theory, but to consider whether it was proper for the courts below to apply a rebuttable presumption of reliance, supported in part by the fraud-on-the—market theory.

This case required resolution of several common questions of law and fact concerning the falsity or misleading nature of the three public statements made by Basic, the presence or absence of scienter, and the materiality of the misrepresentations, if any. In their amended complaint, the named plaintiffs alleged that in reliance on Basic's statements they sold their shares of Basic stock in the depressed market created by petitioners. Requiring proof of individualized reliance from each member of the proposed plaintiff class effectively would have prevented respondents from proceeding with a class action, since individual issues then would have overwhelmed the common ones. The District Court found that the presumption of reliance created by

---

We recognize that trading (and profit making) by insiders can serve as *an* indication of materiality, see *SEC v. Texas Gulf Sulphur Co.,* 401 F.2d, at 851. We are not prepared to agree, however, that "[i]n cases of the disclosure of inside information to a favored few, determination of materiality has a different aspect than when the issue is, for example, an inaccuracy in a publicly disseminated press release." *SEC v. Geon Industries, Inc.,* 531 F.2d 39, 48 (C.A.2 1976). Devising two different standards of materiality, one for situations where insiders have traded in abrogation of their duty to disclose or abstain (or for that matter when any disclosure duty has been breached), and another covering affirmative misrepresentations by those under no duty to disclose (but under the ever-present duty not to mislead), would effectively collapse the materiality requirement into the analysis of defendant's disclosure duties.

84. [By the Court] See, *e.g., SEC v. Shapiro,* 494 F.2d 1301, 1306–1307 (C.A.2 1974) (in light of projected very substantial increase in earnings per share, negotiations material, although merger still less than probable); *Holmes v. Bateson,* 583 F.2d 542, 558 (C.A.1 1978) (merger negotiations material although they had not yet reached point of discussing terms); *SEC v. Gaspar,* CCH Fed.Sec.L.Rep. (1984–1985 Transfer Binder) ¶ 92,004, pp. 90,-977–90,978 (SDNY 1985) (merger negotiations material although they did not proceed to actual tender offer); *Dungan v. Colt Industries, Inc.,* 532 F.Supp. 832, 837 (N.D.Ill.1982) (fact that defendants were seriously exploring the sale of their company was material); *American General Ins. Co. v. Equitable General Corp.,* 493 F.Supp. 721, 744–745 (E.D.Va.1980) (merger negotiations material four months before agreement-in-principle reached).

the fraud-on-the-market theory provided "a practical resolution to the problem of balancing the substantive requirement of proof of reliance in securities cases against the procedural requisites of [Federal Rule of Civil Procedure] 23." The District Court thus concluded that with reference to each public statement and its impact upon the open market for Basic shares, common questions predominated over individual questions, as required by Federal Rule of Civil Procedure 23(a)(2) and (b)(3).

Petitioners and their *amici* complain that the fraud-on-the-market theory effectively eliminates the requirement that a plaintiff asserting a claim under Rule 10b–5 prove reliance. They note that reliance is and long has been an element of common-law fraud, see *e.g.,* Restatement (Second) of Torts § 525 (1977), and argue that because the analogous express right of action includes a reliance requirement, see, *e.g.,* § 18(a) of the 1934 Act, as amended, so too must an action implied under § 10(b).

We agree that reliance is an element of a Rule 10b–5 cause of action. Reliance provides the requisite causal connection between a defendant's misrepresentation and a plaintiff's injury. There is, however, more than one way to demonstrate the causal connection. Indeed, we previously have dispensed with a requirement of positive proof of reliance, where a duty to disclose material information had been breached, concluding that the necessary nexus between the plaintiffs' injury and the defendant's wrongful conduct had been established. Similarly, we did not require proof that material omissions or misstatements in a proxy statement decisively affected voting, because the proxy solicitation itself, rather than the defect in the solicitation materials, served as an essential link in the transaction. See *Mills v. Electric Auto–Lite Co.,* 396 U.S. 375, 384–385 (1970).

The modern securities markets, literally involving millions of shares changing hands daily, differ from the face-to-face transactions contemplated by early fraud cases, and our understanding of Rule 10b–5's reliance requirement must encompass these differences.

> In face-to-face transactions, the inquiry into an investor's reliance upon information is into the subjective pricing of that information by that investor. With the presence of a market, the market is interposed between seller and buyer and, ideally, transmits information to the investor in the processed form of a market price. Thus the market is performing a substantial part of the valuation process performed by the investor in a face-to-face transaction. The market is acting as the unpaid agent of the investor, informing him that given all the information available to it, the value of the stock is worth the market price. *In re LTV Securities Litigation,* 88 F.R.D. 134, 143 (N.D.Tex.1980).

Accord, *e.g., Peil v. Speiser,* 806 F.2d, at 1161 ("In an open and developed market, the dissemination of material misrepresentations or withholding of material information typically affects the price of the stock, and purchasers generally rely on the price of the stock as a reflection of its value"); *Blackie v. Barrack,* 524 F.2d 891, 908 (C.A.9 1975) ("[T]he same causal nexus can be adequately established indirectly, by proof of materiality coupled with the common sense that a stock purchaser does not ordinarily seek to purchase a loss in the form of artificially inflated stock"), cert. denied, 429 U.S. 816 (1976).

B

Presumptions typically serve to assist courts in managing circumstances in which direct proof, for one reason or another, is rendered difficult. See, *e.g.*, 1 D. Louisell & C. Mueller, Federal Evidence 541–542 (1977). The courts below accepted a presumption, created by the fraud-on-the-market theory and subject to rebuttal by petitioners, that persons who had traded Basic shares had done so in reliance on the integrity of the price set by the market, but because of petitioners' material misrepresentations that price had been fraudulently depressed. Requiring a plaintiff to show a speculative state of facts, *i.e.*, how he would have acted if omitted material information had been disclosed, or if the misrepresentation had not been made, would place an unnecessarily unrealistic evidentiary burden on the Rule 10b–5 plaintiff who has traded on an impersonal market.

Arising out of considerations of fairness, public policy, and probability, as well as judicial economy, presumptions are also useful devices for allocating the burdens of proof between parties. The presumption of reliance employed in this case is consistent with, and, by facilitating Rule 10b–5 litigation, supports, the congressional policy embodied in the 1934 Act. In drafting that Act, Congress expressly relied on the premise that securities markets are affected by information, and enacted legislation to facilitate an investor's reliance on the integrity of those markets:

> No investor, no speculator, can safely buy and sell securities upon the exchanges without having an intelligent basis for forming his judgment as to the value of the securities he buys or sells. The idea of a free and open public market is built upon the theory that competing judgments of buyers and sellers as to the fair price of a security brings *[sic]* about a situation where the market price reflects as nearly as possible a just price. Just as artificial manipulation tends to upset the true function of an open market, so the hiding and secreting of important information obstructs the operation of the markets as indices of real value. H.R.Rep. No. 1383, at 11.[85]

The presumption is also supported by common sense and probability. Recent empirical studies have tended to confirm Congress' premise that the market price of shares traded on well-developed markets reflects all publicly available information, and, hence, any material misrepresentations.[86] It has been noted that "it is hard to imagine that there ever is a buyer or seller who does not rely on market integrity. Who would knowingly roll the dice in a crooked crap game?" *Schlanger v. Four–Phase Systems Inc.*, 555 F.Supp. 535,

---

85. [By the Court] Contrary to the dissent's suggestion, the incentive for investors to "pay attention" to issuers' disclosures comes from their motivation to make a profit, not their attempt to preserve a cause of action under Rule 10b–5. Facilitating an investor's reliance on the market, consistently with Congress' expectations, hardly calls for "dismantling the federal scheme which mandates disclosure."

86. [By the Court] See *In re LTV Securities Litigation*, 88 F.R.D. 134, 144 (N.D.Tex.1980) (citing studies); Fischel, Use of Modern Finance Theory in Securities Fraud Cases Involving Actively Traded Securities, 38 Bus.Law. 1, 4, n. 9 (1982) (citing literature on efficient-capital-market theory). We need not determine by adjudication what economists and social scientists have debated through the use of sophisticated statistical analysis and the application of economic theory. For purposes of accepting the presumption of reliance in this case, we need only believe that market professionals generally consider most publicly announced material statements about companies, thereby affecting stock market prices.

538 (S.D.N.Y.1982). Indeed, nearly every court that has considered the proposition has concluded that where materially misleading statements have been disseminated into an impersonal, well-developed market for securities, the reliance of individual plaintiffs on the integrity of the market price may be presumed.[87] Commentators generally have applauded the adoption of one variation or another of the fraud-on-the-market theory.[88] An investor who buys or sells stock at the price set by the market does so in reliance on the integrity of that price. Because most publicly available information is reflected in market price, an investor's reliance on any public material misrepresentations, therefore, may be presumed for purposes of a Rule 10b–5 action.

C

The Court of Appeals found that petitioners "made public, material misrepresentations and [respondents] sold Basic stock in an impersonal, efficient market. Thus the class, as defined by the district court, has established the threshold facts for proving their loss." 786 F.2d, at 751. The court acknowledged that petitioners may rebut proof of the elements giving rise to the presumption, or show that the misrepresentation in fact did not lead to a distortion of price or that an individual plaintiff traded or would have traded despite his knowing the statement was false.

Any showing that severs the link between the alleged misrepresentation and either the price received (or paid) by the plaintiff, or his decision to trade at a fair market price, will be sufficient to rebut the presumption of reliance. For example, if petitioners could show that the "market makers" were privy to the truth about the merger discussions here with Combustion, and thus that the market price would not have been affected by their misrepresentations, the causal connection could be broken: the basis for finding that the fraud had been transmitted through market price would be gone.[89] Similarly, if, despite petitioners' allegedly fraudulent attempt to manipulate market price, news of the merger discussions credibly entered the market and dissipated the effects of the misstatements, those who traded Basic shares after the corrective statements would have no direct or indirect connection with the fraud.[90] Petitioners also could rebut the presumption of reliance as to plaintiffs who would have divested themselves of their Basic shares without relying on the integrity of the market. For example, a plaintiff who believed that Basic's statements were false and that Basic was indeed engaged in merger discussions, and who consequently believed that Basic stock was artificially underpriced, but sold his shares nevertheless because of other

---

87. [By the Editor] The Court cites seven appellate decisions, all after 1978.

88. [By the Court] See, *e.g.*, Black, Fraud on the Market: A Criticism of Dispensing with Reliance Requirements in Certain Open Market Transactions, 62 N.C.L.Rev. 435 (1984).

89. [By the Court] By accepting this rebuttable presumption, we do not intend conclusively to adopt any particular theory of how quickly and completely publicly available information is reflected in market price. Furthermore, our decision today is not to be interpreted as addressing the proper measure of damages in litigation of this kind.

90. [By the Court] We note there may be a certain incongruity between the assumption

that Basic shares are traded on a well-developed, efficient, and information-hungry market, and the allegation that such a market could remain misinformed, and its valuation of Basic shares depressed, for 14 months, on the basis of the three public statements. Proof of that sort is a matter for trial, throughout which the District Court retains the authority to amend the certification order as may be appropriate. Thus, we see no need to engage in the kind of factual analysis the dissent suggests that manifests the "oddities" of applying a rebuttable presumption of reliance in this case.

unrelated concerns, *e.g.*, potential antitrust problems, or political pressures to divest from shares of certain businesses, could not be said to have relied on the integrity of a price he knew had been manipulated. * * *

The judgment of the Court of Appeals is vacated, and the case is remanded to that court for further proceedings consistent with this opinion.

It is so ordered.

THE CHIEF JUSTICE, JUSTICE SCALIA, and JUSTICE KENNEDY took no part in the consideration or decision of this case.

JUSTICE WHITE, with whom JUSTICE O'CONNOR joins, concurring in part and dissenting in part.

I join Parts I–III of the Court's opinion, as I agree that the standard of materiality we set forth in *TSC Industries, Inc. v. Northway, Inc.*, 426 U.S. 438, 449 (1976), should be applied to actions under § 10(b) and Rule 10b–5. But I dissent from the remainder of the Court's holding because I do not agree that the "fraud-on-the-market" theory should be applied in this case.

I

Even when compared to the relatively youthful private cause-of-action under § 10(b), see *Kardon v. National Gypsum Co.*, 69 F.Supp. 512 (E.D.Pa. 1946), the fraud-on-the-market theory is a mere babe.[91] Yet today, the Court embraces this theory with the sweeping confidence usually reserved for more mature legal doctrines. In so doing, I fear that the Court's decision may have many adverse, unintended effects as it is applied and interpreted in the years to come.

A

At the outset, I note that there are portions of the Court's fraud-on-the-market holding with which I am in agreement. Most importantly, the Court rejects the version of that theory, heretofore adopted by some courts, which equates "causation" with "reliance," and permits recovery by a plaintiff who claims merely to have been *harmed* by a material misrepresentation which altered a market price, notwithstanding proof that the plaintiff did not in any way *rely* on that price. I agree with the Court that if Rule 10b–5's reliance requirement is to be left with any content at all, the fraud-on-the-market presumption must be capable of being rebutted by a showing that a plaintiff did not "rely" on the market price. For example, a plaintiff who decides, months in advance of an alleged misrepresentation, to purchase a stock; one who buys or sells a stock for reasons unrelated to its price; one who actually sells a stock "short" days before the misrepresentation is made—surely none of these people can state a valid claim under Rule 10b–5. Yet, some federal courts have allowed such claims to stand under one variety or another of the fraud-on-the-market theory.[92]

91. [By the Justice] The earliest Court of Appeals case adopting this theory cited by the Court is *Blackie v. Barrack*, 524 F.2d 891 (C.A.9 1975), cert. denied, 429 U.S. 816 (1976). Moreover, widespread acceptance of the fraud-on-the-market theory in the Courts of Appeals cannot be placed any earlier than five or six years ago.

92. [By the Justice] *Abrams v. Johns–Manville Corp.*, [1981–1982] CCH Fed.Sec.L.Rep. ¶ 98,348, p. 92,157 (SDNY 1981) * * *.

The *Abrams* decision illustrates the particular pliability of the fraud-on-the-market presumption. In *Abrams*, the plaintiff represented a class of purchasers of defendant's stock who were allegedly misled by defendant's misrepre-

Happily, the majority puts to rest the prospect of recovery under such circumstances. A nonrebuttable presumption of reliance—or even worse, allowing recovery in the face of "affirmative evidence of nonreliance," *Zweig v. Hearst Corp.,* 594 F.2d 1261, 1272 (C.A.9 1979) (Ely, J., dissenting)—would effectively convert Rule 10b–5 into "a scheme of investor's insurance." *Shores v. Sklar,* 647 F.2d 462, 469, n. 5 (C.A.5 1981) (en banc), cert. denied, 459 U.S. 1102 (1983). There is no support in the Securities [Exchange] Act, the Rule, or our cases for such a result.

B

But even as the Court attempts to limit the fraud-on-the-market theory it endorses today, the pitfalls in its approach are revealed by previous uses by the lower courts of the broader versions of the theory. Confusion and contradiction in court rulings are inevitable when traditional legal analysis is replaced with economic theorization by the federal courts.

In general, the case law developed in this Court with respect to § 10(b) and Rule 10b–5 has been based on doctrines with which we, as judges, are familiar: common-law doctrines of fraud and deceit. Even when we have extended civil liability under Rule 10b–5 to a broader reach than the common law had previously permitted, we have retained familiar legal principles as our guideposts. The federal courts have proved adept at developing an evolving jurisprudence of Rule 10b–5 in such a manner. But with no staff economists, no experts schooled in the "efficient-capital-market hypothesis," no ability to test the validity of empirical market studies, we are not well equipped to embrace novel constructions of a statute based on contemporary microeconomic theory.[93]

* * * [T]he Court today ventures into this area beyond its expertise, beyond—by its own admission—the confines of our previous fraud cases. Even if I agreed with the Court that "modern securities markets * * * involving millions of shares changing hands daily" require that the "understanding of Rule 10b–5's reliance requirement" be changed, I prefer that such changes come from Congress in amending § 10(b). The Congress, with its superior

---

sentations in annual reports. But in a deposition taken shortly after the plaintiff filed suit, she testified that she had bought defendant's stock primarily because she thought that favorable changes in the federal tax code would boost sales of its product (insulation).

Two years later, after the defendant moved for summary judgment based on the plaintiff's failure to prove reliance on the alleged misrepresentations, the plaintiff resuscitated her case by executing an affidavit which stated that she "certainly [had] assumed that the market price of Johns–Manville stock was an accurate reflection of the worth of the company" and would not have paid the then-going price if she had known otherwise. Based on this affidavit, the District Court permitted the plaintiff to proceed on her fraud-on-the-market theory.

Thus, *Abrams* demonstrates how easily a *post hoc* statement will enable a plaintiff to bring a fraud-on-the-market action—even in the rare case where a plaintiff is frank or

foolhardy enough to admit initially that a factor other than price led her to the decision to purchase a particular stock.

93. [By the Justice] This view was put well by two commentators who wrote a few years ago:

> Of all recent developments in financial economics, the efficient capital market hypothesis ('ECMH') has achieved the widest acceptance by the legal culture.* * * Yet the legal culture's remarkably rapid and broad acceptance of an economic concept that did not exist twenty years ago is not matched by an equivalent degree of *understanding.*

Gilson & Kraakman, The Mechanisms of Market Efficiency, 70 Va.L.Rev. 549, 549–550 (1984) (footnotes omitted; emphasis added).

While the fraud-on-the-market theory has gained even broader acceptance since 1984, I doubt that it has achieved any greater understanding.

resources and expertise, is far better equipped than the federal courts for the task of determining how modern economic theory and global financial markets require that established legal notions of fraud be modified. In choosing to make these decisions itself, the Court, I fear, embarks on a course that it does not genuinely understand, giving rise to consequences it cannot foresee.[94]

For while the economists' theories which underpin the fraud-on-the-market presumption may have the appeal of mathematical exactitude and scientific certainty, they are—in the end—nothing more than theories which may or may not prove accurate upon further consideration. Even the most earnest advocates of economic analysis of the law recognize this. Thus, while the majority states that, for purposes of reaching its result it need only make modest assumptions about the way in which "market professionals generally" do their jobs, and how the conduct of market professionals affects stock prices, I doubt that we are in much of a position to assess which theories aptly describe the functioning of the securities industry.

Consequently, I cannot join the Court in its effort to reconfigure the securities laws, based on recent economic theories, to better fit what it perceives to be the new realities of financial markets. I would leave this task to others more equipped for the job than we.

C

At the bottom of the Court's conclusion that the fraud-on-the-market theory sustains a presumption of reliance is the assumption that individuals rely "on the integrity of the market price" when buying or selling stock in "impersonal, well-developed market[s] for securities." Even if I was prepared to accept (as a matter of common sense or general understanding) the assumption that most persons buying or selling stock do so in response to the market price, the fraud-on-the-market theory goes further. For in adopting a "presumption of reliance," the Court *also* assumes that buyers and sellers rely—not just on the market price—but on the *"integrity"* of that price. It is this aspect of the fraud-on-the-market hypothesis which most mystifies me.

To define the term "integrity of the market price," the majority quotes approvingly from cases which suggest that investors are entitled to " 'rely on the price of a stock as a reflection of its value' " (quoting *Peil v. Speiser,* 806 F.2d 1154, 1161 (C.A.3 1986)). But the meaning of this phrase eludes me, for it implicitly suggests that stocks have some "true value" that is measurable by a standard other than their market price. While the Scholastics of Medieval times professed a means to make such a valuation of a commodity's "worth," I doubt that the federal courts of our day are similarly equipped.

Even if securities had some "value"—knowable and distinct from the market price of a stock—investors do not always share the Court's presump-

94. [By the Justice] For example, Judge Posner in his Economic Analysis of Law § 15.8, pp. 423–424 (3d ed. 1986), submits that the fraud-on-the-market theory produces the "economically correct result" in Rule 10b–5 cases but observes that the question of damages under the theory is quite problematic. Notwithstanding the fact that "[a]t first blush it might seem obvious," the proper calculation of damages when the fraud-on-the-market the-ory is applied must rest on several "assumptions" about "social costs" which are "difficult to quantify." *Ibid.* Of course, answers to the question of the proper measure of damages in a fraud-on-the-market case are essential for proper implementation of the fraud-on-the-market presumption. Not surprisingly, the difficult damages question is one the Court expressly declines to address today.

tion that a stock's price is a "reflection of [this] value." Indeed, "many investors purchase or sell stock because they believe the price *inaccurately* reflects the corporation's worth." See Black, Fraud on the Market: A Criticism of Dispensing with Reliance Requirements in Certain Open Market Transactions, 62 N.C.L.Rev. 435, 455 (1984) (emphasis added). If investors really believed that stock prices reflected a stock's "value," many sellers would never sell, and many buyers never buy (given the time and cost associated with executing a stock transaction). As we recognized just a few years ago: "[I]nvestors act on inevitably incomplete or inaccurate information, [consequently] there are always winners and losers; but those who have 'lost' have not necessarily been defrauded." *Dirks v. SEC,* 463 U.S. 646, 667, n. 27 (1983). Yet today, the Court allows investors to recover who can show little more than that they sold stock at a lower price than what might have been.[95]

I do not propose that the law retreat from the many protections that § 10(b) and Rule 10b–5, as interpreted in our prior cases, provide to investors. But any extension of these laws, to approach something closer to an investor insurance scheme, should come from Congress, and not from the courts. * * *

III

Finally, the particular facts of this case make it an exceedingly poor candidate for the Court's fraud-on-the-market theory, and illustrate the illogic achieved by that theory's application in many cases.

Respondents here are a class of sellers who sold Basic stock between October 1977 and December 1978, a 14–month period. At the time the class period began, Basic's stock was trading at $20 a share (at the time, an all-time high); the last members of the class to sell their Basic stock got a price of just over $30 a share. It is indisputable that virtually every member of the class made money from his or her sale of Basic stock.

The oddities of applying the fraud-on-the-market theory in this case are manifest. First, there are the facts that the plaintiffs are sellers and the class period is so lengthy—both are virtually without precedent in prior fraud-on-the-market cases. * * * [T]hese two facts render this case less apt to application of the fraud-on-the-market hypothesis.

Second, there is the fact that in this case, there is no evidence that petitioner's officials made the troublesome misstatements for the purpose of manipulating stock prices, or with any intent to engage in underhanded trading of Basic stock. Indeed, during the class period, petitioners do not appear to have purchased or sold *any* Basic stock whatsoever. I agree with *amicus* who argues that "[i]mposition of damages liability under Rule 10b–5 makes little sense * * * where a defendant is neither a purchaser nor a seller of securities." In fact, in previous cases, we had recognized that Rule 10b–5 is concerned primarily with cases where the fraud is committed by one trading

---

95. [By the Justice] This is what the Court's rule boils down to in practical terms. For while, in theory, the Court allows for rebuttal of its "presumption of reliance"—a proviso with which I agree—in practice the Court must realize, as other courts applying the fraud-on-the-market theory have, that such rebuttal is virtually impossible in all but the most extraordinary case.

Consequently, while the Court considers it significant that the fraud-on-the-market presumption it endorses is a rebuttable one, the majority's implicit rejection of the "pure causation" fraud-on-the-market theory rings hollow. In most cases, the Court's theory will operate just as the causation theory would, creating a nonrebuttable presumption of "reliance" in future Rule 10b–5 actions.

the security at issue. And it is difficult to square liability in this case with § 10(b)'s express provision that it prohibits fraud *"in connection with* the purchase or sale of any security."

Third, there are the peculiarities of what kinds of investors will be able to recover in this case. As I read the District Court's class certification order, there are potentially many persons who did not purchase Basic stock until *after* the first false statement (October 1977), but who nonetheless *will* be able to recover under the Court's fraud-on-the-market theory. Thus, it is possible that a person who heard the first corporate misstatement and *disbelieved* it—*i.e.,* someone who purchased Basic stock thinking that petitioners' statement was false—may still be included in the plaintiff-class on remand. How a person who undertook such a speculative stock-investing strategy—and made $10 a share doing so (if he bought on October 22, 1977, and sold on December 15, 1978)—can say that he was "defrauded" by virtue of his reliance on the "integrity" of the market price is beyond me.[96] And such speculators may not be uncommon, at least in this case.

Indeed, the facts of this case lead a casual observer to the almost inescapable conclusion that many of those who bought or sold Basic stock during the period in question flatly disbelieved the statements which are alleged to have been "materially misleading." Despite three statements denying that merger negotiations were underway, Basic stock hit record-high after record-high during the 14–month class period. It seems quite possible that, like Casca's knowing disbelief of Caesar's "thrice refusal" of the Crown,[97] clever investors were skeptical of petitioners' three denials that merger talks were going on. Yet such investors, the savviest of the savvy, will be able to recover under the Court's opinion, as long as they now claim that they believed in the "integrity of the market price" when they sold their stock (between September and December 1978). Thus, persons who bought after hearing and relying on the *falsity* of petitioners' statements may be able to prevail and recover money damages on remand.

And who will pay the judgments won in such actions? I suspect that all too often the majority's rule will "lead to large judgments, payable in the last analysis by innocent investors, for the benefit of speculators and their lawyers." Cf. *SEC v. Texas Gulf Sulphur Co.,* 401 F.2d 833, 867 (C.A.2 1968) (en banc) (Friendly, J., concurring), cert. denied, 394 U.S. 976 (1969). This Court and others have previously recognized that "inexorably broadening * * * the class of plaintiff[s] who may sue in this area of the law will ultimately result in more harm than good." *Blue Chip Stamps v. Manor Drug Stores, supra,* at 747–748. See also *Ultramares Corp. v. Touche,* 255 N.Y. 170, 179–180, 174 N.E. 441, 444–445 (1931) (Cardozo, C.J.). Yet such a bitter harvest is likely to be reaped from the seeds sewn by the Court's decision today. * * *

Notes

(1) Two preliminary aspects of this case should be noted. First, Justice Blackmun's opinion is a plurality opinion. Five of the nine sitting Justices did not

---

96. [By the Justice] The Court recognizes that a person who *sold* his Basic shares believing petitioners' statements to be false may not be entitled to recovery. Yet it seems just as clear to me that one who *bought* Basic stock under this same belief—hoping to profit from the uncertainty over Basic's merger plans—should not be permitted to recover either.

97. [By the Justice] See W. Shakespeare, Julius Caesar, Act I, Scene II.

sign this opinion, either by disqualification or dissent. Second, assuming that the various issues remanded by Justice Blackmun are resolved in favor of the plaintiffs, the defendants may be held liable for damages to all members of a class of plaintiffs who traded in Basic stock over a relatively long period. Depending on the number of members of the class and how damages are computed, the monetary liability of the defendants may be very substantial even though none of them apparently traded in Basic stock or benefited from the violations. May the defendants who are directors take advantage of Del.Gen.Corp.Law § 102(a)(7), discussed at p. 703 supra?

(2) A controversial aspect of *Basic* is the stinging dissent by Justice White. William J. Carney, The Limits of the Fraud on the Market Doctrine, 44 Bus.Law. 1259, 1265–66, 1272–73, 1277 (1989)[98] attempts to respond to Justice White:

> The dissent in *Basic Inc. v. Levinson* expressed concerns over the pitfalls into which some lower courts have fallen "when traditional legal analysis is replaced with economic theorization by the federal courts" which, "with no staff economists, no experts schooled in the 'efficient-capital-market hypothesis,' no ability to test the validity of empirical market studies, * * * are not well equipped to embrace novel constructions of a statute based on contemporary microeconomic theory." The dissent expressed concern that while these theories had the appearance of mathematical exactitude, "they are—in the end—nothing more than theories which may or may not prove accurate upon further consideration."
>
> These remarks evidence an unwarranted suspicion of the knowledge on which the fraud on the market doctrine is based and of the use of this knowledge, which is only for the purpose of establishing a rebuttable presumption. All of our understanding of cause and effect is built upon observations of events and construction of theories, or hypotheses, to explain relationships between them. The "laws" of physics were not always laws. At one time the relationships now explained by these laws were mysteries to mankind. It took scientists such as Newton to hypothesize that a force called gravity explained certain phenomena in the physical world. Since we cannot observe the forces themselves, but only the effects of these forces, our explanations, theories, and hypotheses can only be established by determining whether they have explanatory power. The power of the gravity hypothesis has been demonstrated by untold millions of observations that are consistent with the hypothesis. Yet these observations do not "prove" the truth of the gravity hypothesis, in a strict sense; they only corroborate it further. In non-scientific terms, such a thoroughly corroborated explanation of physical forces becomes a law of gravity. But a careful philosopher of science would avoid such usage. In any event, the presumptions about such well established relationships are generally conclusive, in the interest of judicial economy. Disputes about such hypotheses should first be raised in the laboratories and academic journals before the courts need concern themselves with the question of whether the presumption should only be rebuttable.
>
> The Efficient Capital Markets Hypothesis ("ECMH") is a much younger hypothesis than Newton's. Questions remain about the extent to which markets operate efficiently.[99] Nevertheless, ECMH has been described as one

98. Copyright 1989 by the American Bar Association. All rights reserved. Reprinted with the permission of the American Bar Associa-tion and its Section of Corporation, Banking and Business Law.

99. [By the Author] The market crash of October 1987 raised questions about how

of the best established hypotheses in all the social sciences.[100] * * * There is powerful evidence that "open and developed" capital markets operate quickly to reflect new information in security prices. It is also obvious that those prices influence prices paid and received by all traders. If all trading activity blindly relied on the fairness of market prices and nothing more, then an irrebuttable presumption of causation might be appropriate. But because human motives are complex and because traders operate on different information sets, the presumption established in *Basic* is only rebuttable. * * *

There are misunderstandings about what ECMH teaches about prices. The plurality opinion in *Basic* referred to legislative history suggesting that market processes lead to some kind of "fair" or "just" price. Justice White's dissent expressed doubts about expressions of reasonable reliance on the "integrity" of a market price and about statements that investors are entitled to "rely on the price of a stock as a reflection of its value." Justice White also expressed concern that questions of "true value" raise issues more suited to theologians than judges, noting that there are always individuals who decline to sell at the market price because they believe market prices are "inaccurate" reflections of value. The fact that sales occur at all in actively traded securities raises questions about the meaning of market prices. An understanding of what "value" means in this context is critical to understanding why it is reasonable for traders to rely on such prices. In this setting, it is fair to agree with the cynic who described an economist as one who knows the price of everything and the value of nothing, if by value something more than an individual's revealed reservation price is meant.

To say that prices reflect a security's "value" in the context of modern financial economics only means that the price is set in an unbiased manner and reflects a consensus view of its value. If a stock is perceived to be a bargain by a sufficient number of traders, they will proceed to buy it and sell others, until its price is driven up to the point where it is no longer a bargain, relative to other stocks.

Once this equilibrium is reached, a buyer ought to be able to sell any stock for exactly the price paid for it, if no changes take place. The number of traders who believe it is a bargain will be offset by those who think it is overpriced, so that for every willing buyer at that price there will always be a willing seller. Relative prices will change only upon the revelation of new information, which flows constantly and keeps stock prices in a state of flux. Thus a statement that price is "fair" is true at the moment of purchase but is no guarantee that a security will hold its value relative to the market as news about the issuer develops. * * *

stocks could be fairly priced before and after October 19, 1987. One response is that virtually all stocks fell in proportion to their beta factors, thus retaining relative relationships to each other, but that response only avoids the larger issue of whether stocks were fairly priced with respect to other available investments. This is the fundamental criticism of Gordon & Kornhauser, Efficient Markets, Costly Information, and Securities Research, 60 N.Y.U.L.Rev. 761 (1985). * * * The difficulty in responding to arguments that stock prices do not fairly reflect value with respect to all other possible substitutes is that the hypothesis can be neither proved nor disproved, since the only reliable way of measuring value ex ante is through prices, rather than ex post, through results. The absence of trading rules that allow investors systematically to earn above normal returns from "bargains" suggests the global efficiency of stock prices, even though there may be moments when, in hindsight, it appears that prices did not fairly reflect relative values.

100. [By the Author] Jensen, The Takeover Controversy: Analysis and Evidence, 4 Midland Corp.Fin.J., No. 2, at 6, 11 (1986). See also Gilson & Kraakman, The Mechanisms of Market Efficiency, 70 Va.L.Rev. 549, 549–50 (1984) (ECMH has wide acceptance).

The *Basic* plurality opinion not only quoted congressional language concerning market prices as "just" prices but also stated, "An investor who buys or sells stock at the price set by the market does so in reliance on the integrity of that price." Justice White expressed mystification at that remark. The mystification is probably a product of the confusion of the fairness of average stock prices with the fairness of particular stock prices.

Some lower courts have noted the distinction between reliance on the integrity of the market in a stock and reliance on the integrity of the market price of that stock. Relying on prices of particular stocks set by trading on publicly available information by itself provides no assurance that particular prices are honest with respect to real values. Market processes only assure that these prices are honest with respect to the news in the market. If all of the news is fraudulent, so are all of the prices based upon it. The problem of the emperor's new clothes could be universal if fraud were widespread. * * *

For a strong defense of the "fraud on the market" thesis, see Daniel R. Fischel, Use of Modern Finance Theory in Securities Fraud Cases Involving Actively Traded Securities, 38 Bus.Law. 1 (1982). Professors Carney and Fischel are both strongly identified with the "Chicago school" of law and economics. On the other hand, some post-*Basic* legal literature expresses serious reservations about the broad validity of the efficient capital market hypothesis and the desirability of the fraud on the market doctrine. See Donald C. Langevoort, Theories, Assumptions, and Securities Regulation: Market Efficiency Revisited, 140 U. Pa. L.Rev. 851, 853–54 (1992) ("In the 1980s, using more sophisticated data sets and computer technology, a number of economists began to question the accuracy of the tests that were thought to validate the efficiency model. * * * [T]he idea of strong capital market efficiency [is now] a legitimately debatable issue"); Carol Goforth, The Efficient Capital Market Hypothesis—An Inadequate Justification for the Fraud–on–the–Market Presumption, 27 Wake Forest L.Rev. 895, 897 (1992) ("While substantial empirical data supports certain aspects of the ECMH, much of the data is anomalous, and numerous aspects of the theory have not been researched adequately").

(3) Liability may be avoided, of course, if the defendants can establish that the misrepresented or undisclosed information was not material. The information in *Basic* dealt with merger negotiations; is there any chance at all of the defendants establishing lack of materiality of such an important development? Consider the comments of Judge Easterbrook in Flamm v. Eberstadt, 814 F.2d 1169, 1174 (7th Cir.1987):

> From one perspective this conclusion [that merger negotiations were not material] is simply another cause for wonderment at the legal mind. Investors were looking at potential prices from $11.75 (if Microdot had defeated all bids) to $17 (if General Cable's bid had succeeded) to $21 (under Northwest's bid), and maybe more if a better bid were available. This is almost a 100% range. Only an addlepated investor would consider a 100% difference in price unimportant in deciding what to do.

Does this reasoning make all preliminary merger inquiries at attractive prices material? What about extremely preliminary or tentative inquiries? Might premature disclosure "chill" other possible bidders? Or might it attract competing offers? If negotiations are disclosed before an agreement in principle is reached, might there be liability to a different class of plaintiffs—those who purchased on the basis of the announcement—if no agreement is ultimately reached? To handle these types of problems, Justice Blackmun substitutes a "fact-specific" inquiry into the significance the reasonable investor would place on the withheld or misrepresented information for the more mechanical "agreement in principle" test adopted by the lower court. Can you see any practical problems with the test applied by Justice Blackmun? Assume you are the general counsel of a corporation that receives a "feeler" from a third party; what do you have the corporation say and when should it say it? See Dennis J. Karjala, A Coherent Approach to Misleading Corporate Announcements, Fraud, and Rule 10b–5, 52 Alb. L.Rev. 957, 977 (1988):

> A related potential problem with the materiality approach, especially likely to occur if an affirmative disclosure scheme is adopted, is determining the extent of disclosure necessary for completeness and the frequency of updates required to maintain it. Assuming, under the *Levinson* analysis, that someone inside the company has made a mistake by saying something more than "no comment" to an inquiry, the problem is not solved simply by saying that the company must now make "full disclosure." Even if the company announces, truthfully, that it is negotiating with corporation X concerning a possible merger and that X has been talking in terms of $50 per share while the company is seeking $70, what are the company's obligations when X raises its still tentative offer to $52, or $55 coupled with a more severe condition on closing or some other new term? When an investment banker calls to say that he or she has a client who is considering offering $60? When a key high-tech engineer informs management that he or she does not want to work for X? There is virtually no end to the number of subsidiary events that can occur during this period that are arguably material. Do we really want to force litigation of these kinds of issues under a fact-specific test that, if properly applied, should almost invariably require a trial?

Given these problems, is not the only sensible approach to say "no comment" in response to all inquiries? And, thus, is not the practical consequence of Justice Blackmun's opinion to choke off rather than improve the flow of information into the market?

(4) Rule 10b–5 is described in the leading Supreme Court decisions of the 1970s is that it is an "antifraud" provision. See, for example, Ernst & Ernst v. Hochfelder, p. 823 supra. A rereading of Justice Blackmun's opinion in *Basic* from the beginning of Part II onward, however, reveals that he has a somewhat different perception of the function of rule 10b–5. Justice Blackmun emphasizes the "fundamental purpose" of the securities acts as "full disclosure" of material facts. "Antifraud" and "full disclosure" are related but distinguishable concepts. See, for example, Roeder v. Alpha Indus., Inc., 814 F.2d 22 (1st Cir.1987) (fact that corporation and its managers would probably be indicted for paying a bribe was "material" information for investors but failure to disclose that information was not actionable under rule 10b–5 since that rule is an antifraud provision and there is no duty to disclose material information in absence of inaccurate, incomplete, or misleading prior disclosures). See also In re Time Warner Inc. Securities Litigation, 9 F.3d 259, 267 (2d Cir.1993) ("But a corporation is not required to disclose a fact merely because a reasonable investor would very much like to know that fact. Rather, an omission is actionable under the securities laws only when the corporation is subject to a duty to disclose the omitted facts.") The language of Rule 10b–5(b) that refers to an omission "to state a material fact necessary in order to make the statements made, in the light of the circumstances under which they were made, not misleading" has been construed to require affirmative disclosure in only limited situations:

(a) Disclosure is required if undisclosed information renders previous public statements by the corporation misleading.

(b) Disclosure is required if the corporation has reason to believe that individuals are engaged in trading in the securities markets on the basis of the information that has not been disclosed.

(c) Disclosure is required if there are rumors swirling through the brokerage community that are generally (though incorrectly) being attributed to the issuer.

On the other hand, one should not make too much of the distinction between "antifraud" and "full disclosure." Registration under § 12 of the 1934 Act carries with it substantial affirmative disclosure obligations. A failure to disclose merger negotiations or other major developments may render statements in these disclosure documents misleading or, equally likely, the affirmative disclosure requirements will themselves require prompt disclosure. For example, in the Roeder case, it is likely that the impending indictments would have to be disclosed in the next public filing in response to Item 103 of Regulation S–K requiring disclosure of material legal proceedings "known to be contemplated by government authorities" with respect to corporate officials. For discussion of the limited obligation to make affirmative disclosures under rule 10b–5 see Symposium, Affirmative Disclosure Obligations under the Securities Laws, 46 Md.L.Rev. 907 (1987).

(3) Except to the extent required by the MD&A, disclosure of projections remains voluntary rather than mandatory,[101] and many issuers routinely do not make public their projections of future earnings or cash flow, though such information may be disclosed to securities analysts and others. In In re Lyondell Petrochemical Co. Sec. Litig., 984 F.2d 1050, 1052–53 (9th Cir.1993), the Court held that forward-looking statements that had been made to a lender did not have to be disclosed to the general public: "A corporation may be called upon to make confidential projections for a variety of sound purposes where public disclosure would be harmful. For example, a bank concerned about the security of its loan might require the corporation to provide a worst-case prediction which may or may not happen. A far-reaching disclosure requirement might not be in the best interests of the market, the corporation's legitimate business plans and, ultimately, investors such as Plaintiffs." See generally Harvey L. Pitt & Matt T. Morley, Through a Glass Starkly: A Practical Guide for Management's Forward–Looking Disclosures, Insights, Vol. 7, No. 6, at 3 (June 1993).

(4) Many companies, particularly in the "high tech" area, as a matter of company policy, do regularly publish projections and estimates of future earnings. These companies adopt this policy in an effort to maintain a market price for its securities for purposes of acquisition or merger; these companies are particularly likely to find themselves as defendants in securities class action suits if the projections turn out to have been overly-optimistic.

(5) New York Stock Exchange Listed Company Manual, §§ 202.03–202.06 has well-established disclosure policies for NYSE-listed companies:

---

101. [By the Editor] The question whether a failure to disclose projections constitutes a violation of SEC regulations has arisen in a significant number of cases and various courts of appeals have adopted quite different approaches. Before the SEC changed its policy to encourage projections, courts faced with this question uniformly answered this question in the negative; since then, however, several courts of appeals have found an obligation to disclose projections in specific circumstances. See, e.g., Flynn v. Bass Bros. Enter., Inc., 744 F.2d 978 (3d Cir.1984). Other courts have disagreed, though under different circumstances.

202.03   Dealing With Rumors or Unusual Market Activity

The market activity of a company's securities should be closely watched at a time when consideration is being given to significant corporate matters. If rumors or unusual market activity indicate that information on impending developments has leaked out, a frank and explicit announcement is clearly required. If rumors are in fact false or inaccurate, they should be promptly denied or clarified. A statement to the effect that the company knows of no corporate developments to account for the unusual market activity can have a salutary effect. It is obvious that if such a public statement is contemplated, management should be checked prior to any public comment so as to avoid any embarrassment or potential criticism. If rumors are correct or there are developments, an immediate candid statement to the public as to the state of negotiations or of development of corporate plans in the rumored area must be made directly and openly. Such statements are essential despite the business inconvenience which may be caused and even though the matter may not as yet have been presented to the company's Board of Directors for consideration. * * *

202.04   Exchange Market Surveillance

The Exchange maintains a continuous market surveillance program through its Market Surveillance and Evaluation Division. An "on-line" computer system has been developed which monitors the price movement of every listed stock—on a trade-to-trade basis—throughout the trading session. * * * If the price movement of a stock exceeds a predetermined guideline, it is immediately "flagged" and review of the situation is immediately undertaken to seek the causes of the exceptional activity. Under these circumstances, the company may be called by its Exchange representative to inquire about any company developments which have not been publicly announced but which could be responsible for unusual market activity. Where the market appears to reflect undisclosed information, the company will normally be requested to make the information public immediately. Occasionally it may be necessary to carry out a review of the trading after the fact, and the Exchange may request such information from the company as may be necessary to complete the inquiry.

The Listing Agreement provides that a company must furnish the Exchange with such information concerning the company as the Exchange may reasonably require. * * *

202.05   Timely Disclosure of Material News Developments

A listed company is expected to release quickly to the public any news or information which might reasonably be expected to materially affect the market for its securities. This is one of the most important and fundamental purposes of the listing agreement which the company enters into with the Exchange.

A listed company should also act promptly to dispel unfounded rumors which result in unusual market activity or price variations.

202.06   Procedure for Public Release of Information

(A) Immediate Release Policy

The normal method of publication of important corporate data is by means of a press release. This may be either by telephone or in written form. Any release of information that could reasonably be expected to have an impact on the market for a company's securities should be given to the wire services and the press *"For Immediate Release."* * * *

(B) Telephone Alert to the Exchange

When the announcement of news of a material event or a statement dealing with a rumor which calls for immediate release is made shortly before the opening or during market hours (presently 9:30 A.M. to 5:00 P.M., New York time), it is recommended that the company's Exchange representative be notified by telephone at least ten minutes prior to release of the announcement to the news media. If the Exchange receives such notification in time, it will be in a position to consider whether, in the opinion of the Exchange, trading in the security should be temporarily halted. A delay in trading after the appearance of the news on the Dow Jones or Reuters news wires provides a period of calm for public evaluation of the announcement. * * * A longer delay in trading may be necessary if there is an unusual influx of orders. The Exchange attempts to keep such interruptions in the continuous auction market to a minimum. However, where events transpire during market hours, the overall importance of fairness to all those participating in the market demands that these procedures be followed.

(C) Release to Newspapers and News Wire Services

News which ought to be the subject of immediate publicity must be released by the fastest available means. The fastest available means may vary in individual cases and according to the time of day. Ordinarily, this requires a release to the public press by telephone, telegraph, or hand delivery, or some combination of such methods. Transmittal of such a release to the press solely by mail is not considered satisfactory. Similarly, release of such news exclusively to the local press outside of New York City would not be sufficient for adequate and prompt disclosure to the investing public.

To insure adequate coverage, releases requiring immediate publicity should be given to Dow Jones & Company, Inc., and to Reuters Economic Services.

Companies are also encouraged to promptly distribute their releases to Associated Press and United Press International as well as to newspapers in New York City and in cities where the company is headquartered or has plants or other major facilities. * * *

In 1970, the SEC issued a general release entitled "Timely Disclosure of Material Corporate Developments," SEC Rel. No. 8995, 35 Fed.Reg. 16733 (Oct. 15, 1970), to much the same effect.

In the 1980s and early 1990s the number of class action lawsuits of the *Basic* type alleging securities fraud increased dramatically in the federal courts. Most of the cases were brought against the issuer and its officers and directors alleging fraud or misrepresentation in corporate disclosures, particularly in connection with projections or estimates of future events. The class consisted of all persons who bought (or sold, depending on the nature of the claimed misrepresentation) shares of the issuer during the period between the alleged false statements and the release of corrective information. The triggering event was typically an unexpected or unpredicted decline in the market price of the company's stock; plaintiffs' lawyers would then seek to find positive public statements or predictions by corporate officials on which a claim of fraud could be made. There was sometimes an unseemly "race to the courthouse" by lawyers, since courts usually gave control over class action litigation to the first to file.

Motions to dismiss were regularly filed in these cases on the bases that the claimed misrepresentations were not material, that projections were made in good faith and were protected by SEC Rule 3b–6, and that, in any event, scienter was lacking. The plaintiffs' response was to make detailed discovery requests, which in turn were met by the defendants' motion for a protective order pending resolution of the motion to dismiss. In some instances, companies may have decided to settle simply because of the cost to respond to discovery requests. Commenting on this type of litigation, the Court in In re Time Warner Inc. Sec. Litig., 9 F.3d 259 (2d Cir.1993), observed:

> Cases of this sort present an inevitable tension between two powerful interests. On the one hand, there is the interest in deterring fraud in the securities markets and remedying it when it occurs. That interest is served by recognizing that the victims of fraud often are unable to detail their allegations until they have had some opportunity to conduct discovery of those reasonably suspected of having perpetrated a fraud. Consistent with that interest, modern pleading rules usually permit a complaint to survive dismissal unless, in the familiar phrase, "it appears beyond doubt that the plaintiff can prove no set of facts in support of his claim which would entitle him to relief." See Conley v. Gibson, 355 U.S. 41, 45–46, 78 S.Ct. 99, 101–02, 2 L.Ed.2d 80 (1957).

> On the other hand, there is the interest in deterring the use of the litigation process as a device for extracting undeserved settlements as the price of avoiding the extensive discovery costs that frequently ensue once a complaint survives dismissal, even though no recovery would occur if the suit were litigated to completion. It has never been clear how these competing interests are to be accommodated, and the adjudication process is not well suited to the formulation of a universal resolution of the tensions between them. In the absence of a more refined statutory standard than the vague contours of section 10(b) or a more detailed attempt at rule-making than the SEC has managed in Rule 10b–5, despite 50 years of unavailed opportunity, courts must adjudicate the precise cases before them, striking the balance as best they can.

> In doing so, we do well to recognize several consequences of this common law approach to what is supposed to be a statutory standard. First, our outcomes will not necessarily evolve a discernible pattern. Second, the absence of a clear pattern will inevitably create uncertainty in the fields of both securities and litigation. Third, however sensitively we strike the balance in a particular case, we will not avoid the risks of adverse consequences: in the aftermath of any ruling that upholds the dismissal of a 10b–5 suit, there will be some opportunity for unremedied fraud; in the aftermath of any ruling that permits a 10b–5 suit to progress beyond a motion to dismiss, there will be some opportunity to

extract an undeserved settlement. Unattractive as those prospects are, they neither indicate a sound basis for decision nor permit avoidance of decision.

If the motion to dismiss was denied, the case almost invariably is settled at some time thereafter, arguably not based on the merits. Janet Cooper Alexander, Do The Merits Matter? A Study of Settlements in Securities Class Actions, 43 Stan. L.Rev. 497 (1991), concluded that cases generally settled at about 25 percent of the damage exposure without regard to the merits. While the validity of this study has been questioned, Leonard Simon and William Dato, Legislating on a False Foundation: The Erroneous Academic Underpinnings of the Private Securities Litigation Reform Act of 1995, 33 San Diego L.Rev. 959 (1996), companies used this study to complain bitterly that class action securities litigation had in effect become a species of legalized extortion.

Faced with an overcrowded docket, lower federal courts understandably were inclined to dismiss complex class actions that appear to be long on rumor or allegation but short on actual evidence of misrepresentation or scienter. For example, cases alleging that projections were misleading were quite regularly dismissed on the ground that there is no evidence that the projections were made otherwise than in good faith or that sufficient cautionary statements were included to make reliance unreasonable. See Chapter 9, Section D, page 605 supra. Cases that alleged fraud through citation of anonymous and unattributed statements in press reports were dismissed on the ground that there is no indication that the statements originated with the defendants. See In re Time Warner Inc. Securities Litigation, 9 F.3d 259, (2d Cir.1993). Various courts of appeal adopted different standards for pleading fraud and scienter, with the Second Circuit having the most stringent test and the Ninth Circuit, among the most lenient.

Is the real problem with litigation of this type the imposition of personal liability on defendants who neither traded nor profited in the securities during the period of the misrepresentation or failure to disclose? Or was it the uncritical acceptance of the fraud-on-the-market theory? Jennifer Arlen & William J. Carney, Vicarious Liability for Fraud on Securities Markets: Theory and Evidence, 1992 U. Ill. L.Rev. 691, 694–95 (fraud on the market cases usually involve attempts by officers and directors to present an artificially favorable financial picture in order to "conceal from the market, and from the firm's shareholders, that the firm is ailing in an attempt to save their jobs and their investments in the firm;" on the average, "the magnitude of potential claims in Fraud on the Market class actions is so great that, in many cases, the use of enterprise liability could wipe out nearly all shareholder equity").

Concern over the claimed abuses of securities class actions led to enactment by Congress of the Private Securities Litigation Reform Act of 1995, Pub.Law 104–67, 109 Stat. 737)(PSLRA),[102] probably the most significant securities-related legislation since the original enactment of the securities acts

---

102. [By the Editor] Legislation dealing with securities fraud cases was part of the Republican "Contract with America." President Clinton vetoed this legislation but his veto was promptly overridden by Congress.

in the early 1930s. The changes made by this legislation are so sweeping that their full impact can only be assessed after several years of experience.

EDWARD A. FALLONE, SECTION 10(B) AND THE VAGARIES OF FEDERAL COMMON LAW: THE MERITS OF CODIFYING THE PRIVATE CAUSE OF ACTION UNDER A STRUCTURALIST APPROACH

1997 U.Ill.L.Rev.71, 81–88 (1997).*

The [Private Securities Litigation Reform] Act, as originally drafted, was intended to revolutionize the manner in which private actions are brought under Rule 10b–5. Early drafts of the legislation contained many procedural reforms, some of them novel in character, intended to discourage the filing of meritless claims. For example, the original draft of the House bill contained a "loser pays" system that would have required unsuccessful parties to reimburse the attorneys' fees of prevailing parties.[103] Other provisions were intended to redefine the scope of conduct that could give rise to liability under Rule 10b–5. The original House bill would have eliminated liability for reckless conduct, thereby codifying a more restrictive scienter requirement than is currently applied. The same draft also would have required the plaintiff in a private cause of action to demonstrate actual knowledge of and reliance upon a misstatement, thereby eliminating the "fraud on the market" theory as a basis for liability under Section 10(b).

However, the final legislation, as it developed in congressional subcommittees and eventually in conference committee, largely confines itself to procedural reforms and avoids questions relating to the definition of fraudulent conduct. As it relates to the Securities Exchange Act, the law contains eight general reforms to private litigation.[104] Few of the reforms relate in any meaningful way to the actual scope of liability to be imposed under Rule 10b–5.

1. CLASS ACTION PROCEDURES

The Act contains procedural provisions designed to reduce the ability of the plaintiffs' bar to serve as the instigator of class action filings and to diminish the likelihood that owners of a small economic stake in the defendant corporation will become the class representative in a suit brought under Rule 10b–5. In furtherance of this goal, the Act requires all plaintiffs seeking to serve as representatives in class actions under the Securities Exchange Act to file sworn certifications stating, among other things, that they have reviewed the complaints, that they did not purchase stock at the direction of counsel in order to qualify as class representatives, and that they will not

103. [By the Author] See John W. Avery, Securities Litigation Reform: The Long and Winding Road to the Private Securities Litigation Reform Act of 1995, 51 Bus. Law. 335, at 348 (1996).

104. [By the Author] The following discussion is limited to those aspects of the new law that directly affect securities fraud actions under the Securities Exchange Act. The Private Securities Litigation Reform Act also modifies the Securities Act of 1933 in several similar respects and contains an important modification to the Racketeer Influenced and Corrupt Organizations Act (RICO).

accept any payment for serving as class representatives.[105] The Act also contains new procedures for the appointment of lead plaintiff in a securities class action and requires courts to presume that the plaintiff with the "largest financial stake in the relief sought" is the most appropriate lead plaintiff.[106] In addition, Section 21D(a)(3) of the Act also provides that the lead plaintiff appointed under these procedures will be responsible for selecting and retaining lead counsel, and it contains provisions limiting the capacity of any person to serve as a lead plaintiff more than five times over any three-year period. All of these provisions serve to enhance the independence of the lead plaintiff from the attorney for the class.

The class action attorney's influence and control over the course of the litigation is further diminished by provisions in the Act that limit the lead plaintiff's recovery to a pro rata share of the final judgment, thereby reducing the prospect of the lead plaintiff being co-opted by class counsel.[107] A provision that bars the filing of settlements under seal without "good cause" operates to discourage self-serving settlements on the part of counsel.[108] All proposed and final settlements now must be disseminated to the members of the class in a new format designed to include all of the information deemed necessary to permit the class to evaluate the settlement.[109] In addition, the lead attorney's fees are capped at a "reasonable percentage" of the amount of damages and interest actually paid to the class, thus tying the attorney's compensation more closely to the interests of the class.[110]

2. DELAY OF FACT DISCOVERY

The Act contains provisions designed to delay the onset of litigation costs associated with fact discovery until after the defendant has had the opportunity to bring a motion to dismiss.[111] Section 21D(b)(3)(B) provides that all discovery must be stayed during the pendency of a motion to dismiss, except for discovery of particular facts necessary to preserve evidence or to prevent undue prejudice to a party.[112] By delaying fact discovery in this manner, the Act reduces the likelihood that either side will use the discovery process as a fishing expedition to bolster uncertain claims or as a bludgeon to coerce a settlement.

---

105. [By the Author] * * * For ease of reference, this article will use the citation "Securities Exchange Act § ___" to denote the Securities Exchange Act as amended by the Private Securities Litigation Reform Act of 1995

106. [By the Author] Securities Exchange Act § 21D(a)(3). See generally Joseph A. Grundfest & Michael A. Perino, The Pentium Papers: A Case Study of Collective Institutional Investor Activism in Litigation, 38 Ariz. L. Rev. 559 (1996). In July 1996, the State of Wisconsin Investment Board asserted its rights as a class action member under this provision and successfully filed a motion seeking to replace class counsel with counsel of its own choosing. See Dean Starkman, Fund Displaces Law Firm to Lead CellStar Lawsuit, Wall St. J., Oct. 2, 1996, at B9. The Wisconsin Investment Board is among the largest institutional

investors to date to utilize this new statutory provision. See Keith Johnson, Deployment of Institutions in the Securities Class Action Wars, 38 Ariz. L. Rev. 627, 631 (1996).

107. [By the Author] See id. § 21D(a)(4).

108. [By the Author] See id. § 21D(a)(5).

109. [By the Author] See id. § 21D(a)(7).

110. [By the Author] See id. § 21D(a)(6).

111. [By the Author] See H.R. Conf. Rep. No. 104–369, at 736 (1995).

112. [By the Author] See Securities Exchange Act § 21D(b)(3)(B); see also Medhekar v. United States Dist. Court for the N. Dist. of Cal., 99 F.3d 325, 328 (9th Cir.1996) (concluding that initial disclosure requirements under Federal Rule of Civil Procedure 26(a)(1) are subject to the Act's stay provisions).

3. IMPOSITION OF PROPORTIONATE LIABILITY

The Act alters the present system of joint and several liability in order to limit the circumstances under which one defendant is required to pay for injuries caused by the conduct of another defendant.[113] A new system of "fair share" proportionate liability is instituted whereby, under certain circumstances, a particular defendant may be held liable solely for the portion of the judgment for which he is adjudged responsible. Proportionate liability applies where the defendant has been found liable for a non-knowing (i.e., reckless) violation of the Securities Exchange Act and, in addition, neither of the following scenarios exists: (a) the plaintiff has a net worth of less than $200,000 and is entitled to damages in excess of ten percent of her net worth, or (b) a codefendant is insolvent and cannot pay his share of damages.[114] Joint and several liability remains the rule in most other circumstances, including cases where the defendants have been found liable for a knowing or intentional violation of the law.[115]

4. STRENGTHENING RULE 11

The Act strengthens the application of Rule 11 of the Federal Rules of Civil Procedure to private securities actions in order to better deter frivolous filings.[116] The law now requires the court, upon final adjudication of the action, to enter findings in the record concerning each attorney's compliance with his or her obligations under Rule 11 in connection with the lawsuit.[117] Where the court determines that the requirements of Rule 11 have been violated, the Act requires the imposition of sanctions, with the rebuttable presumption that sanctions will take the form of attorneys' fees and costs. In a class action, the court has the authority to require an advance undertaking from the attorney for the class to provide for the payment of any fees and expenses ultimately awarded under Rule 11.[118]

5. HEIGHTENED PLEADING REQUIREMENTS

The Act heightens the pleading standards necessary in any complaint under the Securities Exchange Act that requires an allegation of the defendant's state of mind. The goal of the Act is to "establish uniform and more stringent pleading requirements to curtail the filing of meritless lawsuits."[119] Wherever liability is dependent upon the defendant having acted with a particular state of mind, the complaint must contain particularized facts that give rise to a "strong inference" that the defendant possessed the requisite scienter.[120] It remains to be seen whether courts will interpret this new standard in a manner that is meaningfully different from previous pleading requirements.[121]

---

113. [By the Author] See H.R. Conf. Rep. No. 104–369, at 736–37.

114. [By the Author] See Securities Exchange Act § 21D(g).

115. [By the Author] See Donald C. Langevoort, The Reform of Joint and Several Liability Under the Private Securities Litigation Reform Act of 1995: Proportionate Liability, Contribution Rights and Settlement Effects, 51 Bus. Law. 1157, 1162 (1996).

116. [By the Author] See H.R. Conf. Rep. No. 104–369, at 738; see, e.g., Katz v. Household Int'l, Inc., 91 F.3d 1036 (7th Cir.1996).

117. [By the Author] See Securities Exchange Act § 21D(c).

118. [By the Author] See id. § 21D(a)(8).

119. [By the Author] H.R. Conf. Rep. No. 104–369, at 740.

120. [By the Author] Securities Exchange Act § 21D(b)(2).

121. [By the Author] See John C. Coffee, Jr., The Future of the Private Securities Liti-

In addition, the Act underscores the requirement that the plaintiff must plead and prove loss causation as an element of her case.[122] Although the language of the Act states only that the plaintiff in a private action has the burden of proving loss causation,[123] the legislative history of the Act evidences an intent to require an allegation of loss causation in the complaint itself.[124] Therefore, a general allegation of transaction (or "but for") causation would appear insufficient to survive a motion to dismiss.

6. New Measure of Damages

The Act introduces a new method for calculating damages once liability has been ascertained in a case alleging securities fraud. The goal of Congress was to reduce the uncertainty involved in calculating damages using the market price of the security at issue at the time that the misrepresentation was publicly disclosed. Congress feared that the use of the market price in calculating damages often leads to an overestimation of the plaintiff's damages, due to the possibility that the price at the time of disclosure resulted from market conditions unconnected to the fraud.[125] Therefore, the Act contains provisions that no damage award based on the market price of a security may exceed the difference between the purchase (or sale) price of the security and the mean trading price at which the security traded within the ninety-day period immediately following the disclosure of corrective information.[126]

7. New Statutory Duties for Auditors

The Act imposes explicit new duties on corporate auditors to identify and report suspected illegal conduct. These duties include obligations to investigate possible illegalities that come to the attention of the auditor during its engagement, obligations to report instances of illegal conduct to the appropriate level of management and to the board of directors, and obligations, under certain circumstances, to report instances of illegal conduct to the Securities

---

gation Reform Act: Or, Why the Fat Lady Has Not Yet Sung, 51 Bus. Law. 975, 977–85 (1996)(suggesting that courts retain discretion to avoid the harsh effects of a heightened pleading standard); Elliott J. Weiss, The New Securities Fraud Pleading Requirement: Speed Bump or Road Block?, 38 Ariz. L. Rev. 675, 706–07 (1996) (stating that "the principal effect of sec. 21D(b)(2) may be to add unnecessarily to motion practice in open market fraud cases, not to eliminate meritorious claims").

122. [By the Author] See H.R. Conf. Rep. No. 104–369, at 740. Prior to the enactment of this provision, a growing number of federal court opinions had dismissed complex securities fraud claims on the basis of the plaintiffs' failure to adequately allege and prove the element of loss causation. See Thomas L. Hazen, The Law of Securities Regulation 818–20 (3d ed. 1996). These courts reasoned that common-law fraud principles counsel in favor of a strict requirement that the plaintiff establish loss causation. Plaintiffs in a private 10b–5 action must therefore show that their entire loss was directly caused by the subject matter of the misrepresentation before they may recover. It

is not sufficient to show that the misrepresentation induced the purchase or sale of the stock and that events unrelated to the defendants caused the loss. See id. Some critics have questioned the validity of loss causation as a separate element of the cause of action in light of the remedial congressional purposes underlying the Securities Exchange Act of 1934. See Theresa A. Gabaldon, Causation, Courts, and Congress: A Study of Contradiction in the Federal Securities Laws, 31 B.C. L. Rev. 1027, 1083 (1990); Michael J. Kaufman, Loss Causation: Exposing a Fraud on Securities Law Jurisprudence, 24 Ind. L. Rev. 357, 397 (1991); Andrew L. Merritt, A Consistent Model of Loss Causation in Securities Fraud Litigation: Suiting the Remedy to the Wrong, 66 Tex. L. Rev. 469, 492 (1988).

123. [By the Author] See Securities Exchange Act § 21D(b)(4).

124. [By the Author] See H.R. Conf. Rep. No. 104–369, at 740.

125. [By the Author] See id. at 741.

126. [By the Author] See Securities Exchange Act § 21D(e).

and Exchange Commission.[127] These new auditor obligations serve as a counterweight to the procedural restrictions contained elsewhere in the Act.[128] Procedural restrictions may be detrimental to an enforcement system that relies heavily on the threat of litigation by private attorneys general to deter fraud, but the new duties imposed on auditors indicate an overall attempt by Congress to compensate for these restrictions by shifting some of the enforcement burden toward independent accountants.

8. New Safe Harbor for Forward–Looking Information * * * [Editor: This material is described at page 606, supra]

D.   WHAT THE REFORM ACT DOES NOT DO

The Act is actually change on a modest scale.[129] Its most significant reforms are reforms of the procedural limitations placed on the class action plaintiff and her attorney in a securities fraud lawsuit. The primary goals of the legislation are transparent: to allow more claims to be dismissed at the pleading stage, to place greater control over litigation in the hands of large shareholder plaintiffs (as opposed to the owners of single shares and their "strike suit" lawyers), and to enact penalties for filing a lawsuit without an adequate factual investigation of the asserted claims. With the exception of the safe harbor provisions, the Act could well have been entitled "The Class Action Reform Act." Most of its goals could have been addressed via changes to the Federal Rules of Civil Procedure as opposed to amendments to the Securities Exchange Act.

Despite the passage of the Act, it is readily apparent that most of the preexisting judge-made law concerning the scope of the Rule 10b–5 cause of action remains untouched. The Act does touch upon the scope of liability in the following ways: (1) the previously recognized existence of loss causation as a separate element of the plaintiff's case is reaffirmed; (2) the measure of damages and the application of proportionate liability are modified for certain cases; and (3) one change to existing standards of liability is effectuated through the creation of a safe harbor for forward-looking statements.

The Act purposefully avoids defining the state of mind required for imposition of liability for securities fraud. It leaves for another day the issues raised by the "fraud on the market" theory. The sole meaningful change to the scope of conduct giving rise to liability is the creation of a new safe harbor of limited availability, which may act to foreclose liability under some circumstances where the judicially created "bespeaks caution" doctrine does not.[130]

---

127. [By the Author] See id. § 10A.

128. [By the Author] See [Richard M. Phillips & Gilbert C. Miller, The Private Securities Litigation Reform Act of 1995: Rebalancing Litigation Risks and Rewards for Class Action Plaintiffs, Defendants and Lawyers, 51 Bus. Law. 1009] at 1062–64. (1996).

129. [By the Author] In the wake of the Reform Act's passage, one attorney observer has noted that new securities fraud filings in federal court have not slowed significantly and "to a large extent, it's business as usual." Phyllis Diamond, California Initiative Could Undermine Reform Legislation, Lawyers Warn, 28 Sec. Reg. & Law Rep. (BNA) 971, 972 (Aug.

9, 1996); see also Dean Starkman, Securities Class–Action Suits Seem Immune to Effects of a New Law, Wall St. J., Nov. 12, 1996, at B7. But see Stephen F. Black et al., The Private Securities Litigation Reform Act of 1995: A Preliminary Analysis, 24 Sec. Reg. L.J. 117, 141 (1996) ("The Reform Act is an ambitious effort to curb the costs and burdens imposed by private federal securities litigation on issuers and others.").

130. [By the Author] See John C. Coffee, Jr., The Future of the Private Securities Litigation Reform Act: Or, Why the Fat Lady Has Not Yet Sung, 51 Bus. Law. 975, at 989–96 (1996)(discussing ambiguities concerning the

By failing to do little more than fiddle with the elements of the cause of action as currently defined, the Act avoids the fundamental question underlying recent Supreme Court jurisprudence in this area: What types of conduct should give rise to a private cause of action under Section 10(b) and Rule 10b–5? Although the new legislation will make it more difficult for certain types of "professional plaintiffs" and their attorneys to assert claims, it will have little effect on the ability of plaintiffs in general to recover under a law whose boundaries are currently uncertain.[131] Even after Congress's recent effort to reassert itself in the arena of securities fraud, the primary expositor of the scope of conduct that constitutes a violation of Section 10(b) remains the federal judiciary. It is therefore appropriate to review the history of the judiciary's interpretation of the private cause of action.

Notes

(1) Much of the information about the impact of PSLRA on actual litigation is available from the Stanford Securities Class Action Clearinghouse website (http://securities.stanford.edu).[132] The conclusions set forth below are drawn from information appearing on this website. After two years' experience the effect of this statute can be best described as an example of the law of unintended consequences in action. The following generalizations are justified:

(a) The total number of securities fraud class actions has not decreased significantly. Between December 22, 1995 and November 18, 1997, 237 companies have been sued for securities fraud in federal courts. Annual figures for pre-PSLRA years are as follows: 1993–158, 1994–220, 1995–162. In addition, the number of cases disposed of finally on motions to dismiss have not increased substantially.

(b) The number of securities fraud class action suits filed in state courts has increased dramatically since December, 1995. Before PSLRA, relatively few of these class action suits were brought in state court; however, from January 1, 1996 through June 30, 1997, 92 companies were sued in state court.[133] Of this number, 54 were sued only in state court while 38 were sued simultaneously in both federal and state courts. Written Testimony of Michael A. Perino, Before the Subcommittee on Securities of the Committee on Banking, Housing, and Urban Affairs, United States Senate, July 24, 1997 (posted on the Stanford website). A variety of possible explanations exist for this movement to state courts: An effort to avoid the pleading standards, automatic stay and lead plaintiff rules imposed by the PSLRA, a longer statute of limitations, a desire to bring suit for aiding and

extent to which the new statutory safe harbor provides protections beyond the bespeaks caution doctrine); see also Wallman Cites Lack of Consensus Within SEC on Safe Harbor Disclosure, 28 Sec. Reg. & L. Rep. (BNA) 1368–69 (Nov. 8, 1996) (same).

131. [By the Author] It is unrealistic to expect federal judges to police abusive securities fraud litigation solely through procedural mechanisms such as Rules 9(b) or 11 of the Federal Rules of Civil Procedure and to leave the substantive contours of liability untouched. But cf. Lawrence A. Cunningham, "Firm–Specific" Information and the Federal Securities Laws: A Doctrinal, Etymological, and Theoretical Critique, 68 Tul. L. Rev. 1409 at 1445 n.149, (1994). To a great extent, the parties before the court frame the issues to be decided.

A judge faced with a claim that he or she perceives to be without merit may not wish to punish the attorney for arguing a good faith extension of the law, but nonetheless may be influenced in deciding the substantive question at issue by a desire to foreclose similar arguments in the future.

132. [By the Editor] A competitive website has been created by the Milberg Weiss law firm, the principal plaintiffs firm involved in securities fraud litigation. MW Securities Class Action Designated Internet Site (http://securities.milberg.com).

133. [By the Editor] Since federal jurisdiction over Rule 10b–5 cases is exclusive, these cases have been brought under state blue sky or anti-fraud statutes.

abetting against "deep pocket" defendants, and availability of non-unanimous verdicts, to name a few. This shift in litigation to the state courts has not only rejuvenated an area of state law that had largely atrophied because of Rule 10b–5, but also has led to proposals that Congress should preempt much if not all of this state litigation. The enactment of such legislation in 1998 is likely.

(c) The new safe harbor for forward looking statements appears not to have changed the amount of voluntary disclosure by issuers but has led to the multiplication of cautionary statements in documents filed with the SEC.

(d) The "lead plaintiff/lead counsel" provisions of PSLRA have led to several highly publicized incidents in which plaintiffs' attorneys who filed the litigation have been replaced (or have been made joint lead counsel with) counsel selected by large institutional investors, usually pension funds. However, institutional investors have rarely stepped forward to become lead plaintiffs, and when they do, they have usually been vigorously attacked by traditional plaintiffs' counsel. Indeed, the preliminary skirmishing over lead plaintiffs and lead counsel has been one of the most visible changes wrought by PSLRA.

(e) Cases appear to be taking longer to litigate and to involve more pretrial motions practice than before PSLRA.

(f) Many of the innovative provisions of PSLRA that relate to damage measurement, proportionate liability, attorney sanctions, and so forth, appear not to have arisen. Further, major issues with respect to the pleading standards and the safe harbor have been litigated in federal district courts but remain to be definitively resolved nearly two years after PSLRA became effective.

(2) In Medhekar v. United States District Court, 99 F.3d 325 (9th Cir. 1996) it was held that the mandatory stay applies to disclosures required by Rule 26(a)(1) of the Federal Rules. For early litigation involving the pleading requirements under PSLRA see Marksman Partners L.P. v. Chantal Pharmaceutical Corp., 927 F.Supp. 1297 (C.D.Cal.1996); In re Silicon Graphics, Inc. Sec. Litigation, 970 F.Supp. 746 (N.D.Cal.1997). The latter case appears to be the leading candidate for appellate review of these standards. Among the issues involved in this litigation is the question whether recklessness constitutes scienter under the standards of PSLRA. In the *Silicon Graphics* litigation the SEC filed an amicus brief urging the California district court to recognize that that the basic standard of responsibility was not changed by the 1995 legislation.

(3) Denis T. Rice, A Practitioner's View of the Private Securities Litigation Reform Act of 1995, 31 U.San Fran.L.Rev. 283 (1997) suggests that the most important change effected by PSLRA was the substitution of proportionate liability for joint and several liability for non-knowing defendants.

(4) See also Lynn A. Stout, Type I Error, Type II Error, and the Private Securities Litigation Reform Act, 38 Ariz. L.Rev. 711 (1996):*

> If I may inflict some theory on you, scholars generally divide error into two categories. The first category of legal error is called Type I error, or the "false positive." In securities litigation, an example of a Type I false positive would be a judicial finding that a defendant had fraudulently misrepresented something, when in fact no fraud occurred. The second type of error is called Type II error, or the "false negative." A Type II false negative occurs when a court trying to decide whether the defendant has committed fraud mistakenly finds there has been no fraud, even though fraud actually occurred.

---

* * * Congress in drafting Section 21D(b)(2) was concerned with both Type I error (allowing meritless suits to proceed) and Type II error (keeping legitimate fraud claims out of court). But Congress was particularly concerned about a form of Type I error: the so-called "strike suit."

Professor Stout suggests that Type I errors in securities litigation involve hundreds of millions of dollars each year while Type II errors involve hundreds of billions of dollars.

E.   TRANSACTIONS IN CONTROLLING SHARES

ZETLIN v. HANSON HOLDINGS, INC.

Court of Appeals of New York, 1979.
48 N.Y.2d 684, 421 N.Y.S.2d 877, 397 N.E.2d 387.

Memorandum

The order of the Appellate Division should be affirmed, with costs.

Plaintiff Zetlin owned approximately 2% of the outstanding shares of Gable Industries, Inc., with defendants Hanson Holdings, Inc., and Sylvestri together with members of the Sylvestri family, owning 44.4% of Gable's shares. The defendants sold their interests to Flintkote Co. for a premium price of $15 per share, at a time when Gable was selling on the open market for $7.38 per share. It is undisputed that the 44.4% acquired by Flintkote represented effective control of Gable.

Recognizing that those who invest the capital necessary to acquire a dominant position in the ownership of a corporation have the right of controlling that corporation, it has long been settled law that, absent looting of corporate assets, conversion of a corporate opportunity, fraud or other acts of bad faith, a controlling stockholder is free to sell, and a purchaser is free to buy, that controlling interest at a premium price (see Barnes v. Brown, 80 N.Y. 527; Levy v. American Beverage Corp., 265 App.Div. 208, 38 N.Y.S.2d 517; Essex Universal Corp. v. Yates, 2nd Cir., 305 F.2d 572).

Certainly, minority shareholders are entitled to protection against such abuse by controlling shareholders. They are not entitled, however, to inhibit the legitimate interests of the other stockholders. It is for this reason that control shares usually command a premium price. The premium is the added amount an investor is willing to pay for the privilege of directly influencing the corporation's affairs.

In this action plaintiff Zetlin contends that minority stockholders are entitled to an opportunity to share equally in any premium paid for a controlling interest in the corporation. This rule would profoundly affect the manner in which controlling stock interests are now transferred. It would require, essentially, that a controlling interest be transferred only by means of an offer to all stockholders, i.e., a tender offer. This would be contrary to existing law and if so radical a change is to be effected it would best be done by the Legislature.

Cooke, C.J., and Jasen, Gabrielli, Jones, Wachtler, Fuchsberg and Meyer, JJ., concur in memorandum.

DEBAUN v. FIRST W. BANK AND TRUST CO.

Court of Appeals of California, 1975.
46 Cal.App.3d 686, 120 Cal.Rptr. 354.

THOMPSON, ASSOCIATE JUSTICE.

This appeal primarily concerns the duty of a majority shareholder to the corporation whose shares he holds in selling the shares when possessed of facts establishing a reasonable likelihood that the purchaser intends to exercise the control to be acquired by him to loot the corporation of its assets. We conclude that in those circumstances the majority shareholder owes a duty of reasonable investigation and due care to the corporation.

FACTS

Alfred S. Johnson Incorporated (Corporation) was incorporated by Alfred S. Johnson in 1955 to process color photographs to be reproduced in printed form. All of the 100 outstanding shares of Corporation were originally owned by Johnson. Subsequently, Johnson sold 20 of his shares to James DeBaun, Corporation's primary salesman, and 10 shares to Walter Stephens, its production manager. In November of 1964, Johnson was seriously ill so that managerial control of Corporation was assumed by DeBaun, Stephens, and Jack Hawkins, Corporation's estimator.

Johnson died testate on January 15, 1965. His will named appellant First Western Bank and Trust Company (Bank) as executor and trustee of a trust created by the will. The 70 shares of Corporation owned by Johnson at the time of his death passed to the testamentary trust. George Furman, an employee of Bank, was charged with the direct administration of the trust. While Bank took no hand in the management of Corporation leaving it to the existing management team, Furman attended virtually all directors' meetings. Bank, through its nominee, voted the 70 shares at stockholders' meetings.

Under the guidance of DeBaun and Stephens, the net after tax profit of Corporation increased dramatically as illustrated by the following table:

Fiscal year ending August 31	Net Profit
1964	$15,903
1965	$42,316
1966	$58,969
1967	$37,583
1968 (10 mos.)	$56,710

On October 27, 1966, Bank's trust department determined that the investment in Corporation was not appropriate for the trust and decided to sell the 70 shares. Bank also decided that no one connected with Corporation should be made aware of its decision to sell until a sale was firm. It caused an appraisal of Corporation to be made by General Appraisal Company which estimated the value of Corporation as a going concern at $326,000. Bank retained W.H. Daum Investment Company (Daum) to find a buyer and to assist it in the sale.

DeBaun and Stephens were not told of the Bank's plans. In March of 1968, a competitor of Corporation showed DeBaun a letter from Daum indicating that Corporation was for sale. Subsequently, both DeBaun and Stephens were contacted by two potential buyers who sought to purchase their shares. They refused to sell, agreeing to hold their shares because they had " * * * a good job * * * and percentage of the company * * * "At the request of Daum's representative, DeBaun submitted an offer for the 70 shares held by Bank. The offer was rejected as inadequate.

On May 15 and 20, 1968, Bank received successive offers for the 70 shares from Raymond J. Mattison, acting in the name of S.O.F. Fund, an inter vivos revocable trust of which he was both settlor and trustee. A sketchy balance sheet of S.O.F. Fund was submitted with the second offer. The offers were rejected. Anticipating a further offer from Mattison and his trust, Furman, acting for Bank, ordered a Dun & Bradstreet report on Mattison and the fund. The report was received on May 24, 1968. It noted pending litigation, bankruptcies, and tax liens against corporate entities in which Mattison had been a principal, and suggested that S.O.F. Fund no longer existed.

As of May 24, I. Earl Funk, a vice-president of Bank, had personal knowledge that: (1) on October 24, 1957, the Los Angeles Superior Court had entered a judgment against Mattison in favor of Bank's predecessor in interest for compensatory and punitive damages as the result of Mattison's fraudulent misrepresentations and a fraudulent financial statement to obtain a loan; and (2) the judgment remained unsatisfied in 1968 and was an asset of Bank acquired from its predecessor in an acquisition of 65 branch banks.

On May 27, 1968, Mattison submitted a third offer to purchase the 70 shares of Corporation held by Bank. The offer proposed that S.O.F. Fund would pay $250,000 for the shares, $50,000 in marketable securities as a down payment with the balance payable over a five-year period. Bank made a counter offer, generally accepting the terms of the Mattison proposal but providing that: (1) the $200,000 balance of the purchase price was to be secured by a pledge of marketable securities valued at a like amount; and (2) Corporation would pay no dividends out of "pre-sale" retained earnings. On June 4, 1968, representatives of Bank met with Oroville McCarrol, who had been a trust officer of Bank's predecessor in interest and was counsel for Mattison. McCarrol proposed that Corporation use its assets to secure the unpaid balance of the purchase price rather than Mattison supplying the security in the form of marketable securities. He proposed also the elimination of the restriction against dividends from pre-sale retained earnings. Despite reservations by Bank personnel on the legality of the use of corporate assets to secure an obligation of a major shareholder, Bank determined to pursue the McCarrol modification further. Troubled by the Dun & Bradstreet report, personnel of Bank met with Mattison and McCarrol on June 27. Mattison explained that it had been his practice to take over failing companies so that the existence of the litigation and tax liens noted in the Dun & Bradstreet report was not due to his fault. Not entirely satisfied, Furman wrote to McCarrol requesting a written report on the status of all pending litigation in which Mattison was involved. McCarrol telephoned his response, declining to represent the status of the litigation but noting that the information was publicly available. Partly because Ralph Whitsett, Furman's immediate superior at Bank, knew McCarrol as a former trust officer of Bank's predecessor in interest, and partly because during a luncheon with Mattison at the Jonathan Club Robert Q. Parsons, the officer at Daum in charge of the transaction, had noted that Mattison was warmly received by his fellow members and reported that fact to Furman, Bank did not pursue its investigation into the public records of Los Angeles County where a mass of derogatory information lay.

As of July 1, 1968, the public records of Los Angeles County revealed 38 unsatisfied judgments against Mattison or his entities totalling $330,886.27, and 54 pending actions claiming a total of $373,588.67 from them. The record also contained 22 recorded abstracts of judgments against Mattison or his entities totalling $285,704.11, and 18 tax liens aggregating $20,327.97. Bank did not investigate the public record and hence was unaware of Mattison's financial track record.

While failing to pursue the investigation of the known information adverse to Mattison, Bank's employees knew or should have known that if his proposal through McCarrol were accepted the payment of the $200,000 balance of the purchase price would necessarily come from Corporation. They assumed that the payments would be made by Mattison from distributions of the Corporation which he would cause it to make after assuming control. They were aware that Corporation would not generate a sufficient aftertax cash flow to pay dividends in a sufficient amount to permit the payments of interest and principal on the $200,000 balance as scheduled in the McCarrol proposal, and knew that Mattison could make those payments only by resorting to distribution of "pre-sale" retained earnings and assets of Corporation.

On July 11, 1968, Bank accepted the McCarrol modification by entering into an exchange agreement with S.O.F. Fund. The agreement obligated S.O.F. to retain a working capital of not less than $70,000, to refrain from intercompany transactions except in the ordinary course of business for adequate consideration, and to furnish monthly financial statements and a certified annual audit report to Bank. It provides that Bank is to transfer its 70 shares of Corporation to Mattison as trustee of S.O.F. Fund, and that the stock will be held by Bank in pledge to secure the fund's obligation. There is provision for acceleration of the unpaid balance of the purchase price if Mattison defaults in any provision of the agreement. The contract obligated Mattison to cause Corporation to execute a security agreement to secure Mattison's obligation to Bank covering all "furniture, fixtures and equipment of [Corporation]." Mattison agreed also to cause Corporation's principal banking business to be maintained with Bank.

The exchange agreement having been executed, Bank gave Mattison a proxy to vote the 70 shares of Corporation at a special meeting of shareholders of Corporation to be held on July 11 at 3 p.m. Furman attended that meeting and an ensuing directors' meeting, as did Mattison. At the shareholders' meeting, DeBaun and Stephens were told that the shares of Corporation owned by Bank had been sold by it on an installment basis to Mattison and that Bank intended to take a pledge of those shares. A new board of directors was elected of which Mattison had control although DeBaun and Stephens remained as directors. DeBaun and Stephens were informed by Furman that a security agreement had been signed to protect Corporation in the event of death or default of Mattison and that in such an event Bank would "foreclose on the stock." Furman did not supply DeBaun or Stephens with a copy of the security agreement or inform them that in fact [it] hypothecated corporate assets as security for Mattison's debt to Bank. Relying upon Furman's statement of the effect of the agreement and misled by his failure to disclose its material terms, and by the further representation that the document was simply a formal requirement of Mattison's purchase of the majority shares, DeBaun and Stephens participated in a unanimous vote approving the execution by Corporation of the security agreement. A directors' meeting was then convened at which Mattison was elected president of Corporation.

At the moment of Bank's sale of the controlling shares to Mattison, Corporation was an eminently successful going business with a bright future. It had cash of $76,126.15 and other liquid assets of over $122,000. Its remaining assets were worth $60,000. Its excess of current assets over current liabilities and reserve for bad debts was $233,391.94, and its net worth about $220,000. Corporation's earnings indicated a pattern of growth. Mattison immediately proceeded to change that situation. Beginning with the date that he acquired control, Mattison implemented a systematic scheme to loot Corporation of its assets. His first step was to divert $73,144 in corporate cash to himself and to MICO, a shell company owned by Mattison. The transfer was made in exchange for unsecured noninterest bearing notes but for no other consideration. On August 2, 1968, Mattison caused Corporation to assign to MICO all of Corporation's assets, including its receivables in exchange for a fictitious agreement for management services. He diverted all corporate mail to a post office box from which he took the mail, opened it, and extracted all incoming checks to the corporation before forwarding the mail on. He ceased paying trade creditors promptly, as had been Corporation's practice, delaying payment of trade creditors to the last possible moment and, to the extent he could, not paying some at all. He delayed shipments on new orders. To cover his activities, Mattison removed the corporate books and records.

In September 1968, DeBaun left Corporation's employ as a salesman because of Mattison's policy of not filling orders and because Mattison had drastically reduced DeBaun's compensation. * * * Mattison continued to loot the corporation, although at a reduced pace by reason of its depleted assets. He collected payments from employees to pay premiums on a voluntary health insurance plan although the policy covering the plan was terminated in September for failure to pay premiums. He issued payroll checks without sufficient funds and continued not to pay trade creditors. Mattison did not supply Bank with the financial reports required by the exchange agreement.

While Bank was not aware of the initial transfer of cash to MICO, it did learn of the other misconduct of Mattison as it occurred. Although the conduct was a breach of the exchange agreement, Bank took no action beyond seeking an oral explanation from Mattison. In December 1968, Stephens also left Corporation's employ.

Bank took no action in the matter until April 25, 1969. On that date, it filed an action in the superior court seeking the appointment of a receiver. On April 30, Bank called a special shareholders' meeting of Corporation at which it voted its shares with those of DeBaun and Stephens to elect a new board of directors replacing the Mattison group. Faced with resistance from Mattison,

Bank pursued neither its receivership nor its ouster of the board until June 20, 1969, when it shut down the operations of Corporation. By that time, Corporation was hopelessly insolvent. Its debts exceeded its assets by over $200,000, excluding its contingent liability to Bank, as a result of the fraudulently obtained hypothecation of corporate assets to secure Mattison's debt. Both the federal Internal Revenue Service and California State Board of Equalization had filed liens upon corporate assets and notices to withhold funds. A trade creditor had placed a keeper on the corporate premises.

On July 10, 1969, Bank, pursuant to the security agreement, sold all of Corporation's then remaining assets for $60,000. $25,000 of the proceeds of sale was paid to release the federal tax lien while the remaining $35,000 was retained by Bank. After the sale, Corporation had no assets and owed $218,426 to creditors.

Respondents filed two related actions against Bank. One asserted their right to recover, as shareholders, for damage caused by Bank. The other was a stockholders' derivate [sic] action brought on behalf of Corporation * * *. The two cases were consolidated. Bank demurred to both complaints. In the demurrer to the first action, it contended that respondents DeBaun and Stephens, as shareholders, lacked capacity to pursue their claim. In the demurrer to the second complaint, Bank took the opposite tack, contending that its liability did not run to Corporation. The demurrer to the first complaint was sustained without leave to amend, and the demurrer to the second complaint was overruled. The case at bench proceeded to trial before a judge as a derivate [sic] action. The trial court held for respondents, finding that Bank had breached duties it owed as a majority controlling shareholder to the corporation it controlled. It assessed monetary damages in the amount of $473,836, computed by adding to $220,000, the net asset value of the corporation as the date of transfer of the shares to Mattison, an amount equal to anticipated after-tax earnings of the corporation for the ensuing 10–year period, taking into account an 8 percent growth factor. The court additionally awarded Corporation an amount equal to the sum it would be required to pay and the cost of defending valid claims existing against it when it became defunct. Pursuant to Fletcher v. A.J. Industries, Inc., 266 Cal.App.2d 313, 320–321, 72 Cal.Rptr. 146, the trial court awarded counsel for respondents attorneys' fees payable from the fund recovered for Corporation's benefit. It denied respondents' claim for punitive damages. This appeal from the resulting judgment followed. * * *

BREACH OF DUTY

Early case law held that a controlling shareholder owed no duty to minority shareholders or to the controlled corporation in the sale of his stock. (See e.g., Ryder v. Bamberger, 172 Cal. 791, 158 P. 753.) Decisional law, however, has since recognized the fact of financial life that corporate control by ownership of a majority of shares may be misused. Thus the applicable proposition now is that "In any transaction where the control of the corporation is material," the controlling majority shareholder must exercise good faith and fairness "from the viewpoint of the corporation and those interested therein." (Remillard Brick Co. v. Remillard–Dandini, 109 Cal.App.2d 405, 420, 241 P.2d 66, 75 quoted in Jones v. H.F. Ahmanson & Co., 1 Cal.3d 93, 110, 81 Cal.Rptr. 592, 600, 460 P.2d 464, 472.) That duty of good faith and fairness encompasses an obligation of the controlling shareholder in possession of facts "[s]uch as to awaken suspicion and put a prudent man on his guard [that a potential buyer of his shares may loot the corporation of its assets to pay for the shares purchased] * * * to conduct a reasonable adequate investigation [of the buyer]." (Insuranshares Corporation v. Northern Fiscal Corp. (E.D.Pa. 1940) 35 F.Supp. 22, 25.)

Here Bank was the controlling majority shareholder of Corporation. As it was negotiating with Mattison, it became directly aware of facts that would have alerted a prudent person that Mattison was likely to loot the corporation. Bank knew from the Dun & Bradstreet report that Mattison's financial record was notable by the failure of entities controlled by him. Bank knew that the only source of funds available to Mattison to pay it for the shares he was purchasing lay in the assets of the corporation. The after-tax net income from the date of the sale would not be sufficient to permit the payment of dividends to him which would permit the making of payments. An officer of Bank possessed personal knowledge that Mattison, on at least one occasion, had been guilty of a fraud perpetrated on Bank's predecessor in interest and had not satisfied a judgment Bank held against him for damages flowing from that conduct.

Armed with knowledge of those facts, Bank owed a duty to Corporation and its minority shareholders to act reasonably with respect to its dealings in the controlling shares with Mattison. It breached that duty. Knowing of McCarrol's refusal to express an opinion on litigation against Mattison and his entities, and that the information could be obtained from the public records, Bank closed its eyes to that obvious source. Rather, it relied upon Mattison's friendly reception by fellow members of the Jonathan Club and the fact that he was represented by a lawyer who had been a trust officer of Bank's predecessor in interest to conclude that indicators that Mattison was a financial bandit should be ignored. Membership in a club, whether it be the Jonathan or the informal group of ex-trust officers of Bank, does not excuse investigation. Nor can Bank be justified in accepting Mattison's uncorroborated statement that the past financial disasters of his entities reported by Dun & Bradstreet were due to his practice of acquiring failing companies. Only one who loots a failed company at the expense of its creditors can profit from its acquisition. Mattison's constantly repeated entry into the transactions without ever pulling a company from the morass was a strong indication that he was milking the companies profitably. Had Bank investigated, as any prudent man would have done, it would have discovered from the public records the additional detail of Mattison's long, long trail of financial failure that would have precluded its dealings with him except under circumstances where his obligation was secured beyond question and his ability to loot Corporation precluded. * * *

Measure of Damages

Appellant contends finally that the trial court improperly multiplied the measure of damages by adding to net asset value on the date of Bank's tortious conduct an estimate for future net profit and an obligation that Bank discharge the valid existing obligations of Corporation. The record refutes the contention.

The trial judge arrived at a value of the corporation as a going concern at the time of appellant's breach by adding to the value of Corporation's tangible assets a goodwill factor computed on the basis of future net income reasonably to be anticipated from the Corporation's past record. This the trial court was authorized to do in determining "the amount which will compensate for all the detriment proximately caused * * * "by appellant's breach of duty. Appellant's breach damaged Corporation not only in the loss of its assets but also in the loss of its earning power. Since the trial court's determination of loss of earning power was based upon a past record of earnings and not speculation, it is supported by substantial evidence. The trial court's order requiring appellant to pay all valid claims of creditors against Corporation is also proper as necessary to restore Corporation to the condition in which it existed prior to the time that Bank contributed to its destruction. Prior to Bank's action, Corporation was a going concern with substantial net assets. As a proximate result of Bank's dereliction of duty, Corporation acquired a negative net worth of about $218,000. Total damage to Corporation is thus the sum necessary to restore the negative net worth, plus the value of its tangible assets, plus its going business value determined with reference to its future profits reasonably estimated. That is the measure which the trial court applied. Since the derivative action is equitable in nature, the court properly framed part of its judgment in terms of an obligation dependent upon future contingencies rather than at a fixed dollar amount.

DISPOSITION

The judgment is affirmed. The matter is, however, remanded to the trial court with directions to hold a hearing to determine the additional amount payable to respondents from the fund recovered by them for benefit of Corporation for counsel fees due for services on this appeal.

Notes

(1) What is the source of the duty owed by the bank to the plaintiffs in the principal case? As a practical matter, if you were advising an owner of a business who was planning to sell his controlling interest to unknown purchasers, how would you go about meeting this duty?

(2) The American Law Institute, Principles of Corporate Governance: Analysis and Recommendations § 5.16,[134] provides:

> A controlling shareholder has the same right to dispose of voting equity securities as any other shareholder, including the right to dispose of those securities for a price that is not made proportionally available to other shareholders, but the controlling shareholder does not satisfy the duty of fair dealing to the other shareholders if:
>
> (a) The controlling shareholder does not make disclosure concerning the transaction to other shareholders with whom the controlling shareholder deals in connection with the transaction; or
>
> (b) It is apparent from the circumstances that the purchaser is likely to violate the duty of fair dealing under Part V in such a way as to obtain a significant financial benefit for the purchaser or an associate.

---

134. Copyright (1994) by The American   of The American Law Institute.
Law Institute. Reprinted with the permission

Would "it [be] apparent" to the First Western Bank that Mattison was likely to loot the Alfred S. Johnson Corporation? Is not the ALI test too lax? The Comment to § 5.16 discusses the language of § 5.16(b) further:

> [T]he circumstances in which the controlling shareholder is required to forgo a transfer because of the risk that the prospective purchaser will violate its fiduciary duty [must] be clearly specified. Otherwise, uncertainty alone can result in deterring transfers that ought not to be restricted. To avoid this result, § 5.16(b) specified that liability will not be imposed unless it is apparent from the circumstances that the purchaser is likely to violate the duty of fair dealing to obtain a significant financial benefit.

> Affirmative investigation by the controlling shareholder is not required in the absence of facts that would alert a reasonable person to the need for further inquiry. What is necessary to trigger that inquiry, however, must be determined in the context of the transaction. The mere fact that the controlling shareholder receives a substantial premium for its shares, or that the purchaser has a general reputation for aggressive acquisitions, is not itself sufficient to trigger such an inquiry. What is required are facts sufficient to put the controlling shareholder on notice that it would be imprudent to proceed with the transaction without making further inquiry as to the purchaser and its motives for acquiring control of the corporation.

Does the commentary set forth a stricter test than § 5.16(b)?

(3) The leading decision in Delaware as to liability for sale to a looter is *Harris v. Carter*, 582 A.2d 222, 235 (Del.Ch.1990). The test suggested there is:

> Thus, I conclude that while a person who transfers corporate control to another is surely not a surety for his buyer, when the circumstances would alert a reasonably prudent person to a risk that his buyer is dishonest or in some material respect not truthful, a duty devolves upon the seller to make such inquiry as a reasonably prudent person would make, and generally to exercise care so that others who will be affected by his actions should not be injured by wrongful conduct.

Is that test the same as the one set forth in § 5.16(b)? As the test applied in *DeBaun* ?

(4) Many cases involve a purchase price that seems unreasonably high given the business being purchased. Should the manifest willingness of an unknown purchaser to pay an unreasonably high price be a suspicious circumstance? Some courts have refused to draw an adverse inference even though the premium seems extreme. In *Clagett v. Hutchison*, 583 F.2d 1259 (4th Cir.1978), for example, the majority shareholder was offered $43.75 per share at a time when the price in a "thinly traded * * * public market" varied between $7.50 and $10.00 per share; the Court held that this price "cannot be said to be so unreasonable as to place [the seller] on notice of the likelihood of fraud on the corporation or the remaining stockholders." 583 F.2d at 1262. One Judge dissented.

(5) Frank H. Easterbrook & Daniel R. Fischel, The Economic Structure of Corporate Law 126, 129–31 (1991):[135]

> Sales of controlling blocs of shares provide a good example of transactions in which the movement of control is beneficial. The sale of control may lead to

135. Reprinted by permission of the publishers from *The Economic Structure of Corporate Law* by Frank H. Easterbrook and Daniel R. Fischel, Cambridge, Mass.: Harvard University Press, Copyright 1991 by the President and Fellows of Harvard College.

new offers, new plans, and new working arrangements with other firms that reduce agency costs and create gains from new business relationships. The premium price received by the seller of the control bloc amounts to an unequal distribution of the gains. Sales at a premium are lawful, and the controlling shareholder generally has no duty to spread the bounty. * * * [T]his unequal distribution may cut the costs to purchasers of control, increasing the number of beneficial control transfers by the incentive for inefficient controllers to relinquish their positions. * * *

A specter of "looting" haunts opinions about corporate control transactions. * * * If it were feasible to detect looters in advance—if they all wore yellow carnations and pinkie rings, and smelled of sulfur—it might make sense to forbid the sellers of control to allow shares to pass to scoundrels (or even to the honest but inept). Certainly the sellers of control can detect knavery at a lower cost than the public shareholders who are not parties to the transaction. Yet it is difficult if not impossible to detect looters early on. Looting is by nature a one-time transaction. Once looters have plundered one firm, their reputation (or their residence in jail) prevents them from doing so again. But when they first obtain control, the may appear innocuous. Any rule that blocks sales in advance is equivalent to a program of preventive detention for people who have never robbed banks but have acquisitive personalities.

Although sellers could spend substantial sums investigating buyers and investors and still more in litigating over the quality of investigation, almost all of these efforts would be wasted. If investigations blocked transfers, most of these refusals would be false positives. That is, they would be refusals that reduced the gains available from transferring control. * * *

We do not suggest that the legal system should disregard looting, but the best remedies are based on deterrence rather than prior scrutiny. Looters, when caught, may be fined or imprisoned. Penalties could be made high enough to be effective, making the transaction unprofitable *ex ante*. The costs of deterrence are less than the costs of dealing with looting through a system of prior scrutiny that would scotch many valuable control shifts as a by-product.

(6) Robert W. Hamilton, Private Sale of Control Transactions: Where We Stand Today, 36 Case W.Res.L.Rev. 248, 267–68 (1985):

It is possible that Easterbrook and Fischel are correct when they infer that the costs of an *ex ante* requirement exceed its benefits, but I doubt it. In the first place, in my personal experience, it is not true that looters abscond and only first-time looters ply their trade. Rather, persons on the fringe of the law often quietly merge into the general economy and surface from time to time, hoping that their background is not discovered, and if it is, quietly disappear again. As a result, routine and inexpensive credit checks on persons offering to buy asset-rich companies often turn up substantially negative factors. * * *

Second, while it is possible that the *ex ante* investigation would turn up some "false positives," I do not see why this should be so. What is supposed to be investigated is not whether the purchaser has dismantled companies in the past, but whether he has a reputation for honesty and the apparent wherewithal to finance a transaction of the magnitude under consideration without recourse to the corporation's assets in a way that defrauds creditors and minority shareholders. If a person does not meet this standard, one wonders whether he is really a "false positive."

Finally, the *ex post* deterrence proposed by Easterbrook and Fischel in the form of criminal sanctions is not very attractive. Even if it is assumed that punishment for this type of conduct will be quick and sure—hardly characteristics of current criminal sanctions against white-collar crime—the result is that the innocent shareholders and others "left behind" will usually suffer the entire economic loss, while the majority shareholders who sold to the thieves may keep the entire purchase price, premium and all. The thieves, of course, go to jail. This result seems so obviously unjust from the standpoint of the minority shareholders that it seems unreasonable to embrace it on the basis of entirely theoretical considerations of economic "efficiency."

PERLMAN v. FELDMANN

United States Court of Appeals, Second Circuit, 1955.
219 F.2d 173.

CLARK, CHIEF JUDGE.

This is a derivative action brought by minority stockholders of Newport Steel Corporation to compel accounting for, and restitution of, allegedly illegal gains which accrued to defendants as a result of the sale in August, 1950, of their controlling interest in the corporation. The principal defendant, C. Russell Feldmann, who represented and acted for the others, members of his family,[136] was at that time not only the dominant stockholder, but also the chairman of the board of directors and the president of the corporation. Newport, an Indiana corporation, operated mills for the production of steel sheets for sale to manufacturers of steel products, first at Newport, Kentucky, and later also at other places in Kentucky and Ohio. The buyers, a syndicate organized as Wilport Company, a Delaware corporation, consisted of end-users of steel who were interested in securing a source of supply in a market becoming ever tighter in the Korean War. Plaintiffs contend that the consideration paid for the stock included compensation for the sale of a corporate asset, a power held in trust for the corporation by Feldmann as its fiduciary. This power was the ability to control the allocation of the corporate product in a time of short supply, through control of the board of directors; and it was effectively transferred in this sale by having Feldmann procure the resignation of his own board and the election of Wilport's nominees immediately upon consummation of the sale.

The present action represents the consolidation of three pending stockholders' actions in which yet another stockholder has been permitted to intervene. Jurisdiction below was based upon the diverse citizenship of the parties. Plaintiffs argue here, as they did in the court below, that in the situation here disclosed the vendors must account to the nonparticipating minority stockholders for that share of their profit which is attributable to the sale of the corporate power. Judge Hincks denied the validity of the premise, holding that the rights involved in the sale were only those normally incident

---

136. [By the Court] The stock was not held personally by Feldmann in his own name, but was held by the members of his family and by personal corporations. The aggregate of stock thus had amounted to 33% of the outstanding Newport stock and gave working control to the holder. The actual sale included 55,552 additional shares held by friends and associates of Feldmann, so that a total of 37% of the Newport stock was transferred.

to the possession of a controlling block of shares, with which a dominant stockholder, in the absence of fraud or foreseeable looting, was entitled to deal according to his own best interests. Furthermore, he held that plaintiffs had failed to satisfy their burden of proving that the sales price was not a fair price for the stock per se. Plaintiffs appeal from these rulings of law which resulted in the dismissal of their complaint.

The essential facts found by the trial judge are not in dispute. Newport was a relative newcomer in the steel industry with predominantly old installations which were in the process of being supplemented by more modern facilities. Except in times of extreme shortage Newport was not in a position to compete profitably with other steel mills for customers not in its immediate geographical area. Wilport, the purchasing syndicate, consisted of geographically remote end-users of steel who were interested in buying more steel from Newport than they had been able to obtain during recent periods of tight supply. The price of $20 per share was found by Judge Hincks to be a fair one for a control block of stock, although the over-the-counter market price had not exceeded $12 and the book value per share was $17.03. But this finding was limited by Judge Hincks' statement that "[w]hat value the block would have had if shorn of its appurtenant power to control distribution of the corporate product, the evidence does not show." It was also conditioned by his earlier ruling that the burden was on plaintiffs to prove a lesser value for the stock.

Both as director and as dominant stockholder, Feldmann stood in a fiduciary relationship to the corporation and to the minority stockholders as beneficiaries thereof. Pepper v. Litton, 308 U.S. 295, 60 S.Ct. 238, 84 L.Ed. 281. His fiduciary obligation must in the first instance be measured by the law of Indiana, the state of incorporation of Newport. Although there is no Indiana case directly in point, the most closely analogous one emphasizes the close scrutiny to which Indiana subjects the conduct of fiduciaries when personal benefit may stand in the way of fulfillment of trust obligations. In Schemmel v. Hill, 91 Ind.App. 373, 169 N.E. 678, 682, 683, McMahan, J., said: "Directors of a business corporation act in a strictly fiduciary capacity. Their office is a trust. When a director deals with his corporation, his acts will be closely scrutinized. Directors of a corporation are its agents, and they are governed by the rules of law applicable to other agents, and, as between themselves and their principal, the rules relating to honesty and fair dealing in the management of the affairs of their principal are applicable. They must not, in any degree, allow their official conduct to be swayed by their private interest, which must yield to official duty. In a transaction between a director and his corporation, where he acts for himself and his principal at the same time in a matter connected with the relation between them, it is presumed, where he is thus potential on both sides of the contract, that self-interest will overcome his fidelity to his principal, to his own benefit and to his principal's hurt." And the judge added: "Absolute and most scrupulous good faith is the very essence of a director's obligation to his corporation. The first principal duty arising from his official relation is to act in all things of trust wholly for the benefit of his corporation."

In Indiana, then, as elsewhere, the responsibility of the fiduciary is not limited to a proper regard for the tangible balance sheet assets of the corporation, but includes the dedication of his uncorrupted business judgment for the sole benefit of the corporation, in any dealings which may adversely affect it. Irving Trust Co. v. Deutsch, 2 Cir., 73 F.2d 121, certiorari denied 294 U.S. 708, 55 S.Ct. 405, 79 L.Ed. 1243; Meinhard v. Salmon, 249 N.Y. 458, 164 N.E. 545, 62 A.L.R. 1. Although the Indiana case is particularly relevant to Feldmann as a director, the same rule should apply to his fiduciary duties as majority stockholder, for in that capacity he chooses and controls the directors, and thus is held to have assumed their liability. Pepper v. Litton, supra, 308 U.S. 295, 60 S.Ct. 238. This, therefore, is the standard to which Feldmann was by law required to conform in his activities here under scrutiny.

It is true, as defendants have been at pains to point out, that this is not the ordinary case of breach of fiduciary duty. We have here no fraud, no misuse of confidential information, no outright looting of a helpless corporation. But on the other hand, we do not find compliance with that high standard which we have just stated and which we and other courts have come to expect and demand of corporate fiduciaries. In the often-quoted words of Judge Cardozo: [The Court quotes the classic language from Meinhard v. Salmon]. The actions of defendants in siphoning off for personal gain corporate advantages to be derived from a favorable market situation do not betoken the necessary undivided loyalty owed by the fiduciary to his principal.

The corporate opportunities of whose misappropriation the minority stockholders complain need not have been an absolute certainty in order to support this action against Feldmann. If there was possibility of corporate gain, they are entitled to recover. * * *

This rationale is equally appropriate to a consideration of the benefits which Newport might have derived from the steel shortage. In the past Newport had used and profited by its market leverage by operation of what the industry had come to call the "Feldmann Plan." This consisted of securing interest-free advances from prospective purchasers of steel in return for firm commitments to them from future production. The funds thus acquired were used to finance improvements in existing plants and to acquire new installations. In the summer of 1950 Newport had been negotiating for cold-rolling facilities which it needed for a more fully integrated operation and a more marketable product, and Feldmann plan funds might well have been used toward this end.

Further, as plaintiffs alternatively suggest, Newport might have used the period of short supply to build up patronage in the geographical area in which it could compete profitably even when steel was more abundant. Either of these opportunities was Newport's, to be used to its advantage only. Only if defendants had been able to negate completely any possibility of gain by Newport could they have prevailed. It is true that a trial court finding states: "Whether or not, in August, 1950, Newport's position was such that it could have entered into 'Feldmann Plan' type transactions to procure funds and financing for the further expansion and integration of its steel facilities and whether such expansion would have been desirable for Newport, the evidence does not show." This, however, cannot avail the defendants, who—contrary to the ruling below—had the burden of proof on this issue, since fiduciaries always have the burden of proof in establishing the fairness of their dealings with trust property. Pepper v. Litton, supra.

Defendants seek to categorize the corporate opportunities which might have accrued to Newport as too unethical to warrant further consideration. It is true that reputable steel producers were not participating in the gray market brought about by the Korean War and were refraining from advancing their prices, although to do so would not have been illegal. But Feldmann plan transactions were not considered within this self-imposed interdiction; the trial court found that around the time of the Feldmann sale Jones & Laughlin Steel Corporation, Republic Steel Company, and Pittsburgh Steel Corporation were all participating in such arrangements. In any event, it ill becomes the defendants to disparage as unethical the market advantages from which they themselves reaped rich benefits.

We do not mean to suggest that a majority stockholder cannot dispose of his controlling block of stock to outsiders without having to account to his corporation for profits or even never do this with impunity when the buyer is an interested customer, actual or potential, for the corporation's product. But when the sale necessarily results in a sacrifice of this element of corporate good will and consequent unusual profit to the fiduciary who has caused the sacrifice, he should account for his gains. So in a time of market shortage, where a call on a corporation's product commands an unusually large premium, in one form or another, we think it sound law that a fiduciary may not appropriate to himself the value of this premium. Such personal gain at the expense of his coventurers seems particularly reprehensible when made by the trusted president and director of his company. In this case the violation of duty seems to be all the clearer because of this triple role in which Feldmann appears, though we are unwilling to say, and are not to be understood as saying, that we should accept a lesser obligation for any one of his roles alone.

Hence to the extent that the price received by Feldmann and his code-fendants included such a bonus, he is accountable to the minority stockholders who sue here. And plaintiffs, as they contend, are entitled to a recovery in their own right, instead of in right of the corporation (as in the usual derivative actions), since neither Wilport nor their successors in interest should share in any judgment which may be rendered. See Southern Pacific Co. v. Bogert, 250 U.S. 483, 39 S.Ct. 533, 63 L.Ed. 1099. Defendants cannot well object to this form of recovery, since the only alternative, recovery for the corporation as a whole, would subject them to a greater total liability.

The case will therefore be remanded to the district court for a determination of the question expressly left open below, namely, the value of defendants' stock without the appurtenant control over the corporation's output of steel. We reiterate that on this issue, as on all others relating to a breach of fiduciary duty, the burden of proof must rest on the defendants. Judgment should go to these plaintiffs and those whom they represent for any premium value so shown to the extent of their respective stock interests.

The judgment is therefore reversed and the action remanded for further proceedings pursuant to this opinion.

SWAN, CIRCUIT JUDGE (dissenting).

With the general principles enunciated in the majority opinion as to the duties of fiduciaries I am, of course, in thorough accord. But, as Mr. Justice Frankfurter stated in Securities and Exchange Comm. v. Chenery Corp., 318 U.S. 80, 85, 63 S.Ct. 454, 458, 87 L.Ed. 626, "to say that a man is a fiduciary only begins analysis; it gives direction to further inquiry. To whom is he a fiduciary? What obligations does he owe as a fiduciary? In what respect has he failed to discharge these obligations?'' My brothers' opinion does not specify precisely what fiduciary duty Feldmann is held to have violated or whether it was a duty imposed upon him as the dominant stockholder or as a director of Newport. Without such specification I think that both the legal profession and the business world will find the decision confusing and will be unable to foretell the extent of its impact upon customary practices in the sale of stock.

The power to control the management of a corporation, that is, to elect directors to manage its affairs, is an inseparable incident to the ownership of a majority of its stock, or sometimes, as in the present instance, to the ownership of enough shares, less than a majority, to control an election. Concededly a majority or dominant shareholder is ordinarily privileged to sell his stock at the best price obtainable from the purchaser. In so doing he acts on his own behalf, not as an agent of the corporation. If he knows or has reason to believe that the purchaser intends to exercise to the detriment of the corporation the power of management acquired by the purchase, such knowledge or reasonable suspicion will terminate the dominant shareholder's privilege to sell and will create a duty not to transfer the power of management to such purchaser. The duty seems to me to resemble the obligation which everyone is under not to assist another to commit a tort rather than the obligation of a fiduciary. But whatever the nature of the duty, a violation of it will subject the violator to liability for damages sustained by the corporation. Judge Hincks found that Feldmann had no reason to think that Wilport would use the power of management it would acquire by the purchase to injure Newport, and that there was no proof that it ever was so used. Feldmann did know, it is true, that the reason Wilport wanted the stock was to put in a board of directors who would be likely to permit Wilport's members to purchase more of Newport's steel than they might otherwise be able to get. But there is nothing illegal in a dominant shareholder purchasing from his own corporation at the same prices it offers to other customers. That is what the members of Wilport did, and there is no proof that Newport suffered any detriment therefrom.

My brothers say that "the consideration paid for the stock included compensation for the sale of a corporate asset", which they describe as "the ability to control the allocation of the corporate product in a time of short supply, through control of the board of directors; and it was effectively transferred in this sale by having Feldmann procure the resignation of his own board and the election of Wilport's nominees immediately upon consummation of the sale." The implications of this are not clear to me. If it means that when market conditions are such as to induce users of a corporation's product to wish to buy a controlling block of stock in order to be able to purchase part of the corporation's output at the same mill list prices as are offered to other customers, the dominant stockholder is under a fiduciary duty not to sell his stock, I cannot agree. For reasons already stated, in my opinion Feldmann was not proved to be under any fiduciary duty as a stockholder not to sell the stock he controlled.

Feldmann was also a director of Newport. Perhaps the quoted statement means that as a director he violated his fiduciary duty in voting to elect Wilport's nominees to fill the vacancies created by the resignations of the former directors of Newport. As a director Feldmann was under a fiduciary duty to use an honest judgment in acting on the corporation's behalf. A director is privileged to resign, but so long as he remains a director he must be faithful to his fiduciary duties and must not make a personal gain from performing them. Consequently, if the price paid for Feldmann's stock included a payment for voting to elect the new directors, he must account to the corporation for such payment, even though he honestly believed that the men he voted to elect were well qualified to serve as directors. He can not take pay for performing his fiduciary duty. There is no suggestion that he did do so, unless the price paid for his stock was more than its value. So it seems to me that decision must turn on whether finding 120 and conclusion 5 of the district judge are supportable on the evidence. They are set out in the margin.[137]

Judge Hincks went into the matter of valuation of the stock with his customary care and thoroughness. He made no error of law in applying the principles relating to valuation of stock. Concededly a controlling block of stock has greater sale value than a small lot. While the spread between $10 per share for small lots and $20 per share for the controlling block seems rather extraordinarily wide, the $20 valuation was supported by the expert testimony of Dr. Badger, whom the district judge said he could not find to be wrong. I see no justification for upsetting the valuation as clearly erroneous. Nor can I agree with my brothers that the $20 valuation "was limited" by the last sentence in finding 120. The controlling block could not by any possibility be shorn of its appurtenant power to elect directors and through them to control distribution of the corporate product. It is this "appurtenant power" which gives a controlling block its value as such block. What evidence could be adduced to show the value of the block "if shorn" of such appurtenant power, I cannot conceive, for it cannot be shorn of it. * * *

The final conclusion of my brothers is that the plaintiffs are entitled to recover in their own right instead of in the right of the corporation. This appears to be completely inconsistent with the theory advanced at the outset of the opinion, namely, that the price of the stock "included compensation for the sale of a corporate asset." If a corporate asset was sold, surely the corporation should recover the compensation received for it by the defendants. Moreover, if the plaintiffs were suing in their own right, Newport was not a proper party. The case of Southern Pacific Co. v. Bogert, 250 U.S. 483, 39 S.Ct. 533, 63 L.Ed. 1099, relied upon as authority for the conclusion that the plaintiffs are entitled to recover in their own right, relates to a situation so different that the decision appears to me to be inapposite.

I would affirm the judgment on appeal.

Notes

(1) On remand, Judge Hincks took a deep breath and concluded that the "enterprise value" of a share of Newport stock was $14.67, so that Feldmann had

---

137. [By the Judge] "120. The 398,927 shares of Newport stock sold to Wilport as of August 31, 1950, had a fair value as a control block of $20 per share. What value the block would have had if shorn of its appurtenant power to control distribution of the corporate product, the evidence does not show."

"5. Even if Feldmann's conduct in cooperating to accomplish a transfer of control to Wilport immediately upon the sale constituted a breach of a fiduciary duty to Newport, no part of the moneys received by the defendants in connection with the sale constituted profits for which they were accountable to Newport."

received a premium of $5.33 per share, or a total premium of $2,126,280. The plaintiffs, representing sixty-three percent of the stock, were therefore entitled to a judgment of $1,339,769, plus interest. Perlman v. Feldmann, 154 F.Supp. 436 (D.Conn.1957).

(2) Accepting Judge Hincks' allocation, why should the recovery go to the plaintiffs personally rather than to the corporation, as would normally be the case with derivative suit recoveries? The ALI's Corporate Governance Project lists nine similar cases, and generalizes them in § 7.18(e) as follows:

> (e) The court having jurisdiction over a derivative action may direct that all or a portion of the award be paid directly to individual shareholders, on a pro-rata basis, when such a payment is equitable in the circumstances and adequate provision has been made for the creditors of the corporation.

The American Law Institute, Principles of Corporate Governance: Analysis and Recommendations § 7.18(e).[138] The explanatory text states:

> In general, when a substantial portion of the shares are held either by persons who had aided or abetted the defendants to commit the fiduciary breach or by non-contemporaneous holders who had suffered no injury because they had bought their shares at a price reflecting the injury done to the corporation, the case for a pro-rata recovery in favor of the other eligible shareholders will be strongest. However, it should not be assumed that pro-rata recovery should be granted merely because persons who committed or aided the breach remain as shareholders.
>
> A corporate recovery in such an instance does not mean that the defendants will receive unjust enrichment. To the contrary, proration of a partial recovery among other shareholders reduces the damages defendants must pay and thereby minimizes both the sanction against them and the amount of compensation that will benefit creditors and others affected by an injury to the corporation. * * *
>
> Another instance in which a pro-rata recovery is justified arises when shareholders who were earlier injured by a wrong for which they have not been adequately compensated have been eliminated as the result of a fundamental corporate change. In these circumstances, a derivative action is a more practical means by which to address such a wrong than is the appraisal remedy, because the appraisal remedy grants relief only against the corporation (and thus indirectly against its current shareholders) rather than against the alleged wrongdoer. * * *

The American Law Institute, Principles of Corporate Governance: Analysis and Recommendations Illustrations to § 7.18, at 232.

(3) In Birnbaum v. Newport Steel Corp., 193 F.2d 461 (2d Cir.1952), cert. denied, 343 U.S. 956, 72 S.Ct. 1051, 96 L.Ed. 1356 (1952), Judge A. Hand offered the following description of the facts of this case as alleged in a complaint under rule 10b–5:

> * * * [During the period June to August 1950] Follansbee Steel Corporation and Newport were negotiating for a merger of the two corporations, which merger, on the terms offered by Follansbee, would have been highly profitable to all the stockholders of Newport. However, in August of 1950, Feldmann,

---

138. Copyright (1994) by The American Law Institute. Reprinted with the permission of The American Law Institute.

acting in his official capacity as president of Newport, rejected the Follansbee offer, and on August 31, 1950, sold his stock to the defendant Wilport Company * * *. Immediately following the sale, Feldmann and the other directors of Newport resigned and * * * [persons who] were officers of and directors of Wilport took their place. * * *

Does this brief description suggest an alternative basis for grounding recovery against Feldmann? Incidentally, the rule 10b–5 complaint was ultimately dismissed because the plaintiff was neither a purchaser nor a seller of securities.

(4) Is it desirable for courts to evolve a single, consistent position with respect to premiums paid for controlling shares? (To date they have not done so.) At least the following arguments seem defensible:

(a) In the absence of fraud or foreseeable looting, a person may sell his or her property for what he can get or refuse to sell it at all. That is what economic freedom is all about. (A number of cases, like *Zetlin*, have adopted this position which is the dominant position today.)

(b) A purchaser is really seeking control of the corporate assets when he buys the controlling shares. If he wants the assets, he should buy them from the corporation, in which case, all the shareholders would receive the same amount per share. In effect, this translates all sale of control cases into corporate opportunity cases. (Some courts have adopted this position, particularly where the purchasers first approached the corporation seeking to buy its assets, and the controlling shareholder proposes a stock deal. See, e.g., Commonwealth Title Ins. & Trust Co. v. Seltzer, 227 Pa. 410, 76 A. 77 (1910).)

(c) If it is part of the deal for the selling shareholder to resign his position with the corporation (as it almost always is), that is what the premium *really* is for. This approach in effect translates virtually all sale of control cases into sale of corporate office cases. (Some courts have tried this approach, particularly where the premium is set aside and its payment is made contingent on the resignations. E.g., Porter v. Healy, 244 Pa. 427, 91 A. 428 (1914).)

(d) It is simply immoral for a shareholder knowingly to take a greater price for his shares than other shareholders, since each share is actually identical with every other share. The additional amount must be for the control and that should belong to the corporation. See, e.g., David Cowan Bayne, The Noninvestment Value of Control Stock, 45 Ind.L.J. 317 (1970).

(5) William D. Andrews, The Stockholder's Right to Equal Opportunity in the Sale of Shares, 78 Harv.L.Rev. 505, 515–17 (1965)[139]; suggests the following "rule":

> The rule to be considered can be stated thus: whenever a controlling stockholder sells his shares, every other holder of shares (of the same class) is entitled to have an equal opportunity to sell his shares, or a prorata part of them, on substantially the same terms. Or in terms of the correlative duty: before a controlling stockholder may sell his shares to an outsider he must assure his fellow stockholders an equal opportunity to sell their shares, or as high a proportion of theirs as he ultimately sells of his own. * * *

> Now let us look briefly at what the rule means. First, it neither compels nor prohibits a sale of stock at any particular price; it leaves a controlling stockholder wholly free to decide for himself the price above which he will sell and below which he will hold his shares. The rule only says that in executing

---

139. Copyright © 1965 by the Harvard Law Review Association.

his decision to sell, a controlling stockholder cannot sell pursuant to a purchase offer more favorable than any available to other stockholders. Second, the rule does not compel a prospective purchaser to make an open offer for all shares on the same terms. He can offer to purchase shares on the condition that he gets a certain proportion of the total. Or he can even make an offer to purchase 51 percent of the shares, no more and no less. The only requirement is that his offer, whatever it may be, be made equally or proportionately available to all stockholders. * * *

Do you think this is a sensible solution to the control premium problem? Several courts have rejected the rule, one describing it as, "while nice theoretically, * * * simply not the law;" Clagett v. Hutchison, 583 F.2d 1259 (4th Cir.1978).

(9) Frank H. Easterbrook & Larry R. Fischel, The Economic Structure of Corporate Law 117–18 (1991):

A sharing requirement also may make an otherwise profitable transaction unattractive to the prospective seller of control. Suppose the owner of a control bloc of shares finds that his perquisites or the other amenities of his position are worth $10. A prospective acquirer of control concludes that, by eliminating these perquisites and other amenities, it could produce a gain of $15. The shareholders in the company benefit if the acquirer pays a premium of $11 to the owner of the controlling bloc, ousts the current managers, and makes the improvements. The net gains of $4 inure to each investor according to his holdings, and although the acquirer obtains the largest portion because it holds the largest bloc, no one is left out. If the owner of the control bloc must share the $11 premium with all of the existing shareholders, however, the deal collapses. The owner will not part with his bloc for less than a $10 premium. A sharing requirement would make the deal unprofitable to him, and the other investors would lose the prospective gain from the installation of better managers.

Compare Robert W. Hamilton, Private Sale of Control Transactions: Where We Stand Today, 36 Case Western Res.L.Rev. 248, 256–57 (1985):

There are several problems with this kind of analysis, however. The hypothetical the authors create assumes the correctness of their thesis. The assumption [is] that the purchasers of control will reduce the "perquisites or the other amenities" enjoyed as a result of the seller's position by $10, thereby producing a corporate gain of $15, * * *. One can equally plausibly assume that the buyer feels that he can enjoy the same "perquisites or the other amenities" as the seller enjoyed, and even increase them to, for instance, $14. On this assumption, the minority shareholders are clearly worse off as a result of the sale, and both the purchaser and seller of the control shares are benefiting at the minority shareholders' expense. * * *

There is another problem with the Easterbrook–Fischel hypothetical. Assume that the control stock sold in the hypothetical consists of 55% of the outstanding shares; if the buyers are content to allow the $15 increase in value to remain in the corporation, they will obtain 55% of the $15 increase in value by reason of their 55% stock ownership, or $8.25. In other words, if they abandon the "perquisites and other amenities," they will pay $11 in order to obtain an increase in investment value of only $8.25. They would obviously be better off if they retain the sellers' "percs" worth $10 and seek to squeeze out another couple of dollars here and there from additional "percs," rather than eliminating the "percs." * * *

The basic question is: If the new purchasers are rational profit maximizers, why should they share the $15 increase in value with the minority? It is not true that minority shareholders always share ratably in all increases in value with the majority shareholders. It would appear to be rational (and certainly practical) to place the minority shareholders on "starvation returns" from the corporation while increasing salaries or other "percs" to the new controlling shareholders in order to obtain all the additional $15 in gains. Why should the minority be given any of it? Starvation returns may also persuade the minority to sell their shares at low prices to the majority so that at some time thereafter the purchasers may own all of the outstanding shares and obtain all of the benefits of their skills. In short, I do not view hypothetical examples, such as those put forth by Easterbrook and Fischel, to prove anything more than that there *may be* idealized situations where everyone is better off as a result of the transfer of control; they do not prove that there are such situations, or their frequency.

(10) For a fresh analysis of all aspects of the sale of control issue, see Einer Elhauge, The Triggering Function of Sale of Control Doctrine, 59 U. Chi. L. Rev. 1465 (1992). Professor Elhauge suggests that present doctrine—apparently riven between two inconsistent approaches, represented on the one hand by equal sharing and on the other by the deregulatory school—in fact works satisfactorily in practice. Elhauge argues that the choice that courts must make when selecting between the two approaches is based on a classification of cases that effectively avoids, on the one hand, underdeterring harmful transfers of control and, on the other, overdeterring beneficial transfers of control.

PETITION OF CAPLAN

Supreme Court of New York, Appellate Division, First Department, 1964.
20 A.D.2d 301, 246 N.Y.S.2d 913.

STEUER, JUSTICE.

On March 8, 1963, Defiance Industries, Inc. entered into a transaction with Roy Cohn which, though unusual in form, amounted to a deferred sale of 55,000 shares of Lionel Corporation then owned by Cohn. * * * The 55,000 shares constituted 3% of the outstanding stock of Lionel Corporation.

The board of directors of Lionel consisted of ten directors, of whom Cohn was one. Six of the other directors were his nominees. Just how his holdings, amounting to 3%, enabled him to have this representation does not appear. Immediately after making the contract, these six directors resigned and their places were filled by nominees of Defiance.

On October 9, 1963, Defiance sold its interest in the above-described contract to A.M. Sonnabend, the transaction to close October 23, 1963. It was a condition of that agreement that prior to closing the six Defiance directors should be replaced by nominees of Sonnabend. On October 16 this was done. On November 14, 1963, Cohn resigned as a director and was replaced by a Sonnabend nominee. All of these changes in the board were effected by the directors filling the vacancy as each was created by resignation.

This proceeding is brought by a stockholder of Lionel to set aside and vacate the elections of the seven directors so elected. Special Term found the elections to be illegal and vacated them. With this finding and disposition we are in accord. The underlying principle is that the management of a corporation is not the subject of trade and cannot be bought apart from actual stock control (McClure v. Law, 161 N.Y. 78, 55 N.E. 388). Where there has been a transfer of the majority of the stock, or even such a percentage as gives working control, a change of directors by resignation and filling of vacancies is proper (Barnes v. Brown, 80 N.Y. 527). Here no claim was made that the stock interest which changed hands even approximated the percentage necessary to validate the substitution. * * *

All concur.

Notes

(1) Carter v. Muscat, 21 A.D.2d 543, 251 N.Y.S.2d 378 (1964), involved seriatim resignations of directors in connection with transfer of 9.7 percent of the outstanding shares. Full disclosure of the change in control was made to the shareholders and some of the new directors were thereafter reelected at annual shareholders meetings. After quoting from *Petition of Caplan,* the Court said: "When a situation involving less than 50% of the ownership of stock exists, the question of what percentage of ownership of stock is sufficient to constitute working control is likely to be a matter of fact, at least in most circumstances." 21 A.D.2d at 545, 251 N.Y.S.2d at 381. The change in control was upheld, the Court relying on the disclosure, the absence of objection, and the subsequent election of directors as "endorsements" of the substituted directors.

(2) The independence of directors, of course, has increased significantly since the early 1960s. What would happen today if a modern board of directors predominantly composed of outside directors (many of whom are CEOs or former CEOs of other corporations) were presented by management with the request that they resign seriatim and vote to replace sitting directors with a new slate of individuals who are strangers to the board members?

(3) The validity of contract provisions requiring seriatim resignations of directors in connection with sales of small percentages of voting shares also may arise in the context of breach of contract suits between the buyer and seller, rather than suits brought by shareholders not party to the contract. The leading case is Essex Universal Corp. v. Yates, 305 F.2d 572 (2d Cir.1962), involving a contract to sell about 28 percent of the stock of the corporation with the additional requirement that sellers deliver the resignations of a majority of the board of directors and cause the election of successors nominated by the purchaser at the closing. The defendants argued that the contract was against public policy because of the provisions relating to the transfer of directorships. The case was complicated by reason of the *Erie* doctrine: The panel of the Second Circuit was forced to divine New York law in the absence of any really controlling precedent. A majority of the panel refused to find the contract invalid on its face. Judge Friendly, starting from a somewhat different perspective, suggested tentatively that "if I were sitting on the New York Court of Appeals, I would hold a provision like Paragraph 6 violative of public policy save when it was entirely plain that a new election would be a mere formality, such as where the seller owned more than 50% of the stock." See also Goode v. Powers, 97 Ariz. 75, 397 P.2d 56 (1964), where the purchasers of a 25 percent interest in the voting shares of an insurance company were sued for the balance of the agreed purchase price. The defendants argued that the stock was only inherently worth $200 per share, but was sold for $500 per share because of the transfer of control provisions. Not surprisingly, this argument was rejected by the Court. In general terms, there seems to be no reason to permit a party to a contract to avoid its commitment on the theory that

the agreement may injure other parties unless those parties actually complain of injury.

(4) Section 14(f) of the Securities Exchange Act of 1934, added in 1970, provides that if there is an "arrangement or understanding" with persons acquiring more than five percent of the stock of an issuer by tender offer or purchase, by which "any persons are to be elected or designated as directors of the issuer, otherwise than at a meeting of security holders, and the persons so elected or designated will constitute a majority of the directors," the issuer must disseminate certain information to all holders of record entitled to vote at a meeting (and to the SEC). The information must identify the persons to whom control was transferred, describe the transaction by which control was transferred, the source of any consideration paid, the identity of the new directors, transactions with the issuer, the remuneration to be paid to directors and management, and the amount of securities held by principal shareholders. Rule 14f–1, 17 C.F.R. § 240.14f–1 (1997). Do you believe that such disclosure provides ample protection? What other kind of approach might be adopted by courts or by Congress? What about *Petition of Caplan,* where control was based on three percent of the outstanding shares?

Chapter Thirteen

INDEMNIFICATION AND INSURANCE

A. A. Sommer, Jr., Review of Olson and Hatch, Director and Officer Liability: Indemnification and Insurance, 47 Bus. Law. 355, 355–56 (1991),[1] captures the importance of the principles discussed in this Chapter:

> Before the onset of * * * litigation, directors are usually unconcerned with the mundane details of the corporation's indemnification provisions, the limitations upon indemnification permitted under state law or the terms of the corporation's directors' and officers' liability policy ("lawyer stuff!", they say). Let the complaint be filed naming him (or her), and here this reviewer speaks from personal experience as a director, and then those matters assume consuming importance, for on them may depend the prosperity of the director's future and the comfort of his or her retirement years. At that point limits on the ability of the corporation to indemnify, or even to advance expenses (most important given the costs of litigation and the increasing insistence by lawyers upon ongoing payments), and the exclusionary clauses of the D & O policy are examined with all the attention and devotion, and parsed as carefully for every nuance, as were once youthful love letters.

MERRITT–CHAPMAN & SCOTT CORP. v. WOLFSON

Superior Court of Delaware, 1974.
321 A.2d 138.

BALICK, JUDGE.

These actions arise over claims of Louis Wolfson, Elkin Gerbert, Joseph Kosow and Marshal Staub (claimants) for indemnification by Merritt–Chapman & Scott Corporation (MCS) against expenses incurred in a criminal action. All parties seek summary judgment.

Claimants were charged by indictment with participation in a plan to cause MCS to secretly purchase hundreds of thousands of shares of its own common stock. Count one charged all claimants with conspiracy to violate federal securities laws. Count two charged Wolfson and count three charged Gerbert with perjury before the Securities and Exchange Commission (SEC).

---

1. Copyright (1991) by the American Bar Association. All rights reserved. Reprinted with permission of the American Bar Association and its Section of Corporation, Banking and Business Law.

Counts four and five charged Wolfson, Gerbert, and Staub with filing false annual reports for 1962 and 1963 respectively with the SEC and New York Stock Exchange.

At the first trial the court dismissed part of the conspiracy count but the jury returned guilty verdicts on all charges against all claimants. At that stage this court held that Wolfson, Gerbert, and Kosow were not entitled to partial indemnification. Merritt–Chapman & Scott v. Wolfson, 264 A.2d 358 (Del.Super.1970). Thereafter the convictions were reversed. United States v. Wolfson, 437 F.2d 862 (2d Cir.1970).

There were two retrials of the perjury and filing false annual report charges against Wolfson and Gerbert. At the first retrial the court entered a judgment of acquittal on count four at the end of the State's case, and the jury could not agree on the other counts. At the second retrial the jury returned a guilty verdict on count three, but could not agree further.

The charges were then settled as follows: Wolfson entered a plea of *nolo contendere* to count five and the other charges against him were dropped. He was fined $10,000 and given a suspended sentence of eighteen months. Gerbert agreed not to appeal his conviction of count three, on which he was fined $2,000 and given a suspended sentence of eighteen months, and the other charges against him were dropped. The prosecution also dropped the charges against Kosow and Staub.

Indemnification of corporate agents involved in litigation is the subject of legislation in Delaware. Title 8 Delaware Code § 145. Subsection (a), which permits indemnification, and subsection (c), which requires indemnification, provide as follows:

(a) A corporation may indemnify any person who was or is a party or is threatened to be made a party to any threatened, pending or completed action, suit or proceeding, whether civil, criminal, administrative or investigative (other than an action by or in the right of the corporation) by reason of the fact that he is or was a director, officer, employee or agent of the corporation, or is or was serving at the request of the corporation as a director, officer, employee or agent of another corporation, partnership, joint venture, trust or other enterprise, against expenses (including attorneys' fees), judgments, fines and amounts paid in settlement actually and reasonably incurred by him in connection with such action, suit or proceeding if he acted in good faith and in a manner he reasonably believed to be in or not opposed to the best interests of the corporation, and, with respect to any criminal action or proceeding, had no reasonable cause to believe his conduct was unlawful. The termination of any action, suit or proceeding by judgment, order, settlement, conviction, or upon a plea of *nolo contendere* or its equivalent, shall not, of itself, create a presumption that the person did not act in good faith and in a manner which he reasonably believed to be in or not opposed to the best interests of the corporation, and, with respect to any criminal action or proceeding, had reasonable cause to believe that his conduct was unlawful. * * *

(c) To the extent that a director, officer, employee or agent of a corporation has been successful on the merits or otherwise in defense of any action, suit or proceeding referred to in [subsection (a)], or in defense of any claim, issue or matter therein, he shall be indemnified against expenses (including attorneys' fees) actually and reasonably incurred by him in connection therewith.

The policy of the statute and its predecessor has been described as follows, Folk, The Delaware General Corporation Law, 98 (1972):

The invariant policy of Delaware legislation on indemnification is to "promote the desirable end that corporate officials will resist what they consider" unjustified suits and claims, "secure in the knowledge that their reasonable expenses will be borne by the corporation they have served if they are vindicated." Beyond that, its larger purpose is "to encourage capable men to serve as corporate directors, secure in the knowledge that expenses incurred by them in upholding their honesty and integrity as directors will be borne by the corporation they serve."

MCS argues that the statute and sound public policy require indemnification only where there has been vindication by a finding or concession of innocence. It contends that the charges against claimants were dropped for practical reasons, not because of their innocence, and that in light of the conspiracy charged in the indictment, the judgment of acquittal on count four alone is not vindication.

The statute requires indemnification to the extent that the claimant "has been successful on the merits or otherwise." Success is vindication. In a criminal action, any result other than conviction must be considered success. Going behind the result, as MCS attempts, is neither authorized by subsection (c) nor consistent with the presumption of innocence.

The statute does not require complete success. It provides for indemnification to the extent of success "in defense of any claim, issue or matter" in an action. Claimants are therefore entitled to partial indemnification if successful on a count of an indictment, which is an independent criminal charge, even if unsuccessful on another, related count. * * *

Notes

(1) In its opinion in the earlier proceeding, 264 A.2d 358, 360 (Del.Super.1970), the Court described the purpose of § 145 as follows:

Indemnification statutes were enacted in Delaware, and elsewhere, to induce capable and responsible businessmen to accept positions in corporate management. [§ 145] is a new statute, enacted to clarify its predecessor, and to give vindicated directors and others involved in corporate affairs a judicially enforcible right to indemnification.

It would be anomalous, indeed, and diametrically opposed to the spirit and purpose of the statute and sound public policy to extend the benefits of indemnification to these defendants under the circumstances of this case. * * *

If the corporation had wished, could it have indemnified Wolfson and Gerbert for the expenses incurred in connection with the claims on which they pleaded nolo contendere? See MBCA § 8.51(c).

(2) As a practical matter, the grant of broad indemnification rights to directors is important—nay, virtually essential—if a publicly held corporation is to persuade desirable individuals to serve as directors. Such individuals are usually

experienced, relatively affluent, and able to command significant salaries in their chosen professions. They are also apt to be relatively risk adverse and quite aware of the growth in litigation against directors, particularly in situations involving defensive tactics in takeovers in derivative litigation involving judicial review of difficult business decisions generally. While fees paid to directors may seem relatively generous, they do not begin to cover the out-of-pocket costs, incurred by a director who is named as a defendant in any major litigation. The decision by the Delaware Supreme Court in *Van Gorkom* (p. 684 supra) doubtless contributed to the concern of directors about personal liability generally and the need for iron-clad indemnification rights against the corporation in particular. The elimination of most due care liability by statutory provisions such as Del.Gen.Corp.Law § 102(b)(7) obviously helps to reduce the overall risk but does not entirely eliminate the need for indemnification from the standpoint of a person considering whether to become a director of a publicly held corporation. Why not?

(3) The need for indemnification to attract directors seems clearest in the case of litigation that ultimately vindicates the actions of the director on the merits. However, reflection should also indicate that a test requiring complete vindication on the merits is too narrow. For example, should directors be entitled to indemnification for costs if a settlement is available that involves a relatively nominal payment to the plaintiffs and their attorneys? Should not the corporation and the defendant directors be able to settle nuisance suits by nominal payments to or on behalf of the plaintiffs without shifting litigation costs from the corporation back to the defendant directors? Can one distinguish such settlements from situations where directors settle because the probability that they will lose is high? Should there be indemnification in such cases? Questions such as these raise the fundamental issue of what should be the outside limits of the power of indemnification.

(4) In In re Landmark Land Co. of Carolina, Inc., 76 F.3d 553 (4th Cir.1996), the board of directors of a bank holding company adopted a resolution determining that directors had acted in good faith and should be indemnified shortly before the board was replaced by directors appointed by the Resolution Trust Company. The new board withdrew the earlier resolutions. The court held that a determination of good faith by a board of directors was not conclusive, that a court may draw an inference of bad faith from the facts found by the court and that improper indemnification payments could be recovered by the corporation. In another case involving similar issues, the Court held that a director who settles an administrative proceeding by the voluntary payment of a fine has conclusively established that he did not act in good faith and indemnification is not permitted (even though apparently authorized by a broadly phrased by-law provision). Waltuch v. Conticommodity Services, Inc., 88 F.3d 87 (2d Cir. 1996). The *Waltuch* court also held that success "on the merits or otherwise" means not being required to pay anything; the fact that other similarly situated defendants did make payments in a settlement was not relevant.

(5) Subchapter E of Chapter 8 of the MBCA (§§ 8.50–8.59) attempts to define the scope of permissible indemnification. This subchapter is a complex series of sections that should be read carefully: It cannot be adequately digested in a single reading, or even in two readings. These sections are similar to § 146 of the Delaware statute, quoted in part in *Wolfson*; the division of a single section into ten separate sections was designed to improve its readability and comprehensibility. Subchapter E was significantly amended in 1994 to integrate it with MBCA § 2.02(b)(4), authorizing a corporation to limit the liability of directors by charter amendments:

Liability limitation insulates the director from personal liability for acts or omissions that have not yet occurred but that might otherwise give rise to personal liability. Indemnification protects the director from personal liability for acts or omissions that occurred in the past. Both liability limitation and indemnification shift from the director to the corporation the ultimate economic cost for the director's acts or omissions. Both liability limitations and indemnification, therefore, are addressed to the issue of allocation, between the directors and the corporation, of the economic cost of certain actual or alleged wrongful conduct by a director.

Is this analogy a plausible basis for establishing principles for indemnification for prior acts or omissions?

(6) The policy considerations underlying the MBCA indemnification provisions are described as follows:

Indemnification (including advance for expenses) provides financial protection by the corporation for its directors against exposure to expenses and liabilities incurred by them in connection with legal proceedings based on an alleged breach of duty in their service to or on behalf of the corporation. Today, when both the volume and the cost of litigation have increased dramatically, it would be difficult to persuade responsible persons to serve as directors if they were compelled to bear personally the cost of vindicating the propriety of their conduct in every instance in which it might be challenged. While reasonable people may differ as to what constitutes a meritorious case, almost all would agree that corporate directors should have some protection against personal risk and that the rule of *New York Dock Co. v. McCollom*, 173 Misc. 106, 16 N.Y.S.2d 844 (Sup.Ct.1939), which denied reimbursement to the directors who successfully defended their case on the merits, should as a matter of policy be overruled by statute.

The concept of indemnification recognizes that there will be situations in which the director does not satisfy all of the elements of the standard of conduct set forth in section 8.30(a) or the requirements of some other applicable law but where the corporation should nevertheless be permitted (or required) to absorb the economic costs of any ensuing litigation. A carefully constructed indemnification statute should identify these situations.

If permitted too broadly, however, indemnification may violate equally basic tenets of public policy. It is inappropriate to permit management to use corporate funds to avoid the consequences of certain conduct. For example, a director who intentionally inflicts harm on the corporation should not expect to receive assistance from the corporation for legal or other expenses and should be required to satisfy from his personal assets not only any adverse judgment but also expenses incurred in connection with the proceeding. Any other rule would tend to encourage socially undesirable conduct.

A further policy issue is raised in connection with indemnification against liabilities or sanctions imposed under state or federal civil or criminal statutes. A shift of the economic cost of these liabilities from the individual director or officer to the corporation by way of indemnification may in some instances frustrate the public policy of those statutes.

The fundamental issue that must be addressed by an indemnification statute is the establishment of policies consistent with these broad principles: to ensure that indemnification is permitted only where it will further accepted corporate policies and to prohibit indemnification where it might protect or encourage wrongful or improper conduct. As phrased by one commentator, the goal of indemnification is to "seek the middle ground between encouraging fiduciaries to violate their trust, and discouraging them from serving at all." Joseph F. Johnston, "Corporate Indemnification and Liability Insurance for Directors and Officers," 33 Bus.Law 1993, 1994 (1978). The increasing number of suits against directors, the increasing cost of defense, and the increasing emphasis on diversifying the membership of boards of directors all militate in favor of workable arrangements to protect directors against liability to the extent consistent with broad public policy.

Introductory Comment to Subchapter E.[2]

(7) When read carefully, Subchapter E contains some surprises and some questionable value judgments about the circumstances in which indemnification may be permitted, the persons who can decide whether to grant indemnification, and the time when indemnification payments may be made.

(a) Compare MBCA §§ 8.51, 8.52, and 8.53. What are the relationships among these three sections?

(b) MBCA § 8.52 requires that a corporation indemnify a director "who was wholly successful, on the merits or otherwise." The word "wholly" was added to reverse the result in the principal case. Does it? More basically, consider the phrase "on the merits *or otherwise.*" Does this really mean what it says? For example, assume that a director is charged with egregious criminal conduct that seriously harms the corporation. She concedes that she engaged in the conduct but defends successfully on the ground that the statute of limitations has run. Should she be entitled to indemnification as a matter of right? She clearly is under MBCA § 8.52, the theory being that a person with a valid procedural defense should not be required to proceed to a trial on the merits, which may be prolonged and expensive, in order to establish eligibility for indemnification.

(c) Consider a director who has probably violated § 16(b). A demand is made, and the director consults an attorney, who advises the director to repay the profits to the corporation and sends a bill for legal services rendered. The director repays the profits and then requests the corporation to pay the attorney. May the corporation do so without court approval under MBCA § 8.51 on the theory that the director acted in "good faith" and in a manner he reasonably believed to be "*not opposed to* [the] best interests [of the corporation]?" MBCA § 8.51(d)(2) was obviously designed to prevent indemnification in § 16(b), rule 10b–5, and other cases where the defendant is found liable after a trial but the corporation is arguably not injured. It seems clear on the literal language of the statute, however, that the director who makes voluntary repayment is not precluded from indemnification in this situation since nothing has been "adjudged," one way or the other.

(d) Who is to make decisions about optional indemnification? See MBCA § 8.55. Is there any requirement that a court or the shareholders be advised that the corporation has decided to indemnify someone? See MBCA § 16.21(a).

(e) Under what circumstances can a director be indemnified for a criminal fine (as contrasted with expenses incurred in connection with a criminal proceeding)? See MBCA §§ 8.51(a)(1)(iii), 8.51(c), 8.54.

2. Reprinted from *Model Business Corporation Act Annotated* (Third Edition) with the permission of Prentice Hall Law & Business.

(f) If a director defends a proceeding to the bitter end and a judgment is entered against him, he is entitled to indemnification for either expenses only, or the judgment plus expenses, only with court approval. See MBCA §§ 8.51(d), 8.54. What if he fears he may lose and offers to settle? Who determines whether he is entitled to indemnification in connection with the settlement? See MBCA § 8.55. Do you think these persons may be more favorably disposed toward the director or officer than a judge?

(g) Assume that a director is called as a witness before a grand jury in connection with corporate matters. He hires counsel, appears as a witness, but is never notified that he is a target of the investigation or indicted. Must his expenses be paid by the corporation? Cf. MBCA § 8.58(d).

(h) Most boards of directors include some directors who are officers of the corporation as well as some who are not. Is there any difference in the power or duty of a corporation to indemnify outside directors as contrasted with director/officers? Between officers who are directors and officers who are not? See MBCA § 8.56. The Official Comment makes clear that the indemnification of officers, employees and agents of a corporation are purely matters of contract: "It would be presumptuous for a corporation statute to seek to limit the indemnification bargain that a corporation may wish to make with those it hires or retains. The same standards applicable to directors and officers may not be appropriate for office workers and hazardous waste workers, brokers and custodians, engineers and farm workers."

(i) Assume that a director is also an executive of a trade association or the trustee of an employee pension trust. Presumably these positions were assumed either at the request of the corporation or with its implicit approval. May that director seek indemnification *from the corporation* for expenses or liabilities incurred while serving the trade association or pension trust? See MBCA §§ 8.50(2), 8.50(6), 8.51(b).

(j) What is the difference between a "determination" of indemnification under MBCA § 8.55(b) and an "authorization" of indemnification under MBCA § 8.55(c)?

(8) What about indemnification of directors in derivative suits brought by shareholders in the name of the corporation? See MBCA § 8.51(d)(1), added in 1994. See also James J. Hanks, Evaluating Recent State Legislation on Director and Officer Liability Limitation and Indemnification, 43 Bus.Law. 1207, 1221, 1240 (1988):

> At least ten states * * * have enacted statutes expanding the right of corporations to indemnify their directors for expenses, settlements, and adverse judgments in derivative suits. * * * The most far-reaching statutory developments affecting derivative suits are provisions eliminating or substantially eliminating the distinction between third-party and derivative suits and permitting indemnification against judgments, settlements, and expenses for any director or officer who meets the general statutory standards for indemnification without a requirement of court approval.[3] * * *

---

3. [By the Author] These standards typically require good faith conduct, reasonable belief that the individual's conduct was in or not opposed to the corporation's best interests, and in a criminal proceeding, no reason to believe the individual's conduct was unlawful. E.g., * * * Model Business Corp. Act § 8.51(a) (1984); Md. Corps. & Ass'ns Code Ann. § 2–418(b)(1) (1985 & Supp.1987). These statutory standards for indemnification differ from the typical statutory standards of conduct for directors by omitting the requirement for the care of an ordinarily prudent person in similar circumstances and by modifying the reasonable

In the absence of any applicable liability limitation, the disadvantage of permitting indemnification against settlements and adverse judgments and derivative suits is its circularity. Any money recovered from the director or officer is paid, less the stockholders' attorneys' fees, by the individual to the corporation, which then returns the money, together with reimbursement for the individual's legal expenses, to the individual as indemnification. Although the individual is made whole, the corporation winds up paying not only the amount of the loss but also the stockholders' and individual's attorneys' fees and costs. Thus, the corporation is actually in a worse economic position than if it had simply sustained the loss without the cost of recovery and consequent reimbursement. The real beneficiaries of circular indemnification are the stockholders' lawyers. Since the corporation's loss really belongs to the stockholders, no rational stockholder would initiate a derivative suit unless the corporation were able to pass the risk along to an insurance company. Of course, it was the unavailability of affordable insurance that gave rise to the search for legislative solutions in the first place.

Moreover, while statutes may permit a corporation to indemnify a director or officer held liable for negligence in a derivative suit, they do not * * * require indemnification. Thus, unless the charter or by-laws require indemnification in such circumstances, the individual is left in a state of uncertainty as to whether indemnification will actually be authorized in his particular case. This type of uncertainty has caused many directors to leave corporate boards. While expanded indemnifiability helps directors and officers by giving them at least one source of reimbursement (assuming the corporation can afford to pay at the time of the loss), it will not provide any relief for the insurance carriers.

Mr. Hanks was discussing developments in indemnification that occurred essentially between 1984 and 1988. These four years were tumultuous times for directors, with widely publicized cases imposing liability on directors, the "drying up" of liability insurance, and the enactment of state statutes limiting the monetary liability of directors.

(9) Mr. Hanks also summarizes developments with respect to exclusivity of the statutory test for indemnification:

At least twenty-nine states have recently expanded the provisions of their indemnification statutes permitting corporations to provide rights [broader] than [statutory] indemnification by charter, by-law, board resolution, contract, or otherwise. * * * The broad form of nonexclusivity provision has been typified by section 145(f) of the Delaware General Corporation Law, which provides that statutory indemnification "shall not be deemed exclusive of any other rights to which those seeking indemnification or advancement of expenses may be entitled under any by-law, agreement * * * or otherwise." * * *

The narrow form of nonexclusivity provision was formerly typified by Maryland, which until earlier this year * * * was based upon [old § 8.58(a) of MBCA (1984) which provided that a provision "is valid only if and to the

belief requirement in the indemnification standards to require only a reasonable belief that the director's conduct "was at least not opposed to [the corporation's] best interests" in the case of conduct not in the director's official capacity. E.g., * * * Model Business Corp. Act § 8.30(a) (1984).

extent the provision is consistent with this subchapter."] The official comment to section 8.58(a) notes that the nonexclusive statutory provisions, such as Delaware's, make "no attempt to limit the non-statutory creation of rights of indemnification. This kind of language is subject to misconstruction * * * since non-statutory conceptions of public policy limit the power of the corporation to indemnify or to contract to indemnify directors." * * *

> The Maryland statute has been changed to state specifically that indemnification "shall not be deemed exclusive of any other rights, by indemnification or otherwise, to which a director [or officer] may be entitled." * * *

> In states like Delaware and Maryland, which have no express limits in their nonexclusivity provisions, there is always the possibility—probably the likelihood—that a court will add its own public policy limits. Thus, the outer parameters of these provisions will always be unclear. * * *

> Finally, in the past two years, Delaware, Maryland, New York, Pennsylvania, and several other states have amended their statutes to add advancement of expenses to indemnification in their nonexclusivity provisions. * * *

43 Bus.Law. at 1224–26. The 1994 amendments explicitly made the MBCA indemnification provisions exclusive. See MBCA § 8.59. Consider, however, MBCA § 8.58. In your judgment, which is preferable: leaving the outer limits to the "wall of public policy," or defining it as in Subchapter E?

(10) Indemnification statutes permit the corporation to purchase insurance for directors and officers "whether or not the corporation would have the power to indemnify * * * against the same liability under this subchapter." MBCA § 8.57. Liability insurance (usually called D & O insurance) is discussed later in this chapter. However, such insurance became extremely expensive (or even not available at any price) during the mid–1980s, and alternative sources of reimbursement essentially amounting to self-insurance were created. Examples include "captive" insurance subsidiaries, "captive" insurance companies formed by industry groups, trust funds, letters of credit, guaranties, and sureties. Virtually all of these devices amount to self-insurance, since the corporation remains the ultimate source of payment. In other words it is indemnification under another name, but with funds set aside in advance or protection purchased in advance from outside sources.

43 Bus.Law. at 1230–31. The justification for these alternative sources of reimbursement may be traced in Louisiana and Texas to the impact of the 1980s decline of oil prices on publicly held but marginally financed energy companies. By the middle of the 1980s, insolvency and bankruptcy reorganization of many of these companies was a strong possibility. What is the status of indemnification rights in bankruptcy? In the absence of alternative reimbursement sources, the answer just about has to be that the director entitled to indemnification is merely one more unsecured creditor. To a potential director in a marginal or shaky corporation, therefore, an unsecured right to indemnification in a marginal company is almost worthless since there can be no assurance that either advance or ultimate indemnification is going to be available when needed. This justification for authorizing alternative sources of reimbursement was persuasive in about ten states.

DIANE H. MAZUR, INDEMNIFICATION OF DIRECTORS IN ACTIONS DIRECTLY BY THE CORPORATION: MUST THE CORPORATION FINANCE ITS OPPONENT'S DEFENSE?

19 J.Corp.L. 201, 202–205 (1994).

Anyone outside the world of corporate law might not believe it. To Public Service Company of New Mexico, the largest public corporation in the state, it was all too serious. Public Service Company of New Mexico, commonly known as 'PNM' within the state, had sued three of its former executives, including its former president and chairman of the board of directors, for breach of their duties of loyalty to the corporation. The company alleged that the former executives had diverted approximately five million dollars of corporate funds for their personal benefit in the form of improper bonuses, personal consulting contracts, and retirement benefits.

However, six months after the company filed suit, the state district court hearing the case ruled that the company would have to pay dearly for the opportunity to recover the money. Under the court's interpretation of New Mexico statutory law, the company's bylaws, and the executives' contracts with the company, PNM would have to pay all attorneys' fees and expenses for all the defendants, in addition to its own. The defendants would not even have to 'run a tab' for reimbursement at a later date; the company was ordered to pay all legal bills submitted by the defendants' three law firms on a monthly basis, within two days of demand.

Although the company filed suit against its former executives in 1991, the suit arose out of prior litigation that began almost two years earlier. PNM is a utility company providing electric, gas, and water service throughout New Mexico. In early 1989, a class-action group of shareholders sued PNM for securities law violations, alleging that PNM either misrepresented or failed to disclose material facts in its public documents, resulting in an artificially inflated value of PNM stock. The alleged misrepresentations and omissions largely fell in two areas: PNM's excess electric generating capacity and PNM's investments in real estate and other non-utility businesses.

PNM anticipated that shareholder derivative suits alleging mismanagement in the same two areas were soon to come, and as a result, the company appointed a 'special litigation committee' (SLC) to investigate the potential claims.[4] * * *

[I]n the process of investigating the non-utility investment claims, the SLC also reviewed the compensation paid to senior executives, an issue which the shareholders had not raised. The SLC concluded that several executives had steered corporate funds to themselves through improper bonuses, personal consulting contracts, and retirement benefits. The committee directed PNM to file its own suit for recovery.

In response to the suit that charged them with improper personal benefit, the executives demanded that PNM begin to finance their defense. They

---

4. [By the Author] Report of the Special Litigation Committee of the Board of Directors of Public Service Company of New Mexico at 5, Kaplan v. Geist, No. CIV–89–1033JC (D.N.M. filed January 31, 1991) (hereinafter SLC Report).

contended that PNM was obligated to pay all attorneys' fees needed to defend the action, and that PNM was obligated to pay those fees as soon as they were incurred. The former executives relied on New Mexico law, PNM's bylaws, and separate contracts they had with PNM in support of their demands.

Although New Mexico statutory law gives corporations the power to indemnify if they choose, the law does not obligate corporations to indemnify. However, corporations are free to grant stronger indemnification rights to directors through corporate bylaws or separate contracts. In the case of PNM, the corporation had granted further indemnification rights to its executives by both methods.[5]

The defendants argued that all three sources of indemnification rights—New Mexico law, PNM bylaw, and contract—entitled them to payment of all attorneys' fees on demand. The corporation balked at paying defense costs

---

5. [By the Editor: This footnote is taken from a later portion of the text of the article] [PNM's] indemnification bylaw was standard, obligating PNM to indemnify 'to the full extent of the authority of the Company to so indemnify as authorized by the law of New Mexico.' * * * The separate indemnification contracts executed by PNM were more specific, granting a number of special procedural protections:

"2. Basic Indemnification Arrangement.

"(a) In the event Indemnitee was, is or becomes a party to * * * a Claim * * * the Company shall indemnify Indemnitee to the fullest extent permitted by law as soon as practicable but in any event no later than thirty days after written demand is presented to the Company, against any and all Expenses, judgments, fines, penalties and amounts paid in settlement * * * of such Claim. If so requested by Indemnitee, the Company shall advance (within two business days of such request) any and all Expenses to Indemnitee (an 'Expense Advance').

"(b) Notwithstanding the foregoing, * * * the obligations of the Company * * * shall be subject to the condition that the Reviewing Party shall not have determined * * * that Indemnitee would not be permitted to be indemnified under applicable law * * * provided, however, that if Indemnitee has commenced or thereafter commences legal proceedings * * * to secure a determination that Indemnitee should be indemnified under applicable law, any determination made by the Reviewing Party * * * shall not be binding and Indemnitee shall not be required to reimburse the Company for any Expense Advance until a final judicial determination is made with respect thereto (as to which all rights of appeal therefrom have been exhausted or lapsed). If there has not been a Change in Control, the Reviewing Party shall be selected by the Board of Directors, and if there has been such a Change in Control * * * the Reviewing Party shall be the Independent Legal Counsel * * * If there has been no determination by the Re-

viewing Party or if the Reviewing Party determines that Indemnitee substantively would not be permitted to be indemnified * * * under applicable law, Indemnitee shall have the right to commence litigation * * * seeking an initial determination by the Court or challenging any such determination by the Reviewing Party * * * including the legal and factual bases therefor. * * *

"6. Burden of Proof. In connection with any determination by the Reviewing Party or otherwise as to whether Indemnitee is entitled to be indemnified hereunder, the burden of proof shall be on the Company to establish that Indemnitee is not so entitled.

"7. No Presumptions * * * (N)either the failure of the Reviewing Party to have made a determination as to whether Indemnitee has met any particular standard of conduct or had any particular belief, nor an actual determination by the Reviewing Party that Indemnitee has not met such standard of conduct or did not have such belief, prior to the commencement of legal proceedings by Indemnitee to secure a judicial determination that Indemnitee should be indemnified under applicable law shall be a defense to Indemnitee's claim or create a presumption that Indemnitee has not met any particular standard of conduct or did not have any particular belief."

All PNM directors received the same form of indemnification contract, which had been drafted by the New York law firm of Skadden, Arps, Slate, Meagher & Flom. The contract provides several common procedural protections that, in general, raise no public policy concerns: 1) time limits on the corporation's response to an indemnification demand; 2) a wide choice of persons who can make the indemnification decision on behalf of the corporation (the 'Reviewing Party'); and 3) the option for a de novo evaluation of conduct by a court. * * * [Under the contract, a Reviewing Party can be 'any appropriate person or body' who is not a party to the litigation.

under these circumstances. It was not that PNM considered the statutes, bylaws, or contracts unenforceable. In fact, PNM had paid defense costs incurred by the individual defendants in the numerous class action and derivative suits. However, in those actions, financing the individual costs of defense was an appropriate use of corporate funds.

* * * To PNM, the suit to recover corporate funds that had been improperly diverted for personal benefit was another story entirely. The corporation had brought those claims only after a long investigation, and it believed that the directors had forfeited any right to indemnification because they had failed to serve PNM in good faith. Certainly they were not entitled to payment of attorneys' fees in advance of trial because 'the facts then known' to PNM showed a clear lack of good faith.

The court disagreed. It ruled that under New Mexico law, PNM's bylaws, and the separate contracts, PNM had no right to deny immediate payment to the defendants' attorneys, no matter what the circumstances. PNM could not deny attorneys' fees on the basis of its investigation into wrongful conduct; it had to pay the defense lawyers until the defendants' conduct was proved wrongful. Even if PNM prevailed at trial, it would have to continue to pay all defense costs until the verdict was upheld on appeal. In essence, by finding that PNM was obligated to pay the attorneys for all parties, PNM would be forced to finance an action both for and against itself if it hoped to recover any improperly paid compensation.

According to The New Mexico Lawyer, the court's ruling that the company had to finance every party to its lawsuit was 'the turning point' in the case:[6]

> As a practical matter, the ruling meant that the trio of defendants could now litigate almost endlessly, because they were tapped directly into PNM's coffers to pay their legal bills. Because they paid no money out of pocket, there would also be little incentive for them to settle on unfavorable terms.

The case was settled within four months of the ruling on attorneys' fees. * * *

[S]ome of these procedural protections are so extreme and so skewed in favor of the director that they, in practice, undermine substantive statutory restrictions. * * * For example, the contract requires PNM to make expense advances within two days of demand. To the extent that a two-day time limit makes any reasonable evaluation of conduct impossible, the provision allows the corporation to ignore the conduct standard and is not enforcible.

Second, all presumptions and burdens of proof for entitlement to indemnification under the contract are in favor of the director. If those presumptions and burdens of proof allow the corporation to grant indemnification by default, instead of on the basis of a conduct evaluation, they violate public policy.

Third, if the Reviewing Party concludes that a director's conduct fails to meet the required standard, the contract essentially silences the corporation

---

6. [By the Author] Michael Haederle, PNM Settlement Began with Legal Gamble, N.M. Law., June 1992, at 5.

on that issue until the end of the litigation. If the Reviewing Party decides against the director, as it did in the PNM case, the contract states that the Reviewing Party's finding "shall not be binding" and cannot be used by the corporation as a defense to the director's claim for indemnification. The contract goes on to provide that the director "shall not be required to reimburse the Company for any Expense Advance until a final judicial determination is made with respect thereto," including all rights of appeal. This contractual right can be read (as it apparently was by the PNM court) to require the corporation to make expense advances throughout trial and appeal even though the corporation's investigation found that the director breached a fiduciary duty. * * *

Notes

(1) There are obviously two sides to the advancement of expenses issue. Consider the position of a director who has been named as a defendant and must incur expenses to prepare her defense. These initial expenditures may be very substantial and absolutely essential if the director is to be vindicated. To preclude any payment to the director until after the matter has been finally resolved may create a serious hardship as well as creating invidious discrimination against directors with smaller pocketbooks. Indeed, if a person is considering becoming a director and is concerned about the possible risks of liability, the right to obtain advances for expenses—either from insurance or from the corporation—may be so important as to determine whether or not she agrees to serve. On the other hand, as PNM's unfortunate experience graphically demonstrates, advances for expenses may dramatically change the dynamics of litigation, possibly to such an extent as to make meritorious litigation impractical.

(2) MBCA § 8.53 makes it clear that a corporation has the option to advance expenses if the director meets the minimal requirements of that section. The director must file with the corporation an undertaking to repay the advances if it is ultimately determined that she is not entitled to indemnification, but that undertaking need not be secured and "may be accepted without reference to financial ability to make repayment." The theory, like the theory underlying advancement of expenses generally, is that it is not fair to favor wealthy directors over directors whose financial resources are modest. Obviously, a director with modest financial resources may lack the resources either to provide security or to give assurance that she is capable of repaying the advances.

(3) An optional provision authorizing advances of expenses is satisfactory as a practical matter only if management of the corporation remains friendly to the defendant director. If there has been a change in control, perhaps following an intense struggle with the ousted management, there is a real risk that the new board of directors may decline to advance expenses to a defeated adversary if the provision is optional. Denial of advances may be justified on the ground that there was no corporate benefit received from the actions of the defendant director now being litigated. Thus, as a practical matter, an optional provision authorizing advances is likely to provide no protection at all when it is needed the most. Recognizing this, sophisticated directors insist that advances should be made mandatory to the maximum extent possible and such provisions are very common in modern articles of incorporation and bylaws. Statutes generally make these provisions enforceable. See MBCA § 8.58(a). Indeed, the last sentence of this section goes a step further and routinely ties mandatory advances of expenses to agreements to provide mandatory indemnification to the maximum extent possi-

ble. Is this wise? The Official Comment to § 8.58 warns of the potential PNM problem as follows:

> Also, a corporation should consider whether obligatory expense advance is intended for direct suits by the corporation as well as for derivative suits by shareholders in the right of the corporation. In the former case, assuming compliance with subsections (a) and (b) of section 8.53, the corporation could be required to fund the defense of a defendant director even where the board of directors has already concluded that he has engaged in significant wrongdoing.

Is this warning sufficient? Or was the problem in PNM an apparent unthinking acceptance of procedural requirements that were clearly drafted to make mandatory advances automatically available in all circumstances?

(4) In Fidelity Fed. Sav. & Loan Ass'n v. Felicetti, 830 F.Supp. 262 (E.D.Pa., 1993), the court found a conflict between the fiduciary obligation of directors to act only in the corporation's best interest and a bylaw provision that mandated advancement of expenses in all events. The court concluded that "the only reasonable interpretation requires that the directors abide by their fiduciary obligations to act only as they believe is in the best interest of the corporation. Accordingly, [the corporation] is not required to advance the funds necessary for Felicetti and Scarcia to defend themselves in this action. * * *" 830 F.Supp. at 269. Most courts, however, have rejected this approach in which preliminary judgments are made about the merits. In Ridder v. CityFed Financial Corp., 47 F.3d 85 (3d Cir.1995), for example, the Court said:

> * * * Because of the perceived strength of the RTC's case against the appellants in the related litigation, the trial court concluded that appellants had failed to demonstrate a likelihood of success on the merits. And, in view of the fact that CityFed is in receivership and the rights of other creditors are implicated, the court felt that the harm to appellants from denial of the injunction was outweighed by the public interest in assuring equal treatment to all of CityFed's creditors, and that appellants' claim should not be accorded priority by the issuance of a preliminary injunction. 853 F.Supp. 131. We conclude that neither reason suffices to justify denial of the relief plainly mandated by the by-laws and the Delaware statute.

> The issue before the district court was not whether appellants were likely to prevail in the RTC litigation, but whether they were likely to prevail in their assertion that CityFed should advance the costs of defense. Under Delaware law, appellants' right to receive the costs of defense in advance does not depend upon the merits of the claims asserted against them, and is separate and distinct from any right of indemnification they may later be able to establish. See Joseph Warren Bishop, Jr., Law of Corporate Officers and Directors Indemnification and Insurance, ¶ 6.27 (1981 & Supp.1993). Indeed, the provisions in both Article XI of CityFed's by-laws and § 145(e) of the Delaware corporation law, conditioning the obligation to advance defense costs upon an undertaking "to repay such amount if it shall ultimately be determined that [the officer] is not entitled to be indemnified by the corporation" leaves no room for argument on that score.

> CityFed urges us to adopt the approach taken by the district court in Fidelity Federal Savings & Loan Assn. v. Felicetti, 830 F.Supp. 262 (E.D.Pa. 1993) * * * We respectfully disagree. * * * [W]e find the reasoning in Felicetti unpersuasive. Rarely, if ever, could it be a breach of fiduciary duty on

the part of corporate directors to comply with the requirements of the corporation's by-laws, as expressly authorized by statute.

The statutory provisions authorizing the advancement of defense costs, conditioned upon an agreement to repay if a right of indemnification is not later established, plainly reflect a legislative determination to avoid deterring qualified persons from accepting responsible positions with financial institutions for fear of incurring liabilities greatly in excess of their means, and to enhance the reliability of litigation-outcomes involving directors and officers of corporations by assuring a level playing field. It is not the province of judges to second-guess these policy determinations.

Appellants made a strong showing that, unless defense costs were advanced to them, their ability to defend the RTC action would be irreparably harmed. * * *

(5) Where advancement of expenses is not mandatory, the decision by the board of directors is to be judged by the standards of the business judgment rule. In this respect, an evaluation (1) of the likelihood the defendants will be able to satisfy their commitments to reimburse the corporation if they are found not eligible for indemnification and (2) whether ultimately the advancement would on balance be likely to promote the corporation's interests, are required. Advanced Mining Systems v. Fricke, 623 A.2d 82, 84 (Del.Ch.1992). In Havens v. Attar, 1997 WL 55957 (Del.Ch.1997), the Court held that a decision to advance expenses to a majority of the board of directors without considering the financial abilities of the individuals was not protected by the business judgment rule.

The 1984 MBCA did not contemplate mandatory advancement of expenses and required in every case "a determination that the facts then known to those making the determination would not preclude indemnification under this chapter." This requirement was eliminated in 1994. Was this deletion desirable?

Consider MBCA § 8.57. Even in states without express authorization, the purchase of D & O insurance may be implicit in other corporate powers relating to the compensation of officers and directors. Is such insurance erosive of the public policy underlying the securities acts and other rules providing for liability? Of course, § 8.57 is only enabling, and there are significant exceptions, exclusions, and public policy limitations applicable to such insurance.

McCULLOUGH v. FIDELITY & DEPOSIT CO.

United States Court of Appeals, Fifth Circuit, 1993.
2 F.3d 110.

Before GOLDBERG, HIGGINBOTHAM, AND DAVIS, CIRCUIT JUDGES.

W. EUGENE DAVIS, CIRCUIT JUDGE:

The Federal Deposit Insurance Corporation (FDIC) filed a declaratory judgment action against Fidelity and Deposit Company of Maryland (F & D) to determine whether F & D provided coverage under a directors' and officers' liability policy. The district court found no coverage under F & D's policy and granted summary judgment to F & D. Because the insured failed to give F &

D adequate notice to trigger coverage under the "claims made" insurance policy, we affirm.

I.

F & D issued four directors' and officers' (D & O) liability policies to four affiliate banks, including Harris County Bankshares, Inc. and three of its subsidiaries (banks). The policy covers claims made against the insured officers and directors if the required notice is given to the insurer during the policy period. This coverage is expanded by Section 6(a) of the policy to cover claims made after expiration of the policy term if the insured gives F & D certain written notice during the policy period of potential claims. Section 6 of the policy provides, in pertinent part:

(a) If during the policy period, or during the extended discovery period * * * the Bank or the Directors and Officers shall:

(1) receive written or oral notice from any party that it is the intention of such party to hold the Directors and Officers, or any of them, responsible for a specified Wrongful Act; or

(2) become aware of any *act, error, or omission* which *may subsequently give rise to a claim* being made against the Directors and Officers, or any of them, for a *specified Wrongful Act*;

and shall during such period give written notice thereof to the Company as soon as practicable and prior to the date of termination of the policy, then any claim which may subsequently be made against the Directors and Officers arising out of such Wrongful Act shall, for the purpose of this policy, be treated as a claim made during the Policy Year or the extended discovery period in which such notice was first given. (emphasis added).

The summary judgment evidence focused on information the banks furnished F & D about their lending activities. The parties disagreed about whether that information was adequate to put F & D on notice of a potential claim under § 6 of the policy.

As requested by F & D, the banks provided F & D with June 1984—March 1985 Call Reports[7] that described increasing loan losses and delinquencies. In conjunction with the 1985 renewal of the policies, the banks provided F & D a 1984 annual report. Footnote M of that report referred to the issuance of a cease and desist order to one of the subsidiaries by its primary regulator, the Office of the Comptroller of the Currency (OCC). The bank did not send the order itself.

F & D continued to express concern about the banks' financial condition and continued to request Call Reports and other information. In one of F & D's letters, they expressed concern about the banks' "problem with the Feds." In September 1985, in response to the increasing loan losses, F & D informed the banks that it intended to cancel their policies mid-term, effective October 9.

After a merger of the subsidiary banks, the OCC declared the bank insolvent in February 1988 and declared the FDIC as Receiver. FDIC sued the

---

7. [By the Court] A Call Report is a quarterly report of financial condition that each insured institution is required to furnish its primary regulator.

banks' directors and officers for improperly or illegally making, administering, or collecting loans. F & D denied coverage to the officers and directors under the D & O policies. FDIC then filed its declaratory judgment action against F & D, seeking a determination that F & D provided coverage under the D & O liability policies.

In the declaratory judgment action, * * * [t]he court found that FDIC had failed to show that F & D received written notice of a potential claim under § 6(a)(2) of the policy, and on reconsideration it entered final judgment for F & D. FDIC timely appealed.

II.

FDIC * * * [argues] that a genuine issue of fact exists regarding whether, pursuant to § 6(a)(2) of the "claims made" policy, they provided F & D sufficient written notice of potential claims during the policy period. * * *

A.

The parties first contest the type of notice the policy requires the banks to give to F & D. F & D contends that the policy requires the bank to notify it of "specified Wrongful Acts" of directors and officers having claim potential. FDIC argues that the notice can be in the broader form of "any act, error or omission" which may give rise to a claim for specified wrongful acts.

We agree with F & D that the policy requires the insured to give notice of specified wrongful acts of officers and directors. First, the plain language supports F & D's argument. § 6 of the policy provides that coverage will be provided if the Bank notifies the insurer of:

> any act, error, or omission which may subsequently give rise to a claim being made against Directors and Officers, or any of them, for a specified Wrongful Act * * *

F & D contends, and this court agrees, that "specified" modifies "Wrongful Act" and not "claim." The word "specified" is meaningless if it is read to modify "claim"; we cannot envision an *unspecified* claim. The policy language thus makes sense only if we read it to require notice of specified wrongful acts, errors, or omissions that may give rise to a claim.

Notice, as provided in the policy, is required in a claims made policy to trigger coverage. Notice in a claims made policy therefore serves a very different function than prejudice-preventing notice required under an "occurrence" policy. If the policy requirement for notice of specified wrongful acts is relaxed, then policy coverage actually expands. For example, if notice that an insured attorney has a poor docket control system is accepted as coverage triggering notice of the attorney's wrongful act, the attorney's malpractice coverage would be triggered for any number of suits predicated on missed deadlines.[8] For all of the above reasons, we are persuaded that the policy requires the insured to give the insurer notice of specified wrongful acts to trigger coverage.

---

8. [By the Court] See *Hirsch v. Texas Lawyers' Ins. Exchange*, 808 S.W.2d 561, 565 (Tex. Ct.App.1991) (court reluctant to permit expansion of "claims made" coverage through relaxation of coverage-triggering notice requirements).

B.

We next must determine whether the insureds gave adequate notice of specified wrongful acts. FDIC argues that even if notice of specified wrongful acts is required, a genuine issue of fact exists regarding whether it provided this notice. FDIC contends that reference to the cease and desist order and the reports of the banks' deteriorating financial condition put F & D on notice of acts or omissions of directors and officers which could later give rise to claims for specified wrongful acts. They argue that the policies define "wrongful act" to include a breach of duty, and the information they furnished F & D was adequate to inform F & D that the insureds breached their duty to properly supervise the banks' lending operations.

Critically, the banks did not furnish F & D with a copy of the cease and desist order. The banks' annual report simply referred to it. But even if we assume that notice of the issuance of a cease and desist order informs the insurer that the bank is having some difficulty, the issuance of such an order does not identify specified wrongful acts. The banks gave F & D no notice of the particular subsidiary involved, the particular agents, officers, or directors involved, the time period during which the events occurred, the identity of potential claimants, and the specific unsound practices made the basis of the order.

We agree with the district court that the insureds failed to give F & D adequate notice of specific wrongful acts to trigger coverage under § 6(a). Notice of an institution's worsening financial condition is not notice of an officer's or director's act, error, or omission. See *American Casualty Co. v. FDIC*, 944 F.2d 455, 460 (8th Cir.1991) and *California Union Ins. Co. v. American Diversified Savings Bank*, 914 F.2d 1271, 1277–78 (9th Cir.1990), cert. denied, 498 U.S. 1088, 111 S.Ct. 966, 112 L.Ed.2d 1052 (1991). Rising delinquencies and bad loan portfolios, especially in light of falling real estate prices, are insufficient to constitute such notice. The district court correctly granted summary judgment. * * *

AFFIRMED.

Notes

(1) Do you understand the difference between a "claims made" policy and an "occurrence" policy? The former provides coverage for claims first made against an insured during the policy period, while the latter provides coverage for injuries that take place during the policy period regardless of when the claim is asserted. Originally, D & O policies were occurrence-based, but the practical difficulties created by the possibility that claims may be asserted many years later caused all companies to shift to claims made policies. For example, it is reported that many of the problems of Lloyds of London arose because of the issuance of occurrence policies covering asbestos liability and similar long-term events. Claims under these policies were asserted years after the close of the year for which the insurance was purchased.

(2) Claims made insurance opens up the possibility that an insured who retires or leaves an employer may not have any insurance in force (or may be insured by an entirely different insurer) at the time a claim arising out of an earlier period is first asserted. For example, a claim that arise from conduct in 1997 may first be asserted in 1999; such a claim is covered only by the 1999 claims

made policy. An employee who was covered in 1997 but has retired may not have any coverage in 1999.

(3) Insurers also offer "discovery" or "awareness" clauses as an amelioration of the "claims made" concept. An awareness or discovery clause allows an insured to report to the insurer circumstances or incidents that may reasonably be expected to give rise to a claim in the future; once any later claim based on those circumstances or incidents are "locked in" and covered by the writer of the policy for that period.

(4) Some policies also allow the insured to purchase "tail" or "extended reporting" periods to permit the reporting of claims following the close of the period. Obviously, these periods only extend the time for reporting of claims and do not provide coverage for events that occur during the extended reporting or tail periods.

JOSEPH P. MONTELEONE & JOHN F. McCARRICK, DI-RECTORS' AND OFFICERS' LIABILITY, A D & O POLI-CY ROAD MAP: THE COVERAGE EXCLUSIONS

Insights, Vol. 7, No. 7, at 8 (July 1993).[9]

A discussion of exclusions typically contained in directors' and officers' liability (D & O) policies may seem a curious place to begin an evaluation of D & O coverage. However, the unique nature of D & O policies and the potentially broad scope of this coverage suggest that it may be easier to identify what is not covered than to spell out what *is* covered.

At the outset, an analysis of exclusions in a D & O policy cannot be limited to a review of the "Exclusions" section of the policy. Coverage limitations that, as a practical matter, constitute exclusions exist throughout the policy form. They may be found in the insuring agreement, in various policy definitions, and even in the policy application.

It is also important to recognize that, unlike general liability policies which typically are derived from common industry wording developed by the Insurance Services Office (ISO), D & O policies largely have developed through each D & O insurer's loss experience. Therefore, the coverage distinctions between various D & O policies may be significant. Further, different policy forms reflect the exposure risks to the niche markets being underwritten. For example, to the extent D & O coverage is available to a biotechnology or high-technology public company (generally perceived as high-risk D & O exposures), the policy terms, conditions and exclusions are likely to be more restrictive than those contained in a policy issued to a *Fortune 100* company. Accordingly, each policy form should be carefully reviewed to identify specific coverage limitations. * * *

There are generally three categories of exclusions in D & O policies. "Conduct" exclusions seek to eliminate coverage for certain conduct which is deemed to be sufficiently self-serving or egregious that insurance protection is considered inappropriate. The personal profit and advantage, dishonesty, remuneration, and § 16(b) exclusions are examples. The "other insurance"

9. Reprinted from *Insights,* July 1993, Volume 7, Number 7, with the permission of Prentice Hall Law & Business.

category of exclusions implements the concept that the D & O policy is the ultimate "backstop" protection for directors and officers. If a corporation can purchase another type of insurance to cover a specific D & O risk, the D & O insurer expects that other insurance to be purchased and therefore the D & O policy will not cover that risk. Examples of exclusions in this category include the exclusions for bodily injury/property damage, ERISA, libel and slander, notice under a prior policy and (at least historically) pollution. Finally, the "laser" exclusions are intended to address specific risks unique to the insured corporation which the insurer has identified as inconsistent with its underwriting principles. * * *

In light of the "claims-made" nature of D & O policies, policy applications typically inquire whether any claims against directors and officers currently are pending, or whether any director or officer has knowledge of facts or circumstances which might give rise to a claim in the future. If, however, the insurer simply is offering renewal terms, these questions likely will not be asked unless the insureds are seeking a higher limit of liability or otherwise are seeking to expand their coverage.

As a general rule, material misrepresentations made by an insured on the policy application may provide grounds for the insurer to subsequently rescind and treat the policy as void *ab initio*.[10] However, the question inquiring whether any director or officer has knowledge of facts or circumstances which might subsequently give rise to a claim is usually followed by a statement to the effect that if any insureds have such knowledge or such information exists, then any resulting claim will be excluded from coverage. This exclusion differs from the rescission remedy in that a rescission of the policy voids coverage for all claims regardless of whether or not any claim arises from the materially misrepresented facts. The application exclusion, on the other hand, excludes coverage only for those claims arising from the known or existing facts or circumstances. * * *

By limiting the scope of defined terms, insurers also may limit the scope of coverage under D & O policies. For example, the term "loss" typically is defined to exclude penalties imposed by law or matters uninsurable under the law pursuant to which the policy is construed. Also, depending upon the policy form, the definition of "loss" may exclude: (1) punitive or exemplary damages; (2) treble damages; (3) taxes; (4) amounts for which the directors and officers are not personally liable (*i.e.*, nonrecourse settlements); (5) amounts incurred by a special committee in the investigation or evaluation of a claim by or on behalf of the corporation; (6) the multiple portion of any multiplied damages award; or (7) any costs, charges or expenses incurred in connection with a grand jury or criminal proceeding. * * *

The term "wrongful act" typically is defined to exclude claims brought against an insured director or officer in an uninsured capacity. For example, if a lawsuit includes allegations against a director who also performs some outside function (*e.g.*, outside counsel), coverage may not be available for that

---

10. [By the Author] *See, e.g., Shapiro v. American Home Assurance Co.*, 584 F.Supp. 1245 (D.Mass.1984) (a material misrepresentation by a company's president in an application for D & O insurance invalidated the D & O policy as to all insureds, innocent and otherwise); *accord INA Underwriters Ins. Co. v. D.H. Forde & Co.*, 630 F.Supp. 76 (W.D.N.Y. 1985).

director to the extent the claim does not relate to his or her position solely as a director. * * *

In the early days of D & O policies, D & O coverage was afforded under two separate policies: one policy which insured the corporation for its indemnification obligations to its directors and officers (often referred to as "corporate reimbursement" coverage), and a second policy ensuring the directors and officers in those instances where the corporation either would not or could not provide indemnification (often referred to as "D & O" or "direct" coverage). Because the various state indemnification statutes were understood to prohibit indemnification of inappropriate conduct, including dishonesty and unentitled personal profit, there was no perceived need to apply exclusions relating to such conduct to the corporate reimbursement coverage. However, since the policies offering direct coverage contained no such underlying protection, exclusions relating to such conduct as "unentitled personal profit" and "dishonesty" were added to the direct policies. Eventually, the two separate policies evolved into a single policy with alternative insuring agreements. Some policy forms still retain the distinction and apply these so-called "conduct" exclusions only to the direct insuring agreement. Most policy forms, however, ignore the historical distinction and apply all exclusions to both insuring agreements.

Some of the more common exclusions found in the exclusions section of D & O policies include the following.

Personal profit or advantage exclusion. Most D & O policies exclude claims based upon or attributable to directors or officers gaining any personal profit or advantage to which they were not legally entitled. Some policy forms require that the personal profiting be established "in fact"[;] other policy forms require an adjudication of unentitled personal profit in the underlying litigation.

Dishonesty exclusion. Given the liberal pleading requirements in virtually every federal and state court, the dishonesty exclusion has potential applicability to virtually all D & O claims and, therefore, is frequently identified in insurers' reservation of rights letters as a potential coverage defense. First, the scope of the exclusion varies among different D & O policy forms in several respects. The conduct falling within the exclusion also may vary. Some policy forms exclude claims brought about or contributed to by the "dishonest" or the "fraudulent, dishonest or criminal" acts of the insureds. Other forms exclude "deliberately fraudulent" or "deliberately dishonest" conduct or a "willful violation of any statute, rule or regulation."

Second, the triggering conditions for the applicability of dishonesty exclusions vary. Some policy forms require a judgment or other final adjudication which establishes that "acts of active and deliberate dishonesty" were committed "with actual dishonest purpose and intent." Other forms simply require the requisite conduct to have occurred "in fact," while yet other forms have no expressed triggering condition. As to policy forms requiring a final adjudication, courts have consistently held that the adjudication must occur in the underlying D & O proceeding (and cannot be established in separate coverage litigation) and, therefore, the exclusion is inapplicable if the underlying D & O litigation is settled prior to a final adjudication. If the exclusion does not expressly require an adjudication, the exclusion has potential applicability even where the underlying lawsuit is settled.

Bodily injury/property damage exclusion. All D & O policies exclude coverage with respect to claims for bodily injury, sickness, disease or death, or property damage. More recent policy forms also may exclude emotional or mental distress, violation of a person's right of privacy, wrongful entry, eviction, false arrest and assault and battery, as well as libel, slander and defamation.

ERISA exclusion. Almost all D & O policy forms exclude claims arising under ERISA or a similar federal or state law. Given this wording, the D & O insurers' intent with respect to this exclusion appears to be to avoid providing overlapping coverage with that typically provided by fiduciary liability insurance. The exclusion may also be deemed sufficiently broad to apply to a claim for benefits in connection with a wrongful termination claim whether or not the claim for benefits is explicitly based on an alleged violation of ERISA.

Section 16(b) ("short-swing profit") exclusion. * * * Since the issue of intent or conduct is not relevant in determining whether liability should be imposed, D & O insurers typically separately exclude claims arising under Section 16(b) regardless of whether or not the trading constituted "personal profit" or "dishonesty."

Return of illegal remuneration exclusion. This exclusion was developed in response to D & O insurers' concerns that if a director or officer is forced to return to the corporation profits or excessive compensation, insureds might seek to obtain those funds under a D & O policy. Like the "short-swing profit" exclusion, it is not necessary that there be a factual finding or adjudication of "personal profit" or "dishonesty" in order for the D & O insurer to invoke this exclusion. Recent policies combine this exclusion with the "personal profit" exclusion.

Pollution exclusion. Virtually every D & O insurance policy contains a "broad form" pollution exclusion, although substantial variations in exclusionary wording exist among policy forms. The intent of most insurers is to exclude coverage for any type of direct or indirect pollution or environmental exposure. Some exclusions are drafted to be more comprehensive than others. Under the most commonly used "broad form" pollution exclusions, coverage is excluded not only for claims by parties seeking recovery for pollution damages, but also for secondary suits, such as shareholder derivative and nondisclosure suits against directors and officers arising out of environment-related losses incurred by the corporation.

In some instances, insureds may be able to obtain an exception to this exclusion through negotiation with D & O insurers and obtain coverage for non-indemnifiable secondary pollution suits.

Insured v. insured exclusion. Prior to the mid–1980s, most D & O policies did not exclude claims brought by the corporation or by some directors and officers against other directors and officers. However, in light of suits brought by corporations against their directors and officers under circumstances which created an appearance that the entities simply were converting their D & O policies to cash by suing their own directors and officers, virtually all D & O policy forms now exclude claims brought against directors and officers by other directors and officers or by the company. Most newer policy forms incorporate this exclusion into the Exclusions section of the policy. Older policy forms generally add this exclusion by endorsement.

The "insured v. insured" exclusion varies significantly from policy to policy, with the primary differences relating to which claims are excepted from the exclusion (and are therefore covered). Almost all policy forms contain an exception to the "insured v. insured" exclusion to provide coverage for derivative lawsuits brought without the solicitation, assistance or participation of an insured. Other exceptions to the "insured v. insured" exclusion may preserve coverage for claims for wrongful termination and claims for contribution or indemnity.

In recent years, the "insured v. insured" exclusion has been frequently litigated in the context of claims brought by the regulatory banking agencies against directors and officers of failed financial institutions. Courts have reached different results as to whether the "insured v. insured" exclusion applies to these claims. * * *

D & O policies typically exclude coverage for claims which may be covered under other insurance policies. This exclusion may be found in the exclusions section of the policy in some policy forms, or in separate provisions in other forms. Some policy forms apply this exclusion only to the extent of actual payments under other policies; others limit the exclusion to other "valid" or "valid and collectible" insurance. In virtually all policies, the exclusion applies only to the amount of such other insurance, with the D & O insurance policy affording coverage in excess of such other insurance.

ENDORSEMENTS

In addition to policy exclusions contained in standardized policy forms, D & O insurers may add further exclusions to the policy by endorsement and thus tailor the policy coverage to a specific risk or industry. The following are some commonly found endorsement exclusions.

Pending/prior litigation exclusion. When an insurer first issues a D & O policy to a corporation, an exclusion is frequently included which eliminates coverage for claims arising from pending or prior litigation or from any facts or circumstances involved in such litigation. In this way, the insurer's intent is to avoid exposure for a claim already in progress or which is likely to arise from existing litigation. The "pending/prior litigation" exclusion typically will reference a date frequently the inception date of the policy which is used to determine whether the litigation is "pending or prior." In evaluating different policy forms, one important inquiry should be which party is the subject of the pending or prior litigation. Some forms of this exclusion limit the scope of the exclusion to litigation, claims, demands, or proceedings *against* the insured directors and officers and, in some forms, the corporation. Other forms apply the exclusion to *any* pending or prior litigation, claims, demands or proceedings whether or not the corporation or any insured is a party or even knows of the existence of the matter.

Depending upon the specific wording, the "pending/prior litigation" exclusion may broadly apply and, therefore, may create inadvertent coverage gaps. For example, if the prior litigation asserts claims against only the corporation (or under the broader form of this exclusion, against only a third party), and insured directors and officers subsequently are named as defendants in the litigation or are subsequently subject to separate litigation based upon the same matters as alleged in the pending litigation, it is likely that no coverage will exist under the newly-issued policy. Thus, unless a notice of circumstances referencing the matters alleged in the prior litigation was submitted to the prior D & O insurer, if any, the defendant directors and officers may well be without any D & O coverage for such claims.

Regulatory exclusion. Although potentially applicable to any corporation subject to regulation by a governmental agency, this exclusion is most commonly endorsed onto D & O policies issued to financial institutions—and particularly where there are concerns that the institution may be taken over by regulators. Beginning in the late 1980s, some courts ruled that this exclusion was unenforceable as being ambiguous and against public policy because it frustrated the broad powers and duties bestowed upon financial institution regulators. During the past two years, however, courts have almost unanimously upheld the enforceability of this exclusion.[11] * * *

Notes

(1) A D & O survey in 1996 indicated that 88 percent of companies with assets of more than $100 million had D & O insurance. The median premium was $255,000, 30 percent of the surveyed companies had had claims filed against them, with the average claim being $5.24 million.

(2) In a modern D & O policy, advancements of expenses to defend insureds usually reduce the available coverage by the amount of the payment. As a result, extended litigation may deplete the policy and limit the protection available to insureds. Not all policies are structured in this fashion.

(3) Significant problems arise when litigation involves claims brought simultaneously against directors and officers who are insured and persons who are not insured: corporate agents and employees and the corporation itself. (The traditional policy covered only the indemnification obligations of the corporation itself and not its direct liability; some new policies now insure the corporation itself as well as directors and officers.) If a settlement is reached, the insurer must allocate the settlement payment between the insureds and the uninsureds based on relative fault or culpability. Not surprisingly, litigation has arisen over the propriety of specific allocations. See Caterpillar v. Great American Ins. Co., 62 F.3d 955 (7th Cir.1995); Safeway Stores v. Nat'l Union Fire Ins. Co., 64 F.3d 1282 (9th Cir.1995). Somewhat similar issues arise when the corporation is insolvent, and settlement is proposed for some but not all the defendants. See Joseph P. Monteleone and John F. McCarrick, Settlement Issues in Securities Litigation Involving Officers and Directors, Insights, Vol. 7, No. 9, Sept. 1996, at 7.

---

11. [By the Authors] Indeed, the only four federal circuit courts that have addressed the issue have agreed that the regulatory exclusion is enforceable. *See FDIC v. American Casualty Co.,* [995 F.2d 471] (4th Cir., Jan.4, 1993); *Fidelity & Deposit Co. of Maryland v. Conner,* 973 F.2d 1236 (5th Cir.1992); *St. Paul Fire and Marine Ins. Co. v. FDIC,* 968 F.2d 695 (8th Cir.1992); *American Casualty Co. v. FDIC,* 944 F.2d 455 (8th Cir.1991); *FDIC v. American Casualty Co.,* 975 F.2d 677 (10th Cir.1992).

Chapter Fourteen

THE TAKEOVER MOVEMENT

The era of the modern takeover movement during which large, publicly held corporations virtually became objects of commerce began sometime in the late 1960s. It paused for an appreciable period—quite abruptly—in the early 1990s but then resumed in modified form in the mid–1990s. Between the late 1960s and 1990, immense economic enterprises were (1) bought and sold; (2) bought, recapitalized, and then reintroduced to the public markets as a new and quite different publicly held corporation; or (3) bought, broken up and individual components sold. During the 1980s, the takeover movement impressed its image on the decade in much the same way as the flappers impressed their image on the 1920s.

Before the pause in the early 1990s, the takeover movement was largely defined by aggressive bidders seeking to acquire controlling interests in publicly held corporations over the opposition and resistance of the incumbent management. While some similar bids have occurred during the takeover movement of the mid–1990s, they are relatively uncommon; most takeover bids today are negotiated directly with incumbent management, and are consensual transactions rather than brutal, no-holds-barred battles. The principal reason for this shift in tactics is that defensive strategies developed during the 1980s have proved to be exceptionally durable and difficult to overcome.

This Chapter is intended to give an impressionistic and somewhat over-simplified picture of the takeover movement and to describe the legal rules of the takeover game as it is played in the 1990s.

A. THE BEGINNINGS

WILLIAM ALLEN, U.S. CORPORATE GOVERNANCE IN A POST–MANAGERIAL AGE

Text of speech given as the Fifth Distinguished Lecture in International
Business and Trade Law, University of Toronto Faculty of Laws.
Pp. 6–12 (Oct. 20, 1993).

You know the managerialist idea as well as I. It surely wasn't invented by * * * John Kenneth Galbraith but he may have given this conception its most popular, if critical, treatment 25 years ago in his book, *The New Industrial State*. Professor Galbraith saw the social landscape dominated by huge, virtually autonomous business institutions, under the control of an elite corps of professional managers. These corporations—or what, in this view, amounted to the same thing, these senior managers—had largely freed themselves from the constraints imposed by product markets by their programs of manipulative advertising. We consumers no longer acted as a real constraint. We had been domesticated by advertising; taught to want what we were told we needed. Corporations had, as well, freed themselves from the constraints of capital markets by internally generating required funds. Berle and Means had long since shown that the modern U.S. corporation was managed free of constraint from shareholders, who—widely dispersed and diversified—could be counted upon to affirm any proposal that management offered. The picture of autonomous management was completed by reference to long-term labor contracts in which management entered into peace treaties with labor and by the co-opting of the regulatory processes of government through revolving door employment practices. Atop these large and powerful institutions, of course, sat self-perpetuating hierarchies of senior management.

Galbraith saw these powerful corporations of 25 years ago—General Motors, IBM, the Pennsylvania Railroad, U.S. Steel, etc.—as impervious, nearly governmental in nature and nearly permanent. We now know that this vision badly underestimated the power of markets, but at the time it reflected what I take to have been a widely held perception.

Businessmen and women, I feel sure, never felt control over their environment to the degree that Mr. Galbraith posited. But the view of the corporation as a quasi-public institution was quite consistent with the dominant view among managers. If they did not view the public corporation as impervious to markets, business leader did see the large scale business enterprise as a quasi-public institution. This was the dogma of managerialism. It was one of managerial authority and managerial responsibility. It implied, of course, that corporations did not exist in a brutally competitive world * * *. It implicitly assumed that there was room for discretionary judgment concerning who got what out of the enterprise. And that discretion was seen as imposing a duty of fairness towards all those involved in or effected by the corporation.

But changes began to undermine the secure suppositions of the managerialist ideology. Those changes included innovation and growth in credit markets and the evolution of takeover entrepreneurs; the explosive growth of pension funds and other institutional shareholders and the striking emergence of a global market place. These forces came together by the early 1980s to trigger a period of significant restructuring in the private sector of the U.S. economy. In that process the premises of the managerialist vision of the corporation were directly challenged by a device that might have come straight out of a neo-classical economics textbook: the hostile cash tender offer.

In 1967, when Professor Galbraith published *The New Industrial State*, devices existed by which inefficient or dishonest corporate managers could be removed. In a few instances, individual shareholders or families owned sufficient shares to influence directly the decisions of boards of directors.

Palace coups were also a possibility. In some instances, publicly held corporations in dire financial straits voluntarily agreed to be taken over by more successful entities. A highly aggressive corporation rebuffed by management of a target corporation might obtain voting control over the target by going over the heads of incumbent management and the board of directors and approaching shareholders of the target with a proposal to exchange shares issued by the aggressor for the target's voting shares. Such an offer is a public offering of securities by the aggressor that requires registration under the Securities Act of 1933 and historically has been viewed as a high risk strategy that was unlikely to be successful.

The best-known device used to oust incumbent managers who insisted on remaining independent—a device much more talked about than actually used—was the proxy fight. A traditional proxy fight was a struggle for control of a public corporation in which most of the high cards were held by management. The nonmanagement group—the "insurgents"—competed with management in an effort to obtain sufficient proxy votes to elect a majority (or all) of the board of directors, and thereby take over control of the corporation. The insurgent group usually made open market purchases of shares before openly announcing its intentions, and in some instances assembled a major block of shares before management became aware that someone was accumulating its shares. In order to solicit proxies successfully, the insurgents had to obtain a list of shareholders, which usually involved a trip to the courthouse. Proxies were solicited by mailings, by personal contact, and by newspaper and radio commercials. Even though institutional investors did not have the holdings they do today, they were often individually courted. Specialized proxy solicitation firms assisted both the insurgents and management in what was essentially a political campaign for control of the corporation, somewhat similar to an election for public office.

Proxy fights obviously were expensive if the number of shareholders was large. The accepted view was that such fights were not feasible at all in very large corporations with hundreds of thousands of shareholders since the cost of solicitation was prohibitive. Usually, incumbent management could have the corporation assume most (or all) of its costs while the insurgents had to finance their campaign entirely out of their own pockets. Furthermore, the expenses of an unsuccessful proxy fight were from the outset sunk costs that were simply lost if the proxy fight failed, so that the insurgents had more to lose than management.

There is a fair amount of law on the appropriateness of charging proxy contest expenses to the corporation. Delaware has adopted a "policy/personality" distinction that permits management to charge expenses relating to the development of policy issues but prohibits them from doing so when the issue is purely a personality contest. Palumbo v. Deposit Bank, 758 F.2d 113 (3d Cir.1985); Levin v. Metro–Goldwyn–Mayer, Inc., 264 F.Supp. 797 (S.D.N.Y. 1967). Can one draw a meaningful distinction between "policy" and "personality"? Cannot all personality disputes be formulated in terms of a policy disagreement? New York narrowly avoided adopting a more stringent test in Rosenfeld v. Fairchild Engine & Airplane Corp., 309 N.Y. 168, 128 N.E.2d 291 (1955), but there was no agreement on what the test should be. So far as the insurgents are concerned, the rule is "no reimbursement" if the insurgents are unsuccessful (since it is highly unlikely that successful incumbent management that has fended off insurgents will volunteer to pay their expenses). On the other hand, if the insurgents are successful, they have provided a benefit to the corporation that usually entitles them to reimbursement. Since the former incumbents presumably charged their expenses to the corporation before they were removed from office, the usual result was that the corporation paid the expenses of both sides where a proxy contest led to the ouster of incumbent management. Academic commentary has suggested that these rules are less than optimal, but there appears to be no movement to try to change them. Lucian Arye Bebchuk & Marcel Kahan, A Framework for Analyzing Legal Policy Towards Proxy Contests, 78 Cal. L.Rev. 1071 (1990); Franklin C. Latcham & Frank D. Emerson, Proxy Contest Expenses and Shareholder Democracy, 4 Western Res. L.Rev. 5 (1952). Is there a socially useful function in providing for reimbursement of unsuccessful insurgents if their campaign leads to beneficial changes in issuer policy? What kinds of restrictions or limitations might be built into such a plan to prevent abuse by publicity seekers, cranks, and the like? Should there be stricter limitations on reimbursement of expenses by management? If the "policy/personality" line is too indefinite, what kind of standard can be devised?

The SEC has promulgated special regulations applicable to proxy contests in corporations subject to § 14. 17 C.F.R. § 240.14a–11 (1997). These regulations require "participants" other than management in a proxy contest to file specified information with the SEC and the securities exchanges at least five days before a solicitation begins. "Participant" is defined so as to include anyone who contributes more than $500 for the purpose of financing the contest. The information that must be disclosed relates to the identity and background of the participants, their interests in securities of the corporation, when they were acquired, financing arrangements, participation in other proxy contests, and understandings with respect to future employment with the corporation. The solicitation of majority consents is also subject to these third-party proxy solicitation rules, as is a solicitation by an institutional investor to more than ten other institutional investors to act in concert on a matter relating to shareholder voting.

The general philosophy of these contested proxy regulations is well-expressed by Judge Clark:

> Appellants' fundamental complaint appears to be that stockholder disputes should be viewed in the eyes of the law just as are political contests, with each side free to hurl charges with comparative unrestraint, the assumption being that the opposing side is then at liberty to refute and thus effectively deflate the "campaign oratory" of its adversary. Such, however, was not the policy of Congress as enacted in the Securities Exchange Act. There Congress has clearly entrusted to the Commission the duty of protecting the investing public against misleading statements made in the course of a struggle for corporate control.

Securities and Exch. Comm'n v. May, 229 F.2d 123, 124 (2d Cir.1956).

The number of proxy fights subject to SEC jurisdiction historically has been rather small. For example, only thirty-seven companies were involved in proxy contests for the election of directors in fiscal 1977. Control was involved in twenty-six instances; in eight of these, management retained control, three were settled by negotiation, five were won by nonmanagement factions, and ten were pending at the end of the year. In eleven instances, representation, not control, was sought; management retained all places on the board in six contests and opposition candidates won places on the board in five cases. 1977 S.E.C. Annual Report, at 107. Similar SEC data are not available for more recent years. The proxy fight was largely eclipsed as a takeover mechanism by the cash tender offer that evolved in the late 1950s. During the late 1980s, however, there was a resurgence of contested proxy or consent solicitation campaigns in connection with purchase-type takeover attempts. During the period between October 1984 and September 1990, there were 165 proxy contests seeking full or partial control of the board of directors. Joseph A. Grundfest, Just Vote No: A Minimalist Strategy for Dealing with Barbarians Inside the Gates, 45 Stan. L. Rev. 857, 862 n. 17 (1993). In some of these instances, the target was simply too big for the aggressor to finance the purchase of a majority of the shares. If the aggressor had financial resources to acquire only fifteen or twenty percent of the outstanding equity, a proxy fight might be instituted in an effort to attract sufficient additional proxies to oust incumbent management without purchasing an outright majority of the voting stock or, at least, mount a viable proxy fight threat to encourage the target to negotiate. A well-known example of this strategy was Carl Icahn's proxy fight against the incumbent management of Texaco, Inc. in 1986. In other instances, takeover defenses proved to be impregnable against an outside cash tender offer, and the aggressor attempted an end run by launching a proxy fight or consent solicitation in order to compel the removal of the defenses. See Christopher Power, Why the Proxy Fight is Back, Bus. Wk., Mar. 7, 1988, at 32; Whose Company Is It Anyway? Judith Dobrzynski, et al., Proxy Fights are Spreading as Shareholders Seek More Power, Bus. Wk., Apr. 25, 1988, at 60. In yet another type of case, proxy fights or majority consent solicitations were launched in an effort to persuade a target corporation to enter into a recapitalization or financial restructuring that involved an extraordinary distribution to shareholders. In about 50 percent of these situations, the insurgents were wholly or partially successful.[1] Grundfest, supra at 863 n. 17. In 1990, financing for all-cash takeovers began to dry up, and there was a spurt of more than a dozen proxy fights instituted against major corporations. This trend, however, did not last. The number of proxy fights again declined markedly by 1993.[2] Aggressors in these latter-day proxy fights had to combat sophisticated defensive techniques developed against cash tender offers. See generally Randall Thomas, Judicial Review of Defensive Tactics in Proxy Contests: When Is Using a Rights Plan Right? 46 Vand. L.Rev. 503 (1993); Irvin H. Warren & Kevin G. Abrams, Evolving Standards of Judicial Review of Procedural Defenses in Proxy Contests, 47 Bus. Law. 647 (1992); Mark A. Stach, An Overview of Legal and Tactical Considerations in Proxy Contests: The Primary Means of Effecting Fundamental Corporate Change in the 1990s, 13 George Mason U.L.Rev. 745 (1991). While the proxy

---

1. [By the Editor] The major successful proxy fight during this period was won by a group headed by Robert Gintel, who began with a 21.6 percent voting interest in Xtra Corporation, and obtained sufficient proxy votes to oust the incumbent management. See Randall Smith, Storming the Barricades with a Proxy: Takeover Defenses Prove to be Flimsy, Wall St. J., May 10, 1990, at C1. In the situa-

tions where these proxy fights were not directly successful, the target often felt the pressure of this tactic in its negotiations with the insurgents or with other possible aggressors.

2. [By the Editor] By 1992, the number of proxy fights had shrunk to less than half of the 1989 peak. Grundfest, supra at 863, n. 17.

fight deflected some of the takeover defenses that had been created to protect against all-cash offers, its overall success was decidedly mixed.

B. THE EARLY PERIOD OF CASH TENDER OFFERS

The classic cash tender offer developed in the late 1960s. At this time, there was essentially no governmental regulation of such offers. In this early period, large pools of capital had not developed for takeover attempts, so aggressors generally concentrated on smaller publicly held businesses which appeared to be vulnerable either because their management was weak or their shares appeared to be depressed in price. A cash tender is essentially a public invitation to the shareholders of the target corporation to tender their shares to the aggressor for purchase for cash. As developed during the late 1960s, the offering price was usually set 15 to 20 percent higher than the current market price for the target's shares. The offer was made by public advertisement, press release, and mailings to all known shareholders. The aggressor almost always sought enough shares to ensure working control of the target corporation, though sometimes the aggressor sought a higher percentage or all of the outstanding shares. The public offer invited tenders of shares but the aggressor was not obligated to purchase any shares unless the required amount was tendered. A few offers were made on an "any or all" basis but they were relatively uncommon. If the stated number of shares was tendered, the aggressor would purchase them and instantly own a controlling interest in the target. If an excess of shares was tendered, the offeror had the option of purchasing all the tendered shares or purchasing the stated amount on either a first-come-first served or pro rata basis and returning the balance. Aggressors tended to prefer first-come-first served offers since they encouraged (or stampeded) large holders to tender early, thereby increasing the probability of success. Tender offerors also promised generous commissions to brokers who persuaded customers to tender shares. The mechanical aspects of a tender offer, receiving shares with properly executed powers of attorney and dispensing funds to sellers were usually handled by banks.

In addition to first-come-first-served offers, aggressors often provided short time periods during which tenders would be accepted. These short periods also encouraged or stampeded shareholders to tender quickly, thereby increasing the probability of success; such offers were called "Saturday night specials."

These takeover techniques developed in lieu of the classic proxy fight because the probability of success in proxy fights was perceived to be low. Initially, the probability of success of a tender offer appeared to be greater than a proxy fight, primarily because of the element of surprise. During this period, it was not uncommon for management of target companies to learn of the offer only when the Wall Street Journal blossomed with full page ads announcing the precise details of the offer. Since offers often remained open only for a brief period, little time was available to incumbent management to respond and shareholders were panicked into tendering quickly lest they lose out on the offer entirely. Further, a cash tender offer was attractive because the individual shareholder's decision was an investment type of decision rather than a choice between competing factions for control. An unsophisticated shareholder thought in terms of "I paid X for this stock; I am now offered Y. Should I sell?" Or more rationally, "Yesterday this stock was at $50; I am now offered $65. Should I sell?" On the other hand, in a proxy contest, the shareholder's choice was pretty clearly a choice between competing factions for the right to run the corporation in which he would have a continuing interest, and the chances of an immediate financial gain were remote.

When a cash tender offer was made the open market price for the shares immediately increased dramatically. (Whether it equaled or exceeded the tender offer price depended on factors such as the probability that a competing offer at a higher price might be made, whether the offer was likely to be oversubscribed, whether it was on a first-come-first-served basis, and so forth.) Persons owning shares thus had the choice of immediately selling their shares in the open market at a price well above the market price just a day or so earlier, retaining them, or tendering them. Most shares sold on the open market ultimately were tendered. A group of speculators, known as arbitrageurs or risk arbitrageurs, purchased shares in the open market at prices below the tender offer price in order to tender them and profit by the difference between the two prices. In some tender offers, the volume of transactions effected by arbitrageurs was very substantial—involving more than 25 percent or more of the tendered shares. The accepted Wall Street wisdom was that all shares sold into the market would be purchased by someone who would tender the shares. Thus, shareholders who sold into the market indirectly helped the aggressor.

In this era, an important variation of the cash tender offer was the public exchange offer in which the aggressor offered to exchange a package of its own securities for the shares of the target. The package usually consisted of both debt and equity interests, and might include highly speculative warrants or options to acquire further equity interests in the aggressor. Such interests sometimes were referred to derogatorily as "funny money." Arbitrageurs were also active in public exchange offers, buying the target corporation's shares and at the same time selling short or on a "when issued" basis the package of the aggressor's securities. While shareholders of the target corporation who accepted the aggressor's offer received securities rather than cash, the availability of a public market for the aggressor's securities permitted target shareholders to liquidate their positions promptly after the exchange was completed, though not always at the value claimed by the aggressor for the original package. In any event, cash tender offers and public exchange offers could be utilized by different aggressors seeking control of a single target corporation. For example, in the fight for Armour & Co. in the late 1960s, a cash tender offer by Greyhound Lines, Inc. was met with a public exchange offer by General Host Corporation.

In a broad sense, public exchange offers can be viewed as a type of financing device by aggressors. An aggressor might sell its own securities to create a pool of capital in order to make offers to shareholders of a target corporation to buy shares for cash. Alternatively, the aggressor might offer its own securities directly to the target shareholders in a public exchange offer, eliminating the cash-raising step and making the target shareholders the source of capital for the takeover.

C. THE WILLIAMS ACT

This classic picture of the tender offer was significantly modified by the enactment of the "Williams Act" in 1968, with amendments in 1970. Pub. L. 90–439, 82 Stat. 454 (1968). This statute amended §§ 13 and 14 of the Securities Exchange Act of 1934 to deal with the perceived problems of cash tender offers. It combined full disclosure obligations with a set of "rules of fair play" in tender offers. A fundamental purpose was to eliminate the advantages of surprise so as to permit the shareholders to make a reasoned choice about the offer being made to them. Thus, § 13(d) was added to require a public filing by any person or group that acquires five percent or more of the voting securities of a registered company. Section 14(e) was added to prohibit the use of false or misleading information in connection with tender offers. The Act also requires tender offers to remain open for at least 20 days and requires that oversubscribed offers be taken up on a prorated rather than a first-come-first-served basis. Because of the economic pressures in the takeover area, however, considerable ingenuity has led to the development of a number of devices to avoid or minimize the impact of these rules of fair play. These devices in turn have sometimes been followed by decisions by the SEC to promulgate regulations designed to modify or eliminate the devices in question, by enactment of state statutes to limit some tactics by aggressors and, most importantly, by innovative defensive tactics. The overall result of these developments has been the creation of a regulatory scheme for tender offers of increasing, and sometimes bewildering, complexity.

The enactment of the Williams Act could have had a major effect on the history and development of the takeover movement, largely by judicializing the process. The reason that it did not can be traced to judicial decisions by federal courts that reflected a strong deference to the marketplace as the court of last resort to determine who should manage large publicly held corporations. This deference is seen strongly in two early Supreme Court opinions. Rondeau v. Mosinee Paper Corp., 422 U.S. 49, 95 S.Ct. 2069, 45 L.Ed.2d 12 (1975) (limiting the economic impact of inadvertent violations of § 13(d)); Piper v. Chris–Craft Indus., Inc., 430 U.S. 1, 97 S.Ct. 926, 51 L.Ed.2d 124 (1977)(holding that a competitor for control did not have standing to attack violations of § 14(e)).

D. THE 1970s AND 1980s

Important changes in takeover practices occurred during the 1970s and 1980s. The underlying development that spurred these changes was the growth of huge pools of capital that could be readily tapped by aggressors in order to make all-cash offers either for working control or for all of the shares of increasingly large corporations. Furthermore, the providers of capital began to look to the cash flow of the target as the source of profit on takeovers. In order to utilize this cash flow, however, it became necessary to eliminate all publicly held shareholders from the target. Thus, two-step takeover process became the norm: the first step is a cash acquisition of a majority interest in the target, and the second step is a cash-out merger that eliminates the shareholders who did not sell their shares during the first step.

As takeover transactions developed, the tactics of both aggressors and targets became increasingly sophisticated. Corporations were put "into play" by a takeover bid or by a "bear hug." Putting a corporation into play might lead to a frantic search to find a more congenial merger partner, a "white knight." The accepted wisdom of Wall Street became that any corporation put "into play" would end up being acquired by someone. Defensive tactics also became increasingly sophisticated—this is the world of poison pills, lockups, sales of crown jewels, and so forth. Indeed, defensive tactics became so effective that they completely reshaped the takeover movement.

Notes

People who are specialists in any area develop their own vocabulary or slang references to the phenomena they deal with every day. This vocabulary is often revealing as to how the participants themselves view their activities. Persons who specialized in tender and exchange offers—attorneys representing either targets or aggressors, financial advisers, brokers, proxy solicitation firm employees, and others—were no exception. Consider the following:

(a) "Saturday night special"—a pre-Williams Act surprise tender offer which expires in one week. Designed to capitalize on panic and haste, such an offer may be made Friday afternoon to take advantage of the fact that markets and most offices are closed on Saturday and Sunday.

(b) "Bear hug"—a takeover attempt that consists of a proposal made to the directors. The proposal may be for a merger or for a cash tender or exchange offer not opposed by management. Though the approach may be friendly, there is a veiled or explicit threat that if the target chooses not to negotiate, an unfriendly offer may result.

(c) "White knight"—a friendly suitor solicited by the target following a bear hug.

(d) "Gray knight"—a bidder not solicited by a target who opportunistically tries to take advantage of the resistance of the target.

(e) "Smoking gun"—a mistake by the aggressor that may be used by the target to gain additional time.

(f) "Show stopper"—a smoking gun that is so serious that the entire takeover attempt must be canceled.

(g) "Arbs"—arbitrageurs.

(h) "Shark repellent"—originally the state tender offer statutes described below; more generally amendments to articles of incorporation or other defensive preparation in advance of a tender offer to make tender offers more difficult.

(i) "Porcupine provisions"—defensive provisions in articles of incorporation or bylaws designed to make unwanted takeover attempts impossible or impractical without the consent of the target's management. Porcupine provisions are also discussed below.

(j) "Lockup"—the setting aside of securities for purchase by friendly interests in order to defeat or make more difficult a takeover attempt. An option giving friendly interests the right to buy a "crown jewel" at a favorable price is also referred to as a "lockup." Another example of a lockup was the purchase of shares in Trans Union by Pritzker at slightly above the then market price before the contingent sale to him was announced. See page 000, supra.

(k) "Golden parachutes"—lucrative employment and fringe benefit contracts given to top management in target corporations. The purposes of such contracts in part may be to assure the continued loyalty of management in stressful situations, and in part to increase the cost of a successful takeover by increasing the costs chargeable to the target corporation after it is taken over.

(*l*) "Pac-man defense"—a counter tender offer by the target for the aggressor's shares as a device to fend off an unwanted takeover attempt.

(m) "Scorched earth defense"—the strategy of entering into commitments to dispose of the target's most desirable assets on condition that the takeover succeeds. The object is to deprive a successful aggressor of the asset he is seeking, thereby deterring unwanted takeovers.

(n) "Crown jewel"—the most prized asset of a corporation, i.e., that which makes it an attractive takeover target. A defensive tactic against a hostile tender offer may be to sell this asset to another party, thereby removing the assets that the unfriendly bidder was hoping to acquire and encouraging it to cease its offer without purchasing any shares of the subject company.

(*o*) "Poison pill"—a class of securities of the target company convertible upon consummation of any merger or similar transaction into more valuable rights or interests; poison pills may be "neutralized" or "disarmed" by the board of directors if they approve the transaction. See page 1034 infra.

(p) "Greenmail"—the purchase of a substantial block of the subject company's securities by an unfriendly suitor with the primary purpose of coercing the subject company into repurchasing the block at a premium over the amount paid by the suitor. In 1987, Congress enacted a special 50 percent nondeductible "antigreenmail" excise tax. Some state statutes also attempt to make greenmail unprofitable.

(q) "Bust-up" or "breakup" takeovers—takeovers with the stated intention of breaking up the target and selling component parts. Bust-up takeovers assume that the sum of the parts are often greater than the value of the whole.

(r) "Lollypop"—an offer to all shareholders except the aggressor to repurchase for cash or debt a portion of each shareholder's holding. (A "lollypop" tastes good to all the shareholders except the hostile bidder.)

(s) "Bridge loans"—financing provided by investment bankers, usually from their own resources, that is viewed as temporary loans to be refinanced at a later date, usually by the issuance of junk bonds.

(t) "Junk"—junk bonds or other securities that are below investment grade and used by aggressors as a substitute for cash.

(u) "LBO"—a leveraged buyout, discussed in the following section.

(v) "MBO"—an LBO instituted by management or one in which management is a major participant.

(w) "Mezzanine financing"—a type of bridge loan.

(x) "Standstill agreement"—a contract between a former aggressor and a target in which the aggressor agrees not to acquire additional shares of the target for a specified period without the consent of the target's management.

During the late 1980s, both the size and number of transactions increased dramatically. Mergers and acquisition activity on a worldwide basis grew from nearly $34 billion in 1980 to more than $500 billion in 1989. The previously little-known securities firm of Drexel Burnham Lambert Inc., and the investment firm of Kohlberg Kravis Roberts & Co., became highly visible major players with access to billions of dollars for the purchase of large publicly owned corporations. In the 1960s and early 1970s, a few insurance companies had financed takeover activity. By the mid–1980s, the game had changed completely: Huge buyout funds had been amassed by investment banking firms and specialized leveraged buyout firms, attracting participants ranging from state and corporate pension funds to individual and foreign investors. Multi-billion dollar all-cash transactions became commonplace. The complacent view by the largest Fortune 500 companies that they were too big to be taken over evaporated; even the very largest corporation instituted defensive strategies. The manageralistic era of the 1960s was dead.

Corporate law firms thrived during the 1980s as never before. Lawyers were close to the center of the takeover movement, charting strategy, devising defenses, and documenting and effectuating the transactions as they occurred. Immense acquisition transactions required structuring, the production of legal documents, of legal opinions, of tax analysis, and so forth. Securities and banking lawyers also played key roles in negotiating the financing of major transactions: the suppliers of huge amounts of capital required legal teams whose size rivaled those of the target and the aggressor. And finally there was the litigation that surrounded virtually every major takeover. Suits were often simultaneously pending in Delaware and six or seven other states as the target attempted to evade the grasp of the aggressor.

The largest takeover transaction ever attempted—the 1988 leveraged buyout of RJR–Nabisco, Inc. by the KKR firm—involved a cash price of $24.8 billion and reflected both the high point and culmination of a movement that had shaken large American enterprise to its roots.

E. LEVERAGED BUYOUTS

The 1980s saw the development of a different type of transaction, the leveraged buyout (LBO), which at the time appeared to be not only the logical outcome of the creation of huge pools of capital available for investment in takeover bids, but also the development of a new business form.

An LBO may be described as follows: An acquirer, which may be existing management, another corporation, or a corporate raider, purchases all or most of the outstanding stock of the target corporation, usually for a substantial premium over market price. The acquisition is financed through loans that initially might involve short-term mezzanine or bridge loans and low-grade high interest debt instruments—noninvestment-grade junk bonds. The transaction is structured so that the repayment of this debt ultimately becomes the obligation of the target corporation. It is the essence of a bootstrap transaction; the proceeds of the debt assumed by the target are used directly or indirectly to purchase the publicly held shares of the target but the debt is repaid by the target. The new debt assumed by the target may be discharged by the sale of components of the target's business or out of the target's subsequent cash flow, including tax savings arising from the deductions for interest payments made on the new debt. In making the financial calculations to see how much debt a target could carry, the standard measure is "EBIT"—earnings before interest and taxes—because the tax obligation is thereafter eliminated by the interest deductions for payments on the new debt. When the debt is paid down sufficiently, the target may again become a publicly held corporation through the sale of shares to the general public. In the best of all worlds, everyone benefits. In the worst, the corporation is unable to carry the load of the new debt and goes into bankruptcy; at that point the issue becomes whether the LBO transaction itself may be attacked as a fraudulent conveyance.

ROBERT W. HAMILTON AND RICHARD A. BOOTH, BUSINESS BASICS FOR LAW STUDENTS: ESSENTIAL TERMS AND CONCEPTS[3]

Pp. ___, ___–___ (1997).

It is important to recognize that even if the bidder acquires over 50 percent of the outstanding shares and replaces the target's board of directors and management, it does not have a free hand with respect to the target's assets. The target is still a publicly owned company with the public owning 49.9 percent; the presence of this minority interest sharply circumscribes and limits what the bidder can do with the target's assets. For example, the bidder may not simply distribute to itself * * * $50,000,000 in excess cash or combine a manufacturing division owned by the target with a similar division owned by the bidder. Transactions of these types would almost certainly be viewed as in breach of the fiduciary duty new management has assumed to the former target company and would likely give rise to immediate shareholder derivative suits. Transactions between the bidder and its new partially owned subsidiary must be made at arms length and, even then, there is a substantial opportunity for distracting litigation brought by minority shareholders of the target. * * *

* * * However, it is not possible, as practical matter, to acquire 100 percent of the shares of a publicly held corporation by a tender offer. Even in an irresistibly attractive tender offer for all shares, a few shareholders always fail to tender by reason of inadvertence or inattention, and there always are a few small shareholders who hold out and refuse to accept an offer at any price. A follow-up transaction to eliminate the remaining shareholders is an essential step where 100 percent ownership is desired. These follow-up transactions, often called back-end or mop-up transactions, are statutory mergers. A back-end transaction is not necessary if the bidder is willing to accept the status of a majority shareholder in a publicly held corporation with minority shareholders.

In a public cash tender offer, the bidder may make the back-end transaction an affirmative weapon. The bidder may make a partial tender offer, seeking to acquire a controlling interest but less than all of the target's outstanding shares, and at the same time announce, as part of its takeover strategy, the terms of the back-end merger that will eliminate all of the remaining outstanding shares if the original partial offer is successful. Such an offer is known as a two-step offer or two-tier offer. The terms of the back-end part of the two-step offer, moreover, may be less attractive than the terms of the original cash tender offer, thereby encouraging (or coercing) all share-

3. Reprinted with permission of Aspen Law & Business/Panel Publishers, a division of As-   pen Publishers, Inc. The text set forth is subject to further revision.

holders to tender promptly to avoid the less attractive terms of the follow-up transaction. Such an offer is known as a front-end loaded offer and is sometimes referred to as a coercive offer (although coercion comes in many forms). Many states have enacted statutes restricting back-end transactions.

HAMILTON, CORPORATE MERGERS AND ACQUISITIONS
The Guide to American Law Yearbook.*
Pp. 66, 72–75 (1990).

Most acquisition transactions since 1985 have involved all-cash purchases of the stock of the target corporation. * * * Even transactions involving little-known companies routinely involve all-cash transactions of hundreds of millions of dollars. The amounts involved in these transactions are so large as to have been almost unimaginable in a private transaction just two decades ago. An important question is that of where all the money is coming from.

In one sense, the answer is very simple: Most of the capital that goes into modern takeover attempts is borrowed. Borrowed money is what makes the modern takeover world go round; if that source of funding disappeared, the present takeover movement would stop instantly. It is true that aggressors such as Conoco and Texaco have immense operations of their own and can accumulate large amounts of cash, but even companies of that size cannot readily finance a multibillion dollar takeover entirely from internal sources. It is not uncommon for more speculative purchasers to borrow virtually all of the capital needed to purchase a going company.

Loans from commercial banks are the source of most of the borrowed capital in large takeover bids, but other sources of high-risk financing also exist. During the 1980s, a market for high-risk, below-investment-grade debt instruments or "bonds," usually called "junk bonds," was largely created by Drexel Burnham Lambert, Inc. This market has grown to the point that it is able to absorb several billion dollars of high-risk debt to finance specific takeover bids. Many institutional investors are active in this market because junk bonds pay interest at rates considerably higher than can be obtained from the less risky "investment-grade" bonds.

In addition, a major source of equity capital has been created by takeover firms such as KKR, which has attracted takeover funds from sophisticated investors, including many institutional investors. The proposed financing by KKR of its purchase of RJR Nabisco illustrates the operation of these modern financing sources. KKR needed $20.1 billion in cash to purchase RJR. (The remaining $4.8 billion was represented by the debt securities being issued to tendering RJR shareholders.) KKR raised the $20.1 billion from the following sources:

    1. Bank loans were obtained from a large consortium of domestic and foreign (largely Japanese) banks—$13.3 billion.

    2. Five billion dollars in "bridge financing" was provided by the brokerage houses of Drexel Burnham Lambert, Inc. ($3.5 billion) and

* Reprinted with permission of the West Publishing Corporation.

Merrill Lynch & Company ($1.5 billion). This bridge financing was to be refinanced within a year by the sale of junk bonds to investors.

3. KKR limited partners put up $1.5 billion in equity capital. KKR itself put up only $15 million, or 1 percent of the entire risk capital and a tiny fraction of the total purchase price. Altogether, KKR raised $25.7 billion to cover the purchase price and expenses but invested only about $15 million of its own capital in order to acquire the nation's nineteenth largest commercial enterprise!

Why do banks and others agree to make such large loans to fund buyouts? For one thing, the return is good—interest rates on both takeover-directed bank loans and junk bonds are well above those available from other alternative investments. For another thing, fees for making loan commitments are earned whether or not the sale actually occurs. In the RJR Nabisco transaction, Merrill Lynch & Company and Drexel Burnham Lambert, Inc., received fees of about $200 million for their commitment to invest $5 billion, while the banks received a somewhat larger amount in commitment fees for making their much larger commitments. These fees are earned and paid when the commitment is made and are not dependent on the success of the bid.

Yet when all is said and done, commitment fees and high interest rates alone do not explain the attractiveness of these loans. One does not make money even from large loan commitment fees and high interest rates if the loans are so risky that they are unlikely to be repaid. These transactions are attractive because the risks are not as great as they first appear. An essential attribute of the ability of KKR and other takeover firms to raise immense amounts of capital is that these loans are in effect secured by the assets and cash flow of the target corporation itself. Such transactions are called "leveraged buyouts" or "bootstrap transactions." Approximately one-half of the recent takeover transactions were of this type. The banks were willing to lend more than $13 billion to KKR to purchase RJR Nabisco common stock because they were assured that, if the transaction succeeded, the assets and cash flow of RJR Nabisco would be used to pay the interest on and secure the repayment of the loans and junk bonds used to finance the purchase.

Of course, RJR Nabisco already had some indebtedness on its books. The new debt was simply added onto this existing debt and it is expected to repay the entire amount. Needless to say, Nabisco's existing creditors were not happy at these new obligations being assumed by RJR Nabisco. Since the proceeds of the new loans were used to pay shareholders, they did not benefit RJR Nabisco, and loans owed to existing creditors now were less secure and considerably more risky. But there was not very much they could do about the transaction.

After a leveraged buyout, the target may find that its total debt obligations greatly exceed its ability to repay them if business is continued as usual. Such a corporation may find it necessary to make Herculean efforts to reduce costs and increase cash flow. It may be compelled to sell portions of its business to third parties in order to liquidate at least a portion of the new indebtedness and permit the corporation to remain solvent. Transactions in which such later sales of components of the original business are contemplated at the time of the offer are called "bust-up transactions" or "bust-up acquisitions." Improvements in earnings and cash flow may also be achieved from the savings inherent in not being a reporting publicly-held corporation, from the immense tax deductions arising from the interest payments on its debt, from the elimination of dividends, and from economic improvements to the target's business. Indeed, the disciplinary effect of the increase in debt has been cited by some observers as a major benefit arising from leveraged transactions since it encourages increased efficiency and control of costs.

Many established businesses that have been acquired in leveraged buy-outs have proven that they are able to carry large increases of indebtedness during periods of high economic activity. However, the recent spate of multibillion dollar leveraged buyouts, bust-up transactions, and junk bond financing—because of the immense sums of money involved—has caused concern among regulatory agencies, legislators, and the general public. The principal concern that has been expressed about the growth of such leveraged transactions generally is whether most of these debt-burdened businesses can survive when there is an economic downturn. Since there was no significant downturn during the 1980s, no one really knows the answer to this question. A secondary concern that has sometimes been expressed is whether the large investments by commercial banks and institutional investors in leveraged buyout loans and investments may harm the public's confidence in the nation's financial institutions during an economic downturn. If such a downturn occurs, the future of the spectacular mergers and acquisitions examined here will be in grave doubt.

Notes

(1) Consider Michael C. Jensen, Eclipse of the Public Corporation, 67 Harv. Bus.Rev., No. 5 (Sept.–Oct.1989) 61, 61–64[4]:

> The publicly held corporation, the main engine of economic progress in the United States for a century, has outlived its usefulness in many sectors of the economy and is being eclipsed. New organizations are emerging in its place—organizations that are corporate in form but have no public shareholders and are not listed or traded on organized exchanges. These organizations use public and private debt, rather than public equity, as their major source of capital. Their primary owners are not households but large institutions and entrepreneurs that designate agents to manage and monitor on their behalf and bind those agents with large equity interests and contracts governing the use and distribution of cash.

> Takeovers, corporate breakups, divisional spin-offs, leveraged buyouts, and going-private transactions are the most visible manifestations of a massive organizational change in the economy. These transactions have inspired criticism, even outrage, among many business leaders and government officials, who have called for regulatory and legislative restrictions. The backlash is understandable. Change is threatening; in this case, the threat is aimed at the senior executives of many of our largest companies.

> Despite the protests, this organizational innovation should be encouraged. By resolving the central weakness of the public corporation—the conflict between owners and managers over the control and use of corporate resources—these new organizations are making remarkable gains in operating

4. Reprinted by permission of *Harvard Business Review*. Excerpts from "Eclipse of the Public Corporation" by Michael C. Jensen (September–October 1989). Copyright © by the President and Fellows of Harvard College; all rights reserved.

efficiency, employee productivity, and shareholder value. Over the long term, they will enhance U.S. economic performance relative to our most formidable international competitor, Japan, whose companies are moving in the opposite direction. The governance and financial structures of Japan's public companies increasingly resemble U.S. companies of the mid–1960s and early 1970s—an era of gross corporate waste and mismanagement that triggered the organizational transformation now under way in the United States. * * *

Developments as striking as the restructuring of our financial markets and major industries reflect underlying economic forces more fundamental and powerful than financial manipulation, management greed, reckless speculation, and the other colorful epithets used by defenders of the corporate status quo. The forces behind the decline of the public corporation differ from industry to industry. But its decline is real, enduring, and highly productive. It is not merely a function of the tax deductibility of interest. Nor does it reflect a transitory LBO phase through which companies pass before investment bankers and managers cash out by taking them public again. Nor, finally, is it premised on a systematic fleecing of shareholders and bondholders by managers and other insiders with superior information about the true value of corporate assets.

(2) Developments since 1990 have not been favorable to Jensen's thesis. A significant number of LBOs have found it impossible to meet the additional debt obligations and have taken refuge in Chapter 11 of the Bankruptcy Code. The gains from increased efficiency proved to be marginal, and the tax savings fell short of compensating for the high interest and principal payments. The heavy debt load effectively prevented the corporation from being able to deal with the normal fluctuations of the business cycle.

(3) Allan H. Ickowitz & Geoffrey D. Genz, Lender Fraud? Courts Sift Through LBO Suits, Nat'l L. J., Nov. 30, 1992, at 27:[5]

From the perspective of unsecured creditors in a bankruptcy proceeding, the presence of an LBO transaction raises serious issues. Not only is it likely that the LBO contributed to the company's failure, but in addition the claims of unsecured creditors have been rendered all but valueless, as the valuable assets of the debtor corporation have been pledged as security to the LBO lender for loans. The proceeds of these loans went directly to the selling shareholders.

In other words, the traditional positions of shareholders and creditors are reversed after an LBO. The shareholders, normally last in priority to claim any interest in the assets of the debtor's estate, have already been paid, while the unsecured creditors, who ordinarily have a high priority claim, have nothing left after the LBO lender's secured claims are satisfied. * * *

Predictably, creditors of LBO-depleted companies sought a device to avoid their unexpected descent to the bottom of the bankruptcy priority ladder. The Statute of Elizabeth, and now codified in some form in every state—such as in the Uniform Fraudulent Transfer Act—as well as in the U.S. Bankruptcy Code.

---

5. Reprinted with the permission of the   New York Law Publishing Company.
National Law Journal, Copyright 1992, The

(4) The application of the fraudulent transfer statutes to LBO transactions has been controversial. Ickowitz & Genz, Lender Fraud? Courts Sift Through LBO Suits, Nat'l L. J., Nov. 30, 1992, at 27, 28–32:

> Persuading courts to apply the concepts in these statutes at first glance presented no real obstacle. When creditors successfully demonstrated that LBOs, in many instances, satisfied the statutory definition of a fraudulent conveyance, courts could not justify creating an explicit exception to the statutes for LBOs without a legislative directive to do so, despite the urging of some commentators.

> But, * * * decisions indicate a reluctance by the courts to apply the harsh remedy of undoing an LBO to truly legitimate business transactions. This reluctance is magnified when the defendant is the LBO lender, perhaps because the lender in many cases has fared as badly as or worse than other creditors, having paid out substantial sums in loan proceeds that cannot be recovered even after liquidating the remaining assets—or because the lender has received little more than a fair rate of return on the borrowed funds.

> Accordingly, although judges have purported to analyze LBOs under the letter of the fraudulent conveyance statutes, they have stretched to interpret the requirements of those statutes in a manner that protects legitimate LBO transactions. In defense of this approach, such stretching arguably has been necessary to conform to the original intent of the statutes—to prevent intentionally *fraudulent* conveyances.

> Courts have not hesitated to impose liability on LBO lenders when there is clear evidence of intent to defraud creditors.

For cases justifying this divergent treatment of failed LBO transactions, compare Lippi v. City Bank, 955 F.2d 599 (9th Cir.1992), and Kupetz v. Wolf, 845 F.2d 842 (9th Cir.1988).

F. ARE TAKEOVERS GOOD OR BAD?

JOHN C. COFFEE, JR., REGULATING THE MARKET FOR CORPORATE CONTROL, A CRITICAL ASSESSMENT OF THE TENDER OFFER'S ROLE IN CORPORATE GOVERNANCE[6]

84 Colum.L.Rev. 1145, 1162–73 (1984).

Those who have sought to explain the phenomenon of the hostile takeover have usually begun with its most striking fact: bidders have been willing to pay extraordinarily high premiums (sometimes over 100%) for the stock of target corporations,[7] even though the securities so solicited were presumably efficiently priced because they were typically traded on major stock exchanges.

---

6. Copyright © 1984 by the Directors of the Columbia Law Review Association, Inc. All rights reserved. This article originally appeared at 84 Colum.L.Rev. 1145 (1984). Reprinted by permission.

7. [By the Author] Professor Bradley has computed the average premium in a successful tender offer (based on market price two months prior to the offer's announcement) to be 49%. See Bradley, Interfirm Tender Offers and the Market for Corporate Control, 53 J.Bus. 545 (1980). A later study by Professors Jarrell and Bradley estimated that the average cash tender premium had risen to "about 73%" in the wake of state takeover statutes; this percentage was computed based on the target's share price 40 days prior to the offer. See Jarrell and Bradley, The Economic Effects of Federal and State Regulations of Cash Tender Offers, 23 J.Law & Econ. 371, 373 (1980).

Why are such lucrative premiums paid? Most of the explanations can be grouped under one of the following four headings:

1.   *The Disciplinary Hypothesis*. Viewed through the lens supplied by the "market for corporate control" thesis, the role of the tender offer is to replace inefficient management. The bidder, it is argued, pays a premium over the market price because it believes that the target's assets have not been optimally utilized and that under superior management they would earn a higher return, thereby justifying the tender offer premium. In this light, the higher the premium, the greater the degree of mismanagement that the bidder must perceive. So viewed, the hostile tender offer appears a benign and socially desirable phenomenon, which benefits both the bidder and the target's stockholders, who simply divide among themselves the value that the incumbent management's inefficiency denied them. * * *

2.   *The Synergy Hypothesis*. An alternative explanation of the hostile takeover views the takeover premium as justified not by the suboptimal performance of the target, but rather as the result of the target's having a unique value to the bidder that is in excess of its value to the market generally. Put simply, the value of the combined enterprise is expected to be greater than the sum of its separate parts as independent companies. Such "synergistic gains" may be the result of a variety of factors that are independent of the inefficient management thesis: unique product complementarity between the two companies, specialized resources possessed by the target, economies of scale, cost reductions, lowered borrowing costs, or the capital market's response to the combined enterprise. * * * [This hypothesis] is subject to two important objections. First, studies of postacquisition experiences of acquiring companies have typically found that the expected synergy seldom materializes in the form of higher profits. Second, this theory gives little attention to the disciplinary or deterrent impact of hostile takeovers. These flaws do not invalidate the theory, but do suggest that it is only a partial explanation.

3.   *The Empire Building Hypothesis*. A more skeptical explanation for high takeover premiums begins from the obvious possibility that the bidder simply may have overpaid. Those who take a "behavioral" view of the modern corporation have long argued that firms tend to maximize size, not profits. Management may pursue size maximization, even when it is not in the interests of shareholders, for any of a variety of reasons: (1) greater size tends to correspond with higher compensation for management; (2) increased size implies greater security from a takeover or other control contest; (3) enhanced prestige and psychic income are associated with increased size and national visibility; (4) greater size often translates into oligopolistic market power; or, finally, (5) expansion offers opportunities for advancement to the executive staff of the bidding firm. Under this "empire building" thesis, the high premiums paid in tender offers are less an indication of the potential latent in the target's assets than of an overly optimistic assessment by the bidder of its own capabilities as a manager. From this perspective, the takeover process may result not in greater efficiency, but only in a net transfer of wealth from the bidder's shareholders to those of the target. Much empirical data suggest that these wealth transfers occur frequently, but it is considerably more

difficult to argue that they predominate.[8] Nonetheless, the Empire Building Hypothesis suggests that the most important conflict of interests in corporate control contests may be on the bidder's side of the transaction—between the interests of the bidder's management and those of its own shareholders. In any case, as a model which explains takeover activity, the Empire Building Hypothesis focuses singlemindedly on only one variable (the effect on the bidder) and therefore cannot be taken as more than a partial explanation.

4. *The Exploitation Hypothesis.* Gain to the bidder in a takeover can come either through the creation of new value or through the transfer of existing value from other investors. Recent commentators have suggested that such wealth transfers may result from the target shareholders being trapped in a classic "prisoner's dilemma" in which they are faced with a choice between an unsatisfactory current price offered by the bidder and a potentially even lower price in the future.[9]

Two distinct scenarios have been suggested to explain how exploitation might occur. Professor Carney has pointed to the recent appearance of the two-tier bid, in which a high premium is paid in a partial bid for 51% of the target's stock, but then a takeout merger is eventually effected at a price below the pre-tender offer market price, with the result that the average price received amounts to a net loss for the target's shareholders. Actual transactions in which the bidder acquires the target at an average price below the pre-tender trading price remain exceedingly rare, however.

Another, more popular form of the exploitation thesis argues that bidders overreach target shareholders by exploiting temporary depressions in the target's stock price in order to seize control of the target in a bargain purchase. A variation on this same theme views the recent high rate of takeover activity as the product of systematic undervaluation on the part of the stock market * * *.

REINIER KRAAKMAN, TAKING DISCOUNTS SERIOUSLY: THE IMPLICATIONS OF "DISCOUNTED" SHARE PRICES AS AN ACQUISITION MOTIVE[10]

88 Colum.L.Rev. 891, 891–93 (1988).

Assume that the Acme Oil Company has 100,000 shares of stock trading at $10 per share, no debt, and a proven oil well as its only asset; how much

---

8. [By the Author] It is undisputed that in some cases bidder-shareholders have experienced dramatic declines in stock values in response to a takeover bid. * * * Nonetheless, after averaging the results of several studies, one survey has found bidders to average a gain in stock price of 3.8% (after adjustment for general market movement). This average figure is open to question on a variety of methodological grounds, both because it does not include extensive postacquisition experience and because alternate methodological approaches have been developed, which call into question much of the data so averaged. Based on this different approach to the computation of the gains, [one] study found that acquirers suffer significant losses in mergers.

9. [By the Author] Prisoner's dilemmas arise when the affected shareholders are unable to communicate or coordinate their actions to resist a tender offer. In the case of the two-tier takeover, the inability of shareholders to coordinate their actions and resist the initial partial tender offer at an attractive premium leaves them vulnerable to the second stage merger at a price below market. Rational investors, had they been able to coordinate, might have rejected the tender offer.

should an identical firm pay to acquire Acme's oil well? Businessmen might fail the quiz, but finance students would probably answer: "Not more than $1,000,000 ($10 × 100,000), excluding synergy gains or tax savings."

This answer echoes a common presumption in the finance literature that informed securities prices credibly estimate the underlying value of corporate assets. Firms whose share prices fall below the market value of their assets—for example, many closed-investment funds, holding companies, or natural resource firms—are frequently tagged as anomalies on this view.[11] But these "anomalous" firms happen to be the only firms whose asset values are readily visible. Here, then, is the rub: The direct evidence, as far as it goes, is more consistent with the conjecture that securities prices *often* "discount"—or underprice—expected cash flows from corporate assets than with the standard presumption that share prices fully value these assets. If discounts are widespread, however, they have significant consequences for many areas of corporate behavior, including, above all, acquisition behavior and the takeover market.

As the Acme hypothetical suggests, the presumption that share prices fully value corporate assets carries a basic implication for acquisition premia. If share prices already reflect the value of targets' assets, then takeover premia, which now average over 50% of prebid share prices, must reflect something else of value that bidders bring to acquisitions: for example, better management or synergy gains. An astute acquirer would never pay $1,500,000 for Acme's shares unless it could earn at least $500,000, on a present value basis, more than what Acme already expects to earn. By contrast, on the view that share prices may discount asset values, takeover premia have an alternative source in the *existing* value of targets' assets. Acme's acquirer might pay $1,500,000 simply because Acme's oil well was reliably appraised at, say, $1,700,000. In this case, the "premium" received by Acme's shareholders might be more accurately described as a recaptured discount.

The discount claim conforms to an intuition, deeply rooted in corporate law and business practice, that share prices often diverge from asset values.[12] I will argue that this intuition is credible for important classes of acquisitions. Nevertheless, the discount claim is an incomplete account of acquisition gains absent an explanation of how share discounts might arise. Here, at least two familiar but divergent hypotheses are possible. One—the "misinvestment" hypothesis—holds that investors rationally expect managers of target firms to misinvest the future returns on corporate assets, and discount the value of these assets accordingly. The second hypothesis—the "market" hypothesis—asserts that share prices themselves may be noisy or skewed. On this view, market prices simply fail to reflect informed estimates of likely cash flows generated by target firms. Both discount hypotheses predict similar acquisition behavior and carry similar implications for other corporate behavior,

11. [By the Author] * * * Of course, discrepancies between share prices and asset values would always be anomalies in a theoretical world of perfect capital and asset markets, no matter how pervasive they were in actual markets.

12. [By the Author] See, e.g., Smith v. Van Gorkom, 488 A.2d 858, 875–76 (Del.1985)(large premium, or spread between offer price and market price, may still undervalue corporate assets). A basic feature of the share contract is a redemption or appraisal right, triggered by fundamental corporate changes, against the going-concern value of the firms. See, e.g., Rosenblatt v. Getty Oil Co., 493 A.2d 929, 930 (Del. 1985).

including the influence of financial policy on share prices. Nevertheless, the distinction between these hypotheses is crucial, since the choice of a discount hypothesis will govern the regulatory implications of the discount claim. * * *

Three possibilities might occur to an observer who first learned that acquirers routinely pay large premia over share price for the assets of target firms: (1) acquirers may be discovering more valuable uses for target assets; (2) share prices may "underprice" these assets; or, finally, (3) acquirers may simply be paying too much. These same possibilities point to a useful typology of current explanations of acquisition gains. A broad class of "traditional" gains hypotheses assumes that acquirers can create or claim new value to pay for acquisition premia. These explanations accord with the assumption that informed share prices fully reflect asset values. They include all ways in which acquirers might expect to increase the net cash flows of targets, for example, by improving management or redeploying assets. A second class of "discount" hypotheses asserts that while acquirers' bid prices reflect real private gains, these gains result because share prices discount the underlying value of target assets. Finally, a third and more troubling class of "overbidding" hypotheses questions whether bid prices and takeover premia reflect real opportunities for acquisition gains at all. Under these theories, managers of acquiring firms may misperceive or misvalue targets out of "hubris," or they may pursue distinctly managerial interests such as corporate growth at great cost to shareholder interests.

JOHN C. COFFEE, JR., THE UNCERTAIN CASE FOR TAKEOVER REFORM: AN ESSAY ON STOCKHOLDERS, STAKEHOLDERS AND BUST–UPS[13]

1988 Wisc.L.Rev. 435, 443–51 (1988).

This is an argumentative essay, longer on speculation than substantiation. * * * Modern institutional economics views the corporation as a "nexus of contracts"—a complex institutional mechanism, which is designed, at least in part, to uphold (and thus permit reliance upon) "implicit contracts" reached between the shareholders and other "stakeholders" in the corporation (e.g., managers, creditors, employees and possibly certain suppliers). * * *

For present purposes, the differences among these "implicit contract" theories are of secondary importance, because in common all recognize the possibility that shareholders could opportunistically breach the implicit contract. [I]n theory, the gains accruing to shareholders in takeovers could simply be wealth transfers from other stakeholders in the corporation (for example, creditors, managers, etc.). Indeed, the social loss could easily exceed the private gain. Such an example has been forcefully posed by Professors Summers and Shleifer, who focus on the ripple effect when plants are closed in a small, one-company town (e.g., Bartlesville, Oklahoma, or Findley, Ohio— the bases of Phillips Petroleum and Marathon Oil, respectively).[14] Not only do

---

13. Copyright 1988, by the Board of Regents of the University of Wisconsin System. Reprinted by permission of Wisconsin Law Review.

14. [By the Author] See A. Shleifer & C. Summers, Hostile Takeovers as Breaches of Trust 4–7, 17–20 (National Bureau of Economic Research Working Paper on The Economic

employees lose salary, but the fixed investments of local suppliers and indeed the local infrastructure are jeopardized. Moreover, other firms are also affected because they may thereafter find it more difficult to induce other suppliers to make fixed investments or to encourage their employees to invest in "firm-specific" human capital. Finally, even if there is no net social loss, any wealth transfer here is probably in an anti-egalitarian direction, because employees are losing as shareholders gain. If we assume that money has a decreasing marginal utility—that the poor value one additional dollar more than the rich—then such transfers have negative social utility, even if there is no net financial loss. * * *

The claim that takeover gains are accounted for by the losses of other stakeholders remains unproven. No clear pattern is evident with respect to creditors,[15] and managerial losses are difficult to estimate. Conversely, * * * the scale of recent takeover gains (roughly $167 billion according to one recent study) cannot be plausibly explained simply on the basis of cost savings to shareholders from opportunistic breaches of implicit contracts. This becomes clearer if we consider takeovers on the micro level. Today, the average takeover premium is around 40 to 50 percent. One cannot generally explain a rational bidder paying $1.5 billion for a target whose prior aggregate stock market value was $1 billion, simply in terms of the cost savings that managerial layoffs are likely to effect. Indeed, for such a takeover to be rational on this basis, given both the risks and the notoriously high transaction costs, the bidder would have to expect to realize cost savings considerably greater than this $500 million premium in order for it to earn a reasonable profit. Although the total losses to third parties, such as local communities and suppliers, may conceivably approach this level, these losses do not necessarily make the bidder better off; the bidder is not one dollar richer because local store owners will sell less when the local plant closes. Moreover, there will be social gains elsewhere where new plants are opened and new suppliers hired, although this may occur abroad and thus not offset national social wealth loss. Given this asymmetry between private gains and social losses, social losses cannot by themselves explain the bidder's motivation.

Notes

Carley, Battle Tactics: Carl Icahn's Strategies In His Quest for TWA Are a Model for Raiders, Wall St.J., June 20, 1985, at 1, col. 6:[16]

NEW YORK—In a half-deserted bar at the Waldorf–Astoria Hotel last month, Carl Icahn leaned across a table toward C.E. Meyer, the president of Trans World Airlines. Mr. Icahn had been trying to take over TWA, and Mr. Meyer had been stoutly resisting.

After a series of verbal thrusts about the best interests of stockholders, the conversation turned bitter. As Mr. Icahn described it in a federal court deposition in New York City later last month, the talk went like this:

Effects of Mergers and Acquisitions, Feb. 1987).

15. [By the Author] One recent survey estimates that bondholders have lost as much as $530 million in 1986 as the result of mergers, acquisitions and recapitalizations. See IRRC, Bondholders Fight Back Against Takeover Losses, 4 Corp. Governance Bull. 156 (Sept./ Oct. 1987). Financial economists have, however, generally found no net losses. Id. at 157.

16. Reprinted by permission of the Wall Street Journal, © Dow Jones & Company, Inc. (1985). All Rights Reserved.

He [Mr. Meyer] said, "All you want is a fast buck. That's all you have ever done in any of these [corporate raids], go for a fast buck."

I said, "If we are psychoanalyzing each other, why don't you admit * * * what you really care about is your job, and you are afraid I am going to take it away from you."

Then, according to Mr. Icahn, "We just sort of looked at each other."

Is not this exchange a realistic explanation of the motivations that really drive the takeover movement—prestige, power, and money?

ROBERTA ROMANO, A GUIDE TO TAKEOVERS: THEORY, EVIDENCE AND REGULATION
9 Yale J. on Reg. 119, 120, 125–25, 129–31, 133–38, 141–45, 155 (1992).

There is a voluminous economic literature seeking to explain takeovers. There is also substantial regulation. This article relates the one to the other, and is a guide to both. It reviews the economic literature in order to facilitate an evaluation of the efficacy of current regulation. The premise is that if some explanations of takeovers are more plausible than others, then certain regulatory regimes make more sense than others. I refer to explanations in the plural because we do not have a comprehensive theory of takeovers. Different theories do well at explaining various subsets of acquisitions, but no theory satisfactorily explains all.

The empirical evidence is most consistent with value-maximizing, efficiency-based explanations of takeovers. * * *

A.   Value–Maximizing Efficiency Explanations

There are two efficiency explanations of takeovers: to realize synergy gains and to reduce agency costs.

1.   Synergy Gains

One value-maximizing efficiency explanation of takeovers is to achieve synergy gains: the value of the combined firm is greater than the value of the two firms (target and acquirer) separately. The increased value may be generated by real operating efficiencies, or it may be due to financial synergies.

2.   Reducing Agency Costs

A reduction in agency costs is the other efficiency explanation for takeovers. Corporate law is concerned with principal-agent problems, the alignment of managers' incentives with shareholders' interests. A takeover is, in this framework, a backstop remedy when other corporate governance devices that monitor performance, such as the board of directors, fail at effective incentive-alignment.

a.   Replacement of Inefficient Management

The most important agency cost explanation of takeovers is that they reduce managerial slack by replacing inefficient management. Manne put forth this view in a classic article over 20 years ago, and it is one of the central insights in corporate law scholarship.[17] Manne maintained that takeovers are the market for corporate control's key mechanism for disciplining managers because, unlike mergers, which require the approval of the target firm's board, the takeover bypasses target management and goes directly to the target shareholders for approval. Takeovers accordingly keep the capital market competitive, and constrain managers to work in the shareholders' interest.

A number of studies provide support for this explanation. For example, acquired firms earn low rates of return prior to mergers and acquiring companies are above average in profitability. Morck, Shleifer, and Vishny find that targets of hostile takeovers, in which managers are more likely to be replaced, are poor performers, as measured by low Tobin's q ratios, compared to targets of friendly acquisitions.[18] Moreover, target firms have, on average, low q ratios, and the gains from takeovers increase when bidders with high q ratios acquire targets with low q ratios. Finally, Mitchell and Lehn find that bad bidders make good targets: firms that experience negative abnormal returns from acquisitions are more likely to be acquired than firms that do not. These studies all indicate that takeovers discipline management, because they are focused on firms with poor performance.

In addition, management turnover is much higher after a takeover than it is when there is no change in control or when firms engage in a friendly merger. Most importantly, Martin and McConnell find that takeover targets whose managers are replaced earned negative abnormal returns before the takeover, as measured against their industry, while targets whose managers are retained earned positive abnormal returns. Of course, turnover does not necessarily indicate that the departing managers are of poorer quality than their replacements. But if we did not observe turnover at the top after takeovers, and if such turnover was unrelated to the targets' performance, then the inefficient management explanation would be in serious jeopardy.

Finally, there is evidence that after mergers, firms' cash flows improve as a result of increased asset productivity. Because the cash flow improvements do not differ across related and unrelated-firm acquisitions, the gains do not appear to come from the realization of operating synergies. This finding suggests that acquirers are better able to manage target assets. I therefore consider it to be consistent with the inefficient management explanation of takeovers.

The inefficient management explanation cannot, however, explain all restructuring transactions. It cannot, for example, explain acquisitions in which the acquirer retains incumbent management, a pattern that appears to have been common in large acquisitions by conglomerate firms. In particular,

---

17. [By the Author] Henry G. Manne, Mergers and the Market for Corporate Control, 73 J. Pol.Econ. 110 (1965).

18. [By the Author] Randall Morck, Andrei Shleifer & Robert W. Vishny, *Characteristics of Targets of Hostile and Friendly Takeovers, in* Corporate Takeovers: Causes and Consequences 101 (Alan J. Auerbach ed., 1988). Tobin's q is the ratio of a firm's market value to the replacement cost of its physical assets. It thus measures the firm's intangible assets—

goodwill, future growth opportunities, quality of management. As Servaes puts it, Tobin's q "measures the market's assessment of the value of the assets in place and * * * future investment opportunities [and a]s such it is a measure of managerial performance." Henri Servaes, Tobin's Q, Agency Costs and Corporate Control 1 (1989) (unpublished manuscript, on file with the author). A low q (q _ 1) indicates poor performance.

it cannot explain management-led leveraged buyouts (MBOs), because in these transactions top management is part of the acquiring group and stays on the job. However, even in these transactions, there are often subsequent management changes.[19]

b. Free Cash Flow

An alternative explanation that views takeovers as a mechanism for reducing agency costs but does not predict management's replacement is Jensen's "free cash flow" theory. Jensen contends that a cause of takeover activity, especially in the petroleum industry, is the agency cost associated with the conflict between managers and shareholders over the payout of free cash flow. Free cash flow is cash flow in excess of the amount required to fund all of the firm's projects that have a positive net present value. If these funds are paid out to shareholders, managers will have fewer resources under their control, and will thus be unable to waste cash by investing in projects with negative net present values. In addition, eliminating free cash flow subjects managers to capital market monitoring when they need to finance new projects, further constraining their ability to undertake negative net present value transactions.

This explanation stands the financial synergy (reduction of the cost of capital) explanation on its head, both because it is the target and not the acquiring firm with excess cash, and because external financing is deemed preferable to internal financing, due to incentive problems. But in contrast to the other efficiency explanations, an acquiring firm is not needed to realize this operating improvement. Incumbent managers can eliminate free cash flow on their own through a financial restructuring, which increases the firm's leverage and pays the borrowed cash out to the shareholders. * * *

B. VALUE-MAXIMIZING EXPROPRIATION EXPLANATIONS

Expropriation explanations of takeovers focus on four distinct groups: taxpayers, bondholders, employees, and consumers.

1. Tax Benefits

Tax benefits provide another value-maximizing explanation for takeovers. Because interest is deductible, this is a more obvious explanation for leveraged acquisitions than the monitoring story of free cash flows: the increased debt load shelters more income, motivating the transaction. * * *

The tax explanation of takeovers is not compelling theoretically. The interest deduction is a tax benefit that does not require an acquisition to be realized—a target firm can leverage its capital structure on its own. This is therefore not an equilibrium story for it implies that the firm had a suboptimal capital structure pre-takeover. Consequently, to be plausible the increased interest-deduction tax explanation of takeovers must be merged with

19. [By the Author] The majority buyer in a leveraged buyout often replaces the retained incumbent management within a year or so of the MBO. *See, e.g.,* Roberts v. General Instrument Corp., 1990 WL 118356 (Del.Ch.1990) (3 of 5 Forstmann–Little buyout firms canvassed by defendant had new, i.e., non-incumbent, chief executive officers). In addition, 12% of the firms in Smith's sample of MBOs replaced a chief executive officer under age 65 within 2 years of the buyout. Abbie J. Smith, *Corporate Ownership Structure and Performance: The Case of Management Buyouts,* 27 J. Fin. Econ. 162 (1990). These data suggest that MBOs may well be driven by Manne's explanation.

an agency cost explanation: target management has failed to maximize firm value by carrying too little debt and paying too much in taxes. * * *

2. Bondholder Expropriation

* * * Leveraged acquisitions may simply be mechanisms for expropriating the wealth of bondholders, rather than taxpayers. When a firm increases its leverage, the value of preexisting debt decreases because it is now a riskier investment (the firm's cash flows may not cover the new debt load). As the bondholders are not compensated for this increased risk, the leveraged transaction redistributes wealth to the shareholders. Bondholders can and do, however, protect themselves from losses upon a leveraged acquisition by event-risk indenture provisions.

Several studies have sought to measure the effects of leveraged acquisitions on target debt. Although bond ratings are typically lowered after a leveraged buyout, studies find either no significant bond price effects or a small negative effect which is nowhere near the magnitude of the premium paid to the shareholders. Bonds without restrictive covenants, such as event-risk provisions, which protect debtholders' investment against leverage increases, experience the greatest losses: for example, Asquith and Wizman find that unprotected bonds experienced negative abnormal returns of 5% whereas protected bonds had positive abnormal returns of 2%. In addition, the size of the shareholders' gain is not correlated with the amount of outstanding debt. Bondholder expropriation cannot, therefore, be driving acquisitions because the bondholders' losses are simply too small compared to takeover premiums.

3. Expropriation From Labor

The expropriation explanation of takeovers that attracts the most attention involves labor as the victim. The most sophisticated version of this explanation is Shleifer and Summers' breach of implicit contract explanation of hostile takeovers.

In Shleifer and Summers' scenario, shareholders initially hire trustworthy individuals as managers, in order to make credible long-term contract commitments to workers. The long-term commitments are implicit, rather than explicit contracts. After employees are hired, shareholders will want to breach the implicit contract, in order to increase their returns by lowering labor's share. A trustworthy management prevents them from doing so by honoring the informal agreements. A hostile takeover will, however, permit shareholders to behave opportunistically because, unlike trustworthy incumbents, a raider will not hesitate to break implicit contracts, cutting costs and releasing the pent-up value of the firm to shareholders.

Rosett tests Shleifer and Summers' breach of contract explanation more directly by examining union wage contracts before and after takeovers. He finds no support for their thesis: there is, in fact, a positive gain in union wealth levels after hostile acquisitions. Although there are losses after friendly acquisitions, even then the losses are insignificant relative to the premiums (when measured over 18 years after the takeover, the union losses in friendly acquisitions equal approximately 5% of the shareholders' gain). Bhagat, Shleifer, and Vishny also find that layoffs occur infrequently, affect high-level white collar workers, are higher when management successfully defeats a bid (either by remaining independent or by finding a white knight) than when a hostile bidder succeeds and, most important, result in losses that are small compared to takeover premiums (10–20%). In sum, while we would need counterfactual data to test the labor expropriation hypothesis fully—we need to know how many workers would have been laid off or what the wage profile would have looked like if the firm had not been acquired—what we do know suggests that expropriation from labor does not motivate takeovers.

C.   Value-Maximizing Market Inefficiency Explanations

The final value-maximizing (that is, beneficial to acquirers' shareholders) explanation of takeover gains is premised on market inefficiency, the view that stock prices do not reflect firms' "fundamental value." According to this explanation, which is probably as widely-circulated in the popular press as the labor expropriation explanation, acquirers exploit market inefficiency by identifying undervalued firms, and presumably capture a large share of the gains by paying premiums below the correct valuation. There are two distinct market inefficiency explanations: general underpricing of stocks and myopia (overvaluation of current profits and excessive discounting of future profits).

1.   *Underpricing*

* * * There is no evidence supporting the underpricing explanation of takeover gains. In particular, if this explanation was correct, then once a bidder identified a target, its price would rise and remain at the higher true value, regardless of whether the acquisition occurred. Several studies find, however, that the stock price of takeover targets that are not acquired returns to its lower pre-bid price. Takeovers therefore do not merely provide an inefficient market with the information necessary for revaluing stock prices. More generally, the large body of event studies examining numerous events in corporate finance besides acquisitions casts doubt on this explanation, as the studies are supportive of market efficiency.

2.   *Market Myopia*

The market myopia inefficiency explanation is more sophisticated than the underpricing hypothesis. In this explanation, investors are short-sighted and behave myopically to sacrifice long-term benefits for immediate profits. As a consequence, firms that engage in long-term planning and make substantial investments in research and development (R & D) are supposedly undervalued by the market and become takeover targets. To avoid undervalued stock, managers thus also behave myopically and shift from profitable long-term investments to more easily valued short-term projects. * * *

There is, however, no empirical support for a myopia explanation. First, there is no evidence of market myopia regarding long-term investment. The market responds positively to announcements of increases in R & D and other capital investment expenditures. Second, there is scant evidence of the posited manager myopia. Firms that protect themselves from takeovers by adopting defensive charter amendments, thus ostensibly freeing themselves from market myopia, actually decrease their R & D expenditures after taking such action. In addition, targets (especially of LBOs) are in industries with low levels of R & D activity, and there are no significant differences in R & D intensity (the ratio of R & D expenditures to sales) between acquiring and acquired firms. Finally, there are no significant differences in the growth of R

& D (as measured by intensity or employment levels) between firms involved in acquisitions and those that are not.

* * * I * * * read the literature as most consonant with the value-maximizing, efficiency-enhancing explanations of takeovers. However, different takeover theories each explain best only subsets of acquisitions and, though empirical studies might point in a particular direction, none are conclusive. There may be, then, instances of non-value-maximizing acquisitions as well as acquisitions which transfer wealth from particular groups to target shareholders, but these should be viewed as the exception, rather than the rule.

G. THE RESPONSE OF STATE LEGISLATURES

WILLIAM ALLEN, U.S. CORPORATE GOVERNANCE IN A POST–MANAGERIAL AGE

Text of Speech Given as the Fifth Distinguished Lecture in International
Business and Trade Law, University of Toronto Faculty of Laws.
Pp. 12–14 (Oct. 20, 1993).

I need not now reprise the causes and effects of the hostile takeover phenomena in the U.S. I note only that during the 1980s, that element of U.S. corporate governance structure represented by the market for corporate control became super heated. In general, academic lawyers and economists approved, believing, generally that these voluntary transactions increased efficiency in the system, created wealth and improved human welfare.

But the polity in general could not, in the end be convinced by the efficiency enhancing account that economists and financiers gave of these tumultuous transactions. By the close of the 1980s there was in the U.S. widespread disenchantment, and indeed anger, at the hostile takeover movement and the dislocations it was thought to cause. The antipathy to takeovers that became evident by the close of the 1980s is quite understandable, of course. Dynamic market systems produce losers as well as winners, even when they increase total wealth. The redistributional impacts of hostile takeovers were seen as significant, and large scale redistribution, or the appearance of it, is disruptive and politically significant.

These dislocations, disruptions and redistributions ultimately did cause profound legislative backlash, not in our federal Congress but in the state legislatures across the U.S. State legislators with no responsibility for the national economy, but with an exquisite sensitivity to the pain that radical restructuring of large corporations seemed to cause to local constituents, were easily enlisted on the side of the status quo. In a remarkably short period towards the end of the 1980s more than 25 separate jurisdictions amended their corporation law to include so-called corporate stakeholder or constituency statutes. These statutes were designed to thwart hostile takeovers. * * *

CTS CORP. v. DYNAMICS CORP. OF AMERICA

Supreme Court of the United States, 1987.
481 U.S. 69, 107 S.Ct. 1637, 95 L.Ed.2d 67.

JUSTICE POWELL delivered the opinion of the Court.

This case presents the questions whether the Control Share Acquisitions Chapter of the Indiana Business Corporation Law, Ind.Code § 23–1–42–1 *et seq.* (Supp.1986), is preempted by the Williams Act or violates the Commerce Clause of the Federal Constitution, Art. I, § 8, cl. 3.

I

A

On March 4, 1986, the Governor of Indiana signed a revised Indiana Business Corporation Law, Ind.Code § 23–1–17–1 *et seq.* (Supp.1986). That law included the Control Share Acquisitions Chapter (Indiana Act or Act). Beginning on August 1, 1987, the Act will apply to any corporation incorporated in Indiana, § 23–1–17–3(a), unless the corporation amends its articles or incorporation or bylaws to opt out of the Act, § 23–1–42–5. Before that date, any Indiana corporation can opt into the Act by resolution of its board of directors. § 23–1–17–3(b). The Act applies only to "issuing public corporations." The term "corporation" includes only businesses incorporated in Indiana. See § 23–1–20–5. An "issuing public corporation" is defined as:

"a corporation that has:

"(1)   one hundred (100) or more shareholders;

"(2)   its principal place of business, its principal office, or substantial assets within Indiana; and

"(3)   either:

"(A)   more than ten percent (10%) of its shareholders resident in Indiana;

"(B)   more than ten percent (10%) of its shares owned by Indiana residents; or

"(C)   ten thousand (10,000) shareholders resident in Indiana." § 23–1–42–4(a).[20]

The Act focuses on the acquisition of "control shares" in an issuing public corporation. Under the Act, an entity acquires "control shares" whenever it acquires shares that, but for the operation of the Act, would bring its voting power in the corporation to or above any of three thresholds: 20%, 33⅓%, or 50%. § 23–1–42–1. An entity that acquires control shares does not necessarily acquire voting rights. Rather, it gains those rights only "to the extent granted by resolution approved by the shareholders of the issuing public corporation." § 23–1–42–9(a). Section 23–1–42–9(b) requires a majority vote of all disinterested[21] shareholders holding each class of stock for passage

---

20. [By the Court] These thresholds are much higher than the 5% threshold acquisition requirement that brings a tender offer under the coverage of the Williams Act.

21. [By the Court] "Interested shares" are shares with respect to which the acquiror, an officer, or an inside director of the corporation "may exercise or direct the exercise of the voting power of the corporation in the election of directors." § 23–1–42–3. If the record date passes before the acquiror purchases shares pursuant to the tender offer, the purchased shares will not be "interested shares" within

the meaning of the Act; although the acquiror may own the shares on the date of the meeting, it will not "exercise ... the voting power" of the shares.

As a practical matter, the record date usually will pass before shares change hands. Under Securities and Exchange Commission (SEC) regulations, the shares cannot be purchased until 20 business days after the offer commences. 17 CFR § 240.14e–1(a) (1986). If the acquiror seeks an early resolution of the issue—as most acquirors will—the meeting required by the Act must be held no more than

of such a resolution. The practical effect of this requirement is to condition acquisition of control of a corporation on approval of a majority of the pre-existing disinterested shareholders.

The shareholders decide whether to confer rights on the control shares at the next regularly scheduled meeting of the shareholders, or at a specially scheduled meeting. The acquiror can require management of the corporation to hold such a special meeting within 50 days if it files an "acquiring person statement,"[22] requests the meeting, and agrees to pay the expenses of the meeting. See § 23–1–42–7. If the shareholders do not vote to restore voting rights to the shares, the corporation may redeem the control shares from the acquiror at fair market value, but it is not required to do so. § 23–1–42–10(b). Similarly, if the acquiror does not file an acquiring person statement with the corporation, the corporation may, if its bylaws or articles of incorporation so provide, redeem the shares at any time after 60 days after the acquiror's last acquisition. § 23–1–42–10(a).

B

On March 10, 1986, appellee Dynamics Corporation of America (Dynamics) owned 9.6% of the common stock of appellant CTS Corporation, an Indiana corporation. On that day, six days after the Act went into effect, Dynamics announced a tender offer for another million shares in CTS; purchase of those shares would have brought Dynamics' ownership interest in CTS to 27.5%. Also on March 10, Dynamics filed suit in the United States District Court for the Northern District of Illinois, alleging that CTS had violated the federal securities laws in a number of respects no longer relevant to these proceedings. On March 27, the board of directors of CTS, an Indiana corporation, elected to be governed by the provisions of the Act, see § 23–1–17–3.

Four days later, on March 31, Dynamics moved for leave to amend its complaint to allege that the Act is preempted by the Williams Act, and violates the Commerce Clause, Art. I, § 8, cl. 3. Dynamics sought a temporary restraining order, a preliminary injunction, and declaratory relief against CTS' use of the Act. On April 9, the District Court ruled that the Williams Act preempts the Indiana Act and granted Dynamics' motion for declaratory relief. 637 F.Supp. 389 (N.D.Ill.1986). Relying on Justice White's plurality opinion in *Edgar v. MITE Corp.*, 457 U.S. 624, 102 S.Ct. 2629, 73 L.Ed.2d 269 (1982), the court concluded that the Act "wholly frustrates the purpose and objective of Congress in striking a balance between the investor, management, and the takeover bidder in takeover contests." 637 F.Supp., at 399. A week later, on April 17, the District Court issued an opinion accepting Dynamics' claim that the Act violates the Commerce Clause. This holding rested on the

50 calendar days after the offer commences, about three weeks after the earliest date on which the shares could be purchased. See § 23–1–42–7. The Act requires management to give notice of the meeting "as promptly as reasonably practicable ... to all shareholders of record as of the record date set for the meeting." § 23–1–42–8(a). It seems likely that management of the target corporation would violate this obligation if it delayed setting the record date and sending notice until after 20 business days had passed. Thus, we assume that the record date usually will be set before the date on which federal law first permits purchase of the shares.

22. [By the Court] An "acquiring person statement" is an information statement describing, *inter alia*, the identity of the acquiring person and the terms and extent of the proposed acquisition. See § 23–1–42–6.

court's conclusion that "the substantial interference with interstate commerce created by the [Act] outweighs the articulated local benefits so as to create an impermissible indirect burden on interstate commerce." *Id.*, at 406. The District Court certified its decisions on the Williams Act and Commerce Clause claims as final under Federal Rule of Civil Procedure 54(b). Ibid.

CTS appealed the District Court's holdings on these claims to the Court of Appeals for the Seventh Circuit. Because of the imminence of CTS' annual meeting, the Court of Appeals consolidated and expedited the two appeals. On April 23rd—23 days after Dynamics first contested application of the Act in the District Court—the Court of Appeals issued an order affirming the judgment of the District Court. The opinion followed on May 28. 794 F.2d 250 (C.A.7 1986).

After disposing of a variety of questions not relevant to this appeal, the Court of Appeals examined Dynamics' claim that the Williams Act preempts the Indiana Act. The court looked first to the plurality opinion in *Edgar v. MITE Corp., supra,* in which three Justices found that the Williams Act preempts state statutes that upset the balance between target management and a tender offeror. The court noted that some commentators had disputed this view of the Williams Act, concluding instead that the Williams Act was "an anti-takeover statute, expressing a view, however benighted, that hostile takeovers are bad." 794 F.2d, at 262. It also noted:

> [I]t is a big leap from saying that the Williams Act does not itself exhibit much hostility to tender offers to saying that it implicitly forbids states to adopt more hostile regulations.... But whatever doubts of the Williams' Act preemptive intent we might entertain as an original matter are stilled by the weight of precedent. *Ibid.*

Once the court had decided to apply the analysis of the *MITE* plurality, it found the case straightforward:

> Very few tender offers could run the gauntlet that Indiana has set up. In any event, if the Williams Act is to be taken as a congressional determination that a month (roughly) is enough time to force a tender offer to be kept open, 50 days is too much; and 50 days is the minimum under the Indiana act if the target corporation so chooses. *Id.*, at 263.

The court next addressed Dynamic's Commerce Clause challenge to the Act. Applying the balancing test articulated in *Pike v. Bruce Church, Inc.,* 397 U.S. 137, 90 S.Ct. 844, 25 L.Ed.2d 174 (1970), the court found the Act unconstitutional:

> Unlike a state's blue sky law the Indiana statute is calculated to impede transactions between residents of other states. For the sake of trivial or even negative benefits to its residents Indiana is depriving nonresidents of the valued opportunity to accept tender offers from other nonresidents.
>
> * * * Even if a corporation's tangible assets are immovable, the efficiency with which they are employed and the proportions in which the earnings they generate are divided between management and shareholders depends on the market for corporate control—an interstate, indeed international, market that the State of Indiana is not authorized to opt out of, as in effect it has done in this statute. 794 F.2d, at 264.

Finally, the court addressed the "internal affairs" doctrine, a "principle of conflict of laws ... designed to make sure that the law of only one state shall govern the internal affairs of a corporation or other association." It stated:

> We may assume without having to decide that Indiana has a broad latitude in regulating those affairs, even when the consequence may be to make it harder to take over an Indiana corporation. * * * But in this case the effect on the interstate market in securities and corporate control is direct, intended, and substantial.* * * [T]hat the mode of regulation involves jiggering with voting rights cannot take it outside the scope of judicial review under the commerce clause. *Ibid.*

Accordingly, the court affirmed the judgment of the District Court.

Both Indiana and CTS filed jurisdictional statements. We noted probable jurisdiction and now reverse. * * *

II

The first question in these cases is whether the Williams Act preempts the Indiana Act. As we have stated frequently, absent an explicit indication by Congress of an intent to preempt state law, a state statute is preempted only

> 'where compliance with both federal and state regulations is a physical impossibility.* * *,' *Florida Lime & Avocado Growers, Inc. v. Paul*, 373 U.S. 132, 142–143 (83 S.Ct. 1210, 1217, 10 L.Ed.2d 248) (1963), or where the state 'law stands as an obstacle to the accomplishment and execution of the full purposes and objectives of Congress.' *Hines v. Davidowitz*, 312 U.S. 52, 67 (61 S.Ct. 399, 404, 85 L.Ed. 581) (1941).* * * *Ray v. Atlantic Richfield Co.*, 435 U.S. 151, 158, 98 S.Ct. 988, 994, 55 L.Ed.2d 179 (1978).

Because it is entirely possible for entities to comply with both the Williams Act and the Indiana Act, the state statute can be preempted only if it frustrates the purposes of the federal law.

A

Our discussion begins with a brief summary of the structure and purposes of the Williams Act. Congress passed the Williams Act in 1968 in response to the increasing number of hostile tender offers. Before its passage, these transactions were not covered by the disclosure requirements of the federal securities laws. See *Piper v. Chris–Craft Industries, Inc.*, 430 U.S. 1, 22, 97 S.Ct. 926, 939–940, 51 L.Ed.2d 124 (1977). The Williams Act, backed by regulations of the SEC, imposes requirements in two basic areas. First, it requires the offeror to file a statement disclosing information about the offer, including: the offeror's background and identity; the source and amount of the funds to be used in making the purchase; the purpose of the purchase, including any plans to liquidate the company or make major changes in its corporate structure; and the extent of the offeror's holdings in the target company.

Second, the Williams Act, and the regulations that accompany it, establish procedural rules to govern tender offers. For example, stockholders who tender their shares may withdraw them during the first 15 business days of the tender offer and, if the offeror has not purchased their shares, any time after 60 days from commencement of the offer. The offer must remain open for at least 20 business days. If more shares are tendered than the offeror sought to purchase, purchases must be made on a pro rata basis from each tendering shareholder. Finally, the offeror must pay the same price for all purchases; if the offering price is increased before the end of the offer, those who already have tendered must receive the benefit of the increased price.

B

The Indiana Act differs in major respects from the Illinois statute that the Court considered in *Edgar v. MITE Corp.,* 457 U.S. 624, 102 S.Ct. 2629, 73 L.Ed.2d 269 (1982). After reviewing the legislative history of the Williams Act, Justice White, joined by Chief Justice Burger and Justice Blackmun (the plurality), concluded that the Williams Act struck a careful balance between the interests of offerors and target companies, and that any state statute that "upset" this balance was preempted. *Id.,* at 632–634, 102 S.Ct., at 2635–2636.

The plurality then identified three offending features of the Illinois statute. Justice White's opinion first noted that the Illinois statute provided for a 20–day precommencement period. During this time, management could disseminate its views on the upcoming offer to shareholders, but offerors could not publish their offers. The plurality found that this provision gave management "a powerful tool to combat tender offers." *Id.,* at 635, 102 S.Ct., at 2637. This contrasted dramatically with the Williams Act; Congress had deleted express precommencement notice provisions from the Williams Act. According to the plurality, Congress had determined that the potentially adverse consequences of such a provision on shareholders should be avoided. Thus, the plurality concluded that the Illinois provision "frustrate[d] the objectives of the Williams Act." *Ibid.* The second criticized feature of the Illinois statute was a provision for a hearing on a tender offer that, because it set no deadline, allowed management " 'to stymie indefinitely a takeover,' " *id.,* at 637, 102 S.Ct., at 2638. * * * The plurality noted that " 'delay can seriously impede a tender offer,' " 457 U.S., at 637, 102 S.Ct., at 2638 (quoting *Great Western United Corp. v. Kidwell,* 577 F.2d 1256, 1277 (C.A.5 1978) (Wisdom, J.)), and that "Congress anticipated that investors and the takeover offeror would be free to go forward without unreasonable delay," 457 U.S., at 639, 102 S.Ct., at 2639. Accordingly, the plurality concluded that this provision conflicted with the Williams Act. The third troublesome feature of the Illinois statute was its requirement that the fairness of tender offers would be reviewed by the Illinois Secretary of State. Noting that "Congress intended for investors to be free to make their own decisions," the plurality concluded that " '[t]he state thus offers investor protection at the expense of investor autonomy—an approach quite in conflict with that adopted by Congress.' " *Id.,* at 639–640, 102 S.Ct., at 2639 (quoting *MITE Corp. v. Dixon, supra,* at 494).

C

As the plurality opinion in *MITE* did not represent the views of a majority of the Court, we are not bound by its reasoning. We need not question that reasoning, however, because we believe the Indiana Act passes muster even under the broad interpretation of the Williams Act articulated by Justice White in *MITE.* As is apparent from our summary of its reasoning, the overriding concern of the *MITE* plurality was that the Illinois statute considered in that case operated to favor management against offerors, to the detriment of shareholders. By contrast, the statute now before the Court protects the independent shareholder against both of the contending parties. Thus, the Act furthers a basic purpose of the Williams Act, " 'plac[ing] investors on an equal footing with the takeover bidder,' " *Piper v. Chris–Craft Industries,* 430 U.S., at 30, 97 S.Ct., at 943 (quoting the Senate Report accompanying the Williams Act, S.Rep. No. 550, 90th Cong., 1st Sess., 4 (1967)).[23]

The Indiana Act operates on the assumption, implicit in the Williams Act, that independent shareholders faced with tender offers often are at a disadvantage. By allowing such shareholders to vote as a group, the Act protects them from the coercive aspects of some tender offers. If, for example, shareholders believe that a successful tender offer will be followed by a purchase of nontendering shares at a depressed price, individual shareholders may tender their shares—even if they doubt the tender offer is in the corporation's best interest—to protect themselves from being forced to sell their shares at a depressed price. As the SEC explains: "The alternative of not accepting the tender offer is virtual assurance that, if the offer is successful, the shares will have to be sold in the lower priced, second step." Two–Tier Tender Offer Pricing and Non–Tender Offer Purchase Programs, SEC Exchange Act Rel. No. 21079 (June 21, 1984) (hereinafter SEC Release No. 21079). See Lowenstein, Pruning Deadwood in Hostile Takeovers: A Proposal for Legislation, 83 Colum.L.Rev. 249, 307–309 (1983). In such a situation under the Indiana Act, the shareholders as a group, acting in the corporation's best interest, could reject the offer, although individual shareholders might be inclined to accept it. The desire of the Indiana Legislature to protect shareholders of Indiana corporations from this type of coercive offer does not conflict with the Williams Act. Rather, it furthers the federal policy of investor protection.

In implementing its goal, the Indiana Act avoids the problems the plurality discussed in *MITE.* Unlike the *MITE* statute, the Indiana Act does not give either management or the offeror an advantage in communicating with the shareholders about the impending offer. The Act also does not impose an indefinite delay on tender offers. Nothing in the Act prohibits an offeror from consummating an offer on the 20th business day, the earliest day permitted under applicable federal regulations. Nor does the Act allow the state government to interpose its views of fairness between willing buyers and sellers of shares of the target company. Rather, the Act allows *shareholders* to evaluate the fairness of the offer collectively.

23. [By the Court] Dynamics finds evidence of an intent to favor management in several features of the Act. * * *

The Act * * * imposes some added expenses on the offeror, requiring it, *inter alia,* to pay the costs of special shareholder meetings to vote on the transfer of voting rights, see § 23–1–42–7(a). In our view, the expenses of such a meeting fairly are charged to the offeror. A corporation pays the costs of annual meetings that it holds to discuss its affairs. If an offeror—who has no official position with the corporation—desires a special meeting solely to discuss the voting rights of the offeror, it is not unreasonable to have the offeror pay for the meeting.

Of course, by regulating tender offers, the Act makes them more expensive and thus deters them somewhat, but this type of reasonable regulation does not alter the balance between management and offeror in any significant way. The principal result of the Act is to grant shareholders the power to deliberate collectively about the merits of tender offers. This result is fully in accord with the purposes of the Williams Act.

D

The Court of Appeals based its finding of pre-emption on its view that the practical effect of the Indiana Act is to delay consummation of tender offers until 50 days after the commencement of the offer. 794 F.2d, at 263. As did the Court of Appeals, Dynamics reasons that no rational offeror will purchase shares until it gains assurance that those shares will carry voting rights. Because it is possible that voting rights will not be conferred until a shareholder meeting 50 days after commencement of the offer, Dynamics concludes that the Act imposes a 50-day delay. This, it argues, conflicts with the shorter 20-business-day period established by the SEC as the minimum period for which a tender offer may be held open. We find the alleged conflict illusory.
* * *

Finally, we note that the Williams Act would preempt a variety of state corporate laws of hitherto unquestioned validity if it were construed to preempt any state statute that may limit or delay the free exercise of power after a successful tender offer. State corporate laws commonly permit corporations to stagger the terms of their directors. See Model Business Corp. Act § 37 (1969 draft) in 3 Model Business Corp. Act Ann. (2d ed. 1971) (hereinafter MBCA); American Bar Foundation, Revised Model Business Corp. Act § 8.06 (1984 draft)(1985) (hereinafter RMBCA).[24] By staggering the terms of directors, and thus having annual elections for only one class of directors each year, corporations may delay the time when a successful offeror gains control of the board of directors. Similarly, state corporation laws commonly provide for cumulative voting. See MBCA § 33, par. 4; RMBCA § 7.28. By enabling minority shareholders to assure themselves of representation in each class of directors, cumulative voting provisions can delay further the ability of offerors to gain untrammeled authority over the affairs of the target corporation. See Hochman & Folger, Deflecting Takeovers: Charter and By-Law Techniques, 34 Bus.Law. 537, 538–539 (1979).

In our view, the possibility that the Indiana Act will delay some tender offers is insufficient to require a conclusion that the Williams Act preempts the Act. The longstanding prevalence of state regulation in this area suggests that, if Congress had intended to preempt all state laws that delay the acquisition of voting control following a tender offer, it would have said so explicitly. The regulatory conditions that the Act places on tender offers are consistent with the text and the purposes of the Williams Act. Accordingly, we hold that the Williams Act does not preempt the Indiana Act.

III

As an alternative basis for its decision, the Court of Appeals held that the Act violates the Commerce Clause of the Federal Constitution. We now address this holding. * * * [The Court concludes that the Indiana Act does not discriminate against interstate commerce nor does it adversely affect interstate commerce by subjecting activities to inconsistent regulations.]

C

The Court of Appeals * * * [found] the Act unconstitutional * * * [because of] its view of the Act's potential to hinder tender offers. We think

---

24. [By the Court] Every State except Arkansas and California allows classification of directors to stagger their terms of office. See 2   Model Business Corp. Act Ann. § 8.06, p. 830 (3d ed., Supp.1986).

the Court of Appeals failed to appreciate the significance for Commerce Clause analysis of the fact that state regulation of corporate governance is regulation of entities whose very existence and attributes are a product of state law. As Chief Justice Marshall explained:

> A corporation is an artificial being, invisible, intangible, and existing only in contemplation of law. Being the mere creature of law, it possesses only those properties which the charter of its creation confers upon it, either expressly, or as incidental to its very existence. These are such as are supposed best calculated to effect the object for which it was created. *Trustees of Dartmouth College v. Woodward*, 4 Wheat. 518, 636, 4 L.Ed. 518 (1819).

Every State in this country has enacted laws regulating corporate governance. By prohibiting certain transactions, and regulating others, such laws necessarily affect certain aspects of interstate commerce. This necessarily is true with respect to corporations with shareholders in States other than the State of incorporation. Large corporations that are listed on national exchanges, or even regional exchanges, will have shareholders in many States and shares that are traded frequently. The markets that facilitate this national and international participation in ownership of corporations are essential for providing capital not only for new enterprises but also for established companies that need to expand their businesses. This beneficial free market system depends at its core upon the fact that a corporation—except in the rarest situations—is organized under, and governed by, the law of a single jurisdiction, traditionally the corporate law of the State of its incorporation.

These regulatory laws may affect directly a variety of corporate transactions. Mergers are a typical example. In view of the substantial effect that a merger may have on the shareholders' interests in a corporation, many States require supermajority votes to approve mergers. See, *e.g.,* MBCA * * * 11.03 (requiring approval of a merger by a majority of all shares, rather than simply a majority of votes cast) * * *. By requiring a greater vote for mergers than is required for other transactions, these laws make it more difficult for corporations to merge. State laws also may provide for "dissenters' rights" under which minority shareholders who disagree with corporate decisions to take particular actions are entitled to sell their shares to the corporation at fair market value. See, *e.g.,* MBCA § 13.02. By requiring the corporation to purchase the shares of dissenting shareholders, these laws may inhibit a corporation from engaging in the specified transactions.[25]

---

25. [By the Court] Numerous other common regulations may affect both nonresident and resident shareholders of a corporation. Specified votes may be required for the sale of all of the corporation's assets. See MBCA § 12.02. The election of directors may be staggered over a period of years to prevent abrupt changes in management. See MBCA § 8.06. Various classes of stock may be created with differences in voting rights as to dividends and on liquidation. See MBCA § 6.01(c). Provisions may be made for cumulative voting. See MBCA § 7.28. Corporations may adopt restrictions on payment of dividends to ensure that specified ratios of assets to liabilities are maintained for

the benefit of the holders of corporate bonds or notes. See MBCA * * * 6.40 (noting that a corporation's articles of incorporation can restrict payment of dividends) * * *. Where the shares of a corporation are held in States other than that of incorporation, actions taken pursuant to these and similar provisions of state law will affect all shareholders alike wherever they reside or are domiciled.

Nor is it unusual for partnership law to restrict certain transactions. For example, a purchaser of a partnership interest generally can gain a right to control the business only with the consent of other owners. See Uniform Partnership Act § 27, Revised Uniform Limit-

It thus is an accepted part of the business landscape in this country for States to create corporations, to prescribe their powers, and to define the rights that are acquired by purchasing their shares. A State has an interest in promoting stable relationships among parties involved in the corporations it charters, as well as in ensuring that investors in such corporations have an effective voice in corporate affairs.

There can be no doubt that the Act reflects these concerns. The primary purpose of the Act is to protect the shareholders of Indiana corporations. It does this by affording shareholders, when a takeover offer is made, an opportunity to decide collectively whether the resulting change in voting control of the corporation, as they perceive it, would be desirable. A change of management may have important effects on the shareholders' interests; it is well within the State's role as overseer of corporate governance to offer this opportunity. The autonomy provided by allowing shareholders collectively to determine whether the takeover is advantageous to their interests may be especially beneficial where a hostile tender offer may coerce shareholders into tendering their shares.

Appellee Dynamics responds to this concern by arguing that the prospect of coercive tender offers is illusory, and that tender offers generally should be favored because they reallocate corporate assets into the hands of management who can use them most effectively.[26] See generally Easterbrook & Fischel, The Proper Role of a Target's Management in Responding to a Tender Offer, 94 Harv.L.Rev. 1161 (1981). * * * Indiana's concern with tender offers is not groundless. Indeed, the potentially coercive aspects of tender offers have been recognized by the SEC, see SEC Release No. 21079, and by a number of scholarly commentators, see, *e.g.,* Bradley & Rosenzweig, Defensive Stock Repurchases, 99 Harv.L.Rev. 1377, 1412–1413 (1986). * * * The Constitution does not require the States to subscribe to any particular economic theory. We are not inclined "to second-guess the empirical judgments of lawmakers concerning the utility of legislation," *Kassel v. Consolidated Freightways Corp.,* 450 U.S., at 679, 101 S.Ct., at 1321 (Brennan, J., concurring in judgment). In our view, the possibility of coercion in some takeover bids offers additional justification for Indiana's decision to promote the autonomy of independent shareholders.

Dynamics argues in any event that the State has " 'no legitimate interest in protecting the nonresident shareholders.' " Dynamics relies heavily on the statement by the *MITE* Court that "[i]nsofar as the ... law burdens out-of-state transactions, there is nothing to be weighed in the balance to sustain the law." 457 U.S., at 644, 102 S.Ct., at 2641. But that comment was made in reference to an Illinois law that applied as well to out-of-state corporations as

---

ed Partnership Act §§ 702, 704. These provisions—in force in the great majority of the States—bear a striking resemblance to the Act at issue in this case.

26. [By the Court] It is appropriate to note when discussing the merits and demerits of tender offers that generalizations usually require qualification. No one doubts that some successful tender offers will provide more effective management or other benefits such as needed diversification. But there is no reason to *assume* that the type of conglomerate corporation that may result from repetitive takeovers necessarily will result in more effective management or otherwise be beneficial to shareholders. The divergent views in the literature—and even now being debated in the Congress—reflect the reality that the type and utility of tender offers vary widely. Of course, in many situations the offer to shareholders is simply a cash price substantially higher than the market price prior to the offer.

to in-state corporations. We agree that Indiana has no interest in protecting nonresident shareholders *of nonresident corporations.* But this Act applies only to corporations incorporated in Indiana. We reject the contention that Indiana has no interest in providing for the shareholders of its corporations the voting autonomy granted by the Act. Indiana has a substantial interest in preventing the corporate form from becoming a shield for unfair business dealing. Moreover, unlike the Illinois statute invalidated in *MITE,* the Indiana Act applies only to corporations that have a substantial number of shareholders in Indiana. See Ind.Code § 23–1–42–4(a)(3) (Supp.1986). Thus, every application of the Indiana Act will affect a substantial number of Indiana residents, whom Indiana indisputably has an interest in protecting.

D

Dynamics' argument that the Act is unconstitutional ultimately rests on its contention that the Act will limit the number of successful tender offers. There is little evidence that this will occur. But even if true, this result would not substantially affect our Commerce Clause analysis. We reiterate that this Act does not prohibit any entity—resident or nonresident—from offering to purchase, or from purchasing, shares in Indiana corporations, or from attempting thereby to gain control. It only provides regulatory procedures designed for the better protection of the corporations' shareholders. We have rejected the "notion that the Commerce Clause protects the particular structure or methods of operation in a ... market." *Exxon Corp. v. Governor of Maryland,* 437 U.S., at 127, 98 S.Ct., at 2215. The very commodity that is traded in the securities market is one whose characteristics are defined by state law. Similarly, the very commodity that is traded in the "market for corporate control"—the corporation—is one that owes its existence and attributes to state law. Indiana need not define these commodities as other States do; it need only provide that residents and nonresidents have equal access to them. This Indiana has done. Accordingly, even if the Act should decrease the number of successful tender offers for Indiana corporations, this would not offend the Commerce Clause.

IV

On its face, the Indiana Control Share Acquisitions Chapter evenhandedly determines the voting rights of shares of Indiana corporations. The Act does not conflict with the provisions or purposes of the Williams Act. To the limited extent that the Act affects interstate commerce, this is justified by the State's interests in defining the attributes of shares in its corporations and in protecting shareholders. Congress has never questioned the need for state regulation of these matters. Nor do we think such regulation offends the Constitution. Accordingly, we reverse the judgment of the Court of Appeals.

It is so ordered.

Justice Scalia, concurring in part and concurring in the judgment.

* * * [H]aving found * * * that the Indiana Control Share Acquisitions Chapter neither "discriminates against interstate commerce," nor "create[s] an impermissible risk of inconsistent regulation by different States," I would conclude without further analysis that it is not invalid under the dormant Commerce Clause. * * * Whether the control shares statute "protects shareholders of Indiana corporations," or protects incumbent management seems

to me a highly debatable question, but it is extraordinary to think that the constitutionality of the Act should depend on the answer. Nothing in the Constitution says that the protection of entrenched management is any less important a "putative local benefit" than the protection of entrenched shareholders, and I do not know what qualifies us to make that judgment—or the related judgment as to how effective the present statute is in achieving one or the other objective—or the ultimate (and most ineffable) judgment as to whether, given importance-level x, and effectiveness-level y, the worth of the statute is "outweighed" by impact-on-commerce z. * * *

I also agree with the Court that the Indiana Control Shares Act is not preempted by the Williams Act, but I reach that conclusion without entering into the debate over the purposes of the two statutes. The Williams Act is governed by the antipreemption provision of the Securities Exchange Act of 1934, 15 U.S.C. § 78bb(a), which provides that nothing it contains "shall affect the jurisdiction of the securities commission (or any agency or officer performing like functions) of any State over any security or any person insofar as it does not conflict with the provisions of this chapter or the rules and regulations thereunder." Unless it serves no function, that language forecloses preemption on the basis of conflicting "purpose" as opposed to conflicting "provision." Even if it does not have literal application to the present case (because, perhaps, the Indiana agency responsible for securities matters has no enforcement responsibility with regard to this legislation), it nonetheless refutes the proposition that Congress meant the Williams Act to displace *all* state laws with conflicting purpose. And if any are to survive, surely the States' corporation codes are among them. It would be peculiar to hold that Indiana could have pursued the purpose at issue here through its blue-sky laws, but cannot pursue it through the State's even more sacrosanct authority over the structure of domestic corporations. Prescribing voting rights for the governance of state-chartered companies is a traditional state function with which the Federal Congress has never, to my knowledge, intentionally interfered. I would require far more evidence than is available here to find implicit preemption of that function by a federal statute whose provisions concededly do not conflict with the state law.

I do not share the Court's apparent high estimation of the beneficence of the state statute at issue here. But a law can be both economic folly and constitutional. The Indiana Control Share Acquisitions Chapter is at least the latter. I therefore concur in the judgment of the Court.

JUSTICE WHITE, with whom JUSTICE BLACKMUN and JUSTICE STEVENS join as to Part II, dissenting.

The majority today upholds Indiana's Control Share Acquisitions Chapter, a statute which will predictably foreclose completely some tender offers for stock in Indiana corporations. I disagree with the conclusion that the Chapter is neither preempted by the Williams Act nor in conflict with the Commerce Clause. The Chapter undermines the policy of the Williams Act by effectively preventing minority shareholders, in some circumstances, from acting in their own best interests by selling their stock. In addition, the Chapter will substantially burden the interstate market in corporate ownership, particularly if other States follow Indiana's lead as many already have done. The Chapter, therefore, directly inhibits interstate commerce, the very economic consequences the Commerce Clause was intended to prevent. The opinion of the Court of Appeals is far more persuasive than that of the majority today, and the judgment of that court should be affirmed. * * *

Given the impact of the Control Share Acquisitions Chapter, it is clear that Indiana is directly regulating the purchase and sale of shares of stock in interstate commerce. Appellant CTS' stock is traded on the New York Stock Exchange, and people from all over the country buy and sell CTS' shares daily. Yet, under Indiana's scheme, any prospective purchaser will be effectively precluded from purchasing CTS' shares if the purchaser crosses one of the Chapter's threshold ownership levels and a majority of CTS' shareholders refuse to give the purchaser voting rights. This Court should not countenance such a restraint on interstate trade. * * *

Notes

(1) Prior to the decision in the principal case, and based largely on language in the plurality opinion in *MITE,* a number of academic scholars of the Chicago "law and economics school" argued that an interstate market for corporate control existed that states were powerless to regulate. Under this approach, state statutes regulating tender offers seemed clearly unconstitutional and it appeared that even traditional state corporation law provisions might be invalidated if they unreasonably restricted or interfered with the market for corporate control. This type of argument was accepted by Judge Posner in the opinion reversed by the Supreme Court in the principal case. The "market for corporate control" idea was clearly appealing to economists but was troublesome to many lawyers because it seemed to be a "slippery slope" that could federalize much of the state law of corporations to the extent applied to publicly held corporations. The CTS opinion is of major importance in the corporate area because of its dicta about the relative rules of federal and state law in this area.

(2) Donald Langevoort, The Supreme Court and the Politics of Corporate Takeovers: A Comment on *CTS Corp. v. Dynamics Corp. of America*, 101 Harv. L.Rev. 96, 106–108 (1987):[27]

The Indiana law of corporations presumably applies to all corporations chartered there. The Control Shares Acquisition statute, by contrast, applies only to Indiana corporations with (1) their principal place of business, principal office, or substantial assets in Indiana, and (2) a certain concentration of shareholders in Indiana. If the legislature was genuinely concerned with protecting *shareholders*—the predicate for the statute's commerce clause validity—why would it deny its "protection" to the shareholders of Indiana corporations just because the principal activities and assets of the firm happen to be in Ohio or New York?

From this, one is drawn to the conclusion that Indiana's real interest was in protecting *local businesses* from the rigors of the interstate market for corporate control and that the state was using the claim of shareholder protection largely as a means to that end, hoping that the Act would indeed have a chilling effect. This observation, coupled with the implausibility of the shareholder protection rationale in the first place, strongly suggests that the Indiana statute only creates the illusion of true corporation law. Such a subterfuge is not surprising; the history of tender offer regulation (state and federal) is one of using shareholder protection as a justification for regulation

---

27. Copyright © (1987) by the Harvard Law Review Association.

that is really motivated by other objections to hostile bids, notwithstanding the intuitively compelling point that, financially, shareholders are substantial net gainers from the takeover phenomenon. * * *

The Court's reluctance to question the state's motive may have stemmed from its inability to formulate a workable test to identify legislative motive in the corporate context. The variety of motivations underlying a statute makes it nearly impossible to isolate accurately the impact of protectionist sentiment. To force the courts to determine actual motivation would set them adrift in a lawmaking process characterized by immense special interest pressure, minimal direct voice for shareholder interests, and, perhaps most powerfully, competition among states to retain jurisdiction over local corporations and to attract new ones—any one of which may by itself explain legislation like Indiana's.

(3) Roberta Romano, The Future of Hostile Takeovers: Legislation and Public Opinion, 57 U.Cin.L.Rev. 457, 461–63 (1988):

Although more than twenty states enacted second generation statutes in the years between the *MITE* and *CTS* decisions, legislators and lobbyists were often reluctant to promote legislation for fear of constitutional infirmities. The most frequently adopted version of a second generation statute was therefore one with limited regulatory scope. After the *CTS* decision, however, the pace and scope of legislation changed: fourteen new statutes were adopted within approximately six months. More important, several of the new statutes strengthened less restrictive second generation statutes by using Indiana as a model, and many test *CTS*'s limits by mandating constraints on bidders that go further than the Indiana statute.

The political history of second generation takeover statutes is similar across the states. The statutes are typically enacted rapidly, with virtually unanimous support and little public notice, let alone discussion. They are frequently pushed through the legislature at the behest of a major local corporation that is the target of a hostile bid or apprehensive that it will become a target.[28] This phenomenon is consistent with the positive correlation between the enactment of state statutes and tender offer activity, for as the overall number of takeovers increases, the probability that any one state will be the home of a target, and hence discover the need for a takeover law, may increase. * * *

---

28. [By the Author] There are at least a dozen examples among second generation statutes: Connecticut for Aetna; Florida for Harcourt Brace Jovanovich (hostile bid by Robert Maxwell); Massachusetts for Gillette (hostile bid by Revlon Group); North Carolina for Burlington Industries (hostile bid by Dominion Textile and Asher Edelman); Kentucky for Ashland Oil (hostile bid by the Belzberg brothers); Pennsylvania for Scott Paper (hostile stockholder Brascan Ltd. trying to increase stake); Ohio for Goodyear Tire & Rubber (hostile bid by Sir Oliver Goldsmith); Ohio for Federated Department Stores (hostile bid by Campeau Corp., statute regulating foreign bidders); Arizona for Greyhound; Minnesota for Dayton Hudson (hostile bid by Dart Group); Wisconsin for G. Heileman Brewing Co. (hostile bid by Bond Holdings); Washington for Weyerhauser; Indiana for Arvin Industries (hostile bid by the Belzbergs), AMOCO also promoted bill; Illinois for an unidentified corporation, see McKenna & Bitner, The "Fair Price Amendment" in the Illinois Business Corporation Act, 67 Chicago Bar Rec., 64, 74 n. 59 (1986) ("one prominent Illinois Corporation" promoted statute); Maine for an unidentified corporation, see Maine Legislative Record—House, June 3, 1985, at 918 (remarks of Rep. Stevens, referring to the "corporation that was the instigator" of the bill); Washington for Boeing (facing possible hostile bid by T. Boone Pickens, statute for foreign resident corporation); Missouri for TWA (hostile bid by Carl Icahn, statute for foreign resident corporation). In addition, one proposed statute was not enacted in large part because it was being pushed by a target of a hostile bid at the time: New York for CBS (hostile bid by Ted Turner).

The statutes are not, however, as some might intuit, promoted by a broad coalition of business, labor, and community leaders who fear that a firm's takeover will have a detrimental effect on the local economy. While some legislators may be concerned about such an effect, labor and community groups are not at the forefront in the attack on takeovers. In fact, the organization most actively involved in promoting the legislation besides corporate management and business groups, in nearly all states, is the local bar association. * * * There is no doubt that the corporate bar's interest can differ from that of managers and shareholders. For example, corporate lawyers profit from takeover litigation, and a statute that prevented all hostile takeovers would, presumably, also eliminate the lawsuits. A factor mitigating the incentive for maintaining some modicum of takeover activity is that a merged firm typically retains the acquiror's legal counsel. Because the acquiror and, correspondingly, its counsel are quite often out-of-state entities, the local bar's interest will be similar to that of incumbent management, in seeking to block takeovers. As we can conjecture plausible, diverse incentives for corporate lawyers independent of their clients' interests, we cannot identify *a priori* what motivates their behavior. * * *

NORMAN VEASEY, ET AL., THE DELAWARE TAKE-OVER LAW: SOME ISSUES, STRATEGIES AND COMPARISONS[29]

43 Bus.Law. 865, 866–69 (1988).

Some states have followed the Indiana model, while others adopted different approaches. For example, New York in 1986 and New Jersey in 1987 adopted statutes prohibiting an acquiror from accomplishing a second-step "business combination"—such as a merger—with the target for a period of five years. Concern was raised that states were trying to outdo each other in their attempts to regulate tender offers of corporations domiciled in other states (notably Delaware), thus leading to a worrisome balkanization of state tender offer statutes. In *TLX Acquisition Corp. v. Telex Corp.,* the federal district court sitting in Oklahoma held that an Oklahoma statute that purported to regulate the tender offer process and thus the internal affairs of a Delaware corporation was unconstitutional even though there were substantial contacts with Oklahoma.[30] * * *

The major question in that national puzzle was whether Delaware would adopt any legislation and, if so, how far it would go. Delaware, of course, is the principal architect and steward of a "national corporation law" since it is the domicile of over 180,000 corporations, many of which are major, national public corporations with no substantial operations in Delaware. Indeed, over half of the Fortune 500 companies are Delaware corporations. As at least one commentator has noted, Delaware has always been wary of antitakeover legislation for at least three reasons: doubts about constitutionality (at least pre–*CTS*); concerns over preemption; and the fact that such statutes simply don't fit comfortably into the mold of a state enabling statute governing

---

30. [By the Authors] TLX Acquisition Corp. v. Telex Corp., 679 F.Supp. 1022 (W.D.Okla.1987).

internal corporate affairs.[31]

Nevertheless, there was an expectation following *CTS* that Delaware would do something, and it did. After a lengthy "on-again, off-again" process stretching from May 1987 through January 1988, the Delaware State Bar Association proposed a new takeover statute,[32] which was adopted in late January substantially in *haec verba* by the Delaware General Assembly. It became effective with the signature of Governor Castle on February 2, 1988. The statute is codified as new section 203 of the Delaware General Corporation Law. Section 203 is a modified "business combination" statute based on the concept, adopted in New York and New Jersey,[33] of regulating second-step transactions between acquirors and the corporation rather than regulating the initial acquisition of stock or voting rights.

With the enactment of section 203, Delaware became the twenty-eighth state to enact a post-*MITE* takeover statute. About half of these statutes were adopted in the wake of the Supreme Court opinion in *CTS*. California is the only major state (in terms of the number of incorporations) without a takeover law.

OPERATION OF SECTION 203

Section 203 is not an enabling (or "opt-in") provision * * * Rather, section 203 is an "opt-out" statute. It automatically applies (with certain exceptions) to every public corporation formed under the laws of Delaware

31. [By the Authors] See Black, Why Delaware Is Wary of Anti–Takeover Law, Wall St. J., July 10, 1987, at 18, col. 3.

Although Delaware prides itself on being a leader in corporation law, it has always been wary of laws regulating tender offers. For one thing, such laws have never fit well in corporation statutes. For another, they don't work. Efforts to regulate tender offers at the federal level under the Williams Act have distorted the process. Since the Williams Act was enacted in 1968, the Securities and Exchange Commission (and the states, through such acts as the now-validated Indiana law) has played an endless game of catch up, adopting rules that seem to fix one problem only to give rise to another.

32. [By the Authors] The Delaware statute is the product of a lengthy study by the Corporation Law Section of the Delaware State Bar Association. In June 1987, following the *CTS* decision, the section studied and sought national comment on a draft control share acquisition statute of the type upheld by the Supreme Court in that case. CTS Corp. v. Dynamics Corp. of America, 107 S.Ct. 1637 (1987). There were many uncertainties regarding the operation and effect of such legislation, including concern that it may, ironically, help put "in play" corporations which might not otherwise become takeover targets. Accordingly, the section determined that it would not be appropriate to propose such a statute for Delaware. Nevertheless, because of continued interest in takeover legislation, the council of the section began a new study in

the late summer of 1987. An exposure draft of a "business combination statute" was released for public comment in November. Over 150 comment letters were received from corporations, lawyers, Commissioners of the Securities and Exchange Commission and the Federal Trade Commission, executives, institutional investors, academics, and many others. Some comments were based on broad policy grounds, some made narrower policy suggestions, and still others recommended drafting changes. During the bar association debate and the legislative process, some law firms represented specific clients and took positions as a firm. Richards, Layton & Finger [the firm in which the authors are partners] did not take a position as a firm and would not accept representation by a client to lobby for or against the bill. Each lawyer in the firm had the freedom to express his or her own personal view since the clients of the firm had divergent views. Some members of the firm fully supported the statute; others supported it with a few specific reservations (for example whether 85% should be 80% and whether the grandfather date should be the effective date); others opposed it on broad policy grounds. Governor Castle strongly supported the legislation, but he said that the issue is "neither black nor white, but gray."

33. [By the Authors] New York Bus.Corp. Law § 912 (McKinney 1986); N.J.Stat.Ann. § 14A:10A (West Supp.1987), *as amended by* 1988 N.J.Laws 380 (effective Jan. 8, 1988).

unless (i) the corporation's original charter contains a provision opting out of the protection of the statute, or (ii) within ninety days of the effective date of the statute (February 2, 1988), the board of directors adopts a by-law opting out of the statute. In addition, the holders of a majority of shares entitled to vote can opt out by amending the certificate or the by-laws. Although such an amendment can be adopted at any time, it will not become effective for twelve months and will not apply to a business combination with a person who was an interested stockholder at or prior to the time of the amendment.

Assuming the statute is applicable and the corporation has not opted out, its operative effect can be briefly summarized as follows. If a person acquires fifteen percent or more of a corporation's voting stock (thereby becoming an "interested stockholder"), he may not engage in a wide range of transactions with the corporation [for three years], unless the board has approved the transaction or exempted the stockholder before he reaches the fifteen-percent threshold or unless one of two exceptions is satisfied: (i) Upon consummation of the transaction which resulted in such person becoming an interested stockholder, the interested stockholder owned at least eighty-five percent of the corporation's voting stock outstanding at the time the transaction commenced (excluding shares owned by officer-directors and shares owned by employee stock plans in which participants do not have the right to determine confidentially whether shares will be tendered in a tender or exchange offer); or (ii) after the acquiror becomes an interested stockholder, the business combination is approved by the board of directors and authorized by the affirmative vote (at an annual or special meeting, and not by written consent) of at least two-thirds of the outstanding voting stock excluding that owned by the interested stockholder. * * *

Notes

(1) Suits attacking the constitutionality of § 203 have been unsuccessful. Black & Decker Corp. v. American Standard Inc., 679 F.Supp. 1183 (D.Del.1988); SWT Acquisition Corp. v. TW Services, Inc., 700 F.Supp. 1323 (D.Del.1988). However, Wisconsin has a business combination statute that is even more restrictive than Delaware's. Under this statute, no Wisconsin corporation having its headquarters, substantial operations, 10 percent of its shares or 10 percent of its shareholders in Wisconsin may enter into a "business combination" with an interested shareholder (defined as one with a ten percent interest in the corporation) for a period of three years after the interested shareholder acquires his or her stock unless the board of directors has approved the business combination before the interested shareholder's acquisition of shares. In Amanda Acquisition Corp. v. Universal Foods Corp., 877 F.2d 496 (7th Cir.1989), cert. denied, 493 U.S. 955, 110 S.Ct. 367, 107 L.Ed.2d 353 (1989), the Court, per Easterbrook, C.J., upheld this statute despite the "almost hermetic separation of bidder and target for three years after the bidder obtains 10 percent of the stock—unless the target's board consented before then. No matter how popular the offer, the ban applies: obtaining 85% (even 100%) of the stock held by non-management shareholders won't allow the bidder to engage in a business combination, as it would under Delaware law." 877 F.2d at 498. After expressing its distaste for the economics and policies that Wisconsin has apparently embraced, Judge Easterbrook concluded that the Wisconsin law is constitutional under *CTS:*

At the end of the day, however, it does not matter whether these countermeasures are "enough". The Commerce Clause does not demand that states leave bidders a "meaningful opportunity for success". * * * A state with the power to forbid mergers has the power to defer them for three years. Investors can turn to firms incorporated in states committed to the dominance of market forces, or they can turn on legislators who enact unwise laws. The Constitution has room for many economic policies. "[A] law can be both economic folly and constitutional." *CTS,* 481 U.S. at 96–97, 107 S.Ct. at 1653–54 (Scalia, J., concurring). Wisconsin's law may well be folly; we are confident that it is constitutional.

877 F.2d at 508–09.

(2) Is the process followed by Delaware consistent with the criticism voiced by Professor Romano that states have adopted post-*CTS* statutes at the behest of individual companies and without consideration of all interests?

(3) In addition to control share acquisition statutes of the Indiana type and restrictions on "second step" transactions of the Delaware/New York/New Jersey type, other types of statutes exist. Most of these statutes were enacted during the interim period after *MITE* and before *CTS* when any state legislation in the takeover area was under a constitutional cloud. The most popular of these statutes are "fair price" and "supermajority voting" requirements for second step transactions with interested shareholders patterned after the Maryland statutes (Md.Corps. & Ass'ns Code Ann. §§ 3–601 to 3–603) and adopted by about fifteen states. Other statutes provide for an appraisal type "cash out" privilege for minority shareholders upon the acquisition of a specified percentage of the corporation's shares. See, e.g., Pa.Bus.Corp.L. §§ 2542–2548 (acquisition of 20 percent or more of voting shares [subject to certain exceptions] triggers buyout right).

H. JUDICIAL REVIEW OF DEFENSIVE TACTICS

Assuming that a takeover offer—either all cash or cash and marketable securities—is made, does incumbent management have a duty to oppose it? To support it? To remain neutral and neither support nor oppose it? These questions raise fundamental issues about the role of shareholders and of management that are at the center of the modern debate over takeovers. If, as will normally be the case, the aggressor has the financial strength to carry out the contemplated offer, shareholders of the target corporation will almost certainly realize more for their shares if the offer succeeds than if it fails. If one accepts the basic proposition that the sole goal of management should be to maximize shareholder wealth, does it not follow that management certainly should not be permitted to actively oppose an offer, and that very probably it should further have an affirmative obligation either to support the offer or at least remain neutral with respect to it? One possible exception might be that management should oppose the offer to the limited extent of finding even more favorable offers from other sources.

On the other hand, the underlying justification for the twenty-odd state statutes that authorize consideration of non-shareholder constituencies (see Chapter 9, Section A) is to free management from the chains of this apparently compelling theoretical argument that they have a duty to maximize the financial interests of the shareholders.

It is clear that acceptance of a takeover bid is often not value-maximizing to incumbent management in a most fundamental way: Individuals face the loss of prestigious positions, seven-figure salaries, desirable "percs," lucrative fringe benefits, and the loss of power to control a large enterprise. Thus, it is not surprising that management usually feels it is a matter of the highest urgency to defeat uninvited takeover bids at all costs. Defensive tactics that involve purely an effort to defeat the offer in order to preserve one's position are usually described by the derogatory term "entrenchment." Entrenchment is a breach of the fiduciary duty of loyalty (since the tactics are not for a corporate purpose but to preserve the position of the managers). Open descriptions of one's motive to entrench and preserve one's position therefore are clear losers; other justifications to defeat the offer must be developed. Examples might include (1) the offered price is too low and does not reflect the "true" value of the corporation's business; (2) the offeror's reputation for sound fiscal management is not good; (3) the aggressor is assuming debt obligations which it probably cannot meet without using the target's assets, thereby injuring remaining common shareholders or senior security or debt holders; (4) it is simply in the best long-run interests of the shareholders for the corporation to remain independent (the "just say no" defense); (5) management has already embarked on long-range plans to improve the corporation's profits and stock price, and the decision to pursue those plans is protected by the business judgment rule; (6) the proposed transaction would result in the violation of the antitrust laws or some other federal or state statute; or (7) the offer is a partial one and is structured in a way that makes it unfair to shareholders by "coercing" them to tender. Whether or not such arguments are persuasive or even plausible obviously depends on the facts of the particular takeover. If one accepts the general explanation that takeovers occur primarily to weed out less efficient managers, the conclusion that management should be sharply restricted in the defensive tactics it may employ in order to let basic economic forces work is considerably strengthened.

The economic stakes in a takeover battle are so great that litigation to test the validity of any defenses employed by management—at least in the 1980s—was a virtual certainty. This litigation traditionally is in the form of suits for equitable relief based either on violations of the Williams Act or on breaches of the duty of care or loyalty by management, or both. However, where management has effectively defeated a tender offer without providing an offsetting management buyout or leveraged recapitalization to replace some or all of the lost value to shareholders, there inevitably has been a precipitous decline in the market price of the target stock and litigation has been brought on the theory that the directors should be held personally liable for the losses since they opposed the takeover not for the benefit of the corporation generally or its shareholders but to preserve their positions with the corporation. Litigation on this theory first foundered on the business judgment rule in its more permissive form. The leading case is Panter v. Marshall Field & Co., 646 F.2d 271 (7th Cir.1981), cert. denied, 454 U.S. 1092, 102 S.Ct. 658, 70 L.Ed.2d 631 (1981), where Marshall Field successfully fended off an unwanted takeover bid from Carter Hawley Hale (CHH), a national retail chain that operated Nieman–Marcus and other stores. Marshall Field adopted and vigorously pursued a policy of independence; among other things, it adopted an expansion program that led to Marshall Field stores coming into direct competition with Nieman–Marcus in several markets.

When CHH withdrew its bid in part because of the antitrust complications, the price of the Marshall Field common stock precipitously declined from about $34 per share to $19 per share. The Court held that the business judgment rule and the presumption of good faith was applicable: "The plaintiffs also contend that the 'defensive acquisitions' of the five Liberty House stores and the Galleria were imprudent, and designed to make Field's less attractive as an acquisition, as well as to exacerbate any antitrust problems created by the CHH merger. It is precisely this sort of Monday-morning-quarterbacking that the business judgment rule was intended to prevent." 646 F.2d at 297.

This approach was too much for Judge Cudahy:

> Unfortunately, the majority here has moved one giant step closer to shredding whatever constraints still remain upon the ability of corporate directors to place self-interest before shareholder interest in resisting a hostile tender offer for control of the corporation. There is abundant evidence in this case to go to the jury on the state claims for breach of fiduciary duty. I emphatically disagree that the business judgment rule should clothe directors, battling blindly to fend off a threat to their control, with an almost irrebuttable presumption of sound business judgment, prevailing over everything but the elusive hobgoblins of fraud, bad faith or abuse of discretion. * * *

> Addressing first the state law claims of breach of fiduciary duty by the Board, the majority has adopted an approach which would virtually immunize a target company's board of directors against liability to shareholders, provided a sufficiently prestigious (and expensive) array of legal and financial talent were retained to furnish *post hoc* rationales for fixed and immutable policies of resistance to takeover. Relying on several recent decisions interpreting the Delaware business judgment rule, the majority fails to make the important distinction between the activity of a corporation in managing a business enterprise and its function as a vehicle for collecting and using capital and distributing profits and losses. The former involves corporate functioning in competitive business affairs in which judicial interference may be undesirable. *The latter involves only the corporation-shareholder relationship, in which the courts may more justifiably intervene to insist on equitable behavior.*

Note, *Protection for Shareholder Interests in Recapitalizations of Publicly Held Companies,* 58 Colum.L.Rev. 1030, 1066 (1958) (emphasis supplied).

The theoretical justification for the "hands off" precept of the business judgment rule is that courts should be reluctant to review the acts of directors in situations where the expertise of the directors is likely to be greater than that of the courts. But, where the directors are afflicted with a conflict of interest, relative expertise is no longer crucial. Instead, the great danger becomes the channeling of the directors' expertise along the lines of their personal advantage—sometimes at the expense of the corporation and its stockholders. Here courts have no rational choice but to subject challenged conduct of directors and questioned corporate transactions to their own disinterested scrutiny. Of course, the self-protective bias of interested directors may be entirely devoid of corrupt motivation, but it may nonetheless constitute a serious threat to stockholder welfare. * * *

Directors of a New York Stock Exchange-listed company are, at the very least, "interested" in their own positions of power, prestige and prominence (and in their not inconsequential perquisites). They are "interested" in defending against outside attack the management which they have, in fact, installed or maintained in power—"their" management (to which, in many cases, they owe their directorships). And they are "interested" in maintaining the public reputation of their own leadership and stewardship against the claims of "raiders" who say that they can do better. Thus, regardless of their technical "independence," directors of a target corporation are in a very special position, where the slavish application of the majority's version of the good faith presumption is particularly disturbing.

Whether or not Panter v. Marshall Field involved a proper application of the business judgment rule may be debated. To some extent the decision may have been influenced by the threatened imposition of immense liabilities on outside directors who did not materially benefit from the transaction.[34]

———

Powerful defensive tactics have been developed that are directed squarely against the aggressor and its offer. These tactics are so effective that they caused the Delaware courts to reject the almost simplistic application of the business judgment rule of *Panter*, and to make a more balanced analysis of the equities of the situation. In Unocal v. Mesa Petroleum Co., 493 A.2d 946 (Del.1985), Mesa launched a takeover fight against Unocal, a major oil company. Mesa offered $54 per share for 64,000,000 shares, just enough to bring its ownership to 50 percent. The bulk of the $3.4 billion purchase price was to be borrowed in the form of junk bonds. At the same time, Mesa announced that if it were successful in the tender offer, it would thereafter purchase the balance of the Unocal stock it did not already own through a second-step merger in which the holders would receive "highly subordinated securities" (presumably subordinated to the borrowings needed to raise the initial $3.4 billion) with a value that the Delaware Supreme Court stated was "purportedly" also $54 per share. Unocal's ultimate defense was a flatly discriminatory proposal: an "exchange offer" that provided that if Mesa bought the 64,000,000 shares it sought, the remaining Unocal shareholders could exchange all of their remaining shares for debt securities worth $72 per share that would be senior to Mesa's junk bond financing. The exchange offer expressly provided that Mesa and persons affiliated with Mesa were not eligible to participate in the offer. The effect of the "Mesa exclusion"—the provision allowing Unocal to offer debt securities to all of its shareholders other than Mesa—devastated Mesa's financing. If it completed its tender offer and obtained control of Unocal, the remaining Unocal shareholders would swap their shares for senior Unocal debt, and Mesa would end up owning

---

34. [By the Editor] This type of litigation against directors for damages is probably not precluded by Del.Gen.Corp.L. § 102(a)(7) (discussed at page 000, supra) because it involves an arguable breach of the duty of loyalty or the receipt of an improper, personal benefit. It may be barred by some statutes enacted after *Van Gorkom.*

virtually 100 percent of a corporation that was awash in debt. Indeed, this defense involves such strong medicine and is so devastatingly effective that it seems ill-matched with the very permissive business judgment rule. The Delaware Supreme Court evolved a new standard for evaluating such proposals:

> In the board's exercise of corporate power to forestall a takeover bid our analysis begins with the basic principle that corporate directors have a fiduciary duty to act in the best interests of the corporation's stockholders. Guth v. Loft, Inc., Del.Supr., 5 A.2d 503, 510 (1939). As we have noted, their duty of care extends to protecting the corporation and its owners from perceived harm whether a threat originates from third parties or other shareholders.[35] But such powers are not absolute. A corporation does not have unbridled discretion to defeat any perceived threat by any Draconian means available.
>
> The restriction placed upon a selective stock repurchase is that the directors may not have acted solely or primarily out of a desire to perpetuate themselves in office. See Cheff v. Mathes, 199 A.2d 548, 556 (1964).
>
> Of course, to this is added the further caveat that inequitable action may not be taken under the guise of law. Schnell v. Chris–Craft Industries, Inc., Del.Supr., 285 A.2d 437, 439 (1971).[36] The standard of proof established in Cheff v. Mathes * * * is designed to ensure that a defensive measure to thwart or impede a takeover is indeed motivated by a good faith concern for the welfare of the corporation and its stockholders, which in all circumstances must be free of any fraud or other misconduct. Cheff v. Mathes, 199 A.2d at 554–55. However, this does not end the inquiry.
>
> A further aspect is the element of balance. If a defensive measure is to come within the ambit of the business judgment rule, it must be reasonable in relation to the threat posed. This entails an analysis by the directors of the nature of the takeover bid and its effect on the corporate enterprise. Examples of such concerns may include: inadequacy of the price offered, nature and timing of the offer, questions of illegality, the impact on "constituencies" other than shareholders (i.e., creditors, customers, employees, and perhaps even the community generally), the risk of nonconsummation, and the quality of securities being offered in the exchange. 40 Bus.Law. 1403 (1985). While not a controlling factor, it also seems to us that a board may reasonably consider the basic stockholder interests at stake, including those of short term speculators, whose actions may have fueled the coercive aspect of the offer at the expense of the long term investor.[37] Here, the threat posed was viewed by the Unocal

---

35. [By the Court]. It has been suggested that a board's response to a takeover threat should be a passive one. Easterbrook & Fischel, 36 Bus.Law. at 1750. However, that clearly is not the law of Delaware, and as the proponents of this rule of passivity readily concede, it has not been adopted either by courts or state legislatures. Easterbrook & Fischel, supra, 94 Harv.L.Rev. at 1194.

36. [By the Editor] The facts of *Schnell* are discussed in the notes following this excerpt.

37. [By the Court] There has been much debate respecting such stockholder interests. One rather impressive study indicates that the stock of over 50 percent of target companies, who resisted hostile takeovers, later traded at higher market prices than the rejected offer price, or were acquired after the tender offer

board as a grossly inadequate two-tier coercive tender offer coupled with the threat of greenmail. * * *

In adopting the selective exchange offer, the board stated that its objective was either to defeat the inadequate Mesa offer or, should the offer still succeed, provide the 49% of its stockholders, who would otherwise be forced to accept "junk bonds", with $72 worth of senior debt. We find that both purposes are valid.

However, such efforts would have been thwarted by Mesa's participation in the exchange offer. First, if Mesa could tender its shares, Unocal would effectively be subsidizing the former's continuing effort to buy Unocal stock at $54 per share. Second, Mesa could not, by definition, fit within the class of shareholders being protected from its own coercive and inadequate tender offer.

Thus, we are satisfied that the selective exchange offer is reasonably related to the threats posed. It is consistent with the principle that "the minority stockholder shall receive the substantial equivalent in value of what he had before." Sterling v. Mayflower Hotel Corp., Del.Supr., 93 A.2d 107, 114 (1952). This concept of fairness, while stated in the merger context, is also relevant in the area of tender offer law. Thus, the board's decision to offer what it determined to be the fair value of the corporation to the 49% of its shareholders, who would otherwise be forced to accept highly subordinated "junk bonds", is reasonable and consistent with the directors' duty to ensure that the minority stockholders receive equal value for their shares.

Notes

(1) See generally Ronald Gilson & Reinier Kraakman, Delaware's Intermediate Standard for Defensive Tactics: Is There Substance to Proportionality Review? 44 Bus.Law. 247 (1989).

(2) Shortly after the Delaware Supreme Court's opinion in *Unocal*, the SEC adopted rule 14d–10, 17 C.F.R. § 240.14d–10 (1989), 51 Fed.Reg. 25,882 (1986), popularly known as the "All Holders Rule," which required that an offer be open to all security holders of the same class of securities. It is clear that the purpose of this rule was to eliminate the *Unocal* strategy, though the SEC explained its purpose as follows:

A major aspect of the legislative effort to protect investors was to avoid favoring either management or the takeover bidder. In implementing this policy of neutrality, the Commission has administered the Williams Act in an even-handed fashion favoring neither side in a contest. Also implicit in these provisions, and necessary for the functioning of the Williams Act are the requirements that a bidder make a tender offer to all security holders of the

was defeated by another company at a price higher than the offer price. See Lipton, 35 Bus.Law. at 106–109, 132–133. Moreover, an update by Kidder Peabody & Company of this study, involving the stock prices of target companies that have defeated hostile tender offers during the period from 1973 to 1982 demonstrates that in a majority of cases the target's shareholders benefited from the defeat. The stock of 81% of the targets studied has, since the tender offer, sold at prices higher than the tender offer price. When adjusted for the time value of money, the figure is 64%. The thesis being that this strongly supports application of the business judgment rule in response to takeover threats. There is, however, a rather vehement contrary view. See Easterbrook & Fischel, supra 36 Bus.Law. at 1739–1745.

class of securities which is the subject of the offer and that the offer made to all holders on the same terms.

The investor protection purposes of the Exchange Act would not be achieved without these requirements because tender offers could be extended to some security holders but not to others or to all security holders but on different terms. * * *

SEC Rel. No. 34–22,198, 50 Fed.Reg. 27,976, 27,977 (1985). The SEC also stated in its accompanying release that the all holders rule "codifies existing interpretations by the Commission's staff." Is the all holders rule really neutral as between the aggressor and management?

(3) In Polaroid Corp. v. Disney, 862 F.2d 987 (3d Cir.1988), the Court upheld the all holders rule on the theory that it broadly related to disclosure. The Court also held that disadvantaged shareholders had standing to enjoin violations of the all holders rule by a third party but that the issuer did not have standing to sue on its own behalf. The Court noted, however, that the question was "a difficult one" and that since it was likely that disadvantaged shareholders would intervene if the issuer were not able to maintain a suit on their behalf, the issuer should be accorded standing on the theory of jus tertii, or the right to sue on behalf of a related third party.

(4) Does the all holders rule principle cover the private repurchase of shares at a premium, i.e., "greenmail"? Should it?

(5) From a relatively early time, courts have indicated that more or less brazen attempts to perpetuate incumbent management in office would be enjoined. The leading case is Schnell v. Chris–Craft Industries, Inc., 285 A.2d 430 (Del.Ch.1971), reversed, 285 A.2d 437 (Del.1971), discussed in *Unocal*. Incumbent management was facing a difficult proxy fight. It exercised the power it possessed under Delaware law to change the date of the meeting from January 11, 1972 to December 8, 1971, thereby cutting down the period the insurgents had to obtain approval by the SEC of their proxy solicitation materials and to solicit proxies. It also moved the meeting site to an "isolated town in up-state New York." The defendants attempted to justify these changes on the ground of "weather conditions in Cortland, New York, in January, as opposed to early December, * * * [and] the normal delays in delivery of notices to stockholders resulting from Christmas mails." 285 A.2d at 439. The Supreme Court of Delaware concluded that the record revealed "that management has attempted to utilize the corporate machinery and the Delaware Law for the purpose of obstructing the legitimate efforts of dissident shareholders in the exercise of their rights to undertake a proxy contest against management. These are inequitable purposes, contrary to established principles of corporate democracy * * * and may not be permitted to stand." Id. The Court also responded to an argument that actions taken by management were lawful if they were taken strictly in compliance with Delaware law with the rather tart observation that "inequitable action does not become permissible simply because it becomes legally possible." Id. Later cases have struggled with the *Schnell* principle in the takeover context. Aprahamian v. HBO & Co., 531 A.2d 1204 (Del.Ch.1987), enjoined a change of the date of the annual meeting after directors learned that a dissident shareholder had successfully obtained a large number of proxies. Blasius Indus., Inc. v. Atlas Corp., 564 A.2d 651 (Del.Ch.1988), enjoined the addition of two new persons to a staggered board that had the effect of making impractical a transaction that was being proposed in a pending consent solicitation. In both of these cases, the enjoined actions would clearly have been protected by the business judgment rule in the absence of

pending shareholder action on the same subject and an intention to defeat the shareholder-initiated action. Stroud v. Grace, 606 A.2d 75 (Del.1992), declined to apply the *Schnell* principle in a situation where the board of directors was not under a threat.

(6) *Stroud* and several other recent Delaware cases involve bylaw amendments that require names of potential board of director candidates to be submitted to the management in advance of the meeting date. Nomad Acquisition Corp. v. Damon Corp., 1988 WL 383667, 14 Del.J.Corp.L. 814 (Del.Ch.1988), holds that such a provision is not invalid on its face, but it is clear from Lerman v. Diagnostic Data., 421 A.2d 906 (Del.Ch.1980), and Hubbard v. Hollywood Park Realty Enter., Inc., 1991 WL 3151, 17 Del. J. Corp. L. 238 (Del.Ch.1991), that such a provision cannot be applied inequitably in the heat of a takeover contest.

MORAN v. HOUSEHOLD INT'L, INC.

Supreme Court of Delaware, 1985.
500 A.2d 1346.

McNEILLY, JUSTICE.

This case presents to this Court for review the most recent defensive mechanism in the arsenal of corporate takeover weaponry—the Preferred Share Purchase Rights Plan ("Rights Plan" or "Plan"). The validity of this mechanism has attracted national attention. *Amici curiae* briefs have been filed in support of appellants by the Security and Exchange Commission ("SEC")[38] and the Investment Company Institute. An *amicus curiae* brief has been filed in support of appellees ("Household") by the United Food and Commercial Workers International Union.

In a detailed opinion, the Court of Chancery upheld the Rights Plan as a legitimate exercise of business judgment by Household. Moran v. Household International, Inc., Del.Ch., 490 A.2d 1059 (1985). We agree, and therefore, affirm the judgment below.

I

* * * A review of the basic facts is necessary for a complete understanding of the issues.

On August 14, 1984, the Board of Directors of Household International, Inc. adopted the Rights Plan by a fourteen to two vote.[39] The intricacies of the Rights Plan are contained in a 48–page document entitled "Rights Agreement". Basically, the Plan provides that Household common stockholders are entitled to the issuance of one Right per common share under certain triggering conditions. There are two triggering events that can activate the Rights. The first is the announcement of a tender offer for 30 percent of Household's shares ("30% trigger") and the second is the acquisition of 20 percent of Household's shares by any single entity or group ("20% trigger").

38. [By the Court] The SEC split 3–2 on whether to intervene in this case. The two dissenting Commissioners have publicly disagreed with the other three as to the merits of the Rights Plan. 17 Securities Regulation & Law Report 400; The Wall Street Journal, March 20, 1985, at 6.

39. [By the Court] Household's Board has ten outside directors and six who are members of management. Messrs. Moran (appellant) and Whitehead voted against the Plan. The record reflects that Whitehead voted against the Plan not on its substance but because he thought it was novel and would bring unwanted publicity to Household.

If an announcement of a tender offer for 30 percent of Household's shares is made, the Rights are issued and are immediately exercisable to purchase $\frac{1}{100}$ share of new preferred stock for $100 and are redeemable by the Board for $.50 per Right. If 20 percent of Household's shares are acquired by anyone, the Rights are issued and become non-redeemable and are exercisable to purchase $\frac{1}{100}$ of a share of preferred. If a Right is not exercised for preferred, and thereafter, a merger or consolidation occurs, the Rights holder can exercise each Right to purchase $200 of the common stock of the tender offeror for $100. This "flip-over" provision of the Rights Plan is at the heart of this controversy.

Household is a diversified holding company with its principal subsidiaries engaged in financial services, transportation and merchandising. HFC, National Car Rental and Vons Grocery are three of its wholly-owned entities.

Household did not adopt its Rights Plan during a battle with a corporate raider, but as a preventive mechanism to ward off future advances. The Vice–Chancellor found that as early as February 1984, Household's management became concerned about the company's vulnerability as a takeover target and began considering amending its charter to render a takeover more difficult. After considering the matter, Household decided not to pursue a fair price amendment.

In the meantime, appellant Moran, one of Household's own Directors and also Chairman of the Dyson–Kissner–Moran Corporation, ("D–K–M") which is the largest single stockholder of Household, began discussions concerning a possible leveraged buy-out of Household by D–K–M. D–K–M's financial studies showed that Household's stock was significantly undervalued in relation to the company's break-up value. It is uncontradicted that Moran's suggestion of a leveraged buy-out never progressed beyond the discussion stage.

Concerned about Household's vulnerability to a raider in light of the current takeover climate, Household secured the services of Wachtell, Lipton, Rosen and Katz ("Watchell, Lipton") and Goldman, Sachs & Co. ("Goldman, Sachs") to formulate a takeover policy for recommendation to the Household Board at its August 14 meeting. After a July 31 meeting with a Household Board member and a pre-meeting distribution of material on the potential takeover problem and the proposed Rights Plan, the Board met on August 14, 1984.

Representatives of Wachtell, Lipton and Goldman, Sachs attended the August 14 meeting. The minutes reflect that Mr. Lipton explained to the Board that his recommendation of the Plan was based on his understanding that the Board was concerned about the increasing frequency of "bust-up" takeovers, the increasing takeover activity in the financial service industry, such as Leucadia's attempt to take over Arco, and the possible adverse effect this type of activity could have on employees and others concerned with and vital to the continuing successful operation of Household even in the absence of any actual bust-up takeover attempt. Against this factual background, the Plan was approved.

Thereafter, Moran and the company of which he is Chairman, D–K–M, filed this suit. On the eve of trial, Gretl Golter, the holder of 500 shares of Household, was permitted to intervene as an additional plaintiff. The trial was held, and the Court of Chancery ruled in favor of Household. Appellants now appeal from that ruling to this Court.

II

The primary issue here is the applicability of the business judgment rule as the standard by which the adoption of the Rights Plan should be reviewed. Much of this issue has been decided by our recent decision in Unocal Corp. v. Mesa Petroleum Co., Del.Supr., 493 A.2d 946 (1985). In *Unocal,* we applied the business judgment rule to analyze Unocal's discriminatory self-tender. We explained:

> When a board addresses a pending takeover bid it has an obligation to determine whether the offer is in the best interests of the corporation and its shareholders. In that respect a board's duty is no different from any other responsibility it shoulders, and its decisions should be no less entitled to the respect they otherwise would be accorded in the realm of business judgment.

Id. at 954 (citation and footnote omitted).

Other jurisdictions have also applied the business judgment rule to actions by which target companies have sought to forestall takeover activity they considered undesirable. See Gearhart Industries, Inc. v. Smith International, 5th Cir., 741 F.2d 707 (1984) (sale of discounted subordinate debentures containing springing warrants); Treco, Inc. v. Land of Lincoln Savings and Loan, 7th Cir., 749 F.2d 374 (1984) (amendment to by-laws); Panter v. Marshall Field, 7th Cir., 646 F.2d 271 (1981) (acquisitions to create antitrust problems); Johnson v. Trueblood, 3d Cir., 629 F.2d 287 (1980), cert. denied, 450 U.S. 999, 101 S.Ct. 1704, 68 L.Ed.2d 200 (1981) (refusal to tender); Crouse–Hinds Co. v. InterNorth, Inc., 2d Cir., 634 F.2d 690 (1980) (sale of stock to favored party); Treadway v. Care Corp., 2d Cir., 638 F.2d 357 (1980) (sale to White Knight), Enterra Corp. v. SGS Associates, E.D.Pa., 600 F.Supp. 678 (1985) (standstill agreement); Buffalo Forge Co. v. Ogden Corp., S.D.N.Y., 555 F.Supp. 892, aff'd, 717 F.2d 757 (2d Cir.), cert. denied, 464 U.S. 1018, 104 S.Ct. 550, 78 L.Ed.2d 724 (1983) (sale of treasury shares and grant of stock option to White Knight); Whittaker Corp. v. Edgar, N.D.Ill., 535 F.Supp. 933 (1982) (disposal of valuable assets); Martin Marietta Corp. v. Bendix Corp., D.Md., 549 F.Supp. 623 (1982) (Pac–Man defense).

This case is distinguishable from the ones cited, since here we have a defensive mechanism adopted to ward off possible future advances and not a mechanism adopted in reaction to a specific threat. This distinguishing factor does not result in the Directors losing the protection of the business judgment rule. To the contrary, pre-planning for the contingency of a hostile takeover might reduce the risk that, under the pressure of a takeover bid, management will fail to exercise reasonable judgment. Therefore, in reviewing a pre-planned defensive mechanism it seems even more appropriate to apply the business judgment rule. See Warner Communications v. Murdoch, D.Del., 581 F.Supp. 1482, 1491 (1984).

Of course, the business judgment rule can only sustain corporate decision making or transactions that are within the power or authority of the Board. Therefore, before the business judgment rule can be applied it must be determined whether the Directors were authorized to adopt the Rights Plan.

III

Appellants vehemently contend that the Board of Directors was unauthorized to adopt the Rights Plan. First, appellants contend that no provision of the Delaware General Corporation Law authorizes the issuance of such Rights. Secondly, appellants, along with the SEC, contend that the Board is unauthorized to usurp stockholders' rights to receive hostile tender offers. Third, appellants and the SEC also contend that the Board is unauthorized to fundamentally restrict stockholders' rights to conduct a proxy contest. We address each of these contentions in turn.

A.

While appellants contend that no provision of the Delaware General Corporation Law authorizes the Rights Plan, Household contends that the Rights Plan was issued pursuant to 8 *Del.C.* §§ 151(g) and 157. It explains that the Rights are authorized by § 157[40] and the issue of preferred stock underlying the Rights is authorized by § 151.[41] Appellants respond by making several attacks upon the authority to issue the Rights pursuant to § 157.

Appellants begin by contending that § 157 cannot authorize the Rights Plan since § 157 has never served the purpose of authorizing a takeover defense. Appellants contend that § 157 is a corporate financing statute, and that nothing in its legislative history suggests a purpose that has anything to do with corporate control or a takeover defense. Appellants are unable to demonstrate that the legislature, in its adoption of § 157, meant to limit the applicability of § 157 to only the issuance of Rights for the purposes of corporate financing. Without such affirmative evidence, we decline to impose such a limitation upon the section that the legislature has not. Compare Providence & Worchester Co. v. Baker, Del.Supr., 378 A.2d 121, 124 (1977) (refusal to read a bar to protective voting provisions into 8 *Del.C.* § 212(a)).

As we noted in *Unocal:*

> [O]ur corporate law is not static. It must grow and develop in response to, indeed in anticipation of, evolving concepts and needs. Merely because the General Corporation Law is silent as to a specific matter does not mean that it is prohibited.

493 A.2d at 957. See also Cheff v. Mathes, Del.Supr., 199 A.2d 548 (1964).

---

40. [By the Court] The power to issue rights to purchase shares is conferred by 8 *Del.C.* § 157 which provides in relevant part:

Subject to any provisions in the certificate of incorporation, every corporation may create and issue, whether or not in connection with the issue and sale of any shares of stock or other securities of the corporation, rights or options entitling the holders thereof to purchase from the corporation any shares of its capital stock of any class or classes, such rights or options to be evidenced by or in such instrument or instruments as shall be approved by the board of directors.

41. [By the Court] 8 *Del.C.* § 151(g) provides in relevant part:

When any corporation desires to issue any shares of stock of any class or of any series of any class of which the voting powers,

designations, preferences and relative, participating, optional or other rights, if any, or the qualifications, limitations or restrictions thereof, if any, shall not have been set forth in the certificate of incorporation or in any amendment thereto but shall be provided for in a resolution or resolutions adopted by the board of directors pursuant to authority expressly vested in it by the provisions of the certificate of incorporation or any amendment thereto, a certificate setting forth a copy of such resolution or resolutions and the number of shares of stock of such class or series shall be executed, acknowledged, filed, recorded, and shall become effective, in accordance with § 103 of this title.

Secondly, appellants contend that § 157 does not authorize the issuance of sham rights such as the Rights Plan. They contend that the Rights were designed never to be exercised, and that the Plan has no economic value. In addition, they contend the preferred stock made subject to the Rights is also illusory, citing *Telvest, Inc. v. Olson,* Del.Ch., C.A. No. 5798, Brown, V.C. (March 8, 1979).

Appellants' sham contention fails in both regards. As to the Rights, they can and will be exercised upon the happening of a triggering mechanism, as we have observed during the current struggle of Sir James Goldsmith to take control of Crown Zellerbach. See Wall Street Journal, July 26, 1985, at 3, 12. As to the preferred shares, we agree with the Court of Chancery that they are distinguishable from sham securities invalidated in *Telvest,* supra. The Household preferred, issuable upon the happening of a triggering event, have superior dividend and liquidation rights. * * *

[Next], appellants contend that if § 157 authorizes the Rights Plan it would be unconstitutional pursuant to the Commerce Clause and Supremacy Clause of the United States Constitution * * * since it is an obstacle to the accomplishment of the policies underlying the Williams Act. Appellants put heavy emphasis upon the case of Edgar v. MITE Corp., 457 U.S. 624, 102 S.Ct. 2629, 73 L.Ed.2d 269 (1982), in which the United States Supreme Court held that the Illinois Business Takeover Act was unconstitutional, in that it unduly burdened interstate commerce in violation of the Commerce Clause. We do not read the analysis in *Edgar* as applicable to the actions of private parties. The fact that directors of a corporation act pursuant to a state statute provides an insufficient nexus to the state for there to be state action which may violate the Commerce Clause or Supremacy Clause. See Data Probe Acquisition Corp. v. Datatab, Inc., 2d Cir., 722 F.2d 1, 5 (1983).

Having concluded that sufficient authority for the Rights Plan exists in 8 *Del.C.* § 157, we note the inherent powers of the Board conferred by 8 *Del.C.* § 141(a), concerning the management of the corporation's "business and *affairs*" (emphasis added), also provides the Board additional authority upon which to enact the Rights Plan.

B.

Appellants contend that the Board is unauthorized to usurp stockholders' rights to receive tender offers by changing Household's fundamental structure. We conclude that the Rights Plan does not prevent stockholders from receiving tender offers, and that the change of Household's structure was less than that which results from the implementation of other defensive mechanisms upheld by various courts.

Appellants' contention that stockholders will lose their right to receive and accept tender offers seems to be premised upon an understanding of the Rights Plan which is illustrated by the SEC *amicus* brief which states: "The Chancery Court's decision seriously understates the impact of this plan. In fact, as we discuss below, the Rights Plan will deter not only two-tier offers, but virtually all hostile tender offers."

The fallacy of that contention is apparent when we look at the recent takeover of Crown Zellerbach, which has a similar Rights Plan, by Sir James Goldsmith. Wall Street Journal, July 26, 1985, at 3, 12. The evidence at trial also evidenced many methods around the Plan ranging from tendering with a condition that the Board redeem the Rights, tendering with a high minimum condition of shares and Rights, tendering and soliciting consents to remove the Board and redeem the Rights, to acquiring 50% of the shares and causing Household to self-tender for the Rights. One could also form a group of up to 19.9% and solicit proxies for consents to remove the Board and redeem the Rights. These are but a few of the methods by which Household can still be acquired by a hostile tender offer.

In addition, the Rights Plan is not absolute. When the Household Board of Directors is faced with a tender offer and a request to redeem the Rights, they will not be able to arbitrarily reject the offer. They will be held to the same fiduciary standards any other board of directors would be held to in deciding to adopt a defensive mechanism, the same standard as they were held to in originally approving the Rights Plan.

In addition, appellants contend that the deterrence of tender offers will be accomplished by what they label "a fundamental transfer of power from the stockholders to the directors." They contend that this transfer of power, in itself, is unauthorized.

The Rights Plan will result in no more of a structural change than any other defensive mechanism adopted by a board of directors. The Rights Plan does not destroy the assets of the corporation. The implementation of the Plan neither results in any outflow of money from the corporation nor impairs its financial flexibility. It does not dilute earnings per share and does not have any adverse tax consequences for the corporation or its stockholders. The Plan has not adversely affected the market price of Household's stock.

Comparing the Rights Plan with other defensive mechanisms, it does less harm to the value structure of the corporation than do the other mechanisms. Other mechanisms result in increased debt of the corporation. See Whittaker Corp. v. Edgar, supra (sale of "prize asset"), Cheff v. Mathes, supra, (paying greenmail to eliminate a threat), Unocal Corp. v. Mesa Petroleum Co., supra, (discriminatory self-tender).

There is little change in the governance structure as a result of the adoption of the Rights Plan. The Board does not now have unfettered discretion in refusing to redeem the Rights. The Board has no more discretion in refusing to redeem the Rights than it does in enacting any defensive mechanism.

The contention that the Rights Plan alters the structure more than do other defensive mechanisms because it is so effective as to make the corporation completely safe from hostile tender offers is likewise without merit. As explained above, there are numerous methods to successfully launch a hostile tender offer.

C.

Appellants' third contention is that the Board was unauthorized to fundamentally restrict stockholders' rights to conduct a proxy contest. Appellants contend that the "20% trigger" effectively prevents any stockholder from first acquiring 20% or more shares before conducting a proxy contest and further, it prevents stockholders from banding together into a group to solicit proxies if, collectively, they own 20% or more of the stock.[42] In addition, at trial, appellants contended that read literally, the Rights Agreement triggers the Rights upon the mere acquisition of the right to vote 20% or more of the shares through a proxy solicitation, and thereby precludes any proxy contest from being waged.[43]

Appellants seem to have conceded this last contention in light of Household's response that the receipt of a proxy does not make the recipient the "beneficial owner" of the shares involved which would trigger the Rights. In essence, the Rights Agreement provides that the Rights are triggered when someone becomes the "beneficial owner" of 20% or more of Household stock. Although a literal reading of the Rights Agreement definition of "beneficial owner" would seem to include those shares which one has the right to vote, it has long been recognized that the relationship between grantor and recipient of a proxy is one of agency, and the agency is revocable by the grantor at any time. Henn, *Corporations* § 196, at 518. Therefore, the holder of a proxy is not the "beneficial owner" of the stock. As a result, the mere acquisition of the right to vote 20% of the shares does not trigger the Rights.

The issue, then, is whether the restriction upon individuals or groups from first acquiring 20% of shares before waging a proxy contest fundamentally restricts stockholders' right to conduct a proxy contest. Regarding this issue the Court of Chancery found:

> Thus, while the Rights Plan does deter the formation of proxy efforts of a certain magnitude, it does not limit the voting power of individual shares. On the evidence presented it is highly conjectural to assume that a particular effort to assert shareholder views in the election of directors or revisions of corporate policy will be frustrated by the proxy feature of the Plan. Household's witnesses, Troubh and Higgins described recent corporate takeover battles in which insurgents holding less than 10% stock ownership were able to secure corporate control through a proxy contest or the threat of one.

490 A.2d at 1080.

We conclude that there was sufficient evidence at trial to support the Vice–Chancellor's finding that the effect upon proxy contests will be minimal. Evidence at trial established that many proxy contests are won with an insurgent ownership of less than 20%, and that very large holdings are no guarantee of success. There was also testimony that the key variable in proxy contest success is the merit of an insurgent's issues, not the size of his holdings.

IV

Having concluded that the adoption of the Rights Plan was within the authority of the Directors, we now look to whether the Directors have met their burden under the business judgment rule.

---

42. [By the Court] Appellants explain that the acquisition of 20% of the shares trigger the Rights, making them non-redeemable, and thereby would prevent even a future friendly offer for the ten-year life of the Rights.

43. [By the Court] The SEC still contends that the mere acquisition of the right to vote 20% of the shares through a proxy solicitation triggers the rights. We do not interpret the Rights Agreement in that manner.

The business judgment rule is a "presumption that in making a business decision the directors of a corporation acted on an informed basis, in good faith and in the honest belief that the action taken was in the best interests of the company." Aronson v. Lewis, Del.Supr., 473 A.2d 805, 812 (1984) (citations omitted). Notwithstanding, in *Unocal* we held that when the business judgment rule applies to adoption of a defensive mechanism, the initial burden will lie with the directors. The "directors must show that they had reasonable grounds for believing that a danger to corporate policy and effectiveness existed. * * * [T]hey satisfy that burden 'by showing good faith and reasonable investigation * * *' " *Unocal,* 493 A.2d at 955 (citing Cheff v. Mathes, 199 A.2d at 554–55). In addition, the directors must show that the defensive mechanism was "reasonable in relation to the threat posed." *Unocal,* 493 A.2d at 955. Moreover, that proof is materially enhanced, as we noted in *Unocal,* where, as here, a majority of the board favoring the proposal consisted of outside independent directors who have acted in accordance with the foregoing standards. *Unocal,* 493 A.2d at 955; *Aronson,* 473 A.2d at 815. Then, the burden shifts back to the plaintiffs who have the ultimate burden of persuasion to show a breach of the directors' fiduciary duties. *Unocal,* 493 A.2d at 958.

There are no allegations here of any bad faith on the part of the Directors' action in the adoption of the Rights Plan. There is no allegation that the Directors' action was taken for entrenchment purposes. Household has adequately demonstrated, as explained above, that the adoption of the Rights Plan was in reaction to what it perceived to be the threat in the market place of coercive two-tier tender offers. Appellants do contend, however, that the Board did not exercise informed business judgment in its adoption of the Plan. * * * Appellants contend the Delaware counsel did not express an opinion on the flip-over provision of the Rights, rather only that the Rights would constitute validly issued and outstanding rights to subscribe to the preferred stock of the company.

To determine whether a business judgment reached by a board of directors was an informed one, we determine whether the directors were grossly negligent. Smith v. Van Gorkom, Del.Supr., 488 A.2d 858, 873 (1985). Upon a review of this record, we conclude the Directors were not grossly negligent. The information supplied to the Board on August 14 provided the essentials of the Plan. The Directors were given beforehand a notebook which included a three-page summary of the Plan along with articles on the current takeover environment. The extended discussion between the Board and representatives of Wachtell, Lipton and Goldman, Sachs before approval of the Plan reflected a full and candid evaluation of the Plan. Moran's expression of his views at the meeting served to place before the Board a knowledgeable critique of the Plan. The factual happenings here are clearly distinguishable from the actions of the directors of Trans Union Corporation who displayed gross negligence in approving a cash-out merger.

In addition, to meet their burden, the Directors must show that the defensive mechanism was "reasonable in relation to the threat posed". The record reflects a concern on the part of the Directors over the increasing frequency in the financial services industry of "boot-strap" and "bust-up" takeovers. The Directors were also concerned that such takeovers may take the form of two-tier offers.[44] In addition, on August 14, the Household Board was aware of Moran's overture on behalf of D–K–M. In sum, the Directors reasonably believed Household was vulnerable to coercive acquisition techniques and adopted a reasonable defensive mechanism to protect itself.

V

* * * While we conclude for present purposes that the Household Directors are protected by the business judgment rule, that does not end the matter. The ultimate response to an actual takeover bid must be judged by the Directors' actions at that time, and nothing we say here relieves them of their basic fundamental duties to the corporation and its stockholders. Smith v. Van Gorkom, 488 A.2d at 872–73. Their use of the Plan will be evaluated when and if the issue arises.

Affirmed.

Notes

(1) The "Rights Plan" approved in *Moran* is usually called a "poison pill." Michael J. Powell, Professional Innovation: Corporate Lawyers and Private Lawmaking, 18 Law & Soc. Inq. 423, 440–42 (1993):[45]

> Wachtell Lipton [Rosen Katz] was adding new wrinkles to the poison pill even while litigation over its legality was proceeding. In particular, the firm developed a new "flip-in" provision intended to prevent a large shareholder from benefiting from such self-dealing transactions with the target corporation as purchases or sales of assets, or special issuances of stock to the holder. If the purchaser of 20% or more of the stock engaged in self-dealing transactions with the target, other shareholders were entitled to purchase further shares at half their market value thereby effectively diluting the large holder's position both in terms of value and voting power. The self-dealing flip-in was a significant modification to the shareholder rights plan, enhancing its deterrent value by making it difficult for raiders to enjoy the fruits of their conquest. Once introduced, the self-dealing flip-in became a standard feature of the Lipton poison pill. * * *

> [S]everal additional varieties of the poison pill soon appeared in the marketplace, each hawked by different law firms extolling the virtues of their particular model.

> Most of the new varieties included two additional ingredients intended to strengthen the pill's deterrent capacity and increase the flexibility it allowed directors of target corporations. In the first place, they generally included a much broader flip-in provision that would release the poisonous ingredients of the pill simply if a bidder exceeded a certain threshold in purchasing the stock of the target, perhaps as low as 20%, without any requirement of a self-dealing transaction as a trigger. Intended to prevent a "creeping acquisition" in which a raider gained majority control of a corporation but stopped short of completing the merger, this modification clearly expanded the defensive capacity of the poison pill.

---

44. [By the Court] We have discussed the coercive nature of two-tier tender offers in *Unocal*, 493 A.2d at 956, n. 12. We explained in *Unocal* that a discriminatory self-tender was reasonably related to the threat of two-tier tender offers and possible greenmail.

45. Law & Social Inquiry: Journal of the American Bar Foundation. © 1993 American Bar Foundation. Published by the University of Chicago Press.

The second new ingredient common to most of the non-Lipton pills was the inclusion of a window, or a second-look redemption period, intended to increase the options available to the directors of a target corporation when faced with a hostile bid. Providing a waiting period of 10 to 20 days after a raider has crossed the specified threshold before the draconian shareholder rights become nonredeemable, this modification allows the directors more time to respond to, and perhaps negotiate with, the acquirer or to find a white knight to rescue them. Otherwise the directors of the target corporation are as much locked in by the nonredeemable nature of the rights as the acquirer. By providing more time and flexibility for target directors, the window is intended to decrease their liability to disgruntled shareholders. These new refinements of the basic Lipton model pushed the poison pill beyond the boundaries established in the *Moran* decision. * * *

Further development continued in 1987 with Wachtell Lipton developing a "second generation" pill including the now common flip-in provision. Lipton had previously opposed general flip-ins, other than for self-dealing, on the grounds that the courts were likely to view them as discriminatory. But while the earlier Lipton pills with the standard flip-over provisions were effective against two-tier, front-end loaded bids, they could be bypassed by determined bidders. The new Lipton model also provided an option for an acquirer to call for a shareholder referendum on cash offers for any and all shares. This option represented an effort by Lipton to avoid challenges to the poison pill on the grounds that it eliminated shareholder democracy.

In the same year, Skadden Arps [Slate Meagher & Flom] came up with a variation on its standard flip-in pill, reducing the percentage level at which the rights would be triggered to 15%. This was much lower than other pills and was viewed as risky by many observers. A year later another major corporate law firm, Gibson Dunn & Crutcher marketed a poison pill with a new twist: a two-trigger flip-in. In this more exotic and complicated version, an acquirer must pass two thresholds before triggering the classic dramatic consequences. The first trigger point was intended to give hostile acquirers a warning before unleashing the full terror of the poison pill in the hope of encouraging them into the boardroom to negotiate. What is happening with these developments is the ongoing modification and refinement of the poison pill to meet new conditions and to differentiate a particular product from rival versions. Law firms were engaging in research and development, if you like, to come up with the safest and most effective pill.

(2) Takeover defenses, of course, proliferated during the 1980s. Among the simplest and most common was a three-tier plan that included (a) a classification of the board of directors into three groups, with one group being elected each year, (b) a prohibition against removing directors except for cause, and (c) a provision that prohibited certain designated types of amendments to the articles of incorporation or bylaws (which could result in a change of control) unless approved by a supermajority (e.g. 80 percent) of the directors. The effect of these provisions was to prevent an aggressor that acquired even 100 percent of the shares from replacing a majority of the board of directors for two years. Consider MBCA §§ 7.27, 8.06, 8.24(a), and (c), 10.21. Delaware's statute is similar to these provisions except that Del. Gen. Corp. Law § 141(d) authorizes the staggering of elections to the board of directors without regard to the privilege of voting cumulatively. Consider also New York Bus. Corp. Law § 616(c), which requires a two-thirds vote to adopt a supermajority amendment to the articles of incorporation and also requires a conspicuous reference to such a provision on each share

certificate. Do you think that such provisions provide adequate protection to the shareholders or to the public against possible misuse of porcupine provisions?

(3) Other types of defensive provisions that had some degree of popularity during the 1980s included:

(a) A requirement that 80 percent or more of the shareholders be required to approve certain transactions (e.g., mergers) between the corporation and persons that own more than 10 per cent of the corporate shares—adopted by Southwest Airlines and others.

(b) A requirement that a majority of the shares other than shares owned by a party to a proposed transaction approve the proposed transaction—adopted by Baldor Electric, Inc. and others.

(c) A requirement that 95 percent approval of certain transactions between the corporation and large shareholders be obtained unless the transaction meets certain precise price and other substantive terms set forth in the articles or bylaws—adopted by Anchor Hocking Corporation and others.

(d) A provision that allows minority shareholders to redeem their shares for cash from the corporation at a price set forth in the articles or bylaws for a limited period following any transaction in which a person acquires a majority of the outstanding shares or a majority shareholder increases his holdings—adopted by Rubbermaid Corporation and others.

(e) A provision creating special classes of preferred shares to be held by a limited number of holders, and requiring approval of that class of shares of certain classes of transactions—e.g., Outdoor Sports Industries, Inc.

(f) Fair price amendments to articles of incorporation which mandate that shareholders receive equivalent consideration (both in terms of amount and form) on both ends of a two-tiered bid—adopted by numerous corporations.

(g) Anti-greenmail provisions: amendments to articles of incorporation prohibiting the repurchase by the company of stock at a premium from a three percent or greater holder unless the repurchase is approved by a majority vote of the shareholders—adopted by International Minerals & Chemical Corporation and others.

(4) A corporation is of course totally takeover-proof if a majority of its voting shares is held by a single person or entity. Many family owned corporations were once safely takeover-proof even though minority shares were widely held and traded on securities exchanges. Because of deaths of founders, sales by heirs, and the natural desire of many family members to diversify the investment of their inherited wealth, these companies tend to become subject to takeovers over time as family ownership is dissipated. In order to slow this process, some prominent corporations issued supervoting stock (shares with multiple votes per share but a lower dividend) to all shareholders in an effort to guarantee family control over the enterprise despite their now-minority position. The supervoting stock is not itself transferable to third persons but may be converted at the request of the shareholder into the regular common stock that is traded on a national securities exchange. The theory is that public shareholders will naturally convert their supervoting common stock promptly into regular common stock to obtain the larger dividend and liquidity provided by the market, while the family group will retain the higher voting, lower yielding supervoting stock. Two well-known corporations that have issued supervoting stock are the Washington Post Company and Dow Jones, Inc., the publisher of the *Wall Street Journal*. The "tenure

voting" provision approved in Williams v. Geier, see page 470 supra, is another device designed to preserve family control of a publicly held corporation.

(5) The potential of the defensive technique of "parking" supervoting stock in safe hands to guarantee voting control was not lost on managements fearing takeovers. One major restraint on this technique was the longstanding "one share-one vote" rule of the New York Stock Exchange that threatened delisting of corporations that issued nonvoting common shares, shares subject to a voting trust, or shares with "unusual voting provisions." New York Stock Exchange Listed Company Manual, §§ 313.000, 802.00. However, with the growth of the over-the-counter market, particularly NASDAQ and the National Market, which had much more liberal listing requirements, the threat of delisting by the NYSE became less serious and, during the late 1980s, a large number of publicly held corporations seriously considered the creation of supervoting stock as the ultimate antitakeover device.

(6) The dispute over "one share-one vote" was triggered by General Motor's plan to issue a second class of common stock with one-half vote per share. The NYSE proposed to relax its prohibition against unusual voting provisions in order to permit the listing of the new shares, a step that required SEC approval. Rather than acting on the proposed NYSE provision, the SEC instead adopted rule 19c–4, 17 C.F.R. § 240.19c–4 (1997), that prohibited exchanges and national securities associations from listing stock of a corporation that takes any corporate action "with the effect of nullifying, restricting or disparately reducing the per share voting rights" of existing shareholders. S.E.C. Rel. No. 34–25,891 (July 7 and 13, 1988), 53 Fed. Reg. 26,376, 26,394 (1988). Academic commentary on this proposal was mixed, with some professors associated with the law and economics movement opposing it. See, e.g., Ronald Gilson, Evaluating Dual Class Common Stock: The Relevance of Substitutes, 73 Va. L.Rev. 807 (1986); Larry R. Fischel, Organized Exchanges and the Regulation of Dual Class Common Stock, 54 U. Chi. L.Rev. 119 (1987); Joel Seligman, Equal Protection in Shareholder Voting Rights: The One Common Share, One Vote Controversy, 54 Geo. Wash. L.Rev. 687 (1987); Roger Lowenstein, Shareholder Voting Rights: A Response to SEC Rule 19c–4 and to Professor Gilson, 89 Colum. L.Rev. 979 (1989). However, in a stinging rebuke to the SEC, the Court of Appeals for the District of Columbia, in Business Roundtable v. S.E.C, 905 F.2d 406, 411–12 (D.C.Cir.1990), invalidated this rule in its entirety on the theory that it exceeded the powers of the Commission:

> * * * Rule 19c–4 * * * directly interferes with the substance of what the shareholders may enact. It prohibits certain reallocations of voting power and certain capital structures, even if approved by a shareholder vote subject to full disclosure and the most exacting procedural rules. * * * If Rule 19c–4 were validated on [the broad grounds urged by the Commission], the Commission would be able to establish a federal corporate law by using access to national capital markets as its enforcement mechanism. This would resolve a longstanding controversy over the wisdom of such a move in the face of disclaimers from Congress and with no substantive restraints on the power. It would, moreover, overturn or at least impinge severely on the tradition of state regulation of corporate law."

The SEC then successfully persuaded securities exchanges voluntarily to impose a modified or "relaxed" "one share-one vote" rule.

(7) A survey by the Investor Responsibility Research Center in 1989 showed that of the 1,440 largest public corporations (representing some 93 percent of the total capitalization of all companies listed on the NYSE, ASE, and NASDAQ):

(a) 616 companies (43 percent) had poison pills;

(b) 781 companies (54 percent) elected directors to staggered terms;

(c) 455 companies (32 percent) had adopted fair price charter amendments requiring all shareholders to be paid the same price;

(d) 241 companies (17 percent) required a supermajority vote for proposed mergers;

(e) 106 companies (7.4 percent) had dual class capitalization plans with different classes of voting shares;

(f) 266 companies (18.5 percent) provided for cumulative voting;

(g) 324 companies (23 percent) had adopted provisions limiting the power of shareholders to act by written consent without a shareholders' meeting;

(h) 301 companies (21 percent) had adopted charter amendments limiting the power of shareholders to call special shareholders' meetings;

(i) 80 companies (5.6 percent) had enacted charter amendments to discourage greenmail;

(j) 32 companies (2.2 percent) had adopted secret shareholder ballot amendments; and

(k) 86 companies (6 percent) had authorized boards to consider interests other than shareholders in evaluating merger proposals.

Obviously, many companies had adopted more than one of the above proposals. Presumably all 1,140 companies have adopted at least one of the listed forms of protection against unwanted takeover bids. The above data does not take into account state statutes that may automatically make the above provisions applicable to corporations incorporated in specific states. In other words, by the end of the 1980s one could safely assume that every publicly held corporation had in place a bristling arsenal of defenses against unwanted tender offers.

———

Almost immediately following *Unocal* and *Moran*, another major Delaware case involving defensive tactics arose, completing the trilogy of Delaware cases that largely shaped takeovers during the second half of the 1980s. The dispute arose when Pantry Pride made a hostile tender offer for any and all shares of Revlon, Inc. for $47.50 per share. Viewing this price as inadequate, considering the value of Revlon's assets, and receiving information that Pantry Pride planned to break up and sell off Revlon's component businesses, Revlon management instituted a series of defensive tactics, including an offer to purchase 10,000,000 of its own shares in part for notes with poison pill provisions. Pantry Pride then increased its offer in a series of steps, first to $50 per share, then to $53, and then to $56.25, contingent in each case on Pantry Pride waiving the poison pill features of the notes. Faced with this steady pressure, Revlon decided to seek possible alternative purchasers, a white knight. One potential white knight was Forstman Little & Co. After some negotiations with Forstmann (during which Forstmann was given access to financial information about Revlon that had been denied Pantry Pride), a leveraged buyout transaction was agreed upon between Forstmann and Revlon management at a price of $57.25 per share. A critical aspect of the Forstmann agreement was that Forstmann received "a lock-up option to purchase Revlon's Vision Care and National Health Laboratories divisions for $525 million, some $100–$175 million below the value ascribed to them by Lazard Freres, if another acquiror got 40% of Revlon's shares." Revlon, Inc. v. MacAndrews & Forbes Holdings, Inc., 506 A.2d 173 (Del.1985). Pantry Pride then raised its price to $58 per share contingent upon removal not only of the poison pill provisions but also the Forstmann lock-up. When Revlon management decided to go through with the Forstmann sale (apparently in large part because Forstmann promised to support the price of the notes issued earlier by Revlon to create poison pill protection), the decision moved into the Delaware courts. In *Revlon*, the Delaware Supreme Court first upheld Revlon's actions to fight off Pantry Pride's initial inadequate offers but then enunciated a new principle for the later portions of the contest:

> However, when Pantry Pride increased its offer to $50 per share, and then to $53, it became apparent to all that the break-up of the company was inevitable. The Revlon board's authorization permitting management to negotiate a merger or buyout with a third party was a recognition that the company was for sale. The duty of the board had thus changed from the preservation of Revlon as a corporate entity to the maximization of the company's value at a sale for the stockholders' benefit. This significantly altered the board's responsibilities under the *Unocal* standards. It no longer faced threats to corporate policy and effectiveness, or to the stockholders' interests, from a grossly inadequate bid. The whole question of defensive measures became moot. The directors' role changed from defenders of the corporate bastion to auctioneers charged with getting the best price for the stockholders at a sale of the company. * * *

> The original threat posed by Pantry Pride—the break-up of the company—had become a reality which even the directors embraced. Selective dealing to fend off a hostile but determined bidder was no longer a proper objective. Instead, obtaining the highest price for the benefit of the stockholders should have been the central theme guiding director action. Thus, the Revlon board could not make the requisite showing of good faith by preferring the noteholders and ignoring its duty of loyalty to the shareholders. The rights of the former already were fixed by contract. Wolfensohn v. Madison Fund, Inc., Del.Supr., 253 A.2d 72, 75 (1969); Harff v. Kerkorian, Del.Ch., 324 A.2d 215 (1974). The noteholders required no further protection, and when the Revlon board entered into an auction-ending lock-up agreement with Forstmann on the basis of impermissible considerations at the expense of the shareholders, the directors breached their primary duty of loyalty.

> The Revlon board argued that it acted in good faith in protecting the noteholders because *Unocal* permits consideration of other corporate constituencies. Although such considerations may be permissible, there are fundamental limitations upon that prerogative. A board may have regard for various constituencies in discharging its responsibilities, provided there are rationally related benefits accruing to the stockholders. *Unocal*, 493 A.2d at 955. However, such concern for non-stockholder interests is inappropriate when an auction among active bidders is in progress, and the object no longer is to protect or maintain the corporate enterprise but to sell it to the highest bidder. * * *

While Forstmann's $57.25 offer was objectively higher than Pantry Pride's $56.25 bid, the margin of superiority is less when the Forstmann price is adjusted for the time value of money. In reality, the Revlon board ended the auction in return for very little actual improvement in the final bid. The principal benefit went to the directors, who avoided personal liability to a class of creditors to whom the board owed no further duty under the circumstances. Thus, when a board ends an intense bidding contest on an insubstantial basis, and where a significant by-product of that action is to protect the directors against a perceived threat of personal liability for consequences stemming from the adoption of previous defensive measures, the action cannot withstand the enhanced scrutiny which *Unocal* requires of director conduct. * * *

In conclusion, the Revlon board was confronted with a situation not uncommon in the current wave of corporate takeovers. A hostile and determined bidder sought the company at a price the board was convinced was inadequate. The initial defensive tactics worked to the benefit of the shareholders, and thus the board was able to sustain its *Unocal* burdens in justifying those measures. However, in granting an asset option lock-up to Forstmann, we must conclude that under all the circumstances the directors allowed considerations other than the maximization of shareholder profit to affect their judgment, and followed a course that ended the auction for Revlon, absent court intervention, to the ultimate detriment of its shareholders. No such defensive measure can be sustained when it represents a breach of the directors' fundamental duty of care. See Smith v. Van Gorkom, Del.Supr., 488 A.2d 858, 874 (1985). In that context the board's action is not entitled to the deference accorded it by the business judgment rule. * * *

Notes

(1) The Revlon decision permits management to justify poison pills and other defensive tactics because they may slow down an initial offeror and lead to an auction involving additional bidders, thereby producing a better price for shareholders than would a sale to the first serious bidder. For a case in which a poison pill in fact led to this result, see CRTF Corp. v. Federated Dep't Stores, Inc., 683 F.Supp. 422 (S.D.N.Y.1988). Even though poison pills permit management to negotiate with potential aggressors, once the decision to sell the company has been made, the role of management shifts to obtaining the best price for shareholders.

(2) John C. Coffee, Jr., Securities Law: Defining 'Sale' Is Paramount Concern, National Law Journal, November 8, 1993, at 18, 20:[46]

* * * A Cook's tour of the relevant case law begins necessarily with the leading Delaware decisions in *Unocal Corp. v. Mesa Petroleum Co.* and *Revlon Inc. v. MacAndrews & Forbes Holdings, Inc.* as these decisions have been reinterpreted by the Delaware Supreme Court's 1990 decision in *Paramount Communications Inc. v. Time Inc.*[47]

In *Revlon*, decided in 1986, the Delaware Supreme Court placed an outer limit on the permissibility of defensive tactics: once a sale or breakup of the company becomes inevitable, the board must seek to obtain the highest

46. Reprinted with the permission of the National Law Journal, copyright 1993. The New York Law Publishing Company.

47. [By the Author] 571 A.2d 1140 (Del. 1989).

possible price for shareholders and may not consider the interests of other constituencies. * * *

But what specifically triggers the *Revlon* duty to auction the company? The *Revlon* court itself said that the critical moment came at the point when Pantry Pride, the hostile bidder, "increased its offer to $50 per share and then $53," but it is doubtful that the bidder's unilateral act in making a bid or increasing its price ever can trigger a duty to auction.

Thus, the critical fact was probably Revlon's granting of a lockup option to a rival bidder to purchase its Vision Care and National Health Laboratories divisions for a total price of $525 million—some $100 to $175 million less than the value that Revlon's own investment banker had placed on them—because these acts made the breakup of the company highly likely. Ultimately, the *Revlon* court enjoined these lockup options, finding that they went beyond inducing a bidder to enter the contest and had a "destructive effect on the auction process."

(3) The *Revlon* principal is easily stated, but its application in specific situations is difficult. For example, what is a "sale"? Is a management buyout a sale? What about a merger between companies roughly equal in size? How should an auction be conducted to meet the standards set forth in that opinion? When may the board of directors decide that it is concluded? What should the board of directors do if it wishes to accept an unexpected offer at an attractive price? May it simply enter into an agreement with that offeror? Or should it publicly announce its intention, seek additional bids, and conduct an auction? What if a board of directors enters into a contract to be acquired by an offeror, and then a second bidder unexpectedly arrives? Does the board of directors commit a breach of contract if it then conducts a *Revlon* auction? Must it include an "out" clause in the initial contract to guard against this possibility?

(4) Subsequent Delaware Supreme Court cases well illustrate the difficulty of determining an appropriate scope for the *Revlon* principle in light of the competing *Unocal* principal. Two subsequent cases that reflect this difficulty are Paramount Communications Inc. v. Time Inc. 571 A.2d 1140 (Del.1989)(holding that the *Revlon* duty was not triggered when a cash tender offer was substituted for a merger transaction involving an exchange of shares in a strategic combination), and Paramount Communications v. QVC Network, Inc., 637 A.2d 34 (Del.1994)(*Revlon* was triggered when a cash tender offer was substituted for a merger transaction involving an exchange of cash for shares). In the former case, the Court expanded upon the *Revlon* obligation as follows:

Under Delaware law there are, generally speaking and without excluding other possibilities, two circumstances which may implicate *Revlon* duties. The first, and clearer one, is when a corporation initiates an active bidding process seeking to sell itself or to effect a business reorganization involving a clear break-up of the company. See, e.g., *Mills Acquisition Co. v. Macmillan, Inc,* Del.Supr., 559 A.2d 1261 (1989.). However, *Revlon* duties may also be triggered where, in response to a bidder's offer, a target abandons its long-term strategy and seeks an alternative transaction involving the breakup of the company. Thus, in *Revlon,* when the board responded to Pantry Pride's offer by contemplating a "bust-up" sale of assets in a leveraged acquisition, we imposed upon the board a duty to maximize immediate shareholder value and an obligation to auction the company fairly. If, however, the board's reaction to a hostile tender offer is found to constitute only a defensive response and not an abandonment of the corporation's continued existence, *Revlon* duties are not triggered, though *Unocal* duties attach.[48] *See, e.g., Ivanhoe Partners v. Newmont Mining Corp.*, Del.Supr., 535 A.2d 1334, 1345 (1987).

> The plaintiffs insist that even though the original Time–Warner agreement may not have worked "an objective change of control," the transaction made a "sale" of Time inevitable. Plaintiffs rely on the subjective intent of Time's board of directors and principally upon certain board members' expressions of concern that the Warner transaction *might* be viewed as effectively putting Time up for sale. Plaintiffs argue that the use of a lock-up agreement, a no-shop clause, and so-called "dry-up" agreements prevented shareholders from obtaining a control premium in the immediate future and thus violated *Revlon*.

> We agree with the Chancellor that such evidence is entirely insufficient to invoke *Revlon* duties; and we decline to extend *Revlon*'s application to corporate transactions simply because they might be construed as putting a corporation either "in play" or "up for sale." The adoption of structural safety devices alone does not trigger *Revlon*. Rather, as the Chancellor stated, such devices are properly subject to a *Unocal* analysis.

571 A.2d at 1150–51. However, the consistency of these two decisions is not intuitively obvious and the decisions have been criticized, both individually and collectively. See Alan E. Garfield, *Paramount*: The Mixed Merits of Mush, 17 Del. J. Corp. L. 33 (1992) (the Court in *Paramount* "took a decisive turn in takeover jurisprudence in favor of management" and "left no clear standards in its wake"); Marc I. Steinberg, Nightmare On Main Street: The *Paramount* Picture Horror Show, 16 Del. J. Corp. L. 1 (1991) (author was a "wishful thinker" when he earlier expressed the view that shareholders were protected in Delaware); John C. Coffee, Jr., The Battle to Control Paramount is Over, But the Legal and Strategic Questions Raised by This Epic Corporate Struggle May Have Just Begun, National Law Journal, March 28, 1994, at B5. Professor Coffee suggests that *"Paramount* represents a half-step retreat from the Delaware Supreme Court's apparent position in *Time Warner*—that only a breakup or liquidation of the company triggers a duty to auction." The focus of when the *Revlon* duty is triggered, he states, appears to be whether the transaction involves the acquisition of control by a new controlling shareholder but a number of questions remain unanswered.

(5) The apparent activism of the Delaware Supreme Court in this area was greatly tempered by the decision in Unitrin, Inc. v. American General Corp., 651 A.2d 1361 (Del.1995). The target corporation, Unitrin, initiated a major share repurchase plan in the face of an unwanted all-cash tender offer and proxy contest. The Delaware Chancery Court enjoined this maneuver on the ground that it was a disproportionate response to the threat posed by American General's "inadequate" tender offer, but the Supreme Court reversed, applying the following analysis to a defensive tactic:

> This Court has recognized "the prerogative of a board of directors to resist a third party's unsolicited acquisition proposal or offer." Paramount Communications, Inc. v. QVC Network, Inc., Del.Supr., 637 A.2d 34, 43 n. 13

---

48. [By the Court] Within the auction process, any action taken by the board must be reasonably related to the threat posed or reasonable in relation to the advantage sought, see *Mills Acquisition Co. v. Macmillan, Inc.*, Del.Supr., 559 A.2d 1261, 1288 (1988). Thus, a *Unocal* analysis may be appropriate when a corporation is in a *Revlon* situation and *Revlon* duties may be triggered by a defensive action taken in response to a hostile offer. Since *Revlon*, we have stated that differing treatment of various bidders is not actionable when such action reasonably relates to achieving the best price available for the stockholders. *Macmillan*, 559 A.2d at 1286–87.

(1994). The Unitrin Board did not have unlimited discretion to defeat the threat it perceived from the American General Offer by any draconian[49] means available. Pursuant to the Unocal proportionality test, the nature of the threat associated with a particular hostile offer sets the parameters for the range of permissible defensive tactics. Accordingly, the purpose of enhanced judicial scrutiny is to determine whether the Board acted reasonably in "relation * * * to the threat which a particular bid allegedly poses to stockholder interests." Mills Acquisition Co. v. Macmillan, Inc., Del.Supr., 559 A.2d 1261, 1288 (1989).

* * * Courts, commentators and litigators have attempted to catalogue the threats posed by hostile tender offers. Commentators have categorized three types of threats: (i) opportunity loss ... [where] a hostile offer might deprive target shareholders of the opportunity to select a superior alternative offered by target management [or, we would add, offered by another bidder]; (ii) structural coercion,* * * the risk that disparate treatment of non-tendering shareholders might distort shareholders' tender decisions; and (iii) substantive coercion, * * * the risk that shareholders will mistakenly accept an underpriced offer because they disbelieve management's representations of intrinsic value. * * *

More than a century before Unocal was decided, Justice Holmes observed that the common law must be developed through its application and "cannot be dealt with as if it contained only the axioms and corollaries of a book of mathematics." Oliver Wendell Holmes, Jr., The Common Law 1 (1881). As common law applications of Unocal's proportionality standard have evolved, at least two characteristics of draconian defensive measures taken by a board of directors in responding to a threat have been brought into focus through enhanced judicial scrutiny. In the modern takeover lexicon, it is now clear that since Unocal, this Court has consistently recognized that defensive measures which are either preclusive or coercive are included within the common law definition of draconian.

If a defensive measure is not draconian, however, because it is not either coercive or preclusive, the Unocal proportionality test requires the focus of enhanced judicial scrutiny to shift to "the range of reasonableness." Paramount Communications, Inc. v. QVC Network, Inc., Del.Supr., 637 A.2d 34, 45–46 (1994). Proper and proportionate defensive responses are intended and permitted to thwart perceived threats. When a corporation is not for sale, the board of directors is the defender of the metaphorical medieval corporate bastion and the protector of the corporation's shareholders. The fact that a defensive action must not be coercive or preclusive does not prevent a board from responding defensively before a bidder is at the corporate bastion's gate.[50]

---

49. [By the Court] Draconian, adj. Of or pert. to Draco, an archon and member of the Athenian eupatridae, or the code of laws which is said to have been framed about 621 B.C. by him as thesmothete. In them the penalty for most offenses was death, and to a later age they seemed so severe that they were said to be written in blood. Hence, barbarously severe; harsh; cruel. Webster's New International Dictionary 780 (2d ed. 1951).

50. [By the Court] This Court's choice of the term draconian in Unocal was a recogni-

tion that the law affords boards of directors substantial latitude in defending the perimeter of the corporate bastion against perceived threats. Thus, continuing with the medieval metaphor, if a board reasonably perceives that a threat is on the horizon, it has broad authority to respond with a panoply of individual or combined defensive precautions, e.g., staffing the barbican, raising the drawbridge, and lowering the portcullis. Stated more directly, depending upon the circumstances, the board may respond to a reasonably perceived threat

The ratio decidendi for the "range of reasonableness" standard is a need of the board of directors for latitude in discharging its fiduciary duties to the corporation and its shareholders when defending against perceived threats. The concomitant requirement is for judicial restraint. Consequently, if the board of directors' defensive response is not draconian (preclusive or coercive) and is within a "range of reasonableness," a court must not substitute its judgment for the board's. * * *

In this case, the initial focus of enhanced judicial scrutiny for proportionality requires a determination regarding the defensive responses by the Unitrin Board to American General's offer. We begin, therefore, by ascertaining whether the Repurchase Program, as an addition to the poison pill, was draconian by being either coercive or preclusive.

A limited nondiscriminatory self-tender, like some other defensive measures, may thwart a current hostile bid, but is not inherently coercive. Moreover, it does not necessarily preclude future bids or proxy contests by stockholders who decline to participate in the repurchase. * * * A selective repurchase of shares in a public corporation on the market, such as Unitrin's Repurchase Program, generally does not discriminate because all shareholders can voluntarily realize the same benefit by selling. Here, there is no showing on this record that the Repurchase Program was coercive.

We have already determined that the record in this case appears to reflect that a proxy contest remained a viable (if more problematic) alternative for American General even if the Repurchase Program were to be completed in its entirety. Nevertheless, the Court of Chancery must determine whether Unitrin's Repurchase Program would only inhibit American General's ability to wage a proxy fight and institute a merger or whether it was, in fact, preclusive[51] because American General's success would either be mathematically impossible or realistically unattainable. If the Court of Chancery concludes that the Unitrin Repurchase Program was not draconian because it was not preclusive, one question will remain to be answered in its proportionality review: whether the Repurchase Program was within a range of reasonableness?

The Court of Chancery found that the Unitrin Board reasonably believed that American General's Offer was inadequate and that the adoption of a poison pill was a proportionate defensive response. Upon remand, in applying the correct legal standard to the factual circumstances of this case, the Court of Chancery may conclude that the implementation of the limited Repurchase Program was also within a range of reasonable additional defensive responses available to the Unitrin Board. In considering whether the Repurchase Program was within a range of reasonableness the Court of Chancery should take into consideration whether: (1) it is a statutorily authorized form of business decision which a board of directors may routinely make in a non-takeover context; (2) as a defensive response to American General's Offer it was limited and corresponded in degree or magnitude to the degree or

by adopting individually or sometimes in combination: advance notice by-laws, supermajority voting provisions, shareholder rights plans, repurchase programs, etc.

51. [By the Court] The record in this case, when properly understood, appears to reflect that the Repurchase Program's effect on a proxy contest would not be preclusive. Accord

Moran v. Household Int'l, Inc., Del.Supr., 500 A.2d 1346, 1355 (1985). If the stockholders of Unitrin are "displeased with the action of their elected representatives, the powers of corporate democracy" remain available as a viable alternative to turn the Board out in a proxy contest.

magnitude of the threat, (i.e., assuming the threat was relatively "mild," was the response relatively "mild?"); (3) with the Repurchase Program, the Unitrin Board properly recognized that all shareholders are not alike, and provided immediate liquidity to those shareholders who wanted it.

The Court of Chancery's holding in *Shamrock*, * * * appears to be persuasive support for the proportionality of the multiple defenses Unitrin's Board adopted. In *Shamrock*, the Court of Chancery concluded that the Polaroid board had "a valid basis for concern that the Polaroid stockholders [like Unitrin's stockholders] will be unable to reach an accurate judgment as to the intrinsic value of their stock." Shamrock Holdings, Inc. v. Polaroid Corp., 559 A.2d at 290. The Court of Chancery also observed, "the likely shift in the stockholder profile in favor of Polaroid" as a result of the repurchase plan "appears to be minimal." Id. Consequently, the Court of Chancery concluded that Polaroid's defensive response as a whole—the ESOP, the issuance of stock to a friendly third party and the stock repurchase plan—was not disproportionate to the Shamrock threat or improperly motivated, and "individually or collectively will [not] preclude the successful completion of Shamrock's tender offer." Id. at 288. * * *

In this case, the Court of Chancery erred by substituting its judgment, that the Repurchase Program was unnecessary, for that of the Board. The Unitrin Board had the power and the duty, upon reasonable investigation, to protect Unitrin's shareholders from what it perceived to be the threat from American General's inadequate all-cash for all-shares Offer. The adoption of the poison pill and the limited Repurchase Program was not coercive and the Repurchase Program may not be preclusive. Although each made a takeover more difficult, individually and collectively, if they were not coercive or preclusive the Court of Chancery must determine whether they were within the range of reasonable defensive measures available to the Board.

If the Court of Chancery concludes that individually and collectively the poison pill and the Repurchase Program were proportionate to the threat the Board believed American General posed, the Unitrin Board's adoption of the Repurchase Program and the poison pill is entitled to review under the traditional business judgment rule. The burden will then shift "back to the plaintiffs who have the ultimate burden of persuasion [in a preliminary injunction proceeding] to show a breach of the directors' fiduciary duties." In order to rebut the protection of the business judgment rule, the burden on the plaintiffs will be to demonstrate, "by a preponderance of the evidence that the directors' decisions were primarily based on [(1)] perpetuating themselves in office or [(2)] some other breach of fiduciary duty such as fraud, overreaching, lack of good faith, or [(3)] being uninformed." Unocal, 493 A.2d at 958 (emphasis added).

(6) In light of Unitrin, may a target corporation faced with an unwanted all cash tender offer at a price significantly above the prior stock price "just say no" and refuse to withdraw or redeem a poison pill even though more than 70 percent of its shares have been tendered to the aggressor? Moore Corp., Ltd. v. Wallace Computer Services, Inc., 907 F.Supp. 1545 (D.Del.1995) comes close to accepting the "just say no" defense in this situation. The court refused to order the pill withdrawn even though 73 percent of Wallace's shareholders had accepted Moore's offer, and even though Wallace's made no effort to find a more friendly bidder and did not make a share buyback offer as in *Unitrin*. Furthermore, Wallace's had a staggered board of directors, so that proxy fights in two successive

years would have been necessary for Moore to have elected a majority of the directors of Wallace's. This decision, if correct, would appear to eliminate all judicial control over defensive tactics. See Andrew E. Bogen, Are Rights Plans Ever 'Draconian'? 11 Insights, No. 1, January 1997, at 13:

The Zany Economics of Rights Plans

Perhaps a word of explanation is in order for those who are not *cognoscenti* of rights plan architecture. In virtually all current rights plans, the acquisition of more than a specific percentage of the issuer's stock (typically from 10 percent to 20 percent) triggers a slow-fused (up to 10 years) rights offering to all shareholders other than the "acquiring person." In the rights offering, each right is exercisable for that number of shares which has a market value (based upon trading prior to trigger of the rights) equal to two times the rights exercise price. Thus, the only determinants of the magnitude of the rights offering are the exercise price of the rights and the percentage of the rights held by the "acquiring person") since rights held by the acquiring person may not be exercise). If the exercise price of the rights is four times the market price of the stock, and the "acquiring person" holds 25 percent of the outstanding rights, the rights offering will equal three times the entire market capitalization of the issuer. Since the new shares are offered at one-half of their market value, the dilution suffered by the "acquiring person" is dramatic.

Isn't this "Draconian"?

Delaware Decisions Have Not Broached the Issue

So far the Delaware courts have barely interfered with rights plans under the *Unocal* standard. In part, this has been simply a function of circumstances. Very few corporations have relied upon rights plans in the face of a takeover for any purpose other than to maintain control over timing while they explored alternatives. * * *

[In Moore Corp. Ltd., v. Wallace Computer Services, Inc.] Moore argued that the Wallace rights plan had served its legitimate purpose by providing time for the Wallace board to explore alternatives, that they had presented none, that the Wallace stockholders had shown their overwhelming preference for the Moore tender offer, and that there was no threat which could justify retention of the rights. The court, however, was unpersuaded. There remained a threat, it said, that stockholders might tender their shares in the absence of full information as to the prospective earnings improvements from Wallace's past business investments. Why, one might ask, did such a risk remain after a takeover fight and proxy contest that had been going on for more three months? Had not the board more than ample time to provide the shareholders full information? The court's opinion contains no answer.

The court did, however, address the proportionality requirement of *Unocal*. * * * Retention of the rights plan was not coercive because it would have no discriminatory effect on shareholders, "as is generally the result in any situation involving a coercive offer." "Second, and more important, retention of the pill will have no effect on the success of the proxy contest." * * * It may be that *Wallace v. Moore* will prove to have been correctly decided, but it seems a far greater extension of the Delaware precedents than the opinion acknowledges.

See also Andrew R. Brownstein, Face-off on Poison Pills, 11 Insights, No. 1, January 1997, 12, 15: "The Delaware federal district court decision arising out of

Moore Corporation's hostile tender offer for Wallace Computer Services reaffirms the right of a target board of directors to stand behind its pill and 'just say no' even in the face of an all-cash premium bid." Moore then withdrew its bid.

(7) The *Revlon* principle accepts the view that at some point the goal of the corporation is to maximize the return to shareholders, and the interests of other constituencies are subordinate to that goal. Delaware has not broadened its statutes to recognize that boards of directors may consider the interests of other constituencies. In a state that recognizes the right of directors to consider the effects of their decisions on debtholders, employees, and localities, should the auction principle of *Revlon* have any place?

(8) On a broader level, Delaware courts recognize that there is room for judicial review of decisions by boards of directors to adopt defensive tactics in takeover battles. Several other states have legislatively rejected this approach and have provided, directly or indirectly, that courts should accept the business judgment of incumbent directors on essentially the terms set forth in *Panter v. Marshall Field* page 1028, supra. For example, Ohio Rev. Code, § 1701.59(c)(1) provides that there is to be no judicial review of decisions by a board of directors on "a change or potential change in control of the corporation, including a determination to resist a change or potential change in control" unless the plaintiffs show "by clear and convincing evidence" that the directors did not act in good faith. See also Ohio Rev. Code, § 1701.13. Based on this statute, one Ohio court has stated simply that "*Revlon* is not applicable in Ohio." Lewis v. Celina Fin. Corp., 101 Ohio App.3d 465, 475, 655 N.E.2d 1333, 1340 (Ohio App. 1995). A Pennsylvania statute, Pa. C.S.A. § 515(d), provides that "there shall not be any greater obligation to justify, or higher burden of proof with respect to, any act as the board of directors * * * than is applied to any other act as a board of directors," and that "any act * * * relating to or affecting an acquisition or potential or proposed acquisition of control to which a majority of the disinterested directors shall have assented shall be presumed to satisfy the standard [of care] set forth in section 512, unless it is proven by clear and convincing evidence that the disinterested directors did not asset to such act in good faith after reasonable investigation." The term "disinterested director" is broadly defined. Id, § 515(e). And, in perhaps the most direct rebuff to this Delaware jurisprudence, Ind.Bus. Corp.L. § 23–1–35–1(f), states:

> (f) * * * Certain judicial decisions in Delaware and other jurisdictions, which might otherwise be looked to for guidance in interpreting Indiana corporate law, including decisions relating to potential change of control transactions that impose a different or higher degree of scrutiny on actions taken by directors in response to a proposed acquisition of control of the corporation, are inconsistent with the proper application of the business judgment rule under this article. * * *

In light of these statutes, why hasn't there been a wholesale exodus of publicly held corporations from Delaware to Ohio, Pennsylvania, or Indiana?

I. THE 1990s

"The takeover wars are over. Management won." With these dramatic words, Professor Joseph A. Grundfest began his evaluation of the takeover movement as of 1993. "These developments," he added, "carry ramifications that reach far beyond a mere shift of power in the battle for corporate control. With the demise of the hostile takeover, shareholders can no longer expect much help from the capital markets in disciplining or removing inefficient managers. Shareholders are also unable to help themselves at the corporate ballot box: The pure proxy contest has proven an ineffective tool for disciplining incumbent managers. * * * As a result, corporate America is now governed by directors who are largely impervious to capital market or electoral challenges." Joseph A. Grundfest, Just Vote No: A Minimalist Strategy for Dealing with Barbarians Inside the Gates, 45 Stan. L.Rev. 857, 858 (1993).

Between 1990 and the middle of 1993 there had been a very marked decline in the number of attempted takeovers. Professor Grundfest attributed this decline to a "confluence of legal, political, and financial factors," but the principal cause was "a sea change in financial market conditions [in 1989] that tightened the supply of available credit and made capital for hostile takeover activity exceedingly difficult to obtain." Grundfest, supra at 861. This drying up of financing for takeovers was caused by a change in the public mood about takeovers—from admiration and envy to anger and even revulsion. Public disclosure of the excesses of the 1980s were to blame: The savings and loan scandals, the insider trading scandals involving Ivan Boesky and others, the collapse of Drexel Burnham Lambert, Inc., and the criminal indictment of Michael Milkin (the Drexel trader after disclosure that he earned more than $500,000,000 in a single year), to name a few. Also contributing was the unexpected recession that began in the late 1980s and continued into the early 1990s, the decline in interest rates, and stories that some of the largest leveraged buyout transactions that had occurred during the 1980s were in financial difficulty. In 1989 and 1990, many conservative organizations that had invested huge amounts of capital—hundreds of millions of dollars in some instances—in takeover bids quietly withdrew their funds. As a result, some short-term loans for interim financing of takeovers became inadvertently long-term when transactions in progress could not be completed.

In retrospect, it is clear that the first major takeover case in the 1990s (QVC's offer in 1993 to purchase Paramount in direct competition with a negotiated deal between Viacom and Paramount) was the harbinger of a new wave of takeovers. See Paramount Communications, Inc. v. QVC Network, 637 A.2d 34 (Del.1994). From the latter half of 1993 forward, merger activity increased rapidly. The total value of merger transactions in the United States in 1991 and 1992 were below $200 billion each year; the number of transactions rose steadily through 1994 to reach $579 billion in 1995, and $659 billion in 1996, well above the levels of the high-flying 1980s. In 1996, each of two deals exceeded $20 billion while seven other transactions involved more than $10 billion each, and more than 100 transactions involved more than $1 billion each. Not even 1988, the high point of the previous decade, could match those levels.

The average takeover in the 1990s appears to differ significantly from those of the 1980s. Charles v. Bagli, A New Breed of Wolf at the Corporate Door, New York Times, March 19, 1997, at c1, col. 3:*

What a difference a decade makes. In the 1980s, takeover battles were like Wild West shootouts, and descriptions of the strife relied on the imagery of violence: greenmailers and raiders with their bear hugs and Saturday night specials were pitted against white knights and corporate managers who fended off their attackers with poison pills and shark repellent. There was even a "Predators' Ball" to celebrate the mayhem.

Today, a new respectability reigns in the takeover game. No longer do the likes of Mr. Pickens, Ronald O. Perelman and Carl C. Icahn begin raids with high-risk junk bonds only to carve up their acquisitions and sell off the pieces for a quick profit. Instead, corporations seek to forge "strategic alliances" that will enable them to grow and prosper in an increasingly competitive marketplace. And the lexicon of even the most hostile endeavors is filled with sober phrases like synergy, the global marketplace and accretion to earnings.

And almost everybody, it seems is doing it.

The 1980s was a period of finance-oriented transactions, while transactions in the 1990s appear to focus more on operational improvements involving firms in the same or complementary lines of business. The justification for most transactions, in other words, are economic, founded in the business interests of the parties. The purchaser is ordinarily an operating corporation, not an LBO specialist or a raider planning to sell off components of the acquired business. Less than 5 percent of all transactions in the 1990s are of the financial type while approximately one-third of the transactions were of this type in the 1980s. Premiums over pre-transaction stock prices of the target corporation are also significantly lower: about 28 percent in the 1990s while they were often 50 percent or higher in the 1980s. The consideration for the acquisition in the 1990s is more often shares of the acquiring corporation than cash while the opposite was true in the 1980s. Of course, with the dramatic increases in securities prices during much of the 1990s, the attractiveness of payment in stock rather than cash is increased.

Perhaps the most important difference is that most transactions in the 1990s are negotiated by the parties and are not straight hostile takeovers. Hostile bids sometimes occur in connection with the negotiation of a takeover, and in some instances have actually led to the completion of a transaction that might not have occurred voluntarily. However, successful hostile bids of the 1980s variety are rare in the 1990s.

These changes reflect a change in the legal environment since the 1980s. Today, there is essentially no doubt about the enforceability of defensive tactics developed during the 1980s, particularly the "poison pill," the so-called "shareholders' rights plan." As a result, it is generally accepted that as a legal matter a target may effectively block an unwanted bid. Today, the poison pill has become a major device in the negotiation process by which the target corporation seeks to improve the terms of what ultimately becomes a consensual transaction. It is no longer solely a device to fend off unwanted solicitations. Furthermore, the limitations placed by the Delaware courts on the use of defensive tactics have been relaxed, though not entirely eliminated.

Notes

(1) Faced with an unbreakable poison pill and an obdurate management, a bidder may seek to obtain a majority of the board of directors through a proxy

fight and then withdraw or redeem the poison pill to permit the takeover to succeed. In response, some poison pills were revised to provide that they could be with withdrawn only by the vote of "continuing directors"—those who originally authorized the pill or persons nominated by those directors. Bank of New York v. Irving Bank Corp., 139 Misc.2d 665, 528 N.Y.S.2d 482 (Sup.Ct.1988), invalidated such a poison pill. However, in Invacare Corp., v. Healthdyne Technologies, Inc., 968 F.Supp. 1578 (N.D.Ga., 1997) a similar shareholder rights plan—pejoratively called a "dead hand pill"—was upheld under Ga. Code Ann. § 14–2–624(c) that authorized terms of options and similar rights to be set in the "sole discretion" of the board of directors. The Healthdyne poison pill, however, only required the consent of a single "continuing director" to the withdrawal or redemption of the poison pill, a fact relied upon by the Court to establish the reasonableness of the poison pill. The court also invalidated a proposal by Invacare to propose a bylaw at the following shareholders' meeting to eliminate the "continuing directors" aspect of the shareholders rights plan. Is it likely that a "continuing director" poison pill would be upheld in Delaware?

(4) In the 1980s, considerable attention was paid to state control share acquisition statutes, business combination statutes, and the like. The importance of these antitakeover devices at the state level have declined in importance as the poison pill has demonstrated that it is the single most effective anti-takeover device, at least as of 1997, though some litigation continues to arise with respect to these devices.[52]

---

52. See WLR Foods, Inc. v. Tyson Foods, Inc., 65 F.3d 1172 (4th Cir.1995) cert. denied, ___ U.S. ___, 116 S.Ct. 921, 133 L.Ed.2d 850 (1996)(Virginia Business Combination Statute is constitutional and bidder could not conduct discovery into the substance of financial advice obtained by the target); United Dominion In-dustries, Ltd. v. Commercial Intertech Corp., 943 F.Supp. 857 (S.D.Ohio, 1996)(Ohio control share acquisition statute is constitutional despite the complexity of counting votes and proxies to determine who are interested share-holders).

Chapter Fifteen

CORPORATE BOOKS AND RECORDS

Chapter 16 of the MBCA attempts to provide guidelines for a number of issues relating to corporate books and records. Most older corporation statutes are silent on these issues, dealing only with inspection rights of shareholders.

Section 16.01(a) requires every corporation to "keep as permanent records" a minimum set of core documents that reflect decisions made by the directors and shareholders of the corporation. In addition, § 16.01(e) requires every corporation to "keep a copy" of specified basic corporate documents at the principal office of the corporation. These documents must be routinely made available for inspection by any shareholder during regular business hours. MBCA § 16.02(a).

Section 16.01(b) requires every corporation to "maintain appropriate accounting records". The word "maintain" should be contrasted with the word "keep" in §§ 16.01(a) and (e); "keep" means permanent retention while "maintain" refers to current records only and does not address the question of how long financial and other records should be kept. Thus, the retention and destruction of all records other than the limited records the corporation is directed to "keep" by the MBCA, is dictated by considerations or rules independent of the MBCA. In part, specific record retention rules may be established by state or federal tax or regulatory statutes, or perhaps by general state statutes. Many corporations have established internal policies that permit the destruction of records after some suitably long period of time, taking into account statutes of limitations and the possibility that products liability claims may arise long after the records relating to those products were generated.

The word "appropriate" with respect to accounting records in § 16.01(b) reflects a general recognition of the fact that the nature and size of the business largely determines its accounting system, which in turn largely determines its accounting records. The Official Comment suggests that "appropriate" records are "generally records that permit financial statements to be prepared which fairly present the financial position and transactions of the corporation. In some very small businesses operating on a cash basis, however, 'appropriate' accounting records may consist only of a check register, vouchers, and receipts." Increasingly, of course, accounting and financial records are maintained electronically, a development recognized in MBCA § 16.01(d).

Section 16.01(c) requires every corporation to "maintain" a record of its shareholders. In larger corporations, records of shareholders are usually maintained electronically; this function is often delegated to transfer agents that have the responsibility of recording transfers of securities.

Publicly held corporations registered under the Securities Exchange Act of 1934 are required to prepare detailed financial statements that are distributed to shareholders and to the public. See Chapter 9. Historically, state statutes did not contain an analogous requirement, so that shareholders of closely held or unregistered corporations did not have the right to receive routine financial statements from the corporation. However, this is gradually changing. The MBCA first introduced such a requirement in 1979. The current provision, MBCA § 16.20, is carefully constructed so as not to impose onerous requirements on very small corporations and yet to require larger corporations that have financial statements professionally prepared to distribute those statements to shareholders. Every corporation under this provision must furnish at the minimum a balance sheet, an income statement, and a statement of changes in shareholders' equity for the year. Financial statements require accounting principles to be established for their preparation; § 16.20 does not require the use of generally accepted accounting principles (GAAP) or any specific set of accounting principles, but if financial statements are prepared for the corporation on the basis of GAAP, the annual financial statements must likewise be prepared on a GAAP basis. Section 16.20(b) sets forth general principles for disclosing the "basis of preparation" of financial statements and whether the system used was consistent with that used for the preceding year.

Under most state statutes, there are few mandatory disclosure requirements, though some states require the filing of annual reports or tax statements that may be available for inspection by shareholders or the public. See MBCA § 16.22. MBCA § 16.21 requires information to be provided to shareholders about (a) the indemnification of or advancement of expenses to a director, and (b) the issuance of shares for promissory notes or for promises to render services in the future. Why were these two types of transactions singled out for special disclosure treatment?

One issue that is more or less addressed in all state corporation statutes is the extent to which shareholders are entitled to inspect corporate books and records. At common law, shareholders, as ultimate owners of the enterprise, enjoyed qualified rights to inspect the corporate books and records, including shareholder lists, contracts, correspondence, tax returns, and other documents. Harry G. Henn & John R. Alexander, Laws of Corporations and Other Business Enterprises § 199 (3rd ed. 1983). As described below, this qualified common law right continues to exist under the MBCA and in many states; in addition many states supplement the common law right with a statutory right.

At one time, most inspection cases revolved around the list of shareholders required to be maintained by the corporation. This list, of course, is a list of record shareholders only. Most statutes permit a virtually automatic right of inspection of the list of record shareholders entitled to vote at a scheduled shareholders' meeting shortly before and during the meeting itself. See MBCA § 7.20. At other times, a list of shareholders may be inspected only if the shareholder qualifies under the general shareholder inspection statutes. See MBCA § 16.02.

Shareholders continue to seek to obtain shareholder lists in connection with proxy fights or takeover bids for publicly held corporations. However, access to this list by an insurgent or outside bidder has become less important than it was twenty or thirty years ago. This is a result of the widespread use of nominees as record holders (thus limiting the usefulness of the list itself), and the growth of institutional investors, many of whom make information about their entire portfolios a matter of public record. Information about the principal shareholders may often be assembled from these sources. Of course, access to a current shareholders' list may still be essential in situations involving closely held corporations or publicly held corporations with shares held widely by individuals rather than institutional investors.

THOMAS & BETTS CORPORATION v. LEVITON MANUFACTURING CO., INC.

Supreme Court of Delaware, 1996.
681 A.2d 1026.

Before VEASEY, C.J., WALSH and BERGER, JJ.

VEASEY, CHIEF JUSTICE:

In this appeal we affirm the order of the Court of Chancery denying in part and limiting a stockholder's entitlement to inspection of books and records. In doing so, we rest our decision on the fact that the trial court's determination of the stockholder's failure to show a proper purpose turned on legal and credibility assessments well within the proper burden placed on a stockholder seeking an inspection. Such a stockholder has the burden of showing, by a preponderance of the evidence, a proper purpose entitling the stockholder to an inspection of every item sought. Here, the Court of Chancery overstated the burden on the stockholder as a "greater-than-normal evidentiary burden." The burden on the stockholder is a normal burden and this stockholder failed to adduce sufficient evidence to meet that burden.

I. FACTS

Plaintiff below—appellant, Thomas & Betts Corporation ("Thomas & Betts" or "plaintiff"), appeals from a decision of the Court of Chancery granting in part and denying in part its request for inspection of certain books and records of defendant below—appellee, Leviton Manufacturing Co., Inc. ("Leviton" or "defendant").

Leviton is a closely held Delaware corporation engaged in the business of manufacturing electronic components and residential wiring devices. Thomas & Betts is a publicly traded New Jersey corporation engaged in the electronics business. Thomas & Betts and Leviton are not considered to be in competition with one another. This is due, in large part, to Leviton's focus on the residential market. For a number of years, Thomas & Betts has expressed an interest either in acquiring Leviton or engaging in some form of joint venture. During the summer of 1993, Thomas & Betts and Leviton engaged in preliminary negotiations concerning a possible union of the two companies, but no agreement was ever reached. To date, Leviton has not expressed any interest in participating in a change-of-control or joint venture transaction with Thomas & Betts.

Leviton's President and CEO, Harold Leviton, is also the company's majority stockholder. Harold Leviton and his wife control a voting trust which represents 76.45 percent of Leviton's Class A voting stock. He and the other Leviton insiders are members of the Leviton family and most bear some relationship to the company's founder. By all accounts, Harold Leviton is the dominant figure in the corporation, deciding the company's strategy, operations and future goals.

Thomas & Betts decided to seek a minority position in Leviton in order to force a sale of the company to Thomas & Betts. In April of 1994, without the knowledge of Harold Leviton, Thomas & Betts began negotiations with Leviton's former Group Vice President, Thomas Blumberg ("Blumberg"). Blumberg and his wife, who is Harold Leviton's niece, owned approximately 29.1 percent of Leviton's outstanding shares. Negotiations for the sale of the Blumberg stock to Thomas & Betts were clandestine. In furtherance of the transaction, Blumberg provided Thomas & Betts with confidential internal Leviton documents and disclosed various facets of Leviton's internal strategies and accounting figures. Ultimately, Thomas & Betts paid Blumberg $50 million for his Leviton stake, with a promise of up to an additional $20 million if Thomas & Betts were to accomplish its desired acquisition of Leviton. Thomas & Betts indemnified Blumberg against, inter alia, litigation by Leviton, and also agreed to pay up to $7.5 million to Blumberg, in equal quarterly installments, if the sale of his shares were enjoined. At the time of sale, Thomas & Betts was fully aware that Leviton did not pay dividends and that Leviton's accounting practices did not follow Generally Accepted Accounting Principles ("GAAP").

The sale of the Blumberg shares was consummated on July 12, 1994, and Harold Leviton was informed of the sale the following day. Harold Leviton immediately fired Blumberg, only to hire him back and fire him again days later, along with his children and their secretaries. Harold Leviton rebuffed overtures from Thomas & Betts to establish an amicable relationship. Instead, Harold Leviton sought to buy out the interest of Thomas & Betts. From July 1994 to February of 1995, various representatives of Thomas & Betts met with Leviton insiders in an attempt to cultivate a working relationship. On October 6, 1994, Kevin Dunnigan ("Dunnigan"), the CEO of Thomas & Betts, reported to the board of Thomas & Betts on his strategy:

> On the Leviton front, we are moving to the next phase. I will write to Harold Leviton next week to give him a rationale on why it is in everyone's best interests to start a dialogue. We will follow this up with a legal request to review all the books and records of Leviton which will start either a dialogue or a lawsuit.

Harold Leviton, however, remained obstinate in his opposition to Thomas & Betts' ownership position. Although some concessions were made and Thomas & Betts was allowed limited access to Leviton's books and records, by February 1995 it was abundantly clear that Harold Leviton intended to thwart any acquisition of Leviton by Thomas & Betts.

On February 8, 1995, Thomas & Betts served Leviton with a formal demand seeking inspection of the following documents:

1. Leviton's stockholder list,

2. Minutes of Leviton shareholder and directors meetings as well as written consents,

3. Audited financial statements for Leviton and its subsidiaries,

4. Internal financial statements for the current fiscal year provided on a monthly basis,

5. Tax returns filed for Leviton and its subsidiaries,

6. Organizational charts for Leviton and its subsidiaries,

7. Documents relating to interested party transactions between Leviton or its subsidiaries and its shareholders, directors or officers,

8. Documents relating to "key man" life insurance policies taken out by Leviton,

9. Material contracts between Leviton and its subsidiaries,

10. Documents relating to Leviton leases for real estate or equipment.

On February 16, 1995, Dunnigan wrote to Harold Leviton and offered to purchase the balance of Leviton's stock for $250 million, net of expenses. Dunnigan's letter threatened litigation if this final offer were rebuffed:

> You are forcing us down a road where given a choice, I am sure neither of us wants to go. Often, once this process gets started, it ends up with consequences that were never intended. Watch! It won't be long before the lawyers, the government and the courts are completely in charge, and in the end neither you nor I will have much say in the outcome. There will be only victims, but it won't be the lawyers.

On February 17, 1995, Leviton formally refused both Thomas & Betts' acquisition offer and its inspection demand.

On February 27, 1995, Thomas & Betts filed this action in the Court of Chancery seeking to compel inspection of Leviton's books and records pursuant to 8 Del.C. § 220. After a four-day trial, the Court of Chancery determined that: (1) plaintiff's demand was not motivated by its stated purposes of investigating waste and mismanagement, * * * and valuation of those shares; (2) plaintiff's actual motivation was to gain leverage in its efforts to acquire Leviton; (3) this motive was antithetical to the interests of Leviton; (4) despite the initially improper purpose of its demand, Thomas & Betts was entitled to limited inspection so it could value its Leviton shares since a fundamental change of circumstances had occurred; and (5) this inspection should be narrowly circumscribed. From this decision, Thomas & Betts appeals. Leviton has not cross-appealed.

II. PROPER PURPOSE

Thomas & Betts' Demand Letter purported to state [two] separate purposes for its requested inspection of Leviton's books and records. Specifically, plaintiff asserted that the books and records were necessary: (1) to investigate possible waste and mismanagement; * * * and (2) to assist in the valuation of Thomas & Betts' Leviton shares. After trial, the Court of Chancery concluded that plaintiff's articulated purposes were not its actual purposes and that plaintiff's actual purpose was improper.[1] Specifically, the trial court held that Thomas & Betts was attempting to use the Section 220 proceeding as leverage in its efforts to acquire Leviton. The trial court concluded, however, that Thomas & Betts should be allowed to inspect those books and records necessary to value its investment in Leviton in view of the fact that there had been a change in circumstances.

Thomas & Betts now asserts that the * * * [purpose] for inspection not credited by the trial court—investigation of waste and mismanagement— constituted [a] proper purpose under Section 220 and that the trial court erred in refusing inspection of books and records relevant to [this purpose]. These contentions are addressed seriatim below.

"The question of a 'proper purpose' under Section 220(b) of our General Corporation Law is an issue of law and equity which this Court reviews de novo." Compaq Computer Corp. v. Horton, Del.Supr., 631 A.2d 1, 3 (1993) (citing Oberly v. Kirby, Del.Supr., 592 A.2d 445, 462 (1991)); Western Air Lines, Inc. v. Kerkorian, Del.Supr., 254 A.2d 240 (1969)(court reviewed proper purpose determination in stocklist case de novo). "The determination of whether [plaintiff's] . . . stated purpose for the inspection was its primary purpose, is a question of fact warranting deference to the trial court's credibility assessments." State ex rel. Scattered Corp., Del.Supr., No. 444, 1995, Veasey, C.J., 1996 WL 191023 (April 4, 1996)(ORDER); accord CM & M Group v. Carroll, Inc., Del.Supr., 453 A.2d 788, 793 (1982).

III. PLAINTIFF'S CLAIMS OF WASTE AND MISMANAGEMENT

As found by the Court of Chancery, plaintiff's claims of waste and mismanagement are grounded on Leviton's purportedly substandard financial performance, the company's failure to pay dividends, Leviton's poor cash flow and the company's higher than average expenses. As specific instances of misconduct, plaintiff asserted that: "(a) Leviton has paid for the Leviton family's personal expenses, including use of the company's accounting firm for tax and estate planning purposes; (b) Leviton has been overcompensating its officers and directors at the shareholders' expense; and (c) Leviton's lease agreements with members of the Leviton family are self-dealing transactions." The trial court found, however, that these claims "are so lacking in record support" that inspection could not be justified.

Plaintiff contends that the Court of Chancery applied an incorrect legal standard in determining that plaintiff's stated purpose lacked adequate record support. Specifically, Thomas & Betts points to portions of the trial court's

---

1. [By the Court] See, e.g., BBC Acquisition Corp. v. Durr–Fillauer Medical, Inc., Del.Ch., 623 A.2d 85, 88 (1992):

[W]hen seeking inspection of books and records other than the corporate stock ledger or stock list, a shareholder has the burden of proving that his purpose is proper. Since such a shareholder will often have more than one purpose, that requirement has been construed to mean that the shareholder's primary purpose must be proper; any secondary purpose, whether proper or not, is irrelevant. CM & M Group, Inc. v. Carroll, Del.Supr., 453 A.2d 788, 792 (1982); Helmsman Man-

agement Services, Inc. v. A & S Consultants, Inc., Del.Ch., 525 A.2d 160, 164 (1987).

See also Ostrow v. Bonney Forge Corp., Del. Ch., C.A. No. 13270, Allen, C., mem. op., 1994 WL 114807 (April 6, 1994) ("Once a shareholder has established a proper purpose for the demanded inspection, any secondary purpose he or she may have is generally considered to be irrelevant.* * * The primary purpose may not, however, be adverse to the corporation's best interests.)" (citing CM & M Group, Inc. v. Carroll, Del.Supr., 453 A.2d 788, 792 (1982); Skoglund v. Ormand Indus., Inc., Del.Ch., 372 A.2d 204, 207 (1976)).

holding which appear to impose on plaintiff "a greater-than-normal evidentiary burden," to "adduce evidence from which a credible possibility of mismanagement and waste may be inferred" and to "adduce specific evidence of waste and mismanagement."

The Court of Chancery incorrectly articulated the governing legal standard. It is well established that investigation of waste and mismanagement is a proper purpose for a Section 220 books and records inspection. Nodana Petroleum Corp. v. State, Del.Supr., 123 A.2d 243, 246 (1956). When a stockholder seeks inspection of books and records, the burden of proof is on the stockholder to demonstrate that his purpose is proper. CM & M Group, 453 A.2d at 792.[2] In order to meet that burden of proof, a stockholder must present some credible basis from which the court can infer that waste or mismanagement may have occurred. Skouras v. Admiralty Enters., Inc., Del.Ch., 386 A.2d 674, 678 (1978)("more than a general statement is required in order for the Court to determine the propriety of a demand"); Helmsman Management Servs., Inc. v. A & S Consultants, Inc., Del.Ch., 525 A.2d 160, 166 (1987)("A mere statement of a purpose to investigate possible general mismanagement, without more, will not entitle a shareholder to broad § 220 inspection relief. There must be some evidence of possible mismanagement as would warrant further investigation of the matter."); Neely v. Oklahoma Publishing Co., Del.Ch., C.A. No. 5293, Brown, V.C. (Aug. 15, 1977); Everett v. Hollywood Park, Inc., Del.Ch., C.A. No. 14556, Jacobs, V.C., mem. op., 1996 WL 32171 (Jan. 19, 1996)("Where, as here, the plaintiff's purpose is to investigate possible waste or mismanagement, she must also adduce evidence of potential mismanagement sufficient to support her suspicions and to warrant going forward."). While stockholders have the burden of coming forward with specific and credible allegations sufficient to warrant a suspicion of waste and mismanagement, they are not required to prove by a preponderance of the evidence that waste and management are actually occurring.[3]

A general standard that a stockholder seeking inspection of books and records bears "a greater-than-normal evidentiary burden" is unclear and could be interpreted as placing an unduly difficult obstacle in the path of stockholders seeking to investigate waste and mismanagement. Viewed in context, however, the articulation in dispute here accurately describes a stockholder's position in cases such as the one at bar, where substantial evidence supports a finding that plaintiff's primary motives for the inspection are improper.

2. [By the Court] While a stockholder has the burden to show a proper purpose for an inspection of books and records, the corporation has the burden of showing an improper purpose when a stockholder seeks only to inspect the stockholder list. 8 Del.C. § 220(c). The trial court held that plaintiff "has established a proper purpose for seeking inspection of Leviton's shareholder list," and the corporation failed to meet its burden that plaintiff's purpose was improper.

3. [By the Court] The Revised Model Business Corporation Act requires that a stockholder "describe with reasonable particularity his purpose and the records he desires to inspect." Revised Model Business Corp. Act § 16.02(c). See Grimes v. Donald, 673 A.2d 1207, 1217 (1996), for an analogous discussion of the reasonable doubt, or reason to believe, standard in the context of a derivative suit. Contrary to plaintiff's assertion in the instant case, this Court in Grimes did not suggest that its reference to a Section 220 demand as one of the "tools at hand" was intended to eviscerate or modify the need for a stockholder to show a proper purpose under Section 220. Id. at 1216 n. 11 (noting that Section 220 can be used to secure information to support demand futility).

In the final analysis, the decision of the trial court did not turn solely on a legal conclusion that Thomas & Betts had failed to meet an elevated evidentiary burden. As discussed further, infra, the trial court's determination turned, in large part, on the Vice Chancellor's determination that plaintiff's witnesses were not credible. According appropriate deference to the factual findings of the Court of Chancery, we conclude that plaintiff failed to satisfy the appropriate standard for inspection of the books and records with regard to the claim of waste and mismanagement. Levitt v. Bouvier, Del.Supr., 287 A.2d 671, 673 (1972)("When the determination of facts turns on a question of credibility and the acceptance or rejection of 'live' testimony by the trial judge, his findings will be approved upon review."); State ex rel. Scattered Corp., Del.Supr., No. 444, 1995, Veasey, C.J. (April 4, 1996)(ORDER)("The determination of whether Scattered's stated purpose for the inspection was its primary purpose, is a question of fact warranting deference to the trial court's credibility assessments.") * * *

More significantly, the trial court did not exclude this testimony. Rather, the Vice Chancellor heard the testimony and found it unworthy of belief. In this posture, plaintiff's evidentiary objections carry little weight. Similarly, Thomas & Betts' citation to Skoglund v. Ormand Industries is unavailing. Skoglund, 372 A.2d at 208, 211–13. As in the case at bar, the Skoglund court allowed hearsay testimony regarding statements made by a corporate insider. Unlike the instant case, however, the trial court in Skoglund chose to credit that testimony as worthy of belief.

Finally, plaintiff's arguments ignore the underlying posture of this case. Unlike the cases relied on by plaintiff, this case does not involve a typical uninformed stockholder seeking to protect his or her investment. Thomas & Betts acquired its shares in Leviton with the acknowledged purpose of acquiring the company. Moreover, Thomas & Betts did so with full knowledge that Leviton's CEO would likely oppose any such transaction. Thomas & Betts first praised Harold Leviton for his expert management of the company, seeking an amicable union of the two corporations. When Thomas & Betts' friendly overtures proved unavailing, it filed an inspection demand to create leverage. Its self-avowed acquisition motives cast serious doubt on the genuineness of its claim that it seeks the books and records to investigate waste and mismanagement.

These facts were properly before the Court of Chancery. See, e.g., Helmsman Management Servs., 525 A.2d at 164 ("The propriety of a demanding shareholder's purpose must be determined from the facts in each case, and the burden of proving a proper purpose is upon the shareholder."). The Court of Chancery concluded that "Thomas & Betts' initial primary purpose in seeking a books and records inspection was * * * to exert pressure on Harold Leviton to negotiate a sale of his controlling interest or, alternatively, the entire company." Ultimately, the Court of Chancery found Thomas & Betts' articulated purpose to be "highly opportunistic" and unworthy of belief. Thomas & Betts has provided no reason for this Court to revisit those factual determinations and credibility assessments. * * *

V. THE SCOPE OF THE INSPECTION

After trial, the Court of Chancery found that Thomas & Betts had failed to meet its burden of establishing that it sought inspection in furtherance of its concerns regarding * * * mismanagement. The trial court found that Thomas & Betts' primary purpose for inspection was to further its plans for acquiring Leviton and that this interest was antithetical to the interests of the corporation. Despite Thomas & Betts' initially improper motives, the Court acknowledged that Thomas & Betts had experienced a fundamental change of circumstances. The court reasoned that, owing to Harold Leviton's unwillingness to negotiate a change-of-control transaction, Thomas & Betts was now in the unenviable position of a "locked-in" minority stockholder. Based on this fact, the trial court allowed inspection of certain Leviton books and records, but limited the scope of that inspection to those documents which are "essential and sufficient" to Thomas & Betts' valuation purpose. Thomas & Betts now contends that the Court of Chancery abused its discretion in limiting the scope of its inspection of Leviton's books and records.

Absent any apparent error of law, this Court reviews for abuse of discretion the decision of the trial court regarding the scope of a stockholder's inspection of books and records. 8 Del.C. § 220(c); CM & M Group, 453 A.2d at 794. The plaintiff bears the burden of proving that each category of books and records is essential to accomplishment of the stockholder's articulated purpose for the inspection. Helmsman Management Servs., 525 A.2d at 168.

The plain language of 8 Del.C. § 220(c) provides that "[t]he Court may, *in its discretion*, prescribe any limitations or conditions with reference to the inspection." (emphasis supplied). The responsibility of the trial court to narrowly tailor the inspection right to a stockholder's stated purpose is well established. See BBC Acquisition Corp., 623 A.2d at 88–89 (entitlement is restricted to those books and records needed to perform the task). In discharging this responsibility, the trial court has wide latitude in determining the proper scope of inspection. Undergirding this discretion is a recognition that the interests of the corporation must be harmonized with those of the inspecting stockholder.

Here, the trial court has found that Thomas & Betts' primary purpose for inspection is at odds with the interests of the corporation. In this posture, it was entirely appropriate for the Court of Chancery to limit plaintiff's inspection to those documents which are essential and sufficient to its valuation purpose.

Moreover, even in a case where no improper purpose has been attributed to the inspecting stockholder, the burden of proof is always on the party seeking inspection to establish that each category of the books and records requested is essential and sufficient to the stockholder's stated purpose. Helmsman Management Servs., 525 A.2d at 167. The trial court specifically found that Thomas & Betts had not met its burden of proof as to certain of the books and records of Leviton. This finding is supported by the record and is the product of an orderly and logical deductive process. Accordingly, the finding of the Court of Chancery and its concomitant decision to limit inspection will not be disturbed on appeal.

VI. CONCLUSION

We AFFIRM the order of the Court of Chancery.

Notes

(1) Why should a shareholder's right of inspection be so limited? If a shareholder suspects that improper conduct may have occurred, should he not have the right to make a general search of corporate records and documents to see if his suspicions are justified? More colloquially, should he not have the right to conduct a "fishing expedition" looking for misconduct? In a word, the answer is "no." The right of inspection reflects a balancing between the shareholder's right to have information about his investment and the fealty of "his" agents in managing the affairs of the corporation, on the one hand, see Shaw v. Agri–Mark, Inc., 663 A.2d 464, 467 (Del.1995), and the competing interest of the corporation to be free from harassment by unhappy investors, see Randall S. Thomas, Improving Shareholder Monitoring and Corporate Management by Statutory Access to Information, 38 Ariz.L.Rev. 331, 334 (1996).

(2) Even if generalized purposes for an inspection are not acceptable, many cases state that a "proper purpose" is to examine financial records in order to determine the value of one's own shares. See, e.g., CM & M Group, Inc. v. Carroll, 453 A.2d 788 (Del.1982).

(3) All states adopt a "proper purpose" or similar test for shareholder inspection of records. Hundreds of cases have classified specific purposes as set forth in trial testimony or deposition as "proper" or "not proper." In resolving these disputes, as in the principal case, courts tend to look beyond the formal statements of purpose put forth and inquire into the shareholder's motive and relationship with the corporation. For a good example in the publicly held corporation context, see State ex rel. Pillsbury v. Honeywell, Inc., 291 Minn. 322, 191 N.W.2d 406 (1971), where, at the height of the Vietnam War, an individual purchased shares of Honeywell and then requested that it produce its shareholders' list and its corporate records relating to production of weapons and munitions. It appeared that the plaintiff was an antiwar activist primarily concerned with Honeywell's manufacture of napalm, but he had the financial resources to institute a proxy contest on this or any other issue if he chose to do so. The Court concluded that the plaintiff had not established a proper purpose to inspect these corporate records, pointing out that "the power to inspect may be the power to destroy" and that only those "with a bona fide interest in the corporation" should be permitted to inspect corporate records. 291 Minn. at 328, 191 N.W.2d at 410.

(4) In this area where "purpose" intersects with "motive," a shareholder who is well versed in the legal tests may be able to establish a "proper" purpose, while someone less sophisticated who is questioned about his "real" intent is likely to say something that indicates his purpose is to some extent personal and not a "bona fide interest in the corporation." In this respect, written communications such as those sent by Mr. Dunnigan in the principal case (apparently without being reviewed by his attorney) may be decisive in a negative way. However, it is the general view of attorneys familiar with litigation over inspection rights that in most instances objections based on purpose are likely to fail, and that at most such objections only delay the inspection.

(5) Of course the right of inspection is only one avenue to the information. See MBCA § 16.02(e)(1). In modern litigation, broad discovery rights exist and these rights appear to be independent of the statutory or common law inspection right of shareholders. Could Thomas & Betts frame a direct suit that would make relevant the information it failed to obtain through the inspection right? If so, in this plenary suit, might it be able to obtain financial information through

discovery? Should the scope of discovery in litigation be limited because the shareholder has also made an inspection demand?

PARSONS v. JEFFERSON–PILOT CORP.

Supreme Court of North Carolina, 1993.
333 N.C. 420, 426 S.E.2d 685.

MITCHELL, JUSTICE.

Louise Price Parsons, a shareholder in Jefferson–Pilot Corporation, initiated this action by filing a complaint and motion for preliminary injunction seeking to compel the defendant corporation to allow her to inspect, *inter alia*, its accounting records and records of shareholder and director action. The defendant answered and filed a motion for summary judgment and for sanctions under Rule 11 of the North Carolina Rules of Civil Procedure.

The evidence introduced at a hearing on the defendant's motion tended to show the following. The plaintiff, Louise Price Parsons, is a shareholder of Jefferson–Pilot Corporation and owns 300,000 shares of its stock, which are worth several million dollars. On 14 February 1991, the plaintiff sent a letter to the defendant corporation requesting that it allow her to inspect and copy designated corporate records that would enable her to communicate with its other shareholders. The defendant allowed the plaintiff to inspect and copy certain records. However, the defendant refused to provide the plaintiff with a list of beneficial owners of its stock, stating that it did not possess such information or maintain such a list. In her letter of 14 February 1991, the plaintiff also requested that the defendant allow her to inspect and copy certain "accounting records" so that she could determine "any possible mismanagement of the company or any possible misappropriation of the company's assets." In refusing the plaintiff's request, the defendant stated that such records "are not within the scope of N.C.G.S. § 55–16–02(b)."[4] On 4

---

4. [By the Editor] North Carolina has adopted MBCA § 16.02 with modifications. As of the time this case was decided, § 55–16–02 of the North Carolina Business Corporation Act was virtually identical to MBCA § 16.02 with the exception of amendments made to § 16.02(a), (b), (c), and the addition of new subsections (g) and (h). Set forth below is § 55–16–02 with the additions from § 16.02 italicized and language in MBCA § 16.02 that does not appear in § 55–16–02 marked through:

(a) ~~Subject to section 16.03(c),~~ ~~a~~A *qualified* shareholder of a corporation is entitled to inspect and copy, during regular business hours at the corporation's principal office, any of the records of the corporation described in ~~section 16.01(e)~~ *G.S. 55–16–01(e)* if he gives the corporation written notice of his demand at least five business days before the date on which he wishes to inspect and copy.

(b) A *qualified* shareholder of a corporation is entitled to inspect and copy, during regular business hours at a reasonable location specified by the corporation, any of the

following records of the corporation if the shareholder meets the requirements of subsection (c) and gives the corporation written notice of his demand at least five business days before the date on which he wishes to inspect and copy:

(1) ~~excerpts from minutes of any meeting of the board of directors, r~~Records of any *final* action *taken with or without a meeting by the board of directors, or by* ~~of~~ a committee of the board of directors while acting in place of the board of directors on behalf of the corporation, minutes of any meeting of the shareholders, and records of action by the shareholders ~~or board of directors~~ without a meeting, to the extent not subject to inspection under section ~~16.02(a)~~ *G.S.55–16–02(a)*;

(2) ~~a~~Accounting records of the corporation; and

(3) ~~t~~*T*he record of shareholders~~.~~*;*

provided that a shareholder of a public corporation shall not be entitled to inspect or copy any accounting records of the corporation or any records of the corporation with respect to

March 1991, the plaintiff sent another letter to the defendant narrowing her request for accounting records to those dealing with "compensation paid to, perquisites made available to and relationships with only the executive officers and directors of the company, their family members and companions." The defendant still refused to allow the plaintiff to inspect and copy any "accounting records." As a result, on 6 May 1991, the plaintiff filed a motion for preliminary injunction seeking, among other things, an order directing the defendant to give her access to its accounting records and to give her a list of beneficial owners of its stock.

At the conclusion of the hearing, Judge Allen entered an order denying the defendant's motion for summary judgment and Rule 11 sanctions, concluding that the defendant must permit the plaintiff to inspect its accounting records and records of shareholder and director action. Judge Allen also found that the defendant, Jefferson–Pilot Corporation, did not have the names of the non-objecting beneficial owners of its stock in its possession and, therefore, that the plaintiff was not entitled to an order requiring that the defendant provide her with a list of such individuals. Both parties appealed to the Court of Appeals.

The Court of Appeals affirmed the trial court's order to the extent that the order indicated that the plaintiff was not entitled to require the defendant corporation to obtain the names of non-objecting beneficial owners of the defendant's shares or to provide the plaintiff with a list of such non-objecting beneficial owners (NOBO list), where the defendant had neither the names nor a list of such individuals in its possession. The Court of Appeals also affirmed that part of the trial court's order which had concluded that the plaintiff's written demands to inspect other corporate records described her purpose and the records she sought with "reasonable particularity." However, the Court of Appeals reversed that part of the trial court's order which had

any matter which the corporation determines in good faith may, if disclosed, adversely affect the corporation in the conduct of its business or may constitute material nonpublic information at the time the shareholder's notice of demand to inspect is received by the corporation.

(c) A *qualified* shareholder may inspect and copy the records ~~identified~~ *described* in subsection (b) only if:

(1) ~~h~~*H*is demand is made in good faith and for a proper purpose;

(2) ~~h~~*H*e describes with reasonable particularity his purpose and the records he desires to inspect; and

(3) ~~t~~*T*he records are directly connected with his purpose.

(d) The right of inspection granted by this section many not be abolished or limited by a corporation's articles of incorporation or by-laws.

(e) This section does not affect:

(1) ~~t~~*T*he right of a shareholder to inspect records under ~~section 7.20~~ *G.S.55-7-20* or, if the shareholder is in litigation with the cor-

poration, to the same extent as any other litigant;

(2) ~~t~~*T*he power of a court, independently of this ~~Act~~ *chapter*, to compel the production of corporate records for examination.

(f) For purposes of this section "shareholder" includes a beneficial owner whose shares are held in a voting trust or by a nominee on his behalf *and whose beneficial ownership is certified to the corporation by that voting trust or nominee.*

(g) For purposes of this section, a "qualified shareholder" of a corporation is a person who shall have been a shareholder in the corporation for at least six months immediately preceding his demand or who shall be the holder of at least five percent (5%) of the corporation's outstanding shares of any class.

(h) A qualified shareholder of a corporation that has the power to elect, appoint, or designate a majority of the directors of another domestic or foreign corporation or of a domestic or foreign nonprofit corporation, shall have the inspection rights provided in this section with respect to the records of that other corporation.

concluded that the plaintiff had the right to inspect the defendant's accounting records. The Court of Appeals remanded the case to the trial court for its determination of whether the records the plaintiff sought were "directly connected" to her described purpose in seeking them and for a determination as to whether certain records sought by the plaintiff were in fact "accounting records." This Court allowed both the plaintiff's and the defendant's petitions for discretionary review on 3 September 1992.

I.

By her first assignment of error, the plaintiff contends that the Court of Appeals erroneously concluded that N.C.G.S. § 55–16–02(b) abrogated a shareholder's common law right to inspect the accounting records of a public corporation. The statute provides, in pertinent part, that a qualified shareholder of any corporation is entitled to inspect and copy accounting records of the corporation if she gives the corporation written notice of her demand at least five days before the date on which she wishes to inspect and copy such records. This right as guaranteed by the statute is limited, however, by its proviso that a shareholder of a public corporation[5] shall not be entitled to inspect or copy any accounting records of the corporation. The Court of Appeals concluded that this proviso restricts a shareholder's statutory right *and abrogates any common law right* to inspect a public corporation's accounting records. We disagree.

Under common law, a shareholder of a corporation has a right to make reasonable inspection of its books and records. *White v. Smith*, 256 N.C. 218, 123 S.E.2d 628 (1962); *Carter v. Wilson Construction Co.*, 83 N.C.App. 61, 348 S.E.2d 830 (1986). This Court has expressly recognized that the shareholders of a corporation have a common law right to make a reasonable inspection of its books to assure themselves of efficient management. We have also noted that the rationale behind the common law right of inspection is that those in charge of the corporation are merely agents of the shareholders, and a shareholder's right to inspect a corporation's books and records is only the right to inspect and examine that which is his own. *Cooke v. Outland*, 265 N.C. 601, 610, 144 S.E.2d 835, 841 (1965).

In light of the controlling case law, it is clear that a common law right to inspect the accounting records of a corporation existed in 1990 when the North Carolina Business Corporation Act, 1989 N.C.Sess.Laws ch. 265, took effect. The issue to be resolved here, then, is whether that common law right to inspect accounting records has been abrogated by N.C.G.S. § 55–16–02(b) or, to the contrary, has been preserved by N.C.G.S. § 55–16–02(e)(2), which provides that section 16–02 does not affect "the power of a court, independently of this Chapter, to compel the production of corporate records for examination."

The North Carolina Business Corporation Act, *inter alia*, provides shareholders certain rights of inspection of corporate records which did not exist under the common law. For example, the Act provides shareholders of corporations other than "public corporations" a new right to an *expedited*

---

5. [By the Court] The term "public corporation" as used in the North Carolina Business Corporation Act "means any corporation that has a class of shares registered under Section 12 of the Securities Exchange Act of 1934, as amended (15 U.S.C. § 78l)." N.C.G.S. § 55–1–40(18a) (Supp.1992).

inspection of a corporation's accounting records *within five business days* after making a proper demand. N.C.G.S. § 55–16–02(b) (Supp.1992). There seems to be general agreement, however, that the General Assembly did not intend the granting of such new or expanded rights of inspection under the Act to abrogate shareholders' rights of inspection already existing at common law; instead, it intended that N.C.G.S. § 55–16–02(e)(2) preserve all existing common law rights of inspection of corporate records. In this regard, one leading commentator has correctly noted:

> The North Carolina Business Corporation Act * * * prescribes statutory inspection rights in detail. Those statutory rights are nonexclusive because the present Act expressly provides that they do not affect the power of a court, independent of the Act, to compel the production of corporate records for examination; they also do not affect discovery rights in litigation.

Robinson [on North Carolina Corporation Law (4th ed. 1990) § 10.1, at 174 (footnotes omitted) (citing N.C.G.S. § 55–16–02(e)(1) and (2)). Both the Official Comment and the North Carolina Commentary to N.C.G.S. § 55–16–02 concur in this view. * * *

N.C.G.S. § 55–16–02(e)(2) expressly provides that "this section" (section 16–02) does not affect "the power of a court, independently of this Chapter, to compel the production of corporate records for examination." The Official Comment states that "Section 16.02(e) provides that the right of inspection granted by section 16.02 is an independent right of inspection that is not a substitute for or in derogation of rights of inspection that may exist * * * as a 'common law' right of inspection, if any is found to exist by a court, to examine corporate records. Section 16.02(e) simply preserves whatever independent right of inspection exists * * *." N.C.G.S. § 55–16–02 official cmt. 4 (1990). *Accord* N.C.G.S. § 55–16–02 North Carolina Commentary (ii) (1990) ("Subsection (e) of this section merely preserves any common law inspection right that may exist * * * "). We find the conclusion expressed in the Official Comment inescapable and are compelled to conclude that the North Carolina Business Corporation Act "was intended to leave in effect any common law rights of inspection existing in North Carolina, and the North Carolina cases have confirmed the existence of such rights in reasonably broad scope." *Robinson* § 10.4, at 181.

We conclude that N.C.G.S. § 55–16–02(e)(2) preserves a shareholder's common law rights of inspection, including the right to make reasonable inspections of the accounting records of a public corporation for proper purposes. *Cooke*, 265 N.C. at 610, 144 S.E.2d at 841. Further, a shareholder who seeks to exercise her common law right—as opposed to a statutory right—to examine corporate records for a proper purpose also has a common law right[6] to utilize the mandamus power of the courts to compel a reluctant corporation to disclose its corporate records pertinent to that purpose. *State ex rel. Lillie v. Cosgriff Co.*, 240 Neb. 387, 482 N.W.2d 555 (1992). Therefore, we reverse that part of the Court of Appeals' opinion which concluded that the

---

6. [By the Court] Shareholders have a statutory right to court-ordered inspection when a corporation fails or refuses to permit them to exercise the rights of inspection granted them by N.C.G.S. § 55–16–02. N.C.G.S. § 55–16–04 (1990).

plaintiff in the present case did not retain these common law rights after the adoption of the North Carolina Business Corporation Act.

II.

By her next assignment of error, the plaintiff shareholder contends that the Court of Appeals erred in failing to compel the defendant corporation to provide her with a NOBO list for inspection. A NOBO list is a list of beneficial owners of a corporation's stock who do not object to the disclosure of their names and addresses by the registered owner of the stock (typically, a stock broker or a bank) to the corporation itself for the limited purpose of allowing direct communication on corporate matters. Only recently have NOBO lists been recognized under federal law. When creating the rules requiring banks, stock brokers and dealers to create such lists upon requests by issuing corporations, the Securities Exchange Commission reviewed the question of whether a corporation's shareholders should themselves be granted the right to compel the production of a NOBO list on the same terms as the issuer of the shares. See Exchange Act Release No. 34–22533, 50 Fed.Reg. 42, 672 (Oct. 22, 1985). However, the Commission has not promulgated any rule providing shareholders with such a right.

A qualified shareholder has a statutory right to inspect a "record of shareholders." N.C.G.S. § 55–16–02(b)(3) (1990). The plaintiff contends that the record of shareholders made available by this statute includes a NOBO list. Our Court of Appeals concluded in the present case that the defendant corporation does not have to provide the plaintiff shareholder with a NOBO list, because the defendant corporation does not have the information needed to create such a list and does not use such a list in communicating with shareholders. We agree.

Other courts have held that where a corporation has obtained a NOBO list and is or will be using it to solicit shareholders, a shareholder should be allowed the same channel of communication. *E.g., Shamrock Associates v. Texas American Energy*, 517 A.2d 658 (Del.Ch.1986); *Bohrer v. International Banknote Co.*, 150 A.D.2d 196, 540 N.Y.S.2d 445 (1989). However, there is a paucity of cases addressing the issue before us in the present case—whether a corporation must provide a shareholder a NOBO list even though the corporation does not have in its possession the names of its non-objecting beneficial owners and does not use such information to solicit shareholders. * * *

We believe that the legislative intent embodied in N.C.G.S. § 55–16–02(b)(3) is that shareholders be entitled to the information concerning the identity of shareholders which is *possessed by the corporation* in order that they may have the same opportunity as the corporation to communicate with the other shareholders. In order to effectuate that legislative goal, it is necessary that shareholders have access to NOBO lists or other information which the corporation itself has in its possession; however, a shareholder is not granted a right under the statute to require a corporation to obtain NOBO lists or the information necessary to compile NOBO lists when the corporation does not possess or use such information. Since the defendant corporation does not have in its possession a NOBO list or the information needed to compile a NOBO list, it is not required to obtain that information simply because the plaintiff shareholder has requested that it do so for an otherwise proper purpose. Therefore, we affirm that part of the opinion of the

Court of Appeals which affirmed the trial court's holding that the defendant corporation was not required to provide the plaintiff with a NOBO list.

III.

In its sole assignment of error, the defendant contends that the Court of Appeals erred in concluding that the plaintiff had satisfied the "reasonable particularity" requirement of N.C.G.S. § 55–16–02(c)(2). This statute provides that a "qualified shareholder may inspect and copy the records described in subsection (b) only if" she describes with reasonable particularity her purpose and the records she desires to inspect. N.C.G.S. § 55–16–02(c)(2) (1990). In her demand, the plaintiff requested

> for the purpose of determining any possible mismanagement of the Company or any possible misappropriation, misapplication or improper use of any property or asset of the Company, all records of any final action taken, with or without a meeting, by the Board of Directors of the Company, or by a committee of the Board of Directors of the Company while acting in place of the Board of Directors of the Company on behalf of the Company, minutes of any meeting of the shareholders of the Company and records of action taken by the shareholders of the Company without a meeting.

Since no court has yet construed the "reasonable particularity" requirement of N.C.G.S. § 55–16–02(c)(2), we find it helpful to consider the interpretation placed upon the "reasonable particularity" requirement contained in Rule 34(b) of the Federal Rules of Civil Procedure. In determining whether the "reasonable particularity" requirement of this federal rule governing document production has been satisfied, it has been recognized that

> the test must be a relative one, turning on the degree of knowledge that a movant in a particular case has about the documents he requests. In some cases he has such exact and definite knowledge that he can designate, identify, and enumerate with precision the documents to be produced. This is the ideal designation, since it permits the party responding to go at once to his files and without difficulty produce the document for inspection. But the ideal is not always attainable and Rule 34 does not require the impossible. Even a generalized designation should be sufficient when the party seeking discovery cannot give a more particular description and the party from whom discovery is sought will have no difficulty in understanding what is wanted. The goal is that the designation be sufficient to apprise a man of ordinary intelligence what documents are required.

8 Charles A. Wright & Arthur R. Miller, *Federal Practice and Procedure* § 2211, at 628–31 (1970). This test is in line with the Official Comment to N.C.G.S. § 55–16–02(c)(2), which provides that under the "reasonable particularity" requirement, a shareholder should make more meaningful statements of purpose and the desired records when "feasible." Whether a shareholder has described his purpose or the desired records with reasonable particularity necessarily depends upon the facts and circumstances of each case.

In the present case, the record does not show that the plaintiff had any specific knowledge of corporate mismanagement or of any improper use of corporate assets at the time that she made the demand. The record shows only that the plaintiff was dissatisfied with the return on her investment in the defendant corporation. In light of the plaintiff's actual knowledge at the time of the demand, it would not have been feasible to state her purpose with any greater particularity. In addition, the plaintiff specifically described the desired records in her demand. The plaintiff sought "all records of any final action taken by the Board or by a committee of the Board, the minutes of any meeting of the shareholders, and records of action taken by the shareholders of the Company without a meeting." Although the plaintiff's demand was broad, we agree with the Court of Appeals' determination that there is nothing in this record to show that the plaintiff could have described the desired records with any greater particularity than she did, and the defendant company should not have had any trouble understanding what the plaintiff desired. Assuming *arguendo* that N.C.G.S. § 55–16–02(c) controls situations in which a shareholder exercises a common law right of inspection, as well as situations in which the statutory right is being exercised, we conclude that the plaintiff described both her purpose and the desired records with the "reasonable particularity" required by that statute. This assignment of error is overruled. * * *

Affirmed in part; reversed in part; and remanded.

Notes

(1) *Parsons* was decided on March 12, 1993. On October 1, 1993, North Carolina added the following new paragraph (i) to § 55–16–02:

(i) Notwithstanding the provisions of this section, or any other provisions of this Chapter or interpretations thereof to the contrary, a shareholder of a public corporation shall have no common law rights to inspect or copy any accounting records of the corporation or any other records of the corporation that may not be inspected or copied by a shareholder of a public corporation as provided in G.S. 55–16–02(b).

Do you believe that the addition of this section is desirable? As a result of this amendment, may a shareholder ever obtain more complete information about a public corporation's financial affairs than provided in the SEC-required disclosures?

(2) NOBOs are discussed in Chapter 9, section B(3). See also Randall S. Thomas, Improving Shareholder Monitoring and Corporate Management by Expanding Statutory Access to Information, 38 Ariz.L.Rev. 331, 332, n. 8 (1996).

(3) Enforcement of inspection rights has long been a problem. Consider the position of management when it receives a request to inspect a list of shareholders or accounting records. Is it not clear that such a request always comes from a potentially unfriendly source, and that any information provided is likely to be used against incumbent management? Prior to the enactment of statutes dealing specifically with shareholder inspection rights, the normal reaction of management to an inspection request was to refuse to provide anything, requiring the shareholder to go to court. In an effort to make the inspection right more meaningful and less costly to shareholders, statutory inspection rights were created. Some placed the burden of showing an improper purpose on the corporation while others imposed penalties on corporate officers that failed to accord inspection rights without reasonable cause. Some statutes required the corpora-

tion to pay a successful shareholder's expenses. The MBCA now addresses the enforcement problem in MBCA § 16.04.

(4) A related problem arises with respect to the scope of the inspection itself. An inspection is not very useful to a shareholder if, for example, the corporation produces a list of 26,000 shareholders of record at the corporation's principal office, but then refuses a request that a copy be provided, refuses a further request that the shareholder be permitted to make a xerographic copy of the list and, in effect, tells the shareholder that he may freely make longhand notes or enter the data on his laptop on his own, if he wishes. An inspection right is also of limited usefulness if the corporation refuses to permit the shareholder to be accompanied by his attorney and accountant when inspecting the records. MBCA § 16.03 is intended to provide comprehensive answers to such problems.

(5) Statutory inspection rights were created in large part to avoid the enforcement and scope of inspection issues discussed in the two preceding notes. Many states adopting streamlined inspection rights limited them to "eligible" shareholders, usually defining eligibility as shareholders holding a specified number of shares or holding any number of shares for some period of time. The Model Act did not include these restrictions on the theory that they were not effective, but North Carolina retained these restrictions through its definition of "qualified shareholder" in § 55–16–02(g). Do you think that the drafters of the Model Act should have retained these restrictions?

(6) The North Carolina statute accepts the idea in MBCA § 16.02(f) that beneficial holders of shares and holders of shares in voting trusts (as well as record shareholders) should be eligible to inspect records. It adds, however, an additional clause requiring the record owner to certify the identity of the beneficial owner to the corporation. See § 55–16–02(f), n. 4 supra. Do you think this amendment is desirable? Might a voting trustee sympathetic to management decline to make such a certification? If so, what, if anything, could the beneficial holder do about it?

(7) The North Carolina statute also adds a new subsection (h) that does not appear in the Model Act. See § 55–16–02(h), n. 4 supra. At what problem was this subsection addressed? Should it be added to the Model Act?

(8) Delaware Gen.Corp.Law § 220(b) permits inspection of not only the corporation's shareholders' lists but also of "its other books and records." In contrast, MBCA § 16.02(b) limits inspection to minutes, shareholder lists, and accounting records of the corporation. Has not the MBCA unreasonably narrowed the inspection right? For example, assume that a shareholder has reason to believe that the CEO of a corporation has privately entered into side agreements with a major supplier of raw materials. The shareholder wishes to inspect the correspondence between the CEO and that supplier to verify if his suspicions are accurate. Might not such records be subject to inspection under the Delaware statute but not under the MBCA, since correspondence hardly falls within the phrase "accounting records"?

(9) In some instances, a dissident director rather than a shareholder may seek to inspect records of the corporation. This may occur, for example, in closely held corporations in which cumulative voting is mandatory and a minority faction has sufficient voting power to elect one or more directors. Does a director have inspection rights greater than those of a shareholder? See Pilat v. Broach Systems, Inc., 108 N.J.Super. 88, 94, 96–97, 260 A.2d 13, 16–18 (1969):

The cases, however, distinguish between the right of a shareholder and those of a director of a corporation. * * * Some hold that a director may be denied the right to examine the corporate records where it is shown that he has a hostile or improper motive. * * *

Other jurisdictions, however, have held a director's right of inspection to be unqualified. In the New York case of Davis v. Keilsohn Offset Co., 273 App.Div. 695, 79 N.Y.S.2d 540 (1948), it was held that:

> The petitioner, as a director of the corporation, has an absolute right to [inspection]. All that he need show is that he is a director of the company; that he has demanded permission to examine and that his demand has been refused. It is the duty of the petitioner to keep himself informed of the business of the corporation. To perform this duty intelligently he has the unqualified right to inspect its books and records. It is of no consequence that petitioner may be hostile to the corporation. His object in seeking the examination is immaterial. His right of inspection is not dependent upon his being able to satisfy other officers of the corporation that his motives are adequate. [79 N.Y.S.2d, at 541]

Even if this court were to follow the reasoning of the first-mentioned jurisdictions, there is no showing of plaintiff's hostile intent so as to preclude him from inspection. Nevertheless, this court must follow the New Jersey decisions and it is therefore held that a director has an absolute, unqualified right to inspect the corporate books and records of account, irrespective of motive, and that in the instant case plaintiff is entitled to such inspection either with or without an attorney or accountant, as soon as conveniently possible. * * *

(10) The American Law Institute, Principles of Corporate Governance: Analysis and Recommendations § 3.03.[7]

(a) Every director has the right, within the limits of § 3.03(b) (and subject to other applicable law), to inspect and copy all books, records, and documents of every kind, and to inspect the physical properties, of the corporation and of its subsidiaries, domestic or foreign, at any reasonable time, in person or by an attorney or other agent.

(b)(1) A judicial order to enforce such right should be granted unless the corporation establishes that the information to be obtained by the exercise of the right is not reasonably related to the performance of directorial functions and duties, or that the director or the director's agent is likely to use the information in a manner that would violate the director's fiduciary obligation to the corporation.

(2) An application for such an order should be decided expeditiously and may be decided on the basis of affidavits.

(3) Such an order may contain provisions protecting the corporation from undue burden or expense, and prohibiting the director from using the information in a manner that would violate the director's fiduciary obligation to the corporation.

(4) A director who makes an application for such an order after the corporation has denied a request should, if successful, be reimbursed by the

corporation for expenses (including attorney's fees) reasonably incurred in connection with the application.

(11) The MBCA is silent on the question of the inspection rights of directors. In view of the diverse views on this issue, was this not an oversight?

Chapter Sixteen

FUNDAMENTAL CHANGES: CORPORATION LAW ASPECTS

BOVE v. COMMUNITY HOTEL CORP. OF NEWPORT, RHODE ISLAND

Supreme Court of Rhode Island, 1969.
105 R.I. 36, 249 A.2d 89.

JOSLIN, JUSTICE.

This civil action was brought in the superior court to enjoin a proposed merger of The Community Hotel Corporation of Newport, Rhode Island, a defendant herein, into Newport Hotel Corp. Both corporations were organized under the general corporation law of this state and are hereinafter referred to respectively as "Community Hotel" and "Newport." No oral testimony was presented and a trial justice sitting without a jury decided the case on the facts appearing in the exhibits and as assented to by the parties in the pretrial order. The case is here on the plaintiffs' appeal from a judgment denying injunctive relief and dismissing the action.

Community Hotel was incorporated on October 21, 1924, for the stated purpose of erecting, maintaining, operating, managing and leasing hotels; and it commenced operations in 1927 with the opening of the Viking Hotel in Newport. Its authorized capital stock consists of 6,000 shares of $100 par value six percent prior preference cumulative preferred stock, and 6,000 shares of no par common stock of which 2,106 shares are issued and outstanding. The plaintiffs as well as the individual defendants are holders and owners of preferred stock, plaintiffs having acquired their holdings of approximately 900 shares not later than 1930. At the time this suit was commenced, dividends on the 4,335 then-issued and outstanding preferred shares had accrued, but had not been declared, for approximately 24 years, and totaled about $645,000 or $148.75 per share.

Newport was organized at the instance and request of the board of directors of Community Hotel solely for the purpose of effectuating the merger which is the subject matter of this action. Its authorized capital stock consists of 80,000 shares of common stock, par value $1.00, of which only one share has been issued, and that to Community Hotel for the consideration of $10.

1079

The essentials of the merger plan call for Community Hotel to merge into Newport, which will then become the surviving corporation. Although previously without assets, Newport will, if the contemplated merger is effectuated, acquire the sole ownership of all the property and assets now owned by Community Hotel. The plan also calls for the outstanding shares of Community Hotel's capital stock to be converted into shares of the capital stock of Newport upon the following basis: Each outstanding share of the constituent corporation's preferred stock, together with all accrued dividends thereon, will be changed and converted into five shares of the $1.00 par value common stock of the surviving corporation; and each share of the constituent corporation's no par common stock will be changed and converted into one share of the common stock, $1.00 par value, of the surviving corporation.

Consistent with the requirements of G.L.1956, § 7–5–3,[1] the merger will become effective only if the plan receives the affirmative votes of the stockholders of each of the corporations representing at least two-thirds of the shares of each class of its capital stock. For the purpose of obtaining the required approval, notice was given to both common and preferred stockholders of Community Hotel that a special meeting would be held for the purpose of considering and voting upon the proposed merger. Before the scheduled meeting date arrived, this action was commenced and the meeting was postponed to a future time and place. So far as the record before us indicates, it has not yet been held.

The plaintiffs argue that the primary, and indeed, the only purpose of the proposed merger is to eliminate the priorities of the preferred stock with less than the unanimous consent of its holders. Assuming that premise, a preliminary matter for our consideration concerns the merger of a parent corporation into a wholly-owned subsidiary created for the sole purpose of achieving a recapitalization which will eliminate the parent's preferred stock and the dividends accumulated thereon, and whether such a merger qualifies within the contemplation of the statute permitting any two or more corporations to merge into a single corporation.

It is true, of course, that to accomplish the proposed recapitalization by amending Community Hotel's articles of association under relevant provisions of the general corporation law[2] would require the unanimous vote of the

---

1. [By the Court] Section 7–5–3 in pertinent part provides:

"Said agreement shall be submitted to the stockholders of each constituent corporation at a meeting thereof called separately for the purpose of taking the same into consideration. * * * At said meeting said agreement shall be considered and the stockholders of said corporation shall vote by ballot, in person or by proxy, for the adoption or rejection of the said agreement, each share entitling the holder thereof to one (1) vote, and if the votes of the stockholders of each such corporation representing at least two-thirds of the shares of each class of its capital stock shall be for the adoption of said agreement * * * the agreement so adopted and certified * * * shall thence be taken and deemed to be the agreement and act of consolidation or merger of said corporations * * *."

2. [By the Court] Section 7–2–18, as amended, provides that a corporation may "* * * from time to time when and as desired amend its articles of association * * *"and § 7–2–19, as amended, provides that "Unless otherwise provided in the articles of association, every such amendment shall require the affirmative vote of the following proportion of the stockholders, passed at a meeting duly called for the purpose:

(a) * * *

(b) Where the amendment diminishes the stipulated rate of dividends on any class of stock or the stipulated amount to be paid thereon in case of call or liquidation, the unanimous vote of the stockholders of such class and the vote of a majority in interest of all other stockholders entitled to vote."

preferred shareholders, whereas under the merger statute, only a two-third vote of those stockholders will be needed. Concededly, unanimity of the preferred stockholders is unobtainable in this case, and plaintiffs argue, therefore, that to permit the less restrictive provisions of the merger statute to be used to accomplish indirectly what otherwise would be incapable of being accomplished directly by the more stringent amendment procedures of the general corporation law is tantamount to sanctioning a circumvention or perversion of that law.

The question, however, is not whether recapitalization by the merger route is a subterfuge, but whether a merger which is designed for the sole purpose of cancelling the rights of preferred stockholders with the consent of less than all has been authorized by the legislature. The controlling statute is § 7–5–2. Its language is clear, all-embracing and unqualified. It authorizes any two or more business corporations *which were or might have been organized* under the general corporation law to merge into a single corporation; and it provides that the merger agreement shall prescribe " * * * the terms and conditions of consolidation or merger, the mode of carrying the same into effect * * * *as well as the manner of converting the shares of each of the constituent corporations into shares or other securities of the corporation resulting from or surviving such consolidation or merger,* with such other details and provisions as are deemed necessary."[3] (italics ours) Nothing in that language even suggests that the legislature intended to make *underlying purpose* a standard for determining permissibility. Indeed, the contrary is apparent since the very breadth of the language selected presupposes a complete lack of concern with whether the merger is designed to further the mutual interests of two existing and nonaffiliated corporations or whether alternatively it is proposed solely upon effecting a substantial change in an existing corporation's capital structure.

Moreover, that a possible effect of corporate action under the merger statute is not possible, or is even forbidden, under another section of the general corporation law is of no import, it being settled that the several sections of that law may have independent legal significance, and that the validity of corporate action taken pursuant to one section is not necessarily dependent upon its being valid under another. Hariton v. Arco Electronics, Inc., 40 Del.Ch. 326, 182 A.2d 22, aff'd, 41 Del.Ch. 74, 188 A.2d 123.

We hold, therefore, that nothing within the purview of our statute forbids a merger between a parent and a subsidiary corporation even under circumstances where the merger device has been resorted to solely for the purpose of obviating the necessity for the unanimous vote which would otherwise be required in order to cancel the priorities of preferred shareholders. Federal United Corp. v. Havender, supra; Hottenstein v. York Ice Machinery Corp., 3 Cir., 136 F.2d 944.

A more basic problem, narrowed so as to bring it within the factual context of this case, is whether the right of a holder of cumulative preferred stock to dividend arrearages and other preferences may be canceled by a statutory merger. That precise problem has not heretofore been before this

---

3. [By the Court] The quoted provision is substantially identical to the Delaware merger statute (Del.Rev.Code (1935) C. 65, § 2091) construed in Federal United Corp. v. Havender, 24 Del.Ch. 318, 11 A.2d 331.

court, but elsewhere there is a considerable body of law on the subject. There is no need to discuss all of the authorities. For illustrative purposes it is sufficient that we refer principally to cases involving Delaware corporations. That state is important as a state of incorporation, and the decisions of its courts on the precise problem are not only referred to and relied on by the parties, but are generally considered to be the leading ones in the field.

The earliest case in point of time is Keller v. Wilson & Co., 21 Del.Ch. 391, 190 A. 115 (1936). Wilson & Company was formed and its stock was issued in 1925 and the law then in effect protected against charter amendments which might destroy a preferred shareholder's right to accumulated dividends. In 1927 that law was amended so as to permit such destruction, and thereafter the stockholders of Wilson & Company, by the required majorities, voted to cancel the dividends which had by then accrued on its preferred stock. In invalidating that action the rationale of the Delaware court was that the right of a holder of a corporation's cumulative preferred stock to eventual payment of dividend arrearages was a fixed contractual right, that it was a property right in the nature of a debt, that it was vested, and that it could not be destroyed by corporate action taken under legislative authority subsequently conferred, without the consent of all of the shareholders.

Consolidated Film Industries v. Johnson, 22 Del.Ch. 407, 197 A. 489 (1937), decided a year later, was an almost precisely similar case. The only difference was that Consolidated Film Industries, Inc. was not created until after the adoption of the 1927 amendment, whereas in the earlier case the statutory amendment upon which Wilson & Company purported to act postdated both its creation and the issuance of its stock. Notwithstanding the *Keller* rationale that an investor should be entitled to rely upon the law in existence at the time the preferred stock was issued, the court in this case was " * * * unable to discover a difference in principle between the two cases." In refusing to allow the proposed reclassification, it reasoned that a shareholder's fixed contractual right to unpaid dividends is of such dignity that it cannot be diminished or eliminated retrospectively even if the authorizing legislation precedes the issuance of its stock.

Two years elapsed before Federal United Corp. v. Havender, supra, was decided. The issue was substantially the same as that in the two cases which preceded. The dissenting stockholders had argued, as might have been expected, that the proposed corporate action, even though styled a "merger," was in effect a *Keller* type recapitalization and was entitled to no different treatment. Notwithstanding that argument, the court did not refer to the preferred stockholder's right as "vested" or as "a property right in the nature of a debt." Neither did it reject the use of *Keller*-type nomenclature as creating "confusion" or as "substitutes for reason and analysis" which are the characterizations used respectively in Davison v. Parke, Austin & Lipscomb, Inc., 285 N.Y. 500, 509, 35 N.E.2d 618, 622; Meck, Accrued Dividends on Cumulative Preferred Stocks; The Legal Doctrine, 55 Harv.L.Rev. 7, 76. Instead, it talked about the extent of the corporate power under the merger statute; and it held that the statute in existence when Federal United Corp. was organized had in effect been written into its charter, and that its preferred shareholders had thereby been advised and informed that their rights to accrued dividends might be extinguished by corporate action taken pursuant thereto.

Faced with a question of corporate action adjusting preferred stock dividends, and required to apply Delaware law under Erie R.R. v. Tompkins, 304 U.S. 64, 58 Sup.Ct. 817, 82 L.Ed. 1188, it is understandable that a federal court in Hottenstein v. York Ice Machinery Corp., 3 Cir., 136 F.2d 944, 950, found *Keller, Johnson* and *Havender* irreconcilable and said,

> If it is fair to say that the decision of the Supreme Court of Delaware in the Keller case astonished the corporate world, it is just to state that the decision of the Supreme Court in Havender astounded it, for shorn of rationalization the decision constitutes a repudiation of principles enunciated in the Keller case and in Consolidated Film Industries v. Johnson, supra. at 950.[4]

With Keller's back thus broken, *Hottenstein* went on to say that under Delaware law a parent corporation may merge with a wholly-owned inactive subsidiary pursuant to a plan canceling preferred stock and the rights of holders thereof to unpaid accumulated dividends and substituting in lieu thereof stock of the surviving corporation.

Only four years intervened between *Keller* and *Havender,* but that was long enough for Delaware to have discarded "vested rights" as the test for determining the power of a corporation to eliminate a shareholder's right to preferred stock dividend accumulation, and to have adopted in its stead a standard calling for judicial inquiry into whether the proposed interference with a preferred stockholder's contract has been authorized by the legislature. The *Havender* approach is the one to which we subscribe as being the sounder, and it has support in the authorities.

The plaintiffs do not suggest, other than as they may have argued that this particular merger is a subterfuge, that our merger statute will not permit in any circumstances a merger for the sole reason that it affects accrued, but undeclared, preferred stock dividends. Rather do they argue that what should control is the date of the enactment of the enabling legislation, and they point out that in *Havender,* Federal United Corp. was organized and its stock was issued subsequent to the adoption of the statute authorizing mergers, whereas in this case the corporate creation and the stock issue preceded adoption of such a statute. That distinguishing feature brings into question what limitations, if any, exist to a state's authority under the reserved power to permit by subsequent legislation corporate acts which affect the preferential rights of a stockholder. More specifically, it raises the problem of whether subsequent legislation is repugnant to the federal and state constitutional prohibitions against the passage of laws impairing the obligations of contracts, because it permits elimination of accumulated preferred dividends by a lesser vote than

---

4. [By the Court] To the same effect the court in Western Foundry Co. v. Wicker, 403 Ill. 260, said at 277, 85 N.E.2d 722 at 730:

"Thus, what was formerly regarded as an almost inviolable vested property right was now considered a mere defeasible right, subject to cancellation by merger by reason of the consent of the preferred shareholders granted at the time the stock was originally issued. There being little or no difference between a recapitalization by corporate amendment and recapitalization by merger of a parent corporation with a wholly-owned subsidiary, the present status of the *Keller* case is obscure. While not expressly overruled, the theory of the *Keller* case was entirely repudiated. Consequently, as an authority for the proposition that the power to change the 'rights' of preferred stock does not include the right to cancel unpaid cumulative dividends, Keller v. Wilson & Co. is highly questionable."

was required under the law in existence at the time of the incorporation and when the stock was issued.

The mere mention of the constitutional prohibitions against such laws calls to mind Trustees of Dartmouth College v. Woodward, 17 U.S. 518, 4 Wheaton 518, 4 L.Ed. 629, where the decision was that a private corporation charter granted by the state is a contract protected under the constitution against repeal, amendment or alteration by subsequent legislation. Of equal significance in the field of corporation law is Mr. Justice Story's concurring opinion wherein he suggested that application of the impairment clause upon acts of incorporation might be avoided if a state legislature, coincident with granting a corporate charter, reserved as a part of that contract the right of amendment or repeal. With such a reservation, he said, any subsequent amendment or repeal would be pursuant, rather than repugnant, to the terms of the contract and would not therefore impair its obligation.

Our own legislature was quick to heed Story's advice, and in the early part of the 19th century, when corporations were customarily created by special act, the power to alter, amend, or revoke was written directly into each charter. Later, when the practice changed and corporations, instead of being created by special enactment, were incorporated under the general corporation law, the power to amend and repeal was reserved in an act of general application, and since at least as far back as 1844 the corporation law has read in substance as it does today viz., " * * * The charter or articles of association of every corporation hereafter created may be amended or repealed at the will of the general assembly." Section 7–1–13.

The language in which the reserved power is customarily stated is not, however, self-explaining, and the extent of the legislative authority under it has frequently been a source of difficulty. Recognizing that problem, but not answering it, the United States Supreme Court said in a frequently quoted passage:

> The authority of a state under the so-called reserve power is wide; but it is not unlimited. The corporate charter may be repealed or amended, and, within limits not now necessary to define, the interrelations of state, corporation and stockholders may be changed; but neither vested property rights nor the obligation of contracts of third persons may be destroyed or impaired. Coombes v. Getz, 285 U.S. 434, 441–442, 52 S.Ct. 435, 436, 76 L.Ed. 866, 871. * * *

On the one side, there is a body of law which speaks of the threefold nature of the stockholder's contract and, while agreeable to an exercise of the reserved power affecting only the contractual relationship between the state and the corporation, rejects as unconstitutional any exercise which affects the relationship between the stockholder and the corporation or between the stockholders inter sese. Under this view, subsequent legislation purporting to permit a corporate act to cancel accrued preferred dividends would obviously be an improper exercise of the power inasmuch as the essence of a preferred stockholder's contract is its definition of his relationship with the corporation and with the other stockholders vis-à-vis such matters as the distribution of the profits of the enterprise or the division of its capital and surplus account in the event of liquidation.

The other side of the argument considers that the question is primarily one of statutory construction and that so long as the statute authorizes the corporate action, it should make no difference whether its enactment preceded or postdated the birth of the corporation or the issuance of its stock.[5] The basis for this viewpoint is that the terms of the preferred stockholder's contractual relationship are not restricted to the specifics inscribed on the stock certificate, but include also the stipulations contained in the charter or articles of association as well as the pertinent provisions of the general corporation law. One of those provisions is, of course, the reserved power; and so long as it is a part of the preferred shareholder's contract, any subsequent legislation enacted pursuant to it, even though it may amend the contract's original terms, will not impair its obligation in the constitutional sense. It is as if the stock certificate were inscribed with the legend "All of the terms and conditions hereof may be changed by the legislature acting pursuant to the power it has reserved in G.L.1956, § 7–1–13." * * *

On the basis of our own precedents we conclude that the merger legislation, notwithstanding its effect on the rights of its stockholders, did not necessarily constitute an improper exercise of the right of amendment reserved merely because it was subsequent.

In addition to arguing that the proposed plan suffers from a constitutional infirmity, plaintiffs also contend that it is unfair and inequitable to them, and that its consummation should, therefore, be enjoined. By that assertion they raise the problem of whether equity should heed the request of a dissenting stockholder and intervene to prevent a merger notwithstanding that it has received the vote[6] of the designated proportions of the various classes of stock of the constituent corporations.

In looking to the authorities for assistance on this question, we avoided those involving recapitalization by charter amendment where a dissident's only remedy against allegedly unfair treatment was in equity. In those situations the authorities generally permit equitable intervention to protect against unfair or inequitable treatment. They are founded on the concept that otherwise there might be confiscation without recompense. The same rationale, however, is not available in the case of a merger, because there the dissenting stockholders usually can find a measure of protection in the statutory procedures giving them the option to compel the corporation to purchase their shares at an appraised value. This is a significant difference and is ample reason for considering the two situations as raising separate and distinct issues.

This case involves a merger, not a recapitalization by charter amendment, and in this state the legislature, looking to the possibility that there might be those who would not be agreeable to the proposed merger, provided a means whereby a dissatisfied stockholder might demand and the corporation be

5. [By the Court] This, in substance was the basis for the decision in Consolidated Firm Industries, Inc. v. Johnson. The corporation there, as distinguished from the one in Keller v. Wilson & Co., was created subsequent to the amendment which permitted recapitalization. Nonetheless, the court was " * * * unable to discover a difference in principle between the two cases."

6. [By the Court] For purposes of this proceeding we have accepted the implied assumption of all of the parties that the proposed merger will receive the required vote and we have not sua sponte suggested that the suit might more properly have awaited that eventuality.

compelled to pay the fair value of his securities. G.L.1956, §§ 7–5–8 through 7–5–16 inclusive. Our inquiry then is to the effect of that remedy upon plaintiff's right to challenge the proposed merger on the ground that it is unfair and inequitable because it dictates what shall be their proportionate interests in the corporate assets. Once again there is no agreement among the authorities. Vorenberg, "Exclusiveness of the Dissenting Stockholder's Appraisal Right," 77 Harv.L.Rev. 1189. Some authorities appear to say that the statutory remedy of appraisal is exclusive. Beloff v. Consolidated Edison Co., 300 N.Y. 11, 87 N.E.2d 561. Others say that it may be disregarded and that equity may intervene if the minority is treated oppressively or unfairly, Barnett v. Philadelphia Market Co., 218 Pa. 649, 67 A. 912; or if the merger is tainted with fraud or illegality, Adams v. United States Distributing Corp., 184 Va. 134, 147, 34 S.E.2d 244, 250, 162 A.L.R. 1227. To these differing views must also be added the divergence of opinion on whether those in control or those dissenting must bear the burden of establishing that the plan meets whatever the required standard may be. Vorenberg, supra; 77 Harv. L.Rev. 1189, 1210–1215.

In this case we do not choose as between the varying views, nor is there any need for us to do so. Even were we to accept that view which is most favorable to plaintiffs we still would not be able to find that they have been either unfairly or inequitably treated. The record insofar as it relates to the unfairness issue is at best sparse. In substance it consists of the corporation's balance sheet as of September 1967, together with supporting schedules. That statement uses book, rather than the appraised, values, and neither it nor any other evidentiary matter in any way indicates, except as the same may be reflected in the surplus account, the corporation's earning history or its prospects for profitable operations in the future.

Going to the figures we find a capital and surplus account of $669,948 of which $453,000 is allocable to the 4,530 issued and outstanding shares of $100 par value preferred stock and the balance of $316,948 to surplus. Obviously, a realization of the book value of the assets in the event of liquidation, forced or otherwise, would not only leave nothing for the common stockholders, but would not even suffice to pay the preferred shareholders the par value of their stock plus the accrued dividends of $645,000.

If we were to follow a rule of absolute priority, any proposal which would give anything to common stockholders without first providing for full payment of stated value plus dividend accruals would be unfair to the preferred shareholders. It could be argued that the proposal in this case violates that rule because an exchange of one share of Community Hotel's preferred stock for five shares of Newport's common stock would give the preferred shareholders securities worth less than the amount of their liquidation preference rights while at the same time the one to one exchange ratio on the common would enrich Community Hotel's common stockholders by allowing them to participate in its surplus.

An inherent fallacy in applying the rule of absolute priority to the circumstances of this case, however, is its assumption that assets would be liquidated and that nothing more than their book value will be realized. But Community Hotel is not in liquidation. Instead it is a going concern which, because of its present capitalization, cannot obtain the modern debt-financing needed to meet threatened competition. Moreover, management, in the call of the meeting at which it was intended to consider and vote on the plan, said that the proposed recapitalization plan was conceived only " * * * after careful consideration by your Board of Directors and a review of the relative values of the preferred and common stocks by the independent public accountants of the Corporation. The exchange ratio of five new common shares for each share of the existing preferred stock was determined on the basis of the book and market values of the preferred and the inherent value of the unpaid preferred dividends." Those assertions are contained in a document admitted as an exhibit and they have testimonial value.

When the varying considerations—both balance sheet figures and management's assertions—are taken into account, we are unable to conclude, at least at this stage of the proceedings, that the proposed plan is unfair and inequitable, particularly because plaintiffs as dissidents may avail themselves of the opportunity to receive the fair market value of their securities under the appraisal methods prescribed in § 7–5–8 through § 7–5–16 inclusive.

The plaintiffs argue that due consideration will not be given to their dividend accruals under the appraisal. We do not agree. Jeffrey v. American Screw Co., 98 R.I. 286, 201 A.2d 146, requires that the securities of a dissident invoking the statute must be appraised by a person "versed in the intricacies of corporate finance." Such a person will find when he looks to *Jeffrey* for guidance that the evaluation process requires him to consider " * * * all relevant value factors including market value, book value, asset value, and other intrinsic factors probative of value." Certainly, unpaid dividend arrearages fall within that directive and are a relevant factor to be considered in arriving at the full and fair cash value of the plaintiffs' preferred stock. While we make no decision one way or the other on the exclusiveness of appraisal as a remedy for a dissident, we do decide that its availability is an element or a circumstance which equity should weigh before intervening. When that is done in this case, we find no ground for intervention.

For the reasons stated, the judgment appealed from is affirmed.

Notes

(1) The notion that certain rights of securities holders are "vested property rights" is superficially appealing and, as indicated in the principal case, has been judicially adopted in a few instances. The effect of it, however, is to require unanimous consent for transactions, and that is usually impractical. Most modern corporation law commentators accept the idea that rights of securities holders may be modified over their individual objections by appropriate corporate action. Such modifications may be made only by following statutory procedures that give some protection to the shareholder: particularly the right to vote as a class in certain situations, the right to dissent and receive in cash a judicially determined "fair market value" in certain instances, and the requirement in many state statutes that more than a majority vote is needed to approve certain proposals. The provision in the Rhode Island statute referred to in n.2 requiring unanimous consent for a certain type of amendment is atypical. See MBCA §§ 10.03, 10.04, 13.02. In addition to these statutory protections, minority shareholders may rely on the fiduciary duties of controlling shareholders and directors in connection with the treatment of minority interests.

(2) In considering fundamental or organic changes, it is important to recognize that there is usually more than one way to skin a cat. Essentially the same final result may often be obtained through several different routes. These routes may involve transactions specifically authorized by statute (e.g., amendments to articles of incorporation, mergers, or share exchanges), nonstatutory transactions (e.g., the purchase of shares or assets in exchange for stock), or a combination of statutory and nonstatutory transactions. The route that is followed is important because some of the fundamental protections of minority interests described in the preceding paragraph—particularly class voting by senior securities and appraisal rights—are literally available only in connection with certain types of statutory transactions. Fiduciary duties of controlling shareholders and directors, of course, are more generally applicable to all transactions.

(3) It is also important to recognize that equality of treatment is often not guaranteed in statutory transactions. See Weinberger v. UOP, Inc., supra at 778. Under most merger statutes, for example, some shareholders in a corporation may be compelled to accept cash while other shareholders receive stock in the continuing venture. See, e.g., MBCA §§ 11.01(b)(3), 11.04(b)(2).

FARRIS v. GLEN ALDEN CORP.

Supreme Court of Pennsylvania, 1958.
393 Pa. 427, 143 A.2d 25.

COHEN, JUSTICE.

We are required to determine on this appeal whether, as a result of a "Reorganization Agreement" executed by the officers of Glen Alden Corporation and List Industries Corporation, and approved by the shareholders of the former company, the rights and remedies of a dissenting shareholder accrue to the plaintiff.

Glen Alden is a Pennsylvania corporation engaged principally in the mining of anthracite coal and lately in the manufacture of air conditioning units and fire-fighting equipment. In recent years the company's operating revenue has declined substantially, and in fact, its coal operations have resulted in tax loss carryovers of approximately $14,000,000. In October 1957, List, a Delaware holding company owning interests in motion picture theaters, textile companies and real estate, and to a lesser extent, in oil and gas operations, warehouses and aluminum piston manufacturing, purchased through a wholly owned subsidiary 38.5% of Glen Alden's outstanding stock.[7] This acquisition enabled List to place three of its directors on the Glen Alden board.

On March 20, 1958, the two corporations entered into a "reorganization agreement," subject to stockholder approval, which contemplated the following actions:

> 1. Glen Alden is to acquire all of the assets of List, excepting a small amount of cash reserved for the payment of List's expenses in connection with the transaction. These assets include over $8,000,000 in cash held chiefly in the treasuries of List's wholly owned subsidiaries.

> 2. In consideration of the transfer, Glen Alden is to issue 3,621,703 shares of stock to List. List in turn is to distribute the stock to its

---

7. [By the Court] Of the purchase price of $8,719,109, $5,000,000 was borrowed.

shareholders at a ratio of five shares of Glen Alden stock for each six shares of List stock. In order to accomplish the necessary distribution, Glen Alden is to increase the authorized number of its shares of capital stock from 2,500,000 shares to 7,500,000 shares without according preemptive rights to the present shareholders upon the issuance of any such shares.

3. Further, Glen Alden is to assume all of List's liabilities including a $5,000,000 note incurred by List in order to purchase Glen Alden stock in 1957, outstanding stock options, incentive stock options plans, and pension obligations.

4. Glen Alden is to change its corporate name from Glen Alden Corporation to List Alden Corporation.

5. The present directors of both corporations are to become directors of List Alden.

6. List is to be dissolved and List Alden is to then carry on the operations of both former corporations.

Two days after the agreement was executed notice of the annual meeting of Glen Alden to be held on April 11, 1958, was mailed to the shareholders together with a proxy statement analyzing the reorganization agreement and recommending its approval as well as approval of certain amendments to Glen Alden's articles of incorporation and bylaws necessary to implement the agreement. At this meeting the holders of a majority of the outstanding shares, (not including those owned by List), voted in favor of a resolution approving the reorganization agreement.

On the day of the shareholders' meeting, plaintiff, a shareholder of Glen Alden, filed a complaint in equity against the corporation and its officers seeking to enjoin them temporarily until final hearing, and perpetually thereafter, from executing and carrying out the agreement.

The gravamen of the complaint was that the notice of the annual shareholders' meeting did not conform to the requirements of the Business Corporation Law, in three respects: (1) It did not give notice to the shareholders that the true intent and purpose of the meeting was to effect a merger or consolidation of Glen Alden and List; (2) It failed to give notice to the shareholders of their right to dissent to the plan of merger or consolidation and claim fair value for their shares, and (3) it did not contain copies of the text of certain sections of the Business Corporation Law as required.[8]

By reason of these omissions, plaintiff contended that the approval of the reorganization agreement by the shareholders at the annual meeting was invalid and unless the carrying out of the plan were enjoined, he would suffer irreparable loss by being deprived of substantial property rights.[9]

---

8. [By the Court] The proxy statement included the following declaration:

    Appraisal Rights.

    In the opinion of counsel, the shareholders of neither Glen Alden nor List Industries will have any rights of appraisal or similar rights of dissenters with respect to any mat-

ter to be acted upon at their respective meetings.

9. [By the Court] The complaint also set forth that the exchange of shares of Glen Alden's stock for those of List would constitute a violation of the preemptive rights of Glen Alden shareholders as established by the law of Pennsylvania at the time of Glen Alden's incor-

The defendants answered admitting the material allegations of fact in the complaint but denying that they gave rise to a cause of action because the transaction complained of was a purchase of corporate assets as to which shareholders had no rights of dissent or appraisal. For these reasons the defendants then moved for judgment on the pleadings.[10]

The court below concluded that the reorganization agreement entered into between the two corporations was a plan for a *de facto* merger, and that therefore the failure of the notice of the annual meeting to conform to the pertinent requirements of the merger provisions of the Business Corporation Law rendered the notice defective and all proceedings in furtherance of the agreement void. Wherefore, the court entered a final decree denying defendants' motion for judgment on the pleadings, entering judgment upon plaintiff's complaint and granting the injunctive relief therein sought. This appeal followed.

When use of the corporate form of business organization first became widespread, it was relatively easy for courts to define a "merger" or a "sale of assets" and to label a particular transaction as one or the other. But prompted by the desire to avoid the impact of adverse, and to obtain the benefits of favorable, government regulations, particularly federal tax laws, new accounting and legal techniques were developed by lawyers and accountants which interwove the elements characteristic of each, thereby creating hybrid forms of corporate amalgamation. Thus, it is no longer helpful to consider an individual transaction in the abstract and solely by reference to the various elements therein determine whether it is a "merger" or a "sale". Instead, to determine properly the nature of a corporate transaction, we must refer not only to all the provisions of the agreement, but also to the consequences of the transaction and to the purposes of the provisions of the corporation law said to be applicable. We shall apply this principle to the instant case.

Section 908 subd. A of the Pennsylvania Business Corporation Law provides: "If any shareholder of a domestic corporation which becomes a party to a plan of merger or consolidation shall object to such plan of merger or consolidation * * * such shareholder shall be entitled to * * * [the fair value of his shares upon surrender of the share certificate or certificates representing his shares]." 15 P.S. § 2852–908, subd. A.[11]

This provision had its origin in the early decision of this Court in Lauman v. Lebanon Valley R.R. Co., 1858, 30 Pa. 42. There a shareholder who objected to the consolidation of his company with another was held to have a right in

poration in 1917. The defendants answered that under both statute and prior common law no preemptive rights existed with respect to stock issued in exchange for property.

10. [By the Court] Counsel for the defendants concedes that if the corporation is required to pay the dissenting shareholders the appraised fair value of their shares, the resultant drain of cash would prevent Glen Alden from carrying out the agreement. On the other hand, plaintiff contends that if the shareholders had been told of their rights as dissenters, rather than specifically advised that they had no such rights, the resolution approving the

reorganization agreement would have been defeated.

11. [By the Court] Furthermore, section 902, subd. B provides that notice of the proposed merger and of the right to dissent thereto must be given the shareholders. "There shall be included in, or enclosed with * * * notice [of meeting of shareholders to vote on plan of merger] a copy or a summary of the plan of merger or plan of consolidation, as the case may be, and * * * a copy of subsection A of section 908 and of subsections B, C and D of section 515 of this act."

the absence of statute to treat the consolidation as a dissolution of his company and to receive the value of his shares upon their surrender.

The rationale of the Lauman case, and of the present section of the Business Corporation Law based thereon, is that when a corporation combines with another so as to lose its essential nature and alter the original fundamental relationships of the shareholders among themselves and to the corporation, a shareholder who does not wish to continue his membership therein may treat his membership in the original corporation as terminated and have the value of his shares paid to him.

Does the combination outlined in the present "reorganization" agreement so fundamentally change the corporate character of Glen Alden and the interest of the plaintiff as a shareholder therein, that to refuse him the rights and remedies of a dissenting shareholder would in reality force him to give up his stock in one corporation and against his will accept shares in another? If so, the combination is a merger within the meaning of section 908, subd. A of the corporation law.

If the reorganization agreement were consummated plaintiff would find that the "List Alden" resulting from the amalgamation would be quite a different corporation than the "Glen Alden" in which he is now a shareholder. Instead of continuing primarily as a coal mining company, Glen Alden would be transformed, after amendment of its articles of incorporation, into a diversified holding company whose interests would range from motion picture theaters to textile companies. Plaintiff would find himself a member of a company with assets of $169,000,000 and a long-term debt of $38,000,000 in lieu of a company one-half that size and with but one-seventh the long-term debt.

While the administration of the operations and properties of Glen Alden as well as List would be in the hands of management common to both companies, since all executives of List would be retained in List Alden, the control of Glen Alden would pass to the directors of List; for List would hold eleven of the seventeen directorships on the new board of directors.

As an aftermath of the transaction plaintiff's proportionate interest in Glen Alden would have been reduced to only two-fifths of what it presently is because of the issuance of an additional 3,621,703 shares to List which would not be subject to pre-emptive rights. In fact, ownership of Glen Alden would pass to the stockholders of List who would hold 76.5% of the outstanding shares as compared with but 23.5% retained by the present Glen Alden shareholders.

Perhaps the most important consequence to the plaintiff, if he were denied the right to have his shares redeemed at their fair value, would be the serious financial loss suffered upon consummation of the agreement. While the present book value of his stock is $38 a share after combination it would be worth only $21 a share. In contrast, the shareholders of List who presently hold stock with a total book value of $33,000,000 or $7.50 a share, would receive stock with a book value of $76,000,000 or $21 a share.

Under these circumstances it may well be said that if the proposed combination is allowed to take place without right of dissent, plaintiff would have his stock in Glen Alden taken away from him and the stock of a new company thrust upon him in its place. He would be projected against his will into a new enterprise under terms not of his own choosing. It was to protect dissident shareholders against just such a result that this Court one hundred years ago in the Lauman case, and the legislature thereafter in section 908, subd. A, granted the right of dissent. And it is to accord that protection to the plaintiff that we conclude that the combination proposed in the case at hand is a merger within the intendment of section 908, subd. A.

Nevertheless, defendants contend that the 1957 amendments to sections 311 and 908 of the corporation law preclude us from reaching this result and require the entry of judgment in their favor. Subsection F of section 311 dealing with the voluntary transfer of corporate assets provides: "The shareholders of a business corporation which acquires by sale, lease or exchange all or substantially all of the property of another corporation by the issuance of stock, securities or otherwise shall not be entitled to the rights and remedies of dissenting shareholders * * *."

And the amendment to section 908 reads as follows: "The right of dissenting shareholders * * * shall not apply to the purchase by a corporation of assets whether or not the consideration therefor be money or property, real or personal, including shares or bonds or other evidences of indebtedness of such corporation. The shareholders of such corporation shall have no right to dissent from any such purchase."

Defendants view these amendments as abridging the right of shareholders to dissent to a transaction between two corporations which involves a transfer of assets for a consideration even though the transfer has all the legal incidents of a merger. They claim that only if the merger is accomplished in accordance with the prescribed statutory procedure does the right of dissent accrue. In support of this position they cite to us the comment on the amendments by the Committee on Corporation Law of the Pennsylvania Bar Association, the committee which originally drafted these provisions. The comment states that the provisions were intended to overrule cases which granted shareholders the right to dissent to a sale of assets when accompanied by the legal incidents of a merger.[12] Whatever may have been the intent of the *committee,* there is no evidence to indicate that the *legislature* intended the 1957 amendments to have the effect contended for. But furthermore, the language of these two provisions does not support the opinion of the committee and is inapt to achieve any such purpose. The amendments of 1957 do not provide that a transaction between two corporations which has the effect of a

---

12. [By the Court] "The amendment to Section 311 expressly provides that a sale, lease or exchange of substantially all corporate assets in connection with its liquidation or dissolution is subject to the provisions of Article XI of the Act, and that no consent or authorization of shareholders other than what is required by Article XI is necessary. The recent decision in Marks v. Autocar Co., D.C.E.D.Pa., [153 F.Supp. 768] is to the contrary. This amendment, together with the proposed amendment to Section 1104 expressly permitting the directors in liquidating the corporation to sell only such assets as may be required to pay its debts and distribute any assets remaining among shareholders (Section 1108, [subd.] B now so provides in the case of receivers) have the effect of overruling Marks v. Autocar Co., * * * which permits a shareholder dissenting from such a sale to obtain the fair value of his shares. The Marks case relies substantially on Bloch v. Baldwin Locomotive Works, 75 [Pa.] Dist. & Co. R. 24, also believed to be an undesirable decision. That case permitted a holder of stock in a corporation which *purchased* for stock all the assets of another corporation to obtain the fair value of his shares. That case is also in effect overruled by the new Sections 311 [subd.] F and 908 [subd.] C." 61 Ann.Rep.Pa.Bar Ass'n, 277, 284 (1957).

merger but which includes a transfer of assets for consideration is to be exempt from the protective provisions of section 908, subd. A and 515. They provide only that the shareholders of a corporation which acquires the property or purchases the assets of another corporation, *without more,* are not entitled to the right to dissent from the transaction. So, as in the present case, when as part of a transaction between two corporations, one corporation dissolves, its liabilities are assumed by the survivor, its executives and directors take over the management and control of the survivor, and, as consideration for the transfer, its stockholders acquire a majority of the shares of stock of the survivor, then the transaction is no longer simply a purchase of assets or acquisition of property to which sections 311, subd. F and 908, subd. C apply, but a merger governed by section 908, subd. A of the corporation law. To divest shareholders of their right of dissent under such circumstances would require express language which is absent from the 1957 amendments.

Even were we to assume that the combination provided for in the reorganization agreement is a "sale of assets" to which section 908, subd. A does not apply, it would avail the defendants nothing; we will not blind our eyes to the realities of the transaction. Despite the designation of the parties and the form employed, Glen Alden does not in fact acquire List, rather, List acquires Glen Alden, and under section 311, subd. D[13] the right of dissent would remain with the shareholders of Glen Alden.

We hold that the combination contemplated by the reorganization agreement, although consummated by contract rather than in accordance with the statutory procedure, is a merger within the protective purview of sections 908, subd. A and 515 of the corporation law. The shareholders of Glen Alden should have been notified accordingly and advised of their statutory rights of dissent and appraisal. The failure of the corporate officers to take these steps renders the stockholder approval of the agreement at the 1958 shareholders' meeting invalid. The lower court did not err in enjoining the officers and directors of Glen Alden from carrying out this agreement.[14]

Decree affirmed at appellants' cost.

Notes

(1) Is the holding of the principal case that shareholder appraisal rights must be recognized whenever it is possible to structure a transaction as a statutory merger?

(2) Compare Hariton v. Arco Elec., Inc., 41 Del.Ch. 74, 188 A.2d 123 (1963), where the Court upheld a plan of reorganization involving a two-step transaction:

13. [By the Court] "If any shareholder of a business corporation which sells, leases or exchanges all or substantially all of its property and assets otherwise than (1) in the usual and regular course of its business, (2) for the purpose of relocating its business, or (3) in connection with its dissolution and liquidation, shall object to such sale, lease or exchange and comply with the provisions of section 515 of this act, such shareholder shall be entitled to the rights and remedies of dissenting shareholders as therein provided."

14. [By the Court] Because of our disposition of this appeal, it is unnecessary for us to consider whether the plaintiff had any preemptive rights in the proposed issuance of newly authorized shares as payment for the transfer of assets from List, or whether amended sections 908 subd. C and 311 subd. F of the corporation law may constitutionally be applied to the present transaction to divest the plaintiff of his dissenter's rights.

(a) First, Corporation A sells its assets to Corporation B (a larger corporation) in exchange for common stock of Corporation B; and

(b) Second, Corporation A dissolves, distributing the common stock of Corporation B to its shareholders.

The Court refused to apply the *de facto* merger doctrine because it would "create uncertainty in the law and invite litigation." 41 Del.Ch. at 77, 188 A.2d at 125. The Court also stated that "the framers of a reorganization plan may resort to either type of corporate mechanics to achieve the desired end." 41 Del.Ch. at 76, 188 A.2d at 125. In commenting approvingly on this decision, Professor Folk has stated that the decision "displays, consciously or unconsciously, a profound distrust of appraisal rights." He continues:

> The basic premise implicitly adopted in *Hariton* may perhaps be stated more affirmatively. One does not invest in a unique corporate entity or even a particular business operation, but rather in a continuous course of business which changes over a long period of time. Certainly the best investments are growth investments—investments in enterprises which change with time, technology, business opportunities, and altered demand; and the worst investments are those which diminish in value because the type of business has lost importance and the corporation has been unable to adapt to the changed conditions. Although a shareholder's enthusiasm dwindles when an enterprise changes internally for the worst, no one suggests that he should have an option to compel the return of his investment. Viewed this way, the fact that the change—for better or for worse—comes through marriage, whether by merger or assets sale, seems purely incidental. The fact that the corporate entity in which one invested disappears as a result of a merger or of a sale of assets coupled with dissolution is also beside the point. One's investment may gain immortality when it takes a new form, i.e., a share in a successor enterprise. The fact is that, closely held corporations aside, an investment in a corporation is really an investment in the judgment, business acumen, integrity, and vigor of management, whose personnel and policy change over time. Management ability may have its finest hour in negotiating and implementing arrangements which conceptually change the shareholder's investment and his original relationship to the corporation and its shareholders, but which actually improve his investment.

> This is not meant to be a paean in praise of management. It does not mean that management (with or without a majority or more of the shareholders) should be omnipotent or that every distinctive Delaware doctrine, e.g., the narrow scope of fraud, the light treatment of preferred stock rights, is sound. It does seem, however, that an unrealistic importance has been attached to the investor's interest in changes in corporate form. Certainly, "fundamental corporate change" is too undiscriminating a basis on which to adopt a *de facto* merger concept, and in so far as *Hariton* rejects such a basis, the decision seems entirely sound.

Ernest L. Folk III, De Facto Mergers in Delaware: *Hariton v. Arco Electronics, Inc.*, 49 Va.L.Rev. 1261, 1278, 1280–81 (1963). Do you agree with this point of view?

(3) There are relatively few recent cases in which the de facto merger doctrine has been invoked in an effort to obtain the procedural protections that would be available if the transaction were cast as a merger. One recent attempt is Irving Bank Corp. v. Bank of New York Co., Inc., 140 Misc.2d 363, 530 N.Y.S.2d 757 (Sup.1988), where the Irving Bank unsuccessfully argued that Bank of New

York's takeover attempt (involving open market purchases, a cash tender offer, and a cash-out merger) constituted a de facto merger that required the affirmative vote of two-thirds of Bank of New York's shareholders.

(4) Presumably this decline of cases involving the de facto merger doctrine is attributable in part to the systemization of the procedures relating to the approval of mergers and economically equivalent transactions. Under the MBCA, for example, there is no immediate procedural advantage in structuring an acquisition in the form of a sale of assets for stock followed by the distribution of the stock to shareholders of the selling corporation and dissolution of that corporation. The shareholders of the selling corporation have the right to vote on the sale of assets, and shareholders opposing that transaction have the right of dissent and appraisal. However, not all states follow this pattern. Delaware and a handful of other states require that a shareholder vote on sales of substantially all the assets of a corporation but do not grant dissenters' rights to shareholders voting against a sale of assets. In addition, other procedural rights in some states may be involved in the characterization of the procedure as a "merger" or as something else. It is therefore likely that cases involving the de facto merger doctrine will arise from time to time even though such attempts to restructure transactions should lose if the reasoning of *Hariton* is accepted.

(5) A few states have statutes that attempt to negate the de facto merger doctrine. See, for example, Tex.Bus.Corp.Act Ann. art. 5.10B (Vernon Supp. 1997).

B. A disposition of any, all, or substantially all, of the property and assets of a corporation, whether or not it requires the special authorization of the shareholders of the corporation, affected under Section A of this article or under Article 5.09 of this Act or otherwise:

(1) is not considered to be a merger or conversion pursuant to this Act or otherwise; and

(2) except as otherwise expressly provided by another statute, does not make the acquiring corporation, foreign corporation, or other entity responsible or liable for any liability or obligation of the selling corporation that the acquiring corporation, foreign corporation, or other entity did not expressly assume.

The original Bar Committee Comment to this Section states that its purpose "is to preclude the application of the doctrine of *de facto* merger in any sale, lease, exchange or other disposition of all or substantially all the property and assets of a corporation requiring authorization [of shareholders] * * *."

(6) One class of cases in which the de facto merger doctrine regularly continues to be discussed (and occasionally applied) involves successor liability. The phrase "de facto merger" appears in more than 200 cases decided since 1989, the great bulk of which involve successor liability. The paradigm situation— though by no means the only one—is the products liability case, where a plaintiff is injured by the use of an allegedly defective product; investigation reveals that the manufacturer of the product voluntarily dissolved more than two years earlier following a sale of all of its assets to a purchaser which is a solvent corporation that is continuing the business of the manufacturer, often manufacturing the same product under the same brand name, using the same plant and many of the same personnel. The asset acquisition agreement contains clauses that unambiguously state that the purchaser only acquired assets and did not assume any liabilities of the seller except those specifically enumerated in the agreement. Subsequently arising products liability claims not only are not enumerated, but

are also specifically disclaimed as being among the classes of liabilities *not* being assumed. The sales proceeds have long since been distributed by the dissolved corporation to its shareholders. While a claim against the shareholders of the dissolved corporation to recover the distributions that were made without making any allowance or provision for subsequently arising tort claims may be possible, it is much more attractive to sue the solvent purchaser on a theory of de facto merger or a related doctrine, such as "mere continuation of enterprise" or "product line." In part motivated by sympathy for the seriously injured plaintiff who apparently has no recourse, a number of decisions have permitted recovery on a theory that views the sale of assets/dissolution as a de facto merger of the acquired corporation into the acquirer (which would, of course, result in the acquiring corporation being liable for all the obligations of the acquired corporation). See e.g., Cargill, Inc. v. Beaver Coal & Oil Co., 424 Mass. 356, 676 N.E.2d 815 (1997); Corbin v. Farmex, Inc., 227 Ga.App. 620, 490 S.E.2d 395 (1997); Harashe v. Flintkote Co., 848 S.W.2d 506 (Mo.App.1993); Simmers v. American Cyanamid Corp., 394 Pa.Super. 464, 576 A.2d 376 (1990); Cab–Tek, Inc. v. E.B.M., Inc., 153 Vt. 432, 571 A.2d 671 (1990); Dayton v. Peck, Stow and Wilcox Co. (Pexto), 739 F.2d 690 (1st Cir.1984); Grant–Howard Assoc. v. General Housewares Corp., 115 Misc.2d 704, 454 N.Y.S.2d 521 (Sup.1982); Ray v. Alad Corp., 19 Cal.3d 22, 136 Cal.Rptr. 574, 560 P.2d 3 (1977); Turner v. Bituminous Cas. Co., 397 Mich. 406, 244 N.W.2d 873 (1976). Indeed, cases holding the successor liable in such circumstances are so common that in many jurisdictions attorneys refuse to express a firm opinion as to whether the asset purchaser will in fact be free of product liability and similar claims despite clear contractual language to that effect. These cases have in turn shaped post-acquisition procedures, as lawyers recommend to purchasers that they take steps to avoid the appearance of merely continuing the old enterprise producing the same product under the same name at the same location with the same personnel. Plants might be closed down and production moved elsewhere, the product may be redesigned or renamed, production may be discontinued for a year or more, and so forth. Whether as a result of this strategy or for other reasons, many cases refuse to impose liability on the purchaser, thus giving effect to the contractual language that protects the defendants. See, e.g., Johnston v. Amsted Indus., Inc., 830 P.2d 1141, 1146 (Colo.App. 1992) (arguments for successor liability have been "rejected by an overwhelming majority" of courts); Fox v. Sunmaster Prod., Inc., 63 Wash.App. 561, 821 P.2d 502 (1991); Kaleta v. Whittaker Corp., 221 Ill.App.3d 705, 164 Ill.Dec. 651, 583 N.E.2d 567 (1991); Weaver v. Nash Int'l, Inc., 730 F.2d 547 (8th Cir.1984). For a case applying the de facto merger doctrine in a situation unrelated to products liability claims, see Cox v. Public Serv. Comm'n, 188 W.Va. 736, 426 S.E.2d 528 (1992)(lease agreement between certified carriers constituted de facto merger and therefore violated statute prohibiting mergers of such carriers without the consent of the Commission).

(7) MBCA § 14.07 attempts to address the general problem of successor liability by broadening the right to proceed against the shareholders of the disappearing corporation receiving liquidating distributions rather than addressing the issue of successor liability directly. The Official Comment to § 14.07 states that "[t]he solution adopted in section 14.07 is to continue the liability of a dissolved corporation for subsequent claims for a period of five years after it publishes notice of dissolution. It is recognized that a five year cut-off is itself arbitrary, but it is believed that the great bulk of post dissolution claims will arise during this period. This provision is therefore believed to be a reasonable compromise between the competing considerations of providing a remedy to injured

plaintiffs and providing a period of repose after which dissolved corporations may distribute remaining assets free of all claims and shareholders may receive them secure in the knowledge that they may not be reclaimed." A more ambitious effort appears in Del. Gen. Corp. Law §§ 280–282, as amended in 1987. The first case arising under these sections, In re RegO Co., 623 A.2d 92 (Del.Ch.1992), describes the basic structure of these sections as follows:

> This is an action under recently enacted provisions of the Delaware General Corporation Law creating a procedure by which a dissolved Delaware corporation may achieve, after a judicial proceeding, court approval of a plan of security for corporate claimants. The effects of such approval include (1) the preclusion of liability on the part of the directors of the dissolved corporation to claimants of the dissolved corporation for matters arising out of the making of liquidation distributions, (2) the limitation of potential liability of stockholders to the lesser of a *pro rata* share of each claim against the corporation, or the amount distributed in dissolution, and (3) the establishment of a limitations period for actions against stockholders on claims against the corporation.

> These statutory provisions are innovative. They provide a judicial mechanism designed to afford fair treatment to foreseeable future, yet unknown claimants of a dissolved corporation, while providing corporate directors with a mechanism that will both permit distributions on corporate dissolution, and avoid risk that a future corporate claimant will, at some future time, be able to establish that such distribution was in violation of any duty owed to the corporation's creditors on dissolution.

Appendix One

AN INTRODUCTION TO AGENCY PRINCIPLES

ROBERT W. HAMILTON, BUSINESS ORGANIZATIONS:
UNINCORPORATED BUSINESSES AND CLOSELY
HELD CORPORATIONS (1997)

Chapter 2.[1]

§ 2.1 Introduction

Basic agency and employment relationships underlay virtually all commercial dealings in the modern world. Agency relationships by and large do not themselves create new business forms; rather they are the glue that holds * * * businesses together. As such, they define the rights and responsibilities of individuals who work for or on behalf of businesses. It is surprising that this essential subject today receives relatively little attention, since modern business is conducted almost entirely by agents or employees. To take an obvious example, a corporation, an artificial legal construct that has no physical being of its own, can act only through agents for everything it does. Whenever one person performs services for, or acts on behalf of, someone else, the principles of agency define the relationships and the responsibilities of both participants and of persons who deal with them. The most common agency relationship is the employment relationship,[2] but agency law is applicable in many other situations as well.

Thirty years ago, virtually every law school in the country required a course in agency. * * * Today, agency as a separate course has disappeared from virtually all law school curricula * * * (and) there is usually no systematic treatment of the subject. * * *

Because of the lack of systematic exposure to agency law, it is not uncommon for a newly minted lawyer to be unable to respond to relatively simple agency questions: for example, an employee acting within the scope of her employment violates specific instructions of her employer, leading to an injury to a third person. Is the employer liable? If the employer has a liability

---

1. Reprinted with permission of Aspen Law and Business.

2. [By the Author] Many aspects of employment law are of course governed by statutes or common law principles independent of agency law. The employment at will doctrine is a common law doctrine that addresses a most basic characteristic of the employment relationship. Statutes of long standing govern such matters as minimum wages, overtime pay, pay periods, and the like. Other statutes govern matters relating to the workplace, e.g., safety, sexual harassment, and a variety of other subjects.

insurance policy that expressly excludes coverage for "intentional torts," and the act of the employee constitutes an intentional tort, (e.g., she falsely imprisons a customer on the belief he is a shoplifter), is the intention of the employee imputed to the employer so that the event is not covered by the employer's insurance? Answers to these questions are not intuitively obvious.[3] * * * Agency law readily lends itself to illustration by example.

§ 2.2 Basic Concepts

The principal source of agency law today is probably the Restatement of Agency, Second, published in 1957. (A new edition, with Professor Deborah DeMott as reporter, is being prepared.) The Restatement is useful particularly because it provides a comprehensive set of definitions for the subject. It defines *agency* as the "fiduciary relation which results from the manifestation of consent by one person to another that the other shall act on his behalf and subject to his control, and consent by the other so to act."[4] The person who is acting for another is the *agent*; the person for whom the agent is acting is the *principal*.

An agency relationship is based on conduct by the principal and agent, the principal manifesting that he is willing to have another act for him and the agent manifesting a willingness to act. The relationship may be contractual, but it need not be. Persons acting as agents without compensation are still agents.[5] Thus, agency is basically a consensual relationship in which one person agrees to act for the benefit of another.

Artificial entities such as corporations, trusts, partnerships, or limited liability companies may act as principals or as agents. The relationships are not limited to natural persons. An artificial entity can in turn act only through agents. Thus, the law of agency is involved whenever a corporation acts, whether it be writing a check, selling a product, or entering into a multi-billion dollar merger. Partnerships similarly involve the law of agency, with each partner being an agent for the partnership.

§ 2.3 Fiduciary Duties

An agency relationship has the important characteristic of being a *fiduciary* relationship. The agent is a fiduciary with respect to matters within the scope of his agency.[6] Basically, this means that the agent is accountable to the principal for any profits arising out of the transactions he is to conduct on the principal's behalf[7] and that he breaches his duty to the principal if he acts either to benefit himself or someone else other than the principal.[8] This *fiduciary duty* also prevents an agent either from acting adversely to the interest of the principal[9] or assisting an adverse party to the principal in connection with the agency.[10] An agent also may not compete with his

---

3. [By the Author] In case you are interested, the answer to the first question is clearly yes. See Restatement, (Second) of Agency § 219(1) (1957). The answer to the second question is also yes, at least if the action was within the scope of employment and the employee was attempting to benefit the employer. See id. § 272.

4. [By the Author] Id. § 1.

5. [By the Author] These agents may be called "unpaid" or "gratuitous" agents.

6. Id. § 13.

7. [By the Author] Id. § 388.

8. [By the Author] Id. § 387.

9. [By the Author] Id. § 389.

10. [By the Author] Id. § 391.

principal concerning the subject matter of the agency.[11] In addition, the agent must act to preserve and protect property entrusted to his care by the principal, and is liable for its loss if he disposes of the property without authority to do so, or it is lost or destroyed because of his neglect or because he intermingles it with his own property.[12] The agent may be required to account for his actions or for property of the principal entrusted to him.

The scope of the agency is usually determined by contract between the principal and agent or by the nature of the instructions given by the principal to the agent. The scope of the agent's fiduciary duty may be shaped by these terms, but the fiduciary obligation exists even though the contract is silent as to the duties of the agent or purports to abolish this duty.

When parties are dealing at arms-length, one party usually does not have a duty to volunteer information to the other. This is not true, however, if one owes the other a fiduciary duty.

Example: *M* is looking for a site for his plant. He learns that *O* has a site for sale. The asking price is $250,000. *M* and *O* negotiate and agree upon a price of $247,500. In this negotiation, *O* does not disclose that he purchased the site for $150,000 a few days before, information that would have been relevant to *M*'s decision to agree to the $247,500 price. *O*'s failure to disclose this information is not a breach of duty and M may not rescind the transaction.

Example: *P* retains *A* to purchase a suitable manufacturing site for him. *A* owns a suitable site which he offers to *P* for $250,000, a fair price. *A* tells *P* all relevant facts except that a short time previously he purchased the site for $150,000. *A* has breached his fiduciary duty and the transaction may be rescinded by *P*.[13]

§ 2.4   Other Duties of the Agent

In addition to the broad fiduciary duty, an agent must act with reasonable care in carrying out the agency and must meet at least the standard of competence and skill in the locality for work of the character he is obligated to perform. An unpaid agent may have a lesser duty than one who is paid.

Example: *X*, a person in the community who does odd jobs for homeowners, agrees to construct a chimney for *Y*, a homeowner. *X* has not previously had experience building chimneys on his own, though he has assisted other masons in building chimneys. He places a row of bricks incorrectly in the chimney with the result that the chimney does not draw properly. *X* has breached his duty to *Y*.

Presumably, if *Y* knows that *X* has had no experience building chimneys, a different result would be reached. In that situation, *Y* reasonably can expect only that *X* will do the best he can.

§ 2.5   Duties of the Principal to the Agent

The principal owes duties to the agent. These duties are different from the agent's duties since the basic fiduciary duty only runs from the agent to the principal. A principal must perform his commitments to the agent, act in

---

11. [By the Author] Id. § 393.
12. [By the Author] Id. §§ 402–404A.

13. [By the Author] Id. § 390, illustration 2.

good faith, cooperate with the agent, and not interfere with or make more difficult the agent's performance of his duties. Implicit in the arrangement may be an obligation by the principal to give the agent work, an opportunity to earn a reasonable compensation, or an opportunity to find additional work. * * *

In addition, if the agent incurs expenses or spends his own funds on behalf of the principal, the principal may have a duty to repay or indemnify the agent.[14]

§ 2.6 The Right to Control: Independent Contractors and Servants

In general terms, the principal has the right to control the conduct of the agent with respect to matters entrusted to him.[15] The principal can determine what the ultimate goal is, and the agent must strive to meet that goal. The degree of control that the principal has over the acts of the agent, may vary widely within the agency relationship. In this respect, the Restatement distinguishes between a master/servant relationship and an independent contractor relationship.[16] A master is a principal who "employs an agent to perform service in his affairs *and who controls or has the right to control the physical conduct of the other* in the performance of the service." (Emphasis added.) A servant is an agent so employed by a master. In a way, the use of the words master and servant for this relationship is unfortunate, because those words may imply servility, household service, or manual labor. Under these definitions, most employment relationships are technically master/servant relationships.

Example: General Motors Corporation employs an individual to serve as head designer of a new automobile. His salary is $300,000 per year. The designer is a "servant" in the Restatement terminology and General Motors is his "master."[17]

An *independent contractor* is a "person who contracts with another to do something for him but who is not controlled by the other nor subject to the other's right to control with respect to his physical conduct in the performance of the undertaking."[18] An independent contractor may or may not be agent.

Example: An attorney agrees to represent hundreds of persons on a contingency basis seeking to recover damages for injuries arising from exposure to asbestos. The attorney is an independent contractor, but not an agent.[19]

---

14. [By the Author] Id. §§ 432–469.

15. [By the Author] Id. § 12.

16. [By the Author] Id. § 2.

17. [By the Author] Do you have any doubt about the correctness of this conclusion? If you do, consider this possible scenario: The chief executive officer of General Motors comes to the designer and says, "John, the board of directors liked your sketches for the new convertible. They feel, however, that it looks a little boxy and they think the headlights are too conspicuous. Please streamline it a little more and move the headlights into the front fenders." What should the head designer do? He makes the changes that are requested, thereby indicating clearly that he is a servant.

18. [By the Author] Id. § 2(3).

19. [By the Author] Do you agree that the attorney is not an agent in this situation? Does he "consent to act subject to the control of" the client? See § 2.2. The attorney may be an agent in other roles, e.g., when negotiating a contract on behalf of his client.

Example: A builder enters into a contract with the owner of a lot to build a house on the lot in accordance with certain plans and specifications prepared by an architect. The builder is an independent contractor, but he is not an agent. He is employed merely to accomplish a specific result and is not otherwise subject to the owner's control.

Example: A broker enters into a contract to sell goods for a manufacturer. His arrangement involves the receipt of a salary plus a commission on each sale, but the broker has discretion as to how to conduct his business. He determines which cities to visit and who to contact. He uses his own automobile to visit prospects. The broker is an agent, but is not a servant. Rather, he is an independent contractor.

Example: A customer of a brokerage firm directs the firm to sell on the New York Stock Exchange at the best price obtainable 100 shares of XYZ Stock owned by the customer. The brokerage firm, when executing this instruction, is both an agent and an independent contractor.

Example: Acme Superstores, a chain of grocery stores, enters into a contract with Gene's Pheasant Farm, Inc., by which Gene's promises to supply Acme with killed and dressed pheasants for sale by Acme. The contract gives Acme the power to direct Gene's operations to assure a continuing supply of fresh, high-quality pheasants. Acme is the principal and Gene's is an agent. Gene's may also be a servant if the degree of control maintained by Acme means that Acme may "control the physical conduct of" Gene's.

The distinction between an independent contractor who is an agent and one who is not depends on the degree and character of control exercised over the work being done by the independent contractor. In some instances, there may be doubt as to whether an independent contractor is also an agent. Similarly, uncertainty may sometimes exist as to whether an agent is also a servant. The Restatement of Agency contains a somewhat dated provision that gives guidelines as to the latter issue.[20]

§ 2.7 The Responsibility of a Principal for his Agent's Torts

The classification of an agent as a servant or as an independent contractor is important primarily because different rules apply with respect to the liability of the principal for physical harm caused by the agent's conduct. A master is liable for torts committed by a servant within the scope of his

---

20. [By the Editor] In determining whether one acting for another is a servant or an independent contractor, the following matters of fact, among others, are considered:

(a) the extent of control which, by the agreement, the master may exercise over the details of the work;

(b) whether or not the one employed is engaged in a distinct occupation or business;

(c) the kind of occupation, with reference to whether, in the locality, the work is usually done under the direction of the employer or by a specialist without supervision.

(d) the skill required in the particular occupation;

(e) whether the employer or the workman supplies the instrumentalities, tools, and the place of work for the person doing the work;

(f) the length of time for which the person is employed;

(g) the method of payment, whether by the time or by the job;

(h) whether or not the work is a part of the regular business of the employer;

(i) whether or not the parties believe they are creating the relation of master and servant; and

(j) whether the principal is or is not in business.

employment, while a principal is not liable for torts committed by an independent contractor in connection with his work.

Example: *P*, the owner of a successful retail operation with two stores, hires *D* to drive her delivery truck and deliver goods to her two stores. Before doing so, *P* checks *D*'s driving record and arranges for him to go to a driving school for truck drivers. *D*'s record shows that he has had no accidents for 20 years, and he completes the driving school program without difficulty. Three weeks later, while driving *P*'s delivery truck, *D* is negligent and has a serious accident, injuring *X*. *P* is liable to *X* for his injuries.

In this example, *D* is a servant, and *P*'s liability is independent of whether *P* exercised due care in hiring *D*, or even whether she knew that *D* was her employee at all. P's liability in this situation may be described as "vicarious liability" and the consequence of "respondeat superior." *Respondeat superior* is a Latin phrase that means "let the master respond." It is important to recognize that P's liability only applies to actions within the scope of D's employment, though nice questions about coverage may arise as to whether the specific trip was a "detour" that was nevertheless part of the agent's duties to the principal or a "frolic" by the agent on his own. * * *

Example: The broker who is selling on commission in one of the above illustrations has an automobile accident while driving his own car to visit a prospect. The manufacturer is not liable for injuries to third persons arising from the accident. The same would be true of a person injured by the contractor in the above illustration while working on the owner's house.

Of course, the broker and the contractor would both be personally liable for the injuries in these illustrations. *D*, the servant in the above illustration, would also be personally liable for *X*'s injuries, since he too is a *tortfeasor*. The reason that respondeat superior is applied in numerous cases is because the chances are very good that the servant is judgment proof, has no insurance of his own, and therefore *X*'s only recourse is against *P*.

§ 2.8 The Power of an Agent To Affect The Principal's Legal Rights and Duties in General

An agent has power to affect the legal rights and duties of the principal in various ways. The tort liability of the principal for acts of the agent discussed in the previous section is one illustration. In other respects, to the extent the agent acts within the scope of his agency his acts are viewed as the acts of the principal and therefore affect the contractual or property rights and duties of the principal accordingly. However, the power of the agent is broader than this. An agent may also affect the principal's rights and duties to some extent even when the agent is acting in direct violation of the principal's instructions or beyond the scope of the agency relationship, or in some cases even when he is not really an agent at all.

The power of the agent to affect the principal's rights and duties is known as the agent's authority. The law of agency deals with three quite different, but interrelated, sources of authority that one person may have to bind another. These sources of power are discussed in the following sections.

§ 2.9 Actual Authority

Actual authority (often described as *express authority* or simply by the words "authority" or "authorized") arises from the manifestation of a principal *to an agent* that the agent has power to deal with others as a representative of the principal. An agent who agrees to act in accordance with that manifestation has actual authority to so act, and his actions without more bind the principal.

Example: P, the owner of two retail stores, employs C to serve as credit manager. C has authority to review and approve requests from customers for the extension of credit. C reviews the application of Y and approves him for the extension of credit. P is bound by C's decision, though that decision may be revoked by P at any time.

When an agent acts within the scope of her authority, she is not personally liable to the third person on the obligation so created (though, of course, the parties may agree otherwise).

Example: C approves of a sale of a washing machine to Z, a customer, $100 down and $50 per month until a total of $600 is paid. This action is within the scope of C's authority. P, the owner, refuses to deliver the washing machine to Z unless Z pays the $600 in cash immediately. P is liable for breach of contract, but C has no responsibility to Z and is not personally liable when P refuses to permit Z to purchase the machine on the terms agreed upon.

In this situation, P is bound by C's decision even though Z is totally unaware of who P is, or erroneously believes that C is the owner of the stores.

Example: T knows that P owns a horse he is thinking of buying and which A, P's agent is offering to sell him. A says, "This horse is only three years old and is sound in every respect." On these facts alone, P is liable if A's warranty turns out to be false, but A is not.[21]

Different rules may be applicable if the principal is not known to the third person. These rules are considered briefly below.

§ 2.10 Apparent Authority

Apparent authority arises from the manifestation *of a principal to a third party* (directly or indirectly) that another person is authorized to act as an agent for the principal.[22] That other person has apparent authority and an act by him within the scope of that apparent authority binds the principal to a third party who is aware of the manifestation by the principal and believes the person is authorized to act on behalf of the principal. The person with power to act in this situation should perhaps be called an "apparent agent" but typically he is simply described as an agent, one with apparent authority to act.

Apparent authority arises when a person represents that someone else is his agent when that is not the case, or, more commonly, creates or permits the creation of the impression that broad authority exists when it in fact does not. The theory is that if a third person relies on the representation or appearance of authority, that person may hold the putative principal liable for the action of the putative agent. The principal is bound by the agent's act within the scope of his apparent authority in this situation even though the act was not in fact authorized by the principal.

21. [By the Author] Restatement (Second) of Agency § 320, illustration 1.

22. [By the Author] Id. § 27.

Example: *P* gives *A*, an agent who is authorized to sell a piece of property on behalf of the principal, specific instructions as to the minimum price ($300,000) *P* is willing to accept as well as other terms. *P* informs possible buyers that *A* is his agent but obviously does not communicate *A*'s specific instructions to anyone but *A* (since to do so would be a virtual blueprint to possible buyers as to how to buy the property as cheaply as possible). *A* has actual authority only to enter a contract to sell the property at a price equal to or higher than $300,000 but he has apparent authority to sell the property at any price since the principal has represented to possible buyers that *A* is his agent.

Example: *A* actually signs a contract on behalf of *P* to sell *P*'s property to *TP* for $275,000. *P* is bound on that contract because the action was within *A*'s apparent authority but *A* has violated his instructions and is liable to *P* for the loss incurred.

The difference between apparent and actual authority can be most easily envisioned in that actual authority flows directly from the principal to the agent while apparent authority flows from the impression created by (or permitted to exist by) the principal in the mind of a third person.

Apparent authority *cannot* be created by the mere representation of the putative agent. Not even the most convincing and persuasive person can create an agency or apparent agency relationship entirely on his own.

Example: *A* approaches John's Buicks, Inc., a new car dealer and falsely explains that he is *P*'s agent, and that *P* desires to test drive a new Buick. Since *P* has been a good customer of John's Buicks in the past, and *A* is unusually convincing, John's entrusts *A* with a new Buick automobile, which *A* misappropriates. *P* is not liable for *A*'s conduct.

Example: John is a smooth-talking con man. He becomes friends with *X* and represents to *X* that he is an agent for General Motors seeking possible owners of new car franchises. John is very convincing, showing forged letters on GM letterhead, a forged identification card, and so forth. He persuades *X* that he will obtain a franchise for *X* if *X* will post $250,000. *X* does so. John converts the money to his own use, and disappears. General Motors is not liable for *X*'s loss.

While the conclusion reached in these two examples may seem self-evident, it is surprising in real life how often a third person relies upon representations by a putative agent of the scope of the agent's authority.

In many instances, the scope of apparent authority is as broad as an agent's actual authority—for example, where identical letters describing the scope of the agent's authority are sent both to the agent and to the third party. However, this is not necessarily so, and it is important to recognize that the power to affect the principal's legal rights and obligations may arise either from statements by the principal to the agent (actual authority) or statements made directly or indirectly by the principal to a third party (apparent authority). Apparent authority is related to concepts of estoppel based on the principal's conduct. In order to establish apparent authority, the third party must establish that it was reasonable for him to believe that the agent was authorized to act, based on what the principal said or on the impression that the principal created. If he can do so, the principal is bound even though he never intended to make *A* his agent or to enter into a contract with that third person.

In one aspect, apparent authority is broader than traditional estoppel. Liability arises under apparent authority even if the relying party has not changed his position in reliance on the representation. In other words, in the two examples in this section relating to the sale of land where *A* violates his instructions and sells the land for $275,000 rather than $300,000, *P* is bound to the contract with *TP* as soon as it is negotiated between *TP* and *A* even though *TP* has not relied in any material way on the contract and shortly thereafter learns that *A* was not authorized to sell the land for $275,000.

§ 2.11 Inherent and Incidental Authority

Inherent authority arises from the *agency itself and without regard to either actual or apparent authority*. Inherent authority may be viewed as authority arising by implication from the authority actually or apparently granted.[23]

Example: *P* hires *A* to operate a branch store of P's retail operations. *A* has authority to manage the store on a day-to-day basis but is told expressly that he has no authority to mark down the prices of goods without the prior approval of *P*. *A* nevertheless marks down slow-moving goods which are sold to third persons. There is neither actual nor apparent authority (because there was no manifestation of authority to the customers) but *P* is bound since a manager of a store has inherent authority based on his position to set prices of goods.

In many instances actual authority is coextensive with inherent authority based on the nature of the agency, but again this is not necessarily so.

Incidental authority is simply authority to do incidental acts that relate to a transaction that is authorized.[24]

Example: *P* authorizes *A* to purchase and obtain goods for him but does not provide him with funds to pay for them. It is implicit that *A* has authority to purchase goods on P's credit.

Obviously, the lines between apparent, inherent, and incidental authority may not always be clear-cut.

§ 2.12 Implied Authority

One complicating factor about the classification of authority as actual or apparent is that in either case the existence of authority may be implied rather than express. Indeed, the same conduct may often be relied upon to prove the existence of implied actual authority and implied apparent authority. Authority may be inferred from a prior course of conduct by the principal. Such conduct may be the basis for implying that the agent has continuing actual authority to act on the principal's behalf. If known to a third party, the very same conduct may lead to an inference that apparent authority exists.

Example: *P* is an elderly person living alone. He is befriended by *A*, a neighbor. *A* does errands for *P*, going to the store, helping *P* go to the doctor, and so forth. *P* has long had a charge account at the local grocery store that *A*

---

23. [By the Author] Id. § 8A.   **24.** [By the Author] Id. § 35.

has used frequently to charge groceries. Originally, the owner of the grocery store checked with P before accepting the charges but has stopped doing so since the relationship between A and P is well known to the owner. When A charges groceries, P is bound to pay for them. This result may be reached on the basis of either implied actual authority or implied apparent authority. The approval by P of A's prior transactions justifies a conclusion that A has actual authority to buy groceries for P (implied actual authority). The holding out in the past by P of A as his agent to the grocer also justifies an inference by the grocer that authority exists no matter what the actual state of relations is between P and A (implied apparent authority).

Apparent authority is destroyed if the third party knows, or has reason to know that A is no longer authorized to act for A.

Example: P and A have an argument and P tells A that he wants nothing more to do with him. The grocer, knowing this, nevertheless sells groceries to A on credit. P is not obligated to pay for them.

§ 2.13   Disclosed and Undisclosed Principals

This section deals with the common situation in which an agent is dealing with a third party on behalf of a principal under circumstances in which the third party may not know that the agent is acting for someone else. There are basically three different situations: the disclosed principal, the partially disclosed principal, and the completely undisclosed principal.

A principal is disclosed if the third party knows the identity of the principal at the time the transaction is entered into. It may be, of course, that in a specific situation, a third person does not actually know who the principal is, but should be able reasonably to infer the identity of the principal from the information on hand. That is still a disclosed principal situation. All of the prior discussion in this chapter has assumed that the principal is disclosed. When a transaction is entered into on behalf of a disclosed principal, the principal becomes a party to that contract. Equally importantly, the agent does not become a party to such a contract unless there is an agreement to the contrary.

A *partially disclosed principal* is one whose identity is unknown but the third person is on notice that the agent is in fact acting on behalf of some principal.[25]

Example: A offers to sell goods to TP, truthfully advising him that he is the manufacturer's representative for a well-known manufacturer. The identity of the manufacturer is not disclosed. The manufacturer is a partially disclosed principal.

Typically, the partially disclosed principal becomes immediately bound to any authorized contracts entered into by the agent. However, the agent also becomes bound to the third party unless there is an agreement by the third party to look solely to the partially disclosed principal. The third party's right to hold the agent responsible on such contracts is based on the common sense notion that the third party normally would not agree to look solely to a person whose identity is not known for performance of the contract. Thus, in the above example, if A's representation accurately describes his instructions from

---

25.   [By the Author] Id. § 321.

P, and *TP* places an order with *A*, both *A* and the manufacturer are personally bound to fill that order. Generally, the agent is not released from liability if *TP* elects to sue the manufacturer for nonperformance—the agent and principal are both liable on the contract, though the third party obviously is entitled to only a single recovery, and in some situations may be required to make an election as to which defendant he prefers to pursue.

A principal is *undisclosed* if the third party is not aware that the agent is acting on behalf of anyone when in fact the agent is acting on behalf of a principal. In effect, the third party is dealing with the agent as though the agent is the sole party in interest.[26] Clearly, in this situation the agent is personally liable to the third person on any contracts negotiated by him since the third party believes he is dealing directly and solely with the agent as the real party in interest. In addition, the agent has the rights and remedies available to any party to a contract, and he may, for example, settle with the third party or release that party from the contract.[27]

The undisclosed principal is also liable on the contract to the third party if the agent was acting within the scope of his *actual* authority. This is because of the basic agency concept that the authorized act of an agent binds the principal. It may seem a bit odd that the third party may have entered into a contract with a person he is unaware of, and be able to enforce that contract against that person, but it really is not, since that person can ignore the undisclosed principal and hold liable the agent with whom he was actually dealing. On the other hand, the right of the undisclosed principal to directly enforce a claim against the third party is circumscribed: the principal has only the rights an assignee of the contract would have, though, of course, the agent may enforce the contract directly against the third party on behalf of the undisclosed principal.

There is generally no room in the same transaction for concepts of apparent authority and an undisclosed principal. However, an agent for an undisclosed principal may have inherent or incidental power from the agency relationship to bind the principal since these types of agency power are based on actual authority.

§ 2.14 Termination of Agency Relationships

As indicated earlier, the relationship between an agent and a principal is a consensual relationship. That relationship terminates when the objective of the relationship has been achieved,[28] when the agent dies or becomes incompetent, or in a variety of other circumstances. The relationship may terminate either when the event occurs or when the other party has notice of the event, depending on how the relationship is formulated.

The relationship also terminates when the principal or agent determines to end it. However, if the relationship is based on contract, the decision to terminate it may be a breach of that contract. Nevertheless, the relationship has ended, even though contractual liability may exist for its termination.

---

26. [By the Author] Id. § 322.

27. [By the Author] Id. §§ 186, 205, et seq. If the agent violates his instructions when he releases the third party from the contract, the principal is bound by the agent's action but has a claim against the agent for the loss thereby incurred.

28. [By the Author] Restatement (Second) of Agency, § 106, et seq.

Since an inference of apparent authority may be based on the existence of prior actual authority, the termination of the relationship does not of itself eliminate the apparent authority of the agent. Notice may have to be given to third persons who may have dealt with the agent or otherwise believe that the principal has authorized the agent to act.[29]

§ 2.15 Managerial Employees

A managerial employee—a high-level employee who is typically in charge of a department or division of a firm and oversees the activities of a number of lower-level employees—is technically a "servant" in the quaint nomenclature of the Restatement of Agency. Theoretically, servants are subject to the right of the master to "control the physical conduct" of the servant's performance. Servants also owe "fiduciary duties" to the master. What do these phrases mean when we are talking about a senior manager that is responsible, say, for the operation of a complex plant with hundreds of employees?

It should be apparent that such an employee is expected to use skilled judgment and discretion in managing his part of the business at a profitable level. It is very unlikely that the "master" (who may be an intangible entity such as a corporation) can oversee and direct in any meaningful way how a managerial-level employee performs his normal work. He is in fact expected to perform much as an owner would in the day-to-day management of his part of the business. This relationship creates problems of *agency cost*[30] as the managerial employee may be tempted to maximize his own personal utility rather than the utility of the owners of the business. Managerial employees lack the incentives of owners to maximize the owners' personal utility.

Employers usually attempt to assure the fidelity of managerial employees through devices that provide incentives to them to perform as though they were owners of the enterprise. Such employees may be given employment contracts that assure some tenure and security even if risks taken by the employees do not work out. Most importantly, at least part of the expected compensation of managerial employees must be based on a series of incentives. The more superior the performance, the greater the income of the employee. In order to have an effective incentive compensation system, there must be a definition of the goal that the managerial employee is to strive for, and some way of measuring how close the employee came to meeting that goal. These arrangements may be difficult to negotiate since there are serious problems of definition and measurement, particularly when other factors beyond the control of the managerial employee may increase the difficulty of achieving his goal.

Of course, it is often possible to place limits on the discretion of even managerial employees. For example, the managerial employee may be instructed that he must obtain approval from one of the owners or an even

---

29. [By the Author] Id. § 125, et seq.

30. [By the Author] "Agency costs" is a term coined by economists to describe the costs incurred by a principal who entrusts decision-making to an agent where the agent reaches decisions in light of his own personal preferences and desires rather than those of the principal. Agency costs may be broken down into "monitoring expenditures," "bonding expenditures," and losses incurred from misappropriations by the agent. Agency costs are reduced by various techniques, as described in the text.

more senior manager for all transactions that involve more than x thousand dollars. It is also possible to impose external restraints by imposing procedures involving employees not under the control of the managerial employee. Inventory records may be kept by persons not under the direction of the sales manager, for example. Managerial employees may also be bonded to protect against misappropriation or theft.

* * * Lawyers are often called upon to draft or review proposed contracts for managerial employees, either on behalf of the firm or on behalf of the employee. In considering the terms of such a contract, it must be recognized that the interests of the employer to some extent diverge from the interests of the managerial employee. For example, the employee wishes job security, a form of tenure which assures him that he will keep his job even if things go badly. The employer, on the hand wishes to have freedom to change managerial employees inexpensively if it loses confidence in the specific managerial employee. These conflicts are right at the surface of the negotiation and must be directly addressed by the firm. All of these methods of providing incentives and ensuring honesty involve real costs from the standpoint of the business.

In addition to managerial employees, similar problems may arise with respect to other classes of employees, particularly purchase agents and individual members of the sales force, since oversight of the activities of these employees is often difficult or impossible. Incentive compensation arrangements are very common to assure that they will exert their best efforts on behalf of their employers. Indeed, compensating sales personnel in part through commissions based on sales volume is probably the norm in most businesses. * * *

Appendix Two

PROXY STATEMENT

BARNES & NOBLE, INC.

122 Fifth Avenue.
New York, New York 10011.

PROXY STATEMENT FOR ANNUAL MEETING OF STOCKHOLDERS TO BE HELD ON JUNE 4,1997

INTRODUCTION

This Proxy Statement and enclosed Proxy Card are being furnished commencing on or about May 2, 1997 in connection with the solicitation by the Board of Directors of Barnes & Noble, Inc., a Delaware corporation (the "Company"), of proxies for use at the Annual Meeting of Stockholders to be held on June 4, 1997 (the "Meeting") for the purposes set forth in the accompanying Notice of Annual Meeting of Stockholders. Any proxy given pursuant to such solicitation and received in time for the Meeting will be voted as specified in such proxy. If no instructions are given, proxies will be voted **FOR** the election of the nominees listed below under the caption "Election of Directors Information Concerning the Directors and Nominees–Nominees for Election as Director," **FOR** the ratification of the appointment of BDO Seidman, LLP as independent certified public accountants for the Company's fiscal year ending January 31, 1998 (collectively, the "Proposals"), and in the discretion of the proxies named on the Proxy Card with respect to any other matters properly brought before the Meeting and any adjournments thereof Any proxy may be revoked by written notice received by the Secretary of the Company at any time prior to the voting thereof by submitting a subsequent proxy or by attending the Meeting and voting in person.

Only holders of record of the Company's voting securities as of the close of business on April 16, 1997 are entitled to notice of and to vote at the Meeting. As of the record date, 33,252,341 shares of Common Stock, par value $.001 per share ("Common Stock"), were outstanding. Each share of Common Stock entitles the record holder thereof to one vote on each of the Proposals and on all other matters properly brought before the Meeting. The presence of a majority of the combined outstanding shares of the Common Stock represented in person or by proxy at the Meeting will constitute a quorum.

Proxy solicitations will be made primarily by mail, but may also be made by telephone or personal interviews conducted by officers or employees of the Company not specifically employed for this purpose. All costs of solicitations, including printing and mailing of this Proxy Statement and accompanying materials, and the reimbursement of brokerage firms and others for their expenses in forwarding solicitation material to the beneficial owners of the Common Stock, will be borne by the Company.

The three nominees for Director receiving the highest vote totals will be elected as Directors of the Company to serve until the 2000 annual meeting of stockholders. The proposal to ratify the Company's independent certified public accountants, and all other matters to be voted on at the Meeting, will be decided by the affirmative vote of a majority of the shares of Common Stock voting on the proposal in person or by proxy at the Meeting. Thus, abstentions and broker non-votes will not be included in vote totals with respect to such proposals and will have no effect on the outcome of the votes with respect thereto. It should be noted that all of the Directors and executive officers of the Company, together with principal stockholders of the Company with which they are affiliated, own or control the voting power of approximately 23.4% of the Common Stock outstanding as of April 16, 1997, and have advised the Company that they intend to vote in favor of all of the Proposals.

A Proxy Card is enclosed for your use. YOU ARE SOLICITED ON BEHALF OF THE BOARD OF DIRECTORS TO COMPLETE, SIGN, DATE AND RETURN THE PROXY CARD IN THE ACCOMPANYING ENVELOPE, which is postage paid if mailed in the United States.

NO PERSON IS AUTHORIZED TO GIVE ANY INFORMATION OR TO MAKE ANY REPRESENTATIONS OTHER THAN THOSE CONTAINED IN THIS PROXY STATEMENT, AND, IF GIVEN OR MADE, SUCH INFORMATION MUST NOT BE RELIED UPON AS HAVING BEEN AUTHORIZED. THE DELIVERY OF THIS PROXY STATEMENT SHALL, UNDER NO CIRCUMSTANCES, CREATE ANY IMPLICATION THAT THERE HAS BEEN NO CHANGE IN THE AFFAIRS OF THE COMPANY SINCE THE DATE OF THIS PROXY STATEMENT.

ELECTION OF DIRECTORS

Proposal I

Information Concerning the Directors and Nominees

The Board of Directors currently consists of nine Directors. The Directors currently are divided into three classes, consisting of three members whose terms expire at the Meeting, three members whose terms expire at the 1998 annual meeting of stockholders and three members whose terms expire at the 1999 annual meeting of stockholders.

Background information with respect to the Board of Directors and nominees for election as Directors, all of whom are incumbent Directors, appears below. See "Security Ownership of Certain Beneficial Owners and Management" for information regarding such persons' holdings of equity securities of the Company.

Name	Age	Director Since	Position
Leonard Riggio (1)	56	1986	Chairman of the Board and Chief Executive Officer
Irene R. Miller	45	1995	Vice Chairman and Chief Financial Officer
Stephen Riggio	42	1997	Chief Operating Officer and Director
Matthew A. Berdon (2)(3)	77	1992	Director
William Dillard, II (1)	52	1993	Director
Jan Michiel Hessels (2)	54	1990	Director
Margaret T. Monaco (2)	49	1995	Director
Michael N. Rosen	56	1986	Secretary and Director
William Sheluck, Jr. (1)(2)(3)	56	1993	Director

(1) Member of Nominating Committee
(2) Member of Compensation Committee
(3) Member of Audit Committee

At the Meeting, three Directors will be elected, each to hold office for a term of three years and until his or her successor is elected and qualified. Irene R. Miller, William Dillard, II and Michael N. Rosen are nominees for election as Directors at the Meeting, each to hold office for a term of three years until the annual meeting of stockholders to be held in 2000. The terms of Leonard Riggio, Jan Michiel Hessels and William Sheluck, Jr. expire in 1998; and the terms of Stephen Riggio, Matthew A. Berdon and Margaret T. Monaco expire in 1999. Although management does not anticipate that Ms. Miller, Mr. Dillard or Mr. Rosen will be unable or unwilling to stand for election, in the event of such an occurrence, proxies may be voted for a substitute designated by the Board of Directors.

In April 1997 William C.J. Angenent resigned as a Director of the Company. The remaining Directors appointed Stephen Riggio, Chief Operating Officer of the Company, to fill the vacancy created by the resignation of Mr. Angenent. Stephen Riggio's term as Director will expire in 1999.

Nominees for Election as Director

The following individuals are nominees for Director at the Meeting:

Irene R. Miller was appointed Vice Chairman of the Company in September 1995, and has been a Director of the Company since May 1995. She has been Chief Financial Officer of the Company since September 1993 and was previously Executive Vice President, Corporate Finance. She joined the Company in January 1991. From July 1986 to December 1990, Ms. Miller held various positions in the Retail Industry Group for Morgan Stanley & Co. Incorporated's Investment Banking Department, most recently as a Principal. From 1982 to 1986, she was a Vice President of Corporate Finance at Rothschild, Inc. Ms. Miller is also a director of Oakley, Inc.

William Dillard, II has been a Director of the Company since November 1993. Mr. Dillard is the President and Chief Operating Officer of Dillard Department Stores, Inc., a U.S. retailing corporation ("Dillard's"), positions he has held since 1977, and he has been a director of Dillard's since 1968. Mr. Dillard also Is a director of Simon Property Group, Texas Commerce Bancshares Inc. and Acxiom Corp.

Michael N. Rosen has been Secretary and a Director of the Company since its inception in 1986 and a senior member of Robinson Silverman Pearce Aronsohn & Berman LLP, counsel to the Company, for more than the past five years. Mr. Rosen is also a director of Barnes & Noble College Bookstores, Inc. ("B & N College"), one of the largest operators of college bookstores in the country, and MBS Textbook Exchange, Inc. ("MBS"), one of the nation's largest wholesalers of college textbooks.

The Board of Directors recommends that the stockholders vote FOR the election of each nominee for Director named above. Proxies solicited hereby will be voted FOR each nominee named above unless a vote against a nominee or an abstention is specifically indicated.

Other Directors whose Terms of Office Continue after the Meeting

Leonard Riggio has been Chairman of the Board, Chief Executive Officer and a principal stockholder of the Company since its inception in 1986. Since 1965, Mr. Riggio has been Chairman of the Board, Chief Executive Officer and the principal stockholder of B & N College. For more than the past five years, Mr. Riggio has been Chairman of the Board and a principal beneficial owner of MBS. Mr. Riggio is also the principal member and sole Manager of Babbage's Etc. LLC, a national retailer of personal computer software and video games.

Stephen Riggio became a Director of the Company in April 1997 and has been Chief Operating Officer of the Company since February 1995. He was President of B. Dalton Bookseller, Inc. ("B. Dalton"), a wholly-owned subsidiary of the Company, from July 1993 to February 1995, and he was Executive Vice President, Merchandising of the Company from January 1987 to February 1995. For 13 years prior to January 1987, Mr. Riggio held various merchandising and marketing positions at B & N College. Mr. Riggio is Leonard Riggio's brother.

Jan Michiel Hessels has been a Director of the Company since October 1990. Mr. Hessels has been the Chief Executive Officer of Vendex International N.V. ("Vendex") since June 1990. Vendex is a multi-billion dollar Netherlands-based corporation with substantial international retailing operations. From January 1985 until January 1990, Mr. Hessels was President and Chief Executive Officer of N.V. Deli–Maatschappij, an international trading company, as well as a director of **its** parent company, Universal Corp. Mr. Hessels is also a director of Dillard's, BAM Holding N.V., Yule Catto Pic., Schiphol Airport, Royal Van Ommeren and Staal Bank.

Matthew A. Berdon has been a Director of the Company since June 1992. Mr. Berdon has been a partner in the certified public accounting firm of Ferro Berdon & Company for more than the past five years. Mr. Berdon is also a director of B & N College.

Margaret T. Monaco has been a Director of the Company since May 1995. Ms. Monaco has been the Principal of Probus Advisors, a management and financial consulting firm, since July 1993. She previously had been the Vice President and Treasurer of The Limited, Inc., a national specialty retailing firm, since 1987. Ms. Monaco is also a director of Crown American Realty Trust and Cooker Restaurant Corporation.

William Sheluck, Jr. has been a Director of the Company since November 1993. Mr. Sheluck formerly was the President, Chief Executive Officer and a director of Nationar, a New York Statechartered commercial bank providing services to financial institutions and corporations, from 1983 until his retirement in April 1993. Mr. Sheluck is also the Treasurer and a director of New Life of New York City, Inc., a not-for-profit organization which provides services to disadvantaged teenagers.

Meetings and Committees of the Board

The Board of Directors met four times during the fiscal year ended February 1, 1997 and acted by unanimous written consent on one additional occasion. All Directors attended at least 75% of all of the meetings of the Board of Directors and the committees thereof on which they served during the fiscal year ended February 1, 1997, except Mr. Hessels who was unable to attend two of the meetings of the Board of Directors.

The Board of Directors has three standing committees: the Audit Committee, the Compensation Committee and the Nominating Committee. In March 1997, the Incentive Plan Committee of the Board of Directors was merged into the Compensation Committee.

Audit Committee. The Audit Committee has the principal function of reviewing the adequacy of the Company's internal system of accounting controls, conferring with the independent certified public accountants concerning the scope of their examination of the books and records of the Company, recommending to the Board of Directors the appointment of independent certified public accountants, reviewing related party transactions and considering other appropriate matters regarding the financial affairs of the Company. The current members of the Audit Committee are Messrs. Sheluck (Chairman) and Berdon, none of whom is, or has ever been, an officer or employee of the Company. The Audit Committee met three times during the fiscal year ended February 1, 1997.

Compensation Committee. The principal function of the Compensation Committee is to make recommendations to the Board of Directors with respect to matters regarding the approval of employment agreements, management and consultant hiring and executive compensation. The current members of the Compensation Committee are Mr. Berdon (Chairman), Mr. Hessels, Ms. Monaco and Mr. Sheluck, none of whom is, or has ever been, an officer or employee of the Company. Ms. Monaco joined the Compensation Committee in March 1997 upon the merger of that Committee with the former Incentive Plan Committee. The Compensation Committee met once during the fiscal year ended February 1, 1997. In addition, as of March 1997, the Compensation Committee assumed the principal function of the former Incentive Plan Committee which is to make grants of options to purchase Common Stock and of restricted shares of Common Stock under the Barnes & Noble, Inc. 1991 Employee Incentive Plan and the Barnes & Noble, Inc. 1996 Incentive Plan. The members of the former Incentive Plan Committee were Mr. Berdon (Chairman), Ms. Monaco and Mr. Sheluck. The former Incentive Plan Committee acted by unanimous written consent on two occasions during the fiscal year ended February 1, 1997.

Nominating Committee. The function of the Nominating Committee is to seek qualified individuals as Directors of the Company. The current members of the Nominating Committee are Messrs. Riggio (Chairman), Dillard and Sheluck. The Nominating Committee met once during the fiscal year ended February 1, 1997.

Compensation of Directors

Non-employee Directors receive an annual fee of $20,000 with no additional fees for attendance at Board or committee meetings. All Directors of the Company are reimbursed for travel, lodging and related expenses incurred in attending Board meetings. On January 16, 1996, each non-employee Director received options to purchase 20,000 shares of Common Stock at a price of $24.375 per share. Of these options, 5,000 became exercisable on May 29, 1996, an additional 5,000 became exercisable on January 1, 1997 and an additional 5,000 become exercisable on each of January 1, 1998 and January 1, 1999, subject in each case to the recipient remaining a Director of the Company.

Executive Officers

The Company's executive officers, as well as additional information with respect to such persons, is set forth in the table below:

Name	Age	Position
Leonard Riggio	56	Chairman of the Board and Chief Executive Officer
Irene R. Miller	45	Vice Chairman and Chief Financial Officer
Stephen Riggio	42	Chief Operating Officer
Mitchell S. Klipper	39	Executive Vice President and President of Barnes & Noble Development
Thomas A. Tolworthy	42	Vice President and President of Barnes & Noble Superstores
David K. Cully	44	Vice President and President of Barnes & Noble Distribution
Richard J. Kish	38	Chief Information Officer
David S. Deason	38	Vice President, Real Estate
Maureen H. Golden	46	Vice President, General Merchandise Manager
Michael N. Rosen	56	Secretary

Information with respect to executive officers of the Company who also are Directors is set forth in "Information Concerning the Directors and Nominees" above.

Mitchell S. Klipper has been President of Barnes & Noble Development, the group responsible for selecting the Company's new store locations, since December 1995 and is an Executive Vice President of the Company. From March 1993 to December 1995, Mr. Klipper was President of Barnes & Noble Superstores, Inc. ("B & N Superstores"), a wholly-owned subsidiary of the Company. Until September 1993, Mr. Klipper also was Chief Financial Officer of the Company, a position to which he was elected in September 1988. He was Vice President, Chief Financial **Officer** of B & N College from June 1986 to September 1988. Prior to June 1986, Mr. Klipper was an Audit Manager at the certified public accounting firm of KMG Main Hurdman.

Thomas A. Tolworthy became President of B & N Superstores in December 1995 and is also a Vice President of the Company. Prior to December 1995, Mr. Tolworthy was President of B. Dalton. He was Vice President of Store Operations of B. Dalton from September 1991 to February 1995 and was a Regional Director of B. Dalton from July 1989 to September 1991. Prior to 1989, Mr. Tolworthy was Stores Director for Duckwall/Alco Stores, Inc., a general merchandise retailer.

David K. Cully has been Vice President of the Company and President of Barnes & Noble Distribution, the group responsible for the Company's distribution center operations, since June 1992. Prior to June 1992, he was Vice President, General Merchandise Manager of the Company. Prior to joining the Company in 1989, Mr. Cully was Executive Vice President, General Merchandise Manager for Egghead Discount Software, Inc., a software retailer.

Richard J. Kish became Chief Information Officer in April 1997. Prior to that, he was Vice President, Information Technology of the Company since February 1995. He was Vice President, Information Technology for Waldenbooks, a national book retailer, from 1989 to January 1995.

David S. Deason joined the Company in January 1990 as a Director of Real Estate and became Vice President, Real Estate in January 1997. Prior to joining the Company, Mr. Deason was a Director of Real Estate for S & A Restaurant Corporation, a national restaurant chain.

Maureen H. Golden has been Vice President, General Merchandise Manager of the Company since June 1992. She joined B & N College in July 1976 and has held various positions in buying and merchandising for the Company since 1987 and for B & N College from 1976 to 1987.

The Company's officers are elected annually by the Board of Directors and hold office at the discretion of the Board of Directors.

Security Ownership of Certain Beneficial Owners and Management

The following table sets forth information regarding the beneficial ownership of shares of Common Stock, as of April 16, 1997, by each person known by the Company to own beneficially more than five percent of the Company's outstanding Common Stock, by each Director and nominee for Director, by each executive officer named in the Summary Compensation Table contained in "Executive Compensation," and by all Directors and executive officers of the Company as a group. Except as otherwise noted, each person named in the table has sole voting and investment power with respect to all shares of Common Stock shown as beneficially owned by him her or it.

Name and Address of Beneficial Owner	Shares Beneficially Owned (1)	Percent of Shares Beneficially Owned (1)
Leonard Riggio .... c/o Barnes & Noble, Inc. 122 Fifth Avenue New York, New York 10011	8,391,751(2)	24.7%
Forstmann–Leff Associates, Inc. .... 55 East 52nd Street New York, NY 10055	3,761,965(3)	11.3%

Name and Address of Beneficial Owner	Shares Beneficially Owned (1)	Percent of Shares Beneficially Owned (1)
Leon G. Cooperman .... c/o Omega Advisors, Inc. 88 Pine Street Wall Street Plaza, 31st Floor New York, NY 10005	1,709,600(4)	5.1%
Investment Advisors, Inc. .... 3700 First Bank Place P.O. Box 357 Minneapolis, MN 55440	1,688,250(5)	5.1%
Irene R. Miller	348,351(6)	1.0%
Stephen Riggio	1,062,161(6)	3.1%
Mitchell S. Klipper	896,259(6)	2.6%
Thomas A. Tolworthy	40,423(6)	*
Matthew A. Berdon	43,500(7)	*
William Dillard, II	20,000(6)	*
Jan Michiel Hessels	11,000(8)	*
Margaret T. Monaco	13,000(8)	*
Michael N. Rosen	16,000(9)	*
William Sheluck, Jr.	26,000(10)	*
All directors and executive officers as a group (15 persons)	10,991,604(11)	30.1%

* Less than 1%.

(1) Shares of Common Stock that an individual or group has a right to acquire within 60 days after April 16, 1997 pursuant to the exercise of options, warrants or other rights are deemed to be outstanding for the purpose of computing the percentage ownership of such individual or group, but are not deemed to be outstanding for computing the percentage ownership of any other person or group shown in the table.

(2) Includes (i) 1,326,167 shares owned by B&N College (Mr. Riggio owns substantially all of the voting securities of B&N College), (ii) 720,000 shares owned by The Riggio Foundation, a charitable trust established by Mr. Riggio, with himself and his wife as trustees, and (iii) 659,375 shares issuable upon the exercise of stock options.

(3) Forstmann–Leff Associates, Inc. ("FLA"), a New York corporation, is a registered investment adviser under Section 203 of the Investment Advisers Act of 1940 (the–1940 Act"), and has sole voting power with respect to 2,554,465 of its shares. FLA shares voting power with respect to 56,450 of its shares, and dispositive power with respect to 770,800 of its shares, with its subsidiary, FLA Asset Management, Inc., a registered investment adviser under the 1940 Act. FLA shares voting and dispositive power with respect to 89,900 of its shares with its subsidiary Stamford Advisers Corp., a registered investment adviser under the 1940 Act. FLA shares voting and dispositive power with respect to 51,200 of its shares with Forstmann-Leff Associates, L.P., a registered investment adviser under the 1940 Act. FLA Asset Management, Inc. is the general partner of Forstmann–Leff Associates L.P. The foregoing information is based upon a Schedule 13G filed by FLA with the Company in February 1997.

(4) Leon G. Cooperman ("Cooperman"), Managing Member of Omega Associates, L.L.C. ("Associates"), has sole voting and dispositive power with respect to 1,372,400 of its shares. Associates is a private investment firm formed to invest in and act as general partner of investment partnerships or similar

investment vehicles. Cooperman is the President and majority stockholder of Omega Advisors, Inc., ("Advisors"), a Delaware corporation engaged **in** providing investment management. Cooperman shares voting and dispositive power **with** unrelated third parties as to 337,200 of its shares in a Managed Account of Advisors. The foregoing information is based upon a Schedule 13G **filed** by Cooper-man with the Company **in** February 1997.

(5) Investment Advisers, Inc. ("IAI"), a registered investment adviser under Section 203 of the 1940 Act, has sole voting and dispositive power with respect to 1,486,300 of its shares. IAI shares voting and dispositive power with respect to 201,950 of its shares held by various custodian banks for various clients of IAI. The foregoing information is based upon a Schedule 13G filed by IAI with the Company in January 1997.

(6) All of these shares are issuable upon the exercise of stock options.

(7) Of these shares, 20,000 are issuable upon the exercise of stock options. Five hundred shares are owned by Mr. Berdon's wife. Mr. Berdon disclaims any beneficial ownership of those shares.

(8) Of these shares, 10,000 are issuable upon the exercise of stock options.

(9) Of these shares, 10,000 shares are issuable upon the exercise of stock options. Of the other 6,000 shares, 5,000 are owned by Mr. Rosen's wife and 1,000 are owned by Mr. Rosen's daughter. Mr. Rosen disclaims any beneficial ownership of these shares.

(10) Of these shares, 20,000 are issuable upon the exercise of stock options. Of the other 6,000 shares, Mr. Sheluck shares voting and dispositive power with respect to 5,000 of these shares with his wife, and the remaining 1,000 shares are owned by a minor child of Mr. Sheluck.

(11) Includes 3,219,728 shares issuable upon the exercise of stock options.

Compensation Committee Interlocks and Insider Participation

The current members of the Compensation Committee of the Board of Directors are Messrs. Berdon (Chairman), Hessels and Sheluck, none of whom is an officer or employee or former officer or employee of the Company. See "Meetings and Committees of the Board–Compensation Committee."

Executive Compensation

The following table summarizes the compensation paid or accrued by the Company for services rendered during the years indicated to the Company's Chief Executive Officer and the Company's four other most highly compensated executive officers. The Company did not grant any restricted stock awards or free-standing stock appreciation fights or make any long-term incentive plan payouts during the years indicated.

Summary Compensation Table

Name and Principal Position	Fiscal Year Ended on or About January 31	Annual Compensation Salary	Bonus	Long–Term Compensation Awards Securities Underlying Options/SARs	All Other Compensation (1)
Leonard Riggio	1997	$900,000 (2)	$540,000	——	$ ——
Chairman of the Board and	1996	900,000	405,000	——	——
Chief Executive Officer	1995	900,000	270,000	——	——
Irene R. Miller	1997	448,462 (2)	276,000	7,192	3,512
Vice Chairman and Chief	1996	379,808	180,000	340,195	3,462
Financial Officer..................	1995	295,000	177,000	6,505	2,042
Stephen Riggio	1997	448,462 (2)	276,000	7,192	9,636 (3)
Chief Operating Officer	1996	385,577	180,000	6,045	5,061
	1995	325,000	195,000	7,166	3,795
Mitchell S. Klipper................	1997	448,462 (2)	276,000	7,192	8,279 (4)
Executive Vice President	1996	395,192	180,000	6,975	8,506
and President of Barnes &........	1995	375,000	225,000	8,269	6,450
Noble Development					
Thomas A. Tolworthy	1997	300,000 (2)	120,000	5,394	3,135
Vice President and...............	1996	295,266	60,000	74,650	3,346
President of Barnes &.............	1995	175,000	35,000	3,859	1,813
Noble Superstores					

(1) Except as set forth in notes 3 and 4 below, "All Other Compensation" for the fiscal year ended February 1, 1997 is comprised of the Company's contributions to the Barnes & Noble, Inc. 401(k) Savings Plan (the "401(k) Plan").

(2) Reflects annual salary for a 52–week period. The Company's fiscal year ended February 1, 1997 included 53 weeks. Salaries paid for that 53–week period were $917,308 for Leonard Riggio; $457,308 for each of Irene R. Miller, Stephen Riggio and Mitchell S. Klipper; and $305,769 for Thomas A. Tolworthy.

(3) Represents (a) $3,512 paid by the Company as a contribution to Mr. Riggio's 401(k) Plan, (b) $1,857 paid by the Company as a premium on a term life insurance policy for the benefit of Mr. Riggio and (c) $4,267 paid to Mr. Riggio for length of service award.

(4) Represents (a) $3,295 paid by the Company as a contribution to Mr. Klipper's 401(k) Plan, (b) $1,857 paid by the Company as a premium on a term life insurance policy for the benefit of Mr. Klipper and (c) $3,127 paid by the Company as a premium on a long-term disability insurance policy for the benefit of Mr. Klipper.

The following table sets forth certain information concerning options granted during the 53 weeks ended February 1, 1997 to the executive officers named in the Summary Compensation Table above. The Company did not grant any free-standing stock appreciation rights during the 53 weeks ended February 1, 1997.

Option/SAR Grants in Last Fiscal Year

	Individual Grants				
Name	Number of Securities Underlying Options/SARs Granted	Percentage of Total Options/SARs Granted to Employees in Fiscal 1996	Exercise Price Per Share	Expiration Date	Present Value of Grant Using the Black-Scholes Model (1)
Leonard Riggio	—	—%	$ —		$ —
Irene R. Miller	7,192	1.6%	34.875	5/31/06	105,291
Stephen Riggio	7,192	1.6%	34.875	5/31/06	105,291
Mitchell S. Klipper.......	7,192	1.6%	34.875	5/31/06	105,291
Thomas A. Tolworthy	5,394	1.2%	34.875	5/31/06	78,968

(1) Calculated using the Black–Scholes option-pricing model with the following assumption volatility of 28.0%, risk-free interest rate of 6.70% and an expected life of six years. The BlackScholes option valuation model was developed for use in estimating the fair value of traded; options which have no vesting restrictions and are fully transferable. In addition, option valuation, models require the input of highly subjective assumptions including the expected stock prim volatility. Because the Company's stock options have characteristics significantly different from those traded options, and because changes in the subjective input assumptions can materially A= the fair value estimate, in management's opinion, the Black–Scholes model does not necessarily provide a reliable measure of the fair value of its stock options.

The following table sets forth information concerning option exercises and the value of unexercised options as of February 1, 1997 for the executive officers named in the Summary Compensation Table above.

Aggregated Option/SAR Exercises in Last Fiscal Year
and
Fiscal Year End Option/SAR Values

Name	Shares Acquired on Exercise	Value Realized	Number of Unexercised Options/SARs at February 1, 1997		Value of Unexercised In-the-Money Options/SARs at February 1, 1997	
			Exercisable	Unexercisable	Exercisable	Unexercisable
Leonard Riggio	—	$ —	659,375	—	$ 4,911,424	$ —
Irene R. Miller	75,000	2,000,351	341,956	124,589	4,230,794	772,667
Stephen Riggio	—	—	1,055,359	13,612	14,306,806	21,563
Mitchell S. Klipper......	75,000	1,983,441	888,780	14,599	10,261,417	24,875
Thomas A. Tolworthy ...	—	—	30,788	58,115	193,815	254,537

Employees' Retirement Plan

The Company's Employees' Retirement Plan (the "Retirement Plan") is a defined benefit pension plan covering all employees whose services are performed within the United States (including Puerto Rico) who are at least 21 years of age and who have completed at least one year of service and work a minimum of 1,000 hours per year. Vesting occurs after five years of service. The Retirement Plan provides Company-funded benefits based upon an employee's years of service and highest average annual salary for any five consecutive years in the last ten years of service.

A participant's annual benefit is determined for an employee, including an officer, generally as (i) 0.7% of the participant's average annual pay as determined in accordance with the Retirement Plan up to Social Security-covered compensation, multiplied by the participant's years of credited service, plus (ii) 1.3% of the participant's average annual pay as determined in accordance with the Retirement Plan in excess of Social Security-covered compensation, multiplied by the participant's years of credited service. A participant's maximum benefit is limited pursuant to Section 415 of the Code to $120,000 for 1996, indexed annually. Compensation recognized under the Retirement Plan is limited to $150,000 for 1996 and $160,000 for 1997, indexed annually in accordance with Section 404(l) of the Code.

Credited years of service under the Retirement Plan as of February 1, 1997 for the individuals named in the Summary Compensation Table above are: Leonard Riggio–9 years; Irene R. Miller6 years; Stephen Riggio—9 years; Mitchell S. Klipper–8 years; and Thomas A. Tolworthy–8 years. For the purposes of determining a participant's benefits in the Retirement Plan, the average annual pay of a participant includes any bonuses paid to such participant.

The following table illustrates the maximum annual amounts payable at age 65 under the Retirement Plan, based on various levels of highest average annual salary and years of credited service:

Assumed Highest Average Salary	Years of Credited Service				
	15	20	25	30	35
$100,000	$16,800	$22,400	$28,000	$33,600	$39,200
$125,000	21,675	28,900	36,125	43,350	50,575
$150,000	26,550	35,400	44,250	53,100	61,950
$160,000 and above (1)	28,500	38,000	47,500	57,000	66,500

(1) The benefits shown corresponding to this compensation reflect the compensation limit under Section 401 (a)(] 7) of the Code. A participant's compensation in excess of $150,000 (as adjusted to reflect cost-of-living increases) is disregarded for purposes of determining highest average earnings in plan years beginning in 1994 through 1996; a participant's compensation in excess of $160,000 (as adjusted to reflect cost-of-living increases) is disregarded for purposes of determining highest average earnings in plan years beginning in or after 1997. Benefits accrued as of the last day of the plan year beginning in 1993 on the basis of compensation in excess of $150,000 are preserved.

Employment Agreements

The Company entered into five-year employment agreements with Stephen Riggio (as of July 15, 1993) and Mitchell S. Klipper (as of April 1, 1993). The agreements with Mr. Riggio and Mr. Klipper provide for their employment at an annual salary determined by the Company, subject to certain minimums. Each is entitled to an annual bonus determined in accordance with the Barnes & Noble, Inc. Supplemental Compensation Plan. The agreements also provide for life and long-term disability insurance, a two-year severance arrangement and a two-year post-employment, non-competition agreement.

COMPENSATION COMMITTEE REPORT ON EXECUTIVE COMPENSATION

The Company's executive officer compensation program is administered by the Compensation Committee of the Board of Directors, consisting of the four non-employee directors listed below. The program is based upon the following guiding principles:

1. The pay and benefits provided by the Company to its executive officers should be competitive and allow the Company to attract and retain individuals whose skills are critical to the long-term success of the Company.

2. The compensation offered by the Company should reward and motivate individual and team performance in attaining business objectives and maximizing stockholder value.

The Compensation Committee reviews the Company's executive compensation program each year. This review includes a comparison of the Company's executive compensation, corporate performance, stock appreciation and total return to the stockholders with that of other companies, including other retailers.

The key elements of the Company's executive compensation package consist of base salary, annual bonus and stock options. The Company's policies with respect to each of these elements are discussed below. In addition, while the elements of compensation described below are considered separately, the Compensation Committee also considers and reviews the full compensation package afforded by the Company to its executive officers, including pension, insurance and other benefits. The Compensation Committee makes its determinations after receiving and considering the recommendations of the Company's chief executive officer.

Base Salaries. An executive officer's base salary is determined by evaluating the responsibilities of the position held, the individual's experience and the competitive marketplace for executive talent. The base salary is intended to be competitive with base salaries paid to executive officers with comparable qualifications, experience and responsibilities at other companies.

Annual Bonuses. In addition to a base salary, each executive officer is eligible for an annual cash bonus. Bonuses for senior executive officers of the Company are based upon annual net earnings of the Company and are determined pursuant to the Barnes & Noble, Inc. Supplemental Compensation Plan (the "Supplemental Compensation Plan").

The Supplemental Compensation Plan provides that senior executive officers designated by the Compensation Committee are entitled to a cash bonus in accordance with a sliding scale formula based on the extent to which a preestablished earnings-per-share target is attained. In general, not later than 90 days after the commencement of each fiscal year of the Company (and before 25% of the relevant period of service has elapsed), the Compensation Committee establishes in writing a target earnings per-share (the "Target"), the attainment of which is substantially uncertain. The Target which is established for each fiscal year must exceed the earnings-per-share for the immediately previous fiscal year. Targets are subject to adjustment for recapitalizations, dividends, stock splits and reverse splits, reorganizations, issuances of additional shares, redemptions of shares, option or warrant exercises, reclassifications, significant acquisitions and divestitures and other extraordinary events.

Each participating executive officer is entitled to receive a cash bonus based on a percentage of his or her base salary for the fiscal year ("Base Salary") as follows:

If actual earnings–per–share are:	Then the Amount of the Cash Bonus is:
Less than 80% of Target	None
80% or more but less than 91% of Target	30% of Base Salary
91% or more but less than 100% of Target	45% of Base Salary
100% or more but less than 109% of Target	60% of Base Salary
109% or more but less than 118% of Target	70% of Base Salary
118% or more of Target	80% of Base Salary

Notwithstanding the foregoing, in no event will the maximum cash bonus payable to any participating executive officer under the Supplemental Compensation Plan exceed $900,000 with respect to any fiscal year. In addition, no participating executive officer is entitled to receive any bonus under the Supplemental Compensation Plan with respect to any fiscal year unless the Company's actual earnings-per-share for such fiscal year (subject to adjustment as provided above) exceeds earnings-per-share for the prior fiscal year.

No bonuses are paid until the Compensation Committee certifies the extent to which the Target has been attained.

Leonard Riggio, Irene R. Miller, Stephen Riggio and Mitchell S. Klipper are the senior executive officers of the Company currently participating in the Supplemental Compensation Plan.

Stock Options. The general purpose of long-term awards, currently in the form of stock options, is to align the interests of the executive officers with the interests of the Company's stockholders. Additionally, long-term awards offer executive officers an incentive for the achievement of superior performance over time and foster the retention of key management personnel. In determining annual stock option grants, the Incentive Plan Committee has based its decision on the individual's performance and potential to improve stockholder value. The issuance of options at 100 percent of the fair market value also assures that executives will receive a benefit only when the stock price increases.

Compensation of Chief Executive Officer. Leonard Riggio's compensation is determined pursuant to the principles noted above, including a bonus as determined by the Supplemental Compensation Plan. Specific consideration is given to Mr. Riggio's responsibilities and experience in the industry and the compensation package awarded to chief executive officers of other comparable companies.

Impact of Section 162(m) of the Internal Revenue Code. The Compensation Committee has considered the potential impact of Section 162(m) of the Internal Revenue Code of 1986, as amended (the "Code"), adopted under the Revenue Reconciliation Act of 1993. This section disallows a tax deduction for any publicly held corporation, for individual compensation exceeding $1,000,-000 in any taxable year paid to its chief executive officer or any of its four other highest paid officers unless (i) the compensation is payable solely on account of the attainment of performance goals, (ii) the performance goals are determined by a compensation committee of two or more outside directors, (iii) the material terms under which compensation is to be paid are disclosed to and approved by stockholders and (iv) the compensation committee certifies that the performance goals were met. Because it is in the best interests of the Company to qualify to the maximum extent possible the compensation of its executives for deductibility under applicable tax laws, the Company has implemented the Supplemental Compensation Plan, which provides for the payment of compensation in compliance with the above guidelines.

> COMPENSATION COMMITTEE
> Matthew A. Berdon, *Chairman*
> Jan Michiel Hessels
> Margaret T. Monaco
> William Sheluck, Jr.

PERFORMANCE GRAPH

Performance Graph. The following table compares the cumulative total stockholder return on the Common Stock for the period commencing September 28, 1993 (the date on which the Common Stock commenced trading on the New York Stock Exchange) through January 31, 1997 (the last trading date during the Company's last completed fiscal year) with the cumulative total return on the Standard & Poor's 500 Stock Index ("S & P 500") and the Dow Jones Retailers, Other Specialty Industry Group Index (the "Dow Jones Specialty Retailers Index") over the same period. Total return values were calculated based on cumulative total return assuming (i) the investment of $100 in the Common Stock, the S & P 500 and the Dow Jones Specialty Retailers Index on September 28, 1993 and (ii) reinvestment of dividends.

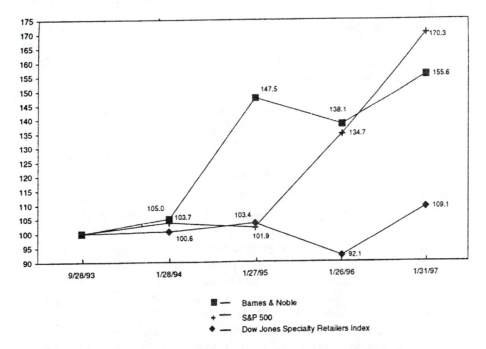

■ — Barnes & Noble
+ — S&P 500
♦ — Dow Jones Specialty Retailers Index

CERTAIN RELATIONSHIPS AND RELATED TRANSACTIONS

The Company leases space for its executive offices in properties in which a principal shareholder/director/executive officer of the company has a minority interest. The space was rented at an aggregate annual rent, including real estate taxes, of approximately $1,307,000 during fiscal 1996. Such space is rented under leases expiring in 1997 and 1998.

Marboro Books Corp., the Company's mail-order subsidiary, leases a 76,000 square foot office/warehouse from a partnership in which a principal shareholder/director/executive officer of the Company has a 50% interest, pursuant to a 15–year lease dated August 1987 requiring an annual rent of $700,000.

The Company utilizes the LTA Group, Inc. ("LTA") as one of its freight consolidators and carriers. A brother of a principal shareholder/director/executive officer of the Company owns a 20% interest in LTA. During fiscal 1996, the Company paid LTA $9,100,000 for freight consolidation and deliveries, which represented approximately 15% of the Company's freight costs.

B & N College, a company owned substantially by a principal shareholder/director/executive officer of the Company, allocated certain expenses it incurred on behalf of the Company for salaries, employee benefit plan expenses and office support services approximating $115,000 during fiscal 1996.

The Company uses a jet aircraft owned by B & N College and pays for the costs and expenses of operating the aircraft based upon the Company's usage. Such costs, which include fuel, insurance, personnel and other costs, approximated $1,685,000 during fiscal 1996.

The Company leases retail space in a building in which B & N College subleases space for its executive offices. Occupancy costs allocated by the Company to B & N College for this space totaled $544,000 during fiscal 1996.

During fiscal 1996, Software Etc. Stores, Inc. ("Software"), a company in which two principal shareholders/directors had an ownership interest, operated retail software departments within the Company's bookstores for which Software was required to pay the Company license fees for the use of such space. Software also operated, and paid all costs associated with, retail software stores that B. Dalton opened when Software was a division of B. Dalton and for which B. Dalton remained primarily liable for rent and other lease costs. On July 29, 1996, the Company purchased the inventory in all but 14 of the retail software departments located within the Company's bookstores from Software for approximately $9,000,000, and the Company assumed the operations of such software departments.

On November 27, 1996, Babbage's Etc. LLC ("Babbage's"), a newly formed company owned by two principal shareholders/directors of the Company, acquired substantially all of Software's assets. Babbage's assumed the operations of the remaining 14 retail software departments located within the Company's bookstores and the 27 retail software stores, the leases for which B. Dalton is primarily liable. As of November 27, 1996, the Company pays all rent related to these leases and receives license fees from Babbage's equal to 7.0% or 8.0% of the gross sales of such departments and stores for Babbage's use of such properties. Like it did with Software, the Company provides real estate and construction services to Babbage's and purchases business insurance on its behalf for which the Company is reimbursed its costs to provide such services. The Company charged Software and Babbage's, on a combined basis, $1,282,000 during fiscal 1996 for such services, license fees and insurance costs.

Michael N. Rosen, the Secretary and a Director of the Company, is a senior member of Robinson Silverman Pearce Aronsohn & Berman LLP, which law firm has represented the Company since its organization.

The Company believes that the transactions discussed above, as well as the terms of any future transactions and agreements (including renewals of any existing agreements) between the Company and its affiliates, are and will be at least as favorable to the Company as could be obtained from unaffiliated parties. The Board of Directors will be advised in advance of any such proposed transaction or agreement and will utilize such procedures in evaluating the terms and provisions of such proposed transaction or agreement as are appropriate in light of the fiduciary duties of directors under Delaware law. In addition, the Board of Directors has established an Audit Committee, which consists of two independent directors. One of the responsibilities of the Audit Committee is to review related party transactions. See "Election of Directors– Meetings and Committees of the Board–Audit Committee."

RATIFICATION OF APPOINTMENT OF INDEPENDENT CERTIFIED PUBLIC ACCOUNTANTS

Proposal 2

The Board of Directors has appointed the firm of BDO Seidman, LLP, which firm was engaged as independent certified public accountants for the fiscal year ended February 1, 1997, to audit the financial statements of the Company for the fiscal year ending January 31, 1998. A proposal to ratify this appointment is being presented to the stockholders at the Meeting. A representative of BDO Seidman, LLP will be present at the Meeting and will have the opportunity to make a statement and will be available to respond to appropriate questions.

The Board of Directors considers BDO Seidman, LLP to be well qualified and recommends that the stockholders vote FOR ratification. Proxies solicited hereby will be voted FOR the proposal unless a vote against the proposal or abstention is specifically indicated.

OTHER MATTERS

The Company does not intend to present any other business for action at the Meeting and does not know of any other business intended to be presented by others. If any matters other than the matters described in the Notice of Annual Meeting of Stockholders and this Proxy Statement should be presented for stockholder action at the Meeting, it is the intention of the persons designated in the proxy to vote thereon according to their best judgment.

Proxy Solicitation. Solicitation may be made personally, by telephone, by telegraph or by mail by officers and employees of the Company who will not be additionally compensated therefor. The Company will request persons such as brokers, nominees and fiduciaries holding stock in their names for others, or holding stock for others who have the right to give voting instructions, to forward proxy materials to their principals and request authority for the execution of the proxy. The Company will reimburse such persons for their expenses in so doing.

Financial and Other Information. The Company's Annual Report for the fiscal year ended February 1, 1997, including financial statements, is being sent to stockholders together with this Proxy Statement.

Compliance with Section 16(a) of the Securities Exchange Act. Section 16(a) of the Exchange Act requires the Company's executive officers and Directors, and persons who own more than ten percent of a registered class of the Company's equity securities, to **file** initial statements of beneficial ownership (Form 3), and statements of changes in beneficial ownership (Forms 4 and 5), of Common Stock of the Company with the Securities and Exchange Commission. Executive officers, Directors and greater than ten-percent stockholders are required to furnish the Company with copies of all such forms they file.

To the Company's knowledge, based solely on its review of the copies of such forms received by it, or written representations from certain reporting persons that no additional forms were required, all filing requirements applicable to its executive officers, Directors, and greater than ten-percent stockholders were complied with.

Stockholder Proposals. Proposals of stockholders intended to be presented at the Annual Meeting of Stockholders to be held in 1998 must be received by the Secretary, Barnes & Noble, Inc., 122 Fifth Avenue, New York, New York I 00 I 1, no later than January 2, 1998.

Stockholders are urged to forward their proxies without delay. A prompt response will be greatly appreciated.

> By Order of the Board of Directors
> Leonard Riggio
> *Chairman*

May 2, 1997

Index

References are to Pages